Alan Greenwood launched *Vintage Guitar* magazine in 1986. *Vintage Guitar* is the largest monthly publication for guitar collectors, enthusiasts, and dealers. He also publishes *Vintage Guitar*® Online at www.Vintage-Guitar.com, the free email newsletter *VG Overdrive*, *VG Acoustic*, and *VG Signal Chain*, and *The Official Vintage Guitar Price Guide* which he started in 1990. His collection includes several vintage instruments from the '20s to the '80s, as well as newer production and custom-made guitars, amps, effects, lap steels, and ukuleles. He lives in Bismarck, North Dakota.

Gil Hembree began collecting guitars in 1966 while working at Kitt's Music, in Washington, D.C. Familiarity with the professional musicians playing on Georgetown's M-Street allowed him to dabble in early buy-sell, but his academic interest in finance led to a corporate job in Michigan. Throughout his financial career he played in bands and searched for original-owner vintage guitars in Flint, Saginaw, Bay City, Port Huron, Pontiac, Battle Creek, and Kalamazoo. In 2000, freshly retired from corporate finance, he became the co-author of *The Official Vintage Guitar Price Guide*. In 2007, Hal Leonard released his biography of Ted McCarty: *Gibson Guitars: Ted McCarty's Golden Era: 1948-1966*. After residing in Michigan for 35 years, Hembree and his wife, Jane, relocated to Austin, Texas.

The Official Vintage Guitar® magazine Price Guide

By Alan Greenwood and Gil Hembree

Vintage Guitar Books
An imprint of Vintage Guitar Inc., PO Box 7301, Bismarck, ND 58507, (701) 255-1197, Fax (701) 255-0250, publishers of *Vintage Guitar*® magazine and Vintage Guitar® Online at www.VintageGuitar.com. Vintage Guitar is a registered trademark of Vintage Guitar, Inc.

ISBN: 978-1-884883-28-6

Cover: Joe Bonamassa's 1959 Les Paul Standard: Rick Gould. 1958 Gibson Les Paul Jr Plectrum: Lark Street Music. 1957 Gibson Les Paul Junior. 1959 Gibson Les Paul. 1957 Gibson Les Paul Model. 1961 Les Paul Standard (SG Body). 1957 Gibson Les Paul (Goldtop). 1973 Gibson Les Paul Recording.
Back: Silvertone archtop acoustic and Model 1474 Twin Twelve amp courtesy of Arnold Jordan. All photos property of Vintage Guitar, Inc.

Cover Design: Doug Yellow Bird/Vintage Guitar, Inc.

Printed in the United States of America

EXCLUSIVELY DISTRIBUTED BY

HAL•LEONARD® CORPORATION
7777 W. BLUEMOUND RD. P.O. BOX 13819
MILWAUKEE, WISCONSIN 53213

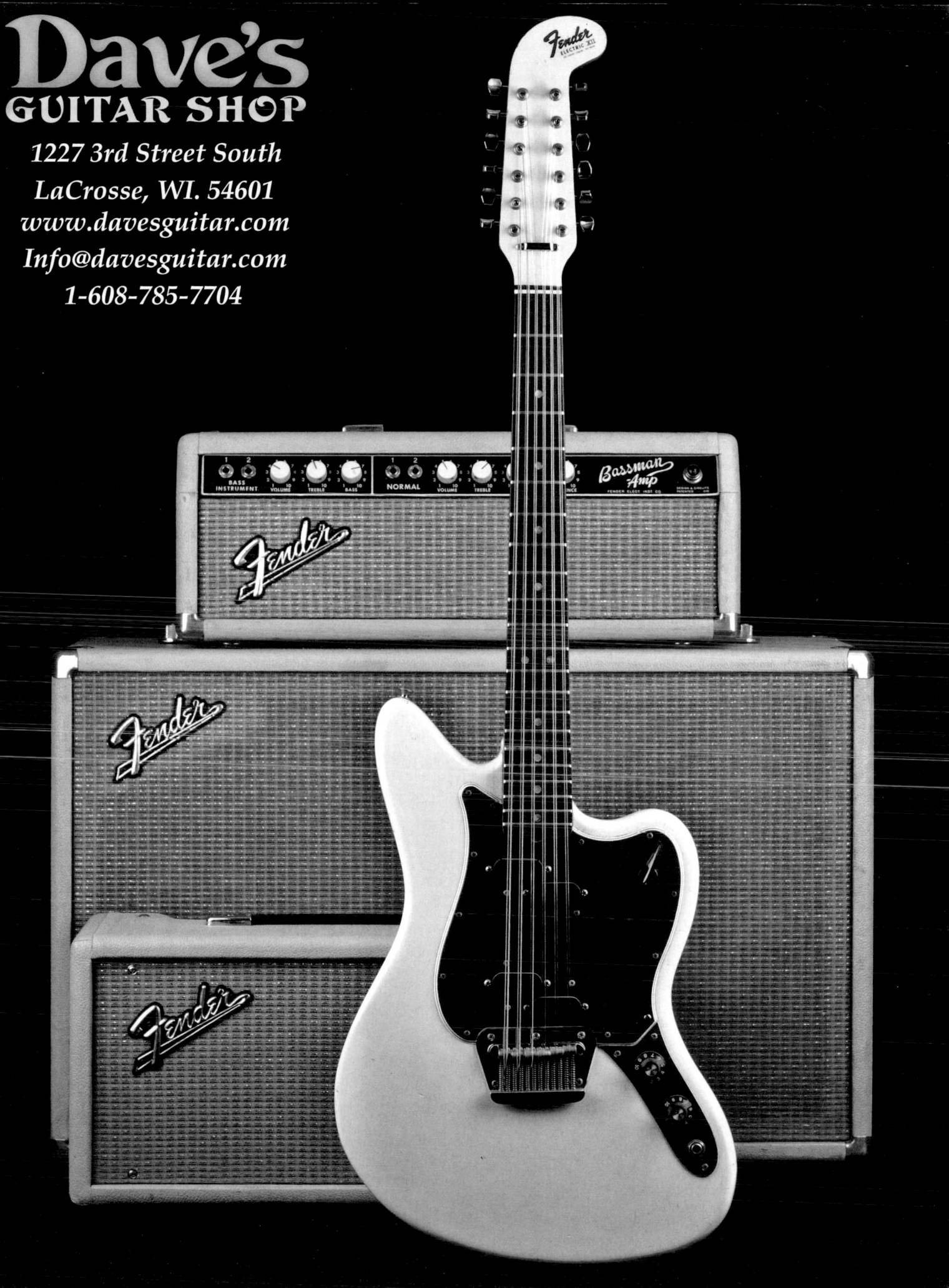

TABLE OF CONTENTS

1970 Uni-Vibe 1968 Vox Clyde McCoy wah wah 1970 Dallas Arbiter Fuzz Face, and 1980 Roger Mayer Octavia: Mike Piera.

A Fanatical Obsession with Details

True Historic from Gibson Custom. As Close As You Can Come to Owning an Original.

The latest in the evolution of Gibson Custom Historic Reissue guitars represents a fine-grain attention to detail unheard of in the guitar industry. From the scientific analysis of materials to determine their original formulations, to the hands-on study of countless vintage Gibson guitars and their nuances, the commitment to getting everything right is exhaustive. Once again using all available resources including the vintage community, players, and original engineering data, Gibson Custom started with the simple assumption that nothing was impossible and everything must be explored.

Molecular Level Accuracy-True Historic Plastic

True Historic guitars feature re-formulated plastics based on lab analysis of original parts that were provided for study by the vintage guitar community. Each part has been recreated with the sole purpose of being exactly the right color, made from the right materials, and to look, feel, and perform as if they were plucked from an original 1950's Gibson guitar. Even the tooling marks and original part numbers are recreated. True Historic plastics include the Toggle Washer, Cream Jackplate, Cream Pickguard, Pickup Mounting Rings and Toggle Switch Cap.

True Historic Knobs-Blacklight Tested

True Historic Les Paul knobs are now made from the same materials as the originals and are hand-painted in a two-part process by filling the numbers from the inside of the knob in one pass, then the knob's color in a second pass. Evidence of their accuracy comes in the way of "the backlight test", a common test for the authenticity of vintage Gibson knobs. Because the True Historic knobs are recreated based on lab analysis of original, 50's counterparts, they too glow subtly under blacklight. They've also been redesigned so their splines line up properly to fit the shaft of the CTS potentiometers. All of this required completely new engineering and tooling.

Double-Carved Top-Carved Twice & Hand Sanded to Retain Proper Dish Shape

To recapture the top carve profile of original Vintage Gibson Les Pauls, all True Historic Les Pauls are double-carved by CNC, with the final shape of their dish carve achieved through a hand-sanding process. This replaces the single-pass carving and "slack-belting" process previously in place, and retains the more prominent dish carve and softer edges as found on Les Pauls of the 1950's.

True Historic Neck-Hand Sanded Profile, Rounded Fingerboard Binding

Like the new top carve process, the necks on all True Historic guitars are double-carved and then hand-sanded to achieve that legendary vintage Gibson neck profile; the "beefy", solid feel of a beautifully hand-crafted Les Paul that rests in the player's hand like no other guitar.

Rounded Fingerboard Binding-All About Feel

To make playability a dream, each neck's fingerboard binding is rounded by hand to capture the feel of a broken-in vintage Les Paul. The result is an effortless, smooth playing experience, the likes of which we've found on the best of vintage, original Les Pauls. It's a small but key detail when it comes to putting the closest thing to an original in your hands.

True Historic

Historically accurate peghead thickness

Historically accurate switch tip

Historically accurate switch washer

Historically accurate pickup rings

Historically accurate pickup covers

Historically accurate top carve

Historically accurate original-style thin lacquer finish

Historically accurate perimeter shape

Historically accurate back edge radius

Historically accurate pick guard

Historically accurate knobs

These are just a few examples of how far Gibson Custom has gone in its quest to bring you as close as possible to the ownership experience one gets with an original 1950's Les Paul. Pick up a True Historic Les Paul and feel it resonate through you, and how the neck seems to be made for your hand. Plug it in and hear it growl when you lean on it then chime when you lay back. You'll find that "that" guitar that everyone's been talking about for nearly sixty years can now be yours too, and for a couple of hundred thousand dollars less.

USING THE GUIDE

UNDERSTANDING THE VALUES

The values presented in *The Official Vintage Guitar Price Guide* are for excellent-condition, all-original instruments. Our definition of excellent condition allows for some wear, but the instrument should be well-maintained, with no significant blemishes, wear, repairs, or damage. All-original means the instrument has the parts and finish it had when it left the factory. Replacement parts and refinishes can greatly affect value, as can the appropriate case (or cover) in excellent condition. In many instances, a "wrong" case will not greatly affect value, but with the top-dollar collectibles, it can.

We use a range of excellent-condition values, as there is seldom agreement on a single price point for vintage and used instruments. A tighter range suggests there is a general consensus, while a wide range means the market isn't in strict agreement. A mint-condition instrument can be worth more than the values listed here, and anything in less-than-excellent condition will have a reduced value. And, of course, when dealing with high-end collectibles, values can quickly change.

Repairs affect value differently. Some repair is necessary to keep an instrument in playable condition. The primary concern is the level of expertise displayed in the work and an amateurish repair will lower the value more than one that is obviously professional. A refinished guitar, regardless of the quality of the work, is generally worth 50% or less of the values shown in *The Guide*. A poorly executed neck repair or significant body repair can mean a 50% reduction in a guitar's value. A professional re-fret or minor, nearly invisible body repair will reduce a guitar's value by only 5%.

The values in the *The Guide* are for unfaded finishes. Slight color fade reduces the value by only 5%, but heavily faded examples can reduce the value by 25% to 50%.

FINDING THE INFORMATION

The table of contents shows the major sections and each is organized in alphabetical order by brand, then by model. In a few instances, there are separate sections for a company's most popular models, especially when there is a large variety of similar instruments. Examples include Fender's Stratocasters, Telecasters, Precision and Jazz basses, and Gibson's Les Pauls. The outer top corner of each page uses a dictionary-type header that tells the models or brands on that page. This provides a quick way to navigate each section.

The Guide has excellent brand histories and in most cases the guitar section has the most detailed information for each brand. When possible, *The Guide* lists each model's years of availability and any design changes that affect values.

More information on many of the brands covered in *The Guide* is available in the pages of *Vintage Guitar* magazine and on the "Features" section of our website, www.VintageGuitar.com.

The authors of *The Guide* appreciate your help, so if you find any errors or have additional information on certain brands or models, we'd like to hear from you. We are especially looking for info on any brand not yet listed. Whatever you may have to contribute, feel free to drop us a line at Alan@VintageGuitar.com.

NEW RETAIL PRICING INFORMATION

The Guide continues to add information on individual luthiers and smaller shops. It's difficult to develop values on used instruments produced by these builders because much of their output is custom work, production is low, and/or they haven't been producing for a period of time sufficient to see their instruments enter the used/resale market. To give you an idea about their instruments, we've developed five grades of retail values for new instruments. These convey only the prices charged by the builder, and are not indicative of the quality of construction. *The Guide* applies this scale to all builders and manufacturers of new instruments.

The five retail-price grades are:
Budget - up to $250,
Intermediate - $251 to $1,000,
Professional - $1,001 to $3,000,
Premium - $3,001 to $10,000,
Presentation - more than $10,000.

The Guide uses the terms "production" and "custom" to differentiate between builders who do true custom work versus those who offer standard production models. "Production" means the company offers specific models, with no variations. "Custom" means they do only custom orders, and "production/custom" indicates they do both. Here's an example:

Herring Guitars
2008-present. Premium grade, custom, solidbody guitars built by luthier Dawn Herring in Bismarck, North Dakota. She also builds basses.

This tells who the builder is, the type of instruments they build, where they build them, how long they've been operating under that brand, that they do only custom work, and that they ask between $3,000 and $10,000 for their guitars (premium-grade).

We've applied the retail price grades and production and/or custom labels to most new-instrument manufacturers.

INTRODUCTION

This is the 25th year that we have published *The Official Vintage Guitar Price Guide.* As we compile each edition, we notice trends. While there's always a degree of subjectivity in such discussions, we offer these observations on some of the hottest-selling instruments.

Among Fender models, the 2004-'06 Robin Trower Custom Shop (by Todd Krause) Artist Signature Series is up 25%, as are Jeff Beck Signature Stratocasters from the '90s and early 2000s. 1980 and '81 models like Stratocasters and Custom Telecasters IIs are finding new favor and pulling closer to similar '78 and '79 models due to their moderate price point and evolving market demographics. All colors and all variations of '60s Fender Coronado models are up 25%, and sunburst versions have pulled even with the solid-color finishes.

Also up 25% are '90s Fender Jag-Stang models (perhaps reflecting Kurt Cobain's lasting popularity), '60s Fender acoustics like the King, Kingman, Malibu, Newporter, Palomino, and Shenandoah, and the '90s Stratocaster XII; historically a $650 guitar, it now regularly fetches $900.

The '80s and early-'90s Japanese-made Fender Esquire Customs are gaining popularity because of their high quality and playability at a reasonable price.

The mid-'90s Gibson Les Paul Special (reissue) has increased in value by 25%; in general, instruments from the '90s continue to gain popularity. At $1,000, it's affordable, is 25 years old, and has appeal for a new generation of collectors. The Melody Maker ¾ has also increased dramatically, as players and collectors pay less attention to the differences between the ¾ body and the full-size models of the early '60s.

The early-'80s Gibson B.B. King Custom is up 10%, sitting equal to the re-named Lucille. The Corvus also continues to move up.

The 2007 Gibson DG-335 Dave Grohl (Inspired By series) continues to increase in value and is a good example of a piece that can fetch more than its retail price when new.

The 1969-'71 Gibson Citation is up 25%. An instrument with an interesting history, in recent years it was very hot and became hard to find for sale. Now, they are reappearing and prices vary according to the degree of figure in their tops.

Those lucky enough to own a '74 Gibson Les Paul Custom 20th

This year's cover of *The Guide* features "Spot," a '59 Gibson Les Paul Standard belonging to guitarist (and *Vintage Guitar* 2014 Artist of the Year) Joe Bonamassa, who regularly tours the world with a bevy of highly collectible vintage instruments. He gave Spot its name because of the deep-red shading on its lower bout, near the strap button. "There's an obvious sonic difference between it and any other guitar I own," he said. "It's the only 'Burst I have with its pickup covers popped off, and when people hear it... game over! It's a great guitar and a true road dog." Spot is surrounded by a 1957 Gibson Les Paul Junior (left) and another '59 Standard (right). Mixed in the background are a '61 Les Paul (SG) Standard, a '57 Les Paul goldtop, a '58 Les Paul Junior plectrum, and a Les Paul Recording from 1973.

Joe Bonamassa photo: Rick Gould.

THE 42 INDEX

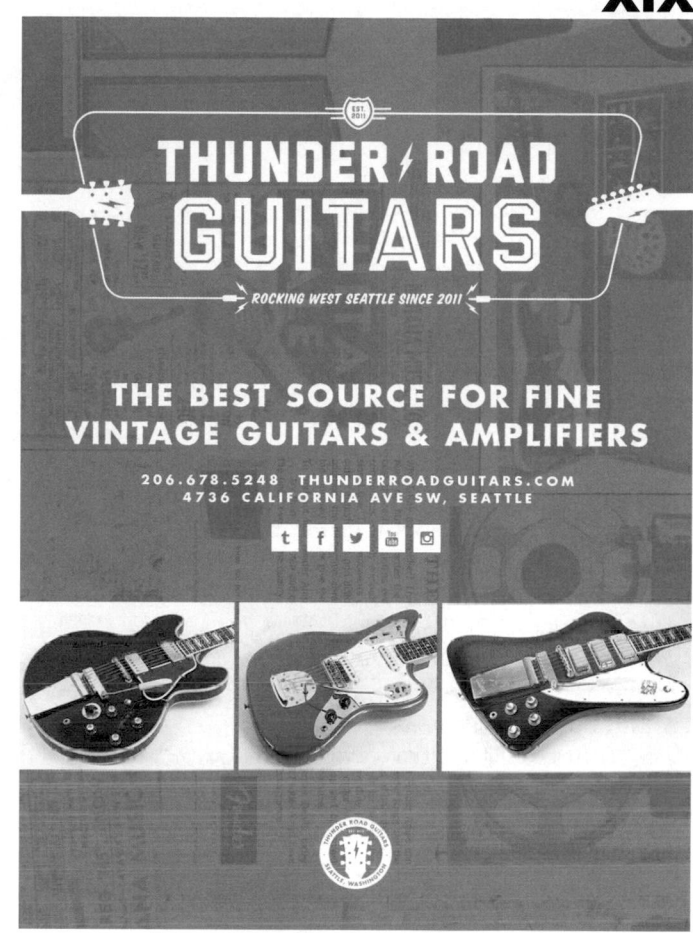

Anniversary Model with black finish will find a 25% increase in value. The cherry sunburst and natural-finish models also saw an increase, but have a slightly lower value.

The '40s Southern Jumbo (SJ) family is up by 25% to 40% including the war-era "banner headstock" and later non-banner models.

In the over-$6,000 segment, the Gibson ES-350N and ES-350 (sunburst) from the '40s and '50s increased in value by more than 25%.

For many years, Martin's electric flat-tops from the '50s have been undervalued. This year, the 00-18E, D-18E, and D-28E increased 20%. Experts have always discounted their amplified sounds, but enthusiasts today apparently disagree.

Other guitars up 20% to 25% include '60s Supro Folkstar, Dean's U.S.-made '70s and '80s ML, V, and Z, Brian Moore's C-series from the '90s/2000s, Pensa-Suhr Classic, Custom, and Standard models from the '80s and '90s, and PRS' Custom 22 12-strings with 10-tops from the 2000s.

In the bass market, Charvels from the '80s and '90s have become popular, with increases in the 25% range across the board. Fender Bass VIs are up, thanks to their '70s cool (*and* '70s affordability!), and among Epiphone instruments, the '60s Embassy Deluxe (with Wilshire body), the '79-'80 Genesis, and the '60s Rivoli (cousin of the Gibson EB-2) are all up.

Always-popular Marshall amps have seen increases, most notably those made since the late '80s, such as the JTM 45 Model 1987 reissue,

(LEFT) Vintage Guitar publisher and *The Guide* co-author, Alan Greenwood, with his '66 Gibson ES-335. (RIGHT) *The Guide* co-author Gil Hembree with an '85 Blue Flower Telecaster and a '85 Pink Paisley Stratocaster.

which increased 50%. Meanwhile, the original JTM 45, made in 1962, has not changed in value over the last four years. More money is flowing into recently built amplifiers than the vintage pieces because old amps are out of range for most buyers. This phenomenon also effects the guitar market, where certain high-quality U.S.- and Japanese-made models made from '85 to '99 are seeing higher appreciation than some from the '50s and '60s.

A popular part of *The Guide* is The 42 Guitar Index, designed to offer an overview of the market via an easy-to-understand graphic. The Index is comprised of 42 collectible models from the '60s or earlier – 14 each from Fender, Gibson, and Martin and it tracks pricing data on

GUITAR DEALER PARTICIPANTS

The information refined on these pages comes from several sources, including the input of many knowledgeable guitar dealers. Without the help of these individuals, it would be very hard for us to provide the information here and in each issue of Vintage Guitar magazine. We deeply appreciate the time and effort they provide.

Andy Eder
Andy's Guitars
Brian Goff
Bizarre Guitars
Les Haynie & Tim Grear
Blue Moon Music
Dave Belzer
Burst Brothers
Walter Carter & Christie Carter
Carter Vintage
David Kalt
Chicago Music Exchange
Dave Rogers
Dave's Guitar Shop
Drew Berlin
Drew Berlin's Vintage Guitars

Stan Werbin & S.J. "Frog" Forgey
Elderly Instruments
Dewey Bowen
Freedom Guitar
Rick Hogue
Garrett Park Guitars
Richard Johnston
Gryphon Strings
Vallis Kolbeck
GuitarVille (Seattle)
Kennard Machol & Leonard Coulson
Intermountain Guitar & Banjo
Jim Singleton
Jim's Guitars
Dave Hinson
Killer Vintage

Kevin Borden & Ben Sopranzetti
Kebo's BassWorks
Timm Kummer
Kummer's Vintage Instruments
Buzzy Levine
Lark Street Music
Larry Wexer
Laurence Wexer, Ltd.
Jim Baggett
Mass Street Music
Artie Leider
McKenzie River Music
Neal Shelton
Neals Music (California)

Lowell Levinger
Players Vintage Instruments
Howie Statland
Rivington Guitars
Mike Reeder
Mike's Music
Eliot Michael
Rumble Seat Music
Mike Rock
Sam Ash Music Stores
Eric Schoenberg
Schoenberg Guitars
Richard Friedman & David Davidson
We Buy Guitars
Nate Westgor
Willie's American Guitars

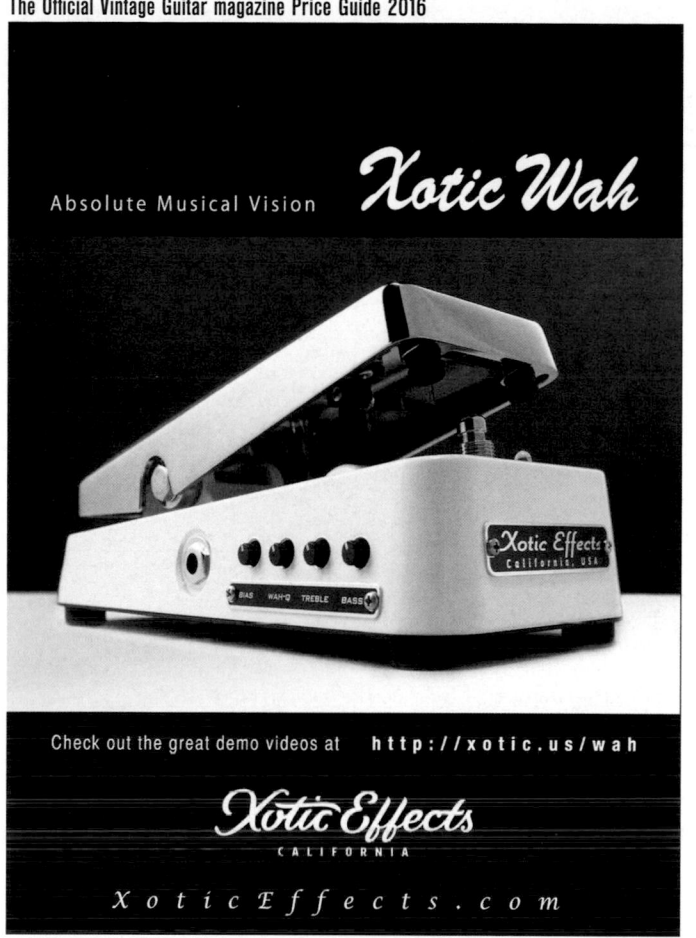

those instruments going back to 1991. In the list of the instruments, please note the Index excludes the highest-end instruments made by each company (i.e. '58 Les Paul Standard, pre-war Martin D-45, and early custom-color Fender Strats) because they are outside the norm and more affected by speculation.

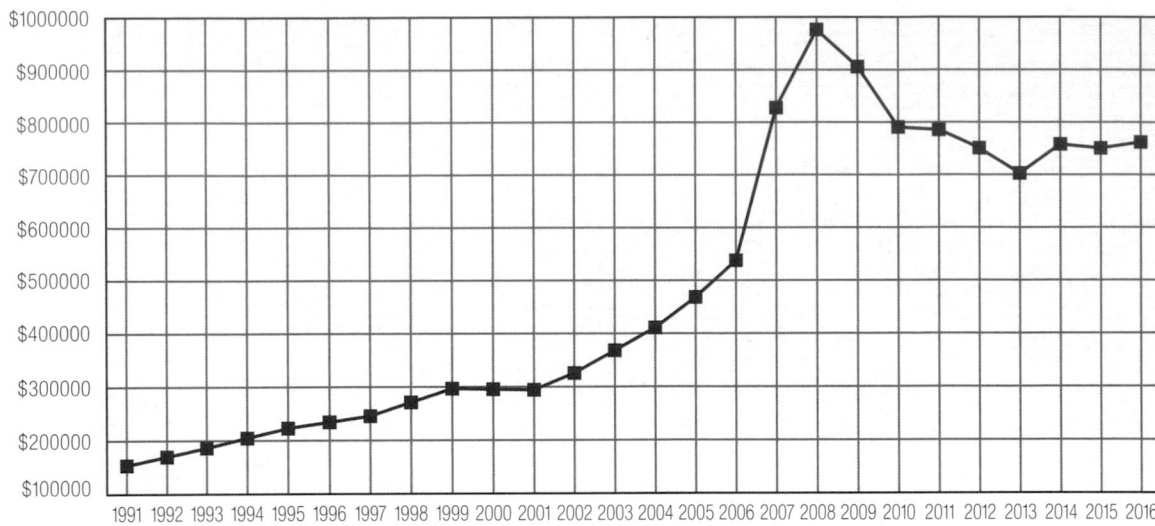

The 42 Guitar Index 1991 - 2016

Through 1999, the Index saw an average yearly increase of a healthy 8.6 percent. Following a two-year plateau, it experienced a faster rise over the next five years followed by an amazing increase in 2007 and '08. There were many reasons, but the primary factor was a strong economy that brought increased interest in all types of investments – homes, stocks, art, and guitars. All of those were affected by the recession beginning 2008, and the 42 Index declined over the next five years. This year, the Index increased by 1.5%. Sixty-seven percent of the 42 guitars increased in value, but that positive trend was diminished by large valuation declines in two expensive Gibson models – the '58 Les Paul Custom and '58 ES-335N. Both declined by 15%.

MORE INFORMATION

VintageGuitar.com has a vast amount of information and articles from the 30-year history of *Vintage Guitar* magazine, including interviews with noted guitarists, reviews of new gear and recordings, and historical information on many of the brands and models covered in this book. Plus, you can sign up for one or all of our free e-mail

newsletters - *VG* Overdrive for general guitar interest, *VG* Acoustic, and *VG* Signal Chain on effects – which each offer more of the type of the articles you get each month in *VG*. You can also read more on classic guitars and your favorite players each month in *Vintage Guitar*, now also offered in digital. Subscribe online at our website or find it on the newsstand. Find us on Facebook, Twitter and Instagram where we talk guitars and offer prizes. We'd love to have you join us.

If a model is missing from *The Guide*, or if you'd like something clarified, please drop a line to Gil@VintageGuitar.com. If you have information on your favorite brand or are a builder and would like to be included or want to correct your info, email Alan@Vintage-Guitar.com.

ACKNOWLEDGEMENTS

The Guide is a huge undertaking. We use many sources to determine values, but the vintage instrument dealers who give their time and expertise to provide market information play an important role. Many provide info on brands and models, and they are acknowledged on XX.

As always, Randy Klimpert provided values, information and photos for the ukulele section and Michael Dregni provided values and information for the effects section. Stan Werbin, of Elderly Instruments, provided many photos for the banjo section. Hundreds of readers and builders have contributed other photos.

Several people at *VG* play an important role, as well. This project would not be possible without the efforts of Wanda Huether, Assistant Editor of The Guide. The amazing covers, layout, and design of the book are from Doug Yellow Bird, *VG*'s Creative Director. Jeanine Shea does most of the proofreading. We thank all of them for their usual fine work.

We welcome suggestions, criticisms, and ideas to improve future editions of The Guide. Contact us at Vintage Guitar, Inc., PO Box 7301, Bismarck, ND 58507, or by e-mail to Gil@VintageGuitar.com or Alan@VintageGuitar.com.

Thank you,
Alan Greenwood and Gil Hembree

BUILDER UPDATES AND CORRECTIONS

If you produce instruments for sale and would like to be included in the next edition of *The Guide*, send your infomation to Alan@VintageGuitar.com. Include info on the types of instruments you build, model names and prices, yearly production, the year you started, where you are located and a short bio about yourself.

If you spot errors in the information about brands and models in this guide, or have information on a brand you'd like to see included, please contact us at the above email address. Your help is appreciated.

GUITARS

GUITARS

Abel Axe

Alan Carruth Mahogany SJ

MODEL YEAR	FEATURES	EXC. COND. LOW	HIGH

17th Street Guitars

2004-2009. Founded by Dave Levine and Colin Liebich. Professional grade, production/custom, solidbody guitars built by luthier John Carruthers in Venice, California.

A Fuller Sound

1998-present. Professional and premium grade, custom nylon and steel-string flat-tops built by Luthier Warren Fuller in Oakland, California.

Abel

1994-present. Custom aircraft-grade aluminum body, wood neck, guitars built by twins Jim and Jeff Abel in Evanston, Wyoming. They offered the Abel Axe from '94-'96 and 2000-'01, and still do custom orders. They also made the Rogue Aluminator in the late '90s.

Axe

1994-1996. Offset double-cut aluminum body with dozens of holes in the body, wood neck, various colors by annodizing the aluminum body. Abel Axe logo on the headstock.

1994-1996	Non-trem or trem	$625	$775

Abilene

Budget and intermediate grade, production, acoustic and electric guitars imported by Samick.

Abyss

See listing under Pederson Custom Guitars.

Acme

1960s. Imported inexpensive copy electric guitar models for the student market.

Acoustic

Ca. 1965-ca. 1987, 2001-2005, 2008-present. Mainly known for solidstate amps, the Acoustic Control Corp. of Los Angeles, California, did offer guitars and basses from around '69 to late '74. The brand has been revived on a new line of amps.

Black Widow

1969-1970, 1972-1974. Double-cut body, 2 pickups, and protective pad on back. The early version (AC500) had 22 frets, ebonite 'board and later one was 24 frets, rosewood 'board. Acoustic outsourced production, possibly to Japan, but final 200 or so guitars produced by Semie Moseley. The AC700 Black Widow 12-string was also available for '69-'70.

1969-1970	2 pickups	$1,100	$1,375
1972-1974	1 pickup	$1,000	$1,275

Agile

1985-present. Budget grade, production, acoustic and electric guitars imported by Rondo Music of Union, New Jersey. They also offer mandolins.

Aims

Ca. 1972-ca. 1976. Aims (American International Music Sales, Inc.) instruments, distributed by Ran-

MODEL YEAR	FEATURES	EXC. COND. LOW	HIGH

dall Instruments in the mid-'70s, were copies of classic American guitar and bass models. They also offered a line of Aims amps during the same time.

Airline

Ca. 1958-1968, 2004-present. Airline originally was a brand used by Montgomery Ward on acoustic, electric archtop and solidbody guitars and basses, amplifiers, steels, and possibly banjos and mandolins. Instruments manufactured by Kay, Harmony and Valco. In '04, the brand was revived on a line of imported intermediate grade, production, reissues from Eastwood guitars.

Acoustic Res-O-Glas Resonator

1964. Res-o-glas, coverplate with M-shaped holes, asymmetrical peghead.

1964		$750	$950

Amp-In-Case Model

1960s. Double-cut, single pickup, short scale guitar with amplifier built into the case, Airline on grille.

1960s		$625	$775

Archtop Acoustic

1950s-1960s. Various models.

1950s-60s	Higher-end	$300	$500
1950s-60s	Lower-end	$125	$300

Electric Hollowbody

1950s-1960s. Various models.

1950s	Kay Barney Kessel Artist copy	$700	$875
1960s	ES-175 copy	$500	$625
1960s	Harmony H-54 Rocket II copy	$500	$625
1960s	Harmony H-75 copy	$550	$675
1960s	Harmony H-76 Rocket III copy	$900	$1,125
1960s	Kay Barney Kessel Swingmaster copy	$700	$875
1960s	Kay Swingmaster copy	$425	$525
1960s	Kay Tuxedo copy	$700	$875
1960s	National Town & Country copy	$650	$800

Electric Res-O-Glas

1960s. Res-o-glas is a form of fiberglass. The bodies and sometimes the necks were made of this material.

1960s	Model 7283 Jack White style, 3 on a side tuners,	$1,800	$2,200
1960s	Model 7283, JB Hutto style, 6 on side tuners, red	$1,800	$2,200
1960s	Other styles, 1 pickup	$400	$800
1960s	Other styles, 2 pickups	$950	$1,200
1960s	Other styles, 3 pickups	$1,800	$2,200

Electric Res-O-Glas Resonator

1960s. Res-o-glas is a form of fiberglass. These models have resonator cones in the body.

1960s		$775	$975

MODEL YEAR	FEATURES	EXC. COND. LOW	HIGH

Electric Solidbody (Standard Lower-End)
1950s-1960s. Various models.

1950s-60s		$150	$375

Electric Solidbody (Deluxe Higher-End)
1950s-1960s. Appointments may include multiple pickups, block inlays, additional logos, more binding.

1950s		$725	$900
1960s		$650	$800

Flat-Top Acoustic
1950s-1960s. Various models.

1950s-60s	Higher-end, 14"-15" body	$300	$500
1950s-60s	Lower-end, 13" body	$125	$300

Alamo
1947-1982. Founded by Charles Eilenberg, Milton Fink, and Southern Music, San Antonio, Texas, and distributed by Bruno & Sons. Alamo started out making radios, phonographs, and instrument cases. In '49 they added amplifiers and lap steels. From '60 to '70, the company produced beginner-grade solidbody and hollow-core body electric Spanish guitars. The amps were all-tube until the '70s. Except for a few Valco-made examples, all instruments were built in San Antonio.

Electric Hollowbody

1950s-70s	Higher-end	$475	$600
1950s-70s	Lower-end	$300	$475

Electric Solidbody

1950s-70s	Higher-end	$475	$600
1950s-70s	Lower-end	$300	$475

Alamo Guitars
1999-2008. The Alamo brand was revived for a line of handcrafted, professional grade, production/custom, guitars by Alamo Music Products, which also offered Robin and Metropolitan brand guitars and Rio Grande pickups.

Tonemonger
2002-2005. Ash or African Fakimba offset double cut solidbody, 3 single coils, tremolo.

2002-2005		$700	$875

Alan Carruth
1970-present. Professional and premium grade, production/custom, classical and archtop guitars built by luthier Alan Carruth in Newport, New Hampshire. He started out building dulcimers and added guitars in '74. He also builds violins and harps.

Albanus
Late 1950s-1973. Luthier Carl Albanus Johnson built around 100 high quality archtop guitars in Chicago, Illinois. He died in '73. He also built violins.

Alberico, Fabrizio
1998-present. Luthier Fabrizio Alberico builds his premium grade, custom, flat-top and classical guitars in Cheltenham, Ontario.

Alden
2005-present. Budget and intermediate grade, production, acoustic and electric guitars, and basses designed by Alan Entwhistle and imported from China.

Alden (Chicago)
1960s. Chicago's Alden was a department store and mail-order house offering instruments from Chicago builders such as Harmony.

H-45 Stratotone
1960s. Alden's version of the H45 Stratotone Mars model, single plain cover pickup.

1960s		$450	$600

Alembic
1969-present. Premium and presentation grade, production/custom, guitars, baritones, and 12-strings built in Santa Rosa, California. They also build basses. Established in San Francisco by Ron and Susan Wickersham, Alembic started out as a studio working with the Grateful Dead and other bands on a variety of sound gear. By '70 they were building custom basses, later adding guitars and cabinets. By '73, standardized models were being offered.

California Special
1988-2009. Double-cut neck-thru solidbody, six-on-a-side tuners, various colors.

1988-2009		$2,100	$2,625

Orion
1990-present. Offset double-cut glued neck solidbody, various colors.

1990-2014		$2,100	$2,600

Series I
Early-1970s-present. Neck-thru, double-cut solidbody, bookmatched koa, black walnut core, 3 pickups, optional body styles available, natural.

1970s-2013	12-string	$4,300	$5,300
1970s-2014	6-string	$4,100	$5,100

Alfieri Guitars
1990-present. Luthier Don Alfieri builds his premium and presentation grade, custom/production, acoustic and classical guitars in Long Island, New York.

Alhambra
1930s. The Alhambra brand was most likely used by a music studio (or distributor) on instruments made by others, including Regal-built resonator instruments.

Allen Guitars
1982-present. Premium grade, production resonators, steel-string flat-tops, and mandolins built by Luthier Randy Allen, Colfax, California.

Alleva-Coppolo Basses and Guitars
1995-present. Professional and premium grade, custom/production, solidbody electric guitars and

Alembic Orion

Allen Resophonic

AlumiSonic 1100-FR

Alvarez 5024
Doug Brazzell

MODEL YEAR	FEATURES	EXC. COND. LOW	HIGH

basses built by luthier Jimmy Coppolo in Dallas, Texas for '95-'97, in New York City for '98-2008, and since in Upland, California.

Aloha

1935-1960s. Private branded by Aloha Publishing and Musical Instruments Company, Chicago, Illinois. Made by others. There was also the Aloha Manufacturing Company of Honolulu which made musical instruments from around 1911 to the late '20s.

Alosa

1947-1958. Luthier Alois Sandner built these acoustic archtop guitars in Germany.

Alpha

1970s-1980s. One of the brand names of guitars built in the Egmond plant in Holland. Sold by Martin for a while in the 1980s.

Alray

1967. Electrics and acoustics built by the Holman-Woodell guitar factory in Neodesha, Kansas, who also marketed similar models under the Holman brand.

Alternative Guitar and Amplifier Company

2006-present. Intermediate grade, custom/production, solidbody electric guitars and basses made in Piru, California, by luthiers Mal Stich and Sal Gonzales and imported from Korea under the Alternative Guitar and Amplifier Company, and Mal n' Sal brands.

AlumiSonic

2006-present. Luthier Ray Matter builds his production/custom, professional grade, aluminum/wood hybrid electric guitars in Bohemia and West Islip, New York.

Alvarez

1965-present. Intermediate and professional grade, production, acoustic guitars imported by St. Louis Music. They also offer lap steels, banjos and mandolins. Initially high-quality handmade guitars Yairi made by K. (Kazuo) Yairi were exclusively distributed, followed by lower-priced Alvarez line. In '90 the Westone brand used on electric guitars and basses was replaced with the Alvarez name; these Alvarez electrics were offered until '02. Many Alvarez electric models designed by luthier Dana Sutcliffe; several models designed by Dan Armstrong.

Classic I, II, III

1994-1999. Designs based on classic solidbody American models.

1994-1999		$200	$300

Flat-Top (Lower-End)

1966-present. Beginner-grade instruments, solid or laminate tops, laminate back and sides, little or no extra appointments. Some are acoustic/electric.

1970s-90s		$75	$150

Flat-Top (Mid-Level)

1966-present. Solid tops, laminated back and sides, lower appointments such as bound 'boards and headstocks, nickel hardware and pearl inlay.

1970s-90s		$100	$225

Flat-Top (Mid-to-Higher-End)

1966-present. Solid spruce tops, solid mahogany or rosewood backs, laminated mahogany or rosewood sides, may have scalloped bracing, mid-level appointments like abalone headstock inlay, soundhole rosettes and herringbone body binding.

1970s-90s		$225	$400

Flat-Top (Higher-End)

1966-present. Solid rosewood and/or mahogany backs and sides, solid spruce tops, may have dovetail neck joint, highest appointments like abalone inlay and real maple binding.

1980s-90s		$400	$650

Alvarez Yairi

1966-present. Alvarez Yairi guitars are hand-crafted and imported by St. Louis Music.

Flat-Top (Mid-Level)

Solid top of cedar or spruce, depending on model, mid-level appointments.

1970s-90s		$300	$500
2000s		$300	$500

Flat-Top (Higher-End)

Solid top of cedar or spruce, depending on model, higher-end appointments.

1970s-90s		$600	$800
2000s		$600	$800

Alvarez, Juan

1952-present. Professional and premium grade, production/custom, classical and flamenco guitars made in Madrid, Spain, originally by luthier Juan Alvarez Gil and now by son Juan Miguel Alvarez.

American Acoustech

1993-2001. Production steel string flat-tops made by Tom Lockwood (former Guild plant manager) and Dave Stutzman (of Stutzman's Guitar Center) as ESVL Inc. in Rochester, New York.

American Archtop Guitars

1995-present. Premium and presentation grade, custom 6- and 7-string archtops by luthier Dale Unger, in Stroudsburg, Pennsylvania.

American Conservatory (Lyon & Healy)

Late-1800s-early-1900s. Guitars, mandolins and harp guitars built by Chicago's Lyon & Healy and sold mainly through various catalog retailers. Mid-level instruments above the quality of Lyon & Healy's Lakeside brand, and generally under their Washburn brand.

Acoustic

1920s	Spanish 6-string	$500	$625
1920s	Tenor 4-string	$500	$625

MODEL YEAR	FEATURES	EXC. COND. LOW	HIGH

G2740 Monster Bass

Early-mid-1900s. Two 6-string neck (one fretless), acoustic flat-top harp guitar, spruce top, birch back and sides with rosewood stain, natural. Their catalog claimed it was "Indispensable to the up-to-date mandolin and guitar club."

1917		$3,200	$4,000

Style G Series Harp Guitar

Early-1900s. Two 6-string necks with standard tuners, 1 neck fretless, rosewood back and sides, spruce top, fancy rope colored wood inlay around soundhole, sides and down the back center seam.

1917	Natural	$3,200	$4,000

American Showster

1986-2004, 2010-2011. Established by Bill Meeker and David Haines, Bayville, New Jersey, building guitars shaped like classic car tailfins or motorcycle gas tanks. The Custom Series was made in the U.S.A., while the Standard Series (introduced in '97) was made in Czechoslovakia. They also made a bass. Bill Meeker started production again around 2010 until his death in late '11.

AS-57 Classic

1987-2004. American-made until 2000, body styled like a '57 Chevy tail fin, basswood body, bolt-on neck, 1 humbucker or 3 single-coils, various colors.

1987-1999	U.S.-made	$3,700	$4,600

AS-57 Classic

1987-2004. American-made until 2000, body styled like a '57 Chevy tail fin, basswood body, bolt-on neck, 1 humbucker or 3 single-coils, various colors.

2000-2004	Import	$1,700	$2,200

Ampeg

1949-present. Founded in '49 by Everett Hull as the Ampeg Bassamp Company in New York and has built amplifiers throughout its history. In '62 the company added instruments with the introduction of their Baby Bass and from '63 to '65, they carried a line of guitars and basses built by Burns of London and imported from England. In '66 the company introduced its own line of basses. In '67, Ampeg was acquired by Unimusic, Inc. From '69-'71 contracted with Dan Armstrong to produce lucite "see-through" guitars and basses with replaceable slide-in pickup design. In '71 the company merged with Magnavox. Beginning around '72 until '75, Ampeg imported the Stud Series copy guitars from Japan. Ampeg shut down production in the spring of '80. MTI bought the company and started importing amps. In '86 St. Louis Music purchased the company. In '97 Ampeg introduced new and reissue American-made guitar and bass models. They discontinued the guitar line in '01, but offered the Dan Armstrong plexi guitar again starting in '05, adding wood-bodied versions in '08. They also offer a bass. In '05 LOUD Technologies acquired SLM and the Ampeg brand.

AMG1

1999-2001. Dan Amstrong guitar features, but with mahogany body with quilted maple top, 2 P-90-style or humbucker-style pickups.

1999-2001	Humbuckers, gold hardware	$625	$800
1999-2001	Kent Armstrong pickups	$375	$475
1999-2001	P-90s, standard hardware	$375	$475

Dan Armstrong Lucite Guitar

1969-1971. Clear plexiglas solidbody, with interchangable pickups, Dan Armstrong reports that around 9,000 guitars were produced, introduced in '69, but primary production was in '70-'71, reissued in '98.

1969-1971	Clear	$2,100	$2,700
1969-1971	Smoke	$2,500	$3,200

Dan Armstrong Plexi Guitar

1998-2001, 2006-2011. Reissue of Lucite guitar, produced by pickup designer Kent Armstrong (son of Dan Armstrong), offered in smoked (ADAG2) or clear (ADAG1). Latest version is Japanese-made ADA6.

1998-2011	Clear or smoke	$800	$1,000

Heavy Stud (GE-150/GEH-150)

1973-1975. Import from Japan, single-cut body, weight added for sustain, single-coils or humbuckers (GEH).

1973-1975		$400	$500

Sonic Six (By Burns)

1964-1965. Solidbody, 2 pickups, tremolo, cherry finish, same as the Burns Nu-Sonic guitar.

1964-1965		$450	$575

Stud (GE-100/GET-100)

1973-1975. Import from Japan, double-cut, inexpensive materials, weight added for sustain, GET-100 included tremolo

1973-1975		$400	$500

Super Stud (GE-500)

1973-1975. Double-cut, weight added for sustain, top-of-the-line in Stud Series.

1973-1975		$400	$500

Thinline (By Burns)

1963-1964. Semi-hollowbody, 2 f-holes, 2 pickups, double-cut, tremolo, import by Burns of London, same as the Burns TR2 guitar.

1963-1964		$625	$775

Wild Dog (By Burns)

1963-1964. Solidbody, 3 pickups, shorter scale, tremolo, sunburst finish, import by Burns of London, same as the Burns Split Sound.

1963-1964		$675	$850

Wild Dog De Luxe (By Burns)

1963-1964. Solidbody, 3 pickups, bound neck, tremolo, sunburst finish, import by Burns of London, same as the Burns Split Sonic guitar.

1963-1964		$700	$875

Anderberg

2002-present. Professional and premium grade, production/custom, electric guitars and basses built by luthier Michael Anderberg in Jacksonville, Florida.

American Archtop Guitars American Legend

1996 American Showster AS-57 Classic

Billy White, Jr.

To get the most from this book, be sure to read "Using *The Guide*" in the introduction.

Andrew White Steel String

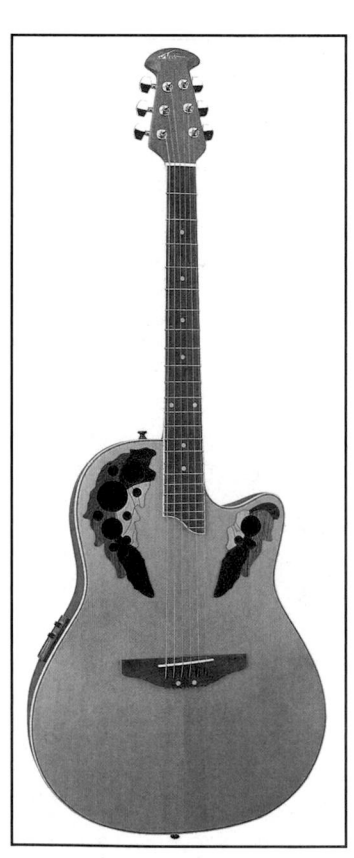

Applause AE148

MODEL YEAR	FEATURES	EXC. COND. LOW	HIGH

Andersen Stringed Instruments

1978-present. Luthier Steve Andersen builds premium and presentation grade, production/custom flat-tops and archtops in Seattle, Washington. He also builds mandolins.

Andreas

1995-2004. Luthier Andreas Pichler built his aluminum-necked, solidbody guitars and basses in Dollach, Austria.

Andrew White Guitars

2000-present. Premium and presentation grade, custom, acoustic flat-top guitars built by luthier Andrew White in Morgantown, West Virginia. He also imports a production line of intermediate and professional grade, acoustic guitars from his factory in Korea.

Andy Powers Musical Instrument Co.

1996-2010. Luthier Andy Powers built his premium and presentation grade, custom, archtop, flat-top, and semi-hollow electric guitars in Oceanside, California. He also built ukes and mandolins.

Angelica

Ca. 1967-1972. Entry-level guitars and basses imported from Japan.

Acoustic

1967-1972		$150	$200

Electric Solidbodies

1967-1972		$200	$275

Angus

1976-present. Professional and premium grade, custom-made steel and nylon string flat-tops built by Mark Angus in Laguna Beach, California.

Antares

1980s-1990s. Korean-made budget electric and acoustic guitars imported by Vega Music International of Brea, California.

Acoustic

1980s-90s	Various models	$100	$175

Double Neck 6/4

1990s. Cherry finish double-cut.

1990s		$450	$575

Solidbody

1980s-90s	Various models	$150	$200

Antique Acoustics

1970s-present. Luthier Rudolph Blazer builds production/custom flat-tops, 12 strings, and archtops in Tubingen, Germany.

Antonio Hermosa

2006-present. Imported budget grade, production, acoustic and acoustic/electric classical guitars from The Music Link.

MODEL YEAR	FEATURES	EXC. COND. LOW	HIGH

Antonio Lorca

Intermediate and professional grade, production, classical guitars made in Valencia, Spain.

Apollo

Ca. 1967-1972. Entry-level guitars imported by St. Louis Music. They also offered basses and effects.

Electric

1967-1972. Japanese imports.

1967-1972	Advanced model, 4 pickups	$375	$475
1967-1972	Mid-range model	$250	$325
1967-1972	Standard model, less features	$175	$250

Applause

1976-present. Budget grade, production, acoustic and acoustic/electric guitars, basses, mandolins and ukes and previously solidbody electrics. Originally Kaman Music's entry-level Ovation-styled brand, it is now owned by Drum Workshop, Inc. The instruments were made in the U.S. until around '82, when production was moved to Korea. On the U.S.-made guitars, the back of the neck was molded Urelite, with a cast aluminum neck combining an I-beam neck reinforcement, fingerboard, and frets in one unit. The Korean models have traditional wood necks.

AA Models

1976-1990s. Acoustic, laminate top, plastic or composition body. Specs and features can vary on AA Models.

1976-1981	U.S.-made	$175	$225
1980s-90s	Import	$100	$150

AE Models

1976-present. Acoustic/electric, laminate top, plastic or composition body. Specs and features can vary on AE Models.

1976-1981	U.S.-made	$225	$275
1980s-90s	Import	$125	$175
2000-2014	Import	$125	$175

Applegate

2001-present. Premium grade, production/custom, acoustic and classical guitars built by luthier Brian Applegate in Minneapolis, Minnesota.

APS Custom

2005-present. Luthier Andy Speake builds his production/custom, professional and premium grade, solidbody guitars in Victoria, British Columbia.

Arbor

1983-ca. 2013. Budget and intermediate grade, production, classical, acoustic, and solid and semi-hollow body electric guitars imported by Musicorp (MBT). They also offered basses.

Acoustic

1980s-2013	Various models	$75	$125

Electric

1980s-2013	Various models	$150	$200

GUITARS

MODEL YEAR	FEATURES	EXC. COND. LOW	HIGH

Arch Kraft

1933-1934. Full-size acoustic archtop and flat-top guitars. Budget brand produced by the Kay Musical Instrument Company and sold through various distributors.

Acoustic (Archtop or Flat-Top)

1933-1934		$200	$300

Aria Diamond

1960s. Brand name used by Aria in the '60s.

Electric

1960s. Various models and appointments in the '60s.

1960s		$425	$550

Aria/Aria Pro II

1956-present. Budget, intermediate and professional grade, production, electric, acoustic, acoustic/electric, and classical guitars. They also make basses, mandolins, and banjos. Aria was established in Japan in '56 and started production of instruments in '60 using the Arai, Aria, Aria Diamond, and Diamond brands. The brand was renamed Aria Pro II in '75. Aria Pro II was used mainly on electric guitars, with Aria used on others. Over the years, they have produced acoustics, banjos, mandolins, electrics, basses, amplifiers, and effects. Around '87 production of cheaper models moved to Korea, reserving Japanese manufacturing for more expensive models. Around '95 some models were made in U.S., though most contemporary guitars sold in U.S. are Korean. In '01, the Pro II part of the name was dropped altogether.

Early Arias don't have serial numbers or pot codes. Serial numbers began to be used in the mid '70s. At least for Aria guitars made by Matsumoku, the serial number contains the year of manufacture in the first one or two digits (Y##### or YY####). Thus, a guitar from 1979 might begin with 79####. One from 1981 might begin with 1#####. The scheme becomes less sure after 1987. Some Korean-made guitars use a serial number with year and week indicated in the first four digits (YYWW####). Thus 9628#### would be from the 28th week of 1996. However, this is not the case on all guitars, and some have serial numbers which are not date-coded.

Models have been consolidated by sector unless specifically noted.

Acoustic Solid Wood Top

1960s-present. Steel string models, various appointments, generally mid-level imports.

1960s-2014		$300	$375

Acoustic Veneer Wood Top

1960s-present. Steel string models, various appointments, generally entry-level imports.

1960s-2014		$175	$225

Classical Solid Wood Top

1960s-present. Various models, various appointments, generally mid-level imports.

1960s-2014		$250	$325

Classical Veneer Wood Top

1960s-present. Various models, various appointments, generally entry-level imports.

1960s-2014		$150	$200

Fullerton Series

1995-2000. Various models with different appointments and configurations based on the classic offset double-cut soldibody.

1995-2000		$250	$325

Herb Ellis (PE-175/FA-DLX)

1978-1987 (Model PE-175) and 1988-1993 (Model FA-DLX). Archtop hollowbody, ebony 'board, 2 humbuckers.

1978-1993		$475	$600

Solidbody

1960s-present. Various models, various appointments, generally mid-level imports.

1960s-2014		$350	$600

Titan Artist TA Series

1967-2012. Double cut, semi-hollow bodies, 2 pickups, various models.

1967-2012		$350	$600

Aristides

2010-present. Dutch engineer Aristides Poort developed the material (arium) used to build production/custom, premium grade, solidbody electric guitars in the Netherlands. They also build basses.

ARK - New Era Guitars

2006-present. Luthier A. R. Klassen builds his professional and premium grade, production/custom, reproductions of vintage Larson Brothers instruments in Chesterton, Indiana.

Armstrong, Rob

1971-present. Custom steel- and nylon-string flat-tops, 12 strings, and parlor guitars made in Coventry, England by luthier Rob Armstrong. He also builds mandolins and basses.

Arpeggio Korina

1995-present. Professional, premium and presentation grade, production/custom, korina wood solidbody guitars built by luthier Ron Kayfield in Pennsylvania.

Art & Lutherie

Budget and intermediate grade, production, steel- and nylon-string acoustic and acoustic/electric guitars. Founded by luthier Robert Godin, who also has the Norman, Godin, Seagull, and Patrick & Simon brands of instruments.

Artesano

Intermediate and professional grade, production, classical guitars built in Valencia, Spain, and distributed by Juan Orozco. Orozco also made higher-end classical Orozco Models 8, 10 and 15.

Aristides 020 Model

ARK - New Era Guitars Prairie State

Asher Ultra Tone T Deluxe

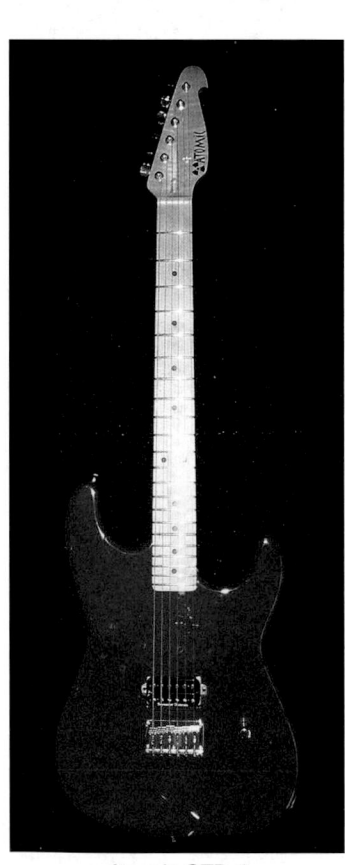

Atomic STD 1

MODEL YEAR	FEATURES	EXC. COND. LOW	HIGH

Artinger Custom Guitars

1997-present. Luthier Matt Artinger builds his professional and premium grade, production/custom, hollow, semi-hollow, and chambered solidbody guitars and basses in Emmaus, Pennsylvania.

Artur Lang

1949-1975. German luthier Artur Lang is best known for his archtops, but did build classicals early on. His was a small shop and much of his output was custom ordered. The instruments were mostly unbranded, but some have L.A. engraved on the headstock.

Asama

1970s-1980s. Some models of this Japanese line of solidbody guitars featured built-in effects. They also offered basses, effects, drum machines and other music products.

Ashborn

1848-1864. James Ashborn, of Wolcottville, Connecticut, operated one of the largest guitar making factories of the mid-1800s. Models were small parlor-sized instruments with ladder bracing and gut strings. Most of these guitars will need repair. Often of more interest as historical artifacts or museum pieces versus guitar collections.

Model 2

1848-1864. Flat-top, plain appointments, no position markers on the neck, identified by Model number.

1855	Fully repaired	$525	$650

Model 5

1848-1864. Flat-top, higher appointments.

1855	Fully repaired	$1,250	$1,550

Asher

1982-present. Luthier Bill Asher builds his professional grade, production/custom, solidbody electric guitars in Venice, California. He also builds lap steels.

Ashland

Intermediate grade, production, acoustic and acoustic/electric guitars made by Korea's Crafter Guitars.

Astro

1963-1964. The Astro AS-51 was a 1 pickup kit guitar sold by Rickenbacker. German luthier Arthur Strohmer also built archtops bearing this name.

Asturias

Professional and premium grade, production, classical guitars built on Kyushu island, in Japan.

Atkin Guitars

1993-present. Luthier Alister Atkin builds his production/custom steel and nylon string flat-tops in Canterbury, England. He also builds mandolins.

MODEL YEAR	FEATURES	EXC. COND. LOW	HIGH

Atlas

Archtop guitars, and possibly other types, built in East Germany and by Zero Sette in Italy.

Atomic

2006-present. Production/custom, intermediate and professional grade, solidbody electric guitars and basses built by luthiers Tim Mulqueeny and Harry Howard in Peoria, Arizona.

Audiovox

Ca. 1935-ca. 1950. Paul Tutmarc's Audiovox Manufacturing, of Seattle, Washington, was a pioneer in electric lap steels, basses, guitars and amps. Tutmarc was a talented Hawaiian steel guitarist and ran a music school and is credited with inventing the electric bass guitar in '35, which his company started selling in the late '30s.

Austin

1999-present. Budget and intermediate grade, production, acoustic, acoustic/electric, resonator, and electric guitars, basses, amps, mandolins, ukes and banjos imported by St. Louis Music.

Acoustic Flat-Top

1999-2014	Various models	$100	$200

Solidbody Electric

1999-2014	Various models	$150	$225

Austin Hatchet

Mid-1970s-mid-1980s. Trademark of distributor Targ and Dinner, Chicago, Illinois.

Hatchet

1981. Travel guitar.

1981		$350	$450

Solidbody Electric

1970s-1980s. Various classic designs.

1970s-80s		$225	$300

Avalon

1920s. Instruments built by the Oscar Schmidt Co. and possibly others. Most likely a brand made for a distributor.

Avalon (Ireland)

2002-present. Luthiers Stevie Graham, Mark Lyttle, Ernie McMillan, Balazs Prohaszka and Robin Thompson build premium and presentation grade, production/custom, steel-string and classical, acoustic and electro-acoustic guitars in Northern Ireland. In '04-'05 their Silver series was imported from South Korea, and '05 the Gold series from Czech Republic.

Avante

1997-2007. Intermediate grade, production, imported sharp cutaway acoustic baritone guitars designed by Joe Veillette and Michael Tobias and offered by MusicYo. Originally higher priced instruments offered by Alvarez, there was the baritone, a 6-string and a bass.

MODEL		EXC. COND.	
YEAR	FEATURES	LOW	HIGH

AV-2 Baritone
1997-2007. Baritone guitar tuned B to B, solid spruce cutaway top, mahogany sides and back.

1997-2007		$275	$350

Avanti
1964-late 1960s. Italian-made guitar brand imported by European Crafts, of Los Angeles. Earlier models were plastic covered; later ones had paint finishes.

Electric Solidbody
1960s. Solidbody, 3 single-coils, dot markers.

1960s		$200	$275

Avar
Late-1960s. Import copy models from Japan, not unlike Teisco, for the U.S. student market.

Solidbody Electric

1969		$225	$300

Aztec
1970s. Japanese-made copy guitars imported into Germany by Hopf.

B.C. Rich
Ca. 1966/67-present. Budget, intermediate, and premium grade, production/custom, import and U.S.-made, electric and acoustic guitars. They also offer basses. Founded by Bernardo Chavez Rico in Los Angeles, California. As a boy he worked for his guitar-maker father Bernardo Mason Rico (Valencian Guitar Shop, Casa Rico, Bernardo's Guitar Shop), building first koa ukes and later, guitars, steel guitars and Martin 12-string conversions. He started using the BC Rich name ca. '66-'67 and made about 300 acoustics until '68, when first solidbody electric made using a Fender neck.

Rich's early models were based on Gibson and Fender designs. First production instruments were in '69 with 10 fancy Gibson EB-3 bass and 10 matching Les Paul copies, all carved out of single block of mahogany. Early guitars with Gibson humbuckers, then Guild humbuckers, and, from '74-'86, DiMarzio humbuckers. Around 150 BC Rich Eagles were imported from Japan in '76. Ca. '76 or '77 some bolt-neck guitars with parts made by Wayne Charvel were offered. Acoustic production ended in '82 (acoustics were again offered in '95).

For '83-'86 the BC Rich N.J. Series (N.J. Nagoya, Japan) was built by Masan Tarada. U.S. Production Series (U.S.-assembled Korean kits) in '84. From '86 on, the N.J. Series was made by Cort in Korea. Korean Rave and Platinum series begin around '86. In '87, Rich agrees to let Class Axe of New Jersey market the Korean Rave, Platinum and N.J. Series. Class Axe (with Neal Moser) introduces Virgin in '87 and in '88 Rave and Platinum names are licensed to Class Axe. In '89, Rico licensed the BC Rich name to Class Axe. Both imported and American-made BC Riches are offered during Class Axe management. In 2000, BC Rich became a division of Hanser Music Group.

During '90-'91, Rico begins making his upscale Mason Bernard guitars (approx. 225 made). In '94, Rico resumes making BC Rich guitars in California. He died in 1999.

First 340-360 U.S.-built guitars were numbered sequentially beginning in '72. Beginning in '74, serial numbers change to YYZZZ pattern (year plus consecutive production). As production increased in the late-'70s, the year number began getting ahead of itself. By '80 it was 2 years ahead; by '81 as much as 4 years ahead. No serial number codes on imports.

The American B.C. Rich company was first and foremost a custom shop, therefore surprising variants are possible for the models described below, especially in the early years of the company. Many of the first models were offered as either a Standard (also called Deluxe) model or as an upgrade called the Supreme model.

The Deluxe or Standard model has diamond markers, unbound rosewood fretboard, three-on-a-side tuners, generally solid mahogany body, some rare examples with maple body or other woods, some with runners or stringers of alternate exotic wood.

The Supreme model has specific options including cloud markers, fully bound ebony fretboard and three-on-a-side headstock, various woods including solid koa, maple, highly-figured maple (birdseye, quilted, curly), other exotic woods offered, most models with runners or stringers of alternating exotic wood, also available as single solid wood, mid-1980s with original Kahler tremolo unit option, custom colors and sunburst finishes generally on a custom order basis, certain custom colors are worth more than the values shown, early models circa '75-'82 had a Leo Quan Badass bridge option and those models are highly favored by collectors, early style control knobs had silver metal inserts and full electronics with Varitone and PreAmp and Grover Imperial bullseye tuners, the earliest models had red head mini-switches (later became silver-chrome switches). Technically speaking the Supreme model only applied to the Mockingbird, Eagle, Bich, and Wave.

The prime collector's market for B.C. Rich is the '72-'85 era. The Seagull, Eagle, Mockingbird, Bich, and Wave models are the true vintage models from that epoch.

Pre-1985 BC Rich Standard Finishes were Natural, Gloss White, Black, Competition Red, Medium Blue, Metallic Red, and Cherry. Any other finish would be a Custom Color. Most custom colors started appearing in late 1978. Prior to '78, guitars had two tone transparent burst finishes, natural finishes and occasional one color paint schemes. Custom Color finishes are worth 10% more than standard finish colors. Special thanks to Matt Touchard for his help with specifications.

Avante AV-2

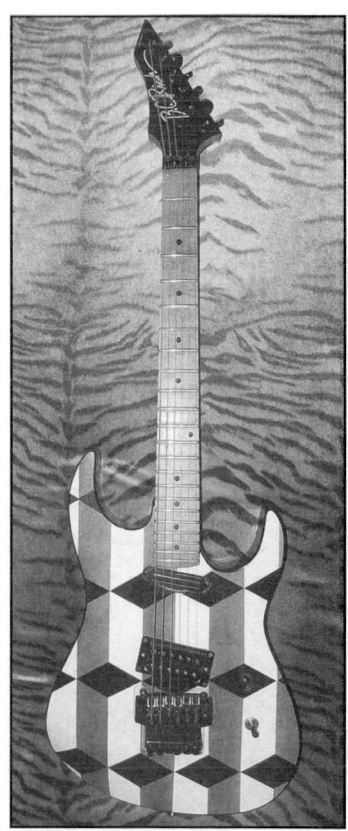

1988 B.C. Rich Assassin
Mike Greco

1980s B.C. Rich Bich

B.C. Rich Exclusive

Rebecca Apodaca

MODEL YEAR	FEATURES	EXC. COND. LOW	HIGH

Assassin
1986-1998, 2000-2010. Double-cut body, 2 humbuckers, maple thru-neck dot markers, various colors.

1986-1989	1st Rico era	$750	$950
1989-1993	Class Axe era, neck-thru	$750	$950
1994-1998	2nd Rico era USA, neck-thru	$650	$850
2000-2010	Includes QX & PX	$280	$360

B-28 Acoustic
Ca.1967-1982. Acoustic flat-top, hand-built, solid spruce top, rosewood back and sides, herringbone trim, pearl R headstock logo.

1967-1982		$800	$1,000

B-30 Acoustic
Ca.1967-1982. Acoustic flat-top.

1967-1982		$800	$1,000

B-38 Acoustic
Ca.1967-1982. Acoustic flat-top, cocobolo back and sides, herringbone trim.

1967-1982		$800	$1,000

B-41 Acoustic
1970s. Brazilian rosewood.

1970s		$1,500	$2,000

B-45 Acoustic
1970s. Hand-built, D-style rosewood body.

1970s		$2,000	$2,500

Beast (U.S.A. Custom Shop)
1999-present. Exaggerated four point cutaway body, flamed or quilted top.

1999-2014		$1,100	$1,375

Bich (U.S.A. Assembly)
1978-1998. Four-point sleek body, came in Standard top or Supreme with highly figured maple body and active EQ.

1978-1979	Standard/Deluxe	$1,900	$2,400
1978-1979	Supreme	$3,200	$4,000
1980-1985	Standard/Deluxe	$1,600	$2,100
1980-1985	Supreme	$2,800	$3,600
1986-1988	Standard/Deluxe	$1,075	$1,400
1986-1988	Supreme	$2,300	$3,000
1989-1993	Class Axe era	$900	$1,125
1994-1998	2nd Rico era USA, bolt-on	$750	$950

Bich 10-String
1977-present. Doubles on 4 low strings.

1977-1982	Highly flamed, koa or koa/maple	$4,300	$5,400
1985	Highly quilted	$4,300	$5,400

Black Hole
1988. Bolt neck, rosewood 'board, integrated pickup design, Floyd Rose.

1988		$250	$325

Body Art Collection
2003-2006. Imports with different exotic graphics on different models issued each month from January '03 to March '04, 25th Anniversary model available into '06, headstock logo states Body Art Collection.

2003	Boris Beast	$215	$275
2003	Skull Pile	$245	$325
2003	Space Face Ironbird	$245	$325
2003	Spiro Light	$215	$275
2003	Torchy ASM	$215	$275
2004	40 Lashes Mockingbird	$245	$325
2004	Umethar Jr. V	$215	$275

Bronze Series
2001-2007. Made in China. Includes 2 models; Mockingbird and Warlock.

2001-2007		$70	$90

Doubleneck Models
1980-1988. Doublenecks were sporadically made and specs (and values) may vary.

1980-1988	Bich	$5,400	$6,700
1980-1988	Eagle	$5,800	$7,300
1980-1988	Iron Bird	$4,400	$5,400
1980-1988	Mockingbird	$5,800	$7,200
1980-1988	Seagull	$6,300	$7,800

Eagle
1975-1982, 2000-2004. Made in USA, often called the Eagle model, but also called Eagle Deluxe or Eagle Standard, features include diamond inlays, unbound rosewood fretboard, 3-on-a-side tuners, generally solid mahogany body, some rare examples with maple body or other woods, some with runners or stringers of alternate exotic wood. (See additional notes in the Eagle Supreme listing.)

1975-1976	Custom Shop	$2,500	$3,100
1977		$2,500	$3,100
1978-1979		$2,300	$2,900
1980-1982		$2,200	$2,800

Eagle Special (U.S.A.)
1977-1982. A variant of the Eagle with even more switches and electronic options, the extra options are not particularly considered an advantage in the BC Rich collector community, therefore an Eagle Special is worth less than the Standard or Eagle Supreme.

1977-1982		$2,000	$2,500

Eagle Supreme
1975-1982, 2000-2004. Made in USA, Eagle body style with specific options including cloud inlays, fully bound ebony fretboard, 3-on-a-side headstock, various woods including solid koa, maple, highly-figured maple (birdseye, quilted, curly), other exotic woods offered, most with runners or stringers of alternating exotic wood, also available as single solid wood, mid-'80s with original Kahler tremolo unit option, custom colors and sunburst finishes generally on a custom order basis, certain custom colors are worth more than the values shown, early models ca. '75-'82 had a Leo Quan Badass bridge option and those models are highly favored by collectors, early style control knobs with silver metal inserts, full electronics with Varitone and PreAmp and Grover Imperial bullseye tuners, the earliest models had red head mini-switches (later became silver-chrome switches).

1975-1976	Custom Shop	$3,900	$4,900
1977		$3,900	$4,900
1978-1979		$3,700	$4,600
1980-1982		$3,600	$4,500
2000-2004		$2,200	$2,750

MODEL		EXC. COND.	
YEAR	FEATURES	LOW	HIGH

Eagle Supreme Condor

1983-1987. Less than 50 made, simplified electronics system based on customer's requests, features can include cloud inlays, fully bound ebony fretboard neck, bound 3-on-a-side headstock, bookmatched figured maple top over solid mahogany body with slight arch, no runners or stringers, basic electronics with master volume, master tone, and pickup switch, also commonly called Condor Supreme.

| 1983-1987 | Common color | $1,600 | $2,000 |

Elvira

2001. Elvira (the witch) photo on black Warlock body, came with Casecore coffin case.

| 2001 | | $500 | $650 |

Exclusive EM I (Platinum Series)

1996-2004. Offset double-cut, bound top, 2 humbuckers.

| 1996-2004 | | $160 | $210 |

Gunslinger

1987-1999. Inverted headstock, 1 (Gunslinger I) or 2 (Gunslinger II) humbuckers, recessed cutout behind Floyd Rose allows player to pull notes up 2 full steps.

1987-1989	Standard finish	$750	$950
1987-1989	Various graphic		
	designs	$800	$1,000
1989-1993	Class Axe era	$750	$950
1994-1999	2nd Rico era,		
	bolt-on	$650	$850
1994-1999	2nd Rico era,		
	neck-thru	$650	$850

Ironbird

1983-2004. Pointy body and headstock.

1983-1989		$1,100	$1,450
1989-1993	Class Axe era	$1,000	$1,250
1994-1998	2nd Rico era,		
	bolt-on	$925	$1,175

Kerry King Wartribe 1 Warlock

2004-present. Tribal Fire finish, 2 pickups.

| 2004-2014 | | $160 | $200 |

Mockingbird

1976-present. Made in USA, often called the Mockingbird model, but also called the Mockingbird Standard or Mockingbird Deluxe, features include diamond inlays, unbound rosewood fretboard, 3-on-a-side tuners, generally solid mahogany body, some rare examples with maple body or other woods, some with runners or stringers of alternate exotic wood. (See additional notes in the Mockingbird Supreme listing.)

1976		$2,900	$3,600
1977-1978	Short horn	$2,800	$3,500
1979-1983	Long horn	$2,800	$3,500
1984-1985		$2,400	$3,100
1986-1989	Last of 1st		
	Rico era	$1,800	$2,300
1989-1993	Class Axe era	$1,700	$2,200
1994-1999	2nd Rico era,		
	bolt-on	$1,550	$1,975

Mockingbird Ice Acrylic

2004-2006. See-thru acrylic body.

| 2004-2006 | | $290 | $365 |

Mockingbird Supreme

1976-1989. Made in USA, Mockingbird body style with specific options including cloud inlays, fully bound ebony fretboard, 3-on-a-side headstock, various woods including solid koa, maple, highly-figured maple (birdseye, quilted, curly), other exotic woods offered, most with runners or stringers of alternating exotic wood, also available as single solid wood, mid-'80s with original Kahler tremolo unit option, custom colors and sunburst finishes generally on a custom order basis, certain custom colors are worth more than the values shown, early models ca. '76-'82 had a Leo Quan Badass bridge option and those models are highly favored by collectors, early style control knobs with silver metal inserts, full electronics with Varitone and PreAmp and Grover Imperial bullseye tuners, the earliest models had red head mini-switches (later became silver-chrome switches).

1976	Earlier short horn	$3,200	$4,000
1976-1978	Supreme short horn	$3,100	$3,900
1977-1978	Earlier short horn	$3,100	$3,900
1979	Later long horn	$2,900	$3,700
1980-1983		$2,900	$3,700
1984-1985		$2,500	$3,200
1986-1989		$1,900	$2,400
1989-1993	Class Axe era	$1,800	$2,300
1994-1999	2nd Rico era,		
	bolt-on	$1,650	$2,075

Nighthawk

1978-ca.1982. Eagle-shaped body with bolt neck.

| 1978-1982 | | $750 | $950 |

NJ Series/NJC Series

1983-2006. Earlier models made in Japan. Made in Korea '86 forward. All NJ models fall within the same price range. Models include; Assassin, Beast, Bich, Ironbird, Eagle, Mockingbird, Outlaw, ST III, Virgin, Warlock. C for Classic added in '06.

1983-1984	Early NJ Japan	$375	$700
1985-1986	Later Japan	$275	$500
1986-2006	Korea	$125	$300

Phoenix

1977-ca.1982. Mockingbird-shaped with bolt neck.

| 1977-1982 | | $775 | $975 |

Platinum Series

1986-2006. Lower-priced import versions including Assassin, Beast, Bich, Ironbird, ST, Warlock.

| 1986-2006 | | $135 | $280 |

Rave Series

1986-ca. 1990. Korean-made down-market versions of popular models.

| 1986-1990 | | $135 | $175 |

Seagull

1972-1975. Single-cut solidbody, neck-thru, 2 humbuckers.

1972-1973	Earliest, 30 made	$3,600	$4,500
1973-1974		$3,400	$4,200
1975		$3,100	$3,800

Seagull II

1974-1977. Double-cut solidbody, neck-thru, 2 humbuckers. Transitional model in '75 between Seagull and Eagle, Seagull Jr. is used interchangable with

1988 B.C. Rich Gunslinger
Mike Greco

B.C. Rich NJC Series Eagle
Michael Korabek

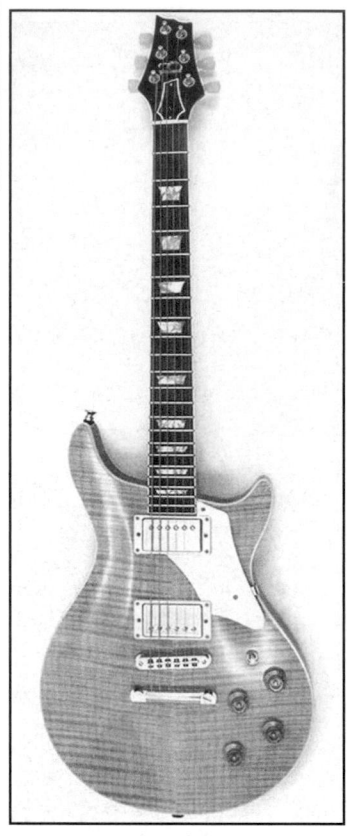

b3 SL

Baden A-Style

MODEL YEAR	FEATURES	EXC. COND. LOW	HIGH

Seagull II, the company made several variants during this period which some collectors consider to be Seagull Jr. while others consider to be Seagull II. The II/Jr. design finally was changed and called the Eagle.

1974	1st 50, Gibson pickups	$3,000	$3,800
1974	Moser, 16 made	$3,000	$3,800
1974	Other from '74	$3,000	$3,800
1976-1977		$2,400	$3,000

Seagull Jr./Seagull II

1975-1977. Another transitional model starting in '75, the model name Seagull Jr. is used interchangable with Seagull II, the company made several variants during this period which some collectors consider to be Seagull Jr. while others consider to be Seagull II. The design finally was changed and called the Eagle.

| 1975-1977 | Jr. and II | $2,400 | $3,000 |

Stealth I Series

1983-1989. Includes Standard (maple body, diamond inlays) and Series II (mahogany body, dot inlays), 2 pickups.

| 1983-1989 | Series II | $1,800 | $2,300 |
| 1983-1989 | Standard | $1,800 | $2,300 |

ST-III (U.S.A.)

1987-1998. Double-cut solidbody, hum/single/single or 2 humbucker pickups, Kahler tremolo.

1987-1989	Bolt-on	$550	$700
1987-1989	Neck-thru	$575	$725
1989-1993	Class Axe era	$550	$700
1994-1998	New Rico era, neck-thru & bolt-on	$550	$700

The Mag

2000. U.S. Handcrafted Series Mockingbird Acoustic Supreme, solid spruce top, quilt maple back and sides, pickup with preamp and EQ optional, dark sunburst.

| 2000 | | $625 | $800 |

Warlock

1981-present. Made in USA, also called Warlock Standard, 4-point sleek body style with widow headstock.

1981-1985	Standard	$1,250	$1,600
1986-1989	Standard	$1,175	$1,500
1990-1999	2nd Rico era, bolt-on	$900	$1,150
1990-1999	2nd Rico era, neck-thru	$900	$1,150

Warlock Ice Acrylic

2004-2006. See-thru acrylic body.

| 2004-2006 | | $250 | $325 |

Wave

1983. U.S.-made, very limited production based upon the Wave bass.

| 1983 | | $3,200 | $4,100 |

b3 Guitars

2004-present. Premium grade, custom/production, solid, chambered and hollow-body guitars built by luthier Gene Baker in Arroyo Grande, California. He previously made Baker U.S.A. guitars.

MODEL YEAR	FEATURES	EXC. COND. LOW	HIGH

Babicz

2004-present. Started by luthier Jeff Babicz and Jeff Carano, who worked together at Steinberger, the company offers intermediate, professional, and premium grade, production/custom, acoustic and acoustic/electric guitars made in Poughkeepsie, New York, and overseas.

Bacon & Day

Established in 1921 by David Day and Paul Bacon, primarily known for fine quality tenor and plectrum banjos in the '20s and '30s. Purchased by Gretsch ca. '40.

Belmont

1950s. Gretsch era, 2 DeArmond pickups, natural.

| 1950s | | $1,300 | $1,600 |

Flat-Top

1930s-1940s. Large B&D headstock logo.

1930s	Fancy appointments	$3,000	$3,700
1930s	Plain appointments	$2,400	$3,000
1940s	Fancy appointments	$2,700	$3,300
1940s	Plain appointments	$2,100	$2,600

Ramona Archtop

1938-1940. Sunburst.

| 1938-1940 | | $1,050 | $1,300 |

Senorita Archtop

1940. Lower-end, sunburst, mahogany back and sides.

| 1940 | | $1,550 | $1,950 |

Style B Guitar Banjo (Bacon)

1920s. 6-string guitar neck on a banjo-resonator body.

| 1920s | Fancy appointments | $2,250 | $2,800 |
| 1920s | Plain appointments | $1,250 | $1,550 |

Sultana I

1930s. Large 18 1/4" acoustic archtop, Sultana engraved on tailpiece, block markers, bound top and back, sunburst.

| 1938 | | $3,100 | $3,800 |

Baden

Founded in 2006, by T.J. Baden, a former vice president of sales and marketing at Taylor guitars, initial production based on six models built in Vietnam, intermediate retail-price grade.

Baker U.S.A.

1997-present. Professional and premium grade, production/custom, solidbody electric guitars. Established by master builder Gene Baker after working at the Custom Shops of Gibson and Fender, Baker produced solid- and hollowbody guitars in Santa Maria, California. They also built basses. Baker also produced the Mean Gene brand of guitars from '88-'90. In September '03, the company was liquidated and the Baker U.S.A. name was sold to Ed Roman. Gene Baker currently builds b3 Guitars.

MODEL YEAR	FEATURES	EXC. COND. LOW	HIGH

B1/B1 Chambered/B1 Hollow
1997-present. Double-cut mahogany body, maple top, with a wide variety of options including chambered and hollowbody construction, set-neck. Gene Baker era USA-made until 2003, Ed Roman era import after.

1997-2003	USA	$1,825	$2,250
2004-2014	Import	$775	$975

BJ/BJ Hollow
1997-2003. Double-cut mahogany body, P-90-type pickups, several options available, set-neck.

1997-2003		$1,725	$2,150

BNT
1997-2000. Mahogany solidbody, maple top, neck-thru body, with various finishes and options.

1997-2000		$1,825	$2,250

Baldwin
1965-1970. Founded in 1862, in Cincinnati, when reed organ and violin teacher Dwight Hamilton Baldwin opened a music store that eventually became one of the largest piano retailers in the Midwest. By 1965, the Baldwin Piano and Organ company was ready to buy into the guitar market but was outbid by CBS for Fender. Baldwin did procure Burns of London in September '65, and sold the guitars in the U.S. under the Baldwin name. Baldwin purchased Gretsch in '67. English production of Baldwin guitars ends in '70, after which Baldwin concentrates on the Gretsch brand.

Baby Bison (Model 560 by Mid-1966)
1966-1970. Double-cut solidbody, V headstock, 2 pickups, shorter scale, tremolo, black, red or white finishes.

1965-1966		$900	$1,100
1966-1970	Model 560	$800	$1,000

Bison (Model 511 by Mid-1966)
1965-1970. Double-cut solidbody, scroll headstock, 3 pickups, tremolo, black or white finishes.

1965-1966		$1,125	$1,400
1966-1970	Model 511	$1,075	$1,350

Double Six (Model 525 by Mid-1966)
1965-1970. Offset double-cut solidbody, 12 strings, 3 pickups, green or red sunburst.

1965-1966		$1,500	$1,875
1966-1970	Model 525	$1,450	$1,800

G.B. 65
1965-1966. Baldwin's first acoustic/electric, single-cut D-style flat-top, dual bar pickups.

1965-1966		$675	$850

G.B. 66 De Luxe
1965-1966. Same as Standard with added density control on treble horn, golden sunburst.

1965-1966		$775	$950

G.B. 66 Standard
1965-1966. Thinline Electric archtop, dual Ultra-Sonic pickups, offset cutaways, red sunburst.

1965-1966		$725	$900

Jazz Split Sound/Split Sound (Model 503 Mid-1966)
1965-1970. Offset double-cut solidbody, scroll headstock, 3 pickups, tremolo, red sunburst or solid colors.

1965-1966		$925	$1,150
1966-1970	Model 503	$775	$950

Marvin (Model 524 by Mid-1966)
1965-1970. Offset double-cut solidbody, scroll headstock, 3 pickups, tremolo, white or brown finish.

1965-1966		$1,125	$1,400
1966-1970	Model 524	$1,075	$1,350

Model 706
1967-1970. Double-cut semi-hollowbody, scroll headstock, 2 pickups, 2 f-holes, no vibrato, red or golden sunburst.

1967-1970		$700	$875

Model 706 V
1967-1970. Model 706 with vibrato.

1967-1970		$750	$925

Model 712 R Electric XII
1967-1970. Double-cut semi-hollow body with regular neck, red or gold sunburst.

1967-1970		$600	$750

Model 712 T Electric XII
1967-1970. Model 712 with thin neck, red or gold sunburst.

1967-1970		$600	$750

Model 801 CP Electric Classical
1968-1970. Grand concert-sized classical with transducer based pickup system, natural pumpkin finish.

1968-1970		$625	$775

Nu-Sonic
1965-1966. Solidbody electric student model, 6-on-a-side tuners, black or cherry finish.

1965-1966		$725	$900

Vibraslim (Model 548 by Late-1966)
1965-1970. Double-cut semi-hollowbody, 2 pickups, tremolo, 2 f-holes, red or golden sunburst. Notable spec changes with Model 548 in '66.

1965-1966		$850	$1,050
1966-1970	Model 548	$775	$950

Virginian (Model 550 by Mid-1966)
1965-1970. Single-cut flat-top, 2 pickups (1 on each side of soundhole), scroll headstock, tremolo, natural.

1965-1966		$1,150	$1,425
1966-1970	Model 550	$1,050	$1,300

Ballurio
2000-present. Luthier Keith Ballurio builds his intermediate, professional, and premium grade, production/custom, solidbody and chambered guitars in Manassas, Virginia.

Baltimore
2007-2008. Budget grade, production, solidbody electric guitars imported by The Music Link.

Bambu
1970s. Short-lived brand name on a line of guitars built by Japan's Chushin Gakki Co., which also built models for several other manufacturers.

Baranik Guitars
1995-present. Premium grade, production/custom steel-string flat-tops made in Tempe, Arizona by luthier Mike Baranik.

Baldwin Double Six

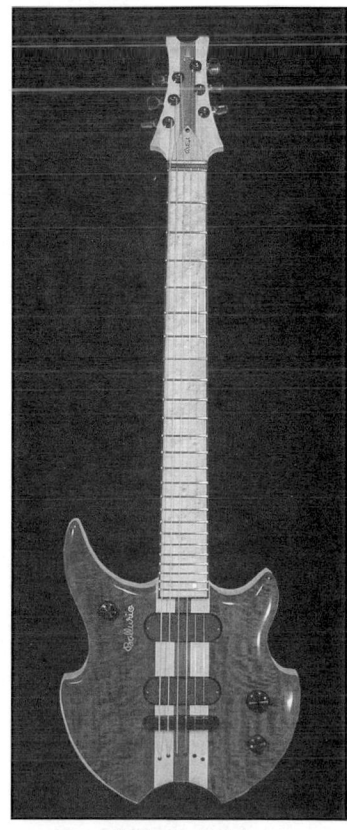

Ballurio Artist

Bashkin Placencia

Bazzolo Classical

MODEL YEAR	FEATURES	EXC. COND. LOW	HIGH

Barclay

1960s. Thinline acoustic/electric archtops, solid-body electric guitars and basses imported from Japan. Generally shorter scale beginner guitars.

Electric Solidbody

1960s. Various models and colors.

| 1960s | | $180 | $230 |

Barcus-Berry

1964-present. Founded by John Berry and Les Barcus introducing the first piezo crystal transducer. Martin guitar/Barcus-Berry products were offered in the mid-'80s. They also offered a line of amps from around '76 to ca. '80.

Barrington

1988-1991. Imports offered by Barrington Guitar Werks, of Barrington, Illinois. Models included solidbody guitars and basses, archtop electrics, and acoustic flat-tops. Barrington Music Products is still in the music biz, offering LA saxophones and other products.

Acoustic/Electric

1988-1991. Acoustic/electric, flat-top single-cut with typical round soundhole, opaque white.

| 1988-1991 | | $160 | $180 |

Solidbody

1988-ca 1991. Barrington's line of pointy headstock, double-cut solidbodies, black.

| 1988-1991 | | $160 | $180 |

Bartell of California

1964-1969. Founded by Paul Barth (Magnatone) and Ted Peckles. Mosrite-inspired designs.

Double Neck

| 1967 | | $1,900 | $2,350 |

Electric 12

1967. Mosrite-style body.

| 1967 | | $1,100 | $1,350 |

Barth

1950s-1960s. Paul Barth was involved with many guitar companies including National, Rickenbacker, Magnatone and others. He also built instruments under his own brand in California, including guitars, lap steels and amps. Most will have either a Barth logo on plastic plate, or decal.

Mark VIII

1959. Double-cut solidbody, 2 pickups, dot markers, Barth headstock logo.

| 1959 | | $2,900 | $3,600 |

Bartolini

1960s. European-made (likely Italian) guitars made for the Bartolini Accordion Company. Similar to Gemelli guitars, so most likely from same manufacturer. Originally plastic covered, they switched to paint finishes by the mid '60s.

Solidbody

| 1960s | | $450 | $550 |

Bashkin Guitars

1998-present. Luthier Michael Bashkin builds his premium grade, custom, steel-string acoustics in Fort Collins, Colorado.

Basone Guitars

1999-present. Luthier Chris Basaraba builds his custom, professional grade, solid and hollowbody electric guitars and basses in Vancouver, British Columbia.

Bauer, George

1894-1911. Luthier George Bauer built guitars, mandolins, and banjos in Philadelphia, Pennsylvania. He also built instruments with Samuel S. Stewart (S.S. Stewart).

Baxendale

1974-present. Luthier Scott Baxendale builds his professional and premium grade, custom, steel-string acoustic and solidbody electric guitars in Athens, Georgia and previously in Colorado, Tennessee and Texas.

Bay State

Ca.1890-ca.1910. Bay State was a trademark for Boston's John C. Haynes & Co., and offered guitars and banjos.

Parlor Guitar

1900s. Small parlor size, mahogany body with salt & pepper binding.

| 1900s | | $800 | $1,000 |

Bazzolo Guitarworks

1983-present. Luthier Thomas Bazzolo began building his premium grade, production/custom, classical and flat-top guitars in Lebanon, Connecticut and since 2008 in Sullivan, Maine.

BC Kingston

1977-present. From 1977 to '96, luthier Brian Kingston built flat-top and semi-hollow acoustic guitars along with a few solidbodies. Presently he builds premium grade, production/custom, archtop jazz and semi-hollow guitars in Prince Edward Island, Canada.

Bear Creek Guitars

1995-present. Luthier Bill Hardin worked for OMI Dobro and Santa Cruz Guitar before introducing his own line of professional and premium grade, custom-made Weissenborn-style guitars, made in Kula, Hawaii. He also builds ukes.

Beardsell Guitars

1996-present. Production/custom flat-tops, classical and electric solidbody guitars built by luthier Allan Beardsell in Toronto, Ontario.

Beaulieu

2006-present. Luthier Hugues Beaulieu builds his production/custom, professional and premium grade, flat-top, flamenco and classical guitars in Pont-Rouge, Quebec.

MODEL YEAR	FEATURES	EXC. COND. LOW	HIGH

Beauregard

1992-present. Luthier Mario Beauregard builds his premium and presentation grade, production/custom, flat-top, archtop and jazz guitars in Montreal, Quebec.

Bedell Guitars

1964-present. Intermediate and premium grade, production/custom, flat-top guitars built in Spirit Lake, Iowa and imported from China, designed by luthier Tom Bedell, Dan Mills and Sophia Yang. They also offer Great Divide Guitars and in 2010 acquired Breedlove.

Behringer

1989-present. The German professional audio products company added budget, production, solidbody guitars in '03, sold in amp/guitar packages. They also offer effects and amps.

Beltona

1990-present. Production/custom metal body resonator guitars made in New Zealand by Steve Evans and Bill Johnson. Beltona was originally located in England. They also build mandolins and ukes.

Beltone

1920s-1930s. Acoustic and resonator guitars made by others for New York City distributor Perlberg & Halpin. Martin did make a small number of instruments for Beltone, but most were student-grade models most likely made by one of the big Chicago builders. They also made mandolins.

Archtop

1920s-30s		$375	$475

Resonator Copy

1930s. Resonator copy but without a real resonator, rather just an aluminum plate on a wooden top, body mahogany plywood.

1938		$400	$500

Beltone (Import)

1950s-1960s. Japan's Teisco made a variety of brands for others, including the Beltone line of guitars, basses and amps. Carvin sold some of these models in the late 1960s. Italy's Welson guitars also marketed marble and glitter-finished guitars in the U.S. under this brand.

Electric Solidbody

1960s. Import from Japan during the import era of the '60s, large B headstock logo with Beltone block lettering on the large B, 4 pickups.

1960s		$250	$350

Benedetto

1968-present. Premium and presentation grade, production/custom archtop and chambered solidbody guitars, built by luthier Robert Benedetto. He has also built a few violins and solidbodies. He was located in East Stroudsburg, Pennsylvania, up to '99; in Riverview, Florida, for '00-'06; and in Savanah, Georgia, since '07. He is especially known for refining the 7-string guitar. From '99 to '06 he licensed the names of his standard models to Fender (see Benedetto FMIC); during that period, Benedetto only made special order instruments. In '06, Howard Paul joined Benedetto as President of the company to begin manufacturing a broader line of more affordable professional instruments.

Benny

1990s-present. Electric chambered single-cut mahogany body, carved spruce top, 2 humbuckers.

1990s-2011	Signed or factory	$2,000	$3,000

Benny Deluxe

1990s-2011. Deluxe version of the Benny.

1990s-2011	Signed or factory	$3,500	$5,200

Bravo Deluxe

2004-present. Electric 1 pickup archtop, laminated back and top, deluxe binding.

2004-2011	Signed or factory	$2,500	$3,800

Cremona

1988-present. Acoustic/electric archtop, single-cut, 17" body, natural.

1988-2011	Signed or factory	$8,500	$13,000

Fratello

1980-present. Electric archtop, single-cut, 17" body, blond or sunburst.

1980-2011	Signed or factory	$6,700	$10,000

La Venezia

1990s-present. Acoustic archtop, single-cut, 17" body, sunburst.

1990s-2011	Signed or factory	$7,200	$10,800

Limelite Custom

1990s. Single-cut, neck pickup, select aged wood, blond.

1990s	Signed or factory	$13,000	$19,500

Manhattan

1989-present. Archtop with 16" body, neck pickup, blond.

1989-2011	Signed or factory	$6,200	$9,300

Manhattan Custom

1990s. Carved 17" body, blond.

1990s	Signed or factory	$8,500	$12,700

Benedetto (FMIC)

1999-2006. Premium and presentation, production/custom, acoustic and electric archtops. From '99 to '06, Bob Benedetto had an agreement with Fender (FMIC) to build Benedetto guitars under his guidance and supervision. The guitars were originally built in the FMIC Guild Custom Shop in Nashville, and later in Fender's Corona, California, facility.

Benedict

1988-present. Founded by Roger Benedict. Professional and premium grade, production/custom, solid and semi-hollow body guitars and basses built by luthier Bill Hager in Cedar, Minnesota.

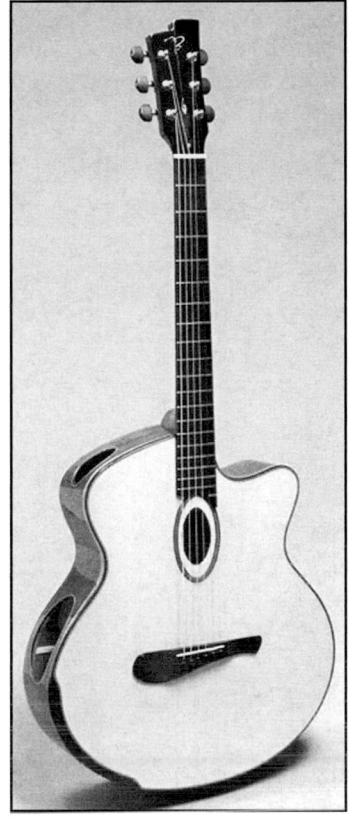

Beardsell 4G

Benedetto Cremona

Beneteau Lucas

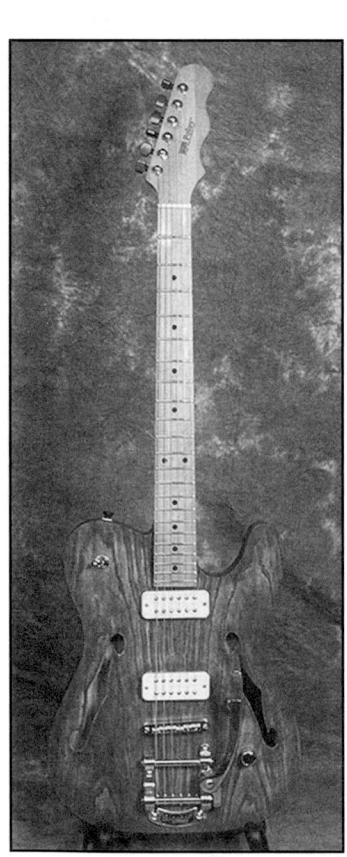

Bill Foley BF-2

MODEL		EXC. COND.	
YEAR	FEATURES	LOW	HIGH

Beneteau

1974-present. Custom, premium grade, classical, baritone and steel string acoustic guitars built first in Ottawa, Ontario, and since 1986 in St. Thomas, Ontario by luthier Marc Beneteau. He also builds ukuleles.

Bennett Music Labs

1998-present. Custom guitars built by luthier Bruce Bennett, who helped design the first Warrior line of instruments with J.D. Lewis. He also built amps and Brown Sound effects and also guitars for J. Backlund Designs.

Bently

Ca.1985-1998. Student and intermediate grade copy style acoustic and electric guitars imported by St. Louis Music Supply. Includes the Series 10 electrics and the Songwriter acoustics (which have a double reversed B crown logo on the headstock). St. Louis Music replaced the Bently line with the Austin brand.

Berkowitz Guitars

1995-present. Luthier David D. Berkowitz builds his premium grade, custom/production, steel string and baritone guitars and basses in Washington, D.C.

Bernie Rico Jr. Guitars

Professional and premium grade, production/custom, solidbody electrics guitars and basses built by luther Bernie Rico, Jr., the son of B.C. Rich founder, in Hesperia, California.

Bertoncini Stringed Instruments

Luthier Dave Bertoncini began building in 1995, premium grade, custom, flat-top guitars, in Olympia, Washington. He has also built solidbody electrics, archtops, mandolins and ukuleles.

Beyond The Trees

1976-present. Luthier Fred Carlson offers a variety of innovative designs for his professional and presentation grade, production/custom 6- and 12-string flat-tops in Santa Cruz, California. He also produces the Sympitar (a 6-string with added sympathetic strings) and the Dreadnautilus (a unique shaped headless acoustic).

Big Lou Guitar

Mid-2010-present. Located in Perris, California, owner Louis Carroll imports his intermediate grade, production, electric guitars from China.

Big Tex Guitars

2000-present. Production/custom, professional grade, vintage-style replica guitars, built for owner Eric Danheim, by luthiers James Love, Mike Simon and Eddie Dale in Houston and Dripping Springs, Texas and Seattle, Washington.

MODEL		EXC. COND.	
YEAR	FEATURES	LOW	HIGH

Bigsby

1946-present. Pedal steel guitars, hollow-chambered electric Spanish guitars, electric mandolins, doublenecks, replacement necks on acoustic guitars, hand vibratos, all handmade by Paul Arthur Bigsby, machinist and motorcycle enthusiast (designer of '30s Crocker motorcycles), in Downey, California. Initially built for special orders.

Bigsby was a pioneer in developing pedal steels. He designed a hand vibrato for Merle Travis. In '48, his neck-through hollow electrics (with Merle Travis) influenced Leo Fender, and Bigsby employed young Semie Moseley. In '56, he designed the Magnatone Mark series guitars and 1 Hawaiian lap steel. He built guitars up to '63.

He built less than 50 Spanish guitars, 6 mandolins, 70 to 150 pedal steels and 12 or so neck replacements. SN was stamped on the end of fingerboard: MMDDYY. In '65, the company was sold to Gibson president Ted McCarty who moved the tremolo/vibrato work to Kalamazoo. Bigsby died in '68. Fred Gretsch purchased the Bigsby company from Ted McCarty in '99. A solidbody guitar and a pedal steel based upon the original Paul Bigsby designs were introduced January, 2002. These were modeled on the 1963 Bigsby catalog, but look very similar to the typical Bigsby solidbodys made since the early 1950s. Early Bigsby guitars command high value on the collectible market and values here assumes authentication by an industry expert.

Standard Solidbody (Spanish)

Late-1940s-1950s, 2002. Standard Guitar, solidbody, natural. Reissue offered in '02.

1948		$200,000	$300,000
1949		$125,000	$290,000
1950-1956		$75,000	$265,000
2002	Reissue	$3,000	$3,700

Bil Mitchell Guitars

1979-present. Luthier Bil Mitchell builds his professional and premium grade, production/custom, flat-top and archtop guitars originally in Wall, New Jersey, and since '02 in Riegelsville, Pennsylvania.

Bill Foley Fine Instruments

2012-present. Luthiers Bill Foley, his son Sam, and Brad Lewis build professional and premium grade, custom electric guitars and basses in Columbus, Ohio.

Bilt Guitars

2010-present. Professional grade, production/custom, solidbody and semi-hollowbody electric guitars built in Des Moines, Iowa by luthiers Bill Henss and Tim Thelen.

Birdsong Guitars

2001-present. Luthiers Scott Beckwith and Jamie Hornbuckle build their professional grade, production/custom, solidbody guitars and basses in Wimberley, Texas.

MODEL YEAR	FEATURES	EXC. COND. LOW	HIGH

Bischoff Guitars

1975-present. Professional and premium-grade, custom-made flat-tops built by luthier Gordy Bischoff in Eau Claire, Wisconsin.

Bishline

1985-present. Luthier Robert Bishline, of Tulsa, Oklahoma, mainly builds banjos, but did build flat-tops and resonators in the past, and still does occasionally.

Black Jack

1960s. Violin-body hollowbody electric guitars and basses, possibly others. Imported from Japan by unidentified distributor. Manufacturers unknown, but some may be Arai.

Blackbird

2006-present. Luthier Joe Luttwak builds his professional grade, production/custom, carbon fiber acoustic guitars in San Francisco, California. He also offers a uke.

Blackshear, Tom

1958-present. Premium and presentation grade, production, classical and flamenco guitars made by luthier Tom Blackshear in San Antonio, Texas.

Blade

1987-present. Intermediate and professional grade, production, solidbody guitars and basses from luthier Gary Levinson and his Levinson Music Products Ltd. located in Switzerland.

California Custom
1994-2010. California Standard with maple top and high-end appointments.

1994-2010		$675	$825

California Deluxe/Deluxe
1994-1995. Standard with mahogany body and maple top.

1994-1995		$500	$625

California Hybrid
1998-1999. Standard with piezo bridge pickup.

1998-1999		$425	$525

California Standard
1994-2007. Offset double-cut, swamp ash body, bolt neck, 5-way switch.

1994-2007		$325	$400

R 3
1988-1993. Offset double-cut maple solidbody, bolt maple neck, 3 single-coils or single/single/humbucker.

1988-1993		$500	$625

R 4
1988-1993. R 3 with ash body and see-thru color finishes.

1988-1992		$575	$725

Texas Series
2003-present. Includes Standard (3 single-coils) and Deluxe (gold hardware, single/single/hum pickups).

2003-2010	Deluxe	$375	$475
2003-2010	Special	$350	$450
2003-2014	Standard	$350	$450

Blanchard Guitars

1994-present. Luthier Mark Blanchard builds premium grade, custom steel-string and classical guitars originally in Mammoth Lakes, California, and since May '03, in northwest Montana.

Blindworm Guitars

2008-present. Luthiers Andrew J. Scott and Steven Sells build premium and presentation grade, production/custom, acoustic, electric and electric-acoustic guitars, basses, mandolins, banjos and others in Colorado Springs, Colorado.

Blount

1985-present. Professional and premium grade, production/custom, acoustic flat-top guitars built by luthier Kenneth H. Blount Jr. in Sebring, Florida.

Blue Star

1984-present. Luthier Bruce Herron builds his production/custom guitars in Fennville, Michigan. He also builds mandolins, lap steels, dulcimers and ukes.

Bluebird

1920s-1930s. Private brand with Bluebird painted on headstock, built by the Oscar Schmidt Co. and possibly others. Most likely made for distributor.

13" Flat-Top

1930s		$160	$200

Bluebird Guitars

2011-present. Luthiers Rob Bluebird and Gian Maria Camponeschi build premium grade, custom, archtop and solidbody guitars in Rome, Italy. They build production resonator guitars in Bali, Indonesia. They also offer basses and ukuleles.

Blueridge

Early 1980s-present. Intermediate and professional grade, production, solid-top acoustic guitars distributed by Saga. In '00, the product line was redesigned with the input of luthier Greg Rich (Rich and Taylor guitars).

Bluesouth

1991-ca. 2006. Custom electric guitars built by luthier Ronnie Knight in Muscle Shoals, Alabama. He also built basses.

Boaz Elkayam Guitars

1985-present. Presentation grade, custom steel, nylon, and flamenco guitars made by luthier Boaz Elkayam in Chatsworth, California.

Boedigheimer Instruments

2000-present. Luthier Brian Boedigheimer builds his professional and premium grade, production/custom, semi-hollowbody electric guitars in Red Wing, Minnesota.

Blackbird Super OM

Blade Texas Series

GUITARS

GUITARS

Boucher Studio Goose

Boulder Creek Solitare ECR2-C

MODEL YEAR	FEATURES	EXC. COND. LOW	HIGH

Bohmann

1878-ca. 1926. Acoustic flat-top guitars, harp guitars, mandolins, banjos, violins made in Chicago Illinois, by Joseph Bohmann (born 1848, in Czechoslovakia). Bohmann's American Musical Industry founded 1878. Guitar body widths are 12", 13", 14", 15". He had 13 grades of guitars by 1900 (Standard, Concert, Grand Concert sizes). Early American use of plywood. Some painted wood finishes. Special amber-oil varnishes. Tuner bushings. Early ovalled fingerboards. Patented tuner plates and bridge design. Steel engraved label inside. Probably succeeded by son Joseph Frederick Bohmann.

Ca. 1896 12" body faux rosewood, 13", 14" and 15" body faux rosewood birch, 12", 13", 14" and 15" body sunburst maple, 12", 13", 14" and 15" body rosewood. By 1900 Styles 0, 1, 2 and 3 Standard, Concert and Grand Concert maple, Styles 1, 2, 3, 4, 5, 6, 7, 8, 9, 10, 11 and 12 in Standard, Concert, and Grand Concert rosewood.

14 3/4" Flat-Top

Solid spruce top, veneered Brazilian rosewood back and sides, wood marquetry around top and soundhole, natural. Each Bohmann should be valued on a case-by-case basis.

1896-1900	Brazilian	$825	$1,025
1896-1900	Other woods	$325	$400

Harp Guitar

1896-1899	All styles	$3,000	$3,700

Bolin

1978-present. Professional and premium grade, production/custom, solidbody guitars and basses built by luthier John Bolin in Boise, Idaho. Bolin is well-known for his custom work. His Cobra guitars are promoted and distributed by Sanderson Sales and Marketing as part of the Icons of America Series.

NS

1996-2011. Slot-headstock, bolt-on neck, single-cut solidbody, Seymour Duncan passive pickups or EMG active, from '96 to the fall of 2001 custom-built serial numbers to 0050 then from the fall of '01 to the present production model build starting with SN 0051.

1996-2001	Custom-built	$1,500	$1,850
2001-2011	Standard production	$700	$875

Bolt

1988-1991. Founded by luthier Wayne Bolt and Jim Dala Pallu in Schnecksville, Pennsylvania, Bolt's first work was CNC machined OEM necks and bodies made for Kramer and BC Rich. In '90, they started building solidbody Bolt guitars, many with airbrushed graphics. Only about 100 to 125 were built, around 40 with graphics.

Bond

1984-1985. Andrew Bond made around 1,400 Electraglide guitars in Scotland. Logo says 'Bond Guitars, London'.

MODEL YEAR	FEATURES	EXC. COND. LOW	HIGH

ElectraGlide

1984-1985. Black carbon graphite 1-piece body and neck, double-cut, 3 single-coils (2 humbuckers were also supposedly available), digital LED controls that required a separate transformer.

1984-1985		$1,000	$1,250

Borges Guitars

2000-present. Luthier Julius Borges builds his premium grade, production/custom, acoustic guitars in Groton, Massachusetts.

Boucher

2005-present. Professional and premium grade, acoustic guitars built by luthier Robin Boucher in Quebec.

Boulder Creek Guitars

2007-present. Intermediate and professional grade, production, imported dreadnought, classical, and 12-string guitars, basses and ukes distributed by Morgan Hill Music of Morgan Hill, California.

Bourgeois

1993-1999, 2000-present. Luthier Dana Bourgeois builds his professional and premium grade, production/custom, acoustic and archtop guitars in Lewiston, Maine. Bourgeois co-founded Schoenberg guitars and built Schoenberg models from '86-'90. Bourgeois' 20th Anniversary model was issued in '97. Bourgeois Guitars, per se, went of business at the end of '99. Patrick Theimer created Pantheon Guitars, which included 7 luthiers (including Bourgeois) working in an old 1840s textile mill in Lewiston, Maine and Bourgeois models continue to be made as part of the Pantheon organization.

Serial Number List: '93 1-70, '94 71-205, '95 206-350, '96 351-665, '97 666-1040, '98 1041-1450, '99 1451-1975.

Blues

1996. D-style, all koa.

1996		$2,600	$3,300

Country Boy

1998-present. Pre-war D-style designed for Ricky Skaggs, Sitka spruce top, mahogany back and sides, Ricky Skaggs label, natural.

1998-2014		$2,200	$2,800

Country Boy Deluxe

2003-present. Country Boy with Adirondack spruce top, rosewood binding.

2003-2014		$2,600	$3,200

D - 20th Anniversary

1997. 20 made, bearclaw spruce top, rosewood back and sides, mother-of-pearl 'board, ornate abalone floral pattern inlay, abalone rosette and border, natural.

1997		$2,600	$3,200

D-150

2002-present. Brazilian rosewood, premium Adirondack, abalone rosette.

2002-2014		$4,800	$6,000

MODEL YEAR	FEATURES	EXC. COND. LOW	HIGH

DBJC

Jumbo cutaway, Indian rosewood back and sides, redwood top, gloss finish.

2007		$2,800	$3,500

Georgia Dreadnought

2003. Mahogany, Adirondack.

| 2003 | | $1,800 | $2,300 |

JOM

1993-present. Jumbo Orchestra Model flat-top, 15 5/8". Model includes one with cedar top, mahogany back and sides, and one with spruce top, Brazilian rosewood back and sides.

1993	Brazilian rosewood	$3,600	$4,600
1993	Mahogany	$1,800	$2,300
1993-2014	Indian rosewood	$1,800	$2,300

JOMC/OMC

1995-present. JOM (jumbo) cutaway.

1995	OMC, figured mahogany	$3,000	$3,800
1995-2014	JOMC200, Indian rosewood	$2,600	$3,300

JR-A

1990s. Artisan Series, 15 5/8", spruce top, rosewood back and sides.

| 1990s | | $1,000 | $1,250 |

LC-4 Archtop Limited Edition

2002. Limited edition of 12, signed and numbered, premium sitka and carved curly maple.

| 2002 | | $9,400 | $11,800 |

Martin Simpson

1997-2003. Grand auditorium with unusual cutaway that removes one half of the upper treble bout, Englemann spruce top, Indian rosewood back and sides, natural.

| 1997-2003 | | $2,100 | $2,600 |

OM

1993-1999. Standard size OM, spruce top, rosewood back and sides.

| 1993-1999 | | $2,800 | $3,500 |

OM Deluxe Artisan

2002. Indian rosewood, sitka.

| 2002 | | $1,700 | $2,200 |

OM Soloist

1990s-present. Full-sized, soft cutaway flat-top, Adirondack spruce top, figured Brick Red Brazilian rosewood back and sides, natural.

| 1990-2014 | | $3,600 | $4,500 |

Ricky Skaggs Signature

1998. D-style, rosewood sides and back, spruce top.

| 1998 | | $2,400 | $3,000 |

Slope D

1993-present. D-size, 16", spruce top, mahogany back and sides.

| 1993-2014 | | $2,000 | $2,500 |

Vintage D

2000-present. Adirondack spruce (Eastern red spruce) top, optional rosewood back and sides.

2000-2014	Indian rosewood	$2,000	$2,500
2000s	Brazilian rosewood	$3,700	$4,700

Vintage OM

2005. Madagascar rosewood and Italian spruce top.

| 2005 | | $2,700 | $3,500 |

Bown Guitars

1981-present. Luthier Ralph Bown builds custom steel-string, nylon-string, baritone, and harp guitars in Walmgate, England.

Bozo

1964-present. Bozo (pronounced Bo-zho) Podunavac learned instrument building in his Yugoslavian homeland and arrived in the United States in '59. In '64 he opened his own shop and has built a variety of high-end, handmade, acoustic instruments, many being one-of-a-kind. He has built around 570 guitars over the years. There were several thousand Japanese-made (K. Yairi shop) Bell Western models bearing his name made from '79-'80; most of these were sold in Europe. He currently builds premium and presentation grade, production/custom guitars in East Englewood, Florida.

Acoustic

1970s-1980s. Indian rosewood.

1970s-80s	12-string	$1,800	$2,250
1970s-80s	6-string	$1,800	$2,250

Classical

1969. Limited production.

| 1969 | | $1,900 | $2,350 |

Cutaway 12-String

1977-1998. Often old world Balkan ornamentation, generally Sitka spruce top, Indian rosewood back and sides, widow-style headstock, ornamentation can vary (standard or elaborate).

1977	Standard	$1,800	$2,250
1993	Elaborate	$3,000	$3,800
1998	Elaborate Custom	$3,700	$4,600

Bradford

Mid-1960s. Brand name used by the W.T. Grant Company, one of the old Five & Ten style retail stores similar to F.W. Woolworth and Kresge. Many of these guitars and basses were made in Japan by Guyatone.

Acoustic Flat-Top

| 1960s | | $150 | $300 |

Electric Solidbody

1960s	1 or 2 pickups	$175	$250
1960s	3 pickups	$225	$300
1960s	4 pickups	$275	$400

Bradley

1970s. Budget Japanese copy models imported by Veneman's Music Emporium.

Brawley Basses

Headquartered in Temecula, California, and designed by Keith Brawley, offering solidbody guitars and basses made in Korea.

Brazen

2005-present. Owner Steve Tsai, along with luthier Eddie Estrada, build professional and premium grade, production, electric guitars in Plainview, New York and assemble them in Covina, California. Steve also imports a line of intermediate grade guitars from China which are set up in Covina.

Bourgeois Ray LaMontagne Signature

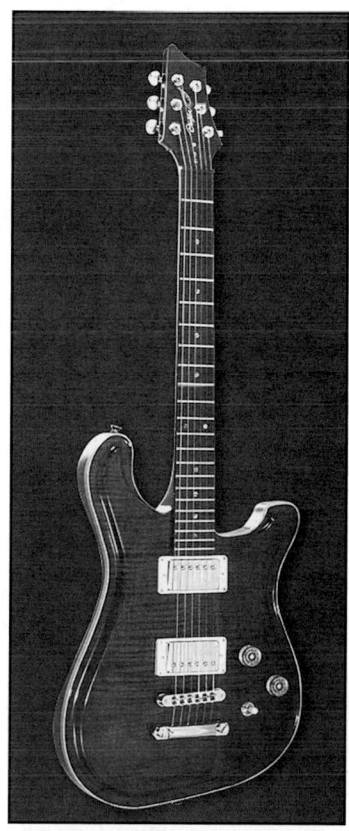

Brazen Fantasy Series

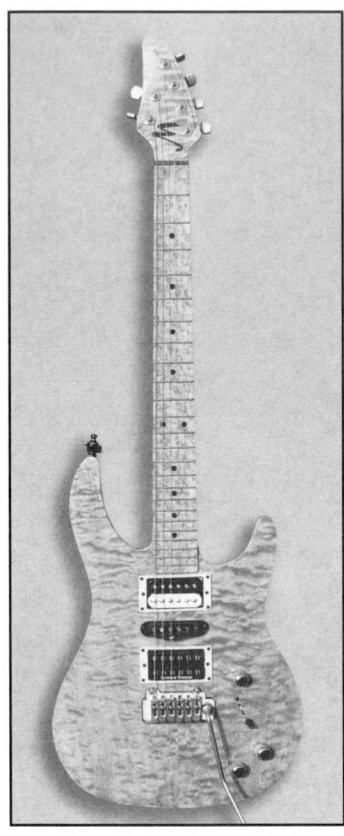

1996 Brian Moore MC1
My Generation Guitars

1920 Bruno and Sons
Parlor Guitar

| MODEL | | EXC. COND. | |
YEAR	FEATURES	LOW	HIGH

Breedlove

1990-present. Founded by Larry Breedlove and Steve Henderson. Intermediate, professional, premium, and presentation grade, production/custom, steel and nylon string flat-top built in Bend, Oregon and imported. They also build mandolins, basses, lapsteels and ukes. Several available custom options may add to the values listed here. They offered chambered electric guitars starting in 2008 but in January 2010, Breedlove discontinued all electric guitar production. Also in '10, they became part of Two Old Hippies.

American Series

2004-2013. American-made, D-, C- and OM-styles, cutaway and non.

2004-2013		$1,200	$2,150

Atlas Series

2004-2013. Imported D and C styles, cutaway and non, steel and nylon, 6 and 12-string.

2004-2013		$275	$525

Bossa Nova

2000-2013. Focus series nylon concert, soft cutaway, rosewood body.

2000-2013		$1,650	$2,100

C Series

1990s-2004. American Concert size models, various options.

1990s-2004		$1,350	$2,550
1990s-2004	Brazilian, high-end	$2,550	$4,000

D Series

2000s. American Dreadnought size models, various options.

2000s		$750	$2,100

Ed Gerhard

1997-2010. Shallow jumbo, soft cut, Indian rosewood body.

1997-2010	Custom	$2,000	$2,450
1997-2010	Signature	$2,000	$2,500

J Series

2001-2004. American Jumbo size models, various options.

2001-2004		$1,900	$2,350

Mark IV Custom

2008-2010. Single-cut chambered body, 2 pickups.

2008-2010		$1,450	$1,800

Myrtlewood Limited 01

1990s-2003. Acoustic/electric, D-size, solid spruce top, solid myrtlewood back and sides.

1995-2003		$1,375	$1,700

N Series

1999-2004. American nylon-string models, various options.

1999-2004		$1,375	$1,825

Pacific

2001-2007, 2011-2013. Sitka spruce, flamed maple, flamed koa binding.

2001-2013		$2,200	$2,700

RD/R Series

1990s-2001. American D-size models, cutaway and non.

1993-2001		$1,100	$1,775

SC Series

1995-2004. American S Series Concert sizes, but with less ornamentation then most premier models.

1995-2004	SC20, Brazilian	$2,025	$2,525
1995-2007	SC20, other	$1,325	$1,625
1995-2007	SC25, other	$1,525	$1,875
1997	SC25-R (Rosewood)	$1,525	$1,875
1998	SC25, Koa		
	Adirondack LE	$2,025	$2,525
1999	SC20 -Z Custom (Zircote)	$1,425	$1,750

SJ Series

1997-2004. American Shallow body Jumbo size models, various options.

1997-2004		$1,350	$2,500

Brentwood

1970s. Student models built by Kay for store or jobber.

K-100

1970s. 13" student flat-top, K-100 label inside back, K logo on 'guard.

1970s		$45	$60

Brian May Guitar Company

2006-present. Guitarist Brian May teamed up with Barry Moorhouse and Pete Malandrone to offer versions of his Red Special Guitar. They also offered a bass.

Brian May Special

2006-present. Mahogany solidbody, 3 pickups, various colors

2006-2014		$375	$465

Brian Moore

1992-present. Founded by Patrick Cummings, Brian Moore and Kevin Kalagher in Brewster, New York; they introduced their first guitars in '94. Initially expensive custom shop guitars with carbon-resin bodies with highly figured wood tops; later went to all wood bodies cut on CNC machines. The intermediate and professional grade, production, iGuitar/i2000series was introduced in 2000 and made in Korea, but set up in the U.S. Currently the premium grade, production/custom, Custom Shop Series guitars are handcrafted in La Grange, New York. They also build basses and electric mandolins.

C-45

1999-2001. Solidbody, mahogany body, bolt neck, 2 P-90-type pickups, natural satin.

1999-2001		$950	$1,200

C-55/C-55P

1997-2004. Solidbody, burl maple body, bolt neck, currently produced as a limited edition. C-55P indicates Piezo option.

1997-2004		$950	$1,200

C-90/C-90P

1996-2011. Solidbody, figured maple top, mahogany body, bolt neck, hum-single-hum pickups, red sunburst. C-90P has Piezo option.

1996-2011	USA	$1,150	$1,500

MODEL		EXC. COND.	
YEAR	FEATURES	LOW	HIGH

DC-1/DC-1P

1997-2011. Quilted maple top, 2 humbuckers, single-cut, gold hardware. DC-1P has Piezo option.

1997-2011		$2,000	$2,500

iGuitar Series

2000-present.

2000-2010	2P	$600	$750
2000-2010	i1	$500	$625
2000-2012	2.13 & 21.13	$625	$775
2000-2014	8.13 & 81.13	$475	$600

MC1

1994-2011. High-end model, quilted maple top, various pickup options including piezo and midi, gold hardware, currently a limited edition with only 12 produced each year. Should be evaluated on a case-by-case basis.

1994-2011		$1,850	$2,250

Brian Stone Classical Guitars

Luthier Brian Stone builds his classical guitars in Corvallis, Oregon.

Briggs

1999-present. Luthier Jack Briggs builds his professional and premium grade, production/custom, chambered and solidbody guitars in Raleigh, North Carolina.

Broman

1930s. The Broman brand was most likely used by a music studio (or distributor) on instruments made by others, including Regal-built resonator instruments.

Bronson

Ca. 1934-early 1960s. George Bronson was a steel guitar instructor in the Detroit area and his instruments were made by other companies. They were mainly lap steels (usually sold with a matching amp), but some other types were also offered.

Honolulu Master Hawaiian

1938		$4,600	$5,600

Student Hawaiian

1930s	13" flat-top	$155	$200

Brook Guitars

1993-present. Simon Smidmore and Andy Petherick build their production/custom Brook steel-string, nylon-strings, and archtops in Dartmoor, England.

Brown's Guitar Factory

1982-present. Luthier John Brown builds professional and premium grade, production/custom, solidbody guitars and basses in Inver Grove Heights, Minnesota.

Bruné, R. E.

1966-present. Luthier Richard Bruné builds his premium and presentation grade, custom, classical and flamenco guitars in Evanston, Illinois. He also offers his professional and premium grade Model 20

and Model 30, which are handmade in a leading guitar workshop in Japan. Bruné's "Guitars with Guts" column appears quarterly in Vintage Guitar magazine.

Bruno and Sons

Distributor Bruno and Sons marketed a variety of brands, including their own. Later became part of Kaman Music.

Harp Guitar

1924		$2,100	$2,600

Hollowbody Electric

1960s-1970s. Various imported models.

1960s		$160	$550

Parlor Guitar

1880-1920. Various woods used on back and sides.

1880-1920	Birch	$425	$525
1880-1920	Brazilian rosewood	$850	$1,050
1880-1920	Mahogany	$450	$550

Buddy Blaze

1985-present. Professional and premium grade, custom/production, solidbody electric guitars built by luthier Buddy Blaze from '85 to '87 in Arlington, Texas, and presently in Kailua Kona, Hawaii. He also designs intermediate grade models which are imported.

Bunker

1961-present. Founder Dave Bunker built custom guitars and basses while performing in Las Vegas in the '60s and developed a number of innovations. Around '92 Bunker began PBC Guitar Technology with John Pearse and Paul Chernay in Coopersburg, Pennsylvania, building instruments under the PBC brand and, from '94-'96, for Ibanez' USA Custom Series. PBC closed in '97 and Bunker moved back to Washington State to start Bunker Guitar Technology and resumed production of several Bunker models. In early 2002, Bunker Guitars became part of Maple Valley Tone Woods of Port Angeles, Washington. Currently Bunker offers intermediate, professional, and premium grade, production/custom, guitars and basses built in Port Angeles. Most early Bunker guitars were pretty much custom-made in low quantities.

Burke

Ca. 1960-ca. 1966. 6- and 12- string electric guitars built by Glen Burke's Tuning Fork Guitar Company in Eugene and Grants Pass, Oregon and mostly sold in kit form. The guitars featured an aluminum neck-thru design with the body portion of the neck shaped being a rectangular box where the body wings are attached. Being kit guitars finishes, pickups, options and build quality will vary.

Burly Guitars

2007-present. Luthier Jeff Ayers builds his professional and premium grade, custom, solid and semi-hollowbody guitars in Land O' Lakes, Wisconsin. He plans on adding basses.

Buddy Blaze Fubar

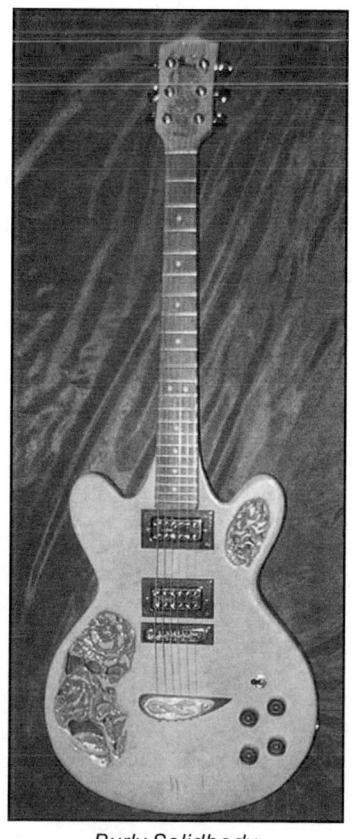

Burly Solidbody

GUITARS

Burns Bison

Byrd Super Avianti

MODEL YEAR	FEATURES	EXC. COND. LOW	HIGH

Burns

1960-1970, 1974-1983, 1992-present. Intermediate and professional grade, production, electric guitars built in England and Asia. They also build basses. Jim Burns began building guitars in the late-'50s and established Burns London Ltd in '60. Baldwin Organ (see Baldwin listing) purchased the company in '65 and offered the instruments until '70. The Burns name was revived in '91 by Barry Gibson as Burns London, with Jim Burns' involvement, offering reproductions of some of the classic Burns models of the '60s. Jim Burns passed away in August '98.

Baby Bison
1965. Double-cut solidbody, scroll headstock, 2 pickups, shorter scale, tremolo.

1965		$950	$1,175

Bison
1964-1965, 2003-present. Double-cut solidbody, 3 pickups, tremolo, black or white, scroll-headstock, replaced flat headstock Black Bison. Has been reissued with both types of headstocks.

1964-1965		$1,225	$1,525
2003-2014	Reissue	$375	$475

Black Bison
1961-1962. Double cut solid, large horns, 4 pickups, flat headstock. Replaced by scroll-headstock Bison.

1961-1962		$1,475	$1,825

Brian May Signature - Red Special
2001-2006. Replica of May's original 'Red Special' but with added whammy-bar, red finish. Korean-made.

2001-2006		$675	$850

Cobra
2004-present. Double-cut solid, 2 pickups.

2004-2014		$130	$175

Double Six
1964-1965, 2003-present. Solidbody 12-string, double-cut, 3 pickups, greenburst. Has been reissued.

1964-1965		$1,600	$2,000
2003-2014		$225	$300

Flyte
1974-1977. Fighter jet-shaped solidbody, pointed headstock, 2 humbucking pickups, silver, has been reissued.

1974-1977		$725	$900

GB 66 Deluxe
1965. Like 66 Standard, but with bar pickups and add Density control.

1965		$825	$1,050

GB 66 Deluxe Standard
1965. Offset double-cut, f-holes, 2 Ultra-Sonic pickups.

1965		$775	$950

Jazz
1962-1965. Offset double-cut solid, shorter scale, 2 pickups.

1962-1965		$975	$1,200

Jazz Split Sound
1962-1965. Offset double-cut solid, 3 pickups, tremolo, red sunburst.

1962-1965		$1,050	$1,300

MODEL YEAR	FEATURES	EXC. COND. LOW	HIGH

Marquee
2000-present. Offset double-cut solid, 3 pickups, scroll headstock

2000-2014		$210	$260

Marvin
1964-1965. Offset double-cut solidbody, scroll headstock, 3 pickups, tremolo, white.

1964-1965		$1,325	$1,625

Nu-Sonic
1964-1965. Solidbody, 2 pickups, tremolo, white or cherry, has been reissued.

1964-1965		$825	$1,050

Sonic
1960-1964. Double shallow cut solid, 2 pickups, cherry.

1960-1964		$725	$900

Split Sonic
1962-1964. Solidbody, 3 pickups, bound neck, tremolo, red sunburst.

1962-1964		$1,000	$1,250

Steer
2000-present. Semi-hollowbody, sound-hole, 2 pickups, non-cut and single-cut versions.

2000-2014		$315	$390

TR-2
1963-1964. Semi-hollow, 2 pickups, red sunburst.

1963-1964		$925	$1,150

Vibraslim
1964-1965. Double-cut, f-holes, 2 pickups, red sunburst.

1964-1965		$925	$1,150

Virginian
1964-1965. Burns of London model, later offered as Baldwin Virginian in '65.

1964-1965		$1,200	$1,500

Vista Sonic
1962-1964. Offset double-cut solid, 3 pickups, red sunburst.

1962-1964		$775	$950

Burnside

1987-1988. Budget solidbody guitars imported by Guild.

Solidbody Electric/Blade
1987-1988. Solidbody, fat pointy headstock.

1987-1988		$160	$200

Burns-Weill

1959. Jim Burns and Henry Weill teamed up to produce three solidbody electric and three solidbody bass models under this English brand. Models included the lower end Fenton, a small single-cutaway, 2 pickups and an elongated headstock and the bizarrely styled RP2G. Henry Weill continued to produce a slightly different RP line under the re-named Fenton-Weill brand.

Burny

1980s-1990s. Solidbody electric guitars from Fernandes and built in Japan, Korea or China.

MODEL YEAR	FEATURES	EXC. COND. LOW	HIGH

Burrell

1984-2010. Luthier Leo Burrell built his professional grade, production/custom, acoustic, semi-hollow, and solidbody guitars and basses in Huntington, West Virginia. Leo retired in '10.

Burton Guitars

1980-present. Custom classical guitars built by luthier Cynthia Burton in Portland, Oregon.

Buscarino Guitars

1981-present. Luthier John Buscarino builds his premium and presentation grade, custom archtops and steel-string and nylon-string flat-tops in Franklin, North Carolina.

Byers, Gregory

1984-present. Premium grade, custom classical and Flamenco guitars built by luthier Gregory Byers in Willits, California.

Byrd

1998-present. Custom/production, professional and premium grade, V-shaped electric guitars, built by luthiers James Byrd and Joe Riggio, in Seattle and several other cities in the state of Washington.

C. Fox

1997-2002. Luthier Charles Fox built his premium grade, production/custom flat-tops in Healdsburg, California. In '02 he closed C. Fox Guitars and moved to Portland, Oregon to build Charles Fox Guitars.

C.F. Mountain

1970s-early 1980s. Japanese copy acoustics made by Hayashi Musical Instrument Ltd with headstock logo that looks very much like that of a certain classic American guitar company.

Acoustic

1970s-80s		$55	$75

CA (Composite Acoustics)

1999-2010, 2011-present. Professional grade, production, carbon fiber composite guitars that were built in Lafayette, Louisiana. The company ceased production in February, '10. At the end of '10 CA was acquired by Peavey, which launched the new Meridian, Mississippi-based line in January, '11.

Califone

1966. Six and 12-string guitars and basses made by Murphy Music Industries (maker of the Murph guitars) for Rheem Califone-Roberts which manufactured tape recorders and related gear. Very few made.

Callaham

1989-present. Professional, production/custom, solidbody electric guitars built by luthier Bill Callaham in Winchester, Virginia. They also make tube amp heads.

Camelli

1960s. Line of solidbody electric guitars imported from Italy.

Solidbody Electric

1960s		$525	$650

Cameo

1960s-1970s. Japanese- and Korean-made electric and acoustic guitars. They also offered basses.

Electric

1960s-70s	Higher-end	$300	$375

Campbell American Guitars

2005-present. Luthier Dean Campbell builds his intermediate and professional grade, production/custom, solidbody guitars originally in Pawtucket, Rhode Island, and currently in Westwood, Massachusetts. From '02 to '05, he built guitars under the Greene & Campbell brand.

Campellone

1978-present. Luthier Mark Campellone builds his premium grade, custom archtops in Greenville, Rhode Island. He also made electrics and basses in the '70s and '80s, switching to archtops around '90.

Deluxe

1990-present. 16" to 18" archtop, middle of the company product line, blond or sunburst.

1990-2014		$4,200	$5,200

Special

1994-present. 16" to 18" archtop, top of the company product line, carved spruce top, carved flamed maple back, flamed maple sides, blond or sunburst.

1994-2014		$5,500	$6,800

Standard

2000-present. 16" to 18" archtop, lower of the 3 model lines offered.

2000-2014		$3,400	$4,200

Canvas

2004-2012. Budget and intermediate grade, production, acoustic and electric guitars and basses imported from China by America Sejung Corp. until '11, then in South Korea.

Carbonaro

1974-present. Luthier Robert Carbonaro builds his premium grade, production/custom, archtop and flat-top guitars in Santa Fe, New Mexico.

Carl Fischer

1920s. Most likely a brand made for a distributor. Instruments built by the Oscar Schmidt Co. and possibly others.

Carlos

Ca.1976-late 1980s. Imported copies of classic American acoustics distributed by Coast Wholesale Music.

Acoustic Flat-Top

1976-1980s	Various models	$60	$200

Buscarino Virtuoso

Carbonaro Dreadnought

Casper CGT-20 Series Classic

Char AJ

MODEL YEAR	FEATURES	EXC. COND. LOW	HIGH

Carvin

1946-present. Intermediate and professional grade, production/custom, acoustic and electric guitars and basses built in San Diego, California. They also offer amps and mandolins. Founded in Los Angeles by Hawaiian guitarist and recording artist Lowell C. Kiesel as the L.C. Kiesel Co. making pickups for guitars. Bakelite Kiesel-brand electric Hawaiian lap steels are introduced in early-'47. Small tube amps introduced ca. '47. By late-'49, the Carvin brand is introduced, combining parts of names of sons Carson and Gavin. Carvin acoustic and electric Spanish archtops are introduced in '54. Instruments are sold by mail-order only. Kiesel brand name revived by Carvin in '15 for use on their guitars.

2,000-4,000 guitars made prior to '70 with no serial number. First serial number appeared in '70, stamped on end of fingerboard, beginning with #5000. All are consecutive. Later SN on neck plates.

Approximate SN ranges include:
1970: First serial number #5000 to 10019 ('79).
'80-'83: 10768 to 15919.
'84-'87: 13666 to 25332.
'88-'90: 22731 to 25683.
'91-'94: 25359 to 42547.
'95-'99: 45879 to 81427.
'00-present: 56162 upward.

Casa Montalvo

1987-present. Intermediate and professional grade, production/custom flamenco and classical guitars made in Mexico for George Katechis of Berkeley Musical Instrument Exchange.

Casio

In 1987 Casio introduced a line of digital MIDI guitars imported from Japan, sporting plastic bodies and synthesizer features. They offered them for just a few years.

DG1
1980s. Squared plastic body.

1980s		$60	$80

DG10
1987-1989. Self-contained digital guitar.

1987-1989		$135	$175

DG20
1987-1989. Midi-capable digital guitar.

1987-1989		$190	$250

MG-500 Series MIDI Guitar
1987-1989. Cut-off teardrop (MG-500) or Strat-shaped (MG-510), basswood body, maple neck, rosewood 'board, 3 pickups.

1987-1989	500 or 510	$575	$725

PG-300
1988-1989. Similar to PG-380, but with less features.

1988-1989		$350	$450

PG-310
1988-1989. Similar to PG-380, but with less features.

1988-1989		$425	$550

MODEL YEAR	FEATURES	EXC. COND. LOW	HIGH

PG-380
1988-1989. Guitar synth, double-cut, over 80 built-in sounds, midi controller capable.

1988-1989		$675	$850

Casper Guitar Technologies

2009-present. Professional grade, production/custom, solidbody electric guitars and basses built by luthier Stephen Casper in Leisure City, Florida.

Cat's Eyes

1980s. Made by Tokai, Cat's Eyes headstock logo, see Tokai guitar listings.

Champion

Ca. 1894-1897. Chicago's Robert Maurer built this brand of instruments before switching to the Maurer brand name around 1897.

Chandler

1984-present. Intermediate and professional grade, production/custom, solidbody electric guitars built by luthiers Paul and Adrian Chandler in Chico, California. They also build basses, lap steels and pickups. Chandler started making pickguards and accessories in the '70s, adding electric guitars, basses, and effects in '84.

555 Model
1992-present. Sharp double-cut, 3 mini-humbuckers, TV Yellow.

1992-2014		$600	$750

Austin Special
1991-1999. Resembles futuristic Danelectro, lipstick pickups, available in 5-string version.

1991-1999		$525	$650

Austin Special Baritone
1994-1999. Nicknamed Elvis, gold metalflake finish, mother-of-toilet-seat binding, tremolo, baritone.

1994-1999		$525	$650

LectraSlide
2001-present. Single-cut, Rezo 'guard, 2 pickups.

2001-2014		$600	$750

Metro
1995-2000. Double-cut slab body, P-90 in neck position and humbucker in the bridge position.

1995-2000		$500	$625

Telepathic
1994-2000. Classic single-cut style, 3 models: Basic, Standard, Deluxe.

1994-2000	Basic	$400	$500
1994-2000	Deluxe 1122 Model	$525	$650
1994-2000	Standard	$475	$600

Chantus

1984-present. Premium grade, production/custom, classical and flamenco guitars built in Austin, Texas, by luthier William King. He also builds ukes.

Chapin

Professional and premium grade, production/custom, semi-hollow, solidbody, and acoustic elec-

MODEL YEAR	FEATURES	EXC. COND. LOW	HIGH

tric guitars built by luthiers Bill Chapin and Fred Campbell in San Jose, California.

Chapman

1970-present. Made by Emmett Chapman, the Stick features 10 strings and is played by tapping both hands. The Grand Stick features 12 strings.

Stick

1970-present. Touch-tap hybrid electric instrument, 10 or 12 strings.

1970-2014	10-string	$1,700	$2,100
1970-2014	12-string	$1,700	$2,100

Char

1985-present. Premium grade, custom, classical and steel string acoustic guitars built in Portland, Oregon by luthier Kerry Char. He also builds harp-guitars and ukuleles.

Charis Acoustic

1996-present. Premium grade, custom/production, steel-string guitars built by luthier Bill Wise in Bay City, Michigan.

Charles Fox Guitars

1968-present. Luthier Charles Fox builds his premium and presentation grade, custom, steel and nylon string guitars in Portland, Oregon. He also produced GRD acoustic and electric guitars for '78-'82 and C. Fox acoustic guitars for '97-'02. He also operates The American School of Lutherie in Portland.

Charles Shifflett Acoustic Guitars

1990-present. Premium grade, custom, classical, flamenco, resonator, and harp guitars, basses and banjos built by luthier Charles Shifflett in High River, Alberta.

Charvel

1976 (1980)-present. Intermediate and professional grade, production, solidbody electric guitars. They also build basses. Founded by Wayne Charvel as Charvel Manufacturing in '76, making guitar parts in Asuza, California. Moved to San Dimas in '78. Also in '78 Grover Jackson bought out Charvel. In '79 or early '80 Charvel branded guitars are introduced. U.S.-made to '85, a combination of imports and U.S.-made post-'85. Charvel also manufactured the Jackson brand.

Charvel licensed its trademark to IMC (Hondo) in '85. IMC bought Charvel in '86 and moved the factory to Ontario, California. On October 25, 2002, Fender Musical Instruments Corp. (FMIC) took ownership of Jackson/Charvel Manufacturing Inc.

Pre-Pro (Pre-Production) Charvels began in November 1980 and ran until sometime in 1981. These are known as 'non-plated' indicating pre-production versus a production neck plate. Production serial-

MODEL YEAR	FEATURES	EXC. COND. LOW	HIGH

ized neck plates are considered to be San Dimas models which have a Charvel logo, serial number, and a PO Box San Dimas notation on the neck plate. These Serialized Plated Charvels came after Pre-Pros. Late '81 and '82 saw the early serialized guitars with 21-fret necks; these are more valuable. During '82 the 22-fret neck was introduced. The so-called Soft Strat-, Tele-, Flying V-, and Explorer-style headstocks are associated with the early San Dimas Charvel models. In late '82 the pointy headstock, called the Jackson style, was introduced. In '82 the Superstrat style with a neck plate was introduced. Superstrats with a Kahler tailpiece have a lower value than the Pre-Pro models (with Fender-style trem tailpiece).

Collectors of vintage Charvels look for the vintage Charvel 3-on-a-side logo. This is a defining feature and a cutoff point for valuations. Bogus builders are replicating early Charvels and attempting to sell them as originals so fakes can be a problem for Charvel collectors, so buyer beware.

Other electric guitar manufacturing info:
1986-1989 Japanese-made Models 1 through 8
1989-1991 Japanese-made 550 XL, 650 XL/ Custom, 750 XL (XL=neck-thru)
1989-1992 Japanese-made Models 275, 375, 475, 575
1990-1991 Korean-made Charvette models
1992-1994 Korean-made Models 325, 425

Early Charvel serial numbers (provided by former Jackson/Charvel associate Tim Wilson):
The first 500 to 750 guitars had no serial number, just marked "Made In U.S.A." on their neckplates. Five digit serial numbers were then used until November '81 when 4-digit number adopted, starting with #1001.
1981: 1001-1095
1982: 1096-1724
1983: 1725-2938
1984: 2939-4261
1985: 4262-5303
1986: 5304-5491

Pre-Pro

November 1980-1981. Pre-Pros came in different configurations of body styles, pickups, and finishes. There are five basic Pre-Pro formats: the Standard Body, the Bound Body, the Graphic Body, the Flamed Top, and the Matching Headstock. It is possible to have a combination, such as a Bound Body and Matching Headstock. Line items are based on body style and can feature any one of four neck/headstock-styles used: the so-called Tele-headstock, Strat-headstock, Flying V headstock, and Explorer headstock. Finishes included white, black, red, metallic Lake Placid Blue, and special graphics. All original parts adds considerable value and it is often difficult to determine what is original on these models, so expertise is required. An original Fender brass trem tailpiece, for example, adds considerable value. The Pre-Pro models were prone to modification such as added Kahler and Floyd Rose trems. Price ranges are wide because this is a relatively

Charis Acoustic SJ

1984 Charvel

GUITARS

Charvel So-Cal Style 1

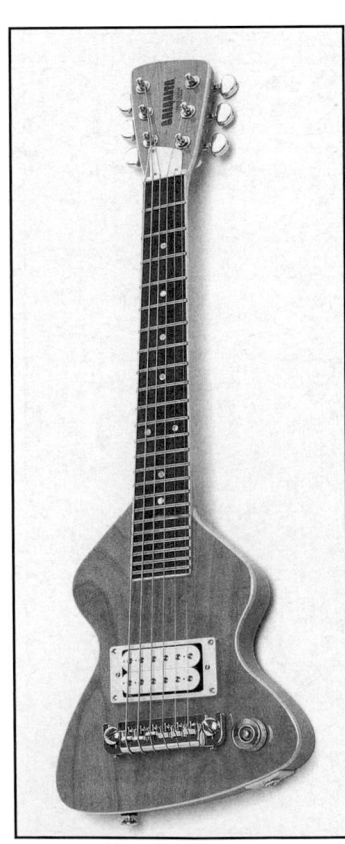

Chiquita Travel Guitar

MODEL YEAR	FEATURES	EXC. COND. LOW	HIGH
new market without mature pricing.			
1980-1981	Bound body	$3,400	$4,200
1980-1981	Flamed top, stained body	$4,400	$5,500
1980-1981	Graphic body	$3,900	$4,850
1980-1981	Matching headstock & body	$4,900	$6,100
1980-1981	Standard body	$2,800	$3,500

275 Deluxe Dinky
1989-1991. Made in Japan, offset double-cut solid-body, 1 single-coil and 1 humbucker, tremolo.

1989-1991		$350	$435

325SL
1992-1994. Dot inlays.

1992-1994		$350	$435

325SLX
1992-1994. Surfcaster-like thinline acoustic/electric, dual cutaways, f-hole, on-board chorus, shark inlays, made in Korea.

1992-1994		$350	$435

375 Deluxe
1989-1991. Maple or rosewood 'board, dot inlays, single-single-humbucker.

1989-1991		$350	$435

475 Deluxe/Special
1989-1991. Introduced as Special, changed to Deluxe in '90, bound rosewood board, shark tooth inlays, 2 oval stacked humbuckers and 1 bridge humbucker. Was also offered as Deluxe Exotic with figured top and back.

1989-1991		$350	$435

525
1989-1994. Acoustic-electric, single-cut.

1989-1994		$350	$435

550XL
1987-1989. Neck-thru (XL), dot markers, 1 single-coil and 1 bridge humbucker.

1987-1989		$400	$500

625-C12
1993-2000. Acoustic-electric cutaway 12-string, spruce top.

1993-2000		$350	$435

625F/625ACEL
1993-1995. Acoustic-electric cutaway, figured maple top.

1993-1995		$350	$435

650XL/Custom
1989-1990. Introduced as neck-thru XL and discontinued as Custom, shark fin markers, 2 stacked oval humbuckers and 1 bridge humbucker, custom version of 550XL.

1989-1990		$700	$875

750XL
1988-1990. Shark fin markers, carved alder archtop body, 2 humbuckers.

1988-1990		$1,000	$1,250

Avenger
1990-1991. Randy Rhoads-style batwing-shaped solidbody, 1 humbucker, 1 single-coil, tremolo, made in Japan.

1990-1991		$425	$525

Charvette
1989-1991. Charvette Series made in Korea, superstrat-style, model number series 100 through 300.

1990-1991		$250	$315

CX Series
1991-1994. Imported offset double cut solidbodies, with body-mounted pickups - HS (192), HSS (292), SSS (392), HSS (692) or HSH (592) - or pickguard mounted pickups - HSS pickups (290, 390) or SSS (291, 391). All with standard tremolo except the 692, 592, 390, and 391 with deluxe locking tremolo.

1991-1994		$250	$315

EVH Art Series
2004-2007. Offset double-cut solidbody, 1 humbucker, striped finish.

2004-2007	Black/white	$1,550	$1,950
2004-2007	White/black on red	$1,750	$2,200
2004-2007	Yellow/black	$1,550	$1,950

Fusion Deluxe
1989-1991. Double-cut solidbody, tremolo, 1 humbucker and 1 single-coil, made in Japan.

1989-1991		$400	$500

Fusion Standard/AS FX 1
1993-1996. Double-cut solidbody, tremolo, 1 regular and 2 mini humbuckers, made in Japan, also named AS FX1.

1993-1996		$350	$425

Model 1/1A/1C
1986-1988. Offset double-cut solidbody, bolt-on maple neck, dot inlays, 1 humbucker, tremolo, made in Japan. Model 1A has 3 single-coils. Model 1C has 1 humbucker and 2 single-coils.

1986-1988		$350	$440

Model 2
1986-1988. As Model 1, but with rosewood 'board.

1986-1988		$350	$440

Model 3/3A/3DR/3L
1986-1989. As Model 2, but with 1 humbucker, 2 single coils. Model 3A has 2 humbuckers. Model 3DR has 1 humbucker and 1 single-coil.

1986-1989		$350	$440

Model 4/4A
1986-1988. As Model 2, but with 1 regular humbucker and 2 stacked humbuckers (no pickguard), active electronics, dots in '86, shark-fin inlays after. Model 4A has 2 regular humbuckers and dot markers.

1986-1988		$450	$575

Model 5/5A
1986-1988. As Model 4A, but neck-thru, with JE1000TG active elctronics. Model 5A is single humbucker and single knob version, limited production, made in Japan.

1986-1988		$450	$575

Model 6
1986-1988. As HSS Model 4, but with shark's tooth inlays, standard or various custom finishes.

1986-1988		$525	$650

Model 7
1988-1989. Single-cut solidbody, bound top, reversed headstock, 2 single-coils, made in Japan.

1988-1989		$525	$650

MODEL YEAR	FEATURES	EXC. COND. LOW	HIGH

Model 88 LTD
1988. Double-cut solidbody, 1 slanted humbucker, shark fin inlay, 1000 built, made in Japan.

1988		$525	$650

Predator
1989-1991. Offset double-cut, bridge humbucker, single-coil neck, bolt-on.

1989-1991		$350	$450

San Dimas Serialized Plated
1981-1986, 1995-1997. U.S.-made with San Dimas neck plate, bolt neck, rounded headstock early production, pointy headstock later, reissued in mid-'90s.

1981-1982	Soft headstock	$2,600	$3,250
1982-1986	Pointy headstock	$1,700	$2,100
1995-1997	Soft headstock	$700	$875

San Dimas LTD 25th Anniversary
2006. About 100 made, 25th Anniversary logo on neck plate with production number, highly figured top, high-end appointments.

2006		$1,700	$2,100

San Dimas Reissue (FMIC)
2004-present. Alder body, bolt neck.

2004-2014		$500	$1,300

San Dimas Style 2 2H
2008-2010. Single cut solidbody, 2 humbuckers, U.S.-made.

2008-2010	Pagan Gold custom color	$700	$875

So-Cal Series
2008-2012. Offset double-cut solidbody.

2008-2012	Various options	$600	$1,000

ST Custom
1990-1991. Offset double-cut ash solidbody, 2 single-coils and 1 humbucker, rosewood 'board, tremolo, made in Japan.

1990-1991		$400	$500

ST Deluxe
1990-1991. Same as ST Custom but with maple 'board.

1990-1991		$375	$475

Standard
2002-2003. Typical offset double-cut Charvel body, 2 Seymour Duncan humbucker pickups, various opaque colors.

2002-2003		$280	$350

Star
1980-1981. The Star is considered by early-Charvel collectors to be Charvel's only original design with its unique four-point body.

1980-1981		$2,800	$3,450

Surfcaster
1991-1994. Offset double-cut, f-hole, various pickup options, bound body, tremolo, made in Japan.

1991-1994	1 single-coil, 1 humbucker	$1,000	$1,300
1991-1994	2 single-coils, hardtail	$1,000	$1,300
1991-1994	2 single-coils, vibrato	$1,000	$1,300
1991-1994	3 single-coils	$1,100	$1,400
1991-1994	Custom color & features	$1,200	$1,500

Surfcaster 12
1991-1995. 12-string version of Surfcaster, no tremolo, made in Japan.

1991-1995		$1,000	$1,300

Surfcaster Double Neck
1992. Very limited production, 6/12 double neck, Charvel logo on both necks, black.

1992		$1,650	$2,100

Surfcaster HT (Model SC 1)
1992-1996. Made in Japan. Hard Tail (HT) non-tremolo version of Surfcaster, has single-coil and bridge humbucker.

1992-1996	Custom color & features	$1,350	$1,675
1992-1996	Standard colors & features	$1,250	$1,575

Chiquita
1979-present. Intermediate grade, production guitars made by Erlewine Guitars in Austin, Texas (see that listing). There was also a mini amp available.

Travel Guitar
1979-present. Developed by Mark Erlewine and ZZ Top's Billy Gibbons, 27" overall length solidbody, 1 or 2 pickups, various colors.

1979-2014		$225	$500

Chris George
1966-present. Professional and premium grade, custom, archtop, acoustic, electric and resonator guitars built by luthier Chris George in Tattershall Lincolnshire, U.K.

Christopher Carrington
1988-present. Production/custom, premium grade, classical and flamenco acoustic guitars built by luthier Chris Carrington in Rockwall, Texas.

Chrysalis Guitars
1998-present. Luthier Tim White builds his premium grade, production/custom Chrysalis Guitar System, which includes interchangeable components that can be quickly assembled into a full-size electric/acoustic guitar, in New Boston, New Hampshire. A variety of instruments may be created, including 6- and 12-string electrics and acoustics, electric and acoustic mandocello and acoustic basses.

Cimar/Cimar by Ibanez
Early-1980s. Private brand of Hoshino Musical Instruments, Nagoya, Japan, who also branded Ibanez. Headstock with script Cimar logo or Cimar by Ibanez, copy models and Ibanez near-original models such as the star body.

Cimar

1982	Classical	$55	$75
1982	Double-cut solidbody	$175	$220
1982	Star body style	$175	$220

Chris George

1975 Cimar

2004 Cimarron MJ
Thomas Ivan

CMG Diane

MODEL		EXC. COND.	
YEAR	FEATURES	LOW	HIGH

Cimarron

1978-present. Luthiers John Walsh and Clayton Walsh build their professional grade, production/custom, flat-top acoustic guitars in Ridgway, Colorado. Between '94 and '98 they also produced electric guitars.

Cipher

1960s. Solidbody electric guitars and basses imported from Japan by Inter-Mark. Generally strange-shaped bodies.

Electric Solidbody

1960s. For any student-grade import, a guitar with any missing part, such as a missing control knob or trem arm, is worth much less.

1960s		$160	$225

Citron

1995-present. Luthier Harvey Citron builds his professional and premium grade, production/custom solidbody guitars and basses in Woodstock, New York. He also builds basses. In '75, Citron and Joe Veillette founded Veillette-Citron, which was known for handcrafted, neck-thru guitars and basses. That company closed in '83.

Clark

1985-present. Custom, professional grade, solidbody electric guitars and basses, built by luthier Ed Clark, first in Amityville, New York ('85-'90), then Medford ('91-'99) and presently Lake Ronkonkoma.

Clifford

Clifford was a brand manufactured by Kansas City, Missouri instrument wholesalers J.W. Jenkins & Sons. First introduced in 1895, the brand also offered mandolins.

Clovis

Mid-1960s. Private brand guitars, most likely made by Kay.

Electric Solidbody

Mid-1960s. Kay slab solidbody, 2 pickups.

1965		$300	$375

CMG Guitars

2012-present. Owner Chris Mitchell imports intermediate grade, acoustic and acoustic-electric guitars from China. He also offers professional grade, production/custom, electric guitars built by luthiers Russell Jones and James Horel in Statesboro, Georgia.

Cole

1890-1919. W.A. Cole, after leaving Fairbanks & Cole, started his own line in 1890. He died in 1909 but the company continued until 1919. He also made mandolins and banjos.

Parlor

1897. Small size, Brazilian rosewood sides and back, spruce top, ebony 'board, slotted headstock, dot markers.

1897		$800	$1,200

MODEL		EXC. COND.	
YEAR	FEATURES	LOW	HIGH

Coleman Guitars

1976-1983. Custom made presentation grade instruments made in Homosassa, Florida, by luthier Harry Coleman. No headstock logo, Coleman logo on inside center strip.

Collings

1986-present. Professional, premium, and presentation grade, production/custom, flat-top, archtop and electric guitars built in Austin, Texas. They also build mandolins and ukuleles. Bill Collings started with guitar repair and began custom building guitars around '73. In '80, he relocated his shop from Houston to Austin and started Collings Guitars in '86. In '06 they moved to a new plant in southwest Austin.

0-1

2005-present. Mother-of-pearl inlays, sitka spruce, mahogany neck, back & sides, ebony 'board and bridge, high gloss lacquer finish.

2005-2014		$2,400	$3,000

0-1A

2010-present. As 0-1 with Adirondack spruce top.

2010-2014		$3,200	$4,100

0-1G

As 0-1 with German spruce top.

2009		$2,700	$3,400

0-1SB

Sitka spruce mahogany.

2006		$2,400	$3,000

00-1G

German spruce.

2009		$3,000	$3,750

00-1MH

All mahogany body.

2010		$2,700	$3,400

00-2H

1999-present. Indian rosewood.

1999-2014		$1,850	$2,300

00-41

2001. Premium Brazilian rosewood back and sides, Adirondack spruce top, abalone top purfling.

2001		$6,400	$8,000

000-1

1990s-present. Mahogany body, spruce top.

1990s	000-1	$2,900	$3,650
1990s-2014	000-1A		
	Adirondack	$3,125	$3,900

000-1 ICC

000-1 with Indian rosewood back and sides.

2000s		$2,100	$2,650

000-1Mh

2006. All mahogany body, 000 size.

2006		$2,100	$2,650

000-2H

1994-present. 15" 000-size, Indian rosewood back and sides, spruce top, slotted headstock, 12-fret neck, dot markers. AAA Koa back and sides in '96.

1994-1995	Indian rosewood	$2,100	$2,650
1996	AAA Koa	$2,450	$3,050
2007-2014	Indian rosewood	$2,100	$2,650

MODEL YEAR	FEATURES	EXC. COND. LOW	HIGH

000-41

1999. Indian rosewood sides and back, Sitka spruce top, slotted headstock.

| 1999 | | $2,800 | $3,500 |

290 Series

2004-present. Solid Honduran mahogany body, East Indian rosewood 'board, 2 P-90 style pickups, '50s style wiring, high gloss lacquer finish.

| 2004-2014 | Deluxe | $1,600 | $2,000 |

AT-17

Collings' archtops are built in limited numbers, AT-17 is a 17" single-cut, with f-holes, Adirondack or European spruce top, premium flamed maple back and sides, and premium appointments, sunburst or blonde. Options include scale length, pickup and bindings.

| 2008-2014 | | $10,000 | $12,500 |

C-10

1986-present. 000-size, mahogany back and sides, spruce top, sunburst or natural.

| 1986-2014 | | $2,600 | $3,300 |

C-10 Custom

Custom built C-10s, various options.

| 2007 | Koa | $3,000 | $3,750 |

C-10 Deluxe

1986-present. C-10 with Indian rosewood back and sides (flamed maple or koa optional), sunburst or natural.

1986-2014	Indian rosewood	$2,600	$3,300
2000s	Flamed maple	$2,600	$3,300
2000s	Koa option	$2,900	$3,600

C-100

1986-1994. Quadruple 0-size, mahogany back and sides, spruce top, natural, replaced by CJ Jumbo.

| 1986-1994 | | $2,100 | $2,600 |

C-100 Deluxe

1986-1994. C-100 with rosewood back and sides.

| 1986-1994 | | $2,500 | $3,100 |

CJ Jumbo

1995-present. Quadruple 0-size, Indian rosewood back and sides, spruce top, natural.

| 1995-2014 | | $2,600 | $3,300 |

CJ Koa ASB

2007. Adirondack spruce top, scalloped bracing ASB, flamed koa sides and back.

| 2007 | | $3,300 | $4,100 |

CL Series

2004-present. City Limits series, fully carved flame maple top, solid Honduran mahogany body, East Indian rosewood 'board, high gloss lacquer finish.

| 2004-2014 | Deluxe | $2,800 | $3,500 |

Clarence White

1989-2000. Brazilian rosewood back and sides, Adirondack top, herringbone trim.

| 1989-2000 | | $6,400 | $8,000 |

D-1 Gruhn

1989. Short run for Gruhn Guitars, Nashville, Gruhn script headstock logo, signed by Bill Collings, choice of Indian rosewood or curly maple back and sides, Engelman spruce top.

| 1989 | | $2,900 | $3,600 |

D-1/D-1SB/D-1A Custom

1992-present. D-size, 15 5/8", mahogany back and sides, spruce top, natural. D-1SB is sunburst option. D-1A Custom upgrades to Adirondack spruce top and higher appointments, natural.

1992-2014	D-1	$2,300	$2,900
1999-2002	D-1A Custom	$3,100	$3,900
2001	D-1SB	$2,300	$2,900

D-2

1986-1995. D-1 with Indian rosewood back and sides, natural.

| 1986-1995 | | $2,300 | $2,900 |

D-2H

1986-present. Dreadnought, same as D-2 with herringbone purfling around top edge.

| 1986-2014 | | $2,400 | $3,000 |

D-2HA

2004-2010. Indian or Brazilian rosewood back and sides, Adirondack spruce top, top herringbone trim, gloss natural finish.

| 2004-2010 | Brazilian rosewood | $6,400 | $8,000 |
| 2004-2010 | Indian rosewood | $3,250 | $4,050 |

D-2HAV

2004-2010. Varnish finish option.

| 2004-2010 | | $3,250 | $4,050 |

D-2HB

1994-2001. Grade AA Brazilian rosewood, spruce top.

| 1994-2001 | Spruce | $5,900 | $7,300 |
| 2005 | Adirondack | $6,400 | $8,000 |

D-2HG SB

German spruce, sunburst varnish.

| 2008 | | $4,500 | $5,600 |

D-2HV

1994. D-2H with V shaped neck.

| 1994 | | $2,200 | $2,700 |

D-3

1990-present. Similar to D-2H but with abalone purfling/rosette.

| 1990-1999 | Brazilian rosewood | $6,000 | $7,400 |
| 2000-2014 | Indian rosewood | $3,000 | $3,700 |

D-42

2000s. Brazilian rosewood back and sides, fancy.

| 2000s | | $6,200 | $7,900 |

DS-1/DS-1A

2004-present. D size, slope shoulders, 12 fret neck, slotted headstock, mahogany back and sides, 1A is Adirondack upgrade.

| 2004-2014 | | $3,000 | $3,800 |

DS-2H

1995-present. D size, slope shoulders, 12 fret neck, slotted headstock.

| 1995-2014 | | $3,000 | $3,800 |

DS-41

1995-2007. Indian rosewood, abalone top trim, snowflake markers.

| 1995-2007 | | $3,600 | $4,500 |

I-35 Deluxe

2007-present. Fully carved flame or quilted maple top, mahogany body, Brazilian or Madagascar rosewood 'board, high Gloss lacquer finish.

| 2007-2014 | | $3,000 | $3,800 |

2008 Collings 000-2H

2004 Collings D-2H
Folkway Music

Collings SOCO DLX

Comins Chester Avenue

MODEL YEAR	FEATURES	EXC. COND. LOW	HIGH

OM-1/OM-1A
1994-present. Grand concert, sitka spruce top, mahogany back and sides, natural. OM-1A includes Adirondack spruce upgrade.

1994-1999	OM-1A	$2,800	$3,500
1994-2014	OM-1	$2,500	$3,100
2000-2014	OM-1 Koa	$2,800	$3,500
2000-2014	OM-1MH Mahogany	$2,200	$2,800
2007-2014	OM-1 Cutaway	$2,700	$3,400
2007-2014	OM-1A Cutaway	$2,900	$3,600

OM-2
2008. Indian rosewood back and sides.

| 2008 | Cutaway | $2,800 | $3,500 |

OM-2H
1990-present. Indian rosewood back and sides, herringbone binding.

| 1990-2014 | | $2,700 | $3,400 |

OM-2H GSS
2008. Indian rosewood sides and back, German spruce top, herringbone trim top.

| 2008 | | $2,800 | $3,500 |

OM-2HAV
1998. Adirondack spruce top, Brazilian rosewood back and sides, ivoroid-bound body.

| 1998 | | $6,000 | $7,400 |

OM-3
1998-present. Brazilian rosewood back and sides, Adirondack spruce top, fancy rosette, later Indian rosewood and figured maple.

1998	Brazilian rosewood	$6,200	$7,700
2002-2014	Indian rosewood	$3,000	$3,700
2003	Figured maple	$3,100	$3,850
2008	Mahogany	$3,100	$3,850

OM-3A
2004-2007. Adirondack, Indian rosewood.

| 2004-2007 | | $3,400 | $4,250 |

OM-3HC
1986-1996. Single rounded cutaway, 15", Indian rosewood back and sides, spruce top, herringbone purfling.

| 1986-1996 | | $3,300 | $4,100 |

OM-41BrzGCut
2007. Brazilian rosewood sides and back, German spruce top, rounded cutaway.

| 2007 | | $6,800 | $8,500 |

OM-42B
Brazilian rosewood back and sides, Adirondack spruce top, fancy rosette and binding.

| 2000 | | $7,100 | $8,900 |

OM-42G
Indian rosewood.

| 1999 | | $3,800 | $4,700 |

SJ
1986-present. Spruce top, quilted maple back and sides or Indian rosewood (earlier option).

| 1986-2014 | Various options | $2,800 | $3,900 |

SJ-41
1996. Brazilian rosewood back and sides, cedar top.

| 1996 | | $6,400 | $8,000 |

MODEL YEAR	FEATURES	EXC. COND. LOW	HIGH

Winfield
2004-2006. D-style, Brazilian rosewood back and sides, Adirondack spruce top, mahogany neck, ebony board.

2004	Indian rosewood	$3,300	$4,100
2005-2006	Brazilian rosewood	$6,600	$8,200
2006	Mahogany	$3,300	$4,100

Columbia
Late 1800s-early 1900s. The Columbia brand name was used on acoustic guitars by New York's James H. Buckbee Co. until c.1987 and afterwards by Galveston's Thomas Goggan and Brothers.

Comins
1992-present. Premium and presentation grade, custom archtops built by luthier Bill Comins in Willow Grove, Pennsylvania. He also builds mandolins and offers a combo amp built in collaboration with George Alessandro.

Commander
Late 1950s-early 1960s. Archtop acoustic guitars made by Harmony for the Alden catalog company.

Concertone
Ca. 1914-1930s. Concertone was a brand made by Chicago's Slingerland and distributed by Montgomery Ward. The brand was also used on other instruments such as ukuleles.

Conklin
1984-present. Intermediate, professional and premium grade, production/custom, 6-, 7-, 8-, and 12-string solid and hollowbody electrics, by luthier Bill Conklin. He also builds basses. Originally located in Lebanon, Missouri, in '88 the company moved to Springfield, Missouri. Conklin instruments are made in the U.S. and overseas.

Conn Guitars
Ca.1968-ca.1978. Student to mid-quality classical and acoustic guitars, some with bolt-on necks, also some electrics. Imported from Japan by band instrument manufacturer and distributor Conn/Continental Music Company, Elkhart, Indiana.

Acoustic
1968-1978. Various models.

| 1968-1978 | | $105 | $175 |

Classical
1968-1978. Various student-level models.

| 1968-1978 | | $80 | $125 |

Electric Solidbody
1970s. Various models.

| 1970-1978 | | $150 | $200 |

Connor, Stephan
1995-present. Luthier Stephan Connor builds his premium grade, custom nylon-string guitars in Waltham, Massachusetts.

MODEL YEAR	FEATURES	EXC. COND. LOW	HIGH

Conrad Guitars

Ca. 1968-1978. Mid- to better-quality copies of glued-neck Martin and Gibson acoustics and bolt-neck Gibson and Fender solidbodies. They also offered basses, mandolins and banjos. Imported from Japan by David Wexler and Company, Chicago, Illinois.

Acoustic 12-String
1970s. Dreadnought size.

1970s		$105	$175

Acoustical Slimline (40080/40085)
1970s. Rosewood 'board, 2 or 3 DeArmond-style pickups, block markers, sunburst.

1970s		$250	$350

Acoustical Slimline 12-String (40100)
1970s. Rosewood 'board, 2 DeArmond-style pickups, dot markers, sunburst.

1970s		$250	$350

Bison (40035/40030/40065/40005)
1970s. 1 thru 4 pickups available, rosewood 'board with dot markers, six-on-side headstock.

1970s		$250	$350

Bumper (40223)
1970s. Clear Lucite solidbody.

1970s		$350	$425

Classical Student (40150)
1970s.

1970s		$95	$115

De Luxe Folk Guitar
1970s. Resonator acoustic, mahogany back, sides and neck, Japanese import.

1970s		$180	$225

Master Size (40178)
1972-1977. Electric archtop, 2 pickups.

1972-1977		$225	$325

Resonator Acoustic
1970s. Flat-top with wood, metal resonator and 8 ports, round neck.

1970s		$360	$435

Violin-Shaped 12-String Electric (40176)
1970s. Scroll headstock, 2 pickups, 500/1 control panel, bass side dot markers, sunburst.

1970s		$350	$425

Violin-Shaped Electric (40175)
1970s. Scroll headstock, 2 pickups, 500/1 control panel, bass side dot markers, vibrato, sunburst.

1970s		$350	$425

White Styrene 1280
1970s. Solid maple body covered with white styrene, 2 pickups, tremolo, bass side dot markers, white.

1970s		$275	$350

Contessa

1960s. Acoustic, semi-hollow archtop, solidbody and bass guitars made in Italy by Zero Sette and imported by Hohner. They also made banjos.

Acoustic

1960s		$80	$200

Electric Solidbody
1967. Various models.

1960s		$225	$350

Contreras

See listing for Manuel Contreras and Manuel Contreras II.

Coral

1967-1969. In '66 MCA bought Danelectro and in '67 introduced the Coral brand of guitars, basses and amps. Special thanks to Brian Conner for his assistance with this brand.

Bellzouki 7021
1967. 12-string electric, modified teardrop shape with body points on treble and bass bouts, 2 pickups.

1967		$1,225	$1,625

Combo/Vincent Bell Combo
1967-1969. Cutaway acoustic/electric,1 or 2 pickups.

1967-1969	V1N6, 1 pickup	$1,850	$2,450
1967-1969	V2N6, 2 pickups	$2,025	$2,700

Firefly
1967-1969. Double-cut, f-holes, 2 pickups, with or without vibrato.

1967-1969	2N, red	$725	$950
1967-1969	2N, sunburst	$650	$875
1967-1969	2V, vibrato, red	$1,100	$1,450
1967-1969	2V, vibrato, sunburst	$1,050	$1,400
1968-1969	F2N12, Electric XII, red	$1,150	$1,525
1968-1969	F2N12, Electric XII, sunburst	$1,100	$1,450

Hornet
1967-1969. Solidbody, 2 or 3 pickups, with or without vibrato, sunburst, black or red.

1967-1969	2N, 2 pickups, black or red	$1,100	$1,450
1967-1969	2N, 2 pickups, sunburst	$950	$1,275
1967-1969	2V, 2 pickups, vibrato, black or red	$1,200	$1,600
1967-1969	2V, 2 pickups, vibrato, sunburst	$1,000	$1,350
1967-1969	3N, 3 pickups, black or red	$1,225	$1,625
1967-1969	3N, 3 pickups, sunburst	$1,100	$1,450
1967-1969	3V, 3 pickups, vibrato, black or red	$1,300	$1,725
1967-1969	3V, 3 pickups, vibrato, sunburst	$1,100	$1,450

Long Horn
1967-1969. Deep double-cut hollowbody, 2 lipstick tube pickups, 6 or 12-string, sunburst.

1967-1969	L2N12, Electric XII	$1,325	$1,775
1967-1969	L2N6, 2 pickups	$1,225	$1,625

Scorpion
1967-1969. Offset double-cut solidbody, 2 or 3 lipstick tube pickups, 12-string.

1967-1969	2N12, 2 pickups, black or red	$1,125	$1,500

Connor Angel Romero

1968 Coral Hornet
Robbie Keene

Córdoba C5

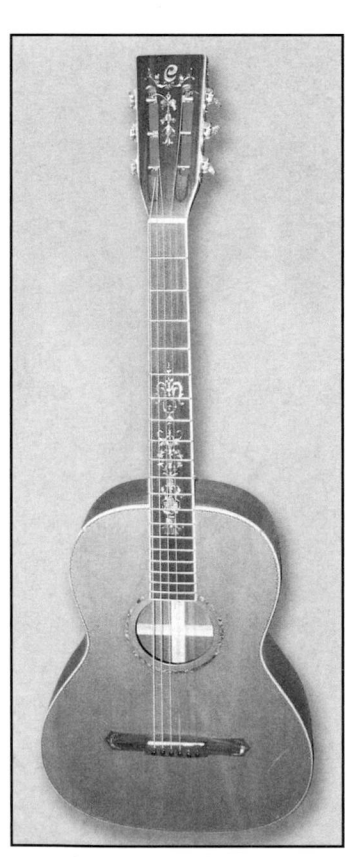

Cort Earth 900 Parlor
Bill Cherensky

MODEL YEAR	FEATURES	EXC. COND. LOW	HIGH
1967-1969	2N12, 2 pickups, sunburst	$925	$1,250
1967-1969	2V12, 2 pickups, vibrato, black or red	$1,225	$1,625
1967-1969	2V12, 2 pickups, vibrato, sunburst	$1,000	$1,350
1967-1969	3N12, 3 pickups, black or red	$1,300	$1,725
1967-1969	3N12, 3 pickups, sunburst	$1,100	$1,450
1967-1969	3V12, 3 pickups, vibrato, black or red	$1,375	$1,825
1967-1969	3V12, 3 pickups, vibrato, sunburst	$1,150	$1,550

Sitar

1967-1969. Six-string guitar with drone strings and 3 pickups (2 under the 6 strings, 1 under the drones), kind of a USA-shaped body.

1967-1969	3S18, 18-string	$2,000	$2,600
1967-1969	3S19, 19-string	$2,100	$2,800
1967-1969	3S9, 9-string	$1,900	$2,500

Teardrop

1967-1969. Teardrop shaped hollowbody, 2 lipstick tube pickups.

1968		$1,800	$2,350

Córdoba

Line of classical guitars handmade in Portugal and imported by Guitar Salon International. By '13, U.S. production was added.

Classical

1999	1A India	$1,700	$2,100
2000s	Gipsy King	$800	$1,000
2000s	Higher-end	$550	$800
2000s	Mid-level	$350	$550
2000s	Student-level	$200	$275

Cordova

1960s. Classical nylon string guitars imported by David Wexler of Chicago.

Grand Concert Model WC-026

1960s. Highest model offered by Cordova, 1-piece rosewood back, laminated rosewood sides, spruce top, natural.

1960s		$230	$300

Corey James Custom Guitars

2005-present. Luthier Corey James Moilanen builds his professional and premium grade, production/custom solidbody guitars and basses in Howell, Michigan.

Coriani, Paolo

1984-present. Production/custom nylon-string guitars and hurdy-gurdys built by luthier Paolo Coriani in Modeila, Italy.

Cort

1973-present. North Brook, Illinois-based Cort offers budget, intermediate and professional grade, production/custom, acoustic and solidbody, semi-hollow, hollow body electric guitars and basses built in Korea.

Cort was the second significant Korean private-label (Hondo brand was the first) to come out of Korea. Jack Westheimer entered into an agreement with Korea's Cort to do Cort-brand, private-label, and Epiphone-brand guitars.

CP Thornton Guitars

1985-present. Luthier Chuck Thornton builds professional and premium grade, production/custom, semi-hollow and solidbody electric guitars in Sumner, Maine. Up to '96 he also built basses.

Crafter

1986-present. Crafter offers budget and intermediate grade, production, classical, acoustic, acoustic/electric, and electric guitars, basses and mandolins made in Korea. They also offer the Cruzer and Ashland brands of instruments. From '72 to '86 they made Sungeum classical guitars.

Crafters of Tennessee

See listing under Tennessee.

Cranium

1996-present. Professional grade, production/custom, hollow, semi-hollow, and solidbody electrics built by luthier Wayne O'Connor in Peterborough, Ontario.

Crescent Moon

Professional grade, production/custom, solidbody guitars and basses built by luthier Craig Muller in Baltimore, Maryland.

Creston

2004-present. Professional grade, custom, solidbody electric guitars and basses built by luthier Creston Lea in Burlington, Vermont.

Crestwood

1970s. Copies of the popular classical guitars, flat-tops, electric solidbodies and basses of the era, imported by La Playa Distributing Company of Detroit.

Acoustic 12-String

1970s		$180	$225

Electric

1970s. Various models include near copies of the 335 (Crestwood model 2043, 2045 and 2047), Les Paul Custom (2020), Strat (2073), Jazzmaster (2078), Tele (2082), and the SG Custom (2084).

1970s		$235	$475

Crimson Guitars

2005-present. Luthiers Benjamin Crowe and Aki Atrill build professional and premium grade, custom, solidbody guitars and basses in Somerset, U.K.

MODEL YEAR	FEATURES	EXC. COND. LOW	HIGH

Cromwell

1935-1939. Budget model brand built by Gibson and distributed by mail-order businesses like Grossman, Continental, Richter & Phillips, and Gretsch & Brenner.

Acoustic Archtop

1935-1939. Archtop acoustic, f-holes, pressed mahogany back and sides, carved and bound top, bound back, 'guard and 'board, no truss rod.

MODEL YEAR	FEATURES	EXC. COND. LOW	HIGH
1935-1939		$650	$1,075
1935-1939	With '30s era pickup	$1,100	$1,400

Acoustic Flat-Top

1935-1939	G-2 (L-00)	$1,500	$1,900

GT-2 Tenor

1935-1939	14.74" flat-top	$650	$1,075

GT-4 Tenor

1935-1939	16" archtop	$650	$1,075

Cromwell (Guild)

1963-1964. Guild imported these 2- or 3-pickup offset double cut solidbodies from Hagstrom. These were basically part of Hagstrom's Kent line with laminated bodies and birch necks. About 500 were imported into the U.S.

Solidbody

1963-1964		$900	$1,125

Crook Custom Guitars

1997-present. Professional grade, custom, solidbody electric guitars and basses built in Moundsville, West Virginia by luthier Bill Crook.

Crossley

2005-present. Professional grade, production/custom, solidbody and chambered electric guitars built in Melbourne, Victoria, Australia by luthier Peter Crossley.

Crown

1960s. Violin-shaped hollowbody electrics, solidbody electric guitars and basses, possibly others. Imported from Japan.

Acoustic Flat-Top

1960s. 6-string and 12-string.

1960s		$105	$150

Electric Archtop

1960s. Double pointed cutaways, 2 humbucking pickups, laminated top, full-depth body.

1960s		$360	$450

Electric Solidbody/Semi-Hollow

1960s. Student-level Japanese import.

1960s	Copy models	$260	$350
1960s	Pointy violin-shaped body	$260	$350
1960s	Standard models	$160	$200

Crucianelli

Early 1960s. Italian guitars imported into the U.S. by Bennett Brothers of New York and Chicago around '63 to '64. Accordion builder Crucianelli

also made Imperial, Elite, PANaramic, and Elli-Sound brand guitars.

Cruzer

Intermediate grade, production, solidbody electric guitars, basses, amps and effects made by Korea's Crafter Guitars.

CSR

1996-present. Father and daughter luthiers Roger and Courtney Kitchens build their premium grade, production/custom, archtop guitars and basses in Byron, Georgia.

Cumpiano

1974-present. Professional and premium grade, custom steel-string and nylon-string guitars, and acoustic basses built by luthier William Cumpiano in Northampton, Massachusetts.

Curbow String Instruments

1994-2007. Premium grade, production/custom, solidbody guitars and basses built by luthier Doug Somervell in Morganton, Georgia. Founded by Greg Curbow who passed away in '05.

Custom

1980s. Line of solidbody guitars and basses introduced in the early '80s by Charles Lawing and Chris Lovell, owners of Strings & Things in Memphis, Tennessee.

Custom Kraft

Late-1950s-1968. A house brand of St. Louis Music Supply, instruments built by Valco and Kay. They also offered basses and amps.

Electric Solidbody

1950s-1960s. U.S.-made or import, entry-level, 1or 2 pickups.

1950s-60s	Import	$150	$225
1950s-60s	USA, Kay, 2 pickups	$425	$550

Sound Saturator

1960s	12-string	$350	$450

Super Zapp

1960s		$400	$500

Thin Twin Jimmy Reed (style)

Late-1950s-early-1960s. Single cut, 2 pickups, 4 knobs and toggle, dot markers.

1959	U.S.-made	$575	$700

Cutler

One of the many guitar brands built by Japan's Matsumoku company.

D.J. Hodson

1994-2007. Luthier David J.Hodson built his professional and premium grade, production/custom, acoustic guitars in Loughborough, Leicestershire, U.K. He also built ukes. He passed away in '07.

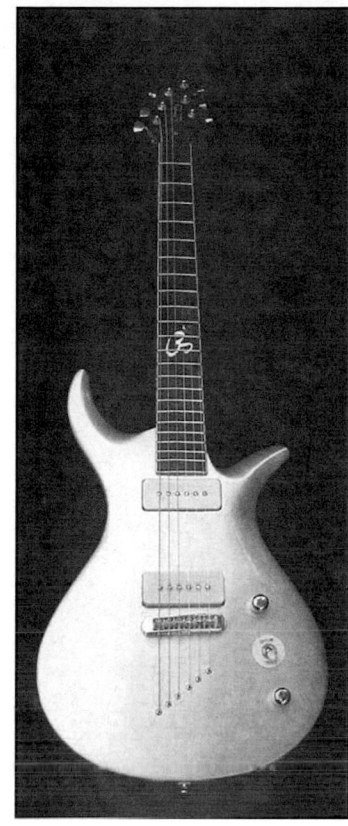

Crossley Goldtop

CSR Serenata

GUITARS

*Daddy Mojo String
Instruments Resophonic*

Daily Classical

MODEL		EXC. COND.	
YEAR	FEATURES	LOW	HIGH

Daddy Mojo String Instruments Inc.

2005-present. Luthiers Lenny Piroth-Robert and Luca Tripaldi build their intermediate and professional grade, production/custom, solidbody electric, resonator and cigar box guitars in Montreal, Quebec.

Dagmar Custom Guitars

2008-present. Luthier Pete Swanson builds custom, premium and presentation grade, acoustic and electric archtop guitars in Niagara, Ontario.

D'Agostino

1976-early 1990s. Acoustic and electric solidbody guitars and basses imported by PMS Music, founded in New York City by former Maestro executive Pat D'Agostino, his brother Steven D'Agostino, and Mike Confortti. First dreadnought acoustic guitars imported from Japan in '76. First solidbodies manufactured by the EKO custom shop beginning in '77. In '82 solidbody production moved to Japan. Beginning in '84, D'Agostinos were made in Korea. Overall, about 60% of guitars were Japanese, 40% Korean. They also had basses.

Acoustic Flat-Top
1976-1990. Early production in Japan, by mid-'80s, most production in Korea.

1976-1990		$160	$250

Electric Semi-Hollowbody
1981-early 1990s. Early production in Japan, later versions from Korea.

1981-1990		$260	$500

Electric Solidbody
1977-early 1990s. Early models made in Italy, later versions from Japan and Korea.

1981-1990		$260	$500

Daily Guitars

1976-present. Luthier David Daily builds his premium grade, production/custom classical guitars in Sparks, Nevada.

Daion

1978-1984. Mid- to higher-quality copies imported from Japan. Original designs introduced in the '80s. Only acoustics offered at first; in '81 they added acoustic/electric and solid and semi-hollow electrics. They also had basses.

Acoustic
1978-1985. Various flat-top models.

1978-1985	Higher-end	$525	$1,000
1978-1985	Lower-end	$325	$400

Electric
1978-1985. Various solid and semi-hollow body guitars.

1978-1985	Higher-end	$525	$1,000
1978-1985	Lower-end	$325	$400

Daisy Rock

2001-present. Budget and intermediate grade, production, full-scale and 3/4 scale, solidbody,

MODEL		EXC. COND.	
YEAR	FEATURES	LOW	HIGH

semi-hollow, acoustic, and acoustic/electric guitars and basses. Founded by Tish Ciravolo as a Division of Schecter Guitars, the Daisy line is focused on female customers.

D'Ambrosio

2001-present. Luthier Otto D'Ambrosio builds his premium grade, custom/production, acoustic and electric archtop guitars in Providence, Rhode Island.

Dan Armstrong

Dan Armstrong started playing jazz in Cleveland in the late-'50s. He moved to New York and also started doing repairs, eventually opening his own store on 48th Street in '65. By the late-'60s he was designing his Lucite guitars for Ampeg (see Ampeg for those listings). He moved to England in '71, where he developed his line of colored stomp boxes. He returned to the States in '75. Armstrong died in '04.

Wood Body Guitar
1973-1975. Sliding pickup, wood body, brown.

1973-1975		$1,700	$2,100

Dan Armstrong Guitars

2015-present. Professional grade, production/custom, acrylic solidbody electrics based on the original Dan Armstrong models, built in Everett, Washington.

Dan Kellaway

1976-present. Production/custom, premium grade, classical and steel string guitars built by luthier Dan Kellaway in Singleton NSW, Australia. He also builds mandolins and lutes.

Danelectro

1946-1969, 1996-present. Founded in Red Bank, New Jersey, by Nathan I. (Nate or Nat) Daniel, an electronics enthusiast with amplifier experience. In 1933, Daniel built amps for Thor's Bargain Basement in New York. In '34 he was recruited by Epiphone's Herb Sunshine to build earliest Electar amps and pickup-making equipment. From '35 to '42, he operated Daniel Electric Laboratories in Manhattan, supplying Epiphone. He started Danelectro in '46 and made his first amps for Montgomery Ward in '47. Over the years, Danelectro made amplifiers, solidbody, semi-hollow and hollowbody electric guitars and basses, electric sitar, and the Bellzouki under the Danelectro, Silvertone, and Coral brands. In '48, began supplying Silvertone amps for Sears (various coverings), with his own brand (brown leatherette) distributed by Targ and Dinner as Danelectro and S.S. Maxwell. He developed an electronic vibrato in '48 on his Vibravox series amps. In '50 he developed a microphone with volume and tone controls and outboard Echo Box reverb unit. In the fall of '54, Danelectro replaced Harmony as provider of Silvertone solidbody

MODEL YEAR	FEATURES	EXC. COND. LOW	HIGH

guitars for Sears. Also in '54, the first Danelectro brand guitars appeared with tweed covering, bell headstock, and pickups under the pickguard. The Coke bottle headstock debuts as Silvertone Lightning Bolt in '54, and was used on Danelectros for '56 to '66. The company moved to Red Bank, New Jersey in '57, and in '58 relocated to Neptune, New Jersey. In '59, Harmony and Kay guitars replace all but 3 Danelectros in Sears catalog. In '66, MCA buys the company (Daniel remains with company), but by mid-'69, MCA halts production and closes the doors. Some leftover stock is sold to Dan Armstrong, who had a shop in New York at the time. Armstrong assembled several hundred Danelectro guitars as Dan Armstrong Modified with his own pickup design.

Rights to name acquired by Anthony Marc in late-'80s, who assembled a number of thinline hollowbody guitars, many with Longhorn shape, using Japanese-made bodies and original Danelectro necks and hardware. In '96, the Evets Corporation, of San Clemente, California, introduced a line of effects bearing the Danelectro brand. Amps and guitars, many of which were reissues of the earlier instruments, soon followed. In early 2003, Evets discontinued offering guitar and amps, but revived the guitar and bass line in '05.

MCA-Danelectro made guitars were called the Dane Series. Dane A model numbers start with an A (e.g. A2V), Dane B models start with a B (e.g. B3V), Dane C (e.g. C2N), and Dane D (e.g. D2N). The least expensive series was the A, going up to the most expensive D. All Dane Series instruments came with 1, 2 or 3 pickups and with hand vibrato options. The Dane Series were made from '67 to '69. MCA did carry over the Convertible, Guitarlin 4123, Long Horn Bass-4 and Bass-6 and Doubleneck 3923. MCA also offered the Bellzouki Double Pickup 7021. Each Dane Series includes an electric 12-string. Danelectro also built the Coral brand instruments (see Coral).

Special thanks to Brian Conner for his assistance with this brand.

Baritone 6-String Reissue
1999-2003, 2008-present. Danelectro has offered several models with 6-string baritone tuning, often with various reissue-year designations, single- or double-cut, 2 or 3 pickups.

1999-2014	Various models	$360	$450

Bellzouki
1963-1969. 12-string electric. Teardrop-shaped body, 1 pickup, sunburst (7010) for '63-'66. Vincent Bell model (7020) with modified teardrop shape with 2 body points on both treble and bass bouts and 2 pickups for '63-'66. Same body as Coral Electric Sitar for '67-'69.

1963-1969	1 pickup, teardrop body	$900	$1,125
1963-1969	2 pickups, pointy body	$1,075	$1,350
1967-1969	2 pickups, sitar body	$1,550	$1,950

Companion
1959-1960. Hollowbody double-cut, 2 pickups, concentric TV knobs.

1959-1960	Pickup installed, rare color	$1,425	$1,800

Convertible
1959-1969. Acoustic/electric, double-cut, guitar was sold with or without the removable single pickup.

1959-1969	Acoustic, no pickup, natural	$325	$400
1959-1969	Pickup installed, natural	$475	$600
1967-1969	Red, white, blue	$775	$975

Convertible Reissue
1999, 2000-2003. The Convertible Pro was offered '00-'03 with upgraded Gotoh tuners and metalflake and pearl finishes.

1999-2003	Blond	$260	$325
1999-2003	Green	$275	$350

Dane A Series
1967-1969. 1or 2 pickups, with or without vibrato (V), solid wood slab body, hard lacquer finish with 4 color options, 12-string also offered.

1967-1969	1N12, Electric XII	$1,300	$1,600
1967-1969	2N12, Electric XII	$1,425	$1,800
1967-1969	N, 6-string, 1 pickup	$1,000	$1,225
1967-1969	N, 6-string, 2 pickups	$1,150	$1,450
1967-1969	V, 6-string, 1 pickup	$1,150	$1,450
1967-1969	V, 6-string, 2 pickups	$1,250	$1,575

Dane B Series
1967-1969. 2 or 3 pickups, with or without vibrato (V), semi-solid Durabody, 6 or 12 strings.

1967-1969	12-string	$1,200	$1,500
1967-1969	6-string, 2 pickups	$925	$1,175
1967-1969	6-string, 3 pickups	$1,100	$1,400

Dane C Series
1967-1969. 2 or 3 pickups, with or without vibrato (V), semi-solid Durabody with 2-tone Gator finish, 6 or 12 strings.

1967-1969	12-string	$1,725	$2,175
1967-1969	6-string	$1,475	$1,850

Dane D Series
1967-1969. 2 or 3 pickups, with or without vibrato (V), solid wood sculptured thinline body, 'floating adjustable pickguard-fingerguide', master volume with 4 switches, 6 or 12 strings.

1967-1969	12-string	$1,275	$1,575
1967-1969	6-string, 2 pickups	$1,100	$1,350
1967-1969	6-string, 3 pickups	$1,275	$1,575

Danoblaster Series
2000-2003. Offset double-cuts, 3 pickups, built-in effects – distortion on the Hearsay, distortion, chorus, trem and echo on Innuendo. Also in 12-string and baritone.

2000-2003		$115	$145

Daisy Rock Classic

Dan Kellaway Rosewood

*Danelectro Deluxe
Double Pickup*

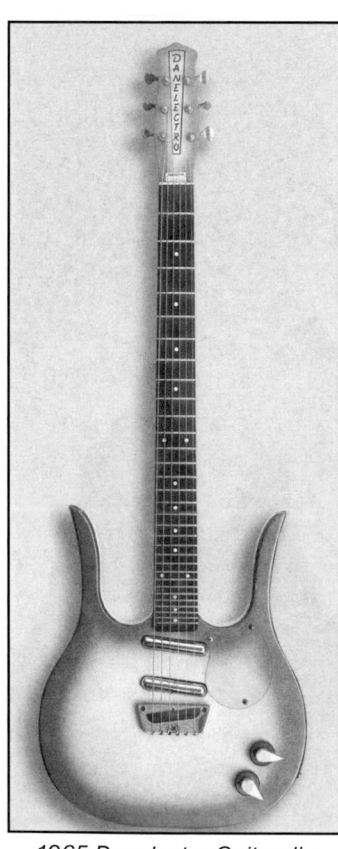

1965 Danelectro Guitaralin

MODEL YEAR	FEATURES	EXC. COND. LOW	HIGH

DC-3/DDC-3
1999-2003. Shorthorn double-cut, 3 pickups, seal-shaped pickguard, Coke bottle headstock, solid and sparkle finishes.

1999-2003		$300	$400

DC-12/Electric XII
1999-2003. 12-string version of 59-DC.

1999-2003		$365	$460

59-DC/'59 Dano (Standard Double Pickup Reissue)
1998-1999, 2007. Shorthorn double-cut, 2 pickups, seal-shaped pickguard, Coke bottle headstock, '07 version called '59 Dano.

1998-1999		$260	$325

Deluxe Single Pickup
1959-1966. Double-cut, Coke bottle headstock, 1 pickup, 2 knobs.

1959-1960	Walnut or white	$1,100	$1,400
1961-1966	Walnut, white, honey	$1,000	$1,250

Deluxe Double Pickup
1959-1966. As Single above, but with 2 pickups, and added master volume on later models.

1959-1960	Walnut or white	$1,150	$1,475
1961-1966	Walnut, white, honey	$1,100	$1,400

Deluxe Triple Pickup
1959-1966. As Single above, but with 3 pickups, 3 knobs, and added master volume on later models.

1959-1960	Walnut or white	$1,250	$1,550
1961-1966	Walnut, white, honey	$1,150	$1,475

Doubleneck (3923)
1958-1966. A shorthorn double-cut, bass and 6-string necks, 1 pickup on each neck, Coke bottle headstocks, white sunburst.

1958-1966		$1,550	$1,950

Doubleneck Reissue
1999-2003. Baritone 6-string and standard 6-string double neck, shorthorn body style, or the 6-12 model with a 6-string and 12-string neck. Price includes $75 for a guitar case, but many sales do not seem to include a guitar case because of unusual body size.

1999-2003		$500	$625

Electric Sitar
1968-1969. Traditional looking, oval-bodied sitar, no drone strings as on the Coral Sitar of the same period.

1968-1969		$1,750	$2,200

Guitaralin (4123)
1958-1966. The Longhorn guitar, 2 huge cutaways, 31-fret neck, 2 pickups.

1958-1960	No neck adjustment	$2,000	$2,500
1961-1966	With neck adjustment	$1,900	$2,400

Hand Vibrato Single Pickup (4011)
1958-1966. Short horn double-cut, 1 pickup, batwing headstock, simple design vibrato, black w/ white guard.

1958-1966		$850	$1,050

MODEL YEAR	FEATURES	EXC. COND. LOW	HIGH

Hand Vibrato Double Pickup (4021)
1958-1960. Same as Single Pickup, but with 2 pickups and larger pickguard.

1963-1966		$950	$1,175

Hawk
1967-1969. Offered with 1 or 2 pickups, vibrato (V models) or non-vibrato (N models), 12-string model also offered.

1967-1969	1N, 1 pickup	$1,000	$1,200
1967-1969	1N12, Electric XII	$1,300	$1,600
1967-1969	1V, 1 pickup	$1,100	$1,500
1967-1969	2N, 2 pickups	$1,100	$1,500
1967-1969	2N12, Electric XII	$1,400	$1,800
1967-1969	2V, 2 pickups	$1,200	$1,600

Hodad/Hodad 12-String
1999-2003. Unique double-cut with sharp horns, 6 or 12 strings, sparkle finish.

1999-2003		$380	$425

Model C
1955. Single-cut, 1or 2 pickups, ginger colored vinyl cover.

1955		$550	$750

Pro 1
1963-1964. Odd-shaped double-cut electric with squared off corners, 1 pickup.

1963-1964		$700	$1,000

Pro Reissue
2007. Based on '60s Pro 1, but with 2 pickups.

2007		$250	$325

Slimline Series
1967-1969. Offset waist double-cut, 2 or 3 pickups, with or without vibrato, 6 or 12 string.

1967-1969	12-string	$1,200	$1,500
1967-1969	6-string, 2 pickups	$900	$1,200
1967-1969	6-string, 3 pickups	$1,100	$1,400

Standard Single Pickup
1958-1966. Nicknamed the Shorthorn, double-cut, 1 pickup, 2 regular control knobs, kidney-shaped pickguard originally, seal-shaped 'guard by ca. 1960, Coke bottle headstock, in black or bronze.

1958-1959	Kidney guard	$800	$1,100
1960-1966	Seal guard	$800	$1,100

Standard Double Pickup
1958-1966. As Single Pickup above but with 2 pickups and 2 stacked, concentric volume/tone controls, in black, bronze and later blond. The black, seal-shaped pickguard version of this guitar is often referred to as the Jimmy Page model because he used one. Reissued in 1998 as 59-DC.

1958-1959	Kidney guard, black	$900	$1,300
1960-1966	Bronze	$850	$1,200
1960-1966	Jimmy Page, black	$1,250	$1,600
1961-1966	Blond	$1,000	$1,400

Standard Triple Pickup
1958. As Single Pickup above but with 3 pickups and 3 stacked, concentric pointer volume/tone controls, in white to bronze sunburst, very rare.

1958		$1,100	$1,500

Tweed Models
1954-1955. First production models, single-cut, bell-shape headstock, 1 or 2 pickups, tweed vinyl cover.

1954-1955	1 pickup	$2,400	$3,000
1954-1955	2 pickups	$2,600	$3,200

MODEL YEAR	FEATURES	EXC. COND. LOW	HIGH

U-1

1955-1958. Single-cut, 1 pickup, 2 regular knobs, bell-shape headstock originally, switching to Coke bottle in late '55. The U Series featured Dano's new 'solid center' block construction.

1955	Enamel, bell headstock	$1,900	$2,350
1956-1957	Enamel, Coke headstock	$1,700	$2,100
1956-1957	Ivory, Coke headstock	$1,800	$2,250
1958	Enamel, Coke headstock	$1,500	$1,900
1958	Ivory, Coke headstock	$1,700	$2,100

U-1 '56 Reissue

1998-1999. Reissue of '56 U-1, various colors.

1998-1999		$175	$225

U-2

1955-1958. As U-1, but with 2 pickups and 2 stacked concentric volume/tone controls.

1955	Enamel, bell headstock	$2,100	$2,600
1956-1957	Enamel, Coke headstock	$1,900	$2,400
1956-1957	Ivory, Coke headstock	$2,000	$2,500
1958	Enamel, Coke headstock	$1,700	$2,100
1958	Ivory, Coke headstock	$1,900	$2,350

U-2 '56 Reissue

1998-2003. Reissue of '56 U-2, various colors.

1998-2003		$225	$275

U-3

1955-1958. As U-2, but with 3 pickups and 3 stacked concentric volume/tone controls.

1958	Enamel, Coke headstock	$1,900	$2,350

U-3 '56 Reissue

1999-2003. Reissue of '56 U-3, various colors.

1999-2003	Common color	$250	$325
1999-2003	Rare color	$300	$400

D'Angelico

John D'Angelico built his own line of archtop guitars, mandolins and violins from 1932 until his death in 1964. His instruments are some of the most sought-after by collectors. The binding on some D'Angelico guitars can become deteriorated and requires replacing. Replaced binding, even if excellent work, reduces the values shown by 20% or more.

D'Angelico (L-5 Snakehead)

1932-1935. D'Angelico's L-5-style with snakehead headstock, his first model, sunburst.

1932-1935		$10,000	$12,500

Excel/Exel (Cutaway)

1947-1964. Cutaway, 17" width, 1- and 3-ply bound f-hole.

1947-1949	Natural, original binding	$31,000	$40,000

1947-1949	Sunburst, original binding	$28,000	$36,000
1950-1959	Natural, original binding	$31,000	$40,000
1950-1959	Sunburst, original binding	$28,000	$36,000
1960-1964	Natural	$31,000	$40,000
1960-1964	Sunburst	$28,000	$36,000

Excel/Exel (Non-Cutaway)

1936-1949. Non-cut, 17" width, 1- and 3-ply bound f-hole, natural finishes were typically not offered in the '30s, non-cut Excels were generally not offered after '49 in deference to the Excel cutaway.

1936-1939	Sunburst, straight f-hole	$15,000	$19,000
1938-1939	Sunburst, standard f-hole	$15,000	$19,000
1940-1949	Natural	$17,000	$22,000
1940-1949	Sunburst, standard f-hole	$15,000	$19,000

New Yorker (Cutaway)

1947-1964. Cutaway, 18" width, 5-ply-bound f-hole, New Yorker non cut orders were overshadowed by the cut model orders starting in '47.

1947-1949	Natural	$45,000	$57,000
1947-1949	Sunburst	$39,000	$49,000
1950-1959	Natural	$45,000	$57,000
1950-1959	Sunburst	$39,000	$49,000
1960-1964	Natural	$39,000	$49,000
1960-1964	Sunburst	$35,000	$44,000

New Yorker (Non-Cutaway)

1936-1949. Non-cut, 18" width, 5-ply-bound f-hole, New Yorker non cut orders were overshadowed by the cut model orders starting in '47.

1936-1939	Sunburst	$22,000	$28,000
1940-1949	Natural	$25,000	$32,000
1940-1949	Sunburst	$22,000	$28,000

New Yorker Special

1947-1964. Also called Excel New Yorker or Excel Cutaway New Yorker Cutaway, 17" width, New Yorker styling, not to be confused with D'Angelico Special (A and B style).

1947-1959	Natural	$29,000	$37,000
1947-1960	Sunburst	$26,000	$34,000
1960-1964	Natural	$26,000	$33,000
1961-1964	Sunburst	$23,000	$29,000

Special (Cutaway)

1947-1964. Generally Style A and B-type instruments made for musicians on a budget, plain specs with little ornamentation, not to be confused with New Yorker Special.

1947-1959	Sunburst	$10,000	$12,500
1960-1964	Sunburst	$9,000	$11,500

Special (Non-Cutaway)

1947-1964. Non-cut Special, not to be confused with New Yorker Special.

1947-1959	Sunburst	$6,000	$7,700
1960-1964	Sunburst	$5,300	$6,800

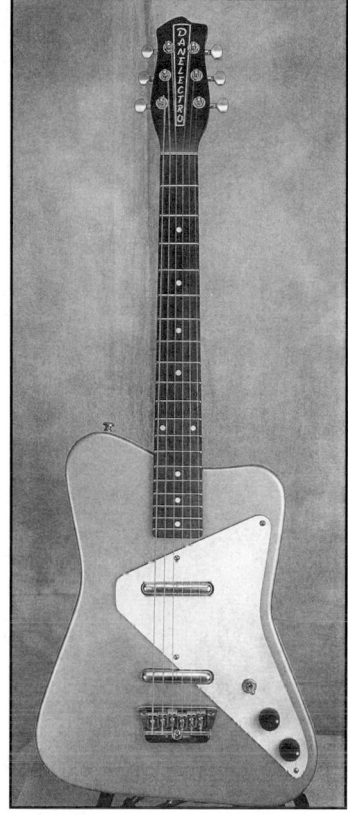

Danelectro Pro Reissue

Late-1930s D'Angelico Style B

Andy Nelson

D'Angelico New Yorker NYL-2

Dave King Louise

MODEL YEAR	FEATURES	EXC. COND. LOW	HIGH

Style A
1936-1945. Archtop, 17" width, unbound f-holes, block 'board inlays, multi-pointed headstock, nickel-plated metal parts.

1936-1939	Sunburst	$8,500	$10,700
1940-1945	Sunburst	$7,500	$9,500

Style A-1
1936-1945. Unbound f-holes, 17" width, arched headstock, nickel-plated metal parts.

1936-1939	Sunburst	$7,500	$9,500
1940-1945	Sunburst	$7,500	$9,500

Style B
1933-1948. Archtop 17" wide, unbound F-holes, block 'board inlays, gold-plated parts.

1936-1939	Sunburst	$10,000	$12,500
1940-1948	Sunburst	$10,000	$12,500

Style B Special
1933-1948. D'Angelico described variations from standard features with a 'Special' designation, Vintage dealers may also describe these instruments as 'Special'.

1936-1939	Sunburst	$11,000	$14,000
1940-1948	Sunburst	$10,000	$12,500

D'Angelico (D'Angelico Guitars of America)
1988-present. Intermediate and professional grade, production/custom, archtop, flat-top, and solidbody guitars made in South Korea and imported by D'Angelico Guitars of America, of Colts Neck, New Jersey. From 1988 to '04, they were premium and presentation grade instruments built in Japan by luthier Hidesato Shino and Vestax. In '12, GTR announced they bought the brand name and are offering premium grade D'Angelicos built in the U.S.

Excel EX-DC
Thinline double-cut.

2005		$1,000	$1,250

New Yorker NYL-2
Japanese 17" single-cut archtop, spruce top, figured maple back and sides.

2001-2004		$2,400	$3,100

D'Angelico (Lewis)
1994-2011. Luthier Michael Lewis built presentation grade, custom/production, D'Angelico replica guitars in Grass Valley, California, under an agreement with the GHS String Company, which owned the name in the U.S. He also builds guitars and mandolins under the Lewis name.

D'Angelico II
Mid-1990s. Archtops built in the U.S. and distributed by Archtop Enterprises of Merrick, New York. Mainly presentation grade copies of Excel and New Yorker models, but also made lower cost similar models.

Jazz Classic
1990s. Electric archtop, cutaway, carved spruce top, figured maple back and sides, single neck pickup, transparent cherry.

1990s		$2,400	$3,100

MODEL YEAR	FEATURES	EXC. COND. LOW	HIGH

Daniel Friederich
1955-present. Luthier Daniel Friederich builds his custom/production, classical guitars in Paris, France.

D'Aquisto
1965-1995. James D'Aquisto apprenticed under D'Angelico until the latter's death, at age 59, in '64. He started making his own brand instruments in '65 and built archtop and flat-top acoustic guitars, solidbody and hollowbody electric guitars. He also designed guitars for Hagstrom and Fender. He died in '95, at age 59.

Avant Garde
1987-1994. 18" wide, non-traditional futuristic model, approximately 5 or 6 instruments were reportedly made, because of low production this pricing is for guidance only.

1990	Blond	$80,000	$100,000

Centura/Centura Deluxe
1994 only. 17" wide, non-traditional art deco futuristic archtop, approximately 10 made, the last guitars made by this luthier, due to the low production this pricing is for guidance only.

1994	Blond	$75,000	$93,000

Excel (Cutaway)
1965-1992. Archtop, 17" width, with modern thin-logo started in '81.

1965-1967	Blond	$31,000	$39,000
1965-1967	Sunburst	$31,000	$39,000
1968-1980	Blond	$31,000	$39,000
1968-1980	Sunburst	$32,000	$40,000
1981-1989	Blond	$32,000	$40,000
1981-1989	Sunburst	$32,000	$40,000
1990-1992	Blond	$32,000	$40,000
1990-1992	Sunburst	$32,000	$40,000

Excel (Flat-Top)
1970s-1980s. Flat-top, 16", flamed maple back and sides, Sitka spruce top, about 15 made, narrow Excel-style headstock, oval soundhole, D'Aquisto script logo on headstock.

1970s-80s		$16,000	$21,000

Hollow Electric
Early model with bar pickup, D'Aquisto headstock, '70s model with humbuckers.

1960s	Sunburst	$14,000	$18,000
1970s	Sunburst	$14,000	$18,000
1980s		$14,000	$18,000

New Yorker Classic (Archtop)
1986. Single-cut acoustic archtop with new modern design features such as large S-shaped soundholes.

1986		$55,000	$70,000

New Yorker Classic (Solidbody)
1980s. Only 2 were reported to be made, therefore this pricing is for guidance only.

1980s		$17,000	$22,000

New Yorker Deluxe (Cutaway)
1965-1992. Most are 18" wide.

1965-1967	Blond	$41,000	$52,000
1965-1967	Sunburst	$41,000	$52,000
1968-1979	Blond	$41,000	$52,000

MODEL YEAR	FEATURES	EXC. COND. LOW	HIGH
1968-1979	Sunburst	$41,000	$52,000
1980-1989	Blond	$43,000	$54,000
1980-1989	Sunburst	$43,000	$54,000
1990-1992	Blond	$43,000	$54,000
1990-1992	Sunburst	$43,000	$54,000

New Yorker Special (7-String)
1980s. Limited production 7-string, single-cut.

1980s		$31,000	$39,000

New Yorker Special (Cutaway)
1966-1992. Most are 17" wide.

1966-1967	Blond	$32,000	$40,000
1966-1967	Sunburst	$32,000	$40,000
1968-1979	Blond	$32,000	$40,000
1968-1979	Sunburst	$32,000	$40,000
1980-1989	Blond	$32,000	$40,000
1980-1989	Sunburst	$32,000	$40,000
1990-1992	Blond	$32,000	$40,000
1990-1992	Sunburst	$32,000	$40,000

Solo/Solo Deluxe
1992-1993. 18" wide, non-traditional non-cut art deco model, only 2 reported made, because of low production this pricing is for guidance only.

1992-1993	Blond	$75,000	$93,000

D'Aquisto (Aria)

May 2002-2013. Premium grade, production, D'Aquisto designs licensed to Aria of Japan by D'Aquisto Strings, Inc., Deer Park, New York.
Various Models

2002-2013		$1,500	$1,850

Dauphin

1970s-late 1990s. Classical and flamenco guitars imported from Spain and Japan by distributor George Dauphinais, located in Springfield, Illinois.

Dave King Acoustics

1980-present. Premium grade, custom/production, acoustic and resonator guitars built by luthier Dave King in Berkshire, U.K.

Dave Maize Acoustic Guitars

1991-present. Luthier Dave Maize builds his professional and premium grade, production/custom, flat-tops and basses in Cave Junction, Oregon.

David Rubio

1960s-2000. Luthier David Spink built his guitars, lutes, violins, violas, cellos and harpsichords first in New York, and after '67, in the U.K. While playing in Spain, he acquired the nickname Rubio, after his red beard. He died in '00.

David Thomas McNaught

1989-present. Professional, premium, and presentation grade, custom, solidbody guitars built by luthier David Thomas McNaught and finished by Dave Mansel in Locust, North Carolina. In '97, they added the production/custom DTM line of guitars.

Davis, J. Thomas

1975-present. Premium and presentation grade, custom, steel-string flat-tops, 12-strings, classicals, archtops, Irish citterns and flat-top Irish bouzoukis made by luthier J. Thomas Davis in Columbus, Ohio.

Davoli

See Wandre listing.

DBZ

2008-present. Solidbody electric guitars from Dean B. Zelinsky, founder of Dean Guitars, and partners Jeff Diamant and Terry Martin. Dean left the partnership February, '12 and established Dean Zelinsky Private Label guitars.

de Jonge, Sergei

1972-present. Premium grade, production/custom classical and steel-string guitars built by luthier Sergei de Jonge originally in Oshawa, Ontario, and since '04 in Chelsea, Quebec.

De Paule Stringed Instruments

1969-1980, 1993-present. Custom steel-string, nylon-string, archtop, resonator, and Hawaiian guitars built by luthier C. Andrew De Paule in Eugene, Oregon.

Dean

1976-present. Intermediate, professional and premium grade, production/custom, solidbody, hollowbody, acoustic, acoustic/electric, and resonator guitars made in the U.S., Korea, the Czech Republic and China. They also offer basses, banjos, mandolins, and amps. Founded in Evanston, Illinois, by Dean Zelinsky. Original models were upscale versions of Gibson designs with glued necks, fancy tops, DiMarzio pickups and distinctive winged headstocks (V, Z and ML), with production beginning in '77. In '80 the factory was relocated to Chicago. Dean's American manufacturing ends in '86 when all production shifts to Korea. In '91 Zelinsky sold the company to Tropical Music in Miami, Florida. For '93-'94 there was again limited U.S. (California) production of the E'Lite, Cadillac and ML models under the supervision of Zelinsky and Cory Wadley. Korean versions were also produced. In '95, Elliott Rubinson's Armadillo Enterprises, of Clearwater, Florida, bought the Dean brand. In '97 and '98, Dean offered higher-end USA Custom Shop models. In '98, they reintroduced acoustics. From 2000 to '08, Zelinsky was once again involved in the company.

Dating American models: first 2 digits are year of manufacture. Imports have no date codes.

Baby ML
1982-1986, 2000-2014. Downsized version of ML model.

1982-1986	Import	$260	$325
1982-1986	U.S.-made	$350	$450

Davis, J. Thomas

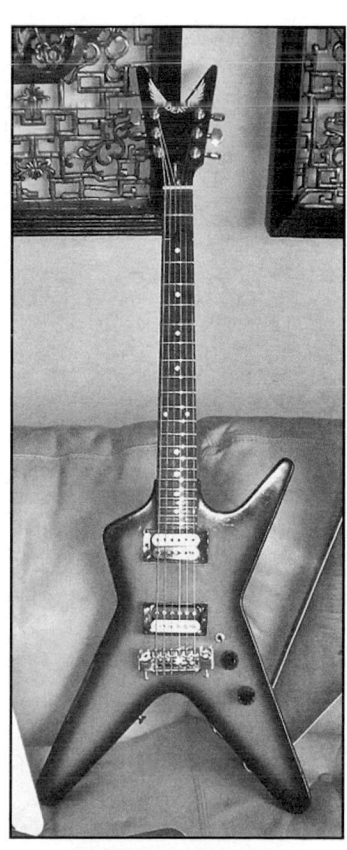

1983 Dean Baby ML
Jeffrey Mallin

GUITARS

1982 Dean Baby V
Jeffrey Mallin

Dean V Standard
Jeffrey Mallin

MODEL YEAR	FEATURES	EXC. COND. LOW	HIGH
Baby V			
1982-1986, 2000-2014. Downsized version of the V model.			
1982-1986	Import	$260	$325
1982-1986	U.S.-made	$350	$450
Baby Z			
1982-1986, 2000-2014. Downsized version of the Z model.			
1982-1986	Import	$260	$325
1982-1986	U.S.-made	$350	$450
Bel Aire			
1983-1984. Solidbody, possibly the first production guitar with humbucker/single/single pickup layout, U.S.-made, an import model was introduced in '87.			
1980s	Import	$260	$325
1983-1984	U.S.-made	$350	$450
Budweiser Guitar			
Ca.1987. Shaped like Bud logo.			
1987		$180	$225
Cadillac (U.S.A.)			
1979-1985. Single long treble horn on slab body.			
1979-1985		$1,500	$1,900
Cadillac 1980			
2006-present. Block inlays, 2 humbuckers, gold hardware.			
2006-2014		$350	$435
Cadillac Deluxe (U.S.A.)			
1993-1994, 1996-1997. Made in U.S., single longhorn shape, various colors.			
1993-1997		$950	$1,200
Cadillac Reissue (Import)			
1992-1994. Single longhorn shape, 2 humbuckers, various colors.			
1992-1994		$275	$340
Cadillac Select			
2009-present. Made in Korea, figured maple top, mahogany, pearl block inlays.			
2009-2014		$300	$375
Cadillac Standard			
1996-1997. Slab body version.			
1996-1997		$1,200	$1,500
Del Sol			
2008. Import, small double-cut thinline semi-hollow, ES-335 style body, rising sun fretboard markers.			
2008		$300	$375
Dime O Flame (ML)			
2005-present. ML-body, Dimebuckers, burning flames finish, Dime logo on headstock.			
2005-2014		$350	$435
Eighty-Eight (Import)			
1987-1990. Offset double-cut solidbody, import.			
1987-1990		$150	$185
E'Lite			
1978-1985, 1994-1996. Single-horn shape.			
1978-1985		$1,000	$1,250
1994-1996		$900	$1,125
E'Lite Deluxe			
1980s. Single-horn shape.			
1980s		$1,050	$1,300

MODEL YEAR	FEATURES	EXC. COND. LOW	HIGH
EVO XM			
2004-present. Single-cut slab body, 2 humbuckers.			
2004-2014		$80	$100
Golden E'Lite			
1980. Single pointy treble cutaway, fork headstock, gold hardware, ebony 'board, sunburst.			
1980		$1,050	$1,300
Hollywood Z (Import)			
1985-1986. Bolt-neck Japanese copy of Baby Z, Explorer shape.			
1985-1986		$105	$125
Jammer (Import)			
1987-1989. Offset double-cut body, bolt-on neck, dot markers, six-on-a-side tuners, various colors offered.			
1987-1989		$105	$125
Leslie West Standard			
2008-present. Flame maple top, mahogany body, rosewood 'board.			
2008-2014		$355	$435
Mach I (Import)			
1985-1986. Limited run from Korea, Mach V with six-on-a-side tunes, various colors.			
1985-1986		$105	$125
Mach V (Import)			
1985-1986. Pointed solidbody, 2 humbucking pickups, maple neck, ebony 'board, locking trem, various colors, limited run from Korea.			
1985-1986		$105	$125
Mach VII (U.S.A.)			
1985-1986. Mach I styling, made in America, offered in unusual finishes.			
1985-1986		$1,050	$1,300
ML (ML Standard/U.S.A.)			
1977-1986. There is a flame model and a standard model.			
1977-1981	Burst flamed top	$1,850	$2,300
1977-1981	Burst plain top	$1,650	$2,050
1977-1981	Common opaque finish	$1,300	$1,650
1982-1986	Burst flamed top	$1,550	$1,925
1982-1986	Burst plain top	$1,650	$2,050
1982-1986	Common opaque finish	$1,300	$1,650
ML (Import)			
1983-1990. Korean-made.			
1983-1990		$375	$450
Soltero SL			
2007-2010. Made in Japan, single-cut solidbody, 2 pickups, flame maple top.			
2007-2010		$1,250	$1,550
USA Time Capsule Exotic V			
2005-2014. Flying V style, solid mahogany body with exotic spalted and flamed maple top, Dean V neck profile (split V headstock).			
2005-2014		$2,000	$2,400
USA Time Capsule Z			
2000-2014. Explorer style body, figured maple top.			
2000-2014		$1,650	$2,050
V Standard (U.S.A.)			
1977-1986. V body, there is a standard and a flame model offered.			
1977-1981	Burst flamed top	$1,850	$2,300

MODEL YEAR	FEATURES	EXC. COND. LOW	HIGH
1977-1981	Burst plain top	$1,650	$2,050
1977-1981	Common opaque finish	$1,300	$1,650
1982-1986	Burst flamed top	$1,550	$1,925
1982-1986	Burst plain top	$1,650	$2,050
1982-1986	Common opaque finish	$1,300	$1,650

Z Standard (U.S.A.)

1977-1986. Long treble cutaway solidbody, 2 humbuckers.

1977-1983	Common finish	$1,300	$1,650
1977-1983	Rare finish	$1,550	$1,925

Z Autograph (Import)

1985-1987. The first Dean import from Korea, offset double-cut, bolt neck, dot markers, offered in several standard colors.

1985-1987		$200	$250

Z Coupe/Z Deluxe (U.S.A. Custom Shop)

1997 1998. Mahogany body offered in several standard colors, Z Deluxe with Floyd Rose tremolo.

1997-1998		$825	$1,025

Z Korina (U.S.A. Custom Shop)

1997-1998. Z Coupe with korina body, various standard colors.

1997-1998		$925	$1,175

Z LTD (U.S.A. Custom Shop)

1997-1998. Z Coupe with bound neck and head-stock, offered in several standard colors.

1997-1998		$925	$1,175

Dean Markley

The string and pickup manufacturer offered a limited line of guitars and basses for a time in the '80s. They were introduced in '84.

Dean Zelinsky Private Label

2012-present. Premium grade, production/custom, hollow, semi-hollow and solidbody electric guitars built in Chicago, Illinois by luthier Dean Zelinsky, founder of Dean Guitars. He also imports a line of intermediate grade guitars from South Korea and Indonesia.

DeArmond Guitars

1999-2004. Solid, semi-hollow and hollow body guitars based on Guild models and imported from Korea by Fender. They also offered basses. The DeArmond brand was originally used on pickups, effects and amps built by Rowe Industries.

Electric

1999-2004. Various import models, some with USA electronic components.

1999-2000	Bajo Jet Baritone	$550	$700
1999-2001	S-65 (S-100)	$350	$450
1999-2004	Jet Star (Polara style)	$450	$575
1999-2004	M-75/M-75T (Bluesbird)	$450	$575
1999-2004	M-77T Duo Jet	$450	$575
1999-2004	Starfire Special, single-cut	$450	$575
1999-2004	Starfire, double-cut	$525	$650

MODEL YEAR	FEATURES	EXC. COND. LOW	HIGH
1999-2004	X135 (Duane Eddy), 1 pickup	$500	$625
1999-2004	X145 (Duane Eddy), 2 pickups	$525	$650
1999-2004	X155 (Duane Eddy)	$550	$700
2000-2001	M-70 (Bluesbird)	$375	$475
2000-2001	M-72 (Bluesbird)	$450	$575

Dearstone

1993-present. Luthier Ray Dearstone builds his professional and premium grade, custom, archtop and acoustic/electric guitars in Blountville, Tennessee. He also builds mandolin family instruments and violins.

Decar

1950s. A private brand sold by Decautur, Illinois music store, Decar headstock logo.

Stratotone H44 Model

1956. Private branded Stratotone with maple neck and fretboard instead of the standard neck/fretboard, 1 pickup and other Harmony H44 Stratotone attributes, bolt-on neck.

1956		$600	$750

DeCava Guitars

1983-present. Professional and premium grade, production/custom, archtop and classical guitars built by luthier Jim DeCava in Stratford, Connecticut. He also builds ukes, banjos, and mandolins.

Decca

Mid-1960s. Acoustic, solid and hollow body guitars, basses and amps made in Japan by Teisco and imported by Decca Records, Decca headstock logo, student-level instruments.

Acoustic Flat-Top

1960s. Decca label on the inside back.

1960s		$75	$175

Electric Solidbody

1960s. Teisco-made in Japan, 3 pickups, sunburst.

1960s		$275	$350

Defil

Based out of Lubin, Poland, Defil made solid and semi-hollowbdy electric guitars at least from the 1970s to the '90s.

DeGennaro

2003-present. Premium grade, custom/production, acoustic, archtop, semi-hollow and solidbody guitars, basses and mandolins built by luthier William DeGennaro in Grand Rapids, Michigan.

Del Oro

1930s-1940s. Flat-top (including cowboy stencil models) and resonator guitars, built by Kay. At least the cowboy stencils were sold by Spiegel.

Small Acoustic

1930s	13" to 14" body	$150	$225

1999 DeArmond M-75

Defil Solidbody

Del Vecchio V01P01

Delirium Bettie Red

MODEL YEAR FEATURES	EXC. COND. LOW	HIGH

Del Pilar Guitars

1956-1986. Luthier William Del Pilar made his classical guitars in Brooklyn, New York.

Classical (Rosewood)

1950s-1980s. Brazilian rosewood back and sides, cedar top, quilt rosette, 9-ply top binding.

| 1950s-80s | $3,000 | $4,000 |

Del Vecchio

1902-present. Casa Del Vecchio builds a variety of Spanish instruments including acoustic and resonator guitars in São Paulo, Brazil.

Delaney Guitars

2004-present. Luthier Mike Delaney builds his professional grade, production/custom, chambered, solidbody, and semi-hollowbody electric guitars and basses in Atlanta, Georgia. Prior to 2008 he built in Florence, Montana.

Delgado

1928-present. Delgado began in Torreon, Coahuila, Mexico, then moved to Juarez in the '30s with a second location in Tijuana. In '48 they moved to California and opened a shop in Los Angeles. Since 2005, Manuel A. Delgado, a third generation luthier, builds his premium and presentation grade, production/custom, classical, flamenco and steel string acoustic guitars in Nashville, Tennessee. He also builds basses, mandolins, ukuleles and banjos.

Delirium Custom Guitars

2008-present. Luthiers Patrick and Vincent Paul-Victor along with Gael Canonne build their professional and premium grade, production/custom, solidbody electric guitars in Paris and Toulouse, France.

Dell'Arte

1997-present. Production/custom Maccaferri-style guitars from John Kinnard and Alain Cola. In '96, luthier John Kinnard opened a small shop called Finegold Guitars and Mandolins. In '98 he met Alain Cola, a long time jazz guitarist who was selling Mexican-made copies of Selmer/Maccaferri guitars under the Dell'Arte brand. Cola wanted better workmanship for his guitars, and in October '98, Finegold and Dell'Arte merged. As of May '99 all production is in California.

Delta Guitars

2005-2010. Acoustic, acoustic/electric, and solidbody electric guitars from Musician's Wholesale America, Nashville, Tennessee.

Dennis Hill Guitars

Premium and presentation grade, production/custom, classical and flamenco guitars built by luthier Dennis Hill in Panama City, Florida. He has also built dulcimers, mandolins, and violins.

MODEL YEAR FEATURES	EXC. COND. LOW	HIGH

Desmond Guitars

1991-present. Luthier Robert B. Desmond builds his premium grade, production/custom classical guitars in Orlando, Florida.

DeTemple

1995-present. Premium grade, production/custom, solidbody electric guitars and basses built by luthier Michael DeTemple in Sherman Oaks, California.

DeVoe Guitars

1975-present. Luthier Lester DeVoe builds his premium grade, production/custom flamenco and classical guitars in Nipomo, California.

Diamond

Ca. 1963-1964. Line of sparkle finish solidbody guitars made in Italy for the Diamond Accordion company.

Ranger

Ca. 1963-1964. Rangers came with 1, 2, 3, or 4 pickups, sparkle finish.

| 1960s | $525 | $650 |

Dick, Edward Victor

1975-present. Luthier Edward Dick currently builds his premium grade, custom, classical guitars in Denver, Colorado (he lived in Peterborough and Ottawa, Ontario until '95). He also operates the Colorado School of Lutherie.

Dickerson

1937-1947. Founded by the Dickerson brothers in '37, primarily for electric lap steels and small amps. Instruments were also private branded for Cleveland's Oahu company, and for the Gourley brand. By '47, the company changed ownership and was renamed Magna Electronics (Magnatone).

Dillion

1996-present. Dillion, of Cary, North Carolina, offers intermediate grade, production, acoustic, acoustic/electric, hollow-body and solidbody guitars, basses and mandolins made in Korea and Vietnam.

Dillon

1975-2006. Professional and premium grade, custom, flat-tops and basses built by luthier John Dillon in Taos, New Mexico, and in Bloomsburg, Pennsylvania ('81-'01).

Dino's Guitars

1995-present. Custom, professional grade, electric solidbody guitars built by a social co-op company founded by Alessio Casati and Andy Bagnasco, in Albisola, Italy. They also build effects.

DiPinto

1995-present. Intermediate and professional grade, production retro-vibe guitars and basses

MODEL		EXC. COND.	
YEAR	FEATURES	LOW	HIGH

from luthier Chris DiPinto of Philadelphia, Pennsylvania. Until late '99, all instruments built in the U.S., since then all built in Korea.

Ditson

1835-1937. Started in Boston by music publisher Oliver Ditson, by the end of the 1800s, the company was one of the east coast's largest music businesses, operating in several cities and was also involved in distribution and manufacturing of a variety of instruments, including guitars and ukes.

From 1916-1930 Ditson guitars were made by Martin. The majority of Martin production was from '16 to '22 with over 500 units sold in '21. Ditson also established Lyon and Healy in Chicago and the John Church Company in Cincinnati.

Concert Models

1916-1922. Similar in size to Martin size 0. Models include Style 1, Style 2 and Style 3.

1916-1922	Style 1	$3,500	$4,400
1916-1922	Style 2	$4,300	$5,400
1916-1922	Style 3	$4,800	$6,000

Standard Models

1916-1922. Small body similar to Martin size 3, plain styling. Models include Style 1, Style 2 and Style 3.

1916-1922	Style 1	$2,100	$2,600
1916-1922	Style 2	$2,600	$3,200
1916-1922	Style 3	$3,700	$4,600

Style 111 Dreadnought

1916-1930. Dreadnought-sized exceeding the Martin 000 size, initially intended to be a 6-string bass guitar, fan bracing (only 7 made) on the top generally requires extensive restoration, X bracing is Martin-made (19 made).

1916-1922	Fan bracing	$17,000	$21,000
1923-1930	X bracing (Martin)	$50,000	$63,000

Style 1-45

1919. Only 4 made.

1919		$22,000	$28,000

D'Leco Guitars

1991-2003. Guitarist Maurice Johnson and luthier James W. Dale built premium grade, production/custom archtops in Oklahoma City, Oklahoma.

DM Darling Guitars

Beginning 2006 luthier Denis Merrill builds professional and premium grade, custom, acoustic, classical, resonator and solidbody guitars in Tacoma, Washington. From 1978 to '06 he built under his own name and Merrill Custom Shop. He also builds mandolin family instruments.

Dobro

1929-1942, ca. 1954-present. Currently, professional and premium grade, production, wood and metal body resophonic guitars offered by Gibson.

Founded 1929 in Los Angeles by John Dopyera, Rudy Dopyera, Ed Dopyera and Vic Smith (Dobro stands for Dopyera Brothers). Made instruments sold under the Dobro, Regal, Norwood Chimes,

Angelus, Rex, Broman, Montgomery Ward, Penetro, Bruno, Alhambra, More Harmony, Orpheum, and Magn-o-tone brands.

Dobro instruments have a single cone facing outward with a spider bridge structure and competed with National products. Generally, model names are numbers referring to list price and therefore materials and workmanship (e.g., a No. 65 cost $65). Because of this, the same model number may apply to various different instruments. However, model numbers are never identified on instruments!

In '30, the company name was changed to Dobro Corporation, Ltd. In '32, Louis Dopyera buys Ted Kleinmeyer's share of National. Louis, Rudy and Ed now hold controlling interest in National, but in '32 John Dopyera left Dobro to pursue idea of metal resophonic violin. In December of '34 Ed Dopyera joins National's board of directors (he's also still on Dobro board), and by March of '35 Dobro and National have merged to become the National Dobro Corporation. Dobro moves into National's larger factory but continues to maintain separate production, sales and distribution until relocation to Chicago is complete. Beginning in early-'36 National Dobro starts relocating its offices to Chicago. L.A. production of Dobros continues until '37, after which some guitars continue to be assembled from parts until '39, when the L.A. operations were closed down.

All resonator production ended in '42. Victor Smith, Al Frost and Louis Dopyera buy the company and change the name to the Valco Manufacturing Company. The Dobro name does not appear when production resumes after World War II.

In mid-'50s - some sources say as early as '54 - Rudy and Ed Dopyera began assembling wood bodied Dobros from old parts using the name DB Original. In about '59, some 12-fret DB Originals were made for Standel, carrying both DB Original and Standel logos. In around '61, production was moved to Gardena, California, and Louis Dopyera and Valco transferred the Dobro name to Rudy and Ed, who produce the so-called Gardena Dobros. At this time, the modern Dobro logo appeared with a lyre that looks like 2 back-to-back '6s'. Dobro Original debuts ca. '62. In late-'64 the Dobro name was licensed to Ed's son Emil (Ed, Jr.) Dopyera. Ed, Jr. designs a more rounded Dobro (very similar to later Mosrites) and has falling out with Rudy over it.

In '66 Semi Moseley acquires the rights to the Dobro brand, building some in Gardena, and later moving to Bakersfield, California. Moseley introduced Ed, Jr's design plus a thinline double-cutaway Dobro. He also made MoBros during this time period. Moseley Dobros use either Dobro or National cones. In '67 Ed, Sr., Rudy and Gabriella Lazar start the Original Music Instrument Company (OMI) and produce Hound Dog brand Dobros. In '68 Moseley goes bankrupt and in '70 OMI obtains the rights to the Dobro brand and begins production of OMI Dobros. In '75 Gabriella's son and daughter, Ron Lazar and Dee Garland, take over OMI. Rudy

*DeTemple Spirit Series
Stellacasta*

*DiPinto Metro Series
Philadelphian*

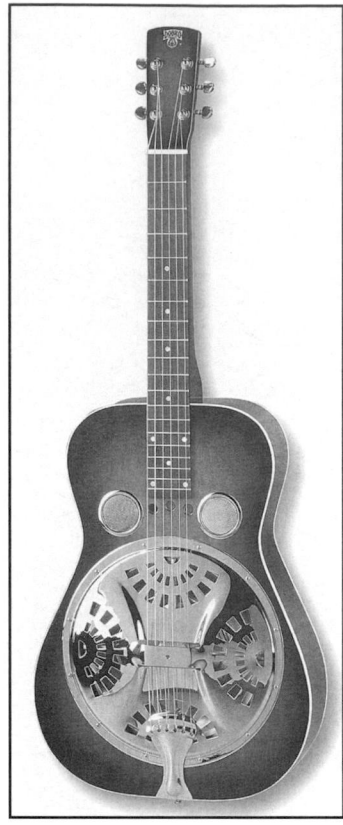

Dobro Classic 60

Dobro Regal Esquire

MODEL YEAR	FEATURES	EXC. COND. LOW	HIGH

Dupyera makes and sells Safari brand resonator mandolins. Ed, Sr. dies in '77 and Rudy in '78. In '84 OMI was sold to Chester and Betty Lizak. Both wood and metal-bodied Dobros produced in Huntington Beach, California. Chester Lizak died in '92. Gibson purchased Dobro in '93 and now makes Dobros in Nashville, Tennessee.

Dobros generally feature a serial number which, combined with historical information, provides a clue to dating. For prewar L.A. guitars, see approximation chart below adapted from "Gruhn's Guide to Vintage Guitars." No information exists on DB Originals.

Gardena Dobros had D prefix plus 3 digits beginning with 100 and going into the 500s (reportedly under 500 made). No information is available on Moseley Dobros.

OMI Dobros from '70-'79 have either D prefix for wood bodies or B prefix for metal bodies, plus 3 or 4 numbers for ranking, space, then a single digit for year (D XXXX Y or B XXX Y; e.g., D 172 8 would be wood body #172 from '78). For '80-'87 OMI Dobros, start with first number of year (decade) plus 3 or 4 ranking numbers, space, then year and either D for wood or B for metal bodies (8 XXXX YD or 8 XXX YB; e.g., 8 2006 5B would be metal body #2008 from '85). From '88-'92, at least, a letter and number indicate guitar style, plus 3 or 4 digits for ranking, letter for neck style, 2 digits for year, and letter for body style (AX XXXX NYYD or AX XXX NYYB).

L.A. Guitars (approx. number ranges, not actual production totals):

1929-30	900-2999
1930-31	3000-3999
1931-32	BXXX (Cyclops models only)
1932-33	5000-5599
1934-36	5700-7699
1937-42	8000-9999

Angelus

1933-1937. Wood body, round or square neck, 2-tone walnut finish, continues as Model 19 in Regal-made guitars.

| 1933-1937 | Round neck | $1,125 | $1,400 |
| 1933-1937 | Square neck | $1,200 | $1,500 |

Artist M-16

1934-1935. German silver alloy body, engraved.

| 1934-1935 | II square neck | $3,400 | $4,200 |
| 1934-1935 | M round neck | $5,400 | $6,700 |

Columbia D-12

1967-1968. Acoustic 12-string, typical Dobro resonator with spider style bridge, made during Dobro-Moseley era.

| 1967-1968 | | $725 | $900 |

Cyclops 45

1932-1933. Bound walnut body, 1 screen hole.

| 1932-1933 | Round neck | $2,500 | $3,100 |
| 1932-1933 | Square neck | $3,000 | $3,700 |

D-40 Texarkana

1965-1967. Mosrite-era (identified by C or D prefix), traditional Dobro style cone and coverplate, dot inlays,

MODEL YEAR	FEATURES	EXC. COND. LOW	HIGH

Dobro logo on headstock, sunburst wood body. Red and blue finishes available.

| 1965-1967 | Sunburst, square neck | $925 | $1,150 |

D-40E Texarkana

1965-1967. D-40 electric with single pickup and 2 knobs.

| 1965-1967 | | $1,000 | $1,250 |

D-100 The Californian

1965-1969. Dobro's version of Mosrite (thus nicknamed the "Mobro") thinline double-cut, resonator, 2 small metal ports, 2 pickups, 2 knobs, sunburst.

| 1965-1969 | | $1,400 | $1,750 |

DM-33 California Girl/DM-33H

1996-2006. Chrome-plated bell brass body, biscuit bridge, spider resonator, rosewood 'board. Girl or Hawaiian-scene (H) engraving.

| 1996-2006 | | $1,275 | $1,600 |

Dobro/Regal Model 19

Ca.1934-1938. In the 1930s Dobro licensed Chicago's Regal Company to build Dobro-style guitars. The headstocks on these models can have a Dobro logo, Regal logo, or no logo at all. The 19 is a lower-end model, round holes in coverplate, square neck.

| 1934-1938 | | $1,000 | $1,250 |

Dobro/Regal Model 46/47

1935-1942. Dobro/Regal 46, renamed 47 in '39, aluminum body, round neck, 14 frets, slotted headstock, silver finish. Degraded finish was a common problem with the Dobro/Regal 47.

| 1935-1938 | Model 46 | $1,400 | $1,750 |
| 1939-1942 | Model 47, original finish | $1,900 | $2,400 |

Dobro/Regal Model 62/65

1935-1942. Renamed Model 65 in '39, nickel-plated brass body, Spanish dancer etching, round or square neck. Note: Dobro/Regal 65 should not be confused with Dobro Model 65 which discontinued earlier.

1935-1938	Model 62, round neck	$2,500	$3,100
1935-1938	Model 62, square neck	$2,800	$3,500
1939-1942	Model 65, round neck	$2,400	$3,000
1939-1942	Model 65, square neck	$2,600	$3,250

Dobro/Regal Tenor Model 27-1/2

1930. Tenor version of Model 27.

| 1930 | | $560 | $700 |

Dobrolektric

1996-2005. Resonator guitar with single-coil neck pickup, single-cut.

| 1996-2005 | | $1,100 | $1,400 |

DS-33/Steel 33

1995-2000. Steel body with light amber sunburst finish, resonator with coverplate, biscuit bridge.

| 1995-2000 | | $925 | $1,150 |

DW-90C

2001-2006. Single sharp cutaway, wood body, metal resonator, f-hole upper bass bout.

| 2001-2006 | | $900 | $1,125 |

MODEL YEAR	FEATURES	EXC. COND. LOW	HIGH

F-60/F-60 S
1986-2005. Round neck (60, discontinued '00) or square neck (60 S), f-holes, brown sunburst.

1986-2005		$1,100	$1,375

Gardena
1968. Electric Dobro body, 2 knobs, single-coil soap bar pickup.

1968		$700	$900

Hound Dog
2002-present. Laminated wood, 10 1/2" spider-bridge resonator.

2002-2014		$400	$500

Hula Blues
1987-1999. Dark brown wood body (earlier models have much lighter finish), painted Hawaiian scenes, round neck.

1987-1999		$1,100	$1,375

Jerry Douglas
1995-2005. Mahogany body, square neck, limited run of 200 with signature, but also sold without signature.

1995-2005		$1,900	$2,400

Josh Graves
1996-2006. Single bound ample body, spider cone, nickel plated.

1996-2006	Unsigned	$1,275	$1,600

Leader 1 4M/14H
1934-1935. Nickel plated brass body, segmented f-holes.

1934-1935	H square neck	$1,900	$2,350
1934-1935	M round neck	$1,550	$1,925

Model 25
1930-1935. Sunburst wood body, f-holes upper bout, large single metal cone, square neck.

1930-1935		$1,500	$1,850

Model 27 (OMI)
1976-1994. Wood body, square neck.

1976-1994		$1,200	$1,500

Model 27 Cyclops
1932-1933.

1932-1933	Round neck	$1,775	$2,200
1932-1933	Square neck	$1,875	$2,300

Model 27 Deluxe
1995-2005. 27 with figured maple top, nicer appointments.

1996-2005		$1,550	$1,950

Model 27/27G
1933-1937. Regal-made, wooden body.

1933-1937	Round neck	$1,400	$1,750
1933-1937	Square neck	$1,700	$2,100

Model 32
1939-1941. Regal-made, wooden body.

1939-1941		$1,950	$2,450

Model 33 (Duolian)
1972. Only made in '72, becomes Model 90 in '73.

1972		$900	$1,125

Model 33 H
1973-1997 (OMI & Gibson). Same as 33 D, but with etched Hawaiian scenes, available as round or square neck.

1980s-90s	Round neck	$1,300	$1,600
1980s-90s	Square neck	$1,300	$1,600

Model 35 (32)
1935-1942. Metal body, called Model 32 (not to be confused with wood body 32) for '35-'38.

1935-1942		$2,000	$2,400

Model 36
1932-1937. Wood body with resonator, round or square neck.

1932-1937	Round neck	$1,125	$1,400
1932-1937	Square neck	$1,600	$2,000

Model 36/36 S
1970s-1997, 2002-2005. Chrome-plated brass body, round or square (S) neck, dot markers, engraved rose floral art.

1970s-2005		$1,400	$1,750

Model 37
1933-1937. Regal-made wood body, mahogany, bound body and 'board, round or square 12-fret neck.

1933-1937	Round neck	$1,225	$1,550
1933-1937	Square neck	$1,600	$2,000

Model 37 Tenor
1933-1937 (Regal). Tenor version of No. 37.

1933-1937		$900	$1,125

Model 45
1934-1939. Regal-made wood body, round or square neck.

1936	Square neck	$1,950	$2,450

Model 55/56 Standard
1929-1931 Model 55 Standard, renamed 56 Standard 1932-1934. Unbound wood body, metal resonator, bound neck, sunburst.

1929-1931	Model 55 square neck	$1,500	$2,500
1929-1931	Model 55 round neck	$1,250	$1,800
1932-1934	Model 56 square neck	$1,500	$2,500
1932-1934	Model 56 round neck	$1,250	$1,800

Model 60
1933-1936. Similar to Model 66/66B.

1933-1936	Round neck	$3,600	$4,500
1933-1936	Square neck	$4,600	$5,700

Model 60 Cyclops
1932-1933.

1932-1933		$3,500	$4,400

Model 60/60 D (OMI)/60 DS
1970-1993. Wood body (laminated maple) with Dobro resonator cone, model 60 until '73 when renamed 60 D, and various 60 model features offered, post-'93 was Gibson-owned production.

1970-1993	Model 60 Series	$900	$1,200

Model 63
1973-1996. Wood body, 8-string, square neck.

1973-1996		$1,050	$1,300

Model 65/66/66 B
1929-1933. Wood body with sandblasted ornamental design top and back, metal resonator, sunburst. Model 66 B has bound top.

1929-1931	Model 65	$2,900	$3,600
1932-1933	Model 66	$2,900	$3,600
1932-1933	Model 66 B	$2,900	$3,600

Dobro Hound Dog

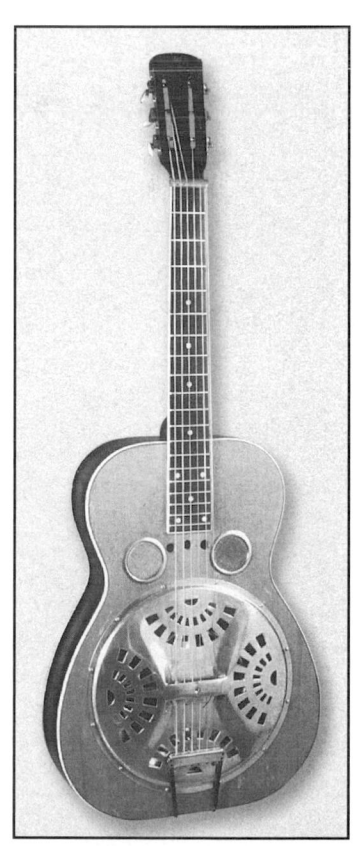

1930s Dobro Model 45

1931 Dobro Model 66

Doolin Jumbo

MODEL YEAR	FEATURES	EXC. COND. LOW	HIGH

Model 66/66 S
1972-1995. Wood body with sandblasted ornamental design top and back, metal resonator, sunburst, round or square (S) neck.

1972-1995		$880	$1,100

Model 75/Lily of the Valley
1972-1997, 2002-2005. Chrome plated bell brass body resonator, round neck, Lily of the Valley engraving.

1972-1997		$1,600	$2,000

Model 85/86
1929-1934. Wood body, triple-bound, round or square neck, renamed 86 in '32.

1929-1934		$3,100	$4,100

Model 90 (Duolian) (OMI)
1972-1995. Chrome-plated, f-holes, etched Hawaiian scene.

1972-1995	Various models	$800	$1,400

Model 90 (Woodbody)/WB90 G/WB90 S
1980s-2005. Maple body with upper bout f-holes or sound holes, round neck, metal resonator with spider bridge, sunburst.

1984-2005		$1,050	$1,300

Model 125 De Luxe
1929-1934. Black walnut body, round or square neck, Dobro De Luxe engraved, triple-bound top, back and 'board, nickel-plated hardware, natural.

1929-1934	Round neck	$5,000	$6,800
1929-1934	Square neck	$9,000	$12,000

Professional 15M/15H
1934-1935. Engraved nickel body, round (M) or square (H) neck, solid peghead.

1934-1935	H square neck	$2,400	$3,000
1934-1935	M round neck	$2,100	$2,600

Dodge
1996-present. Luthier Rick Dodge builds his intermediate and professional grade, production, solidbody guitars with changeable electronic modules in Tallahassee, Florida. He also builds basses.

Doitsch
1930s. Acoustic guitars made by Harmony most likely for a music store or studio.

Domino
Ca. 1967-1968. Solidbody and hollowbody electric guitars and basses imported from Japan by Maurice Lipsky Music Co. of New York, New York, previously responsible for marketing the Orpheum brand. Models are primarily near-copies of EKO, Vox, and Fender designs, plus some originals.

Models were made by Arai or Kawai. Earlier models may have been imported, but this is not yet documented.

Electric
1967-1968. Various models include the Baron, Californian, Californian Rebel, Dawson, and the Spartan.

1967-1968		$250	$400

Dommenget
1978-1985, 1988-present. Luthier Boris Dommenget (pronounced dommen-jay) builds his premium grade, custom/production, solidbody, flat-top, and archtop guitars in Balje, Germany. From '78 to '85 he was located in Wiesbaden, and from '88-'01 in Hamburg. He and wife Fiona also make pickups.

Don Musser Guitars
1976-present. Custom, classical and flat-top guitars built by luthier Don Musser in Cotopaxi, Colorado.

Doolin Guitars
1997-present. Luthier Mike Doolin builds his premium grade, production/custom acoustics featuring his unique double-cut in Portland, Oregon.

Dorado
Ca. 1972-1973. Six- and 12-string acoustic guitars, solidbody electrics and basses. Brand used briefly by Baldwin/Gretsch on line of Japanese imports.

Acoustic Flat-Top/Acoustic Dobro
1972-1973. Includes folk D, jumbo Western, and grand concert styles (with laminated rosewood back and sides), and Dobro-style.

1972-1973	Higher-end models	$200	$325
1972-1973	Lower-end models	$125	$155
1972-1973	Mid-level models	$155	$200

Solidbody Electric
1972-1973. Includes Model 5985, a double-cut with 2 P-90-style pickups. Price for this type of student import assumes the guitar is in all-original, excellent plus condition. Well-used examples with missing parts are worth less than the value shown.

1972-1973		$200	$300

Douglas Ching
1976-present. Luthier Douglas J. Ching builds his premium grade, production/custom, classical, acoustic, and harp guitars currently in Chester, Virginia, and previously in Hawaii ('76-'89) and Michigan ('90-'93). He also builds ukes, lutes and violins.

D'Pergo Custom Guitars
2002-present. Professional, premium, and presentation grade, production/custom, solidbody guitars built in Windham, New Hampshire. Every component of the guitars is built by D'Pergo.

Dragge Guitars
1982-2010. Luthier Peter Dragge builds his custom, steel-string and nylon-string guitars in Ojai, California.

Dragonfly Guitars
1994-present. Professional grade, production/custom, sloped cutaway flat-tops, semi-hollow body electrics, basses and dulcitars built by luthier Dan Richter in Roberts Creek, British Columbia.

MODEL		EXC. COND.	
YEAR	FEATURES	LOW	HIGH

Drive

Ca. 2001-ca. 2011. Budget grade, production, import solidbody electric guitars and basses. They also offered solidstate amps.

DTM

1997-present. See David Thomas McNaught listing.

Dudley Custom Guitars

2005-present. Luthier Peter Dudley builds his custom, premium grade, chambered solidbody electric guitars in Easton, Maryland.

Duelin Guitars

1994-present. Professional grade, production/custom, 6 ½ string guitars designed by Don Scheib of Simi Valley and built by luthier Mike Lipe in Sun Valley, California.

Duesenberg

1995-present. Professional and premium grade, production/custom, solid and hollow body electric guitars and basses built by luthier Dieter Goelsdorf in Hannover, Germany. Rockinger had a Duesenberg guitar in the 1980s.

Dunwell Guitars

1996-present. Professional and premium grade, custom, flat-tops built by luthier Alan Dunwell in Nederland, Colorado.

Dupont

Luthier Maurice Dupont builds his classical, archtop, Weissenborn-style and Selmer-style guitars in Cognac, France.

Dwight

See info under Epiphone Dwight guitar.

Dyer

1902-1939. The massive W. J. Dyer & Bro. store in St. Paul, Minnesota, sold a complete line of music related merchandise though they actually built nothing but a few organs. The Larson Brothers of Chicago were commissioned to build harp guitar and harp mandolin pieces for them somewhat following the harp guitar design of Chris Knutsen, until 1912 when the Knutsen patent expired. Although the body design somewhat copied the Knutsen patent the resulting instrument was in a class by itself in comparison. These harp guitars have become the standard by which all others are judged because of their ease of play and the tremendous, beautiful sound they produce. Many modern builders are using the body design and the same structural ideas evidenced in the Larson originals. They were built in Styles 4 (the plainest), 5, 6, 7 and 8. The ornamentation went from the no binding, dot inlay Style 4 to the full treatment, abalone trimmed, tree-of-life fingerboard of the Style 8. All had mahogany back and sides with ebony fingerboard and

bridge. There are also a very few Style 3 models found of late that are smaller than the standard and have a lower bout body point. Other Dyer instruments were built by Knutsen. Dyer also carried Stetson brand instruments made by the Larson Brothers.

Harp Guitar

1920s	Style 3, smaller, short scale	$6,000	$11,000
1920s	Style 4, no binding	$6,000	$11,000
1920s	Style 5, bound top	$8,000	$14,000
1920s	Style 6, bound top/bottom	$8,000	$14,000
1920s	Style 7, fancy inlays	$8,000	$14,000
1920s	Style 8, tree-of-life	$16,000	$21,000

Dynacord

1950-present. Dynacord is a German company that makes audio and pro sound amps, as well as other electronic equipment. In 1966-'67 they offered solidbody guitars and basses from the Welson Company of Italy. They also had the Cora guitar and bass which is the center part of a guitar body with a tube frame in a guitar outline. They also offered tape echo machines.

Dynelectron

1960s-late 1970s. This Italian builder offered a variety of guitars and basses, but is best known today for their almost exact copies of Danelectro Longhorns of the mid-'60s.

E L Welker

1984-present. Luthier Eugene L. Welker builds his premium and presentation grade, production/custom, leather-wrapped archtop guitars in Claremont, New Hampshire.

E.L. Bashore Guitars

2011-present. Professional grade, custom, steel string and classical acoustic and solidbody electric guitars, basses and banjos built by luthier Eric L. Bashore in Danville, Pennsylvania.

Earthwood

1972-1985. Acoustic designs by Ernie Ball with input from George Fullerton and made in Newport Beach, California. One of the first to offer acoustic basses.

Eastman

1992-present. Intermediate and professional grade, production, archtop and flat-top guitars and basses, mainly built in China, with some from Germany and Romania. Beijing, China-based Eastman Strings started out building violins and cellos. They added guitars in '02 and mandolins in '04.

Eastwood

1997-present. Mike Robinson's company imports budget and intermediate grade, production, solid and semi-hollowbody guitars, many styled after 1960s models. They also offer basses and mandolins.

Dudley Lone Star

Eastwood Airline Espanada

GUITARS

Edward Klein GOSH

EER Custom E-06 Classic

MODEL YEAR	FEATURES	EXC. COND. LOW	HIGH

Eaton, William

1976-present. Luthier William Eaton builds custom specialty instruments such as vihuelas, harp guitars, and lyres in Phoenix, Arizona. He is also the Director of the Robetto-Venn School of Luthiery.

Echopark Guitars

2010-present. Premium and presentation grade, production/custom, solidbody electric guitars built by luthier Gabriel Currie in Los Angeles, California. He originally began building in Echo Park.

Ed Claxton Guitars

1972-present. Premium grade, custom flat-tops made by luthier Ed Claxton, first in Austin, Texas, and currently in Santa Cruz, California.

Eduardo Duran Ferrer

1987-present. Luthier Eduardo Duran Ferrer builds his premium grade, classical guitars in Granada, Spain.

Edward Klein

1998-present. Premium grade, custom, guitars built by luthier Edward Klein in Mississauga, Ontario.

EER Custom

2005-present. Professional and premium grade, custom, soldibody and semi-hollowbody electric guitars built by luthier Ernest E. Roesler in Forks, Washington.

Egmond

1935-1972. Founded by Ulke Egmond, building acoustic, archtop, semi-hollow and solidbody guitars originally in Eindhoven, later in Best Holland. They also made basses. Egmond also produced instruments under the Orpheum (imported into U.S.) Rosetti (England), Miller, Wilson and Lion brand names.

Electric
1960-1972. Solid or semi-hollow bodies.

1960-1972		$400	$500

Ehlers

1968-present. Luthier Rob Ehlers builds his premium grade, production/custom, flat-top acoustic guitars, originally in Oregon and since '06, in Veracruz, Mexico.

15 CRC
Cutaway, Western red cedar top, Indian rosewood back and sides.

1996		$1,925	$2,400

15 SRC
Cutaway, European spruce top, Indian rosewood back and sides.

1998		$1,925	$2,400

MODEL YEAR	FEATURES	EXC. COND. LOW	HIGH

16 BTM
European spruce top, mahogany back and sides, Troubadour peghead, black lacquer finish.

1998		$2,025	$2,500

16 C
16" lower bout, cutaway, flamed maple sides and back, European spruce top.

1990		$2,025	$2,500

16 SK Concert
16" lower bout, relatively small upper bout, small waist, European spruce top, flamed koa back and sides, diamond markers, natural.

1993		$1,825	$2,250

16 SM
European spruce top, mahogany back and sides.

1999		$1,725	$2,125

16 SSC
Cutaway, European spruce top, English sycamore back and sides.

1996		$1,825	$2,275

25 C
Limited Edition Anniversary Model, European spruce top, Indian rosewood back and sides, abalone top border.

2001		$2,725	$3,400

GJ (Gypsy Jazz)

2000s	D-style	$1,725	$2,125

Eichelbaum Guitars

1994-present. Luthier David Eichelbaum builds his premium grade, custom, flat-tops in Santa Barbara, California.

EKO

1959-present. Originally acoustic, acoustic/electric, electric thinline and full-size archtop hollowbody, solidbody electric guitars and basses built by Oliviero Pigini and Company in Recanati, Italy, and imported by LoDuca Brothers, Milwaukee, Radio and Television Equipment Company in Santa Ana, California and others. First acoustic guitars followed by sparkle plastic-covered electrics by '62. Sparkle finishes are gone ca. '66. Pigini dies ca. '67. LoDuca Bros. phases out in early-'70s. By '75 EKO offers some copy guitars and they purchased a custom shop to make other brands by '78. In '85 they ceased production in Italy, continuing the brand for a few years with Asian imports, and continued to distribute other brands. By 2004, the Eko line of guitar was revived with budget and intermediate grade, production, classical, acoustic, acoustic/electric, solidbody, solidbody, and hollowbody guitars made in Asia. They also make basses and amps.

Barracuda VI
1966-ca.1978. Double-cut semi-hollow, 2 pickups, 6-string.

1966-1978		$475	$600

Barracuda XII
1966-ca.1978. Double-cut semi-hollow, 2 pickups, 12-string.

1966-1978		$525	$650

MODEL YEAR	FEATURES	EXC. COND. LOW	HIGH

Cobra I/II/III/XII

1966-1978. Double-cut solidbody, 2 knobs. Cobra I has 1 pickup, II 2 pickups and III 3 pickups. 12-string Cobra XII offered '67-'69, has 2 pickups.

1966-1978	Cobra I	$325	$400
1966-1978	Cobra II	$400	$500
1966-1978	Cobra III	$425	$525
1966-1978	Cobra XII	$425	$525

Commander

1965. Single-cut archtop electric, 1 pickup, 2 controls, EKO logo on upper bass bout, maple body in 'dura-glos' finish.

1965		$350	$450

Condor

1966-ca.1969. Double-cut solidbody with 3 or 4 pickups.

1966-1969		$475	$600

Dragon

1967 ca.1969. Single-cut archtop, 2 f-holes, 3 pickups, tremolo.

1967-1969		$575	$700

Flat-Top Acoustic

1960s. Various student-level flat-top acoustic models.

1960s		$175	$250

Florentine

1964-ca.1969. Double-cut archtop, 2 pickups.

1964-1969		$475	$600

Kadett/Kadett XII

1967-ca.1978. Double-cut solidbody with point on lower bass side of body, 3 pickups, tremolo. 12-string Kadett XII offered '68-'69.

1967-1978	Kadett	$475	$600
1968-1969	Kadett XII	$475	$600

Lancer Stereo

1967-1969. Lancer VI with stereo output (route output to 2 amplifiers requires EKO stereo cable for stereo application).

1967-1969		$375	$475

Lancer VI

1967-ca.1969. Double-cut solidbody, 2 pickups.

1967-1969		$275	$350

Lancer XII

1967-1969. Double-cut solidbody electric, 12-string.

1967-1969		$325	$410

Lark I/II

1970. Thin hollow cutaway, sunburst. Lark I has 1 pickup and Lark II 2.

1970	Lark I	$375	$475
1970	Lark II	$375	$475

Model 180

1960s. Cutaway acoustic archtop.

1960s		$325	$410

Model 285 Modello

1960s. Thinline single-cut, 1 pickup.

1962		$350	$435

Model 290/2V

1963-1965. Maple body and neck, ebony 'board, dot markers, 2 pickups, tremolo, renamed Barracuda in '66.

1963-1965		$475	$600

Model 300/375

1962. Copy of Hofner Club-style electric, single-cut, 2 pickups, set-neck.

1962		$675	$850

Model 500/1 / 500/1V

1961-1965. Plastic covered solidbody, 1 pickup. 500/1 no vibrato, 1V with vibrato.

1961-1965	500/1	$525	$675
1961-1965	500/1V	$600	$775

Model 500/2 / 500/3V

1961-1964. Plastic covered solidbody, plastic sparkle finish. 500/2 no vibrato, 2 pickups. 3V with vibrato, 3 pickups.

1961-1965	500/2	$600	$775
1961-1965	500/3V	$650	$825

Model 500/4 / 500/4V

1961-1964. Plastic covered solidbody, 4 pickups. 500/4 no vibrato, 4V with vibrato.

1961-1965	500/4	$700	$875
1961-1965	500/4V	$750	$950

Model 540 (Classical)

1960s. Nylon-string classical guitar.

1960s		$150	$200

Model 700/3V

1961-1964. Map-shape/tulip-shape body, 3 pickups, vibrato, woodgrain plastic finish.

1961-1964		$900	$1,175

Model 700/4V

1961-1967. Map-shape/tulip-shape body, 4 pickups, multiple switches, vibrato.

1961-1967	Red, blue, silver sparkle	$1,250	$1,550
1961-1967	Standard finish	$900	$1,175

Ranger 6/12

1967-ca.1982. D-size flat top acoustic, large 3-point 'guard, dot inlays, EKO Ranger label. Ranger 12 is 12-string.

1967-1982	Ranger 12	$335	$425
1967-1982	Ranger 6	$335	$425

Ranger 6/12 Electra

1967. Ranger 6/12 with on-board pickup and 2 controls, 6-string with dot markers, 12-string with block markers.

1967	12 Electra	$350	$450
1967	6 Electra	$350	$450

Rocket VI/XII (Rokes)

1967-ca.1969. Rocket-shape design, solidbody, 6-string, says Rokes on the headstock, Rokes were a popular English band that endorsed EKO guitars, marketed as the Rocket VI in the U.S.; and as the Rokes in Europe, often called the Rok. Rocket XII is 12-string.

1967-1969	Rocket VI	$650	$825
1967-1969	Rocket XII	$650	$825

El Degas

Early-1970s. Japanese-made copies of classic America electrics and acoustics, imported by Buegeleisen & Jacobson of New York, New York.

Solidbody

Early-1970s. Copies of classic American models, including the Let's Play model.

1970s		$250	$325

Eichelbaum Grand Concert

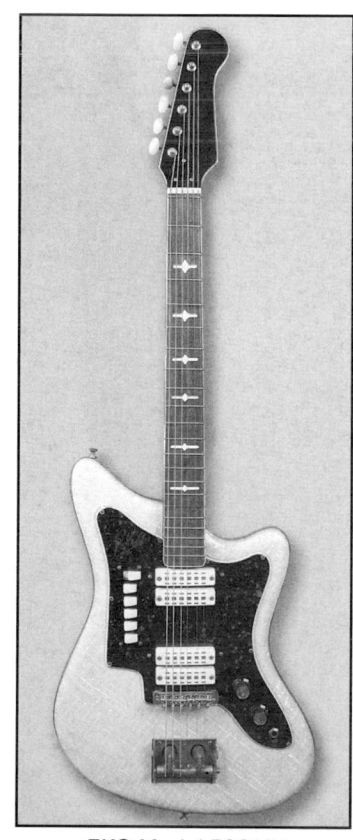

EKO Model 500/4V

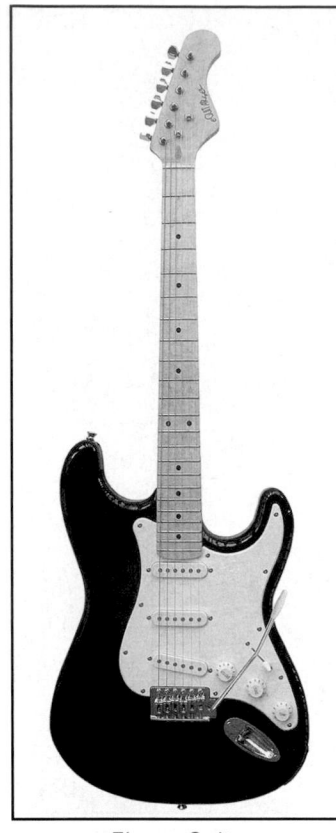

Eleca eGuitar

Late-1970s Electra MPC X320

| MODEL | | EXC. COND. | |
YEAR	FEATURES	LOW	HIGH

El Maya

1970s-1980s. Also labeled Maya. Solidbody, archtop and semi-hollow guitars built by Japan's Chushin Gakki Co., which also built models for several other manufacturers.

Eleca

2004-present. Student/budget level, production, acoustic and electric guitars, imported by Eleca International. They also offer amps, effects and mandolins.

Electar

See Epiphone listing.

Electra

1970-1984, 2013-present. Imported from Japan by St. Louis Music. Most instruments made by Matsumoku in Japan. The Electra line replaced SLM's Japanese-made Apollo and U.S.-made Custom Kraft lines. First guitar, simply called The Electra, was a copy of the Ampeg Dan Armstrong lucite guitar and issued in '70, followed quickly by a variety of bolt-neck copies of other brands. In '75 the Tree-of-Life guitars debut and the line is expanded. Open-book headstocks changed to wave or fan shape by '78. Some Korean production begins in early-'80s. In the fall of '83, the Electra Brand becomes Electra Phoenix. By beginning of '84, the brand becomes Electra-Westone and by the end of '84 just Westone. In 2013, the brand was revived with guitars built by luthiers Ben Chafin and Mick Donner in Tampa, Florida. Matsumoku-made guitars have serial number in which first 1 or 2 digits represent the year of manufacture. Thus a guitar with a serial number beginning in 0 or 80 would be from 1980.

Concert Professional
Late 1970s. Howard Roberts style, single-cut electric flat-top with oval sound hole, single humbucking pickup, fancy markers.

1977		$725	$900

Custom
1970s. Double-cut solidbody, 2 pickups, Custom logo on truss rod, cherry finish.

1970s		$600	$750

Elvin Bishop
1976-ca.1980. Double-cut semi-hollow body, tree-of-life inlay.

1976-1980		$750	$925

Flying Wedge
1970s. V body, six-on-a-side tuners.

1970s		$400	$500

MPC Outlaw
1977-1980. Symmetric horn body, neck-thru, has separate modules (Modular Powered Circuits) that plug in for different effects. Includes X710 (peace sign burned into natural mahogany top), X720 (gray sunburst), X730 (tobacco sunburst) and X 740 (maple top).

1977-1980		$700	$950
1977-1980	MPC plug in module	$80	$110

| MODEL | | EXC. COND. | |
YEAR	FEATURES	LOW	HIGH

MPC X310
1976-1980. MPC model, LP solidbody, 2 humbuckers (bridge w/ exposed zebra bobbins), 4 in-line control knobs plus 2 toggles, gold hardware, black finish.

1976-1980		$625	$800

MPC X320
1976-1980. Same as X310, but with transparent cherry red finish over mahogany top.

1976-1980		$625	$800

MPC X330
1976-1980. Same as X310, but with cherry sunburst finish on maple top.

1976-1980		$625	$800

MPC X340
1976-1980. Same as X310, but with Jacaranda rosewood top.

1976-1980		$625	$800

MPC X350
1977-1980. Same as X310, but with tobacco sunburst on a maple top.

1977-1980		$625	$800

Phoenix
1980-1984. Classic offset double-cut solidbody, Phoenix logo on headstock.

1980-1984		$275	$350

Rock
1971-1973. Single cut solidbody, becomes the Super Rock in '73.

1971-1973		$375	$475

Super Rock
1973-ca.1978. Renamed from Rock ('71-'73).

1973-1978		$500	$650

X135
1982. Offset double-cut solidbody, 2 humbucker pickups.

1982		$300	$375

X145 60th Anniversary
1982. Classic offset double-cut only made one year, Anniversary plate on back of headstock, single/single/hum pickups.

1982		$250	$325

X150
1975. Offset double-cut, 2 humbucker pickups.

1975		$375	$475

X220 Omega
1976-ca. 1980. Single-cut solidbody, block inlays, Omega logo on truss rod, black with rosewood neck, or natural with figured top and maple neck.

1976-1980		$400	$500

X280/X290 Working Man
1980-1984. Modified double-cut solidbody, 2 exposed-coil humbuckers, dot inlays, natural satin finish (X280) or jet black (X290).

1980-1984		$275	$350

X410
1975. Double-cut thinline acoustic archtop, 2 humbucker pickups, large split triangle markers, open-book style headstock shape.

1975		$750	$925

MODEL YEAR	FEATURES	EXC. COND. LOW	HIGH

X420

1978. Double-cut thinline acoustic archtop, 2 humbucker pickups, dot markers, wave-shape style headstock.

1978 $500 $625

X935 Endorser

1983-1984. Double-cut solidbody, 2 humbucker pickups, tune-o-matic, dot markers.

1983-1984 $350 $450

X960 Ultima

1981. Hybrid single-cut with additional soft bass bout cutaway, slab solidbody, dot markers, 2 humbucker pickups, wave-shape style headstock.

1981 $400 $500

Electric Gypsy

See listing under Teye.

Electro

1964-1975. The Electro line was manufactured by Electro String Instruments and distributed by Radio-Tel. The Electro logo appeared on the headstock rather than Rickenbacker. Refer to the Rickenbacker section for models.

Electromuse

1940s-1950s. Mainly known for lap steels, Electromuse also offered acoustic and electric hollowbody guitars. They also had tube amps usually sold as a package with a lap steel.

Elferink

1993-present. Production/custom, premium grade, archtop guitars built in the Netherlands by luthier Frans Elferink.

Elijah Jewel

2009-present. Luthier Michael Kerry builds his professional grade, production/custom, acoustic guitars in Mineola, Texas. He also builds mandolins.

Elite

1960s. Guitars made in Italy by the Crucianelli accordion company, which made several other brands.

Elk

Late-1960s. Japanese-made by Elk Gakki Co., Ltd. Many were copies of American designs. They also offered amps and effects.

Elliott Guitars

1966-present. Premium and presentation grade, custom, nylon-string classical and steel-string guitars built by luthier Jeffrey Elliott in Portland, Oregon.

Ellis

2000-present. Luthier Andrew Ellis builds his production/custom, premium grade, steel string acoustic and resophonic guitars in Perth, Western Australia. In 2008 he also added lap steels.

Elli-Sound

1960s. Guitars made in Italy by the Crucianelli accordion company, which made several other brands.

Ellsberry Archtop Guitars

2003-present. Premium and presentation grade, custom/production, acoustic and electric archtops built by luthier James Ellsberry previously in Torrance and Harbor City, California, and presently in Huntington Beach.

Emperador

1966-1992. Guitars and basses imported from Japan by Westheimer Musical Instruments. Early models appear to be made by either Teisco or Kawai; later models were made by Cort.

Acoustic

1960s   Archtop or flat-top $130 $160

Electric Solidbody

1960s $155 $190

Empire

1997-present. Professional and premium grade, production/custom, solidbody guitars from Lee Garver's GMW Guitarworks of Glendora, California.

Encore

Mid-1960s-present. Budget grade, production, classical, acoustic, and electric guitars imported from China and Vietnam by John Hornby Skewes & Co. in the U.K. They also offer basses.

Engel Guitars

1990-present. Luthier Robert Engel builds his premium grade, production/custom, hollowbody and solidbody guitars in Stamford, Connecticut.

English Electronics

1960s. Lansing, Michigan, company named after owner, some private branded guitars and amps by Valco (Chicago), many models with large English Electronics vertical logo on headstock.

Tonemaster

1960s. National Val-Pro 84 with neck pickup and bridge mounted pickup, black.

1960s $700 $875

Epcor

1967. Hollowbody electirc guitars and basses built by Joe Hall's Hallmark Guitars in Bakersfield, CA for manufacturer's rep Ed Preager (the EP in the name). Only about 35 were built.

Epi

1970s. Typical Japanese copy-import, Epi logo on headstock with capital letter split-E logo, inside label says "Norlin", probably for Japanese domestic market.

Elliott Classical

Encore E-49
Chaz McIntyre

Epiphone B.B. King Lucille

1964 Epiphone Casino

MODEL YEAR	FEATURES	EXC. COND. LOW	HIGH

Acoustic Flat-Top
1970s. D-style, mahogany body.

1970s		$135	$170

Epiphone

Ca. 1873-present. Budget, intermediate, professional and premium grade, production, solidbody, archtop, acoustic, acoustic/electric, resonator, and classical guitars made in the U.S. and overseas. They also offer basses, amps, mandolins, ukes and banjos. Founded in Smyrna, Turkey, by Anastasios Stathopoulos and early instruments had his label. He emigrated to the U.S. in 1903 and changed the name to Stathoupoulo. Anastasios died in '15 and his son, Epaminondas ("Epi") took over. The name changed to House of Stathopoulo in '17 and the company incorporated in '23. In '24 the line of Epiphone Recording banjos debut and in '28 the company name was changed to the Epiphone Banjo Company. In '43 Epi Stathopoulo died and sons Orphie and Frixo took over. Labor trouble shut down the NYC factory in '51 and the company cut a deal with Conn/Continental and relocated to Philadelphia in '52. Frixo died in '57 and Gibson bought the company. Kalamazoo-made Gibson Epiphones debut in '58. In '69 American production ceased and Japanese imports began. Some Taiwanese guitars imported from '79-'81. Limited U.S. production resumed in '82 but sourcing shifted to Korea in '83. In '85 Norlin sold Gibson to Henry Juszkiewicz, Dave Barryman and Gary Zebrowski. In '92 Jim Rosenberg became president of the new Epiphone division.

Alleykat
2000-2010. Single cut small body archtop, 1 humbucker and 1 mini-humbucker.

2000-2010		$275	$350

B.B. King Lucille
1997-present. Laminated double-cut maple body, 2 humbuckers, Lucille on headstock.

1997-2014		$500	$600

Barcelona CE
1999-2000. Classical, solid spruce top, rosewood back and sides, EQ/preamp.

1999-2000		$275	$340

Barcelone (Classical)
1963-1968. Highest model of Epiphone '60s classical guitars, maple back and sides, gold hardware.

1963-1964		$800	$1,000
1965-1968		$700	$875

Bard 12-String
1962-1969. Flat-top, mahogany back and sides, natural or sunburst.

1962-1964		$1,500	$1,800
1965-1969		$1,150	$1,450

Beverly Tenor
1931-1936. Archtop, 4-string.

1931-1936		$825	$1,025

Biscuit
1997-2000, 2002-2010. Wood body resonator, biscuit bridge, round neck.

1997-2010		$275	$340

Blackstone
1931-1950. Acoustic archtop, f-holes, sunburst.

1933-1934	Masterbilt	$1,000	$1,250
1935-1937		$850	$1,050
1938-1939		$725	$900
1940-1941		$675	$850
1948-1950		$575	$725

Broadway (Acoustic)
1931-1958. Non-cut acoustic archtop.

1931-1938	Sunburst, walnut body	$2,350	$2,950
1939-1942	Sunburst, maple body	$2,350	$2,950
1946-1949	Natural	$2,000	$2,500
1946-1958	Sunburst	$1,800	$2,250
1950-1958	Natural	$2,000	$2,500

Broadway Regent (Acoustic Cutaway)
1950-1958. Single-cut acoustic archtop, sunburst.

1950-1958		$2,100	$2,600

Broadway (Electric)
1958-1969. Gibson-made electric archtop, single-cut, 2 New York pickups (mini-humbucking pickups by '61), Frequensator tailpiece, block inlays, sunburst or natural finish with cherry optional in '67 only.

1958-1959	Natural	$2,700	$3,350
1958-1959	Sunburst	$2,400	$3,050
1960-1964	Natural	$2,500	$3,150
1960-1964	Sunburst	$2,300	$2,850
1965	Natural	$2,000	$2,550
1965	Sunburst	$1,850	$2,300
1966-1967	Natural, cherry	$1,850	$2,300
1966-1967	Sunburst	$1,750	$2,200
1968-1969	Natural, cherry	$1,750	$2,200
1968-1969	Sunburst	$1,750	$2,200

Broadway Reissue
1997-present. Full depth acoustic-electric single cut archtop, 2 humbuckers.

1997-2014		$475	$600

Broadway Tenor
1937-1953. Acoustic archtop, sunburst.

1937-1949		$1,250	$1,550
1950-1953		$1,150	$1,450

Byron
1949-ca.1955. Acoustic archtop, mahogany back and sides, sunburst.

1949-1955		$375	$475

C Series Classical (Import)
1995-2006. Nylon-string classical guitars, including C-25 (mahogany back & sides), C-40 (cedar top, mahogany), C-70-CE (rosewood).

1998-2005	C-40	$135	$165

Caiola Custom
1963-1970. Introduced as Caiola, renamed Caiola Custom in '66, electric thinbody archtop, 2 mini-humbuckers, multi-bound top and back, block inlays, walnut or sunburst finish (walnut only by '68).

1963-1964		$3,300	$4,100
1965		$3,000	$3,700
1966-1967		$2,800	$3,500
1968-1970		$2,600	$3,300

MODEL YEAR	FEATURES	EXC. COND. LOW	HIGH
Caiola Standard			

1966-1970. Electric thinbody archtop, 2 P-90s, single-bound top and back, dot inlays, sunburst or cherry.

MODEL YEAR	FEATURES	EXC. COND. LOW	HIGH
1966-1967		$2,400	$3,000
1968-1970		$2,200	$2,800
Casino (1 Pickup)			

1961-1969. Thinline hollowbody, double-cut, 1 P-90 pickup, various colors.

1961		$3,000	$4,000
1962-1964		$3,000	$4,000
1965		$2,500	$3,200
1966-1969		$2,000	$2,600
Casino (2 Pickups)			

1961-1969. Two pickup (P-90) version, various colors. '61-'63 known as Keith Richards model, '64-'65 known as Beatles model.

1961-1964		$5,000	$6,500
1965		$4,500	$6,000
1966-1969		$4,300	$5,400
Casino (Japan)			

1982-1983. Epiphone built a few of its classic models, including the Casino, in Japan from mid-'82 to mid-'83.

1982-1983		$800	$1,000
Casino J.L. U.S.A. 1965			

2003-2006. 1,965 made.

2003-2006		$2,175	$2,700
Casino Reissue			

1995-present. Sunburst.

1995-2014		$425	$525
Casino Revolution			

1999-2005. Limited production 1965 reissue model, with certificate of authenticity, sanded natural.

1999-2005		$2,100	$2,600
Casino 1961 50th Anniversary Limited Edition			

2011. Trapeze (TD) or TremTone vibrato (TDV), total run of 1,961 built.

2011	TDV	$700	$900
2011	Trapeze	$675	$875
Century			

1939-1970. Thinline archtop, non-cut, 1 pickup, trapeze tailpiece, walnut finish, sunburst finish available in '58, Royal Burgundy available '61 and only sunburst finish available by '68.

1939-1948	Oblong shape pickup	$1,100	$1,350
1949	Large rectangular pickup	$1,050	$1,300
1950	New York pickup	$1,000	$1,225
1951-1957	Sunburst	$975	$1,200
1958-1962	Sunburst, P-90 pickup, plate logo	$1,400	$1,750
1963-1964	Sunburst, P-90 pickup, no plate logo	$1,400	$1,750
1965	Sunburst, cherry	$1,200	$1,525
1966-1970	Sunburst, cherry	$1,100	$1,375
Classic (Classical)			

1963-1970.

1963-1964		$475	$600
1965		$400	$500
1966-1970		$350	$450

Collegiate

2004-2005. Les Paul-style body, 1 humbucker, various college graphic decals on body.

2004-2005		$175	$500
Coronet (Electric Archtop)			

1939-1949. Electric archtop, laminated mahogany body, 1 pickup, trapeze tailpiece, sunburst, name continued as an electric solidbody in '58.

1939-1949		$900	$1,100
Coronet (Solidbody)			

1958-1969. Solidbody electric, 1 New York pickup ('58-'59), 1 P-90 ('59-'69), cherry or black finish, Silver Fox finish available by '63, reintroduced as Coronet USA '90-'94, Korean-made '95-'98.

1958-1959		$2,900	$3,600
1960-1964	Various colors	$2,700	$3,400
1965-1966	Custom color (3 options)	$3,400	$4,300
1965-1966	Standard color	$1,850	$2,300
1967-1969	Various colors	$1,600	$2,000
Coronet U.S.A.			

1990-1994. Made in Nashville, reverse banana headstock, typical Coronet styled body, single-coil and humbucker.

1990-1994		$550	$700
Coronet (Import)			

1995-1998. Import version.

1995-1998		$240	$300
Crestwood Custom			

1958-1970. Solidbody, 2 New York pickups ('58-'60), 2 mini-humbuckers ('61-'70), symmetrical body and 3+3 tuners ('58-'62), asymmetrical and 1x6 tuners ('63-'70), slab body with no Gibson equivalent model.

1958-1960	Cherry, NY pickups, 3+3	$4,400	$5,400
1959-1960	Sunburst, NY pickups	$4,400	$5,400
1961-1962	Cherry, mini-humbuckers	$4,100	$5,100
1961-1962	White, mini-humbuckers	$5,000	$6,000
1963-1964	Cherry, 1x6	$3,100	$3,900
1963-1964	Custom color (3 options)	$5,500	$9,500
1965	Cherry	$2,900	$3,500
1965	Custom color (3 options)	$5,400	$7,100
1966-1967	Cherry	$2,700	$3,300
1966-1967	Custom color (3 options)	$3,500	$4,400
1968-1970	Cherry, white	$2,500	$3,100
Crestwood Deluxe			

1963-1969. Solidbody with 3 mini-humbuckers, block inlay, cherry, white or Pacific Blue finish, 1x6 tuners.

1963-1964	Cherry	$3,500	$4,400
1963-1964	Custom color (3 options)	$5,500	$9,500
1965	Cherry	$3,100	$3,900
1965	Custom color (3 options)	$5,300	$9,300

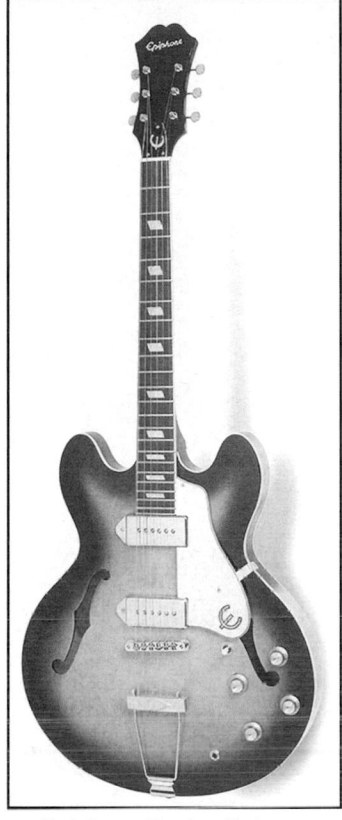

Epiphone Casino Reissue

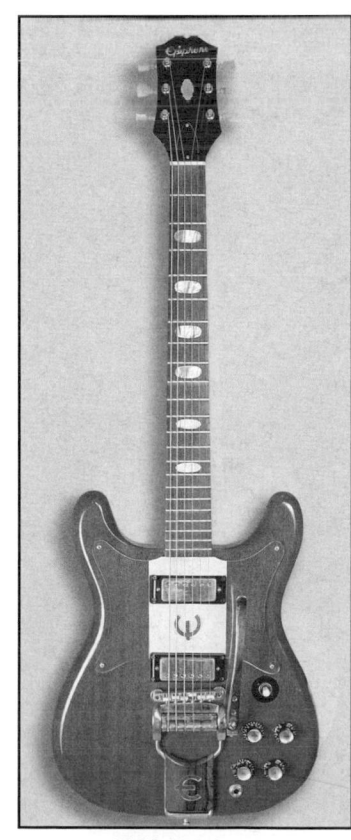

1962 Epiphone Crestwood Custom

1934 Epiphone De Luxe

John DeSilva

Epiphone Elitist Series Casino

MODEL YEAR	FEATURES	EXC. COND. LOW	HIGH
1966-1967	Cherry	$2,800	$3,500
1966-1967	Custom color (3 options)	$3,600	$4,600
1968-1969	Cherry, white	$2,800	$3,500

De Luxe

1931-1957. Non-cut acoustic archtop, maple back and sides, trapeze tailpiece ('31-'37), frequensator tailpiece ('37-'57), gold-plated hardware, sunburst or natural finish.

1931-1934	Sunburst	$3,300	$4,100
1935-1938	Sunburst	$3,200	$4,000
1939-1944	Natural	$3,300	$4,100
1939-1944	Sunburst	$2,900	$3,600
1945-1949	Natural	$2,900	$3,600
1945-1949	Sunburst	$2,500	$3,100
1950-1957	Natural	$2,500	$3,100
1950-1957	Sunburst	$2,200	$2,700

De Luxe Regent (Acoustic Archtop)

1948-1952. Acoustic cutaway archtop, high-end appointments, rounded cutaway, natural finish, renamed De Luxe Cutaway in '53.

1948-1952		$3,300	$4,100

De Luxe Cutaway/Deluxe Cutaway

1953-1970. Renamed from De Luxe Regent, cataloged Deluxe Cutaway by Gibson in '58, special order by '64 with limited production because acoustic archtops were pretty much replaced by electric archtops. There is also a FT Deluxe Cutaway flat-top (see FT listings).

1953-1957	Epiphone NY-made	$3,000	$3,700
1958-1959		$4,500	$5,500
1960-1965	Gibson Kalamazoo, rounded cutaway	$4,500	$5,500
1965-1970	Special order only	$4,000	$5,000

De Luxe Electric (Archtop)

1954-1957. Single-cut electric archtop, 2 pickups, called the Zephyr De Luxe Regent from '48-'54. Produced with a variety of specs, maple or spruce tops, different inlays and pickup combinations.

1954-1957	Natural	$3,000	$3,700
1954-1957	Sunburst	$2,800	$3,500

Del Ray

1995-2000. Offset double-cut body, 2 blade humbuckers, dot markers, tune-o-matic, flamed maple top.

1995-2000		$280	$350

Devon

1949-1957. Acoustic archtop, non-cut, mahogany back and sides, sunburst finish, optional natural finish by '54.

1950-1953	Sunburst	$1,300	$1,600
1954-1957	Natural	$1,300	$1,600
1954-1957	Sunburst	$1,300	$1,600

Don Everly (SQ-180)

1997-2004. Jumbo acoustic reissue, large double 'guard, black gloss finish.

1997-2004		$400	$500

Dot (ES-335 Dot)/Dot Archtop

2000-present. Dot-neck ES-335.

2000-2014		$300	$375

Dot Studio

2004-present. Simplified Dot, 2 control knobs, black hardware.

2004-2014		$225	$280

Dove Limited Edition

2008. Dove Limited Edition logo on label, Dove script logo on truss rod cover, classic dove logo art on 'guard and dove inlay on bridge, cherry or ebony.

2008		$250	$315

Dwight

1963, 1967. Coronet labeled as Dwight and made for Sonny Shields Music of St. Louis, 75 made in '63 and 36 in '67, cherry. National-Supro made Dwight brand lap steels in the '50s.

1963		$2,600	$3,200
1967		$2,300	$2,900

EA/ET/ES Series (Japan)

1970-1979. Production of the Epiphone brand was moved to Japan in '70. Models included the EA (electric thinline) and ET (electric solidbody).

1970-1975	EA-250	$350	$450
1970-1975	ET-270	$450	$550
1970-1975	ET-275	$450	$550
1972	ES-255 Casino	$475	$575
1975-1979	ET-290 Crestwood	$450	$550

EJ160E John Lennon

1997-2013. Based on John's Gibson acoustic/electric, sunburst, signature on body.

1997-2013		$350	$450

El Diablo

1994-1995. Offset double-cut acoustic/electric, onboard piezo and 3-band EQ, composite back and sides, spruce top, cherry sunburst.

1994-1995		$275	$350

Electar Model M

1935-1939. Epiphone's initial entry into the new electric guitar market of the mid-'30s, 14 3/4" laminate maple archtop, horseshoe pickup, trap door on back for electronics, Electar logo on headstock, oblong pickup replaces horseshoe in late-'37.

1935-1936	2 control knobs	$1,300	$1,600
1937-1939	3 control knobs	$1,300	$1,600

Electar Model M Tenor

1937-1939. 4-string electric tenor with Electar specs.

1937-1939	3 knobs, natural	$1,225	$1,525

Elitist Series

2003-present. Made in Japan, higher-grade series, using finer woods and inlays and U.S.-made Gibson pickups.

2003-2004	J-200	$1,300	$1,600
2003-2004	L-00/VS	$1,300	$1,600
2003-2005	'65 Texan	$1,300	$1,600
2003-2005	1961 SG Standard	$1,000	$1,250
2003-2005	Riviera	$1,500	$1,900
2003-2008	1963 ES-335 Dot	$1,450	$1,800
2003-2008	Byrdland/L5	$1,800	$2,250
2003-2009	Broadway	$1,300	$1,600
2003-2009	Casino	$1,300	$1,600
2003-2009	Les Paul Custom	$1,000	$1,250
2003-2009	Les Paul Standard	$1,000	$1,250
2003-2009	Les Paul Standard '57 Goldtop	$1,000	$1,250

MODEL YEAR	FEATURES	EXC. COND. LOW	HIGH
2003-2009	Les Paul Studio	$800	$1,000
2003-2009	Sheraton	$1,500	$1,900
2004-2005	Jim Croce L-00	$875	$1,100
2005	Chet Atkins Country Gentleman	$1,300	$1,600
2007-2009	Les Paul Plus	$1,000	$1,250
2012	Dwight Yoakam Dwight Trash Casino, 250 made	$1,600	$1,950

Emperor (Acoustic Archtop)
1935-1954. Acoustic archtop, non-cut, maple back and sides, multi-bound body, gold-plated hardware, sunburst, optional natural finish by '39.

1935-1938	Sunburst	$4,500	$5,400
1939-1949	Natural	$5,100	$6,300
1939-1949	Sunburst	$4,100	$4,900
1950-1954	Natural	$4,500	$5,600
1950-1954	Sunburst	$3,300	$4,100

Emperor Regent
1948-1953. Acoustic archtop with rounded cutaway, renamed Emperor Cutaway in '53.

1948-1953	Natural	$4,800	$5,900
1948-1953	Sunburst	$4,300	$5,300

Emperor Cutaway
1953-1957. Renamed from Emperor Regent, acoustic archtop, single-cut, maple back and sides, multi-bound body, gold-plated hardware, sunburst or natural.

1953-1957	Natural	$4,800	$5,900
1953-1957	Sunburst	$4,300	$5,300

Emperor Electric
1953-1957. Archtop, single-cut, 3 pickups, multi-bound body, sunburst, called the Zephyr Emperor Regent in '50-'53.

1953-1957		$3,200	$4,000

Emperor (Thinline Electric)
1958-1969. Single-cut, thinline archtop, 3 New York pickups in '58-'60, 3 mini-humbuckers '61 on, multi-bound, gold-plated hardware, sunburst or natural finish until '65 when only sunburst was made.

1958	Natural, 3 NY pickups	$10,000	$12,500
1958	Sunburst, 3 NY pickups	$8,000	$10,000
1959	Natural, 3 pickups	$10,000	$12,500
1959	Sunburst, 3 pickups	$8,000	$10,000
1960-1962	Natural	$9,500	$12,000
1960-1962	Sunburst	$7,500	$9,500
1963-1969	Special order only	$7,000	$8,800

Emperor/Emperor II
1982-1994. Single-cut archtop jazz guitar, 2 humbuckers, blocks, gold hardware. II added to name in '93, became Joe Pass Emperor II (see that listing) in '95, although his name was on the guitar as early as '91.

1982-1989	Matsumoku, Japan	$1,200	$1,500
1990-1994		$500	$650

Entrada (Classical)
1963-1968. Classical, natural.

1963-1964		$475	$600

MODEL YEAR	FEATURES	EXC. COND. LOW	HIGH
1965		$400	$500
1966-1968		$350	$450

ES-295
1997-2001, 2003-2006. Epiphone's version of classic Gibson goldtop.

1997-2006		$500	$650

Espana (Classical)
1962-1968. Classical, U.S.-made, maple back and sides, natural, imported in '69 from Japan.

1962-1964		$700	$875
1965		$650	$800
1966-1968		$600	$750

Exellente
1963-1969, 1994-1995. Flat-top, rosewood back and sides, cloud inlays. Name revived on Gibson Montana insturment in '90s.

1963-1964		$5,700	$7,200
1965		$5,700	$7,200
1966-1969		$5,700	$7,200

1958 Korina Explorer
1998-2011. Explorer with typical appointments, korina body. This guitar was produced with a variety of specs, ranging from maple tops to spruce tops, different inlay markers were also used, different pickup combinations have been seen, natural or sunburst finish.

1998-2011		$350	$435

1958 Gothic Explorer/Flying V
2002-2012. Flat black finish, V ends in 2010.

2002-2012		$350	$435

Firebird
1995-2000. Two mini-humbuckers, Firebird Red, dot markers.

1995-2000		$350	$435

Firebird 300
1986-1988. Korean import, Firebird Red

1986-1988		$350	$435

Firebird 500
1986-1988. Korean import, Firebird Red.

1986-1988		$350	$435

1963 Firebird VII/Firebird VII
2000-2010. Three mini-humbuckers, gold hardware, Maestro-style vibrato, block markers, Firebird Red, reverse body. 1963 dropped from name in '03.

2000-2010		$525	$650

Firebird Studio
2006-2011. Two humbuckers, with worn cherry finish.

2006-2011		$400	$500

Flamekat
1999-2005. Archtop, flame finish, double dice position markers, 2 mini-humbuckers, Epiphone Bigsby.

1999-2005		$300	$375

Flying V/'67 Flying V
1989-1998, 2003-2005. '67 or '58 specs, alder body, natural.

1989-1998	'67 specs	$350	$435
2003-2005	'58 specs	$350	$435

1958 Korina Flying V
1998-2011. Typical Flying V configuration, korina body.

1998-2011		$350	$435

1957 Epiphone Emperor

Epiphone Firebird Studio

*Epiphone Paul McCartney
1964 Texan*

Epiphone G 310

MODEL YEAR	FEATURES	EXC. COND. LOW	HIGH

FT 30
1941-1949. Acoustic flat-top, brown stain, mahogany back and sides, reintroduced as Gibson-made FT 30 Caballero in '58.

1941-1943		$1,175	$1,500
1944-1949		$1,000	$1,300

FT 30 Caballero
1959-1970. Reintroduced from Epiphone-made FT 30, Gibson-made acoustic flat-top, natural, all mahogany body, dot inlay, tenor available '63-'68.

1959-1961		$1,075	$1,325
1962-1964		$850	$1,025
1965		$750	$925
1966-1969		$600	$750
1970		$475	$600

FT 45
1941-1948. Acoustic flat-top, walnut back and sides, cherry neck, rosewood 'board, natural top, reintroduced as Gibson-made FT 45 Cortez in '58.

1941-1943		$1,750	$2,250
1944-1948		$1,400	$1,800

FT 45 Cortez
1958-1969. Reintroduced from Epiphone-made FT 45, Gibson-made acoustic flat-top, mahogany back and sides, sunburst or natural top (sunburst only in '59-'62).

1958-1959	Sunburst	$1,525	$1,900
1960-1964	Sunburst, natural	$1,325	$1,650
1965-1966	Sunburst, natural	$1,000	$1,250
1967-1969	Sunburst, natural	$875	$1,100

FT 79
1941-1958. Acoustic 16" flat-top, square shoulder dreadnought, walnut back and sides until '49 and laminated maple back and sides '49 on, natural, renamed FT 79 Texan by Gibson in '58.

1941-1943	Walnut back & sides	$3,900	$5,100
1944-1949	Walnut back & sides	$3,300	$4,500
1949-1958	Laminated pressed maple body	$3,100	$4,000

FT 79 Texan
1958-1970, 1993-1995. Renamed from Epiphone FT 79, Gibson-made acoustic flat-top, mahogany back and sides, sunburst or natural top, Gibson Montana made 170 in '93-'95.

1958-1959		$2,750	$3,400
1960 1964		$2,750	$3,400
1965		$2,600	$3,200
1966-1967		$2,400	$3,000
1968-1969		$2,300	$2,900
1970		$2,125	$2,700

Paul McCartney 1964 Texan (U.S.A.)
2005-2006. Reproduction of McCartney's '64 Texan made in Gibson's Montana plant, two runs, one of 40 guitars ('05), second of 250 ('05-'06). First 40 were hand-aged and came with Sir Paul's autograph, display case and certificate; the 250 run were not-hand aged, but have signed labels.

2005-2006	250 run	$3,100	$3,900

Paul McCartney 1964 Texan (Japan)
2006-2010. Limited run of 1,964 guitars.

2006-2010		$1,100	$1,350

1964 Texan (Inspired By Series)
2010-present. Imported production model, acoustic/electric, non-adjustable bridge.

2010-2014		$250	$300

FT 85 Serenader 12-String
1963-1969. 12 strings, mahogany back and sides, dot inlay, natural.

1963-1964		$1,075	$1,325
1965-1966		$850	$1,050
1967-1969		$675	$850

FT 90 El Dorado
1963-1970. Dreadnought flat-top acoustic, mahogany back and sides, multi-bound front and back, natural.

1963-1964		$2,500	$3,100
1965		$1,800	$2,200
1966-1967		$1,700	$2,100
1968-1970		$1,600	$2,000

FT 95 Folkster
1966-1969. 14" small body, mahogany back and sides, natural, double white 'guards.

1966-1969		$750	$925

FT 98 Troubadour
1963-1969. 16" square shouldered drednought, maple back and sides, gold-plated hardware, classical width 'board.

1963-1964		$2,200	$2,700
1965-1969		$2,000	$2,500

FT 110
1941-1958. Acoustic flat-top, natural, renamed the FT 110 Frontier by Gibson in '58.

1941-1943	Square shoulder	$3,900	$5,100
1944-1949	Square shoulder	$3,300	$4,500
1949-1954	Round shoulder	$3,100	$4,000
1954-1958	Mahogany neck	$3,100	$4,000

FT 110 Frontier
1958-1970, 1994. Renamed from FT 110, acoustic flat-top, natural or sunburst, Gibson Montana made 30 in '94.

1958-1959		$3,700	$4,900
1960-1964		$3,300	$4,400
1965		$3,150	$3,900
1966-1967		$2,950	$3,700
1968-1970	Maple	$2,950	$3,700

FT Deluxe
1939-1941. Acoustic flat-top, 16.5".

1939-1941		$4,300	$5,600

FT Deluxe Cutaway (FT 210)
1954-1957. Acoustic flat-top, cutaway, 16.5". Some labeled FT 210.

1954-1957		$4,800	$6,300

FT Series (Flat-Tops Japan)
1970s. In '70 Epiphone moved production to Japan. Various 6- to 12-string models were made, nearly all with bolt necks and small rectangular blue labels on the inside back, rangeing from the budget FT 120 to the top-of-the-line FT 570 Super Jumbo.

1970s	Various models	$150	$500

MODEL YEAR	FEATURES	EXC. COND. LOW	HIGH

G 310
1989-present. SG-style model with large 'guard and gig bag.

1989-2014		$175	$225

G 400
1989-2013. SG-style, 2 humbuckers, crown inlays.

1989-2013		$200	$250

G 400 Custom
1998-2000, 2003-2011. 3 humbucker version, gold harware, block inlays.

1998-2011		$300	$375

G 400 Deluxe
1999-2007. Flame maple top version of 2 humbucker 400.

1999-2007		$400	$500

G 400 Limited Edition
2001-2002. 400 with Deluxe Maestro lyra vibrola, cherry red.

2001-2002		$300	$375

G 400 Tony Iommi
2003-2011. SG-style model with cross 'board inlay markers, black finish.

2003-2011		$350	$425

G 1275 Custom Double Neck
1996-2011. SG-style alder body, 6- & 12-string, maple top, mahogany neck, cherry red, set neck. Also offered as bolt-neck Standard for '96-'98.

1996-2011		$550	$700

Genesis
1979-1980. Double-cut solidbody, 2 humbuckers with coil-taps, carved top, red or black, available as Custom, Deluxe, and Standard models, Taiwan import.

1979-1980		$675	$850

Granada (Non-cutaway Thinbody)
1962-1969. Non-cut thinline archtop, 1 f-hole, 1 pickup, trapeze tailpiece, sunburst finish.

1962-1964		$700	$900
1965		$600	$800
1966-1969		$550	$750

Granada (Cutaway)
1965-1970. Single-cut version.

1965-1966		$825	$1,025
1967-1970		$725	$900

Hollywood Masterbilt Tenor
1931-1936. Tenor version of the Triumph, acoustic archtop 15.4", 19-fret Brazilian rosewood 'board, diagonal diamond markers.

1931-1936		$1,800	$2,250

Howard Roberts Standard
1964-1970. Single-cut acoustic archtop, bound front and back, cherry or sunburst finish, listed in catalog as acoustic but built as electric.

1964		$2,600	$3,200
1965-1967		$2,100	$2,600
1968-1970		$1,800	$2,200

Howard Roberts Custom
1965-1970. Single-cut archtop, bound front and back, 1 pickup, walnut finish (natural offered '66 only).

1965-1967		$2,800	$3,400
1968-1970		$2,300	$2,800

Howard Roberts III
1987-1991. Two pickups, various colors.

1987-1991		$400	$500

Inspiration Style A Tenor
1928-1929. Banjo resonator style body with round soundhole, A headstock logo, spruce top, walnut back, sides and neck.

1928-1929		$2,300	$2,850

Joe Pass/Joe Pass Emperor II
1995-present. Single-cut archtop jazz guitar, 2 humbuckers, blocks, gold hardware, natural or sunbusrt, renamed from Emperor II (see that listing). Limited Edition all-gold finish or Wine Red were available early on.

1995-2014		$500	$625

Les Paul 100/LP-100
1993-present. Affordable single-cut Les Paul, bolt-on neck.

1993-2014		$175	$225

Les Paul '56 Goldtop
1998-2013. Based on '56 Goldtop specs with 2 P-90s. Black finish was offered starting in '09.

1998-2013	Gold	$400	$525
2009-2013	Black	$400	$525

Les Paul Ace Frehley
2001. Les Paul Custom 3-pickups, Ace's signature on 22nd fret, lightning bolt markers

2001		$600	$750

Les Paul Alabama Farewell Tour
2003. Limited production, 1 pickup single-cut Jr., American flag and Alabama logo graphics and band signatures on body, Certificate of Authenticity.

2003		$400	$525

Les Paul Black Beauty
1997-present. Classic styling with three gold plated pickups, black finish, block markers.

1997-2014		$400	$525

Les Paul Classic
2003-2005. Classic Les Paul Standard specs, figured maple top, sunburst.

2003-2005		$400	$525

Les Paul Custom
1989-2011. Various colors.

1989-2011		$400	$525

Les Paul Custom Plus (Flame Top)
1998-2010. Flamed maple top version of 2 pickup Custom, gold hardware, sunburst.

1998-2010		$400	$525

Les Paul Custom Silverburst
2007-2008. 2 humbuckers, silverburst finish.

2007-2008		$400	$525

Les Paul Dale Earnhardt
2003. Dale Earnhardt graphics, 1 humbucker.

2003		$325	$425

Les Paul Deluxe
1998-2000. Typical mini-humbucker pickups.

1998-2000		$400	$525

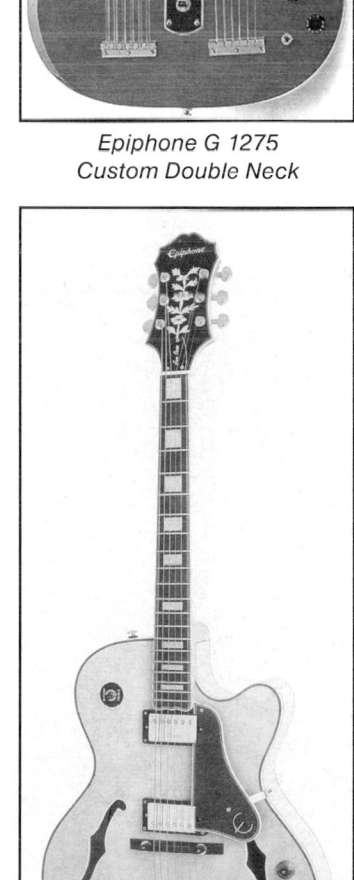

Epiphone G 1275 Custom Double Neck

Epiphone Joe Pass Emperor II

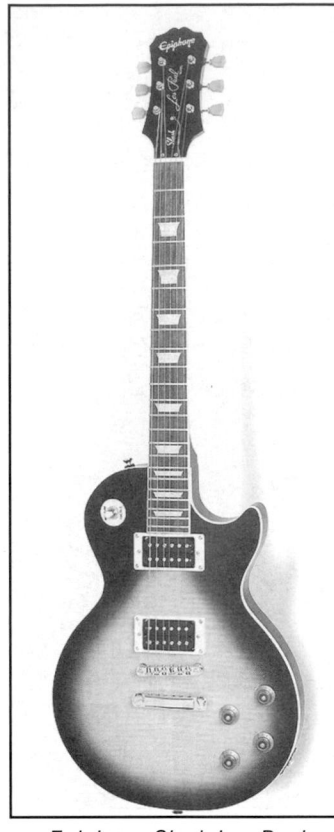

Epiphone Slash Les Paul Standard Plus-Top

Epiphone Zakk Wylde Les Paul Custom

MODEL YEAR	FEATURES	EXC. COND. LOW	HIGH

Les Paul ES Limited Edition
1999-2000. Les Paul semi-hollow body with f-holes, carved maple top, gold hardware, cherry sunburst and other color options.

| 1999-2000 | Custom | $500 | $625 |
| 1999-2000 | Standard | $500 | $625 |

Les Paul Gold Top
1994-1998. Goldtop, 2 humbuckers. Listed as Les Paul Standard Goldtop in '94.

| 1994-1998 | | $375 | $465 |

Les Paul Joe Perry Boneyard
2004-2006. Boneyard logo on headstock, figured Boneyard finish.

| 2004-2006 | | $425 | $525 |

Les Paul Jr. '57 Reissue
2006. '57 Reissue on truss rod cover, logo and script Les Paul Junior stencil on headstock, lower back headstock states 'Epiphone Limited Edition Custom Shop'.

| 2006 | | $275 | $350 |

Les Paul Music Rising
2006-2007. Music Rising (Katrina charity) graphic, 2 humbuckers.

| 2006-2007 | | $275 | $350 |

Les Paul Sparkle L.E.
2001. Limited Edition LP Standard, silver, purple, red (and others) glitter finish, optional Bigsby.

| 2001 | | $400 | $500 |

Les Paul Special
1994-2000. Double-cut, bolt neck.

| 1994-2000 | | $180 | $225 |

Les Paul Special II
1996-present. Economical Les Paul, 2 pickups, single-cut, various colors.

| 1996-2014 | Guitar only | $80 | $100 |
| 1996-2014 | Player Pack with amp | $95 | $120 |

Les Paul Special Limited Edition/TV Special
2006. Copy of single-cut late '50s Les Paul Special with TV finish.

| 2006 | | $225 | $275 |

Les Paul Standard
1989-present. Solid mahogany body, carved maple top, 2 humbuckers.

| 1989-2014 | Various colors | $300 | $375 |

Les Paul Standard Baritone
2004-2005. 27-3/4" long-scale baritone model.

| 2004-2005 | | $350 | $435 |

Les Paul Standard Plus FMT
2003-2012. LP Standard figured curly maple sunburst top.

| 2003-2012 | | $375 | $475 |

Les Paul Standard Ultra/Ultra II
2005-2012. LP Standard with chambered and contoured body, quilted maple top.

| 2005-2012 | Ultra | $375 | $475 |
| 2005-2012 | Ultra II | $475 | $600 |

Les Paul Studio
1995-present. Epiphone's version of Gibson LP Studio.

| 1995-2013 | | $200 | $250 |

MODEL YEAR	FEATURES	EXC. COND. LOW	HIGH

Les Paul XII
1998-2000. 12-string solidbody, trapeze tailpiece, flamed maple sunburst, standard configuration.

| 1998-2000 | | $425 | $525 |

Slash Les Paul
1997-2000. Slash logo on body.

| 1997-2000 | | $600 | $750 |

Slash Les Paul Goldtop
2008-2012. Limited Edition 2,000 made, goldtop finish, Seymour Duncan exposed humbuckers, Slash logo on truss rod cover, includes certificate of authenticity.

| 2008-2012 | With certificate | $850 | $1,050 |

Slash Les Paul Standard Plus-Top
2008-2012. Figured top, exposed humbuckers, includes certificate of authenticity.

| 2008-2012 | With certificate | $900 | $1,125 |

Zakk Wylde Les Paul Custom
2002-present. Bull's-eye graphic, block markers, split diamond headstock inlay.

| 2002-2014 | | $425 | $525 |

Madrid (Classical)
1962-1969. Classical, natural.

1962-1964		$400	$500
1965		$350	$425
1966-1969		$300	$375

MD-30
1993. D-size, round metal resonator, spruce top with dual screens.

| 1993 | | $450 | $550 |

Melody Tenor
1931-1937. 23" scale, bound body.

| 1931-1937 | Masterbilt | $1,200 | $1,500 |

Moderne
2000. Copy of '58 Gibson Moderne design, dot markers, Moderne script logo on 'guard, black.

| 2000 | | $500 | $625 |

Navarre
1931-1940. Flat-top, mahogany back and sides, bound top and back, dot inlay, brown finish.

| 1931-1937 | Hawaiian, Masterbilt label | $1,800 | $2,250 |
| 1938-1940 | Hawaiian, standard label | $1,600 | $2,000 |

Nighthawk Standard
1995-2000. Epiphone's version of the Gibson Nighthawk, single-cut, bolt neck, figured top.

| 1995-2000 | | $275 | $350 |

Noel Gallagher Union Jack/Super Nova
1997-2005. Limited edition, higher-end ES-335. Union Jack with British flag finish (introduced '99) or Supernova in solid blue.

| 1997-2005 | | $1,000 | $1,250 |

Olympic (Acoustic Archtop)
1931-1949. Mahogany back and sides.

| 1931-1949 | | $700 | $900 |

Olympic Tenor (Acoustic Archtop)
1937-1949. 4-string version of the Olympic.

| 1937-1949 | | $700 | $875 |

Olympic Single (Solidbody)
1960-1970. Slab body, the same as the mid-'60s Coronet, Wilshire and Crestwood Series, single-cut

MODEL YEAR	FEATURES	EXC. COND. LOW	HIGH

'60-'62, asymmetrical double-cut '63-'70, 2 Melody maker single-coil pickups, vibrato optional in '64 and standard by '65.

1960-1962	Sunburst, single-cut	$1,250	$1,550
1963-1964	Sunburst, double-cut	$1,100	$1,350
1965-1970	Cherry or sunburst	$1,000	$1,250

Olympic Double (Solidbody)
1960-1969. Slab body, the same as the mid-'60s Coronet, Wilshire and Crestwood Series, single-cut '60-'62, asymmetrical-cut '63-'70, 2 Melody Maker single-coils, vibrato optional in '64 and standard by '65.

1960-1963	Sunburst, single-cut	$2,100	$2,600
1963-1964	Sunburst, double-cut	$1,750	$2,200
1965	Cherry or sunburst	$1,150	$1,450
1966-1969	Cherry or sunburst	$1,100	$1,400

Olympic (3/4 Scale Solidbody)
1960-1963. 22" scale, sunburst.

1960-1963		$725	$900

Olympic Special (Solidbody)
1962-1970. Short neck with neck body joint at the 16th fret (instead of the 22nd), single Melody Maker-style single-coil bridge pickup, small headstock, double-cut slab body, dot markers, Maestro or Epiphone vibrato optional '64-'65, slab body contour changes in '65 from symmetrical to asymmetrical with slightly longer bass horn, sunburst.

1962-1964	Symmetrical	$550	$700
1965-1970	Asymmetrical	$500	$625

PR Series
1980-2004. Budget acoustics, mainly D size but some smaller, cut and non-cut bodies.

1980-2004	Various Models	$200	$400

Pro 1
1989-1996. Solidbody, double-cut, 1 single-coil and 1 humbucking pickup, bolt-on neck, various colors.

1989-1996		$300	$375

Pro 2
1995-1998. Higher-end Pro I with Steinberger DB bridge, set-neck, 2 humbuckers, various colors.

1995-1998		$300	$375

Professional
1962-1967. Double-cut, thinline archtop, 1 pickup, mahogany finish. Values include matching Professional amp.

1962-1964	With matching amp	$2,800	$3,700
1965	With matching amp	$2,400	$3,200
1966-1967	With matching amp	$2,000	$2,700

Recording A
1928-1931. Asymmetrical body flat-top with exaggerated treble bout cutaway, celluloid headstock veneer, dot inlays. All Recording models were offered in concert or auditorium body sizes.

1928-1931	Standard 6-string	$1,700	$2,100
1928-1931	Tenor 4-string	$1,600	$2,000

Recording B
1928-1931. As Recording A but with arched back, bound fingerboard, fancier body binding and zigzagging double slotted-diamond inlays.

1928-1931		$2,250	$2,800

Recording C
1928-1931. As Recording B but with arched top.

1928-1931		$2,750	$3,400

Recording D
1928-1931. As Recording C, but with large cross-hatched block inlays.

1928-1931		$3,250	$4,000

Recording E
1928-1931. As Recording D, but with large floral engraved block inlays.

1928-1931		$4,250	$5,200

Ritz
1940-1949. 15.5" acoustic archtop, large cello f-holes, dot inlays, no headstock ornamentation other than script Epiphone inlay, blond finish.

1940-1949		$775	$975

Riviera
1962-1970. Double-cut thinline archtop, 2 mini-humbuckers, Royal Tan standard finish changing to sunburst in '65, cherry optional by '66-'70, additional 250 were made in Nashville in '93-'94, a Riviera import was available in '82 and for '94-'06.

1962-1964	Tan or custom cherry	$3,600	$4,500
1965	Sunburst or cherry	$3,200	$3,975
1966-1967	Sparkling Burgundy	$3,200	$3,975
1966-1967	Sunburst or cherry	$3,000	$3,750
1967-1968	Walnut	$3,000	$3,750
1968-1970	Sunburst or cherry	$3,000	$3,750

Riviera (U.S.A.)
1993-1994. Made in U.S.A. on back of headstock.

1993-1994		$1,100	$1,400

Riviera Reissue (Korea)
1994-2006. Korean-made contemporary reissue, natural.

1994-2006		$525	$650

Riviera 12-String
1965-1970. Double-cut, 12 strings, thinline archtop, 2 mini-humbuckers, sunburst or cherry.

1965-1970		$1,900	$2,400

Riviera 12-String Reissue (Korea)
1997-2000. Korean-made reissue, natural.

1997-2000		$525	$650

Royal
1931-1935. 15 1/2" acoustic archtop, mahogany back and sides, dot markers, sunburst, bound top, back and neck, Masterbilt headstock logo.

1931-1935		$1,400	$1,750

S-900
1986-1989. Neck-thru-body, locking Bender tremolo system, 2 pickups with individual switching and a coil-tap control.

1986-1989		$300	$375

SC350
1976-1979. Mahogany solidbody, scroll bass horn, rosewood 'board, dot inlays, bolt neck, 2 humbuckers, made in Japan.

1976-1979	Mahogany	$450	$575

SC450
1976-1979. Like SC350, but with maple body, glued neck, and coil tap.

1976-1979	Maple	$450	$575

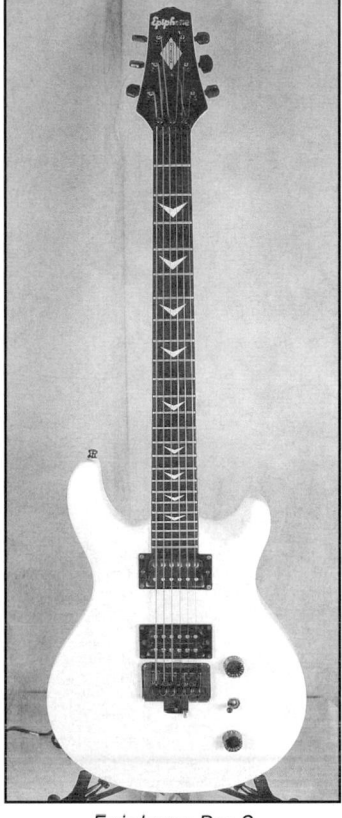

Epiphone Pro 2

1967 Epiphone Riviera
George Healey

GUITARS

Epiphone SG Special

Epiphone Sheraton II

MODEL YEAR	FEATURES	EXC. COND. LOW	HIGH
SC550			

1976-1979. Like SC450, but with gold hardware, block inlays, neck and body binding, and ebony 'board.

| 1976-1979 | Maple, gold hardware | $475 | $600 |

Seville EC-100 (Classical)

1938-1941, 1961-1969 (Gibson-made). Classical guitar, mahogany back and sides, natural, the '61-'63 version also available with a pickup.

1961-1964		$475	$600
1965		$400	$500
1966-1969		$350	$450

SG Special

2000-present. SG body, dot markers, 2 open-coil humbuckers.

| 2000-2014 | Guitar only | $80 | $100 |
| 2000-2014 | Player Pack with amp | $95 | $120 |

Sheraton

1958-1970, 1993-1994. Double-cut thinline archtop, 2 New York pickups '58-'60, 2 mini-humbuckers '61 on, frequensator tailpiece, multi-bound, gold-plated hardware, sunburst or natural finish with cherry optional by '65.

1958-1960	Natural, NY pickups	$11,000	$14,000
1959-1964	Sunburst, mini-humbuckers	$10,500	$13,000
1961-1964	Natural, mini-humbuckers	$11,000	$14,000
1965	Cherry	$7,500	$9,500
1965	Natural	$7,500	$9,500
1965	Sunburst	$5,000	$6,300
1966-1970	Sunburst or cherry	$4,800	$6,000
1967	Natural	$5,500	$6,700

Sheraton (Japan)

1982-1983. Early reissue, not to be confused with Sheraton II issued later, natural or sunburst.

| 1982-1983 | | $1,125 | $1,400 |

Sheraton (Reissue U.S.A.)

1993-1994, 2005. An additional 250 American-made Sheratons were built from '93-'94.

| 1993-1994 | | $1,500 | $1,900 |
| 2005 | | $1,900 | $2,400 |

Sheraton II (Reissue)

1986-present. Contemporary reissue, natural or sunburst.

| 1986-2014 | | $375 | $475 |

Slasher

2001. Reverse offset double cut solidbody, bolt neck, six-on-a-side tuners, 2 pickups, dot markers.

| 2001 | | $250 | $315 |

Sorrento (1 pickup)

1960-1970. Single-cut thinline archtop, 1 pickup in neck position, tune-o-matic bridge, nickel-plated hardware, sunburst, natural or Royal Olive finish, (cherry or sunburst by '68).

1960-1964		$1,425	$1,775
1965-1966		$1,225	$1,525
1967-1970		$1,125	$1,400

MODEL YEAR	FEATURES	EXC. COND. LOW	HIGH
Sorrento (2 pickups)			

1960-1970. Single-cut thinline archtop, 2 pickups, tune-o-matic bridge, nickel-plated hardware, sunburst, natural or Royal Olive finish, (cherry or sunburst by '68).

1960-1964		$2,350	$2,950
1965-1966		$2,000	$2,500
1967-1970		$1,900	$2,400

Sorrento (Reissue)

1994-2000. Reissue of 2 pickup model, import.

| 1994-2000 | | $425 | $525 |

Spartan

1934-1949. Acoustic archtop, 16 3/8", laminated maple body, multi-bound, trapeze tailpiece, sunburst or natural.

1934-1939	Sunburst	$850	$1,050
1940-1949	Sunburst	$775	$950
1941-1947	Natural	$850	$1,050

Special/SG Special (U.S.A.)

1979-1983. SG Special body style, dot markers, 2 exposed humbuckers, Special logo on truss rod cover.

| 1979-1983 | | $650 | $800 |

Spider/The Spider

1997-2000. Wood body resonator, spider bridge, square neck.

| 1997-2000 | | $400 | $500 |

Spirit

1979-1983. U.S.-made electric solidbody, Spirit logo on truss rod cover and new Epiphone U.S.A. designated script logo on headstock, double-cut, carved top with 2 humbuckers, various colors.

| 1979-1983 | | $500 | $625 |

SST

2007-2011. Acoustic/electric solidbody, either Classic (nylon) or Studio (steel). Chet Atkins model also available.

| 2007-2011 | | $225 | $300 |

Tom Delonge Signature ES-333

2008-present. One humbucker, dot inlays.

| 2008-2014 | | $275 | $350 |

Trailer Park Troubadour Airscreamer

2003-2005. Airstream trailer-shaped body, identifying logo on headstock.

| 2003-2005 | | $350 | $450 |

Triumph

1931-1957. 15 1/4" '31-'33, 16 3/8" '33-'36, 17 3/8" '36-'57, walnut back and sides until '33, laminated maple back and sides '33, solid maple back and sides '34, natural or sunburst.

1931-1932	Sunburst, laminated walnut body	$1,350	$1,700
1933	Sunburst, laminated maple body	$1,350	$1,700
1934-1935	Sunburst, solid maple body	$1,450	$1,800
1936-1940	Sunburst 17 3/8" body	$1,500	$1,900
1941-1949	Natural	$1,500	$1,900
1941-1949	Sunburst	$1,400	$1,750
1950-1957	Natural	$1,400	$1,750
1950-1957	Sunburst	$1,300	$1,600

MODEL YEAR	FEATURES	EXC. COND. LOW	HIGH

Triumph Regent (Cutaway)

1948-1969. Acoustic archtop, single-cut, F-holes, renamed Triumph Cutaway in '53, then Gibson listed this model as just the Triumph from '58-'69.

1948-1952	Regent, natural	$2,200	$2,700
1948-1952	Regent, sunburst	$1,900	$2,400
1953-1957	Cutaway, natural	$2,200	$2,700
1953-1957	Cutaway, sunburst	$1,900	$2,400
1958-1959	Sunburst	$2,200	$2,700
1960-1964	Sunburst	$2,200	$2,700
1965	Sunburst	$2,100	$2,600
1966-1969	Sunburst	$2,100	$2,600

USA Map Guitar

1982-1983. U.S.-made promotional model, solidbody electric, mahogany body shaped like U.S. map, 2 pickups, natural.

1982-1983		$2,000	$2,500

USA Map Guitar Limited Edition

2007	Import	$400	$500

Vee-Wee (Mini Flying V)

2003. Mini Flying V, single bridge pickup, gig bag.

2003		$75	$100

Wildkat

2001-present. Thinline, single-cut, hollow-body, 2 P-90s, Bigsby tailpiece.

2001-2014		$300	$375

Wilshire

1959-1970. Double-cut solidbody, 2 pickups, tune-o-matic bridge, cherry.

1959	Symmetrical body	$4,400	$5,600
1960-1962	Thinner-style body, P-90s	$3,000	$3,900
1962	Mini-humbuckers	$3,000	$3,900
1963-1964	Asymmetrical body	$2,500	$3,200
1965-1966	Custom color (3 options)	$3,500	$4,500
1965-1966	Standard color	$2,300	$3,000
1967-1970		$1,800	$2,400

Wilshire 12-String

1966-1968. Solidbody, 2 pickups, cherry.

1966-1968		$2,300	$3,000

Wilshire II

1984-1985. Solidbody, maple body, neck and 'board, 2 humbuckers, 3-way switch, coil-tap, 1 tone and 1 volume control, various colors.

1984-1985		$375	$475

Windsor (1 Pickup)

1959-1962. Archtop, 1 or 2 pickups, single-cut thinline, sunburst or natural finish.

1959-1960	New York pickup, natural	$2,000	$2,550
1959-1960	New York pickup, sunburst	$1,925	$2,450
1961-1962	Mini-humbucker, natural	$2,025	$2,550
1961-1962	Mini-humbucker, sunburst	$1,925	$2,450

Windsor (2 Pickups)

1959-1962. Archtop, 1 or 2 pickups, single-cut thinline, sunburst or natural finish.

1959-1960	New York pickup, natural	$2,550	$3,350
1959-1960	New York pickup, sunburst	$2,450	$3,250
1961-1962	Mini-humbucker, natural	$2,550	$3,350
1961-1962	Mini-humbucker, sunburst	$2,450	$3,250

X-1000

1986-1989. Electric solidbody, Korean-made, various colors.

1986-1989		$225	$280

Zenith

1931-1969. Acoustic archtop, bound front and back, f-holes, sunburst.

1931-1933		$1,600	$2,000
1934-1935	Larger 14 3/4" body	$1,600	$2,000
1936-1949	Still larger 16 3/8" body	$1,600	$2,000
1950-1957	Natural	$1,600	$2,000
1950-1957	Sunburst	$1,300	$1,600
1958-1969		$625	$800

Zephyr

1939-1957. Non-cut electric archtop, 1 pickup, bound front and back, blond or sunburst (first offered '53), called Zephyr Electric starting in '54.

1939-1940	Natural, 16 3/8", metal handrest pickup	$1,300	$1,600
1941-1943	Natural, no metal handrest	$1,300	$1,600
1944-1946	Natural, top mounted pickup	$1,300	$1,600
1947-1948	17 3/8", metal covered pickup	$1,300	$1,600
1949-1952	Natural, New York pickup	$1,200	$1,500
1953-1957	Natural, New York pickup	$1,200	$1,500
1953-1957	Sunburst, New York pickup	$1,100	$1,350

Zephyr Regent

1950-1953. Single-cut electric archtop, 1 pickup, natural or sunburst, called Zephyr Cutaway for '54-'57.

1950-1953	Natural	$2,000	$2,500
1950-1953	Sunburst	$1,800	$2,300

Zephyr Cutaway

1954-1957. Cutaway version of Zephyr Electric, called Zephyr Regent for 1950-'53.

1954-1957	Natural	$2,200	$2,800
1954-1957	Sunburst	$2,000	$2,500

Zephyr Electric (Cutaway)

1958-1964. Gibson-made version, thinline archtop, single-cut, 2 pickups, natural or sunburst.

1958-1959	Natural	$2,300	$2,900
1958-1959	Sunburst	$1,975	$2,475
1960-1964	Natural	$2,175	$2,700
1960-1964	Sunburst	$1,900	$2,375

Ca. 1952 Epiphone Triumph Regent

Epiphone Wildkat

Epiphone Zephyr De Luxe Regent

Esoterik DR1

MODEL YEAR	FEATURES	EXC. COND. LOW	HIGH

Zephyr De Luxe (Non-cutaway)
1941-1954. Non-cut electric archtop, 1 or 2 pickups, multi-bound front and back, gold-plated hardware, natural or sunburst.

1941-1942	Natural	$2,100	$2,600
1945-1949	Natural, 1 pickup	$2,300	$2,900
1945-1949	Natural, 2 pickups	$2,500	$3,100
1950-1954	Natural, 2 pickups	$2,500	$3,100
1950-1954	Sunburst, 2 pickups	$2,300	$2,900

Zephyr De Luxe Regent (Cutaway)
1948-1954. Single-cut electric archtop, 1 or 2 pickups until '50, then only 2, gold-plated hardware, sunburst or natural finish. Renamed Deluxe Electric in '54.

1948-1949	Natural, 1 pickup	$2,500	$3,100
1948-1949	Natural, 2 pickups	$3,200	$3,900
1948-1949	Sunburst, 1 pickup	$2,200	$2,800
1948-1949	Sunburst, 2 pickups	$2,850	$3,550
1950-1954	Natural, 2 pickups	$3,000	$3,700
1950-1954	Sunburst, 2 pickups	$2,700	$3,350

Zephyr Emperor Regent
1950-1954. Archtop, single rounded cutaway, multi-bound body, 3 pickups, sunburst or natural finish, renamed Emperor Electric in '54.

1950-1954	Natural	$4,000	$5,000
1950-1954	Sunburst	$3,700	$4,600

Zephyr Tenor
1940. Natural, figured top.

1940		$1,000	$1,250

Zephyr Blues Deluxe
1999-2005. Based on early Gibson ES-5, 3 P-90 pickups.

1999-2005		$600	$750

Epoch
Economy level imports made by Gibson and sold through Target stores.

Equator Instruments
2006-present. Production/custom, professional and premium grade, solidbody, hollowbody, acoustic and classical guitars built in Chicago, Illinois by luthier David Coleman.

Erlewine
1979-present. Professional and premium grade, production/custom guitars built by luthier Mark Erlewine in Austin, Texas. Erlewine also produces the Chiquita brand travel guitar.

Esoterik Guitars
2010-present. Professional grade, production/custom, electric guitars built in San Luis Obispo, California by luthier Ryan Cook. He plans to add basses.

ESP
1983-present. Intermediate, professional, and premium grade, production/custom, Japanese-made solidbody guitars and basses. Hisatake Shibuya founded Electronic Sound Products (ESP), a chain of retail stores, in '75. They began to produce replacement parts for electric guitars in '83 and in

'85 started to make custom-made guitars. In '87 a factory was opened in Tokyo. In '86 ESP opened a sales office in New York, selling custom guitars and production models. From around '98 to ca. '02 they operated their California-based USA custom shop. In '96, they introduced the Korean-made LTD brand and in '03 introduced the Xtone brand, which was folded into LTD in '10. Hisatake Shibuya also operated 48th Street Custom Guitars during the '90s but he closed that shop in 2003.

20th Anniversary
1995. Solidbody, double-cut, ESP95 inlaid at 12th fret, gold.

1995		$1,000	$1,250

Eclipse Custom (U.S.A.)
1998-2002. U.S. Custom Shop-built, single-cut, mahogany body and maple top, various colors offered.

1998-2002		$625	$775

Eclipse Custom/Custom T (Import)
1986-1988, 2003-2010. Single-cut mahogany solidbody, earliest model with bolt dot marker neck, 2nd version with neck-thru and blocks, the Custom T adds locking trem. Current has quilt maple top.

1986-1987	Bolt, dots	$525	$650
1987-1988	Neck-thru, blocks	$625	$700
1987-1988	Neck-thru, Custom T	$550	$675

Eclipse Deluxe
1986-1988. Single-cut solidbody, 1 single-coil and 1 humbucker, vibrato, black.

1986-1988		$525	$650

Eclipse Series
1995-present. Recent Eclipse models.

1995-2000	Eclipse (bolt neck, mahogany)	$450	$575
1996-2000	Eclipse Archtop	$450	$550

Horizon (Import)
1986, 1996-2001. Double-cut neck-thru, bound ebony 'board, 1 single-coil and 1 humbucker, buffer preamp, various colors, reintroduced '96-'01with bolt neck, curved rounded point headstock.

1986		$550	$700
1996-2001		$550	$700

Horizon Classic (U.S.A.)
1993-1995. U.S.-made, carved mahogany body, set-neck, dot markers, various colors, optional mahogany body with figured maple top also offered.

1993-1995		$1,100	$1,350

Horizon Custom (U.S.A.)
1998-2001. U.S. Custom Shop-made, mahogany body, figured maple top, bolt-on neck, mostly translucent finish in various colors.

1998-2001		$1,100	$1,350

Horizon Deluxe (Import)
1989-1992. Horizon Custom with bolt-on neck, various colors.

1989-1992		$575	$725

Hybrid I (Import)
1986 only. Offset double-cut body, bolt maple neck, dots, six-on-a-side tuners, vibrato, various colors.

1986		$300	$375

The Vintage Guitar Price Guide shows low to high values for items in all-original excellent condition, and, where applicable, with original case or cover.

MODEL YEAR	FEATURES	EXC. COND. LOW	HIGH

Hybrid II (Import)
1980s. Offset double-cut, rosewood 'board on maple bolt neck, lipstick neck pickup, humbucker at bridge, Hybrid II headstock logo.

1980s		$325	$425

LTD EC-GTA Guitarsonist
2008. Flame graphic by Matt Touchard, 100 made.

2008		$1,000	$1,250

LTD EC-SIN Sin City
2008. Vegas graphic by Matt Touchard, 100 made.

2008		$1,550	$1,900

LTD Series
1998-present. Range of prices due to wide range of models.

1998-2014	Various models	$100	$600

Maverick/Maverick Deluxe
1989-1992. Offset double-cut, bolt maple or rosewood cap neck, dot markers, double locking vibrola, six-on-a-side tuners, various colors.

1989-1992		$325	$400

Metal I
1986 only. Offset double-cut, bolt maple neck, rosewood cap, dots, various colors.

1986		$325	$400

Metal II
1986 only. Single horn V body, bolt on maple neck with rosewood cap, dot markers, various colors.

1986		$350	$450

Metal III
1986 only. Reverse offset body, bolt maple neck with maple cap, dot markers, gold hardware, various colors.

1986		$375	$450

M-I Custom
1987-1994. Offset double-cut thru-neck body, offset block markers, various colors.

1987-1994		$575	$700

M-I Deluxe
1987-1989. Double-cut solidbody, rosewood 'board, 2 single-coils and 1 humbucker, various colors.

1987-1989		$550	$650

M-II
1989-1994, 1996-2000. Double-cut solidbody, reverse headstock, bolt-on maple or rosewood cap neck, dot markers, various colors.

1989-1994		$575	$700

M-II Custom
1990-1994. Double-cut solidbody, reverse headstock, neck-thru maple neck, rosewood cap, dot markers, various colors.

1990-1994		$750	$900

M-II Deluxe
1990-1994. Double-cut solidbody, reverse headstock, Custom with bolt-on neck, various colors.

1990-1994		$650	$800

Mirage Custom
1986-1990. Double-cut neck-thru solidbody, 2-octave ebony 'board, block markers, 1 humbucker and 2 single-coil pickups, locking trem, various colors.

1986-1990		$650	$800

Mirage Standard
1986 only. Single pickup version of Mirage Custom, various colors.

1986		$425	$525

Phoenix
1987 only. Offset, narrow waist solidbody, thru-neck mahogany body, black hardware, dots.

1987		$550	$650

Phoenix Contemporary
Late-1990s. 3 pickups vs. 2 on the earlier offering.

1998		$750	$875

S-454/S-456
1986-1987. Offset double-cut, bolt maple or rosewood cap neck, dot markers, various colors.

1986-1987		$425	$525

S-500
1991-1993. Double-cut figured ash body, bolt-on neck, six-on-a-side tuners, various colors.

1991-1993		$500	$600

SV-II
2009-2012. Neck-thru offset v-shaped solidbody, 2 pickups, dot inlays, part of Standard Series, made in Japan.

2009-2012		$1,400	$1,700

Traditional
1989-1990. Double-cut, 3 pickups, tremolo, various colors.

1989-1990		$525	$650

Vintage/Vintage Plus S
1995-1998. Offset double-cut, bolt maple or rosewood cap neck, dot markers, Floyd Rose or standard vibrato, various colors.

1995	20th Anniversary Edition, gold	$750	$950
1995-1998		$700	$850

Viper Series
2004-present. Offset double-cut SG style, 2 humbuckers, various models

2010	300M	$300	$350

Espana
1963-ca. 1973. Primarily acoustic guitars distributed by catalog wholesalers Bugeleisen & Jacobson. Built by Watkins in England.

Classical
1963-1973. Guitars with white spruce fan-braced tops with walnut, mahogany, or rosewood back and sides.

1963-1973		$155	$200

EL (Electric) Series
1963-1973. Various double-cut models, 2 or 3 pickups, tremolo, '63-ca. '68 with nitro finish, ca. '69-'73 poly finish.

1963-1973	EL-30, 2 pickups	$225	$300
1963-1973	EL-31, 3 pickups	$275	$350
1963-1973	EL-32 (XII)	$225	$300
1963-1973	EL-36, 2 pickups	$275	$350

Jumbo Folk
1969-1973. Natural.

1969-1973		$175	$275

ESP Eclipse E-II DB VB

ESP Viper-256

Ca. 1935 Euphonon
Folkway Music

EVH Wolfgang Special

MODEL YEAR	FEATURES	EXC. COND. LOW	HIGH

Essex (SX)

1985-present. Budget grade, production, electric and acoustic guitars imported by Rondo Music of Union, New Jersey. They also offer basses.

Solidbody Electric

1980s-1990s. Copies of classic designs like the Les Paul and Telecaster.

1980s		$105	$130

Este

1909-1939. Luthier Felix Staerke's Este factory built classical and archtop guitars in Hamburg, Germany. They also built high-end banjos. The plant ceased instrument production in '39 and was destroyed in WW II.

Esteban

2002-present. Budget grade, production, acoustic and classical import guitars sold as packages with classical guitarist Esteban's (Stephen Paul) guitar lesson program, other miscellany and sometimes a small amp.

Steel and Nylon Acoustics

2002-2014		$25	$155

EtaVonni

2008-2010. Luthier Ben Williams built premium grade, production/custom, carbon fiber and aluminum electric guitars in Kentwood, Michigan.

Euphonon

1930-1944. A Larson brothers brand, most Euphonons date from 1934-'44. Body sizes range from 13 ½" to the 19" and 21" super jumbos. The larger body 14-fret neck sizes have body woods of Brazilian rosewood, mahogany, or maple. Ornamentation and features are as important to value as rosewood vs. mahogany.

Everett Guitars

1977-present. Luthier Kent Everett builds his premium and presentation grade, production/custom, steel-string and classical guitars in Atlanta, Georgia. From '01 to '03, his Laurel Series guitars were built in conjunction with Terada in Japan and set up in Atlanta. He has also built archtops, semi-hollow and solidbody electrics, resonators, and mandolins.

Evergreen Mountain

1971-present. Professional grade, custom, flat-top and tenor guitars, basses and mandolins built by luthier Jerry Nolte in Cove, Oregon. He also built over 100 dulcimers in the '70s.

Everly Guitars

1982-2001. Luthier Robert Steinegger built these premium grade, production/custom flat-tops in Portland, Oregon (also see Steinegger Guitars).

MODEL YEAR	FEATURES	EXC. COND. LOW	HIGH

EVH

2007-present. Eddie Van Halen works with FMIC to create a line of professional and premium grade, production, solidbody guitars built in the U.S. and imported from other countries. They also build amps.

Wolfgang Special

2010-present. Made in Japan, offset double-cut solidbody, figured maple top over basswood body, birdseye maple 'board, 2 pickups, tremolo.

2010-2014		$825	$1,025

Excelsior

The Excelsior Company started offering accordions in 1924 and had a large factory in Italy by the late '40s. They started building guitars around '62, which were originally plastic covered, switching to paint finishes in the mid '60s. They also offered classicals, acoustics, archtops and amps. By the early '70s they were out of the guitar business. The Excelsior brand was also used ca.1885-ca.1890 on guitars and banjos by Boston's John C. Haynes & Co.

Dyno and Malibu

1960s. Offset, double cut, 2 or 3 pickups, vibrato.

1960s	Dyno I	$185	$230
1960s	Dyno II	$210	$260
1960s	Malibu I	$210	$260
1960s	Malibu II	$210	$260

Exlusive

2008-2013. Intermediate grade, production, electric guitars and basses, imported from Asia and finished in Italy by luthier Galeazzo Frudua.

Fairbuilt Guitar Co.

2000-present. Professional and premium grade, custom/production, archtop and flattop acoustic guitars built by luthiers Martin Fair and Stuart Orser in Loudoun County, Virginia. They also build mandolins and bouzoukis.

Falk

1989-present. Professional and premium grade, production/custom archtop guitars built by luthier Dave Falk, originally in Independence, Missouri, and currently in Amarillo, Texas. He also builds mandolins and dulcimers.

Fano

1995-present. Professional grade, production/custom, solidbody electric guitars and basses built by luthier Dennis Fano in Fleetwood, Pennsylvania.

Farnell

1989-present. Luthier Al Farnell builds his professional grade, production, solidbody guitars and basses in Ontario, California. He also offers his intermediate grade, production, C Series which is imported from China.

MODEL YEAR	FEATURES	EXC. COND. LOW	HIGH

Fat Cat Custom Guitars

2004-present. Intermediate to premium grade, production/custom, solidbody and chambered electric guitars and basses built in Carpentersville, Illinois by luthier Scott Bond.

Favilla

1890-1973. Founded by the Favilla family in New York, the company began to import guitars in 1970, but folded in '73. American-made models have the Favilla family crest on the headstock. Import models used a script logo on the headstock.

Acoustic Classical

1960s-1973. Various nylon-string classical models.

1960s-1969		$155	$400
1970-1973	Import	$155	$400

Acoustic Flat-Top

1960s-1973. Various flat-top models, 000 to D sizes, mahogany to spruce.

1960s-1969	U.S.-made, Crest logo	$155	$400
1970-1973	Import, Script logo	$155	$400

Fell

One of the many guitar brands built by Japan's Matsumoku company.

Fender

1946 (1945)-present. Budget, intermediate, professional and premium grade, production/custom, electric, acoustic, acoustic/electric, classical, and resonator guitars built in the U.S. and overseas. They also build amps, basses, mandolins, bouzoukis, banjos, lap steels, violins, and PA gear. Ca. 1939 Leo Fender opened a radio and record store called Fender Radio Service, where he met Clayton Orr 'Doc' Kauffman, and in '45 they started KF Company to build lap steels and amps. In '46 Kauffman left and Fender started the Fender Electric Instrument Company.

In January '65 CBS purchased the company and renamed it Fender Musical Instruments Corporation. The CBS takeover is synonymous with a perceived decline in quality among musicians and collectors, and Pre-CBS Fenders are more valuable. Fender experienced some quality problems in the late-'60s. Small headstock is enlarged in '65 and the 4-bolt neck is replaced by the 3-bolt in '71. With high value and relative scarcity of Pre-CBS Fenders, even CBS-era instruments are now sought by collectors. Leo Fender was kept on as consultant until '70 and went on to design guitars for Music Man and G&L.

In '82 Fender Japan is established to produce licensed Fender copies for sale in Japan. Also in '82, the Fender Squier brand debuts on Japanese-made instruments for the European market and by '83 they were imported into U.S. In '85, the company was purchased by an investor group headed by Bill Schultz but the purchase does not include the Fullerton factory. While a new factory was being established at Corona, California, all Fender Contemporary Stratocasters and Telecasters were made either by Fender Japan or in Seoul, Korea. U.S. production resumes in

'86 with American Standard Stratocaster. The Fender Custom Shop, run by Michael Stevens and John Page, opens in '87. The Mexican Fender factory is established in '90. In '95, Fender purchased the Guild guitar company. On January 3, 2002, Fender Musical Instruments Corporation (FMIC) recapitalized a minority portion of common stock, with partners including Roland Corporation U.S. and Weston Presidio, a private equity firm in San Francisco. In 2003, Fred Gretsch Enterprises, Ltd granted Fender the exclusive rights to develop, produce, market and distribute Gretsch guitars worldwide. Around the same time, Fender also acquired the Jackson/Charvel Guitar Company. In October, '04, Fender acquired Tacoma Guitars. On January 1, '08, Fender acquired Kaman Music Corporation and the Hamer, Ovation, and Genz Benz brands. The Groove Tubes brand was purchased by Fender in June, '08.

Dating older Fender guitars is an imprecise art form at best. While serial numbers were used, they were frequently not in sequence, although a lower number will frequently be older than a substantially higher number. Often necks were dated, but only with the date the neck was finished, not when the guitar was assembled. Generally, dating requires triangulating between serial numbers, neck dates, pot dates, construction details and model histories.

From '50 through roughly '65, guitars had more-or-less sequential numbers in either 4 or 5 digits, though some higher numbers may have an initial 0 or - prefix. These can range from 0001 to 99XXX.

From '63 into '65, some instruments had serial numbers beginning with an L prefix plus 5 digits (LXXXXX). Beginning in '65 with the CBS takeover into '76, 6-digit serial numbers were stamped on F neckplates roughly sequentially from 10XXXX to 71XXXX. In '76 the serial number was shifted to the headstock decal. From '76-'77, the serial number began with a bold-face 76 or S6 plus 5 digits (76XXXXX).

From '77 on, serial numbers consisted of a 2-place prefix plus 5 digits (sometimes 6 beginning in '91): '77 (S7, S8), '78 (S7, S8, S9), '79 (S9, E0), '80-'81 (S9, E0, E1), '82 (E1, E2, E3), '84-'85 (E4), '85-'86 (no U.S. production), '87 (E4), '88 (E4, E8), '89 (E8, E9), '90 (E9, N9, N0), '91 (N0), '92 (N2).

Serial numbers on guitars made by Fender Japan consist of either a 2-place prefix plus 5 digits or a single prefix letter plus 6 digits: '82-'84 (JV), '83-'84 (SQ), '84-'87 (E), '85-'86+ (A, B, C), '86-'87 (F), '87-'88+ (G), '88-'89 (H), '89-'90 (I, J), '90-'91 (K), '91-'92 (L), '92-'93 (M).

Factors affecting Fender values: The sale to CBS in '65 is a major point in Fender instrument values as CBS made many changes collectors feel affected quality. The '70s introduced the 3-bolt neck and other design changes that aren't as popular with guitarists. Custom color instruments, especially Strats from the '50s and early-'60s, can be valued much more than the standard sunburst finishes. In '75 Fender dropped the optional custom colors and started issuing the guitars in a variety of standard colors.

Custom colors are worth more than standard

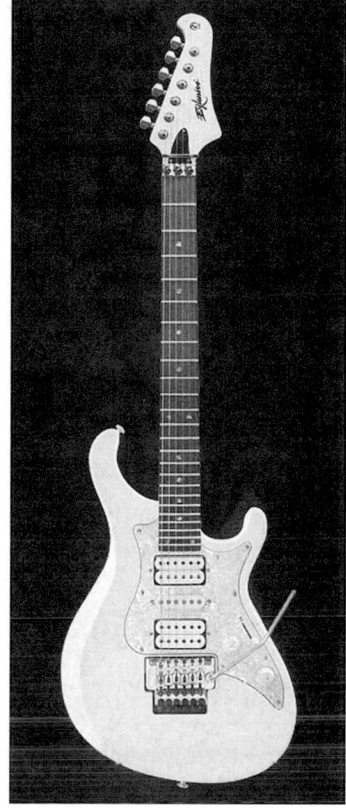

Exlusive Alien

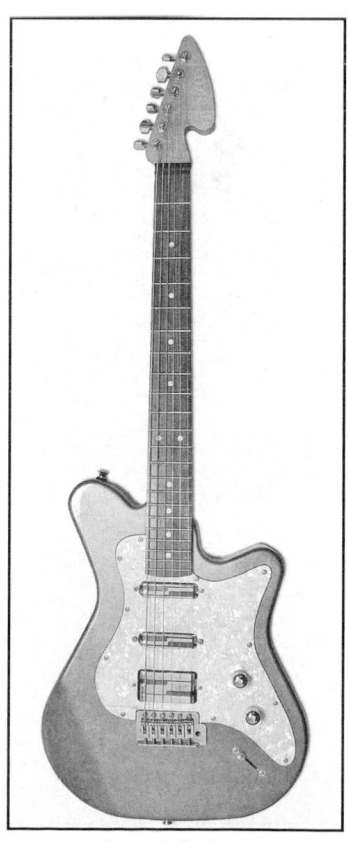

Farnell Guitars

1960 Fender Stratocaster
Folkway Music

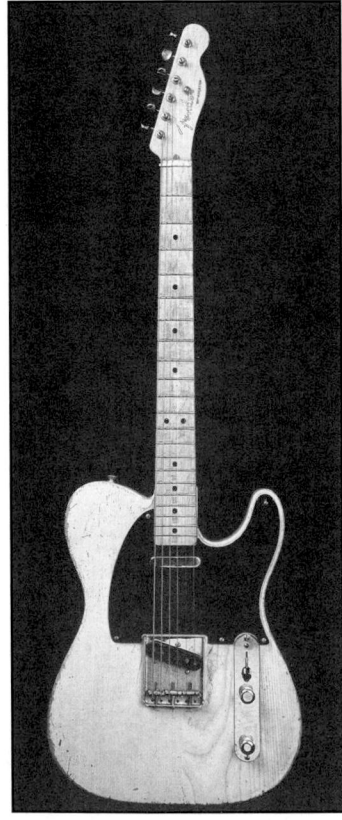

1951 Fender Broadcaster

colors. For a Stratocaster, Telecaster Custom and Esquire Custom the standard color is sunburst, while the Telecaster and Esquire standard color is blond. The first Precision Bass standard color was blond but changed to sunburst in the late 1950s. The Jazz Bass standard color is sunburst. The Telecaster Thinline standard color is natural. To understand a custom color, you need to know what the standard color is. Some custom colors are rarer than others. Below is a list of the custom colors offered in 1960. They are sorted in ascending order with the most valuable color, Shell Pink, listed last. For example, Fiesta Red is typically worth 12% more than a Black or Blond, though all are in the Common Color category. In the Rare Color group, Foam Green is normally worth 8% more than Shoreline Gold. The two Very Rare colors are often worth 30% more than Shoreline Gold. In our pricing information we will list the standard color, then the relative value of a common custom color, and then the value of a rare custom color. Remember that the amount of fade also affects the price. These prices are for custom colors with slight or no fade, which implies a lighter color, but with custom colors a faded example can also be much darker in color. Blue can fade to dark green. White can fade to deep yellow.

The various Telecaster and Stratocaster models are grouped under those general headings.

Common Color:
Black, Blond, Candy Apple Red, Olympic White, Lake Placid Blue, Dakota Red, Daphne Blue, Fiesta Red

Rare Color:
Shoreline Gold, Inca Silver, Burgundy Mist, Sherwood Green, Sonic Blue, Foam Green

Rare (Very Rare) Color
Surf Green, Shell Pink

Fender changed their color options in the 1960s. Below is a list of what was offered.

1960 - 1962
Black, Blond, Burgundy Mist, Dakota Red, Daphne Blue, Fiesta Red, Foam Green, Inca Silver, Lake Placid Blue, Olympic White, Shell Pink, Sherwood Green, Shoreline Gold, Sonic Blue, Sunburst, Surf Green

1963 - 1964
Black, Blond, Burgundy Mist, Candy Apple Red, Dakota Red, Daphne Blue, Fiesta Red, Foam Green, Inca Silver, Lake Placid Blue, Olympic White, Sherwood Green, Shoreline Gold, Sonic Blue, Sunburst, Surf Green

1965 - 1969
Black, Blond, Blue Ice, Candy Apple Red, Charcoal Frost, Dakota Red, Fiesta Red, Firemist Gold, Firemist Silver, Foam Green, Lake Placid Blue, Ocean Turquoise, Olympic White, Sonic Blue, Sunburst, Teal Green

1970 - 1971
Black, Blond, Candy Apple Red, Firemist Gold, Firemist Silver, Lake Placid Blue, Ocean Turquoise, Olympic White, Sonic Blue, Sunburst

1972
Black, Blond, Candy Apple Red, Lake Placid Blue, Olympic White, Sonic Blue, Sunburst

MODEL YEAR	FEATURES	EXC. COND. LOW	HIGH
1973			
Black, Blond, Candy Apple Red, Lake Placid Blue, Natural, Olympic White, Sunburst, Walnut			
1974 - 1977			
Black, Blond, Natural, Olympic White, Sunburst, Walnut			
1978 - 1979			
Antigua, Black, Blond, Natural, Olympic White, Sunburst, Walnut, Wine			

Arrow
1969-1972. See listing for Musiclander.

Avalon
1985-1995. California Series, acoustic import, 6-on-a-side tuners, mahogany neck, back and sides (nato after '93), spruce top, various colors.

1985-1995		$215	$265

Balboa
1983-1987. California Series, acoustic import.

1983-1987		$340	$425

Broadcaster
Mid-1950e-early-1951. For a short time in early-'51, before being renamed the Telecaster, models had no Broadcaster decal; these are called No-casters by collectors.

1950	Blond	$45,000	$60,000
1951	Clipped decal, "No Caster"	$30,000	$40,000

Broadcaster Leo Fender Custom Shop
1999 only. Leo Fender script logo signature replaces Fender logo on headstock, Custom Shop Certificate signed by Phyllis Fender, Fred Gretsch, and William Schultz, includes glass display case and poodle guitar case.

1999		$5,800	$7,300

'50s Relic/'51 NoCaster Custom Shop
1995-2014. Called the '50s Relic NoCaster for '96-'99, and '51 NoCaster in NOS, Relic, or Closet Classic versions 2000-'10, with the Relic Series being the highest offering. From June '95 to June '99 Relic work was done outside of Fender by Vince Cunetto and included a certificate noting model and year built, an instrument without the certificate is worth less than the value shown. Blonde or Honey Blonde finish. Also in '09, the Limited '51 NoCaster Relic was offered with Twisted Tele neck pickup, 50 each in 2-tone sunburst or Dakota Red.

1995-1997	Cunetto built Relic	$3,000	$3,700
1997-1999	Cunetto era Closet Classic	$2,000	$2,500
1997-1999	Cunetto era NOS	$1,800	$2,200
1998-1999	Cunetto era Relic	$2,200	$2,800
2000-2009	Closet Classic	$2,000	$2,500
2000-2014	NOS	$1,800	$2,200
2000-2014	Relic	$2,200	$2,800

'51 NoCaster Limited Edition
2009. Custom Shop Limited Edition, as above but with Twisted Tele neck pickup, 50 each in 2-tone sunburst or Dakota Red.

2009	Relic	$2,200	$2,800

MODEL YEAR	FEATURES	EXC. COND. LOW	HIGH
Bronco			
1967-1980. Slab solidbody, 1 pickup, tremolo, red.			
1967-1968	Nitro	$1,400	$1,750
1969-1980	Poly	$1,200	$1,500
Buddy Miller Signature			
2007-2009. Flat-top, Fishman Ellipse Aura, 6-on-a-side tuner headstock.			
2007-2009		$650	$800
Bullet/Bullet Deluxe			
1981-1983. Solidbody, came in 2- and 3-pickup versions (single-coil and humbucker), and single- and double-cut models, various colors. Becomes Squire Bullet in '85.			
1981-1983	Various models	$650	$800
CD (Classic Design) Series			
2006-present. Imported, intermediate grade, various models, acoustic or acoustic-electric, steel or nylon string.			
2006-2014	Higher-end models	$275	$475
2006-2014	Lower-end models	$125	$275
CG (Classical Guitar) Series			
1995-2005. Imported, various nylon-string classical acoustic and acoustic/electric models, label on the inside back clearly indicates the model number, back and sides of rosewood, mahogany or other woods.			
1995-2005		$55	$290
Concert			
1963-1970. Acoustic flat-top slightly shorter than King/Kingman, spruce body, mahogany back and sides (optional Brazilian or Indian rosewood, zebrawood or vermillion), natural, sunburst optional by '68.			
1963-1965	Natural	$775	$975
1966-1970	Natural or sunburst	$775	$975
Concord			
1987-1995. Dreadnought flat-top, 6-on-a-side headstock, natural.			
1987-1995		$105	$130
Coronado I			
1966-1969. Thinline semi-hollowbody, double-cut, tremolo, 1 pickup, single-bound, dot inlay.			
1966-1969	Solid colors	$1,350	$1,700
1966-1969	Sunburst	$1,350	$1,700
Coronado II			
1966-1969 (Antigua finish offered until '70). Thinline semi-hollowbody, double-cut, tremolo optional, 2 pickups, single-bound, block inlay, available in standard finishes but special issues offered in Antigua and 6 different Wildwood finishes (labeled on the pickguard as Wildwood I through Wildwood VI to designate different colors). Wildwood finishes were achieved by injecting dye into growing trees.			
1966-1969	Solid colors	$1,750	$2,200
1966-1969	Sunburst	$1,750	$2,200
1966-1969	Wildwood	$2,500	$3,100
1967-1970	Antigua	$1,950	$2,450
Coronado XII			
1966-1969 (Antigua finish offered until '70). Thinline semi-hollowbody, double-cut, 12 strings, 2 pickups, block inlay, standard, Antigua and Wildwood finishes available.			
1966-1969	Solid colors	$1,750	$2,200

MODEL YEAR	FEATURES	EXC. COND. LOW	HIGH
1966-1969	Wildwood	$2,500	$3,100
1967-1969	Sunburst	$1,750	$2,200
1967-1970	Antigua	$1,950	$2,450
Custom			
1969-1971. Six-string solidbody that used up parts from discontinued Electric XII, asymmetrical-cut, long headstock, 2 split pickups, sunburst. Also marketed as the Maverick.			
1969-1971		$3,100	$3,900
Cyclone			
1998-2006. Mexican import, solidbody, contoured offset waist, poplar body, various colors.			
1998-2006	Various options	$440	$550
D'Aquisto Elite			
1984, 1989-1994, 1994-2002. Part of Fender's Master Series, 16" laminated maple-side archtop, single-cut, glued neck, 1 pickup, gold hardware, made in Japan until '94, in '94 the Fender Custom Shop issued a version that retailed at $6,000, various colors.			
1984		$1,750	$2,200
1989-1994		$1,750	$2,200
D'Aquisto Standard			
1984 (Serial numbers could range from 1983-1985). Like D'Aquisto Elite, but with 2 pickups.			
1984		$1,750	$2,200
D'Aquisto Ultra			
1984, 1994-2000. USA Custom Shop, made under the supervision of James D'Aquisto, solid flamed maple back and sides, spruce top, ebony tailpiece, bridge and 'guard, all hand carved.			
1994-2000		$3,200	$4,000
DG (Dreadnought Guitar) Series			
1995-1999, 2002-2014. Made in China, various lower-end acoustic and acoustic/electric models.			
1995-2014		$75	$350
Duo-Sonic			
1956-1969. Solidbody, 3/4-size, 2 pickups, Desert Sand ('56-'61), sunburst ('61-'63), blue, red or white after, short- and long-scale necks, short-scale necks listed here (see Duo-Sonic II for long-scale), reissued Mexican-made in '94.			
1956-1959	Maple neck	$1,400	$1,750
1960-1963	Rosewood 'board	$1,300	$1,600
1963	Sunburst (rare)	$1,300	$1,600
1964	Blue, red or white	$1,300	$1,600
1965	Blue, red or white	$1,100	$1,350
1966-1969	Blue, red or white	$1,050	$1,300
Duo-Sonic II			
1965-1969. Solidbody, 2 pickups, blue, red or white, long-scale neck, though the long-scale neck Duo-Sonic was not known as the Duo-Sonic II until '65, we have lumped all long-scales under the II for the purposes of this Guide.			
1965		$1,300	$1,600
1966-1969		$1,200	$1,500
Duo-Sonic Reissue			
1993-1997. Made in Mexico, black, red or white.			
1994-1997		$200	$250
Electracoustic			
1993-1995, 2000-2005, 2007-present. Thin body acoustic-electric, available with Jazzmaster, Strato-			

Fender Classic Design CD-230SCE

1964 Fender Duo-Sonic
Robbie Keene

1965 Fender Electric XII

Richard F. Johnson

1956 Fender Esquire

MODEL YEAR	FEATURES	EXC. COND. LOW	HIGH

caster and Telecaster body and neck shapes, spruce top, maple sides and back, Fishman Classic IV MB electronics with top-mounted pickup, sunburst and various color options.

MODEL YEAR	FEATURES	EXC. COND. LOW	HIGH
2007-2010	JZM Deluxe	$350	$425
2007-2010	Stratacoustic Deluxe	$400	$500
2007-2010	Telecoustic Deluxe	$400	$500
2007-2014	Stratacoustic Standard	$250	$325
2007-2014	Telecoustic Standard	$250	$325

Electric XII

1965-1969. Solidbody, 12 strings, long headstock, 2 split pickups. Custom colors can fade or become darker; for example Lake Placid Blue changes to green. The price ranges below are for instruments that are relatively unfaded. Many older guitars have some color fade and minor fade is factored into these values. Each custom color should be evaluated on a case-by-case basis.

Custom color Fenders can be forged and bogus finishes have been a problem. As the value of custom color Fenders has increased, so has the problem of bogus non-original finishes. The prices in the Guide are for factory original finishes in excellent condition. The prices noted do not take into account market factors such as fake instruments, which can have the effect of lowering a guitar's market value unless the guitar's provenance can be validated. Please refer to the Fender Guitar Intro Section for details on Fender color options.

1965	Sunburst, blocks	$2,900	$3,600
1965-1966	Common colors	$3,200	$4,000
1965-1966	Rare colors	$4,000	$5,600
1965-1966	Sunburst, dots	$2,900	$3,600
1966	Sunburst, blocks	$2,700	$3,400
1967-1968	Sunburst	$2,900	$3,600
1967-1969	Common colors	$3,200	$4,000
1967-1969	Rare colors	$4,000	$5,600
1969	Sunburst, blocks	$2,700	$3,400

Ensenada Series

2005-2007. Made in Mexico acoustics, solid top, back and sides, A (grand auditorium), D (dreadnought), M (mini jumbo) and V (orchestra) sizes, E suffix denotes on-board electronics.

2005-2007	Acoustic	$400	$500
2005-2007	Acoustic-electric	$475	$600

Esprit Elite

1984. Master Series, made in Japan, double-cut, semi-hollow, carved maple top, 2 humbuckers, 4 controls, bound rosewood 'board, snowflake inlays.

1983-1985		$1,300	$1,650

Esprit Standard

1984. Like Esprit Elite, but with dot inlays, 2 controls.

1983-1985		$1,200	$1,500

Esprit Ultra

1984. Like Esprit Elite, but with bound ebony 'board, split-block inlays, gold hardware.

1984		$1,350	$1,700

Esquire

1950-1970. Ash body, single-cut, 1 pickup, maple neck, black 'guard '50-'54, white 'guard '54 on. Please refer to the Fender Guitar Intro Section for details on Fender color options.

1950	Blond, black 'guard	$32,000	$40,000
1951	Blond, black 'guard	$32,000	$40,000
1952	Blond, black 'guard	$28,000	$35,000
1953	Blond, black 'guard	$28,000	$35,000
1954	Blond, black 'guard	$25,000	$32,000
1954	Blond, white 'guard	$21,000	$27,000
1955	Blond, white 'guard	$20,000	$26,000
1956	Blond	$19,000	$25,000
1957	Blond	$14,000	$19,000
1958	Blond, backloader	$13,000	$17,000
1958	Blond, frontloader	$13,000	$17,000
1959	Blond, maple 'board	$13,000	$17,000
1959	Blond, rosewood 'board	$13,000	$17,000
1960	Blond	$12,000	$15,100
1960	Sunburst	$14,000	$17,600
1961	Blond, slab 'board	$11,000	$14,100
1961	Custom colors	$18,000	$37,000
1961	Sunburst, slab 'board	$14,000	$17,600
1962	Blond, curved 'board	$10,000	$12,500
1962	Blond, slab 'board	$11,000	$14,000
1962	Custom colors	$17,000	$34,000
1962	Sunburst, curved 'board	$10,500	$13,000
1962	Sunburst, slab 'board	$13,000	$16,500
1963	Blond	$10,000	$12,500
1963	Common colors	$17,000	$24,000
1963	Rare colors	$23,000	$33,000
1963	Sunburst	$13,000	$16,500
1964	Blond	$9,000	$11,500
1964	Common colors	$15,000	$21,000
1964	Rare colors	$21,000	$29,000
1964	Sunburst	$11,000	$14,000
1965	Blond	$7,000	$9,500
1965	Common colors	$12,000	$16,500
1965	Rare colors	$16,500	$23,000
1965	Sunburst	$9,000	$11,300
1966	Blond	$6,300	$7,900
1966	Common colors	$10,000	$13,800
1966	Rare colors	$13,800	$19,000
1966	Sunburst	$8,000	$10,000
1967	Blond	$6,000	$7,500
1967	Blond, smuggler cavity	$8,500	$10,600
1967	Common colors	$10,000	$13,800

MODEL YEAR	FEATURES	EXC. COND. LOW	HIGH
1967	Rare colors	$13,800	$19,000
1967	Sunburst	$7,800	$9,600
1968	Blond	$6,000	$7,500
1968	Common colors	$10,000	$13,800
1968	Rare colors	$13,800	$19,000
1968	Sunburst	$7,200	$9,000
1969	Blond	$5,900	$7,400
1969	Common colors	$10,000	$13,800
1969	Rare colors	$13,800	$19,000
1969	Sunburst	$6,200	$7,700
1970	Blond	$4,000	$5,000
1970	Common colors	$6,800	$9,300
1970	Rare colors	$9,300	$13,000
1970	Sunburst	$4,300	$5,300

Esquire (Japan)
1985-1994. Made in Japan, '54 specs.

1985-1986		$800	$1,000
1987-1994	'50s Esquire	$650	$825

'50s Esquire (Mexico)
2005-2010. Maple neck, ash body.

2005-2010		$500	$625

'52 Esquire
2012. Custom Shop model, price includes Certificate of Authenticity.

2012	NOS	$1,800	$2,200

'53 Esquire
2012. Custom Shop model, price includes Certificate of Authenticity.

2012	NOS	$1,800	$2,200

'59 Esquire
2003-2007, 2013. Custom Shop model, Relic version lasted to '07, then came back in '13 for limited run.

2003-2006	Closet Classic	$2,000	$2,500
2003-2006	NOS	$1,800	$2,200
2003-2007	Relic	$2,200	$2,800

'60 Esquire
Custom Shop model, NOS.

2010		$1,800	$2,200

'70 Esquire
2008. Custom Shop model, only 20 made.

2008	Relic	$2,200	$2,800

Custom Esquire '95

1995		$2,000	$2,500

Esquire Custom
1959-1970. Same as Esquire, but with bound alder sunburst body and rosewood 'board.

1959	Sunburst	$23,000	$29,000
1960	Custom colors	$26,000	$60,000
1960	Sunburst	$22,000	$28,000
1961	Custom colors	$26,000	$60,000
1961	Sunburst	$21,000	$27,000
1962	Custom colors	$22,000	$50,000
1962	Sunburst, curve	$16,000	$20,000
1962	Sunburst, slab	$20,000	$25,000
1963	Custom colors	$22,000	$40,000
1963	Sunburst	$17,000	$21,000
1964	Custom colors	$20,000	$37,000
1964	Sunburst	$13,500	$20,000
1965	Custom colors	$17,000	$32,000
1965	Sunburst	$11,000	$17,000
1966	Custom colors	$13,000	$23,000

MODEL YEAR	FEATURES	EXC. COND. LOW	HIGH
1966	Sunburst	$10,000	$13,000
1967	Sunburst	$9,000	$12,000
1968	Sunburst	$9,000	$12,000
1969	Sunburst	$8,500	$11,000
1970	Sunburst	$8,000	$10,000

Esquire Custom (Import)
1983-1994. Made in Japan with all the classic bound Esquire features, sunburst.

1983-1989		$775	$1,000
1990-1994		$675	$900

Esquire Custom GT/Celtic/Scorpion
2003. Made in Korea, single-cut solidbody, 1 humbucker, 1 knob (volume), set-neck, solid colors.

2003		$400	$500

Esquire Z
2001. Custom Shop, black body and headstock, curly maple neck, ebony 'board, 25 made.

2001		$5,300	$6,800

Jeff Beck Tribute Esquire (Custom Shop)
2006. Also called Beck Artist Esquire or Tribute Series Jeff Beck Esquire, specs include an extremely lightweight 2-piece offset ash body with Beck's original contours, distressed for an appearance like Beck's original Esquire that was used on many Yardbird records.

2006		$6,900	$8,700

Flame Elite
1984. Master Series, made in Japan, neck-thru, offset double-cut, solidbody, 2 humbuckers, rosewood 'board, snowflake inlays.

1984-1988		$1,400	$1,750

Flame Standard
1984-1988. Like Flame Elite, but with dot inlays.

1984-1988		$1,300	$1,650

Flame Ultra
1984. Like Flame Elite, but with split block inlays (some with snowflakes), gold hardware.

1984-1988		$1,350	$1,700

FR-48 Resonator
2003-2009. Made in Korea, steel body.

2003-2009		$240	$300

FR-50 Resonator
2000-present. Spruce top, mahogany back and sides, sunburst, optional square-neck.

2000-2014		$240	$300

FR-50CE Resonator
2000-present. Same as FR-50 with cutaway and pickups.

2009-2014		$270	$335

FR-55 Hawaiian Resonator
2012-2013. Bell brass nickel-plated body etched with scenes of South Seas.

2012-2013		$320	$400

F-Series Dreadnought Flat-Top
1969-1981. The F-Series were Japanese-made flat-top acoustics, included were Concert- and Dreadnought-size instruments with features running from plain to bound necks and headstocks and fancy inlays, there was also a line of F-Series classical, nylon-string guitars. A label on the inside indicates the model. FC-20 is a classical with Brazilian rosewood. There was

1957 Fender Esquire

Fender FR-55 Hawaiian Resonator

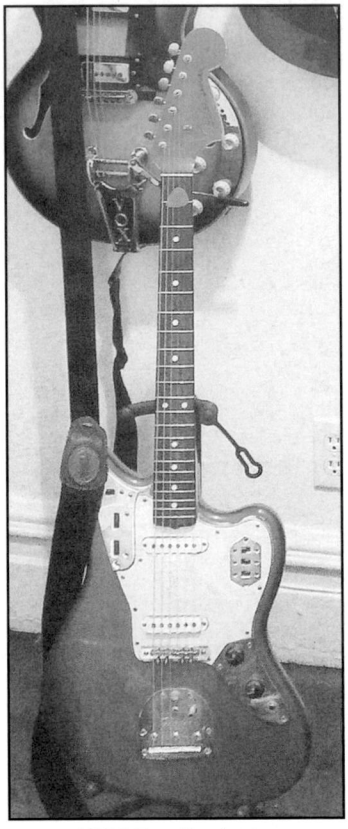

1964 Fender Jaguar
Dave McDermott

*Fender Jaguar Classic
Player Special*

MODEL YEAR	FEATURES	EXC. COND. LOW	HIGH

also an Asian (probably Korean) import Standard Series for '82-'90 where the models start with a F.

1969-1981	Higher-end solid top	$150	$350
1969-1981	Lower-end laminated	$50	$150
1972-1981	FC-20 Classical	$150	$350

GA (Grand Auditorium) Series

2001-2009. Various grand auditorium models, an oval label on the inside back clearly indicates the model number.

2001-2009		$125	$525

GC (Grand Concert) Series

1997-2009. Various grand concert models, an oval label on the inside back clearly indicates the model number.

1997-2009		$110	$140

GDO (Global Design Orchestra) Series

2004-2008. Various orchestra-sized acoustic models, an oval label on the inside back clearly indicates the model number.

2004-2008		$320	$400

Gemini Series

1983-1990. Korean-made flat-tops, label on inside indicates model. I is classical nylon-string, II, III and IV are dreadnought steel-strings, there is also a 12-string and an IIE acoustic/electric.

1984-1987	Gemini II	$140	$175
1984-1988	Gemini I	$125	$155
1987-1988	Gemini III	$155	$195
1987-1990	Gemini IIE	$165	$210
1987-1990	Gemini IV	$165	$210

GN (Grand Nylon) Series

2001-2007. Various grand nylon acoustic models, an oval label on the inside back clearly indicates the model number.

2001-2007		$320	$400

Harmony-Made Series

1970-1973. Harmony-made with white stencil Fender logo, mahogany, natural or sunburst.

1970-1973		$65	$120

Jag-Stang

1996-1999, 2003-2004. Japanese-made, designed by Curt Cobain, body similar to Jaguar, tremolo, 1 pickup, oversize Strat peghead, Fiesta Red or Sonic Blue.

1996	1st issue, 50th Anniv. Label	$675	$850
1997-1999		$675	$850
2003-2004		$600	$800

Jaguar

1962-1975. Reintroduced as Jaguar '62 in '95-'99. Custom colors can fade and often the faded color has very little similarity to the original color. The values below are for an instrument that is relatively unfaded. Each custom color should be evaluated on a case-by-case basis. As the value of custom color Fenders has increased, so has the problem of bogus non-original finishes. The prices in the Guide are for factory original finishes in excellent condition. Please refer to the Fender Guitar Intro Section for details on Fender color options.

1962	Common colors	$4,300	$5,500
1962	Rare colors	$5,500	$7,900
1962	Sunburst	$3,800	$4,700
1963	Common colors	$3,800	$4,800
1963	Rare colors	$4,800	$7,500
1963	Sunburst	$3,100	$3,900
1964	Common colors	$3,900	$4,900
1964	Rare colors	$4,900	$7,500
1964	Sunburst	$3,100	$3,900
1965	Common colors	$3,700	$4,700
1965	Rare colors	$5,000	$6,500
1965	Sunburst	$2,700	$3,400
1966	Common colors	$3,500	$4,400
1966	Rare colors	$4,800	$6,000
1966	Sunburst, block markers	$2,600	$3,200
1966	Sunburst, dot markers	$2,700	$3,400
1967-1969	Common colors	$3,500	$4,400
1967-1969	Rare colors	$4,400	$6,000
1967-1969	Sunburst	$2,500	$3,100
1970	Common colors	$3,500	$4,500
1970	Rare colors	$4,100	$5,500
1970-1975	Sunburst	$2,400	$3,100
1971-1974	Custom colors	$2,600	$3,500
1975	Custom colors	$2,500	$3,200

Jaguar '62

1986-2012. Reintroduction of Jaguar, Japanese-made until '99, then U.S.-made American Vintage series, basswood body, rosewood 'board, various colors.

1986-1999	Import	$850	$1,050
1999-2012	U.S.A.	$1,050	$1,300

Jaguar HH/Special Edition Jaguar HH

2005-2014. Japan, 2 Dragster humbuckers, matching headstock, chrome knobs and pickup covers.

2005-2014		$450	$550

50th Anniversary Jaguar

2012. USA, modeled after '62, classic 24" scale, new one-degree neck-angle pocket, repositioned tremolo plate, redesigned hot Jaguar single-coils, lacquer finish in Lake Placid Blue, Candy Apple Red, or burgundy.

2012		$1,100	$1,350

Blacktop Jaguar HH

2010-2014. Stripped-down electronics with 2 humbuckers, 1 volume, 1 tone, single 3-way switch, maple neck, rosewood 'board, black 'guard, black or silver.

2010-2014		$300	$375

Jaguar Baritone Special HH

2005-2010. Japan, limited edition, Baritone Special logo on matching headstock, 2 humbuckers, no trem, black.

2005-2010		$450	$550

Jaguar Classic Player Special

2009-present. Classic Player series, classic Jag look, tremolo, 2 single-coils.

2009-2014		$550	$700

Jaguar Classic Player Special HH

2009-present. Classic Player series. 2 humbucker version.

2009-2014		$550	$700

Jaguar FSR Classic '66 Reissue

2008-2010. Fender Special Run, '66 specs, block inlays, black logo, custom colors, limited edition.

2008-2010		$1,000	$1,250

MODEL YEAR	FEATURES	EXC. COND. LOW	HIGH

Modern Player Jaguar
2012-2014. Mahogany body, maple neck, rosewood 'board, 2-color chocolate burst, trans red or trans black.

2012-2014		$275	$350

Jazzmaster
1958-1980. Contoured body, 2 pickups, rosewood 'board, clay dot inlay, reintroduced as Japanese-made Jazzmaster '62 in '94.

Custom color Fenders can be forged and bogus finishes have been a problem. As the value of custom color Fenders has increased, so has the problem of bogus non-original finishes. The prices in the Guide are for factory original finishes in excellent condition. Please refer to the Fender Guitar Intro Section for details on Fender color options.

1958	Sunburst	$8,000	$10,000
1958	Sunburst, rare maple 'board	$7,000	$8,700
1959	Custom colors, includes rare	$8,700	$13,000
1959	Sunburst	$7,800	$9,800
1960	Common colors	$7,800	$9,800
1960	Rare colors	$9,800	$15,000
1960	Sunburst	$5,800	$7,200
1961	Common colors	$7,300	$8,800
1961	Rare colors	$8,800	$13,700
1961	Sunburst	$5,000	$6,300
1962	Common colors	$7,300	$8,800
1962	Rare colors	$8,800	$13,700
1962	Sunburst	$4,000	$5,000
1963	Common colors	$5,000	$7,000
1963	Rare colors	$7,000	$12,000
1963	Sunburst	$4,000	$5,000
1964	Common colors	$4,800	$6,900
1964	Rare colors	$6,900	$11,000
1964	Sunburst	$4,000	$5,000
1965	Common colors	$4,400	$6,700
1965	Early '65, Sunburst	$3,900	$4,800
1965	Late '65, Sunburst	$3,700	$4,600
1965	Rare colors	$6,700	$9,900
1966	Common colors	$4,000	$6,500
1966	Rare colors	$6,500	$9,000
1966	Sunburst, block markers	$3,600	$4,500
1966	Sunburst, dot markers	$3,700	$4,600
1967-1969	Common colors	$3,700	$5,000
1967-1969	Rare colors	$5,000	$7,000
1967-1969	Sunburst	$3,600	$4,500
1970	Common colors	$3,700	$4,800
1970	Rare colors	$5,000	$6,900
1970-1980	Sunburst	$2,600	$3,300
1971-1974	Custom colors	$3,000	$4,000
1975-1980	Custom colors	$2,700	$3,400

Jazzmaster '62
1986-2012. Japanese-made reintroduction of Jazzmaster, basswood body, rosewood 'board, from '99 U.S.-made American Vintage series, various colors.

1986-1989	Import	$900	$1,125
1990-1998	Import	$800	$1,000
1999-2012	U.S.A.	$1,225	$1,525

Jazzmaster '69
1986-1990s. Made in Japan.

1986-1989		$900	$1,125
1990s		$800	$1,000

Blacktop Jazzmaster HS
2010-2014. Stripped-down electronics with a single-coil and a humbucker, 1 volume, 1 tone, single 3-way switch, maple neck, rosewood 'board, black or sunburst.

2010-2014		$300	$375

Classic Player Jazzmaster Special
2008-present. Alder body, maple neck, rosewood 'board, 2 single-coils, 3-color sunburst or black.

2008-2014		$500	$675

Jazzmaster Elvis Costello (Artist Series)
2008-2010. Walnut stain, '70s neck, vintage style tremolo.

2008-2010		$1,400	$1,750

Jazzmaster J Mascis (Artist Series)
2007 2009. Purple sparkle finish, matching headstock, Adjusto-Matic bridge, reinforced tremolo arm.

2007-2009		$875	$1,100

Jazzmaster Sonic Youth Signature
2009-2010. Lee Ranaldo and Thurston Moore Signature models based on their modified Jazzmasters which basically removed the standard control layout and replaced it with a 3-way switch.

2009-2010	Lee Ranaldo	$1,025	$1,275
2009-2010	Thurston Moore	$1,025	$1,275

Jazzmaster The Ventures Limited Edition
1996. Japanese-made, ash body, 2 pickups, block inlay, transparent purple/black.

1996		$950	$1,200

Katana
1985-1986. Japanese-made wedge-shaped body, 2 humbuckers, set neck, triangle inlays, black.

1985-1986		$560	$700

King
1963-1965. Full-size 15 5/8" wide acoustic, natural. Renamed Kingman in '65.

1963-1965	Brazilian rosewood option	$2,100	$2,600
1963-1965	Indian, Zebra, Vermillion	$1,250	$1,550

Kingman
1965-1971, 2006-present. Full-size 15 5/8" wide acoustic, slightly smaller by '70, offered in 3 Wildwood colors, referred to as the Wildwood acoustic which is a Kingman with dyed wood. Reissued as import in '06.

1965-1968		$1,150	$1,450
1969-1971		$1,100	$1,400

Kingman "C" USA Select
2012. Custom Shop limited edition of 150, Engelmann spruce top, mahogany back and sides, vintage C-shaped maple neck, rosewood 'board, Fiesta Red, certificate of authenticity.

2012		$950	$1,200

Kingman SCE
2008-present. Cutaway electric dreadnought, spruce top, mahogany back and sides, rosewood 'board, natural.

2008-2014		$305	$380

Fender Jazzmaster J Mascis
Keith Myers

1985 Fender Katana

GUITARS

1968 Fender Malibu

Tim Fleck

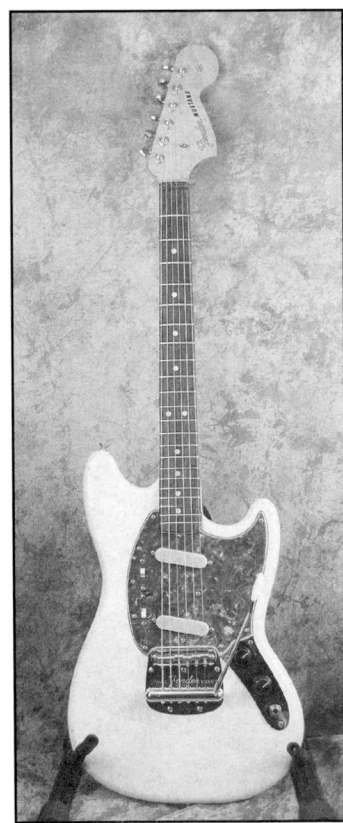

1965 Fender Mustang

Robbie Keene

MODEL YEAR	FEATURES	EXC. COND. LOW	HIGH

Kingman/Elvis Kingman
2012-2013. Wildwood model as used by Elvis Presley in the '67 film 'Clambake', spruce top, mahogany back and sides, rosewood 'board, natural.

2012-2013		$280	$350

Lead I
1979-1982. Double-cut solidbody with 1 humbucker, maple or rosewood 'board, black or brown.

1979-1982		$500	$625

Lead II
1979-1982. Lead with 2 pickups, black or brown.

1979-1982		$675	$850

Lead III
1982. Lead with 2 split-coil humbuckers, 2 3-way switches, various colors.

1982		$750	$950

LTD
1969-1975. Archtop electric, single-cut, gold-plated hardware, carved top and back, 1 pickup, multi-bound, bolt-on neck, sunburst.

1969-1975		$2,600	$3,200

Malibu
1965-1971. Flat-top, spruce top, mahogany back and sides, black, mahogany or sunburst. Later version is import.

1965-1971		$850	$1,050

Malibu (California Series)
1983-1995. Made first in Japan, then Korea in '85.

1983-1995		$225	$275

Malibu SCE
2006-2013. Imported single-cut acoustic/electric, solid spruce top, laminated mahogany back and sides, block inlays.

2006-2013		$325	$405

Marauder
1965 only. The Marauder has 3 pickups, and some have slanted frets, only 8 were made, thus it is very rare. 1st generation has hidden pickups, 2nd has exposed.

1965	1st generation	$8,300	$10,300
1965	2nd generation	$5,900	$7,300

Marauder (Modern Player Series)
2011-2014. Jazzmaster-type body, 1 jazzmaster pickup and 1 Triple Bucker, rosewood 'board.

2011-2014		$240	$300

Montara (California Series)
1990-1995. Korean-made single-cut acoustic/electric flat-top, natural, sunburst or black. Maple with flamed sides starting '92.

1990-1992		$375	$475

Montego I/II
1968-1975. Electric archtop, single-cut, bolt-on neck, 1 pickup (I) or 2 pickups (II), chrome-plated hardware, sunburst.

1968-1975	I	$1,900	$2,400
1968-1975	II	$2,100	$2,600

Musiclander
1969-1972. Also called Swinger and Arrow, solidbody, 1 pickup, arrow-shaped headstock, no model name on peghead, red, white, and blue.

1969-1972		$2,500	$3,100

MODEL YEAR	FEATURES	EXC. COND. LOW	HIGH

Musicmaster
1956-1980. Solidbody, 1 pickup, short-scale (3/4) neck, Desert Sand ('56-'61), sunburst ('61-'63), red, white or blue after. Regular-scale necks were optional and are called Musicmaster II from '64 to '69, after '69 II is dropped and Musicmaster continues with regular-scale neck.

1956-1959	Blond	$1,200	$1,500
1960-1964	Blond	$1,100	$1,400
1964-1965	Nitro, red, white, blue	$1,100	$1,400
1966-1969	Nitro, red, white, blue	$900	$1,150
1969-1972	Poly, red, white, blue	$800	$1,000
1973-1980	Red, white, blue	$800	$1,000

Musicmaster II
1964-1969. Solidbody, 1 pickup, long regular-scale neck version of Musicmaster, red, white, or blue.

1964-1965		$1,100	$1,400
1966-1969		$900	$1,150

Mustang
1964-1982, 1997-1998. Solidbody, 2 pickups. Reissued as '69 Mustang in 1990s, name changed back to Mustang '97-'98. Dakota Red, Daphne Blue and Olympic White with Competition Red, Blue and Orange finishes with a racing stripe on the front of the body added '69-'73 (with matching headstock for '69-'70).

1964-1965	Red, white, or blue	$1,500	$1,900
1966-1969	Red, white, or blue	$1,500	$1,900
1969-1970	Competition colors	$1,900	$2,400
1970-1979	Various colors	$1,250	$1,575
1978-1980	Antigua	$1,500	$1,900
1980-1982	Various colors	$925	$1,150

Mustang '65 Reissue
2006-present. Made in Japan, Classic Series.

2006-2014		$575	$725

Mustang '69 Reissue
1986-1998, 2005. Japanese-made, blue or white.

1986-1998		$560	$700

Mustang Kurt Cobain
2012-present. Artist Series, rosewood 'board, Fiesta Red finish.

2012-2014		$570	$710

Newporter
1965-1971. Acoustic flat-top, mahogany back and sides. Reissued as import.

1965-1968	Spruce top	$525	$650
1968-1971	Mahogany top	$475	$600

Newporter (California Series)
1983-1995. Made first in Japan, then Korea in '85.

1983-1995		$150	$185

Palomino
1968-1971. Acoustic flat-top, spruce top, mahogany back and sides, triple-bound, black or mahogany.

1968-1971		$850	$1,050

Pawn Shop Series
2011-2014. All-new designs with diverse Fender components and the philosophy "guitars that never were but should have been".

2011	Fender '51	$450	$575
2011-2012	Fender '72	$475	$600
2011-2014	Mustang Special	$560	$700

MODEL YEAR	FEATURES	EXC. COND. LOW	HIGH

Performer
1985-1986. Imported Swinger-like body design, 2 slanted humbuckers.

1985-1986		$950	$1,175

Prodigy
1991-1993. US-made, electric solidbody, double-cut, chrome-plated hardware, 2 single-coil and 1 humbucker pickups, blue or black.

1991-1993		$575	$725

Redondo
1969-1970. Mid-size flat-top, 14 3/8" wide, replaces Newport spruce top model.

1969-1970		$625	$775

Redondo (California Series)
1983-1995. Made first in Japan, then Korea in '85.

1983-1995		$165	$205

Robben Ford
1989-1994. Symmetrical double-cut, 2 pickups, glued-in neck, solidbody with tone chambers, multibound, gold-plated hardware, sunburst. After '94 made in Fender Custom Shop.

1989-1994		$1,400	$1,750
1995	Custom Shop	$2,350	$3,050

Shenandoah 12-String
1965-1971. Acoustic flat-top, spruce top, mahogany back and sides.

1965-1968	Antigua	$1,125	$1,400
1965-1968	Blond	$950	$1,175
1969-1971	Antigua	$1,050	$1,300
1969-1971	Blond	$800	$1,000

Showmaster (Import)
2003-2007. Off-set double-cut solidbody, set neck, various models.

2003	Celtic, 1 bridge humbucker	$340	$425
2003-2007	HH, 2 humbuckers	$360	$450
2004-2006	3 single coils	$360	$450

Showmaster FMT (Custom Shop)
2000-2007. Bound figured maple top (FMT), 2 single-coil pickups and a bridge position humbucker, maple neck, Custom Shop certificate.

2000-2007		$1,600	$2,000

Sonoran SCE (California Series)
2006-present. Cutaway flat-top acoustic, 6-on-a-side tuners, spruce top, laminated mahogany back and sides, rosewood 'board, electronics options.

2006-2014		$200	$250

Squier Series

The following are all Squier Series instruments from Fender, listed alphabetically. Fender Japan was established in '82 with Squier production beginning that same year. Production was shifted to Korea in '87 and later allocated to China, India (Squier II '89–'90), Mexico and other countries.

Squier '51
2004-2006. Korean-made, Strat-style body with a Tele-style neck, various colors.

2004-2006		$60	$75

Squier Bullet
1983-1988, 1995-1996, 2000-2011. Strat style, early with Tele headstock, 1980s' models include H-2 ('83-'86, 2 humbuckers), S-3 ('83-'86, 3 single-coils), S-3T ('83-'88, 3 single-coils, vibrato). Name revived in 1995 (3 SC, vib.) and in 2000 on various models with 3 SC or 2 HB pickups.

1983-1984	H-2	$350	$440
1983-1984	S-3, T	$350	$440
1985-1986	H-2	$250	$310
1985-1988	S-3, T	$250	$310
2000-2011		$60	$100

Squier Classic Vibe Duo-Sonic '50s
2008-2010. Made in China.

2008-2010		$200	$250

Squier Katana
1985-1987. Wedge-shaped body, 1 humbucker, bolt neck, dot inlays.

1985-1987		$560	$700

Squier Showmaster Series
2002-2005. Various models, various pickup configs, made in China.

2002-2005		$100	$125

Squier Stagemaster HH
1999-2002. 2 humbuckers, reverse headstock, 6- or 7-string.

1999-2002		$125	$160

Squier Affinity Stratocaster
1997-present. Lower priced versions, made in China.

1997-2014		$50	$80

Squier Classic Vibe Stratocaster '50s
2008-present. Alder body, maple 'board, white pickguard, 2-tone sunburst, Lake Placid Blue or Oly White.

2008-2014		$225	$280

Squier Classic Vibe Stratocaster '60s
2008-present. As '50s Classic Vibe but with rosewood 'board, tortoise pickguard, 3-tone sunburst or candy apple red.

2008-2014		$225	$280

Squier Standard Fat Strat
1996-2006. Hum/single/single pickups. Replaced by the HSS.

1996-2006		$120	$150

Squier Standard Double Fat Strat
1999-2007. 2 humbucker pickups.

1999-2007		$120	$150

Squier Standard Floyd Rose Stratocaster
1992-1996. Floyd Rose tailpiece, foto flame finish or black or white, Fender and Squier headstock logos.

1992-1996	Foto Flame	$275	$340

Squier Stratocaster Pro-Tone
1996-1998. Korean-made, higher-end Squier series with solid ash bodies, one-piece maple necks, alnico single-coils.

1996-1998		$375	$475

Squier Standard Stratocaster
1982-present. Standard Series represent the classic designs.

1982-1983	1st logo, JV serial	$1,000	$1,250
1984	1st logo, JV serial	$900	$1,150
1985-1989	2nd logo, SQ serial	$450	$600
1990-1999	Mexico	$300	$375
2000-2014	Indonesia	$100	$125

Fender Squier Classic Vibe Stratocaster

2002 Fender Squier Standard Stratocaster

GUITARS

*Fender Squier
Telecaster Standard*

*Fender Squier Affinity
Telecaster*

MODEL YEAR	FEATURES	EXC. COND. LOW	HIGH

Squier Tom Delonge Stratocaster
2002-2003. Hardtail, 1 humbucker.

2002-2003		$250	$310

Squier II Stratocaster
1988-1992. Squier II models were targeted at a lower price point than regular Squier series. Mainly built in Korea but some early ones from India. Line was replaced by other models under regular Squier instruments.

1988-1992		$160	$200

Squier Affinity Telecaster
1998-present. Lower priced versions, made in China.

1998-2014		$75	$95

Squier Standard Telecaster
1982-present. Standard Series represent the classic designs.

1982-1984	1st logo, JV serial	$900	$1,125
1985-1989	2nd logo, SQ serial	$475	$600
1990-1999	Mexico	$300	$375
2000-2014	Indonesia	$100	$125

Squier Standard Tele Special
2004-2007. Made in Indonesia, 1 humbucker, 1 single-coil.

2004-2007		$100	$125

Squier Telecaster Custom
2003-present. 2 humbuckers, Custom II has 2 soapbar single-coils.

2003-2014		$100	$125

Squier Telecaster Thinline
2004-present. Thinline body with f-hole, set neck, 2 humbuckers.

2004-2014		$190	$240

Squier Venus
1997-1998. Offset double-cut solidbody, 2 pickups, co-designed by Courtney Love, also offered as 12-string.

1997-1998		$425	$525

Squier Vintage Modified Series
2012-present. Imported, various models, large script Squier logo and small Fender logo on headstock.

2012-2014	'70s Stratocaster	$160	$200
2012-2014	Jazzmaster Special	$160	$200
2012-2014	Stratocaster HSS	$160	$200
2012-2014	Surf Stratocaster	$160	$200
2012-2014	Telecaster Special	$160	$200

Starcaster
1974-1980, 2013-present. Offset double-cut, thinline semi-hollowbody, arched maple top and back, 2 humbuckers, 5 knobs (2 tone, 2 volume, 1 master volume), originally offered in tobacco sunburst, natural, walnut, black, white or custom blond finish. Model revived as part of Modern Player Series in '13. Fender also recently used the Starcaster name as a brand on a line of budget guitars.

1974	White	$4,000	$5,000
1974-1980	Blond, highly flamed maple	$4,000	$5,000
1974-1980	Sunburst, moderate flame	$2,900	$3,900
1977	Antigua, plain top	$3,800	$4,800

MODEL YEAR	FEATURES	EXC. COND. LOW	HIGH

Starcaster by Fender
2000s. Fender used the Starcaster brand on a line of budget versions of the Strat, Tele, and J- and P-Bass. They also offered small solid state amps and guitar packages with nylon- or steel-string acoustic or a Strat/amp combo. Sold in Costco and other discounters.

2000s	Acoustic	$80	$110
2000s	Electric guitar only	$70	$80
2000s	Pack with guitar, amp, stand	$85	$100

Stratocaster
The following are all variations of the Stratocaster. The first five listings are for the main American-made models and the '85 interim production Japanese model. All others are listed alphabetically after that in the following order:

Stratocaster
Standard Stratocaster (includes "Smith Strat")
American Standard Stratocaster
American Series Stratocaster
American Standard Series Stratocaster
25th Anniversary Stratocaster
30th Anniversary L.E. Guitar Center Strat
35th Anniversary Stratocaster
40th Anniversary 1954 Stratocaster Limited Edition
40th Anniversary American Standard Stratocaster
40th Anniversary Stratocaster (Japan)
40th Anniversary Stratocaster Diamond Dealer
'50s Stratocaster/Classic Series '50s Stratocaster
Classic Player '50s Stratocaster
Road Worn '50s Stratocaster
50th Anniversary 1954 Stratocaster
50th Anniversary American Deluxe Strat (USA)
50th Anniversary American Series Stratocaster
50th Anniversary Stratocaster
50th Anniversary Stratocaster (Mexico)
50th Anniversary Stratocaster Relic
'54 Stratocaster
'54 Stratocaster FMT
'55 Stratocaster
'55 Rocking Dog Stratocaster
'56 Stratocaster
American Vintage '56 Stratocaster
'57 Special Stratocaster
'57 Stratocaster
'57 Stratocaster (Custom Shop)
George Fullerton 50th Anniversary '57 Strat Ltd Ed. Set
'57 Commemorative Stratocaster
'57 Stratocaster (USA)
'57 Vintage Stratocaster (Japan)
American Vintage '57 Stratocaster
Wildwood "10s" 1957 Limited Stratocaster HSS Relic
'58 Stratocaster
'58 Stratocaster (Dakota Red)
'59 Rocking Dog Stratocaster
Wildwood "10s" 1959 Limited Stratocaster Relic

'60 FMT Stratocaster
'60 Stratocaster
'60s Stratocaster/'60 Stratocaster
Custom 1960 Stratocaster
'60s Stratocaster/Classic Series '60s Stratocaster
Classic Player '60s Stratocaster
Road Worn '60s Stratocaster
60th Anniversary American Stratocaster
60th Anniversary Commemorative Stratocaster
60th Anniversary Classic Player '50 Stratocaster
60th Anniversary Standard Stratocaster
'61 Stratocaster
'62 Stratocaster (USA)
'62 Commemorative Stratocaster
'62 Vintage Stratocaster (Japan)
'62 Heavy Relic Stratocaster
'62 Stratocaster ST62US Reissue
American Vintage '62 Stratocaster
Deluxe Vintage Player '62 Stratocaster
'65 Stratocaster
'65 Vintage Stratocaster
'66 Stratocaster
'68 Reverse Strat Special (USA)
'68 Stratocaster (Japan)
'69 Stratocaster
'70s Stratocaster American Vintage
'70s Stratocaster/Classic Series '70s Stratocaster
'72 Stratocaster (Japan)
'72 Stratocaster Limited Edition (Japan)
Acoustasonic Stratocaster
Aerodyne Stratocaster
Aluminum Stratocaster American Standard
Aluminum Stratocaster Custom Shop
American Classic Holoflake Stratocaster
American Classic Stratocaster
American Deluxe Stratocaster
American Deluxe Fat Stratocaster HSS
American Deluxe Stratocaster HSS
American Deluxe Stratocaster FMT HSS
American Series HSS/HH Stratocaster
American Special Stratocaster
American Standard Stratocaster HSS
American Standard Stratocaster Limited Edition
Antigua Stratocaster
Antigua Stratocaster FSR
Big Apple Stratocaster
Big Block Stratocaster
Bill Carson Stratocaster
Billy Corgan Stratocaster
Blackie Stratocaster (Custom Shop 1987)
Blackie Stratocaster (Custom Shop)
American Standard Limited Edition Blackout
   Stratocaster
Blacktop Stratocaster HH/HSH/HH Floyd Rose
Blue Flower Stratocaster
Bonnie Raitt Stratocaster
Bowling Ball/Marble Stratocaster
Buddy Guy Stratocaster (Mexico)
Buddy Guy Stratocaster (Signature)
Buddy Holly Tribute Stratocaster
California Fat Stratocaster
California Stratocaster
Classic Player Stratocaster

Collector's Edition Stratocaster ('62 Reissue)
Contemporary Stratocaster
Contemporary Stratocaster (Import)
Crash Stratocaster
Custom Classic Stratocaster
Custom Shop Masterbuild Stratocaster
David Gilmour Signature Stratocaster
Deluxe Lone Star Stratocaster
Deluxe Players Special Edition Stratocaster
Deluxe Players Stratocaster
Deluxe Strat Plus
Dick Dale Stratocaster
Elite Stratocaster
Eric Clapton Gold Leaf Stratocaster
Eric Clapton Stratocaster
Eric Clapton Stratocaster (Custom Shop)
Eric Johnson Stratocaster
Floyd Rose Classic Relic Stratocaster
Floyd Rose Classic Stratocaster (Strat HSS)
   (Strat HH)
Ford Shelby GT Stratocaster
Foto Flame Stratocaster
Freddy Tavares Aloha Stratocaster
Gold Stratocaster
Gold Elite Stratocaster
Gold Stratocaster (CS)
Hank Marvin Stratocaster
Hank Marvin 40th Anniversary Stratocaster
Harley-Davidson 90th Anniversary Stratocaster
Highway One Stratocaster/HSS
HM Stratocaster (USA/Import)
Homer Haynes HLE Stratocaster
Hot Wheels Stratocaster
HRR Stratocaster/ Floyd Rose HRR (Japan)
Ike Turner Tribute Stratocaster
Jeff Beck Signature Stratocaster (CS)
Jeff Beck Stratocaster
Jerry Donahue Hellecaster Stratocaster
Jim Root Signature Stratocaster
Jimi Hendrix Monterey Pop Stratocaster
Jimi Hendrix Tribute Stratocaster
Jimi Hendrix Voodoo 29th Anniversary Strato-
   caster
Jimi Hendrix Voodoo Stratocaster
Jimmie Vaughan Tex-Mex Stratocaster
John Jorgenson Hellecaster Stratocaster
John Mayer Stratocaster
Kenny Wayne Shepherd Stratocaster
Koa Stratocaster
Kon Tiki Stratocaster
Lenny Stratocaster
Lite Ash Stratocaster Special Edition
Lone Star Stratocaster
Mark Knopfler Stratocaster
Milonga Deluxe Stratocaster
Modern Player Stratocaster HSH/HSS
Moto Limited Edition Stratocaster
Moto Set Stratocaster
Orange Krush Limited Edition Stratocaster
Paisley Stratocaster
Playboy 40th Anniversary Stratocaster
Powerhouse/Powerhouse Deluxe Stratocaster
Proud Stratocaster

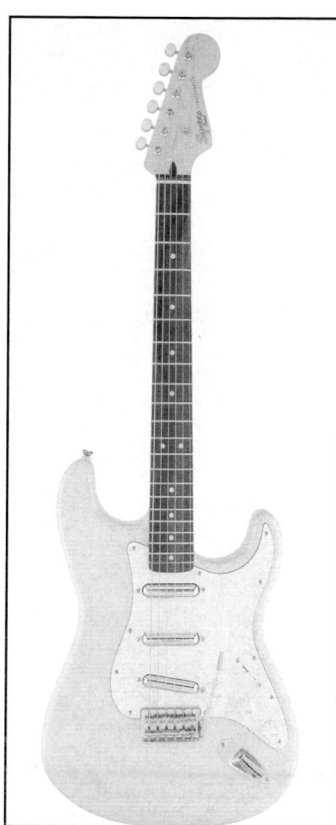

Fender Squire Vintage
Modified Surf Stratocaster

1955 Fender Stratocaster

GUITARS

1960 Fender Stratocaster

Mario Vilas

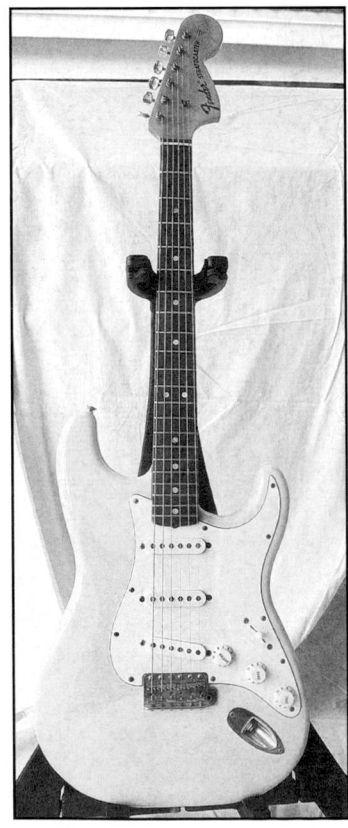

1971 Fender Stratocaster

Rod Highsmith

Richie Sambora Stratocaster
Ritchie Blackmore Stratocaster
Ritchie Blackmore Tribute Stratocaster
Roadhouse Stratocaster
Roadhouse Stratocaster (Mexico)
Robert Cray Signature Stratocaster
Robert Cray Stratocaster (Mexico)
Robin Trower Signature Stratocaster
Rory Gallagher Tribute Stratocaster
Select Stratocaster
Set-Neck Stratocaster
Short-Scale (7/8) Stratocaster
So-Cal Speed Shop L.E. Stratocaster
Special Edition Stratocaster
Splatter Stratocaster
Standard Fat Strat
Standard Fat Strat Floyd Rose
Standard Roland Ready Stratocaster
Standard Stratocaster (Japan)
Standard Stratocaster (Mexico)
Standard Stratocaster HH
Standard Stratocaster HSS
Standard Stratocaster HSS Floyd Rose
Standard Stratocaster HSS Swirl
Standard Stratocaster Satin Finish
Stevie Ray Vaughan Stratocaster
Stevie Ray Vaughan Tribute #1 Stratocaster
Strat Plus
Strat Pro Closet Classic
Stratacoustic/Strtacoustic Deluxe
Stratocaster Junior
Stratocaster Special
Stratocaster XII
Strat-o-Sonic
Sub Sonic Stratocaster
Super Strat
Tanqurey Tonic Stratocaster
Texas Special Stratocaster
The Strat
Tie-Dye Stratocaster
Tom Delonge Stratocaster
Tree of Life Stratocaster
Turquoise Sparkle Stratocaster
U.S. Ultra / Ultra Plus Stratocaster
Ventures Limited Edition Stratocaster
VG Stratocaster
Vintage Hot Rod Stratocaster
Walnut Elite Stratocaster
Walnut Stratocaster
Western Stratocaster
Yngwie Malmsteen Stratocaster

Stratocaster

1954-1981. Two-tone sunburst until '58, 3-tone after. Custom color finishes were quite rare in the '50s and early-'60s and are much more valuable than the standard sunburst finish. By the '70s, color finishes were much more common and do not affect the value near as much. In '75 Fender dropped the optional custom colors and started issuing the guitars in a variety of standard colors (sunburst, blond, white, natural, walnut and black).

Custom color Fenders can be forged and bogus finishes have been a problem. As the value of custom color Fenders has increased, so has the problem of bogus non-original finishes. The prices in the Guide are for factory original finishes in excellent condition. One color, Shell Pink, is notable because many vintage authorities wonder if a Shell Pink Strat even exists? An ultra-rare custom color should have strong documented provenance and be verifiable by at least one (preferable two or more) well-known vintage authorities. Please refer to the Fender Guitar Intro Section for details on Fender color options.

Three-bolt neck '72-'81, otherwise 4-bolt. Unless noted, all Stratocasters listed have the Fender tremolo system. Non-tremolo models (aka hardtails) typically sell for less. Many guitarists feel the tremolo block helps produce a fuller range of sound. On average, many more tremolo models were made. One year, '58, seems to be a year where a greater percentage of non-tremolo models were made. Tremolo vs. non-tremolo valuation should be taken on a brand-by-brand basis; for example, a pre-'65 Gibson ES-335 non-tremolo model is worth more than a tremolo equipped model.

From '63-'70, Fender offered both the standard Brazilian rosewood fretboard and an optional maple fretboard. Prices listed here, for those years, are for the rosewood 'board models. Currently, the market considers the maple 'board to be a premium, so guitars with maple, for those years, are worth 10% to 15% more than the values shown.

See Standard Stratocaster for '82-'84 (following listing), American Standard Stratocaster for '86-2000, and the American Series Stratocaster for 2000-'07. Currently called again the American Standard Stratocaster.

MODEL YEAR	FEATURES	EXC. COND. LOW	EXC. COND. HIGH
1954	Very first '54, rare features	$80,000	$150,000
1954	Early-mid '54, typical features	$50,000	$80,000
1954	Sunburst, later production	$45,000	$75,000
1955	Blond, nickel hardware, late '55	$44,000	$55,000
1955	Sunburst	$30,000	$40,000
1956	Blond, nickel hw	$43,000	$53,000
1956	Mary Kaye, gold hw	$57,000	$72,000
1956	Sunburst, alder body	$28,000	$38,000
1956	Sunburst, ash body	$29,000	$39,000
1956	Sunburst, non-trem	$20,000	$26,000
1957	Blond, nickel hw	$43,000	$53,000
1957	Mary Kaye, gold hw	$57,000	$72,000
1957	Sunburst	$27,000	$35,000
1957	Sunburst, non-trem	$20,000	$26,000
1958	Blond, nickel hw	$36,000	$45,000
1958	Mary Kaye, gold hw	$52,000	$65,000

MODEL YEAR	FEATURES	EXC. COND. LOW	HIGH
1958	Sunburst 2-tone	$27,000	$34,000
1958	Sunburst 2-tone, non-trem	$19,000	$24,000
1958	Sunburst 3-tone	$25,000	$32,000
1958	Sunburst 3-tone, non-trem	$18,000	$23,000
1959	Blond, nickel hw, maple 'board	$36,000	$45,000
1959	Blond, nickel hw, slab 'board	$35,000	$44,000
1959	Custom colors	$43,000	$60,000
1959	Mary Kaye, gold hw, maple	$52,000	$65,000
1959	Mary Kaye, gold hw, slab	$51,000	$64,000
1959	Sunburst, maple	$24,000	$30,000
1959	Sunburst, non-trem, slab	$17,000	$21,000
1959	Sunburst, slab	$23,000	$29,000
1960	Common colors	$26,000	$35,000
1960	Rare colors	$35,000	$60,000
1960	Sunburst	$22,000	$28,000
1961	Common colors	$26,000	$35,000
1961	Rarc colors	$35,000	$60,000
1961	Sunburst	$21,000	$27,000
1962	Common colors, curve	$22,000	$29,000
1962	Common colors, slab	$26,000	$35,000
1962	Rare color, curve	$29,000	$40,000
1962	Rare color, slab	$35,000	$50,000
1962	Sunburst, curve	$16,000	$20,000
1962	Sunburst, slab	$20,000	$25,000
1963	Common colors	$23,000	$30,000
1963	Rare colors	$30,000	$40,000
1963	Sunburst	$17,000	$21,000
1964	Common colors	$21,000	$27,000
1964	Rare colors	$27,000	$37,000
1964	Sunburst, spaghetti logo	$16,000	$20,000
1964	Sunburst, transition logo	$13,500	$18,000
1965	Common colors	$17,000	$22,000
1965	Rare colors	$22,000	$32,000
1965	Sunburst, F-plate	$11,000	$14,000
1965	Sunburst, green 'guard	$13,000	$17,000
1965	Sunburst, white 'guard	$12,000	$16,000
1966	Common colors	$13,000	$16,000
1966	Rare colors	$16,000	$23,000
1966	Sunburst	$10,000	$13,000
1967	Common colors	$12,000	$15,000
1967	Rare colors	$15,000	$20,000
1967	Sunburst	$9,000	$12,000
1968	Common colors	$10,000	$14,000
1968	Rare colors	$14,000	$20,000
1968	Sunburst	$9,000	$12,000
1969	Common colors	$9,500	$13,500
1969	Rare colors	$13,500	$19,000
1969	Sunburst	$8,500	$11,000

MODEL YEAR	FEATURES	EXC. COND. LOW	HIGH
1970	Common colors	$9,000	$12,500
1970	Rare colors	$12,500	$14,500
1970	Sunburst	$8,000	$10,000
1971	Common colors	$8,000	$10,500
1971	Early-mid '71, sunburst, 4-bolt	$7,000	$9,000
1971	Late '71, sunburst, 3-bolt	$3,700	$4,600
1971	Rare colors	$10,500	$13,500
1972	Common colors, 3-bolt	$4,500	$5,700
1972	Rare colors, 3-bolt	$5,700	$7,000
1972	Sunburst, 3-bolt	$3,700	$4,600
1973	Black, blond, blue, Olympic White	$4,100	$5,100
1973	Natural	$2,500	$3,300
1973	Rare colors	$5,100	$6,400
1973	Sunburst	$3,400	$4,200
1973	Walnut	$2,800	$3,600
1974	Black, blond, Olympic White	$3,500	$4,400
1974	Natural	$2,400	$3,000
1974	Sunburst, white parts	$2,900	$3,600
1974	Walnut	$2,600	$3,300
1975	Black, blond, Olympic White (black parts)	$2,400	$3,000
1975	Black, blond, Olympic White (white parts)	$3,200	$4,000
1975	Natural	$2,200	$2,800
1975	Sunburst, black parts	$2,200	$2,800
1975	Sunburst, white parts	$2,600	$3,200
1975	Walnut	$2,200	$2,800
1976	Black, blond, Olympic White	$2,000	$2,500
1976	Natural	$2,000	$2,500
1976	Sunburst	$2,000	$2,500
1976	Walnut	$2,000	$2,500
1977	Black, blond, Olympic White	$2,200	$2,500
1977	Natural	$2,000	$2,500
1977	Sunburst	$2,000	$2,500
1977	Walnut	$2,000	$2,500
1978	Antigua	$2,000	$2,500
1978	Black, blond, Olympic White, Wine	$2,000	$2,500
1978	Natural	$2,000	$2,500
1978	Sunburst	$2,000	$2,500
1978	Walnut	$2,000	$2,500
1979	Antigua	$2,000	$2,500
1979	Black, blond, Olympic White, Wine	$2,000	$2,500
1979	Natural	$2,000	$2,500
1979	Sunburst	$2,000	$2,500
1979	Walnut	$2,000	$2,500

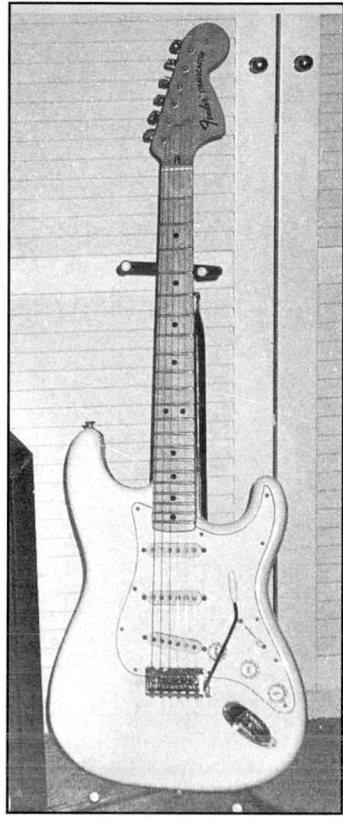

1974 Fender Stratocaster

1977 Fender Stratocaster

To get the most from this book, be sure to read "Using *The Guide*" in the introduction.

GUITARS

*Fender American
Standard Stratocaster*

Serge Small

Fender '56 NOS Stratocaster

Philip Naessens

MODEL YEAR	FEATURES	EXC. COND. LOW	HIGH
1980	Antigua	$2,000	$2,500
1980	Black, Olympic White, Wine	$2,000	$2,500
1980	International colors	$2,000	$2,500
1980	Natural	$2,000	$2,500
1980	Sunburst	$2,000	$2,500
1981	Black, Olympic White, Wine	$1,950	$2,450
1981	International colors	$1,950	$2,450
1981	Sunburst	$1,950	$2,450

Standard Stratocaster (includes "Smith Strat")

1981-1984. Replaces the Stratocaster. Renamed the American Standard Stratocaster for '86-'00 (see next listing). Renamed American Series Stratocaster in '00. From '81/'82 to mid-'83, 4 knobs same as regular Strat but with 4-bolt neck. In August '81, Dan Smith was hired by Bill Schultz and Fender produced an alder body, 4-bolt neck, 21-fret, small headstock Standard Stratocaster that has been nicknamed the Smith Strat (made from Dec. '81-'83). Mid-'83 to the end of '84 2 knobs and 'guard mounted input jack. Not to be confused with current Standard Stratocaster, which is made in Mexico.

1981	Smith Strat	$1,850	$2,300
1982	Smith Strat	$1,850	$2,300
1983	Smith Strat	$1,850	$2,300
1983-1984	Sunburst, 2-knob	$1,175	$1,475
1983-1984	Various colors, 2-knob	$1,175	$1,475

American Standard Stratocaster

1986-2000. Fender's new name for the American-made Strat when reintroducing it after CBS sold the company. The only American-made Strats made in 1985 were the '57 and '62 models. See Stratocaster and Standard Stratocaster for earlier models, renamed American Series Stratocaster in

1986-1989	SN: E series	$800	$1,000
1990-1999	Various colors	$800	$1,000

American Series Stratocaster

2000-2007. Ash or alder body, rosewood or maple 'board, dot markers, 3 staggered single-coils, 5-way switch, hand polished fret edges. Renamed the American Standard Stratocaster again in '08.

2000-2007		$800	$1,000

American Standard Series Stratocaster

2008-present. New bridge, neck and body finish, alder or ash body, rosewood or maple 'board, 3 single-coils.

2008-2014		$800	$1,000

25th Anniversary Stratocaster

1979-1980. Has ANNIVERSARY on upper body horn, silver metallic or white pearlescent finish.

1979-1980		$1,900	$2,500

30th Anniversary L.E. Guitar Center Strat

1994. Commemorates Guitar Center's opening in '64, 250 made, 30th Anniversary Limited Edition Guitar Center logo on neck plate, quilted top, sunburst.

1994		$1,000	$1,250

35th Anniversary Stratocaster

1989-1991. Custom Shop model, 500 made, figured maple top, Lace Sensor pickups, Eric Clapton preamp circuit.

1989-1991		$2,200	$2,800

40th Anniversary 1954 Stratocaster Limited Edition

1994. Standard production (not Custom Shop), 1,954 made, "40th Anniversary STRATOCASTER 1994" neck plate, serial number series xxxx of 1954, spaghetti logo, tremolo, Kluson tuners, solid maple neck, 2-tone sunburst semi-transparent finish on ash body.

1994		$1,850	$2,300

40th Anniversary American Standard Stratocaster

1994 only. US-made, American Standard model (not Custom Shop), plain top, appearance similar to a '54 maple-neck Strat, sunburst, 2 neck plates offered "40th Anniversary" and "40th Anniversary and still rockin'".

1994	"...and still rockin'" neck plate	$1,000	$1,250
1994	"40th Anniversary" neck plate	$900	$1,150

40th Anniversary Stratocaster (Japan)

1994 only. Made in Japan, '62 reissue specs.

1994		$800	$1,000

40th Anniversary Stratocaster Diamond Dealer

1994 only. Custom Shop model, 150 made, 40th Anniversary headstock inlay, flamed maple top on ash body, '54-'94 inlay at 12th fret, gold etched 'guard, gold hardware, sunburst.

1994		$3,200	$4,000

'50s Stratocaster/Classic Series '50s Stratocaster

1985-present. 'Made in Japan' logo until 'Crafted in Japan' logo mid-'97, basswood body, then mid-'99 made in Mexico with poplar or alder body. Foto-Flame finish offered '92-'94.

1985-1996	Made in Japan	$650	$800
1992-1994	Foto-flame	$625	$775
1997-1999	Crafted in Japan	$550	$700
1999-2014	Mexico	$475	$600

Classic Player '50s Stratocaster

2006-present. U.S.-made components but assembled in Mexico, alder body, maple neck and 'board, vintage-style pickups.

2006-2014		$575	$725

Road Worn '50s Stratocaster

2009-present. Maple 'board, '50s specs, aged finish.

2009-2014		$575	$725

50th Anniversary 1954 Stratocaster

2004-2005. Custom Shop, celebrates 50 years of the Strat, 1954 specs and materials, replica form-fit case, certificate, Fender took orders for these up to December 31, 2004.

2004-2005		$3,200	$4,000

50th Anniversary American Deluxe Strat (USA)

2004. U.S.-made, Deluxe series features, engraved neck plate, tweed case.

2004		$1,050	$1,325

50th Anniversary American Series Stratocaster

2004. U.S. made, '54 replica pickups, engraved neck plate, tweed case.

2004		$850	$1,050

MODEL YEAR	FEATURES	EXC. COND. LOW	HIGH

50th Anniversary Stratocaster
1995-1996. Custom Shop model, flame maple top, 3 vintage-style pickups, gold hardware, gold 50th Anniversary (of Fender) coin on back of the headstock, sunburst, 2500 made.

| 1995-1996 | | $1,425 | $1,775 |

50th Anniversary Stratocaster (Mexico)
2004. Made in Mexico, Aztec gold finish, no logo on guitar to indicate 50th Anniv., CE on neck plate to indicate import.

| 2004 | | $450 | $575 |

50th Anniversary Stratocaster Relic
1995-1996. Custom Shop Relic model, aged played-in feel, diamond headstock inlay, Shoreline Gold finish, 200 units planned.

| 1995-1996 | | $2,600 | $3,300 |

'54 Stratocaster
1992-1998. Custom Shop Classic reissue, ash body, Custom '50s pickups, gold-plated hardware.

| 1992-1998 | Various options | $2,300 | $2,900 |

'54 Stratocaster FMT
1992-1998. Custom Classic reissue, Flame Maple Top, also comes in gold hardware edition

| 1992-1998 | | $2,000 | $2,500 |

'55 Stratocaster
2006, 2013. Custom Shop model, 1st version is Limited Edition of 100 Relics with 2-tone sunburst; 2nd version is CS Closet Classic. Both include certificate of authenticity.

| 2006 | Relic | $2,200 | $2,800 |
| 2013 | Closet Classic | $2,000 | $2,500 |

'55 Rocking Dog Stratocaster
2007. Custom Shop, various colors.

| 2007 | | $2,600 | $3,400 |

'56 Stratocaster
1996-2014. Custom Shop model, most detailed replica (and most expensive to date) of '56 Strat, including electronics and pickups, offered with rosewood or maple 'board, gold hardware is +$100.

1996-1998	Cunetto built relic	$3,000	$3,900
1997-1998	Cunetto era (staff built)	$2,300	$2,900
1999-2010	Closet Classic	$2,000	$2,500
1999-2010	NOS	$1,800	$2,200
1999-2014	Relic	$2,200	$2,800

American Vintage '56 Stratocaster
2013-present. Vintage '56 style, maple 'board, black, Shell Pink or aged white blonde.

| 2013-2014 | | $1,100 | $1,400 |

'57 Special Stratocaster
1992-1993. Custom Shop model, flamed maple top, birdseye maple neck, run of 60 made, sunburst.

| 1992-1993 | | $2,200 | $2,800 |

'57 Stratocaster
1994-1996. Custom Shop model, replaced by the more authentic, higher-detailed '56 Custom Shop Stratocaster by '99, Custom Shop models can be distinguished by the original certificate that comes with the guitar.

| 1994-1996 | Various colors | $2,300 | $2,900 |

'57 Stratocaster (Custom Shop)
2007, 2010-present. Heavy Relic (2007, '15-present), Closet Classic ('10-'13), NOS Dealer Select program ('13-present) where models are built for specific dealers.

2007	Relic	$2,200	$2,800
2010-2013	Closet Classic	$2,000	$2,500
2013-2015	NOS	$1,800	$2,200

George Fullerton 50th Anniversary '57 Strat Ltd. Ed. Set
2007. 150 made, '57 Strat with matching relic Pro Junior tweed amp, certificates of authenticity signed by Fullerton, commemorative neck plate.

| 2007 | | $3,000 | $3,700 |

'57 Commemorative Stratocaster
2007. Limited production, part of American Vintage Series, 1957-2007 Commemorative logo neckplate.

| 2007 | | $1,100 | $1,400 |

'57 Stratocaster (USA)
1982-2012. U.S.-made at the Fullerton, California plant ('82-'85) and at the Corona, California plant ('85-present), American Vintage series.

1982-1984	SN: V series	$2,500	$3,400
1986-1989		$1,200	$1,500
1986-1989	Rare colors	$1,500	$1,900
1990-1999		$1,200	$1,500
1990-1999	Rare colors	$1,500	$1,900
2000-2012		$1,100	$1,400

'57 Vintage Stratocaster (Japan)
1984-1985. Japanese-made, various colors.

| 1984-1985 | | $1,100 | $1,400 |

American Vintage '57 Stratocaster
2007-2012. Alder body (except ash on white blonde), maple neck.

| 2007-2012 | | $1,200 | $1,500 |

Wildwood "10s" 1957 Limited Stratocaster HSS Relic
2014-present. Custom Shop Dealer Select model for Wildwood Music, '57 specs with hum-single-single pickups.

| 2014-2015 | | $2,800 | $3,500 |

'58 Stratocaster
1996-1999. Custom Shop model, ash body, Fat '50s pickups, chrome or gold hardware (gold is +$100.), Custom Shop models can be distinguished by the original certificate that comes with the guitar.

| 1996-1999 | Various colors | $2,300 | $2,900 |

'58 Stratocaster (Dakota Red)
1996. Custom Shop model, run of 30 made in Dakota Red with matching headstock, maple neck, Texas special pickups, gold hardware.

| 1996 | | $2,300 | $2,900 |

'59 Rocking Dog Stratocaster
2007. Custom Shop, commissioned by Garrett Park Guitars, based on '59 rosewood 'board Strat, various colors.

| 2007 | | $2,600 | $3,400 |

Wildwood "10s" 1959 Limited Stratocaster Relic
2011-present. Custom Shop, quartersawn maple neck, rosewood 'board, 3 pickups, faded 3-color sunburst. Limited Edition neck plate, decal, and certificate of authenticity.

| 2011-2014 | | $4,200 | $5,000 |

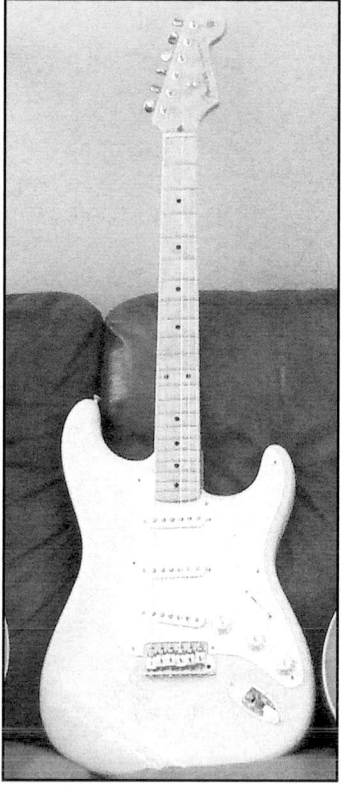

Fender American Vintage '57 Commemorative Stratocaster

Dan Drozdik

Fender Wildwood "10s" 1959 Limited Stratocaster Relic

GUITARS

Fender Classic Series
'60s Stratocaster

Fender Road Worn
'60s Stratocaster

MODEL YEAR	FEATURES	EXC. COND. LOW	HIGH

'60 FMT Stratocaster
1997-1999. Custom Shop model, flame maple top.

1997-1999		$1,850	$2,300

'60 Stratocaster
1992-1999. Custom Shop, 3 Texas Special pickups, various colors, optional gold hardware is +$100, with certificate of authenticity. In 2000 the '60 Stratocaster name was applied to the Time Machine model (see following).

1992-1999		$2,300	$2,900

'60s Stratocaster/'60 Stratocaster
1996-2014. Custom Shop Relic/Time Machine. For '96-'99 was called the '60s Stratocaster, in 2000, name was changed to '60 Stratocaster. Optional gold hardware is +$100. Vince Cunetto and company did the aging of the guitars to mid-1999. The price includes the original Certificate of Authenticity, a guitar without the original certificate is worth less than the values shown.

1996-1998	Cunetto built relic	$3,000	$3,900
1997-1999	Cunetto era (staff built)	$2,300	$2,900
1999-2010	Closet Classic	$2,000	$2,500
1999-2010	NOS	$1,800	$2,200
1999-2014	Relic	$2,200	$2,800

Custom 1960 Stratocaster
1994. Short run of 20 custom ordered and specified instruments that have 1960 specs along with other specs such as a pearloid 'guard, came with Certificate of Authenticity, matching headstock color.

1994		$1,850	$2,300

'60s Stratocaster/Classic Series '60s Stratocaster
1985-present. 'Made in Japan' logo until 'Crafted in Japan' logo mid-'97, basswood body, then mid-'99 made in Mexico with poplar or alder body. Foto-Flame finish offered '92-'94.

1985-1996	Made in Japan	$650	$800
1992-1994	Foto-flame	$625	$775
1997-1999	Crafted in Japan	$550	$700
1999-2014	Mexico	$575	$725

Classic Player '60s Stratocaster
2006-present. U.S.-made components but assembled in Mexico, alder body, maple neck, rosewood 'board, vintage-style pickups.

2006-2014		$650	$800

Road Worn '60s Stratocaster
2009-present. Rosewood 'board, '60s specs, aged finish.

2009-2014		$600	$750

60th Anniversary American Stratocaster
2006-2007. Celebrates Fender's 60th, US-made, 'Sixty Years' decal logo on headstock, engraved 60th Anniversary neck plate, Z-series serial number, coin on back of headstock, paperwork.

2006-2007		$950	$1,200

60th Anniversary Commemorative Stratocaster
2014. Celebrates the Strat's 60th, US-made, 60th Anniversary neckplate, 60th medallion on back of headstock, gold hardware, special case, commemorative book.

2014		$950	$1,200

60th Anniversary Classic Player '50 Stratocaster
2014. Maple neck, anodized guard, 60th medallion on back of headstock, Desert Sand finish.

2014		$575	$725

60th Anniversary Standard Stratocaster
2006. Mexico, engraved 60th Anniversary neck plate, 60th Anniversary Gig Bag.

2006		$300	$375

'61 Stratocaster
2001. Custom Shop model, Relic, white, Certificate of Authenticity.

2001		$2,000	$2,500

'62 Stratocaster (USA)
1982-2012. Made at Fullerton plant ('82-'85) then at Corona plant ('86-present), American Vintage series.

1982-1984	SN: V series	$2,500	$3,400
1986-1989		$1,200	$1,500
1986-1989	Rare colors	$1,500	$1,900
1990-1999	Common colors	$1,200	$1,500
1990-1999	Rare colors	$1,500	$1,900
2000-2012		$1,100	$1,400

'62 Commemorative Stratocaster
2007. Limited production, part of American Vintage Series, 1957-2007 Commemorative logo neckplate.

2007		$1,200	$1,500

'62 Vintage Stratocaster (Japan)
1982-1985. Japanese-made, various colors.

1982-1985		$1,100	$1,400

'62 Heavy Relic Stratocaster
2007-2010. Custom Shop, Dealer Select model, extreme Relic work.

2007-2010		$2,200	$2,800

'62 Stratocaster ST62US Reissue
2008-2012. Made by Fender Japan for that market, US-made 'vintage' pickups.

2008-2012		$550	$700

American Vintage '62 Stratocaster
2007-2012. Alder body, rosewood 'board.

2007-2012		$1,100	$1,400

Deluxe Vintage Player '62 Stratocaster
2005-2006. Vintage and modern features based upon '62 specs, 3 Samarium Cobalt Noiseless pickups, Deluxe American Standard electronics, limited edition, Olympic White or Ice Blue Metallic.

2005-2006		$925	$1,150

'65 Stratocaster
1998-1999, 2003-2006, 2010 (no Closet Classic). Custom Shop model, '65 small-headstock specs, rosewood or maple cap 'board, transition logo, offered in NOS, Relic, or Closet Classic versions.

1998-1999	Cunetto era (staff built)	$2,300	$2,900
2003-2006	Closet Classic	$2,000	$2,500
2003-2006	NOS	$1,800	$2,200
2003-2006	Relic	$2,200	$2,800
2010	NOS	$1,800	$2,200
2010	Relic	$2,200	$2,800

MODEL YEAR	FEATURES	EXC. COND. LOW	HIGH

'65 Vintage Stratocaster
2013-present. American Vintage, flash coat finish, V serial number.

2013-2015		$1,375	$1,700

'66 Stratocaster
2004-2008. Custom Shop model, offered in Closet Classic, NOS or Relic versions.

2004-2008	Closet Classic	$2,000	$2,500
2004-2008	NOS	$1,800	$2,200
2004-2008	Relic	$2,200	$2,800

'68 Reverse Strat Special (USA)
2001-2002. With special reverse left-hand neck, large headstock (post-CBS style).

2001-2002		$2,000	$2,500

'68 Stratocaster (Japan)
1994-1999, 2013. '68 specs including large headstock, part of Collectables Series, sunburst, natural, Olympic White.

1994-1999		$700	$900
2013		$700	$900

'69 Stratocaster
1997-2009. Custom Shop model, large headstock, U-shaped maple neck with rosewood or maple cap options, '69-style finish, gold hardware is +$100, since 2000, offered in NOS, Relic, or Closet Classic (no CC in '09) versions.

1997-1999	Cunetto era (staff built)	$2,300	$2,900
2000-2008	Closet Classic	$2,000	$2,500
2000-2009	NOS	$1,800	$2,200
2000-2009	Relic	$2,200	$2,800

'70s Stratocaster American Vintage
2009-2012. US-made, large '70s headstock, early '70s white pickups and knobs, 3-bolt neck.

2009-2012		$1,050	$1,300

'70s Stratocaster/Classic Series '70s Stratocaster
1999-present. Made in Mexico, large headstock, white pickups and knobs, rosewood 'board.

1999-2014		$475	$600

'72 Stratocaster (Japan)
1985-1996. Basswood body, maple 'board, large headstock, various colors (does not include the Paisley '72).

1985-1989		$800	$1,000
1990-1996		$700	$900

'72 Stratocaster Limited Edition (Japan)
2013. Made in Japan for US domestic sales, 144 made, large headstock, bullet truss rod, 3-bolt maple neck, 21 frets, 3 Alnico pickups.

2013		$525	$675

Acoustasonic Stratocaster
2003-2009. Hollowed out alder Strat body with braceless graphite top, 3 in-bridge Fishman piezo pickups, acoustic sound hole.

2003-2009		$550	$700

Aerodyne Stratocaster
2004-2009. Import Strat with Aerodyne body profile, bound body, black.

2004-2009		$700	$875

Aluminum Stratocaster American Standard
1994-1995. Aluminum-bodied American Standard with anodized finish in blue marble, purple marble or red, silver and blue stars and stripes. Some with 40th Anniversary designation. There is also a Custom Shop version.

1994-1995	Marble patterns	$1,600	$2,000
1994-1995	Red-silver-blue flag option	$2,000	$2,500

Aluminum Stratocaster Custom Shop
1994. Custom Shop aluminum bodies, chrome body with black 'guard, black body with chrome 'guard, or green with black lines and red swirls. There are also several Custom Shop one-offs with aluminum bodies.

1993-1994	Chrome	$2,600	$3,300

American Classic Holoflake Stratocaster
1992-1993. Custom Shop model, splatter/sparkle finish, pearloid 'guard.

1992-1993		$1,600	$2,000

American Classic Stratocaster
1992-1999. Custom Shop version of American Standard, 3 pickups, tremolo, rosewood 'board, nickel or gold-plated hardware, various colors.

1992-1999	See-thru blond ash	$1,600	$2,000
1992-1999	Various colors & options	$1,600	$2,000

American Deluxe Stratocaster
1998-present. Made in USA, premium alder or ash body, noiseless pickups.

1998-2014		$875	$1,100

American Deluxe Fat Stratocaster HSS
1998-2003. Made in USA, Fender DH-1 bridge humbucker and 2 single-coils, premium alder or ash body. Basically replaced by the American Deluxe Strat HSS.

1998-2003	Ash body, trans finish	$925	$1,150
1998-2003	Various colors	$925	$1,150

American Deluxe Stratocaster HSS
2004-present. Deluxe features, hum/single/single pickups.

2004-2014		$950	$1,200

American Deluxe Stratocaster FMT HSS
2004-2009. Flame maple top version of the HSS.

2004-2009		$1,100	$1,400

American Series HSS/HH Stratocaster
2003-2007. Made in U.S., HSS has humbucker/single/single, HH ('03-'05) 2 humbuckers. Renamed American Standard Strat HSS in '08.

2003-2007	Alder or ash body	$800	$1,000

American Special Stratocaster
2010-present. Large '70s headstock with post-CBS black Stratocaster logo, satin (early were gloss) urethane finish, Texas Special pickups (SSS or HSS).

2010-2014		$550	$675

American Standard Stratocaster HSS
2008-present. Renamed from American Series Stratocaster HSS.

2008-2014		$800	$1,000

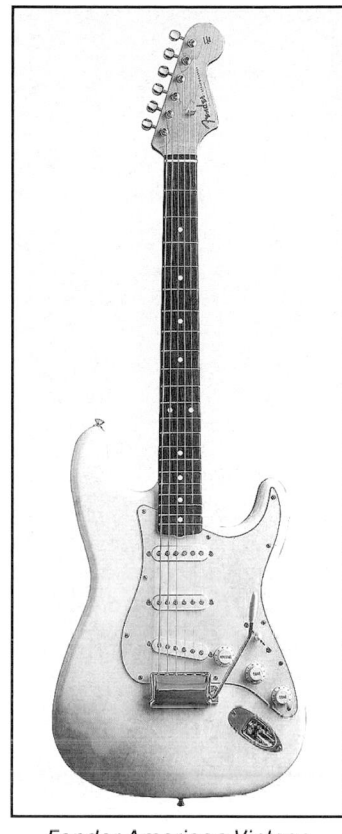

Fender American Vintage '62 Stratocaster

Fender American Deluxe Stratocaster

GUITARS

Fender Billy Corgan Stratocaster

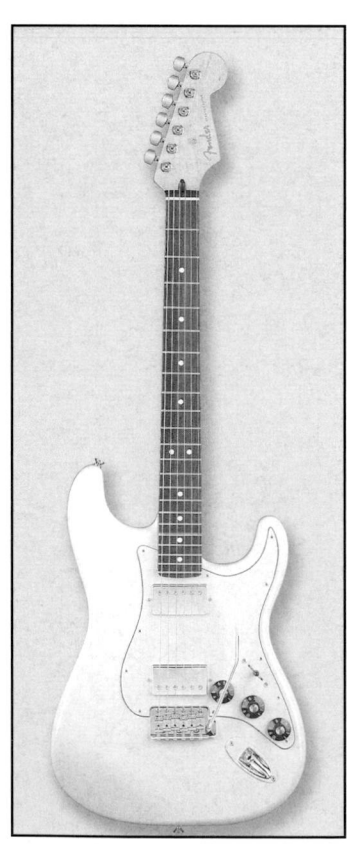

Fender Blacktop Stratocaster HH

MODEL YEAR	FEATURES	EXC. COND. LOW	HIGH

American Standard Stratocaster Limited Edition
1995. 1950s style headstock decal, Ocean Turquoise or Candy Apple Red with matching headstock.

1995		$1,050	$1,300

Antigua Stratocaster
2004. Made in Japan, limited-edition reissue, '70s features and antigua finish.

2004		$625	$800

Antigua Stratocaster FSR
2012. Fender Special Run (FSR), 380 made, large headstock, bullet rod.

2012		$525	$650

Big Apple Stratocaster
1997-2000. Two humbucking pickups, 5-way switch, rosewood 'board or maple neck, non-tremolo optional.

1997-2000	Various colors	$775	$950

Big Block Stratocaster
2005-2006. Pearloid block markers, black with matching headstock, 2 single coils (neck, middle) 1 humbucker (bridge), vintage style tremolo.

2005-2006		$600	$750

Bill Carson Stratocaster
1992. Based on the '57 Strat, birdseye maple neck, Cimarron Red finish, 1 left-handed and 100 right-handed produced, serial numbers MT000-MT100, made in Fender Custom Shop, and initiated by The Music Trader (MT) in Florida.

1992		$1,700	$2,100

Billy Corgan Stratocaster
2008-2012. US-made, 3 DiMarzio pickups, string-thru hardtail bridge.

2008-2012		$1,250	$1,550

Blackie Stratocaster (Custom Shop 1987)
1987. 12 made, includes Certificate of Authenticity.

1987		$2,400	$3,000

Blackie Stratocaster (Custom Shop)
November 2006. 185 instruments for U.S. market, 90 made for export, original retail price $24,000.

2006		$12,000	$15,000

American Standard Limited Edition Blackout Stratocaster
2015. Mystic Black finish, ebony 'board.

2015		$1,100	$1,400

Blacktop Stratocaster HH/HSH/HH Floyd Rose
2011-present. Alder body, maple neck, rosewood or maple 'board, 2 humbucker pickups, various finish options. HSH includes 1 Tele single-coil. Floyd Rose version also available.

2011-2014		$300	$375

Blue Flower Stratocaster
1984-1997, 2002-2004. Made in Japan, '72 Strat reissue with a '68 Tele Blue Floral finish.

1984	1st issue	$1,300	$1,600
1985		$1,200	$1,500
1986-1994		$1,100	$1,350
1995-1999		$750	$950
2002-2004	2nd issue	$550	$675

Bonnie Raitt Stratocaster
1995-2000. Alder body, often in blueburst, Bonnie Raitt's signature on headstock.

1995-2000		$1,350	$1,700

Bowling Ball/Marble Stratocaster
1984. Standard Strat with 1 tone and 1 volume control, jack on 'guard, called Bowling Ball Strat due to the swirling, colored finish.

1984	Blue	$2,500	$3,100
1984	Red	$2,500	$3,100
1984	Yellow	$2,500	$3,100

Buddy Guy Stratocaster (Mexico)
1996-present. Maple neck, polka-dot finish.

1996-2014		$475	$600

Buddy Guy Stratocaster (Signature)
1995-2009. Maple neck, 3 Gold Lace Sensor pick-ups, ash body, signature model, blond or sunburst.

1995-2009		$1,100	$1,375

Buddy Holly Tribute Stratocaster
2012. Custom Shop model, 50 made, '55 specs, with certificate of authenticity.

2012		$7,000	$8,800

California Fat Stratocaster
1997-1998. 2 single-coils with humbucker in bridge position.

1997-1998		$625	$775

California Stratocaster
1997-1999. Made in the U.S., painted in Mexico, 3 single coils, various colors.

1997-1999		$625	$775

Classic Player Stratocaster
2000. Custom Shop model, Standard Stratocaster with useful 'player-friendly features' such as noiseless stacked single-coil pickups and factory Sperzel locking tuners, made in the Custom Shop, black, gold anodized 'guard.

2000		$1,500	$1,900

Collector's Edition Stratocaster ('62 Reissue)
1997. Pearl inlaid '97 on 12th fret, rosewood 'board, alder body, gold hardware, tortoise 'guard, nitro finish, sunburst, 1997 made.

1997		$1,300	$1,625

Contemporary Stratocaster
1989-1998. Custom Shop model, 7/8 scale body, hum/single/single pickups, various colors.

1989-1998		$1,200	$1,500

Contemporary Stratocaster (Import)
1985-1987. Import model used while the new Fender reorganized, black or natural headstock with silver-white logo, black or white 'guard, 2 humbucker pickups or single-coil and humbucker, 2 knobs and slider switch.

1985-1987		$600	$750

Crash Stratocaster
2005-2007. Master Built Custom Shop model, hand painted by John Crash Matos, approximately 50, comes with certificate, the prices shown include the original certificate.

2005-2007		$3,200	$4,000

The ***Vintage Guitar Price Guide*** shows low to high values for items in all-original excellent condition, and, where applicable, with original case or cover.

MODEL YEAR	FEATURES	EXC. COND. LOW	HIGH

Custom Classic Stratocaster
2000-2008. Custom Shop version of American Standard Strat.

2000-2008		$1,425	$1,775

Custom Shop Masterbuild Stratocaster
2006-present. Various models and builders, specific identification to builder, must include certificate of authenticity.

2006-2014	Various models	$3,000	$8,000

David Gilmour Signature Stratocaster
2008-present. Custom Shop model, based on Gilmour's '70 black Stratocaster, certificate of authenticity.

2008	Relic	$3,000	$3,750
2008-2014		$3,000	$3,750

Deluxe Lone Star Stratocaster
2007-present. Reissue of Lone Star Strat, made in Mexico, 1 humbucker and 2 single-coils, rosewood 'board.

2007-2014		$400	$500

Deluxe Players Special Edition Stratocaster
2007. Made in Mexico, Special Edition Fender oval sticker on back of headstock along with 60th Anniversary badge.

2007		$350	$450

Deluxe Players Stratocaster
2004-present. Made in Mexico, 3 noiseless single-coils, push-button switching system.

2004-2014		$400	$500

Deluxe Strat Plus
1987-1998. Three Lace Sensor pickups, Floyd Rose, alder (poplar available earlier) body with ash veneer on front and back, various colors, also see Strat Plus.

1987-1998		$1,100	$1,375

Dick Dale Stratocaster
1994-present. Custom Shop signature model, alder body, reverse headstock, sparkle finish.

1994-2014		$1,850	$2,350

Elite Stratocaster
1983-1984. The Elite Series feature active electronics and noise-cancelling pickups, push buttons instead of 3-way switch, Elite script logo on 4-bolt neck plate, various colors. Also see Gold Elite Stratocaster and Walnut Elite Stratocaster.

1983-1984		$1,700	$2,100

Eric Clapton Gold Leaf Stratocaster
2004. Custom Shop model, special build for Guitar Center, 50 made, 23k gold leaf finish/covering.

2004		$5,000	$6,400

Eric Clapton Stratocaster
1988-present. U.S.-made, '57 reissue features, had Lace Sensor pickups until '01, when switched to Vintage Noiseless. Black versions have added "Blackie" decal on headstock.

1988-1989		$1,300	$1,600
1990-2000	Lace Sensor	$1,150	$1,450
2001-2014	Noiseless	$1,150	$1,450

Eric Clapton Stratocaster (Custom Shop)
2004-present. Custom Shop model, standard non-active single-coil pickups, black or blue finish.

2004-2014		$2,400	$3,000

Eric Johnson Stratocaster
2005-present. '57 spec body and soft-v-neck, maple or, since '09, rosewood 'board, special design pickups, vintage tremolo with 4 springs, EJ initials and guitar-player figure engraved neck plate..

2005-2014		$1,250	$1,550

Floyd Rose Classic Relic Stratocaster
1998. Custom Shop model, late '60s large headstock, 1 humbucker and 1 Strat pickup.

1998		$2,000	$2,500

Floyd Rose Classic Stratocaster (Strat HSS) (Strat HH)
1992-2002. Two single-coils, bridge humbucker, Floyd Rose tremolo, becomes Floyd Rose Classic Strat HSS or HH (2 humbuckers) in '98.

1992-2002		$1,125	$1,400

Ford Shelby GT Stratocaster
2007. 200 made, black with silver Shelby GT racing stripe.

2007	200 made	$2,000	$2,500

Foto Flame Stratocaster
1994-1996, 2000. Japanese-made Collectables model, alder and basswood body with Foto Flame (simulated woodgrain) finish on top cap and back of neck.

1994-1996		$625	$775
2000		$625	$775

Freddy Tavares Aloha Stratocaster
1993-1994. Custom Shop model, hollow aluminum body with hand engraved Hawaiian scenes, custom inlay on neck, 153 made.

1993-1994		$5,000	$6,200

Gold Stratocaster
1981-1983. Gold metallic finish, gold-plated brass hardware, 4-bolt neck, maple 'board, skunk strip, trem.

1981-1983		$2,000	$2,500

Gold Elite Stratocaster
1983-1984. The Elite series feature active electronics and noise-cancelling pickups, the Gold Elite has gold hardware and pearloid tuner buttons, also see Elite Stratocaster and Walnut Elite Stratocaster.

1983-1984		$1,700	$2,100

Gold Stratocaster (CS)
1989. Custom Shop model, 500 made, gold finish with gold anodized and white 'guards included.

1989		$2,000	$2,500

Hank Marvin Stratocaster
1995-1996. Custom Shop model, Feista Red.

1995-1996		$2,200	$2,800

Hank Marvin 40th Anniversary Stratocaster
1998. Custom Shop logo with '40 Years 1958-1998' marked on back of headstock, Fiesta Red, only 40 made, Custom Shop certificate.

1998		$5,500	$6,900

Harley-Davidson 90th Anniversary Stratocaster
1993. Custom Shop, 109 total made, Harley-Davidson and Custom Shop V logo on headstock (Diamond Edition, 40 units), 9 units produced for

Fender Deluxe Lone Star Stratocaster

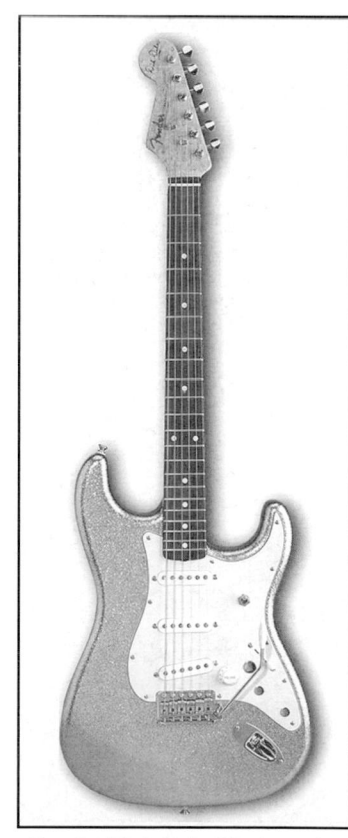

Fender Dick Dale Stratocaster

Fender John Mayer Stratocaster

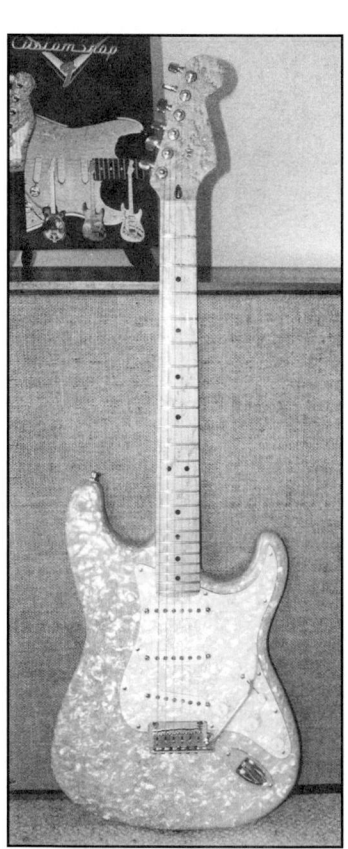

1995 Fender Moto Stratocaster

MODEL YEAR	FEATURES	EXC. COND. LOW	HIGH

the Harley-Davidson company without diamond logo, 60 units were not Diamond Edition, chrome-plated engraved metal body, engraved 'guard, Custom Shop Certificate important attribute.

| 1993 | | $10,500 | $13,000 |

Highway One Stratocaster/HSS

2002-2011. U.S.-made, alder body, satin lacquer finish, HSS version has humbucker/single/single pickups.

| 2002-2011 | | $525 | $650 |

HM Stratocaster (USA/Import)

1988-1992 ('88 Japanese-made, '89-'90 U.S.- and Japanese-made, '91-'92 U.S.-made). Heavy Metal Strat, Floyd Rose, regular or pointy headstock, black hardware, H, HH, SH, or SSH pickup options. Later models have choice of SHH or SSH.

| 1988-1990 | Import | $725 | $900 |
| 1989-1992 | U.S.A. | $725 | $900 |

Homer Haynes HLE Stratocaster

1988-1989. Custom Shop model, limited edition of 500, '59 Strat basics with gold finish, gold anodized guard and gold hardware.

| 1988-1989 | | $2,550 | $3,150 |

Hot Wheels Stratocaster

2003. Custom Shop model commissioned by Hot Wheels, 16 made, orange flames over blue background, large Hot Wheels logo.

| 2003 | | $1,900 | $2,400 |

HRR Stratocaster/ Floyd Rose HRR (Japan)

1990-1994. Japanese-made, hot-rodded vintage-style Strat, Floyd Rose tremolo system, H/S/S pickups, maple neck, sunburst or colors. Called the Floyd Rose HRR for '92-'94 (with optional Foto Flame finish).

| 1990-1994 | | $650 | $800 |

Ike Turner Tribute Stratocaster

2005. Custom Shop model, 100 made, replica of Ike Turner's Sonic Blue Strat.

| 2005 | | $2,000 | $2,500 |

Jeff Beck Signature Stratocaster (CS)

2004-present. Custom Shop, 3 Noiseless dual-coils, Olympic White or Surf Green.

| 2004-2014 | | $1,700 | $2,100 |

Jeff Beck Stratocaster

1991-present. Alder body, originally 4 Lace Sensors (H/S/S) changing to 3 Noiseless dual-coils in '01, rosewood 'board, Olympic White and Surf Green (Midnight Purple until '02).

1991 1993	1st issue, larger headstock	$1,400	$1,750
1994-2009		$1,200	$1,500
2010-2014	Artist Series	$1,150	$1,450

Jerry Donahue Hellecaster Stratocaster

1997. Made in the Fender Japan Custom Shop as one part of the 3-part Hellecasters Series, limited edition, Seymour Duncan pickups, maple, blue with blue sparkle guard.

| 1997 | | $800 | $1,000 |

Jim Root Signature Stratocaster

2010-present. Mahogany body, ebony or maple 'board, 2 active pickups, black hardware, black or white finish.

| 2010-2014 | | $900 | $1,100 |

MODEL YEAR	FEATURES	EXC. COND. LOW	HIGH

Jimi Hendrix Monterey Pop Stratocaster

1997-1998. Custom Shop model, near replica of Monterey Pop Festival sacrifice guitar, red psychedelic-style finish.

| 1997-1998 | | $8,000 | $10,000 |

Jimi Hendrix Tribute Stratocaster

1997-2000. Left-handed guitar strung right-handed, maple cap neck, Olympic White finish. Fender headstock logo positioned upside down, made for right-handed player to look as if they are playing a left-handed guitar flipped over.

| 1997-2000 | | $1,500 | $2,000 |

Jimi Hendrix Voodoo 29th Anniversary Stratocaster

1993. Fender Custom Shop made only 35 for Guitar Center, large 'Guitar Center 29th Anniversary' logo on neckplate, right-handed body with reverse left-handed headstock and reversed Fender headstock logo, purple sparkle finish.

| 1993 | | $2,000 | $2,500 |

Jimi Hendrix Voodoo Stratocaster

1997-2002. Right-handed body with reverse peghead, maple neck, sunburst, Olympic White, or black.

| 1997-1998 | 1st years | $1,500 | $2,000 |
| 1999-2002 | | $1,500 | $2,000 |

Jimmie Vaughan Tex-Mex Stratocaster

1997-present. Poplar body, maple 'board, signature on headstock, 3 Tex-Mex pickups, various colors.

| 1997-2014 | | $525 | $650 |

John Jorgenson Hellecaster Stratocaster

1997. Fender Japan Custom Shop, part of the 3-part Hellecasters Series, limited edtion, Seymour Duncan pickups, gold sparkle 'guard, gold hardware, split single-coils, rosewood 'board.

| 1997 | | $975 | $1,225 |

John Mayer Stratocaster

2005-2014. Alder body, special scooped mid-range pickups, vintage tremolo, special design gigbag with pocket for laptop computer.

| 2005-2014 | | $1,100 | $1,350 |

Kenny Wayne Shepherd Stratocaster

2009-present. Based on Shepherd's '61, rosewood 'board, jumbo frets, Artic White with cross, black with racing stripes or 3-color sunburst.

| 2009-2014 | | $525 | $650 |

Koa Stratocaster

2006-2008. Made in Korea, Special Edition series, sunburst over koa veneer top, plain script Fender logo, serial number on back of headstock with.

| 2006-2008 | | $460 | $575 |

Kon Tiki Stratocaster

2003. Custom Shop model, limited run of 25, Tiki Green including Tiki 3-color art work on headstock.

| 2003 | | $2,000 | $2,500 |

Lenny Stratocaster

Introduced Dec. 12, 2007 by Guitar Center stores, Custom Shop model, 185 guitars made, initial product offering price was 17K.

| 2007 | | $7,900 | $9,900 |

MODEL YEAR	FEATURES	EXC. COND. LOW	HIGH

Lite Ash Stratocaster Special Edition
2007. Korea, light ash body, birds-eye maple neck.

2007		$400	$500

Lone Star Stratocaster
1996-2001. Alder body, 1 humbucker and 2 single-coil pickups, rosewood 'board or maple neck, various colors.

1996	50th Anniv. Badge	$750	$925
1997-2001		$750	$925

Mark Knopfler Stratocaster
2003-2013. '57 body with '62 maple neck.

2003-2013		$1,100	$1,400

Milonga Deluxe Stratocaster
2005. Special Edition made in Mexico, Vintage Noiseless pickups, rosewood 'board, Olympic White, gold hardware.

2005		$400	$500

Modern Player Stratocaster HSH/HSS
2013-present. Hum-single-hum or hum-single-single, China.

2013-2014		$325	$400

Moto Limited Edition Stratocaster
1995. Custom Shop model, pearloid cover in various colors, includes Certificate of Authenticity, not to be confused with white pearloid Moto Strat which is part of a guitar and amp set (as listed below).

1995		$2,300	$2,900

Moto Set Stratocaster
1995-1996. Custom Shop set including guitar, case, amp and amp stand, white pearloid finish.

1995-1996	Red (few made)	$4,000	$5,000
1995-1996	White	$4,000	$5,000

Orange Krush Limited Edition Stratocaster
1995. Custom Shop, 25 made, based on '57 Strat, orange finish with matching headstock, certificate of authenticity.

1995		$2,000	$2,500

Paisley Stratocaster
1984-1997, 2002-2004, 2008. Japanese-made '72 Strat reissue with a reissue '68 Tele Pink Paisley finish, large headstock until mid-'94, 'Made in Japan' logo used until early-'97, 'Crafted in Japan' after.

1984-1987	1st issue	$1,200	$1,500
1988-1997		$1,100	$1,350
2002-2004		$650	$800
2008	2nd issue, 200 made	$650	$800

Playboy 40th Anniversary Stratocaster
1994. Custom Shop model, nude Marilyn Monroe graphic on body.

1994		$13,500	$17,000

Powerhouse/Powerhouse Deluxe Stratocaster
1997-2010. Made in Mexico, Standard Strat configuration with pearloid 'guard, various colors.

1997-2010		$375	$475
2005	Powerbridge, TRS stereo	$425	$525

Proud Stratocaster
2003. Custom Shop, 3 made to commemorate

United Way and Rock & Roll Hall of Fame project, body painted in detail by Fender's artist.

2003		$2,800	$3,500

Richie Sambora Stratocaster
1993-2002. Alder body, Floyd Rose tremolo, maple neck, sunburst. There was also a cheaper Richie Sambora Standard Stratocaster in blue or white.

1993-2002	USA	$2,400	$3,000
1994-2002	Import	$375	$475

Ritchie Blackmore Stratocaster
2009-present. Based on Blackmore's '70s large headstock model, scalloped rosewood 'board, Duncan Quarter Pound Flat pickups, Olympic White.

2009-2014		$725	$900

Ritchie Blackmore Tribute Stratocaster
2013. Custom Shop model, '68 specs, maple neck.

2013		$5,100	$6,400

Roadhouse Stratocaster
1997 2000. U.S.-made, poplar body, tortoise shell 'guard, maple 'board, 3 Texas Special pickups, various colors.

1997-2000		$750	$925

Roadhouse Stratocaster (Mexico)
2008-present. Deluxe series reissue, Texas Special pickups.

2008-2014		$375	$475

Robert Cray Signature Stratocaster
1991-present. Custom Shop, rosewood 'board, chunky neck, lighter weight, non-trem, alder body, gold-plated hardware, various colors.

1991-2014		$1,100	$1,400

Robert Cray Stratocaster (Mexico)
1996 present. Artist series, chrome hardware.

1996-2014		$475	$600

Robin Trower Signature Stratocaster
2004-2006. Custom Shop, 100 made, large headstock (post '65-era), with '70s logo and 3-bolt neck, bullet truss rod, white.

2004-2006		$1,900	$2,400

Rory Gallagher Tribute Stratocaster
2005. Custom Shop, heavily distressed '61 model based on Gallagher's guitar, price includes the original certificate.

2005		$2,450	$3,050

Select Stratocaster
2012-present. Select Series, figured top, rear-headstock 'Fender Select' medallion, gloss-lacquer finish, various colors.

2012-2014		$1,500	$1,900

Set-Neck Stratocaster
1992-1999. Custom Shop model, mahogany body and figured maple top, 4 pickups, glued-in neck, active electronics, by '96 ash body.

1992-1999		$1,800	$2,250

Short-Scale (7/8) Stratocaster
1989-1995. Similar to Standard Strat, but with 2 control knobs and switch, 24" scale vs. 25" scale, sometimes called a mini-Strat, Japanese import, various colors.

1989-1995		$500	$625

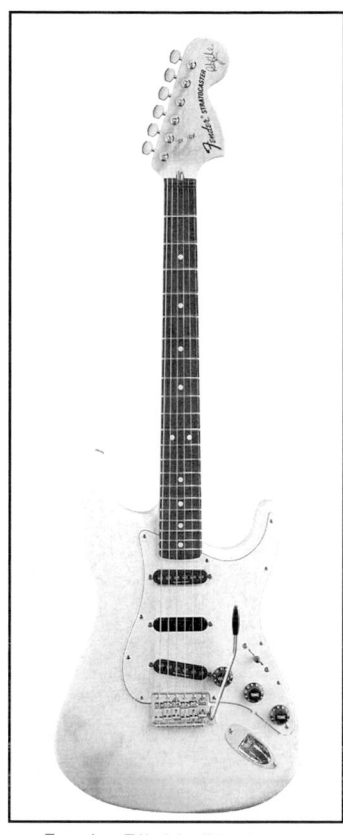

Fender Ritchie Blackmore Stratocaster

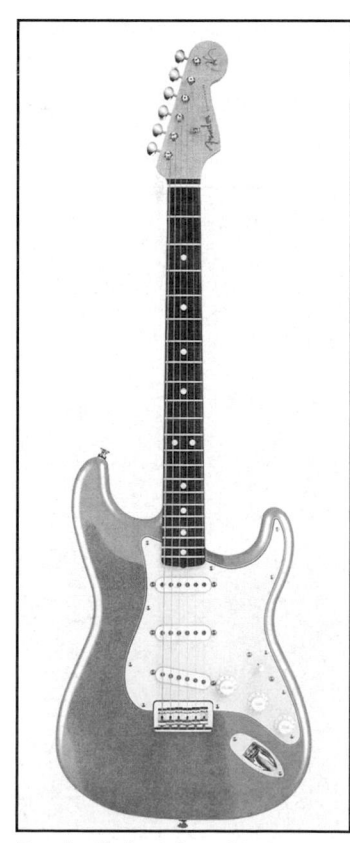

Fender Robert Cray Stratocaster

GUITARS

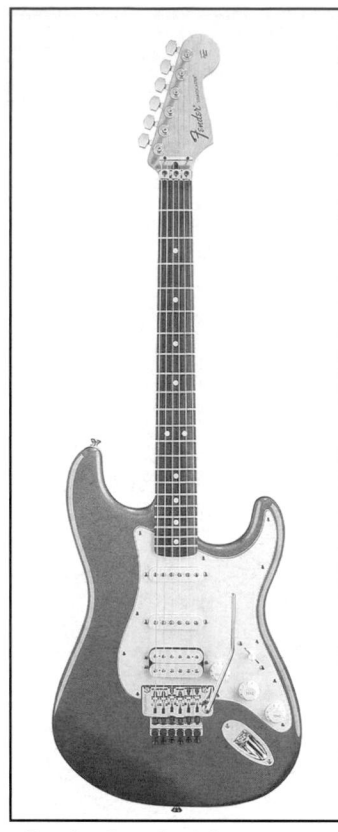

Fender Standard Stratocaster HSS Floyd Rose

1991 Fender Strat U.S. Ultra
Danny Lester

So-Cal Speed Shop L.E. Stratocaster

2005-2006. Limited edition for Musician's Friend, red, white, and black So-Cal paint job, basswood body, rosewood 'board, 1 humbucker, So-Cal Speed Shop decal.

2005-2006	$500	$625

Special Edition Stratocaster

2004-2009. Special Edition oval logo on back of headstock, import model, various styles offered, '50s or '60s vintage copy specs, maple fretboard, ash or koa body, see-thru or opaque finish.

2004-2009	$375	$475

Splatter Stratocaster

2003. Made in Mexico, splatter paint job, various color combinations, with gig bag.

2003	$525	$675

Standard Fat Strat

1999-2003. Made in Mexico (vs. California Fat Strat). Renamed Standard Strat HSS in '04.

1999-2003	$300	$375

Standard Fat Strat Floyd Rose

1999-2003. With Floyd Rose tremolo. Renamed Standard Strat HSS w/ Floyd Rose in '04.

1999-2003	$300	$375

Standard Roland Ready Stratocaster

1998-2011. Made in Mexico, built-in Roland pickup system and 3 single-coils.

1998-2011	$475	$600

Standard Stratocaster (Japan)

1985-1989. Interim production in Japan while the new Fender reorganized, standard pickup configuration and tremolo system, 3 knobs with switch, traditional style input jack, traditional shaped headstock, offered in black, red or white.

1985-1989	$600	$750

Standard Stratocaster (Mexico)

1990-present. Fender Mexico started guitar production in '90. Not to be confused with the American-made Standard Stratocaster of '81-'84. High end of range includes a hard guitar case, while the low end of the range includes only a gig bag, various colors.

1989-2005		$300	$375
2006-2014	Thicker bridge block	$300	$375

Standard Stratocaster HH

2004-2006. Tex Mex Fat Strat humbuckers, 1 volume and 2 tone control knobs.

2004-2006	$300	$375

Standard Stratocaster HSS

2004-present. Made in Mexico, humbucker and 2 singles.

2004-2014	$325	$400

Standard Stratocaster HSS Floyd Rose

2004-present. With Floyd Rose tremolo. Currently called HSS with Locking Tremolo.

2004-2014	$325	$400

Standard Stratocaster HSS Swirl

2013. Made in Mexico, swirl finish.

2013	$350	$435

Standard Stratocaster Satin Finish

2003-2006. Basically Mexico-made Standard with satin finish.

2003-2006	$250	$315

Stevie Ray Vaughan Stratocaster

1992-present. U.S.-made, alder body, sunburst, gold hardware, SRV 'guard, lefty tremolo, Brazilian rosewood 'board (pau ferro by '93).

1992	1st year	$1,100	$1,375
1993-2014		$1,100	$1,375

Stevie Ray Vaughan Tribute #1 Stratocaster

2004. Custom Shop model limited edition recreation of SRV's #1 made by Master Builder John Cruz in the Custom Shop, 100 made, $10,000 MSRP, includes flight case stenciled "SRV - Number One," and other goodies.

2004	$10,500	$13,000

Strat Plus

1987-1999. Three Lace Sensor pickups, alder (poplar available earlier) body, tremolo, rosewood 'board or maple neck, various colors. See Deluxe Strat Plus for ash veneer version.

1987-1999	Common colors	$1,075	$1,325
1987-1999	Rare colors	$1,200	$1,700

Strat Pro Closet Classic

2006-2013. Custom Shop, ash body, early '60s neck, rosewood or maple board, solid or sunburst finish.

2006-2013	$1,750	$2,200

Stratacoustic/Strtacoustic Deluxe

2000-present. Thinline acoustic/electric, single-cut, spruce top, fiberglass body.

2000-2014	$160	$200

Stratocaster Junior

2004-2006. Import, short 22.7" scale, Alder body, non-trem hardtail bridge.

2004-2006	$260	$325

Stratocaster Special

1993-1995. Made in Mexico, a humbucker and a single-coil pickup, 1 volume, 1 tone.

1993-1995	$300	$375

Stratocaster XII

1988-1997, 2003-2010. 1st version Japanese-made, alder body, 22-fret rosewood 'board. 2nd version is 21-fret Classic Series model for 2 years then Classic Series.

1988-1997	$800	$1,000
2003-2010	$800	$1,000

Strat-o-Sonic

2003-2006. American Special Series, Stratocaster-style chambered body, includes Strat-o-Sonic Dove I (1 pickup, '03 only), Dove II/DV II (2 black P-90s, '03-'06) and HH (2 humbuckers, '05-'06).

2003	Dove I	$775	$975
2003-2006	Dove II/DV II	$900	$1,125
2003-2006	HH	$900	$1,125

Sub Sonic Stratocaster

2000-2001. Baritone model, offered in 2 production models - HH (2 humbuckers, 2000-'01), HSS (hum-single-single, '01) - and in a Custom Shop version of the HSS (2000-'01).

2000-2001		$900	$1,125
2000-2001	Custom Shop, COA	$2,000	$2,500

MODEL YEAR	FEATURES	EXC. COND. LOW	HIGH

Super Strat
1997-2003. Deluxe series, made in Mexico, 3 Super Fat single-coils, Super Switching gives 2 extra pickup options, gold tremolo.

1997-2003		$400	$500

Tanqurey Tonic Stratocaster
1988. Made for a Tanqurey Tonic liquor ad campaign giveaway in '88, Tanqurey Tonic Green; many were given to winners around the country, ads said that they could also be purchased through Tanqurey, but that apparently didn't happen.

1988		$1,200	$1,500

Texas Special Stratocaster
1991-1992. Custom Shop model, 50 made, state of Texas map stamped on neck plate, Texas Special pickups, maple fretboard, sunburst.

1991-1992		$1,900	$2,400

The Strat
1980-1983. Alder body, 4-bolt neck, large STRAT on painted peghead, gold-plated brass hardware, various colors.

1980-1983		$1,500	$1,900

Tie-Dye Stratocaster
2004-2005. Single-coil neck and humbucker bridge pickups, Band of Gypsies or Hippie Blue tie-dye pattern poly finish.

2004-2005 Band of Gypsies	$400	$500

Tom Delonge Stratocaster
2001-2004. 1 humbucker, rosewood back and sides. Also in Squier version.

2001-2004		$500	$625

Tree of Life Stratocaster
1993. Custom Shop model, 29 made, tree of life fretboard inlay, 1-piece quilted maple body.

1993		$5,500	$7,000

Turquoise Sparkle Stratocaster
2001. Custom Shop model, limited run of 75 for Mars Music, turquoise sparkle finish.

2001		$1,200	$1,500

U.S. Ultra / Ultra Plus Stratocaster
1990-1997. Alder body with figured maple veneer on front and back, single Lace Sensor pickups in neck and middle, double Sensor at bridge, ebony 'board, sunburst.

1990-1997		$1,475	$1,850

Ventures Limited Edition Stratocaster
1996. Japanese-made tribute model, matches Jazzmaster equivalent, black.

1996		$1,050	$1,300

VG Stratocaster
2007-2009. American Series, modeling technology using Roland's VG circuitry, 5 guitar tone banks deliver 16 sounds.

2007-2009		$1,000	$1,250

Vintage Hot Rod Stratocaster
2007-2014. Vintage styling with modern features, '07-'13 named '57 Strat and '62 Strat, in '14 changed to '50s and '60s.

2007-2014 '57, '62, '50s or '60s	$1,100	$1,400

Walnut Elite Stratocaster
1983-1984. The Elite Series features active electronics and noise-cancelling pickups, Walnut Elite has a walnut body and neck, gold-plated hardware and pearloid tuner buttons. Also see Elite Stratocaster and Gold Elite Stratocaster.

1983-1984		$1,700	$2,100

Walnut Stratocaster
1981-1983. American black walnut body and 1-piece neck and 'board.

1981-1983		$1,800	$2,300

Western Stratocaster
1995. Custom Shop model, only 5 made, featured in Fender Custom Shop book from the 1990s.

1995		$7,000	$9,500

Yngwie Malmsteen Stratocaster
1988-present. U.S.-made, maple neck, scalloped 'board, 3 single-coil pickups, blue, red, white.

1988-2014		$950	$1,200

Swingcr
1969-1972. See listing for Musiclander.

TC-90/TC-90 Thinline
2004. Made in Korea, semi-hollow thinline, double-cut, Duncan SP 90 pickups stop bar and tune o matic tailpiece.

2004		$600	$750

Telecaster
The following are all variations of the Telecaster. Broadcaster and Nocaster models are under Broadcaster. The first four listings are for the main American-made models. All others are listed alphabetically after that in the following order:

Telecaster
Standard Telecaster
American Standard Telecaster
American Series Telecaster
30th Anniversary Guitar Center Tree of Life Telecaster
40th Anniversary Telecaster
'50 Custom Telecaster
'50s Telecaster/Classic Series '50s Telecaster
Road Worn '50s Telecaster
50th Anniversary Spanish Guitar Set Custom Shop
50th Anniversary Telecaster
'52 Telecaster/American Vintage '52 Telecaster
'52 Telecaster (Custom Shop)
'58 Telecaster (Custom Shop)
'60s Telecaster Custom
'60s Telecaster/Classic Series '60s Telecaster
'60 Telecaster Custom
60th Anniversary American Telecaster
60th Anniversary Telecaster Limited Edition
60th Anniversary Telecaster (USA)
'61 Telecaster Custom
'62 Telecaster Custom (Import)
'62 Telecaster Custom (USA)
'62 Mod Squad Custom Telecaster
'62 Telecaster Reissue (Japan)
Junkyard Dog 1962 Telecaster Relic
Vintage Hot Rod '62 Telecaster

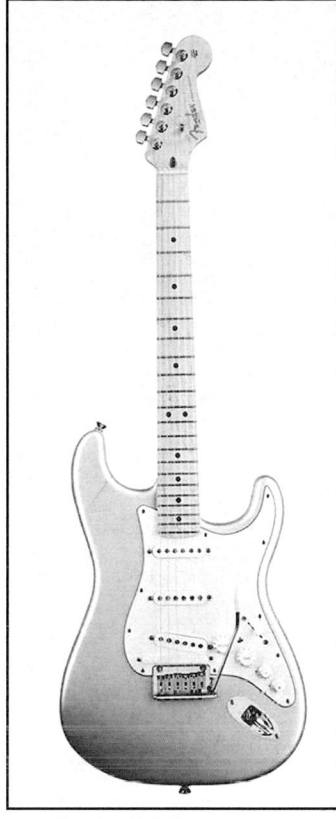

Fender VG Stratocaster

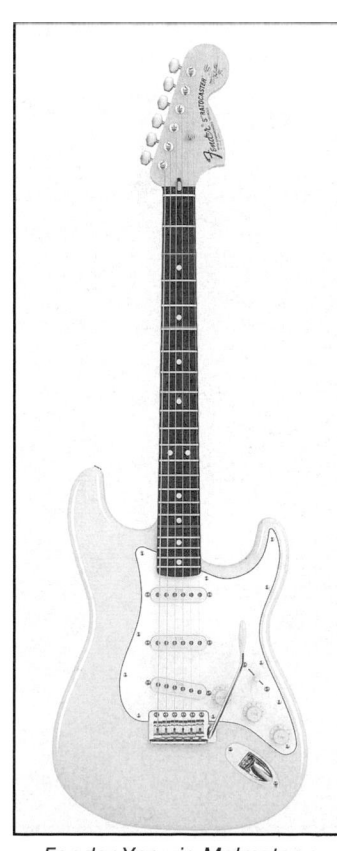

Fender Yngwie Malmsteen Stratocaster

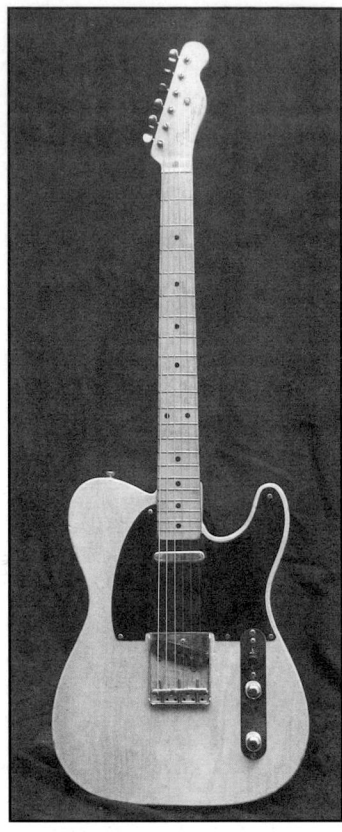

1954 Fender Telecaster

Tom Siska

1957 Fender Telecaster

Tom Siska

'63 Telecaster
'63 Telecaster Custom Relic LTD
'64 Telecaster Limited Relic
American Vintage '64 Telecaster (USA)
'67 Telecaster
'68 Telecaster Rosewood
'69 Tele/Telecaster Thinline (Import)
'69 Telecaster Thinline (Custom Shop)
'72 Custom Telecaster (Import)
'72 Telecaster Reissue (Japan)
'72 Telecaster Deluxe
'72 Telecaster Thinline (Import)
'72 Telecaster Thinline American Vintage
1998 Collectors Edition Telecaster
'90s Tele Thinline
'90s Telecaster Deluxe (Foto-Flame)
Aerodyne Telecaster
Albert Collins Telecaster
Aluminum Telecaster
American Classic Holoflake Telecaster
American Classic Telecaster
American Deluxe HH Telecaster
American Deluxe Power Telecaster
American Deluxe Telecaster
American Special Telecaster
Andy Summers Masterbuilt Tribute Telecaster
Antigua Telecaster
Big Block Telecaster
Bigsby Telecaster
Blacktop Telecaster Series
Blue Flower Telecaster
Bowling Ball/Marble Telecaster
Brown's Canyon Redwood Telecaster
Buck Owens Limited Edition Telecaster
Cabronita Telecaster
Cabronita Telecaster Classic Player
California Fat Telecaster
California Telecaster
Chambered Mahogany Telecaster
Classic Player Baja Telecaster
Collector's Edition Telecaster
Contemporary Telecaster (Import)
Custom Shop Masterbuild Telecaster
Custom Telecaster
Danny Gatton Telecaster
Deluxe Nashville Power Telecaster
Deluxe Nashville Telecaster (Mexico)
Deluxe Telecaster (USA)
Elite Telecaster
Fat Telecaster
Foto Flame Telecaster
G.E. Smith Telecaster
Graham Coxon Telecaster
Highway One Telecaster/Texas Telecaster
HMT Telecaster (Import)
J5 Triple Telecaster Deluxe
James Burton Standard Telecaster
James Burton Telecaster
Jerry Donahue JD Telecaster
Jerry Donahue Telecaster
Jim Adkins JA-90 Telecaster Thinline
Jim Root Telecaster
Jimmy Bryant Tribute Telecaster

Joe Strummer Telecaster
John Jorgenson Telecaster
Jr. Telecaster
Koa Telecaster
Matched Set Telecaster
Merle Haggard Signature Telecaster
Moto Limited Edition Telecaster
Muddy Waters Signature Telecaster Custom
Nashville Telecaster
NHL Premier Edition Telecaster
Old Pine Telecaster
Paisley Telecaster
Plus/Plus Deluxe Telecaster
Rosewood Telecaster
Rosewood Telecaster (Japan)
Select Telecaster
Set-Neck Telecaster
Sparkle Telecaster
Special Telecaster/Telecaster Special
Standard Telecaster (Japan)
Standard Telecaster (Mexico)
Telecaster (Japanese Domestic)
Telecaster Custom
Telecaster Custom (Japan)
Telecaster Custom FMT HH (Korea)
Telecaster Stratocaster Hybrid
Telecaster Thinline
Tele-Sonic
Texas Special Telecaster
Twisted Telecaster Limited Edition
Vintage Hot Rod Telecaster
Waylon Jennings Tribute Telecaster
Will Ray Jazz-A-Caster
Will Ray Mojo Telecaster

Telecaster

1951-1982. See Standard Telecaster (following listing) for '82-'85, American Standard Telecaster for '88-2000 and American Series Telecaster for 2000-'07. Renamed American Standard Telecaster again in '08. In the late '60s and early '70s Fender began to increase their use of vibrato tailpieces. A vibrato tailpiece for this period is generally worth about 13% less than the values shown. Please refer to the Fender Guitar Intro Section for details on Fender color options. The "rare color" listing have a wide range due to the various colors included in that category.

From '63-'70, Fender offered both the standard Brazilian rosewood fretboard and an optional maple fretboard. Prices listed here, for those years, are for the rosewood 'board models. Currently, the market considers the maple 'board to be a premium, so guitars with maple, for those years, are worth 10% to 15% more than the values shown.

MODEL YEAR	FEATURES	EXC. COND. LOW	HIGH
1951	Blond, black 'guard	$33,000	$41,000
1952	Blond, black 'guard	$32,000	$40,000
1953	Blond, black 'guard	$29,000	$37,000
1954	Blond, black 'guard	$26,000	$33,000

MODEL YEAR	FEATURES	EXC. COND. LOW	HIGH
1954	Blond, white 'guard	$24,000	$30,000
1955	Blond, white 'guard	$23,000	$29,000
1956	Blond	$20,000	$26,000
1957	Blond	$17,000	$22,200
1958	Blond, backloader	$16,000	$20,200
1958	Blond, top loader	$15,000	$19,200
1958	Sunburst, backloader	$18,500	$23,500
1958	Sunburst, top loader	$17,000	$22,000
1959	Blond, maple	$15,000	$19,200
1959	Blond, slab	$14,000	$18,200
1959	Custom colors	$30,000	$45,000
1959	Sunburst, maple	$18,000	$22,000
1959	Sunburst, slab	$17,000	$21,000
1960	Blond, slab	$14,000	$18,000
1960	Common colors	$20,000	$28,000
1960	Rare colors	$28,000	$42,000
1960	Sunburst, slab	$16,500	$20,500
1961	Blond, slab	$13,000	$16,700
1961	Common colors	$18,000	$25,000
1961	Rare colors	$25,000	$37,000
1961	Sunburst, slab	$16,000	$19,500
1962	Blond, curved	$11,000	$14,200
1962	Blond, slab	$12,000	$15,200
1962	Common colors	$17,000	$24,000
1962	Rare colors	$24,000	$34,000
1962	Sunburst, curved	$14,000	$18,000
1962	Sunburst, slab	$15,500	$19,000
1963	Blond	$11,000	$14,200
1963	Common colors	$17,000	$24,000
1963	Rare colors	$23,000	$33,000
1963	Sunburst	$14,000	$18,000
1964	Blond	$9,500	$12,200
1964	Common colors	$15,000	$21,000
1964	Rare colors	$21,000	$29,000
1964	Sunburst	$12,000	$15,000
1965	Blond	$8,000	$10,500
1965	Common colors	$12,000	$16,500
1965	Rare colors	$16,500	$23,000
1965	Sunburst	$9,500	$11,800
1966	Blond	$6,500	$8,000
1966	Common colors	$10,000	$13,800
1966	Rare colors	$13,800	$19,000
1966	Sunburst	$8,300	$10,400
1967	Blond	$6,000	$7,500
1967	Blond, smuggler	$8,700	$10,800
1967	Common colors	$10,000	$13,800
1967	Rare colors	$13,800	$19,000
1967	Sunburst	$7,800	$9,600
1968	Blond	$6,000	$7,500
1968	Blue Flower	$10,500	$13,200
1968	Common colors	$10,000	$13,800
1968	Rare colors	$13,800	$19,000
1968	Red (Pink) Paisley	$10,500	$13,200
1968	Sunburst	$7,200	$9,000
1969	Blond	$5,900	$7,400
1969	Blue Flower	$10,500	$13,200
1969	Common colors	$10,000	$13,800

MODEL YEAR	FEATURES	EXC. COND. LOW	HIGH
1969	Rare colors	$13,800	$19,000
1969	Red (Pink) Paisley	$10,500	$13,200
1969	Sunburst	$6,200	$7,700
1970	Blond	$4,000	$5,000
1970	Common colors	$7,000	$9,300
1970	Rare colors	$9,300	$13,000
1970	Sunburst	$4,300	$5,300
1971	Blond	$3,500	$4,300
1971	Common colors	$6,000	$7,000
1971	Rare colors	$7,000	$9,000
1971	Sunburst	$3,600	$4,500
1972	Blond	$3,500	$4,300
1972	Common colors	$3,800	$4,700
1972	Rare colors	$4,700	$6,500
1972	Sunburst	$3,600	$4,500
1973	Black, Olympic White	$3,500	$4,300
1973	Blond	$3,500	$4,300
1973	Natural	$2,400	$3,000
1973	Rare colors	$4,000	$6,000
1973	Sunburst	$3,000	$3,800
1973	Walnut	$2,800	$3,600
1974	Black, blond, Olympic White	$3,300	$4,100
1974	Natural	$2,300	$2,900
1974	Sunburst	$2,600	$3,300
1974	Walnut	$2,500	$3,200
1975	Black, blond, Olympic White	$2,200	$2,800
1975	Natural	$2,200	$2,800
1975	Sunburst	$2,200	$2,800
1975	Walnut	$2,200	$2,800
1976	Black, blond, Olympic White	$2,200	$2,800
1976	Natural	$2,200	$2,800
1976	Sunburst	$2,200	$2,800
1976	Walnut	$2,200	$2,800
1977	Antigua	$2,200	$2,800
1977	Black, blond, Olympic White	$2,200	$2,800
1977	Natural	$2,200	$2,800
1977	Sunburst	$2,200	$2,800
1977	Walnut	$2,200	$2,800
1978	Antigua	$2,200	$2,800
1978	Black, blond, Olympic White, Wine	$2,200	$2,800
1978	Natural	$2,200	$2,800
1978	Sunburst	$2,200	$2,800
1978	Walnut	$2,200	$2,800
1979	Antigua	$2,000	$2,500
1979	Black, blond, Olympic White, Wine	$2,000	$2,500
1979	Natural	$2,000	$2,500
1979	Sunburst	$2,000	$2,500
1979	Walnut	$2,000	$2,500
1980	Antigua	$2,000	$2,500
1980	Black, blond, Olympic White, Wine	$1,800	$2,300

1973 Fender Telecaster
Bob Ohsiek

1978 Fender Telecaster
Robbie Keene

To get the most from this book, be sure to read "Using *The Guide*" in the introduction.

GUITARS

*1982 Fender American
Vintage '52 Telecaster*

Billy White Jr.

Fender '60 Telecaster Custom

MODEL YEAR	FEATURES	EXC. COND. LOW	HIGH
1980	International colors	$2,000	$2,500
1980	Natural	$1,500	$1,900
1980	Sunburst	$1,500	$1,900
1981	Black and Gold	$1,700	$2,200
1981	Black, blond, Olympic White, Wine	$1,700	$2,200
1981	International colors	$1,950	$2,450
1981	Sunburst	$1,500	$1,900

Standard Telecaster

1982-1984. See Telecaster for '51-'82, and American Standard Telecaster (following listing) for '88-2000. Not to be confused with the current Standard Telecaster, which is made in Mexico.

1982-1984	Blond, sunburst	$1,175	$1,475

American Standard Telecaster

1988-2000, 2008-present. Name used when Fender reissued the standard American-made Tele after CBS sold the company. The only American-made Tele available for '86 and '87 was the '52 Telecaster. See Telecaster for '51-'81, and Standard Telecaster for '82-'84. All '94 models have a metal 40th Anniversary pin on the headstock, but should not be confused with the actual 40th Anniversary Telecaster model (see separate listing), all standard colors. Renamed the American Series Telecaster in 2000, then back to American Standard Telecaster in '08.

1988-2000		$800	$1,000
2008-2013		$800	$1,000

American Series Telecaster

2000-2007. See Telecaster for '51-'81, Standard Telecaster for '82-'84, and American Standard for '88-'99. Renamed American Standard again in '08.

2000-2007		$800	$1,000

30th Anniversary Guitar Center Tree of Life Telecaster

1994. Produced for 30th anniversary of Guitar Center, engraved neckplate with GC logo, tree-of-life 'board inlay.

1994		$3,800	$4,800

40th Anniversary Telecaster

1988, 1999. Custom Shop model limited edition run of 300, 2-piece flamed maple top, gold hardware ('88), flamed maple top over ash body, gold hardware ('99).

1988	1st run, higher-end	$5,000	$6,300
1999	2nd run, plain top	$4,000	$5,000

'50 Custom Telecaster

1997. Custom Shop model, limited run of 10, humbucker neck pickup, standard unbound body, highly figured maple neck, blackguard specs.

1997		$1,800	$2,200

'50s Telecaster/Classic Series '50s Telecaster

1990-present. Made in Japan (basswood body) until mid '99, then in Mexico with ash body. Foto-Flame finish offered in '94 (see separate listing).

1990-1999	Japan	$700	$900
1999-2014	Mexico	$500	$625

Road Worn '50s Telecaster

2009-present. Maple 'board, '50s specs, aged finish.

2009-2014		$575	$725

50th Anniversary Spanish Guitar Set Custom Shop

1996. 50 sets made, Tele Prototype reproduction with similar era copy of woodie amp.

1996		$4,600	$5,800

50th Anniversary Telecaster

1995-1996. Custom Shop model, flame maple top, 2 vintage-style pickups, gold hardware, sunburst, gold 50th Anniversary coin on back of the headstock, 1250 made.

1995-1996		$1,400	$1,750

'52 Telecaster/American Vintage '52 Telecaster

1982-present. Ash body, maple neck or rosewood 'board, blond.

1982-1984		$2,450	$3,050
1986-1999		$1,225	$1,525
1990-1999	Copper (limited number)	$1,100	$1,375
2000-2014		$1,100	$1,375

'52 Telecaster (Custom Shop)

2004-present. Custom Shop Dealer Select model, changed to Heavy Relic in '15.

2004-2012	NOS	$1,800	$2,200
2004-2014	Relic	$2,200	$2,800
2010	Heavy relic	$2,200	$2,800

'58 Telecaster (Custom Shop)

2008. Custom Shop, Relic and Heavy Relic.

2008		$2,200	$2,800

'60s Telecaster Custom

1997-1999. Custom Shop, bound alder body, sunburst, black or custom colors, nickel or gold hardware.

1997-1999		$2,000	$2,500

'60s Telecaster/Classic Series '60s Telecaster

1992-present. Made in Japan (basswood body) until mid '99, then in Mexico with ash body. Foto-Flame finish offered in '94 (see separate listing).

1999-2014		$550	$700

'60 Telecaster Custom

2003-2004. Custom Shop Time Machine, bound alder body, offered in NOS, Closet Classic and Relic versions and in sunburst, CA Red and Sonic Blue.

2003-2004	Closet Classic	$1,900	$2,400
2003-2004	NOS	$1,800	$2,300
2003-2004	Relic	$2,000	$2,500

60th Anniversary American Telecaster

2006-2007. Special Edition commemorating Fender's 60th year, banner headstock 60th logo, neck plate reads Diamond Anniversary 1946-2006, made in U.S.A., rosewood 'board, sunburst.

2006-2007		$900	$1,125

60th Anniversary Telecaster Limited Edition

2006. Limited Edition of 1,000, 60 Diamond Anniversary 1946-2006 logo engraved in neck plate, American Flag logo on pickguard, '51 NoCaster pickup layout, 60 wood inlay on the face below bridge, clear nitro finish on natural ash body, silver guitar case with Fender 60 logo on inside lid.

2006		$1,300	$1,625

MODEL YEAR	FEATURES	EXC. COND. LOW	HIGH

60th Anniversary Telecaster (USA)
2011-2012. Celebrating 60 years of the Tele, commemorative chrome neck plate, ash body, blonde thin-skin finish.

2011-2012		$900	$1,125

'61 Telecaster Custom
2010-2012. Custom Shop Dealer Select model, bound body Custom, NOS, Relic or Heavy Relic.

2010-2012	Closet Classic	$2,000	$2,500
2010-2012	NOS	$1,800	$2,200
2010-2012	Relic	$2,200	$2,700

'62 Telecaster Custom (Import)
1985-1999. Made in Japan, bound top and back, rosewood 'board, sunburst or red.

1985-1989		$900	$1,125
1990-1999		$800	$1,000

'62 Telecaster Custom (USA)
1999-2012. American Vintage Series, rosewood board.

1999-2012		$800	$1,000

'62 Mod Squad Custom Telecaster
2013. Custom Shop, Broadcaster bridge pickup and Duncan neck humbucker.

2013		$2,200	$2,800

'62 Telecaster Reissue (Japan)
1989-1990, 2005-2006. Made by Fender Japan.

1989-1990		$800	$1,000
2005-2006		$700	$875

Junkyard Dog 1962 Telecaster Relic
2014-present. Custom Shop Dealer Select series, ash body, rosewood neck and 'board, white guard, Vintage Blonde.

2014		$2,600	$3,400

Vintage Hot Rod '62 Telecaster
2007-2014. Vintage styling with modern features.

2007-2014		$1,050	$1,300

'63 Telecaster
1999-2010. Custom Shop, alder body (or blond on ash), original spec pickups, C-shaped neck, rosewood 'board.

1999-2010	Closet Classic	$2,000	$2,500
1999-2010	NOS	$1,800	$2,200
2007	Relic	$2,200	$2,800

'63 Telecaster Custom Relic LTD
2006. Custom Shop, Limited Edition.

2006		$2,200	$2,700

'64 Telecaster Limited Relic
2009. Custom Shop, rosewood 'board, thin nitro finish, 50 each of black, aged white, and 3-tone chocolate sunburst.

2009		$2,200	$2,800

American Vintage '64 Telecaster (USA)
2013-present. Rounded rosewood 'board.

2013-2014		$1,275	$1,600

'67 Telecaster
2005-2008, 2010-2011. Custom Shop, alder body, rosewood or maple 'board, Relic, NOS or Closet Classic, 2010 and later is rosewood 'board, Relic or NOS.

2005-2008	Closet Classic	$2,000	$2,500
2005-2011	NOS	$1,800	$2,200
2005-2011	Relic	$2,200	$2,800

'68 Telecaster Rosewood
Custom Shop, rosewood body.

2007	NOS	$1,800	$2,200

'69 Tele/Telecaster Thinline (Import)
1986-present. Import, Classic Series, 2 Tele pickups.

1986-1989	Japan	$875	$1,100
1990-1999	Japan	$750	$925
2000-2014	Mexico	$550	$675

'69 Telecaster Thinline (Custom Shop)
2005-2006. Semi-hollow mahoganhy body, maple neck with maple 'board.

2005-2006		$1,900	$2,400

'72 Custom Telecaster (Import)
1986-present. Import, Classic Series, 1 humbucker and 1 single-coil, 2 humbuckers after '99.

1986-1989	Japan	$900	$1,125
1990-1999	Japan	$800	$1,000
2000-2014	Mexico	$500	$700

'72 Telecaster Relssue (Japan)
1994. Made by Fender Japan for Japanese domestic market.

1994		$700	$900

'72 Telecaster Deluxe
2004-present. Classic Series, large Deluxe 'guard, 2 humbuckers.

2004-2014		$475	$600

'72 Telecaster Thinline (Import)
1986-present. Import, Classic Series, 2 humbuckers, f-hole.

1986-1999	Japan	$750	$925
2000-2014	Mexico	$500	$625

'72 Telecaster Thinline American Vintage
2012-2013. US-made, American Vintage FSR model, f-hole, 2 humbuckers.

2012-2013		$1,000	$1,250

1998 Collectors Edition Telecaster
1998. 1,998 made, 1998 logo inlay on 'board, maple, gold hardware.

1998		$1,250	$1,575

'90s Tele Thinline
1998-2001. Bound semi-hollow ash body, f-hole, white or brown shell 'guard, 2 single-coils, sunburst, black, natural, or transparent crimson.

1998-2001		$1,800	$2,250

'90s Telecaster Deluxe (Foto-Flame)
1995-1998. Import, 1 Tele-style bridge pickup and 2 Strat-style pickups, rosewood 'board, Foto Flame '95-'97 and standard finishes '97-'98.

1995-1997	Foto-Flame	$625	$775
1997-1998	Standard finish	$625	$775

Aerodyne Telecaster
2004-2009. Imported Tele with Aerodyne body profile, bound body, black.

2004-2009		$600	$750

Albert Collins Telecaster
1990-present. U.S.-made Custom Shop signature model, bound swamp ash body, humbucker pickup in neck position.

1990-2013	Natural	$1,200	$1,500
1995	Silver sparkle	$1,300	$1,600

Fender '72 Telecaster Thinline American Vintage

Fender Albert Collins Telecaster

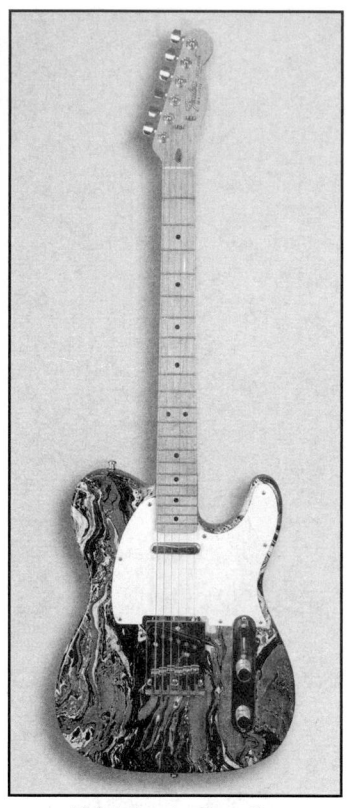

1984 Fender Bowling Ball Telecaster

'Lone Wolf'

Fender Danny Gatton Telecaster

MODEL YEAR	FEATURES	EXC. COND. LOW	HIGH
Aluminum Telecaster			
1994-1995. Aluminum-bodied American Standard with anodized finish in blue marble, purple marble or red, silver and blue stars and stripes.			
1994-1995	Marble patterns	$1,600	$2,000
1994-1995	Red-silver-blue flag option	$2,000	$2,500
American Classic Holoflake Telecaster			
1996-1999. Custom Shop model, splatter/sparkle finish, pearloid 'guard.			
1996-1999		$1,300	$1,600
American Classic Telecaster			
1996-1999. Custom Shop model, handcrafted version of American Standard, thin lacquer-finished ash body, maple or rosewood 'board, various options and colors, earlier versions had gold hardware and custom-color options.			
1996-1999		$1,300	$1,600
American Deluxe HH Telecaster			
2004-2006. Rosewood, maple top, 2 humbucker pickups.			
2004-2006		$1,000	$1,250
American Deluxe Power Telecaster			
1999-2001. Made in USA, with Fishman power bridge piezo pickups.			
1999-2001		$1,000	$1,250
American Deluxe Telecaster			
1998-present. Premium ash or alder body with see-thru finishes.			
1998-2014		$1,000	$1,250
American Special Telecaster			
2010-present. Alder body, gloss finish, Texas Special pickups.			
2010-2014		$600	$750
Andy Summers Masterbuilt Tribute Telecaster			
2009. Custom shop, based on Summer's '61 Tele, heavy relic, 250 made, custom electronics rear-mounted overdrive unit controlled by a third knob, includes DVD, strap and Andy Summer's logo travel guitar case.			
2009		$7,000	$9,000
Antigua Telecaster			
2004. Made in Japan, limited edition (400 made) reissue, '70s features and antigua finish.			
2004		$625	$800
Big Block Telecaster			
2005-2006. Pearloid block markers, black with matching headstock, 3 single-coils with center pickup reverse wound.			
2005-2006		$600	$750
Bigsby Telecaster			
2003. Made in Mexico, standard Tele specs with original Fender-logo Bigsby tailpiece.			
2003		$525	$650
Blacktop Telecaster Series			
2012-present. Includes 2 humbucker HH and hum-single-single Baritone.			
2012-2014		$300	$375
Blue Flower Telecaster			
1985-1993, 2003-2004. Import, Blue Flower finish.			
1985-1993	1st issue	$1,100	$1,350
2003-2004	2nd issue	$500	$625

MODEL YEAR	FEATURES	EXC. COND. LOW	HIGH
Bowling Ball/Marble Telecaster			
1984. Standard Tele, called Bowling Ball Tele due to the swirling, colored finish.			
1984	Blue	$2,500	$3,100
1984	Red	$2,500	$3,100
1984	Yellow	$2,500	$3,100
Brown's Canyon Redwood Telecaster			
2011. For Fender's 60th anniversary in 2011, they released 12 limited edition U.S.-made Tele-bration Telecasters, including this one with body made from 1890s California redwood.			
2011		$1,300	$1,650
Buck Owens Limited Edition Telecaster			
1998. Red, white and blue sparkle finish, gold hardware, gold 'guard, rosewood 'board.			
1998-2002		$1,400	$1,775
Cabronita Telecaster			
2011. For Fender's 60th anniversary in 2011, they released 12 limited edition U.S.-made Tele-bration Telecasters, including this one with 2 TV Jones Filter'Trons.			
2011		$900	$1,200
Cabronita Telecaster Classic Player			
2014-present. Mexico version.			
2014-2015		$325	$400
California Fat Telecaster			
1997-1998. Alder body, maple fretboard, Tex-Mex humbucker and Tele pickup configuration.			
1997-1998		$625	$775
California Telecaster			
1997-1998. Alder body, maple fretboard, sunburst, Tex-Mex Strat and Tele pickup configuration.			
1997-1998		$625	$775
Chambered Mahogany Telecaster			
2006. U.S.-made, chambered mahogany body, Delta Tone System.			
2006		$950	$1,200
Classic Player Baja Telecaster			
2007-present. Made in Mexico, Custom Shop designed neck plate logo, thin gloss poly blond finish.			
2007-2014		$500	$600
Collector's Edition Telecaster			
1998. Mid-1955 specs including white 'guard, offered in sunburst with gold hardware (which was an option in '55), 1,998 made.			
1998		$1,300	$1,625
Contemporary Telecaster (Import)			
1985-1987. Japanese-made while the new Fender reorganized, 2 or 3 pickups, vibrato, black chrome hardware, rosewood 'board.			
1985-1987		$600	$750
Custom Shop Masterbuild Telecaster			
2006-present. Various models and builders, specific identification to builder, must include certificate of authenticity.			
2006-2014	Various models	$3,000	$6,000
Custom Telecaster			
1972-1981. One humbucking and 1 Tele pickup, standard colors, see Telecaster Custom for 2 Tele pickup/bound body version.			
1972		$2,800	$3,500

MODEL YEAR	FEATURES	EXC. COND. LOW	HIGH
1973		$2,700	$3,400
1974-1979		$2,700	$3,400
1980-1981		$2,500	$3,200

Danny Gatton Telecaster
1990-present. Custom Shop model, like '53 Telecaster, maple neck, 2 humbuckers.

1990-1999	Frost Gold	$2,200	$2,800
2000-2014	Various colors	$1,800	$2,200

Deluxe Nashville Power Telecaster
1999-2014. Like Deluxe Nashville, but with piezo transducer in each saddle.

1999-2014		$525	$650

Deluxe Nashville Telecaster (Mexico)
1997-present. Tex-Mex Strat and Tele pickup configuration, various colors.

1997-2014		$460	$575

Deluxe Telecaster (USA)
1972-1981. Two humbuckers, various colors Mexican-made version offered starting in 2004.

1972		$2,800	$3,600
1973		$2,700	$3,500
1974-1981		$2,500	$3,300

Elite Telecaster
1983-1985. Two active humbucker pickups, 3-way switch, 2 volume knobs, 1 presence and filter controls, chrome hardware, various colors.

1983-1985		$1,700	$2,100

Fat Telecaster
1999-2001. Humbucker pickup in neck, Tele bridge pickup.

1999-2001		$550	$700

Foto Flame Telecaster
1994-1996. Import, sunburst or transparent.

1994-1996		$650	$800

G.E. Smith Telecaster
2007-2014. Swamp ash body, vintage style hardware, U-shaped neck, oval and diamond inlays.

2007-2014		$1,000	$1,250

Graham Coxon Telecaster
2011, 2013-2014. Blond, Tele bridge and humbucker neck pickup, rosewood 'board, limited run in 2011.

2011		$900	$1,100

Highway One Telecaster/Texas Telecaster
2003-2011. U.S.-made, alder body, satin lacquer finish, Texas version (introduced in '04) has ash body and Hot Vintage pickups.

2003-2011		$525	$650

HMT Telecaster (Import)
1990-1993. Japanese-made Metal-Rock Tele, available with or without Floyd Rose tremolo, 1 Fender Lace Sensor pickup and 1 DiMarzio bridge humbucker pickup, black.

1990-1993		$350	$425

J5 Triple Telecaster Deluxe
2007-present. John 5 model, made in Mexico, 3 humbuckers, medium jumbo frets.

2007-2014		$550	$800

James Burton Standard Telecaster
1995-present. Mexico, 2 Texas Special Tele pickups, standard colors (no paisley).

1995-2014		$450	$575

James Burton Telecaster
1990-present. Ash body, 3 Fender Lace pickups, available in black with Gold Paisley, black with Candy Red Paisley, Pearl White, and Frost Red until '05. In '06 in black with red or blue flame-shaped paisley, or Pearl White.

1990-2005	Black & gold paisley, gold hw	$1,400	$1,750
1990-2005	Black & red paisley, black hw	$1,050	$1,325
1990-2010	Frost Red or Pearl White	$925	$1,150
2006-2014	Paisley flames	$925	$1,150

Jerry Donahue JD Telecaster
1993-1999. Made in Japan, Custom Strat neck pickup and Custom Tele bridge pickup, basswood body, special "V" shaped maple neck.

1993-1999		$800	$1,000

Jerry Donahue Telecaster
1992-2001. Custom Shop model designed by Donahue, Tele bridge pickup and Strat neck pickup, birdseye maple neck, top and back, gold hardware, passive circuitry, sunburst, transparent Crimson Red or Sapphire Blue. There was also a Japanese-made JD Telecaster.

1992		$1,500	$1,900
1993-1999		$1,300	$1,625

Jim Adkins JA-90 Telecaster Thinline
2008-present. Rosewood 'board, vintage-style P-90 soapbars.

2008-2014		$525	$650

Jim Root Telecaster
2007-present. Made in Mexico, black hardware, mahogany body.

2007-2014		$850	$1,050

Jimmy Bryant Tribute Telecaster
2004-2005. Custom Shop model, hand-tooled leather 'guard overlay with JB initials.

2004-2005		$2,000	$2,500

Joe Strummer Telecaster
2007-2009. Limited edition, heavily relic'd based on Strummer's '66 Tele, Fender offered a limited edition art customization kit as part of the package.

2007-2009		$650	$825

John Jorgenson Telecaster
1998-2001. Custom Shop, korina body, double-coil stacked pickups, sparkle or black finish.

1998-2001	Sparkle	$2,000	$2,500

Jr. Telecaster
1994, 1997-2000. Custom Shop model, transparent blond ash body, 2 P-90-style pickups, set neck, 11 tone chambers, 100 made in '94, reintroduced in '97.

1994		$1,900	$2,400
1997-2000		$1,750	$2,200

Koa Telecaster
2006-2008. Made in Korea, Special Edition series, standard Tele specs, koa veneer top over basswood body, pearloid 'guard, sunburst.

2006-2008		$400	$500

Fender Deluxe Nashville Power Telecaster

2008 Fender Joe Strummer Telecaster

Rick Hanson

*Fender Merle Haggard
Signature Telecaster*

Fender Telecaster Custom

Travis Adkinson

MODEL YEAR	FEATURES	EXC. COND. LOW	HIGH

Matched Set Telecaster
1994. Matching Tele and Strat Custom Shop models, model name on certificate is "Matched Set Telecaster", 3 sets were built, each set has serial number 1, 2, or 3.

1994		$3,100	$3,800

Merle Haggard Signature Telecaster
2009-present. Custom Shop, figured maple body and neck, maple 'board, 2-color sunburst.

2009-2014		$2,900	$3,700

Moto Limited Edition Telecaster
1990s. Custom Shop model, pearloid cover in various colors. There were also Strat and Jag versions.

1990s		$2,300	$2,900

Muddy Waters Signature Telecaster Custom
2001-2009. Mexico, Fender amp control knobs, Telecaster Custom on headstock, Muddy Waters signature logo on neck plate, Candy Apple Red.

2001-2009		$700	$900

Nashville Telecaster
1995. Custom Shop model, 3 pickups.

1995		$1,900	$2,400

NHL Premier Edition Telecaster
1999-2000. Limited edition of 100 guitars with NHL hockey art logo on the top.

1999-2000	All models	$1,400	$1,750

Nokie Edwards Telecaster
1996. Made in Japan, limited edition, book matched flamed top, multi-lam neck, Seymour Duncan pickups, gold hardware, zero fret, tilted headstock.

1996		$1,600	$2,000

Old Pine Telecaster
2011. For Fender's 60th anniversary in 2011, they released 12 limited edition U.S.-made Tele-bration Telecasters, including this one with 100-year-old pine body, 300 made.

2011		$1,300	$1,600

Paisley Telecaster
1986-1998, 2003-2004, 2008. Import, 'Made in Japan' logo used until '98, 'Crafted in Japan' after, Pink Paisley finish.

1986-1987		$1,200	$1,500
1988-1998		$1,100	$1,350
2003-2004		$650	$800
2008	600 made	$650	$800

Plus/Plus Deluxe Telecaster
1990-1997. Tele with Strat 3-pickup combination, Deluxe has added Strat-style tremolo system, various colors.

1990-1997	2 pickups	$1,400	$1,800
1990-1997	3 pickups	$1,400	$1,800

Rosewood Telecaster
1969-1972. Rosewood body and neck.

1969-1972		$10,000	$15,000

Rosewood Telecaster (Japan)
1986-1996. Japanese-made reissue, rosewood body and neck.

1986	1st year	$2,500	$3,100
1987-1996		$2,300	$2,900

MODEL YEAR	FEATURES	EXC. COND. LOW	HIGH

Select Telecaster
2012-2013. Select Series, carved figured top, rear-headstock 'Fender Select' medallion, gloss-lacquer finish, various colors.

2012-2013		$1,500	$1,900

Set-Neck Telecaster
1990-1996. Glued-in neck, Custom Shop, 2 humbucking pickups, Set-Neck CA (Country Artist) has 1 humbucker and 1 Tele pickup, various colors.

1990-1996		$1,800	$2,250

Sparkle Telecaster
1993-1995. Custom Shop model, poplar body, white 'guard, sparkle finish: champagne, gold, silver.

1993-1995		$1,650	$2,050

Special Telecaster/Telecaster Special
2004-2008. Made in Mexico, Special Edition logo with star logo sticker on back of headstock, special features like 6-way bridge and modern tuners.

2004-2008		$450	$560

Standard Telecaster (Japan)
1985-1989. In '85, the only Teles were interim production in Japan while the new Fender reorganized, no serial number, Japan headstock logo in '85, back of neck '86-'89

1985		$700	$900
1986-1989		$600	$800

Standard Telecaster (Mexico)
1990-present. Guitar production at the Mexico facility started in '90. High end of range includes a hard guitar case, while the low end of the range includes only a gig bag, various colors.

1990-1999		$300	$375
2000-2014		$300	$375

Telecaster (Japanese Domestic)
1982-1997. Made in Japan for Japanese domestic market (not for export), suffix serial numbers JV5 ('82-'84) and A6 through V6 ('84-'97).

1982-1984	JV serial	$900	$1,100
1985-1997		$600	$750

Telecaster Custom
1959-1972. Body bound top and back, rosewood 'board, 2 Tele pickups, see Custom Telecaster for the 1 Tele/1 humbucker version. Please refer to the Fender Guitar Intro Section for details on Fender color options.

1959	Sunburst, maple	$23,000	$29,000
1960	Custom colors	$26,000	$60,000
1960	Sunburst	$22,000	$28,000
1961	Custom colors	$26,000	$60,000
1961	Sunburst	$21,000	$27,000
1962	Custom colors	$22,000	$50,000
1962	Sunburst, curved	$16,000	$20,000
1962	Sunburst, slab	$20,000	$25,000
1963	Custom colors	$22,000	$40,000
1963	Sunburst	$17,000	$21,000
1964	Custom colors	$20,000	$37,000
1964	Sunburst	$13,500	$20,000
1965	Custom colors	$17,000	$32,000
1965	Sunburst	$11,000	$17,000
1966	Custom colors	$13,000	$23,000
1966	Sunburst	$10,000	$13,000

MODEL YEAR	FEATURES	EXC. COND. LOW	HIGH
1967	Custom colors	$12,000	$20,000
1967	Sunburst	$9,000	$12,000
1968	Custom colors	$12,000	$20,000
1968	Sunburst	$9,000	$12,000
1969	Custom colors	$9,500	$19,000
1969	Sunburst	$8,500	$11,000
1970	Custom colors	$9,000	$14,500
1970	Sunburst	$8,000	$10,000
1971	Custom colors	$8,000	$13,500
1971	Sunburst, 3-bolt	$3,700	$4,600
1971	Sunburst, 4-bolt	$7,000	$9,000
1972	Custom colors, 3-bolt	$4,500	$6,800
1972	Sunburst, 3-bolt	$3,700	$4,600

Telecaster Custom (Japan)

1985. Made in Japan during the period when Fender suspended all USA manufacturing in '85, Tele Custom specs including bound body.

1985		$900	$1,125

Telecaster Custom FMT HH (Korea)

2003-present. Part of Special Edition, Korean-made, flamed maple top, 2 humbuckers.

2003-2014		$575	$725

Telecaster Stratocaster Hybrid

2006. Custom Shop model, Tele body shape, Strat pickup system and wiring, Strat headstock shape, dot markers on rosewood board, reissue tremolo, includes Custom Shop Certificate that reads "Telecaster Stratocaster Hybrid".

2006		$2,000	$2,500

Telecaster Thinline

1968-1980. Semi-hollowbody, 1 f-hole, 2 Tele pickups, ash or mahogany body, in late-'71 the tilt neck was added and the 2 Tele pickups were switched to 2 humbuckers. Please refer to the Fender Guitar Intro Section for details on Fender color options.

1968	Common colors	$10,000	$13,800
1968	Natural ash	$6,700	$8,400
1968	Natural mahogany	$6,700	$8,400
1968	Rare colors	$13,800	$19,000
1968	Sunburst	$8,000	$10,000
1969	Common colors	$10,000	$13,800
1969	Natural ash	$6,700	$8,400
1969	Natural mahogany	$6,700	$8,400
1969	Rare colors	$13,800	$19,000
1969	Sunburst	$8,000	$10,000
1970	Common colors	$7,000	$9,300
1970	Natural ash	$4,000	$5,000
1970	Natural mahogany	$4,000	$5,000
1970	Rare colors	$9,300	$13,000
1970	Sunburst	$4,800	$6,000
1971	Color option, 3-bolt, humbuckers	$3,600	$5,600
1971	Color option, 4-bolt	$7,000	$12,000
1971	Natural ash, 3-bolt	$3,000	$3,800
1971	Natural ash, 3-bolt, humbuckers	$3,100	$3,800
1971	Natural ash, 4-bolt	$3,500	$4,300
1971	Natural mahogany, 3-bolt	$3,000	$3,800

MODEL YEAR	FEATURES	EXC. COND. LOW	HIGH
1971	Natural mahogany, 3-bolt, humbuckers	$3,100	$3,800
1971	Natural mahogany, 4-bolt	$3,500	$4,300
1971	Sunburst, 3-bolt, humbuckers	$3,000	$3,800
1971	Sunburst, 4-bolt	$4,100	$5,000
1972	Common colors	$3,600	$4,500
1972	Mahogany	$3,100	$3,800
1972	Natural ash	$3,100	$3,800
1972	Rare colors	$4,500	$5,600
1972	Sunburst	$3,000	$3,800
1973	Color option	$3,300	$4,100
1973	Mahogany	$2,900	$3,600
1973	Natural ash	$2,900	$3,600
1973	Sunburst	$2,900	$3,600
1974	Color option	$3,300	$4,100
1974	Mahogany	$2,500	$3,200
1974	Natural ash	$2,500	$3,200
1974	Sunburst	$2,500	$3,200
1975-1978	Color option	$3,300	$4,100
1975-1978	Natural ash	$2,500	$3,200
1975-1978	Sunburst	$2,500	$3,200

Tele-Sonic

1998-2000. U.S.A., chambered Telecaster body, 2 DeArmond pickups, dot markers, upper bass bout 3-way toggle switch.

1998-2000		$850	$1,050

Texas Special Telecaster

1991-1992. Custom Shop model, 60 made, state of Texas outline on the 'guard, ash body with Texas Orange transparent finish, large profile maple neck, with certificate of authenticity.

1991-1992		$1,900	$2,400

Twisted Telecaster Limited Edition

2005. Custom Shop, 50 built by Master Builder Yuriy Shishkov, 100 built by the Custom Shop team, top loaded Bigsby.

2005	Shishkov built	$2,900	$3,700
2005	Team built	$2,200	$2,700

Vintage Hot Rod Telecaster

2007-2014. Vintage styling with modern features, '07-'13 named '52 Tele and '62 Tele, in '14 changed to '50s, and '60s.

2007-2014	'52, '62, '50s or '60s	$1,100	$1,400

Waylon Jennings Tribute Telecaster

1995-2003. Custom Shop, black with white leather rose body inlays.

1995-2003		$5,800	$7,500

Will Ray Jazz-A-Caster

1997. Made in Fender Japan Custom Shop as one part of the three part Hellecasters Series, limited edition, Strat neck on a Tele body with 2 soap-bar Seymour Duncan Jazzmaster-style pickups, gold leaf finish.

1997		$1,000	$1,250

Will Ray Mojo Telecaster

1998-2001. Custom Shop, ash body, flamed maple Strat neck, locking tuners, rosewood 'board, skull inlays, double coil pickups, optional Hipshot B bender.

1998-2001		$2,500	$3,100

1972 Fender Telecaster Custom
Robbie Keene

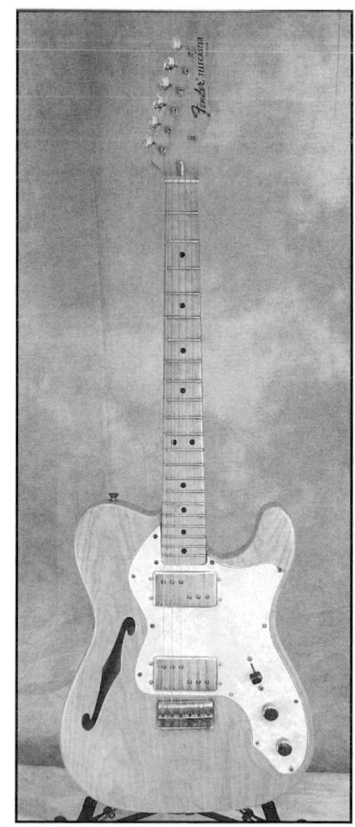

1972 Fender Telecaster Thinline

2012 Fender California Series Villager 12-String

Fine Resophonic Custom Model 2

MODEL YEAR	FEATURES	EXC. COND. LOW	HIGH

Toronado
1998-2006. Deluxe Series made in Mexico, 2 humbuckers.

1998-2006		$475	$625

Villager 12-String
1965-1969, 2011-present. Acoustic flat-top, spruce top, mahogany back and sides, 12 strings, natural. Reintroduced in '11 (California Series) with on-board Fishman System, made in China.

1965-1969		$800	$1,000
2011-2014	Reintroduced	$275	$350

Violin - Electric
1958-1976, 2013. Violin-shape, solidbody, sunburst is the standard finish.

1958-1959		$1,625	$2,025
1960-1969		$1,525	$1,900
1970-1976		$1,425	$1,800
2013		$485	$615

Wildwood
1963-1971. Acoustic flat-top with Wildwood dyed top.

1966-1971	Various (unfaded)	$1,700	$2,100

Fenix
Late 1980s-mid 1990s. Brand name of Korean manufacturer Young Chang, used on a line of original-design and copy acoustic, electric and bass guitars. They also built Squier brand guitars for Fender during that period.

Fenton-Weill
See info under Burns-Weill.

Fernandes
1969-present. Established in Tokyo. Early efforts were classical guitars, but they now offer a variety of intermediate grade, production, imported guitars and basses.

Nomad Travel/Nomad Deluxe
1998-present. Unusual body style, extra large banana headstock, built-in effects, amp and speaker. Deluxe models have added features.

1998-2014	Standard	$180	$225
2000-2009	Deluxe	$400	$500
2010-2012	Deluxe, Digitech FX	$525	$650

Fina
Production classical and steel-string guitars and acoustic basses built in Huiyang City, Guang Dong, China.

Finck, David
1986-present. Luthier David Finck builds his production/custom, professional and premium grade, acoustic guitars, presently in Valle Crucis, North Carolina. In the past, he has built in Pittsburg, Kansas and Reader, West Virginia.

Fine Resophonic
1988-present. Professional and premium grade, production/custom, wood and metal-bodied resophonic guitars (including reso-electrics) built by luthiers Mike Lewis and Pierre Avocat in Vitry Sur Seine, France. They also build ukes and mandolins.

First Act
1995-present. Budget and professional grade, production/custom, acoustic, solid and semi-hollow body guitars built in China and in their Custom Shop in Boston. They also make basses, violins, and other instruments.

Firth Pond & Company
1822-1867. An east coast retail distributor that sold Martin and Ashborn private brand instruments. The company operated as Firth and Hall from 1822-1841 (also known as Firth, Hall & Pond) in New York City and Litchfield, Connecticut. Most instruments were small parlor size (11" lower bout) guitars, as was the case for most builders of this era. Sometimes the inside back center seam will be branded Firth & Pond. Brazilian rosewood sides and back instruments fetch considerably more than most of the other tone woods and value can vary considerably based on condition. Guitars from the 1800s are sometimes valued more as antiques than working vintage guitars. In 1867 Firth & Sons sold out to Oliver Ditson Company.

Flammang Guitars
1990-present. Premium grade, custom/production, steel string guitars built by luthier David Flammang in Greene, Iowa and previously in East Hampton and Higganum, Connecticut.

Flaxwood
2004-present. Professional grade, production/custom, solid and semi-hollow body guitars built in Finland, with bodies of natural fiber composites.

Fleishman Instruments
1974-present. Premium and presentation grade, custom flat-tops made by luthier Harry Fleishman in Sebastopol, California. He also offers basses and electric uprights. Fleishman is the director of Luthiers School International.

Fletcher Brock Stringed Instruments
1992-present. Custom flat-tops and archtops made by luthier Fletcher Brock originally in Ketchum, Idaho, and currently in Seattle, Washington. He also builds mandolin family instruments.

Flowers Guitars
1993-present. Premium grade, custom, archtop guitars built by luthier Gary Flowers in Baltimore, Maryland.

Floyd Rose
2004-2006. Floyd Rose, inventor of the Floyd Rose Locking Tremolo, produced a line of intermediate and professional grade, production, solidbody guitars from '04 to '06. They continue to offer bridges and other accessories.

MODEL YEAR	FEATURES	EXC. COND. LOW	HIGH

Foggy Mountain

2005-present. Intermediate grade, production, steel and nylon string acoustic and acoustic/electric guitars imported from China.

Fontanilla Guitars

1987-present. Luthier Allan Fontanilla builds his premium grade, production/custom, classical guitars in San Francisco, California.

Fouilleul

1978-present. Production/custom, classical guitars made by luthier Jean-Marie Fouilleul in Cuguen, France.

Fox Hollow Guitars

2004-present. Luthier Don Greenough builds his professional and premium grade, custom, acoustic and electric guitars in Eugene, Oregon. He also builds mandolins.

Fox or Rocking F

1983-present. Premium grade, custom, steel string acoustic guitars built in Seattle, Washington by luthier Cat Fox.

Foxxe

1990-1991. Short-lived brand of solidbodies offered by the same company that produced Barrington guitars, Korean-made.

Frame Works

1995-present. Professional grade, production/custom, steel and nylon string guitars built by luthier Frank Krocker in Burghausen, Germany. The instruments feature a neck mounted on a guitar-shaped frame. Krocker has also built traditional archtops, flat-tops, and classicals.

Framus

1946-1977, 1996-present. Professional and premium grade, production/custom, guitars made in Markneukirchen, Germany. They also build basses, amps, mandolins and banjos. Frankische Musikindustrie (Framus) founded in Erlangen, Germany by Fred Wilfer, relocated to Bubenreuth in '54, and to Pretzfeld in '67. Begun as an acoustic instrument manufacturer, Framus added electrics in the mid-'50s. Earliest electrics were mostly acoustics with pickups attached. Electric designs begin in early-'60s. Unique feature was a laminated maple neck with many thin plies. By around '64-'65 upscale models featured the organtone, often called a spigot, a spring-loaded volume control that allowed you to simulate a Leslie speaker effect. Better models often had mutes and lots of switches.

In the '60s, Framus instruments were imported into the U.S. by Philadelphia Music Company. Resurgence of interest in ca. '74 with the Jan Akkermann hollowbody followed by original mid-'70s design called the Nashville, the product of an alli-

ance with some American financing.

The brand was revived in '96 by Hans Peter Wilfer, the president of Warwick, with production in Warwick's factory in Germany.

Amateur
Early 1960s to mid-1970s. Model 5/1, small flat-top, early without pickguard, plain, dot markers.

1960s-70s		$200	$250

Atilla Zoller AZ-10
Early-1960s-early-1980s. Single-cut archtop, 2 pickups, neck glued-in until the '70s, bolt-on after, sunburst. Model 5/65 (rounded cutaway, made until late '60s) and Model 5/67 (sharp cutaway).

1960s	Model 5/65	$625	$800
1960s-70s	Model 5/67	$625	$800

Atlantic
Ca. 1965-ca. 1970. Model 5/110, single-cut thin body electric archtop, 2 pickups, tremolo optional.

1965-1970	Model 5/110	$550	$725

Atlantic (08000) Elec-12
Mid to late 1960s. Model 5/011 and 5/013, double cut semi-hollow, 2 pickups, 12-string.

1960s	Model 5/013	$550	$725

Big 18 Doubleneck
Late 1960s. Model 5/200 is a solidbody and Model 5/220 is acoustic.

1960s	Model 5/200	$675	$875
1960s	Model 5/220	$675	$875

Caravelle
Ca.1965-ca. 1975. Double-cut archtop, tremolo, model 5/117-52 has 2 pickups and 5/117-54 has 3.

1965-1975		$650	$825

Gaucho
Late 1960s-mid 1970s. Lower grade flat-top, concert size, spruce top, mahogany sides and back, rosewood bridge and 'board, sunburst or natural finish.

1960s-70s	Model 5/194	$200	$250

Hollywood
1960s. Double-cut, 3 pickups, red sunburst.

1960s	Model 5/132	$725	$925

Jan Akkerman
1974-1977. Single-cut semi-hollowbody, 2 pickups, gold hardware.

1974-1977		$325	$400

Jumbo
1963-late 1970s. Models earlier 5/97, later 5/197, jumbo flat-top, mahogany or maple sides and back.

1960s		$450	$600

Jumbo 12-String
Late 1960s-mid 1970s. 12-string version.

1960s-70s	Model 5/297	$450	$600

Missouri (E Framus Missouri)
Ca.1955-ca. 1975. Originally non-cut acoustic archtop until early '60s when single-cut archtop with 1 or 2 pickups added.

1960s	Model 5/60	$475	$625

New Sound Series
1960s. Double-cut semi-hollowbody, model 5/116-52 has 2 pickups and 5/116-54 has 3.

1960s		$650	$850

Foggy Mountain

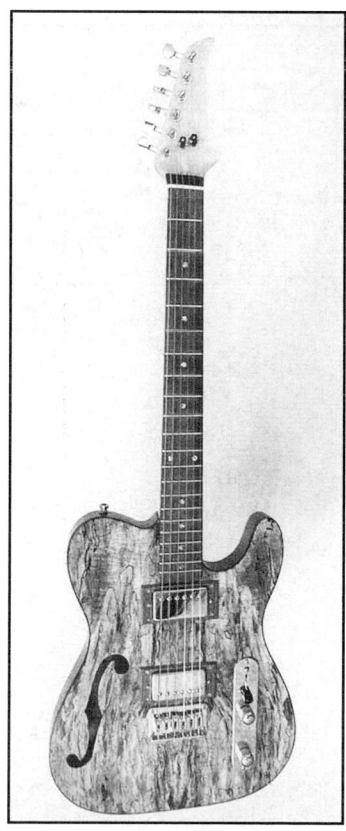

Fox Hollow

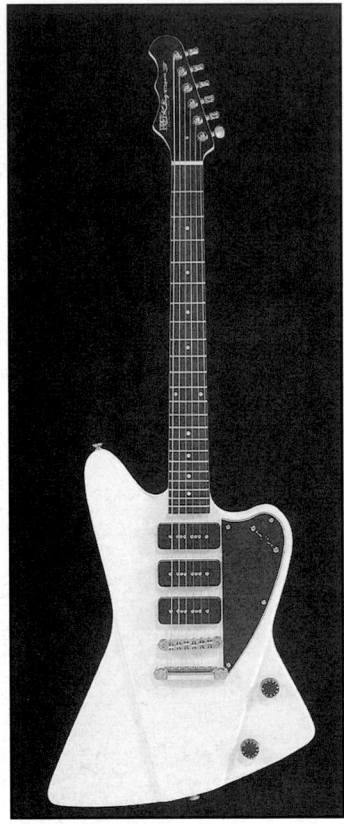

Fret-King Blue Label Esprit 3

Franklin Guitar Company OM

MODEL YEAR	FEATURES	EXC. COND. LOW	HIGH

Sorella Series
Ca.1955-mid 1970s. Single-cut, Model 5/59 is acoustic archtop (with or without single pickup), 5/59-50 is 1-pickup electric archtop, 5/59-52 is electric 2-pickup.

1955-1975	Model 5/59	$550	$725
1965-1972	Model 5/59-50	$600	$800
1965-1972	Model 5/59-52	$625	$825

Sorento
Ca.1963-ca. 1970. Thinline archtop, single-cut, 2 pickups, organ effect, f-holes.

1963-1970	Model 5/112-53	$600	$800

Sorento 12
Ca.1963-ca. 1970. 12-string version.

1963-1970	Model 5/012	$700	$900

Sport
Early 1950s-mid-1970s. Small beginner flat-top, plain appointments, dot markers.

1950s-70s	Model 50/1	$180	$225

Strato de Luxe 12 String
Ca. 1963-ca. 1970. Model 5/067(metal pickguard) and 5/068 (wood grain pickguard and large gold cover plates), 2 pickups, tremolo.

1963-1970	Model 5/068	$600	$800

Strato de Luxe Series
Ca.1964-ca. 1970. 1, 2 (5/155, 5/167-52, 5/168-52) or 3 (5/167-54, 5/168-54) pickups, some models have gold hardware.

1960s	2 pickups	$525	$675
1960s	3 pickups	$625	$800

Strato Super
Early to late 1960s. Offset double-cut, 2 pickups.

1960s	Model 5/155-52	$600	$800

Studio Series
Late 1950s-mid 1970s. Model 5/51 (a.k.a. 030) is non-cut acoustic archtop (some with pickup - 5/51E), 5/108 is electric archtop, 1 pickup.

1960s-70s	Model 5/51	$200	$250
1960s-70s	Model 5/51E	$250	$325

Television Series
Early to late 1960s. Model 5/118-52 2 pickups and 5/118-54 3 pickups, offset double-cut thinline hollowbody.

1960s	Model 5/118-52	$550	$725
1960s	Model 5/118-54	$650	$850

Texan Series
Late 1960s-early 1980s. Model 5/196, 5/196E (with pickup) and 5/296 12-string flat-top, mahogany back and sides. 6-string ends in late '70s.

1960s-70s	6-string	$260	$325
1960s-80s	12-string	$260	$325

Western
1960s. Model 5/195, grand concert size, lower grade flat-top, spruce top, maple sides and back.

1960s	Model 5/195	$200	$250

Franklin Guitar Company
1974-present. Premium and presentation grade, custom, flat-top steel string guitars built first in Franklin, Michigan and since 2003 in Rocheport, Missouri by luthier Nick Kukich. He also built in Idaho, Washington and Oregon.

Fraulini
2001-present. Luthier Todd Cambio builds his professional and premium grade, primarily custom, early 20th century style guitars, in Madison, Wisconsin.

FreeNote
Intermediate to professional grade, the innovative FreeNote 12-Tone Ultra Plus provides two frets for every traditional fret placement which provides an unlimited number of playable notes.

Fresher
1973-1985. The Japanese-made Fresher brand models were mainly copies of popular brands and limited numbers were imported into the U.S. They also made basses.

Solidbody Electric
1970s. Import from Japan.

1970s		$230	$300

Fret-King
2008-present. Luthier Trev Wilkinson builds professional and premium grade, production, solid-body and semi-hollow electric guitars and basses in Yorkshire, U.K., and also offers a line imported from Korea.

Fritz Brothers
1988-present. Premium grade, production/custom, acoustic, semi-hollow, and solidbody guitars and basses built by luthier Roger Fritz, originally in Mobile, Alabama, then in Mendocino, California. In 2013 he again relocated to Mobile.

Froggy Bottom Guitars
1974-present. Luthier Michael Millard builds his premium and presentation grade, production/custom flat-tops in Newfane, Vermont (originally in Hinsdale, New York, and until '84 production was in Richmond, New Hampshire).

Frudua Guitar Works
1988-present. Luthier Galeazzo Frudua builds his intermediate to premium grade, production/custom, electric guitars, basses and amps in Imola, Italy.

Fukuoka Musical Instruments
1993-present. Custom steel- and nylon-string flat-tops and archtops built in Japan.

Furch
See listing for Stonebridge.

Furnace Mountain Guitar Works
1995-1999. Instruments built by luthier Martin Fair in New Mexico. He currently builds under the Fairbuilt Guitar Co. brand.

MODEL YEAR	FEATURES	EXC. COND. LOW	HIGH

Fury

1962-present. Founded by Glenn McDougall in Saskatoon, Saskatchewan, Fury currently offers production, solidbody electrics guitars and basses. They have built hollow and semi-hollow body guitars in the past.

Futurama

1957-mid to late 1960s. Futurama was a brand name used by Selmer in the United Kingdom. Early instruments made by the Drevokov Cooperative in Czechoslovakia, models for '63-'64 made by Sweden's Hagstrom company. Some later '60s instruments may have been made in Japan. Beatles fans will recognize the brand name as Beatle George Harrison's first electric.

Futurama/II/III

1957-1969. Offset double-cut, 2- or 3-pickup versions available, large Futurama logo on headstock with the reverse capital letter F. George Harrison purchased his Futurama in '59; maple neck, 3 pickups, 3 push button levels, 2 knobs, Futurama logo on 'guard. The price shown for the Harrison model assumes an all-original, excellent condition that exactly matches his '59 model.

1959	III, Harrison specs	$1,500	$5,500
1959	III, rosewood, 3 pickups	$800	$1,000
1960-1962	II, 2 pickups	$800	$1,000

Fylde Guitars

1973-present. Luthier Roger Bucknall builds his professional and premium grade, production/custom acoustic guitars, basses, mandolins, mandolas, bouzoukis, and citterns in Penrith, Cumbria, UK.

G & L

1980-present. Intermediate and professional grade, production/custom, solidbody and semi-hollowbody electric guitars made in the U.S. and overseas. They also make basses. Founded by Leo Fender and George Fullerton following the severance of ties between Fender's CLF Research and Music Man. Company sold to John MacLaren and BBE Sound, when Leo Fender died in '91. In '98 they added their Custom Creations Department. In '03 G & L introduced the Korean-made G & L Tribute Series. George Fullerton died in July, '09.

ASAT

1986-1998. Called the Broadcaster in '85. Two or 3 single-coil or 2 single-coil/1 humbucker pickup configurations until early-'90s, 2 single-coils after.

1986		$1,100	$1,350
1987	Leo sig. on headstock	$1,300	$1,600
1988-1991	Leo sig. on body	$1,200	$1,475
1992-1998	BBE era	$825	$1,025

ASAT 20th Anniversary

2000. Limited Edition run of 50, ash body, tinted birdseye maple neck, 2-tone sunburst.

2000		$1,200	$1,475

ASAT '50

1999. Limited edition of 10.

1999		$1,300	$1,600

ASAT Bluesboy Limited Edition

1999. Limited edition of 20.

1999		$1,200	$1,475

ASAT Bluesboy Semi-Hollow Limited Edition

1999. Limited edition of 12, thin semi-hollow.

1999		$1,300	$1,600

ASAT Classic

1990-present. Two single-coil pickups, individually adjustable bridge saddles, neck-tilt adjustment and tapered string posts.

1990-1991	Leo sig. on body	$1,200	$1,500
1992-1997	3-bolt neck	$900	$1,125
1997-2014	4-bolt neck	$900	$1,125

ASAT Classic B-Bender

1997. 12 made with factory-original B-Bender.

1997		$1,300	$1,600

ASAT Classic Bluesboy

2001-present. Humbucker neck pickup, single-coil at bridge.

2001-2014		$975	$1,225

ASAT Classic Bluesboy Rustic

2010-present. Classic Bluesboy with Rustic aging and refinements.

2010-2014		$1,325	$1,650

ASAT Classic Bluesboy Semi-Hollow

1997-present. Chambered Classic with f-hole.

1997-2014		$975	$1,225

ASAT Classic Commemorative

1991-1992. Leo Fender signature and birth/death dating.

1991-1992	Australian lacewood, 6 made	$5,000	$6,200

ASAT Classic Custom

1996-1997, 2002-2013. Large rectangular neck pickup, single-coil bridge pickup.

1996-1997	1st version	$950	$1,200
2002-2013	2nd version, 4-bolt neck	$950	$1,200

ASAT Classic Custom Semi-Hollow

2002-2013. Custom with f-hole.

2002-2013		$925	$1,150

ASAT Classic S

2007. Limited run of 50, certificate, swamp ash body, 3 single-coil pickups, Nashville pickup configuration.

2007		$975	$1,200

ASAT Classic Semi-Hollow

1997-present. With f-hole.

1997-2014		$975	$1,200

ASAT Classic Three

1998. Limited Edition run of 100.

1998		$1,275	$1,575

ASAT Custom

1996. No pickguard, 25 to 30 made.

1996		$950	$1,175

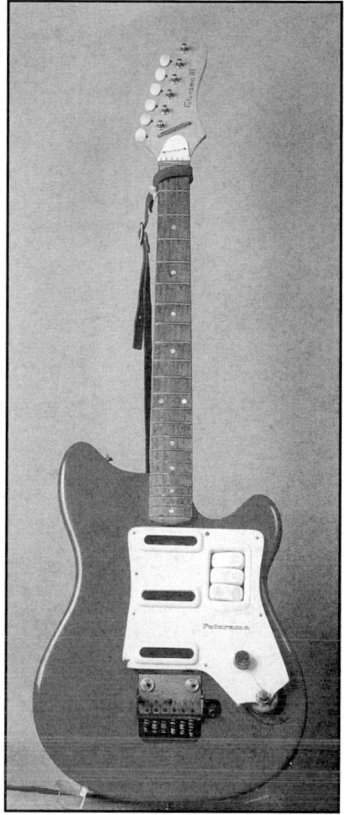

Futurama III

G & L ASAT Classic

G & L F-100 Model I

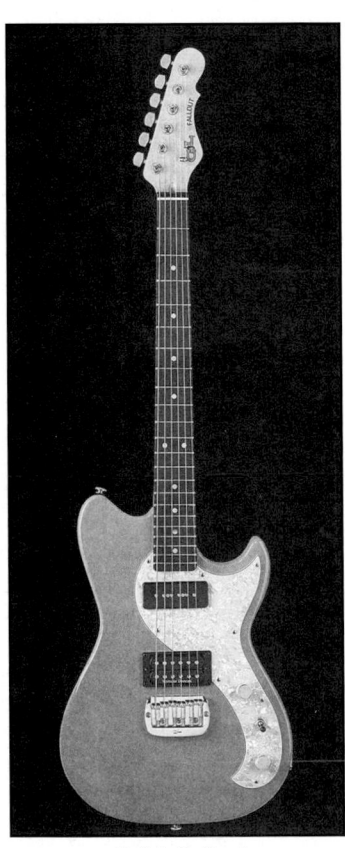

G & L Fallout

MODEL YEAR	FEATURES	EXC. COND. LOW	HIGH
ASAT Deluxe			
1997-present. Flamed maple top, bound body, 2 humbuckers.			
1997	3-bolt neck, less than 100 made	$1,200	$1,450
1997-1999	4-bolt neck	$1,200	$1,450
2000-2014	4-bolt neck	$1,100	$1,350
ASAT Deluxe Semi-Hollow			
1997-present. Two humbuckers.			
1997-2014		$1,200	$1,450
ASAT III			
1988-1991, 1996-1998. Single-cut body, 3 single-coil pickups.			
1988-1991	1st version, Leo era, 150 made	$1,250	$1,500
1996-1998	Post Leo era	$1,200	$1,450
ASAT JD-5/Jerry Donahue JD-5			
2004-2007. Jerry Donahue model, single-cut, 2 single-coils, special wired 5-way switch.			
2004-2007		$1,200	$1,450
ASAT Junior			
1998-1999. Limited Edition run of 250, single-cut semi-hollowbody, 2 single-coils.			
1998-1999		$1,175	$1,450
ASAT S-3			
1998-2000. Three soap-bar single-coil pickups, limited production.			
1998-2000		$925	$1,150
ASAT Special			
1992-present. Like ASAT, but with 2 larger P-90-type pickups, chrome hardware, various colors.			
1992-1997	3-bolt neck	$925	$1,150
1997-2014	4-bolt neck	$925	$1,150
ASAT Special Semi-Hollow			
1997-present. Semi-hollow version of ASAT Special.			
1997-2014		$925	$1,150
ASAT Special Deluxe			
2001-present. No 'guard version of the Special with figured maple top.			
2001-2014		$1,000	$1,250
ASAT Z-2 Limited Edition			
1999. Limited edition of 10 instruments, semi-hollow construction, natural ash, tortoise bound, engraved neckplate.			
1999		$1,150	$1,425
ASAT Z-3			
1998-present. Three offset-style Z-3 high output pickups, sunburst.			
1998-2014		$900	$1,125
ASAT Z-3 Semi-Hollow			
1998-present. F-hole version of Z-3.			
1998-2014		$900	$1,125
Broadcaster			
1985-1986. Solidbody, 2 single-coils with adjustable polepieces act in humbucking mode with selector switch in the center position, black parts and finish, name changed to ASAT in early-'86.			
1985-1986	Kahler	$875	$1,075
1985-1986	Signed by Leo, ebony 'board	$2,100	$2,600
1985-1986	Signed by Leo, maple 'board	$2,100	$2,600

MODEL YEAR	FEATURES	EXC. COND. LOW	HIGH
Cavalier			
1983-1986. Offset double-cut, 2 humbuckers, 700 made, sunburst.			
1983-1986		$950	$1,200
Climax			
1992-1996. Offset double-cut, bolt maple neck, six-on-a-side tuners, double locking vibrato, blue.			
1992-1996		$850	$1,050
Climax Plus			
1992-1996. Two humbuckers replace single-coils of the Climax, plus 1 single-coil.			
1992-1996		$850	$1,050
Climax XL			
1992-1996. Two humbuckers only.			
1992-1996		$850	$1,050
Comanche V			
1988-1991. Solidbody, 3 Z-shaped single-coil humbuckers, maple neck in choice of 3 radii, rosewood 'board, vibrato, fine tuners, Leo Fender's signature on the body, sunburst.			
1988-1991		$1,050	$1,300
Comanche VI			
1990-1991. Leo Fender's signature on the body, 6 mini-toggles.			
1990-1991		$1,200	$1,500
Comanche (Reintroduced)			
1998-present. Reissue with either swamp ash or alder body, bolt-on maple neck, 3 Z-coil pickups, standard or premium finish options.			
1998-2014	Premium finish, flame top	$1,025	$1,275
1998-2014	Standard finish	$900	$1,125
Commemorative			
1992-1997. About 350 made, Leo Fender signature on upper bass bout.			
1991	Cherryburst	$2,000	$2,500
1992-1997	Sunburst	$1,800	$2,300
F-100 (Model I and II)			
1980-1986. Offset double-cut solidbody, 2 humbuckers, natural. Came in a I and II model - only difference is the radius of the 'board.			
1980-1986		$800	$1,000
F-100 E (Model I and II)			
1980-1982. Offset double-cut solidbody, 2 humbuckers, active electronics, pre-amp, natural. Came in a I and II model - only difference is the radius of the 'board.			
1980-1982		$850	$1,050
Fallout			
2013-present. SC-2 body style, P-90 and humbucker, swamp ash body on premier and alder on standard finishes, maple neck, maple or rosewood 'board.			
2013-2014		$800	$1,000
G-200			
1981-1982. Mahogany solidbody, maple neck, ebony 'board, 2 humbucking pickups, coil-split switches, natural or sunburst, 209 made.			
1981-1982		$1,850	$2,300
GBL-LE (Guitars by Leo Limited Edition)			
1999. Limited edition of 25, semi-hollowbody, 3 pickups.			
1999		$1,100	$1,350

MODEL YEAR	FEATURES	EXC. COND. LOW	HIGH

George Fullerton Signature
1995-2007. Double-cut solidbody, sunburst.

| 1995-1997 | 3-bolt neck | $1,000 | $1,250 |
| 1997-2007 | 4-bolt neck | $1,000 | $1,250 |

HG-1
1982-1983. Offset double-cut, 1 humbucker, dot inlays. Very rare as most were made into HG-2s.

| 1982-1983 | | $1,500 | $1,900 |

HG-2
1982-1984. 2-humbucker HG, body changes to classic offset double-cut in '84.

| 1982-1983 | Mustang-body | $1,250 | $1,550 |
| 1984 | S-body | $1,250 | $1,550 |

Interceptor
1983-1991. To '86 an X-shaped solidbody, either 3 single-coils, 2 humbuckers, or 1 humbucker and 2 single-coils, '87-'89 was an offset double-cut solidbody.

1983-1985	1st X-body, 70 made	$2,000	$2,500
1985-1986	2nd X-body, 12 made	$2,000	$2,500
1987-1991	Double-cut	$1,300	$1,625

Invader
1984-1991, 1998-present. Double-cut solidbody, 2 single-coil and 1 humbucker pickups.

| 1984-1991 | 1st version | $850 | $1,050 |
| 1998-2014 | 2nd version | $850 | $1,050 |

Invader Plus
1998-present. Two humbuckers and single blade pickup in the middle position.

| 1998-2014 | | $800 | $1,000 |

Invader XL
1998-present. Fancy top, 2 humbuckers.

| 1998-2014 | | $1,000 | $1,250 |

John Jorgenson Signature Model ASAT
1995. About 190 made, Silver Metalflake finish.

| 1995 | | $1,100 | $1,375 |

Legacy
1992-present. Classic double-cut configuration, various colors.

1992-1994	3-bolt neck, Duncan SSLs	$700	$875
1995-1997	3-bolt neck, Alnicos	$700	$875
1998-1999	4-bolt neck, Alnicos	$700	$875
2000-2014		$700	$875

Legacy 2HB
2001-present. Two humbucker pickups.

| 2001-2014 | | $700 | $875 |

Legacy Deluxe
2001-present. No 'guard, figured maple top.

| 2001-2014 | | $800 | $1,000 |

Legacy HB
2001-present. One humbucker pickup at bridge position plus 2 single-coil pickups.

| 2001-2014 | | $700 | $875 |

Legacy Special
1993-present. Legacy with 3 humbuckers, various colors.

| 1992-1997 | 3-bolt neck | $700 | $875 |
| 1998-2014 | 4-bolt neck | $700 | $875 |

25th Anniversary Limited Edition
2006. G&L Custom Creations, 250 made, combines appearance of '81 F-100 with contours and control layout of ASAT Super, single-cut mahogany body, 2 custom wound MFD humbuckes, custom blend 'root beer' finish.

| 2006 | | $1,000 | $1,250 |

Nighthawk
1983. Offset double-cut solidbody, 3 single-coil pickups, 269 made, sunburst, name changed to Skyhawk in '84.

| 1983 | | $800 | $1,000 |

Rampage
1984-1991. Offset double-cut solidbody, hard rock maple neck, ebony 'board, 1 bridge-position humbucker pickup, sunburst. Currently available as Jerry Cantrell Signature Model.

| 1984-1991 | Common color | $1,000 | $1,250 |
| 1984-1991 | Rare color | $1,500 | $1,850 |

Rampage (Reissue)
2000. Limited Edition run of 70, supplied with gig bag and not hard case, ivory finish.

| 2000 | | $625 | $775 |

S-500
1982-present. Double-cut mahogany or ash solidbody, maple neck, ebony or maple 'board, 3 single-coil pickups, vibrato.

1982-1987		$1,000	$1,250
1988-1991	Mini-toggle, Leo sig. on body	$900	$1,125
1992-1997	3-bolt neck	$725	$900
1997-2014	4-bolt neck	$725	$900

S-500 Deluxe
2001-present. Deluxe Series features, including no 'guard and flamed maple top, natural.

| 2001-2014 | Flame & solid tops | $875 | $1,100 |

SC-1
1982-1983. Offset double-cut solidbody, 1 single-coil pickup, tremolo, sunburst, 250 made.

| 1981-1982 | | $800 | $1,000 |

SC-2
1982-1983, 2010-present. Offset double-cut solidbody, 2 MFD soapbar pickups, about 600 made in original run, reissue maple or rosewood 'board.

1982-1983	Shallow cutaway	$1,000	$1,250
1983	Deeper, pointed cutaway	$1,000	$1,250
2010-2014	Reissue	$550	$675

SC-3
1982-1991. Offset double-cut solidbody, 3 single-coil pickups, tremolo.

1982-1983	Shallow cutaway	$875	$1,075
1984-1987	Deeper cutaway, no 'guard	$875	$1,075
1988-1991	Deeper cutaway, 'guard	$800	$1,000

Skyhawk
1984-1991. Renamed from Nighthawk, offset double-cut, 3 single-coils, signature on headstock '84-'87, then on body '88-'91.

| 1984-1987 | Dual-Fulcrum or saddle lock | $800 | $1,000 |

G & L S-500
Kevin Ferby

1982 G & L SC-2
Mark Deweese

G & L Will Ray Signature Model

Gallagher A-70

MODEL YEAR	FEATURES	EXC. COND. LOW	HIGH
1984-1987	Kahler	$650	$800
1988-1991	Dual-Fulcrum or saddle lock	$650	$800
1988-1991	Kahler	$600	$750

Superhawk
1984-1987. Offset double-cut, maple neck, ebony 'board, G&L or Kahler tremolos, 2 humbuckers, signature on headstock.

1984-1987		$725	$900

Tribute Series
2003-present. Import versions of regular models.

2003-2014		$300	$500

Trinity
2006. Only 25 made, ASAT-style with 3 new style single-coils, designed by Tim Page of Buffalo Brothers, the last G&L to have COA signed by George Fullerton.

2006		$1,550	$1,900

Will Ray Signature Model
2002-present. Will Ray signature on headstock, 3 Z-coil pickups, Hipshot B-Bender.

2002-2014		$675	$850

G.L. Stiles
1960-1994. Built by Gilbert Lee Stiles primarily in the Miami, Florida area. First solidbody, including pickups and all hardware, built by hand in his garage. Stiles favored scrolls, fancy carving and walnut fingerboards. His later instruments were considerably more fancy and refined. He moved to Hialeah, Florida by '63 and began making acoustic guitars and other instruments. Only his solidbodies had consecutive serial numbers. Stiles, who died in '94, made approximately 1000 solidbodies and 500 acoustics.

Gabriel's Guitar Workshop
1979-present. Production/custom steel- and nylon-stringed guitars built by luthier Gabriel Ochoteco in Germany until '84 and in Brisbane, Australia since.

Gadotti Guitars
1997-present. Luthier Jeanfranco Biava Gadotti builds his premium grade, custom/production, nylon- and steel-string, carved, chambered solidbodies in Orlando, Florida.

Gadow Guitars
2002-present. Luthier Ryan Gadow builds his professional and premium grade, custom/production, solid and semi-hollow body guitars and basses in Durham, North Carolina.

Gagnon
1998-present. Luthier Bill Gagnon builds his premium and presentation grade, production/custom, archtop guitars in Beaverton, Oregon.

Galanti
Ca.1962-ca.1967. Electric guitars offered by the longtime Italian accordion maker, some built by Zero Sette. They may have also offered acoustics.

MODEL YEAR	FEATURES	EXC. COND. LOW	HIGH
Electric			
1962-1967. Solidbody or hollowbody.			
1962-1967	Fancy features	$525	$750
1962-1967	Plain features	$275	$500

Galiano
New Yorkers Antonio Cerrito and Raphael Ciani offered guitars under the Galiano brand during the early part of the last century. They used the brand both on guitars built by them and others, including The Oscar Schmidt Company. They also offered mandolins.

Gallagher
1965-present. Professional and premium grade, production/custom, flat-top guitars built in Wartrace, Tennessee. J. W. Gallagher started building Shelby brand guitars in the Slingerland Drum factory in Shelbyville, Tennessee in '63. In '65 he and his son Don made the first Gallagher guitar, the G-50. Doc Watson began using Gallagher guitars in '68. In '76, Don assumed operation of the business when J. W. semi-retired. J. W. died in '79.

71 Special
1970s-present. Rosewood back and sides, spruce top, herringbone trim, bound ebony 'board, natural.

1970s-2014		$1,650	$2,075

72 Special
1977-present. Rosewood back and sides, spruce top, abalone trim, bound ebony 'board, natural.

1977-2014		$3,000	$3,700

A-70 Ragtime Special
1978-present. Smaller auditorium/00 size, spruce top, mahogany back and sides, G logo, natural.

1978-2014		$1,175	$1,475

Custom 12-String
Introduced in 1965-present. Mahogany, 12-fret neck, natural.

1965		$1,175	$1,475

Doc Watson
1974-present. Spruce top, mahogany back and sides, scalloped bracing, ebony 'board, herringbone trim, natural.

1974-2014		$1,700	$2,100

Doc Watson (Cutaway)
1975-2010. Spruce top, mahogany back and sides, scalloped bracing, ebony 'board, herringbone trim, natural.

1975-2010		$1,900	$2,350

Doc Watson 12-String
1995-2000. Natural.

1995-2000		$1,500	$1,875

Doc Watson Signature
2000-present. Signature inlay 12th fret.

2000-2014		$1,900	$2,350

G-45
1970-2008. Mahogany back and sides, spruce top, ebony 'board, natural.

1970-1979		$1,300	$1,650
1980-2008		$1,100	$1,400

MODEL YEAR	FEATURES	EXC. COND. LOW	HIGH

G-50
1960s-present. Mahogany back and sides, spruce top, ebony 'board, natural.

1960s		$2,000	$2,500
1970-2014		$1,400	$1,750

G-65
1980s-present. Rosewood back and sides, spruce top, ebony 'board, natural.

1980s-2014		$1,450	$1,850

G-70
1978-present. Rosewood back and sides, herringbone purfling on top and soundhole, mother-of-pearl diamond 'board inlays, bound headstock, natural.

1978-2014		$1,500	$1,900

G-71
1970s. Indian rosewood, gold tuners.

1970s		$1,800	$2,225

Gallagher, Kevin
1996. Kevin Gallagher, luthier, changed name brand to Omega to avoid confusion with J.W. Gallagher. See Omega listing.

Gallotone
1950s-1960s. Low-end foreign brand similar to 1950s Stellas, the Gallotone Champion, a 3/4 size student flat-top, is associated with John Lennon as his early guitar.

Galloup Guitars
1994-present. Luthier Bryan Galloup builds his professional and premium grade, production/custom flat-tops in Big Rapids, Michigan. He also operates the Galloup School of Lutherie and The Guitar Hospital repair and restoration business.

Galveston
Budget and intermediate grade, production, imported acoustic, acoustic/electric, resonator and solidbody guitars. They also offer basses and mandolins.

Gamble & O'Toole
1978-present. Premium grade, custom classical and steel string guitars built by luthier Arnie Gamble in Sacramento, California, with design input and inlay work from his wife Erin O'Toole.

Ganz Guitars
1995-present. Luthier Steve Ganz builds his professional grade, production/custom classical guitars in Bellingham, Washington.

Garcia
Made by luthier Federico Garcia in Spain until late-1960s or very early-'70s when production moved to Japan.

Classical
1960s-1970s. Mid-level, '60s model is solid spruce top with solid mahogany, rosewood or walnut back and sides, '70s model is Spanish pine top with walnut back and sides.

1960s	Mahogany	$210	$300
1960s	Rosewood	$400	$500
1960s	Walnut	$210	$300
1970s	Spanish pine/ Brazilian rosewood	$500	$700
1970s	Spanish pine/walnut	$210	$300

Garrison
2000-2007. Intermediate and professional grade, production, acoustic and acoustic/electric guitars designed by luthier Chris Griffiths using his Active Bracing System (a single integrated glass-fiber bracing system inside a solid wood body). He started Griffiths Guitar Works in 1993 in St. John's, Newfoundland, and introduced Garrison guitars in 2000. In '07, the Garrison facility was acquired by Gibson.

Gary Kramer
2005-present. Gary Kramer, the founder of the original Kramer brand, started a new business in 2005. The initial line was based upon a half-moon shaped model called the USA Delta Wing. Later import models were added.

Gauge Guitars
2002-present. Luthier Aaron Solomon builds custom, professional and premium grade, solidbody and semi-solid electric guitars in New Jersey.

Gemelli
Early 1960s-ca. 1966. European-made (likely Italian) guitars. Similar to Bartolini guitars, so most likely from same manufacturer. Originally plastic covered, they switched to paint finishes by around '65.

Gemunder
1870s-1910s. New York shop that specialized in reproduction-aged violins, but also made parlor-sized guitars that were similar to Martin guitars of the era. An original label on the inside back identifies August Gemunder and Sons, New York.

Parlor
1870s-1910s. Style 28 appointments, rosewood body, spruce top.

1870-1910s		$1,225	$1,525

George
See listing under Chris George.

German Guitars
2001-present. Luthier Greg German builds his premium grade, custom/production, acoustic archtop guitars in Broomfield, Colorado.

Giannini
1900-present. Classical, acoustic, and acoustic/electric guitars built in Salto, SP, Brazil near Sao Paolo. They also build violas, cavaquinhos and mandolins. Founded by guitar-builder Tranquillo Giannini, an Italian who traveled to Brazil in 1890

Gauge DC

German Guitars

1980 Gibson 335 S DeLuxe
Ken MacSwan

*Gibson Randy Scruggs
Advanced Jumbo Limited Edition*

and discovered the exotic woods of Brazil. The company was producing 30,000 instruments a year by '30. They began exporting their acoustic instruments to the U.S. in '63. They added electric guitars in '60, but these weren't imported as much, if at all. Gianninis from this era used much Brazilian Rosewood.

Classical
Early-1970s. Nylon string import, small body.

MODEL YEAR	FEATURES	EXC. COND. LOW	HIGH
1970s	Brazilian rosewood	$260	$500
1970s	Pau ferro, mahogany	$155	$250

CraViolia
1972-1974, 2004-present. Kidney bean-shaped rosewood body, acoustic, natural, line included a classical, a steel string, and a 12-string.

1972-1974		$450	$575

CraViolia 12-String
1972-1974, 2004-present. Kidney bean-shaped body, 12 strings.

1972-1974		$450	$575
2004-2014		$130	$225

Gibson

1890s (1902)-present. Intermediate, professional, and premium grade, production/custom, acoustic and electric guitars made in the U.S. They also build basses, mandolins, amps, and banjos. Gibson also offers instruments under the Epiphone, Kramer, Steinberger, Dobro, Tobias, Valley Arts, Garrison, Slingerland (drums), Baldwin (pianos), Trace Elliot, Electar (amps), Maestro, Gibson Labs, Oberheim, and Echoplex brands.

Founded in Kalamazoo, Michigan by Orville Gibson, a musician and luthier who developed instruments with tops, sides and backs carved out of solid pieces of wood. Early instruments included mandolins, archtop guitars and harp guitars. By 1896 Gibson had opened a shop. In 1902 Gibson was bought out by a group of investors who incorporated the business as Gibson Mandolin-Guitar Manufacturing Company, Limited. The company was purchased by Chicago Musical Instrument Company (CMI) in '44. In '57 CMI also purchased the Epiphone guitar company, transferring production from Philadelphia to the Gibson plant in Kalamazoo. Gibson was purchased by Norlin in late-'69 and a new factory was opened in Nashville, Tennessee in '74. The Kalamazoo factory ceased production in '84. In '85, Gibson was sold to a group headed by Henry Juskewiscz. Gibson purchased the Flatiron Company in '87 and built a new factory in '89, moving acoustic instrument production to Bozeman, Montana.

The various models of Firebirds, Flying Vs, Les Pauls, SGs, and Super 400s are grouped together under those general headings. Custom Shop and Historic instruments are listed with their respective main model (for example, the '39 Super 400 Historical Collection model is listed with the Super 400s).

Model specifications can cross model years. For example, it is possible that an early '60 Gibson guitar might have a specification, such as a wider-rounder neck, which is typically a '59 spec. In that case it is possible for the early '60 model to be valued more closely to the late '59 model than to a mid to late '60 model with a thinner-flatter neck profile.

Orville Gibson
1894-1902. Hand-made and carved by Orville Gibson, various models and sizes most with standard printed white rectangle label "O.H. Gibson" with photo of Orville Gibson and lyre-mandolin. Prices are for fully functional original or refurbished examples. It is almost expected that a black Orville Gibson instrument has been refinished, and most of those were done by Gibson.

MODEL YEAR	FEATURES	EXC. COND. LOW	HIGH
1894-1902	Basic plain model	$4,000	$6,000
1894-1902	Fancy rare model	$20,000	$25,000
1894-1902	Very rare, historical	$25,000	$60,000

335 S Custom
1980-1981. Solidbody, 335-shaped, mahogany body, unbound rosewood 'board, 2 exposed Dirty Finger humbuckers, coil-tap, TP-6 tailpiece. Also available in natural finish, branded headstock Firebrand version.

1980-1981		$1,100	$1,400

335 S Deluxe
1980-1982. Same as 335 S Custom but with bound ebony 'board, brass nut.

1980-1982		$1,100	$1,400

335 S Limited Run
2011-2013. Maple body and neck, rosewood 'board, nitro-finish sunburst.

2011-2013		$875	$1,100

335 S Standard
1980-1981. Same as 335 S Custom except stop tailpiece, no coil-tap. Also available in natural finish, branded headstock Firebrand version.

1980-1981		$1,100	$1,400

Advanced Jumbo
1936-1940. Dreadnought, 16" wide, round shoulders, Brazilian rosewood back and sides, sunburst, reintroduced '90-'97.

1936-1940		$48,000	$63,000

Advanced Jumbo (Reissue)
1990-1999, 2002-present. Issued as a standard production model, but soon available only as a special order for most of the '90s; currently offered as standard production. Renamed 1936 Advanced Jumbo for 1997-1998. There were also some limited-edition AJs offered during the '90s.

MODEL YEAR	FEATURES	EXC. COND. LOW	HIGH
1990-1999	Reissue	$1,800	$2,250
1990-1999	Special Ed., flamed maple	$2,600	$3,400
1994	Machiche, Mexican rosewood	$2,600	$3,400
2002-2014	Reintroduced	$1,800	$2,250

Advanced Jumbo 75th Anniversary
2011. 75th Anniversary label.

2011		$2,550	$3,150

Advanced Jumbo Koa (Custom Shop)
2006. Custom Shop model, koa back and sides, Adirondack top.

2006		$2,200	$2,800

The Official Vintage Guitar magazine Price Guide 2016   **Gibson** Adv. Jumbo Luthier's Choice — Barney Kessel Cstm.   **105**

GUITARS

MODEL YEAR	FEATURES	EXC. COND. LOW	HIGH

Advanced Jumbo Luthier's Choice (CS)
2000-2005, 2008. Custom Shop model.

| 2000-2005 | Brazilian | $5,200 | $6,500 |
| 2008 | Cocobolo | $3,400 | $4,200 |

Advanced Jumbo Pro
2011-2013. Guitar Center model, Baggs pickup, Sitka top, solid rosewood back and sides.

| 2011-2013 | | $1,300 | $1,650 |

Advanced Jumbo Supreme (CS)
2007. Custom Shop model, Madagascar rosewood back and sides, Adirondack spruce top.

| 2007 | | $2,175 | $2,700 |

Randy Scruggs Advanced Jumbo Limited Edition
2010-present. Sitka spruce top, East Indian rosewood body, king's crown headstock logo on, crown markers, Fishman pickup, vintage sunburst.

| 2010-2014 | | $1,800 | $2,275 |

All American II
1996. Solidbody electric with vague double-cut Melody Maker body style, 2 pickups.

| 1996 | | $500 | $650 |

B.B. King Custom
1980-1988. Lucille on peghead, 2 pickups, multibound, gold-plated parts, Vari-tone, cherry or ebony, renamed B.B. King Lucille in '88.

| 1980-1988 | | $2,075 | $2,575 |

B.B. King Lucille
1988-present. Introduced as B.B. King Custom, renamed B.B. King Lucille. Lucille on peghead, 2 pickups, multi-bound, gold-plated parts, Vari-tone, cherry or ebony. In '07 B.B. King logo and large king's crown on headstock with Lucille logo on truss rod cover.

1988-1999		$2,075	$2,575
2000-2014		$2,075	$2,575
2007-2009	King logo	$2,075	$2,575

B.B. King Standard
1980-1985. Like B.B. King Custom, but with stereo electronics and chrome-plated parts, cherry or ebony.

| 1980-1985 | | $2,075 | $2,575 |

B.B. King Commemorative ES-355 Lucille
2006. Limited edition of 80 guitars, price includes matching serial number/certificate number, matching B.B. King script logo case.

| 2006 | | $4,100 | $5,200 |

B-15
1967-1971. Mahogany, spruce top, student model, natural finish.

| 1967-1971 | | $750 | $950 |

B-20
1971-1972. 14.5" flat-top, mahogany back and sides, dot markers, decal logo, strip in-line tuners with small buttons.

| 1971-1972 | | $650 | $850 |

B-25
1962-1977. Flat-top, mahogany, bound body, cherry sunburst (natural finish is the B-25 N).

1962-1964		$1,750	$2,200
1965		$1,450	$1,800
1966-1968		$1,250	$1,650
1968	Black, white 'guard	$2,400	$3,000
1968	Red, white 'guard	$2,000	$2,500
1969		$1,200	$1,550
1970-1977		$1,000	$1,300

B-25 3/4
1962-1968. Short-scale version, flat-top, mahogany body, cherry sunburst (natural finish is the B-25 3/4 N).

1962-1964		$1,300	$1,650
1965		$1,100	$1,450
1966-1968		$1,000	$1,350

B-25 N
1962-1977. Flat-top, mahogany, bound body, natural (cherry sunburst finish is the B-25).

1962-1964		$1,750	$2,200
1965		$1,450	$1,800
1966-1969		$1,250	$1,550
1970-1977		$1,000	$1,300

B-25 N 3/4
1966-1968. Short-scale version, flat-top, mahogany body, natural (cherry sunburst finish is the B-25 3/4).

| 1966-1968 | | $1,300 | $1,650 |

B-25-12
1962-1970. Flat-top 12-string version, mahogany, bound body, cherry sunburst (natural finish is the B-25-12 N).

1962-1964		$1,300	$1,650
1965		$1,200	$1,550
1966-1969		$1,050	$1,350
1970		$950	$1,200

B-25-12 N
1962-1977. Flat-top 12-string version, mahogany, bound body, natural (cherry sunburst is the B-25-12).

1962-1964		$1,300	$1,650
1965		$1,200	$1,550
1966-1969		$1,050	$1,350
1970-1977		$950	$1,200

B-45-12
1961-1979. Flat-top 12-string, mahogany, round shoulders for '61, square after, sunburst (natural finish is the B-45-12 N).

1961-1962	Round shoulder	$1,350	$1,700
1962-1964	Square shoulder	$1,350	$1,700
1965		$1,250	$1,575
1966-1969		$1,100	$1,350
1970-1979		$950	$1,250

B-45-12 N
1962-1979. Flat-top 12-string, mahogany, natural (cherry sunburst finish is the B-45-12).

1962	Round shoulder	$1,350	$1,700
1962-1964	Square shoulder	$1,350	$1,700
1965		$1,250	$1,575
1966-1969		$1,100	$1,350
1970-1979		$950	$1,250

B-45-12 Limited Edition
1991-1992. Limited edition reissue with rosewood back and sides, natural.

| 1991-1992 | | $1,000 | $1,300 |

Barney Kessel Custom
1961-1973. Double-cut archtop, 2 humbuckers, gold hardware, cherry sunburst.

| 1961 | PAFs | $5,300 | $6,500 |
| 1962 | Black finish | $4,100 | $5,100 |

Gibson B-25 3/4
Rod Highsmith

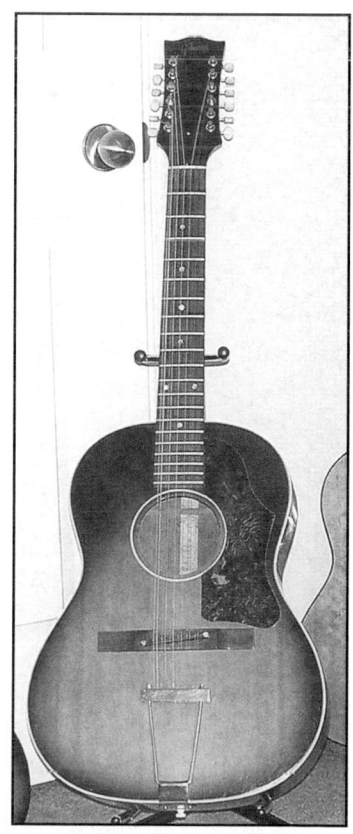

1967 Gibson B-25-12
Frank Thoubboron

GUITARS

1957 Gibson Byrdland

1958 Gibson CF-100 E

MODEL YEAR	FEATURES	EXC. COND. LOW	HIGH
1962-1964	Pat. #	$4,100	$5,100
1965		$3,600	$4,500
1966-1969		$3,300	$4,100
1970-1973		$2,750	$3,400

Barney Kessel Standard
1961-1974. Double-cut archtop, 2 humbuckers, nickel hardware, cherry sunburst.

1961	PAFs	$4,900	$6,100
1962-1964	Pat. #	$3,900	$4,900
1965		$3,300	$4,100
1966-1969		$3,000	$3,700
1970-1973		$2,450	$3,050

Blue Ridge
1968-1979, 1989-1990. Flat-top, dreadnought, laminated rosewood back and sides, natural finish, reintroduced for '89-'90.

1968-1969		$1,200	$1,500
1970-1979		$950	$1,250

Blue Ridge 12
1970-1978. Flat-top, 12 strings, laminated rosewood back and sides, natural finish.

1970-1978		$750	$1,000

Blueshawk
1996-2006. Small single-cut, f-holes, 2 single-coil hum cancelling Blues 90 pickups, 6-way Varitone dial, gold hardware, Bigsby option starts '98.

1996-2006		$800	$1,100

Blues King
2012-2013. Acoustic/electric, non-cut, bubinga back and sides, dot inlays.

2012-2013		$1,500	$1,875

B-SJ Blue Ridge
1989. Model name on label is B-SJ, truss rod covers logo is Blue Ridge, SJ appointments but with narrow peghead shape.

1989		$1,200	$1,525

Byrdland
1955-1992. Thinline archtop, single-cut (rounded until late-'60, pointed '60-late-'69, rounded after '69, rounded or pointed '98-present), 2 pickups, now part of the Historic Collection.

1956-1957	Natural, Alnicos	$9,000	$11,200
1956-1957	Sunburst, Alnicos	$6,900	$8,600
1958-1959	Natural, PAFs	$13,200	$16,300
1958-1959	Sunburst, PAFs	$9,300	$11,500
1960-1962	Natural, PAFs	$11,100	$13,800
1960-1962	Sunburst, PAFs	$8,000	$10,000
1963-1964	Natural, pat. #	$7,000	$8,800
1963-1964	Sunburst, pat. #	$6,100	$7,700
1965	Natural	$6,400	$8,000
1965	Sunburst	$5,900	$7,400
1966	Natural	$5,800	$7,300
1966	Sunburst	$5,800	$7,300
1967-1969	Natural	$5,800	$7,300
1967-1969	Sunburst	$5,600	$6,800
1970-1992	Various colors	$4,200	$5,300

Byrdland Historic Collection
1993-present. Various colors.

1993-2014		$4,800	$6,000

C-0 Classical
1962-1971. Spruce top, mahogany back and sides, bound top, natural.

1962-1964		$475	$600
1965		$400	$500
1966-1971		$350	$450

C-1 Classical
1957-1971. Spruce top, mahogany back and sides, bound body, natural.

1957-1960		$525	$650
1961-1964		$475	$600
1965		$400	$500
1966-1971		$350	$450

C-1 D Laredo
1963-1971. Natural spruce top, mahogany sides and back, upgrade to standard C-1.

1963-1964		$675	$850
1965		$600	$750

C-1 E Classical Electric
1960-1967. C-1 with ceramic bridge pickup, catalog notes special matched amplifier that filters out fingering noises.

1960-1964		$675	$850
1965		$600	$750
1966-1967		$525	$650

C-1 S Petite Classical
1961-1966. Petite 13 1/4" body, natural spruce top, mahogany back and sides.

1961-1964		$475	$600
1965		$400	$500
1966-1967		$350	$450

C-2 Classical
1960-1971. Maple back and sides, bound body, natural.

1960-1964		$575	$725
1965		$500	$625
1966-1971		$450	$575

C-4 Classical
1962-1968. Maple back and sides, natural.

1962-1964		$700	$875
1965		$650	$800
1966-1968		$600	$750

C-5 Classical
1957-1960. Rosewood back and sides, previously named GS-5 Classical in '54-'56.

1957-1960		$800	$1,000

C-6 Classical
1958-1971. Rosewood back and sides, gold hardware, natural.

1958-1959		$1,100	$1,375
1960-1964		$1,000	$1,250
1965		$900	$1,125
1966-1971		$825	$1,050

C-8 Classical
1962-1969. Rosewood back and sides, natural.

1962-1964		$1,400	$1,750
1965		$1,200	$1,475
1966-1969		$1,100	$1,375

C-100 Classical
1971-1972. Slotted peghead, spruce top, mahogany back and sides, ebony 'board, Gibson Master Model label, non-gloss finish.

1971-1972		$350	$450

MODEL YEAR	FEATURES	EXC. COND. LOW	HIGH

C-200 Classical
1971-1972. C-100 with gloss finish.
| 1971-1972 | | $450 | $575 |

C-300 Classical
1971-1972. Similar to C-100, but with rosewood 'board, wood binding, wider soundhole ring.
| 1971-1972 | | $450 | $575 |

C-400 Classical
1971-1972. Rosewood sides and back, spruce top, high-end appointments, chrome hardware.
| 1971-1972 | | $825 | $1,050 |

C-500 Classical
1971-1972. C-400 with gold hardware.
| 1971-1972 | | $925 | $1,150 |

CF-100
1950-1958. Flat-top, pointed cutaway, mahogany back and sides, bound body, sunburst finish.
| 1950-1958 | | $3,200 | $4,000 |

CF-100 E
1951-1958, 2009. CF-100 with a single-coil pickup. Also offered in '94 1950 CF-100 E limited edition and in '07 as a Custom Shop model.
| 1950-1958 | | $3,600 | $4,500 |

CF-100 E Reissue (Custom Shop)
2007. Custom Shop, all maple body, ebony 'board, 24 made.
| 2007 | | $1,900 | $2,450 |

Challenger I
1983-1985. Single-cut Les Paul-shaped solidbody, 1 humbucker, bolt-on maple neck, rosewood 'board, dot markers, silver finish standard.
| 1983-1985 | | $400 | $500 |

Challenger II
1983-1985, 2 humbucker version.
| 1983-1985 | | $450 | $560 |

Challenger III
1984. 3 single-coil version, never cataloged so could be very limited.
| 1984 | | $500 | $625 |

Chet Atkins CE
1981-2005. CE stands for Classical Electric, single-cut, multi-bound body, rosewood 'board until '95, then ebony, standard width nut, gold hardware, various colors.
| 1981-2005 | | $1,425 | $1,800 |

Chet Atkins CEC
1981-2005. Same as CE, but with ebony 'board and 2" classical width nut, black or natural.
| 1981-2005 | | $1,425 | $1,800 |

Chet Atkins Country Gentleman
1987-2005. Thinline archtop, single rounded cutaway, 2 humbuckers, multi-bound, gold hardware, Bigsby. Part of Gibson's Custom line.
| 1987-2005 | | $2,300 | $2,875 |

Chet Atkins SST
1987-2006. Steel string acoustic/electric solidbody, single-cut, bridge transducer pickup, active bass and treble controls, gold hardware.
| 1987-2006 | | $1,175 | $1,475 |

Chet Atkins SST Celebrity
1991-1993. Gold hardware, 200 made, black body with unique white 'guard.
| 1991-1993 | | $1,925 | $2,425 |

Chet Atkins SST-12
1990-1994. 12-string model similar to 6-string, mahogany/spruce body, preamp circuit controls single transducer pickup, natural or ebony finish.
| 1990-1994 | | $1,225 | $1,525 |

Chet Atkins Tennessean
1990-2005. Single rounded cutaway archtop, 2 humbuckers, f-holes, bound body. Part of Gibson's Custom line.
| 1990-2005 | | $1,350 | $1,675 |

Chicago 35
1994-1995. Flat-top dreadnought, round shoulders, mahogany back and sides, prewar script logo.
| 1994-1995 | | $1,000 | $1,275 |

Citation
1969-1971. 17" full-depth body, single-cut archtop, 1 or 2 floating pickups, fancy inlay, natural or sunburst. Only 8 shipped for '69-'71, reissued the first time '79-'83 and as part of the Historic Collection in '93.
| 1969-1971 | Sunburst, natural | $12,000 | $16,000 |

Citation (1st Reissue)
1979-1983. Reissue of '69-'71 model, reintroduced in '93 as part of Gibson's Historic Collection.
| 1979-1983 | Sunburst, natural | $12,000 | $16,000 |

Citation (2nd Reissue)
1993-present. Limited production via Gibson's Historic Collection, natural or sunburst.
| 1994-2014 | Various colors | $11,000 | $14,600 |

CJ-165/CJ-165 Modern Classic
2006-2008. Classic small body non-cutaway flat-top, solid spruce top, maple or rosewood back and sides, originally called J-165.
| 2006-2008 | | $1,500 | $1,875 |

CJ-165 EC Modern Classic
2007-2009. As above, but with single-cut, electronics, maple or rosewood back and sides.
| 2007-2009 | | $1,550 | $1,975 |

CL-10 Standard
1997-1998. Flat-top, solid spruce top, laminated mahogany back and sides.
| 1997-1998 | | $800 | $1,000 |

CL-20 Standard Plus
1997-1998. Flat-top, laminated back and sides, 4-ply binding with tortoiseshell appointments, abalone diamond inlays.
| 1997-1998 | | $1,000 | $1,250 |

CL-30 Deluxe
1997-1998. J-50 style dreadnought, solid spruce top, bubinga back and sides, factory electronics.
| 1997-1998 | | $1,000 | $1,250 |

CL-35 Deluxe
1998. Single cutaway CL-30.
| 1998 | | $1,100 | $1,350 |

CL-40 Artist
1997-1998. Flat-top, gold hardware, rosewood back and sides.
| 1997-1998 | | $1,450 | $1,800 |

CL-45 Artist
1997-1998. Single cutaway CL-40.
| 1997-1998 | | $1,650 | $2,000 |

Gibson Challenger III

*Gibson Chet Atkins
Country Gentleman*
Brett Ivers

Gibson CS-336F
Serge Small

1964 Gibson Dove

MODEL YEAR	FEATURES	EXC. COND. LOW	HIGH

CL-50
1997-1999. Custom Shop model, D-style body, higher-end appointments, offered with Brazilian rosewood.

| 1997-1999 | | $3,500 | $4,500 |

Corvus I
1982-1984. Odd-shaped solidbody with offset V-type cut, bolt maple neck, rosewood 'board, 1 humbucker, standard finish was silver gloss, but others available at an additional cost.

| 1982-1984 | | $800 | $1,000 |

Corvus II
1982-1984. Same as Corvus I, but with 2 humbuckers, 2 volume controls, 1 master tone control.

| 1982-1984 | | $900 | $1,125 |

Corvus III
1982-1984. Same as Corvus I, but with 3 single-coil pickups, master volume and tone control, 5-way switch.

| 1982-1984 | | $1,000 | $1,250 |

Crest Gold
1969-1971. Double-cut thinline archtop, Brazilian rosewood body, 2 mini-humbuckers, bound top and headstock, bound f-holes, gold-plated parts.

| 1969-1971 | | $4,400 | $5,600 |

Crest Silver
1969-1972. Silver-plated parts version of Crest.

| 1969-1972 | | $3,800 | $4,800 |

CS Series
2002-present. Scaled down ES-335 body style, made in Custom Shop.

2002-2003	CS-356 (plain top)	$1,850	$2,300
2002-2008	CS-356F (figured top)	$2,100	$2,600
2002-2010	CS-336F (figured top)	$2,000	$2,500
2002-2014	CS-336 (plain top)	$1,850	$2,300

Dave Grohl DG-335
2007-2008. Inspired By Series, Trini Lopez Standard specs, Certificate of Authenticity, Pelham Blue or black finish.

| 2007-2008 | | $5,500 | $6,900 |

Dove
1962-1996, 1999-2013. Flat-top acoustic, maple back and sides, square shoulders.

1962-1964	Natural	$5,900	$7,500
1962-1964	Sunburst	$5,500	$7,000
1965	Natural, early '65	$4,800	$6,200
1965	Natural, late '65	$3,700	$4,800
1965	Sunburst, early '65	$4,400	$5,700
1965	Sunburst, late '65	$3,600	$4,700
1966	Natural	$3,300	$4,400
1966	Sunburst	$3,000	$3,900
1967-1969	Natural	$2,900	$3,800
1967-1969	Sunburst	$2,900	$3,800
1970-1979	Various colors	$2,500	$3,100
1980-1984	Double X	$2,000	$2,500
1985-1988	Single X	$1,600	$2,000
1989	New specs	$1,600	$2,000
1990-1996	Various colors	$2,000	$2,500
1999-2013	Reissue model	$2,000	$2,500

'60s Dove
1997-2004. Spruce top, maple back and sides, Dove appointments.

| 1997-2004 | | $2,000 | $2,500 |

Dove Commemorative
1994-1996. Commemorates Gibson's 100th anniversary, Heritage or Antique Cherry finish, 100 built.

| 1994-1996 | | $2,000 | $2,500 |

Dove In Flight Limited Edition (Custom Shop)
1996-1997. 250 made, figured maple sides and back, Adirondack top, Certificate of Authenticity, dove inlays on headstock.

| 1996-1997 | | $4,000 | $5,100 |

Doves In Flight (Brazilian)
2003. Custom Shop, only 2 made.

| 2003 | | $10,000 | $13,000 |

Doves In Flight (Production Model)
1996-present. Gibson Custom model, maple back and sides, doves in flight inlays.

| 1996-2014 | | $3,550 | $4,600 |

Dove Elvis Presley Signature
2008-2010. Artist Series, Certificate of Authenticity, black.

| 2008-2010 | | $2,350 | $3,000 |

Super Dove
2009-2012. Cutaway, on-board electronics, sold through certain retailers.

| 2009-2012 | | $2,000 | $2,550 |

Duane Eddy Signature
2004-2009. Single rounded cut, flamed maple top and back, 2 single-coils and piezo, pearl 'moustache' markers, signature engraved on 'guard, Bigsby, Rockabilly Brown finish.

| 2004-2009 L | | $3,500 | $4,400 |

EAS Deluxe
1992-1994. Single-cut flat-top acoustic/electric, solid flamed maple top, bound rosewood 'board, trapezoid inlays, 3-band EQ, Vintage Cherry Sunburst.

| 1992-1994 | | $750 | $950 |

EAS Standard/Classic
1992-1995. Like EAS Deluxe, but with spruce top, unbound top, dot inlays, called EAS Classic for '92.

| 1992-1995 | | $750 | $950 |

EBS(F)-1250 Double Bass
1962-1968. Double-cut SG-type solidbody, double-neck with bass and 6-string, originally introduced as the EBSF-1250 because of a built-in fuzztone, which was later deleted, only 22 made.

1962-1964		$10,200	$12,800
1965		$7,500	$9,500
1966-1968		$7,000	$8,800

EC-10 Standard
1997-1998. Jumbo single-cut, on-board electronics, solid spruce top, maple back and sides.

| 1997-1998 | | $900 | $1,150 |

EC-20 Starburst
1997-1998. Jumbo single-cut, on-board electronics, solid spruce top, maple back and sides, renamed J-185 EC in '99.

| 1997-1998 | | $1,500 | $1,875 |

MODEL YEAR	FEATURES	EXC. COND. LOW	HIGH

EC-30 Blues King Electro (BKE)

1997-1998. Jumbo single-cut, on-board electronics, solid spruce top, maple back and sides, double parallelogram inlays, renamed J-185 EC in '99.

1997-1998		$1,500	$1,875

EDS-1275 Double 12

1958-1967, 1977-1990. Double-cut doubleneck with one 12- and one 6-string, thinline hollowbody until late-'62, SG-style solidbody '62 on.

1958-1961	Custom order	$23,000	$29,000
1962-1967	SG body	$18,000	$23,000
1977-1979	Various colors	$4,600	$5,800
1977-1979	White	$4,600	$5,800
1980-1989	Various colors	$3,700	$4,600
1990	Various colors	$3,000	$3,800

EDS-1275 Double 12 (Historic Collection)

1991-present. Custom Shop Historic Collection reissue.

1991-2009	Various colors	$3,400	$4,200
2010-2014	Various colors	$3,000	$3,800

EDS-1275 Double 12 Centennial

1994. Guitar of the Month (May), gold medallion on back of headstock, gold hardware.

1994	Cherry	$3,400	$4,200

EDS-1275 Double 12 Jimmy Page VOS Signature

2008. Custom Shop model with Certificate of Authenticity, 250 made.

2008		$6,100	$7,600

EMS-1235 Double Mandolin

1958-1968. Double-cut, doubleneck with 1 regular 6-string and 1 short 6-string (the mandolin neck), thinline hollowbody until late-1962, SG-style solidbody '62-'68, black, sunburst or white, total of 61 shipped.

1958-1961	Custom order	$23,000	$29,000
1962-1967	SG body	$18,000	$23,000

ES-5

1949-1955. Single-cut archtop, 3 P-90 pickups, renamed ES-5 Switchmaster in '55.

1949-1955	Natural	$10,000	$12,500
1949-1955	Sunburst	$6,700	$8,300

ES-5 Switchmaster

1956-1962. Renamed from ES-5, single-cut (rounded until late-'60, pointed after) archtop, 3 P-90s until end of '57, humbuckers after, switchmaster control.

1956-1957	Natural, P-90s	$9,300	$11,600
1956-1957	Sunburst, P-90s	$7,000	$8,800
1957-1960	Natural, humbuckers	$13,500	$17,000
1957-1960	Sunburst, humbuckers	$10,000	$12,500
1960-1962	Pointed Florentine cutaway	$8,000	$10,000

ES-5/ES-5 Switchmaster Custom Shop Historic

1995-2006.

1995-2002	ES-5, sunburst, P-90s	$3,200	$4,000
1995-2002	Switchmaster, sunburst, humbuckers	$3,600	$4,500
1995-2002	Switchmaster, Wine Red, humbuckers	$3,000	$3,700
1995-2006	Switchmaster, natural option, humbuckers	$3,600	$4,500

ES-100

1938-1941. Archtop, 1 pickup, bound body, sunburst, renamed ES-125 in '41.

1938-1941		$1,725	$2,150

ES-120 T

1962-1970. Archtop, thinline, 1 f-hole, bound body, 1 pickup, sunburst.

1962-1964		$1,050	$1,300
1965		$950	$1,200
1966-1970		$875	$1,100

ES-125

1941-1943, 1946-1970. Archtop, non-cut, 1 pickup, sunburst, renamed from ES-100.

1941-1943	Blade pickup	$1,800	$2,250
1947-1949	1st non-adj., P-90s	$1,650	$2,050
1950	1st non-adj., P-90s	$1,450	$1,825
1951-1959	Adj. P-90s with poles	$1,450	$1,825
1960-1964		$1,200	$1,500
1965		$1,100	$1,400
1966-1970		$1,000	$1,250

ES-125 C

1966-1970. Wide body archtop, single pointed cut away, 1 pickup, sunburst.

1965-1970		$1,450	$1,825

ES-125 CD

1966-1970. Wide body archtop, single-cut, 2 pickups, sunburst.

1965		$2,000	$2,500
1966-1970		$1,650	$2,100

ES-125 D

1957. Limited production (not mentioned in catalog), 2 pickup version of thick body ES-125, sunburst.

1957		$2,200	$2,700

ES-125 T

1956-1968. Archtop thinline, non-cut, 1 pickup, bound body, sunburst.

1956-1959		$1,450	$1,825
1960-1964		$1,200	$1,500
1965		$1,100	$1,400
1966-1968		$1,000	$1,250

ES-125 T 3/4

1957-1970. Archtop thinline, short-scale, non-cut, 1 pickup, sunburst.

1957-1959		$1,150	$1,450
1960-1964		$1,050	$1,300
1965-1968		$850	$1,075

ES-125 TC

1960-1970. Archtop thinline, single pointed cutaway, bound body, 1 P-90 pickup, sunburst.

1960-1964		$1,700	$2,125
1965		$1,600	$2,025
1966-1970		$1,500	$1,900

1959 Gibson EDS-1275

1965 Gibson ES-120 T

Luis Barrios

GUITARS

1964 Gibson ES-125 TDC

Matthew Leo

Gibson ES-140 3/4 T

Jim Gillivan

MODEL YEAR	FEATURES	EXC. COND. LOW	HIGH

ES-125 TD

1957-1963. Archtop thinline, non-cut, 2 pickups, sunburst.

| 1957-1959 | | $2,300 | $2,875 |
| 1960-1963 | | $2,200 | $2,775 |

ES-125 TDC or ES-125 TCD

1960-1971. Archtop thinline, single pointed cutaway, 2 P-90 pickups, sunburst.

1960-1964		$3,200	$4,000
1965	Early '65	$2,900	$3,600
1965	Late '65	$2,500	$3,100
1966-1971		$2,500	$3,100

ES-130

1954-1956. Archtop, non-cut, 1 pickup, bound body, sunburst, renamed ES-135 in '56.

| 1954-1956 | | $1,750 | $2,175 |

ES-135

1956-1958. Renamed from ES-130, non-cut archtop, 1 pickup, sunburst, name reused on a thin body in the '90s.

| 1957-1959 | | $1,750 | $2,175 |

ES-135 (Thinline)

1991-2003. Single-cut archtop, laminated maple body, 2 humbuckers or 2 P-90s, chrome or gold hardware, sunburst.

| 1991-2003 | Stop tail | $1,150 | $1,450 |
| 1991-2003 | Trapeze | $1,150 | $1,450 |

ES-137 Classic

2002-present. Thin-body electric single cut, trapezoid inlays, 2 humbuckers, f-holes, gold hardware.

| 2002-2014 | | $1,250 | $1,575 |

ES-137 Custom

2002-2011. Like Classic, but with split-diamond inlays and varitone.

| 2002-2011 | | $1,350 | $1,700 |

ES-137 P

2002-2005. Like Classic, but with exposed humbuckers, chrome hardware and very small trapezoid inlays.

| 2002-2005 | | $900 | $1,125 |

ES-139

2013-present. Semi-hollow Les Paul style body, 2 humbuckers, Guitar Center model.

| 2013-2014 | | $900 | $1,150 |

ES-140 (3/4)

1950-1956. Archtop, single-cut, 1 pickup, bound body, short-scale, sunburst or natural option (140N).

| 1950-1956 | Natural option | $2,000 | $2,500 |
| 1950-1956 | Sunburst | $2,000 | $2,500 |

ES-140 3/4 T

1957-1968. Archtop thinline, single-cut, bound body, 1 pickup, short-scale, sunburst.

1956-1959		$1,800	$2,250
1960-1964		$1,650	$2,100
1965		$1,450	$1,800
1966-1968		$1,350	$1,700

ES-140N (3/4) T

1956-1958. Natural finish option, low run production, 57 made.

| 1956-1958 | | $2,000 | $2,500 |

MODEL YEAR	FEATURES	EXC. COND. LOW	HIGH

ES-150

1936-1942, 1946-1956. Historically important archtop, non-cut, bound body, Charlie Christian bar pickup from '36-'39, various metal covered pickups starting in '40, sunburst.

1936-1939	Charlie Christian pickup	$5,200	$6,400
1940-1942	Metal covered pickup	$2,500	$3,100
1946-1949	P-90 pickup	$2,100	$2,650
1950-1956	P-90 pickup	$1,900	$2,400

ES-150 DC

1969-1975. Archtop, double rounded cutaway, 2 humbuckers, multi-bound.

1969	Cherry, walnut	$2,400	$3,000
1969	Natural	$2,600	$3,200
1970-1975	Cherry, walnut	$2,200	$2,800
1970-1975	Natural	$2,400	$3,000

ES-165 Herb Ellis

1991-2011. Single pointed cut hollowbody, 1 humbucker, gold hardware.

| 1991-2011 | | $1,650 | $2,050 |

ES-175/ES-175N

1949-1971. Archtop, single pointed cutaway, 1 pickup (P-90 from '49-early-'57, humbucker early-'57-'71), multi-bound, sunburst or natural option (175N).

1949-1956	Natural, P90	$3,800	$4,800
1949-1956	Sunburst, P-90	$3,600	$4,500
1957-1959	Natural, humbucker	$6,900	$8,650
1957-1962	Sunburst, humbucker	$5,400	$6,700
1963	Sunburst, PAFs	$5,400	$6,700
1964	Sunburst, pat. #	$3,800	$4,800
1965	Sunburst, humbucker	$3,500	$4,400
1966-1969	Sunburst	$3,100	$3,900
1967-1969	Black	$3,300	$4,100
1970-1971	Various colors	$2,400	$3,000

ES-175 D/ES-175N D

1952-present. Archtop, single-cut, 2 pickups (P-90s from '53-early-'57, humbuckers early-'57 on), sunburst or natural option (175N D). Humbucker pickups were converted from PAF-stickers to Pat. No.-stickers in '62. Different models were converted at different times. An ES-175 model, made during the transitional time, with PAFs, will fetch more. In some of the electric-archtop models, the transition period may have been later than '62. Cataloged as the ES-175 Reissue in the '90s, Currently as the ES-175 under Gibson Memphis.

1952-1956	Natural, P-90s	$4,500	$5,700
1952-1956	Sunburst, P-90s	$4,600	$5,800
1957-1959	Natural, humbuckers	$9,800	$12,200
1957-1959	Sunburst, humbuckers	$7,200	$9,000
1960-1961	Natural, humbuckers	$9,600	$12,000
1960-1961	Sunburst, humbuckers	$7,000	$8,800
1962-1963	Natural, PAFs	$9,600	$12,000
1962-1963	Sunburst, PAFs	$7,000	$8,800

The ***Vintage Guitar Price Guide*** shows low to high values for items in all-original excellent condition, and, where applicable, with original case or cover.

MODEL YEAR	FEATURES	EXC. COND. LOW	HIGH
1964	Natural, pat. #	$5,500	$6,800
1964	Sunburst, pat. #	$4,300	$5,400
1965	Natural, humbuckers	$4,500	$5,700
1965	Sunburst, humbuckers	$3,900	$4,900
1966	Natural, humbuckers	$3,700	$4,700
1966	Sunburst, humbuckers	$3,300	$4,100
1967-1969	Black	$3,300	$4,100
1967-1969	Various colors	$3,300	$4,100
1970-1979	Various colors	$2,650	$3,300
1980-1999	Various colors	$2,500	$3,100
2000-2014	Various colors	$2,400	$3,000
2007	Sunburst, natural, Wine	$2,400	$3,000

ES-175 D-AN
1999-2000. P-90s, Antique Natural finish.

1999-2000		$2,200	$2,825

ES-175 CC
1978-1979. 1 Charlie Christian pickup, sunburst or walnut.

1978-1979		$2,400	$3,000

ES-175 T
1976-1980. Archtop thinline, single pointed cutaway, 2 humbuckers, various colors.

1976-1980		$2,400	$3,025

ES-175 SP
2006. Single humbucker version.

2006	Sunburst	$2,200	$2,825

ES-175 Steve Howe
2001-2007. Maple laminate body, multi-bound top, sunburst.

2001-2007		$2,800	$3,525

ES-225 T/ES-225N T
1955-1959. Thinline, single pointed cutaway, 1 P-90 pickup, bound body and neck, sunburst or natural option (225N T).

1955-1959	Natural	$2,700	$3,400
1955-1959	Sunburst	$2,300	$2,900

ES-225 TD/ES-225N TD
1956-1959. Thinline, single-cut, 2 P-90s, bound body and neck, sunburst or natural option (225N TD).

1956-1959	Natural	$4,000	$5,200
1956-1959	Sunburst	$3,500	$4,600

1959 ES-225 Historic
2014-present. Single-cut TD reissue with 2 P-90s, sunburst.

2014		$2,500	$3,100

ES-250/ES-250N
1939-1940. Archtop, carved top, special Christian pickup, multi-bound, high-end appointments, sunburst or natural option (250N).

1939	Natural	$18,200	$24,000
1939	Sunburst	$12,000	$15,000
1940	Natural	$14,000	$18,000
1940	Sunburst	$10,100	$12,600

ES-295
1952-1958. Single pointed cutaway archtop, 2 pickups (P-90s from '52-late-'57, humbuckers after), gold finish, gold-plated hardware.

1952-1957	P-90s	$5,000	$6,300
1957-1958	Humbuckers	$13,000	$17,000

ES-295 Reissue
1990-1993. Gold finish, 2 P-90 pickups, Bigsby.

1990-1993		$2,500	$3,100

ES-295 '52 Historic Collection
1990-2000. Higher-end reissue, Antique Gold finish, 2 P-90 pickups, Bigsby.

1990-2000		$2,725	$3,400

ES-300/ES-300N
1940-1942, 1945-1953. Archtop, non-cut, f-holes, had 4 pickup configurations during its run, sunburst or natural (300N).

1940	Natural, oblong diagonal pickup	$4,500	$5,800
1940	Sunburst, oblong diagonal pickup	$3,500	$4,500
1941-1942	Natural, 1 pickup	$4,500	$5,800
1941-1942	Sunburst, 1 pickup	$3,300	$4,200
1945	Black, 1 pickup	$3,000	$3,900
1945-1949	Sunburst, 1 pickup	$2,800	$3,600
1949-1953	Natural, 2 pickups	$3,700	$4,700
1949-1953	Sunburst, 2 pickups	$3,300	$4,200

ES-320 TD
1971-1974. Thinline archtop, double-cut, 2 single-coil pickups, bound body, cherry, natural, or walnut.

1971-1974		$1,450	$1,800

ES-325 TD
1972-1978. Thinline archtop, double-cut, 2 mini-humbuckers, 1 f-hole, bound body, top mounted control panel, cherry or walnut.

1972-1978		$2,200	$2,700

ES-330 T/ES-330N T
1959-1963. Double rounded cutaway, thinline, 1 pickup, bound body and neck, sunburst, cherry or natural option (330N T). In the '60s came with either an original semi-hard case (better than chip board) or a hardshell case. Prices quoted are for hardshell case; approximately $100 should be deducted for the semi-hard case.

1959-1961	Natural	$5,750	$7,200
1959-1963	Cherry	$3,200	$4,000
1959-1963	Sunburst	$3,200	$4,000

ES-330 TD/ES-330N TD
1959-1972. Double rounded cutaway, thinline, 2 pickups, bound body and neck, sunburst, cherry or natural option (330N TD). In the '60s came with either an original semi-hard case (better than chip board) or a hardshell case. Prices noted for the hardshell case; approximately $100 should be deducted for the semi-hard case.

1959-1961	Natural	$7,600	$9,500
1959-1964	Cherry	$4,100	$5,100
1959-1964	Sunburst	$4,100	$5,100
1965	Sunburst, cherry	$3,300	$4,100
1966-1968	Sunburst, cherry	$2,575	$3,225
1967	Burgundy Metallic (unfaded)	$3,125	$3,900
1968	Burgundy Metallic	$3,125	$3,900
1968	Walnut option	$2,575	$3,225
1969-1972	Various colors, long neck	$2,575	$3,225

1966 Gibson ES-330
Tom Siska

1964 Gibson ES-330 TD
Luis Barrios

To get the most from this book, be sure to read "Using *The Guide*" in the introduction.

1961 Gibson ES-335
David Daviee

1963 Gibson ES-335

ES-330 TDC

1998-2000. Custom Shop model, block markers.

MODEL YEAR	FEATURES	EXC. COND. LOW	HIGH
1998-2000		$2,350	$2,950

ES-330 VOS

2012-present. Custom Shop, late '50s specs and VOS finish in sunburst, natural and cherry.

MODEL YEAR	FEATURES	EXC. COND. LOW	HIGH
2012-2013		$2,350	$2,950

ES-333

2002-2005. Economy ES-335, no 'guard, no headstock inlay, exposed coils, stencil logo, satin finish.

MODEL YEAR	FEATURES	EXC. COND. LOW	HIGH
2002-2005		$1,050	$1,300

ES-335/ES-335N TD

1958-1981. The original design ES-335 has dot 'board inlays and a stop tailpiece, sunburst, cherry or natural option (335N). Block inlays replaced dots in mid-'62, in late-'64 the stop tailpiece was replaced with a trapeze tailpiece. Replaced by the ES-335 DOT in '81.

MODEL YEAR	FEATURES	EXC. COND. LOW	HIGH
1958	Natural, bound neck	$52,000	$65,000
1958	Natural, bound neck, Bigsby	$41,000	$52,000
1958	Natural, unbound neck	$50,000	$65,000
1958	Natural, unbound neck, Bigsby	$39,000	$49,000
1958	Sunburst, bound neck	$25,000	$32,000
1958	Sunburst, bound neck, Bigsby	$21,000	$27,000
1958	Sunburst, unbound neck	$24,000	$31,000
1958	Sunburst, unbound neck, Bigsby	$20,000	$25,000
1959	Cherry (early), stop tail	$27,000	$34,000
1959	Natural, bound neck	$62,000	$80,000
1959	Natural, bound neck, Bigsby	$49,000	$64,000
1959	Sunburst, bound neck	$31,000	$40,000
1959	Sunburst, bound neck, Bigsby	$22,000	$29,000
1960	Cherry, factory Bigsby	$20,000	$25,000
1960	Cherry, factory stop tail	$26,000	$33,000
1960	Natural, factory Bigsby	$31,000	$40,000
1960	Natural, factory stop tail	$49,000	$64,000
1960	Sunburst, factory Bigsby	$20,000	$25,000
1960	Sunburst, factory stop tail	$27,000	$34,000
1961	Cherry, factory Bigsby	$17,000	$21,000
1961	Cherry, factory stop tail	$22,000	$28,000
1961	Sunburst,		

MODEL YEAR	FEATURES	EXC. COND. LOW	HIGH
	factory Bigsby	$17,000	$21,000
1961	Sunburst, factory stop tail	$22,000	$28,000
1962	Cherry, blocks, PAFs	$15,000	$20,000
1962	Cherry, blocks, pat. #	$14,000	$18,500
1962	Cherry, dots, PAFs	$16,000	$21,000
1962	Cherry, vibrola tail	$11,000	$14,500
1962	Sunburst, blocks, PAFs	$15,000	$20,000
1962	Sunburst, blocks, pat. #	$14,000	$18,500
1962	Sunburst, dots, PAFs	$16,000	$21,000
1962	Sunburst, dots, pat. #	$14,000	$18,500
1962	Sunburst, vibrola tail	$11,000	$14,500
1963-1964	Cherry, factory Bigsby	$11,000	$14,000
1963-1964	Cherry, factory Maestro	$11,000	$14,000
1963-1964	Cherry, factory stop tail	$13,500	$18,000
1963-1964	Sunburst, factory Bigsby	$11,000	$14,000
1963-1964	Sunburst, factory Maestro	$11,000	$14,000
1963-1964	Sunburst, factory stop tail	$13,500	$18,000
1965	Early '65, wide neck	$8,500	$10,700
1965	Mid '65, narrow neck	$5,500	$7,300
1966	Cherry, sunburst	$5,000	$6,500
1966	Pelham Blue	$10,000	$13,000
1966	Sparkling Burgundy	$7,500	$10,000
1967	Black	$7,500	$10,000
1967	Cherry, sunburst	$5,000	$6,500
1967	Pelham Blue	$10,000	$13,000
1967	Sparkling Burgundy	$7,500	$10,000
1968	Cherry, sunburst	$5,000	$6,500
1968	Pelham Blue	$10,000	$13,000
1968	Sparkling Burgundy	$7,500	$10,000
1969	Cherry, sunburst	$4,500	$6,000
1969	Walnut finish option	$4,000	$5,000
1970-1976	Cherry or sunburst	$3,500	$4,400
1970-1976	Walnut finish option	$3,300	$4,300
1977-1979	Various colors, coil tap	$3,300	$4,300
1980-1981	Various colors	$2,900	$3,800

MODEL YEAR	FEATURES	EXC. COND. LOW	HIGH

ES-335 TD CRR
1979. Country Rock Regular, 2 stereo pickups, coil-tap, sunburst.

1979		$3,300	$4,300

ES-335 Dot
1981-1990. Reissue of 1960 ES-335 and replaces ES-335 TD. Name changed to ES-335 Reissue. Various color options including highly figured wood.

1981-1990	Cherry, sunburst	$2,400	$3,025
1981-1990	Natural	$3,000	$3,825

ES-335 Dot CMT (Custom Shop)
1983-1985. Custom Shop ES-335 Dot with curly maple top and back, full-length center block, 2 PAF-labeled humbuckers, natural or sunburst.

1983-1985		$3,100	$3,900

ES-335 Reissue/ES-335 '59 Dot Reissue/ES-335
1991-present. Replaced the ES-335 DOT, dot inlays, various color options including highly figured wood. Renamed the 1959 ES-335 Dot Reissue in '98 and currently just ES-335 followed by options - Dot, Block (added in '98), Fat Neck (added in '08), Figured (added in '06), Plain, Satin (added in '06).

1991-2014	Cherry, sunburst, walnut	$2,100	$2,625
1991-2014	Natural	$2,550	$3,150
2006-2013	Satin	$1,400	$1,775
2014-2015	Satin, Memphis	$1,450	$1,825

ES-335 Dot P-90
2007. Custom Shop limited edition with black dog-ear P-90s, stop tailpiece.

2007		$2,400	$3,000

ES-335-12
1965 1971. 12 string version of the 335.

1965-1968		$3,500	$4,400

ES-335 '59 Dot Historic Collection (CS)
1999-2000, 2002-present. Custom Shop model, Historical Series based upon 1959 ES-335 dot neck, figured maple top on early series, plain on later, nickel hardware.

1999-2000	Figured top	$3,000	$3,800
2002-2014	Figured top	$3,000	$3,800
2002-2014	Plain top	$2,700	$3,400

1959 ES-335 Dot Reissue Limited Edition
2009-present. Custom Shop, plain laminated maple top/back/sides, rounded '59 neck profile, '57 Classic humbuckers, Certificate of Authenticity, 250 each to be made in Antique Vintage Sunburst or Antique Natural (standard gloss or V.O.S. treatments).

2009-2014		$2,900	$3,700

ES-335 '60s Block Inlay
2004-2007. Made in Memphis facility, plain maple top, small block markers.

2004-2007		$2,200	$2,700

50th Anniversary 1960 ES-335TD (Custom Shop)
2010-2013. Dot markers, double-ring vintage-style tuners, Antique Faded Cherry, Antique Vintage Sunburst, or Antique Natural.

2010-2013		$3,100	$3,900

50th Anniversary 1963 ES-335
2013-present. Gibson Memphis model, 3-ply maple/poplar/maple body, mahogany neck, rosewood 'board, mother-of-pearl headstock logo, Historic Burst or '60s Cherry finish.

2013-2014		$2,700	$3,400

ES-335 '63 Block Historic Collection (CS)
1998-2000, 2002-2013. Custom Shop model, Historical Series based upon 1963 ES-335 with small block markers, figured maple top on early series, plain on later, nickel hardware.

1998-2000	Figured top	$3,100	$3,900
2002-2013	Figured top	$3,100	$3,900
2002-2013	Plain top	$2,400	$3,000

ES-335 Alvin Lee
2006-2007. Custom Division Nashville, 50 made, features reflect Alvin Lee's Big Red ES-335 complete with decal art, cherry red, includes certificate of authenticity (if missing value is reduced) There is also an unlimited version without certificate.

2006-2007	With certificate	$3,000	$3,800

ES-335 Artist
1981. Off-set dot markers, large headstock logo, metal truss rod plate, gold hardware, 3 control knobs with unusual toggles and input specification.

1981		$2,600	$3,300

ES-335 Centennial
1994. Centennial edition, gold medallion in headstock, diamond inlay in tailpiece, cherry.

1994		$3,000	$3,800

ES-335 Chris Cornell
2012-present. Olive Drab Green or black.

2012-2014		$2,400	$3,000

ES-335 Diamond Edition
2006. Trini Lopez style diamond f-holes, Bigsby tailpiece option, gold hardware, Pelham Blue, pearl white or black pearl.

2006		$2,300	$2,900

ES-335 Eric Clapton Crossroads '64 Reissue
2005. Reissue of EC's, with certificate of authenticity.

2005		$7,000	$9,500

ES-335 Jimmy Wallace Reissue
Special order by Texas Gibson dealer Jimmy Wallace.

1980	Blond	$2,700	$3,450

ES-335 Joe Bonamassa Signature
2012. Based on Joe's '61 335, VOS sunburst.

2012		$2,700	$3,450

ES-335 King of the Blues
2006. Offered through Guitar Center, 150 made, based on B.B.'s Lucille.

2006		$2,050	$2,600

ES-335 Larry Carlton
2002-present. Mr. 335 logo on truss rod cover, block neck like Larry's guitar, vintage (faded) sunburst.

2002-2014		$2,600	$3,250

ES-335 Lee Ritenour
2008. Custom Shop, COA, 50 signed and 100 unsigned, Antique Cherry finish.

2008		$2,400	$3,050

1978 Gibson ES-335
Mark Stander

Gibson ES-335 Larry Carlton

Gibson ES-339

Rob Bernstein

1971 Gibson ES-345 TD

Tom Siska

ES-335 Limited Edition
2001. ES-335 style crown inlay on headstock, P-90 pickups.

2001	$2,300	$2,950

ES-335 Nashville
1994. All serial numbers begin with 94, first year Custom Shop run (not the Centennial).

1994	$2,900	$3,600

ES-335 Pro
1979-1981. Two humbucking pickups with exposed coils, bound 'board, cherry or sunburst.

1979-1981	$2,100	$2,650

ES-335 Rich Robinson
2014-present. Bigsby, small blocks, Cherry VOS finish.

2014	$3,000	$3,750

ES-335 Roy Orbison
2006. About 70 made, RO serial number, black finish.

2006	$2,600	$3,300

ES-335 Showcase Edition
1988. Guitar of the Month series, limited production, transparent white/beige finish, black gothic-style hardware, EMG pickups.

1988	$2,100	$2,750

ES-335 Studio
1986-1991, 2013-present. Bound body, 2 Dirty Finger humbuckers, cherry or ebony. Reissued in '13 by Gibson Memphis using '58 specs but with Vintage Sunburst or ebony finish.

1986-1991	$1,300	$1,650
2013-2014	$1,000	$1,275

ES-335 Warren Haynes
2013-2014. Custom Shop model.

2013-2014	500 made	$2,800	$3,600
2014	1961 Ltd. Ed.	$2,800	$3,600

ES-336
1996-1998. Custom Shop smaller sized ES-335 with smaller headstock, dot markers.

1996-1998	All options	$1,850	$2,400

ES-339
2007-present. Smaller-sized bound 335 body, block inlays, 2 humbuckers.

2007-2014	$1,750	$2,225

ES-339 Studio
2013-present. Stripped-down 339, dot inlays, no binding or pickguard.

2013-2014	$875	$1,100

ES-340 TD
1968-1973. The 335 with a laminated maple neck, master volume and mixer controls, various colors.

1968-1973	Natural	$2,600	$3,300
1968-1973	Walnut	$2,500	$3,200

ES-345 TD/ES-345 TDSV
1959-1983. The 335 with Vari-tone, stereo, 2 humbuckers, gold hardware, double parallelogram inlays, stop tailpiece '59-'64 and '82-'83, trapeze tailpiece '65-'82. Cataloged as ES-345 TDSV by '80.

1959	Cherry, Bigsby	$10,000	$13,500
1959	Cherry, stud tail	$16,000	$22,000
1959	Natural, Bigsby	$25,000	$33,000

MODEL YEAR	FEATURES	EXC. COND. LOW	HIGH
1959	Natural, stud tail	$35,000	$45,000
1959	Sunburst, Bigsby	$10,000	$13,500
1959	Sunburst, stud tail	$16,000	$22,000
1960	Cherry, Bigsby	$9,500	$13,000
1960	Cherry, stud tail	$14,000	$19,000
1960	Natural, Bigsby	$25,000	$33,000
1960	Natural, stud tail	$33,000	$43,000
1960	Sunburst, Bigsby	$9,500	$13,000
1960	Sunburst, stud tail	$14,000	$19,000
1961	Cherry, Bigsby	$9,500	$13,000
1961	Cherry, stud tail	$14,000	$19,000
1961	Sunburst, Bigsby	$9,500	$13,000
1961	Sunburst, stud tail	$14,000	$19,000
1962	Bigsby, PAF	$9,500	$13,000
1962	Stud tail, PAF	$14,000	$19,000
1963-1964	Bigsby, pat. #	$7,400	$10,000
1963-1964	Stud tail, pat. #	$11,500	$15,000
1965	Early '65 wide neck	$5,900	$8,100
1965	Mid '65 narrow neck	$4,500	$6,100
1966-1967	Various colors	$4,400	$6,000
1968-1969	Various colors	$4,000	$5,500
1970-1979	Various colors	$3,300	$4,300
1980-1983	TDSV, Various colors	$2,900	$3,800

ES-345 Historic Collection
1998-1999. Custom Shop, stopbar, Bigsby or Maestro tailpiece, Viceroy Brown, Vintage Sunburst, Faded Cherry or natural.

1998-1999	$3,100	$3,900

ES-345 Reissue
2002-2010. ES-345 features with 6-position Varitone selector, gold hardware, stop tailpiece, various colors.

2002-2010	$2,250	$2,825

ES-346 Paul Jackson Jr.
1997-2006. Custom Shop, 335-like with figured or plain maple top, rosewood 'board, double-parallelogram inlays.

1997-2006	$2,200	$2,900

ES-347 TD/ES-347 S
1978-1985, 1987-1993. 335-style with gold hardware, tune-o-matic bridge, 2 Spotlight double-coil pickups, coil-tap, bound body and neck, S added to name in '87.

1978-1979	TD	$3,300	$4,300
1980-1985	TD	$2,900	$3,800
1987-1993	S	$2,900	$3,800

ES-350/ES-350N
1947-1956. Originally the ES-350 Premier, full body archtop, single-cut, 1 P-90 pickup until end of '48, 2 afterwards, sunburst or natural (350N).

1947-1948	Natural, 1 pickup	$7,500	$9,500
1947-1948	Sunburst, 1 pickup	$6,500	$8,500
1949-1956	Natural, 2 pickups	$8,000	$10,000
1949-1956	Sunburst, 2 pickups	$7,000	$9,000

ES-350 Centennial
1994. Guitar of the Month, sunburst, gold hardware, gold medallion on back of headstock, diamond accents, 101 made with serial numbers from 1984-1994. Included a gold signet ring.s.

1994	$3,500	$4,300

The *Vintage Guitar Price Guide* shows low to high values for items in all-original excellent condition, and, where applicable, with original case or cover.

MODEL YEAR	FEATURES	EXC. COND. LOW	HIGH

ES-350 T/ES-350N T

1955-1963, 1977-1981, 1992-1993. Called the ES-350 TD in early-'60s, thinline archtop, single-cut (round '55-'60 and '77-'81, pointed '61-'63), 2 P-90 pickups '55-'56, humbuckers after, gold hardware. Limited runs were done in 1992-1993.

1956	Natural, P-90s	$7,500	$9,500
1956	Sunburst, P-90s	$5,500	$7,000
1957	Sunburst, humbuckers	$8,000	$10,000
1957-1959	Natural, humbuckers	$10,000	$12,500
1958-1959	Sunburst, humbuckers	$8,800	$11,000
1960-1963	Natural	$9,300	$11,600
1960-1963	Sunburst	$6,200	$7,800
1977-1981	Norlin era, natural	$2,500	$3,100
1977-1981	Norlin era, sunburst	$2,400	$3,000

ES-350 T (Custom Shop)

1998-2000. Historic Collection reissue.

1998-2000		$3,000	$3,800

ES-355 TD

1958-1970. 335-style with large block inlays, multi-bound body and headstock, 2 humbuckers, the 355 model was standard with a Bigsby, sideways or Maestro vibrato, non-vibrato models were an option. The prices shown assume a vibrato tailpiece, a factory stop tailpiece was considered an advantage and will fetch more. Early examples have factory Bigsby vibratos, early '60s have sideways vibratos, and late '60s have Maestro vibratos, cherry finish was the standard finish.

1958-1959	Cherry, PAFs, Bigsby vibrato	$12,000	$15,500
1960-1962	Cherry, PAFs, Bigsby vibrato	$10,500	$14,000
1962	Cherry, PAFs, side-pull vibrato	$10,500	$14,000
1963-1964	Cherry, pat. #, Bigsby vibrato	$10,500	$14,000
1965	Early '65 wide neck	$8,000	$10,500
1965	Mid '65 narrow neck	$5,500	$7,300
1966	Cherry or sunburst	$5,000	$6,500
1966	Sparkling Burgundy	$7,500	$9,700
1967-1968	Cherry or sunburst	$5,000	$6,500
1967-1968	Sparkling Burgundy	$7,500	$10,000
1969-1970	Various colors	$4,500	$6,000

ES-355 TDSV

1959-1982. Stereo version of ES-355 with Vari-tone switch, a mono version was available but few were made, the 355 model was standard with a Bigsby, sideways or Maestro vibrato, non-vibrato models were an option. The prices shown assume a vibrato tailpiece. A factory stop tailpiece was considered an advantage and will fetch more, early examples have factory Bigsby vibratos, early-'60s have sideways vibratos and late-'60s have Maestro vibratos, cherry finish was standard, walnut became available in '69.

1959	Bigsby	$12,100	$15,700
1960	Bigsby	$11,000	$14,300
1961-1962	Sideways, late PAFs	$11,000	$14,300
1962	Maestro, late PAFs	$12,100	$15,700
1963	Sideways, late PAFs	$11,000	$14,300
1963-1964	Maestro, pat. #	$11,000	$14,300
1965	Early '65 wide neck	$8,000	$10,500
1965	Mid '65 narrow neck	$5,500	$7,300
1966	Sparkling Burgundy, Maestro	$7,500	$9,700
1966-1967	Cherry or sunburst, Maestro	$5,000	$6,500
1968	Various colors, Maestro	$5,000	$6,500
1969	Various colors, Bigsby	$4,500	$6,000
1970-1979	Various colors, Bigsby	$3,300	$4,300
1980-1982	Various colors, Bigsby	$2,900	$3,800

ES-355 TDSV/79

1980. No Vari-tone switch, stereo or monaural circuitry.

1980		$3,000	$3,800

ES-355/ES-355 TD

1994, 1997, 2006-2010. Custom Shop model, Mono, Bigsby or stop tail.

1994		$2,900	$3,600
1997		$2,900	$3,600
2006-2010		$2,900	$3,600

ES-355 Centennial

1994. Guitar of the Month, sunburst, gold hardware, gold medallion on back of headstock, diamond accents, 101 made with serial numbers from 1984-1994. Included a gold signet ring.

1994		$3,200	$4,000

ES-355 Alex Lifeson

2008-2010. Custom Shop model, Inspired By series.

2008-2010		$4,400	$5,500

ES-355 Curly Maple Limited Edition

2010-2012. Figured flamed maple top, stop tailpiece, natural finish.

2010-2012		$3,000	$3,800

ES-355 Summer Jam Series

2011. Custom Shop Summer Jam series, 25 made in Bourbon Burst.

2011		$2,300	$2,900

ES-359

2008-present. Custom Shop, ES-335/ES-339 style with LP Custom style appointments, minor-figured top and back, sunburst.

2008-2014		$2,100	$2,700

ES-369

1981-1982. A 335-style with 2 exposed humbucker pickups, coil-tap, sunburst.

1981-1982		$2,200	$2,800

1965 Gibson ES-355 TD
Robbie Keene

Gibson ES-359

Gibson ES-390

1968 Gibson Everly Brothers

Keith Myers

MODEL YEAR	FEATURES	EXC. COND. LOW	HIGH

ES-390

2014-present. Memphis model, thinline hollow-body, rosewood 'board, 2 P-90s, Vintage Dark Burst finish.

2014		$1,900	$2,400

ES-446

1999-2003. Single cut semi-hollow, 2 humbuckers, Bigsby, Custom Shop.

1999-2003	Various colors	$2,300	$2,900

ES-775

1990-1993. Single-cut hollowbody, 2 humbuckers, gold hardware, ebony, natural or sunburst.

1990-1993		$2,400	$3,000

ES-Artist

1979-1985. Double-cut thinline, semi-hollowbody, no f-holes, 2 humbuckers, active electronics, gold hardware, ebony, fireburst or sunburst. Moog electronics includes 3 mini-switches for compressor, expander and bright boost.

1979-1985		$2,800	$3,500

EST-150 (Tenor)

1937-1939. Tenor version of ES-150, renamed ETG-150 in '40, sunburst.

1937-1939		$2,600	$3,300

ETG-150 (Tenor)

1940-1942, 1947-1971. Renamed from EST-150, tenor version of ES-150, 1 pickup, sunburst.

1940-1942		$2,600	$3,300
1947-1959		$2,400	$3,000
1960-1969		$2,000	$2,500
1970-1971		$1,800	$2,300

Everly Brothers

1962-1972. Jumbo flat-top, huge double 'guard, star inlays, natural is optional in '63 and becomes the standard color in '68, reintroduced as the J-180 Everly Brothers in '86.

1962-1964	Black	$10,500	$13,000
1963	Natural option	$10,500	$13,000
1965	Black, early '65, larger neck	$8,800	$10,800
1965	Black, late '65, smaller neck	$7,300	$9,000
1966-1967	Black	$7,300	$9,000
1968-1969	Natural replaces black	$5,600	$6,900
1970-1972	Natural	$4,700	$5,800

Explorer

1958-1959, 1963. Some '58s shipped in '63, korina body, 2 humbuckers. The Explorer market is a very specialized and very small market, with few genuine examples available and a limited number of high-end buyers. The slightest change to the original specifications can mean a significant drop in value. The narrow price ranges noted are for all original examples that have the original guitar case.

1958-1959		$450,000	$580,000
1963		$250,000	$335,000

Explorer (Mahogany)

1975-1982. Mahogany body, 2 humbuckers, black, white or natural.

1975-1979	Black or white	$2,500	$3,100
1975-1979	Natural	$3,000	$3,700

MODEL YEAR	FEATURES	EXC. COND. LOW	HIGH
1980-1982	Black or white	$2,300	$2,900
1980-1982	Natural	$2,800	$3,500

Explorer I

1981-1982. Replaces Explorer (Mahogany), 2 Dirty Finger humbuckers, stoptail or Kahler vibrato, becomes Explorer 83 in '83.

1981-1982		$900	$1,150

Explorer 83/Explorer (Alder)

1983-1989. Renamed Explorer 83 from Explorer I, changed to Explorer in '84, alder body, 2 humbuckers, maple neck, ebony 'board, dot inlays, triangle knob pattern.

1983-1984		$1,300	$1,650
1984-1989	Custom colors, limited run	$1,200	$1,500
1984-1989	Standard finishes	$1,000	$1,250

Explorer II (E/2)

1979-1983. Five-piece maple and walnut laminate body sculptured like V II, ebony 'board with dot inlays, 2 humbuckers, gold-plated hardware, natural finish.

1979-1983	All color options	$1,950	$2,450

Explorer III

1984-1985. Alder body, 3 P-90 pickups, 2 control knobs, chrome or black hardware ('85 only), optional locking trem.

1984-1985		$950	$1,200

Explorer '76/X-plorer/Explorer

1990-2014. Mahogany body and neck, rosewood 'board, dot inlays, 2 humbucking pickups, name changed to X-plorer in 2002 and to Explorer in '09.

1990-1999	Various colors	$1,000	$1,250
2000-2009	Various colors	$1,000	$1,250
2010-2014	Various colors	$950	$1,200

Explorer 90 Double

1989-1990. Mahogany body and neck, 1 single-coil and 1 humbucker, strings-thru-body.

1989-1990		$1,000	$1,250

Explorer Baritone

2011-2013. 28"-scale, 2 exposed humbuckers.

2011-2013		$1,400	$1,800

Explorer Centennial

1994 only. Les Paul Gold finish, 100 year banner inlay at 12th fret, diamonds in headstock and gold-plated knobs, Gibson coin in rear of headstock, only 100 made.

1994		$4,000	$5,000

Explorer CMT/The Explorer

1981-1984. Flamed maple body, bound top, exposed-coil pickups, TP-6 tailpiece.

1981-1984		$2,000	$2,500

Explorer Custom Shop

2003-2012. Custom Shop model with Certificate of Authenticity, Korina body, gold hardware.

2003-2012		$3,300	$4,200

Explorer Designer Series

1983-1985. Custom paint finish.

1983-1985		$1,300	$1,850

Explorer Gothic

1998-2003. Gothic Series with black finish and hardware.

1998-2003		$950	$1,200

Explorer Heritage

1983. Reissue of '58 Explorer, korina body, gold hardware, inked serial number, limited edition.

1983	Black, white, red	$3,000	$3,800
1983	Natural	$3,300	$4,100

Explorer (Limited Edition Korina)

1976. Limited edition korina body replaces standard mahogany body, natural.

1976	$6,000	$7,500

Explorer Korina

1982-1984. Korina body and neck, 2 humbucking pickups, gold hardware, standard 8-digit serial (versus the inked serial number on the Heritage Explorer of the same era).

1982-1984	$3,000	$3,800

Explorer 50th Anniversary '58 Korina

2007-2008. Custom Shop model, natural korina, includes custom colors.

2007-2008	$6,500	$8,000

Explorer 50-Year Commemorative

2008. Guitar of the month Oct. '08, AA figured maple top, higher-end appointments, 50th logo on truss rod cover, Brimstone Burst finish.

2008	$5,000	$6,300

Explorer Pro

2002-2005, 2007-2008. Explorer model updated with smaller, lighter weight mahogany body, 2 humbuckers, ebony or natural.

2002-2008	No production '06	$1,200	$1,500

Dethklok "Thunderhorse" Explorer

2011-2012. Limited Edition of 400, Thunderhorse logo on truss rod cover, silverburst finish.

2011-2012	$1,650	$2,050

Explorer Robot

2008-2012. Announced Sept. '08, Robot Tuning System, trapezoid markers, 2 exposed humbuckers, red finish.

2008-2012	$1,100	$1,400

Explorer Split Headstock Collection

2001. Custom Shop model, 25 made, Explorer body with V-split headstock.

2001	$2,700	$3,400

Explorer Voodoo

2002-2004. Juju finish, red and black pickup coils.

2002-2004	$1,000	$1,250

Explorer XPL

1985. Gibson Custom Shop logo on back of headstock, factory Gibson Kahler tremolo, extra cutaway on lower treble bout.

1985	$975	$1,225

Holy Explorer

2009-2011. Explorer body 7 routed holes, 1 knob, 2 exposed humbuckers, Limited Run Series certificate of authenticity, 350 made.

2009-2011	$925	$1,150

Reverse Explorer

2008. Guitar of the Month Sept. '08, 1,000 made, Antique Walnut finish, includes custom guitar case.

2008	$1,200	$1,500

Sammy Hagar Signature Explorer

2011-2013. Mahogany with Red Rocker finish, ghosted Chickenfoot logo on back.

2011-2013	$1,200	$1,500

Shred X Explorer

2008. Guitar of the Month June '08, 1,000 made, ebony finish, black hardware, 2 EMG 85 pickups, Kahler.

2008	$1,000	$1,250

Tribal Explorer

2009-2011. Black tribal graphics on white body. Limited run of 350.

2009-2011	$850	$1,050

X-Plorer/X-Plorer V New Century

2006-2007. Full-body mirror 'guard, mahogany body and neck, 2 humbuckers, mirror truss rod cover.

2006-2007	$875	$1,100

Firebird I

1963-1969. Reverse body and 1 humbucker '63-mid-'65, non-reversed body and 2 P-90s mid-'65-'69.

1963	Sunburst, reverse, hardtail	$11,400	$14,500
1963	Sunburst, reverse, trem	$6,300	$8,000
1964	Cardinal Red, reverse	$11,400	$14,500
1964	Sunburst, reverse, hardtail	$8,000	$10,000
1964	Sunburst, reverse, trem	$5,500	$7,000
1965	Cardinal Red, reverse	$10,200	$13,000
1965	Custom colors, non reverse	$10,000	$12,500
1965	Sunburst, non-reverse, 2 P-90s	$2,600	$3,300
1965	Sunburst, reverse	$5,100	$6,400
1966	Custom colors, non-reverse	$7,100	$9,000
1966	Sunburst, non-reverse	$2,300	$2,900
1967	Custom colors, non-reverse	$7,100	$9,000
1967	Sunburst, non-reverse	$2,300	$2,900
1968-1969	Sunburst, non-reverse	$2,300	$2,900

Firebird I 1963 Reissue Historic Collection

2000-2006. Neck-thru, reverse body, Firebird logo on 'guard, various colors including sunburst and Frost Blue.

2000-2006	Various colors	$2,200	$2,900

Firebird I Custom Shop

1991-1992. Limited run from Custom Shop, reverse body, 1 pickup, gold-plated, sunburst.

1991-1992	$2,200	$2,700

Firebird 76

1976-1978. Reverse body, gold hardware, 2 pickups.

1976	Bicentennial	$2,500	$3,300
1976	Black	$2,300	$3,100
1976	Sunburst, red/white/blue guard logo	$2,500	$3,300
1977-1978	Sunburst	$2,300	$3,100
1977-1978	White	$2,300	$3,100

Gibson Explorer Designer Series

Justin Cosper

Gibson Shred X Explorer

1964 Gibson Firebird V

1972 Gibson Firebird V Medallion
Tom Mazz

MODEL YEAR	FEATURES	EXC. COND. LOW	HIGH

Firebird I/ Firebird 76
1980-1982. Reintroduced Firebird 76 but renamed Firebird I.

1980-1982		$2,300	$3,100

Firebird II/Firebird 2
1981-1982. Maple body with figured maple top, 2 full size active humbuckers, TP-6 tailpiece.

1981-1982		$2,200	$2,900

Firebird III
1963-1969. Reverse body and 2 humbuckers '63-mid-'65, non-reversed body and 3 P-90s mid-'65-'69.

1963	Cardinal Red	$11,500	$14,500
1963	Golden Mist	$11,500	$14,500
1963	Polaris White	$10,500	$13,000
1963	Sunburst	$6,100	$7,700
1964	Cardinal Red, reverse	$11,500	$14,500
1964	Golden Mist, reverse	$11,500	$14,500
1964	Pelham Blue	$11,500	$14,500
1964	Polaris White, reverse	$9,800	$12,200
1964	Sunburst, reverse	$6,100	$7,700
1965	Cherry, non-reverse, 3 P-90s	$4,400	$5,500
1965	Cherry, reverse	$6,700	$8,500
1965	Frost Blue, non-reverse	$8,900	$11,200
1965	Frost Blue, reverse	$9,800	$12,200
1965	Inverness Green, non-reverse	$11,300	$14,000
1965	Iverness Green, reverse	$9,800	$12,200
1965	Sunburst, non-reverse, 3 P-90s	$4,400	$5,500
1965	Sunburst, reverse, 2 P-90s	$4,400	$5,500
1965	Sunburst, reverse, mini humbuckers	$5,400	$6,800
1966	Polaris White	$6,800	$8,600
1966-1967	Frost Blue	$7,700	$9,600
1966-1969	Pelham Blue	$7,700	$9,600
1966-1969	Sunburst	$3,200	$4,000
1967	Cherry	$4,500	$5,600
1968-1969	Pelham Blue	$9,500	$12,000

Firebird III 1964 Reissue (Custom Shop)
2000-2013. Maestro, mini-humbuckers, sunburst or color option.

2000-2013		$2,200	$2,700

Firebird Non-Reverse
2002-2004. Non-reverse body, 2 humbuckers, standard finishes. There was also a limited edition in '02 with swirl finishes.

2002-2004		$1,500	$1,900

Firebird Studio Non-Reverse
2011-2012. Non-reverse body, 3 tapped P-90 pickups, 5-way pickup selector switch, dot markers, vintage sunburst or Pelham Blue nitrocellulose finish.

2011-2012		$950	$1,200

Firebird Studio/Firebird III Studio
2004-2010. Two humbuckers, dot markers, tune-o-matic and bar stoptail, reverse body, dark cherry finish.

2004-2010		$950	$1,200

Firebird V
1963-1969. Two humbuckers, reverse body '63-mid-'65, non-reversed body mid-'65-'69.

1963	Pelham Blue	$17,600	$22,000
1963	Sunburst	$10,500	$13,000
1964	Cardinal Red, reverse	$15,200	$19,000
1964	Sunburst, reverse	$8,700	$11,000
1965	Cardinal Red, reverse	$14,400	$18,000
1965	Sunburst, non-reverse	$4,400	$5,500
1965	Sunburst, reverse	$6,400	$8,000
1966-1967	Cardinal Red	$8,000	$10,000
1966-1969	Sunburst	$3,500	$4,400

Firebird V 1965 Reissue (Custom Shop)
2000-2013. Reverse body, 2 mini-humbuckers, Maestro tremolo, certificate, sunburst or colors.

2000-2013		$2,000	$2,500

Firebird V Celebrity Series
1990-1993. Reverse body, gold hardware, 2 humbuckers, various colors.

1990-1993		$2,200	$2,900

Firebird V Guitar Trader Reissue
1982. Guitar Trader commissioned Firebird reissue, only 15 made, sunburst or white.

1982		$3,000	$3,900

Firebird V Limited Edition Zebrawood
2007. Limited edition from Gibson USA, 400 made, zebrawood reverse body.

2007		$1,300	$1,625

Firebird V Medallion
1972-1973. Reverse body, 2 humbuckers, Limited Edition medallion mounted on body.

1972-1973		$6,000	$7,500

Firebird V/Firebird V Reissue/Firebird V 2010
1986-1987, 1990-present. Based on Firebird V specs, reverse body, 2 pickups, tune-o-matic bridge, vintage sunburst, classic white or ebony with Cardinal Red optional in '91. Called Reissue for '90-'93, renamed V in '94, then V 2010 in '10.

1986-1987	Common finish	$2,200	$2,900
1990	Common finish	$2,200	$2,900
1991	Cardinal Red	$2,000	$2,700
1991-1999	Common finish	$1,500	$2,000
2000-2014	Common finish	$1,200	$1,600

Firebird V-12
1966-1967. Non-reverse Firebird V-style body with standard six-on-a-side headstock and split diamond headstock inlay (like ES-335-12 inlay), dot markers, special twin humbucking pickups (like mini-humbuckers).

1966-1967	Custom colors	$8,700	$11,000
1966-1967	Sunburst	$4,000	$5,000

The **Vintage Guitar Price Guide** shows low to high values for items in all-original excellent condition, and, where applicable, with original case or cover.

MODEL YEAR	FEATURES	EXC. COND. LOW	HIGH

Firebird VII

1963-1969. Three humbuckers, reverse body '63-mid-'65, non-reversed body mid-'65-'69, sunburst standard.

1963	Sunburst	$12,000	$15,000
1964	Custom colors	$21,800	$27,000
1964	Sunburst	$11,000	$14,000
1965	Custom colors	$13,500	$17,000
1965	Sunburst, non-reverse	$6,000	$7,500
1965	Sunburst, reverse	$10,800	$13,500
1966-1967	Custom colors, non-reverse	$12,000	$15,000
1966-1967	Sunburst, non-reverse	$5,600	$7,000
1968	Custom colors	$7,500	$9,400
1968-1969	Sunburst, non-reverse	$5,600	$7,000

Firebird VII 1965 Reissue (Historic/Custom Shop)

1998-2013. Custom Shop/Historic Collection, 3 mini-humbuckers, Vintage Sunburst or solid colors.

1998-2013	Vintage Sunburst	$2,000	$2,500

Firebird VII (Reissued)

2002-2007. Various production models, reverse and non-reverse, 3 pickups, block markers, vibrola, various color options with matching headstock finish.

2002-2007	Candy Apple Red	$1,700	$2,100
2003	Artic White	$1,700	$2,100

Firebird VII Centennial

1994 only. Headstock medallion, sunburst.

1994		$3,200	$4,000

Firebird X Limited Edition Robot

2011-present. 1800 to be made, lightweight swamp ash body, 1-piece maple neck, curly maple 'board, 3 pickups, robot electronics, nitro lacquer finish in Redolution or Bluevolution.

2011-2014		$1,600	$2,000

Firebird Custom Acoustic

2004-present. Sitka spruce top, quilted maple back and sides, ebony 'board, mother-of-pearl headstock logo with MOP and abalone flames inlay, antique natural finish.

2004-2014		$3,200	$4,000

Elliot Easton "Tikibird" Firebird

2013-present. Reverse body, mahogany, rosewood 'board, 2 pickups, Tiki graphic on 'guard, signature on headstock back, Gold Mist Poly finish.

2013-2015		$1,200	$1,500

Flamenco 2

1963-1967. Natural spruce top, 14 3/4", cypress back and sides, slotted headstock, zero fret.

1963-1967		$1,100	$1,400

Flying V

1958-1959, 1962-1963. Only 81 shipped in '58 and 17 in '59, guitars made from leftover parts and sold in '62-'63, natural korina body, string-thru-body design.

As with any ultra high-end instrument, each instrument should be evaluated on a case-by-case basis. The Flying V market is a very specialized market, with few untouched examples available, and a limited number of high-end buyers. The price ranges noted are for all-original, excellent condition guitars with the original

Flying V case. The slightest change to the original specifications can mean a significant drop in value.

1958-1959		$240,000	$320,000

Flying V (Mahogany)

1966-1970, 1975-1980. Mahogany body, around 200 were shipped for '66-'70. Gibson greatly increased production of Flying Vs in '75. See separate listing for the '71 Medallion V version.

1966-1970	Cherry, sunburst	$17,000	$23,000
1975-1978	Various colors	$3,200	$4,000
1979	Silverburst	$3,600	$4,500
1979	Various colors	$3,200	$4,000
1980	Various colors	$2,800	$3,500
1981	Silverburst	$3,600	$4,500

Flying V (Mahogany string-through-body)

1981-1982. Mahogany body, string-thru-body design, only 100 made, most in white, some red or black possible.

1981	Silverburst	$2,800	$3,600
1981-1982	Black, red, white	$2,200	$2,900

Flying V Heritage

1981-1982. Limited edition based on '58 specs, korina body, 4 colors available.

1981-1982	Natural	$3,300	$4,100
1981-1982	Various colors	$3,000	$3,800

Flying V (Korina)

1983. Name changed from Flying V Heritage, korina body, various colors.

1983		$3,000	$3,800

Flying V I/V '83/Flying V (no pickguard)

1981-1988. Introduced as Flying V I, then renamed Flying V '83 in 1983, called Flying V from '84 on. Alder body, 2 exposed humbuckers, maple neck, ebony 'board, dot inlays, black rings, no 'guard, ebony or ivory finish, designed for lower-end market.

1981-1988		$1,475	$1,850

Flying V Reissue/'67/Factor X/Flying V

1990-2014. Mahogany body, called Flying V Reissue first year, then '67 Flying V '91-'02, V Factor X '03-'08, Flying V '09-'14.

1990-2014	Various colors	$1,000	$1,250

Flying V II

1979-1982. Five-piece maple and walnut laminate sculptured body (1980 catalog states top is either walnut or maple), ebony 'board with dot inlays, 2 V-shaped pickups (2 Dirty Fingers humbuckers towards end of run), gold-plated hardware, natural.

1979-1982		$1,950	$2,450

1958/1959 Korina Flying V (Historic/Custom Shop)

1991-2013. Historic Collection, based on '58/'59 Flying V, gold hardware, natural korina.

1991-2013		$4,000	$5,000

Flying V '67 (Historic/Custom Shop)

1997-2004. Historic Collection, '67 Flying V specs, korina body, natural or opaque colors.

1997-2004		$2,200	$2,700

Flying V (Custom Shop)

2004-2008. A few made each year, figured maple top, options include standard point-headstock or split-headstock.

2004-2008		$4,000	$5,000

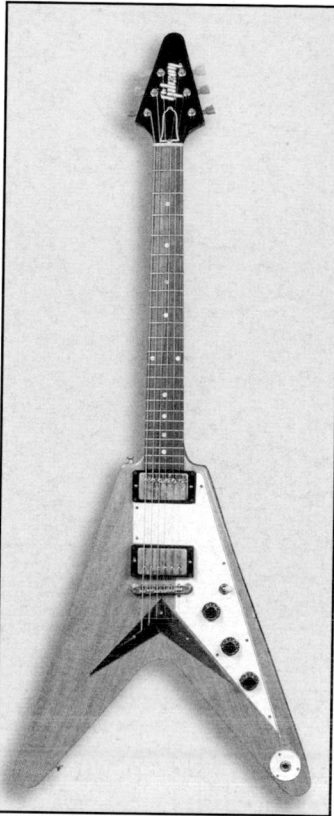

1959 Gibson Flying V

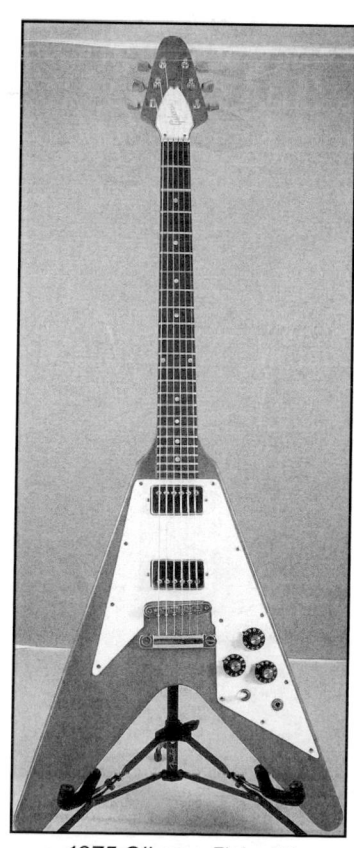

1975 Gibson Flying V
Keith Myers

GUITARS

Gibson Flying V 50-Year Commemorative

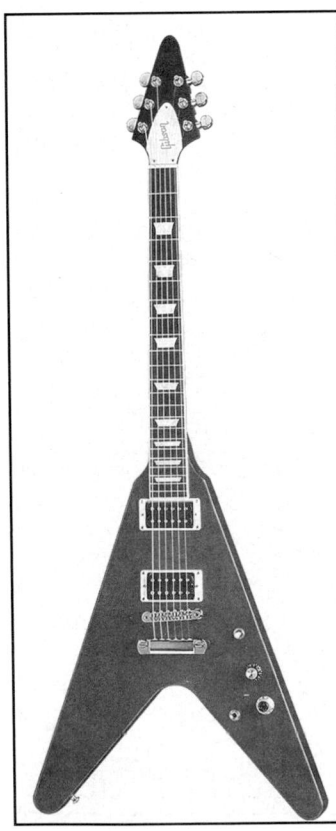

Gibson Flying V Robot

MODEL YEAR	FEATURES	EXC. COND. LOW	HIGH

Flying V 50th Anniversary
2008. Built as replica of '58 square shoulder V, 100 made, natural finish on korina body and neck, rosewood 'board, 8-series serial number, price includes original certificate.

2008		$6,500	$8,000

Flying V 50-Year Commemorative
2008. Guitar of the Month March '08, 1,000 made, AA flamed maple top, higher-end appointments, 50th logo on truss rod cover, Brimstone Burst finish.

2008		$1,200	$1,500

Flying V '90 Double
1989-1990. Mahogany body, stud tailpiece, 1 single-coil and 1 double-coil humbucker, Floyd Rose tremolo, ebony, silver or white.

1989-1990		$1,000	$1,250

Flying V '98
1998. Mahogany body, '58 style controls, gold or chrome hardware.

1998		$975	$1,200

Flying V Centennial
1994 only. 100th Anniversary Series, all gold, gold medalion, other special appointments.

1994		$4,000	$5,000

Flying V CMT/The V
1981-1985. Maple body with a curly maple top, 2 pickups, stud tailpiece, natural or sunburst.

1981-1985		$2,000	$2,500

Flying V Custom (Limited Edition)
2002. Appointments similar to Les Paul Custom, including black finish, only 40 made.

2002		$4,000	$5,000

Flying V Designer Series
1983-1984. Custom paint finish.

1983-1984		$1,300	$1,850

Flying V Faded
2002-2012. Worn cherry finish.

2002-2012		$625	$800

Flying V Gothic/'98 Gothic
1998-2003. Satin black finish, black hardware, moon and star markers.

1998-2003		$950	$1,200

Flying V Hendrix Hall of Fame
Late-1991-1993. Limited Edition (400 made), numbered, black.

1991-1993		$2,200	$2,750

Flying V Hendrix Psychedelic
2006. Hand-painted 1967 Flying V replica, 300 made, includes certificate, instruments without the certificate are worth less than the amount shown.

2006		$6,300	$8,000

Flying V Lenny Kravitz
2002. Custom Shop, 125 made.

2002		$2,600	$3,300

Flying V Lonnie Mack
1993-1995. Mahogany body with Lonnie Mack style Bigsby vibrato, cherry.

1993-1995		$3,800	$4,700

Flying V Medallion
1971. Mahogany body, stud tailpiece, numbered Limited Edition medallion on bass side of V, 350 made

in '71 (3 more were shipped in '73-'74).

1971-1974		$7,000	$8,800

Flying V New Century
2006-2007. Full-body mirror 'guard, mahogany body and neck, 2 humbuckers, Flying V style neck profile, mirror truss rod cover.

2006-2007		$875	$1,100

Flying V Primavera
1994. Primavera (light yellow/white mahogany) body, gold-plated hardware.

1994	Natural yellow/white	$1,500	$1,900
1994	Various special colors	$1,500	$1,900

Flying V Robot
2008-2011. Robot Tuning System.

2008-2011		$1,100	$1,400

Flying V The Holy V
2009. Guitar of the month for Jan. '09, large triangular cutouts in bouts, split diamond markers, 1 humbucker, 1 control knob.

2009		$925	$1,150

Flying V Voodoo
2002-2003. Black finish, red pickups.

2002-2003		$1,000	$1,250

Reverse Flying V
2006-2008. Introduced as part of Guitar of the Week program, reintroduced by popular demand in a '07 limited run, light colored solid mahogany body gives a natural Korina appearance or opaque white or black, V-shaped reverse body, traditional Flying V neck profile.

2006-2008		$1,100	$1,400

Rudolph Schenker Flying V
1993. Only 103 made, black and white body and headstock, signature on 'guard.

1993		$2,000	$2,500

Shred V
2008. Guitar of the Month, 1000 made, EMG humbuckers, Kahler, black.

2008		$1,000	$1,250

Tribal V
2009-2011. Black tribal graphics on white body. Limited run of 350.

2009-2011		$850	$1,050

F-25 Folksinger
1963-1971. 14-1/2" flat-top, mahogany body, most have double white 'guard, natural.

1963-1964		$1,200	$1,500
1965		$1,100	$1,400
1966-1971		$1,000	$1,250

Folk Singer Jumbo (FJN)
1963-1967. Square shoulders, jumbo flat-top, natural finish with deep red on back and sides.

1963-1964		$3,200	$4,000
1965		$2,800	$3,500
1966-1967		$2,400	$3,000

Futura
1982-1984. Deep cutout solidbody, 2 humbucker pickups, gold hardware, black, white or purple.

1982-1984		$1,200	$1,500

The **Vintage Guitar Price Guide** shows low to high values for items in all-original excellent condition, and, where applicable, with original case or cover.

MODEL YEAR	FEATURES	EXC. COND. LOW	HIGH

GB Series Guitar Banjos
See listings in Banjo section of the Price Guide.

GGC-700
1981-1982. Slab single-cut body, 2 exposed humbuckers, dots.

1981-1982		$750	$950

GK-55
1979-1980. LP body style, 2 exposed Dirty Fingers humbuckers, bolt neck, dot markers.

1979-1980		$725	$900

Gospel
1973-1979. Flat-top, square shoulders, laminated maple back and sides, arched back, Dove of Peace headstock inlay, natural.

1973-1979		$750	$950

Gospel Reissue
1992-1997. Laminated mahogany back and sides, natural or sunburst (walnut added in '94, blue and red in '95), changes to old-style script logo and headstock ornamentation in '94.

1992-1993		$1,150	$1,450
1994-1997		$1,200	$1,500

GS-1 Classical
1950-1956. Mahogany back and sides.

1950-1956		$1,000	$1,250

GS-2 Classical
1950-1956. Maple back and sides.

1950-1959		$1,000	$1,250

GS-5 Custom Classic/C-5 Classical
1954-1960. Rosewood back and sides, renamed C-5 Classical in '57.

1954-1960		$1,600	$2,000

GS-35 Classical/Gut String 35
1939-1942. Spruce top, mahogany back and sides, only 39 made.

1939-1942		$2,300	$2,900

GS-85 Classical/Gut String 85
1939-1942. Rosewood back and sides.

1939-1942		$3,800	$4,700

GY (Army-Navy)
1918-1921. Slightly arched top and back, low-end budget model, Sheraton Brown.

1918-1921		$900	$1,125

Harley Davidson Limited Edition
1994-1995. Body 16" wide, flat-top, Harley Davidson in script and logo, black, 1500 sold through Harley dealers to celebrate 100th Anniversary of Harley.

1994-1995		$1,800	$2,250

Heritage
1965-1982. Flat-top dreadnought, square shoulders, rosewood back and sides (Brazilian until '67, Indian '68 on), bound top and back, natural finish.

1965-1967	Brazilian rosewood	$2,800	$3,500
1968-1969	Indian rosewood	$1,400	$1,750
1970-1982	Indian rosewood	$1,350	$1,700

Heritage-12
1968-1971. Flat-top dreadnought, 12 strings, Indian rosewood back and sides, bound top and back, natural finish.

1968-1971		$1,350	$1,700

HG-00 (Hawaiian)
1932-1942. Hawaiian version of L-00, 14 3/4" flat-top, mahogany back and sides, bound top, natural.

1932-1947		$3,500	$4,300

HG-20 (Hawaiian)
1929-1933. Hawaiian, 14 1/2" dreadnought-shaped, maple back and sides, round soundhole and 4 f-holes.

1929-1933		$3,500	$4,300

HG-22 (Hawaiian)
1929-1932. Dreadnought, 14", Hawaiian, round soundhole and 4 f-holes, white paint logo, very small number produced.

1929-1932		$4,000	$5,000

HG-24 (Hawaiian)
1929-1932. 16" Hawaiian, rosewood back and sides, round soundhole plus 4 f-holes, small number produced.

1929-1932		$7,000	$8,700

HG-Century (Hawaiian)
1937-1938. Hawaiian, 14 3/4" L-C Century of Progress, pearloid 'board.

1937-1938		$3,300	$4,100

Howard Roberts Artist
1976-1980. Full body single-cut archtop, soundhole, 1 humbucking pickup, gold hardware, ebony 'board, various colors.

1976-1980		$2,200	$2,800

Howard Roberts Artist Double Pickup
1979-1980. Two pickup version of HR Artist.

1979-1980		$2,400	$3,000

Howard Roberts Custom
1975-1981. Full body single-cut archtop, soundhole, 1 humbucking pickup, chrome hardware, rosewood 'board, various colors.

1975		$2,300	$2,700
1976-1981		$2,200	$2,700

Howard Roberts Fusion/Fusion II/Fusion III
1979-2009. Single-cut, semi-hollowbody, 2 humbucking pickups, chrome hardware, ebony 'board (unbound until '78), TP-6 tailpiece, various colors, renamed Howard Roberts Fusion II in late-'88, and Howard Roberts Fusion III in '91.

1979-1989		$1,900	$2,400
1990-2009		$1,400	$1,750

Hummingbird
1960-present. Flat-top acoustic, square shoulders, mahogany back and sides, bound body and neck.

1960	Cherry Sunburst	$5,000	$6,300
1961-1964	Cherry Sunburst	$4,800	$6,100
1963-1965	Natural	$5,200	$6,500
1965	Cherry Sunburst, early '65	$3,300	$4,100
1965	Cherry Sunburst, late '65	$3,100	$3,800
1966	Cherry Sunburst	$2,800	$3,500
1966	Natural	$3,100	$3,800
1967-1968	Natural, screwed 'guard	$3,100	$3,800
1967-1968	Sunburst, screwed 'guard	$2,800	$3,500

1992 Gibson Howard Roberts Fusion III

1967 Gibson Hummingbird
Garrett Park

*Gibson 50th Anniversary
1960 Hummingbird*

1967 Gibson J-45

MODEL YEAR	FEATURES	EXC. COND. LOW	HIGH
1969-1970	Natural, sunburst	$2,100	$2,600
1971	Natural, sunburst	$2,200	$2,750
1972-1979	Double X, block markers	$2,200	$2,750
1980-1985	Double X, block markers	$1,800	$2,250
1985-1988	Single X	$1,450	$1,800
1989-1999	25 1/2" scale	$1,650	$2,050
1994	100 Years 1894-1994 label	$1,650	$2,050
2000-2014		$1,650	$2,050

50th Anniversary 1960 Hummingbird

2010-2012. 200 made, 50th Anniversary logo on truss rod cover.

2010-2012		$3,200	$4,000

Hummingbird Artist

2007-2011. Plain (no Hummingbird) small 'guard, L.R. Baggs Element, sold through Guitar Center.

2007-2011		$1,500	$1,900

Hummingbird Custom Koa

2004, 2009-present. Highly flamed koa back and sides, spruce top, gloss finish.

2004-2014		$3,400	$4,300

Hummingbird Custom Shop Models

2005-present. Various models from the Custom Shop.

2005-2011	12-string	$2,100	$2,600
2007-2014	Quilt Series, 6-string	$2,700	$3,500

Hummingbird Limited Edition

1993-1994. Only 30 made, quilted maple top and back.

1993-1994		$2,800	$3,600

Hummingbird Modern Classic

2010-2012. Cherry sunburst or ebony finish, L.R. Baggs Element Active pickup system.

2010-2012		$1,800	$2,300

Hummingbird Pro

2010-2013. Non-cut, plain (no Hummingbird) small 'guard, L.R. Baggs Element, Guitar Center.

2010-2013		$1,400	$1,750

Hummingbird Pro EC

2010-2013. Cutaway version, Fishman Prefix Plus-T, Guitar Center.

2010-2013	Cutaway	$1,500	$1,850

Invader

1983-1988. Single cutaway solid mahogany body, two humbucker pickups, four knobs with three-way selector switch, stop tailpiece, bolt-on maple neck.

1983-1988	Black, red, white	$475	$600
1983-1988	Silverburst	$600	$750

J-25

1983-1985. Flat-top, laminated spruce top, synthetic semi-round back, ebony 'board, natural or sunburst.

1983-1985		$525	$650

J-29 Rosewood

2014-present. Sitka spruce top, solid rosewood back and sides.

2014		$1,500	$1,900

J-30

1985-1993. Dreadnought-size flat-top acoustic,

mahogany back and sides, sunburst, renamed J-30 Montana in '94.

1985-1993		$1,100	$1,350

J-30 Cutaway

1990-1995. Cutaway version of J-30, transducer pickup.

1990-1995		$1,100	$1,350

J-30 Montana

1994-1997. Renamed from J-30, dreadnought-size flat-top acoustic, mahogany back and sides, sunburst.

1994-1997		$1,100	$1,350

J-30 RCA Limited Edition

1991. Limited edition for RCA Nashville, RCA logo on headstock.

1991		$1,125	$1,375

J-35

2012-present. Sitka spruce top, mahogany back, sides and neck, rosewood 'board.

2012-2014		$1,300	$1,650

J-40

1971-1982. Dreadnought flat-top, mahogany back and sides, economy satin finish.

1971-1979		$1,000	$1,275
1980-1982		$900	$1,150

J-45

1942-1982, 1984-1993, 1999-present. Dreadnought flat-top, mahogany back and sides, round shoulders until '68 and '84 on, square shoulders '69-'82, sunburst finish (see J-50 for natural version) then natural finish also available in '90s, renamed J-45 Western in '94, renamed Early J-45 in '97 then renamed J-45 in '99. The prices noted are for all-original crack free instruments. A single professionally repaired minor crack that is nearly invisible will reduce the value only slightly. Two or more, or unsightly repaired cracks will devalue an otherwise excellent original acoustic instrument. Repaired cracks should be evaluated on a case-by-case basis.

1942-1945	Banner logo	$8,800	$11,000
1946-1949		$5,400	$7,000
1950-1955		$4,500	$5,600
1956-1959	Standard fixed bridge	$4,500	$5,600
1960-1964		$3,700	$4,800
1965		$2,900	$3,700
1966-1967		$2,700	$3,350
1968	Black, round shoulders	$3,200	$4,000
1968	Cherry, round shoulders	$3,000	$3,800
1968	Sunburst, Gibson 'guard	$2,400	$3,100
1969	Late '69 square D-shape	$1,800	$2,300
1969	Round shoulders	$2,200	$2,900
1970-1979	Sunburst	$1,500	$1,875
1980-1982	Sunburst	$1,400	$1,750
1984-1993	Various colors	$1,400	$1,750
1999-2014	Various colors	$1,400	$1,750

J-45/Early J-45

1997-1998. J-45 model name for '97 and '98.

1997-1998		$1,550	$1,925

The *Vintage Guitar Price Guide* shows low to high values for items in all-original excellent condition, and, where applicable, with original case or cover.

MODEL YEAR	FEATURES	EXC. COND. LOW	HIGH

J-45 1968 Reissue Limited Edition
2004-2007. Special run using '68 specs including Gibson logo 'guard, black or cherry finish.

| 2004-2007 | | $1,400 | $1,750 |

J-45 Brad Paisley
2010-present. Adirondack red spruce top, mahogany back and sides, cherry sunburst.

| 2010-2014 | | $2,600 | $3,200 |

J-45 Buddy Holly Limited Edition
1995-1996. 250 made.

| 1995-1996 | | $2,600 | $3,200 |

J-45 Celebrity
1985. Acoustic introduced for Gibson's 90th anniversary, spruce top, rosewood back and sides, ebony 'board, binding on body and 'board, only 90 made.

| 1985 | | $1,900 | $2,400 |

J-45 Custom
1999-present. Dressed up with abalone trim, Custom logo on truss rod, fancy headstock inlay, maple, mahogany or rosewood body.

| 1999-2014 | Various woods | $1,900 | $2,400 |
| 2013 | Goldtop | $2,000 | $2,500 |

J-45 Custom Vine
1999-2010. Custom Shop, Indian rosewood back and sides, fancy pearl and abalone vine inlay in ebony 'board, pearl Gibson logo and crown, natural gloss finish.

| 1999-2010 | | $3,000 | $3,800 |

J-45 Historic
2005. Limited edition, 670 made, Historic Collection logo rear headstock, sunburst.

| 2005 | | $1,700 | $2,100 |

J-45 Red Spruce Edition
2007. Custom Shop limited edition, only 50 made.

| 2007 | | $2,400 | $3,000 |

J-45 Rosewood
1999-2006. Indian rosewood body, spruce top.

| 1999-2006 | | $1,625 | $2,025 |

J-45 True Vintage
2007-present. Part of Vintage Series, vintage sunburst finish.

| 2007-2014 | | $2,000 | $2,500 |

J-45 Western
1994-1997. Previously called J-45, name changed to Early J-45 in '97.

| 1994-1997 | | $1,600 | $2,000 |

Working Man 45 (J-45)
1998-2005. Soft shoulder J-45 style, gloss finish spruce top, satin finish mahogany back and sides, dot markers, natural.

| 1998-2005 | | $1,200 | $1,500 |

J-50
1942, 1945-1981, 1990-1995, 1998-2008 (present). Dreadnought flat-top, mahogany back and sides, round shoulders until '68, square shoulders after, natural finish (see J-45 for sunburst version). Though not labeled J-50, the J-45 Standard is now also available in natural finish.

1945	Banner logo	$8,000	$10,000
1946-1949		$5,500	$7,000
1950-1955		$4,500	$5,600

MODEL YEAR	FEATURES	EXC. COND. LOW	HIGH
1956	Standard fixed bridge	$4,500	$5,600
1957-1959		$4,500	$5,600
1960-1964		$3,700	$4,800
1965		$2,700	$3,400
1966-1967		$2,400	$3,000
1968	Sunburst, Gibson 'guard	$2,400	$3,000
1969	Round shoulders	$2,200	$2,700
1969	Square shoulders	$1,750	$2,200
1970-1979		$1,400	$1,750
1980-1981		$1,350	$1,700
1990-1995		$1,350	$1,700
1998-2008		$1,350	$1,700

J-55 (Jumbo 55) Limited Edition
1994 only. 16" flat-top, spruce top, mahogany back and sides, 100 made, sunburst.

| 1994 | | $1,450 | $1,850 |

J-55 (Reintroduced)
1973-1982. Flat-top, laminated mahogany back and sides, arched back, square shoulders, sunburst. See Jumbo 55 listing for '39-'43 version.

| 1973-1982 | | $875 | $1,125 |

J-60
1992-1999. Solid spruce top dreadnought, square shoulders, Indian rosewood back and sides, multiple bindings, natural or sunburst.

| 1992-1999 | | $1,400 | $1,775 |

J-60 Curly Maple
1993 and 1996. Curly maple back and sides, limited edition from Montana shop, natural.

| 1993,1996 | | $1,600 | $2,100 |

J 100/J 100 Custom
1970-1974, 1985-1997. Flat-top jumbo, multi-bound top and back, black 'guard, dot inlays, mahogany back and sides, '80s version has maple back and sides, dot inlays and tortoise shell 'guard, '90s model has maple back and sides, no 'guard, and J-200 style block inlays.

| 1970-1974 | Mahogany | $1,300 | $1,675 |
| 1985-1997 | Maple | $1,425 | $1,825 |

J-100 Xtra
1991-1997, 1999-2004. Jumbo flat-top, mahogany back and sides, moustache bridge, dot inlays, various colors, J-100 Xtra Cutaway also available, reintroduced in '99 with maple back and sides and single-bound body.

| 1991-2004 | | $1,225 | $1,550 |

J-150
1999-2005. Super jumbo body, solid spruce top, figured maple back and sides (rosewood in '05), MOP crown inlays, moustache bridge with transducer. Renamed SJ-150.

| 1999-2005 | | $1,700 | $2,100 |

J-160E
1954-1979. Flat-top jumbo acoustic, 1 bridge P-90 pickup, tone and volume controls on front, sunburst finish, reintroduced in '90.

| 1954 | 19 frets, large
bridge dots,
solid top | $5,000 | $6,500 |
| 1955 | 20 frets,
laminated top | $4,500 | $5,800 |

1970 Gibson J-50
Steve Larsen

1965 Gibson J-160E
Torsten Myrgren

To get the most from this book, be sure to read "Using *The Guide*" in the introduction.

Gibson J-160 VS/ John Lennon 70th

1953 Gibson J-200

MODEL YEAR	FEATURES	EXC. COND. LOW	HIGH
1956-1961		$4,500	$5,800
1962-1963	Beatles' vintage June '62	$4,700	$6,100
1964	Lennon's 2nd model	$4,700	$6,100
1965		$3,500	$4,500
1966-1969		$2,400	$3,100
1970-1979		$1,900	$2,500

J-160E Reissue/Standard/VS

1990-1997, 2003-2008. Reintroduced J-160E with solid spruce top, solid mahogany back and sides.

| 1990-1997 | | $1,700 | $2,125 |
| 2003-2008 | | $1,500 | $1,950 |

J-160E John Lennon Peace

2003-2013. J-160E with tortoise 'guard, natural, signature truss rod cover.

| 2003-2013 | | $1,700 | $2,125 |

J-160E John Lennon Peace Model Limited Edition

2009. 750 made, COA.

| 2009 | | $1,825 | $2,300 |

J-160E Montana Special

1995 only.

| 1995 | | $1,500 | $1,950 |

J-160 VS/John Lennon 70th

2010. Commemorative edition for John Lennon's 70th birthday, 500 made, vintage sunburst gloss finish.

| 2010 | | $1,700 | $2,125 |

J-165

2006. Acoustic-electric flat-top 15". See CJ-165.

| 2006 | | $1,600 | $2,000 |

J-180/Everly Brothers/The Everly Brothers

1986-2005. Reissue of the '62-'72 Everly Brothers model, renamed The Everly Brothers ('92-'94), then The Everly ('94-'96), then back to J-180, black.

| 1986-2005 | | $1,850 | $2,300 |

J-180 Billy Jo Armstrong

2011. Certificate of authenticity, 300 made.

| 2011 | | $2,300 | $2,900 |

J-180 Special Edition

1993. Gibson Bozeman, only 36 made, Everly Brother specs, large double white pearloid 'guard.

| 1993 | | $2,400 | $3,000 |

J-185/J-185N

1951-1959. Flat-top jumbo, figured maple back and sides, bound body and neck, sunburst (185) or natural (185N).

| 1951-1959 | Natural | $11,600 | $15,400 |
| 1951-1959 | Sunburst | $9,500 | $12,500 |

J-185 Reissue

1990-1995, 1999-present. Flat-top jumbo, figured maple back and sides, bound body and neck, natural or sunburst, limited run of 100 between '91-'92.

| 1990-1995 | | $1,700 | $2,300 |
| 1999-2014 | | $1,700 | $2,300 |

1951 J-185 (Centennial Model)

1994-1995. Oct. '94 Centennial model, 100 made.

| 1994-1995 | | $2,900 | $3,800 |

J-185 Custom Vine

2004-2012. J-185 with abalone and mother-of-pearl

MODEL YEAR	FEATURES	EXC. COND. LOW	HIGH

vine 'board inlay.

| 2004-2012 | | $2,200 | $2,700 |

J-185 EC

1999-2013. Acoustic/electric, rounded cutaway, maple back and sides. Replaced EC-30 Blues King.

| 1999-2013 | | $1,400 | $1,750 |

J-185 EC Custom

2005. Limited Edition, 200 made, spruce top, figured maple sides and back, pearl double parallelogram markers, Fishman Prefix Plus on-board electronics.

| 2005 | | $1,500 | $1,850 |

J-185 EC Quilt

2002. Quilted maple top, flamed maple body.

| 2002 | | $2,900 | $3,600 |

J-185 EC Rosewood

2006-present. Acoustic/electric, rounded cutaway, Indian rosewood back and sides.

| 2006-2014 | | $1,400 | $1,750 |

J-185-12

2001-2004. 12-string J-185, flamed maple sides and back.

| 2001-2004 | | $1,750 | $2,200 |

J-190 EC Super Fusion

2001-2004. Jumbo single cut acoustic/electric, spruce top, curly maple back and sides, neck pickup and Fishman Piezo.

| 2001-2004 | | $1,325 | $1,650 |

J-200/SJ-200/J-200N/SJ-200N

1946-present. Labeled SJ-200 until ca.'54. Super Jumbo flat-top, maple back and sides, see Super Jumbo 200 for '38-'42 rosewood back and sides model, called J-200 Artist for a time in the mid-'70s, renamed '50s Super Jumbo 200 in '97 and again renamed SJ-200 Reissue in '99. Currently again called the SJ-200. 200N indicates natural option.

1946-1949	Natural option	$10,000	$12,600
1946-1949	Sunburst	$9,400	$11,800
1950-1959	Natural option	$8,200	$11,000
1950-1959	Sunburst	$8,000	$10,500
1960-1964	Natural, sunburst	$7,800	$10,300
1965	Natural, sunburst	$5,800	$7,400
1966-1969	Natural, sunburst	$5,000	$6,500
1970-1979	Natural, sunburst	$2,600	$3,400
1980-1989	Natural, sunburst	$2,200	$2,900
1990-1999	Natural, sunburst	$2,200	$2,900
2000-2014	Natural, sunburst	$2,200	$2,900

J-200 Celebrity

1985-1987. Acoustic introduced for Gibson's 90th anniversary, spruce top, rosewood back, sides and 'board, binding on body and 'board, sunburst, only 90 made.

| 1985-1987 | | $2,700 | $3,350 |

J-200 Custom

2009-2013. Additional abalone trim, gold hardware, sunburst or natural.

| 2009-2013 | | $3,000 | $3,700 |

J-200 Elvis Presley Signature

2002. 250 made, large block letter Elvis Presley name on 'board, figured maple sides and back, gloss natural spruce top, black and white custom designed 'guard after one of Presley's personal guitars.

| 2002 | | $3,800 | $4,700 |

MODEL YEAR	FEATURES	EXC. COND. LOW	HIGH

J-200 Jr.

1991-1996, 2002. Smaller 16" body, sunburst, natural, black or cherry.

1991-1996		$1,700	$2,100

J-200 Koa

1993-1995, 2013. Figured Hawaiian Koa back and sides, spruce top, natural.

1993-1995		$2,600	$3,300
2013		$2,600	$3,300

J-200 M Trophy 75th Anniversary

2012-2013. Quilt maple back and sides, rosewood 'board, abalone crown inlays, antique natural or vintage sunburst nitrocellulose finish.

2012-2013		$2,400	$3,000

J-200 Montana Gold Flame Maple

1998-2012. SJ-200 design, AAA Sitka spruce top with Eastern curly maple back and sides, ebony 'board, Custom Montana Gold banner peghead logo, antique natural.

1998-2012		$2,600	$3,200

J-200 Rose

1994-1995. Centennial Series model, based on Emmylou Harris' guitar, black finish, rose 'guard, gold tuners, 100 built.

1994-1995		$4,000	$5,000

J-200 Studio

2009-present. Studio logo on truss rod cover, unbound 'board, plain 'guard.

2009-2014		$1,925	$2,400

J-200 Western Classic Pre-War

1999-2012. Indian rosewood.

1999-2012		$2,600	$3,400

J-200 Western Classic Pre-War 200 Brazilian

2003. Based on Ray Whitley's 1937 J-200, Custom Shop, limited production, Brazilian rosewood back and sides.

2003		$6,600	$8,200

J-200/SJ-200 Ron Wood

1997. Based on a '57 SJ-200 with Wood's oversized double 'guard on either side of the sound hole, flame-pattern fretboard inlays, script signature inlay on headstock, natural.

1997		$1,675	$2,100

J-250 R

1972-1973, 1976-1978. A J-200 with rosewood back and sides, sunburst, only 20 shipped from Gibson.

1972-1973		$2,400	$3,000
1976-1978		$2,400	$3,000

J-1000/SJ-1000

1992-1994. Jumbo cutaway, spruce top, rosewood back and sides, on-board electronics, diamond-shape markers and headstock inlay.

1992-1994		$1,900	$2,400

J-1500

1992. Jumbo cutaway flat-top, higher-end appointments including Nick Lucas-style position markers, sunburst.

1992		$1,900	$2,400

J-2000/J-2000 Custom/J-2000 R

1986, 1992-1999. Cutaway acoustic, rosewood back and sides (a few had Brazilian rosewood or maple bodies), ebony 'board and bridge, Sitka spruce top, multiple bindings, sunburst or natural. Name changed to J-2000 Custom in '93 when it became available only on a custom-order basis.

1986	J-2000 R, rosewood	$2,600	$3,250
1986	J-2000, maple	$2,600	$3,250
1992	Rosewood	$2,600	$3,250
1993-1996	J-2000 Custom	$2,600	$3,250
1999	J-2000 Custom Cutaway	$2,700	$3,400

Jackson Browne Signature

2011-present. Based on '30s Jumbo style with increased body depth and upgraded tonewoods, Model 1 without pickup, Model A with pickups, Adirondack red spruce top, English walnut back and sides, nitro lacquer sunburst finish.

2011-2014	Model 1	$3,225	$4,000
2011-2014	Model A	$3,425	$4,250

JG-0

1970-1972. Economy square shouldered jumbo, follows Jubilee model in '70.

1970-1972		$850	$1,050

JG-12

1970. Economy square shouldered jumbo 12-string, follows Jubilee-12 model in '70.

1970		$850	$1,050

Johnny A Signature Series

2004-2013. Thinline semi-hollow, sharp double-cut, flamed maple top, humbuckers, gold hardware, Bigsby, sunburst, includes certificate of authenticity.

2004-2013	Includes rare color option	$2,900	$3,600

Johnny Smith

1961-1989. Single-cut archtop, 1 humbucking pickup, gold hardware, multiple binding front and back, natural or sunburst. By '80 cataloged as JS model.

1961-1964		$10,200	$12,700
1965		$8,500	$10,500
1966-1969		$7,500	$9,500
1970-1989		$6,200	$7,700

Johnny Smith Double

1963-1989. Single-cut archtop, 2 humbucking pickups, gold hardware, multiple binding front and back, natural or sunburst. By '80 cataloged as JSD model.

1961-1964		$10,600	$13,200
1965		$9,000	$11,000
1966-1969		$8,500	$10,500
1970-1989		$6,600	$8,200

Jubilee

1969-1970. Flat-top, laminated mahogany back and sides, single bound body, natural with black back and sides.

1969-1970		$950	$1,200

Jubilee Deluxe

1970-1971. Flat-top, laminated rosewood back and sides, multi-bound body, natural finish.

1970-1971		$1,050	$1,300

Jubilee-12

1969-1970. Flat-top, 12 strings, laminated mahogany back and sides, multi-bound, natural.

1969-1970		$950	$1,200

Gibson Jackson Browne Signature

1965 Gibson Johnny Smith Double

GUITARS

Gibson L-4 CES

Gibson L-1 Robert Johnson

MODEL YEAR	FEATURES	EXC. COND. LOW	HIGH

Jumbo
1934-1936. Gibson's first Jumbo flat-top, mahogany back and sides, round shoulders, bound top and back, sunburst, becomes the 16" Jumbo 35 in late-'36.

1934-1936		$18,200	$23,000

Jumbo 35/J-35
1936-1942. Jumbo flat-top, mahogany back and sides, silkscreen logo, sunburst, reintroduced as J-35, square-shouldered dreadnought, in '83.

1936		$12,500	$15,600
1937-1942		$13,000	$16,500

Jumbo 55/J-55
1939-1943. Flat-top dreadnought, round shoulders, mahogany back and sides, pearl inlaid logo, sunburst, reintroduced in '73 as J-55.

1939-1943		$17,000	$21,000

Jumbo Centennial Special
1994. Reissue of 1934 Jumbo, natural, 100 made.

1994		$2,000	$2,500

Junior Pro
1987-1989. Single-cut, mahogany body, KB-X tremolo system 1 humbucker pickup, black chrome hardware, various colors.

1987-1989		$500	$625

Kalamazoo Award Model
1978-1981. Single-cut archtop, bound f-holes, multi-bound top and back, 1 mini-humbucker, gold-plated hardware, woodgrain 'guard with bird and branch abalone inlay, highly figured natural or sunburst.

1978-1981	Natural	$11,000	$13,700
1978-1981	Sunburst	$10,000	$12,500

Keb' Mo' Signature Bluesmaster
2010. Limited run of 300, small-bodied flat-top acoustic, Baggs pickup, soundhole-mounted volume control, vintage sunburst or antique natural finish.

2010		$1,900	$2,400

Kiefer Sutherland KS-336
2007. Custom Shop model inspired by Artist Series.

2007		$3,600	$4,500

KZ II
1980-1981. Double-cut solidbody, 2 humbuckers, 4 knob and toggle controls, tune-o-matic, dot markers, stencil Gibson logo on headstock, KZ II logo on truss rod cover, walnut stain finish.

1980		$750	$950

L-0
1926-1933, 1937-1942. Acoustic flat-top, maple back and sides '26-'27, mahogany after.

1926-1928	13.5", maple	$3,200	$4,100
1928-1930	13.5", mahogany	$3,200	$4,100
1931-1933	14.75"	$3,200	$4,100
1937-1942	Reissue, spruce top	$3,200	$4,100

L-00
1932-1946. Acoustic flat-top, mahogany back and sides, bound top to '36 and bound top and back '37 on.

1932-1946		$3,500	$4,500

L-00 1937 Legend
2006-present. Part of the Vintage Series.

2006-2014		$2,900	$3,700

L-00/Blues King
1991-1997, 1999-present. Reintroduced as L-00,

MODEL YEAR	FEATURES	EXC. COND. LOW	HIGH

called Blues King L-00 for '94-'97, back as L-00 for '99-'02, called Blues King '03-present.

1991-1997	L-00/Blues King	$1,000	$1,250
2003-2011	Blues King	$1,350	$1,700
2012-2013	Blues King	$1,500	$1,900

L-1 (Archtop)
1902-1925. Acoustic archtop, single-bound top, back and soundhole, name continued on flat-top model in '26.

1902-1907	12.5"	$1,700	$2,100
1908-1919	13.5"	$1,700	$2,100
1920-1924	13.5", Loar era	$1,800	$2,250
1925	13.5"	$1,800	$2,250

L-1 (Flat-Top)
1926-1937. Acoustic flat-top, maple back and sides '26-'27, mahogany after.

1925-1929	13.5", 12-fret	$3,300	$4,100
1930-1931	14.75", 13-fret	$3,300	$4,100
1932-1937	14-fret	$3,500	$4,300

L-1 1928 Blues Tribute
2013-present. Adirondack red spruce top, mahogany back and sides, rosewood 'board, faded Vintage Sunburst.

2013-2014		$2,400	$3,000

L-1 Robert Johnson
2007-present. 1926 specs, Robert Johnson inlay at end of 'board.

2007-2014		$1,400	$1,750

L-2 (Archtop)
1902-1926. Round soundhole archtop, pearl inlay on peghead, 1902-'07 available in 3 body sizes: 12.5" to 16", '24-'26 13.5" body width.

1902-1907	12.5"	$1,700	$2,100
1924-1926	13.5"	$1,800	$2,250

L-2 (Flat-Top)
1929-1935. Acoustic flat-top, rosewood back and sides except for mahogany in '31, triple-bound top and back, limited edition model in '94.

1929-1933	12-fret, rosewood	$8,900	$12,000
1931-1932	12-fret, mahogany	$7,500	$10,000
1934-1935	14-fret, mahogany	$10,000	$13,000
1934-1935	14-fret, rosewood	$15,000	$20,000

L-2 1929 Reissue
1994 only. Spruce top, Indian rosewood back and sides, raised 'guard.

1994		$1,900	$2,375

L-3 (Archtop)
1902-1933. Acoustic archtop, available in 3 sizes: 12.5", 13.5", 16".

1902-1907	12.5", round hole	$1,900	$2,400
1908-1919	13.5", round hole	$1,900	$2,400
1920	Loar era	$2,000	$2,500
1921-1926	Loar era	$2,100	$2,700
1927-1928	13.5", oval hole	$2,100	$2,700
1929-1933	13.5", round hole	$2,100	$2,700

L-4
1912-1956. Acoustic archtop, 16" wide.

1912-1919	12-fret, oval hole	$2,300	$2,900
1920-1924	Loar era	$2,500	$3,200
1925-1927	12-fret, oval hole	$2,500	$3,200
1928-1934	14-fret, round hole	$2,500	$3,200

MODEL YEAR	FEATURES	EXC. COND. LOW	HIGH
1935-1946	Fleur-de-lis, f-holes	$2,700	$3,700
1947-1956	Crown, double-parallel	$2,700	$3,700

L-4 A/L-4 A EC

2003-2008. 15 3/4" lower bout, mid-size jumbo, rounded cutaway, factory electronics with preamp.

2003-2008		$1,325	$1,675

L-4 C/L-4 CN

1949-1971. Single-cut acoustic archtop, sunburst or natural (CN)

1949-1959	Natural	$4,000	$5,000
1949-1959	Sunburst	$3,500	$4,400
1960-1964	Natural	$3,500	$4,400
1960-1964	Sunburst	$2,800	$3,500
1965	Natural, sunburst	$2,300	$2,900
1966-1969	Natural, sunburst	$1,850	$2,300
1970-1971	Natural, sunburst	$1,350	$1,700

L-4 CES/L-4 CES Mahogany

1958, 1969, 1986-present. Single pointed cutaway archtop, 2 humbuckers, gold parts, natural or sunburst, maple back and sides '58 and '69, mahogany laminate back and sides for '86-'93, became part of Gibson's Historic Collection with laminated maple back and sides for '94, renamed L-4 CES Mahogany with solid mahogany back and sides in '04, Custom Shop model.

1958	Natural, PAF humbuckers	$9,800	$12,200
1958	Sunburst, PAF humbuckers	$7,200	$9,000
1969	Natural	$3,500	$4,400
1969	Sunburst	$3,200	$4,100
1986-1993	Laminate mahogany	$2,600	$3,300
1994-2003	Laminate maple	$2,600	$3,300
2004-2014	Solid mahogany	$2,900	$3,600

L-4 Special Tenor/Plectrum

Late-1920s. Limited edition 4-string flat-top.

1929		$2,500	$3,100

L-5

1924-1958. Acoustic archtop, non-cut, multiple bindings, Lloyd Loar label in '24, 17" body by '35, Master Model label until '27, sunburst with natural option later.

1924	Lloyd Loar era	$45,000	$60,000
1925	Early '25, Master Model label	$24,500	$31,000
1925	Late '25, Master Model label	$19,500	$25,000
1926-1927	Master Model label	$19,500	$25,000
1928	Carter, banjo tuners	$27,000	$34,000
1928	Non-Carter, no banjo tuners	$16,000	$20,000
1929	Early '29	$11,000	$13,500
1929-1930	Block markers	$10,200	$13,000
1931-1932	Kaufman vibrola	$9,200	$11,800
1931-1932	Standard trapeze	$9,200	$11,800
1933-1939	16" body	$9,000	$11,500
1935-1940	17" body	$7,000	$9,500

MODEL YEAR	FEATURES	EXC. COND. LOW	HIGH
1939-1940	Natural option	$9,000	$11,500
1946-1949	Natural option	$9,000	$11,500
1946-1949	Sunburst	$6,600	$8,300
1950-1958	Natural	$6,700	$8,400
1950-1958	Sunburst	$5,400	$6,900

L-5 '34 Non-Cutaway Historic

1994. 1934 specs including block pearl inlays, bound snakehead peghead, close grained solid spruce top, figured solid maple sides and back, Cremona Brown sunburst finish, replica Grover open back tuners.

1994		$4,000	$5,050

L-5 Premier/L-5 P

1939-1943. Introduced as L-5 Premier (L-5 P) and renamed L-5 C in '48, single rounded cutaway acoustic archtop.

1939-1943	Natural option	$13,200	$17,300
1939-1943	Sunburst	$11,500	$15,000

L-5 C/L-5 CN

1948-1982. Renamed from L-5 Premier (L-5 P), single rounded cutaway acoustic archtop, sunburst or natural option (CN)

1948-1949	Natural	$12,400	$15,600
1948-1949	Sunburst	$11,100	$14,000
1950-1959	Natural	$12,600	$15,900
1950-1959	Sunburst	$11,100	$14,000
1960-1962	Natural	$9,100	$11,400
1960-1962	Sunburst	$7,400	$9,200
1963-1964	Natural	$9,000	$11,300
1963-1964	Sunburst	$7,300	$9,100
1965	Natural	$7,200	$8,900
1965	Sunburst	$6,300	$7,800
1966	Natural	$5,900	$7,400
1966	Sunburst	$5,600	$6,900
1967-1969	Natural	$5,700	$7,200
1967-1969	Sunburst	$5,400	$6,700
1970-1982	Natural, sunburst	$4,800	$6,000

L-5 CES/L-5 CESN

1951-present. Electric version of L-5 C, single round cutaway (pointed mid-'60-'69), archtop, 2 pickups (P-90s '51-'53, Alnico Vs '54-mid-'57, humbuckers after), sunburst or natural (CESN), now part of Gibson's Historic Collection.

1951-1957	Natural, single coils	$16,500	$21,000
1951-1957	Sunburst, single coils	$13,500	$17,000
1958-1959	Natural, PAFs	$20,100	$25,100
1958-1959	Sunburst, PAFs	$17,000	$21,200
1960-1962	Natural, PAFs	$20,100	$25,100
1960-1962	Sunburst, PAFs	$16,100	$20,100
1963-1964	Natural, pat. #	$16,100	$20,100
1963-1964	Sunburst, pat. #	$13,500	$16,900
1965	Natural	$9,200	$11,500
1965	Sunburst	$8,000	$10,000
1966-1969	Natural	$7,500	$9,400
1966-1969	Sunburst	$7,000	$8,700
1970-1972	Natural, sunburst	$5,700	$7,000
1973-1979	Natural, sunburst	$5,400	$6,700
1980-1984	Kalamazoo made	$5,400	$6,700
1985-1992	Nashville made	$5,400	$6,700

1958 Gibson L-5
Tom Siska

1967 Gibson L-5 CES
Greg Perrine

1973 Gibson L-5 S

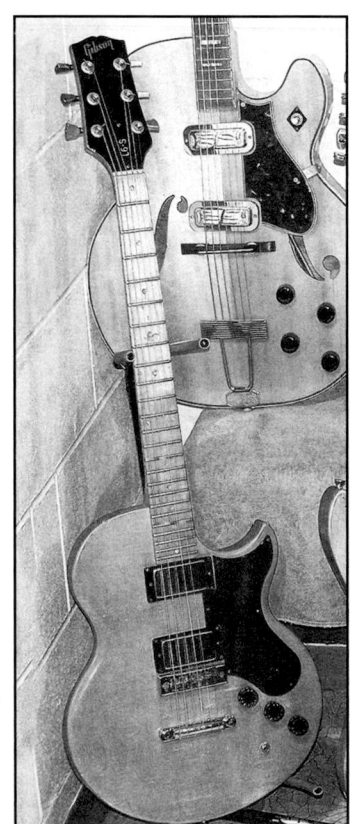

Gibson L-6 S
Tom Pfeifer

MODEL YEAR	FEATURES	EXC. COND. LOW	HIGH

L-5 CES Custom Shop Historic Collection
1994-1997. Historic Collection Series, sunburst or natural.

1994	100th Anniv., black	$4,800	$6,000
1994-1996	Natural, highly figured	$6,000	$7,500
1994-1996	Sunburst	$5,500	$6,800
1997	Wine Red	$5,500	$6,800

L-5 CT (George Gobel)
1959-1961. Single-cut, thinline archtop acoustic, some were built with pickups, cherry.

1959-1961		$16,000	$20,000

L-5 CT Reissue
1998-2007. Historic Collection, acoustic and electric versions, natural, sunburst, cherry.

1998-2007		$5,200	$6,400

L-5 S
1972-1985, 2004-2005. Single-cut solidbody, multi-bound body and neck, gold hardware, 2 pickups (low impedance '72-'74, humbuckers '75 on), offered in natural, cherry sunburst or vintage sunburst. 1 humbucker version issued in '04 from Gibson's Custom, Art & Historic division.

1972-1985	All options	$4,300	$5,400
2004-2005	All options	$4,300	$5,400

L-5 Studio
1996-2000. Normal L-5 dual pickup features, marble-style 'guard, translucent finish, dot markers.

1996-2000		$2,200	$2,750

L-5 Wes Montgomery Custom Shop
1993-present. Various colors.

1993-2009		$6,000	$7,500
2010-2014		$5,300	$6,500

L-6 S
1973-1975. Single-cut solidbody, 2 humbucking pickups, 6 position rotary switch, stop tailpiece, cherry or natural, renamed L-6 S Custom in '75.

1973-1975	Cherry, natural	$1,050	$1,300

L-6 S Custom
1975-1980. Renamed from the L-6 S, 2 humbucking pickups, stop tailpiece, cherry or natural.

1975-1980	Cherry, natural	$1,200	$1,500
1978-1979	Silverburst option	$1,300	$1,600

L-6 S Deluxe
1975-1981. Single-cut solidbody, 2 humbucking pickups, no rotary switch, strings-thru-body design, cherry or natural.

1975-1981		$1,350	$1,700

L-6 S Reissue
2011-2012. With rotary switch, 2 humbuckers, natural or silverburst.

2011-2012	Natural	$875	$1,100

L-7/L-7N
1932-1956. Acoustic archtop, bound body and neck, fleur-de-lis peghead inlay, 16" body '32-'34, 17" body X-braced top late-'34, sunburst or natural (N).

1932-1934	16" body	$4,000	$5,000
1935-1939	17" body, X-braced	$4,000	$5,000
1940-1949	Natural	$3,400	$4,300
1940-1949	Sunburst	$3,000	$3,800

MODEL YEAR	FEATURES	EXC. COND. LOW	HIGH
1950-1956	Natural	$2,900	$3,600
1950-1956	Sunburst	$2,500	$3,100

L-7 C/L-7 CN
1948-1972, 2002-2013. Single-cut acoustic archtop, triple-bound top, sunburst or natural (CN). Gibson revived the L-7 C name for a new acoustic archtop in 2002.

1948-1949	Natural	$4,800	$6,000
1948-1949	Sunburst	$4,000	$5,000
1950-1959	Natural	$4,800	$6,000
1950-1959	Sunburst	$4,000	$5,000
1960-1964	Natural	$4,400	$5,700
1960-1964	Sunburst	$3,600	$4,500
1965	Natural	$4,000	$5,000
1965	Sunburst	$3,200	$4,000
1966-1972	Natural	$3,500	$4,400
1966-1972	Sunburst	$3,000	$3,800

L-7 Custom Electric
1936. L-7 with factory Christian-style pickup, limited production, often custom ordered.

1936		$6,200	$7,800

L-7 E/L-7 CE
1948-1954. L-7 and L-7 C with "McCarty" assembly of pickguard-mounted pickups (1 or 2), sunburst only.

1948-1954	L-7 CE	$4,500	$5,700
1948-1954	L-7 E	$3,500	$4,500

L-7 C Custom Shop
2006. Custom Shop logo, Certificate of Authenticity.

2006		$3,500	$4,400

L-10
1923-1939. Acoustic archtop, single-bound body and 'board.

1923-1934	16", F-holes	$3,800	$5,000
1935-1939	17", X-braced	$3,800	$5,000

L-12
1930-1955. Acoustic archtop, single-bound body, 'guard, neck and headstock, gold-plated hardware, sunburst.

1930-1934	16"	$4,500	$6,000
1935-1939	17", X-braced	$4,500	$6,000
1940-1941	Parallel top braced	$4,500	$6,000
1946-1949	Post-war	$3,500	$4,400
1950-1955		$2,900	$3,600

L-12 Premier/L-12 P
1947-1950. L-12 with rounded cutaway, sunburst.

1947-1950		$4,500	$6,000

L-20 20th Anniversary Limited Edition
2009. Custom Shop, 20 made, "20th Anniversary" logo on back of headstock and on label, Certificate of Authenticity.

2009		$2,900	$3,600

L-20 Special/L-20 K International Special
1993-1994. Rosewood or mahogany back and sides (koa on the K), ebony 'board, block inlays, gold tuners, multi-bound.

1993-1994	L-20, mahogany	$1,900	$2,400
1993-1994	L-20, rosewood	$2,000	$2,500
1993-1994	L-20K, koa	$2,000	$2,500

L-30
1935-1943. Acoustic archtop, single-bound body, black or sunburst.

1935-1943		$900	$1,250

MODEL YEAR	FEATURES	EXC. COND. LOW	HIGH

L-37

1937-1941. 14-3/4" acoustic archtop, flat back, single-bound body and 'guard, sunburst.

| 1937-1941 | | $1,000 | $1,350 |

L-47

1940-1942. Acoustic archtop.

| 1940-1942 | | $1,400 | $1,750 |

L-48

1946-1971. 16" acoustic archtop, single-bound body, mahogany sides, sunburst.

1946-1949		$1,200	$1,600
1950-1959		$1,200	$1,600
1960-1964		$1,000	$1,400
1965		$900	$1,250
1966-1969		$800	$1,100
1970-1971		$700	$1,000

L-50

1932-1971. 14.75" acoustic archtop, flat or arched back, round soundhole or f-holes, pearl logo pre-war, decal logo post-war, maple sides, sunburst, 16" body late-'34.

1932-1934	14.75" body	$2,000	$2,500
1934-1945	16" body	$2,150	$2,700
1946-1949	Maple sides	$1,500	$2,000
1950-1959		$1,500	$2,000
1960-1964		$1,400	$1,900
1965		$1,275	$1,625
1966-1969		$1,150	$1,525
1970-1971		$950	$1,250

L-75

1932-1939. 14.75" archtop with round soundhole and flat back, size increased to 16" with arched back in '35, small button tuners, dot markers, lower-end style trapeze tailpiece, pearl script logo, sunburst.

1932	14.75", dot neck	$2,000	$2,500
1933-1934	14.75", pearloid	$2,000	$2,500
1935-1939	16" body	$2,000	$2,500

L-130

1999-2005. 14 7/8" lower bout, small jumbo, solid spruce top, solid bubinga back and sides, rosewood 'board, factory electronics with preamp.

| 1999-2005 | | $1,000 | $1,250 |

L-140

1999-2005. Like L-130 but with rosewood back and sides, ebony 'board.

| 1999-2005 | | $1,200 | $1,500 |

L-200 Emmylou Harris

2001-present. Smaller and thinner than standard 200, flamed maple sides and back, gold hardware, crest markers, natural or sunburst.

| 2001-2014 | | $2,000 | $2,500 |

L-C Century

1933-1939. Curly maple back and sides, bound body, white pearloid 'board and peghead (all years) and headstock (until '38), sunburst.

| 1933-1939 | | $5,500 | $6,900 |

L-C Reissue

1994. Pearloid headstock and 'board.

| 1994 | | $2,075 | $2,600 |

LC-1 Cascade

2002-2006. LC-Series acoustic/electric, advanced L-00-style, solid quilted maple back and sides.

| 2002-2006 | | $1,350 | $1,675 |

LC-2 Sonoma

2002-2006. Released November '02, LC-Series acoustic/electric, advanced L-00-style, solid walnut back and sides.

| 2002-2006 | | $1,550 | $1,950 |

LC-3 Caldera

2003-2004. 14 3/4" flat-top, soft cutaway, solid cedar top, solid flamed Koa back and sides, fancy appointments.

| 2003-2004 | | $1,650 | $2,100 |

Le Grande

1993-2010. Electric archtop, 17", formerly called Johnny Smith.

| 1993-2010 | | $5,800 | $7,200 |

Les Paul

Following are models bearing the Les Paul name, beginning with the one that started it all, the original Les Paul Model. All others are then listed pretty much alphabetically as follows:

Les Paul Model
'52 Les Paul Goldtop
'52 Les Paul Tribute
'54 Les Paul Goldtop
'54 Les Paul Wildwood
'55 Les Paul Goldtop Hot-Mod Wraptail
'56 Les Paul Goldtop
'57 Les Paul Goldtop
'57 Les Paul Goldtop (R-7 wrap-around)
1957 Les Paul Junior Single Cut (VOS)
'58 Les Paul Figured Top
'58 Les Paul Plaintop (VOS)
1958 Les Paul Junior Double Cut (VOS)
'59 Les Paul Flametop/Reissue/Standard
'59 Les Paul Burst Brothers
'59 Les Paul Plaintop (VOS)
'60 Les Paul Corvette
'60 Les Paul Flametop/Standard
'60 Les Paul Plaintop (VOS)
'60 Les Paul Junior
'60 Les Paul Special
Les Paul 25/50 Anniversary
Les Paul 30th Anniversary
Les Paul 40th Anniversary (from 1952)
Les Paul 40th Anniversary (from 1959)
Les Paul 50th Anniversary 1957 Les Paul Standard Goldtop
Les Paul 50th Anniversary 1960 Les Paul Standard
Les Paul 50th Anniversary '56 Les Paul Standard
Les Paul 50th Anniversary '59 Les Paul Standard
Les Paul 50th Anniversary DaPra
Les Paul 50th Anniversary Korina Tribute
Les Paul 55
Les Paul 295

1941 Gibson L-47
Kevin Ferby

Gibson L-200 Emmylou Harris

GUITARS

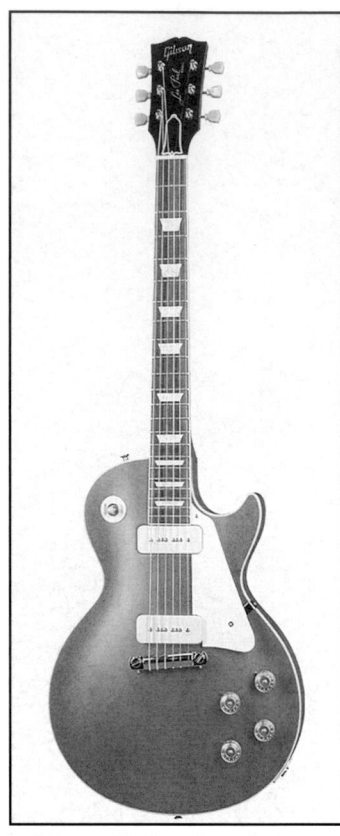

Gibson '54 Les Paul Goldtop

Gibson '56 Les Paul Goldtop

Les Paul Ace Frehley "Budokan" LP Custom
Les Paul Ace Frehley Signature
Les Paul Axcess Alex Lifeson
Les Paul Axcess Standard
Les Paul (All Maple)
Les Paul Artisan and Artisan/3
Les Paul Artist/L.P. Artist/Les Paul Active
Les Paul BFG
Les Paul Billy F. Gibbons Goldtop
Les Paul Bird's-Eye Standard
Les Paul Carved Series
Les Paul Centennial ('56 LP Standard Goldtop)
Les Paul Centennial ('59 LP Special)
Les Paul Class 5
Les Paul Classic
Les Paul Classic Antique Mahogany
Les Paul Classic Custom
Les Paul Classic H-90
Les Paul Classic Limited Edition
Les Paul Classic Mark III/MIII
Les Paul Classic Plus
Les Paul Classic Premium Plus
Les Paul Classic Tom Morgan Limited Edition
Les Paul Cloud 9 Series
Les Paul Collector's Choice Series
Les Paul Custom
Les Paul Custom 20th Anniversary
Les Paul Custom 35th Anniversary
Les Paul Custom '54
Les Paul Custom Historic '54
Les Paul Custom Historic '57 Black Beauty
Les Paul Custom Historic '68
Les Paul Custom Jimmy Page
Les Paul Custom Lite
Les Paul Custom Lite (Show Case Edition)
Les Paul Custom Mick Ronson '68
Les Paul Custom Music Machine
Les Paul Custom Peter Frampton Signature
Les Paul Custom Plus
Les Paul Custom Showcase Edition
Les Paul Custom Silverburst
Les Paul Dale Earnhardt
Les Paul Dale Earnhardt Intimidator
Les Paul Dark Fire
Les Paul DC AA
Les Paul DC Classic
Les Paul DC Pro
Les Paul DC Standard (Plus)
Les Paul DC Studio
Les Paul Deluxe
Les Paul Deluxe #1 Pete Townshend
Les Paul Deluxe #3 Pete Townshend
Les Paul Deluxe #9 Pete Townshend
Les Paul Deluxe 30th Anniversary
Les Paul Deluxe '69 Reissue
Les Paul Deluxe Hall of Fame
Les Paul Deluxe Limited Edition
Les Paul Deluxe Limited Edition AMS
Les Paul Deluxe Reissue
Les Paul Dickey Betts Goldtop
Les Paul Dickey Betts Red Top
Les Paul Don Felder Hotel California 1959
Les Paul Duane Allman (Custom Shop)

Les Paul Dusk Tiger
Les Paul Elegant
Les Paul Elegant Streak Silver
Les Paul Eric Clapton 1960
Les Paul ES-Les Paul
Les Paul Florentine Plus
Les Paul Futura
Les Paul Gary Moore BFG
Les Paul Gary Moore Signature
Les Paul Gary Rossington Signature
Les Paul Goddess
Les Paul GT
Les Paul Guitar Trader Reissue
Les Paul HD.6-X Pro Digital
Les Paul Heritage 80
Les Paul Heritage 80 Award
Les Paul Heritage 80 Elite
Les Paul Heritage 80/Standard 80
Les Paul Indian Motorcycle
Les Paul Jim Beam
Les Paul Jimmy Page (Custom Authentic)
Les Paul Jimmy Page Signature
Les Paul Jimmy Page Signature Custom Shop
Les Paul Jimmy Wallace Reissue
Les Paul Joe Bonamassa Aged Goldtop
Les Paul Joe Bonamassa Skinnerburst 1959
Les Paul Joe Perry 1959 Custom Shop
Les Paul Joe Perry Signature
Les Paul Jumbo
Les Paul Junior
Les Paul Junior 3/4
Les Paul Junior Billie Joe Armstrong Signature
Les Paul Junior DC Hall of Fame
Les Paul Junior Double Cutaway
Les Paul Junior Faded
Les Paul Junior John Lennon LTD
Les Paul Junior Lite
Les Paul Junior Special
Les Paul Junior Special Robot
Les Paul Junior Tenor/Plectrum
Les Paul Katrina
Les Paul KM (Kalamazoo Model)
Les Paul Korina (Custom Shop)
Les Paul Leo's Reissue
Les Paul Limited Edition (3-tone)
Les Paul LP295 Goldtop
Les Paul Menace
Les Paul Michael Bloomfield 1959 Standard
Les Paul Music Machine 25th Anniversary
Les Paul Music Machine Brazilian Stinger
Les Paul Neal Schon Signature
Les Paul Old Hickory
Les Paul Paul Kossoff 1959 Standard
Les Paul Peace
Les Paul Personal
Les Paul Pro Deluxe
Les Paul Pro Showcase Edition
Les Paul Professional
Les Paul Recording
Les Paul Reissue Flametop
Les Paul Reissue Goldtop
Les Paul Richard Petty LTD

The *Vintage Guitar Price Guide* shows low to high values for items in all-original excellent condition, and, where applicable, with original case or cover.

Les Paul SG '61 Reissue
Les Paul SG Standard Authentic
Les Paul SG Standard Reissue
Les Paul Signature
Les Paul Signature/L.P. Signature
Les Paul Slash Appetite
Les Paul Slash Appetite For Destruction
Les Paul Slash Signature
Les Paul SmartWood Exotic
Les Paul SmartWood Standard
Les Paul SmartWood Studio
Les Paul Special
Les Paul Special (Reissue)
Les Paul Special 3/4
Les Paul Special Centennial
Les Paul Special Double Cutaway
Les Paul Special Faded
Les Paul Special New Century
Les Paul Special Robot
Les Paul Special Tenor
Les Paul Special Worn Cherry
Les Paul Spider-Man
Les Paul Spotlight Special
Les Paul Standard (Sunburst)
Les Paul Standard (SG body)
Les Paul Standard (reintroduced then re-
   named)
Les Paul Standard 2008
Les Paul Standard '82
Les Paul Standard Billy Gibbons 'Pearly
   Gates'
Les Paul Standard Faded
Les Paul Standard Lite
Les Paul Standard Plus
Les Paul Standard Premium Plus
Les Paul Standard Raw Power
Les Paul Standard Robot
Les Paul Standard Sparkle
Les Paul Strings and Things Standard
Les Paul Studio
Les Paul Studio '50s Tribute
Les Paul Studio '60s Tribute
Les Paul Studio Baritone
Les Paul Studio BFD
Les Paul Studio Custom
Les Paul Studio Deluxe '60s
Les Paul Studio Faded Vintage Mahogany
Les Paul Studio Faded/Les Paul Studio Pro
   Faded
Les Paul Studio Gem
Les Paul Studio Gothic
Les Paul Studio Gothic Morte
Les Paul Studio Limited Edition
Les Paul Studio Lite
Les Paul Studio MLB Baseball
Les Paul Studio Platinum
Les Paul Studio Platinum Plus
Les Paul Studio Plus
Les Paul Studio Premium Plus
Les Paul Studio Raw Power
Les Paul Studio Robot
Les Paul Studio Shred
Les Paul Studio Swamp Ash

Les Paul Supreme
Les Paul Tie Dye (St. Pierre)
Les Paul Tie Dye Custom Shop
Les Paul Traditional Pro
Les Paul Traditional/Plus
Les Paul TV
Les Paul TV 3/4
Les Paul Ultima
Les Paul Vixen
Les Paul Voodoo/Voodoo Les Paul
Les Paul XR-I/XR-II/XR-III
Les Paul Zakk Wylde Signature
The Les Paul
The Paul
The Paul Firebrand Deluxe
The Paul II

Les Paul Model

1952-1958. The Goldtop, 2 P-90 pickups until mid-'57, humbuckers after, trapeze tailpiece until late-'53, stud tailpiece/bridge '53-mid-'55, Tune-o-matic bridge '55-'58, renamed Les Paul Standard in '58. All gold option add +10% if the neck retains 90% of the gold paint. All gold option with ugly green wear on the neck is equal to or below the value of a standard paint job. Some instruments had all mahogany bodies which did not have the maple cap. These instruments are of lower value than the standard maple on mahogany bodies. The all mahogany version, although more rare, has a 10% lower value. A factory installed Bigsby tailpiece will reduce value by 30%. A non-factory installed Bigsby will reduce value up to 50%.

MODEL YEAR	FEATURES	EXC. COND. LOW	HIGH
1952	1st made, unbound neck	$15,000	$19,500
1952	5/8" knobs, bound neck	$11,600	$15,200
1953	1/2" knobs, early-'53 trapeze tailpiece	$11,600	$15,200
1953	1/2" knobs, late-'53 stud tailpiece	$18,000	$24,000
1954	Stud tailpiece, wrap-around	$18,000	$24,000
1955	Stud tailpiece, wrap-around, early-'55	$21,000	$27,000
1955	Tune-o-matic tailpiece, late-'55	$31,000	$39,300
1956	Tune-o-matic tailpiece	$29,000	$37,000
1957	P-90s, early-'57	$28,500	$36,300
1957	PAFs, black plastic	$67,000	$80,000
1957	PAFs, white plastic	$77,000	$95,000
1958	PAFs	$77,000	$95,000

'52 Les Paul Goldtop

1997-2002. Goldtop finish, 2 P-90s, '52-style trapeze tailpiece/bridge.

MODEL YEAR	FEATURES	EXC. COND. LOW	HIGH
1997-2002		$2,000	$2,500
1997-2002	Murphy aged	$2,200	$2,750

2004 Gibson '59 Les Paul Flametop

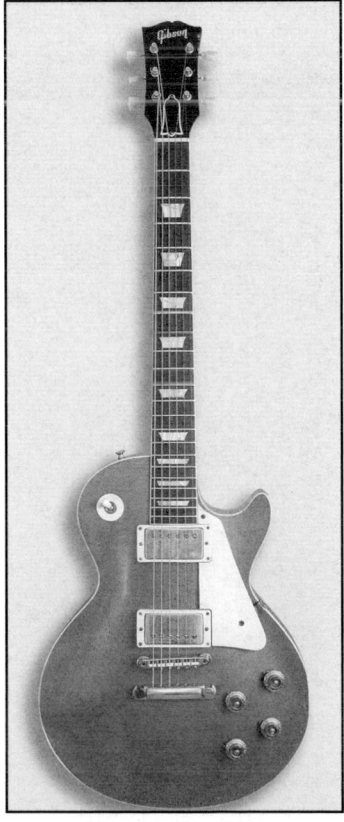

1957 Gibson Les Paul
Dave Hinson

GUITARS

2007 Gibson '58 Les Paul Plaintop

David Carver

2007 '60 Les Paul Standard

Rob Bernstein

MODEL YEAR	FEATURES	EXC. COND. LOW	HIGH

'52 Les Paul Tribute
2009. Recreation of '52 Les Paul Goldtop model, 564 made, special serialization, each guitar has 'prototype' impressed on back of headstock, Tribute designation logo on truss rod, includes COA booklet with serialized COA and tribute dates 1915-2009.

2009		$2,000	$2,500

'54 Les Paul Goldtop
1996-2013. Goldtop finish, 2 P-90s, '53-'54 stud tailpiece/bridge.

1996-2000		$2,400	$3,000
2001-2003	R-4 (very accurate)	$2,200	$2,750
2003	Brazilian rosewood	$4,500	$5,600
2004-2006	VOS	$2,200	$2,750
2007	R-4, limited, 1/4 sawn fleck	$2,200	$2,750
2007-2013	VOS	$2,200	$2,750

'54 Les Paul Wildwood
2012. Wildwood guitars special run, '54 specs, wraparound tailpiece, 2 P-90 pickups, plaintop sunburst.

2012		$2,400	$3,000

'55 Les Paul Goldtop Hot-Mod Wraptail
2010. Musician's Friend, based on '55 LP Humbucking Pickup Test Guitar, '55 specs, aged nitrocellulose gold finish, includes COA.

2010		$2,400	$3,000

'56 Les Paul Goldtop
1991-present. Renamed from Les Paul Reissue Goldtop. Goldtop finish, 2 P-90 pickups, Tune-o-matic, now part of Gibson's Historic Collection, Custom Authentic aging optional from '01, Vintage Original Specs aging optional from '06.

1991-1999		$2,400	$3,000
2000-2005		$2,200	$2,750
2003	Brazilian rosewood	$4,500	$5,600
2006-2014	VOS	$2,200	$2,750

'57 Les Paul Goldtop
1993-present. Goldtop finish, 2 humbuckers, now part of Gibson's Historic Collection.

1993-1999		$2,400	$3,000
2000-2005		$2,200	$2,750
2003	Brazilian rosewood	$4,900	$6,100
2006-2014	VOS	$2,200	$2,750

'57 Les Paul Goldtop (R-7 wrap-around)
2007. Special run with wrap-around bar tailpiece/bridge similar to tailpiece on an original '54 Les Paul Goldtop.

2007		$2,300	$2,900

1957 Les Paul Junior Single Cut (VOS)
1998-2014. Custom Shop, certificate of authenticity, nickel-plated hardware, Vintage Original Spec aging optional from '06.

1998-2014		$1,350	$1,700

'58 Les Paul Figured Top
1996-2000, 2002-2003, 2009-2012. Less top figure than '59 Reissue, Custom Shop, sunburst.

1996-2003		$3,900	$5,000
2003	Brazilian rosewood	$8,400	$11,000
2009-2012		$3,500	$4,500

'58 Les Paul Plaintop (VOS)
1994-1999, 2003-2012. Custom Shop model, plain maple top version of '58 Standard reissue, sunburst,

VOS model starts in '04. Replaced by the 1958 Les Paul Reissue with a non-chambered body.

1994-2003		$2,300	$2,900
2004-2012	VOS, non-chambered	$2,300	$2,900
2006-2012	VOS, chambered	$2,300	$2,900

1958 Les Paul Junior Double Cut (VOS)
1998-2013. Custom Shop, nickel plated hardware, Vintage Original Spec aging optional from '06.

1998-2013		$1,350	$1,700

'59 Les Paul Flametop/Reissue/Standard
1993-present. Renamed from Les Paul Reissue Flametop, for 2000-'05 called the 1959 Les Paul Reissue, in '06 this model became part of Gibson's Vintage Original Spec series and is called the '59 Les Paul Standard VOS. Flame maple top, 2 humbuckers, thick '59-style neck, sunburst finish, part of Gibson's Historic Collection, the original certificate authenticity adds value, an instrument without the matching certificate has less value. By '98 Gibson guaranteed only AAA Premium grade maple tops would be used.

Collectors of Historic Collection instruments tend to buy and store these instruments, maintaining them in near mint to New Old Stock (NOS) mint condition. In recent years, NOS instruments that are up to five years old, but in like-new mint condition, have been sold at prices that are higher than instruments in excellent condition, which is the usual condition that VG Price Guide values are given. Because of that trend, the prices shown here give consideration to the numerous NOS instruments that have sold. The inclusion of both excellent condition instruments and mint NOS instruments creates a wider than normal price range, but the high-side of the range is very realistic for NOS instruments.

1993	Custom Shop decal, early '93	$5,500	$7,200
1993	Historic decal, late '93	$4,900	$7,000
1994-1999	Aged	$4,900	$7,000
1996-1999	Figured top	$4,900	$7,000
2000-2014	Aged	$4,800	$6,000
2000-2014	Figured top	$4,400	$5,500
2003	Brazilian, aged	$9,300	$11,600
2003	Brazilian, highly figured	$9,000	$12,000
2003	Brazilian, low figured	$8,000	$10,500

'59 Les Paul Burst Brothers
2009-2010. Limited edition created with Dave Belzer and Drew Berlin, sold through Guitar Center, wood-figure was selected to reflect the nature of a '50s LP Standard rather than using only AAA best-quality flame, 1st run of 34 (ser. # series BB 9 001-034) with dark Madagascar rosewood 'board, 2nd run had 37 (ser. # series BB 0 001-037).

2009	1st run, 34 made	$6,300	$7,700
2010	2nd run, 37 made	$5,100	$6,300

'59 Les Paul Plaintop (VOS)
2006-2013. Custom Shop, very little or no-flame.

2006-2013		$3,200	$4,000

MODEL YEAR	FEATURES	EXC. COND. LOW	HIGH

'60 Les Paul Corvette
1995-1997. Custom Shop Les Paul, distinctive Chevrolet Corvette styling from '60, offered in 6 colors.

1995-1997		$4,400	$5,600

'60 Les Paul Flametop/Standard
1991-present. Renamed from Les Paul Reissue Flametop, flame maple top, 2 humbuckers, thinner neck, sunburst finish, part of Gibson's Historic Collection, in '06 this model became part of Gibson's Vintage Original Spec series and is called the '60 Les Paul Standard VOS.

1991-2014	Figured top	$3,900	$4,900
1994-2014	Aged	$4,400	$5,500
2003	Brazilian, aged	$9,100	$11,500
2003	Brazilian, figured	$9,000	$12,000

'60 Les Paul Plaintop (VOS)
2006-2010. Plain maple top version of '60 Standard reissue, certificate of authenticity, cherry sunburst.

2006-2010		$2,500	$3,100

'60 Les Paul Junior
1992-2003. Historic Collection reissue.

1992-2003		$1,600	$2,000

'60 Les Paul Special
1998-2012. Historic Collection reissue, limited edition, single-cut or double-cut.

1998-2012		$1,850	$2,300
2007	Murphy aged	$2,050	$2,550

Les Paul 25/50 Anniversary
1978-1979. Regular model with 25/50 inlay on headstock, sunburst.

1978-1979	Moderate flame	$3,200	$4,000
1978-1979	Premium flame	$3,500	$4,300

Les Paul 30th Anniversary
1982-1984. Features of a 1958 Les Paul Goldtop, 2 humbuckers, 30th Anniversary inlay on 19th fret.

1982-1984		$2,000	$2,500

Les Paul 40th Anniversary (from 1952)
1991-1992. Black finish, 2 soapbar P-100 pickups, gold hardware, stop tailpiece, 40th Anniversary inlay at 12th fret.

1991-1992		$2,000	$2,500

Les Paul 40th Anniversary (from 1959)
1999. Reissue Historic, humbuckers, highly figured top, price includes 40th Anniversary Edition Certificate of Authenticity with matching serial number, a guitar without the certificate is worth less.

1999		$3,500	$4,300

Les Paul 50th Anniversary 1957 Les Paul Standard Goldtop
2007. Limited run of 150, humbucker pickups, large gold 50th Anniversary headstock logo.

2007		$3,700	$4,600

Les Paul 50th Anniversary 1960 Les Paul Standard
2010-2011. Limited Edition, offered in Heritage Cherry Sunburst, Heritage Dark Burst, Sunset Tea Burst and Cherry Burst.

2010-2011		$4,000	$5,000

Les Paul 50th Anniversary '56 Les Paul Standard
2006. Custom Shop, '56 tune-o-matic P-90 specs.

2006		$2,000	$2,500

Les Paul 50th Anniversary '59 Les Paul Standard
2009-2011. Custom Shop, highly figured top, certificate of authenticity.

2009-2011		$4,000	$5,000

Les Paul 50th Anniversary DaPra
2009. Limited run of 25 made for Vic DaPra of Guitar Gallery, '59 Historic R9.

2009		$4,000	$5,000

Les Paul 50th Anniversary Korina Tribute
2009. Custom Shop model, 100 made, single-cut Korina natural finish body, 3 pickups, dot markers, V-shaped Futura headstock, Custom logo on truss rod cover, slanted raised Gibson logo on headstock.

2009		$4,000	$5,000

Les Paul 55
1974, 1976-1981. Single-cut Special reissue, 2 pickups. By '78 the catalog name is Les Paul 55/78.

1974	Sunburst	$1,500	$1,900
1974	TV limed yellow	$1,500	$1,900
1976-1981	Sunburst	$1,500	$1,900
1976-1981	Wine Red	$1,500	$1,900

Les Paul 295
2008. Guitar of the Month, Les Paul Goldtop with ES295 appointments.

2008		$2,200	$2,800

Les Paul Ace Frehley "Budokan" LP Custom
2012-2013. Custom Shop, limited edition of 50 hand-aged signed by Frehley, 100 hand-aged unsigned and 150 additional with VOS finish.

2012-2013	VOS	$2,100	$2,600

Les Paul Ace Frehley Signature
1997-2001. Ace's signature inlay at 15th fret, 3 humbuckers, sunburst.

1997-2001		$2,500	$3,100

Les Paul Axcess Alex Lifeson
2011-present. Custom Shop, push-pull volume pots, nitrocellulose lacquer finish in Royal Crimson or Viceroy Brown Sunburst, first 25 of each color signed by Lifeson with additional production unsigned, certificate of authenticity.

2011	Signed	$4,700	$5,900
2011-2014	Unsigned	$3,000	$3,800

Les Paul Axcess Standard
2009-present. Custom Shop, new neck joint carve allows access to high frets, Floyd Rose, slightly thinner body, nitro lacquer Iced Tea Burst or Gun Metal Gray.

2009-2014		$2,000	$2,500

Les Paul (All Maple)
1984. Limited run, all maple body, Super 400-style inlay, gold hardware.

1984		$2,400	$3,000

Les Paul Artisan and Artisan/3
1976-1982. Carved maple top, 2 or 3 humbuckers, gold hardware, hearts and flowers inlays on 'board and headstock, ebony, sunburst or walnut.

1976-1982	2 pickups	$2,500	$3,100
1976-1982	3 pickups	$2,600	$3,200

2007 Gibson Les Paul 50th Anniversary '57 Les Paul Standard Goldtop

Paul Harbinson

Gibson Les Paul Axcess Alex Lifeson

Gibson Les Paul Artist

Mark Menna

Gibson Les Paul Billy F. Gibbons Goldtop

Les Paul Artist/L.P. Artist/Les Paul Active

1979-1982. Two humbuckers (3 optional), active electronics, gold hardware, 3 mini-switches, multibound, Fireburst, ebony or sunburst.

1979-1982		$2,200	$2,725

Les Paul BFG

2006-2008. Burstbucker 3 humbucker at bridge and P-90 at neck, 2 volume and 1 tone knobs, figured maple top over mahogany body.

2006-2008		$725	$900
2008	Silverburst	$750	$950

Les Paul Billy F. Gibbons Goldtop

2014-present. Custom Shop, mahogany neck with maple spline, rosewood 'board, holly headstock, 2 Duncan Pearly Gates pickups, Goldtop VOS or Goldtop Aged.

2014		$6,800	$8,500

Les Paul Bird's-Eye Standard

1999. Birdseye top, gold hardware, 2 humbucking pickups, transparent amber.

1999		$1,900	$2,400

Les Paul Carved Series

2003-2005. Custom Shop Standards with relief-carved tops, one in diamond pattern, one with flame pattern.

2003-2005	Carved Diamond (top)	$1,800	$2,250

Les Paul Centennial ('56 LP Standard Goldtop)

1994. Guitar of the Month, limited edition of 100, Goldtop mahogany body, gold hardware, gold truss rod plate, gold medallion, engraved light-gold 'guard, with COA.

1994		$3,200	$4,000

Les Paul Centennial ('59 LP Special)

1994. Guitar of the Month, limited edition of 100, slab body Special-style configuration, gold hardware, P-90s, gold medallion, commemorative engraving in 'guard, cherry, with COA.

1994		$2,900	$3,600

Les Paul Class 5

2001-2006. Custom Shop, highly flamed or quilt top, or special finish, 1960 profile neck, weight relieved body, Burst Bucker humbucking pickups, several color options.

2001-2006		$2,700	$3,400
2001-2006	Stars and Stripes, 50 made	$2,700	$3,400

Les Paul Classic

1990-1998, 2000-2008, 2014-present. Early models have 1960 on pickguard, 2 exposed humbucker pickups, Les Paul Model on peghead until '93, Les Paul Classic afterwards. Limited run of Ebony finish in 2000, 2014 and 2015 have those years in the model name.

1990	Goldtop, 1st year	$1,450	$1,800
1990	Various colors, 1st year	$1,450	$1,800
1991-1998	Goldtop, all gold	$1,450	$1,800
1991-2008	Various colors, plain top	$1,450	$1,800
1998-2008	Goldtop, standard back	$1,450	$1,800
2000	Ebony limited run	$1,450	$1,800
2014-2015		$1,450	$1,800

Les Paul Classic Antique Mahogany

2007. All mahogany body, exposed humbuckers, Guitar of the Week, limited run of 400 each of cherry (week 27) and sunburst (week 33).

2007		$1,500	$1,900

Les Paul Classic Custom

2007-2008. Ebony, 'board, 2 exposed humbuckers, black finish on maple top, gold hardware.

2007-2008		$1,450	$1,950

Les Paul Classic H-90

2008. Guitar of the Week, 400 made, gold hardware, H-90 soapbar pickups.

2008		$1,325	$1,650

Les Paul Classic Limited Edition

2000. Limited Edition logo on back of headstock, Les Paul Classic stencil logo, 3 exposed humbuckers, gold hardware, black finish.

2000		$1,800	$2,250

Les Paul Classic Mark III/MIII

1991-1993. Les Paul Classic features, no 'guard, exposed-coil humbuckers at neck and bridge and single-coil at middle position, 5-way switch, coil-tap.

1991-1993		$1,800	$2,250

Les Paul Classic Plus

1991-1996, 1999-2003. Les Paul Classic with fancier maple top, 2 exposed humbucker pickups. Price depends on top figure.

1991-2003		$2,000	$2,500

Les Paul Classic Premium Plus

1993-1996, 2001-2002. Les Paul Classic with AAA-grade flame maple top, 2 exposed humbucker pickups. Price depends on top figure.

1993-2002		$2,150	$2,700

Les Paul Classic Tom Morgan Limited Edition

2007. 400 made, custom finish top, black finish back/sides, Classic logo on truss rod cover.

2007		$1,500	$1,850

Les Paul Cloud 9 Series

2003-2006. Special lightweight Les Paul series run for three dealers, Music Machine, Dave's Guitar Shop, and Wildwood Guitars, '59 Les Paul body specs, CR serial series number, '59 or '60 neck profile options, various colors, other reissue models available.

2003-2004	'59 or '60 models	$3,500	$4,300
2003-2006	'52, '54, '56, '57, '58 models	$2,700	$3,300

Les Paul Collector's Choice Series

2010-present. Custom models based on Gibson replicas of one-of-a-kind historic guitars.

2010	#1 '59 Gary Moore	$5,900	$7,400
2010	#1 '59 Melvyn Franks	$4,200	$5,300
2010-2014	#2 '59 Goldie	$4,900	$6,100
2010-2014	#3 '60 The Babe	$4,300	$5,400
2010-2014	#4 '59 Sandy	$4,900	$6,100
2010-2014	#6 '59 Les Paul	$4,200	$5,300

Les Paul Custom

1953-1963 (renamed SG Custom late-1963), 1968-present (production moved to Custom Shop in 2004). Les Paul body shape except for SG body '61-'63, 2 pickups (3 humbuckers mid-'57-'63 and '68-'70, 3 pickups were optional various years after), '75 Price List shows a Les Paul Custom (B) model which is equipped with a Bigsby tailpiece versus a wraparound. By '80 offered as Les Paul Custom/Gold Parts and /Nickel Parts, because gold plating wears more quickly and is therefore less attractive there is no difference in price between an '80s Gold Parts and Nickel Parts instrument.

MODEL YEAR	FEATURES	EXC. COND. LOW	HIGH
1953	Early NSN model	$21,000	$29,000
1954-1957	Single coils	$23,000	$31,000
1954-1957	Single coils, factory Bigsby	$14,000	$18,000
1957-1961	Bigsby	$40,000	$50,000
1957-1961	Stoptail	$46,000	$60,000
1961	White, SG body, side-pull vibrato	$9,000	$11,200
1961-1963	Black option, SG body, factory stop tail	$14,500	$18,000
1961-1963	Black option, SG body, side-pull vibrato	$10,000	$12,500
1961-1963	White, SG body, Maestro vibrola	$12,000	$15,000
1961-1963	White, SG body, Maestro, ebony block	$12,000	$15,000
1962-1963	White, SG body, factory stop tail	$14,500	$18,000
1962-1963	White, SG body, Maestro tail	$12,000	$15,000
1962-1963	White, SG body, side-pull vibrato	$9,000	$11,200
1968	Black, 1-piece body	$10,500	$15,000
1968	Black, 3-piece body	$8,000	$10,500
1969	Black, 1-piece body	$9,700	$13,000
1969	Black, 3-piece body	$7,500	$9,700
1970-1974	Volute, 2 pickups	$2,700	$3,600
1970-1974	Volute, 3 pickups	$2,700	$3,600
1975	Maple fretboard, 2 pickups	$2,700	$3,600
1975	Maple fretboard, 3 pickups	$2,700	$3,600
1975	Volute, 2 pickups	$2,500	$3,300
1975	Volute, 3 pickups	$2,500	$3,300
1976	Maple fretboard, 2 pickups	$2,700	$3,600
1976	Maple fretboard, 3 pickups	$2,700	$3,600
1976	Volute, 2 pickups	$2,500	$3,300
1976	Volute, 3 pickups	$2,500	$3,300
1977	Maple fretboard, 2 pickups	$2,700	$3,600
1977	Volute, 2 pickups	$2,500	$3,300
1977	Volute, 3 pickups	$2,500	$3,300
1978	Maple fretboard, 2 pickups	$2,700	$3,600
1978	Volute, 2 pickups	$2,500	$3,300
1978	Volute, 3 pickups	$2,500	$3,300
1979	2 pickups	$2,500	$3,300
1979	3 pickups	$2,500	$3,300
1979-1984	Silverburst, volute, 2 pickups	$3,100	$4,000
1980-1982	2 pickups	$2,650	$3,300
1980-1982	3 pickups	$2,650	$3,300
1983-1985	Silverburst, 2 pickups	$3,100	$4,000
1983-1986	2 pickups	$2,550	$3,200
1983-1986	3 pickups	$2,550	$3,200
1987-1989	Various colors	$2,550	$3,200
1990-1999	Limited Edition color series	$2,550	$3,200
1990-1999	Various colors	$2,200	$2,800
2000	Silverburst, 300 made	$1,900	$2,500
2000-2010	Various colors	$1,700	$2,400
2003	Silverburst	$1,900	$2,500
2007-2010	Silverburst reissue, certificate	$1,900	$2,500
2008-2014	Black	$1,700	$2,400

Les Paul Custom 20th Anniversary

1974. Regular 2-pickup Custom, with 20th Anniversary inlay at 15th fret, black or white.

1974	Black	$4,100	$5,100
1974	Cherry Sunburst	$3,700	$4,600
1974	Natural	$3,700	$4,600

Les Paul Custom 35th Anniversary

1989. Gold hardware, 3 pickups, carved, solid mahogany body and neck, 35th Anniversary inlay on headstock, black.

1989		$2,700	$3,400

Les Paul Custom '54

1972-1973. Reissue of 1954 Custom, black finish, Alnico V and P-90 pickups.

1972-1973		$4,800	$5,900

Les Paul Custom Historic '54

1991-2013. Custom Shop Historic Collection, 1954 appointments and pickup configuration, black, gold hardware.

1991-2013		$2,700	$3,400

Les Paul Custom Historic '57 Black Beauty

1991-2013. Black finish, gold hardware, 2 or 3 humbucker pickups, part of Gibson's Historic Collection.

1991-2012	2 pickups	$2,700	$3,400
1991-2013	3 pickups	$2,700	$3,400
2007	3 pickups, goldtop	$2,700	$3,400
2007	3 pickups, Murphy aged	$2,900	$3,600

Les Paul Custom Historic '68

1999-2007. Custom Shop Historic Collection, flamed maple top, 2 pickups.

1999-2007		$3,000	$3,750

Les Paul Custom Jimmy Page

2008. Based on Page's '60 LP Custom with 3 pickups, stop tailpiece or Bigsby option, certificate of authenticity, black finish.

2008	Bigsby option	$5,500	$7,100

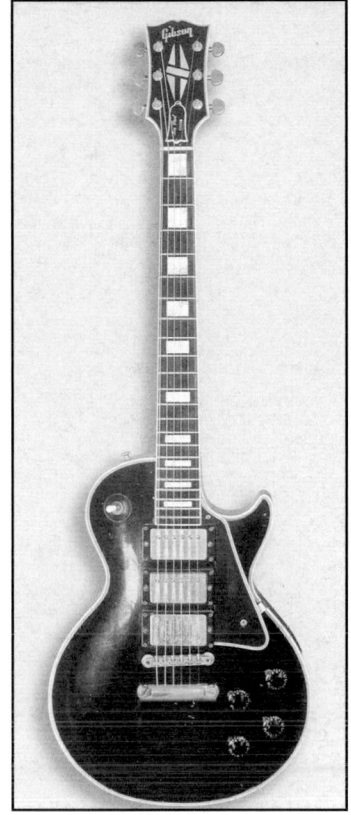

1958 Gibson Les Paul Custom

2004 Gibson Les Paul Custom Historic '68

Robbie Keene

GUITARS

1979 Gibson Les Paul Deluxe
Robbie Keene

1981 Gibson Les Paul Deluxe
Tom Pfeifer

MODEL YEAR	FEATURES	EXC. COND. LOW	HIGH
Les Paul Custom Lite			
1987-1990. Carved maple top, ebony 'board, pearl block inlays, gold hardware, PAF pickups, bound neck, headstock and body.			
1987-1990		$2,000	$2,500
1987-1990	Floyd Rose	$1,500	$1,900
Les Paul Custom Lite (Show Case Edition)			
1988. Showcase Edition, only 200 made, gold top.			
1988		$1,700	$2,100
Les Paul Custom Mick Ronson '68			
2007. Custom Shop, includes certificate and other authentication material.			
2007		$3,300	$4,100
Les Paul Custom Music Machine			
2003. Custom run for dealer Music Machine with special serial number series, chambered body style for reduced body weight, quilt tops.			
2003	Brazilian, figured top	$5,000	$6,300
2003	Quilt top	$3,100	$3,900
Les Paul Custom Peter Frampton Signature			
2008. Limited Edition 3-pickup version of Frampton's LP Custom, PF serial number series, black.			
2008		$3,300	$4,100
Les Paul Custom Plus			
1991-1998. Regular Custom with figured maple top, sunburst finish or colors.			
1991-1998		$2,300	$2,900
Les Paul Custom Showcase Edition			
1988. Showcase Edition logo on back of headstock, goldtop, black hardware.			
1988		$2,400	$3,000
Les Paul Custom Silverburst			
2007-2014. Custom Shop Limited Edition.			
2007-2012		$2,900	$3,600
2013-2014		$2,800	$3,500
Les Paul Dale Earnhardt			
1999. 333 made, Dale's image and number 3 on front and headstock, signature script on fretboard, several pieces of literature and an original certificate are part of the overall package, a lower serial number may add value.			
1999		$2,600	$3,300
1999	Early number, NOS condition	$3,700	$4,600
Les Paul Dale Earnhardt Intimidator			
2000. 333 made, Dale's 'Goodwrench' car on the front of the body, The Intimidator inlay on the fretboard, includes certificate, chrome hardware.			
2000		$2,600	$3,300
2000	Early number, NOS condition	$3,700	$4,600
Les Paul Dark Fire			
2009. Limited edition, 1st run of Les Pauls with Robot 2 Chameleon tone Technology designed to produce various classic guitar tones, completely computer interactive, Burstbucker3 bridge pickup, P-90H neck pickup and 6 Piezo pickups.			
2009		$2,200	$2,800

MODEL YEAR	FEATURES	EXC. COND. LOW	HIGH
Les Paul DC AA			
2007. Double A flamed top.			
2007		$1,700	$2,100
Les Paul DC Classic			
1992-1993. Gold finish.			
1992-1993		$1,400	$1,750
Les Paul DC Pro			
1997-1998, 2006-2007. Custom Shop, body like a '59 Les Paul Junior, carved highly figured maple top, various options. Name revived in '06 but not a Custom Shop model.			
1997-1998		$1,600	$2,000
2006-2007		$1,325	$1,675
Les Paul DC Standard (Plus)			
1998-1999, 2001-2006. Offset double-cut, highly flamed maple top, translucent lacquer finishes in various colors, reintroduced as Standard Lite in '99 but without Les Paul designation on headstock or truss rod cover.			
1998-1999		$1,200	$1,500
2001-2006		$1,200	$1,500
Les Paul DC Studio			
1997-1999. DC Series double-cut like late '50s models, carved maple top, 2 humbucker pickups, various colors.			
1997-1999		$750	$950
Les Paul Deluxe			
1969-1985. In 1969, the Goldtop Les Paul Standard was renamed the Deluxe. Two mini-humbuckers (regular humbuckers optional in mid-'70s). Mid-'70s sparkle tops are worth more than standard finishes. The market slightly favors the Goldtop finish, but practically speaking condition is more important than finish, such that all finishes fetch about the same amount (with the exception of the sparkle finish). Initially, the Deluxe was offered only as a Goldtop and the first year models are more highly prized than the others. Cherry sunburst was offered in '71, cherry in '71-'75, walnut in '71-'72, brown sunburst in '72-'79, natural in '75, red sparkle in '73-'75 only, blue sparkle in '73-'77, wine red/see-thru red offered '75-'85. In '99, the Deluxe was reissued for its 30th anniversary.			
1969	Goldtop	$4,800	$6,000
1970	Goldtop	$3,600	$4,500
1971-1975	Goldtop	$2,800	$3,500
1971-1975	Natural	$2,200	$2,800
1971-1975	Red (solid)	$2,200	$2,800
1971-1975	Sunburst	$2,200	$2,800
1971-1975	Wine	$2,200	$2,800
1973-1975	Red sparkle, fewer made	$3,400	$4,300
1973-1977	Blue sparkle, more made	$3,000	$3,800
1976-1979	Goldtop	$2,400	$3,000
1976-1985	Various colors	$2,200	$2,800
Les Paul Deluxe #1 Pete Townshend			
2006. Limited to 75, red.			
2006		$6,300	$8,000
Les Paul Deluxe #3 Pete Townshend			
2006. Limited to 75, goldtop.			
2006		$6,300	$8,000

The *Vintage Guitar Price Guide* shows low to high values for items in all-original excellent condition, and, where applicable, with original case or cover.

MODEL YEAR	FEATURES	EXC. COND. LOW	HIGH

Les Paul Deluxe #9 Pete Townshend
2006. Limited to 75, cherry burst.

2006		$6,300	$8,000

Les Paul Deluxe 30th Anniversary
1999. Limited Edition logo on the lower back of the headstock, Deluxe logo on truss rod cover, Wine Red.

1999		$1,750	$2,200

Les Paul Deluxe '69 Reissue
2000-2005. Mini-humbuckers, gold top

2000-2005		$1,300	$1,650

Les Paul Deluxe Hall of Fame
1991. All gold finish.

1991		$1,750	$2,200

Les Paul Deluxe Limited Edition
1999-2002. Limited edition reissue with Les Paul Standard features and Deluxe mini-humbuckers, black.

1999-2002		$1,750	$2,200

Les Paul Deluxe Limited Edition AMS
2014. Limited edition chocolate finish, offered only by American Musical Supply.

2014		$500	$625

Les Paul Deluxe Reissue
2012. Mini-humbuckers, chambered body.

2012		$1,775	$2,225

Les Paul Dickey Betts Goldtop
2001-2003. Aged gold top.

2001-2003		$5,800	$7,200

Les Paul Dickey Betts Red Top
2003. Transparent red, gold hardware.

2003		$3,900	$4,800

Les Paul Don Felder Hotel California 1959
2010. Custom Shop, '59 sunburst specs, 50 aged and signed by Felder, 100 aged, and 150 in VOS finish.

2010	Murphy aged, signed	$5,300	$6,500

Les Paul Duane Allman (Custom Shop)
2013. Custom Shop certificate, Murphy Aged or VOS, 150 made of each.

2013	Aged	$6,800	$8,500
2013	VOS	$6,200	$7,800

Les Paul Dusk Tiger
Late-2009-2012. Limited edition, 1000 to be made, features Gibson's Robot Technology, Burstbucker bridge, P-90H neck and 6 Piezo pickups.

2009-2012		$2,100	$2,700

Les Paul Elegant
1996-2004. Custom Shop, highly flamed maple top, abalone crown markers and Custom Shop headstock inlay.

1996-2004		$2,200	$2,800

Les Paul Elegant Streak Silver
1999. Custom Shop, Flow Silver finish, made for Mars Music.

1999		$1,800	$2,300

Les Paul Eric Clapton 1960
2011. Nicknamed the Beano Burst, '60 thinner 'Clapton' neck profile, Custom Bucker pickups, nickel-plated Grover kidney button tuners, lightly figured maple cap, traditional 17 degree angled headstock, total of 500 made; 55 Murphy Aged and signed by Clapton,

95 unsigned Murphy Aged, 350 finished with Gibson's VOS treatment.

2011	Aged	$8,700	$10,700
2011	Aged and signed	$17,500	$21,500
2011	VOS	$5,500	$6,800

Les Paul ES-Les Paul
2014-present. Semi-hollow Les Paul body with f-holes, 3-ply maple/basswood/maple top and back, mahogany neck with maple spline, dark rosewood 'board, 2 pickups, light burst or black.

2014		$2,100	$2,600

Les Paul Florentine Plus
1997-2001. Custom Shop model, hollowbody with f-holes, higher-end appointments.

1997-2001		$3,000	$3,775

Les Paul Futura
2014-present. Light weight, unbound, Min-Etune, various bright colors.

2014		$950	$1,200

Les Paul Gary Moore BFG
2009-2012. Plain appointment BFG specs, P-90 neck pickup and Burstbucker 3 bridge pickup.

2009-2012		$1,100	$1,375

Les Paul Gary Moore Signature
2000-2002. Signature Series model, Gary Moore script logo on truss rod cover, flamed maple top.

2000-2002		$2,900	$3,600

Les Paul Gary Rossington Signature
2002. GR serial number, replica of his '59 LP Standard, Custom Shop, aged finish, 250 made, includes display case with backdrop photo of Rossington, price includes certificate with matching serial number.

2002		$5,500	$6,900

Les Paul Goddess
2006-2007. Maple carved top, trapezoid inlays, smaller body, 2 humbuckers, 2 controls, tune-a-matic bridge.

2007		$1,300	$1,625

Les Paul GT
2007. Includes over/under dual truss rods, GT logo on truss rod cover, several specs designed to add durability during heavy professional use.

2007		$1,425	$1,775

Les Paul Guitar Trader Reissue
1982-1983. Special order flametop Les Paul by the Guitar Trader Company, Redbank, New Jersey. Approximately 47 were built, the first 15 guitars ordered received original PAFs, all were double black bobbins (except 1 Zebra and 1 double white), 3 of the guitars were made in the '60-style. The PAF equipped models were based on order date and not build date. The serial number series started with 9 1001 and a second serial number was put in the control cavity based upon the standard Gibson serial number system, which allowed for exact build date identification. Gibson's pickup designer in the early-'80s was Tim Shaw and the pickups used for the last 32 guitars have been nicknamed Shaw PAFs. After Gibson's short run for Guitar Trader, 10 non-Gibson replica Les Pauls were made. These guitars have a poorly done Gibson logo and other telltale issues.

1982-1983	Actual PAFs installed	$8,000	$10,000

Gibson Les Paul ES-Les Paul

Gibson Les Paul Gary Moore BFG

1982 Gibson Les Paul Jimmy Wallace Reissue

1957 Gibson Les Paul Junior
Frank Thoubboron

MODEL YEAR	FEATURES	EXC. COND. LOW	HIGH
1982-1983	Shaw PAFs, highly flamed	$4,000	$5,000
1982-1983	Shaw PAFs, low flame	$3,500	$4,400

Les Paul HD.6-X Pro Digital

2008-2009. Digital sound system, hex pickups.

2008-2009		$2,100	$2,600

Les Paul Heritage 80

1980-1982. Copy of '59 Les Paul Standard, curly maple top, mahogany body, rosewood 'board, nickel hardware, sunburst. In '80 cataloged as Les Paul Standard-80 without reference to Heritage, the catalog notes that the guitar has Heritage Series truss rod cover.

1980-1982	Figured top	$3,200	$4,000
1980-1982	Plain top	$2,500	$3,100

Les Paul Heritage 80 Award

1982. Ebony 'board, 1-piece mahogany neck, gold-plated hardware, sunburst.

1982	Figured	$4,000	$5,000
1982	Highly figured	$5,300	$6,600

Les Paul Heritage 80 Elite

1980-1982. Copy of '59 Les Paul Standard, quilted maple top, mahogany body and neck, ebony 'board, chrome hardware, sunburst. In '80 cataloged as Les Paul Standard-80 Elite without reference to Heritage, the catalog notes that the guitar has the distinctive Heritage Series truss rod cover.

1980-1982	Quilted	$4,000	$5,000

Les Paul Heritage 80/Standard 80

1982. Based on '57 Les Paul Standard Goldtop, Heritage Series Standard 80 logo on truss rod cover.

1982		$2,900	$3,600

Les Paul Indian Motorcycle

2002. 100 made, has Indian script logo on fretboard and chrome cast war bonnet on the body, crimson red and cream white.

2002		$3,100	$3,900

Les Paul Jim Beam

Ca. 2002-2003. Custom Shop, JBLP serial number series, several versions of Jim Beam logo art on top of guitar, award-ribbon-style B Bean logo on headstock, around 75 made.

2002-2003		$950	$1,200

Les Paul Jimmy Page (Custom Authentic)

2004-2006. Custom Shop, includes certificate.

2004-2006		$5,500	$6,800

Les Paul Jimmy Page Signature

1995-1999. Jimmy Page signature on 'guard, mid-grade figured top, push-pull knobs for phasing and coil-tapping, Grover tuners, gold-plated hardware. This is not the '04 Custom Shop Jimmy Page Signature Series Les Paul (see separate listing).

1995	1st year, highly figured	$5,300	$6,600
1995	1st year, low to moderate figure	$4,000	$5,000
1996-1999	Highly figured	$4,800	$6,000
1996-1999	Low to moderate figure	$3,600	$4,500

Les Paul Jimmy Page Signature Custom Shop

2004. January '04 NAMM Show, 175 planned production, the first 25 were personally inspected, played-in, and autographed by Jimmy Page. Initial retail price for first 25 was $25,000, the remaining 150 instruments had an initial retail price of $16,400. Cosmetically aged by Tom Murphy to resemble Page's No. 1 Les Paul in color fade, weight, top flame, slab cut attribution on the edges, neck size and profile.

2004	1st 25 made	$15,000	$19,000
2004	Factory order 25-150	$12,000	$15,000

Les Paul Jimmy Wallace Reissue

1978-1997. Les Paul Standard '59 reissue with Jimmy Wallace on truss rod cover, special order by dealer Jimmy Wallace, figured maple top, sunburst.

1978-1983	Kalamazoo-made, highly flamed	$3,600	$4,500
1978-1983	Kalamazoo-made, low flame	$3,000	$3,700
1983-1989	Nashville-made	$3,200	$4,000
1990-1997		$3,200	$4,000

Les Paul Joe Bonamassa Aged Goldtop

2008. Inspired By Series, LP Standard aged goldtop with black trim (including black pickup rings), serial number starts with BONAMASSA.

2008		$2,300	$2,800

Les Paul Joe Bonamassa Skinnerburst 1959

2014. Custom Shop, recreation of '59 Les Paul, 150 Murphy aged (first 50 signed by Joe) and 150 VOS, faded Dirty Lemon finish.

2014		$5,000	$6,300

Les Paul Joe Perry 1959 Custom Shop

2013. Custom Shop, recreation of '59 Les Paul, 150 Murphy aged (first 50 signed by Perry) and 150 VOS, faded Tobacco Sunburst finish.

2013		$9,300	$11,600

Les Paul Joe Perry Signature

1997-2001. Unbound slab body with push-pull knobs and Joe Perry signature below bridge, Bone-Yard logo model with typical Les Paul Standard bound body, configuration and appointments.

1997-2001	Bone-Yard option with logo	$2,000	$2,500
1997-2001	Unbound standard model	$1,350	$1,700

Les Paul Jumbo

1969-1970. Single rounded cutaway, flat-top dread-nought acoustic/electric, 1 pickup, rosewood back and sides, natural.

1969-1970		$3,000	$3,900

Les Paul Junior

1954-1963, 1986-1992, 2001-2002, 2005-2013. One P-90 pickup, single-cut solidbody '54-mid-'58, double-cut '58-early-'61, SG body '61-'63, renamed SG Jr. in '63, reintroduced as single-cut for '86-'92, reissued as the 1957 Les Paul Jr. Single Cutaway in '98. Headstock repair reduces the value by 40%-50%. Reinstalled tuners reduces the value by 5% to 10%. Replaced tuner

The Official Vintage Guitar magazine Price Guide 2016 **Gibson** LP Junior 3/4 — Music Machine Brazilian Stinger **139**

GUITARS

MODEL YEAR	FEATURES	EXC. COND. LOW	HIGH
buttons reduces the value by 5% to 10%.			
1954-1958	Sunburst, single-cut	$3,500	$4,700
1958-1961	Cherry, double-cut	$4,300	$5,400
1961-1963	Cherry, SG body	$3,200	$4,000
1986-1992	Sunburst, single-cut, Tune-o-matic	$725	$900
1998-2013	Sunburst, single-cut, stop tail	$725	$900

Les Paul Junior 3/4
1956-1961. One P-90 pickup, short-scale, single-cut solidbody '54-mid-'58, double-cut '58-early-'61.

1956-1958	Sunburst, single-cut	$2,400	$3,000
1958-1961	Cherry, double-cut	$2,400	$3,000

Les Paul Junior Billie Joe Armstrong Signature
2006-2013. 1956 LP Junior specs.

2006-2013		$950	$1,175

Les Paul Junior DC Hall of Fame
1990-1992. Part of Hall of Fame Series, limited run of LP Junior Double Cutaway but with P-100 pickup.

1990-1992		$750	$950

Les Paul Junior Double Cutaway
1986-1992, 1995-1996. Copy of '50s double-cut Jr., cherry or sunburst, reissued as the 1958 Les Paul Jr. Double Cutaway in '98.

1986-1989		$800	$1,000

Les Paul Junior Faded
2010-2012. Single-cut, faded cherry finish.

2010-2012		$575	$725

Les Paul Junior John Lennon LTD
2008. Custom Shop, 300 made, Charlie Christian neck pickup and P-90 bridge as per Lennon's modified Junior, aged-relic finish, certificate, book and New York t-shirt.

2008		$3,100	$4,100

Les Paul Junior Lite
1999-2002. Double-cut, Tune-o-matic, 2 P-100 pickups, stop tail, mini-trapezoid markers, burnt cherry gloss finish.

1999-2002		$575	$700

Les Paul Junior Special
1999-2004. LP Jr. single-cut slab body with 2 P-90s (making it a Special) instead of the standard single P-90, double pickup controls, cherry, tinted natural or sunburst.

1999-2004		$625	$775

Les Paul Junior Special Robot
2008. P-90s, TV Yellow.

2008		$700	$900

Les Paul Junior Tenor/Plectrum
Late-1950s. Four string neck on Junior body, cherry.

1959		$3,700	$4,700

Les Paul Katrina
2005. 300 made in cooperation with Music Rising Foundation and the Edge U2.

2005		$2,400	$3,000

Les Paul KM (Kalamazoo Model)
1979. Regular Les Paul Standard with 2 exposed humbuckers, KM on headstock, sunburst, approximately 1500 were made in the Kalamazoo plant.

1979		$2,400	$3,000

Les Paul Korina (Custom Shop)
1999. Limited run with figured Korina top, Custom Shop logo on back of headstock.

1999		$3,000	$3,700

Les Paul Leo's Reissue
1980-1985. Special order from Gibson's Nashville facility for Leo's Music, Oakland, California. Identified by serial number with L at the beginning, flamed maple top. About 800 guitars were made, with about 400 being exported to Japan. Kalamazoo-made Leo's have a 2nd serial number in the control cavity, Nashville-made Leo's do not have a 2nd serial number.

1980-1983	Kalamazoo-made, highly flamed	$3,600	$4,500
1980-1983	Kalamazoo-made, lower-level flame	$3,000	$3,700
1983-1985	Nashville-made	$3,200	$4,000

Les Paul Limited Edition (3-tone)
1997. Limited Edition stamped on the back of the headstock, Les Paul Standard configuration with cloud inlay markers, 2-piece 3-tone sunburst finish over non-figured maple top.

1997		$1,900	$2,400

Les Paul LP295 Goldtop
2008. Guitar of the Month (April, '08), limited run of 1000, Les Paul body style, goldtop, 2 humbuckers, ES-295 appointments such as 'guard and fretboard markers, Bigsby tailpiece option.

2008		$2,000	$2,500

Les Paul Menace
2006-2007. Carved mahogany body, 2 humbucker pickups.

2006-2007		$550	$700

Les Paul Michael Bloomfield 1959 Standard
2009-2011. Custom Shop, limited production of 100 Murphy-aged and 200 VOS, matching certificate of authenticity.

2009-2011	VOS	$5,500	$6,900

Les Paul Music Machine 25th Anniversary
2002. Custom run for dealer Music Machine with special serial number series, 14 flame top and 14 quilt top instruments were produced, Music Machine 25th Anniversary logo on truss rod cover, special cherry sunburst finish

2002	Flame top	$4,100	$5,900
2002	Quilt top	$4,100	$5,900

Les Paul Music Machine Brazilian Stinger
2003. Custom run for dealer Music Machine with special serial number series, Brazilian rosewood 'board, black stinger paint on back of neck-headstock, '59 or '60 reissue body and neck profile options, highly figured flame or quilt top options, other reissue options available.

2003	'54, '56 or '58, figured flame or quilt	$6,000	$7,600
2003	'54, '56 or '58, goldtop	$4,000	$5,000
2003	'59 or '60, figured flame or quilt	$8,000	$10,000
2003	'59 or '60, plain top	$4,800	$6,000

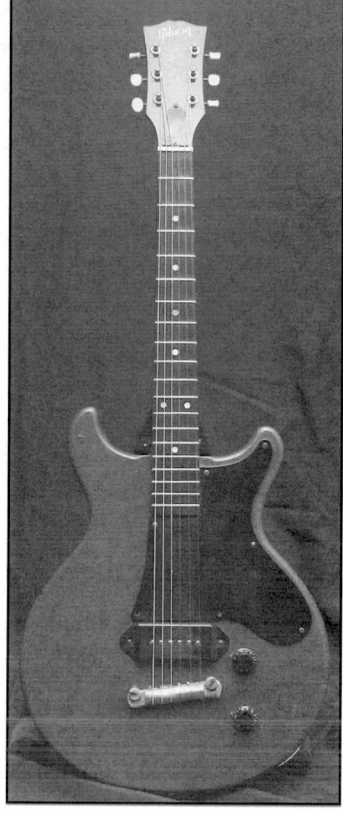

1962 Gibson Les Paul Junior 3/4
Tom Siska

2010 Gibson Les Paul Michael Bloomfield '59 Standard

GUITARS

*1969 Gibson Les Paul
Professional*

Pete Pensec

*2010 Gibson Les Paul
Slash Appetite*

Derek Sasaki

MODEL YEAR	FEATURES	EXC. COND. LOW	HIGH

Les Paul Neal Schon Signature
2005. Custom Shop, Floyd Rose tremolo, signature on truss rod cover, certificate of authenticity, black.

2005		$9,500	$12,000

Les Paul Old Hickory
1998 only. Limited run of 200, tulip poplar body wood from The Hermitage, Custom-style trim.

1998		$3,100	$3,900

Les Paul Paul Kossoff 1959 Standard
2012-2013. Custom Shop, 100 aged and 250 VOS made, without matching certificate of authenticity is worth less.

2012-2013	VOS	$4,800	$6,000

Les Paul Peace
2014-present. AA top, rosewood 'board, 2 pickups, various color finishes.

2014-2015		$1,550	$1,950

Les Paul Personal
1969-1972. Two angled, low impedance pickups, phase switch, gold parts, walnut finish.

1969-1972		$2,100	$2,600

Les Paul Pro Deluxe
1978-1982. Chrome hardware, 2 P-90s, various colors. Les Pauls could vary significantly in weight during the '70s and '80s and lighter-weight examples may be worth up to 25% more than these values.

1978-1982		$1,800	$2,250

Les Paul Pro Showcase Edition
1988. Goldtop 1956 specs, Showcase Edition decal, 200 made.

1988		$2,300	$2,850

Les Paul Professional
1969-1971, 1977-1979. Single-cut, 2 angled, low impedance pickups, carved top, walnut or white.

1969-1971	Walnut	$2,000	$2,500
1969-1971	White	$2,800	$3,500

Les Paul Recording
1971-1980. Two angled, low impedance pickups, high/low impedance selector switch, walnut and white '71-'77, natural, ebony and sunburst added '78.

1971-1977	Walnut	$2,100	$2,600
1975-1980	White	$2,600	$3,200
1978-1980	Various	$2,100	$2,600

Les Paul Reissue Flametop
1983-1990. Flame maple top, 2 humbuckers, thicker '59-style neck, sunburst finish, renamed '59 Les Paul Flametop in '91.

1983-1990	Highly figured	$3,500	$4,400

Les Paul Reissue Goldtop
1983-1991. Goldtop finish, 2 P-100 pickups, renamed '56 Les Paul Goldtop in '91.

1983-1991		$2,000	$2,500

Les Paul Richard Petty LTD
2003. Richard Petty's image on front and back, 'The King' inlay on fretboard.

2003		$3,100	$3,800

Les Paul SG '61 Reissue
1993-2003. Renamed the Les Paul SG '61 Reissue from SG '62 Reissue, early '60s Les Paul Standard SG specs with small guard, trapezoid markers, heritage cherry finish, by 2003 the Les Paul script marking was

MODEL YEAR	FEATURES	EXC. COND. LOW	HIGH

not on the truss rod cover, renamed to SG '61 Reissue.

1993-2003	Stud tail	$1,300	$1,625

Les Paul SG Standard Authentic
2005. SG '61 specs, small guard, Les Paul truss rod logo, stud tailpiece.

2005		$2,025	$2,525

Les Paul SG Standard Reissue
2000-2004. Reissue of early-'60s specs including Deluxe Maestro vibrato with lyre tailpiece (stop bar tp offered), small 'guard, holly head veneer, standard color faded cherry, available in Classic White or TV Yellow, becomes the SG Standard Reissue by '05.

2000-2004	Maestro	$1,825	$2,325

Les Paul Signature
2014-present. Chambered solidbody, 2 exposed split-coil humbuckers, "Les Paul" signature on 'guard, Min-Etune.

2014		$1,400	$1,725

Les Paul Signature/L.P. Signature
1973-1978. Thin semi-hollowbody, double-cut, 2 low impedance pickups, f-holes, various colors. The Price List refers to it as L.P. Signature.

1973-1978		$2,100	$2,600

Les Paul Slash Appetite
2010-2012. Figured maple top, Slash artwork headstock logo, 2 Alnico II Pro Slash pickups, Appetite Amber finish.

2010-2012		$3,300	$4,300

Les Paul Slash Appetite For Destruction
2010. Custom Shop, figured maple top, 2 Duncan Slash pickups, butterscotch finish available as VOS or Aged.

2010	VOS	$6,900	$9,100

Les Paul Slash Signature
2007. Slash logo on truss rod, SL serial number series.

2007		$2,550	$3,300

Les Paul SmartWood Exotic
1998-2001. Full-depth Les Paul-style built with eco-friendly woods, Muiracatiara (or Muir) top, mahogany back, Preciosa 'board, pearloid dots.

1998-2001		$875	$1,100

Les Paul SmartWood Standard
1996-2002. Smartwood Series, figured maple top, mahogany body, Smartwood on truss rod cover, antique natural.

1996-2002		$700	$875

Les Paul SmartWood Studio
2002-2006. Muiracatiara (Muir) top and mahogany back, Preciosa (Prec) 'board, Studio appointments including pearl-style dot markers.

2002-2006		$675	$850

Les Paul Special
1955-1959. Slab solidbody, 2 pickups (P-90s in '50s, P-100 stacked humbuckers on later version), single-cut until end of '58, double in '59, the '89 reissue is a single-cut, renamed SG Special in late-'59.

1955-1959	TV Yellow	$10,000	$12,500
1959	Cherry (mid- to late-'59)	$8,000	$10,000

MODEL YEAR	FEATURES	EXC. COND. LOW	HIGH

Les Paul Special (Reissue)

1989-1998, 2002-2006. Briefly introduced as Les Paul Junior II but name changed to Special in the first year, single-cut, 2 P-100 stacked humbuckers, TV Yellow, in '90 there was a run of 300 with LE serial number, renamed Special SL in '98.

1989-1998	P-100s	$800	$1,000
2002-2006	Humbuckers	$650	$825

Les Paul Special 3/4

1959. Slab solidbody, 2 P-90 pickups, double-cut, short-scale, cherry finish, renamed SG Special 3/4 in late-'59.

1959		$5,000	$6,300

Les Paul Special Centennial

1994 only. 100 made, double-cut, cherry, 100 year banner at the 12th fret, diamonds in headstock and in gold-plated knobs, gold-plated Gibson coin in back of headstock.

1994		$2,700	$3,400

Les Paul Special Double Cutaway

1976-1979, 1993-1994. Double-cut, 2 P-90s, 1990s version was made in Custom Shop and was reintroduced as the '60 Les Paul Special Historic in '98.

1976-1979		$1,700	$2,100
1993-1994	Custom Shop	$1,100	$1,400

Les Paul Special Faded

2005-2010. Double-cut, dot markers, 2 P-90s, Special logo on truss rod cover, faded TV limed mahogany or cherry finish.

2005-2010		$625	$775

Les Paul Special New Century

2006-2008. Full-body mirror 'guard, 2 exposed humbuckers, single-cut LP Special body, mirror truss rod cover.

2006-2008		$800	$1,000

Les Paul Special Robot

2008. Two P-90 pickups, various colors.

2008	TV Yellow	$775	$975

Les Paul Special Tenor

1959. Four-string electric tenor, LP Special body, TV Yellow.

1959		$5,000	$6,300

Les Paul Special Worn Cherry

2003-2006. Single-cut, non-bound LP Special with 2 humbuckers.

2003-2006		$625	$775

Les Paul Spider-Man

2002. Custom Shop, superhero depicted on the body, red spider logo, gold hardware, Standard appointments. 15 guitars were produced as a Gibson/Columbia TriStar Home Entertainment/Tower Records promotion, while a larger batch was sold at retail.

2002		$2,800	$3,500

Les Paul Spotlight Special

1983-1984. Curly maple and walnut top, 2 humbuckers, gold hardware, multi-bound top, Custom Shop Edition logo, natural or sunburst.

1983-1984	Figured top	$4,500	$5,700
1983-1984	Highly figured	$5,700	$7,000

Les Paul Standard (Sunburst)

1958-1960, special order 1972-1975. Les Paul Sunbursts from '58-'60 should be individually valued

based on originality, color and the amount and type of figure in the maple top, changed tuners or a Bigsby removal will drop the value. Approximately 15% came with the Bigsby tailpiece. The noted price ranges are guidance valuations. Each '58-'60 Les Paul Standard should be evaluated on a case-by-case basis. As is always the case, the low and high ranges are for an all original, excellent condition, undamaged guitar. About 70% of the '58-'60 Les Paul Standards have relatively plain maple tops. The majority of '58-'60 Les Paul Standards have moderate or extreme color fade.

Wider fret wire was introduced in early-'59. White bobbins were introduced in early- to mid-'59. Double ring Kluson Deluxe tuners were introduced in late-'60. It has been suggested that all '58-'60 models have 2-piece centerseam tops. This implies that 1-piece tops, 3-piece tops and off-centerseam tops do not exist.

The terminology of the 'Burst includes: arching medullary grain, swirling medullary grain, ribbon-curl, chevrons, Honey-Amber, receding red aniline, pinstripe, bookmatched, double-white bobbins, zebra bobbins, black bobbins, fiddleback maple, sunburst finish, Honeyburst, lemon drop, quarter sawn, blistered figure, width of gradation, flat sawn, Teaburst, Bigsby-shadow, rift sawn, heel size, aged clear lacquer, 3-dimensional figure, intense fine flame, tag-shadow, red pore filler, Eastern maple fleck, medium-thick flame, shrunk tuners, wave and flame, flitch-matched, elbow discoloration, ambered top coat, natural gradation, grain orientation, script oxidation, asymmetrical figure Tangerineburst, Greenburst, and birdseye.

The bobbins used for the pickup winding were either black or white. The market has determined that white bobbin PAFs are the most highly regarded. Generally speaking, in '58 bobbins were black, in '59 the bobbin component transitioned to white and some guitars have 1 white and 1 black bobbin (aka zebra). In '60, there were zebras and double blacks returned.

Rather than listing separate line items for fade and wood, the Guide lists discounts and premiums as follows. The price ranges shown below are for instruments with excellent color, excellent wood, with the original guitar case. The following discounts and premiums should be considered.

An instrument with moderate or total color fade should be discounted about 10%.

One with a factory Bigsby should be discounted about 10%-15%.

Original jumbo frets are preferred over original small frets and are worth +10%.

1958	Highly figured	$300,000	$400,000
1958	Minor figured	$225,000	$310,000
1958	Plain top, no figuring	$150,000	$200,000
1959	Highly figured	$325,000	$430,000
1959	Minor figured	$245,000	$330,000
1959	Plain top, no figuring	$160,000	$215,000
1960	Early '60, fat neck, highly figured	$255,000	$340,000

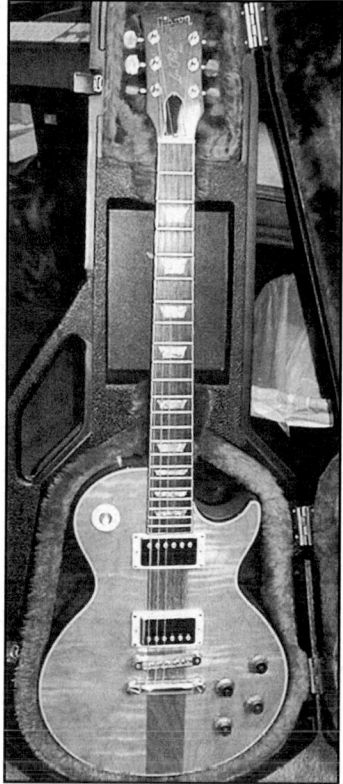

1983 Gibson Les Paul Spotlight Special

Greg Moran

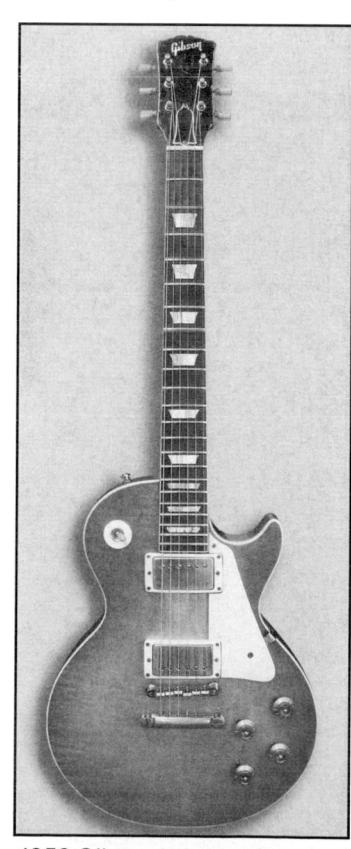

1959 Gibson Les Paul Standard

Keith Nelson

2005 Gibson Les Paul Standard

Dan Drozdik

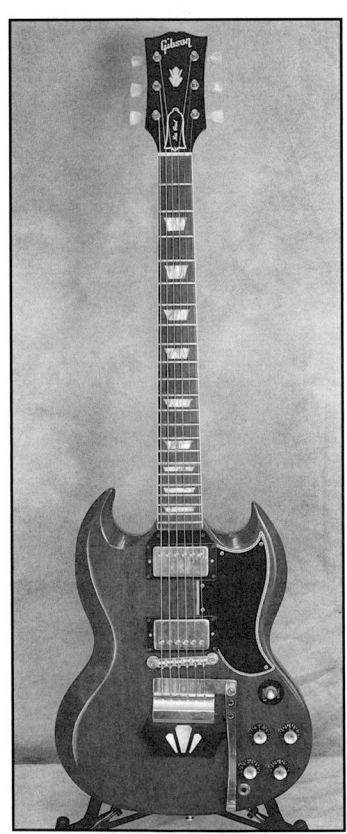

1962 Gibson Les Paul Standard (SG body)

MODEL YEAR	FEATURES	EXC. COND. LOW	HIGH
1960	Early '60, fat neck, minor figured	$215,000	$300,000
1960	Early '60, fat neck, plain top	$120,000	$160,000
1960	Late '60, flat neck, highly figured	$245,000	$325,000
1960	Late '60, flat neck, minor figured	$185,000	$250,000
1960	Late '60, flat neck, plain top	$112,000	$150,000

Les Paul Standard (SG body)

1961-1963 (SG body those years). Renamed SG Standard in late-'63.

MODEL YEAR	FEATURES	EXC. COND. LOW	HIGH
1961-1963	Cherry, side vibrola, PAFs	$11,200	$14,000
1962-1963	Cherry, side vibrola, pat. #	$9,000	$12,000
1962-1963	Ebony block, SG, PAFs, deluxe vibrola	$11,200	$14,000
1962-1963	Ebony block, SG, pat. #, deluxe vibrola	$10,000	$13,000

Les Paul Standard (reintroduced then renamed)

1968-1969. Comes back as a goldtop with P-90s for '68-'69 (renamed Les Paul Deluxe, '69), available as special order Deluxe '72-'76.

MODEL YEAR	FEATURES	EXC. COND. LOW	HIGH
1968	P-90s, large headstock	$6,800	$8,600
1968	P-90s, small headstock	$11,200	$14,600
1969	P-90s, large headstock	$6,600	$8,400

Les Paul Standard (reintroduced)

1976-July 2008, 2012-present. Available as special order Deluxe '72-'76, reintroduced with 2 humbuckers '76-present. The '75 Price List shows a Les Paul Standard (B) model which is equipped with a Bigsby tailpiece versus a wraparound, also shows a Les Paul Standard (B) with palm pedal. Replaced by Les Paul Standard 2008 in August '08. Name revived in '12 on chambered-body version with tapped Burstbucker pickups, available in AAA tops, black, Gold Top or Blue Mist finishes.

MODEL YEAR	FEATURES	EXC. COND. LOW	HIGH
1971	Early special order goldtop, P-90s	$5,250	$6,600
1972-1974	Special order goldtop, P-90s	$3,750	$4,700
1972-1974	Special order sunburst, P-90s	$3,750	$4,700
1974-1975	Special order sunburst, humbuckers	$3,750	$4,700
1976	Sunburst, 4-piece pancake body	$2,700	$3,500
1976	Wine Red or natural	$2,700	$3,500
1977	Sunburst	$2,700	$3,500
1977	Various colors	$2,700	$3,500
1978	Natural	$2,700	$3,500
1978	Sunburst	$2,700	$3,500

MODEL YEAR	FEATURES	EXC. COND. LOW	HIGH
1978	Various colors	$2,700	$3,500
1979	Brown Sunburst	$2,700	$3,500
1979	Cherry Sunburst	$2,700	$3,500
1979	Goldtop	$2,700	$3,500
1979	Natural	$2,700	$3,500
1979	Wine Red	$2,700	$3,500
1980-1983	Natural	$2,150	$2,800
1980-1986	Black	$2,150	$2,800
1980-1989	White (R.Rhoads)	$2,500	$3,100
1980-85	Wine Red	$2,150	$2,800
1980-86	Sunburst	$2,150	$2,800
1981-1982	Goldtop	$2,150	$2,800
1982	Brown Sunburst	$2,150	$2,800
1982	Candy Apple Red, gold hardware, LD	$2,150	$2,800
1982	Cherry Sunburst	$2,150	$2,800
1987-1989	Various colors	$2,150	$2,800
1990-1993	Limited Edition colors with sticker	$2,200	$2,850
1990-1999	Various colors	$1,650	$2,050
1990-1999	White (R.Rhoads)	$2,000	$2,500
2000-2008	Opaque solid color	$1,600	$2,000
2000-2008	Transparent figured wood	$1,750	$2,175
2000-2008	Transparent plain top	$1,650	$2,050
2012-2014	New radius & switching, transparent top	$1,650	$2,050
2012-2014	Opaque solid color	$1,600	$2,000

Les Paul Standard 2008

August 2008-2012. 2008 added to name, chambered mahogany body, new asymmetrical neck profile, locking grovers, plain or AA flamed maple top, Ebony, Gold Top, various sunbursts.

MODEL YEAR	FEATURES	EXC. COND. LOW	HIGH
2008-2012	Figured top	$1,800	$2,350
2008-2012	Gold top	$1,475	$1,900
2008-2012	Plain top	$1,450	$1,875

Les Paul Standard '82

1982. Standard 82 on truss rod cover, made in Kalamazoo, Made in USA stamp on back of the headstock, generally quilted maple tops.

MODEL YEAR	FEATURES	EXC. COND. LOW	HIGH
1982		$2,000	$2,500

Les Paul Standard Billy Gibbons 'Pearly Gates'

2009-2011. Aged - 50 made, Aged and signed - 50 made, V.O.0S. - 250 made.

MODEL YEAR	FEATURES	EXC. COND. LOW	HIGH
2009-2011	Aged	$6,800	$8,500
2009-2011	VOS	$6,200	$7,800

Les Paul Standard Faded

2005-2008. Figured top, exposed humbuckers, faded satin finish.

MODEL YEAR	FEATURES	EXC. COND. LOW	HIGH
2005-2008		$1,475	$1,825

Les Paul Standard Lite

1999-2001. DC body-style, renamed from DC Standard in '99, reintroduced as Les Paul Standard DC Plus in 2001, various translucent finishes, available in 2004 under this name also.

MODEL YEAR	FEATURES	EXC. COND. LOW	HIGH
1999-2001		$1,200	$1,500

MODEL YEAR	FEATURES	EXC. COND. LOW	HIGH

Les Paul Standard Plus

1995-2008. Gibson USA model, figured maple top, Vintage Sunburst, Heritage Cherry Sunburst or Honeyburst finish.

| 1995-2008 | | $1,900 | $2,400 |

Les Paul Standard Premium Plus

1999-2007. Premium plus flamed maple top.

| 1999-2007 | | $2,100 | $2,625 |

Les Paul Standard Raw Power

2000-2001, 2006-2007. Natural gloss finish on maple top, appears to have been a Musician's Friend version in '06-'07.

| 2000-2001 | | $1,400 | $1,750 |

Les Paul Standard Robot

| 2007 | Blueburst | $1,100 | $1,400 |

Les Paul Standard Sparkle

2001. Sparkle holoflake top, reflective back, Standard logo on truss rod.

| 2001 | | $2,000 | $2,500 |

Les Paul Strings and Things Standard

1975-1978. Special order flamed maple top Les Paul Standard model, built for Chris Lovell, owner of Strings and Things, a Gibson dealer in Memphis, approximately 28 were built, authentication of a Strings and Things Les Paul is difficult due to no diffinitive attributes, valuation should be on a case-by-case basis, sunburst.

| 1975-1978 | 2-piece top | $4,700 | $5,900 |
| 1975-1978 | 3-piece top | $3,000 | $3,800 |

Les Paul Studio

1983-present. Non bound mahogany body, (early models have alder body), 2 humbuckers, various colors.

1983-1999		$800	$1,000
2000-2014		$800	$1,000
2009-2012	Silverburst	$850	$1,075

Les Paul Studio '50s Tribute

2010-present. '56 LP Goldtop specs, P-90s, '50s neck, Tune-o-matic, stopbar tailpiece, chambered unbound body, worn finishes. Also Humbucker version.

| 2010-2014 | | $800 | $1,000 |

Les Paul Studio '60s Tribute

2011-present. Similar to '50s Tribute except for '60 slim taper neck. Also Darkback version (but no humbucker one).

| 2011-2014 | | $800 | $1,000 |

Les Paul Studio Baritone

2004-2012. 28" baritone scale, maple top, mahogany back and neck, 2 pickups, nitro gloss honeyburst finish.

| 2004-2012 | | $900 | $1,125 |

Les Paul Studio BFD

2007. Studio specs but with BFD electronics.

| 2007 | | $550 | $700 |

Les Paul Studio Custom

1984-1985. 2 humbucking pickups, multi-bound top, gold-plated hardware, various colors.

| 1984-1985 | | $850 | $1,050 |

Les Paul Studio Deluxe '60s

2010-2012. Exposed pickups, Deluxe logo on truss rod cover, plain top, sunburst.

| 2010-2012 | | $975 | $1,300 |

Les Paul Studio Faded Vintage Mahogany

2007-2010. Vintage mahogany with faded satin.

| 2007-2010 | | $575 | $725 |

Les Paul Studio Faded/Les Paul Studio Pro Faded

2005-2012. Faded sunburst tops. Name changes to Studio Pro Faded in '12, then ends production.

| 2005-2012 | | $525 | $700 |

Les Paul Studio Gem

1996-1998. Limited edition with Les Paul Studio features, but using P-90 pickups instead of humbucker pickups, plus trapezoid markers and gold hardware.

| 1996-1998 | | $850 | $1,050 |

Les Paul Studio Gothic

2000-2001. Orville Gibson image on back of headstock, single Gibson crescent and star neck marker, Gothic Black with black hardware.

| 2000-2001 | | $750 | $925 |

Les Paul Studio Gothic Morte

2011-2012. All-mahogany body, African Obeche 'board, 2 humbuckes, satin ebony finish.

| 2011-2012 | | $650 | $800 |

Les Paul Studio Limited Edition

1997. P-100 pickups, black.

| 1997 | | $675 | $850 |

Les Paul Studio Lite

1987-1998. Carved maple top, mahogany back and neck, 2 humbucker pickups, various colors.

| 1987-1998 | | $675 | $850 |

Les Paul Studio MLB Baseball

2008. Major League Baseball graphics on body, only 30 made, satin finish, dot markers.

| 2008 | | $1,400 | $1,725 |

Les Paul Studio Platinum

2004-2006. 2 Humbuckers, no position markers, brushed metal hardware, body, neck and headstock in satin platinum finish, matching platinum hardshell case.

| 2004-2006 | | $1,000 | $1,250 |

Les Paul Studio Platinum Plus

2004-2006. Same as Platinum but with trapezoid markers and black hardshell case.

| 2004-2006 | | $1,100 | $1,375 |

Les Paul Studio Plus

2002-2007. Two-piece AA flamed unbound top, gold hardware, Desert Burst or see-thru black.

| 2002-2007 | | $950 | $1,175 |

Les Paul Studio Premium Plus

2006-2008. AAA flamed-maple top.

| 2006-2008 | | $1,100 | $1,375 |

Les Paul Studio Raw Power

April 2009-2012. Unbound maple top on chambered maple body, 2 humbuckers, dot markers, offered in several satin finishes.

| 2009-2012 | | $700 | $875 |

Les Paul Studio Robot

2007-2011. Robot tuning, trapezoid inlays, silverburst, fireburst, wine red, black, red metallic, green metallic.

| 2007-2011 | | $800 | $1,000 |

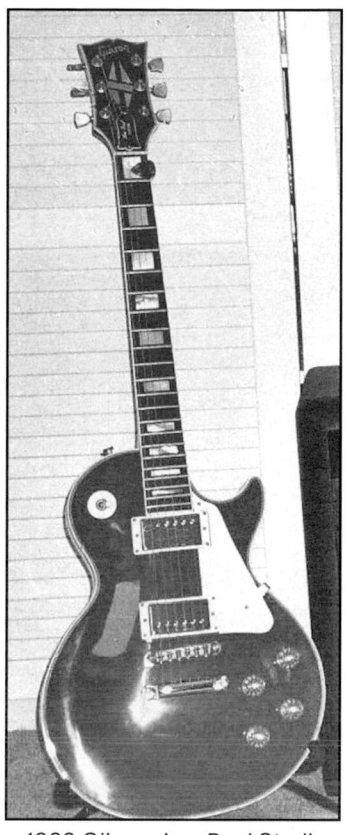

1983 Gibson Les Paul Studio

Gibson Les Paul Studio '60s Tribute

GUITARS

2012 Gibson Les Paul Studio Shred

Gibson Les Paul Supreme

MODEL YEAR	FEATURES	EXC. COND. LOW	HIGH

Les Paul Studio Shred
2012. Unbound body, trapazoid markers, 2 hum-buckers. Floyd Rose, high-gloss ebony nitro finish.

| 2012 | | $800 | $1,000 |

Les Paul Studio Swamp Ash
2004-2012. Studio model with swamp ash body.

| 2004-2012 | | $725 | $900 |

Les Paul Supreme
2003-present. Highly figured AAAA maple top and back on translucent finishes only, custom binding, deluxe split style pearl inlay markers, chambered mahogany body, globe logo on headstock, solid colors available by '06.

| 2003-2014 | AAAA top | $2,200 | $2,750 |
| 2003-2014 | Various colors | $2,200 | $2,750 |

Les Paul Tie Dye (St. Pierre)
1996-1997. Hand colored by George St. Pierre, just over 100 made.

| 1996-1997 | | $2,350 | $2,950 |

Les Paul Tie Dye Custom Shop
2002. Limited series of one-off colorful finishes, Custom Shop logo.

| 2002 | | $1,900 | $2,350 |

Les Paul Traditional Pro
2010-2011. Exposed tapped coil humbuckers, sun-bursts, goldtop, ebony or wine red.

| 2010-2011 | | $1,300 | $1,600 |

Les Paul Traditional/Plus
2008-present. Traditional on truss rod, '80s styl-ing with weight-relief holes in an unchambered body, Standard appointments. Figured maple (Plus) or opaque color top.

| 2008-2014 | Figured maple | $1,750 | $2,150 |
| 2008-2014 | Opaque or plain top | $1,600 | $2,000 |

Les Paul TV
1954-1959. Les Paul Jr. with limed mahogany (TV Yellow) finish, single-cut until mid-'58, double-cut after, renamed SG TV in late-'59.

| 1954-1958 | Single-cut | $6,900 | $8,700 |
| 1958-1959 | Double-cut | $6,500 | $8,200 |

Les Paul TV 3/4
1954-1957. Limed mahogany (TV Yellow) Les Paul Jr. 3/4, short-scale, single-cut.

| 1954-1957 | | $5,000 | $6,300 |

Les Paul Ultima
1996-2007. Custom Shop model, flame or quilted sunburst top, fancy abalone and mother-of-pearl tree of life, harp, or flame fingerboard inlay, multi abalone bound body.

| 1996-2007 | | $4,600 | $5,800 |

Les Paul Vixen
2006-2007. Les Paul Special single-cut slab body, dot markers, 2 humbuckers, 2 controls, wrap-around bridge.

| 2006-2007 | | $725 | $900 |

Les Paul Voodoo/Voodoo Les Paul
2004-2005. Single-cut, swamp ash body, 2 exposed humbuckers, black satin finish.

| 2004-2005 | | $1,000 | $1,250 |

MODEL YEAR	FEATURES	EXC. COND. LOW	HIGH

Les Paul XR-I/XR-II/XR-III
1981-1983. No frills model with Dirty Finger pickups, dot markers, Les Paul stencil logo on headstock, gold-burst, silverburst and cherryburst finishes.

1981-1983	XR-I, goldburst	$900	$1,150
1981-1983	XR-II	$900	$1,150
1981-1983	XR-III	$900	$1,150

Les Paul Zakk Wylde Signature
1999, 2003-present. Custom shop, black and antique-white bullseye graphic finish.

1999	Black/white bullseye	$2,800	$3,550
2003-2014	Black/white bullseye	$2,300	$2,950
2003-2014	Green Camo bullseye option	$2,300	$2,950

The Les Paul
1976-1979. Figured maple top, 2 humbuckers, gold hardware, rosewood binding, 'guard, 'board, knobs, cover plates, etc., natural or rosewood finishing, natural only by '79.

| 1976-1979 | Natural or rosewood | $7,500 | $9,500 |

The Paul
1978-1982. Offered as The Paul Standard with solid walnut body and The Paul Deluxe with solid mahogany body, 2 exposed humbuckers.

| 1978-1982 | Walnut or mahogany | $825 | $1,025 |

The Paul Firebrand Deluxe
1980-1982. Single-cut mahogany solidbody, rough natural finish, Gibson branded in headstock, 2 ex-posed humbuckers.

1980-1982	Black	$675	$850
1980-1982	Pelham Blue	$675	$850
1980-1982	Rough natural	$675	$850

The Paul II
1996-1998. Mahogany body, 2 humbucking pickups, rosewood dot neck, renamed The Paul SL in '98.

| 1996-1998 | | $475 | $600 |

LG-0
1958-1974. Flat-top acoustic, mahogany, bound body, rosewood bridge '58-'61 and '68-'74, plastic bridge '62-'67, natural.

1958-1961	Rosewood bridge	$950	$1,200
1962-1964	Plastic bridge	$750	$1,000
1965	Plastic bridge	$700	$900
1966	Plastic bridge	$600	$800
1967-1969	Rosewood bridge	$600	$800
1970-1974		$500	$675

LG-1
1943-1968. Flat-top acoustic, spruce top, mahogany back and sides, bound body, rosewood bridge '43-'61, plastic bridge after, examples seen to '74, sunburst.

1943-1945		$1,750	$2,300
1946-1949		$1,600	$2,150
1950-1959	Rosewood bridge	$1,400	$2,000
1960-1961	Rosewood bridge	$1,200	$1,650
1962-1964	Plastic bridge	$1,100	$1,450
1965		$1,000	$1,300
1966-1968		$900	$1,200

MODEL YEAR	FEATURES	EXC. COND. LOW	HIGH

LG-2

1942-1962. Flat-top acoustic, spruce top, mahogany back and sides (some with maple '43-'46), banner headstock '42-'46, bound body, X-bracing, sunburst finish, replaced by B-25 in '62.

1942-1945	Banner	$4,400	$5,500
1946-1949		$4,000	$5,000
1950-1959		$3,400	$4,200
1960-1961	Rosewood bridge	$3,000	$3,750
1962	Ajustable bridge	$2,000	$2,500

LG-2 3/4

1949-1962. Short-scale version of LG-2 flat-top, wood bridge, sunburst.

1949-1959		$2,400	$3,000
1960-1961	Rosewood bridge	$2,200	$2,750
1962	Ajustable bridge	$1,800	$2,250

LG-2 3/4 Arlo Guthrie

2003, 2005-present. Vintage replica finish.

2003-2014		$1,375	$1,700

LG-2 American Eagle

2013-2014. Sitka top, mahogany back and sides, L.R. Baggs.

2013-2014		$1,100	$1,375

LG-2 Banner

2013. All mahogany, only 50 made.

2013		$1,525	$1,875

LG-2 H

1945-1955. Flat-top, Hawaiian, natural or sunburst.

1944-1945		$4,200	$5,300
1946-1949		$3,600	$4,500
1950-1955		$3,100	$3,900

LG-3

1942-1964. Flat-top acoustic, spruce top, mahogany back and sides, bound body, natural finish, replaced by B-25 N.

1942-1945	Banner	$5,000	$6,200
1946-1949		$4,200	$5,200
1950-1959		$3,700	$4,600
1960-1961	Wood bridge	$3,400	$4,200
1962-1964	Plastic bridge	$2,150	$2,700

Longhorn Double Cutaway

2008. Guitar of the Month for July '08, AA figured maple top, 2 active pickups, piezo pickup, sunburst or transparent finishes.

2008		$1,300	$1,650

M III Series

1991-1996, 2013-present. Double-cut solidbody with extra long bass horn, six-on-a-side tuners on a reverse pointy headstock, dot markers, reverse Gibson decal logo. Reissued in '13 with natural finish on 'board and choice of Cosmic Cobalt, Electric Lime, Vibrant Red, or Orange Glow.

1991-1992	Deluxe	$1,400	$1,775
1991-1996	Standard	$1,050	$1,325
2013-2014	Reissue	$900	$1,150

Mach II

1990-1991. Renamed from U-2, offset double-cut, 2 single coils and 1 humbucking pickup.

1990-1991		$750	$975

Map Guitar

1983, 1985. Body cutout like lower 48, 2 humbuckers, limited run promotion, '83 version in natural

mahogany or red, white and blue, '85 version red, white and blue stars and stripes on a white background. This model can often be found in better than excellent condition because the instrument is as much a show piece as it is a player guitar, and the price range reflects that.

1983	Natural	$2,500	$3,150
1983	Red, white & blue	$3,000	$3,800

Marauder

1975-1980. Single-cut solidbody, pointed headstock, 2 pickups, bolt-on neck, various colors.

1975-1980		$1,100	$1,425

Marauder Custom

1976-1977. Marauder with 3-way selector switch, bound 'board, block markers, bolt-on neck, Marauder logo on truss rod cover, sunburst.

1976-1977		$1,200	$1,525

Melody Maker

1959-1971, 1986-1993. Slab solidbody, 1 pickup, single-cut until '61, double '61-'66, SG body '66-'71, reintroduced as single-cut in '86-'93. A single-cut Les Paul Melody Maker was offered from '03-'06.

1959-1961	Sunburst, single-cut	$1,450	$1,800
1962-1963	Sunburst or cherry, double-cut	$1,300	$1,600
1964	Cherry, double-cut	$1,300	$1,600
1965	Cherry, double cut	$1,200	$1,500
1966	Cherry, double-cut	$1,100	$1,400
1966-1971	Various colors, SG body	$1,350	$1,700
1986-1993	Reintroduced as single-cut	$625	$800

Melody Maker 3/4

1959-1970. Short-scale version.

1959-1961		$1,350	$1,700
1962-1963		$1,200	$1,500

Melody Maker D

1960-1970. Two pickup version of Melody Maker, reintroduced as Melody Maker Double in '77.

1960-1961	Sunburst, single-cut	$2,100	$2,700
1961-1964	Sunburst or cherry, double-cut	$1,850	$2,400
1965	Sunburst or cherry, double-cut	$1,550	$2,000
1966	Sunburst or cherry, double-cut	$1,450	$1,850
1966-1970	Various colors, SG body	$1,550	$2,000

Melody Maker Double

1977-1983. Reintroduction of Melody Maker D, double-cut solidbody, 2 pickups, cherry or sunburst.

1977-1983	Bolt-on	$650	$825
1977-1983	Set-neck	$825	$1,050

Melody Maker III

1967-1971. SG-style double-cut solidbody, 3 pickups, various colors.

1967-1971		$1,650	$2,100

Melody Maker 12

1967-1971. SG-style solidbody, 12 strings, 2 pickups, red, white or Pelham Blue.

1967-1971		$1,550	$1,950

1944 Gibson LG-2 Banner
Folkway Music

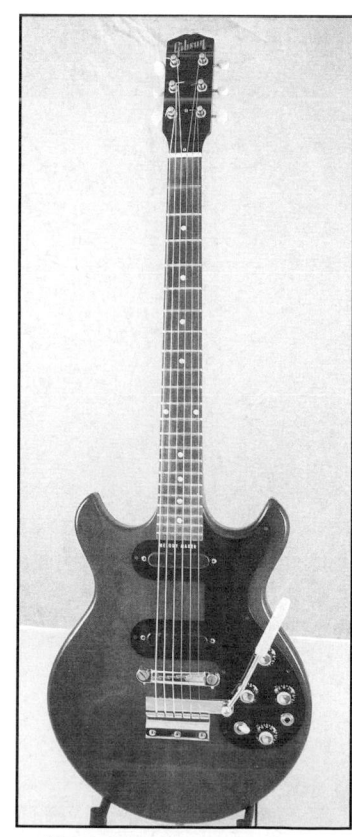

1965 Gibson Melody Maker
Keith Myers

Gibson Melody Maker Joan Jett Signature Blackheart

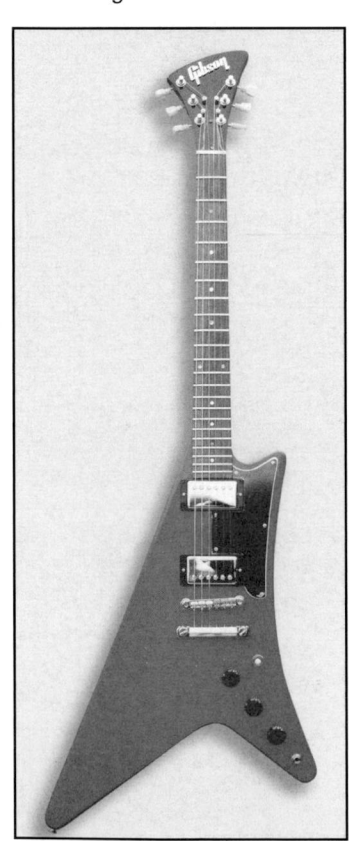

1981 Gibson Moderne Heritage
My Generation Guitars

MODEL YEAR	FEATURES	EXC. COND. LOW	HIGH

Melody Maker Faded

2003. Les Paul Jr. styling, single-cut, 1 P-90 style pickup, Nashville tune-o-matic bridge, black satin finish.

2003		$350	$445

Les Paul Melody Maker

2003-2008. Slab single-cut solidbody, one P-90, tune-o-matic bridge, dot markers, 2 knobs. Revised in '07 with 1 single-coil (2 also offered), wrap around tailpiece, 1 knob, pickguard mounted jack.

2003-2006		$320	$410
2007-2008	2 pickup option	$375	$485
2007-2008	Revised specs	$320	$410

Melody Maker Joan Jett Signature

2008-2012. Double-cut, worn-white (til '11), 1 Burstbucker 3. Blackheart version in black with red dots starts '10.

2008-2012		$850	$1,075

Midnight Special

1974-1975. L-6S body style, maple 'board, dot markers, 2 humbucker pickups, custom colors.

1974-1975		$1,350	$1,750

Midtown Custom

2012-2014. 335-style semi-hollow, 2 humbuckers, block markers.

2011-2014		$1,050	$1,350

Midtown Standard P-90

2012-2014. Like Midtown Custom, but with dots, P-90s.

2012-2014		$950	$1,200

MK-35

1975-1978. Mark Series flat-top acoustic, mahogany back and sides, black-bound body, natural or sunburst, 5226 made.

1975-1978		$650	$850

MK-53

1975-1978. Mark Series flat-top acoustic, maple back and sides, multi-bound body, natural or sunburst, 1424 made.

1975-1978		$675	$875

MK-72

1975-1978. Mark Series flat-top acoustic, rosewood back and sides, black-bound body, chrome tuners, natural or sunburst, 1229 made.

1975-1978		$700	$900

MK-81

1975-1978. Mark Series flat-top acoustic, rosewood back and sides, multi-bound body, gold tuners, high-end appointments, natural or sunburst, 431 made.

1975-1978		$725	$950

Moderne

2012. Mahogany body and neck, dual '57 Classic humbuckers, trans amber or ebony finish.

2012		$1,300	$1,650

Moderne Heritage

1981-1983. Limited edition, korina body, 2 humbucking pickups, gold hardware.

1981-1983	Black or white	$3,800	$4,900
1981-1983	Natural	$3,800	$4,900

Nick Lucas

1928-1938. Flat-top acoustic, multi-bound body and neck, sunburst, reintroduced in '91 and '99. Also

MODEL YEAR	FEATURES	EXC. COND. LOW	HIGH

known as Nick Lucas Special and Gibson Special.

1927-1928	Mahogany, 12-fret, 13 1/3"	$10,100	$12,600
1927-1928	Rosewood, 12-fret, 13 1/2"	$13,500	$17,000
1929	Mahogany, 12-fret, 14 3/4"	$10,100	$12,600
1929	Rosewood, 12-fret, 14 3/4"	$13,500	$17,000
1930-1933	Rosewood, 13-fret, 14 3/4", pin bridge	$20,000	$26,000
1930-1933	Rosewood, 13-fret, 14 3/4", trapeze	$20,000	$26,000
1934-1938	Maple, 14-fret, 14 3/4"	$31,000	$40,000
1934-1938	Maple, tenor 4-string	$9,500	$12,500

Nick Lucas Reissue

1991-1992, 1999-2004. Limited edition flat-top acoustic, sunburst.

1991-1992		$2,000	$2,600
1999-2004		$2,000	$2,600

Nick Lucas Elite

2003-2005. Ebony 'board, abalone inlay, gold tuners.

2003-2005		$3,100	$4,000

Nighthawk Custom

1993-1998. Flame maple top, ebony 'board, gold hardware, fireburst, single/double/mini pickups.

1993-1998		$1,300	$1,700

Nighthawk 2009

2009. Dot markers, figured top, limited run.

2009		$900	$1,175

Nighthawk 2010

2010-2012. AAA quilted maple top, chambered poplar body, 3 pickups.

2010-2012		$900	$1,175

Nighthawk Special

1993-1998. Single-cut solidbody, figured maple top, double-coil and mini-pickup or with additional single-coil options, dot marker inlay, cherry, ebony or sunburst.

1993-1998		$1,100	$1,450

Nighthawk Standard

1993-1998. Single-cut solidbody, figured maple top, 2 or 3 pickups, double-parallelogram inlay, amber, fireburst or sunburst.

1993-1998		$1,200	$1,600

Nighthawk Studio

2011-2012. AAA quilted maple top, dots.

2011-2012		$600	$800

Nouveau NV6T-M

1986-1987. A line of Gibson flat-tops with imported parts assembled and finished in the U.S., acoustic dreadnought, bound maple body, natural.

1986-1987		$400	$515

Original Jumbo (Custom Shop)

2003. 16" jumbo body, Adirondack top, mahogany sides and back, butterbean tuner buttons, deep sunburst finish on complete body, Custom Art Historic.

2003		$2,000	$2,600

MODEL YEAR	FEATURES	EXC. COND. LOW	HIGH

Pat Martino Custom/Signature

1999-2006. Sharp single-cut thinline, f-holes, 2 humbuckers, flamed cherry sunburst maple top, small snakehead style headstock, Pat Martino logo on truss rod cover.

1999-2006		$2,000	$2,600

PG-00

1932-1937. Plectrum neck, flat-top.

1932-1937		$2,600	$3,300

PG-1

1928-1938. Plectrum neck, flat-top.

1929		$2,800	$3,600

PG-175

1950. Acoustic/electric with ES-175 bobdy and 4-string plectrum neck, bow-tie markers, sunburst.

1950		$5,000	$6,300

Q-100

1985-1986. Offset double-cut solidbody, Kahler trem, 6-on-a-side tuners, 1 humbucker, black hardware.

1985-1986		$450	$600

Q-200/Q2000

1985-1986. Like Q-100, but with 1 single and 1 hum, black or chrome hardware. Name changed to 2000 late '85.

1985-1986		$600	$800

Q-300/Q3000

1985-1986. Like Q-100, but with 3 single-coils, black or chrome hardware. Name changed to 3000 late '85.

1985-1986		$600	$800

Q-3000 Custom Shop

1985. Limited Custom production, 3 single-coil pickups.

1985		$1,200	$1,600

Q-400/Q4000

Late-1985-1987. Limited custom production, like Q-100, but with 2 singles and 1 hum, black hardware, Name changed to 400 late '85. Ferrari Red or Pink Panther finish as 4000, ebony as 400.

1985-1987		$1,200	$1,600

RD Artist CMT

1981. Figured top.

1981		$2,500	$3,200

RD Artist/77

1980. The 77 model has a 25.5" scale versus 24.75".

1980		$1,675	$2,100

RD Artist/79

1978-1982. Double-cut solidbody, 2 humbuckers, TP-6 tailpiece, active electronics, ebony 'board, block inlays, gold-plated parts, various colors, called just RD (no Artist) in '81 and '82.

1978-1982		$1,675	$2,100

RD Custom

1977-1979. Double-cut solidbody, 2 humbuckers, stop tailpiece, active electronics, dot inlays, maple 'board, chrome parts, natural or walnut.

1977-1979		$1,725	$2,150

RD Standard

1977-1979. Double-cut solidbody, 2 humbuckers, stop tailpiece, rosewood 'board, dot inlays, chrome parts, natural, sunburst or walnut.

1977-1979		$1,300	$1,650

RD Standard Reissue

2007, 2009, 2011. 400 Silverburst made in '07. Black or Trans Amber Red versions offered as limited run in '09 in Japan and in U.S. in '11.

2007	Silverburst	$1,050	$1,350
2009, '11	Black, Trans Amber Red	$1,050	$1,350

Roy Smeck Radio Grande Hawaiian

1934-1939. Dreadnought acoustic flat-top, rosewood back and sides, bound body and neck, natural.

1934-1939		$14,000	$18,000

Roy Smeck Radio Grande Hawaiian Reissue

1996. Part of SmartWood Series, Grenadillo back and sides.

1996		$2,250	$2,900

Roy Smeck Radio Grande Hawaiian Limited

1994. Centennial Guitar of the Month in '94, 100 made, Indian rosewood.

1994		$2,250	$2,900

Roy Smeck Stage Deluxe Hawaiian

1934-1942. Dreadnought acoustic flat-top, mahogany back and sides, bound body, natural.

1934-1942		$6,700	$8,500

S-1

1976-1980. Single-cut solidbody, pointed headstock, 3 single-coil pickups, similar to the Marauder, various colors.

1976-1980		$800	$1,000

SG

Following are models, listed alphabetically, bearing the SG name.

SG I

1972-1978. Double-cut, mahogany body, 1 mini-humbucker (some with SG Jr. P-90), wraparound bridge/tailpiece, cherry or walnut.

1972-1978		$950	$1,200

SG II

1972-1979. SG I with 2 mini-humbuckers (some in '75 had regular humbuckers), 2 slide switches, cherry or walnut.

1972-1979		$1,000	$1,250

SG III

1972-1977. SG II with sunburst and tune-o-matic.

1972-1977		$1,050	$1,300

SG-3

2007-2008. SG styling, SG Standard appointments, 3 gold humbuckers or 3 single coils, 1 rotor switch, 2 knobs, stop tail.

2007-2008	3 humbuckers	$1,050	$1,300
2007-2008	3 single coils	$725	$900

SG '61 Reissue

2003-present. Renamed from Les Paul SG '61 Reissue, no Les Paul script on truss rod, small 'guard, stop bar tailpiece (no Deluxe Maestro vibrato), '60 slim-taper neck profile.

2003-2014		$1,300	$1,625

Gibson Pat Martino Custom/Signature

2006 Gibson SG '61 Reissue

Gibson SG Carved Top - Autumn Burst

Gibson SG Classic

MODEL YEAR	FEATURES	EXC. COND. LOW	HIGH

SG '62 Reissue/SG Reissue
1986-1991. Trapezoid markers, stop bar, 2 humbuckers, called SG Reissue '86-'87, SG '62 Reissue '88-'91. Reintroduced as Les Paul SG '61 Reissue for '93-'03 and SG '61 Reissue '03-present, cherry.

1986-1991		$1,200	$1,500

SG '62 Reissue Showcase Edition
1988. Guitar of the Month, bright blue opaque finish, 200 made.

1988		$1,575	$1,950

Les Paul '63 Corvette Sting Ray
1995-1997. Custom Shop SG-style body carved to simulate split rear window on '63 Corvette, Sting Ray inlay, 150 made, offered in black, white, silver or red.

1995-1997		$3,700	$4,700

SG-90 Double
1988-1990. SG body, updated electronics, graphite reinforced neck, 2 pickups, cherry, turquoise or white.

1988-1990		$675	$850

SG-90 Single
1988-1990. SG body, updated electronics, graphite reinforced neck, 1 humbucker pickup, cherry, turquoise or white.

1988-1990		$650	$825

SG-100
1971-1972. Double-cut solidbody, 1 pickup, cherry or walnut.

1971-1972	Melody Maker pickup	$950	$1,200
1971-1972	P-90 pickup option	$950	$1,200
1971-1972	Sam Ash model	$950	$1,200

SG-200
1971-1972. Two pickup version of SG-100 in black, cherry or walnut finish, replaced by SG II.

1971-1972	Melody Maker pickups	$1,000	$1,250

SG-250
1971-1972. Two-pickup version of SG-100 in cherry sunburst, replaced by SG III.

1971-1972	Melody Maker pickups	$1,050	$1,300

SG-400/SG Special 400
1985-1987. SG body with 3 toggles, 2 knobs (master volume, master tone), single-single-humbucker pickups, available with uncommon opaque finishes.

1985-1987		$850	$1,050

SG Carved Top - Autumn Burst
2009. Limited run of 350, highly flamed carved maple top, rosewood 'board, certificate of authenticity.

2009		$1,450	$1,800

SG Classic/SG Classic Faded
1999-2001, 2003-2013. Late '60s SG Special style, Classic on truss rod cover, large 'guard, black soapbar single-coil P-90s, dot markers, stop bar tailpiece, cherry or ebony stain.

1999-2001		$725	$900
2003-2013		$725	$900

SG Custom
1963-1980. Renamed from Les Paul Custom, 3 humbuckers, vibrato, made with Les Paul Custom plate from '61-'63 (see Les Paul Custom), white finish

until '68, walnut and others after.

1963-1964	White, pat. #, Maestro	$11,600	$14,700
1965	Early '65, white	$10,100	$12,600
1965	Late '65, white	$8,800	$11,200
1966-1968	White	$6,200	$7,800
1969	Walnut, lyre, 1-piece neck	$4,600	$5,700
1969	Walnut, lyre, 3-piece neck	$3,600	$4,500
1969	White, lyre, 1 piece neck	$5,000	$6,200
1969	White, lyre, 3 piece neck	$4,000	$5,000
1970-1973	Walnut	$3,300	$4,100
1970-1973	White option	$4,000	$5,000
1974-1979	Various colors	$2,400	$3,000
1980	Various colors	$2,200	$2,800

SG Custom 30th Anniversary
1991. Custom Shop, block inlay, 3 57 Classic humbuckers, engraved 30th Anniversary headstock logo, gold hardware, darker TV yellow.

1991		$2,400	$3,000

SG Custom '67 Reissue/Les Paul SG '67 Custom
1991-1993. The SG Custom '67 Reissue has a wine red finish, the Les Paul SG '67 Custom ('92-'93) has a wine red or white finish.

1991-1993		$1,675	$2,100

SG Custom Elliot Easton Signature
2006-2007. Custom Shop, SG Custom specs, Maestro deluxe vibrola, Pelham Blue or white, includes Certificate of Authenticity.

2006-2007		$2,800	$3,500

SG Deluxe
1971-1972, 1981-1985, 1998-1999. The '70s models were offered in cherry, natural or walnut finishes, reintroduced in '98 with 3 Firebird mini-humbucker-style pickups in black, Ice Blue or red finishes.

1971-1972	Cherry	$1,400	$1,750
1971-1972	Natural, walnut	$1,275	$1,600
1981-1985	Various colors	$1,050	$1,300
1998-1999	Various colors	$1,050	$1,300

SG Diablo
2008. Guitar of the Month for Dec. '08, 1,000 made, '61 specs, metallic silver finish with matching headstock, 1 volume, 1 tone knob, 3-way toggle, 24 frets.

2008		$1,100	$1,375

SG Diablo Premium Plus
2012-2013. AAA maple top.

2012-2013		$1,200	$1,475

SG Dickey Betts
2012. Custom, 75 hand-aged made include a leather certificate of authenticity signed by Betts, 250 VOS include unsigned COA, Vintage Red finish.

2012	Aged	$5,000	$6,300
2012	VOS	$3,000	$3,800

SG Elegant
2004-2013. Custom Shop, quilt maple top, gold hardware, Blue Burst, Firemist and Iguana Burst finishes.

2004-2013		$2,000	$2,500

MODEL		EXC. COND.	
YEAR	FEATURES	LOW	HIGH

SG Exclusive

1979. SG with humbuckers, coil-tap and rotary control knob, block inlay, pearl logo (not decal), black/ebony finish.

| 1979 | | $1,800 | $2,250 |

SG Firebrand

1980-1982. Double-cut mahogany solidbody, rough natural finish, Gibson branded in headstock, 2 exposed humbuckers, Firebrand logo on The SG (Standard) model.

| 1980-1982 | | $900 | $1,125 |

SG Goddess

2007. SG Goddess logo on truss rod cover, only 2 control knobs versus standard 4, exposed humbuckers.

| 2007 | | $850 | $1,075 |

SG Gothic

2000-2003. SG Special with satin black finish, moon and star marker on 12th fret, black hardware.

| 2000-2003 | | $625 | $775 |

SG Gothic Morte

2011-2012. Solid mahogany body, African Obeche 'board, 2 pickups, satin ebony finish

| 2011 2012 | | $350 | $435 |

SG GT

2006-2007. '61 specs with racing stripes paint job and removable tailpiece hood scoop, locking tuners, Candy Apple Red, Daytona Blue, or Phantom Black.

| 2006-2007 | | $1,400 | $1,750 |

SG Jeff Tweedy Signature

2012. SG Standard with Maestro vibrola, mahogany body and neck, rosewood 'board, Blue Mist.

| 2012 | | $1,400 | $1,725 |

SG Judas Priest Signature

2003. Custom Shop, 30 made, dot markers, exposed '57 classic humbucker and EMG58 pickups, black, large chrome metal 'guard, also sold as a set with Flying V Judas Priest, includes certificate of authenticity.

| 2003 | | $1,750 | $2,150 |

SG Judas Priest Signature Set With Flying V

2003. Custom Shop, 30 sets made.

| 2003 | | $4,000 | $5,000 |

SG Junior

1963-1971, 1991-1994. One pickup, solidbody. Prices are for an unfaded finish, cherry finish faded to brown reduces the value by 30%.

1963	Cherry	$2,600	$3,300
1963	White	$3,400	$4,200
1964	Cherry	$2,600	$3,300
1964	White	$3,400	$4,200
1965	Early-'65, cherry	$2,600	$3,300
1965	Late-'65, cherry	$2,000	$2,500
1965	Pelham Blue	$4,000	$5,000
1965	White	$2,600	$3,200
1966	Cherry	$1,800	$2,250
1966	White	$2,400	$3,000
1967	Cherry	$1,800	$2,250
1967	White	$2,400	$3,000
1968	Cherry	$1,800	$2,250
1968	White	$2,400	$3,000
1969	Cherry	$1,800	$2,250
1970	Cherry	$1,650	$2,050
1971	Cherry or walnut	$1,650	$2,050
1991-1994	Various colors	$675	$850

SG Junior P-90

2007. Single P-90 pickup, large 'guard, stop tail, cherry finish.

| 2007 | | $675 | $850 |

SG Les Paul '61 Custom Reissue

1997-2005. 1961 specs, SG body style, 3 humbuckers, Deluxe Maestro vibrato or stud with tune-o-matic bridge, white or silver option.

| 1997-2005 | | $1,800 | $2,250 |

SG Les Paul '62 Custom

1986-1990. 1962 specs, 3 humbuckers.

| 1986-1990 | | $1,675 | $2,075 |

SG Les Paul '62 Custom (Custom Shop)

2003. Custom Shop, Maestro vibrato, small 'guard, white.

| 2003 | | $1,675 | $2,075 |

SG Les Paul '90 Custom

1990-1992. 1962 specs, 3 humbuckers.

| 1990-1992 | | $1,675 | $2,075 |

SG Les Paul Custom 30th Anniversary

1991. SG body, 3 humbuckers, gold hardware, TV Yellow finish, 30th Anniversary on peghead.

| 1991 | | $2,100 | $2,600 |

SG Menace

2006-2007. Carved mahogany body, 2 exposed humbuckers, flat black finish, black hardware, single brass knuckle position marker, gig bag.

| 2006-2007 | | $625 | $800 |

SG Music Machine Stinger

2003. Custom run for dealer Music Machine, special serial number series, SG Custom with 2 pickups and SG Standard models available, black stinger paint job on neck/headstock, various colors.

| 2003 | SG Custom | $2,300 | $2,900 |
| 2003 | SG Standard | $2,100 | $2,600 |

SG Pete Townshend Signature (Custom Shop)

2000. SG Special with '69 specs, large 'guard, 2 cases, cherry red, COA, limited edition of 250.

| 2000 | Includes certificate | $1,325 | $1,675 |

SG Platinum

2005. A mix of SG Special and SG Standard specs, platinum paint on the body, back of neck, and headstock, no crown inlay, Gibson stencil logo, exposed humbucker pickups, large plantium-finish 'guard, special plantium colored Gibson logo guitar case.

| 2005 | | $600 | $750 |

SG Pro

1971-1974. Tune-o-matic bridge, vibrato, 2 P-90 pickups, cherry, mahogany or walnut.

| 1971-1974 | | $1,400 | $1,750 |

SG R1/SG Artist

1980-1982. Active RD-era electronics. SG style but thicker body, no 'guard, ebony 'board, black finish, dot markers, renamed SG Artist in '81.

| 1980 | SG-R1 | $750 | $935 |
| 1981-1982 | SG Artist | $750 | $935 |

1965 Gibson SG Junior
David Daviee

2006 Gibson SG Menace

1965 Gibson SG Special

Don Tucker

Gibson SG Special Faded

MODEL YEAR	FEATURES	EXC. COND. LOW	EXC. COND. HIGH

SG Reissue
1986-1987. Standard early to mid-'60s small guard SG specs, stop tailpiece with tune-o-matic bridge, no designation on truss rod cover, cherry finish, renamed SG '62 Reissue in '88.

1986-1987	Small 'guard	$1,100	$1,400
1986-1987	Stop bar	$1,100	$1,400

SG Select
2007. Made in Nashville, TN, carved solid book-matched AAA flame maple, 3-piece flamed maple neck, described as the most exquisite SG offered to date, 2 humbuckers, gold hardware.

2007		$1,850	$2,300

SG Silverburst Limited
2010. 400 made, standard tuners.

2010		$1,125	$1,400

SG Special
1959-1978, 1985-present. Rounded double-cut for '59-'60, switched to SG body early-'61, 2 P-90s '59-'71, 2 mini-humbuckers '72-'78, 2 regular humbuckers on current version, reintroduced in '85. Prices are for an unfaded finish, cherry finish faded to brown reduces the value by 20%-30%. Instruments with stop tailpieces vs. Maestro tailpiece have the same value.

1959	Cherry, slab, high neck pickup	$5,600	$7,000
1960	Cherry, slab, lower neck pickup	$5,600	$7,000
1961-1962	Cherry, SG body	$4,600	$5,700
1962	White, SG body	$5,400	$6,700
1963-1964	Cherry, Maestro or stop	$4,600	$5,700
1963-1964	White	$5,400	$6,700
1965	Cherry	$3,600	$4,500
1965	White	$4,200	$5,300
1966	Cherry, large 'guard	$2,900	$3,600
1966	Cherry, small 'guard	$3,100	$3,900
1966	White, large 'guard	$3,300	$4,100
1966	White, small 'guard	$3,700	$4,600
1967	Cherry	$2,900	$3,600
1967	White	$3,300	$4,100
1968-1969	Cherry	$2,900	$3,600
1970-1971	Cherry	$2,600	$3,200
1972-1978	Cherry or walnut	$1,400	$1,750

SG Special (redesigned)
1985-1996. In mid-'85 Gibson introduced a redesigned SG Special model with 2 control knobs (1 pickup) or 3 control knobs (2 pickups) versus the previously used 4-knob layout.

1985-1986	1 pickup, 2 knobs	$575	$725
1985-1989	2 pickups, 3 knobs	$600	$750
1990-1996	2 pickups, 3 knobs	$550	$675

SG Special (reintroduced)
1996-present. In '96 Gibson reintroduced the original 4-knob layout, 2 humbucker pickups, dot markers.

1996-2007		$580	$725
2008-2015		$580	$725

SG Special 3/4
1961. Only 61 shipped.

1961		$2,500	$3,100

SG Special '60s Tribute
2011-present. '60s specs including small guard, dot markers, dual P-90s, Slim Taper '60s neck profile, 4 worn-finish options.

2011-2014		$575	$725

SG Special Faded (3 pickups)
2007. Made in Nashville, TN, 3 exposed 490 humbuckers, dot markers, stop tail, SG initials on truss rod cover, 2 knobs and 6-position selector switch, hand-worn satin finish.

2007		$550	$675

SG Special Faded/Faded SG Special
2002-present. Aged worn cherry finish.

2002-2005	Half moon markers	$550	$675
2003-2014	Dot markers	$550	$675

SG Special I
1983-1985. Dot markers, 1 exposed-coil humbucker pickup with 2 knobs, called by various names including Gibson Special ('83), Special I, and SG Special I.

1983-1985		$550	$700

SG Special II
1983-1985. Dot markers, 2 exposed-coil humbucker pickups with 3 knobs, called by various names including Gibson Special ('83), Special II, SG Special II.

1983-1985		$550	$700

SG Special II EMG
2007. EMG humbucker pickups, no position markers, standard 4-knob and 3-way toggle switch SG format, black satin finish over entire guitar, black hardware.

2007		$700	$875

SG Special New Century
2006-2008. Full-body mirror 'guard, 2 exposed humbuckers, SG body, mirror truss rod cover.

2006-2008		$800	$1,000

SG Special Robot
2008-2012. Dot markers, robot tuning.

2008-2012		$700	$900

SG Special Robot Limited
2008. Limited run with trapezoid markers, robot tuning.

2008		$800	$1,000

SG Special Robot Limited Silverburst
2008. Limited run of 400.

2008		$850	$1,075

SG Special VOS Reissue
2006-2013. Custom Shop, mahogany body and neck, bound rosewood 'board, dot inlays, 2 P-90s, certificate, white, TV yellow, or faded cherry finish.

2006-2013		$1,750	$2,175

SG Standard
1963-1981, 1983-present. Les Paul Standard changes to SG body, 2 humbuckers, some very early models have optional factory Bigsby. Prices are for an unfaded finish, a cherry finish faded to brown reduces the value by 30% or more.

1963-1964	Cherry, small 'guard, deluxe vibrato	$9,000	$12,000

MODEL YEAR	FEATURES	EXC. COND. LOW	HIGH
1964	Pelham Blue, small 'guard, deluxe vibrato	$14,700	$18,400
1965	Cherry, small 'guard, deluxe vibrato	$8,800	$11,500
1965	Pelham Blue, small 'guard, deluxe vibrato	$13,000	$16,400
1966	Early '66 cherry, small 'guard, deluxe vibrato	$6,500	$8,200
1966	Late '66, cherry, large 'guard	$5,400	$6,800
1967	Burgundy Metallic	$5,900	$7,400
1967	Cherry	$5,100	$6,500
1967	White	$5,900	$7,400
1968	Cherry, engraved lyre	$5,100	$6,500
1969	Engraved lyre, 1-piece neck	$5,100	$6,500
1969	Engraved lyre, 3-piece neck	$3,500	$4,500
1970	Cherry, non-lyre tailpiece	$2,500	$3,100
1970	Engraved lyre, 3-piece neck	$2,700	$3,400
1970	Walnut, non-lyre tailpiece	$2,200	$2,700
1971	Cherry, non-lyre tailpiece	$2,300	$2,900
1971	Engraved lyre, 3-piece neck	$2,700	$3,400
1972-1979	Blocks, mini 'guard, top mount	$1,700	$2,200
1980-1986	New colors, small blocks	$1,600	$2,100
1992-1999	New specs	$900	$1,150
2000-2014	Standard colors, large 'guard, stoptail	$800	$1,025
2006-2007	Silverburst, 400 made	$925	$1,150
2010	Silverburst	$925	$1,150

SG Standard '61 Reissue

2004-present. Small 'guard, stop tail, Nashville tune-o-matic bridge, Gibson Deluxe Keystone tuners, standard Gibson logo and crown inlay, no Les Paul logo, Vintage Original Spec aging optional from '06.

2004-2014		$1,300	$1,625

SG Angus Young

2010-present. Like Angus Signature but with small guard, stop tailpiece and tune-o-matic, Aged Cherry.

2010-2014		$1,500	$1,925

SG Angus Young Signature

2000-2009. Late-'60s Std specs with large 'guard, Deluxe Maestro lyre vibrato with Angus logo, aged cherry finish.

2000-2009		$1,375	$1,725

SG Standard 24 50th Anniversary

2011. Limited run, mother-of-pearl Gibson logo with gold 50th Anniversary silkscreen, 2 '57 classic pickups, antique ebony finish.

2011		$850	$1,050

MODEL YEAR	FEATURES	EXC. COND. LOW	HIGH

SG Standard Celebrity Series

1991-1992. SG Standard with large 'guard, gold hardware, black finish.

1991-1992		$1,400	$1,750

SG Standard Gary Rossington Signature

2004. '63-'64 SG Standard specs with Deluxe Maestro vibrola, '60 slim taper neck, limited edition, faded cherry aged by Tom Murphy.

2004		$3,300	$4,100

SG Standard Korina

1993-1994. Korina version of SG Standard, limited run, natural.

1993-1994		$2,000	$2,500

SG Standard Limited Edition

2000. Limited Edition logo back of headstock, 2 humbuckers, large pearloid guard, gold hardware, dark opaque finish.

2000		$950	$1,175

SG Standard Limited Edition (3 pickups)

2007. Guitar of the Week, 400 made, 3 single-coil blade pickups, 6-position rotator switch with chickenhead knob, SG logo on truss rod cover, large 'guard, satin finish.

2007		$800	$1,000

SG Standard Reissue

2004-present. Reissue of near '63-'64 specs with Deluxe Maestro lyre vibrato and small 'guard, also offered with stop bar tailpiece, cherry finish, '60 slim taper neck, smooth neck heel joint, trapezoid markers, unmarked truss rod cover without Les Paul designation, formerly called Les Paul SG Standard Reissue, by 2005 part of Gibson's 'Vintage Original Spec' Custom Shop series.

2004-2007	VOS, Maestro, COA	$1,800	$2,300
2007-2014	VOS, stoptail, COA	$1,800	$2,300
2008-2009	Maestro, LP logo	$1,800	$2,300

SG Standard Robby Krieger

2009. Custom Shop model, Inspired By series, based on Krieger's '67 SG, limited run of 150 with 50 aged and signed, 100 with V.O.S. finish treatment, certificate of authenticity.

2009	Aged, signed	$3,400	$4,200
2009	VOS	$2,800	$3,500

SG Standard Robby Krieger 50th Anniversary

2012. Mahogany body and neck, rosewood 'board, 2 '57 classic Alnico II pickups, Maestro tailpiece, Heritage Cherry finish.

2012		$1,350	$1,700

SG Supreme

2004-2007. '57 humbuckers, flamed maple top, split-diamond markers, various colors.

2004-2007		$1,550	$1,950

SG Tommy Iommi Signature (Historic/Custom Shop)

2001-2003. Custom Shop higher-end, signature humbuckers without poles, cross inlays, ebony or Wine Red.

2001-2003		$3,700	$4,600

SG Tommy Iommi Signature (Production)

2002-2003. Standard production model.

2002-2008		$1,750	$2,200

1966 Gibson SG Standard

Robbie Keene

Gibson SG Standard 24 50th Anniversary

2009 Gibson SG Zoot Suit

1959 Gibson SJN
Country Western
Rod Highsmith

MODEL YEAR	FEATURES	EXC. COND. LOW	HIGH

SG TV

1959-1968. Les Paul TV changed to SG body, double rounded cutaway solidbody for '59-'60, SG body '61-'68, 1 pickup, limed mahogany (TV yellow) finish. Prices are for unfaded finish, a faded finish reduces the value by 20%-30%.

1959-1961	TV Yellow, slab body	$5,300	$6,600
1961-1963	White, SG body	$3,700	$4,600

SG Voodoo/Voodoo SG

2002-2004. Carved top, black hardware, voodoo doll inlay at 5th fret, Juju finish (black with red wood filler).

2002-2004		$925	$1,175

SG-X (All American I)

1995-2000. Renamed the SG-X in '98, previously part of the All American series, SG body with single bridge humbucker, various colors.

1995-1999		$625	$775

SG-X Tommy Hilfiger

1998. Hilfiger logo on front, dot markers, plain headstock like a SG Special, dark blue finish, 100 made.

1998		$500	$625

SG Zoot Suit

2009-2010. Body of individual dyed strips of birch.

2009-2010		$950	$1,200

SG-Z

1998. Z-shaped string-thru tailpiece, 2 humbuckers, split diamond markers.

1998		$1,550	$1,950

The SG

1979-1983. Offered as The SG Standard (walnut body) and The SG Deluxe (mahogany), ebony 'board, 2 humbuckers.

1979-1983	Walnut or mahogany	$700	$875

Sheryl Crow Signature

2001-2014. Artist Series, based on Sheryl Crow's 1962 Country and Western with Hummingbird influences.

2001-2014		$1,700	$2,100

Sheryl Crow Southern Jumbo Special Edition

2013-present. Adirondack red spruce top, mahogany back and sides, rosewood 'board, with signed certificate of authenticity, Montana Sunsetburst finish. Limited production in '13.

2013-2014		$2,800	$3,500

SJ (Southern Jumbo)

1942 1969,1991-1996. Flat-top, sunburst standard, natural optional starting in '54 (natural finish version called Country-Western starting in '56), round shoulders (changed to square in '62), catalog name changed to SJ Deluxe in '70, refer to that listing.

1942-1944	Banner	$12,000	$16,000
1945-1946		$9,800	$12,500
1947-1949		$6,500	$8,300
1950-1953		$5,300	$6,750
1954-1956	Natural option	$5,300	$6,750
1954-1956	Sunburst	$5,300	$6,750
1957-1959		$5,300	$6,750
1960-1962	Round shoulder (ends)	$4,800	$6,000

MODEL YEAR	FEATURES	EXC. COND. LOW	HIGH
1962-1964	Square shoulder (begins)	$4,300	$5,500
1965	Cherry Sunburst	$2,700	$3,500
1965	Tobacco Sunburst	$3,550	$4,500
1966	Tobacco Sunburst	$3,200	$4,075
1966-1968	Cherry Sunburst	$2,650	$3,375
1969	Below belly bridge	$1,800	$2,250

SJ Deluxe (Southern Jumbo)

1970-1978. SJ name changed to SJ Deluxe in catalog, along with a series of engineering changes.

1970-1971	Non-adj. saddle	$1,900	$2,350
1972-1973	Unbound 'board	$1,450	$1,825
1974-1978	4-ply to binding	$1,400	$1,775

SJN (Country-Western)

1956-1969. Flat-top, natural finish version of SJ, round shoulders '56-'62, square shoulders after, called the SJN in '60 and '61, the SJN Country Western after that, catalog name changed to SJN Deluxe in '70, refer to that listing.

1956-1959		$5,300	$6,750
1960-1962	Round shoulder (ends)	$4,000	$5,500
1962-1964	Square shoulder (begins)	$3,200	$4,050
1965-1968		$2,400	$3,050
1969	Below belly bridge, SJN logo	$2,000	$2,500

SJN Deluxe (Country-Western Jumbo)

1970-1978. SJN name changed to SJN Deluxe in catalog, along with a series of engineering changes.

1970-1971	Non-adj. saddle	$1,900	$2,350
1972-1973	Unbound 'board	$1,450	$1,825
1974-1978	4-ply to binding	$1,400	$1,775

SJ 1942 Reissue (Southern Jumbo)

2000. Custom Shop, mahogany back and sides, '42 SJ appointments, 'Only A Gibson is Good Enough' banner logo.

2000		$2,200	$2,800

SJ Reissue (Southern Jumbo)

2003-2007. Sunburst.

2003-2007		$1,575	$1,975

SJ Hank Williams Jr. Hall of Fame (Southern Jumbo)

1997. Custom Shop, mahogany back and sides, SJ appointments.

1997		$2,200	$2,725

SJ Kristofferson (Southern Jumbo)

2009-2012. Limited run of 300, AAA Sitka top, mahogany back and sides, Indian rosewood 'board, aged vintage sunburst.

2009-2012		$1,900	$2,375

SJ True Vintage (Southern Jumbo)

2007-2008. "Only A Gibson Is Good Enough" headstock banner, sitka spruce top, dark mahogany back and sides, dual parallelogram markers.

2007-2008		$2,000	$2,500

SJ Woody Guthrie (Southern Jumbo)

2003-present. Single-bound round shoulder body, mahogany back and sides, parallelogram inlays.

2003-2014		$2,000	$2,500

MODEL YEAR	FEATURES	EXC. COND. LOW	HIGH

SJ-100
2008. Jumbo body, dot markers, crown headstock inlay, inlaid Gibson logo, natural.

| 2008 | | $1,000 | $1,250 |

SJ-100 1939 Centennial
1994. Acoustic flat-top, limited edition, sunburst.

| 1994 | | $1,900 | $2,400 |

SJ-100 1941
2013-present. Sitka spruce top, mahogany back, sides and neck, rosewood 'board, Vintage Sunburst.

| 2013-2014 | | $1,800 | $2,250 |

SJ-150 Maple
2006-2008. Acoustic-electric 17" Jumbo, flamed maple back and sides, gloss natural finish.

| 2006-2008 | | $1,450 | $1,800 |

SJ-200 Centennial Limited Edition
1994. Made in Bozeman, Montana, 100 made, 'guard specs based on '38 design, inside label "Gibson 100 Years 1894-1994", includes Certificate of Authenticity.

| 1994 | | $2,650 | $3,300 |

SJ-200 Elite
1998-2007. Gibson Custom Shop Bozeman, maple sides and back.

| 1998-2007 | | $3,000 | $3,700 |

SJ-200 Pete Townshend Limited
2004-2012. Gibson Custom Shop Bozeman, maple sides and back.

| 2004 | Signed 1st 50 made | $6,500 | $8,000 |
| 2004-2012 | | $3,200 | $4,000 |

SJ-200 Ray Whilley/J-200 Custom Club
1994-1995. Based on Ray Whitley's late-1930s J-200, including engraved inlays and initials on the truss rod cover, only 37 made, one of the limited edition models the Montana division released to celebrate Gibson's 100th anniversary.

| 1994-1995 | | $9,200 | $11,500 |

SJ-200 Summer Jam Koa
2006. Custom Shop, only 6 made, offered to attendees of Gibson Guitar Summer Jam, highly figured koa back/sides.

| 2006 | | $4,250 | $5,300 |

SJ-200 True Vintage
2007-present. AAA Adirondack red spruce top, AAA Eastern curly maple back and sides, rosewood 'board, tortoise 'guard, nitrocellulose finish.

| 2007-2014 | | $3,300 | $4,100 |

SJ-200 Vine
2002. Custom Shop, Sitka spruce top, Eastern curly maple back/sides, abalone vine inlay in 'board, abalone body trim.

| 2002 | | $5,200 | $6,800 |

SJ-300
2007-2010. Super Jumbo with Indian rosewood back and sides, ebony 'board, abalone crown inlays and rosette, gold imperial tuners, active transducer.

| 2007-2010 | | $2,700 | $3,350 |

Sonex-180 Custom
1980-1982. Two Super humbuckers, coil-tap, maple neck, ebony 'board, single-cut, body of Multi-Phonic synthetic material, black or white.

| 1980-1982 | | $750 | $950 |

Sonex-180 Deluxe
1980-1984. Hardwood neck, rosewood 'board, single-cut, body of Multi-Phonic synthetic material, 2 pickups, no coil-tap, various colors.

1980-1984	Ebony	$675	$850
1982-1984	Red or Fireburst	$675	$850
1982-1984	Silverburst	$675	$850

Sonex-180 Standard
1980. Dirty-fingers pickups, rosewood 'board, ebony finish.

| 1980 | | $800 | $1,000 |

Songbird Deluxe
1999-2002. Solid rosewood back, sides and 'board, on-board electronics. Renamed Songwriter Deluxe.

| 1999-2002 | | $1,225 | $1,525 |

Songwriter Deluxe
2003-2008. Solid rosewood back and sides, trapezoid inlays, cutaway or non-cutaway, on-board electronics.

| 2003-2008 | | $1,325 | $1,675 |

Songwriter Deluxe 12-String
2006-2008. 12-string version, non-cut.

| 2006-2008 | | $1,325 | $1,675 |

Songwriter Deluxe Koa
2009. Custom Shop, all koa, cutaway.

| 2009 | | $1,925 | $2,400 |

Songwriter Deluxe Standard
2009-2012. Solid rosewood back and sides, bound ebony 'board, diamond and arrows inlays, cutaway or non-cutaway.

| 2009-2012 | | $1,625 | $2,025 |

Songwriter Deluxe Studio
2009-present. Like Standard, but with bound rosewood 'board and double parallelogram inlays, cutaway or non-cutaway.

| 2009-2014 | | $1,225 | $1,550 |

Songwriter Special
2007. Mahogany sides and back, dark opaque finish.

| 2007 | | $1,125 | $1,400 |

Songwriter Studio
2003-2012. Non-cutaway or cutaway.

| 2003-2012 | | $1,425 | $1,800 |

Special 400
1985. Double-cut SG body, exposed humbucker and 2 single-coils, Kahler locking tremolo, coil tap.

| 1985 | | $700 | $875 |

Spirit I
1982-1987. Double rounded cutaway, 1 pickup, chrome hardware, various colors.

| 1982-1987 | | $650 | $825 |

Spirit I XPL
1985-1986. Spirit I with 6-on-a-side Explorer-style headstock.

| 1985-1986 | | $650 | $825 |

Spirit II
1982-1987. Spirit I with 2 pickups, bound top.

| 1982-1987 | | $725 | $900 |

Spirit II XPL
1985-1986. 2 pickup version.

| 1985-1986 | | $725 | $900 |

1963 Gibson SJN Country Western

Travis Adkinson

2010 Gibson SJ Kristofferson

GUITARS

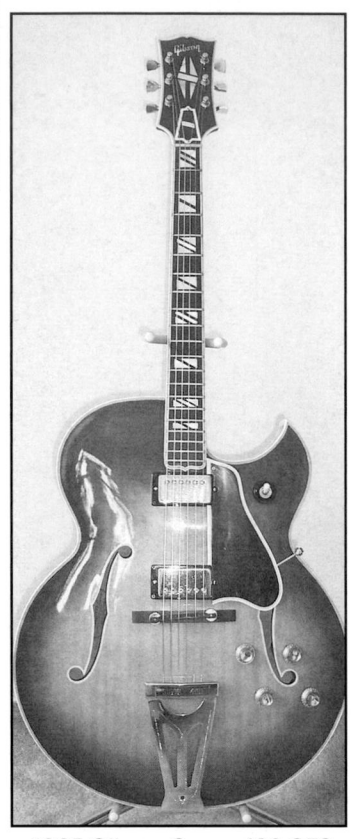

1965 Gibson Super 400 CES

Ray Prosser

Gibson Super 400 CES

MODEL YEAR	FEATURES	EXC. COND. LOW	HIGH

SR-71
1987-1989. Floyd Rose tremolo, 1 humbucker, 2 single-coil pickups, various colors, Wayne Charvel designed.

| 1987-1989 | | $800 | $1,000 |

Star
1992. Star logo on headstock, star position markers, single sharp cutaway flat-top, sunburst.

| 1991-1992 | | $1,150 | $1,450 |

Starburst Standard/Flame
1992-1994. Single-cut acoustic/electric, star inlays, figured maple back and sides.

| 1992-1994 | | $1,350 | $1,675 |

Style O
1902-1925. Acoustic archtop, oval soundhole, bound top, neck and headstock, various colors.

1902-1906	Paddle headstock	$4,200	$5,300
1902-1906	Paddle headstock, fancy	$6,000	$7,500
1906-1908	Slotted headstock	$4,200	$5,300
1908-1913	Solid headstock	$4,200	$5,300
1914-1921	Scroll variation	$4,200	$5,300
1922-1924	Loar era	$5,200	$6,500
1925	Scroll, truss rod	$5,200	$6,500

Style O-1
1902. Acoustic archtop, celluloid binding.

| 1902 | | $6,000 | $7,500 |

Style O-2
1902. Acoustic archtop, pearl/ebony binding.

| 1902 | | $6,500 | $8,100 |

Style O-3
1902. Acoustic archtop, green/white binding.

| 1902 | | $6,500 | $8,100 |

Style R Harp Guitar
1902-1907. Acoustic 6-string, with 6 sub-bass strings, walnut back and sides, bound soundhole.

| 1902-1907 | | $6,800 | $8,500 |

Style R-1 Harp Guitar
1902. Style R with fancier pearl and ivory rope pattern binding.

| 1902 | | $7,400 | $9,200 |

Style U Harp Guitar
1902-1939. Acoustic 6-string, with 10 or 12 sub-bass strings, walnut (until about '07) or birch back and sides, bound soundhole, black.

| 1902-1939 | | $7,500 | $9,500 |

Style U-1 Harp Guitar
1902-1907. Slightly fancier Style U.

| 1902-1907 | | $8,500 | $10,500 |

Super 300
1948-1955. Acoustic archtop, non-cut, bound body, neck and headstock, sunburst.

| 1948-1949 | | $4,000 | $5,000 |
| 1950-1955 | | $3,800 | $4,700 |

Super 300 C
1954-1958. Acoustic archtop, rounded cutaway, bound body, neck and headstock, sunburst with natural option.

| 1954-1958 | Sunburst | $4,900 | $6,100 |

Super 400
1935-1941, 1947-1955. Introduced early '35 as Super L-5 Deluxe. Acoustic archtop, non-cut, multi-bound,

MODEL YEAR	FEATURES	EXC. COND. LOW	HIGH

f-holes, sunburst (see Super 400 N for natural version).

1935	Early, Super L-5 Deluxe, highly flamed maple	$16,000	$21,000
1935	Early, Super L-5 Deluxe, plain maple	$14,000	$18,000
1935	Late, Super 400, highly flamed maple	$14,000	$18,500
1935	Late, Super 400, plain maple	$11,000	$14,000
1936-1941	Highly flamed maple	$12,000	$15,500
1936-1941	Plain maple	$9,600	$12,500
1947-1949	Highly flamed maple	$8,500	$11,000
1947-1949	Plain maple	$7,000	$9,000
1950-1955		$6,500	$8,300

Super 400 N
1940, 1948-1955. Natural finish version of Super 400, non-cut, acoustic archtop.

1940		$14,000	$18,000
1948-1949		$10,000	$13,000
1950-1955		$8,500	$11,000

Super 400 P (Premier)
1939-1941. Acoustic archtop, single rounded cutaway, '39 model 'board rests on top, sunburst finish.

| 1939-1941 | | $17,000 | $21,500 |

Super 400 PN (Premier Natural)
1939-1940. Rounded cutaway, '39 'board rests on top, natural finish.

| 1939-1940 | | $24,000 | $31,000 |

Super 400 C
1948-1982. Introduced as Super 400 Premier, acoustic archtop, single-cut, sunburst finish (natural is called Super 400 CN).

1948-1949		$10,500	$13,000
1950-1959		$10,000	$12,500
1960-1964		$8,800	$11,000
1965		$7,000	$8,800
1966-1969		$6,300	$7,900
1970-1979		$5,300	$6,700
1980-1982		$5,300	$6,700

Super 400 CN
1950-1987. Natural finish version of Super 400 C.

1950-1959		$12,000	$15,000
1960-1964		$10,400	$13,000
1965		$9,500	$12,000
1966-1969		$8,500	$10,500

Super 400 CES
1951-present. Electric version of Super 400 C, archtop, single-cut (round '51-'60 and '69-present, pointed '60-'69), 2 pickups (P-90s '51-'54, Alnico Vs '54-'57, humbuckers '57 on), sunburst (natural version called Super 400 CESN), now part of Gibson's Historic Collection.

1951-1953	P-90s	$16,000	$20,000
1954-1957	Alnico Vs	$16,000	$20,000
1957-1959	PAFs	$20,000	$25,000
1960	PAFs	$19,000	$24,000

MODEL YEAR	FEATURES	EXC. COND. LOW	HIGH
1961-1962	PAFs, sharp cut intro.	$14,700	$18,200
1963	Pat. #	$13,700	$17,200
1964	Pat. #	$12,700	$16,000
1965		$9,500	$11,800
1966-1969		$8,000	$10,000
1970-1979		$7,000	$8,800
1980-2014		$6,500	$8,000

Super 400 CESN

1952-present. Natural version of Super 400 CES, now part of Gibson's Historic Collection.

1952-1953	P-90s	$18,000	$23,000
1954-1956	Alnico Vs	$18,000	$23,000
1957-1960	PAFs	$22,000	$27,000
1961-1962	PAFs, sharp cut intro.	$16,000	$20,000
1963	Pat. #	$15,000	$19,000
1964	Pat. #	$14,000	$18,000
1965		$10,500	$13,500
1966-1969		$8,800	$11,000
1970-1979		$7,000	$8,800
1980-2014		$6,500	$8,000

'39 Super 400

1993-1997. Part of Historic Collection, reissue of non-cut '39 version, various colors.

1993-1997		$6,500	$8,000

Super Jumbo 100

1939-1943. Jumbo flat-top, mahogany back and sides, bound body and neck, sunburst, reintroduced as J-100 with different specs in '84.

1939-1940		$30,000	$40,000
1941	Early '41	$30,000	$40,000
1941	Late '41	$23,000	$30,000
1942-1943		$23,000	$30,000

Super Jumbo/Super Jumbo 200

1938-1942. Initially called Super Jumbo in '38 and named Super Jumbo 200 in '39. Name then changed to J-200 (see that listing) by '47 (with maple back and sides) and SJ-200 by the '50s. Named for super large jumbo 16 7/8" flat-top body, double braced with rosewood back and sides, sunburst finish.

1938-1940		$90,000	$125,000
1941	Early '41	$90,000	$125,000
1941	Late '41	$85,000	$105,000
1942		$85,000	$105,000

Super V CES

1978-1993. Archtop, L-5 with a Super 400 neck, 2 humbucker pickups, natural or sunburst.

1978-1993		$7,000	$8,800

Super V BJB

1978-1983. A Super V CES but with a single floating pickup.

1978-1983		$7,000	$8,800

Tal Farlow

1962-1971, 1993-2006. Full body, single-cut archtop, 2 humbuckers, triple-bound top, reintroduced '93, now part of Gibson's Historic Collection.

1962-1971	Viceroy Brown	$7,000	$8,700
1993-2006	Various colors	$3,000	$3,700

TG-0 (L-0 based)

1927-1933. Acoustic tenor based on L-0, mahogany body, light amber.

1927-1933		$2,200	$2,700

TG-0 (LG-0 based)

1960-1974. Acoustic tenor based on LG-0, mahogany body, natural.

1960-1964		$1,000	$1,250
1965		$750	$950
1966-1969		$675	$850
1970-1974		$575	$725

TG-00 (L-00 based)

1932-1943. Tenor flat-top based on L-00.

1932-1943		$2,200	$2,700

TG-1/L-1 Tenor/L-4 Tenor (and Plectrum)

1927-1937. Acoustic flat-top, tenor or plectrum guitar based on L-1, mahogany back and sides, bound body, sunburst.

1927-1937		$2,100	$2,600
1928-1932	Rare Lucas/ Johnson body	$3,500	$4,300

TG-7

1934-1940. Tenor based on the L-7, sunburst.

1934-1940		$4,050	$5,050

TG-25/TG-25 N

1962-1970. Acoustic flat-top, tenor guitar based on B-25, mahogany back and sides, sunburst or natural (25 N).

1962-1964		$1,000	$1,250
1965		$900	$1,100
1966-1970		$800	$1,000

TG-50

1934-1940, 1947-1961, 1963. Acoustic archtop, tenor guitar based on L-50, mahogany back and sides, sunburst.

1934-1940		$1,600	$2,000
1947-1963		$1,450	$1,825

Traveling Songwriter EC

2005-present. Solid spruce top, solid mahogany sides and back, soft cutaway, on-board electronics and F.Q.

2005-2014		$1,500	$1,900

Trini Lopez Standard

1964-1970. Double rounded cutaway, thinline archtop, 2 humbuckers, tune-o-matic bridge, trapeze tailpiece, single-bound, cherry, Sparkling Burgundy and Pelham Blue finishes.

1964	Cherry	$5,100	$6,300
1965	Cherry	$4,500	$5,600
1965-1966	Pelham Blue	$5,200	$6,700
1965-1966	Sparkling Burgundy	$4,400	$5,500
1966	Cherry	$4,000	$5,200
1967-1969	Cherry	$4,000	$5,000
1967-1969	Sparkling Burgundy, Pelham Blue	$4,100	$5,100
1970	Cherry	$3,300	$4,200
1970	Sparkling Burgundy, Pelham Blue	$3,500	$4,300

Gibson Traveling Songwriter EC

Gibson Trini Lopez Standard

MODEL YEAR	FEATURES	EXC. COND. LOW	HIGH

2007 Gibson Vegas High Roller

2008 Gibson Zakk Wylde ZV Buzzsaw

Trini Lopez Standard (Custom Shop)
2010-2011. Custom Shop reissue of thinline Trini Lopez Standard, diamond f-holes, 6-on-a-side tuners, trapeze tailpiece, Certificate of Authenticity, cherry red.

2010-2011		$2,500	$3,300

Trini Lopez Deluxe
1964-1970. Double pointed cutaway archtop, 2 humbuckers, triple-bound, sunburst.

1964		$5,100	$6,300
1965		$4,300	$5,400
1966-1969		$4,000	$5,000
1970		$3,300	$4,200

U-2
1987-1989. Double-cut, 1 humbucker and 2 single-coil pickups, ebony or red, renamed Mach II in '90-'91.

1987-1991		$600	$800

U-2 Showcase Edition
1988. November 1988 Guitar of the Month series, 250 made.

1988		$700	$900

US-1/US-3
1986-1991. Double-cut maple top with mahogany back, 3 humbucker pickups (US-1), or 3 P-90s (US-3), standard production and Custom Shop.

1986-1991		$600	$800

Vegas Standard
2006-2007. Flat-top semi-hollowbody thinline, slim neck, 2 humbuckers, f-holes, split diamond inlays.

2006-2007		$1,300	$1,650

Vegas High Roller
2006-2007. Upgraded version, AAA maple top, gold hardware and frets, block inlays.

2006-2007		$1,500	$1,850

Victory MV II (MV 2)
1981-1984. Asymetrical double-cut with long horn, 3-way slider, maple body and neck, rosewood 'board, 2 pickups.

1981-1984		$775	$975

Victory MV X (MV 10)
1981-1984. 3 humbuckers, 5-way switch, various colors.

1981-1984		$850	$1,050

XPL Custom
1985-1986. Explorer-like shape, exposed humbuckers, locking tremolo, bound maple top, sunburst or white.

1985-1986		$1,000	$1,250

Y2K Dwight Yoakam Signature
2005. Limited run of 200, small body jumbo, spruce top, highly figured maple sides and back, 2-piece flamed maple neck, double 'guard, gloss natural finish.

2005		$1,650	$2,050

Zakk Wylde ZV Buzzsaw
2008. Custom Shop Inspired By series, limited run of 50, Flying V wings with SG horns, 2 humbuckers.

2008		$2,600	$3,300

Gibson Baldwin
2005-Ca. 2013. Entry-level electric and acoustic guitars, basses, amps and accessories made in China for discount store market and sold under the Signature, Maestro, Echelon, and Genesis brand names. Models include Les Paul and SG copies. Guitars have Music - Gibson logo on neckplate and brand logo on headstock.

Giffin
1977-1988, 1997-present. Professional and premium grade, production/custom, hollow-, semi-hollow-, and solidbody guitars built by luthier Roger Giffin in West San Fernando Valley, California. For '77-'88, Giffin's shop was in London. From '88 to '93, he worked for the Gibson Custom Shop in California as a Master Luthier. In '97, Giffin set up shop in Sweden for a year, moving back to California in the Spring of '98. He also built small numbers of instruments during '67-'76 and '94-'96 (when he had a repair business).

Gigliotti
2000-present. Premium grade, production/custom, electric guitars with a metal plate top and tone chambers and designed by Patrick Gigliotti in Tacoma, Washington.

Gila Eban Guitars
1979-present. Premium grade, custom, classical guitars built by luthier Gila Eban in Riverside, Connecticut.

Gilbert Guitars
1965-present. Custom classical guitars by luthiers John Gilbert and William Gilbert in Paso Robles, California. Son William has handled all production since 1991.

Gilchrist
1978-present. Currently known more for his mandolins, luthier Steve Gilchrist, of Warrnambool, Australia, has also built premium and presentation grade, custom, guitars.

Acoustic Archtop
1978-1995. Very limited production.

1978-1995		$17,000	$22,000

Gilet Guitars
1976-present. Luthier Gerard Gilet builds production/custom, premium grade, acoustic, classical, flamenco, and wooden bodied resonator guitars in Botany, Sydney, New South Wales, Australia. He also builds lap steels.

Girl Brand Guitars
1996-2012. Premium-grade, production/custom, guitars built by luthier Chris Larsen in Tucson, Arizona. Larsen now builds under the Larsen Guitar Mfg. name.

Gitane
2003-present. Intermediate and professional grade, production, classic Selmer-Maccaferri style jazz guitars made in China for Saga.

MODEL YEAR	FEATURES	EXC. COND. LOW	HIGH

Gittler

1974-ca.1985. Minimalistic electric guitar designed by Allan Gittler, consisting basically of a thin rod with frets welded to it. A total of 560 were built, with Gittler making the first 60 in the U.S. from '74 to the early '80s. The remainder were made around '85 in Israel by the Astron corporation under a licensing agreement. Three Gittler basses were also built. Gittler emigrated to Israel in the early '80s and changed his name to Avraham Bar Rashi. He died in 2002. A U.S.-made Gittler is the only musical instrument in the Museum of Modern Art in New York.

Metal Skeleton
1971-1999.

1971-1982		$2,600	$3,200
1982-1999		$2,300	$2,900

GJ2

2012-present. Gold Jackson Enterprises LLC, a partnership between luthier Grover Jackson and Jon Gold, builds professional and premium grade, production/custom, solidbody electric guitars in Laguna Hills, California.

Glendale

2004-present. Professional grade, production/custom, solidbody guitars built by luthier Dale Clark in Arlington, Texas.

GLF

1991-1997. Solidbody electric guitars built by luthier Kevin Smith in Minnesota. In '97 he started building his ToneSmith line of guitars.

Glick Guitars

1996-present. Premium grade, production/custom, acoustic and electric archtop, and acoustic guitars built in Santa Barbara, California by luthier Mike Glick.

Global

Late-1960s-1970s. Budget copy models, not unlike Teisco, imported from Asia for the student market. They also offered amps.

Electric Solidbody
Late-1960s-1970s.

1968		$80	$175

GMP

1990-2005. Professional and premium grade solidbody electric guitars built by GM Precision Products, Inc. of San Dimas, California. Original owners were Gary and Cameron Moline, Dave Pearson and Glenn Matjezel. Many guitars featured fancy tops or custom graphics. They also made basses. Overall production is estimated at 1120 guitars and basses. GMP reopened in '10 under new ownership (see following).

GMP (Genuine Musical Products)

2010-present. The GMP brand was acquired by Dan and Kim Lawrence in '08. Since '10, Dan along with fellow luthiers Glenn Matjezel and William Stempke build professional and premium grade, production/custom, electric guitars in San Dimas, California. They also build basses.

GMW

1998-present. Professional grade, production/custom, solidbody guitars from Lee Garver's GMW Guitarworks of Glendora, California.

Godin

1987-present. Intermediate and professional grade, production, solidbody electrics and nylon and steel string acoustic/electrics from luthier Robert Godin. They also build basses and mandolins. Necks and bodies are made in La Patrie, Quebec with final assembly in Berlin, New Hampshire. Godin is also involved in the Seagull, Norman, Richmond, Art & Lutherie, and Patrick & Simon brand of guitars. SA on Godin models stands for Synth Access.

5th Avenue Kingpin
2008-present. Full-size non-cut electric archtop, 1 or 2 P-90 pickups, plain or highly flamed top, premium price for highly flamed.

2008-2014		$625	$775

5th Avenue Uptown
2012-present. Archtop cutaway with Bigsby, f-holes, Canadian wild cherry top, back and sides, silver leaf maple neck, various colors

2012-2014		$625	$775

A Series
1990s-present. Multiac-style body.

1990s-2014	A-12, 12-string	$500	$625
1990s-2014	A-6, 6-string	$475	$600

Acousticaster (6)
1987-present. Thin line single-cut chambered maple body, acoustic/electric, maple neck, 6-on-a-side tuners, spruce top.

1987-2014		$425	$525

Acousticaster 6 Deluxe
1994-2008. Acousticaster 6 with mahogany body.

1994-2008		$475	$600

Artisan ST I/ST I
1992-1998. Offset double-cut solidbody, birdseye maple top, 3 pickups.

1992-1998		$325	$400

Flat Five X
2002-2004. Single-cut, semi-hollow with f-holes, 3-way pickup system (magnetic to transducer).

2002-2004		$625	$775

Freeway Classic/Freeway Classic SA
2004-present. Offset double-cut solidbody, birdseye maple top on translucent finishes, hum-single-hum pickups.

2004-2014		$425	$525

Gilbert Classical

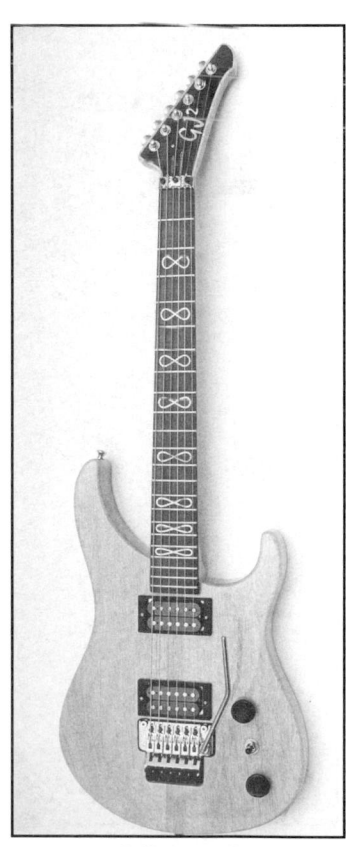

GJ2 Arete 5

Gold Tone PBS8

Goodall Grand Concert

MODEL		EXC. COND.	
YEAR	FEATURES	LOW	HIGH

G-1000/G-2000/G-3000
1993-1996. Offset double-cut solidbody, extra large bass horn, various pickup options.
| 1993-1996 | | $225 | $300 |

Glissentar A11
2000-present. Electric/acoustic nylon 11-string, solid cedar top, chambered maple body, fretless, natural.
| 2000-2014 | | $575 | $725 |

Jeff Cook Signature
1994-1995. Quilted maple top, light maple back, 2 twin rail and 1 humbucker pickups.
| 1994-1995 | | $550 | $675 |

L.R. Baggs Signature
1990s. Single-cut chambered thinline electric, spruce top, mahogany body, EQ.
| 1990s | | $425 | $525 |

LG/LGT
1995-2011. Single-cut carved slab mahogany body, 2 Tetrad Combo pickups ('95-'97) or 2 Duncan SP-90 pickups ('98-present), various colors, satin lacquer finish. LGT with tremolo.
| 1995-2011 | | $325 | $400 |

LGX/LGXT/LGX-SA
1996-present. Single-cut maple-top carved solidbody, 2 Duncan humbuckers, various quality tops offered. LGXT with tremolo.
1996-2014	Standard top	$600	$725
1997-2014	SA synth access	$800	$1,000
1998-2014	AA top	$800	$1,000
1998-2014	AAA top	$900	$1,100

Montreal
2004-present. Chambered body carved from solid mahogany, f-holes, 2 humbuckers, saddle transducer, stereo mixing output.
| 2004-2014 | | $700 | $875 |

Multiac Series
1994-present. Single-cut, thinline electric with solid spruce top, RMC Sensor System electronics, available in either nylon string or steel string versions, built-in EQ, program up/down buttons.
| 1994-2014 | Various models | $700 | $1,000 |

Radiator
1999-2013. Single-cut, dual pickup, pearloid top, dot markers.
| 1999-2013 | | $225 | $300 |

Redline Series
2007-present. Maple body and neck, rosewood 'board, Redline 1 has 1 pickup, 2 and 3 have 2 pickups (3 has Floyd Rose), various colors.
| 2007-2011 | Redline 1 | $325 | $400 |
| 2008-2014 | Redline 3 | $350 | $440 |

SD Series
1990s-2012.
| 1990-2012 | SD 22, SD 24 | $230 | $285 |

Solidac - Two Voice
2000-2009. Single-cut, 2-voice technology for electric or acoustic sound.
| 2000-2009 | | $275 | $350 |

TC Signature
1987-1999. Single-cut, quilted maple top, 2 Tetrad Combo pickups.
| 1987-1999 | | $425 | $525 |

MODEL		EXC. COND.	
YEAR	FEATURES	LOW	HIGH

Velocity
2007-2011. Offset double-cut, hum/single/single.
| 2007-2011 | | $425 | $525 |

Gold Tone
1993-present. Wayne and Robyn Rogers build their intermediate and professional grade, production/custom guitars and basses in Titusville, Florida. They also build lap steels, mandolins, ukuleles, banjos and banjitars.

Goldbug Guitars
1997-present. Presentation grade, production/custom, acoustic and electric guitars built by luthier Sandy Winters in Delavan, Wisconsin.

Golden Hawaiian
1920s-1930s. Private branded lap guitar most likely made by one of the many Chicago makers for a small retailer, publisher, cataloger, or teaching studio.
Guitars
| 1920-1930s Sunburst | | $475 | $600 |

Goldentone
1960s. Guitars made by Ibanez most likely in the mid to late '60s. Often have a stylized I (for Ibanez) on the tailpiece or an Ibanez logo on the headstock.

Goldon
German manufacturer of high-quality archtops and other guitars before and shortly after W W II. After the war, they were located in East Germany and by the late 1940s were only making musical toys.

Goodall
1972-present. Premium grade, custom flat-tops and nylon-strings, built by luthier James Goodall originally in California and, since '92, in Kailua-Kona, Hawaii.
Classical
1986. Brazilian and cedar.
| 1986 | BC425 | $5,500 | $6,800 |

Concert Jumbo
1998-present. Various woods.
| 2007-2014 | Red cedar/ Indian rosewood | $2,800 | $3,500 |
| 2007-2014 | Sitka/figured koa | $2,800 | $3,500 |

Concert Jumbo Cutaway
2004-present. Rosewood.
| 2004-2014 | | $3,150 | $3,950 |

Jumbo KJ
1995-2011. Sitka, koa.
| 1995-2014 | | $2,800 | $3,500 |

RS Rosewood Standard
1989-1997. Indian rosewood back and sides.
| 1989-1997 | | $2,300 | $2,900 |

Standard
1980s-present. Jumbo-style with wide waist, mahogany back and sides, sitka spruce top.
| 1980s-2014 | | $2,100 | $2,600 |

MODEL YEAR	FEATURES	EXC. COND. LOW	HIGH

Goodman Guitars

1975-present. Premium grade, custom/production, archtop, flat-top, classical, and electric guitars built by luthier Brad Goodman in Brewster, New York. He also builds mandolins.

Goran Custom Guitars

1998-present. Luthier Goran Djuric builds his professional and premium grade, custom, electric guitars in Belgrade, Serbia. He also builds effects.

Gordon-Smith

1979-present. Intermediate and professional grade, production/custom, semi-hollow and solidbody guitars built by luthier John Smith in Partington, England.

Gower

1955-1960s. Built in Nashville by Jay Gower, later joined by his son Randy. Gower is also associated with Billy Grammer and Grammer guitars.

G-55-2 Flat-Top

1960s. Square shoulder-style flat-top, triple abalone rosette, abalone fretboard trim, small block markers, natural.

1960s		$725	$900

G-65 Flat-Top

1960s. Square shoulder-style flat-top, lower belly bridge with pearl dots on bridge, dot markers, sunburst.

1960s		$525	$650

G-100 Flat-Top

1960s	Brazilian rosewood	$775	$975

Solidbody Electric

1960s. Mosrite influenced odd-shaped body, 2 single-coils, bolt neck, Bigsby bridge.

1960s		$525	$650

Goya

1952-1996. Brand initially used by Hershman Musical Instrument Company of New York City, New York, in mid-'50s for acoustic guitars made in Sweden by Levin, particularly known for its classicals. From '58 to '61 they imported Hagstrom- and Galanti-made electrics labeled as Goya; in '62 they offered electrics made by Valco. In '67 they again offered electrics, this time made by Zero Sette in Castelfidardo, Italy. By '63 the company had become the Goya Musical Instrument Corporation, marketing primarily Goya acoustics. In '67 they again offered electrics, this time made by Zero Sette in Castelfidardo, Italy. Goya was purchased by Avnet, Inc., prior to '66, when Avnet purchased Guild Guitars. In '69, Goya was purchased by Kustom which offered the instruments until '71. Probably some '70s guitars were made in Japan. The brand name was purchased by C.F. Martin in '76, with Japanese-made acoustic guitars, solidbody electric guitars and basses, banjos and mandolins imported in around '78 and continuing into the '90s.

Classical

1950s-1980s. Various models.

1955-60s	G Series	$100	$1,200
1980s	Japan	$350	$550

Flamenco

1955-1960s. Various models.

1955-60s	FL Series	$300	$600

Folk

1950s-1980s. Various models.

1955-60s	F Series	$200	$600

Model 80/Model 90

1959-1962. Single-cut body, replaceable modular pickup assembly, sparkle top.

1959-1962		$1,000	$1,250

Panther S-3

1967-1968. Double-cut solidbody, 3 pickups, Panther S-3 Goya logo, volume and tone knobs with 6 upper bass bout switches, bolt-on neck.

1967-1968		$1,000	$1,250

Rangemaster

1967-1968. Wide variety of models.

1967-1968		$800	$1,000

Steel

1955-1960s. Various models.

1955-60s	M and S Series	$100	$300

Graf

See listing under Oskar Graf Guitars.

Grammer

1965-1971. Acoustic guitars built in Nashville. Founded by country guitarist Bill Grammer, music store owner Clyde Reid and luthier J.W. Gower (who also built his own line). Grammer sold the company to Ampeg in '68 who sold it again in '71, but it quickly creased business. Originally the Grammer headstock logo had an uppercase G, Ampeg-made instruments have a lower-case one.

G-10

1965-1970. Solid Brazilian rosewood back and sides, solid spruce top, large crown-shaped bridge, pearl dot markers, natural.

1965-1967	Grammer era	$1,450	$1,800
1968-1970	Ampeg era	$1,250	$1,550

G-20

1965-1970. Natural.

1965-1967	Grammer era	$1,450	$1,800
1968-1970	Ampeg era	$1,250	$1,550

G-30

1965-1970. Natural.

1965-1967	Grammer era	$1,450	$1,800
1968-1970	Ampeg era	$1,250	$1,550

G-50

1965-1970. Top-of-the-line Grammer, Brazilian rosewood back and sides, Adirondack spruce top.

1965-1967	Grammer era	$1,800	$2,250
1968-1970	Ampeg era	$1,600	$2,000

S-30

1965-1970. Solid spruce top, solid ribbon mahogany back and sides.

1965-1967	Grammer era	$1,300	$1,600
1968-1970	Ampeg era	$1,100	$1,375

2007 Gordon-Smith GS-1

Jon Way

1974 Grammer S-20

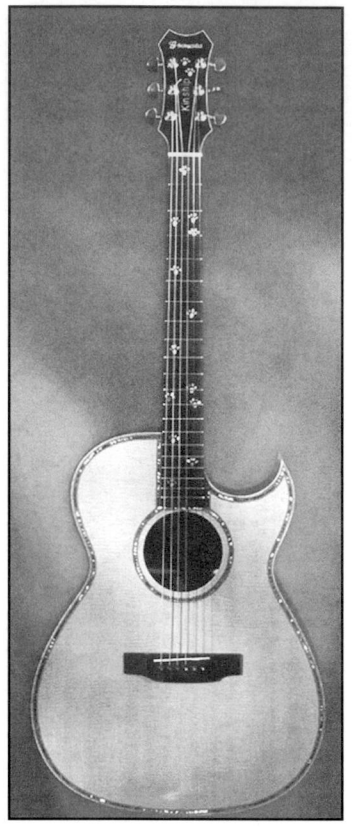

Granata SJ-C

1979 Greco EG700
Jon Way

MODEL YEAR	FEATURES	EXC. COND. LOW	HIGH

Granada

1970s-1980s. Japanese-made acoustic, electric solid, semi-hollow and hollowbody guitars, many copies of classic American models. They also offered basses.

Acoustic

1970-1979. Import from Japan, various copy models.

1970-1979		$110	$160

Electric

1970-1979. Import from Japan, various copy models.

1970-1979		$160	$210

Granata Guitars

1989-present. Luthier Peter Granata builds his professional grade, custom, flat-top and resonator guitars in Oak Ridge, New Jersey.

Graveel

Production/custom, solidbody guitars built by luthier Dean Graveel in Indianapolis, Indiana.

Grazioso

1950s. Grazioso was a brand name used by Selmer in England on instruments made in Czechoslovakia. They replaced the brand with their Futurama line of guitars.

GRD

1978-1982. High-end acoustic and electric guitars produced in Charles Fox's Guitar Research & Design Center in Vermont. GRD introduced the original thin-line acoustic-electric guitar to the world at the '78 Winter NAMM show.

Great Divide Guitars

2009-2011. Budget and intermediate grade, production, flat-top guitars imported from China, designed by luthier Tom Bedell, Dan Mills and Sophia Yang. They also offer Bedell Guitars.

Greco

1960s-present. Brand name used in Japan and owned by Kanda Shokai. Fuji Gen Gakki, maker of many Hoshino/Ibanez guitars, also made many Greco models during the '70s; thus often Greco guitars are similar to Ibanez. During the '70s the company sold many high-quality copies of American designs, though by '75 they offered many weird-shaped original designs, including the Iceman and carved people shapes. By the late-'70s they were offering neck-through-body guitars. Currently offering solidbody, hollowbody and acoustic guitars and basses, including models licensed by Zemaitis.

Green, Aaron

1990-present. Premium and presentation grade, custom, classical and flamenco guitars built by luthier Aaron Green in Waltham, Massachusetts.

Greene & Campbell

2002-2005. Luthier Dean Campbell built his intermediate and professional grade, production/custom, solidbody guitars in Westwood, Massachusetts. Founding partner Jeffrey Greene left the company in '04; Greene earlier built guitars under his own name. In '05, Campbell changed the name to Campbell American Guitars.

Greene, Jeffrey

2000-2002. Professional grade, production/custom, electric solidbody guitars built by luthier Jeffrey Greene in West Kingston, Rhode Island. He went to work with Dean Campbell building the Greene & Campbell line of guitars.

Greenfield Guitars

1996-present. Luthier Michael Greenfield builds his production/custom, presentation grade, acoustic steel string, concert classical and archtop guitars in Montreal, Quebec.

Gretsch

1883-present. Currently Gretsch offers intermediate, professional, and premium grade, production, acoustic, solidbody, hollowbody, double neck, resonator and Hawaiian guitars. They also offer basses, amps and lap steels. In 2012 they again started offering mandolins, ukuleles and banjos.

Previous brands included Gretsch, Rex, 20th Century, Recording King (for Montgomery Ward), Dorado (Japanese imports). Founded by Friedrich Gretsch in Brooklyn, New York, making drums, banjos, tambourines, and toy instruments which were sold to large distributors including C. Bruno and Wurlitzer. Upon early death of Friedrich, son Fred Gretsch, Sr. took over business at age 15. By the turn of the century the company was also making mandolins. In the '20s, they were distributing Rex and 20th Century brands, some made by Gretsch, some by others such as Kay. Charles "Duke" Kramer joined Gretsch in '35. '40 Gretsch purchased Bacon & Day banjos. Fred Gretsch, Sr. retired in '42 and was replaced by sons Fred, Jr. and Bill. Fred departs for Navy and Bill runs company until his death in '48, when Fred resumes control. After the war the decision was made to promote the Gretsch brand rather than selling to distributors, though some jobbing continues. Kramer becomes Chicago branch manager in '48.

In '67 Baldwin of Cincinnati buys Gretsch. During '70-'72 the factory relocates from Brooklyn to Booneville, Arkansas and company headquarters moves to Cincinnati. A '72 factory fire drastically reduces production for next two years. In '78 Baldwin buys Kustom amps and sells Gretsch to Kustom's Charlie Roy, and headquarters are moved to Chanute, Kansas. Duke Kramer retires in '80. Guitar production ends '80-'81. Ca. '83 ownership reverts back to Baldwin and Kramer was asked to arrange the sale of the company. In '84 Fred Gretsch III was contacted and in '85 Gretsch guitars came back to the Gretsch family and Fred Gretsch Enterprises, Ltd (FGE). Initial

MODEL YEAR	FEATURES	EXC. COND. LOW	HIGH

Gretsch Enterprise models were imports made by Japan's Terada Company. In '95, some U.S.-made models were introduced. In 2003, Gretsch granted Fender the rights to develop, produce, market and distribute Gretsch guitars worldwide, including development of new products.

Binding rot can be a problem on 1950s models and prices shown are for fully original, unrestored bindings.

12-String Electric Archtop (6075/6076)
1967-1972. 16" double-cut, 2 Super Tron pickups, 17" body option available, sunburst (6075) or natural (6076).

| 1967-1972 | Natural | $1,850 | $2,300 |
| 1967-1972 | Sunburst | $1,750 | $2,200 |

12-String Flat-Top (6020)
1969-1972. 15 1/5" body, mahogany back and sides, spruce top, slotted headstock, dot markers.

| 1969-1972 | | $900 | $1,125 |

Anniversary (6124/6125)
1958-1972, 1993-1999. Single-cut hollowbody archtop, 1 pickup (Filtron '58-'60, Hi-Lo Tron '61 on), bound body, named for Gretsch's 75th anniversary. 6125 is 2-tone green with 2-tone tan an option, 6124 sunburst. Model numbers revived in '90s.

1958-1959	Green 2-tone	$2,100	$2,600
1958-1959	Sunburst	$1,500	$1,900
1960-1961	2-tone green or tan	$2,000	$2,500
1960-1961	Sunburst	$1,400	$1,800
1962-1964	2-tone green or tan	$1,725	$2,150
1962-1964	Sunburst	$1,300	$1,650
1965-1966	Various colors	$1,300	$1,650
1967-1969	Various colors	$1,100	$1,400
1970-1972	Various colors	$1,000	$1,250

Anniversary Tenor (6124)
1958-1971. Gretsch offered many models with the 4-string tenor option and also made small batches of tenors, with the same colors and pickups as standard models.

| 1958-1971 | | $1,400 | $1,750 |

Anniversary Reissue (6124/6125)
1993-1999. 1 pickup Anniversary reissue, 6124 in sunburst, 6125 2-tone green.

| 1993-1999 | | $1,100 | $1,400 |

Anniversary Reissue (6117/6118)
1993-present. 2 pickup like Double Anniversary, 6118 in 2-tone green with (T) or without Bigsby, 6117 is sunburst.

| 1993-2014 | 6117 | $1,300 | $1,700 |
| 1993-2014 | 6118 | $1,300 | $1,700 |

Astro-Jet (6126)
1965-1967. Solidbody electric, double-cut, 2 pickups, vibrato, 4/2 tuner arrangement, red top with black back and sides.

| 1965-1967 | | $1,600 | $2,000 |

Atkins Axe (7685/7686)
1976-1980. Solidbody electric, single pointed cutaway, 2 pickups, ebony stain (7685) or red rosewood stain (7686), called the Super Axe with added onboard effects.

| 1976-1980 | | $1,000 | $1,250 |

Atkins Super Axe (7680/7681)
1976-1981. Single pointed cutaway solidbody with built-in phaser and sustain, five knobs, three switches, Red Rosewood (7680) or Ebony (7681) stains.

| 1976-1981 | | $1,750 | $2,200 |

Bikini (6023/6024/6025)
1961-1962. Solidbody electric, separate 6-string and bass neck-body units that slide into 1 of 3 body butterflies - 1 for the 6-string only (6023), 1 for bass only (6024), 1 for double neck (6 and bass - 6025). Components could be purchased separately.

| 1961-1962 | 6023/6024, single neck | $775 | $975 |
| 1961-1962 | 6025, double neck | $1,550 | $1,900 |

Billy-Bo Jupiter Thunderbird (6199)
2005-present. Billy Gibbons and Bo Diddley influenced, chambered mahogany body, laminate maple top, 2 pickups.

| 2005-2014 | | $1,500 | $1,900 |

Black Falcon (6136BK/TBK/DSBK)
1992-1997, 2003-present. Black version of Falcon, single-cut, 2.75" body, oversize f-holes, G tailpiece, DSBK with DynaSonic pickups replaces Filter'Tron BK in '06. Had the Limited Edition 1955 designation for '96-'97. Bigsby-equipped TBK offered '04-present.

| 1992-2014 | | $1,750 | $2,200 |

Black Falcon (7594BK)
1992-1998. Black version of G7594 Falcon, double-cut, 2" thick body, Bigsby.

| 1992-1998 | | $1,750 | $2,200 |

Black Falcon I (7593BK)
1993-1998, 2003-2005. G63136BK with Bigsby and standard f-holes. Came back in '03 as Black Falcon I with wire handle Gretsch Bigsby tailpiece.

| 1993-1998 | | $1,750 | $2,200 |

Black Hawk (6100/6101)
1967-1972. Hollowbody archtop, double-cut, 2 pickups, G tailpiece or Bigsby vibrato, bound body and neck, sunburst (6100) or black (6101).

1967-1969	6100, sunburst	$2,000	$2,500
1967-1969	6101, black	$2,000	$2,500
1970-1972	6100, sunburst	$2,000	$2,500
1970-1972	6101, black	$2,000	$2,500

Black Penguin (6134B)
2003-present. Jet black version.

| 2003-2014 | | $1,750 | $2,200 |

Bo Diddley (1810/5810)
2000-present. Korean-made version.

| 2000-2014 | | $185 | $230 |

Bo Diddley (6138)
1999-present. Reproduction of rectangle-shaped, semi-hollow guitar originally made for Diddley by Gretsch, Firebird Red.

| 1999-2014 | | $1,400 | $1,750 |

Broadkaster (Hollowbody)
1975-1980. Double-cut archtop, hollowbody, 2 pickups, natural or sunburst.

1975-1977	7603, Bigsby, natural	$750	$925
1975-1977	7604, Bigsby, sunburst	$750	$925
1975-1977	7607, G tailpiece, natural	$750	$925

Greenfield The Dragonfly

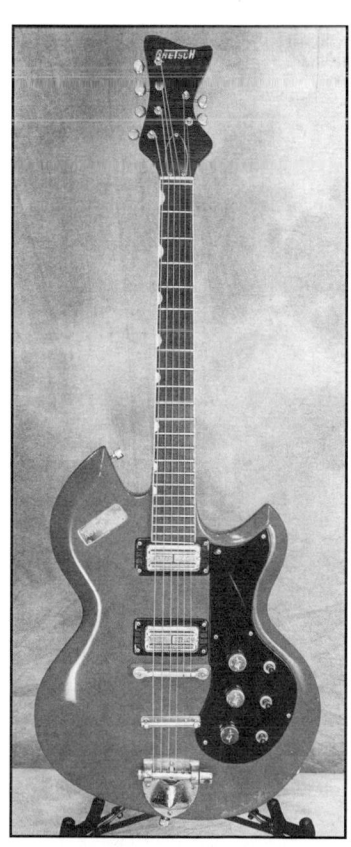

1966 Gretsch Astro-Jet
Willie's American Guitars

1959 Gretsch Chet Atkins 6120

*2009 Gretsch Brian
Setzer Nashville*

MODEL YEAR	FEATURES	EXC. COND. LOW	HIGH
1975-1977	7608, G tailpiece, sunburst	$700	$875
1977-1980	7609, red	$700	$875

Broadkaster (Solidbody)

1975-1979. Double-cut, maple body, 2 pickups, bolt-on neck, natural (7600) or sunburst (7601).

1975-1979		$650	$825

BST 1000 Beast

1979-1980. Single-cut solidbody, bolt-on neck, mahogany body, available with 1 pickup in walnut stain (8210) or red stain (8216) or 2 pickups in walnut (7617, 8215, 8217) or red stain (8211).

1979-1980		$475	$600

BST 2000 Beast

1979. Symmetrical double-cut solidbody of mahogany, 2 humbucking pickups, bolt-on neck, walnut stain (7620 or 8220) or red stain (8221).

1979		$550	$700

BST 5000 Beast

1979-1980. Asymmetrical double-cut solidbody, neck-thru, walnut and maple construction, 2 humbucker pickups, stud tailpiece, natural walnut/maple (8250).

1979-1980		$650	$800

Burl Ives (6004)

1949-1955. Flat-top acoustic, mahogany back and sides, bound body, natural top (6004).

1949-1955		$600	$750

Chet Atkins Country Gentleman (6122/7670)

1957-1981. Hollowbody, single-cut to late-'62 and double after, 2 pickups, painted f-holes until '72, real after, mahogany finish (6122). Model number changes to 7670 in '71. Guitars made during and after '64 might have replaced body binding which reduces the value shown by about 10% or more.

1957-1959		$8,000	$10,000
1960		$6,700	$8,500
1961		$6,300	$8,000
1962-1963	George Harrison specs	$4,600	$5,700
1964		$3,700	$4,600
1965		$3,500	$4,300
1966		$2,600	$3,300
1967-1970		$2,500	$3,100
1971-1981	7670	$2,300	$2,900

Chet Atkins Country Gentleman (6122-1958)

2007-present. Single-cut reissue of '58.

2007-2014		$1,600	$2,000

Chet Atkins Country Gentleman (6122-1962)

2007-present. Double-cut reissue of '62, double muffler (mutes) system, Filter'Trons.

2007-2014		$1,600	$2,000

Chet Atkins Hollowbody (6120)

1954-1966, 2007-present. Archtop electric, single-cut to '61, double after, 2 pickups, vibrato, f-holes (real to '61 and fake after), cactus and cows engraved block inlays '54-early '56, G brand on top '54-'56, orange finish (6120). Renamed Chet Atkins Nashville in '67. Reissued single-cut in '07.

1954-1956	G brand, engraved blocks	$10,000	$12,500

MODEL YEAR	FEATURES	EXC. COND. LOW	HIGH
1956	G brand, non-engraved blocks	$8,000	$10,000
1957-1959	No G brand	$7,500	$9,500
1960		$6,500	$8,100
1961	Single-cut	$6,500	$8,100
1961-1965	Double-cut	$3,200	$4,000
1966	Double-cut	$2,500	$3,100
2007-2014	Single-cut	$1,500	$1,900

Chet Atkins Nashville (6120/7660)

1967-1980. Replaced Chet Atkins Hollowbody (6120), electric archtop, double-cut, 2 pickups, amber red (orange). Renumbered 7660 in '72, reissued in '90 as the Model 6120 Nashville.

1967	6120	$2,200	$2,800
1968	6120	$2,100	$2,600
1969	6120	$2,000	$2,500
1970-1971	6120	$1,800	$2,250
1972-1980	7660	$1,700	$2,150

Brian Setzer Hot Rod (6120SHx)

1999-present. Like SSL, but with only pickup switch and 1 master volume control.

1999-2014		$1,450	$1,800

Brian Setzer Nashville (6120SSL, etc.)

1993-present. Hollowbody electric, double-cut, 2 Alnico PAF Filtertron pickups, based on the classic Gretsch 6120.

1993-2014	Western Orange	$1,400	$1,750

Chet Atkins Junior

1970. Archtop, single-cut, 1 pickup, vibrato, open f-holes, double-bound body, orange stain.

1970		$875	$1,100

Duane Eddy (6120DE)

1997-2003. 2 DeArmond single coils, Bigsby, orange.

1997-2003		$1,700	$2,100

Duane Eddy Signature Hollow Body (6120DE)

2011-present. Single-cut, Western Orange stain lacquer finish.

2011-2014		$1,700	$2,100

Keith Scott Nashville (6120KS)

1999-2013. Hump-back inlays, gold hardware, metallic gold finish.

1999-2014		$1,500	$1,850

Nashville Double Neck 6/12 (6120)

1997-2002. Built in Japan, few made, all gold hardware, necks are maple with ebony 'boards, orange finish.

1997-2002		$2,100	$2,800

New Nashville (6120N)

2001-2003. Single-cut, humptop inlays, gold hardware.

2001-2003		$1,800	$2,250

Reverend Horton Heat (6120RHH)

2005-present. Cows and cactus inlays, TV jones pickups.

2005-2014		$2,000	$2,500

Chet Atkins Solidbody (6121)

1955-1963. Solidbody electric, single-cut, maple or knotty pine top, 2 pickups, Bigsby vibrato, G brand

The Official Vintage Guitar magazine Price Guide 2016   **Gretsch** Chet Atkins Tennessean — Country Club 1955 R.I.   **163**

GUITARS

MODEL YEAR	FEATURES	EXC. COND. LOW	HIGH

until '57, multi-bound top, brown mahogany, orange finish (6121).

1955-1956		$11,000	$14,000
1957	G brand	$8,500	$10,800
1957-1959	No G brand	$8,300	$10,300
1960		$6,000	$7,500
1961-1963		$5,700	$7,200

Chet Atkins Tennessean (6119/7655)

1958-1980. Archtop electric, single-cut, 1 pickup until '61 and 2 after, vibrato. Renumbered as the 7655 in '71.

1958-1959		$2,475	$3,075
1960-1961	1 pickup	$2,200	$2,800
1961-1964	2 pickups	$2,475	$3,075
1965-1967		$2,375	$2,975
1968-1970		$2,075	$2,575
1971-1980	7655	$2,000	$2,500

Chet Atkins Tennessee Rose (6119-1959, 1962)

1995-present. Import, 16" maple body, maple neck, dual FilterTron pickups.

| 1995-2014 | | $1,400 | $1,750 |

Clipper (6185/6186/6187/7555)

1958-1975. Archtop electric, single-cut, sunburst, 1 pickup (6186) until '72 and 2 pickups (6185) from '72-'75, also available in 1 pickup natural (6187) from '59-'61.

1958-1961	6186	$900	$1,125
1959-1961	6187	$1,000	$1,250
1962-1967	6186	$875	$1,100
1968-1971	6186	$750	$950
1972-1975	7555	$1,000	$1,250

Committee (7628)

1977-1980. Neck-thru electric solidbody, double-cut, walnut and maple body, 2 pickups, 4 knobs, natural.

| 1977-1980 | | $725 | $900 |

Constellation

1955-1960. Renamed from Synchromatic 6030 and 6031, archtop acoustic, single-cut, G tailpiece, humped block inlay.

1955-1956		$1,500	$1,875
1957-1958		$1,400	$1,750
1959-1960		$1,300	$1,600

Convertible (6199)

1955-1958. Archtop electric, single-cut, 1 pickup, multi-bound body, G tailpiece, renamed Sal Salvadore in '58.

| 1955-1958 | | $2,000 | $2,500 |

Corsair

1955-1960. Renamed from Synchromatic 100, archtop acoustic, bound body and headstock, G tailpiece, available in sunburst (6014), natural (6015) or burgundy (6016).

| 1955-1959 | | $850 | $1,050 |
| 1960-1965 | | $800 | $1,000 |

Corvette (Hollowbody)

1955-1959. Renamed from Electromatic Spanish, archtop electric, 1 pickup, f-holes, bound body, Electromatic on headstock, non-cut, sunburst (6182), natural or Jaguar Tan (6184), and ivory with rounded cutaway (6187).

1955-1959	6182, sunburst	$1,200	$1,500
1955-1959	6184, Jaguar Tan	$1,500	$1,875
1955-1959	6184, natural	$1,500	$1,875
1957-1959	6187, ivory	$1,500	$1,875

Corvette (Solidbody)

1961-1972, 1976-1978. Double-cut slab solidbody. Mahogany 6132 and cherry 6134 1 pickup for '61-'68. 2 pickup mahogany 6135 and cherry 7623 available by '63-'72 and '76-'78. From late-'61 through '63 a Twist option was offered featuring a red candy stripe 'guard. Platinum Gray 6133 available for '61-'63 and the Gold Duke and Silver Duke sparkle finishes were offered in '66.

1961-1962	Mahogany, cherry	$1,100	$1,400
1961-1963	Platinum Gray	$2,000	$2,500
1961-1963	Twist 'guard	$2,000	$2,500
1963-1965	Custom color	$1,800	$2,250
1963-1965	Mahogany, cherry, 1 pickup	$800	$1,000
1963-1965	Mahogany, cherry, 2 pickups	$1,200	$1,500
1966	Gold Duke	$2,000	$2,500
1966	Silver Duke	$2,000	$2,500
1966-1968	Mahogany, cherry, 1 pickup	$600	$750
1966-1972	Mahogany, cherry, 2 pickups	$1,000	$1,250
1976-1978	7623, 2 pickups	$800	$1,000

Corvette/CVT (5135)

2006-present. Like double-cut solidbody Corvette, 2 Mega'Tron pickuups, Bigsby, becomes the CVT in '10.

| 2006-2014 | | $500 | $625 |

Country Classic I/II (6122 Reissue)

1989-2006. Country Gentleman reissue in '58 (I) and '62 (II) specs. Also cataloged as G6122-1958 and G6122-1962 Country Classic.

| 1989-2006 | '58, single-cut | $1,700 | $2,100 |
| 1989-2006 | '62, double-cut | $1,700 | $2,100 |

Country Classic II Custom Edition (6122)

2005. Reissue of George Harrison's 2nd 6122 Country Gentleman, the Custom Edition has TV Jones Filtertron pickups.

| 2005 | | $1,700 | $2,100 |

Country Club

1954-1981. Renamed from Electro II Cutaway, archtop electric, single-cut, 2 pickups (Filter Trons after '57), G tailpiece, multi-bound, various colors.

1954-1959	Cadillac Green	$4,000	$5,000
1954-1959	Natural	$3,700	$4,600
1954-1959	Sunburst	$3,400	$4,200
1960-1962	Cadillac Green	$3,300	$4,100
1960-1962	Natural	$2,600	$3,300
1960-1963	Sunburst	$2,300	$2,900
1964	Cadillac Green	$3,000	$3,700
1964	Sunburst	$2,000	$2,500
1965-1969	Sunburst or walnut	$1,900	$2,400
1970-1981	Various colors	$1,900	$2,400

Country Club 1955 Reissue (6196-1955) (FGE)

1995-1999. U.S.-made reissue of Country Club, single-cut, 2 DeArmond pickups, hand-rubbed lacquer finish.

| 1995-1999 | | $1,700 | $2,100 |

Gretsch Duane Eddy Signature Hollow Body (6120DE)

1959 Gretsch Clipper
Custom Amp Covers, inc.

1967 Gretsch Double Anniversary
Angelo Guarini

Gretsch Duo Jet Reissue 6128T
David Carver

MODEL YEAR	FEATURES	EXC. COND. LOW	HIGH

Country Club (6196, etc.)

2001-present. Includes Cadillac Green (G6196, '01-present), sunburst (G6192, '03-'08), amber natural (G6193,'03-'08), Bamboo Yellow (G6196TSP-BY, '09-'13), and smoky gray and violet 2-tone (G6196TSP-2G, '09-'12) T means Bigsby.

| 2001-2014 | Cadillac Green | $1,700 | $2,100 |
| 2009-2013 | Bamboo Yellow | $1,700 | $2,100 |

Country Roc (7620)

1974-1978. Single-cut solidbody, 2 pickups, belt buckle tailpiece, western scene fretboard inlays, G brand, tooled leather side trim.

| 1974-1978 | | $1,900 | $2,400 |

Custom (6117)

1964-1968. Limited production, smaller thinner version of Double Anniversary model, 2 pickups, cat's eye soundholes, red or black finish.

1964		$2,700	$3,400
1965-1966		$2,300	$2,900
1967-1968		$2,000	$2,500

Deluxe Chet (7680/7681)

1972-1974. Electric archtop with rounded cutaway, Autumn Red (7680) or brown walnut (7681) finishes.

| 1972-1974 | | $2,000 | $2,500 |

Deluxe Flat-Top (7535)

1972-1978. 16" redwood top, mahogany back and sides.

| 1972-1978 | | $1,600 | $2,000 |

Double Anniversary Mono (6117/6118)

1958-1976. Archtop electric, single-cut, 2 pickups, stereo optional until '63, sunburst (6117) or green 2-tone (6118). Reissued in '93 as the Anniversary 6117 and 6118.

1958-1961	Green 2-tone	$2,300	$2,900
1958-1961	Sunburst	$1,700	$2,100
1962-1964	Green 2-tone or tan	$1,900	$2,300
1962-1964	Sunburst	$1,500	$1,900
1965-1966	Various colors	$1,400	$1,750
1967-1969	Various colors	$1,200	$1,500
1970-1976	Various colors	$1,100	$1,375

Double Anniversary Stereo (6111/6112)

1961-1963. One stereo channel/signal per pickup, sunburst (6111) or green (6112).

| 1961-1963 | Green | $2,000 | $3,000 |
| 1961-1963 | Sunburst | $1,500 | $2,100 |

Duo-Jet (6128)

1953-1971. Solidbody electric, single-cut until '61, double after, 2 pickups, block inlays to late '56, then humptop until early '58, then thumbprint inlays, black (6128) with a few special order Cadillac Green, sparkle finishes were offered '63-'66, reissued in '90.

1953-1956	Black, single-cut	$5,100	$6,400
1956-1958	Black, humptop	$6,200	$7,700
1956-1958	Cadillac Green	$7,500	$9,300
1958-1960	Black, thumbprint	$4,400	$5,600
1961-1964	Black, double-cut	$3,600	$4,500
1963-1964	Sparkle, double-cut	$4,500	$5,600
1965-1966	Sparkle, double-cut	$3,600	$4,500
1965-1967	Black	$3,000	$3,800
1968-1971	Black	$2,800	$3,500

Duo-Jet Reissue (6128/6128T)

1990-present. Reissue of the '50s solidbody, black, optional Bigsby (G6128T).

| 1990-2014 | | $1,700 | $2,100 |

Duo-Jet Tenor

1959-1960. Electric tenor, 4 strings, block inlays, black.

| 1959-1960 | | $4,000 | $5,000 |

Eldorado (6040/6041)

1955-1970, 1991-1997. This is the larger 18" version, renamed from Synchromatic 400, archtop acoustic, single-cut, triple-bound fretboard and peghead, sunburst (6040) or natural (6041). Reintroduced in '91, made by Heritage in Kalamazoo, as the G410 Synchromatic Eldorado in sunburst or natural (G410M).

1955-1959	Natural	$2,700	$3,400
1955-1959	Sunburst	$2,200	$2,700
1960-1963	Natural	$2,000	$2,500
1960-1963	Sunburst	$1,800	$2,250
1964-1965	Natural	$1,700	$2,100
1964-1965	Sunburst	$1,600	$2,000
1966-1967	Natural	$1,600	$2,000
1966-1967	Sunburst	$1,500	$1,900
1968-1969	Sunburst	$1,450	$1,850
1991-1997	Natural	$1,600	$2,000
1991-1997	Sunburst	$1,300	$1,600

Eldorado (6038/6039)

1959-1968. The smaller 17" version, named Fleetwood from '55 to '58, sunburst (6038) or natural (6039), also available as a full body non-cutaway.

| 1959-1965 | Natural or sunburst | $1,200 | $1,600 |
| 1966-1968 | Natural or sunburst | $1,000 | $1,250 |

Electro Classic (6006/6495)

1969-1973. Classical flat-top with piezo pickup.

| 1969-1970 | 6006 | $600 | $750 |
| 1971-1973 | 6495 | $500 | $625 |

Electro II Cutaway (6192/6193)

1951-1954. Archtop electric, single-cut, Melita bridge by '53, 2 pickups, f-holes, sunburst (6192) or natural (6193). Renamed Country Club in '54.

| 1951-1954 | 6192 | $2,400 | $3,100 |
| 1951-1954 | 6193 | $2,800 | $3,500 |

Electro II Non-Cutaway (6187/6188)

1951-1954. 16" electric archtop, 2 DeArmonds, large f-holes, block markers, 6187 sunburst, 6188 natural, label is Model 6187-8, verticle Electromatic logo on headstock.

| 1951-1954 | 6187 | $950 | $1,200 |
| 1951-1954 | 6188 | $1,050 | $1,300 |

Electromatic Hollow Body (5120/5125-29/5420)

2005-present. Single-cut, 2 dual-coils, Bigsby, black, Aspen Green, sunburst or orange. With Filter'Tron pickups in '13 (5420).

| 2005-2013 | | $475 | $600 |

Electromatic Hollow Body (5122/5422)

2009-present. Double-cut version of G5120, 2 dual-coils, Bigsby, black, trans red or walnut. With Filter'Tron pickups in '13 (5422).

| 2009-2014 | | $475 | $600 |

MODEL YEAR	FEATURES	EXC. COND. LOW	HIGH

Tim Armstrong Signature Electromatic (5191BK)
2013-present. Hollow body, single-cut, all maple, 2 Filter'Tron pickups, black.

2013-2014		$600	$750

Electromatic Spanish (6185/6185N)
1940-1955. Hollowbody, 17" wide, 1 pickup, sunburst (6185) or natural (6185N). Renamed Corvette (hollowbody) in '55.

1940-1949	Sunburst	$1,050	$1,325
1950-1955	Natural	$1,050	$1,325
1950-1955	Sunburst	$950	$1,200

Fleetwood (6038/6039)
1955-1958. Named Synchromatic prior to '55, single-cut, sunburst (6038) or natural (6039). Renamed Eldorado in '59, available by custom order.

1955-1958	Natural	$2,700	$3,400
1955-1958	Sunburst	$2,200	$2,700

Folk/Folk Singing (6003/7505/7506)
1963-1975. Lower-model of Gretsch flat-tops, 14 1/4", mahogany back and sides. Renamed from Jimmie Rodgers model, renamed Folk Singing in '63.

1963-1965		$625	$775
1966-1969		$500	$625
1970-1975		$450	$560

Golden Classic (Hauser Model/Model 6000)
1961-1969. Grand Concert body size, nylon-string classical, 14 1/4" spruce top, mahogany back and sides, multiple inlaid sound hole purfling, inlaid headstock.

1961-1969		$425	$525

Grand Concert (6003)
1955-1959. Lower-model of Gretsch flat-tops, 14 1/4", mahogany back and sides. Renamed from Model 6003 and renamed Jimmie Rodgers in '59.

1955-1959		$525	$650

Guitar-Banjo
1920s. 6-string guitar neck on banjo body, slotted headstock, open back.

1920s		$575	$725

Jet 21
Late-1940s. 16" acoustic archtop, Jet 21 engraved logo on headstock, bound top and back, white 'guard, jet black finish.

1947-1948		$475	$600

Jet Firebird (6131)
1955-1971. Solidbody electric, single-cut until '61, double '61-'71, 2 pickups, black body with red top, block inlays to late '56, then humptop until early '58, then thumbprint inlays.

1955-1960	Single-cut	$5,100	$6,400
1961-1964	Double-cut	$3,600	$4,500
1965-1967		$2,500	$3,100
1968-1971	Super Trons	$2,300	$2,900

Jet Firebird Reissue/Power Jet Firebird (6131/6131T)
1989-1997, 2003-present. Single-cut '58 specs, red top, 2 FilterTrons, thumbprint markers, gold hardware for '91-'05, currently chrome. Bigsby available (T). Non-Bigsby 6131 ends in '05. DynaSonic-equipped TDS starts in '05 and TV Jones PowerTrons (TVP) in '06.

2003-2014		$1,100	$1,400

MODEL YEAR	FEATURES	EXC. COND. LOW	HIGH

Jimmie Rodgers (6003)
1959-1962. 14" flat-top with round hole, mahogany back and sides, renamed from Grand Concert and renamed Folk Singing in '63.

1959-1962		$650	$800

Jumbo Synchromatic (125F)
1947-1955. 17" flat-top, triangular soundhole, bound top and back, metal bridge anchor plate, adjustable wood bridge, natural top with sunburst back and sides or optional translucent white-blond top and sides.

1947-1955	Natural	$1,900	$2,400
1947-1955	White-blond	$2,100	$2,600

Model 25 (Acoustic)
1933-1939. 16" archtop, no binding on top or back, dot markers, sunburst.

1933-1939		$550	$700

Model 30 (Acoustic)
1939-1949. 16" archtop, top binding, dot markers, sunburst.

1939-1949		$625	$800

Model 35 (Acoustic)
1933-1949. 16" archtop, single-bound top and back, dot markers, sunburst.

1933-1949		$700	$875

Model 40 Hawaiian (Acoustic)
1936-1949. Flat-top, bound top and neck, diamond inlays.

1936-1949		$775	$950

Model 50/50R (Acoustic)
1936-1949. Acoustic archtop, f-holes. Model 50R (1936-'39) has round soundhole.

1936-1939	TG-50 Tenor	$700	$875
1936-1949	50/50R	$800	$1,000

Model 65 (Acoustic)
1933-1939. Archtop acoustic, bound body, amber.

1933-1939		$875	$1,100

Model 75 Tenor (Acoustic)
1933-1949. 4-string tenor.

1933-1949		$700	$875

Model 6003
1951-1955. 14 1/4", mahogany back and sides, renamed Grand Concert in '55.

1951-1954		$625	$775

Monkees
1966-1969. Hollowbody electric, double-cut, 2 pickups, Monkees logo on 'guard, bound top, f-holes and neck, vibrato, red.

1966-1969		$2,700	$3,400

New Yorker
Ca.1949-1970. Archtop acoustic, f-holes, sunburst.

1949-1951		$850	$1,050
1952-1954		$800	$1,000
1955-1959		$750	$925
1960-1965		$675	$825
1966-1969		$600	$750
1970		$500	$625

New Yorker Tenor (6050)
1950s. 4-string tenor version.

1950s		$600	$800

1957 Gretsch Jet Firebird (6131)
Tom Siska

1955 Gretsch New Yorker
Tim Fleck

To get the most from this book, be sure to read "Using *The Guide*" in the introduction.

GUITARS

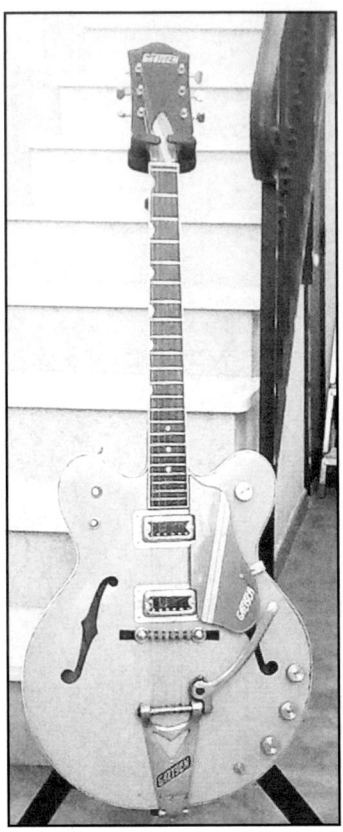

1967 Gretsch Rally
Angelo Guarini

1955 Gretsch Round-Up 6130

MODEL YEAR	FEATURES	EXC. COND. LOW	HIGH

Ozark/Ozark Soft String (6005)
1965-1968. 16" classical, rosewood back and sides.
| 1965-1968 | | $500 | $625 |

Princess (6106)
1963. Corvette-type solidbody double-cut, 1 pickup, vibrato, gold parts, colors available were white/grape, blue/white, pink/white, or white/gold, often sold with the Princess amp.
| 1963 | | $1,500 | $1,900 |

Rally (6104/6105)
1967-1969. Archtop, double-cut, 2 pickups, vibrato, racing stripe on truss rod cover and pickguard, Rally Green (6104) or Bamboo Yellow (6105).
| 1967-1969 | 6104 or 6105 | $1,900 | $2,350 |

Rambler (6115)
1957-1961. Small body electric archtop, single-cut, 1 DeArmond pickup '57-59, then 1 Hi-Lo 'Tron '60-'61, G tailpiece, bound body and headstock.
| 1957-1959 | DeArmond | $1,250 | $1,550 |
| 1960-1961 | Hi-Lo 'Tron | $975 | $1,225 |

Rancher
1954-1980. Flat-top acoustic, triangle soundhole, Western theme inlay, G brand until '61 and '75 and after, Golden Red (orange), reissued in '90.
1954-1957	G brand	$4,000	$5,000
1958-1961	G brand	$3,500	$5,000
1962-1964	No G brand	$2,800	$3,500
1965-1966	No G brand	$2,400	$3,000
1967-1969	No G brand	$2,000	$2,500
1970-1974	No G brand	$1,800	$2,300
1975-1980	G brand	$1,800	$2,300

Roc I/Roc II (7635/7621)
1974-1976. Electric solidbody, mahogany, single-cut, Duo-Jet-style body, 1 pickup (7635) or 2 pickups (7621), bound body and neck.
| 1974-1976 | Roc I | $1,150 | $1,400 |
| 1974-1977 | Roc II | $1,300 | $1,600 |

Roc Jet
1969-1980. Electric solidbody, single-cut, 2 pickups, adjustamatic bridge, black, cherry, pumpkin or walnut.
1970-1972		$2,000	$2,500
1973-1976		$1,700	$2,100
1977-1980		$1,400	$1,750

Round-Up (6130)
1954-1960. Electric solidbody, single-cut, 2 pickups, G brand, belt buckle tailpiece, maple, pine, knotty pine or orange. Reissued in '90.
1954-1956	Knotty pine (2 knots)	$12,000	$16,000
1954-1956	Knotty pine (4 knots)	$14,000	$18,000
1954-1956	Mahogany (few made)	$11,000	$13,500
1954-1956	Maple	$11,000	$13,500
1954-1956	Pine	$12,500	$15,200
1957-1959	Orange	$11,000	$13,500
1960	Orange	$8,000	$11,000

Round-Up Reissue (6121/6121W)
1989-1995, 2003-2006. Based on the '50s model, Bigsby, Western Orange, G brand sticker.
| 1989-2006 | | $1,400 | $1,750 |

Roundup (G6130)
2006. Higher-end reissue of '55 Roundup, G branded in top, steer inlays, tooled western leather trim on sides, gold 'guard and hardware.
| 2006 | | $1,500 | $1,850 |

Sal Fabraio (6117)
1964-1968. Double-cut thin electric archtop, distinctive cats-eye f-holes, 2 pickups, sunburst, ordered for resale by guitar teacher Sal Fabraio.
| 1964-1968 | | $1,650 | $2,050 |

Sal Salvador (6199)
1958-1968. Electric archtop, single-cut, 1 pickup, triple-bound neck and headstock, sunburst.
1958-1959		$2,500	$3,100
1960-1962		$2,000	$2,500
1963-1964		$1,600	$2,000
1965-1966		$1,500	$1,850
1967-1968		$1,300	$1,600

Sho Bro (Hawaiian/Spanish)
1969-1978. Flat-top acoustic, multi-bound, resonator, lucite fretboard, Hawaiian version non-cut, square neck and Spanish version non- or single-cut, round neck.
| 1969-1978 | Hawaiian | $650 | $800 |
| 1969-1978 | Spanish | $600 | $750 |

Silver Classic (Hauser Model/Model 6001)
1961-1969. Grand Concert body size, nylon-string classical. Similar to Golden Classic but with less fancy appointments.
| 1961-1969 | | $300 | $375 |

Silver Falcon (6136SL) (1955) (T)
1995-1999, 2003-2005. Black finish, silver features, single cut, G tailpiece available until '05, T for Bigsby available starting 2'05. Had the 1955 designation in the '90s.
| 1995-1999 | | $1,750 | $2,200 |

Silver Falcon (7594SL)
1995-1999. Black finish and silver features, double-cut, 2" thick body.
| 1995-1999 | | $1,750 | $2,200 |

Silver Jet (6129)
1954-1963. Solidbody electric, single-cut until '61, double '61-'63, 2 pickups, Duo-Jet with silver sparkle top, reissued in '89. Optional sparkle colors were offered but were not given their own model numbers; refer to Duo-Jet listing for optional colors.
| 1954-1960 | Single-cut | $5,500 | $7,200 |
| 1961-1963 | Double-cut | $4,500 | $5,900 |

Silver Jet 1957 Reissue (6129-1957)
1989-present. Reissue of single-cut '50s Silver Jet, silver sparkle. '1957' added to name in '94.
| 1989-2014 | | $1,400 | $1,750 |

Silver Jet 1962 Reissue (6129-1962)
1996-2009. Reissue of '60s double-cut Silver Jet, silver sparkle.
| 1996-2009 | | $1,400 | $1,750 |

Songbird (Sam Goody 711)
1967-1968. Standard body thinline double cutaway with G soundholes, offered by Sam Goody of New York.
| 1967-1968 | | $1,900 | $2,450 |

MODEL YEAR	FEATURES	EXC. COND. LOW	HIGH

Southern Belle (7176)
1983. Electric archtop, walnut, parts from the late-'70s assembled in Mexico and U.S., 5 made with all original parts, several others without pickguard and case.

1983		$1,000	$1,250

Sparkle Jet (6129/6129T)
1995-present. Duo-Jet with sparkle finishes other than Silver, single-cut, 2 pickups. Many different colors offered over the years.

1995-2014		$1,400	$1,750

Streamliner Single Cutaway (6189/6190/6191)
1955-1959. Electric archtop, single-cut, maple top, G tailpiece, 1 pickup, multi-bound, Jaguar Tan (6189), sunburst (6190), or natural (6191), name reintroduced as a double-cut in '68.

1955-1959	6189	$2,000	$2,600
1955-1959	6190	$1,300	$1,700
1955-1959	6191	$1,700	$2,300

Streamliner Double Cutaway (6102/6103)
1968-1973. Reintroduced from single-cut model, electric archtop, double-cut, 2 pickups, G tailpiece, cherry or sunburst.

1968-1969		$1,250	$1,600
1970-1973		$1,150	$1,500

Sun Valley (6010/7515/7514)
1959-1977. Flat-top acoustic, laminated Brazilian rosewood back and sides, multi-bound top, natural or sunburst.

1959-1964	6010	$800	$1,000
1965-1970	6010	$650	$800
1971-1972	7515	$600	$750
1973-1977	7514	$600	$750

Super Chet (7690/7690-B/7691/7691-B)
1972-1980. Electric archtop, single rounded cutaway, 2 pickups, gold hardware, mini control knobs along edge of 'guard, Autumn Red or walnut.

1972-1980		$1,700	$2,200

Supreme (7545)
1972-1978. Flat-top 16", spruce top, mahogany or rosewood body options, gold hardware.

1972-1978	Mahogany	$1,200	$1,500
1972-1979	Rosewood	$1,500	$1,850

Synchromatic (6030/6031)
1951-1955. 17" acoustic archtop, becomes Constellation in '55.

1951-1955		$1,000	$1,275

Synchromatic (6038/6039)
1951-1955. 17" acoustic archtop, single-cut, G tailpiece, multi-bound, sunburst (6038) or natural (6039), renamed Fleetwood in '55.

1951-1955	6038 or 6039	$1,100	$1,400

Synchromatic 75
1939-1949. Acoustic archtop, f-holes, multi-bound, large floral peghead inlay. Tenor available.

1939-1949		$700	$900
1939-1949	Tenor	$500	$650

Synchromatic Jr. (3900)
2000-2003. Historic Series, 15" single-cut archtop acoustic.

2000-2003		$775	$975

Synchromatic 100 (6014/6015)
1939-1955. Renamed from No. 100F, acoustic archtop, double-bound body, amber, sunburst (6014) or natural (6015), renamed Corsair in '55.

1939-1949	Natural	$650	$850
1939-1949	Sunburst	$575	$750
1950-1955	Natural	$600	$800

Synchromatic 160 (6028/6029)
1939-1943, 1947-1951. Acoustic archtop, cats-eye soundholes, maple back and sides, triple-bound, natural or sunburst.

1939-1943	Sunburst	$1,000	$1,250
1947-1951	Sunburst	$900	$1,150
1948-1951	Natural	$1,000	$1,250

Synchromatic 200
1939-1949. Acoustic archtop, cats-eye soundholes, maple back and sides, multi-bound, gold-plated hardware, amber or natural.

1939-1949		$1,100	$1,450

Synchromatic 300
1939-1955. Acoustic archtop, cats-eye soundholes until '51 and f-holes after, multi-bound, natural or sunburst.

1939-1949	Natural	$2,000	$2,700
1939-1949	Sunburst	$1,700	$2,300
1950-1955	Natural	$1,700	$2,300
1950-1955	Sunburst	$1,600	$2,200

Synchromatic 400
1940-1955. Acoustic archtop, cats-eye soundholes until '51 and f-holes after, multi-bound, gold hardware, natural or sunburst.

1940-1949	Natural	$4,000	$5,300
1940-1949	Sunburst	$3,700	$4,900
1950-1955	Natural	$3,700	$4,900
1950-1955	Sunburst	$4,500	$5,600

Synchromatic 400/400C
1990-2008. Acoustic archtop, full-body, non-cut (400) or single-cut (C), sunburst.

1990-2008	400C	$900	$1,125

Synchromatic 400F/6042 Flat-Top
1947-1955. 18" flat-top, renamed 6042 in the late '40s.

1947-1948	400F	$4,000	$5,000
1949-1955	6042	$3,500	$4,400

Synchromatic Limited (450/450M)
1997. Acoustic archtop, hand carved spruce (G450) or maple (G450M) top, floating pickup, sunburst, only 50 were to be made.

1997	Maple	$1,000	$1,250
1997	Spruce	$900	$1,125

Synchromatic Sierra
1949-1955. Renamed from Synchromatic X75F (see below), acoustic flat-top, maple back and sides, triangular soundhole, sunburst.

1949-1955		$1,200	$1,500

Synchromatic X75F
1947-1949. Acoustic flat-top, maple back and sides, triangular soundhole, sunburst, renamed Synchromatic Sierra in '49.

1947-1949		$1,200	$1,500

Gretsch Silver Jet 1957 Reissue (6129-1957)

1955 Gretsch Synchromatic
Pete Mann

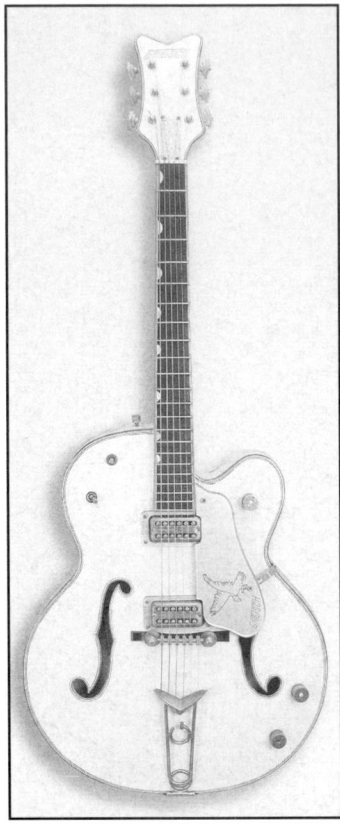

1958 Gretsch White Falcon Mono

Gretsch White Falcon I

MODEL YEAR	FEATURES	EXC. COND. LOW	HIGH

TK 300 (7624/7625)
1977-1981. Double-cut maple solidbody, 1 humbucker, bolt-on neck, six-on-a-side tuners, hockey stick headstock, Autumn Red or natural.

1977-1981		$575	$725

Town and Country (6021)
1954-1959. Renamed from Jumbo Synchromatic 125 F, flat-top acoustic, maple back and sides, triangular soundhole, multi-bound.

1954-1959		$1,600	$2,000

Traveling Wilburys (TW300T)
1988-1990. Promotional guitar, solidbody electric, single-cut, 1 and 2 pickups, 6 variations, graphics.

1988-1990		$325	$410

Van Eps 6-String (6081/6082)
1968-1971. Electric archtop, single-cut, 2 pickups, 6 strings.

1968-1971		$2,800	$3,500

Van Eps 7-String (6079/6080)
1968-1978. Electric archtop, single-cut, 2 pickups, 7 strings, sunburst or walnut.

1968-1978		$2,800	$3,500

Viking (617/6188/6189)
1964-1975. Electric archtop, double-cut, 2 pickups, vibrato, sunburst (6187), natural (6188) or Cadillac Green (6189).

1964-1967	Cadillac Green	$4,000	$4,900
1964-1967	Natural	$3,500	$4,300
1964-1967	Sunburst	$2,500	$3,100
1968-1970	Cadillac Green	$3,000	$3,700
1968-1970	Natural	$2,800	$3,500
1968-1970	Sunburst	$2,200	$2,700
1971-1972	Various colors	$2,000	$2,500
1973-1975	Various colors	$1,900	$2,400

Wayfarer Jumbo (6008)
1969-1971. Flat-top acoustic dreadnought, non-cut, maple back and sides, multi-bound, Wayfarer and sailing ship logo on 'guard.

1969-1971		$750	$950

White Falcon Mono (6136/7594)
1955-1981. Includes the single-cut 6136 of '55-'61, the double-cut 6136 of '62-'70, and the double-cut 7594 of '71-'81.

1955-1961	Single-cut 6136	$18,000	$23,000
1962-1964	Double-cut 6136	$10,000	$12,500
1965-1969		$7,000	$8,800
1970		$5,500	$6,900
1971-1972	7594	$5,000	$6,300
1973-1979		$4,000	$5,000
1980-1981		$3,600	$4,500

White Falcon Stereo (6137/7595)
1958-1981. Features Project-O-Sonic Stereo, includes Includes the single-cut 6137 of '58-'61, the double-cut 6137 of '62-'70, and the double-cut 7595 of '71-'81.

1958-1961	Single-cut 6137	$18,000	$23,000
1962-1964	Double-cut 6137	$10,000	$12,500
1965-1969		$7,000	$8,800
1970		$5,500	$6,900
1971-1972	7595	$5,000	$6,300
1973-1979		$4,000	$5,000
1980-1981		$3,600	$4,500

MODEL YEAR	FEATURES	EXC. COND. LOW	HIGH

White Falcon (6136) (T) (DS)
1989-present. Single-cut, white, 2.75" thick body, thumbnail fret markers, Cadillac G tailpiece standard through '05, Bigsby (T) optional starting '04, standard in starting '06. DynaSonic (DS) model starting '06. See Black and Silver Falcons under those listings.

1989-2014		$2,000	$2,500

White Falcon (6136T-LTV)
2007-present. 6136 with TV Jones Classic pickups, Grovers.

2007-2014		$2,000	$2,500

White Falcon (7593) (I)
1989-2013. Similar to 6136, but with block inlays, Bigsby. Called the White Falcon I for '91-'92, the G7593 for '93-ca. '02, and White Falcon I G7593 after.

1989-2013		$2,000	$2,500

White Falcon (7594) (II)
1989-2006. Double-cut, block inlays, white, 2" thick body, Bigsby. Called the White Falcon II for '91-'92, the G7594 for '93-ca. '02, and White Falcon II G7594 after.

1989-2006		$2,000	$2,500

White Falcon Custom U.S.A. (6136-1955)
1995-1999. U.S.-made, single-cut, DynaSonic pickups, gold sparkle appointments, rhinestone embedded knobs, white. In '04, Current U.S. model called G6136CST is released. The import White Falcon has sometimes been listed with the 1955 designation and is not included here.

1995-1999		$2,800	$3,500

White Penguin (6134)
1955-1962. Electric solidbody, single-cut until '61, double '61-'62, 2 pickups (DeArmond until '58 then Filter Tron), fewer than 100 made, white, gold sparkle bound, gold-plated parts. More than any other model, there seems a higher concern regarding forgery.

1956-1962		$95,000	$125,000
1956-1962	With Snow Flake case	$125,000	$150,000

White Penguin (G6134)
1993, 2003-present. White, single-cut, metalflake binding, gold hardware, jeweled knobs, Cadillac G tailpiece.

2003-2014		$1,550	$1,900

Greven
1969, 1975-present. Luthier John Greven builds his premium grade, production/custom, acoustic guitars in Portland, Oregon.

Griffin String Instruments
1976-present. Luthier Kim Griffin builds his professional and premium grade, production/custom, parlor, steel-string, and classical guitars in Greenwich, New York.

Grimes Guitars
1972-present. Premium and presentation grade, custom, flat-tops, nylon-strings, archtops, semi-hollow electrics made by luthier Steve Grimes originally in Port Townsend, Washington, and since '82 in Kula, Hawaii. He also made mandolins early on.

GUITARS

MODEL YEAR	FEATURES	EXC. COND. LOW	HIGH

Grinnell

Late 1930s-early 1940s. Private brand made by Gibson for Grinnell Music of Detroit and Southeast Michigan, which at the time, was the largest music chain in the Detroit area.

KG-14

1940. Gibson-made L-00 flat-top style with maple sides and back, tortoise-style binding on top and back, ladder bracing.

1940		$1,300	$1,650

Groehsl

1890-1921. Chicago's Groehsl Company made guitars for Wards and other mass-marketers. In 1921 the company became Stromberg-Voisinet, which in turn became the Kay Musical Instrument Company.

Groove Tools

2002-2004. Korean-made, production, intermediate grade, 7-string guitars that were offered by Conklin Guitars of Springfield, Missouri. They also offered basses.

Grosh

1993-present. Professional and premium grade, production/custom, solid and semi-hollow body guitars and basses built by luthier Don Grosh originally in Santa Clarita, California and, since '05 in Broomfield, Colorado. He also builds basses. Grosh worked in production for Valley Arts from '84-'92. Guitars generally with bolt necks until '03 when set-necks were added to the line.

Classical Electric

1990s. Single-cut solidbody with nylon strings and piezo-style hidden pickup, highly figured top

1990s		$1,225	$1,525

Custom S Bent Top

2003-present. Offset double-cut, figured maple carved top, 2 pickups.

2003-2014		$1,275	$1,575

Custom T Carve Top

2003-2012. Single-cut, figured maple carved top, 2 pickups.

2003-2012		$1,275	$1,575

ElectraJet Custom

2009-present. Modified offset double-cut, 2 P-90s, 2 hums, or single-single-hum pickups.

2009-2014		$1,225	$1,525

Retro Classic

1993-present. Offset double-cut, 3 pickups.

1993-2014		$1,225	$1,525

Retro Classic Vintage T

1993-present. Single-cut, black 'guard.

1993-2014		$1,225	$1,525

Gruen Acoustic Guitars

1999-present. Luthier Paul Gruen builds his professional grade, custom steel-string guitars in Chapel Hill, North Carolina.

Gruggett

Mid 1960s-2012. In the 1960s, luthier Bill Gruggett worked with Mosrite and Hallmark guitars as well as building electric guitars under his own name in Bakersfield, California. He continued to make his Stradette model for Hallmark guitars until his death in October, 2012.

Guernsey Resophonic Guitars

1989-present. Production/custom, resonator guitars built by luthier Ivan Guernsey in Marysville, Indiana.

Guild

1952-present. Professional and premium grade, production/custom, acoustic and acoustic/electric guitars. They have built solid, hollow and semi-hollowbody guitars in the past. Founded in New York City by jazz guitarist Alfred Dronge, employing many ex-Epiphone workers. The company was purchased by Avnet, Inc., in '66 and the Westerly, Rhode Island factory was opened in '68. Hoboken factory closed in '71 and headquarters moved to Elizabeth, New Jersey. Company was in bankruptcy in '88 and was purchased by Faas Corporation, New Berlin, Wisconsin. The brand was purchased by Fender in '95 and production was moved from Westerly to the Fender plant in Corona, California in 2001. In '05, Fender moved Guild production to their newly-acquired Tacoma plant in Washington. In '08, production moved to the Ovation/Hamer plant in New Hartford, Connecticut. In '14 Fender sold Guild to Cordoba Music Group which set up production in southern California.

With the 2001 move to the Fender Corona plant, Bob Benedetto and Fender veteran Tim Shaw (who previously ran the Nashville-based custom shop) created a line of Guild acoustic guitars that were primarily based on vintage Guild Hoboken designs.

Designs of Tacoma-built Guild product were nothing like Tacoma guitars. The new Guilds were dovetail neck based with nitrocellulose finishes. Later, FMIC Guild introduced the Contemporary Series giving the Tacoma factory another line in addition to the vintage-based F and D model Traditional Series. In '14 Fender sold Guild to Cordoba Music Group, manufacturer of Cordoba acoustic guitars who moved production to Oxnard, California.

A-50

1994-1996. Original A-50 models can be found under the Cordoba A-50 listing, the new model drops the Cordoba name, size 000 flat-top, spruce top, Indian rosewood body.

1994-1996		$900	$1,125

Aragon F-30

1954-1986. Acoustic flat-top, spruce top, laminated maple arched back (mahogany back and sides by '59), reintroduced as just F-30 in '98.

1954-1959		$1,500	$2,000
1960-1969		$1,350	$1,825
1970-1986		$1,200	$1,600

Grimes Kula Rose

1967 Gruggett Model SC6V Stradette

GUITARS

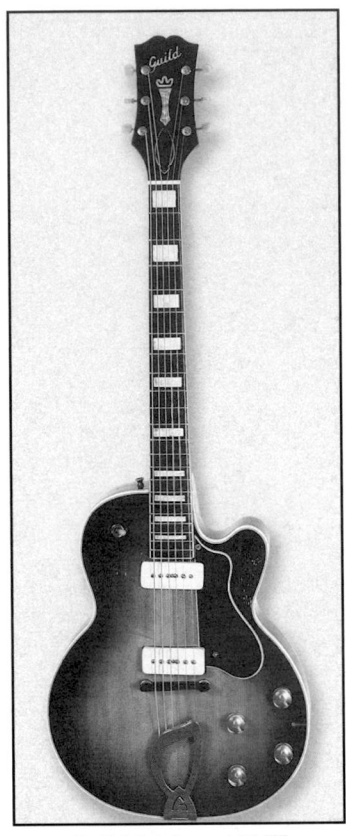

Guild Aristocrat M-75

1971 Guild Bluegrass D-25

Dick Johnson

MODEL YEAR	FEATURES	EXC. COND. LOW	HIGH

Aragon F-30 NT
1959-1985. Natural finish version of F-30.
1959-1969		$1,350	$1,825
1970-1985		$1,200	$1,600

Aragon F-30 R
1973-1995. Rosewood back and sides version of F-30, sunburst.
1973-1979		$1,200	$1,600

Aristocrat M-75
1954-1963. Electric archtop, routed semi-hollow single-cut body, 2 pickups, sunburst, natural (added '59) or cherry (added '61), reintroduced as Bluesbird M-75 in '67.
1954-1959		$3,500	$4,400
1960-1963		$3,300	$4,100

Aristocrat M-75 Tenor
Mid-late 1950s. Tenor version of 6-string Aristocrat electric, dual soapbar pickups, 4 knobs.
1950s		$2,900	$3,600

Artist Award
1961-1999. Renamed from Johnny Smith Award, single-cut electric archtop, floating DeArmond pickup (changed to humbucker in '80), multi-bound, gold hardware, sunburst or natural.
1961-1969		$5,400	$7,000
1970-1999		$4,300	$5,600

Bluegrass D-25/D-25 M
1968-1999. Flat-top, mahogany top until '76, spruce after, mahogany back and sides, various colors, called Bluegrass D-25 M in late-'70s and '80s, listed as D-25 in '90s.
1968-1969		$1,050	$1,300
1970-1979		$950	$1,200
1980-1999		$750	$950

Bluegrass D-25-12
1987-1992, 1996-1999. 12-string version of D-25.
1987-1999		$750	$950

Bluegrass D-35
1966-1988. Acoustic flat-top, spruce top and mahogany back and sides, rosewood 'board and bridge, natural.
1966-1969		$1,250	$1,550
1970-1979		$1,150	$1,450
1980-1988		$1,050	$1,325

Bluegrass F-40
1954-1963, 1973-1983. Acoustic flat-top, spruce top, maple back and sides, rosewood 'board and bridge, natural or sunburst.
1954-1963	F-40	$2,400	$3,000
1973-1983	Bluegrass F-40	$1,250	$1,550

Bluegrass F-47
1963-1976. 16" narrow-waist style, mahogany sides and back, acoustic flat-top, spruce top, mahogany back and sides, bound rosewood 'board and bridge, natural.
1963-1969		$2,500	$3,100
1970-1976		$2,200	$2,750

Bluegrass Jubilee D-40
1963-1992. Acoustic flat-top, spruce top, mahogany back and sides, rosewood 'board and bridge, natural. Has been reissued.
1963-1969		$1,550	$1,950
1970-1979		$1,400	$1,750
1980-1992		$1,250	$1,550

Bluegrass Jubilee D-40 C
1975-1991. Acoustic flat-top, single Florentine cutaway, mahogany back and sides, rosewood 'board and bridge, natural.
1975-1991		$1,250	$1,550

Bluegrass Jubilee D-44
1965-1972. Acoustic flat-top, spruce top, pearwood back and sides, ebony 'board, rosewood bridge.
1965-1969		$1,400	$1,750
1970-1972		$1,250	$1,550

Bluegrass Jubilee D-44 M
1971-1985. Acoustic flat-top, spruce top, maple back & sides, ebony fingerboard, rosewood bridge.
1971-1985		$1,250	$1,550

Bluegrass Special D-50
1963-1993. Acoustic flat-top, spruce top, rosewood back and sides, ebony fretboard, multi-bound.
1963-1968	Brazilian rosewood	$4,000	$5,000
1969-1979	Indian rosewood	$1,200	$1,500
1980-1993	Indian rosewood	$1,100	$1,400

Bluegrass Special D-50 (Reissue)/D-50
1999-2004, 2006-2014. Also available with pickup system, initially listed as D-50.
1999-2014		$1,700	$2,100

Blues 90
2000-2002. Bluesbird single-cut, chambered body, unbound rosewood board, dots, 2 Duncan 2 P-90s.
2000-2002		$900	$1,125

Bluesbird M-75 (Hollowbody)
1967-1970. Reintroduced from Aristocrat M-75, thinbody electric archtop of maple, spruce ('67) or mahogany, single-cut, 2 pickups, Deluxe has gold hardware, Standard chrome. A solidbody Bluesbird was also introduced in '70.
1967-1970		$2,200	$2,700

Bluesbird M-75 (Solidbody)
1970-1978. Solidbody version of Bluesbird M-75, mahogany body, rounded cutaway, 2 pickups.
1970-1978	CS, plain top, chrome hardware	$1,900	$2,400
1970-1978	GS, flamed top, gold hardware	$2,100	$2,600

Bluesbird M-75 (Solidbody) Reintroduced
1984-1988.
1984-1985	3 single-coil pickups	$925	$1,150
1986	EMG pickups	$925	$1,150
1987-1988	DiMarzio pickups	$925	$1,150

Bluesbird (Reintroduced)
1994-2003. Single-cut chambered solidbody, 2 humbuckers, block inlays, available with AAA flamed top.
1994-2004	Standard	$1,250	$1,550
1998-2003	AAA maple	$1,250	$1,550
2001	Fender Custom Shop	$1,875	$2,325

Bluesbird
2011-2012. Single-cut solidbody, Chesterfield headstock logo, flame maple top, block markers, 2 humbuckers, natural finish.
2011-2012		$1,350	$1,700

The **Vintage Guitar Price Guide** shows low to high values for items in all-original excellent condition, and, where applicable, with original case or cover.

MODEL YEAR	FEATURES	EXC. COND. LOW	HIGH

Brian May BHM-1
1984-1987. Electric solidbody, double-cut, vibrato, 3 pickups, bound top and back, red or green, Brian May Pro, Special and Standard introduced in '94.

1984-1987		$2,700	$3,400

Brian May Pro
1994-1995. Electric solidbody, double-cut, vibrato, 3 pickups, bound top and back, various colors.

1994-1995		$2,100	$2,600

Brian May Signature Red Special
1994. Signature initials on truss rod cover, script signature on back of headstock, BM serial number, dot markers, custom Duncan pickups, custom vibrola, red special finish.

1994		$2,100	$2,600

CA-100 Capri
1956-1973. Acoustic archtop version of CE-100, sharp Florentine cutaway, solid spruce top, laminated maple back and sides, rosewood 'board and bridge, nickel-plated metal parts, natural or sunburst.

1956-1959		$1,750	$2,200
1960-1973		$1,600	$2,000

Capri CE-100
1956-1985. Electric archtop, single Florentine cutaway, 1 pickup (2 pickups by '83), maple body, Waverly tailpiece, sunburst, in '59-'82 CE-100 D listed with 2 pickups.

1956-1959		$1,750	$2,200
1960-1985		$1,600	$2,000

Capri CE-100 D
1956-1982. Electric archtop, single Florentine cutaway, 2 pickups, maple body, sunburst, Waverly tailpiece (D dropped, became the Capri CE-100 in '83).

1956-1959		$1,900	$2,400
1960-1982		$1,750	$2,200

Capri CE-100 T Tenor
1950s. Electric-archtop Capri 4-string tenor guitar, sunburst.

1956		$1,600	$2,000

CO-1/CO-1C
2006-2008. Vintage F-30 style, red cedar top, solid mahogany neck/back/sides, rosewood 'board, natural. CO 1C with soft cutaway.

2006-2008		$1,000	$1,250

CO-2/CO-2C
2008. As CO-1 but with red spruce top, ebony 'board, and offered in blonde, Antique Burst or Ice Tea Burst. CO-2C with soft cutaway.

2008		$1,000	$1,250

Cordoba A-50
1961-1972. Acoustic archtop, lowest-end in the Guild archtop line, named Granda A-50 prior to '61.

1961-1965		$950	$1,200
1966-1969		$850	$1,075
1970-1972		$750	$950

Cordoba T-50 Slim
1961-1973. Thinbody version of Cordoba X-50.

1961-1965		$950	$1,200
1966-1969		$850	$1,075
1970-1972		$750	$950

Cordoba X-50
1961-1970. Electric archtop non-cut, laminated maple body, rosewood 'board, 1 pickup, nickel-plated parts.

1961-1965		$950	$1,200
1966-1969		$850	$1,075
1970		$750	$950

CR-1 Crossroads Single E/Double E
1993-2000. Single-cut solidbody acoustic, humbucker (S2 in '93) neck pickup and Piezo bridge, 97 single necks (Single E, '93-'97) and very few 6/12 double necks (Double E, '93, '98-'00) made by Guild custom shop.

1993-1997	Single neck	$1,325	$1,625
1993-2000	Double neck	$2,600	$3,200

Custom F-412 12-String
1968-1986. Special order only from '68-'74, then regular production, 17" wide body 12-string version of F-50 flat-top, spruce top, maple back and sides, arched back, 2-tone block inlays, gold hardware, natural finish.

1968-1969		$1,750	$2,150
1970-1979		$1,600	$1,975
1980-1986		$1,450	$1,800

Custom F-512 12-String
1968-1986, 1990. Rosewood back and sides version of F-412. See F-512 for reissue.

1968-1969		$1,750	$2,150
1970-1979		$1,600	$1,975
1980-1986		$1,450	$1,800

Custom F-612 12-String
1972-1973. Acoustic 12-string, similar to Custom F-512, but with 18" body, fancy mother-of-pearl inlays, and black/white marquee body, neck and headstock binding.

1972-1973	Brazilian rosewood	$3,150	$3,900
1972-1973	Indian rosewood	$1,625	$2,000

Custom Shop 45th Anniversary
1997. Built in Guild's Nashville Custom Shop, all solid wood, spruce top, maple back and sides, with high-end appointments.

1997	Natural, gold hardware	$2,000	$2,500

CV-1/CV-1C
2006-2008. F-40 style, solid Indian rosewood back/sides, rosewood 'board. CV-1C with sharp cutaway.

2006-2008	CV-1	$775	$975
2006-2008	CV-1C	$900	$1,125

CV-2/CV-2C
2008. As CV-1 but with flamed maple back/sides, ebony 'board. CV-2C with sharp cutaway.

2008	CV-2	$775	$975
2008	CV-2C	$900	$1,125

D-4 Series
1991-2002. Dreadnought flat-top, mahogany sides, dot markers.

1991-2002	6-String	$500	$600
1992-1999	12-String	$500	$600

D-6 (D-6 E/D-6 HG/D-6 HE)
1992-1995. Flat-top, 15 3/4", mahogany back and sides, natural satin non-gloss finish, options available.

1992-1995		$500	$625

1970 Guild Bluesbird M-75

1977 Guild Capri CE-100 D
Greg Gagliono

1968 Guild D-35

Guild D-40 Richie Havens

MODEL YEAR	FEATURES	EXC. COND. LOW	HIGH

D-15 Mahogany Rush
1983-1988. Dreadnought flat-top, mahogany body and neck, rosewood 'board, dot inlays, stain finish.

1983-1988		$375	$475

D-15 12-String
1983-1985. 12-string version of Mahogany Rush D-15.

1983-1985		$375	$475

D-16 Mahogany Rush
1984-1986. Like D-15, but with gloss finish.

1984-1986		$450	$575

D-17 Mahogany Rush
1984-1988. Like D-15, but with gloss finish and bound body.

1984-1988		$500	$625

D-25/D-25 M/GAD-25
2003, 2006-2011. Solid mahogany body. Refer to Bluegrass D-25 for earlier models. Reintroduced in '06 as GAD-25.

2003-2011		$550	$700

D-30
1987-1999. Acoustic flat-top, spruce-top, laminated maple back and solid maple sides, rosewood 'board, multi-bound, various colors.

1987-1999		$800	$1,000

D-40
1999-2007. Solid spruce top, mahogany back and sides, rosewood 'board. See earlier models under Bluegrass Jubilee D-40.

1999-2007		$1,225	$1,525

D-40 Bluegrass Jubilee
2006-2014. Indian rosewood, red spruce top, mahogany back and sides, 3-piece neck (mahogany/walnut/mahogany).

2006-2014	No pickup	$1,225	$1,525
2006-2014	With Duncan D-TAR	$1,325	$1,625

D-40 Richie Havens
2003-2014. Richie Havens signature logo on truss rod cover, mahogany sides and back, Fishman Matrix, natural.

2003-2014		$950	$1,175

D-40C NT
1975-1991. Pointed cutaway version.

1975-1991		$1,250	$1,550

D-46
1980-1985. Dreadnought acoustic, ash back, sides and neck, spruce top, ebony 'board, ivoroid body binding.

1980-1985		$800	$1,000

D-55
See TV Model.

D-60
1987-1990, 1998-2000. Renamed from D-66, rosewood back and sides, scalloped bracing, multi-bound top, slotted diamond inlay, G shield logo.

1987-1990		$2,000	$2,500
1998-2000		$2,000	$2,500

D-64
1984-1986. Maple back and side, multi-bound body, notched diamond inlays, limited production.

1984-1986		$2,000	$2,500

MODEL YEAR	FEATURES	EXC. COND. LOW	HIGH

D-66
1984-1987. Amber, rosewood back and sides, 15 3/4", scalloped bracing, renamed D-60 in '87.

1984-1987		$2,000	$2,500

D-70
1981-1985. Dreadnought acoustic, spruce top, Indian rosewood back and sides, multi-bound, ebony 'board with mother-of-pearl inlays.

1981-1985		$2,000	$2,500

D-100
1999. Top-of-the-line dreadnought-size acoustic, spruce top, rosewood back and sides, scalloped bracing.

1999		$2,000	$2,500

D-212 12-String
1981-1983. 12-string version of D-25, laminated mahogany back and sides, natural, sunburst or black, renamed D-25-12 in '87, reintroduced as D-212 '96-present.

1981-1983		$600	$750

D-412 12-String
1990-1997. Dreadnought, 12 strings, mahogany sides and arched back, satin finished, natural.

1990-1997		$700	$875

DC-130
1994-1995. US-made, limited run, D-style cutaway, flamed maple top/back/sides.

1994-1995		$2,000	$2,450

DCE True American
1993-2000. Cutaway flat-top acoustic/electric, 1 with mahogany back and sides, 5 with rosewood.

1993-2000	DCE1, DCE1 T.A.	$475	$600
1994-2000	DCE5	$550	$675

Del Rio M-30
1959-1964. Flat-top, 15", all mahogany body, satin non-gloss finish.

1959		$1,450	$1,800
1960-1964		$1,350	$1,700

Detonator
1987-1990. Electric solidbody, double-cut, 3 pickups, bolt-on neck, Guild/Mueller tremolo system, black hardware.

1987-1990		$450	$575

Duane Eddy Deluxe DE-500
1962-1974, 1984-1987. Electric archtop, single rounded cutaway, 2 pickups (early years and '80s version have DeArmonds), Bigsby, master volume, spruce top with maple back and sides, available in blond (BL) or sunburst (SB).

1962	Natural	$4,700	$5,800
1962	Sunburst	$3,900	$4,800
1963	Natural	$4,600	$5,700
1963	Sunburst	$3,800	$4,700
1964	Natural	$4,600	$5,700
1964	Sunburst	$3,800	$4,700
1965	Natural	$4,000	$4,900
1965	Sunburst	$3,500	$4,300
1966	Natural	$3,600	$4,500
1966	Sunburst	$3,300	$4,100
1967-1969	Various colors	$3,200	$4,000
1970-1974	Various colors	$2,900	$3,600
1984-1987	Various colors	$2,500	$3,100

MODEL YEAR	FEATURES	EXC. COND. LOW	HIGH

Duane Eddy Standard DE-400
1963-1974. Electric archtop, single rounded cutaway, 2 pickups, vibrato, natural or sunburst, less appointments than DE-500 Deluxe.

1963	Natural	$3,200	$4,000
1963	Sunburst	$2,700	$3,400
1964	Natural	$3,000	$3,700
1964	Sunburst	$2,400	$3,000
1965	Natural	$2,700	$3,400
1965	Sunburst	$2,200	$2,700
1966	Natural	$2,400	$3,000
1966	Sunburst	$2,000	$2,500
1967-1969	Various colors	$1,900	$2,400
1970-1974	Various colors	$1,700	$2,100

DV Series
1992-1999, 2007-2011. Acoustic flat-top, mahogany or rosewood back and sides, ebony or rosewood 'board, satin or gloss finish.

1992-2011		$500	$1,500

Economy M-20
1958-1965, 1969-1973. Mahogany body, acoustic flat-top, natural or sunburst satin finish.

1958 1959		$1,350	$1,700
1960-1969		$1,250	$1,600
1970-1973		$1,150	$1,450

F-4 CEHG
1992-2002. High Gloss finish, single-cut flat-top, acoustic/electric.

1992-2002		$525	$650

F-5 CE
1992-2001. Acoustic/electric, single cutaway, rosewood back and sides, dot inlays, chrome tuners.

1992-2001		$525	$650

F-30
1998-2001. Formerly the Aragon F-30, made in Westerly, Rhode Island.

1998-2001		$1,100	$1,375

F-30 R-LS
1990s. Custom Shop model, other F-30 models are listed under Aragon F-30 listing, rosewood sides and back, bearclaw spruce top, limited production.

1990s		$1,200	$1,500

F-45 CE
1983-1992. Acoustic/electric, single cutaway, mahogany or maple back and sides, rosewood 'board, natural.

1983-1992	Flamed maple	$625	$800
1983-1992	Mahogany	$725	$900

F-46 NT
1984. Jumbo body style flat-top, designed for Guild by George Gruhn.

1984		$1,575	$1,950

F-47 M/F-47 MC
2007-present. Made in USA, solid flamed maple sides and back, MC with cutaway.

2007-2014	F-47 M	$1,350	$1,700
2007-2014	F-47 MC	$1,450	$1,800

F-47 R/F-47 RC
2008-2014. Solid rosewood sides and back, available with electronics, RC with cutaway.

2008-2014		$1,350	$1,700

F-47 RCE Grand Auditorium
1999-2003. Cutaway acoustic/electric, rosewood back and sides, block inlays.

1999-2003		$1,275	$1,600

F-50/F-50 R
2002-present. Jumbo, solid spruce top, solid maple sides, arched laminated maple back, abalone rosette. See Navarre F-50/F-50 for earlier models.

2002-2014	F-50, maple	$1,350	$1,700
2002-2014	F-50R, rosewood	$1,350	$1,700

F-65 CE
1992-2001. Acoustic/electric, single cutaway, rosewood back and sides, block inlay, gold tuners.

1992-2001		$1,350	$1,700

F-212 12-String
1964-1982. Acoustic flat-top jumbo, 12 strings, spruce top, mahogany back and sides, 16" body.

1964-1969		$1,150	$1,450
1970-1979		$1,050	$1,300
1980-1982		$900	$1,150

F-212 XL 12-String
1966-1986, 1998-2000. Acoustic flat-top, 17" body, 12 strings, spruce top, mahogany back and sides, ebony fingerboard.

1966-1969		$1,150	$1,450
1970-1979		$1,050	$1,300
1980-1986		$900	$1,150
1998-2000		$875	$1,100

F-312 Artist 12-String
1964-1973. Flat-top, rosewood back and sides, spruce top, no board inlay (but some in '72 may have dots).

1964-1968	Brazilian rosewood	$3,200	$4,000
1969-1973	Indian rosewood	$1,600	$2,000

F-412
2002-present. Solid spruce top, solid maple back and sides, block inlays, 12-string. See Custom F-412 for earlier models.

2002-2014		$1,600	$2,000

F-512
2002-present. Solid spruce top, rosewood back and sides, 12-string. See Custom F-512 for earlier models.

2002-2014		$1,750	$2,225

Freshman M-65
1958-1973. Electric archtop, single-cut, mahogany back and sides, f-holes, 1 single-coil (some with 2), sunburst or natural top.

1958-1959		$1,500	$1,875
1960-1969		$1,275	$1,575
1970-1973		$1,200	$1,475

Freshman M-65 3/4
1958-1973. Short-scale version of M-65, 1 pickup.

1958-1959		$1,100	$1,350
1960-1969		$1,000	$1,250
1970-1973		$900	$1,125

FS-20 CE
1986-1987. Solidbody acoustic, routed mahogany body.

1986-1987		$525	$650

FS-46 CE
1983-1986. Flat-top acoustic/electric, pointed cutaway, mahogany, black, natural or sunburst.

1983-1986		$600	$750

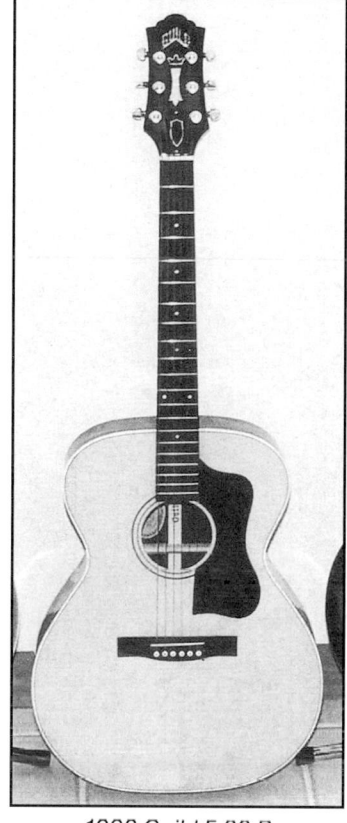

1998 Guild F-30 R
Dennis Morley

1976 Guild F-212
Dick Johnson

1975 Guild G-41

Denns Morley

Guild George Barnes AcoustiLectric

MODEL YEAR	FEATURES	EXC. COND. LOW	HIGH

G-5 P
1988-ca.1989. Handmade in Spain, cedar top, gold-plated hardware.

1988-1989		$600	$750

G-37
1973-1986. Acoustic flat-top, spruce top, laminated maple back and sides, rosewood 'board and bridge, sunburst or natural top.

1973-1986		$700	$875

G-41
1974-1978. Acoustic flat-top, spruce top, mahogany back and sides, rosewood 'board and bridge, 20 frets.

1975-1978		$700	$875

G-45 Hank Williams Jr.
1982-1986, 1993-1996. Hank Williams Jr. logo on 'guard, flat-top.

1982-1996		$900	$1,125

G-75
1975-1977. Acoustic flat-top, 3/4-size version of D-50, spruce top, rosewood back and sides, mahogany neck, ebony 'board and bridge.

1975-1977		$700	$875

G-212 12-String
1974-1983. Acoustic flat-top 12-string version of D-40, spruce top, mahogany back and sides, natural or sunburst.

1974-1979		$700	$875
1980-1983		$625	$800

G-212 XL 12-String
1974-1983. Acoustic flat-top, 12 strings, 17" version of G-212.

1974-1979		$700	$875
1980-1983		$625	$800

G-312 12-String
1974-1987. Acoustic flat-top 12-string version of the D-50, spruce top, rosewood back and sides.

1974-1979		$900	$1,125
1980-1987		$800	$1,025

GAD (Guild Acoustic Design) Series
2004-2014. Imported, all models begin with GAD.

2004-2014		$400	$850

George Barnes AcoustiLectric
1962-1972. Electric archtop, single-cut, solid spruce top, curly maple back and sides, multi-bound, 2 humbuckers, gold-plated hardware, sunburst or natural finish.

1962-1972		$3,200	$4,000

George Barnes Guitar in F
1963-1973. Smaller Electric archtop at 13.5", 2 humbuckers, chrome hardware.

1963-1973		$3,200	$4,000

GF-25
1987-1992. Acoustic flat-top, mahogany back and sides.

1987-1992		$775	$950

GF-25 C
1988-1991. Cutaway GF-25.

1988-1991		$825	$1,025

GF-30
1987-1991. Acoustic flat-top, maple back/sides/neck, multi-bound.

1987-1991		$1,000	$1,250

GF-40
1987-1991. Mahogany back and sides, multi-bound.

1987-1991		$1,000	$1,250

GF-50
1987-1991. Acoustic flat-top, rosewood back and sides, mahogany neck, multi-bound.

1987-1991		$1,000	$1,250

GF-60
1987-1989. Jumbo size, rosewood or maple sides and back, diamond markers.

1987-1989	GF-60M, maple	$1,125	$1,400
1987-1989	GF-60R, rosewood	$1,125	$1,400

GF-60 C
1987-1989. Cutaway GF-60.

1987-1989		$1,175	$1,450

Granada A-50 (Acoustic Archtop)
1956-1960. Lowest-end acoustic archtop in the Guild line, renamed Cordoba A-50 in '61.

1956-1960		$1,050	$1,300

Granada X-50
1954-1961. Electric archtop, non-cut, laminated all maple body, rosewood 'board and bridge, nickel-plated metal parts, 1 pickup, sunburst. Renamed Cordoba X-50 in '61.

1955-1961		$1,250	$1,550

GV Series
1993-1995. Flat-top, rosewood back and sides, various enhancements.

1993-1995	GV-52, gloss	$1,050	$1,300
1993-1995	GV-52, satin	$850	$1,050
1993-1995	GV-70, abalone, gloss	$1,125	$1,400
1993-1995	GV-72, herringbone, gloss	$1,125	$1,400

Jet Star S-50
1963-1970. Electric solidbody, double-cut, mahogany or alder body, 1 pickup, vibrato optional by '65, asymmetrical headstock until '65, reintroduced as S-50 in '72-'78 with body redesign.

1963-1965	3-on-side	$1,500	$1,900
1966-1970	6-in-line	$1,500	$1,900

JF-4 NT
1992-1995. Jumbo flat-top, mahogany, natural.

1992-1995		$650	$800

JF-30
1987-2004. Jumbo 6-string acoustic, spruce top, laminated maple back, solid maple sides, multi-bound.

1987-2004		$1,000	$1,250

JF-30 E
1994-2004. Acoustic/electric version.

1994-2004		$1,050	$1,300

JF-30-12
1987-2004. 12-string version of the JF-30.

1987-2004		$1,200	$1,500

JF-50 R
1987-1988. Jumbo 6-string acoustic, rosewood back and sides, multi-bound.

1987-1988		$1,300	$1,600

JF-55
1989-2000. Jumbo flat-top, spruce top, rosewood body.

1989-2000		$1,500	$1,875

The *Vintage Guitar Price Guide* shows low to high values for items in all-original excellent condition, and, where applicable, with original case or cover.

MODEL YEAR	FEATURES	EXC. COND. LOW	HIGH

JF-55-12
1991-2000. 12-string JF-55.

1991-2000		$1,500	$1,875

JF-65
1987-1994. Renamed from Navarre F-50, Jumbo flat-top acoustic, spruce top, R has rosewood back and sides and M has maple.

1987-1994	JF-65M, maple	$1,400	$1,750
1987-1994	JF-65R, rosewood	$1,400	$1,750

JF-65-12
1987-2001. 12-string, version of JF-65.

1987-2001	JF-65M-12, maple	$1,400	$1,750
1987-2001	JF-65R-12, rosewood	$1,400	$1,750

Johnny Smith Award
1956-1961. Single-cut electric archtop, floating DeArmond pickup, multi-bound, gold hardware, sunburst or natural, renamed Artist Award in '61.

1956-1961		$7,500	$9,300

Johnny Smith Award Benedetto
2004-2006. 18 custom made instruments under the supervision of Bob Benedetto, signed by Johnny Smith, with certificate of authenticity signed by Smith and Benedetto.

2004-2006	18 made	$5,500	$7,000

Liberator Elite
1988. Limited Edition, set-neck, offset double-cut solidbody, figured maple top, mahogany body, rising-sun inlays, 3 active pickups, last of the Guild solidbodies.

1988		$900	$1,125

M-80 CS/M-80
1975-1984. Solidbody, double-cut, 2 pickups, introduced as M-80 CS with bound rosewood 'board and block inlays, shortened to M-80 in '80 with unbound ebony 'board and dots.

1975-1980	M-80CS	$1,000	$1,250
1980-1984	M-80	$900	$1,150

Manhattan X-170 (Mini-Manhattan X-170)
1985-2002. Called Mini-Manhattan X-170 in '85-'86, electric archtop hollowbody, single rounded cutaway, maple body, f-holes, 2 humbuckers, block inlays, gold hardware, natural or sunburst.

1985-2002		$1,400	$1,750

Manhattan X-175 (Sunburst)
1954-1985. Electric archtop, single rounded cutaway, laminated spruce top, laminated maple back and sides, 2 pickups, chrome hardware, sunburst. Reissued as X-160 Savoy.

1954-1959		$1,800	$2,250
1960-1969		$1,600	$2,050
1970-1985		$1,450	$1,850

Manhattan X-175 B (Natural)
1954-1976. Natural finish X-175.

1954-1959		$2,300	$2,800
1960-1969		$2,100	$2,600
1970-1976		$2,000	$2,500

Mark I
1961-1972. Classical, Honduras mahogany body, rosewood 'board, slotted headstock.

1961-1969		$375	$475
1970-1973		$300	$375

Mark II
1961-1987. Like Mark I, but with spruce top and body binding.

1961-1969		$625	$775
1970-1979		$375	$475
1980-1987		$300	$375

Mark III
1961-1987. Like Mark II, but with Peruvian mahogany back and sides and floral soundhole design.

1961-1969		$725	$900
1970-1979		$600	$800
1980-1987		$425	$575

Mark IV
1961-1985. Like Mark III, but with flamed pearwood back and sides (rosewood offered in '61, maple in '62).

1961-1969	Pearwood	$800	$1,000
1970-1979	Pearwood	$700	$900
1980-1985	Pearwood	$525	$700

Mark V
1961-1987. Like Mark III, but with rosewood back and sides (maple available for '61-'64).

1961-1968	Brazilian rosewood	$1,600	$2,000
1969-1979	Indian rosewood	$800	$1,000
1980-1987	Indian rosewood	$525	$700

Mark VI
1962-1973. Rosewood back and sides, spruce top, wood binding.

1962-1968	Brazilian rosewood	$1,800	$2,250
1969-1973	Indian rosewood	$900	$1,125

Mark VII Custom
1968-1973. Special order only, spruce top, premium rosewood back and sides, inlaid rosewood bridge, engraved gold tuners.

1962-1968	Brazilian rosewood	$2,000	$2,500
1969-1973	Indian rosewood	$1,000	$1,250

Navarre F-48
1972-1975. 17", mahogany, block markers.

1972-1975		$1,300	$1,650

Navarre F-50/F-50
1954-1986, 1994-1995. Acoustic flat-top, spruce top, curly maple back and sides, rosewood 'board and bridge, 17" rounded lower bout, laminated arched maple back, renamed JF-65 M in '87. Reissued in '94 and again in '02 as the F-50.

1954-1956		$4,000	$5,000
1957-1962	Pearl block markers added	$3,300	$4,100
1963-1969	Ebony 'board added	$3,100	$3,900
1970-1975		$2,300	$2,900
1976-1979		$2,300	$2,900
1980-1995		$2,150	$2,650

Navarre F-50 R/F-50 R
1965-1987. Rosewood back and side version of F-50, renamed JF-65 R in '87. Reissued in '02 as F-50R.

1965-1968	Brazilian rosewood	$6,200	$7,800
1969-1975	Indian rosewood	$3,000	$3,800
1976-1979		$2,250	$2,800
1980-1987		$2,100	$2,600

1964 Guild Jet Star S-50
Todd Bauer

2002 Guild JF-30-12
Joseph Bradshaw Jr.

GUITARS

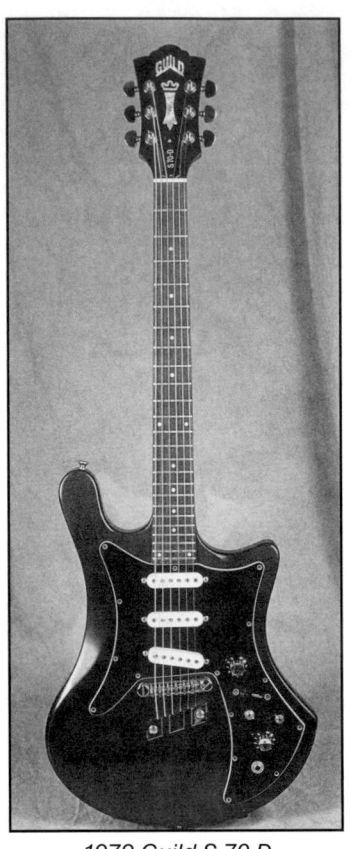

1979 Guild S-70 D

Guild Standard Series F-30

MODEL YEAR	FEATURES	EXC. COND. LOW	HIGH

Nightbird
1985-1987. Single-cut solidbody, tone chambers, 2 pickups, multi-bound, black or gold hardware, renamed Nightbird II in '87.

1985-1987		$1,900	$2,400

Nightbird I
1987-1988. Like Nightbird but with chrome hardware, less binding and appointments.

1987-1988		$1,700	$2,100

Nightbird II
1987-1992. Renamed from Nightbird, with black hardware, renamed Nightbird X-2000 in '92.

1987-1992		$2,000	$2,500

Nightbird X-2000
1992-1996. Renamed from Nightbird II.

1992-1996		$1,700	$2,100

Park Ave X-180
2005. Cutaway acoustic archtop, 2 pickups, block markers.

2005		$1,500	$1,900

Polara S-100
1963-1970. Double-cut mahogany or alder solidbody, rosewood 'board, 2 single coils, built-in stand until '70, asymmetrical headstock, in '70 Polara dropped from title (see S-100), renamed back to Polara S-100 in '97.

1963-1964	2 pickups	$1,600	$2,000
1965-1970	3 pickups	$1,600	$2,000

Roy Buchanan T-200
1986. Single-cut solidbody, 2 pickups, pointed six-on-a-side headstock, poplar body, bolt-on neck, gold and brass hardware.

1986		$525	$650

S-50
1972-1978. Double cut solidbody, 1 single-coil (switched to humbucker in '74), dot inlay.

1972-1973	Single-coil	$1,000	$1,250
1974-1978	Humbucker	$1,000	$1,250

S-60/S-60 D
1976-1981. Double-cut solidbody with long bass horn, 1 humbucker (60) or 2 single-coils (60 D), mahogany body, rosewood 'board

1976-1980	S-60	$1,000	$1,250
1977-1981	S-60D	$1,000	$1,250

S-65 D
1980-1981. S-60 but with 1 DiMarzio Super Distortion pickup.

1980-1981		$1,000	$1,250

S-70 D/S-70 AD
1979-1981. Solidbody (mahogany D, ash AD), rosewood 'board, 3 single-coils.

1979-1981	S-70AD, ash	$1,150	$1,450
1979-1981	S-70D, mahogany	$1,100	$1,350

S-90
1972-1977. Double-cut SG-like body, 2 humbuckers, dot inlay, chrome hardware.

1972-1977		$1,000	$1,250

S-100
1970-1978, 1994-1996. S-100 Standard is double-cut solidbody, 2 humbuckers, block inlays. Deluxe of '72-'75 had added Bigsby. Standard Carved of '74-'77 has

acorns and oakleaves carved in the top.

1970-1978	Standard	$1,400	$1,750
1972-1975	Deluxe	$1,400	$1,750
1974-1977	Standard Carved	$1,400	$1,750

S-100 Reissue
1994-1997. Renamed Polara in '97.

1994-1997		$825	$1,050

S-250
1981-1983. Double-cut solidbody, 2 humbuckers.

1981-1983		$500	$625

S-261
Ca.1985. Double-cut, maple body, black Kahler tremolo, 1 humbucker and 2 single-coil pickups, rosewood 'board.

1985		$400	$500

S-270 Runaway
1985. Offset double-cut solidbody, 1 humbucker, Kahler.

1985		$400	$500

S-271 Sprint
1986. Replaced the S-270.

1986		$400	$500

S-275
1982-1983. Offset double-cut body, 2 humbuckers, bound figured maple top, sunburst or natural.

1982-1983		$400	$500

S-280 Flyer
1983-1984. Double-cut poplar body, 2 humbuckers or 3 single-coils, maple or rosewood neck, dot markers.

1983-1984		$400	$500

S-281 Flyer
1983-1988. Double-cut poplar body S-280 with locking vibrato, optional pickups available.

1983-1988		$400	$500

S-284 Starling/Aviator
1984-1988. Starling (early-'84) and Aviator (late-'84-'88), double-cut, 3 pickups.

1984	Starling	$400	$500
1984-1988	Aviator	$400	$500

S-285 Aviator
1986. Deluxe Aviator, bound 'board, fancy inlays.

1986		$400	$500

S-300 Series
1976-1983. Double-cut mahogany solidbody with larger bass horn and rounded bottom, 2 humbuckers. S-300 A has ash body, D has exposed DiMarzio humbuckers.

1976-1983	S-300	$625	$800
1977-1982	S-300D	$625	$800
1977-1983	S-300A	$625	$800

S-400/S-400 A
1980-1981. Double-cut mahogany (400) or ash (400 A) solidbody, 2 humbuckers.

1980-1981		$900	$1,125

Savoy A-150
1958-1973, 2013-present. Acoustic archtop version of X-150, available with floating pickup, natural or sunburst finish. Reissued in 2013.

1958-1961	Natural	$1,800	$2,250
1958-1961	Sunburst	$1,700	$2,100
2013-2014		$1,200	$1,500

MODEL YEAR	FEATURES	EXC. COND. LOW	HIGH

Savoy X-150

1954-1965. Electric archtop, single rounded cutaway, spruce top, maple back and sides, rosewood 'board and bridge, 1 single-coil pickup, sunburst, blond or sparkling gold finish. Reissued in '98 as X-150 Savoy.

1954	Sunburst	$1,900	$2,400
1955-1959	Sunburst	$1,800	$2,300
1960-1961	Sunburst	$1,700	$2,100

Slim Jim T-100

1958-1973. Electric archtop thinline, single-cut, laminated all-maple body, rosewood 'board and bridge, Waverly tailpiece, 1 pickup, natural or sunburst.

1958-1959		$1,150	$1,450
1960-1964		$1,050	$1,300
1965-1973		$900	$1,125

Slim Jim T-100 D

1958-1973. Semi-hollowbody electric, single Florentine cutaway, thinline, 2-pickup version of the T-100, natural or sunburst.

1958-1959		$1,250	$1,600
1960-1964		$1,225	$1,550
1965-1969		$1,200	$1,500
1970-1973		$1,100	$1,400

Songbird S Series

1984-1991. Designed by George Gruhn, flat-top, mahogany back, spruce top, single pointed cutaway, pickup with preamp, multi-bound top, black, natural or white. Renamed S-4 later in run.

1984-1991		$825	$1,025

Standard F-112 12-String

1968-1982. Acoustic flat-top, spruce top, mahogany back, sides and neck.

1968-1969		$925	$1,150
1970-1979		$775	$950
1980-1982		$675	$850

Standard Series

2010-2014. Imported flat-top acoustics based on classic Guild models, various models.

2010-2014	F-30 Standard	$1,150	$1,450

Starfire I

1960-1964. Electric archtop, single-cut thinline, laminated maple or mahogany body, bound body and neck, 1 pickup.

1960-1961	Starfire Red	$1,375	$1,750
1962-1964		$1,275	$1,650

Starfire II

1960-1976, 1997-2001. Electric archtop, single-cut thinline, laminated maple or mahogany body, bound body and rosewood neck, 2 pickups.

1960-1961	Sunburst	$1,850	$2,300
1962	Emerald Green	$1,925	$2,400
1962-1966	Special color options	$2,000	$2,500
1962-1966	Sunburst, Starfire Red	$1,775	$2,200
1967-1969	Sunburst, Starfire Red	$1,575	$2,000
1970-1975	Sunburst, Starfire Red	$1,475	$1,850
1997-2001	Reissue model	$1,375	$1,725

Starfire III

1960-1974, 1997-2005. Electric archtop, single-cut thinline, laminated maple or mahogany body, bound body and rosewood neck, 2 pickups, Guild or Bigsby vibrato, Starfire Red.

1960-1961		$2,100	$2,600
1962-1974		$2,000	$2,500
1997-2005	Reissue model	$1,375	$1,725

Starfire IV

1963-1987, 1991-2005. Thinline, double-cut semi-hollowbody, laminated maple or mahogany body, f-holes, 2 humbuckers, rosewood 'board, cherry or sunburst.

1963-1975		$2,500	$3,100
1976-1979		$2,300	$2,850
1980-1987		$2,100	$2,600
1991-2005	Reissue model	$1,475	$1,825

Starfire IV Special (Custom Shop)

2001-2002. Nashville Custom Shop.

2001-2002		$1,800	$2,250

Starfire V

1963-1973, 1999-2001. Same as Starfire IV but with block markers, Bigsby and master volume, natural or sunburst finish, reissued in '99.

1963-1966		$2,600	$3,200
1967-1973		$2,500	$3,100
1999-2001	Reissue model	$1,500	$1,900

Starfire VI

1964-1979. Same as Starfire IV but with higher appointments such as ebony 'board, pearl inlays, Guild/Bigsby vibrato, natural or sunburst.

1964-1966		$2,600	$3,200
1967-1979		$2,500	$3,100

Starfire Xii

1966-1973. Electric archtop, 12-string, double-cut, maple or mahogany body, set-in neck, 2 humbuckers, harp tailpiece.

1966-1973		$1,750	$2,200

Stratford A-350

1956-1973. Acoustic archtop, single rounded cutaway, solid spruce top with solid curly maple back and sides, rosewood 'board and bridge (changed to ebony by '60), sunburst.

1956-1959		$2,100	$2,600
1960-1965		$2,000	$2,500
1966-1969		$1,900	$2,400
1970-1973		$1,800	$2,300

Stratford A-350 B

1956-1973. A-350 in blond/natural finish option.

1956-1959		$2,300	$2,900
1960-1965		$2,150	$2,700
1966-1969		$2,100	$2,600
1970-1973		$2,000	$2,500

Stratford X-350

1954-1965. Electric archtop, single rounded cutaway, laminated spruce top with laminated maple back and sides, rosewood 'board, 6 push-button pickup selectors, sunburst finish (natural finish is X-375).

1954-1959		$2,550	$3,200
1960-1965		$2,400	$3,000

1962 Guild Starfire III

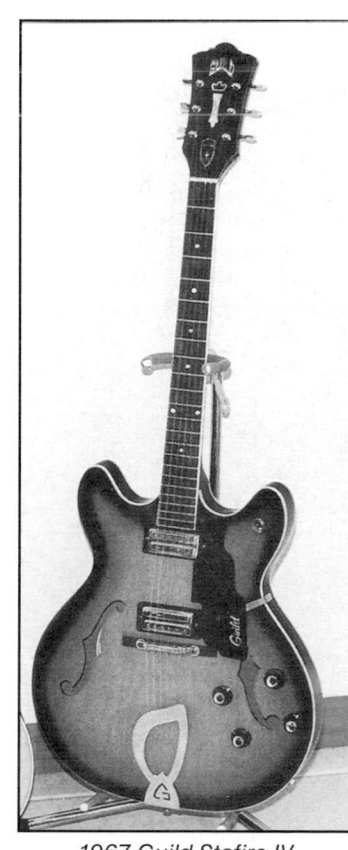

1967 Guild Stafire IV

Denns Morley

GUITARS

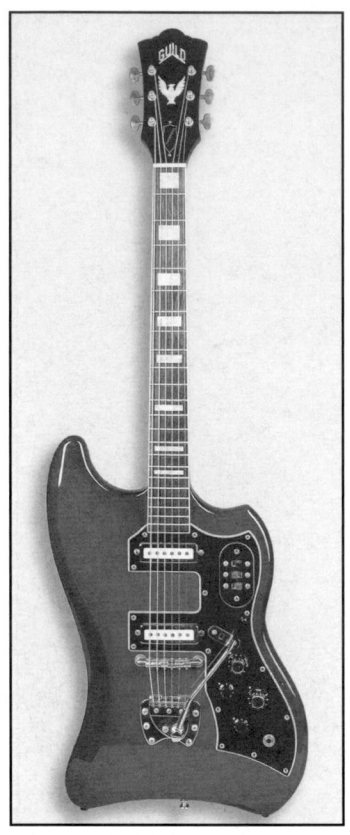

1966 Guild Thunderbird S-200

1958 Guild Troubadour F-20

Robbie Keene

MODEL YEAR	FEATURES	EXC. COND. LOW	HIGH

Stratford X-375/X-350 B
1953-1965. Natural finish version of X-350, renamed X-350 B in '58.

| 1953-1958 | X-375 | $2,700 | $3,400 |
| 1959-1965 | X-350B | $2,500 | $3,100 |

Stuart A-500
1956-1969. Acoustic archtop single-cut, 17" body, A-500 sunburst, available with Guild logo, floating DeArmond pickup.

1956-1959		$2,250	$2,800
1960-1965		$2,150	$2,700
1966-1969		$2,100	$2,600

Stuart A-550/A-500 B
1956-1969. Natural blond finish version of Stuart A-500, renamed A-500 B in '60.

1956-1959		$2,500	$3,100
1960-1965		$2,400	$3,000
1966-1969		$2,300	$2,900

Stuart X-500
1953-1995. Electric archtop, single-cut, laminated spruce top, laminated curly maple back and sides, 2 pickups, sunburst.

1953-1959		$2,800	$3,500
1960-1964		$2,550	$3,200
1965-1969		$2,400	$3,000
1970-1979		$2,200	$2,800
1980-1995		$2,100	$2,600

Stuart X-550/X-500 B
1953-1995. Natural blond finish Stuart X-500, renamed X-500 B in '60.

1953-1959		$2,800	$3,500
1960-1964		$2,550	$3,200
1965-1969		$2,400	$3,000
1970-1979		$2,200	$2,800
1980-1995		$2,100	$2,600

Studio 301/ST301
1968-1970. Thinline, semi-hollow archtop Starfire-style but with sharp horns, 1 pickup, dot inlays, cherry or sunburst.

| 1968-1969 | Single-coil | $1,000 | $1,250 |
| 1970 | Humbucker | $1,175 | $1,475 |

Studio 302/ST302
1968-1970. Like Studio 301, but with 2 pickups.

| 1968-1969 | Single-coils | $1,350 | $1,675 |
| 1970 | Humbuckers | $1,350 | $1,675 |

Studio 303/ST303
1968-1970. Like Studio 301, but with 2 pickups and Guild/Bigsby.

| 1968-1969 | Single-coils | $1,550 | $1,975 |
| 1970 | Humbuckers | $1,550 | $1,975 |

Studio 402/ST402
1969-1970. Inch thicker body than other Studios, 2 pickups, block inlays.

| 1969-1970 | Humbuckers | $1,900 | $2,350 |
| 1969-1970 | Single-coils | $1,900 | $2,350 |

T-250
1986-1988. Single-cut body and pickup configuration with banana-style headstock.

| 1986-1988 | | $600 | $750 |

Thunderbird S-200
1963-1968. Electric solidbody, offset double-cut,

built-in rear guitar stand, AdjustoMatic bridge and vibrato tailpiece, 2 humbucker pickups until changed to single-coils in '66.

| 1963-1965 | Humbuckers | $3,600 | $4,450 |
| 1966-1968 | Single-coils | $3,200 | $4,000 |

Troubadour F-20
1956-1987. Acoustic flat-top, spruce top with maple back and sides (mahogany '59 and after), rosewood 'board and bridge, natural or sunburst.

1956-1959		$1,550	$1,950
1960-1969		$1,450	$1,825
1970-1979		$1,275	$1,600
1980-1987		$1,125	$1,400

TV Model D-55/D-65/D-55
1968-1987, 1990-present (special order only for 1968-1973). Dreadnought acoustic, spruce top, rosewood back and sides, scalloped bracing, gold-plated tuners, renamed D-65 in '87. Reintroduced as D-55 in '90.

1968-1969		$1,925	$2,400
1970-1975		$1,850	$2,300
1976-1979		$1,675	$2,100
1980-1987		$1,575	$2,000
1988-1989	D-65	$1,450	$1,800
1990-1999		$1,450	$1,800
2000-2014	D-55	$1,750	$2,200

Willy Porter Signature
2007-2008. AAA sitka spruce top, solid flamed maple sides and back, special appointments, Fishman Ellipse system.

| 2007-2008 | | $1,100 | $1,375 |

X-79 Skyhawk
1981-1986. Four-point solidbody, 2 pickups, coil-tap or phase switch, various colors.

| 1981-1986 | | $1,100 | $1,400 |

X-80 Skylark/Swan
1982-1985. Solidbody with 2 deep cutaways, banana-style 6-on-a-side headstock, renamed Swan in '85.

| 1982-1985 | | $1,100 | $1,400 |

X-82 Nova/Starfighter
1981-1986. Solidbody, XR-7 humbuckerss, also available with 3 single-coil pickups, Quick Change SP-6 tailpiece, Adjusto-Matic bridge, Deluxe tuning machine.

| 1981-1983 | Nova | $1,100 | $1,400 |
| 1984-1986 | Starfighter | $1,100 | $1,400 |

X-88 D Star
1984-1987. 2 humbucker version X-88.

| 1984-1987 | | $875 | $1,100 |

X-88 Flying Star Motley Crue
1984-1986. Pointy 4-point star body, rocketship meets spearhead headstock on bolt neck, 1 pickup, optional vibrato.

| 1984-1986 | | $875 | $1,100 |

X-92 Citron
1984. Electric solidbody, detachable body section, 3 pickups.

| 1984 | | $700 | $875 |

X-100/X-110
1953-1954. Guild was founded in 1952, so this is a very early model, 17" non-cut, single-coil soapbar neck

MODEL YEAR	FEATURES	EXC. COND. LOW	HIGH

pickup, X-100 sunburst, X-110 natural blond.

| 1953-1954 | X-100 | $1,200 | $1,500 |
| 1953-1954 | X-110 | $1,400 | $1,750 |

X-100 Bladerunner

1985-1987. 4-point body with large cutouts, 1 humbucker, Kahler, script Guild logo on body, cutout headstock.

| 1985-1987 | | $2,700 | $3,400 |

X-150 D Savoy

1998-2003. Savoy with 2 humbuckers.

| 1998-2003 | | $1,200 | $1,500 |

X-150 Savoy

| 1998-2005 | | $1,200 | $1,500 |

X-160 Savoy

1989-1993. No Bigsby, black or sunburst.

| 1989-1993 | | $1,400 | $1,750 |

X-161/X-160B Savoy

1989-1994. X-160 Savoy with Bigsby, black or sunburst.

| 1989-1994 | | $1,400 | $1,750 |

X-200/X-220

1953-1954. Electric archtop, spruce top, laminated maple body, rosewood 'board, non-cut, 2 pickups. X-200 is sunburst and X-220 blond.

| 1953-1954 | X-200 | $1,500 | $1,900 |
| 1953-1954 | X-220 | $1,700 | $2,100 |

X-300/X-330

1953-1954. No model name, non-cut, 2 pickups, X-300 is sunburst and X-330 blond. Becomes Savoy X-150 in '54.

| 1953-1954 | X-300 | $1,500 | $1,900 |
| 1953-1954 | X-330 | $1,700 | $2,100 |

X-400/X-440

1953-1954. Electric archtop, single-cut, spruce top, laminated maple body, rosewood 'board, 2 pickups, X-400 in sunburst and X-440 in blond. Becomes Manhattan X-175 in '54.

| 1953-1954 | X-400 | $2,100 | $2,600 |
| 1953-1954 | X-440 | $2,300 | $2,850 |

X-600/X-660

1953. No model name, single-cut, 3 pickups, X-600 in sunburst and X-660 in blond. Becomes Statford X-350 in '54.

| 1953 | X-600 | $2,800 | $3,500 |
| 1953 | X-660 | $3,200 | $4,000 |

X-700

1994-1999. Rounded cutaway, 17", solid spruce top, laminated maple back and sides, gold hardware, natural or sunburst.

| 1994-1999 | | $1,900 | $2,400 |

Guillermo Roberto Guitars

Professional grade, solidbody electric bajo quintos made in San Fernando, California starting in the year 2000.

Guitar Company of America

1971-present. Professional grade, production, acoustic guitars built by luthier Dixie Michell. Originally built in Tennessee, then Missouri; currently being made in Tulsa, Oklahoma. She also offers mandolins.

Guitar Mill

2006-2011. Luthier Mario Martin built his production/custom, professional grade, semi-hollow and solidbody guitars and basses in Murfreesboro, Tennessee. He also built basses. In '11, he started branding his guitars as Mario Martin.

Gurian

1965-1981. Luthier Michael Gurian started making classical guitars on a special order basis, in New York City. In '69, he started building steel-string guitars as well. 1971 brought a move to Hinsdale, Vermont, and with it increased production. In February, '79 a fire destroyed his factory, stock, and tools. He reopened in West Swanzey, New Hampshire, but closed the doors in '81. Around 2,000 Gurian instruments were built. Dealers have reported that '70s models sometimes have notable wood cracks which require repair.

CL Series

1970-1981. Classical Series, mahogany (M), Indian rosewood (R), or Brazilian rosewood (B).

1970-1981	CLB, Brazilian rosewood	$2,600	$3,300
1970-1981	CLM, mahogany	$1,200	$1,500
1970-1981	CLR, Indian rosewood	$1,400	$1,750

FLC

1970-1981. Flamenco guitar, yellow cedar back and sides, friction tuning pegs.

| 1970-1981 | | $1,500 | $1,900 |

JB3H

| 1970-1981 | Brazilian rosewood | $2,900 | $3,600 |

JM/JMR

1970-1981. Jumbo body, mahogany (JM) or Indian rosewood (JMR), relatively wide waist (versus D-style or SJ-style).

| 1970-1981 | JM | $1,400 | $1,800 |
| 1970-1981 | JMR | $1,400 | $1,800 |

JR3H

1970-1981. Jumbo, Indian rosewood sides and back, 3-piece back, herringbone trim.

| 1970-1981 | | $1,800 | $2,250 |

S2B3H

| 1970-1981 | Brazilian rosewood | $3,000 | $3,750 |

S2M

1970-1981. Size 2 guitar with mahogany back and sides.

| 1970-1981 | | $1,400 | $1,800 |

S2R/S2R3H

1970-1981. Size 2 with Indian rosewood sides and back, R3H has 3-piece back and herringbone trim.

| 1970-1981 | S2R | $1,400 | $1,800 |
| 1970-1981 | S2R3H | $1,500 | $1,900 |

S3B3H

| 1981 | Brazilian rosewood | $3,000 | $3,750 |

S3M

| 1970-1981 | Mahogany | $1,450 | $1,800 |

S3R/S3R3H

1970-1981. Size 3 with Indian Rosewood, S3R3H has has 3-piece back and herringbone trim.

| 1970-1981 | S3R | $1,500 | $1,900 |
| 1970-1981 | S3R3H | $1,600 | $2,000 |

Guild D-55

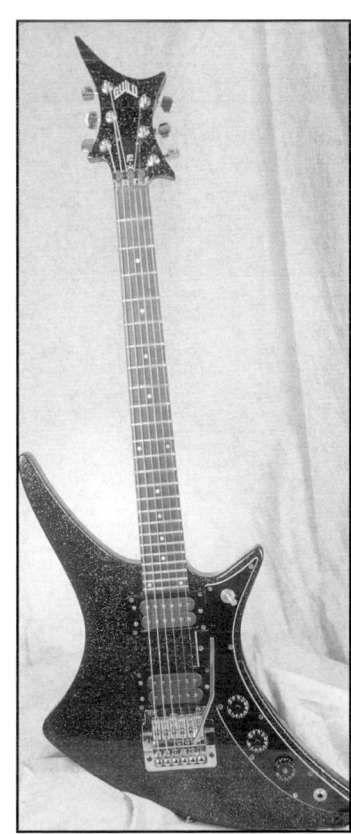

'83 Guild X-79 Skyhawk

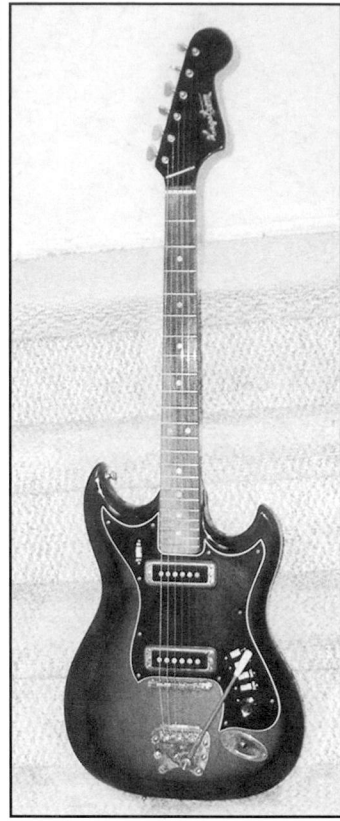

1965 Hagstrom Model II
Bill Cherensky

Halfling Jazz

MODEL YEAR	FEATURES	EXC. COND. LOW	HIGH

Guyatone

1933-present. Made in Tokyo by Matsuki Seisakujo, founded by Hawaiian guitarists Mitsuo Matsuki and Atsuo Kaneko (later of Teisco). Guya brand Rickenbacker lap copies in '30s. After a hiatus for the war ('40-'48), Seisakujo resumes production of laps and amps as Matsuki Denki Onkyo Kenkyujo. In '51 the Guyatone brand is first used on guitars and basses, and in '52 they changed the company name to Tokyo Sound Company. Guyatones are among the earliest U.S. imports, branded as Marco Polo, Winston, Kingston and Kent. Other brand names included LaFayette and Bradford. Production and exports slowed after '68.

Hagenlocher, Henner

1996-present. Luthier Henner Hagenlocher builds his premium grade, custom, nylon-string guitars in Granada, Spain.

Hagstrom

1958-1983, 2004-present. Intermediate, professional, and premium grade, production/custom, solidbody, semi-hollowbody and acoustic guitars made in the U.S. and imported. Founded by Albin Hagström of Älvdalen, Sweden, who began importing accordions in 1921 and incorporated in '25. The name of the company was changed to A.B. Hagström, Inc. in '38, and an American sales office was established in '40. Electric guitar and bass production began in '58 with plastic-covered hollowbody De Luxe and Standard models. The guitars were imported into the U.S. by Hershman Music of New York as Goya 90 and 80 from '58-'61. Bass versions were imported in '61. Following a year in the U.S., Albin's son Karl-Erik Hagström took over the company as exclusive distributor of Fender in Scandinavia; he changed the U.S. importer to Merson Musical Instruments of New York (later Unicord in '65), and redesigned the line. The company closed its doors in '83. In 2004 American Music & Sound started manufacturing and distributing the Hagstrom brand under license from A.B. Albin Hagstrom. In 2009 U.S. Music became involved via its acqustion of JAM, and the 'new' Hagstrom established a Swedish office. A new line of instruments under the Vintage Series (made in China) included classic '60s models. Later the Northen series was introduced with instruments made entirely in Europe.

Corvette/Condor

1963-1967. Offset double-cut solidbody, 3 single-coils, multiple push-button switches, spring vibrato, called the Condor on U.S. imports.

1963-1967		$1,000	$1,250

D'Aquisto Jimmy

1969-1975, 1976-1979. Designed by James D'Aquisto, electric archtop, f-holes, 2 pickups, sunburst, natural, cherry or white. The '69 had dot inlays, the later version had blocks. From '77 to '79, another version with an oval soundhole (no f-holes) was also available.

1969-1975	1st design	$1,000	$1,250
1976-1979	2nd design	$1,000	$1,250

MODEL YEAR	FEATURES	EXC. COND. LOW	HIGH

Deluxe Series

2004-2008. Carved single-cut mahogany body, set-neck, 2 humbuckers, sparkle tops or sunburst.

2004-2014	Various models	$200	$400

F Series (China)

2004-present. Offset double-cut basswood body, 2 or 3 pickups.

2004-2014	Various models	$200	$400

H-12 Electric/Viking XII

1965-1967. Double-cut, 2 pickups, 12 strings.

1965-1967		$475	$625

H-22 Folk

1965-1967. Flat-top acoustic.

1965-1967		$350	$450

Impala

1963-1967. Two-pickup version of the Corvette, sunburst.

1963-1967		$800	$1,000

Kent

1962-1967. Offset double-cut solidbody, 2 pickups.

1962-1967		$475	$600

Model

1965-1971. Small double-cut solidbody, 2 single-coils, early models have plastic top.

1965-1969	Rare finish, 6-on-a-side	$700	$1,000
1965-1969	Standard finish, 6-on-a-side	$400	$625
1970-1971	3-on-a-side	$350	$575

Model II/F-200 Futura/H II

1965-1972, 1975-1976. Offset double-cut slab body with beveled edge, 2 pickups, called F-200 Futura in U.S., Model II elsewhere, '75-'76 called H II. F-200 reissued in 2004.

1965-1970	Rare finish, 6-on-a-side	$700	$1,000
1965-1970	Standard finish, 6-on-a-side	$400	$625
1970-1972	3-on-a-side	$350	$575

Model III/F-300 Futura/H III

1965-1972, 1977. Offset double-cut slab body with beveled edge, 3 pickups, called F-300 Futura in U.S., Model III elsewhere, '77 called H III.

1965-1972		$700	$1,000
1977		$500	$650

Swede

1970-1982, 2004-present. Bolt-on neck, single-cut solidbody, black, cherry or natural, '04 version is set-neck.

1979-1982		$800	$1,000

Super Swede

1979-1983, 2004-present. Glued-in neck upgrade of Swede, '04 version is maple top upgrade of Swede.

1979-1983		$1,000	$1,250
1979-1983	Custom color	$1,350	$1,700
2004-2014	Reissue	$320	$400

Viking/V1

1965-1975, 1978-1979, 2004-present. Double-cut thinline, 2 f-holes, 2 pickups, chrome hardware, dot inlays, also advertised as the V-1. '60s had 6-on-side headstock, '70s was 3-and-3, latest version back to 6-on-side.

1965-1969		$1,000	$1,250
1970-1975		$900	$1,125
2004-2014	Reissue	$320	$400

The *Vintage Guitar Price Guide* shows low to high values for items in all-original excellent condition, and, where applicable, with original case or cover.

MODEL YEAR FEATURES	EXC. COND. LOW	HIGH

Viking Deluxe/V2

1967-1968, 2004-present. Upscale version, gold hardware, block inlays, bound headstock and f-holes. Current version upgrades are blocks and flame maple.

1967-1968	$1,200	$1,500
2004-2014 Reissue	$320	$400

Hahn

2007-present. Professional and premium grade, custom electric guitars built by luthier Chihoe Hahn in Garnerville, New York.

Haight

1989-present. Premium and presentation grade, production/custom, acoustic (steel and classical) guitars built in Scottsdale, Arizona by luthier Norman Haight. He also builds mandolins.

Halfling Guitars and Basses

2003-present. Luthier Tom Ribbecke builds premium grade, production/custom, pin bridge, thinline and jazz guitars and basses in Healdsburg, California.

Hallmark

1965-1967, 2004-present. Imported and U.S.-made, intermediate and premium grade, production/custom, guitars and basses from luthiers Bob Shade and Bill Gruggett, and located in Greenbelt, Maryland. They also make basses. The brand was originally founded by Joe Hall in Arvin, California, in '65. Hall had worked for Semie Moseley (Mosrite) and had also designed guitars for Standel in the mid-'60s. Bill Gruggett, who also built his own line of guitars, was the company's production manager. Joe Hall estimates that less than 1000 original Hallmark guitars were built. The brand was revived by Shade in '04.

Sweptwing

1965-1967. Pointed body, sorta like a backwards Flying V.

1965-1967	$2,000	$2,500

Hamblin Guitars

1996-present. Luthier Kent Hamblin built his premium grade, production/custom, flat-top acoustic guitars in Phoenix, Arizona and Telluride, Colorado, and presently builds in Colorado Springs.

Hamer

1974-2012. Intermediate, professional and premium grade, production/custom, electric guitars made in the U.S. and overseas. Hamer also made basses and the Slammer line of instruments. Founded in Arlington Heights, Illinois, by Paul Hamer and Jol Dantzig. Prototype guitars built in early-'70s were on Gibson lines, with first production guitar, the Standard (Explorer shape), introduced in '75. Hamer was puchased by Kaman Corporation (Ovation) in '88. The Illinois factory was closed and the operations were moved to the Ovation factory in Connecticut in '97. On January 1, '08, Fender acquired Kaman Music Corporation and the Hamer brand. In '90, they started the Korean-import Hamer Slammer series which in '97 became Hamer Import Series (no Slammer on headstock). In '05 production was moved to China and name changed to XT Series (in '07 production moved to Indonesia). The U.S.-made ones have U.S.A. on the headstock. The less expensive import Slammer brand (not to be confused with the earlier Slammer Series) was introduced in '99 (see that listing). Fender suspended production of the Hamer brand at the end of 2012.

Artist/Archtop Artist/Artist Custom

1995-2012. U.S.-made, similar to Sunburst Archtop with semi-solid, f-hole design, sunburst, named Archtop Artist, then renamed Artist (with stop tailpiece)/Artist Custom in '97.

1995-2012	Higher-end specs	$1,000	$1,250
1995-2012	Standard specs	$800	$1,000

Artist 25th Anniversary Edition

1998. Made in USA, 25th Anniversary Edition script logo on headstock.

1998	$800	$1,000

Artist Korina

2001-2012. Double-cut, bass f-hole, korina (limba) body and neck, 2 P-90s or 2 humbuckers (HB), natural gloss finish.

2001-2012	$1,100	$1,350

Blitz

1982-1984 (1st version), 1984-1990 (2nd version). Explorer-style body, 2 humbuckers, three-on-a-side peghead, dot inlays, choice of tremolo or fixed bridge, second version same except has angled six-on-a-side peghead and Floyd Rose tremolo.

1982-1984	3-on-a-side	$950	$1,150
1984-1990	6-on-a-side	$750	$900

Californian

1987-1997. Made in USA, solidbody double cut, bolt neck, 1 humbucker and 1 single-coil, Floyd Rose tremolo.

1987-1989	$1,100	$2,200
1990-1997	$800	$2,000

Californian Custom

1987-1997. Made in USA, downsized contoured body, offset double-cut, neck-thru-body, optional figured maple body, Duncan Trembucker and Trem-single pickups.

1987-1989	$1,000	$2,200
1990-1997	$800	$2,000

Californian Elite

1987-1997. Made in USA, downsized contoured body, offset double-cut, optional figured maple body, bolt-on neck, Duncan Trembucker and Trem-single pickups.

1987-1989	$1,000	$2,200
1990-1997	$800	$2,000

Centaura

1989-1995. Alder or swamp ash offset double-cut, bolt-on neck, 1 humbucker and 2 single-coils, Floyd Rose, sunburst.

1989-1995	$600	$750

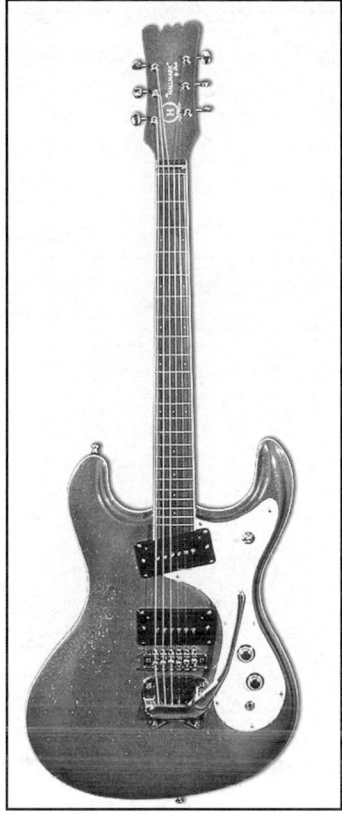

Hallmark 60 Custom

Hamer Artist Korina

Hamer Monaco Elite

1996 Hamer Special
Paul Johnson

MODEL YEAR	FEATURES	EXC. COND. LOW	HIGH

Chaparral
1985-1987 (1st version), 1987-1994 (2nd version). Offset double-cut, glued neck, angled peghead, 1 humbucker and 2 single-coils, tremolo, second version has bolt neck with a modified peghead.

1985-1987	Set-neck	$825	$1,025
1987-1994	Bolt-on neck	$725	$900

Daytona
1993-1997. Offset double-cut, bolt neck, dot inlay, 3 single-coils, Wilkinson tremolo.

1993-1997		$700	$875

Diablo
1992-1997. Offset double-cut, bolt neck, rosewood 'board, dot inlays, reversed peghead '92-'94, 2 pickups, tremolo.

1992-1997		$575	$725

DuoTone
1993-2003. Semi-hollowbody, double-cut, bound top, glued-in neck, rosewood 'board, 2 humbuckers, EQ.

1993-2003		$500	$625

Echotone/Echotone Custom
2000-2002. Thinline semi-hollow archtop, f-holes, 2 humbuckers, trapezoid inlays, gold hardware.

2000-2002		$300	$375

Eclipse
1994-1996. Asymmetrical double-cut slab mahogany body, glued neck, rosewood 'board, 2 Duncan Mini-Humbuckers, cherry.

1994-1996		$600	$750

Eclipse (Import)
1997-1999. Import version.

1997-1999		$240	$300

FB I
1986-1987. Reverse Firebird-style body, glued-in neck, reverse headstock, 1 pickup, rosewood 'board with dot inlays, also available in non-reverse body.

1986-1987		$550	$700

FB II
1986-1987. Reverse Firebird-style, glued-in neck, ebony 'board with boomerang inlays, angled headstock, 2 humbuckers, Floyd Rose tremolo, also available as a 12-string.

1986-1987		$625	$775

Korina Standard
1995-1996. Limited run, Korina Explorer-type body, glued-in neck, angled peghead, 2 humbuckers.

1995-1996		$1,200	$1,500

Maestro
1990. Offset double-cut, 7 strings, tremolo, bolt-on maple neck, 3 Seymour Duncan rail pickups.

1990		$750	$950

Mirage
1994-1998. Double-cut carved figured koa wood top, transparent flamed top, initially with 3 single-coil pickups, dual humbucker option in '95.

1994-1998		$725	$900

Monaco Elite
2003-2012. Single-cut solidbody, 2 humbuckers, mother-of-pearl inlaid 'victory' position markers, mahogany body, flamed maple sunburst.

2003-2012	USA	$1,325	$1,650

Newport Series
1999-2012. USA, double-cut thinline, center block, f-holes, 2 humbuckers (Newport 90 has P-90s), wrap-around bridge tailpiece.

1999-2012	Newport	$1,000	$1,250
1999-2012	Newport Pro	$1,100	$1,375

Phantom A5
1982-1884, 1985-1986 (2nd version). Offset double-cut, glued neck, 3-on-a-side peghead, 1 triple-coil and 1 single-coil pickup, second version same but with 6-on-a-side peghead and Kahler.

1982-1984		$700	$875

Phantom GT
1984-1986. Contoured body, offset double-cut, glued-in fixed neck, six-on-a-side peghead, 1 humbucker, single volume control.

1984-1986		$700	$875

Prototype
1981-1985. Contoured mahogany body, double-cut with 1 splitable triple-coil pickup, fixed bridge, three-on-a-side peghead, Prototype II has extra pickup and tremolo.

1981-1985		$800	$1,000

Scarab I
1984-1986. Multiple cutaway body, six-on-a-side peghead, 1 humbucker, tremolo, rosewood or ebony 'board, dot inlays.

1984-1986		$800	$1,000

Scarab II
1984-1986. Two humbucker version of the Scarab.

1984-1986		$850	$1,050

Scepter
1986-1990. Futuristic-type body, ebony 'board with boomerang inlays, angled six-on-a-side peghead, Floyd Rose tremolo.

1986-1990		$900	$1,125

Slammer Series
1990-1997. Various models imported from Korea, not to be confused with Hamer's current Slammer budget line started in '98.

1990-1997		$175	$400

Special
1980-1983 (1st version), 1984-1985 (Floyd Rose version), 1992-1997 (2nd version). Double-cut solidbody, flame maple top, glued neck, 3-on-a-side peghead, 2 humbuckers, Rose version has mahogany body with ebony 'board, the second version is all mahogany and has tune-o-matic bridge, stop tailpiece and Duncan P-90s, cherry red.

1980-1983	1st version	$850	$1,075
1984-1985	With Floyd Rose	$825	$1,050
1992-1997	2nd version	$800	$1,000

Special FM
1993-1997. Special with flamed maple top, 2 humbuckers, renamed the Special Custom in '97.

1993-1999		$800	$1,000

Standard
1974-1985, 1995-2005. Futuristic body, maple top, bound or unbound body, glued neck, angled headstock, either unbound neck with dot inlays or bound neck with crown inlays, 2 humbuckers. Reissued in '95

MODEL YEAR	FEATURES	EXC. COND. LOW	HIGH

with same specs but unbound mahogany body after '97. Higher dollar Standard Custom still available.

1974-1975	Pre-production, about 20 made	$6,500	$10,000
1975-1977	Production, about 50 made, PAFs	$6,300	$7,800
1977-1979	Dimarzio PAF-copies	$3,700	$5,000
1980-1985		$2,700	$3,500
1995-1999		$2,000	$2,500
2000-2005	USA, flamed top	$2,000	$2,500

Standard (Import, XT)
1998-2012. Import version, 2 humbuckers.

1998-2012		$260	$325

Standard Custom GSTC
2007-2012. Made in USA, flamed maple top, mahogany neck, rosewood 'board.

2007-2012		$2,250	$2,800

Stellar 1
1999-2000. Korean import, double-cut, 2 humbuckers.

1999-2000		$130	$160

Steve Stevens I
1984-1992. Introduced as Prototype SS, changed to Steve Stevens I in '86, contoured double-cut, six-on-a-side headstock, dot or crown inlays, 1 humbucker and 2 single-coil pickups.

1984-1992		$800	$1,000

Steve Stevens II
1986-1987. One humbucker and 1 single-coil version.

1986-1987		$800	$1,000

Studio
1993-2012. Double-cut, flamed maple top on mahogany body, 2 humbuckers, cherry or natural.

1993-2012		$1,000	$1,300

Studio Custom
1997-2012. Carved figured maple, humbuckers, tune-o-matic bridge, stop tailpiece, sunburst.

1997-2012		$1,100	$1,500

Sunburst
1977-1983, 1990-1992. Double-cut bound solidbody, flamed maple top, glue-in neck, bound neck and crown inlays optional, 3-on-a-side headstock, 2 humbuckers.

1977-1979		$2,100	$2,600
1980-1983	Arlington Heights built	$2,000	$2,500
1990-1992		$1,450	$1,800

Sunburst (Import, XT)
1997-2012. Import version of Sunburst, flat-top or archtop, 2 pickups.

1997-2012		$175	$225

Sunburst Archtop
1991-1997. Sunburst model with figured maple carved top, 2 humbuckers, offered under various names: Standard - unbound neck and dot inlays, tune-o-matic and stop tailpiece '91-'93 (replaced by the Studio). Custom - bound neck and crown inlays '91-'93, which became the Archtop for '94-'97 (replaced by the Studio Custom). Archtop GT - Gold top with P-90 soapbar-style pickups '93-'97.

1991-1997	Various models	$1,100	$1,500

T-51
1993-1997. Classic single-cut southern ash body, 2 single-coils.

1993-1997		$875	$1,100

T-62
1991-1995. Classic offset double-cut solidbody, tremolo, pau ferro 'board, Lubritrak nut, locking tuners, 3-band active EQ, various colors.

1991-1995		$875	$1,100

TLE
1986-1992. Single-cut mahogany body, maple top, glued neck, 6-on-a-side headstock, rosewood 'board, dot inlays, 3 pickups.

1986-1992		$925	$1,150

TLE Custom
1986-1992. Bound, single-cut solidbody with maple top, glued-in neck, angled headstock, ebony 'board with boomerang inlays, 3 pickups.

1986-1992		$925	$1,150

Vector
1982-1985. V-style body (optional flame maple top), 3-on-a-side peghead, rosewood 'board, 2 humbuckers, Sustain Block fixed bridge (Kahler or Floyd Rose tremolos may also be used).

1982-1985	Maple top	$950	$1,200
1982-1985	Regular top	$900	$1,125

Vector Limited Edition Korina
1997. 72 built in Hamer's Arlington Heights, Illinois shop, price includes original Hamer Certificate of Authenticity with matching serial number, Flying-V Vector style body, gold hardware, natural finish.

1997		$2,200	$2,750

Hanson
2009-present. Founders John and Bo Pirruccello import intermediate grade, electric guitars which are set up in Chicago, Illinois.

Harden Engineering
1999-present. Professional grade, custom, solidbody guitars built by luthier William Harnden in Chicago, Illinois. He also builds effects pedals.

Harmony
1892-1976, late 1970s-present. Huge, Chicago-based manufacturer of fretted instruments, mainly budget models under the Harmony name or for many other American brands and mass marketers. Harmony was at one time the largest guitar builder in the world. In its glory days, Harmony made over one-half of the guitars built in the U.S., with '65 being their peak year. But by the early-'70s, the crash of the '60s guitar boom and increasing foreign competition brought an end to the company.

The Harmony brand appeared on Asian-built instruments starting in the late '70s to the '90s with sales mainly is mass-retail stores. In 2000, the Harmony brand was distributed by MBT International. In '02, former MBT marketing director Alison Gillette launched Harmony Classic Reissue Guitars and Basses and in '09 the trademark was acquired

Hamer Standard Custom GSTC

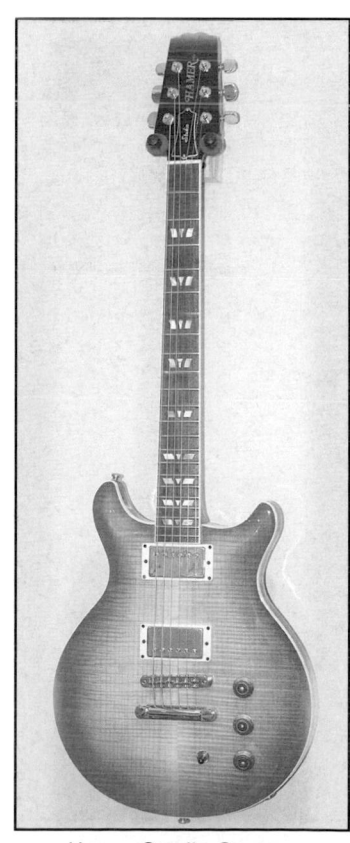

Hamer Studio Custom
Rob Bernstein

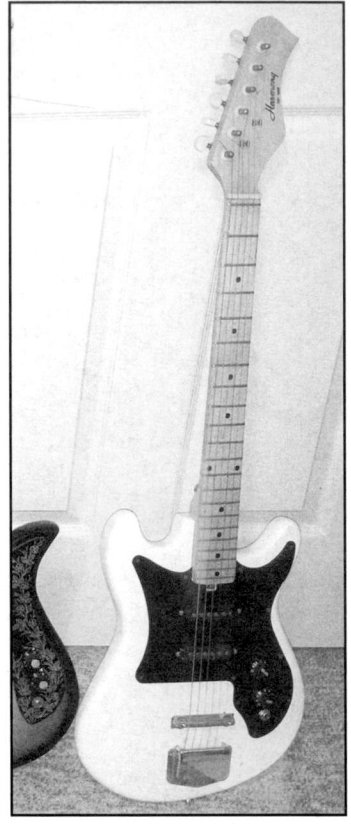

1970s Harmony
Jim Edwards

1938 Harmony Cremona
George Cox

by Westheimer Corporation.

Many Harmony guitars have a factory order number on the inside back of the guitar which often contains the serial number. Most older Harmony acoustics and hollowbodies have a date ink-stamped inside the body. DeArmond made most of the electronic assemblies used on older Harmony electrics, and they often have a date stamped on the underside.

Amplifying Resonator Model 27
1930s. Dobro-licensed with Dobro metal resonator, wood body.

Year	Features	Low	High
1930s		$700	$875

Archtone H1215/H1215 Tenor
1950s. Lower-end archtop, sunburst.

Year	Features	Low	High
1950-1960s	4-string tenor	$250	$335
1950-1960s	6-string	$250	$335

Bob Kat H14/H15
1968. Replaces Silhouette solidbody, H14 has single pickup and 2 knobs, H15 has 2 pickups. When vibrato is added it becomes the H16 model.

Year	Features	Low	High
1968	H14	$325	$400
1968	H15	$425	$525

Brilliant Cutaway H1310/H1311
1962-1965. 16 1/2" body (Grand Auditorium), acoustic archtop cutaway, block markers, sunburst.

Year	Features	Low	High
1962-1965		$625	$775

Broadway H954
1930s-1971. 15-3/4" body, acoustic archtop, dot markers, sunburst.

Year	Features	Low	High
1960-1971		$235	$290

Buck Owens
1969. Acoustic flat-top, red, white and blue. The price shown is for a guitar that has an unblemished finish, paint-wear will reduce the price, prices vary considerable due to the condition of the finish.

Year	Features	Low	High
1969		$1,200	$1,900

Cremona
1930s-1952. Full-size archtop line, Harmony and Cremona logo on headstock, natural. Cutaways became available in '53.

Year	Features	Low	High
1940-1952		$310	$385

D Series (Electric)
Late-1980s-Early-1990s. Classic electric copy models including offset double- and single-cut solidbody and double-cut thin hollowbody (D720), 1 to 3 pickups. All models begin with D, some models part of Harmony Electric series and others the Harmony Igniter series.

Year	Features	Low	High
1980s-90s	Various models	$85	$105

Espanada H63
1950s-1965. Thick body, single-cut, jazz-style double pickups, black finish with white appointments, by early '60s 'Espanada' logo on lower bass bout.

Year	Features	Low	High
1950s-1965		$1,360	$1,700

Folk H165/H6365
1958-1974. Square-shouldered flat-top, all mahogany body. Renamed the H6365 in '72.

Year	Features	Low	High
1958-1974		$400	$500

Grand Concert H165
1948-1957. Flat-top, all mahogany body. Body changed to square-shoulder in '58 (see Folk H165).

Year	Features	Low	High
1948-1957		$400	$500

H/HG Series (Electric)
Late-1980s-Early-1990s. Classic electric copy models including offset double-cut, single-cut and double-cut semi-hollow, 1 to 3 pickups, with or without tremolo. All models begin with H or HG, some models part of Harmony Electric series and others the Harmony Igniter series.

Year	Features	Low	High
1980s-90s	Various models	$55	$100

H60 Double Cutaway Hollowbody
1970. Thinline double-cut, 2 pickups, trapeze tailpiece, sunburst.

Year	Features	Low	High
1970		$775	$975

H62 Blond
1950s-1965. Thin body, dual pickup archtop, curly maple back and sides, spruce top, block markers, blond.

Year	Features	Low	High
1950s-1965		$1,250	$1,575

H62VS (Reissue)
2000s. H62 with sunburst finish.

Year	Features	Low	High
2000s		$835	$1,035

H64 Double Cutaway Electric
1968-1970. Factory Bigsby, dot markers, sunburst.

Year	Features	Low	High
1968-1970		$680	$860

H72/H72V Double Cutaway Hollowbody
1966-1971. Multiple bindings, 2 pickups, cherry red, H72V has Bigsby.

Year	Features	Low	High
1966-1971		$800	$1,000

H73 Double Cutaway Hollowbody
1960s. Double cutaway, 2 pickups.

Year	Features	Low	High
1960s		$575	$725

H74 Thinline
1964. Thinline, partial cutaway on bass bout, full cutaway on treble bout, 2 pickups.

Year	Features	Low	High
1964		$690	$860

H75 Double Cutaway Hollowbody
1960-1970. Three pickups, multi-bound body, 3-part f-holes, block inlays, bolt neck, brown sunburst.

Year	Features	Low	High
1960-1970		$1,025	$1,275

H76 Double Cutaway Hollowbody
1960-1962. H75 with Bigsby.

Year	Features	Low	High
1960-1962		$1,125	$1,375

H77 Double Cutaway Hollowbody
1964-1970. Same as H75, but in cherry sunburst.

Year	Features	Low	High
1964-1970		$900	$1,125

H78 Double Cutaway Hollowbody
Late-1960s. H78 with Bigsby.

Year	Features	Low	High
1960s		$815	$1,015

H79 Double Cutaway Hollowbody 12-String
1966-1970. Unique slotted headstock, cherry finish.

Year	Features	Low	High
1966-1970		$750	$950

H910 Classical
1970s. Beginner guitar, natural.

Year	Features	Low	High
1970s		$80	$100

H1200 Auditorium Series
1948-1975. Moderately-priced acoustic archtop, treble-clef artwork on headstock, model 1213 & 1215 (shaded brown sunburst) and 1214 (blond ivory, ends in '64). Model 1215 was renamed H6415 in '72 and lasted until '75.

Year	Features	Low	High
1948-1964	H1214 blond	$260	$330
1948-1975	H1215 sunburst	$260	$330

MODEL YEAR	FEATURES	EXC. COND. LOW	HIGH

H1270 12-String Flat-Top
1965. 16" deluxe acoustic 12-string flat-top, spruce top, mahogany sides and back, dot markers.

1965		$535	$665

H1310 Brilliant Cutaway
1953-1973. Grand Auditorium acoustic archtop, single rounded cutaway, block inlays, sunburst. Called H6510 in '72.

1953-1973		$610	$760

H1311 Brilliant Cutaway
1953-1962. As H 1310, but in blond.

1953-1963		$660	$810

H4101 Flat-Top Tenor
1972-1976. Mahogany body, 4-string.

1972-1976		$350	$440

Holiday Rocket
Mid-1960s. Similar to H59 Rocket III but with push-button controls instead of rotary selector switch, 3 Goldentone pickups, pickup trim rings, Holiday logo on 'guard, higher model than standard Rocket.

1960s		$1,035	$1,300

Hollywood H37
1960-1961. Electric archtop, auditorium size 15.75" body, 1 pickup, 2-tone gold metallic finish, block markers.

1960-1961		$625	$775

Hollywood H39
1960-1965. Like H37 but with sunburst.

1960-1965		$475	$600

Hollywood H41
1960-1965. Like H37 but with 2 pickups, sunburst.

1960-1965		$490	$610

Igniter Series (D/H/HG)
Late-1980s-Early-1990s. Pointy-headstock electric copy models, offset double-cut, all models begin with D, H, or HG.

1980s-90s	Various models	$90	$110

Lone Ranger
1950-1951. Lone Ranger headstock stencil, Lone Ranger and Tonto stencil on brown body. This model was first introduced in 1936 as the Supertone Lone Ranger with same stencil on a black body.

1950-1951		$290	$360

Master H945
1965-1966. 15" (Auditorium) acoustic archtop, block markers, music note painted logo on headstock, sunburst.

1965-1966		$310	$385

Meteor H70/H71
1958-1966. Single rounded cutaway 2" thin body, 2 pickups, 3-part f-holes, block inlays, bolt neck, H70 sunburst, H71 natural (ended '65), lefty offered '65-'66, reintroduced as H661 and H671 (without Meteor name) in '72-'74.

1958-1965	H71, natural	$1,075	$1,350
1958-1966	H70, sunburst	$1,075	$1,350

Modern Trend H65
1956-1960. Short-scale electric thin body archtop, 1 single-coil, block inlays, sherry blond finish on curly maple grain.

1956-1960		$700	$875

Monterey H950/H952/H1325/H1456/ H1457/H6450
1930s-1974. Line of Auditorium and Grand Auditorium acoustic archtop models.

1950s	H952 Colorama	$370	$460
1950s	Other models	$240	$300
1960s		$240	$300
1970s	H6450	$160	$200

Patrician
1932-1973. Model line mostly with mahogany bodies and alternating single/double dot markers (later models with single dots), introduced as flat-top, changed to archtop in '34. In '37 line expanded to 9 archtops (some with blocks) and 1 flat-top. Flat-tops disappeared in the '40s, with various archtops offered up to '73.

1932-1973		$370	$460

Professional H1252 Hawaiian
1940. Hawaiian acoustic jumbo, high-end appointments, vertical Professional logo on front of headstock, figured koa or mahogany back and sides, spruce top, Brazilian rosewood fretboard, various-shaped fretboard markers.

1940		$2,400	$3,000

Robol H81
1968-1971. Single pickup version of Rebel, brown sunburst.

1968-1971		$290	$360

Rebel H82/H82G
Listed as a new model in 1971. Thin body, hollow tone chamber, double-cut, 2 pickups, H82 sunburst, H82G greenburst avacado shading (renumbered as H682 and H683 in '72).

1970s	H82	$475	$600
1970s	H82G	$530	$660

Rocket H53
1959-1973. Single-cut, f-holes, 1 pickup, trapeze, 2-tone brown sunburst ('59-'62) or red sunburst ('63 on).

1959-1969		$460	$575
1970-1973		$310	$385

Rocket H54
1959-1973. Same as H53 but with 2 pickups.

1959-1969		$700	$875
1970-1973		$450	$550

Rocket H59
1959-1973. Same as H53 but with 3 pickups.

1959-1969		$1,200	$1,500
1970-1973		$1,100	$1,375

Roy Rogers H600
1954-1958. 3/4 size, stencil, sold through Sears.

1954-1958		$270	$335

Roy Smeck Arched Model 1442 (Artiste)
1939-ca. 1942. Grand auditorium acoustic archtop, old style Harmony script logo and Roy Smeck Artiste logo on headstock, split rectangle markers, small button tuners, black finish with white guard.

1939-1942		$575	$725

Roy Smeck H73
1963-1964. Electric hollowbody, Roy Smeck logo on headstock or upper bass bout, single neck position silver bar-style pickup or 2 Harmony pickups, standard 4 knobs and toggle, pickup without poles.

1963-1964		$750	$950

1967 Harmony H79 Double Cutaway Hollowbody 12-String
Bill Ruxton

Harmony Roy Smeck H73
Bill Ruxton

Harmony Sovereign
Dave McDermott

1966 Harptone Acoustic
Harry Anderson Jr.

MODEL YEAR	FEATURES	EXC. COND. LOW	HIGH

Silhouette De Luxe Double H19
1965-1969. Double-cut solidbody, deluxe pickups, block markers, advanced vibrato, sunburst.

1965-1969		$510	$635

Silhouette H14/H15/H17
1964-1967. Double-cut solidbody, H14 single pickup, H15 dual pickup, H17 dual with vibrato (offered until '66).

1965-1966	H17	$400	$500
1965-1967	H14	$270	$335
1965-1967	H15	$370	$460

Singing Cowboys H1057
1950s. Western chuck-wagon scene stencil top, Singing Cowboys stenciled on either side of upper bouts, brown background versus earlier Supertone version that had black background.

1950s		$290	$360

Sovereign Jumbo Deluxe H1266
1960s-1970s. Jumbo nearly D-style, 16" wide body with out-size 'guard, natural.

1960s		$525	$655
1970s		$500	$620

Sovereign Jumbo H1260
1960s-1970s. Jumbo shape, 16" wide body, natural.

1960s		$500	$620
1970s		$450	$560

Sovereign Western Special Jumbo H1203
1960s-1970s. 15" wide body, 000-style.

1960s		$550	$700

Stratotone Deluxe Jupiter H49
1958-1965. Single-cut, tone chamber construction, 2 pickups, bound spruce top, curly maple back and 6 control knobs, blond finish.

1958-1965		$1,000	$1,250

Stratotone Doublet H88
1954-1957. Basically 2 pickup H44.

1954-1957		$1,300	$1,750

Stratotone H44
1953-1957. First edition models had small bodies and rounded cutaway, 1 pickup with plain cover using 2 mounting rivets, sometimes called Hershey Bar pickup, '60s models had slightly larger bodies and sharp cutaways, some with headstock logo Harmony Stratotone with atomic note graphic.

1953-1957		$1,300	$1,750

Stratotone Mars Electric H45/H46
1958-1968. Single-cut, tone chamber construction, sunburst finish, H45 with 1 pickup, H46 with 2 pickups.

1960s	H45	$450	$575
1960s	H46	$450	$575

Stratotone Mercury Electric H47/H48
1958-1968. Single-cut, tone chamber construction, H47 with 1 pickup, block inlay and curly maple sunburst top, H48 is the same with a blond top.

1960s	H47	$625	$800
1960s	H48	$625	$800

Stratotone Newport H42/1 H42/2
1957-1958. Brightly colored, single-cut, Newport headstock logo, 1 single-coil. 42/1 in sunshine yellow, /2 in metallic green.

1957-1958		$1,300	$1,750

MODEL YEAR	FEATURES	EXC. COND. LOW	HIGH

TG1201 Tenor
1950s. Spruce top, two-on-a-side tuners, Sovereign model tenor, natural.

1950s		$325	$425

Vibra-Jet H66
1962-1966. Thinline single-cut, 2 pickups, built-in tremolo circuit and control panel knobs and selection dial, sunburst.

1962-1966		$800	$1,000

Harptone

1893-ca. 1975. The Harptone Manufacturing Corporation was located in Newark, New Jersey. They made musical instrument cases and accessories and got into instrument production from 1934 to '42, making guitars, banjos, mandolins, and tiples. In '66 they got back into guitar production, making the Standel line from '67 to '69. Harptone offered flat-tops and archtops under their own brand until the mid-'70s when the name was sold to the Diamond S company, which owned Micro-Frets.

Acoustic
1966-mid-1970s. Various models.

1966-1970s	Common models	$1,025	$1,275
1966-1970s	Fancy models	$1,400	$1,750

Electric
1966-mid-1970s. Various models.

1966-1970s		$1,300	$1,625

Harrison Guitars

1992-present. Luthier Douglas Harrison builds premium grade, production/custom, archtop and semi-hollowbody jazz guitars in Toronto, Ontario.

Harwood

Harwood was a brand introduced in 1885 by Kansas City, Missouri instrument wholesalers J.W. Jenkins & Sons (though some guitars marked Harwood, New York). May have been built by Jenkins until circa 1905, but work was later contracted out to Harmony.

Parlor
1890s. Slotted headstocks, most had mahogany bodies, some with Brazilian rosewood body, considered to be well made.

1890s	Brazilian rosewood	$800	$1,200
1890s	Mahogany	$400	$600

Hascal Haile

Late 1960s-1986. Luthier Hascal Haile started building acoustic, classical and solidbody guitars in Tompkinsville, Kentucky, after retiring from furniture making. He died in '86.

Hauver Guitar

2001-present. Professional and premium grade, custom, acoustic guitars, built in Sharpsburg, Maryland by luthier Michael S. Hauver.

Hayes Guitars

1993-present. Professional and premium grade, production/custom, steel and nylon string guitars made by luthier Louis Hayes in Paonia, Colorado.

MODEL YEAR	FEATURES	EXC. COND. LOW	HIGH

Hayman

1970-1973. Solid and semi-hollowbody guitars and basses developed by Jim Burns and Bob Pearson for Ivor Arbiter of the Dallas Arbiter Company and built by Shergold in England.

Haynes

1865-early 1900s. The John C. Haynes Co. of Boston also made the Bay State brand.

Heartfield

1989-1994. Founded as a joint venture between Fender Musical Instrument Corporation (U.S.A.) and Fender Japan (partnership between Fender and distributors Kanda Shokai and Yamano Music) to build and market more advanced designs (built by Fuji Gen-Gakki). First RR and EX guitar series and DR Bass series debut in '90. Talon and Elan guitar series and Prophecy bass series introduced in '91. The brand was dead by '94.

Elan
1989-1994. Carved-style bound double-cut body, flamed top, 2 humbuckers, offset headstock

1989-1994		$425	$525

EX/EX II
1990-1994. 3 single-coils, Floyd Rose tremolo.

1990-1994		$425	$525

Talon
1989-1994. Offset double-cut, wedge-triangle headstock, dot markers, hum/single/hum pickups.

1989-1994	I, II, III	$340	$425
1989-1994	IV	$405	$510

Heiden Stringed Instruments

1974-present. Luthier Michael Heiden builds his premium grade, production/custom, flat-top guitars in Chilliwack, British Columbia. He also builds mandolins.

Heit Deluxe

Ca. 1967-1970. Imported from Japan by unidentified New York distributor. Many were made by Teisco, the most famous being the Teisco V-2 Mosrite copy. They also had basses.

Acoustic Archtop
1967-1970. Various models.

1967-1970		$130	$200

Electric Solidbody
1967-1970. Various models.

1967-1970		$160	$350

Electric Thinline Hollowbody
1967-1970. Various models.

1967-1970		$190	$350

Hembry Guitars

2002-present. Professional grade, production/custom, solidbody electric guitars built by luthier Scott Hembry in Shelton, Washington. He also builds basses.

Hemken, Michael

1993-present. Luthier Michael Hemken builds his premium grade, custom, archtops in St. Helena, California.

HenBev

2005-present. Premium grade, production, solid and hollow body electric guitars and basses built by luthier Scotty Bevilacqua in Oceanside, California.

Hendrick

1982-1985. Solidbody guitars built by luthier Kurt Hendrick in Texas, Ohio and Michigan. Less than 100 built, the most popular model was the Generator. Hendrick also worked with Schecter, Fender, Jackson and Epiphone.

Henman Guitars

2010-present. Owners Graham and Paris Henman offer premium grade, production/custom, solidbody and chambered electric guitars and basses built by luthier Rick Turner in Santa Cruz, California.

Heritage

1985-present. Professional, premium, and presentation grade, production/custom, hollow, semi-hollow, and solidbody guitars built in Kalamazoo, Michigan. They have also made banjos, mandolins, flat-tops, and basses in the past.

Founded by Jim Deurloo, Marvin Lamb, J.P. Moats, Bill Paige and Mike Korpak, all former Gibson employees who did not go to Nashville when Norlin closed the original Gibson factory in '84. In 2007, Vince Margol bought out Paige.

Eagle
1986-2009. Single rounded cut semi-hollowbody, mahogany body and neck, bound body, 1 jazz pickup, f-holes, sunburst or natural.

1986-2009		$1,700	$2,100

Eagle Classic
1992-present. Eagle with maple body and neck, bound neck and headstock, gold hardware.

1992-2014		$2,200	$2,700

Gary Moore Model
1989-1991. Single-cut solidbody, 2 pickups, chrome hardware, sunburst.

1989-1991		$1,500	$1,850

Golden Eagle
1985-present. Single-cut hollowbody, back inlaid with mother-of-pearl eagle and registration number, multi-bound ebony 'board with mother-of-pearl cloud inlays, bound f-holes, gold-plated parts, ebony bridge inlaid with mother-of-pearl, mother-of-pearl truss rod cover engraved with owner's name, 1 Heritage jazz pickup, multi-bound curly maple 'guard.

1985-1999	Floating pickup	$2,700	$3,400
1985-1999	Mounted pickup	$2,500	$3,100
2000-2014	Floating pickup	$2,800	$3,500
2000-2014	Mounted pickup	$2,600	$3,200

Heiden OM Model

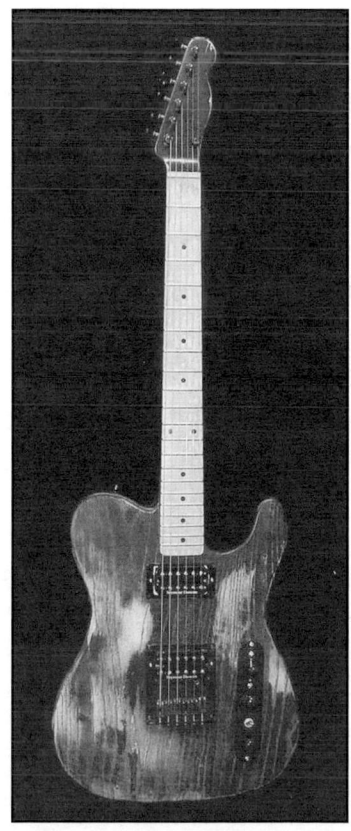

Hembry Ratrod

GUITARS

Heritage Groove Master

Heritage H-150

MODEL		EXC. COND.	
YEAR	FEATURES	LOW	HIGH

Groove Master
2004-present. 16" hollow-body, single rounded cutaway, neck pickup, sunburst.

2004-2014		$1,350	$1,700

H-137
1980s-present. Single-cut solidbody, 2 P-90s, sunburst.

1980s-2014	Sunburst	$800	$1,000
2008	Natural Lime	$900	$1,125

H-140/H-140 CM
1985-2005, 2007-present. Single pointed cutaway solidbody, bound curly maple ('85-'04) or solid gold top ('94-'05), 2 humbuckers, chrome parts.

1985-1996	Black	$900	$1,125
1985-2004	CM, curly maple	$900	$1,125
1994-2005	Goldtop	$900	$1,125
2001	CM, flamed maple	$1,000	$1,250
2007-2014	2nd edition, goldtop	$1,000	$1,250

H-147
1990-1991. Single-cut solidbody, 2 humbuckers, mahogany body, mother-of-pearl block inlays, black with black or gold hardware.

1990-1991		$900	$1,125

H-150 C/H-150 CM
1985-present. Single rounded cutaway solidbody, curly maple top, 2 pickups, chrome parts, cherry sunburst.

1985-2014		$1,325	$1,650
1985-2014	Goldtop	$1,250	$1,550

H-150 Deluxe Limited Edition
1992. 300 made.

1992		$1,350	$1,675

H-157 Ultra
1993-1994. Single-cut solidbody, large block markers, highly figured maple top.

1993-1994		$1,500	$1,900

H-160
1986, 2007. Limited production.

1986		$700	$900
2007	2nd Edition	$800	$1,000

H-170
1980s. Double-cut solidbody, 2 humbuckers, bound carved top, was also a later curly maple top version (H-170CM).

1980s		$1,000	$1,250

H-204 DD
1986-1989. Single-cut solidbody of mahogany, curly maple top, 1-piece mahogany neck, 22-fret rosewood 'board.

1986-1989		$500	$625

H-207 DD
1986-1989. Double-cut solidbody of mahogany, curly maple top, 1-piece mahogany neck, 22-fret rosewood 'board.

1986-1989		$500	$625

H-357
1989-1994. Asymmetrical solidbody, neck-thru.

1989-1994		$1,725	$2,150

H-535
1987-present. Double-cut semi-hollowbody archtop, rosewood 'board, 2 humbucker pickups.

1987-2014		$1,600	$2,000

MODEL		EXC. COND.	
YEAR	FEATURES	LOW	HIGH

H-537
1990. Single-cut, thinline, dots.

1990		$1,200	$1,500

H-550
1990-present. Single-cut hollowbody, laminated maple top and back, multiple bound top, white bound 'guard, f-holes, 2 humbuckers.

1990-2014		$1,350	$1,675

H-555
1989-present. Like 535, but with maple neck, ebony 'board, pearl and abalone inlays, gold hardware.

1989-2014		$1,850	$2,300

H-575
1987-present. Single sharp cut hollowbody, solid maple top and back, cream bound top and back, wood 'guard, f-holes, 2 humbuckers.

1987-2014		$1,775	$2,225

H-576
1990-2004. Single rounded cut hollowbody, laminated maple top and back, multiple bound top, single bound back and f-holes and wood 'guard, 2 humbuckers.

1990-2004		$1,250	$1,550

Henry Johnson Signature
2005-present. Pointed single cut curly maple back and sides hollowbody, 2 humbuckers, block inlays, multi-bound.

2005-2014		$1,300	$1,600

HFT-445
1987-2000. Flat-top acoustic, mahogany back and sides, spruce top, maple neck, rosewood 'board.

1987-2000		$650	$800

Johnny Smith
1989-2001. Custom hand-carved 17" hollowbody, single-cut, f-holes, 1 pickup.

1989-2001	Optional colors & inlays	$2,500	$3,300
1989-2001	Sunburst	$2,300	$2,850

Kenny Burrell KB Groove Master
2004-present. Single-cut 16" hollow body, 1 humbucker, gold hardware, block inlays.

2004-2014		$1,600	$2,000

Millennium Eagle 2000
2000-2009. Single-cut semi-solidbody, multiple bound curly maple top, single-bound curly maple back, f-holes, 2 humbuckers, block inlays.

2000-2009		$1,600	$2,000

Millennium Eagle Custom
2000-2009. Like ME 2000 but with curlier maple, multiple bound neck, split block inlays.

2000-2009		$2,000	$2,500

Millennium SAE
2000-2009. Single-cut semi-solidbody, laminated arch top, single cream bound top and back, f-holes, 2 humbuckers.

2000-2009		$1,000	$1,250

Millennium Standard Ultra
2004-present. Single-cut, ultra curly maple top, mahogany back and sides, 1-piece mahogany neck, f-holes, mother of pearl block inlays.

2004-2014		$1,300	$1,600

The *Vintage Guitar Price Guide* shows low to high values for items in all-original excellent condition, and, where applicable, with original case or cover.

MODEL		EXC. COND.	
YEAR	FEATURES	LOW	HIGH

Parsons Street
1989-1992. Offset double-cut, curly maple top on mahogany body, single/single/hum pickups, pearl block markers, sunburst or natural.

1989-1992		$600	$750

Roy Clark
1992-present. Thinline, single-cut semi-hollow archtop, gold hardware, 2 humbuckers, block markers, cherry sunburst.

1992-2014		$1,500	$1,850

SAE Custom
1992-2000. Single-cut maple semi-hollowbody, f-holes, 2 humbuckers and 1 bridge pickup.

1992-2000		$1,000	$1,250

Super Eagle
1988-present. 18" body, single-cut electric archtop, 2 humbuckers.

1989-2014		$2,800	$3,500

Sweet 16
1987-present. Single-cut maple semi-hollowbody, spruce top, 2 pickups, pearl inlays.

1987-2014		$2,000	$2,500

Hermann Hauser

Born in 1882, Hauser started out building zithers and at age 23 added classical guitars and lutes, most built in his shop in Munich, Germany. He died in 1952. His son and grandson and great-granddaughter, Hermann II and III and Kathrin, continued the tradition. The Hermann Hauser's legacy is based on his innovative approach to bracing and top thickness which gave his instruments their own voice. Hermann I Era instruments are linked with Andres Segovia who used them. Hermann II Era instruments are linked with modern players like Julian Bream. Hermann III builds Segovia style and custom-made instruments. Kathrin Hauser, daughter of Hermann III, is a fourth generation builder. The original Hauser shop in Munich was destroyed by Allied bombing in 1946 and was moved to Reisbach in the Bavaria region, where the shop remains. Hauser instruments used paper labels on the inside back. The labels often stipulate the city of construction as well as the Hermann Hauser name. Labels are easily removed and changed, and an original instrument should be authenticated. Beautiful violin-like clear varnish finish ends in '52, approximately 400 instruments were made by Hermann I. Under Hermann II, nitrocellulose lacquer spray replaces varnish in '52, bracing patterns change in the '60s, which was a welcome change for modern players. Instruments should be evaluated on a case by case basis.

Hermann Hauser II

1952-1988. Born in 1911 and the son of Hermann Hauser I, he built between 500 and 600 classical guitars in Germany during his career. He died in 1988.

Hermann Hauser III

1988-present. Hermann III started build guitars in '74, and took over the family business upon the death of his father in '88. He continues to build Segovia style and custom-made classical guitars in Munich, Germany.

Hess

1872-ca. 1940. Located in Klingenthal, Germany, Hess built acoustic and harp guitars, as well as other stringed instruments and accordians.

Hewett Guitars

1994-present. Luthier James Hewett builds his professional and premium grade, custom/production, steel string, archtop jazz, solidbody and harp guitars in Panorama Village, Texas.

Hill Guitar Company

1972-1980, 1990-present. Luthier Kenny Hill builds his professional and premium grade production/custom, classical and flamenco guitars in Felton, California and Michoacan, Mexico.

Hirade Classical

1968-present. Professional grade, production, solid top, classical guitars built in Japan by Takamine. The late Mass Hirade was the founder of the Takamine workshop. He learned his craft from master luthier Masare Kohno. Hirade represents Takamine's finest craftsmanship and material.

HML Guitars

1997-present. Howard Leese custom-designs premium grade, electric guitars, which are built by luthier Jack Pimentel in Puyallup, Washington.

Hoffman Guitars

1971-present. Premium grade, custom flat-tops and harp guitars built by luthier Charles Hoffman in Minneapolis, Minnesota.

Höfner

1887-present. Budget, intermediate, professional and premium grade, production, solidbody, semi-hollow, archtop, acoustic, and classical guitars built in Germany and the Far East. They also produce basses and bowed-instruments. Founded by Karl Höfner in Schonbach, Germany. The company was already producing guitars when sons Josef and Walter joined the company in 1919 and '21 and expanded the market worldwide. They moved the company to Bavaria in '50 and to Hagenau in '97. The S in Hofner model names usually denotes cutaway.

Beatle Electric Model 459TZ
1966-1967. Violin-shaped 500/1 body, block-stripe position markers, transistor-powered flip-fuzz and treble boost, sunburst.

1966-1967		$1,600	$2,000

Beatle Electric Model 459VTZ
1966-1967. Same as Model 459TZ except with vibrato tailpiece, brown (standard) or blond option.

1966-1967	Blond option	$1,600	$2,000
1966-1967	Brown	$1,400	$1,750

Heritage Millennium Ultra Standard

Hewett Grand Concert

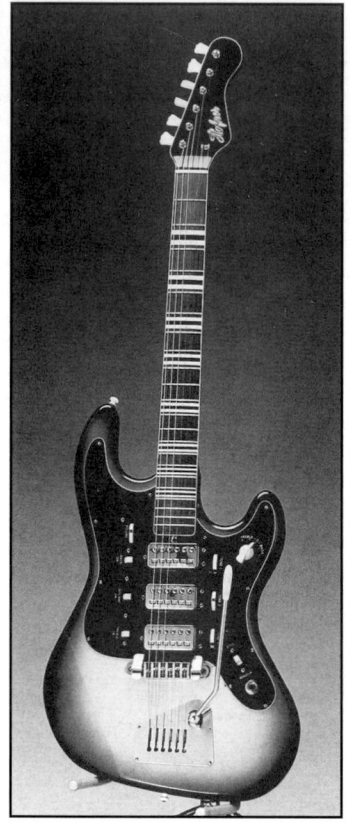

1964 Höfner Deluxe Model 176

Greg Larson

1966 Höfnner Galaxy Model 175

Robbie Keene

MODEL YEAR	FEATURES	EXC. COND. LOW	HIGH

Beatle Electric Model G459TZ Super
1966-1967. Deluxe version of Model 459TZ, flamed maple sides, narrow grain spruce top, gold hardware, elaborate inlays and binding, natural blond.

1966-1967		$1,700	$2,100

Beatle Electric Model G459VTZ Super
1966-1967. Same as G459TZ Super but with vibrato tailpiece.

1966-1967		$1,800	$2,300

Club Model 50
1959-1962. Mid-level of the late '50s 'Club Series', single-cut, 2 pickups, sunburst.

1959-1962		$1,600	$2,000

Club Model 60
1959. Highest model of late '50s 'Club Series', single-cut, 2 black bar pickups, 2 knobs and 2 slider switches on control panel, highest-end split-diamond style markers, natural blond finish.

1959		$1,800	$2,250

Club Model 126
1954-1970. Mid-sized single-cut solidbody, dot markers, flamed maple back and sides, spruce top, sunburst. Listed with Höfner Professional Electric Series.

1954-1958		$850	$1,075

Committee Model 4680 Thin Electric
1961-1968. Thinline single-cut archtop, 2 pickups, split-arrowhead markers, no vibrato, sunburst.

1961-1968		$1,200	$1,500

Deluxe Model 176
1964-1983. Double-cut, 3 pickups, polyester varnished sunburst finish, vibrola tailpiece, similar to Model 175 polyester varnished red and gold version.

1964-1969		$575	$700
1970-1983		$475	$600

Galaxy Model 175
1963-1966. Double-cut, 3 pickups, red and gold vinyl covering, fancy red-patch 'guard, vibrola, similar to Model 176 polyester varnished sunburst version.

1963-1966	Red & gold vinyl	$925	$1,150
1963-1966	Sunburst	$825	$1,050

Golden Höfner
1959-1963. Single-cut archtop, blond, 2 pickups, f-holes.

1959-1963		$7,000	$8,600

Jazzica Custom
2000-2010. Full body, single soft cutaway, acoustic/electric archtop, carved German spruce top, sunburst.

2000-2010		$1,600	$2,000

Model 165
1975-1976. Offset double-cut, S-style body, 2 single-coil pickups, bolt-on neck.

1975-1976		$400	$500

Model 171
1975-1976. Copy of Tele-Thinline.

1975-1976		$350	$450

Model 172 II (R) (S) (I)
1962-1963. Double-cut body, polyester varnished wood (S) or scuff-proof red (R) or white (I) vinyl, 2 pickups, vibrato.

1962-1963		$425	$525

Model 173 II (S) (I)
1962-1963. Double-cut body, polyester varnished wood (S) or scuffproof vinyl (I), 3 pickups, vibrato.

1962-1963	Gold foil vinyl	$550	$700
1962-1963	White vinyl	$550	$700

Model 178
1967-ca. 1969. Offset double-cut solidbody, 2 pickups with an array of switches and push button controls, fancy position markers, vibrola, sunburst. 178 used on different design in the '70s.

1967-1969		$575	$725

Model 180 Shorty Standard
1982. Small-bodied travel guitar, single-cut, solidbody, 1 pickup, travel, the Shorty Super had a built-in amp and speaker.

1982		$300	$375

Model 450S Acoustic Archtop
Mid-1960s. Economy single-cut acoustic archtop in Hofner line, dot markers, Höfner logo on 'guard, sunburst.

1960s		$550	$675

Model 455/S
1950s-1970. Archtop, single-cut, block markers.

1959		$700	$900

Model 456 Acoustic Archtop
1950s-1962. Full body acoustic archtop, f-holes, laminated maple top, sides, back, large pearloid blocks, two color pearloid headstock laminate.

1950s-1962		$725	$900

Model 457 President
1959-1972. Single-cut thinline archtop, 2 pickups, non-vibrato.

1959-1972		$900	$1,125

Model 457/12 12-String Electric
1969-1970. Comfort-thin cutaway archtop, shaded brown.

1969-1970		$700	$900

Model 462 Acoustic Archtop
Ca. 1952-1960s. Single-cut archtop, bound cat's-eye soundholes, 3-piece pearloid headstock overlay, 3-piece large block inlays. Also offered with fingerboard mounted pickup with no controls (EG) and by mid '50s with 1, 2, or 3 pickups with volume and tone knobs/switches (462S/EI, 2, or 3).

1952-1960s	462S	$650	$800
1952-1960s	462SEG	$1,000	$1,250

Model 463
1958-1960. Archtop electric, 2 or 3 pickups.

1958-1960		$1,200	$1,500

Model 470SE2 Electric Archtop
1961-1994. Large single rounded cutaway electric archtop on Höfner's higher-end they call "superbly flamed maple (back and sides), carved top of best spruce," 2 pickups, 3 control knobs, gold hardware, pearl inlay, natural finish only.

1961-1994		$1,000	$1,250

Model 471SE2 Electric Archtop
1969-1977. Large single pointed cutaway electric archtop, flamed maple back and sides, spruce top, black celluloid binding, ebony 'board, pearl inlays, sunburst version of the 470SE2.

1969-1977		$1,000	$1,250

The *Vintage Guitar Price Guide* shows low to high values for items in all-original excellent condition, and, where applicable, with original case or cover.

MODEL		EXC. COND.	
YEAR	FEATURES	LOW	HIGH

Model 490 Acoustic

Late 1960s. 16" body, 12-string, spruce top, maple back and sides, dot markers, natural.

| 1960s | | $265 | $325 |

Model 490E Acoustic Electric

Late 1960s. Flat-top 12-string with on-board pickup and 2 control knobs.

| 1960s | | $360 | $450 |

Model 491 Flat-Top

1960s-1970s. Slope shoulder body style, spruce top, mahogany back and sides, shaded sunburst.

| 1970s | | $360 | $450 |

Model 492 Acoustic

Late 1960s. 16" body, 12-string, spruce top, mahogany back and sides, dot markers.

| 1960s | | $325 | $400 |

Model 492E Acoustic Electric

Late 1960s. Flat-top 12-string with on-board pickup and 2 control knobs.

| 1960s | | $325 | $400 |

Model 496 Jumbo Flat-Top

1960s. Jumbo-style body, selected spruce top, flamed maple back and sides, gold plated hardware, vine pattern 'guard, sunburst.

| 1960s | | $825 | $1,025 |

Model 514-H Classical Concert

1960s. Concert model, lower-end of the Höfner classical line, natural.

| 1960s | | $150 | $225 |

Model 4500 Thin Electric

Late-1960s-early-1970s. Thinline archtop, single-cut, 3 options, laminated maple top and back, dot markers, top mounted controls, brown sunburst.

1960s-70s	E1, 1 pickup	$600	$750
1960s-70s	E2, 2 pickups	$750	$900
1960s-70s	V2, 2 pickups, vibrato	$775	$950

Model 4560 Thin Electric

Late-1960s-early-1970s. Thinline archtop, single-cut, 2 options, laminated maple top and back, 2-color headstock, large block markers, top mounted controls, brown sunburst.

| 1960s-70s | E2 | $800 | $1,000 |
| 1960s-70s | V2, vibrato | $850 | $1,050 |

Model 4574VTZ Extra Thin

Late-1960s-early-1970s. Extra thinline acoustic, 2 pickups.

| 1960s-70s | | $825 | $1,025 |

Model 4575VTZ Extra Thin

Late-1960s-early-1970s. Extra-thinline acoustic, double-cut with shallow rounded horns, 3 pickups, vibrato arm, treble boost and flip-fuzz, straight-line markers.

| 1960s-70s | | $900 | $1,125 |

Model 4578TZ President

1959-1970. Double-cut archtop. 'President' dropped from name by late-'60s and renamed Model 4578 Dual Cutaway, also added sharp horns.

| 1959-1965 | | $850 | $1,075 |
| 1966-1970 | | $750 | $925 |

Model 4600 Thin Electric

Late-1960s-early-1970s. Thinline acoustic, double-

cut, 2 pickups, dot markers, sunburst, V2 with vibrato.

| 1960s-70s | E2 | $750 | $925 |
| 1960s-70s | V2, vibrato | $800 | $975 |

Model 4680 Thin Electric

Late-1960s-early-1970s. Single-cut thinline electric, 2 pickups, 3-in-a-line control knobs, ornate inlays, spruce top, brown sunburst, V2 with vibrato.

| 1960s-70s | E2 | $1,100 | $1,375 |
| 1960s-70s | V2, vibrato | $1,200 | $1,475 |

Model 4700 Thin Electric

Late-1960s-early-1970s. Deluxe version of Model 4680, gold plated appointments and natural finish, V2 with vibrato.

| 1960s-70s | E2 | $1,300 | $1,625 |
| 1960s-70s | V2, vibrato | $1,400 | $1,725 |

Senator Acoustic Archtop

1958-1960s. Floating pickup option available, full body archtop, f-holes, made for Selmer, London.

| 1958-1960 | | $525 | $650 |

Senator E1

1961. Senator full body archtop with single top mounted pickup and controls.

| 1961 | | $775 | $950 |

Verythin Standard

2001-2008. Update of the 1960s Verythin line, 2 humbuckers, f-holes, dot inlays.

| 2001-2008 | | $950 | $1,200 |

Hohner

1857-present. Budget and intermediate grade, production, acoustic and electric guitars and basses. They also have mandolins, banjos and ukuleles. Matthias Hohner, a clockmaker in Trossingen, Germany, founded Hohner in 1857, making harmonicas. Hohner has been offering guitars and basses at least since the early '70s. HSS was founded in 1986 as a distributor of guitars and other musical products. By 2000, Hohner was also offering the Crafter brands of guitars.

Alpha Standard

1987. Designed by Klaus Scholler, solidbody, stereo outputs, Flytune tremolo.

| 1987 | | $175 | $220 |

G 2T/G 3T Series

1980s-1990s. Steinberger-style body, 6-string, neck-thru, locking tremolo.

| 1980s-90s | | $210 | $300 |

Jacaranda Rosewood Dreadnought

1978. Flat-top acoustic.

| 1978 | | $155 | $200 |

Jack

1987-1990s. Mate for Jack Bass. Headless, tone circuit, tremolo, 2 single-coils and 1 humbucker.

| 1987-1992 | | $175 | $220 |

L 59/L 75 Series

Late-1970s-1980s. Classic single-cut solidbody, 2 humbuckers, glued neck, sunburst, 59 has upgrade maple body with maple veneer top.

| 1970s-80s | | $250 | $315 |

Miller Beer Guitar

1985. Solidbody, shaped like Miller beer logo.

| 1985 | | $225 | $280 |

*1967 Höfner Model
457 President*

Clay Harrell

*Late-1950s Höfner Senator
Acoustic Archtop*

Paul Johnson

GUITARS

Hohner GT 76

Holst Arched Flat-Top

MODEL YEAR FEATURES	EXC. COND. LOW	HIGH

Professional
1980s. Single-cut solidbody, maple neck, extra large 'guard, natural.

| 1980s | $230 | $290 |

Professional Series - TE Custom
1980s-1990s. Single-cut solidbody, bolt neck.

| 1980s-90s | $600 | $800 |

Professional Series - TE Prinz
Late 1980s-early 1990s. Based on Prince's No. 1 guitar, 2 single-coils, bolt neck, Professional The Prinz headstock logo, natural.

| 1989-1990 | $600 | $800 |

SE 35
1989-mid-1990s. Semi-hollow thinline, 2 humbuckers, natural.

| 1989 | $310 | $380 |

SG Lion
1980s-1990s. Offset double-cut, pointy headstock, glued neck.

| 1980s-90s | $200 | $250 |

ST Series
1986-1990s. Includes the bolt neck ST 57, ST Special, ST Special S, Viper I, Viper II (snakeskin finish option), ST Victory, ST Metal S, and the ST Custom.

| 1986-1992 | $155 | $200 |

Standard Series - EX Artist
1970s-1980s. Solidbody, 2 humbuckers, gold hardware, neck-thru, solid maple body, rosewood 'board, tremolo.

| 1970s-80s | $200 | $250 |

Standard Series - RR Custom
1970s-1980s. Randy Rhoads V body, 2 humbuckers, chrome hardware, glued neck, mahogany body, rosewood 'board, tremolo.

| 1970s-80s | $200 | $250 |

Standard Series - SR Heavy
1970s-1980s. Hybrid body, 2 humbuckers, neck-thru, solid maple body, rosewood 'board, tremolo.

| 1970s-80s | $200 | $250 |

Holiday
1960s. Electric, acoustic and bass guitars sold by Aldens, a Chicago catalog company. Most models built by Harmony. They also offered mandolins and banjos.

Silhouette Bobcat
1964-1967. Solidbody electric made by Harmony, similar to Harmony Silhouette, offset double-cut, 2 pickups, 4-in-a-row control knobs.

| 1964-1967 | $370 | $460 |

Hollenbeck Guitars
1970-2008. Luthier Bill Hollenbeck built his premium grade, production/custom, hollow and semi-hollow body acoustics and electric guitars in Lincoln, Illinois. Bill passed away in '08.

Hollingworth Guitars
1995-present. Luthier Graham Hollingworth builds his production/custom, premium grade, electric, acoustic and archtop guitars in Mermaid

MODEL YEAR FEATURES	EXC. COND. LOW	HIGH

Beach, Gold Coast, Queensland, Australia. He also builds lap steels.

Holman
1966-1968. Built by the Holman-Woodell guitar factory in Neodesha, Kansas. The factory was started to build guitars for Wurlitzer, but that fell through by '67.

Holst
1984-present. Premium grade, custom, archtop, flat-top, semi-hollow, and classical guitars built in Creswell, Oregon by luthier Stephen Holst. He also builds mandolins. Until '01 he was located in Eugene, Oregon.

Hondo
1969-1987, 1991-2005. Budget grade, production, imported acoustic, classical and electric guitars. They also offered basses, banjos and mandolins. Originally imported by International Music Corporation (IMC) of Fort Worth, Texas, founded by Jerry Freed and Tommy Moore and named after a small town near San Antonio, Texas. Early pioneers of Korean guitarmaking, primarily targeted at beginner market. Introduced their first electrics in '72. Changed brand to Hondo II in '74. Some better Hondos made in Japan '74-'82/'83. In '85 IMC purchases major interest in Jackson/Charvel, and the Hondo line was supplanted by Charvels. 1987 was the last catalog before hiatus. In '88 IMC was sold and Freed began Jerry Freed International and in '91 he revived the Hondo name. Acquired by MBT International in '95, currently part of Musicorp.

Acoustic Flat-Top
1969-1987, 1991-2005.

| 1969-2005 | $80 | $125 |

Electric Hollowbody
1969-1987, 1991-2005.

| 1969-2005 | $160 | $550 |

Electric Solidbody
1969-1987, 1991-2005.

1969-1987	$160	$550
1991-1999	$160	$260
2000-2005	$55	$150

Longhorn 6/12 Doubleneck Copy
1970s-1980s. Copy of Danelectro Longhorn 6/12 Doubleneck guitar, Dano coke bottle-style headstock, white sunburst.

| 1970s-80s | $580 | $715 |

Longhorn Copy
Ca. 1978-1980s. Copy of Danelectro Long Horn guitar, Dano Coke bottle-style headstock, brown-copper.

| 1978-80s | $400 | $500 |

M 16 Rambo-Machine Gun
1970s-1980s. Machine gun body-style, matching machine gun-shaped guitar case, black or red. Price includes original case with form-fit interior; deduct as much as 40% less for non-original case.

| 1970s-80s | $400 | $500 |

MODEL		EXC. COND.	
YEAR	FEATURES	LOW	HIGH

Hopf

1906-present. Intermediate, professional, premium, and presentation grade, production/custom, classical guitars made in Germany. They also make basses, mandolins and flutes.

The Hopf family of Germany has a tradition of instrument building going back to 1669, but the modern company was founded in 1906. Hopf started making electric guitars in the mid-'50s. Some Hopf models were made by others for the company. By the late-'70s, Hopf had discontinued making electrics, concentrating on classicals.

Explorer Standard
1960s. Double-cut semi-hollow, sharp horns, center block, 2 mini-humbuckers.

1960s		$480	$600

Saturn Archtop
1960s. Offset cutaway, archtop-style soundholes, 2 pickups, white, says Saturn on headstock.

1960s		$625	$775

Super Deluxe Archtop
1960s. Archtop, 16 3/4", catseye soundholes, carved spruce top, flamed maple back and sides, sunburst.

1960s		$650	$800

Hopkins

1998-present. Luthier Peter Hopkins builds his presentation grade, custom, hand-carved archtop guitars in British Columbia.

Horabe

Classical and Espana models made in Japan.

Classical

1960-1980s Various models	$250	$650

Hottie

2005-present. In '09, amp builders Jean-Claude Escudie and Mike Bernards added production/custom, professional and premium grade, solidbody electric guitars built by luthier Saul Koll in Portland, Oregon.

House Guitars

2004-present. Luthier Joshua House builds his production/custom, premium grade, acoustic guitars and guitar-bouzoukis in Goderich, Ontario.

Howe-Orme

1897-ca. 1910. Elias Howe and George Orme's Boston-based publishing and distribution buisness offered a variety of mandolin family instruments and guitars and received many patents for their designs. Many of their guitars featured detachable necks.

Hoyer

1874-present. Intermediate grade, production, flat-top, classical, electric, and resonator guitars. They also build basses. Founded by Franz Hoyer, building classical guitars and other instruments. His son, Arnold, added archtops in the late-1940s,

and solidbodies in the '60s. In '67, Arnold's son, Walter, took over, leaving the company in '77. The company changed hands a few times over the following years. Walter started building guitars again in '84 under the W.A. Hoyer brand, which is not associated with Hoyer.

Acoustic
1960s. Acoustic archtop or flat-top.

1960s		$230	$310

Junior
Early-1960s. Solidbody with unusual sharp horn cutaway, single neck pickup, bolt-on neck, dot markers, Arnold Hoyer logo on headstock, shaded sunburst.

1960s		$430	$530

Soloist Electric
1960-1962. Single-cut archtop, 2 pickups, teardrop f-holes, sunburst.

1960-1962		$530	$650

Huerga

1995-present. Professional to presentation grade, production/custom, archtop, flat-top, and metal-front solidbody electric guitars built by luthier Diego Huerga in Buenos Aires, Argentina.

Humming Bird

1947-ca.1975. Japanese manufacturer offering acoustics and electrics. By 1968 making pointy Mosrite inspirations. Probably not imported into the U.S.

Electric Solidbody

1950s		$130	$225

Humphrey, Thomas

1970-2008. Premium and presentation grade, custom, nylon-string guitars built by luthier Thomas Humphrey in Gardiner, New York. In 1996 Humphrey began collaborating with Martin Guitars, resulting in the Martin C-TSH and C-1R. Often the inside back label will indicate the year of manufacture. Humphrey died in April, 2008.

Classical
1976-1984. Brazilian or Indian rosewood back and sides, spruce top, traditionally-based designs evolved over time with Millenium becoming a benchmark design in 1985, values can increase with new designs. Valuations depend on each specific instrument and year and type of construction, price ranges are guidance only; each instrument should be evaluated on a case-by-case basis.

1976-1984		$4,700	$5,800

Millennium (Classical)
1985-2008. Professional performance-grade high-end classical guitar with innovative taper body design and elevated 'board, tops are generally spruce (versus cedar) with rosewood back and sides.

1995-2008		$8,000	$10,000

Steel String
1974. D-style, only 4 made.

1974		$2,600	$3,200

Hopkins Marquis

House Guitars Salvaged Sinker

Hutchins Memphis

Ian A. Guitars Standard

MODEL YEAR	FEATURES	EXC. COND. LOW	HIGH

Huss and Dalton Guitar Company

1995-present. Luthiers Jeff Huss and Mark Dalton build their professional and premium grade flat-tops and banjos in Staunton, Virginia.

Hutchins

2006-present. Gary Hutchins in Sussex, U.K. imports intermediate and professional grade, production, acoustic and electric guitars and basses from China, Germany and Korea.

Ian A. Guitars

1991-present. In the early 1990s luthier Ian Anderson built guitars under his name, in 2005 he began using the Ian A. brand. He builds premium grade, production/custom, solidbody electric guitars in Poway, California.

Ibanez

1932-present. Budget, intermediate, and professional grade, production/custom, acoustic and electric guitars. They also make basses, amps, mandolins, and effects.

Founded in Nagoya, Japan, by Matsujiro Hoshino as book and stationary supply, started retailing musical instruments in 1909, importing them by '21. The company's factories were destroyed during World War II, but the business was revived in '50. The Ibanez name in use by 1957. Junpei Hoshino, grandson of founder, became president in '60; a new factory opened called Tama Seisakusho (Tama Industries). Brand names by '64 included Ibanez, Star, King's Stone, Jamboree and Goldentone, supplied by 85 factories serving global markets. Sold acoustic guitars to Harry Rosenblum of Elger Guitars ('59-ca.'65) in Ardmore, Pennsylvania, in early-'60s. Around '62 Hoshino purchased 50% interest in Elger Guitars, and ca. '65 changed the name to Ibanez.

Jeff Hasselberger headed the American guitar side beginning '73-'74, and the company headquarters were moved to Cornwells Heights, Pennsylvania in '74. By '75 the instruments are being distributed by Chesbro Music Company in Idaho Falls, Idaho, and Harry Rosenblum sells his interest to Hoshino shortly thereafter. Ca. '81, the Elger Company becomes Hoshino U.S.A. An U.S. Custom Shop was opened in '88.

Most glued-neck guitars from '70s are fairly rare. Dating: copy guitars begin ca. '71. Serial numbers begin '75 with letter (A-L for month) followed by 6 digits, the first 2 indicating year, last 4 sequential (MYYXXXX). By '88 the month letter drops off. Dating code stops early-'90s; by '94 letter preface either F for Fuji or C for Cort (Korean) manufacturer followed by number for year and consecutive numbers (F4XXXX=Fuji, C4XXXX=Cort, 1994).

Pickups on Asian import electric guitars from the '50s-'70s are often considered to be the weakest engineering specification on the instrument. Old Ibanez pickups can become microphonic and it is not unusual to see them replaced.

MODEL YEAR	FEATURES	EXC. COND. LOW	HIGH

AE (Acoustic Electric) Series
1983-present. Models include AE, AEF, AEL flat-tops (no archtops).
| 1983-2014 | Various models | $100 | $400 |

AH10 (Allan Holdsworth)
1985-1987. Offset double-cut solidbody, bolt neck, bridge humbucker, dots, various colors.
| 1985-1987 | 1 pickup | $350 | $400 |

AH20 (Allan Holdsworth)
1986. As AH10 but with 2 humbuckers.
| 1986 | 2 pickups | $375 | $425 |

AM Series
1985-1991. Small body archtops, models include AM70, 75, 75T, 100, 225. Becomes Artstar in '92.
| 1985-1991 | Various models | $500 | $800 |

AM Stagemaster Series
1983-1984, 1989-1990. Made in Japan, small double-cut semi-hollow body, 2 humbuckers, models include AM50, 100, 205, 255. Model name used again, without Stagemaster in '89-'90.
| 1983-1984 | | $600 | $750 |

AR50 "Jr. Artist"
1979-1983. Double-cut solidbody, dot markers, 2 humbuckers.
| 1979-1983 | | $450 | $550 |

AR100 Artist
1979-1984. Double-cut solidbody, set neck, maple top, 2 humbuckers.
| 1979-1984 | | $650 | $800 |

AR300 Artist
1979-1982. Symmetrical double-cut, carved maple top.
| 1979-1982 | | $650 | $800 |

AR500 Artist
1979-1982. 2 humbuckers, EQ.
| 1979-1982 | | $800 | $1,000 |

Artcore Series
2002-present. Made in China, hollowbody electric, models include AF, AG, AK, AM, AS and TM.
| 2002-2014 | Various models | $200 | $550 |

AS50 Artist
1980-1981. Made in Japan, semi-acoustic.
| 1980-1981 | | $600 | $700 |

AS50 Artstar
1998-1999. Laminated maple body, bound rosewood 'board, dot inlays, 2 humbuckers.
| 1998-1999 | | $500 | $625 |

AS80 Artstar
1994-2002. Made in Korea, double cut semi-hollow body, dots, 2 humbuckers.
| 1994-2002 | | $500 | $625 |

AS100 Artist
1979-1981. Set neck, gold hardware.
| 1979-1981 | | $1,000 | $1,200 |

AS180 Artstar
1997-1999. Double cut semi-hollow body, plain top, dots, 2 humbuckers.
| 1997-1999 | | $900 | $1,100 |

AS200 Artist
1979-1986. Double-cut semi-acoustic, flamed maple, block markers, gold hardware, 2 humbuckers,

MODEL YEAR	FEATURES	EXC. COND. LOW	HIGH
replaced Artist 2630. Artist dropped from name when model becomes hollowbody archtop in '82.			
1979-1986		$1,300	$1,600
AS200 Artstar			
1992-2000. Flame maple top, gold hardware, 2 humbuckers, block inlays.			
1992-2000		$1,100	$1,400
AW Artwood Series			
1979-present. Electric/acoustics, various models.			
1979-2014	Various models	$150	$500
BL Blazer Series			
1980-1982, 1997-1998. Offset double-cut, 10 similar models in the '80s with different body woods and electronic configurations. Series name returns on 3 models in late '90s.			
1980-1982	Various models	$300	$350
1997-1998	Various models	$250	$300
Bob Weir Model 2681			
1975-1980, 1995. Double-cut ash solidbody, ebony 'board, tree-of-life inlay, gold-plated pickups, limited numbers. Reintroduced as a limited run in '95.			
1975-1980		$1,600	$2,000
Bob Weir Standard Model 2680			
1976-1980. Standard production model of 2681.			
1976-1980		$1,200	$1,500
Bob Weir Model One BWM1 (Cowboy Fancy)			
2005. Double-cut swamp ash solidbody, ebony 'board, pearl vine inlay down neck and part way around body, 30 made.			
2005		$2,800	$3,500
Challenger 2552ASH			
1977-1978. T-style ash solidbody.			
1977-1978		$350	$425
CN100 Concert Standard			
1978-1979. Double-cut solidbody, set neck, 2 humbuckers, chrome hardware, dot markers.			
1978-1979		$250	$300
CN200 Concert Custom			
1978-1979. Carved maple top, mahogany body, 7 layer black/white binding, bolt-on neck, gold hardware, block inlays, 2 Super 80 pickups.			
1978-1979		$400	$500
CN250 Concert			
1978-1979. Like CN200 but with vine inlay.			
1978-1979		$575	$700
DG350 Destroyer II			
1986-1987. X Series, modified X-shaped basswood body, flame maple top, 2 humbuckers, trem.			
1986-1987		$375	$475
DT50 Destroyer II			
1980-1982. Modified alder Explorer body, 6-in-line headstock, bolt neck, 2 humbuckers, thick paint.			
1980-1982		$500	$600
DT150 Destroyer II			
1982-1984. Like DT50 but birch/basswood, 1 humbucker.			
1982-1984		$500	$600
DT155 Destroyer II			
1982-1984. Like DT150 but with 3 humbuckers.			
1982-1984		$800	$1,000

MODEL YEAR	FEATURES	EXC. COND. LOW	HIGH
DT350 Destroyer II			
1984-1985. X Series, opaque finish, 1 humbucker, trem.			
1984-1985		$275	$375
DT400 Destroyer II			
1980-1982. Modified mahogany Explorer body, flame maple top, 6-in-line headstock, set-neck, 2 humbuckers, cherry sunburst. Model changed to DT500 in '82.			
1980-1982		$400	$500
DT500 Destroyer II			
1982-1984. Replaced the DT400, flame maple top.			
1982-1984		$400	$500
DT555 Destroyer II Phil Collen			
1983-1987. Bound basswood solidbody, 3 humbuckers, vibrato, black.			
1983-1987		$1,800	$2,250
DTX120 Destroyer			
2000-2004. X Series, known as the Millennium Destroyer, 2 humbuckers.			
2000-2004		$225	$280
EX Series			
1988-1993. Double-cut solidbodies with long thin horns.			
1988-1993	Various models	$150	$300
FA (Full Acoustic) Series			
1978-1982. Single-cut full body jazz-style.			
1978-1982		$1,000	$1,225
FG-100			
1982-1987. Single-cut archtop, maple top, 2 humbuckers.			
1982-1987		$1,000	$1,225
GAX Series			
1998-2009. Symmetrical double-cut (Gibson SG style) with 2 humbuckers, lower cost of the AX line.			
1998-2009		$90	$175
George Benson GB10			
1977-present. Single-cut, laminated spruce top, flame maple back and sides, 2 humbuckers, 3-piece set-in maple neck, ebony 'board.			
1977-1979	Blond	$1,700	$2,100
1977-1979	Sunburst	$1,700	$2,100
1980-1989	Blond	$1,700	$2,100
1980-1989	Sunburst	$1,500	$1,900
1990-1999	Blond	$1,500	$1,900
1990-1999	Sunburst	$1,300	$1,600
2000-2014	Sunburst	$1,300	$1,600
2004	Blond	$1,500	$1,900
George Benson GB15			
2006-2010. Like GB10, but with 1 humbucker.			
2006-2010		$1,800	$2,250
George Benson GB20			
1978-1982. Larger than GB10, laminated spruce top, flame maple back and sides.			
1978-1982		$1,900	$2,350
George Benson GB100 Deluxe			
1993-1996. GB-10 with flamed maple top, pearl binding, sunburst finish 'guard, pearl vine inlay tailpiece, gold hardware.			
1993-1996		$2,300	$2,850

Ibanez AEL50SERLV

Ibanez George Benson GB10

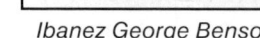

To get the most from this book, be sure to read "Using *The Guide*" in the introduction.

GUITARS

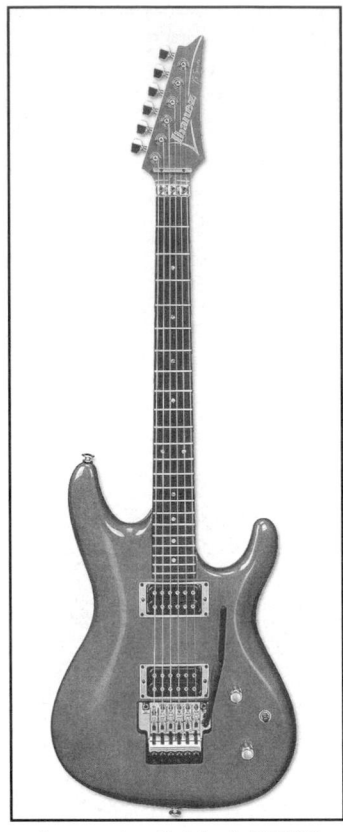

Ibanez Joe Satriani JS1200

Ibanez John Scofield JSM100

MODEL YEAR	FEATURES	EXC. COND. LOW	HIGH

GSA Series
2000-2011. Offset double-cut body.

| 2000-2011 | GSA20/GSA60 | $75 | $125 |

Howie Roberts Model 2453
1974-1977. Single-cut archtop, round soundhole, maple body, set neck, rosewood 'board, block markers, 1 pickup, gold hardware, burgundy or sunburst.

| 1974-1977 | | $1,200 | $1,500 |

Iceman 2663/2663 TC/2663 SL
1975-1978. The original Iceman Series models, called the Flash I, II and III respectively, I has 2 humbuckers, II (TC) and III (SL) have 1 triple-coil pickup.

| 1975-1978 | | $750 | $900 |

Iceman PS10 Paul Stanley
1978-1981. Limited edition Paul Stanley model, abalone trim, Stanley's name engraved at 21st fret, reissued in '95 with upgraded model names.

| 1978-1981 | Korina finish | $2,650 | $3,350 |
| 1978-1981 | Sunburst or black | $2,650 | $3,350 |

Iceman PS10 II Paul Stanley
1995-1996. Reissue of original PS-10.

| 1995-1996 | Black | $1,400 | $1,750 |

Iceman PS10 LTD Paul Stanley
1995-1996. Limited edition, gold mirror appointments, gold hardware, black pearl metalflake finish.

| 1995-1996 | | $3,000 | $3,750 |

Iceman Series
1975-2010. Ibanez unique body styles with hooked lower treble horn body.

1978	IC210	$950	$1,175
1978-1979	IC250	$925	$1,150
1978-1979	IC300 (Korina)	$750	$950
1978-1982	IC400	$850	$1,050
1978-1990	IC200	$750	$950
1981-1982	IC400 CS	$900	$1,150
1994	IC500	$900	$1,150
1994-2003	IC300	$325	$410
1995-1996	IC350	$325	$410

IMG-2010 Guitar Controller MIDI
1985-1987. Similar to Roland GR-707, slim triangle-wedge body with treble horn.

| 1985-1987 | Guitar only | $500 | $625 |

JEM 7 Series
1988-2010. Basswood or alder body, various models, alder 7V offered until '10.

| 1988-2010 | Various colors | $1,350 | $1,850 |

JEM 77 Series
1988-1999, 2003-2010. Basswood body, monkey grip handle, 3 pickups, 'board with tree of life or pyramids inlay, finishes include floral pattern or multicolor swirl. Current version has dot inlays and solid finish. The JEM 77BRMR Bad Horsie was introduced in '05 with a mirror finish.

| 1980-2010 | Various colors | $1,400 | $3,000 |

JEM 555
1994-2000. Basswood, dots and vine inlay, 3 pickups.

| 1994-2000 | | $550 | $700 |

JEM 777 Series
1987-1996. Basswood body, monkey grip 3 pickups, pyramids or vine inlay.

| 1987-1996 | Various colors | $1,400 | $3,000 |

MODEL YEAR	FEATURES	EXC. COND. LOW	HIGH

JEM 10th Anniversary
1996. Limited Edition signature Steve Vai model, bolt neck, vine metal 'guard, vine neck inlays and headstock art.

| 1996 | | $3,850 | $4,800 |

JEM 20th Anniversary
2007. Steve Vai 20th Anniversary JEM model, green acrylic illuminating body, celebrates the 20th year (1987-2007) of the Ibanez JEM series, limited edition.

| 2007 | | $3,850 | $4,800 |

JEM 90th Anniversary
1997. Limited Edition signature Steve Vai model, textured silver finish, chrome 'guard.

| 1997 | | $1,400 | $1,750 |

JEM Y2KDNA (Limited Edition)
2000. Red Swirl marble finish using Steve Vai's blood in the paint.

| 2000 | | $3,300 | $4,100 |

Joe Pass JP20
1981-1990. Full body, single-cut, 1 pickup, abalone and pearl split block inlay, JP inlay on headstock.

| 1981-1990 | Sunburst | $1,700 | $2,100 |

Joe Satriani JS6
1993. Limited production, lightweight mahogany body, non-gloss finish, JS Series headstock logo.

| 1993 | | $1,200 | $1,500 |

Joe Satriani JS100
1994-2014. Offset double cut basswood body, 2 humbuckers, vibrato, red, black, white or custom finish.

| 1994-2014 | Custom finish | $450 | $575 |
| 1994-2014 | Standard finish | $360 | $450 |

Joe Satriani JS1000
1994-1996, 1998-2012. 2 DiMarzio humbuckers, lightweight body.

| 1994-2012 | Various colors | $750 | $1,000 |

Joe Satriani JS1200
2004-present. Candy Apple Red.

| 2004-2014 | | $875 | $1,100 |

Joe Satriani JS 10th Anniversary
1998. Chrome-metal body, Satriani Anniversary script on back cover plate.

| 1998 | | $2,300 | $2,900 |

Joe Satriani JS 20th Anniversary
2008. Opaque finish with alien surfer graphic.

| 2008 | | $2,300 | $2,900 |

Joe Satriani Y2K
2000. Clear see-thru plexi-style body.

| 2000 | | $1,800 | $2,300 |

John Petrucci JPM100 P2
1996. Offset double-cut solidbody, 2 pickups, multi-color graphic.

| 1996 | | $1,700 | $2,100 |

John Petrucci JPM100 P3
1997. As P2 but with same graphic in black and white.

| 1997 | | $1,700 | $2,100 |

John Petrucci JPM100 P4
1998. As P2 but with same graphic in camo colors.

| 1998 | | $1,700 | $2,100 |

John Scofield JSM100
2001-present. Double-cut semi hollow body, 2 humbuckers, ebony 'board, gold hardware.

| 2001-2014 | | $1,500 | $1,850 |

MODEL YEAR	FEATURES	EXC. COND. LOW	HIGH

Lee Ritenour LR10
1981-1987. Flame maple body, bound set neck, Quick Change tailpiece, 2 pickups, dark red sunburst, foam-filled body to limit feedback.

1981-1987		$1,350	$1,700

M310
1982. D-size flat-top, maple back and sides, rosewood 'board.

1982		$170	$210

M340
1978-1979. D-size flat-top, flamed maple back and sides, maple 'board. 'board.

1978-1979		$275	$350

Maxxas
1987-1988. Solidbody (MX2) or with internal sound chambers (MX3, '88 only), 2 pickups, all-access neck joint system.

1987-1988	MX2	$1,100	$1,350
1988	MX3	$1,300	$1,600

MC Musician Series
1978-1982. Solidbodies, various models.

1978-1980	MC500, carved top	$1,200	$1,500
1978-1980	Neck-thru body	$725	$900
1978-1982	Bolt neck	$625	$775

Mick Thompson MTM-1
2006. Seven logo on fretboard, MTM1 logo on back of headstock.

2006		$650	$825

Model 600 Series
1974-1978. Copy era acoustic flat-tops with model numbers in the 600 Series, basically copies of classic American square shoulder dreadnoughts. Includes the 683, 684, 693, and the six-on-a-side 647; there were 12-string copies as well.

1974-1978		$550	$700

Model 700 Series
1974-1977. Upgraded flat-top models such as the Brazilian Scent 750, with more original design content than 600 Series.

1974-1977		$550	$700

Model 900 Series
1963-1964. Offset double-cut solidbody with sharp curving horns, Burns Bison copy.

1963-1964	901, 1 pickup	$200	$250
1963-1964	992, 2 pickups	$225	$285

Model 1453
1971-1973. Copy of classic single-cut hollowbody, replaced by Model 2355 in '73.

1971-1973		$1,300	$1,600

Model 1800 Series
1962-1963. Offset double-cut solidbody (Jazzmaster-style), models came with bar (stud) or vibrato tailpiece, and 2, 3 or 4 pickups.

1962-1963	1830, 2 pickups, bar	$200	$250
1962-1963	1850, 3 pickups, bar	$225	$275
1962-1963	1860, 2 pickups, vibrato	$200	$250
1962-1963	1880, 3 pickups, vibrato	$225	$275

Model 1912
1971-1973. Double-cut semi-hollow body, sunburst finish.

1971-1973		$950	$1,200

Model 2020
1970. Initial offering of the copy era, offset double-cut, 2 unusual rectangular pickups, block markers, raised nailed-on headstock logo, sunburst.

1970		$550	$700

Model 2240M
Early 1970s. Thick hollowbody electric copy, single pointed cutaway, double-parallelogram markers, 2 humbuckers, natural finish.

1971-1973		$1,100	$1,400

Model 2336 Les Jr.
1974-1976. Copy of classic slab solidbody, TV Lime.

1974-1976		$500	$625

Model 2340 Deluxe '59er
1974-1977. Copy of classic single-cut solidbody, Hi-Power humbuckers, opaque or flametop.

1974-1977	Flametop	$650	$800
1974-1977	Opaque	$600	$750

Model 2341 Les Custom
1974-1977. Copy of classic single-cut solidbody.

1974-1977		$650	$800

Model 2342 Les Moonlight/Sunlight Special
1974-1977. Copy of classic slab solidbody, black (Moonlight) or ivory (Sunlight).

1974-1977		$550	$675

Model 2343 FM Jr.
1974-1976. Copy of LP TV Jr.

1974-1976		$500	$625

Model 2343 Jr.
1974-1976. Copy of classic Jr., cherry mahogany.

1974-1976		$500	$625

Model 2344
1974-1976. Copy of classic double-cut solidbody.

1974-1976		$400	$500

Model 2345
1974-1976. Copy of classic sharp double-cut solidbody, set neck, walnut or white, vibrato, 3 pickups.

1974-1976		$600	$750

Model 2346
1974. Copy of classic sharp double-cut solidbody, vibrato, set neck, 2 pickups.

1974		$600	$750

Model 2347
1974-1976. Copy of classic sharp double-cut solidbody, set-neck, 1 pickup.

1974-1976		$500	$650

Model 2348 Firebrand
1974-1977. Copy of classic reverse solidbody, mahogany body, bolt neck, 2 pickups.

1974-1977		$800	$1,000

Model 2350 Les
1971-1977. Copy of classic single-cut solidbody, bolt neck, black, gold hardware, goldtop version (2350G Les) also available. A cherry sunburst finish (2350 Les Custom) was offered by '74.

1971-1977		$600	$750

Ibanez Model 2020

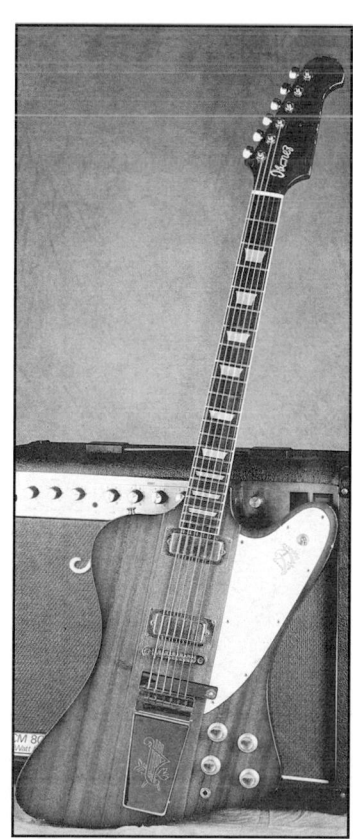

Ibanez Model 2348 Firebrand

MODEL YEAR	FEATURES	EXC. COND. LOW	HIGH

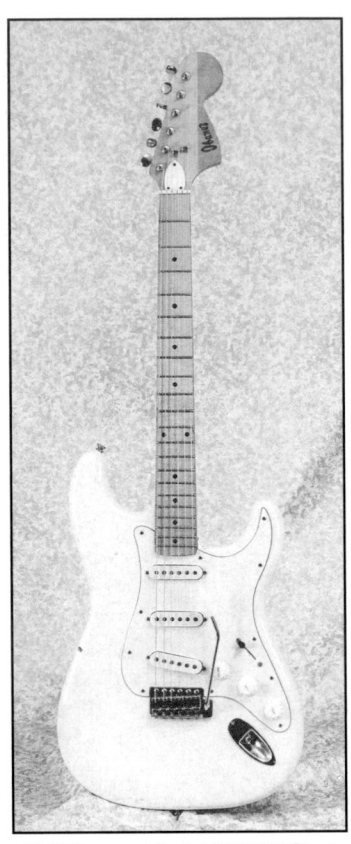

1974 Ibanez Model 2375W Strato

Michael Wright

Model 2351 Les
1974-1977. Copy of classic single-cut solidbody, gold top, 2 pickups.
1974-1977 ... $600 ... $750

Model 2351DX
1974-1977. Copy of classic single-cut solidbody, gold top, 2 mini-humbuckers.
1974-1977 ... $600 ... $750

Model 2351M Les
1974-1977. LP Standard style, sunburst.
1974-1977 ... $600 ... $750

Model 2352 Telly
1974-1978. Copy of early classic single-cut solidbody, 1 bridge pickup, white finish.
1974-1978 ... $600 ... $750

Model 2352CT
1974-1978. Copy of classic single-cut solidbody, single-coil bridge and humbucker neck pickup.
1974-1978 ... $550 ... $700

Model 2352DX Telly
1974-1978. Copy of classic single-cut solidbody, 2 humbuckers.
1974-1978 ... $550 ... $700

Model 2354
1974-1977. Copy of classic sharp double-cut solidbody, 2 humbuckers, vibrato.
1974-1977 ... $550 ... $700

Model 2354S
1972-1977. Stop tailpiece version of 2354.
1972-1977 ... $550 ... $700

Model 2355/2355M
1973-1977. Copy of classic single-cut hollowbody, sunburst or natural maple (M).
1973-1977 ... $1,300 ... $1,600

Model 2356
1973-1975. Copy of classic double pointed cutaway hollowbody, bowtie markers, sunburst. There was another Model 2356 in '74, a copy of a different hollowbody.
1973-1975 ... $850 ... $1,050

Model 2363R
1973-1974. Cherry finish copy of classic varitone double-cut semi-hollow body.
1973-1974 ... $900 ... $1,150

Model 2364 Ibanex
1971-1973. Dan Armstrong see-thru Lucite copy, 2 mounted humbuckers.
1971-1973 ... $700 ... $900

Model 2368 Telly
1973-1978. Copy of classic single-cut thinline, chambered f-hole body, single coil pickup, mahogany body.
1973-1978 ... $550 ... $675

Model 2368F
1973-1974. Classic single-cut black 'guard copy.
1973-1974 ... $550 ... $700

Model 2370
1972-1977. Sunburst version of Model 2363R.
1972-1977 ... $900 ... $1,150

Model 2372 Les Pro/2372DX Les Pro
1972-1977. Copy of classic single-cut solidbody, bolt neck, low impedance pickups, DX with gold hardware

Ibanez Model 2384 Telly

available for '73-'74.
1972-1977 ... $600 ... $750

Model 2374 Crest
1974-1976. Copy of classic double-cut semi-hollow body, walnut finish.
1974-1976 ... $900 ... $1,150

Model 2375 Strato
1971-1978. Strat copy, 3 single-coils, sunburst.
1971-1978 ... $500 ... $625

Model 2375 Strato 6/12
1974-1975. Double neck, 6 and 12 strings.
1974-1975 ... $1,300 ... $1,600

Model 2375ASH Strato
1974-1978. 2375 with ash body.
1974-1978 ... $550 ... $700

Model 2375WH/N/BK Strato
1974-1978. 2375 in white (WH), natural (N), and black (BK) finishes.
1974-1978 ... $500 ... $625

Model 2377
1974-1975. Copy of classic double sharp-cut solidbody, short production run, dot markers.
1974-1975 ... $450 ... $575

Model 2380
1973-1977. Copy of LP Recording, single-cut solidbody, low impedence pickups, small block markers.
1973-1977 ... $600 ... $750

Model 2383
1974-1976. Copy of classic double sharp cut solidbody, white or walnut, 3 humbuckers, gold hardware.
1974-1976 Walnut ... $500 ... $700
1974-1976 White ... $650 ... $750

Model 2384 Telly
1974-1976. Copy of classic single-cut, f-holes, 2 humbuckers, ash body.
1974-1976 ... $500 ... $700

Model 2387 Rocket Roll/Rocket Roll Sr.
1975-1977. Copy of classic v-shaped solidbody, bolt-neck (2387) or set-neck (2387DX/2387CT), dot markers, gold-covered pickups.
1975-1977 ... $1,100 ... $1,350

Model 2390
1974-1976. Copy of classic double-cut semi-hollow body, maple 'board, walnut finish.
1974-1976 ... $800 ... $1,000

Model 2394
Ca. 1974-ca. 1976. SG style, 2 humbuckers, maple 'board, black block inlays.
1974-1976 ... $650 ... $800

Model 2395
1974-1976. Natural finished 2390.
1974-1976 ... $800 ... $1,000

Model 2397
1974-1976. Double-cut semi-hollow body, low impedance electronics, trapezoid markers, goldtop.
1974-1976 ... $800 ... $1,000

Model 2399DX Jazz Solid
1974-1976. Single-cut solidbody, sunburst, set-neck, gold hardware.
1974-1976 ... $750 ... $925

MODEL YEAR	FEATURES	EXC. COND. LOW	HIGH

Model 2401 Signature

1974-1976. Double-cut semi-hollow archtop, gold top, bolt neck.

1974-1976		$800	$1,000

Model 2402/2402DX Double Axe

1974-1977. Double sharp cut solidbody 6/12 double-neck, cherry or walnut, DX model has gold hardware and white finish.

1974-1977	2402, walnut, cherry	$1,000	$1,250
1974-1977	2402DX, white	$1,100	$1,350

Model 2404 Double Axe

1974-1977. Double sharp cut solidbody guitar/bass doubleneck copy, walnut, white available '75 only.

1974-1977		$1,000	$1,250

Model 2405 Custom Agent

1974-1977. Single-cut solidbody, set neck, scroll headstock, pearl body inlay, 2 humbuckers.

1974-1977		$1,000	$1,250

Model 2406 Double Axe

1974-1977. Double sharp cut solidbody doubleneck, two 6-strings, cherry or wlanut.

1974-1977		$1,000	$1,250

Model 2407 Stratojazz 4/6

1974-1975. Half Strat, half Jazz bass, all rock and roll!

1974-1975		$1,000	$1,250

Model 2451

1974-1977. Single-cut solidbody, maple 'board, black or natural, set neck.

1974-1977		$725	$900

Model 2454

1974-1977. Copy of classic double-cut semi-hollow body, set-neck, small block markers, cherry finish over ash.

1974-1977		$800	$1,000

Model 2455

1974-1977. L-5 copy, sharp single-cut archtop, blocks, natural.

1974-1977		$1,300	$1,700

Model 2459 Destroyer

1975-1977. Korina finished mahogany body.

1975-1977		$1,500	$1,900

Model 2460

1975-1977. L-5 copy, rounded cut laminated archtop, blocks, natural.

1975-1977		$1,300	$1,650

Model 2461

1975-1977. Copy of classic single-cut archtop, laminated spruce top, curly maple body, set-neck, ebony 'board, pearl blocks, 2 pickups, gold hardware, sunburst or natural.

1975-1977		$1,400	$1,800

Model 2464

1975-1977. Byrdland copy, rounded single-cut, blocks, natural.

1975-1977		$1,300	$1,650

Model 2469 Futura

1976-1977. Korina finished furturistic model copy.

1976-1977		$1,300	$1,650

Model 2601 Artist

1976-1978. D-style flat-top with fancy appointments.

1976-1978		$200	$250

Model 2612 Artist

1974-1975. Rounded double-cut solidbody, black finish, birch top, gold hardware, bound rosewood 'board, 2 humbuckers, fleur-de-lis inlay.

1974-1975		$800	$1,000

Model 2613 Artist

1974-1975. Natural version of 2612.

1974-1975		$800	$1,000

Model 2616 Artist Jazz

1974-1975. Single-cut curly maple hollow body, f holes, fleur-de-lis, 2 humbuckers.

1974-1975		$1,350	$1,700

Model 2617 Artist

1976-1980. Pointed double-cut natural ash solidbody, set-neck, German carved top, spilt block inlays, bound ebony 'board, 2 humbuckers, later would evolve into the Professional model.

1976-1980		$1,000	$1,250

Model 2618 Artist

1976-1979. Like 2617, but wtth maple and mahogany body and dot markers. Becomes AR200 in '79.

1976-1979		$800	$1,000

Model 2619 Artist

1976-1979. Like 2618, but with split block markers. Becomes AR300 in '79.

1976-1979		$800	$1,000

Model 2622 Artist EQ

1977-1979. EQ, Steve Miller model. Becomes AR500 in '79.

1977-1979		$800	$1,000

Model 2630 Artist Deluxe

1976-1979. Double cut semi hollow body, sunburst, name changed to AS200 in '79.

1976-1979		$1,075	$1,350

Model 2640 Artist/AR1200 Doubleneck

1977-1984. Double-cut solidbody, set 6/12 necks, 4 humbuckers, gold hardware. Called 2640 until '79 when changed to AR1200.

1977-1984		$1,100	$1,375

Model 2662 Super Cutaway

1974-1976. Solidbody, set neck, two dramatic cutaways, block inlays, 2 humbuckers.

1974-1976		$800	$1,000

Model 2671 Randy Scruggs

1976-1978. Single-cut solidbody, tree-of-life inlay, German-carve top.

1976-1978		$1,200	$1,500

Model 2700 Artist Custom

1977-1978. Cutaway, dot markers, gold hardware, natural, black, antique violin or dark satin finish.

1977-1978		$1,500	$1,900

Model 2710 Artist Custom

1978. Like Model 2700 with exotic wood and anvil case.

1978		$1,600	$2,000

Model 2800 Andorra Series

1974-1979. Classical nylon-string guitars, part of Ibanez Andorra Series, all with 2800-2899 model numbers.

1974-1979		$150	$400

Ibanez 2402DX Double Axe

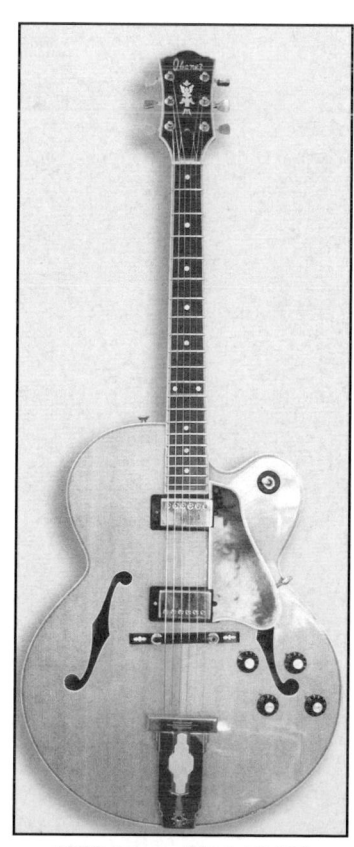

1976 Ibanez Model 2460
My Generation Guitars

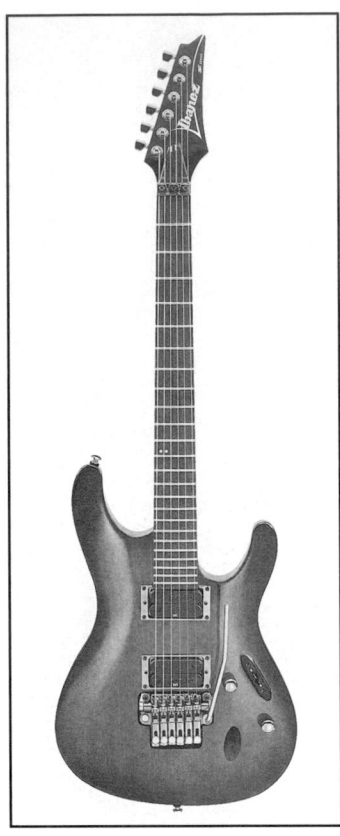

Ibanez S420

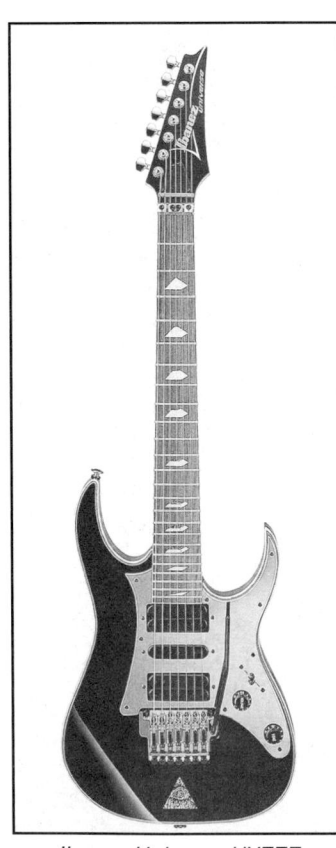

Ibanez Universe UV777

MODEL YEAR	FEATURES	EXC. COND. LOW	HIGH

Model 2900 Andorra Professional Series
1974-1979. Steel-string dreadnought models with solid spruce tops, all with 2909-2912 model numbers.

| 1974-1979 | | $150 | $400 |

Pat Metheny PM
1996-present. Acoustic-electric archtops, single or single/half cutaway, 1 or 2 humbuckers.

1996-2010	PM100	$1,300	$1,625
1997-1999	PM20	$1,000	$1,250
2000-2014	PM120	$1,500	$1,875

Paul Gilbert PGM
1992-2011. Superstrat body style, painted f-holes, appointments vary with model numbers.

1997-2011	PGM300 WH (white)	$1,150	$1,450
1998	PGM 90th	$1,350	$1,700
1998	PGM200 FB	$1,350	$1,700

PF Performer Series Acoustics
1987-present. Mostly dreadnought size flat-tops, various models.

| 1987-2014 | Various models | $75 | $225 |

PF100 Performer Standard
1978-1979. Single-cut solidbody, plain birch top, mahogany body, bolt neck, dot inlays, 2 humbuckers.

| 1978-1979 | | $350 | $450 |

PF200 Performer Custom
1978-1979. Maple top PF100.

| 1978-1979 | | $400 | $500 |

PF300 Performer
1978-1980. Single-cut solidbody, maple top, mahogany body, set neck, 2 humbuckers, Tri-Sound.

| 1978-1980 | | $475 | $600 |

PF400 Performer
1978-1979. Single cut solidbody, flame maple top, alder body, set neck, block inlays, 2 humbuckers, Tri-Sound.

| 1978-1979 | | $525 | $650 |

PL Pro Line Series
1985-1987. Pro Line models begin with PL or PR.

| 1985-1987 | Various models | $275 | $450 |

PR Pro Line Series
1985-1987. Pro Line models begin with PL or PR.

| 1985-1987 | Various models | $250 | $425 |

RBM1 Reb Beach Voyager
1991-1996. Unusual cutaway lower bout, extreme upper bout cutaways, RBM Series logo on headstock.

| 1991-1996 | | $975 | $1,200 |

RG/RS Roadstar Series
1992-present. A large family of guitars whose model identification starts with RG or RS prefix, includes the Roadstar Standard and Roadstar Deluxe models.

1992-2014	Higher-range	$500	$625
1992-2014	Highest-range	$700	$1,500
1992-2014	Low to mid-range	$250	$350
1992-2014	Lower-range	$150	$250
1992-2014	Mid-range	$400	$500

Roadstar II Series
1982-1985. Various offset double-cut solidbodies, 'Roadstar II Series' on headstock, 3 single-coils or 2 humbuckers. Over 40 models appeared in this line, offered in Standard, Deluxe and Custom forms.

| 1982-1985 | Deluxe models | $335 | $420 |
| 1982-1985 | Standard models | $335 | $420 |

Rocket Roll II RR550
1982-1984. Flying V body, six-on-side headstock, pearloid blocks, cherry sunburst, maple top, set neck.

| 1982-1984 | | $900 | $1,150 |

RT Series
1992-1993. Offset double-cut, bolt neck, rosewood 'board, dot markers, various models.

| 1992-1993 | Various models | $250 | $400 |

RX Series
1994-1997. Offset double-cut, solidbodies, various models.

| 1994-1997 | Various models | $70 | $150 |

S Models
1987-present. In '87 Ibanez introduced a new line of highly tapered, ultra-thin body, offset double-cut guitars that were grouped together as the S Models. Intially the S Models were going to be called the Sabre models but that name was trademarked by Music Man and could not be used. The S models will carry an S suffix or S prefix in the model name.

| 1987-2014 | Various models | $250 | $550 |

ST Studio Series
1978-1982. Double-cut solidbodies, lots of natural finishes, various models, even a doubleneck.

| 1979-1981 | Various models | $275 | $525 |

STW Double
1999. Double neck with 7-string and 6-string neck, limited edition.

| 1999 | | $1,650 | $2,050 |

TC/TV Talman Series
1994-1998. Softer double-cut solidbodies, various models.

| 1994-1998 | Various models | $275 | $450 |

Universe UV7/UV7P/UV77 Series
1990-1997. Basswood 7-strings, hum/single/hum pickups. The '90-'93 white 7P and multi-colored 77 have pyramid inlays, the black '90-'97 7 has dots.

| 1990-1997 | Various models | $1,200 | $3,500 |

Universe UV777 Series
1998-2012. Basswood 7-string, pyramid inlays, maple 'board, hum/single/hum pickups.

| 1991-2012 | Various models | $1,200 | $2,000 |

USRG U.S.A. Custom Series
1994-1995. RG style guitars built in the U.S. by PBC Guitar Technology.

| 1994-1995 | Various models | $1,000 | $1,300 |

V300 Vintage Series
1978-1991. Vintage Series acoustic dreadnought, spruce top, mahogany back and sides, sunburst or various colors.

| 1978-1991 | | $150 | $200 |

XV500
1985-1987. Sharply pointed X-body with scalloped bottom.

| 1985-1987 | | $300 | $400 |

Ibanez, Salvador
1875-1920. Salvador Ibanez was a Spanish luthier who operated a small guitar-building workshop. In

MODEL YEAR	FEATURES	EXC. COND. LOW	HIGH

the early 1900s he founded Spain's largest guitar factory. In 1929 Japan's Hoshino family began importing Salvador Ibanez guitars. Demand for the Salvador Ibanez guitars became so great that the Hoshino family began building their own guitars, which ultimately became known as the Ibanez brand. Guitars from 1875-1920 were mostly classical style and often can be identified by a label on the inside back which stipulates Salvador Ibanez.

Ignacio Rozas

1987-present. Luthier Ignacio M. Rozas builds his classical and flamenco guitars in Madrid, Spain. He also offers factory-made guitars built to his specifications.

Illusion Guitars

1992-present. Luthier Jeff Scott builds his premium grade, production/custom, solidbody guitars in Fallbrook, California.

Imperial

Ca.1963-ca.1970. Imported by the Imperial Accordion Company of Chicago, Illinois. Early guitars made in Italy by accordion builder Crucianelli. By ca. '66 switched to Japanese guitars. They also made basses.

Electric Solidbody
1963-1968. Italian-made until '66, then Japanese-made, includes the Tonemaster line.

1963-1968		$210	$260

Imperial (Japan)

1957-1960. Early, budget grade, Japanese imports from the Hoshino company which was later renamed Ibanez.

Infeld

2003-2005. Solidbody guitars and basses offered by string-maker Thomastik-Infeld of Vienna.

Infinox

1980s. Infinox by JTG, of Nashville, offered a line of 'the classic shapes of yesterday and the hi tech chic of today'. Classic shapes included copies of many classic American solidbody designs with the block letter Infinox by JTG logo on headstock, special metallic grafteq paint finish, space-age faux graphite-feel neck, Gotoh tuning machines, Gotoh locking nut tremolo with fine tuners, all models with 1 or 2 humbucker pickups.

Interdonati

1920s-1930s. Guitars built by luthier Philip Interdonati, in New York City, originally professional grade. He also built mandolins.

Size 000 Flat-Top
1920s-1930s.

1920s-30s	Less fancy	$4,600	$5,500
1920s-30s	More fancy	$5,500	$11,100

Island Instruments

2010-present. Luthier Nic Delisle builds professional and premium grade, production/custom, small-bodied acoustic and electric guitars in Montreal, Quebec. He also builds basses.

Italia

1999-present. Intermediate grade, production, solid, semi-solid, and hollow body guitars and basses designed by Trevor Wilkinson and made in Korea.

J Backlund Design

2008-present. Professional and premium grade, custom, electric guitars and basses designed by J. Backlund in Hixson, Tennessee. He also imports Korean-made guitars under the Retronix brand.

J Burda Guitars

Flat-top guitars built by luthier Jan Burda in Berrien Springs, Michigan.

J. Frog Guitars

1978-present. Professional and premium grade, production/custom, solidbody guitars made by Ed Roman Guitars.

J.B. Player

1980s-present. Budget and intermediate grade, production, imported acoustic, acoustic/electric, and solidbody guitars and basses. They also offer banjos and mandolins. Founded in United States. Moved production of guitars to Korea but maintained a U.S. Custom Shop. MBT International/Musicorp took over manufacture and distribution in '89.

J.R. Zeidler Guitars

1977-2002. Luthier John Zeidler built premium and presentation grade, custom, flat-top, 12-string, and archtop guitars in Wallingford, Pennsylvania. He also built mandolins. He died in '02 at age 44.

J.S. Bogdanovich

1996-present. Production/custom, premium grade, classical and steel string guitars built by luthier John S. Bogdanovich in Swannanoa, North Carolina.

J.T. Hargreaves Basses & Guitars

1995-present. Luthier Jay Hargreaves builds his premium grade, production/custom, classical and steel string guitars and basses in Seattle, Washington.

Jack Daniel's

2004-present. Acoustic and electric guitars and basses, some with Jack Daniel's artwork on the body and headstock, built by Peavey for the Jack Daniel's Distillery. There is also an amp model.

Italia Mondial

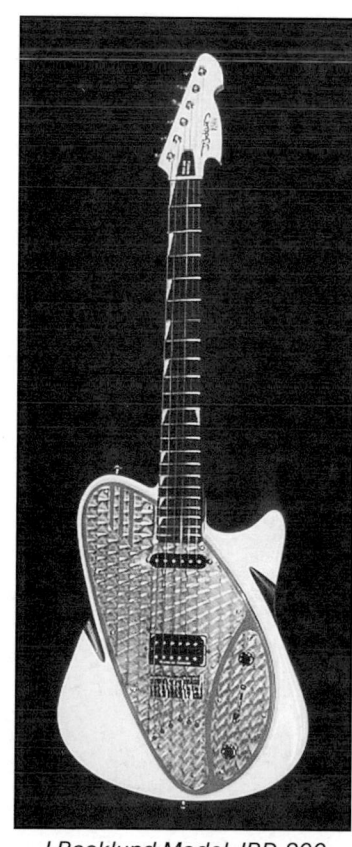

J Backlund Model JBD-200

GUITARS

1999 Jackson Randy Rhoads

Randy Schleyhahn

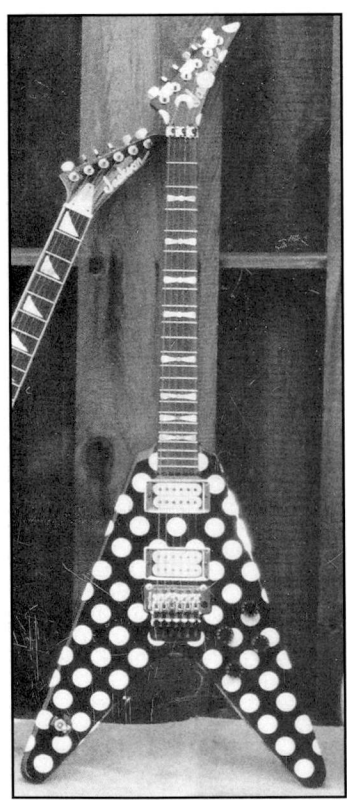

1997 Jackson Randy
Rhoads Tribute

Cort Hullinger

MODEL YEAR	FEATURES	EXC. COND. LOW	HIGH

Jackson

1980-present. Currently Jackson offers intermediate, professional, and premium grade, production, electric guitars. They also offer basses. In '78 Grover Jackson bought out Charvel Guitars and moved it to San Dimas. Jackson made custom-built bolt-on Charvels. In '82 the pointy, tilt-back Jackson headstock became standard. The Jackson logo was born in '80 and used on a guitar designed as Randy Rhoad's first flying V. Jacksons were neck-through construction. The Charvel trademark was licensed to IMC in '85. IMC moved the Jackson factory to Ontario, California in '86. Grover Jackson stayed with Jackson/Charvel until '89 (see Charvel). On October 25, 2002, Fender Musical Instruments Corp (FMIC) took ownership of Jackson/Charvel Manufacturing Inc.

Dinky Reverse

1991	Import	$370	$465

DR2

1996-1998. U.S.-made offset double-cut solidbody, 2 Duncan humbuckers, ebony 'board.

1996-1998	U.S.-made	$675	$845

DR3

1996-2001. Dinky Reverse, double-cut solidbody, reverse headstock, triangle markers, 2 humbuckers, locking vibrato, made in Japan, flamed maple top available.

1996-2001		$270	$340

DR5

1996 only. Offset double-cut solidbody, 2 Kent Armstrong humbuckers, rosewood 'board, dot markers.

1996		$270	$340

DX Series

2000-2007. Standard offset double-cut body, reverse headstock.

2000-2007		$190	$300

Fusion Pro

Late 1980s-early 1990s. Import from Japan.

1980s-90s		$470	$590

Fusion U.S.A.

1992-1994. Jackson with Made In USA logo on headstock, graphics.

1992-1994		$775	$965

Jenna II RX10D Rhoads

2009. Limited production, Rhoads body style, named after performer Jenna Jameson.

2009		$470	$590

JSX94

1994-1995. Offset double-cut solidbody, single/single/hum, rosewood 'board, dot markers.

1994-1995		$240	$300

JTX

1993-1995. Partial offset double-cut, single-coil neck pickup, humbucker bridge pickup, Jackson-Rose double lock vibrato, bolt-on neck, dot markers on maple fretboard, JTX truss rod cover logo.

1993-1995		$325	$400

Kelly Custom

1984-early 1990s. Solidbody, Kahler tremolo, 2

humbuckers, ebony 'board with shark's tooth inlays, bound neck and headstock.

1984-1985		$1,250	$1,550
1986-1993		$1,200	$1,500

Kelly Pro

1994-1995. Pointy-cut solidbody, neck-thru, 2 humbuckers, bound ebony 'board, sharkfin inlays.

1994-1995		$550	$675

Kelly Standard

1993-1995. Pointy cutaway solidbody, bolt neck, 2 humbuckers, dot markers.

1993-1995		$390	$490

Kelly U.S.A. (KE2)

1998-present. Alder solidbody, flame maple top, neck-thru.

1998-2014		$825	$1,025

Kelly XL

1994-1995. Pointy cutaway solidbody, bolt neck, 2 humbuckers, bound rosewood 'board, sharkfin inlays.

1994-1995		$530	$650

King V (KV2)

2003-present. King V Pro reissue, neck-thru, sharkfin markers, Floyd Rose, U.S.-made.

2003-2014		$630	$780

King V Pro

1993-1995. Soft V-shaped neck-thru solidbody, sharkfin markers, 2 humbuckers.

1993-1995		$430	$535

King V STD

1993-1995. Bolt neck version of King V.

1993-1995		$270	$330

Phil Collen

1989-1991, 1993-1995. Offset double-cut maple neck-thru solidbody, six-on-a-side tuners, 1 volume, bound ebony 'board, U.S.-made, early version has poplar body, 1 humbucker; later version with basswood body, 1 single-coil and 1 humbucker.

1993-1995		$1,050	$1,300

Phil Collen PC1 (U.S.A.)

1996-present. Quilt maple top, bolt-on maple neck, maple board, koa body '96-'00, mahogany body '01-present, 1 humbucker and 1 single coil '96-'97, humbucker, stacked humbucker, and single coil '98-present.

1996-2013		$1,150	$1,500

Phil Collen PC3 (Import)

1996-2001. Downscale version of Collen model, poplar body, bolt neck, humbucker\single\single.

1996-2001		$450	$550

PS Performers Series

1994-2003. Some with PS model number on truss rod cover.

1994-1999	PS3 Rhoads body h/h	$250	$310
1994-2000	PS1 Dinky body h/s/h	$250	$310
1994-2003	PS2 Dinky body s/s/h	$250	$310
1995-2001	PS4 Dinky body h/s/h	$250	$310
1995-2001	PS7 h/s/s	$250	$310
1997-2001	PS6/PS6T Kelly body	$250	$310

Randy Rhoads (Import)

1992-2011. Bolt neck import version.

1992-2011		$270	$335

MODEL YEAR	FEATURES	EXC. COND. LOW	HIGH

Randy Rhoads (Japan)
1995-2011.

| 1995-2011 | RR3, bolt-on | $240 | $300 |
| 2001-2011 | RR5, neck-thru | $400 | $500 |

Randy Rhoads (U.S.A.)
1983-present. V-shaped (also referred to as concorde-shaped) neck-thru solidbody, 2 humbuckers, originally made at San Dimas plant, serial numbers RR 0001 to RR 1929, production moved to the Ontario plant by '87, serial numbers RR 1930 to present in sequential order.

1983	Early serial #, no trem	$2,800	$5,000
1983-1986	Kahler trem	$1,600	$2,500
1983-1986	Rose trem or string-thru	$2,000	$2,600
1987-1989	Early Ontario-built	$1,400	$1,800
1990-1992	Early '90s vintage	$1,200	$1,600
1993-1999		$1,200	$1,600
2002-2005	RR5	$750	$950
2002-2014	RR1	$1,200	$1,600

Randy Rhoads Limited Edition
1992 only. Shark fin-style maple neck-thru body, gold hardware, white with black pinstriping, block inlays, six-on-a-side tuners, U.S.-made, only 200 built.

| 1992 | | $5,200 | $6,500 |

Randy Rhoads Relic Tribute
2010-2011. Custom Shop limited edition to celebrate the 30th anniversary of the Randy Rhoads Concorde, 60 made, exacting dimension and design of Rhoads' original custom-made Concorde guitar, relic-treatment to mimic the original.

| 2010-2011 | | $5,600 | $7,000 |

RX Series
2000s-2011. Bolt-on, shark fin inlays.

| 2007-2011 | RX10D Rhoads | $236 | $290 |

San Dimas Serialized Plated
1980-1982. Various custom-built solidbody models, values vary depending on each individual instrument. The values are true for so-called "Serialized Plated" with Jackson neck plate, Jackson logo and serial number.

| 1980-1982 | | $3,300 | $4,100 |

Soloist
1984-1990. U.S.-made, double-cut, neck-thru, string-thru solidbody, 2 humbuckers, bound rosewood 'board, standard vibrato system on Soloist is Floyd Rose locking vibrato, a guitar with Kahler vibrato is worth less. Replaced by the Soloist USA in '90.

1984-1986	Custom order, Floyd Rose	$2,000	$2,500
1984-1986	Custom order, Kahler	$1,800	$2,250
1984-1986	San Dimas-built, Floyd Rose	$1,900	$2,400
1984-1986	San Dimas-built, Kahler	$1,700	$2,150
1986-1990	Custom order features	$1,900	$2,400
1986-1990	Ontario-built	$1,500	$1,900

Soloist Custom
1993-1995. Double-cut, neck-thru solidbody, 1 humbucker and 2 single-coils, bound ebony 'board, shark's tooth inlays, U.S.-made.

| 1993-1995 | | $1,150 | $1,450 |

Soloist Pro
1990-1995. Import version of Soloist, with, shark's tooth inlays.

| 1990-1995 | | $800 | $1,000 |

Soloist Shannon
1998. Shark fin inlays, single-single-hum pickups, Rose, signed by Mike Shannon.

| 1998 | | $1,700 | $2,100 |

Soloist Student J1 (U.S.A.)
1984-1999. Double-cut neck-thru solidbody, Seymour Duncan single-single-hum pickups, rosewood 'board, dot inlays, no binding.

| 1984-1986 | San Dimas-built | $1,050 | $1,300 |
| 1986-1999 | Ontario-built | $1,000 | $1,250 |

Soloist U.S.A./SL Series
1990-present. Replaces Soloist, sharkfin markers.

1990-1999	Various models	$1,250	$1,550
2006	SL1, h/s/s, flamed	$1,500	$1,900
2006	SL1, h/s/s, graphic	$1,500	$1,900
2006	SL1, h/s/s, opaque	$1,100	$1,350
2006-2014	SL2H, h/h	$1,400	$1,750

Stealth EX
1992-late 1990s. Offset double-cut, pointed headstock, H/S/S pickups, offset dot markers, tremolo, Jackson Professional logo.

| 1990s | | $290 | $360 |

Stealth HX
1992-1995. 3 humbucker version of Stealth, string-thru body.

| 1992-1995 | | $420 | $525 |

Stealth XL
1993. Stealth XL truss rod cover logo, 1 humbucker, 2 single-coils, left edge dot markers.

| 1993 | | $420 | $525 |

Surfcaster SC1
1998-2001. Jackson logo on headstock, Charvel Surfcaster styling.

| 1998-2001 | | $825 | $1,025 |

Warrior Pro (Import)
1990-1992. Japanese version.

| 1990-1992 | | $290 | $360 |

Warrior U.S.A.
1990-1992. Four point neck-thru solidbody, 1 humbucker and 1 single-coil, triangle markers, active electronics, U.S.-made, the Warrior Pro was Japanese version.

| 1990-1992 | Red | $825 | $1,050 |

Y2KV Dave Mustaine Signature
2000-2002. V-shaped body, shark tooth markers, neck-thru, 2 humbuckers.

| 2000-2002 | | $2,000 | $2,500 |

Jackson-Guldan/Jay G Guitars
1920s-1960s. The Jackson-Guldan Violin Company, of Columbus, Ohio, mainly built inexpensive

Jackson Phil Collen PC1

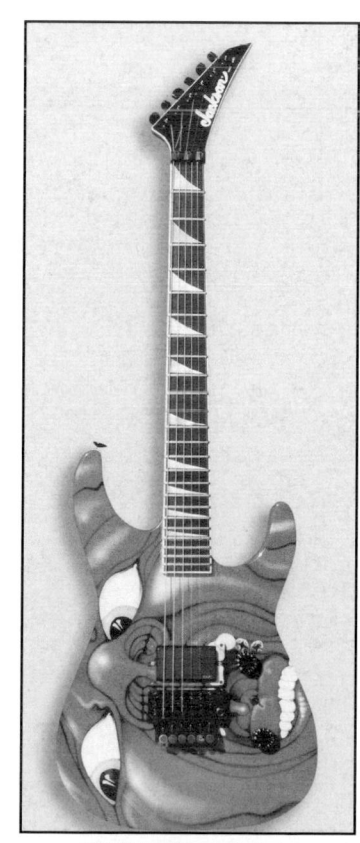

1987 Jackson Soloist
John DeSilva

MODEL		EXC. COND.	
YEAR	FEATURES	LOW	HIGH

MODEL		EXC. COND.	
YEAR	FEATURES	LOW	HIGH

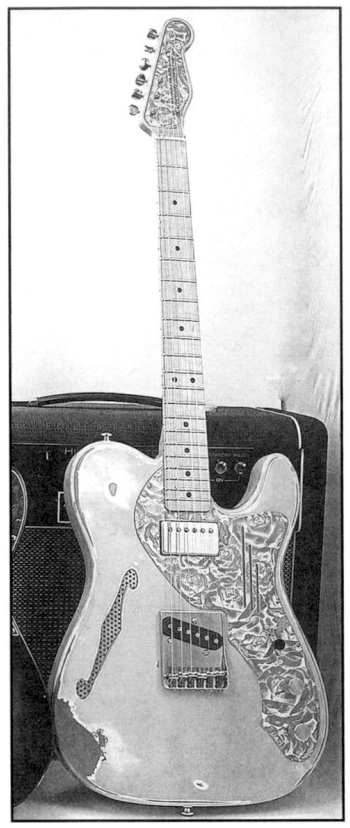

James Trussart Deluxe Steelcaster
Stephen Rabinowitz

violins, violas, cellos, etc. but also offered acoustic guitars in the 1950s and early '60s, some of which were distributed by Wards. Their sales flyers from that era state - Made in America by Jackson-Guldan Craftsman. Very similar to small (13"-14") Stella economy flat-tops. Jay G name with quarter-note logo is sometimes on the headstock. They also offered lap steels and small tube amps early on.

Jacobacci
1930s-1994. Founded in France by Italian Vincent Jacobacci and originally building basso-guitars, banjos, and mandolins. Sons Roger and Andre joined the company and encouraged pop to add lapsteels and electric and regular acoustic guitars around '52. The guitars are sometimes labeled as Jaco and, from ca. '54 to ca. '66, as Jaco Major. In '58 the company introduced aluminum neck models, and in '59 their first solidbodies. In the '60s they also made instruments branded Royal, Texas, Ohio, Star and made instruments for Major Conn and other companies. By the mid '60s, they were producing mainly jazz style guitars.

Jamboree
1960s. Guitar brand exported by Japan's Hoshino (Ibanez).

James Einolf Guitars
1964-present. Production/custom, professional grade, flat-top guitars built in Denver, Colorado by luthier James Einolf.

James R. Baker Guitars
1996-present. Luthier James R. Baker builds his premium grade, custom, archtops in Shoreham, New York.

James Trussart
1980-present. Luthier James Trussart builds his premium grade, custom/production, solid and semi-hollow body electric guitars and basses in Los Angeles, California.

James Tyler
Early 1980s-present. Luthier James Tyler builds his professional and premium grade, custom/production, solidbody guitars and basses in Van Nuys, California, and also has a model built in Japan.

Janofsky Guitars
Production classical and flamenco guitars built by luthier Stephen Janofsky in Amherst, Massachusetts starting in 1978.

Jaros
Beginning 1995 these professional and premium grade, production/custom, solidbody and acoustic/electric guitars were originally built by father and son luthiers Harry and Jim Jaros in Rochester, Pennsylvania. In '01 Ed Roman in Las Vegas,

Jason Z. Schroeder Shorty

bought the brand. He sold it in '04 to Dave Weiler in Nashville. Serial numbers under 1000 were made by the Jaros', numbers 1001-2000 were made by Ed Roman, over 2000 made by Dave Weiler.

Jasmine
1994-present. Budget and intermediate grade, production, steel and classical guitars offered by Takamine Jasmine or Jasmine by Takamine. Student level instruments.

Jason Z. Schroeder Guitars
1994-present. Luthier Jason Schroeder builds professional and premium grade, production/custom, electric guitars in Redding, California.

Jay Turser
1997-present. Budget and intermediate grade, production, imported acoustic, acoustic/electric, electric and resonator guitars and basses. They also amps. Designed and developed by Tommy Rizzi for Music Industries Corp.

JBG (Joe Bochar Guitars)
2009-present. Production/custom, professional grade, solidbody electric guitars built by luthier Joe Bochar in Santa Clarita, California.

JD Bluesville
John Schappell and luthier Davis Millard build their professional grade, custom/production, solidbody electric guitars in Allentown, Pennsylvania.

Jeff Traugott Guitars
1991-present. Premium and presentation grade, custom, flat-top, nylon-string, and acoustic/electric guitars built by luthier Jeff Traugott, in Santa Cruz, California.

Jeremy Locke Guitars
1985-present. Premium grade, production/custom, classical and flamenco guitars built by luthier Jeremy Locke in Coomera, South East Queensland, Australia.

Jeronimo Pena Fernandez
1967-present. Luthier Jeronimo Pena Fernandez started building classical guitars in Marmolejo, Spain, in the '50s. In '67, he went full-time and soon became well-known for his fine work. He is now retired, but still builds a few guitars a year.

Classical
Late 1967-1990s. Brazilian rosewood back and sides, cedar top, full-size classical guitar, higher-end luthier. Prices can vary depending on model specs, each instrument should be evaluated on a case-by-case basis.

1967-1990s		$5,100	$6,400

Jerry Jones
1981-2011. Intermediate grade, production, semi-hollowbody electric guitars and sitars from

MODEL YEAR	FEATURES	EXC. COND. LOW	HIGH

luthier Jerry Jones, built in Nashville, Tennessee. They also built basses. Jones started building custom guitars in '81, and launched his Danelectro-inspired line in '87. He retired in 2011.

Electric Models

Various models include Baritone 6-string ('89-'11); Electric Sitar ('90-'11) with buzz-bar sitar bridge, individual pickup for sympathetic strings and custom color gator finish; Longhorn Guitarlin ('89-'00, '05-'11) with large cutaway Guitarlin-style body, 24 frets in '89 and 31 after;and the Neptune 12-string ('81-'11) single-cut with 3 pickups.

YEAR	MODEL / FEATURES	LOW	HIGH
1981-2011	Neptune Electric 12-string	$725	$900
1989-2011	Baritone 6-string	$725	$900
1989-2011	Longhorn Guitarlin	$725	$900
1990-2011	Baby Sitar	$725	$900
1990-2011	Electric Sitar	$725	$900
1990-2011	Shorthorn	$725	$900

Jersey Girl

1991-present. Premium grade, production/custom, solidbody guitars made in Japan. They also build effects.

JET

1998-present. Premium grade, custom/production, chambered solidbody electric guitars built by luthier Jeffrey Earle Terwilliger in Raleigh, North Carolina.

Jewel

1920s. Instruments built by the Oscar Schmidt Co. and possibly others. Most likely a brand made for a distributor.

JG Guitars

1991-present. Luthier Johan Gustavsson builds his premium and presentation grade, production/custom, solidbody electric guitars in Malmö, Sweden.

Jim Dyson

1972-present. Intermediate, professional and premium grade, production/custom electric guitars and basses built by luthier Jim Dyson in Torquay, Southern Victoria, Australia. He also builds lap steels.

Jim Redgate Guitars

1992-present. Luthier Jim Redgate builds his premium grade, custom, nylon-string classical guitars in Belair, Adelaide, South Australia.

John Le Voi Guitars

1970-present. Production/custom, gypsy jazz, flat-top, and archtop guitars built by luthier John Le Voi in Lincolnshire, United Kingdom. He also builds mandolin family instruments.

John Page Guitars

2006-present. Luthier John Page builds his custom, premium grade, chambered and solidbody electric guitars in Sunny Valley, Oregon.

John Price Guitars

1984-present. Custom classical and flamenco guitars built by luthier John Price in Australia.

Johnson

Mid-1990s-present. Budget, intermediate and professional grade, production, acoustic, classical, acoustic/electric, resonator and solidbody guitars and basses imported by The Music Link, Brisbane, California. Johnson also offers amps, mandolins, ukuleles and effects.

Jon Kammerer Guitars

1997-present. Luthier Jon Kammerer builds his professional and premium grade, custom/production, solidbody, chambered, hollow-body, and acoustic guitars and basses in Keokuk, Iowa.

Jones

See TV Jones listing.

Jordan

1981-present. Professional and premium grade, custom, flat-top and archtop guitars built by luthier John Jordan in Concord, California. He also builds electric violins and cellos.

Jose Oribe

1962-present. Presentation grade, production, classical, flamenco, and steel-string acoustic guitars built by luthier Jose Oribe in Vista, California.

Jose Ramirez

See listing under Ramirez, Jose.

JY Jeffrey Yong Guitars

2003-present. Professional and premium grade, production/custom, classical, acoustic and electric guitars and basses and harp guitars built by Jeffrey Yong in Kuala Lumpur, Malaysia.

K & S

1992-1998. Hawaiian-style and classical guitars distributed by George Katechis and Marc Silber and handmade in Paracho, Mexico. A few 16" wide Leadbelly Model 12-strings were made in Oakland, California by luthier Stewart Port. K & S also offered mandolins, mandolas and ukes. In '98, Silber started marketing guitars under the Marc Silber Guitar Company brand and Katechis continued to offer instruments under the Casa Montalvo brand.

Kakos, Stephen

1972-present. Luthier Stephen Kakos builds his premium grade, production/custom, classical guitars in Mound, Minnesota.

John Page AJ-K

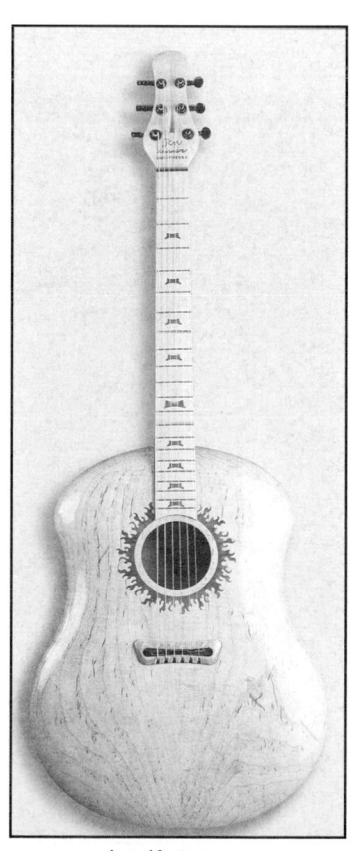

Jon Kammerer

Karol Dragonfly

1950s Kay K27 Jumbo
Curt Huettner

MODEL YEAR	FEATURES	EXC. COND. LOW	HIGH

Kalamazoo

1933-1942, 1965-1970. Budget brand built by Gibson. Made flat-tops, solidbodies, mandolins, lap steels, banjos and amps. Name revived for a line of amps, solidbodies and basses in '65-'67. Playability and string tension will affect values of '60s electrics.

KG-1/KG-1 A
1965-1969. Offset double-cut (initial issue) or SG-shape (second issue), 1 pickup, Model 1 A with spring vibrato, red, blue or white.

1965-1969	Early Mustang body	$400	$525
1965-1969	Later SG body	$425	$550

KG-2/KG-2 A
1965-1970. Offset double-cut (initial shape) or SG-shape, 2 pickups, Model 2 A with spring vibrato, red, blue or white.

1965-1970	Early Mustang body	$425	$550
1965-1970	Later SG body	$475	$625

KG-11
1933-1941. Flat-top, all mahogany, 14" with no 'guard, sunburst.

1933-1941		$1,000	$1,250

KTG-11 Tenor
1936-1940. Tenor version of 11.

1936-1940		$625	$775

KG-12
1940-1941. Rare model, L-00, sunburst.

1940-1941		$1,500	$1,900

KG-14/KG-14 N
1936-1940. Flat-top L-0-size, mahogany back and sides, with 'guard, sunburst or natural (N).

1936-1940		$1,500	$1,900

KTG-14 Tenor
1936-1940. Tenor version of 14.

1936-1940		$925	$1,150

KG-16
1939-1940. Gibson-made archtop, small body, f-hole.

1939-1940		$650	$825

KG-21
1936-1941. Early model 15" archtop (bent, not curved), dot markers, bound top, sunburst.

1936-1941		$650	$825

KTG-21 Tenor
1935-1939. Tenor version of 21.

1935-1939		$600	$750

KG-22
1940-1942. Early model 16" archtop.

1940-1942		$850	$1,075

KG-31
1935-1940. Archtop L-50-size, 16" body, non-carved spruce top, mahogany back and sides.

1935-1940		$850	$1,075

KG-32
1939-1942. Archtop, 16" body.

1939-1942		$850	$1,075

KGN-32 Oriole
1940. 16" acoustic archtop, Kalamazoo brand logo, stencil Oriole-bird picture on headstock, natural.

1940		$1,400	$1,750

MODEL YEAR	FEATURES	EXC. COND. LOW	HIGH

KHG Series
1936-1941. Acoustic Hawaiian guitar (HG), some converted to Spanish set-up.

1936-1940	KHG-11	$725	$875
1936-1941	KHG-14	$1,000	$1,250

Kamico

1947-1951. Flat-top acoustic guitars. Low-end budget brand made by Kay Musical Instrument Company and sold through various distributors. They also offered lap steel and amp sets.

K Stratotone Thin Single
1950s. Similar to Kay Stratotone-style neck-thru solidbody, single slim-tube pickup.

1950s		$1,200	$1,500

Kapa

Ca. 1962-1970. Begun by Dutch immigrant and music store owner Koob Veneman in Hyattsville, Maryland whose father had made Amka guitars in Holland. Kapa is from K for Koob, A for son Albert, P for daughter Patricia, and A for wife Adeline. Crown shield logo from Amka guitars. The brand included some Hofner and Italian imports in '60. Ca. '66 Kapa started offering thinner bodies. Some German Pix pickups ca. '66. Thinlines and Japanese bodies in '69. Kapa closed shop in '70 and the parts and equipment were sold to Micro-Frets and Mosrite. Later Veneman was involved with Bradley copy guitars imported from Japan. Approximately 120,000 Kapa guitars and basses were made.

Electric
1962-1970. Various models include Challenger with 3-way toggle from '62-'66/'67 and 2 on/off switches after; Cobra with 1 pickup; Continental and Continental 12-string; Minstrel and Minstrel 12-string with teardrop shape, 3 pickups; and the Wildcat, mini offset double-cut, 3 pickups and

1962-1970	Various models	$225	$750

Karol Guitars

2001-present. Luthier Tony Karol builds his custom, premium grade, acoustic and electric guitars in Mississauga, Ontario.

Kasha

1967-1997. Innovative classical guitars built by luthier Richard Schneider in collaboration with Dr. Michael Kasha. Schneider also consulted for Gibson and Gretsch. Schneider died in '97.

Kathy Wingert Guitars

1996-present. Luthier Kathy Wingert builds her premium grade, production/custom, flat-tops in Rancho Palos Verdes, California.

Kawai

1927-present. Kawai is a Japanese piano and guitar maker. They started offering guitars around '56 and they were imported into the U.S. carrying many different brand names, including Kimberly and

MODEL YEAR	FEATURES	EXC. COND. LOW	HIGH

Teisco. In '67 Kawai purchased Teisco. Odd-shaped guitars were offered from late-'60s through the mid-'70s. Few imports carrying the Kawai brand until the late-'70s; best known for high quality basses. By '90s they were making plexiglass replicas of Teisco Spectrum 5 and Kawai moon-shaped guitar. Kawai quit offering guitars and basses around 2002.

Acoustic

1956-2002		$225	$350

Electric

1956-2002	Common model	$225	$350
1956-2002	Rare model	$550	$750

Kay

　Ca. 1931 (1890)-present. Originally founded in Chicago, Illinois as Groehsl Company (or Groehsel) in 1890, making bowl-backed mandolins. Offered Groehsl, Stromberg, Kay Kraft, Kay, Arch Kraft brand names, plus made guitars for S.S.Maxwell, Old Kraftsman (Spiegel), Recording King (Wards), Supertone (Sears), Silvertone (Sears), National, Dobro, Custom Kraft (St.Louis Music), Hollywood (Shireson Bros.), Oahu and others.

　In 1921 the name was changed to Stromberg-Voisinet Company. Henry Kay "Hank" Kuhrmeyer joined the company in '23 and was secretary by '25. By the mid-'20s the company was making many better Montgomery Ward guitars, banjos and mandolins, often with lots of pearloid. First production electric guitars and amps are introduced with big fanfare in '28; perhaps only 200 or so made. Last Stromberg instruments seen in '32. Kuhrmeyer becomes president and the Kay Kraft brand was introduced in '31, probably named for Kuhrmeyer's middle name, though S-V had used Kay brand on German Kreuzinger violins '28-'36. By '34, if not earlier, the company is changed to the Kay Musical Instrument Company. A new factory was built at 1640 West Walnut Street in '35. The Kay Kraft brand ends in '37 and the Kay brand is introduced in late-'36 or '37.

　Violin Style Guitars and upright acoustic basses debut in '38. In '40 the first guitars for Sears, carrying the new Silvertone brand, are offered. Kamico budget line introduced in '47 and Rex flat-tops and archtops sold through Gretsch in late-'40s. Kuhrmeyer retires in '55 dies a year later. New gigantic factory in Elk Grove Village, Illinois opens in '64. Seeburg purchased Kay in '66 and sold it to Valco in '67. Valco/Kay went out of business in '68 and its assets were auctioned in '69. The Kay name went to Sol Weindling and Barry Hornstein of W.M.I. (Teisco Del Rey) who began putting Kay name on Teisco guitars. By '73 most Teisco guitars are called Kay. Tony Blair, president of Indianapolis-based A.R. Musical Enterprises Inc. (founded in '73) purchased the Kay nameplate in '79 and currently distributes Kay in the U.S. Currently Kay offers budget and intermediate grade, production, acoustic, semi-hollow body, solidbody, and resonator guitars. They also make amps, basses, banjos, mandolins, ukes, and violins.

K11/K8911 Rhythm Special
1952-1960. Single-cut 17" acoustic archtop, "eighth note" headstock logo, large position markers, white 'guard, became K8911 in '57, sunburst or blond (B).

1953-1961	Blond	$1,050	$1,300
1953-1961	Sunburst	$950	$1,200

K20 Super Auditorium
1939-1942. 16" archtop, solid spruce top, maple back and sides, sunburst.

1939-1942		$275	$375

K20T
1970s. Japanese-made solidbody, 2 pickups, tremolo, model number on neck plate, circle-capital K logo on headstock.

1970s		$125	$160

K21/K21B Cutaway Professional
1952-1956. Single-cut 17" acoustic archtop, split block markers, sunburst or blond (B).

1952-1956	Blond	$1,250	$1,550
1952-1956	Sunburst	$1,150	$1,425

K22 Artist Spanish
1947-1956. Flat-top similar to Gibson J-100 17", spruce top, mahogany back and sides.

1947-1956		$650	$800

K26 Artist Spanish
1947-1951. Flat-top, block markers, natural.

1947-1951		$700	$900

K27 Jumbo
1952-1956. 17" Jumbo flat-top, fancy appointments.

1952-1956		$1,200	$1,500

K37T Spanish Tenor
1952-1956. Mahogany bodied archtop, tenor.

1952-1956		$250	$300

K39 Super Grand Auditorium
1947-1951. Full size acoustic archtop, faux rope binding on top, Kay script logo.

1947-1951		$375	$450

K44 Artist Archtop
1947-1951. Non-cut archtop, solid spruce top, 17" curly maple veneered body, block markers, sunburst.

1947-1951		$500	$600

K45 Professional Master Size Archtop
1952-1954. Non-cut archtop, 17" body, engraved tortoiseshell-celluloid headstock, large block markers, natural.

1952-1954		$600	$750

K45 Travel Guitar
1981. Made in Korea, known as the 'rifle guitar', 'travel guitar', or 'Austin-Hatchet copy', circle K logo.

1981		$325	$400

K46 Master Size Artist Archtop
1947-1951. Non-cut archtop, solid spruce top, 17" curly maple-veneered body, double-eighth note headstock inlay, sunburst.

1947-1951		$525	$635

K48 Master Size Artist Archtop
1947-1951. Non-cut archtop, 17" solid spruce top with figured maple back and sides, split block inlays, sunburst or black.

1947-1951		$875	$1,100

1950 Kay K39
Jim Bame

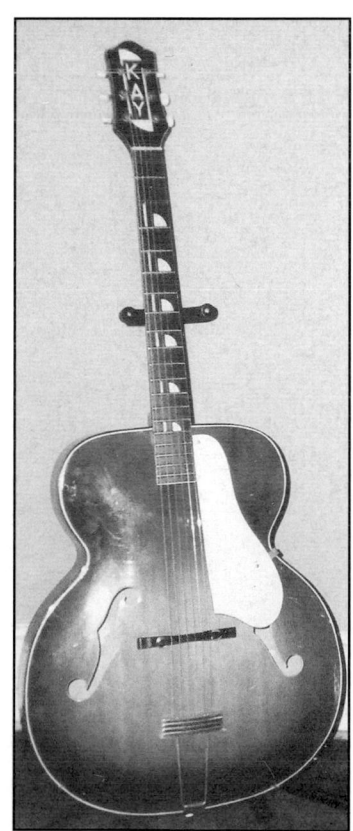

Kay K46
John Neff

Early-1960s Kay K102 Vanguard

Richard Kregear

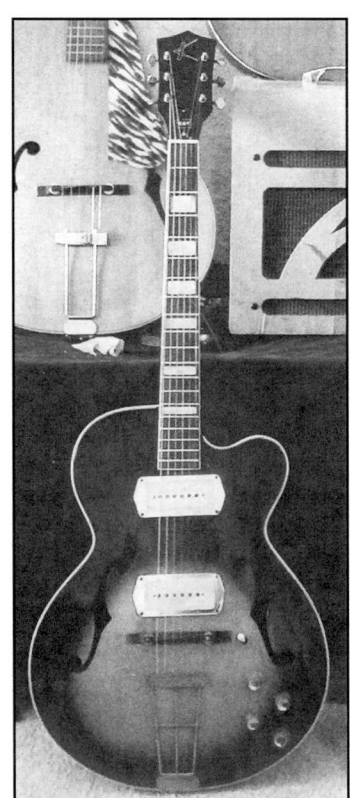

Early-1960s Kay K672 Swingmaster

Jim Bame

MODEL YEAR	FEATURES	EXC. COND. LOW	HIGH

K48/K21 Jazz Special
Late-1960s. Slim solidbody with 3 reflective pick-ups, garden spade headstock, fancy position Circle K headstock logo, white.

1968		$450	$550

K100 Vanguard
1961-1966. Offset double-cut slab solidbody, genuine maple veneered top and back over hardwood body, sunburst.

1961-1966		$275	$350

K102 Vanguard
1961-1966. Double pickup version of the K100, sunburst.

1961-1966		$325	$400

K136 (aka Stratotone)
1955-1957. Small single-cut slab solidbody electric, similar to Harmony Stratotone style, set neck, 1 pickup, trapeze tailpiece, triangle paint graphic in Spring Green and White Mist, matching green headstock, attractive finish adds value to this otherwise lower-end student model.

1955-1957		$1,300	$1,600

K142 (aka Stratotone)
1955-1957. Small slab solidbody, introduced in '55 along with the K136, offered with 1 pickup or 2 pickups (more rare), trapeze tailpiece, copper finish.

1955-1957	1 pickup	$1,000	$1,250
1955-1957	2 pickups	$1,200	$1,500

K161 Thin Twin/Jimmy Reed
1952-1958. Single-cut semi-hollow body, 2 pickups.

1952-1958		$1,250	$1,550

K300 Double Cutaway Solid Electric
1962-1966. Two single-coils, block inlays, some with curly maple top and some with plain maple top, natural.

1962-1966		$425	$525

K535
1961-1965. Thinline double-cut, 2 pickups, vibrato, sunburst.

1961-1965		$500	$650

K550 Dove
1970s. Square shoulder D-style, 2 Dove-style 'guards, capital K logo.

1970s		$100	$125

K571/K572/K573 Speed Demon
1961-1965. Thinline semi-acoustic/electric, single pointed cutaway, some with Bigsby vibrato, with 1 (K571), 2 (K572) or 3 (K573) pickups. There was also a Speed Demon solidbody.

1961-1965	571, 1 pickup	$400	$525
1961-1965	572, 2 pickups	$475	$575
1961-1965	573, 3 pickups	$550	$675

K580 Galaxy
1963. Thinline, single-cut, 1 pickup.

1963		$425	$525

K592 Double Cutaway Thinline
1962-1966. Thinline semi-acoustic/electric, double Florentine cut, 2 or 3 pickups, Bigsby vibrato, pie-slice inlays, cherry.

1962-1966		$500	$625

K672/K673 Swingmaster
1961-1965. Single rounded cutaway semi-hollowbody, with 2 (K672) or 3 (K673) pickups.

1961-1965	672, 2 pickups	$1,000	$1,250
1961-1965	673, 3 pickups	$1,200	$1,450

K775/K776 Jazz II
1961-1966. Electric thinline archtop, double-cut, standard Bigsby vibrato, 2 Gold K pickups, 4 knobs with toggle controls. Replaces Barney Kessel series as top-of-the-line model.

1961-1966	775, shaded	$1,400	$1,700
1961-1966	776, blond	$1,400	$1,700

K797 Acoustic Archtop
1930s. Full size student-intermediate acoustic archtop, 3-on-a-strip tuners, dot markers, sunburst.

1935-1937		$250	$325

K1160 Standard
1957-1964. Small 13" (standard) flat-top, laminated construction.

1957-1964		$50	$65

K1452 Aristocrat
1952. Acoustic-electric archtop, 2 pickups, sunburst.

1952		$800	$1,000

K1700/K1701 Barney Kessel Pro
1957-1960. 13" hollowbody, single-cut, Kelvinator headstock, ebony 'board with pearl inlays, white binding, 1 (K1701) or 2 (K1700) pickups, sunburst.

1957-1960	1700, 2 pickups	$2,250	$2,800
1957-1960	1701, 1 pickup	$2,000	$2,500

K1961/K1962/K1963 Value Leader
1960-1965. Part of Value Leader line, thinline single-cut, hollowbody, identified by single chrome-plated checkered, body-length guard on treble side, laminated maple body, maple neck, dot markers, sunburst, with 1 (K1961), 2 (K1962) or 3 (K1963) pickups.

1960-1965	1961, 1 pickup	$425	$525
1960-1965	1962, 2 pickups	$525	$625
1960-1965	1963, 3 pickups	$575	$675

K1982/K1983 Style Leader/Jimmy Reed
1960-1965. Part of the Style Leader mid-level Kay line. Sometimes dubbed Jimmy Reed of 1960s. Easily identified by the long brushed copper dual guardplates on either side of the strings. Brown or gleaming golden blond (natural) finish, laminated curly maple body, simple script Kay logo, with 2 (K1982) or 3 (K1983) pickups.

1960-1965	1982, 2 pickups	$575	$700
1960-1965	1983, 3 pickups	$650	$800

K3500 Studio Concert
1966-1968. 14 1/2" flat-top, solid spruce top, laminated maple back and sides.

1966-1968		$80	$100

K5113 Plains Special
1968. Flat-top, solid spruce top, laminated mahogany back and sides.

1968		$125	$175

K5160 Auditorium
1957-1965. Flat-top 15" auditorium-size, laminated construction.

1957-1965		$125	$175

The *Vintage Guitar Price Guide* shows low to high values for items in all-original excellent condition, and, where applicable, with original case or cover.

MODEL YEAR	FEATURES	EXC. COND. LOW	HIGH

K6100 Country
1950s-1960s. Jumbo flat-top, spruce x-braced top, mahogany back and sides, natural.
1957-1962 $350 $450

K6116 Super Auditorium
1957-1965. Super Auditorium-size flat-top, laminated figured maple back and sides, solid spruce top.
1957-1965 $200 $250

K6120 Western
1960s. Jumbo flat-top, laminated maple body, pinless bridge, sunburst.
1962 $175 $225

K6130 Calypso
1960-1965. 15 1/2" flat-top with narrow waist, slotted headstock, natural.
1960-1965 $250 $300

K6533/K6535 Value Leader
1961-1965. Value Leader was the budget line of Kay, full body archtop, with 1 (K6533) or 2 (K6535) pickups, sunburst.
1961-1965   6533, 1 pickup $425 $525
1961-1965   6535, 2 pickups $425 $525

K6700/K6701 Barney Kessel Artist
1956-1960. Single-cut, 15 1/2" body, 1 (K6701) or 2 (K6700) pickups, Kelvinator headstock, sunburst or blond.
1956-1960   6700, 2 pickups $2,250 $2,800
1956-1960   6701, 1 pickup $2,000 $2,500

K6878 Style Leader
1966-1968. Full size (15.75) acoustic archtop, circle K logo on 'guard, sunburst.
1966-1968 $225 $285

K7000 Artist
1960-1965. Highest-end of Kay classical series, fan bracing, spruce top, maple back and sides.
1960-1965 $360 $450

K7010 Concerto
1960-1965. Entry level of Kay classical series.
1960-1965 $75 $100

K7010 Maestro
1960-1965. Middle level of Kay classical series.
1960-1965 $200 $275

K8110 Master
1957-1960. 17" master-size flat-top which was largest of the series, laminated construction.
1957-1960 $150 $200

K8127 Solo Special
1957-1965. Kay's professional grade flat-top, narrow waist jumbo, block markers.
1957-1965 $425 $550

K8700/K8701 Barney Kessel Jazz Special
1956-1960. Part of the Gold K Line, top-of-the-line model, 17" single-cut archtop, 1 (K8701) or 2 (K8700) pickups, 4 controls and toggle, Kelvinator headstock with white background, natural or shaded sunburst, Barney Kessel signature logo on acrylic scalloped 'guard, no signature logo on '60 model.
1956-1960   8700, 2 pickups $2,250 $2,800
1956-1960   8701, 1 pickup $2,000 $2,500

K8990/K8995 Upbeat
1956/1958-1960. Less expensive alternative to Barney Kessel Jazz Special, 2 (K8990) or 3 (K8995) pickups, Gold K Line, Kelvinator headstock, sunburst.
1956-1960   8990, 2 pickups $1,500 $2,000
1958-1960   8995, 3 pickups $1,700 $2,200

Wood Amplifying Guitar
1934. Engineered after Dobro/National metal resonator models except the resonator and chamber on this model are made of wood, small production.
1934 $2,400 $3,000

Kay Kraft

1927-1937. First brand name of the Kay Musical Instrument Company as it began its transition from Stromberg-Voisinet Company to Kay (see Kay for more info).

Recording King
1931-1937 $500 $625

Venetian Archtop
1930s. Unique Venetian cutaway body style, acoustic with round soundhole, flower-vine decal art on low bout.
1930s $900 $1,125

KB

1989-present. Luthier Ken Bebensee builds his premium grade, custom, acoustic and electric guitars and basses in North San Juan, California. He was located in San Luis Obispo from '89-'01. He also builds mandolins.

Kel Kroydon (by Gibson)

1930-1933. Private branded budget level instruments made by Gibson. They also had mandolins and banjos. The name has been revived on a line of banjos by Tom Mirisola and made in Nashville.

KK-1
1930-1933. 14 3/4" L-0 sytle body, colorful parrot stencils on body.
1930-1933 $3,000 $3,800

Keller Custom Guitars

Professional grade, production/custom, solid-body guitars built by luthier Randall Keller in Mandan, North Dakota.

Keller Guitars

1975-present. Premium grade, production/custom, flat-tops made by luthier Michael L. Keller in Rochester, Minnesota.

Kelly Guitars

1968-present. Luthier Rick Kelly builds professional grade, custom, solidbody electric guitars in New York, New York.

Ken Franklin

2003-present. Luthier Ken Franklin builds his premium grade, production/custom, acoustic guitars in Ukiah, California.

Kay K8700 Barney Kessel Jazz Special
Dave Linden

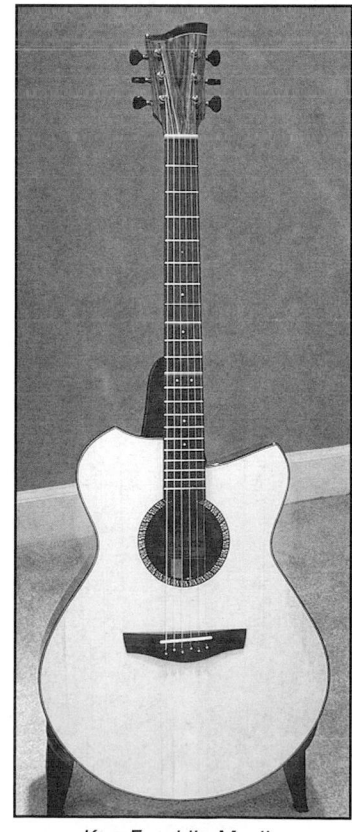

Ken Franklin Merlin

Kevin Ryan Signature Cathedral

Kinal Standard MT

MODEL YEAR	FEATURES	EXC. COND. LOW	HIGH

Kendrick

1989-present. Premium grade, production/custom, solidbody guitars built in Texas. Founded by Gerald Weber in Pflugerville, Texas and currently located in Kempner, Texas. Mainly known for their handmade tube amps, Kendrick added guitars in '94 and also offers speakers and effects.

Kenneth Lawrence Instruments

1986-present. Luthier Kenneth Lawrence builds his premium grade, production/custom, electric solidbody and chambered guitars and basses in Arcata, California.

Kent

1961-1969. Imported from Japan by Buegeleisen and Jacobson of New York, New York. Manufacturers unknown but many early guitars and basses were made by Guyatone and Teisco.

Acoustic Flat-Top
1962-1969. Various models.

1962-1969		$120	$150

Acoustic/Electric
1962-1969. Various models.

1962-1969		$145	$180

Electric 12-String
1965-1969. Thinline electric, double pointy cutaways, 12 strings, slanted dual pickup, sunburst.

1965-1969		$250	$350

Semi-Hollow Electric
1962-1969. Thinline electric, offset double pointy cutaways, slanted dual pickups, various colors.

1962-1969		$250	$350

Solidbody Electric
1962-1969. Models include Polaris I, II and III, Lido, Copa and Videocaster.

1962-1969	Common model	$125	$250
1962-1969	Rare model	$250	$350

Kevin Ryan Guitars

1989-present. Premium grade, custom, flat-tops built by luthier Kevin Ryan in Westminster, California.

KeyKord

Ca. 1929-mid 1930s.. Keykord offered guitars, ukes and banjos that had a push-button mechanism mounted over the fingerboard that "fingered" a different chord for each button. The guitars were built by Chicago's Stromberg-Voisinet (Kay).

Tenor
1920s-1930s. Venetian mahogany body, 4-string, pearloid headstock overlay.

1920s-30s		$475	$600

Kiesel

See Carvin.

Kimbara

1970s-1980s. Japanese line of guitars and basses mainly imported into the U.K. Models were the same as the Fresher brand.

Kimberly

Late-1960s-early-1970s. Private branded import made in the same Japanese factory as Teisco. They also made basses.

May Queen
1960s. Same as Teisco May Queen with Kimberly script logo on headstock and May Queen Teisco on the 'guard.

1960s		$500	$625

Kinal

1969-present. Production/custom, professional and premium grade, solid body electric and archtop guitars and basses built and imported by luthier Michael Kinal in Vancouver, British Columbia.

King's Stone

1960s. Guitar brand exported by Japan's Hoshino (Ibanez).

Kingsley

1960s. Early Japanese imports, Teisco-made.

Soldibody Electric
1960s. Four pickups with tremolo.

1960s		$275	$350

Kingslight Guitars

1980-present. Luthier John Kingslight builds his premium grade, custom/production, steel string guitars and basses in Portage, Michigan (in Taos, New Mexico for '80-'83).

Kingston

Ca. 1958-1967. Guitars and basses imported from Japan by Jack Westheimer and Westheimer Importing Corporation of Chicago, Illinois. Early examples made by Guyatone and Teisco. They also offered mandolins and banjos.

Electric
1958-1967. Various models include: B-1, soldibody, 1 pickup; B-2T/B-3T/B-4T, solidbodies, 2/3/4 pickups and tremolo; SA-27, thin hollowbody, 2 pickups, tremolo.

1958-1967	Common model	$125	$250
1958-1967	Rare model	$250	$350

Kinscherff Guitars

1990-present. Luthier Jamie Kinscherff builds his premium grade, production/custom, flat-top guitars in Austin, Texas.

Kleartone

1930s. Private brand made by Regal and/or Gibson.

Small Flat-Top

1930s		$500	$650

Klein Acoustic Guitars

1972-present. Luthiers Steve Klein and Steven Kauffman build their production/custom, premium and presentation grade flat-tops and basses in Vine, California.

MODEL		EXC. COND.	
YEAR	FEATURES	LOW	HIGH

Klein Electric Guitars

1988-2007. Steve Klein added electrics to his line in '88. In '95, he sold the electric part of his business to Lorenzo German, who continued to produce professional grade, production/custom, solidbody guitars and basses in Linden, California.

K-Line Guitars

2005-present. Professional grade, production/custom, T-style and S-style guitars and basses built by luthier Chris Kroenlein in St. Louis, Missouri. He also builds basses.

Klira

1887-1980s. Founded by Johannes Klira in Schoenbach, Germany, mainly made violins, but added guitars in the 1950s. The guitars of the '50s and '60s were original designs, but by the '70s most models were similar to popular American models. The guitars of the '50s and '60s were aimed at the budget market, but workmanship improved with the '70s models. They also made basses.

Electric

1960s	Common model	$320	$400
1960s	Rare model	$400	$625

Knaggs

2010-present. Luthiers Joseph Knaggs and Peter Wolf build premium and presentation grade, production/custom, acoustic and electric guitars and basses in Greensboro, Maryland.

Knox

Early-mid-1960s. Budget grade guitars imported from Japan, script Knox logo on headstock.

Electric Solidbody

1960s. Student models, 2 pickups, push buttons.

1960s		$100	$150

Knutsen

1890s-1920s. Luthier Chris J. Knutsen of Tacoma and Seattle, Washington, experimented with and perfected Hawaiian and harp guitar models. He moved to Los Angeles, California around 1916, where he also made steels and ukes. Dealers state the glue used on Knutsen instruments is prone to fail and instruments may need repair.

Convertible

1909-1914. Flat-top model with adjustable neck angle that allowed for a convertible Hawaiian or Spanish setup.

1909-1914		$2,950	$3,700

Harp Guitar

1900s. Normally 11 strings with fancy purfling and trim.

1900-1910		$2,400	$3,000

Knutson Luthiery

1981-present. Professional and premium grade, custom, archtop and flat-top guitars built by luthier John Knutson in Forestville, California. He also builds basses, lap steels and mandolins.

Kohno

1960-present. Luthier Masaru Kohno built his classical guitars in Tokyo, Japan. When he died in '98, production was taken over by his nephew, Masaki Sakurai.

Koll

1990-present. Professional and premium grade, custom/production, solidbody, chambered, and archtop guitars and basses built by luthier Saul Koll, originally in Long Beach, California, and since '93, in Portland, Oregon.

Kona

1910s-1920s. Acoustic Hawaiian guitars sold by C.S. Delano and others, with later models made by the Herman Weissenborn Co. Weissenborn appointments are in line with style number, with thicker body and solid neck construction. Kona name currently used on an import line.

Style 2

1927-1928		$2,350	$2,950

Style 3

1920s	Koa	$3,100	$3,900

Style 4

1920s	Hawaiian	$3,800	$4,900
1920s	Spanish	$2,900	$3,800

Kona Guitar Company

2000-present. Located in Fort Worth, Texas, Kona imports budget and intermediate grade, production, nylon and steel string acoustic and solid and semi-hollow body electric guitars and basses. They also offer amps, mandolins and ukes.

Koontz

1970-late 1980s. Luthier Sam Koontz started building custom guitars in the late '50s. Starting in '66 Koontz, who was associated with Harptone guitars, built guitars for Standel. In '70, he opened his own shop in Linden, New Jersey, building a variety of custom guitars. Koontz died in the late '80s. His guitars varied greatly and should be valued on a case-by-case basis.

Kopp String Instruments

2000-present. Located in Republic, Ohio from 2000-2004, luthier Denny Kopp presently builds his professional and premium grade, production/custom, semi-hollow archtop electric and hand-carved archtop jazz guitars in Catawba Island, Ohio.

Kopy Kat

1970s. Budget copy-era solidbody, semi-hollow body and acoustic guitars imported from Japan. They also made basses and mandolins.

Acoustic

1970s	J-200 copy	$125	$175

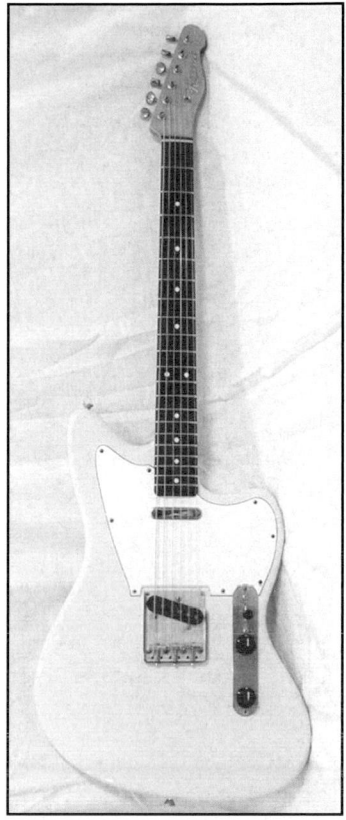

K-Line Texola

*Knaggs Steve Stevens
Signature*

GUITARS

Kragenbrink OM Fingerstylist

1985 Kramer Triax

MODEL		EXC. COND.	
YEAR	FEATURES	LOW	HIGH

Kragenbrink

2001-present. Premium grade, production/custom, steel string acoustic guitars built by luthier Lance Kragenbrink in Vandercook Lake, Michigan.

Kramer

1976-1990, 1995-present. Currently Kramer offers budget and intermediate grade, production, imported acoustic, acoustic/electric, semi-hollow and solidbody guitars. They also offer basses, amps and effects.

Founded by New York music retailer Dennis Berardi, ex-Travis Bean partner Gary Kramer and ex-Norlin executive Peter LaPlaca. Initial financing provided by real estate developer Henry Vaccaro. Parent company named BKL Corporation (Berardi, Kramer, LaPlaca), located in Neptune City, New Jersey. The first guitars were designed by Berardi and luthier Phil Petillo and featured aluminum necks with wooden inserts on back to give them a wooden feel. Guitar production commenced in late-'76. Control passed to Guitar Center of Los Angeles for '79-'82, which recommended a switch to more economical wood necks. Aluminum necks were phased out during the early-'80s, and were last produced in '85. In '84 they added their first import models, the Japanese-made Focus line, followed by the Korean-made Striker line. By 1986 Kramer was the top American electric guitarmaker. In '89, a new investment group was brought in with James Liati as president, hoping for access to Russian market, but the company went of business in late-'90. In '95 Henry Vaccaro and new partners revived the company and designed a number of new guitars in conjunction with Phil Petillo. However, in '97 the Kramer brand was sold to Gibson. In '98, Henry Vaccaro released his new line of aluminum-core neck, split headstock guitars under the Vacarro brand. From 1997 to 2009, sales of Kramer instruments was only through Gibson's MusicYo website. In 2010, Gibson began to distribute the brand through traditional music retail channels with new issues and 1980s legacy models.

Non-U.S.-made models include the following lines: Aerostar, Ferrington, Focus, Hundred (post-'85 made with 3 digits in the 100-900), Showster, Striker, Thousand (post-'85 made with 4 digits in the 1000-9000), XL (except XL-5 made in '80s).

Serial numbers for import models include:

Two alpha followed by 4 numbers: for example AA2341 with any assortment of letters and numbers.

One alpha followed by 5 numbers: for example B23412.

Five numbers: for example 23412.

Model number preceding numbers: for example XL1-03205.

The notation "Kramer, Neptune, NJ" does indicate U.S.A.-made production.

Most post-'85 Kramers were ESP Japanese-made guitars. American Series were ESP Japanese components that were assembled in the U.S.

MODEL		EXC. COND.	
YEAR	FEATURES	LOW	HIGH

The vintage/used market makes value distinctions between U.S.-made and import models. Headstock and logo shape can help identify U.S. versus imports as follows:

Traditional or Classic headstock with capital K as Kramer: U.S.A. '81-'84.

Banana (soft edges) headstock with all caps KRAMER: U.S.A. American Series '84-'86.

Pointy (sharp cut) headstock with all caps KRAMER: U.S.A. American Series '86-'87.

Pointy (sharp cut) headstock with downsized letters Kramer plus American decal: U.S.A. American Series '87-'94.

Pointy (sharp cut) headstock with downsized letters Kramer but without American decal, is an import.

1984 Reissue

2003-2007. Made in the U.S., based on EVH's Kramer, single Gibson humbucker, Rose tremolo, various colors.

2003-2007		$525	$650

250-G Special

1977-1979. Offset double-cut, tropical woods, aluminum neck, dot markers, 2 pickups.

1977-1979		$650	$825

350-G Standard

1976-1979. Offset double-cut, tropical woods, aluminum neck, tuning fork headstock, ebonol 'board, zero fret, 2 single coils, dot inlays. The 350 and 450 were Kramer's first models.

1976-1979		$800	$1,000

450-G Deluxe

1976-1980. Like 350-G, but with block inlays, 2 humbuckers. Became the 450G Deluxe in late '77 with dot inlays.

1976-1980		$900	$1,125

650-G Artist

1977-1980. Aluminum neck, ebonol 'board, double-cut solidbody, 2 humbuckers.

1977-1980		$1,000	$1,250

Baretta

1984-1990. Offset double-cut, banana six-on-a-side headstock, 1 pickup, Floyd Rose tremolo, black hardware, U.S.A.-made.

1984	Non-tilt headstock	$2,400	$3,800
1984-1985	2nd style, angled headstock	$800	$1,000
1984-1985	With graphics	$900	$1,125
1985-1987	3rd style, ESP neck	$450	$550
1985-1987	With graphics	$500	$700
1988-1990	Standard opaque	$450	$550
1988-1990	With graphics	$500	$700
1990	Baretta III hybrid	$400	$500

Baretta '85 Reissue

2006. Made in the U.S., based on 1985 banana headstock model, Rose tremolo.

2006		$600	$750

Baretta II/Soloist

1986-1990. Soloist sleek body with pointed cutaway horns.

1986-1990		$350	$450

MODEL YEAR	FEATURES	EXC. COND. LOW	HIGH

Classic Series
1986-1987. Solidbody copies of the famous Southern California builder, including offset contoured double-cut (Classic I) and slab body single-cut designs (Classic II and Classic III).

1986-1987	Classic I	$400	$500
1986-1987	Classic II	$600	$800
1986-1987	Classic III	$600	$800

Condor
1985-1986. Futuristic 4-point body with large upper bass horn and lower treble horn.

1985-1986		$450	$575

DMZ Custom Series
1978-1981. Solidbody double-cut with larger upper horn, bolt-on aluminum T-neck, slot headstock, models include the 1000 (super distortion humbuckers), 2000 (dual-sound humbuckers), 3000 (3 SDS single-coils), 6000 (dual-sound humbuckers, active DBL).

1978-1981	DMZ-1000	$800	$1,000
1978-1981	DMZ-2000	$800	$1,000
1978-1981	DMZ-3000	$975	$1,225
1978-1981	DMZ-6000	$1,025	$1,275

Duke Custom/Standard
1981-1982. Headless aluminum neck, 22-fret neck, 1 pickup, Floyd Rose tremolo.

1981-1982		$340	$425

Duke Special
1982-1985. Headless aluminum neck, two pickups, tuners on body.

1982-1985		$380	$475

Eliot Easton Pro I
1987-1988. Designed by Elliot Easton, offset double-cut, six-on-a-side headstock, Floyd Rose tremolo, 2 single-coils and 1 humbucker.

1987-1988		$600	$750

Eliot Easton Pro II
1987-1988. Same as Pro I, but with fixed-bridge tailpiece, 2 single-coils.

1987-1988		$525	$650

Ferrington
1985-1990. Acoustic-electric, offered in single- and double-cut, bolt-on electric-style neck, transducers, made in Korea.

1985-1990		$225	$275

Floyd Rose Signature Edition
1983-1984. Four pointed-bout body with deep cutaway below tremolo assembly, Floyd Rose vibrato system.

1983-1984		$600	$750

Focus/F Series (Import)
1983-1989. Kramer introduced the Focus series as import copies of their American-made models like the Pacer, Baretta, Vanguard (Rhoads-V), and Voyager (star body). Model numbers were 1000-6000, plus the Focus Classic I, II, and III. Most models were offset, double-cut solidbodies. In '87 the Focus line was renamed the F-Series. In '88 a neck-through body design, which is noted as NT, was introduced for a short time. The Classic series was offered with over a dozen color options.

1983-1989	Various models	$200	$400

Gene Simmons Axe
1980-1981. Axe-shaped guitar, aluminum neck, 1 humbucker, slot headstock, stop tailpiece, 25 were made.

1980-1981		$5,000	$6,300

Gorky Park (Import)
1986-1989. Triangular balalaika, bolt-on maple neck, pointy droopy six-on-a-side headstock, 1 pickup, Floyd Rose tremolo, red with iron sickle graphics, tribute to Russian rock, reissued in late-'90s.

1986-1989		$225	$275

Hundred Series
1988-1990. Import budget line, most with offset double-cut 7/8th solidbody.

1988-1989	615, bound 610	$260	$325
1988-1990	110, 1 pickup	$180	$225
1988-1990	120	$230	$290
1988-1990	210, 2 pickups	$205	$255
1988-1990	220	$230	$290
1988-1990	310, 3 pickups	$230	$290
1988-1990	410	$230	$290
1988-1990	420, V-body	$260	$325
1988-1990	610, sleek body, 3 pickups	$230	$290
1988-1990	620	$230	$290
1989-1990	111, 2 pickups	$230	$290
1989-1990	112, carved 111	$230	$290
1989-1990	612	$230	$290
1989-1990	710	$230	$290
1989-1990	720, revised 710	$230	$290

Jersey Star
2004-2007. A reissue of the Richie Sambora model.

2004-2007		$700	$875

Liberty '86 Series
1986-1987. Offset double cut arched-top solidbody, pointy head, 2 humbuckers, black, white or flame-maple bound body.

1986-1987	Black or white	$575	$725
1986-1987	Flame maple	$625	$775

Metalist/Showster Series
1989-1990. Korean-made offset double-cut solidbody, metal trim in body design, pointy droopy six-on-a-side headstock, various pickup options, Floyd Rose.

1989-1990		$360	$450

Night Rider
2000-2007. Inexpensive import double-cut semi-hollow, 2 humbuckers.

2000-2007		$75	$100

Nightswan
1987-1990. Offset double-cut, six-on-a-side headstock, 2 Duncan humbuckers, Floyd Rose tremolo, blue metallic.

1987-1990		$1,000	$1,200
1987-1990	Custom color or finish	$1,100	$1,350

Pacer Series
1981-1987. Offset double-cut, six-on-a-side headstock, various pickup options, bolt-on maple neck.

1981-1982	Pacer, 2 pickups, soft headstock	$900	$1,125
1982	Imperial, soft headstock	$500	$625

Kramer Baretta

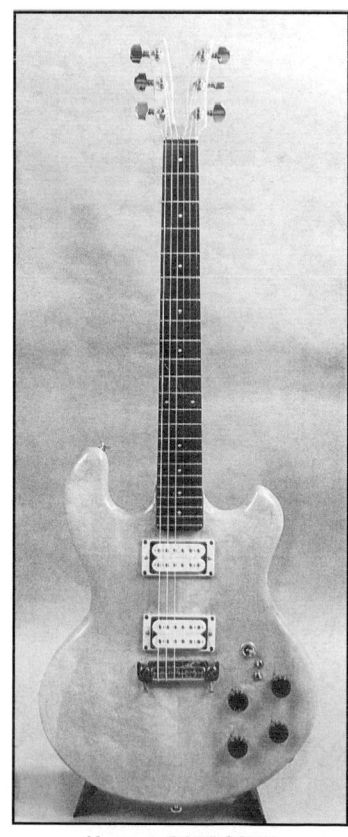

Kramer DMZ-2000

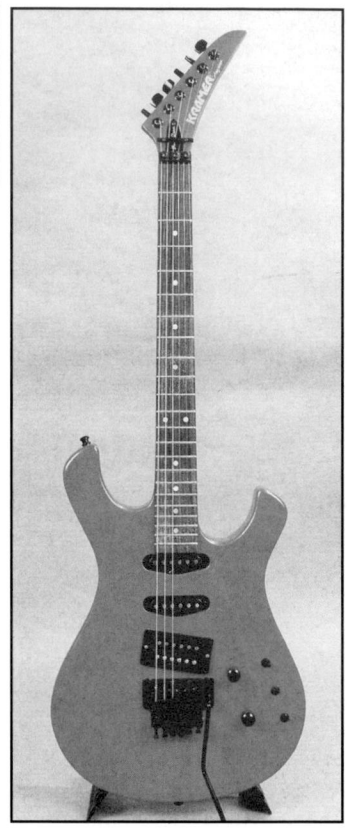

Kramer Paul Dean

*Kramer Stagemaster
Deluxe (U.S.A.)*

MODEL YEAR	FEATURES	EXC. COND. LOW	HIGH
1982	Special, 1 pickup	$450	$575
1982-1984	Carerra, 2 pickups, classic headstock	$575	$725
1982-1984	Pacer, 2 pickups, classic headstock	$550	$675
1983-1984	Custom, classic headstock	$575	$725
1983-1984	Deluxe, classic headstock	$550	$675
1983-1984	Imperial, classic headstock	$500	$625
1984	Pacer, 2 pickups, banana headstock	$575	$725
1985	Carerra USA, 2 pickups, banana headstock	$600	$750
1985	Custom USA, banana headstock	$575	$725
1985	Deluxe USA, banana headstock	$550	$675
1985	Imperial USA, banana headstock	$500	$625
1986	Carerra Japan, 2 pickups, pointy headstock	$600	$750
1986-1987	Custom Japan, pointy headstock	$575	$725
1986-1987	Deluxe USA/Japan, pointy headstock	$550	$675
1986-1987	Imperial USA/ Japan, pointy headstock	$500	$625
1987	Custom II	$575	$725

Paul Dean
1986-1988. Offset double cut, neck-thru, hum/ single/single pickups, droopy pointy head.

1986-1988		$625	$775

ProAxe (U.S.A.)
1989-1990. U.S.A.-made, offset double-cut, sharp pointy headstock, dot markers, 2 or 3 pickups, smaller 7/8ths size body, 3 models offered with slightly different pickup options. The model was discontinued when Kramer went out of business in 1990.

1989-1990	Deluxe	$675	$850
1989-1990	Special	$650	$825
1989-1990	Standard	$625	$775

Richie Sambora
1987-1989. Designed by Sambora, mahogany offset double-cut, maple neck, pointy droopy 6-on-a-side headstock, gold hardware, Floyd Rose, 3 pickups, 2 coil-taps.

1987-1989		$950	$1,175

Ripley Series
1984-1987. Offset double-cut, banana six-on-a-side headstock, 22 frets, hexophonic humbucking pickups, panpots, dual volume, Floyd Rose tremolo, black hardware, stereo output, pointy droopy headstock in '87.

1984-1987		$825	$1,025

Savant/Showster Series
1989-1990. Offset double-cut solidbody, pointy headstock, various pickup options.

1989-1990		$250	$325

Stagemaster Deluxe (U.S.A.)
1981. U.S.-made version.

1981		$1,225	$1,525

Stagemaster Series (Import)
1983-1987. Offset double-cut neck-thru solidbody models, smaller 7/8th body, built by ESP in Japan.

1983-1987	Custom/Custom I	$800	$1,000
1983-1987	Deluxe/Deluxe I	$700	$900
1983-1987	Imperial	$575	$725
1983-1987	Special	$500	$625
1983-1987	Standard/Standard I	$575	$725
1987	Deluxe II	$600	$800

Striker Series (Import)
1984-1989. Korean imports, offset double-cut, various pickup options, series included Striker 100, 200, 300, 400, 600 and 700 Bass.

1984-1989	Various models	$200	$350

Sustainer
1989. Offset double-cut solidbody, reverse pointy headstock, Floyd Rose tremolo.

1989		$650	$800

Vanguard Series
1981-1986. U.S.-made or American Series (assembled in U.S.). V shape, 1 humbucker, aluminum (Special '81-'83) or wood (Custom '81-'83) neck. Added for '83-'84 were the Imperial (wood neck, 2 humbuckers) and the Headless (alum neck, 1 humbucker). For '85-'86, the body was modified to a Jackson Randy Rhoads style V body, with a banana headstock and 2 humbuckers. In '99 this last design was revived as an import.

1981-1983	Custom	$500	$600
1981-1983	Special	$600	$800
1983-1984	Imperial	$500	$600
1985-1986	Rhoads V-body	$400	$500

Vanguard (Reissue)
1999-2014. 2 humbuckers, pointy headstock, licensed Floyd Rose.

1999-2014		$205	$255

Voyager
1982-1985. Wood neck, classic headstock, rosewood 'board, 1 pickup (2 optional), Floyd Rose tremolo, black.

1982-1985	Imperial	$600	$750

XKG-10
1980-1981. Aluminum neck, V-shaped body.

1980-1981		$625	$775

XKG-20
1980-1981. More traditional double-cut body with small horns.

1980-1981		$550	$675

XL Series
1980-1981, 1987-1990. The early-'80s U.S.-made models had aluminum necks and were completely different than the late-'80s wood neck models, which were inexpensive imports.

1980-1981	Aluminum neck	$700	$875
1987-1990	Wood neck	$125	$175

ZX Aero Star Series (Import)
1986-1989. Offset double-cut solidbodies, pointy six-on-a-side headstock. Models include the 1 humbucker ZX-10, 2 humbucker ZX-20, 3 single coil ZX-30, and hum/single/single ZX-30H.

1986-1989		$125	$175

MODEL		EXC. COND.	
YEAR	FEATURES	LOW	HIGH

Kramer-Harrison, William

1977-present. Luthier William Kramer-Harrison builds his premium grade, custom, classical and flat-top guitars in Kingston, New York.

KSM

1988-present. Luthier Kevin S. Moore builds his premium grade, custom/production, solidbody electric guitars in Logan, Utah.

Kubicki

1973-present. Kubicki is best known for their Factor basses, but did offer a few guitar models in the early '80s. See Bass section for more company info.

Kustom

1968-present. Founded by Bud Ross in Chanute, Kansas, and best known for the tuck-and-roll amps, Kustom also offered guitars from '68 to '69. See Amp section for more company info.

Electric Hollowbody

1968-1969. Hollowed-out 2-part bodies; includes the K200A (humbucker, Bigsby), the K200B (single-coils, trapeze tailpiece), and the K200C (less fancy tuners), various colors.

1960s		$900	$1,225

Kwasnycia Guitars

1997-present. Production/custom, premium grade, acoustic guitars built by luthier Dennis Kwasnycia in Chatham, Ontario.

Kyle, Doug

1990-present. Premium grade, custom, Selmer-style guitars made by luthier Doug Kyle in the U.K.

L Benito

Professional grade, steel and nylon string acoustics from luthier Lito Benito and built in Chile.

La Baye

1967. Designed by Dan Helland in Green Bay, Wisconsin and built by the Holman-Woodell factory in Neodesha, Kansas. Introduced at NAMM and folded when no orders came in. Only 45 prototypes made. A few may have been sold later as 21st Century. They also had basses.

2x4 6-String

1967. Narrow plank body, controls on top, 2 pickups, tremolo, 12-string version was also made.

1967		$1,100	$1,400

La Mancha

1996-present. Professional and premium grade, production/custom, classical guitars made in Mexico under the supervision of Kenny Hill and Gil Carnal and distributed by Jerry Roberts of Nashville, Tennessee.

La Patrie

Production, classical guitars. Founded by luthier Robert Godin, who also has the Norman, Godin, Seagull, and Patrick & Simon brands of instruments.

La Scala

Ca. 1920s-1930s. La Scala was another brand of the Oscar Schmidt Company of New Jersey, and was used on guitars, banjos, and mandolins. These were often the fanciest of the Schmidt instruments. Schmidt made the guitars and mandolins; the banjos were made by Rettberg & Lang.

Lace Music Products

1979-present. Intermediate and professional, production, electric guitars from Lace Music Products of Cypress, California, a division of Actodyne General Inc. which was founded by Don Lace Sr., inventor of the Lace Sensor Pickup. In '96, Lace added amplifiers, followed by guitars in 2001 and Rat Fink guitars in '02.

Lacey Guitars

1974-present. Luthier Mark Lacey builds his premium and presentation archtops and flat-tops in Nashville, Tennessee.

Lado

1973-present. Founded by Joe Kovacic, Lado builds professional and premium grade, production/custom, solidbody guitars and basses in Lindsay, Ontario. Some model lines are branded J. K. Lado.

Lafayette

Ca. 1963-1967. Sold through Lafayette Electronics catalogs. Early Japanese-made guitars and basses from pre-copy era, generally shorter scale beginner instruments. Many made by Guyatone, some possibly by Teisco.

Acoustic Thinline Archtop

1963-1967. Various models.

1963-1967		$325	$400

Laguna

2008-present. Guitar Center private label, budget and intermediate grade, production, imported electric and acoustic guitars price range.

Lakeside (Lyon & Healy)

Early-1900s. Mainly catalog sales of guitars and mandolins from the Chicago maker. Marketed as a less expensive alternative to the Lyon & Healy Washburn product line.

Harp Guitar

Early-1900s. Spruce top, rosewood finished birch back and sides, two 6-string necks with standard tuners, 1 neck is fretless without dot markers, rectangular bridge.

1900s	Various models	$2,000	$2,500

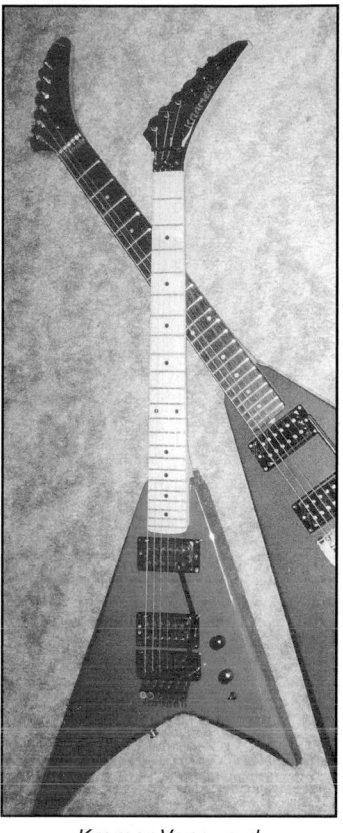

Kramer Vanguard
Rick Walters

Laguna LG300CE

Lakewood J-56 Premium

Larrivee D-40R Legacy

MODEL YEAR	FEATURES	EXC. COND. LOW	HIGH

Lakewood

1986-present. Luthier Martin Seeliger builds his professional and premium grade, production/custom, steel and nylon string guitars in Giessen, Germany. He has also built mandolins.

Langdon Guitars

1997-present. Luthier Jeff Langdon builds his professional and premium grade, production/custom, flat-top, archtop, and solidbody guitars in Eureka, California.

Langejans Guitars

1971-present. Premium grade, production/custom, flat-top, 12-string, and classical guitars built by luthier Delwyn Langejans in Holland, Michigan.

Larrivee

1968-present. Professional and premium grade, production/custom, acoustic, acoustic/electric, and classical guitars built in Vancouver, British Columbia and, since '01, in Oxnard, California. They also offered several acoustic and a few electric basses over the years. Founded by Jean Larrivee, who apprenticed under Edgar Monch in Toronto. He built classical guitars in his home from '68-'70 and built his first steel string guitar in '71. Moved company to Victoria, BC in '77 and to Vancouver in '82. In '83, he began building solidbody electric guitars until '89, when focus again returned to acoustics.

Up to 2002, Larrivee used the following model designations: 05 Mahogany Standard, 09 Rosewood Standard, 10 Deluxe, 19 Special, 50 & 60 Standard (unique inlay), 70 Deluxe, and 72 Presentation. Starting in '03 designations used are: 01 Parlor, 03 Standard, 05 Select Mahogany, 09 Rosewood Artist, 10 Rosewood Deluxe, 19 California Anniv. Special Edition Series, 50 Traditional Series, 60 Traditional Series, E = Electric, R = Rosewood. Larrivee also offers Limited Edition, Custom Shop, and Custom variations of standard models although the model name is the same as the standard model. These Custom models are worth more than the values shown.

0-60
2005. Small fancy rosewood.

2005		$1,675	$2,100

00-05
1996. 14.25", all mahogany.

1996		$1,150	$1,425

00-09
2000s		$1,175	$1,475

00-10
2000s. 00-size 14" lower bout, spruce top, rosewood back and sides, gloss finish.

2000s		$1,350	$1,700

000-50
2008-present. Mahogany back and sides.

2008-2014		$1,450	$1,800

000-60
2006-present. Traditional Series, Indian rosewood.

2006-2014		$1,450	$1,800

MODEL YEAR	FEATURES	EXC. COND. LOW	HIGH

000-60K
Traditional Series, figured koa.

2012		$2,200	$2,800

C-10 Deluxe
Late-1980s-1990s. Sitka spruce top, Indian rosewood back and sides, sharp cutaway, fancy binding.

1980s		$1,500	$1,900

C-72 Presentation
1990s. Spruce top, Indian rosewood back and sides, non-cut Style D, ultra-fancy abalone and pearl hand-engraved headstock.

1990s	Jester headstock	$2,500	$3,100

C-72 Presentation Cutaway
1990s. Spruce top, Indian rosewood back and sides, sharp cutaway, ultra-fancy abalone and pearl hand-engraved headstock.

1990s	Mermaid headstock	$2,900	$3,600

D-03E
2008-present. Solid mahogany back and sides, spruce top, satin finish.

2008-2014		$800	$1,000

D-03R
2002-present. Rosewood.

2002-2014		$800	$1,000

D-03RE
2010-present. Rosewood, on-board electronics.

2010-2014		$850	$1,050

D-04E
2000-2004, 2013-2014. mahogany, on-board electronics.

2013-2014		$1,100	$1,400

D-05-12E
2008-2013. 12 strings.

2008-2013		$1,100	$1,400

D-09
2001-present. Rosewood, spruce top, gloss finish.

2001-2012	Indian or walnut	$1,250	$1,575
2001-2014	Brazilian	$2,400	$3,000

D-10 Deluxe
1990s-present. Spruce top, rosewood, abalone top and soundhole trim.

1995-2014		$1,650	$2,050

D-60
2003-present. Rosewood back and sides.

2003-2014	Indian rosewood	$1,250	$1,575
2000s	Brazilian rosewood	$2,400	$3,000

D-70 Deluxe
1992		$1,700	$2,100

D-Style Classical
1970s. Rosewood body, unicorn inlays.

1970s		$1,525	$1,900

DV Series
2000s	DV-03K, koa	$1,300	$1,650

J-05-12
2000s. Jumbo acoustic-electric 12-string, spruce top, mahogany back and sides.

2000s		$1,200	$1,500

J-09
2008-2009		$1,400	$1,750

J-09-12K
2008-2009		$1,700	$2,100

MODEL YEAR	FEATURES	EXC. COND. LOW	HIGH

J-70
1990s. Jumbo, sitka spruce top, solid Indian rosewood back and sides, presentation grade fancy appointments, limited production.

1994		$1,800	$2,250

JV-05 Mahogany Standard
2000s		$1,100	$1,400

L Series
1990s	L-50	$1,500	$1,900
1990s	L-72 Presentation Custom	$3,000	$3,800
2000s	L-30 (Classical)	$1,200	$1,500

L-0 Standard Series
1980s-present. Models include L-03 (satin finish), L-05 (mahogany) and L-09 (Indian rosewood).

1980s-2014	L-05	$1,175	$1,475
1983-2014	L-09	$1,250	$1,575
1990s-2014	L-03	$750	$950
2000s	L-01	$600	$750
2000s	L-03-12R, 12-string	$750	$950
2008-2012	L-03K, koa	$1,000	$1,250
2008-2014	L-03R, rosewood	$750	$950
2008-2014	L-03RE	$775	$975

LS Series
1998	LS-05, mahogany	$1,100	$1,350
2008-2011	LS-03R, rosewood	$1,100	$1,375

LV Series
1990s-present.

1990s-2014	LV-05, LV-05E	$1,175	$1,475
1990s-2014	LV-09	$1,225	$1,525
2002	LV-19 Special Vine	$2,900	$3,600
2007-2014	LV-03, LV-03E	$950	$1,175
2007-2014	LV-10, LV-10E	$2,000	$2,500

OM Series
1990s-present.

1990-2000s	OM-02	$650	$825
1990-2000s	OM-09R, rosewood	$1,400	$1,750
1990s-2014	OM-03, mahogany, satin	$900	$1,125
1990s-2014	OM-10 Deluxe, rosewood	$1,800	$2,250
1999-2014	OM-05, mahogany	$1,200	$1,500
2000-2014	OM-03R, rosewood	$975	$1,225
2000-2014	OM-50, mahogany	$1,300	$1,700
2000s	OM-09K, koa	$1,600	$2,000
2008-2014	OM-60 Bluegrass, rosewood	$1,400	$1,800

OMV Series
2000s	OMV-50	$1,725	$2,150
2003	OMV-09	$1,425	$1,775
2009	OMV-60	$1,825	$2,275

Parlor Walnut
Early 2000s. Spruce top, solid walnut back and sides.

2002		$575	$725

PV Series
2007-present.

2007	PV-09 Parlor, maple	$1,175	$1,475
2007-2014	PV-09 Parlor, Brazilian	$2,200	$2,800

RS-2 Ventura
2010-present. Mahogany solidbody, rosewood 'board, 1 or 2 pickups, satin finish various colors.

2010-2014		$750	$950

RS-4 CM Carved Top
1988-1989. Carved top solidbody, curly maple top, single-single-humbucker pickups, sunburst or translucent finishes.

1988-1989		$1,200	$1,500

SD Series
2008-present.

2008	SD-03R	$1,300	$1,625
2008-2014	SD-50, mahogany	$1,650	$2,050
2008-2014	SD-60, SD-60E	$1,450	$1,825

Larry Alan Guitars
2003-present. Professional and premium grade, production/custom, acoustic and electric guitars and basses, built by luthier Larry Alan Daft in Lansing, Michigan. He also builds effects pedals.

Larson Brothers
1900-1944. Chicago's Carl and August Larson bought Maurer & Company in 1900 where they built guitars and mandolin family instruments until 1944. Their house brands were Maurer, Prairie State and Euphonon and they also built for catalog companies Wm. C. Stahl and W. J. Dyer & Bro., adding brands like Stetson, a house brand of Dyer. See brand listings for more information.

Laskin
1973-present. Luthier William "Grit" Laskin builds his premium and presentation grade, custom, steel-string, classical, and flamenco guitars in Toronto, Ontario. Many of his instruments feature extensive inlay work.

Laurie Williams Guitars
1983-present. Luthier Laurie Williams builds his premium and presentation grade, custom/production, steel string, classical and archtop guitars on the North Island of New Zealand. He also builds mandolins.

Leach Guitars
1980-present. Luthier Harvey Leach builds his professional and premium grade, custom, flat-tops, archtops, and solidbody electrics, travel guitars and basses in Cedar Ridge, California.

Lehmann Stringed Instruments
1971-present. Luthier Bernard Lehmann builds his professional and premium grade, production/custom, flat-top, archtop, classical and Gypsy guitars in Rochester, New York. He also builds lutes, vielles and rebecs.

Leach VG Franconia

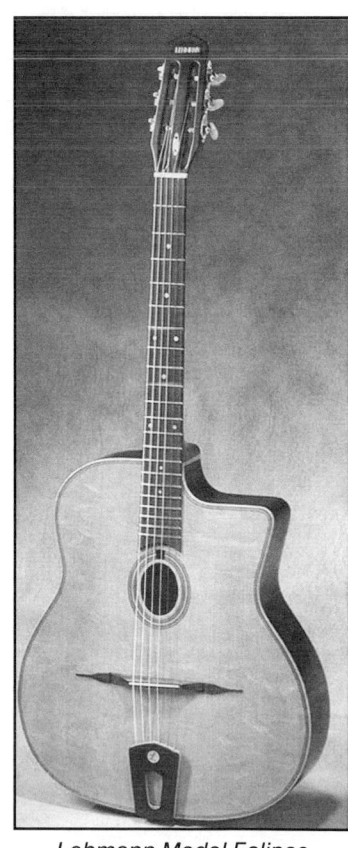

Lehmann Model Eclipse

Liscombe KL74

Lowden Jazz Series

MODEL YEAR	FEATURES	EXC. COND. LOW	HIGH

Lehtela

1993-present. Professional and premium grade, custom/production, acoustic, acoustic/electric, archtop, and solidbody guitars and basses built by luthier Ari Lehtela in Newell, North Carolina.

Lentz

1975-present. Luthier Scott Lentz builds his professional, premium, and presentation grade, custom/production, solidbody electric guitars in San Marcos, California.

Les Stansell Guitars

1980-present. Luthier Les Stansell builds his premium grade, custom, nylon-string guitars in Pistol River, Oregon.

Levin

1900-1973. Founded by Herman Carlson Levin and located in Gothenburg, Sweden, Levin was best known for their classical guitars, which they also built for other brands, most notably Goya from ca. 1955 to the mid '70s. They also built mandolins and ukes.

Levy-Page Special

1930s. Acoustic guitars likely built by Gibson, having many features of Kalamzoo guitars of the era. Possibly made for a distributor.

Lewis

1981-present. Luthier Michael Lewis builds his premium and presentation grade, custom/production, archtop guitars in Grass Valley, California. He also builds mandolins. He also built guitars under the D'Angelico name.

Linc Luthier

1991-present. Professional and premium grade, custom/production, electric and acoustic guitars, basses and double-necks built by luthier Linc Luthier in Upland, California.

Lindberg

Ca. 1950s. Line of guitars produced by Hoyer for Germany's Lindberg music store.

Lindert

1986-2002. Luthier Chuck Lindert made his intermediate and professional grade, production/custom, Art Deco-vibe electric guitars in Chelan, Washington.

Line 6

1996-present. Professional grade, production, imported solidbody and acoustic modeling guitars able to replicate the tones of a variety of instruments. Line 6 also builds effects and amps.

Lion

1960s. One of the brand names of guitars built for others by Egmond in Holland.

Lipe Guitars USA

1983-1989, 2000-present. Custom, professional grade, guitars and basses built in Sun Valley, California by luthier Michael Lipe.

Liscombe

1992-2013. Professional grade, production and limited custom, chambered electric guitars built by luthier Ken Liscombe in Burlington, Ontario.

Loar (The)

2005-present. Professional grade, production, imported archtop acoustic guitars designed by Greg Rich for The Music Link, which also has Johnson and other brands of instruments. They also offer mandolins.

Lollar

1979-present. Luthier Jason Lollar builds his premium grade, production/custom, solidbody and archtop guitars in Vashon, Washington.

Lopez, Abel Garcia

1985-present. Luthier Abel Garcia Lopez builds his premium grade, custom, classical guitars in Mexico.

Loprinzi

1972-present. Professional and premium grade, production/custom, classical and steel-string guitars built in Clearwater, Florida. They also build ukes. Founded by Augustino LoPrinzi and his brother Thomas in New Jersey. The guitar operations were taken over by AMF/Maark Corp. in '73. LoPrinzi left the company and again started producing his own Augustino Guitars, moving his operations to Florida in '78. AMF ceased production in '80, and a few years later, LoPrinzi got his trademarked name back.

Classical

1970s. Various models.

1970s	Brazilian rosewood	$1,600	$2,000
1970s	Indian rosewood	$950	$1,175
1970s	Mahogany	$900	$1,125

Lord

Mid-1960s. Acoustic and solidbody electric guitars imported by Halifax.

Acoustic or Electric Soldibody

1960s	Various models	$80	$150

Lotus

Late-1970s-2004. Budget grade acoustic and electric guitars and basses imported originally by Midco International, of Effingham, Illinois, and most recently by Musicorp. They also offered banjos and mandolins.

Louis Panormo

Early to mid-1800s. Spanish guitars made in London, England by luthier Louis (Luis) Panormo. He was born in Paris in 1784, and died in 1862.

MODEL		EXC. COND.	
YEAR	FEATURES	LOW	HIGH

Lowden

1973-present. Luthier George Lowden builds his premium and presentation grade, production/custom, steel and nylon string guitars in Downpatrick, Northern Ireland. From '80 to '85, he had some models made in Japan.

Flat-Tops

1980s-2000s. Standard models include D, F, O, and S sizes and models 10 thru 32.

1980s-90s	Premium 6-string	$2,700	$3,500
2000s	12-string	$2,000	$2,500
2000s	Premium 6-string	$2,700	$3,500
2000s	Standard 6-string	$2,000	$2,500

LsL Instruments

2008-present. Luthier Lance Lerman builds his production, professional grade, solidbody electric guitars in Los Angeles, California.

LSR Headless Instruments

1988-present. Professional and premium grade, production/custom, solidbody headless guitars and basses made by Ed Roman Guitars.

LTD

1995-present. Intermediate grade, production, Korean made solidbody guitars and basses offered by ESP.

Lucas Custom Instruments

1989-present. Premium and presentation grade, production/custom, flat-tops built by luthier Randy Lucas in Columbus, Indiana.

Lucas, A. J.

1990-present. Luthier A. J. Lucas builds his production/custom, classical and steel string guitars in Lincolnshire, England.

Luis Feu de Mesquita

2000-present. Professional and premium grade, custom, acoustic and flat-top guitars including Spanish, classical and flamenco built in Toronto, Ontario by luthier Luis Feu de Mesquita.

Luna Guitars

2005-present. Located in Tampa, Florida, Yvonne de Villiers imports her budget to professional grade, production, acoustic and electric guitars and basses from Japan, Korea and China. She also added ukuleles in '09 and amps in '10.

Luttrell Guitars

1993-present. Professional and premium grade, production/custom, acoustic, electric and resonator guitars built by luthier Ralph H. Luttrell in Sandy Springs, Georgia.

Lyle

Ca. 1969-1980. Imported by distributor L.D. Heater of Portland, Oregon. Generally higher qual-ity Japanese-made copies of American designs by unknown manufacturers, but some early ones, at least, were made by Arai and Company. They also had basses and mandolins.

Lyon & Healy

1864-present. Founded by George Washburn Lyon and Patrick Joseph Healy, Lyon & Healy was an industry giant, operating a chain of music stores, and manufacturering harps (their only remaining product), pianos, Washburn guitars and a line of brass and wind instruments. See Washburn, American Conservatory, Lakeside, and College brands.

Lyon by Washburn

1990s-2000s. Budget grade, production, solidbody guitars and basses sold by mass merchandisers such as Target.

Lyra

1920s. Instruments built by the Oscar Schmidt Co. and possibly others. Most likely a brand made for a distributor.

Lyric

Luthier John Southern starting building his professional and premium grade, custom, semi-hollow and solidbody and basses guitars in Tulsa, Oklahoma in 1996.

M. Campellone Guitars

See listing under Campellone Guitars

M.Zaganin and N.Zaganin

1989-present. Luthier Márcio Zaganin began his career using the M.Zaganin brand, in 2004 it was changed to N. He builds professional and premium grade, production/custom, semi-hollow and solidbody electric guitars in São Paulo, Brazil. He also builds basses.

Maccaferri

1923-1990. Built by luthier and classical guitarist Mario Maccaferri (b. May 20, 1900, Cento, Italy; d. 1993, New York) in Cento, Italy; Paris, France; New York, New York; and Mount Vernon, New York. Maccaferri was a student of Luigi Mozzani from '11 to '28. His first catalog was in '23, and included a cutaway guitar. He designed Selmer guitars in '31. Maccaferri invented the plastic clothespin during World War II and used that technology to produce plastic ukes starting in '49 and Dow Styron plastic guitars in '53. He made several experimental plastic electrics in the '60s and plastic violins in the late-'80s.

Plastic (Dow Styron)

1950s. Plastic construction, models include Deluxe (archtop, crown logo), Islander (Islander logo), TV Pal (4-string cutaway) and Showtime (Showtime logo).

1950s	Deluxe	$240	$300
1950s	Islander	$220	$275

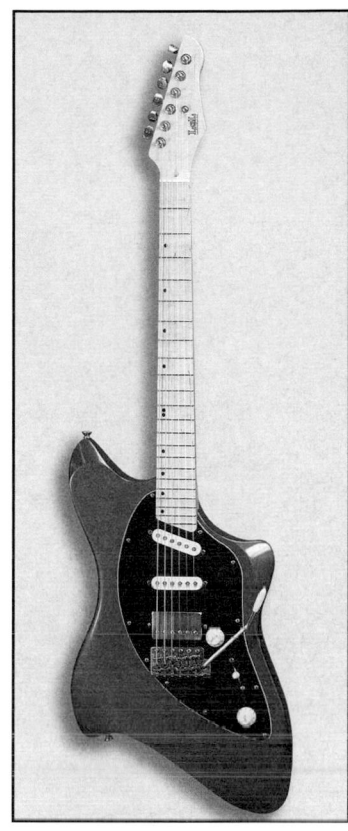

LsL Instruments Del Rey

Lyle 12-string

Peter Najdin

1956 Magnatone
Mark III Standard

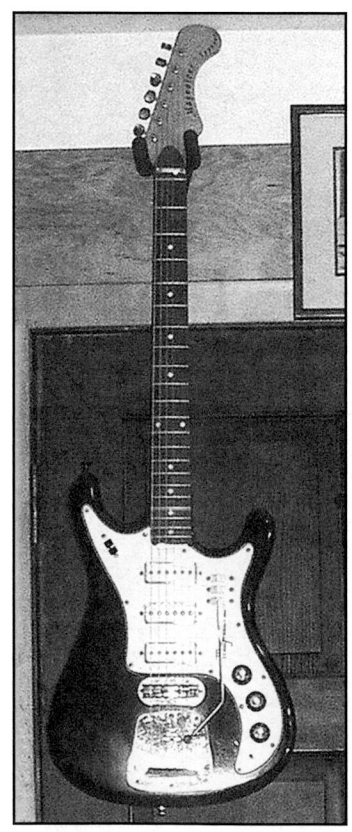

1960 Magnatone Typhoon X-20
Tom Roberts

MODEL YEAR	FEATURES	EXC. COND. LOW	HIGH
1950s	Romancer	$220	$275
1950s	Showtime	$220	$275
1950s	TV Pal	$150	$200

Madeira

1973-ca. 1984, ca. 1990. Imported Budget and intermediate grade acoustic and electric guitars distributed by Guild. The Japanese-made electrics were basically copies of Gibson, Fender and Guild models, the acoustics originally copies of Martin. The electrics only offered first year or so during the '70s run. Name revived again around '90 on imported acoustics and electrics. They also offered mandolins and banjos.

Madrid

1996-present. Luthier Brandon Madrid builds his production/custom, professional and premium grade, acoustic and solidbody electric guitars, in San Diego, California. Prior to 2009 he built in Portland, Oregon.

Maestro

1950s-1970s, 2001-present. Maestro is a brand name Gibson first used on 1950s accordian amplifiers. The first Maestro effects were introduced in the early-'60s and they used the name until the late-'70s. In 2001, Gibson revived the name for a line of effects, banjos and mandolins. Those were dropped in '09, when imported budget and intermediate, production, acoustic and electric guitars and amps were added.

Electric

2009-present. Various student models, Maestro headstock logo, 'By Gibson' logo on truss rod cover.

2009-2014		$55	$100

Magnatone

Ca.1937-1971, 2013-present. Founded as Dickerson Brothers in Los Angeles, California and known as Magna Electronics from '47, with Art Duhamell president. Brands include Dickerson, Oahu (not all), Gourley, Natural Music Guild, Magnatone. In '59 Magna and Estey merged and in '66 the company relocated to Pennsylvania. In '71, the brand was taken over by a toy company. Between 1957 and '67, the company produced four different model lines of Spanish electrics. In 2013, Ted Kornblum revived the Magnatone name on a line of tube amps built in St. Louis, Missouri.

Cyclops

1930s. Dobro-made resonator guitar.

1930s	Round neck	$1,500	$1,850
1930s	Square neck	$1,700	$2,100

Mark Artist Series

1959-1961	More common	$1,000	$1,250
1959-1961	Rare	$1,500	$3,200

Mark Series

1955-1960. Solidbody series made by Paul Bigsby in small quantities, then taken over by Paul Barth at Magnatone in '59.

1955-1959	Mark IV	$3,100	$3,900
1955-1959	Mark V	$3,100	$3,900

MODEL YEAR	FEATURES	EXC. COND. LOW	HIGH
Model Series			
1962	Model 100	$350	$450
1962	Model 150	$350	$450
1962	Model 200, 2 pickups	$350	$450
Tornado X-15			

1965-1966. Offset double-cut body, 3 DeArmond pickups, vibrato.

1965-1966		$725	$900

Typhoon X-20

1965-1966. Double-cut solidbody, 3 DeArmond pickups, vibrato.

1965-1966		$750	$950

Zephyr X-5

1965-1966. Double-cut with 2 DeArmond single-coil pickups, metallic finish, vibrato.

1965-1966		$750	$950

Magno-Tone

1930s. Brand most likely used by a music studio (or distributor) on instruments made by others, including Regal-built resonator instruments.

Mai Kai

1910s. Line of Hawaiian guitars built in Los Angeles, California by the Shireson Brothers.

Mako

1985-1989. Line of budget to lower-intermediate solidbody guitars from Kaman (Ovation, Hamer). They also offered basses and amps.

Solidbody

1985-1989	Various models	$80	$200

Mal n' Sal

See listing for Alternative Guitar and Amplifier Company.

Malinoski

1986-present. Luthier Peter Malinoski builds his production/custom, professional and premium grade, solidbody electric guitars and basses in Hyattsville, Maryland.

Mann

Ca. 1971-ca. 1985. A brand name used in Canada by Japan's Hoshino company on some of the same acoustic and electric models as their Ibanez guitars.

Manne

1987-present. Professional and premium grade, production/custom, semi-acoustic and electric guitars and basses built by luthier Andrea Ballarin in Italy.

Manson Guitar Works

1979-present. Premium grade, production/custom, electric guitars built by luthiers Hugh Manson and Adrian Ashton in Exeter, Devon UK. They also offer a line of professional grade, guitars crafted in the Czech Republic and assembled in UK. They also build basses.

The **Vintage Guitar Price Guide** shows low to high values for items in all-original excellent condition, and, where applicable, with original case or cover.

MODEL		EXC. COND.	
YEAR	FEATURES	LOW	HIGH

Manuel & Patterson

1993-present. Luthiers Joe Manuel and Phil Patterson build professional, premium and presentation grade, production/custom, flat-top, archtop and solidbody electric guitars in Abita Springs, Louisiana. They also offer mandolins.

Manuel Contreras

1962-1994. Luthier Manuel Gonzalez Contreras worked with José Ramírez III, before opening his own shop in Madrid, Spain, in '62.

Manuel Contreras II

1986-present. Professional grade, production/custom, nylon-string guitars made in Madrid, Spain, by luthier Pablo Contreras, son of Manuel.

Manuel Ramirez

See listing under Ramirez, Manuel.

Manuel Rodriguez and Sons, S.L.

1905-present. Professional, premium, and presentation grade, custom flat-top and nylon-string guitars from Madrid, Spain.

Manuel Velázquez

1933-2014. Luthier Manuel Velázquez (d. 2014) built his classical guitars in Puerto Rico ('72-'82), New York City, Virginia, and Florida. His son Alfredo continues to build guitars.

Manzanita Guitars

1993-present. Custom, steel-string, Hawaiian, and resonator guitars built by luthiers Manfred Pietrzok and Moritz Sattler in Rosdorf, Germany.

Manzer Guitars

1976-present. Luthier Linda Manzer builds her premium and presentation grade, custom, steel-string, nylon-string, and archtop guitars in Toronto, Ontario.

Maple Lake

2003-present. Intermediate grade, production, flat-top and acoustic/electric imported guitars from luthier Abe Wechter. Wechter also builds guitars under his own name.

Mapson

1995-present. Luthier James L. Mapson builds his premium and presentation grade, production/custom, archtops in Santa Ana, California.

Marc Silber Guitar Company

1998-present. Intermediate and professional grade, production, flat-top, nylon-string, and Hawaiian guitars designed by Marc Silber and made in Mexico. These were offered under the K & S Guitars and/or Silber brands for 1992-'98. Silber also has ukuleles.

Marchione Guitars

1993-present. Premium and presentation grade, custom, archtops and solidbodies built by Stephen Marchione originally in New York City, but currently in Houston, Texas.

Marcia

1920s. Instruments built by the Oscar Schmidt Co. and possibly others. Most likely a brand made for a distributor.

Marco Polo

1960-ca. 1964. Imported from Japan by Harry Stewart and the Marco Polo Company of Santa Ana, California. One of the first American distributors to advertise inexpensive Japanese guitars and basses. Manufacturers unknown, but some acoustics by Suzuki, some electrics by Guyatone.

Acoustic Hollowbody

1960-1964	Various models	$80	$200

Mario Martin Guitars

2011-present. Luthier Mario Martin builds his production/custom, professional grade, semi-hollow and solidbody guitars and basses in Murfreesboro, Tennessee. From 2006 to '11, he built guitars under the Guitar Mill brand name.

Mark Wescott Guitars

1980-present. Premium grade, custom, flat-tops, built by luthier Mark Wescott in Somers Point, New Jersey.

Marling

Ca. 1975. Budget line guitars and basses marketed by EKO of Recanati, Italy; probably made by them, although possibly imported.

Acoustic

1975. Includes the steel-string S.110, and the dreadnoughts W.354 Western, and W.356 Western.

1975		$80	$200

Electric Soldibody

1975. Includes the E.400 (semi-acoustic/electric), E.490 (solidbody), E.480 (single-cut-style), and the 460 (Manta-style).

1975		$130	$170

Martelle

1934. Private brand attributed to Gibson and some to Kay.

De Luxe

1934. Gibson 12-fret round shoulder Jumbo construction, mahogany back and sides, sunburst, Hawaiian or Spanish option.

1934		$8,800	$11,000

Martin

1833-present. Intermediate, professional, premium, and presentation grade, production/custom, acoustic, acoustic/electric, archtop and resonator guitars. Founded in New York City by Christian

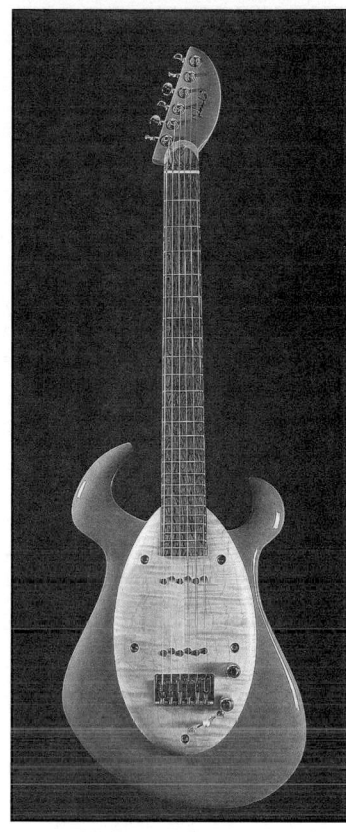

Malinoski Guitar 51

Manne Semiacustica

1970 Martin D-18

Martin 000-18

Frederick Martin, former employee of J. Staufer in Vienna, Austria. Moved to Nazareth, Pennsylvania in 1839. Early guitars were made in the European style, many made with partners John Coupa, Charles Bruno and Henry Schatz. Scalloped X-bracing was introduced in the late-1840s. The dreadnought was introduced in 1916 for the Oliver Ditson Company, Boston; and Martin introduced their own versions in 1931.

Martin model size and shape are indicated by the letter prefix (e.g., 0, 00, 000, D, etc.); materials and ornamentation are indicated by number, with the higher the number, the fancier the instrument (e.g., 18, 28, 35, etc.). Martin offered electric thinline guitars from '61-'68 and electric solidbodies from '78-'82. The Martin Shenandoah was made in Asia and assembled in U.S. Japanese Martin Sigma ('72-'73) and Korean Martin Stinger ('85 on) imported solidbodies.

Most Martin flat-top guitars, particularly Style 18 and above, came with a standard natural finish, therefore Martin guitar finish coloring is generally not mentioned because it is assumed to be see-through natural. Conversely, Gibson's standard finish for their flat-tops during their Golden Era was sunburst. Martin introduced their shaded (sunburst) finish as an option on their Style 18 in 1934 and their Style 28 in 1931. An original Martin shaded factory (sunburst) finish from the 1930's is worth 40% more than the value shown in the Price Guide. A shaded finish option in the 1940s adds 30%, in the 1950s it adds 20%, and in the 1960s it adds 20%. A refinished guitar with a sunburst finish is not included in this analysis, in fact a refinished guitar is generally worth less than one-half that of an original finish guitar. In particular, a refinished sunburst guitar would be worth one-half the value of an original natural finish guitar. The amount of added value associated with a shaded (sunburst) finish for a guitar made between the 1930s and the 1960s also depends on the model. A Style 18 model shaded finish option is more common than some of the other styles, and D-body, OM-body, and 000-body styles can have different premiums for a shaded finish. Braced for steel strings specifications described under certain models are based on current consensus information and data provided by the late Martin employee-historian Mike Longworth, and is for guidance only. Variations from these specs have been found, so "bracing" should be considered on a case-by-case basis.

O-15
1935, 1940-1943, 1948-1961. All mahogany, unbound rosewood 'board, slotted peghead and 12-fret neck until '34, solid peghead and 14-fret neck thereafter, natural mahogany.

MODEL YEAR	FEATURES	EXC. COND. LOW	HIGH
1935	2 made	$2,100	$2,800
1940-1949		$2,100	$2,800
1950-1959		$2,200	$2,800
1960-1961		$2,000	$2,500

O-15 H
1940. Hawaiian neck, all mahogany.

1940		$2,800	$3,500

O-15 M Elderly Instruments 40th Anniversary Limited Editions
2011-2012. Only 10 offered, solid mahogany body and neck, special appointments, inside label signed by Elderly Instruments president Stan Werbin and Martin CEO Chris Martin.

2011-2012		$1,100	$1,400

O-15 T
1960-1963. Tenor with Style 15 appointments, natural mahogany.

1960-1963		$1,300	$1,700

O-16
1961 only. Six made.

1961		$2,150	$2,650

O-16 NY
1961-1977, 1979-1992, 1994. Mahogany back and sides, 12 frets, slotted peghead, unbound extra-wide rosewood 'board, natural.

1961-1965		$2,150	$2,650
1966-1969		$1,850	$2,350
1970-1979		$1,650	$2,050
1980-1989		$1,450	$1,825
1990-1994		$1,375	$1,750

O-17
1906-1917, 1929-1948, 1966-1968. First version has mahogany back and sides, 3 black soundhole rings, rosewood bound back, unbound ebony 'board, 12 frets, slotted peghead. Second version ('29 and on) is all mahogany, 3 white-black-white soundhole rings, top bound until '30, thin black backstripe, 12 frets and slotted peghead until '34, solid peghead and 14 frets thereafter, natural mahogany.

1906-1917	Gut braces	$2,050	$2,550
1929-1933	Steel, 12 fret	$2,300	$2,900
1934	Flat natural finish, 14 fret	$3,100	$3,900
1934-1938	Gloss dark finish, 14 fret	$3,100	$3,900
1939	Early '39, 1.75 neck	$3,100	$3,900
1939	Later '39, 1.68 neck	$2,700	$3,400
1940-1944		$2,400	$3,100
1945-1948		$2,300	$3,000
1966-1968		$1,850	$2,350

O-17 H
1930, 1935-1940. Hawaiian, mahogany back and sides, 12 frets clear of body, natural.

1930	60 made	$2,300	$2,900
1935-1940		$3,100	$3,900

O-17 S
Early 1930s. Limited production style 17 with spruce top, unique 'guard.

1931		$5,000	$6,200

O-17 T
1932-1960. Mahogany back and sides, tenor, natural.

1932-1933		$1,500	$1,875
1934-1939		$2,000	$2,500
1940-1949		$1,550	$2,000
1950-1960		$1,300	$1,700

GUITARS

MODEL YEAR	FEATURES	EXC. COND. LOW	HIGH

O-18

1898-1996. Rosewood back and sides until 1917, mahogany back and sides after, Adirondack spruce top until 1946, slotted peghead and 12 frets until 1934, solid peghead and 14 frets after 1934, braced for steel strings in 1923, improved neck in late-1934, non-scalloped braces appear late-'44, natural.

Year	Features	Low	High
1898-1917	Brazilian rosewood	$3,000	$3,750
1918-1922	Mahogany	$2,300	$2,850
1923-1933	12 fret, steel strings	$3,800	$4,800
1934-1938	14-fret	$4,500	$5,700
1939	Early '39, 1.75 neck	$4,500	$5,700
1939	Later '39, 1.68 neck	$4,200	$5,400
1940-1944		$3,800	$4,700
1945		$3,100	$3,900
1946-1949		$2,900	$3,700
1951-1959		$2,600	$3,300
1960-1964		$2,300	$3,000
1965-1966		$2,000	$2,600
1967-1969		$1,850	$2,350
1970-1979		$1,575	$2,000
1980-1989		$1,350	$1,700
1990-1996		$1,240	$1,550

O-18 G

1960s. Special order classical nylon-string model, natural.

1961		$1,600	$2,000

O-18 K

1918-1935. Hawaiian, all koa wood, T-frets and steel T-bar neck in late-1934, natural.

1918-1933		$3,700	$4,600
1934-1935	14-fret era	$4,800	$6,000

O-18 KH

1927-1928. Hawaiian, koa.

1927-1928		$3,700	$4,600

O-18 T

1929-1932, 1936-1989, 1991-1992, 1994-1995. Mahogany body, spruce top, tenor, natural.

1929-1949		$2,400	$3,000
1950-1959		$1,700	$2,150
1960-1966		$1,500	$1,900
1967-1969		$1,200	$1,525
1970-1979		$1,025	$1,300
1980-1989		$875	$1,100
1991-1995		$800	$1,000

O-18 T Nick Reynolds

2010-2011. Mahogany.

2010-2011		$2,200	$2,800

O-18 TE

1959, 1962. Only 2 made, tenor, 1 pickup.

1959, 1962		$4,500	$5,500

O-18 VS Elderly Instruments 40th Anniversary Limited Edition

2012-2014. Mahogany body, sitka spruce top, slotted headstock, 12-fret neck, inside label signed by C. F. Martin IV and Elderly founder Stan Werbin.

2012-2014		$2,000	$2,500

O-20

1850s.

1850-1859		$4,500	$5,700

O-21

1898-1931, 1934-1938, 1941, 1944, 1946-1948. Rosewood back and sides, Adirondack spruce top until 1946, 12 frets, T-frets and steel T-bar neck in late-1934, non-scalloped braces in late-1944, natural.

Year	Features	Low	High
1898-1920		$4,500	$5,700
1921-1926		$4,500	$5,700
1927-1930		$6,000	$7,500
1930	14-fret (only year)	$7,400	$9,200
1931-1938		$6,000	$7,500
1941		$5,500	$7,000
1944	Non-scalloped	$5,000	$6,300
1946		$4,000	$5,000
1947		$3,900	$4,900
1948		$3,800	$4,800

O-21 K

1919-1929. Koa top, back and sides.

1919-1926		$5,500	$6,700
1927-1929		$6,700	$8,300

O-21 T

1929-1930, 1935, 1961.

1929-1930		$4,300	$5,400
1935		$4,300	$5,400
1961		$2,300	$2,900

O-26

1850-1890. Rosewood back and sides, ivory-bound top, rope-style purfling.

1850-1890		$6,000	$7,500

O-27

1850-1898. Rosewood back and sides, ivory-bound top.

1850-1859	Antique market value	$7,500	$9,500
1890-1898		$6,000	$7,500

O-28

1874-1931, 1937 (6 made), 1969 (1 made). Brazilian rosewood back and sides, herringbone binding until 1937, natural.

Year	Features	Low	High
1874-1895		$6,000	$7,500
1896	Dark orange top (rare)	$8,000	$10,000
1896-1923		$5,900	$7,400
1924-1927	Gut braces	$5,900	$7,400
1925-1927	Steel option	$11,000	$13,500
1928-1929	Steel (standard)	$11,000	$13,500
1930-1937	Belly bridge	$9,500	$11,800
1969	Brazilian	$2,500	$3,100

O-28 Ian Anderson

2004. Adirondack top, scalloped bracing, Indian rosewood back and sides, slotted headstock, 87 made.

2004		$3,000	$3,700

O-28 K

1917-1931, 1935. Hawaiian, all koa wood, braced for steel strings in '23, natural.

1917-1927	Gut braces	$6,000	$7,500
1928-1929	Steel	$8,500	$10,500
1930-1935	Belly bridge	$9,500	$11,800

O-28 T

1930-1931, 1941. Tenor neck.

1930-1931	Steel option	$6,200	$8,000
1941		$5,100	$6,200

1957 Martin 0-15
Folkway Music

1903 Martin 0-28
California Vintage

To get the most from this book, be sure to read "Using *The Guide*" in the introduction.

1955 Martin 00-17

Folkway Music

1952 Martin 00-18

Billy White Jr.

MODEL YEAR	FEATURES	EXC. COND. LOW	HIGH
0-28 VS			
2009-present. Rosewood back and sides, slotted head, 12 fret neck.			
2009-2014		$2,050	$2,550
0-30			
1899-1921. Brazilian rosewood back and sides, ivory-bound body, neck and headstock.			
1899-1921		$6,600	$8,300
0-34			
1885, 1898-1899, 1907. Brazilian rosewood.			
1885-1907		$6,900	$8,600
0-40			
1860s-1898, 1912-1913. Indian rosewood.			
1880-1913		$8,500	$10,500
0-42			
1870s-1924, 1926-1930, 1 each in '34, '38,'42. Brazilian rosewood back and sides, 12 frets, natural.			
1890-1927	Gut braces	$10,000	$12,500
1928-1938	Steel braces	$12,500	$15,500
1942	Steel braces	$12,000	$15,000
0-44 Soloist/Olcott-Bickford Artist Model			
1911-1931. Style 44 guitars were made for guitarist Vahdah Olcott-Bickford in small quantities, Brazilian rosewood, ivory or faux-ivory-bound ebony 'board, 17 made.			
1911-1931		$17,500	$21,500
0-45			
1904-1908, '11, '13, '15, '17-'20, '22-'24, '26-'30, '39. Brazilian rosewood back and sides, natural, special order only for '31-'39.			
1904-1927	Gut braces	$22,500	$28,100
1927-1929	Steel braces	$36,000	$45,000
1930	Steel braces	$41,000	$51,000
1939	Steel braces	$33,000	$41,000
0-45 JB Joan Baez			
1998. Indian rosewood, 59 made.			
1998		$3,800	$4,700
0-45 S Stephen Stills			
2007. 91 made, Madagascar rosewood sides and back, Adirondack spruce top.			
2007		$6,400	$8,000
00-1			
1995-2002. Grand Concert, mahogany.			
1995-2002		$625	$775
00-1 R			
1995-1999. Rosewood version.			
1995-1999		$625	$775
00-15			
1999-2010. Sapele/mahogany.			
1999-2010		$650	$825
00-15 M			
2011-present. All mahogany.			
2011-2014		$825	$1,025
00-15 M Custom Elderly Instruments			
2010-2014. All mahogany, diamond and square inlays, custom-made for Elderly Instruments.			
2010-2014		$975	$1,200
00-15 M Elderly Instruments 40th Anniversary Limited Edition			
2012. Only 10 made, mahogany body and neck, label signed by Elderly's president Stan Werbin and			

MODEL YEAR	FEATURES	EXC. COND. LOW	HIGH
Martin CEO Chris Martin.			
2012		$1,200	$1,500
00-16 C			
1962-1977, 1980-1981. Classical, mahogany back and sides, 5-ply bound top, satin finish, 12 frets, slotted peghead, natural.			
1962-1964		$1,225	$1,525
1965-1966		$1,175	$1,475
1967-1969		$1,100	$1,400
1970-1977		$925	$1,150
1980-1981	2 made	$775	$975
00-16 DB Women and Music Series			
1997-2010. Deep Body, various body materials, electronics available.			
1997-1999	R, rosewood	$1,125	$1,400
1998-1999	M, mahogany	$1,125	$1,400
2000-2005	M, mahogany	$1,025	$1,275
2001-2006	FM, flamed maple	$1,025	$1,275
00-17			
1908-1917, 1930-1960, 1982-1988, 2001-2004. Mahogany back and sides, 12 frets and slotted headstock until '34, solid headstock and 14 frets after '34, natural mahogany, reissued in 2001 with a high gloss finish.			
1908-1917	Gut braces	$2,550	$3,200
1930-1933	Steel, 12-fret	$2,700	$3,400
1934	14-fret, flat natural finish	$3,600	$4,500
1935-1938	14-fret, gloss dark finish	$3,600	$4,500
1939	Early '39, 1.75 neck	$3,600	$4,500
1939	Later '39, 1.68 neck	$3,200	$4,000
1940-1944		$3,200	$4,000
1945-1949		$3,000	$3,750
1950-1959		$2,650	$3,350
1960		$2,250	$2,850
1982-1988		$1,500	$1,950
2000-2004	Reissue model	$1,250	$1,550
00-17 H			
1934-1935. Hawaiian set-up, mahogany body, no binding.			
1934-1935		$3,600	$4,500
00-17 SO Sing Out!			
2000. Limited edition, for 50th anniversary of Sing Out Magazine, folk era logo inlays, SING OUT inlay on 20th fret, mahogany body.			
2000		$1,300	$1,600
00-18			
1898-1995. Rosewood back and sides until 1917, mahogany after, braced for steel strings in 1923, improved neck in late-1934, war-time design changes 1942-1946, non-scalloped braces in late-1944, Adirondack spruce top until 1946, natural.			
1898-1917	Brazilian rosewood	$4,200	$5,250
1918-1922	Mahogany	$3,200	$4,000
1923-1928	Steel strings, 12-fret	$5,400	$6,800
1929-1933	12-fret	$5,400	$6,800
1934-1938	14-fret	$6,400	$8,000
1939	Early '39, 1.75 neck	$6,400	$8,000
1939	Later '39, 1.68 neck	$6,100	$7,700
1940-1941		$5,800	$7,300
1942-1944	Scalloped	$5,800	$7,300

MODEL YEAR	FEATURES	EXC. COND. LOW	HIGH
1944	Non-scalloped	$4,800	$5,900
1945	Non-scalloped	$4,500	$5,600
1946-1949	Non-scalloped	$4,300	$5,400
1950-1952		$3,400	$4,300
1953-1959		$3,200	$4,000
1960-1964		$3,050	$3,825
1965-1966		$2,900	$3,625
1967-1969		$2,675	$3,325
1970-1979		$2,275	$2,800
1980-1989		$1,800	$2,200
1990-1995		$1,500	$1,850

00-18 C

1962-1995. Renamed from 00-18 G in '62, mahogany back and sides, classical, 12 frets, slotted headstock, natural.

1962-1964		$1,300	$1,650
1965-1966		$1,200	$1,550
1967-1969		$1,100	$1,400
1970-1979		$950	$1,200
1980-1989		$875	$1,100
1990-1995		$825	$1,050

00-18 CTN Elizabeth Cotton

2001. Commemorative Edition, 76 made.

2001		$2,050	$2,550

00-18 Custom

2008. Custom Shop run of 75 or more made.

2008		$2,050	$2,550

00-18 E

1959-1964. Flat-top Style 18, single neck pickup and 2 knobs, heavier bracing, natural.

1959-1964		$4,000	$5,500

00-18 G

1936-1962. Mahogany back and sides, classical, natural, renamed 00-18 C in '62.

1936-1939		$2,200	$2,700
1940-1949		$1,850	$2,700
1950-1959		$1,600	$2,000
1960-1962		$1,500	$1,900

00-18 Gruhn Limited Edition

1995. Sitka spruce top, C-shaped neck profile, 25 made.

1995		$1,850	$2,350

00-18 H

1935-1941. Hawaiian, mahogany back and sides, 12 frets clear of body, natural. The Price Guide is generally for all original instruments. The H conversion is an exception, because converting from H (Hawaiian-style) to 00-18 specs is considered by some to be a favorable improvement and something that adds value.

1935-1938		$6,400	$8,000
1940-1941		$6,100	$7,700

00-18 H Geoff Muldaur

2006-2011. Solid Adirondack spruce top, solid mahogany sides and back, sunburst.

2006-2011		$2,050	$2,550

00-18 K

1918-1925, 1934. All koa wood.

1918-1921		$3,800	$4,750
1922-1925		$6,000	$7,500
1934		$6,000	$7,500

00-18 S John Mellencamp

2009-2010. Slotted, 12-fret.

2009-2010		$2,500	$3,100

00-18 SH Steve Howe

1999-2000. Limited edition run of 250.

1999-2000		$1,775	$2,225

00-18 T

1931, 1936, 1938-1940. Tenor version.

1931		$3,900	$4,900
1936-1939		$4,500	$5,600
1940		$4,100	$5,100

00-18 Tim O'Brien Limited Edition Signature

2008-2011. 25.5" scale, label signed by O'Brien.

2008-2011		$3,400	$4,300

00-18 V

1984, 2003-present. Vintage Series, mahogany back and sides, spruce top.

1984	9 made	$1,750	$2,200
2003-2014		$1,700	$2,150

00-18 V/VS Elderly Instruments 40th Anniversary

2012. Limited Edition, solid (V) or slotted (VS) headstock, 12-fret, low profile.

2012-2013	V	$2,000	$2,500
2013	VS	$2,200	$2,750

00-21

1898-1996. Brazilian rosewood back and sides, changed to Indian rosewood in 1970, dark outer binding, unbound ebony 'board until 1947, rosewood from 1947, slotted diamond inlays until '44, dot after, natural.

1898-1926		$5,100	$6,400
1927-1931	Steel braces	$6,200	$7,900
1932-1937	Natural	$6,200	$7,900
1938-1939	Early '39, 1.75 neck	$6,200	$7,900
1940-1943	Scalloped braces	$6,000	$7,600
1944-1945	Non-scalloped	$5,500	$7,000
1946-1949		$5,200	$6,600
1950-1959		$4,500	$5,700
1960-1964		$4,050	$5,100
1965-1966	Brazilian rosewood	$3,850	$4,850
1967-1969	Brazilian rosewood	$3,650	$4,600
1970-1979	Indian rosewood	$2,375	$2,900
1980-1989	Indian rosewood	$1,900	$2,400
1990-1996	Indian rosewood	$1,750	$2,200

00-21 Custom

2005-2006. Custom order size 00 style 21, Brazilian rosewood sides and back.

2005-2006		$3,600	$4,500

00-21 G

1937-1938. Gut string, Brazilian rosewood sides and back.

1937-1938		$2,500	$3,100

00-21 Golden Era

1998. Limited edition, Adirondack spruce top, scalloped braces, rosewood back and sides.

1998-2000		$2,100	$2,600

00-21 H

Hawaiian, special order, limited production.

1914	1 made	$5,100	$6,400
1934		$6,200	$7,900
1952, 1955	1 made each year	$4,500	$5,700

1963 Martin 00-18
Folkway Music

1931 Martin 00-21
Keith Myers

GUITARS

Martin 00-28 VS

1997 Martin 00-40 Stauffer

Steve Zuckerman

MODEL YEAR	FEATURES	EXC. COND. LOW	HIGH
00-21 Kingston Trio LTD			

2007. 50th Anniversary of the Kingston Trio, inspired by Dave Guard's 00-21, 100 made, 12-fret, Indian rosewood, Kingston Trio label and notation "In Memory of Dave Guard 1934-1991".

2007		$3,000	$3,700
00-21 LE			

1987. Guitar of the Month, 19 made.

1987		$2,300	$2,900
00-21 NY			

1961-1965. Brazilian rosewood back and sides, no inlay, natural.

1961-1965		$4,400	$5,500
00-21 S			

1968. Slotted headstock, Brazilian rosewood sides and back.

1968		$5,800	$7,300
00-21 T			

1934. Tenor, Brazilian rosewood back and sides, only 2 made.

1934		$5,500	$6,800
00-25 K			

1980, 1985, 1988. Spruce top, koa back and sides.

1980-1988		$2,000	$2,500
00-25 K2			

1980, 1982-1984, 1987-1989. Koa top, back and sides.

1980-1989		$2,000	$2,500
00-28			

1898-1941, 1958 (1 made), 1977 (1 made), 1984 (2 made). Brazilian rosewood back and sides, changed to Indian rosewood in 1977, herringbone purfling through 1941, white binding and unbound 'board after 1941, no inlays before 1901, diamond inlays from 1901-'41, dot after, natural.

1898-1924	Gut braces	$8,600	$10,800
1925-1931	Steel braces	$14,000	$17,850
1934		$14,000	$17,850
1936-1941	Few made	$16,500	$22,500
1958	1 made	$6,900	$8,600
1977	1 made	$2,100	$2,650
1984	2 made	$1,750	$2,150
00-28 C			

1966-1995. Renamed from 00-28 G, Brazilian rosewood back and sides, changed to Indian rosewood in '70, classical, 12 frets, natural.

1966-1969	Brazilian rosewood	$3,100	$3,900
1970-1979	Indian rosewood	$1,600	$2,000
1980-1989		$1,350	$1,700
1990-1995		$1,250	$1,550
00-28 G			

1936-1962. Brazilian rosewood back and sides, classical, natural, reintroduced as 00-28 C in '66.

1936-1939		$5,500	$6,875
1940-1946		$4,500	$5,625
1947-1949		$4,200	$5,250
1950-1959		$3,600	$4,500
1960-1962		$3,100	$3,900

MODEL YEAR	FEATURES	EXC. COND. LOW	HIGH
00-28 K			

1919-1921, 1926, 1928-1931, 1933. Hawaiian, koa back and sides.

1919-1921	34 made	$10,000	$12,500
1926-1933	1 made per year	$16,500	$21,000
00-28 T			

1931, 1940. Brazilian rosewood back and sides, tenor 4-string neck, only 2 made.

1931, 1940		$8,000	$10,000
00-28 VS			

2009-present. Rosewood back and sides.

2009-2014		$2,150	$2,750
00-28 VS Custom Shop			

2009-present. Various Custom Shop options.

2013		$2,600	$3,300
00-30			

1890s-1921. Rosewood .

1899-1921		$10,800	$13,500
00-34			

1898-1899. 6 made.

1898-1899		$11,900	$14,900
00-37 K2 Steve Miller			

2001. Style 00, 12-fret, all koa, 68 made.

2001		$4,100	$5,100
00-40			

1913, 1917. 4 made.

1913	Brazilian	$19,900	$24,900
1917	Koa	$19,900	$24,900
00-40 H			

1928-1939. Hawaiian, Brazilian rosewood back and sides, 12 frets clear of body, natural. H models are sometimes converted to standard Spanish setup, in higher-end models this can make the instrument more valuable to some people.

1928-1929	Pyramid bridge	$18,000	$22,000
1930-1939	Belly bridge	$18,000	$22,000
00-40 K			

Few were made (only 6), figured koa, natural.

1918	1 made	$20,000	$25,000
1930	5 made	$20,000	$25,000
00-40 Martin Stauffer			

1997. Rosewood/spruce, 35 made.

1997		$5,500	$6,900
00-41 Custom Shop			

2005. Custom Shop model.

2005		$3,400	$4,250
00-42			

1898-1943, 1973 (1 made). Brazilian rosewood back and sides, Indian rosewood in 1973, pearl top borders, 12 frets, ivory bound peghead until 1918, ivoroid binding after 1918, natural.

1898-1926	Pyramid bridge	$18,700	$23,300
1927	Early '27, Pyramid bridge	$18,700	$23,300
1927	Late '27, Belly bridge	$25,000	$31,000
1928-1929	Belly bridge, 12-fret	$25,000	$31,000
1930-1938	14-fret	$26,500	$33,000
1939		$24,000	$30,000
1940-1943		$22,000	$28,000
1973	1 made	$3,000	$3,700

MODEL YEAR	FEATURES	EXC. COND. LOW	HIGH

00-42 G
1936-1939. Gut string slotted headstock classical, only 3 made.

1936-1939	3 made	$9,500	$12,000

00-42 K
1919. Koa body, only 1 made.

1919	1 made	$20,000	$25,000

00-42 K2 Robbie Robertson
2008-2009. Limited Edition, all koa body (K2), 00-12 fret style, high-end appointments.

2008-2009		$4,000	$5,000

00-42 Linda Ronstadt Limited Edition
2009-2010. Madagascar rosewood, slotted headstock.

2009-2010		$5,700	$7,200

00-42 SC John Mayer
2012-present. Sitka spruce top, cocobolo back, sides and headplate, ebony 'board.

2012-2014		$4,200	$5,300

00-44 Soloist/Olcott-Bickford Artist Model
1913-1939. Custom-made in small quantities, Brazilian rosewood, ivory or faux-ivory-bound ebony 'board.

1913-1939	6 made	$35,000	$44,000

00-45
1904-1929, 1970-1982, 1984-1987, 1989-1990, 1992-1993. Brazilian rosewood back and sides, changed to Indian rosewood in '70, 12 frets and slotted headstock until '34 and from '70 on 14 frets, and solid headstock from '34-'70, natural.

1904-1927	Gut braces	$35,000	$44,000
1927-1929	Steel braces	$70,000	$90,000
1970-1979	Reintroduced	$4,600	$5,800
1980-1989		$4,000	$5,000
1990-1993		$3,900	$4,800

00-45 K
1919. Koa body, 1 made.

1919		$48,000	$60,000

00-45 S
1970. Slotted headstock.

1970		$3,800	$4,800

00-45 S Limited Edition
2002. 1902 vintage-pattern with fancy inlays, 00 size style 45, 50 made.

2002		$10,400	$13,000

00-45 SC John Mayer Limited Edition
2012-2013. Only 25 made, slotted headstock, cocobolo.

2012-2013		$11,600	$14,500

00-45 ST Stauffer Commemorative Limited Edition
1997-1998. Six-on-a-side headstock, 45-style appointments, 00 body, Sitka top, Brazilian rosewood back and sides., 25 made.

1997-1998		$10,400	$13,000

00C-16 DBRE
2005-2007. Women and Music Series, rounded cutaway, rosewood back and sides, abalone dot inlays and rosette, Fishman.

2005-2007		$1,500	$1,875

OOCMAE
1999-2001. Single-cut acoustic-electric flat-top, laminate back and sides, made in U.S.

1999-2001		$500	$625

OOCXAE
2000-2013. Single-cut acoustic-electric flat-top, composite laminate back and sides, made in U.S.

2000-2013		$350	$435

00-DB Jeff Tweedy Signature
2011-present. Solid FSC® Certified Mahogany with mahogany burst finish.

2011-2014		$1,550	$1,925

000-1
1994-2005. Solid spruce top with laminated mahogany back and sides.

1994-2005		$650	$800

000-1 E
1994-2005. 000-1 with electronics.

1994-2005		$675	$850

000-1 R
1994-2003. 000-1 with back and sides.

1994-2003		$650	$800

000-15 M
2010-present. All mahogany.

2010-2014		$750	$950

000-15 M Elderly Instruments 40th Anniversary
2012. 10 made, mahogany body and neck, label signed by Elderly Instruments president Stan Werbin and Martin CEO Chris Martin

2012		$1,275	$1,600

000-15 SM
2011-present. Slotted headstock, 12-fret neck, all mahogany.

2011-2014		$850	$1,100

000-15/000-15 S
1999-2009. Mahogany bodies, headstock is solid or slotted (S, first offered in '00). Renamed 000-15 M with solid headstock in '10.

1999-2009	000-15	$750	$950
2000-2009	000-15 S	$900	$1,150

000-16 Series
1989-present. Mahogany back and sides, diamonds and squares inlaid, sunburst, name changed to 000-16 T Auditorium with higher appointments in '96, in 2000-2005 slotted (000-16 S) and gloss finish (000-16 SGT) were offered.

1989	000-16 M	$950	$1,200
1989-1995	000-16	$950	$1,200
1989-2014	000-16 GT	$900	$1,125
1996	000-16 TR	$900	$1,125
1996-1997	000-16 T	$950	$1,200
1996-2002	000-16 R	$900	$1,125
2001-2005	000-16 RGT	$900	$1,125
2003-2004	000-16 SGT	$825	$1,025

000-17
1911, 1952. Mahogany back and sides, 1 made in 1911, 25 more in '52.

1911		$8,500	$10,600
1952		$3,500	$4,400

Martin 000-15 M

1950 Martin 000-18
Billy White Jr.

1955 Martin 000-18
Folkway Music

1956 Martin 000-21

MODEL YEAR	FEATURES	EXC. COND. LOW	HIGH
000-17 S			
2002-2004. All mahogany, slotted headstock, 12 fret neck.			
2002-2004		$1,075	$1,350
000-17 SM			
2013-present. Sitka spruce top, mahogany back and sides, East Indian rosewood headplate, vintage slotted headstock.			
2013-2014		$1,000	$1,250
000-18			
1906, 1911-present (none in 1932-1933). Maple back and sides in '06, then rosewood until '17, and mahogany since, longer scale in '24-'34, 12-fret neck until '33, changed to 14 in '34. Improved neck late-'34, war-time changes '41-'46, non-scalloped braces in late-'44, switched from Adirondack spruce to Sitka spruce top in '46 (though some Adirondack tops in '50s and '60s), natural. Now called the 000-18 Auditorium.			
1906-1917	Gut braces	$8,500	$10,600
1920-1922	Gut braces	$7,600	$9,500
1923-1931	Steel braces	$9,900	$12,300
1934	Early '34, long scale	$18,000	$22,700
1934-1938	14-fret	$16,800	$20,800
1939	Early '39 1.75 neck	$15,800	$19,800
1939	Late '39, 1.68 neck	$14,000	$17,500
1940		$11,900	$14,900
1941		$11,000	$13,500
1942-1944	Scalloped braces	$10,000	$12,500
1944	Non-scalloped	$5,800	$7,200
1945		$5,500	$6,900
1946-1949		$5,200	$6,500
1950-1952		$3,700	$4,700
1953-1959		$3,500	$4,400
1960-1964		$3,500	$4,300
1965-1966		$3,000	$3,750
1967-1969		$2,800	$3,450
1970-1979		$2,200	$2,750
1980-1989		$1,775	$2,250
1990-1999		$1,600	$2,000
2000-2014		$1,400	$1,750
000-18 Authentic 1937			
2008-2011. Natural or sunburst, high-X bracing.			
2008-2011		$4,000	$5,000
000-18 E Retro			
2012-present.			
2012-2014		$1,700	$2,100
000-18 G			
1955. Classical.			
1955		$4,400	$5,500
000-18 Golden Era 1934 Special Edition			
2007. Adirondack red spruce top, scalloped and forward shifted X-bracing, 14-fret V-shaped mahogany neck, 20-fret ebony 'board, old style decal logo.			
2007		$2,400	$3,000
000-18 Golden Era 1937			
2006-2014. Natural. 1937 dropped from name in '12.			
2006-2014		$2,000	$2,500
000-18 Golden Era Sunburst			
2006-2014. Sunburst version.			
2006-2014		$2,000	$2,500

MODEL YEAR	FEATURES	EXC. COND. LOW	HIGH
000-18 Kenny Sultan			
2007-2009. Flamed mahogany sides, diamond and squares inlays, label signed by Sultan.			
2007-2009		$2,400	$3,000
000-18 Norman Blake Signature			
2006-2011. 12 fret neck on 14-fret body.			
2006-2011		$2,400	$3,000
000-18 P			
1930. Plectrum neck.			
1930		$7,000	$8,700
000-18 S			
1976-1977. Slotted, 12-fret.			
1976-1977		$2,750	$3,450
000-18 T			
1930, '34, '36, '38, '41. Tenor.			
1930		$6,400	$8,000
1934-1938		$11,500	$14,500
1941		$7,100	$8,900
000-18 V/VS Elderly Instruments 40th Anniversary			
2012-2013. Limited Edition, solid (V) or slotted (VS) headstock, Sitka top, label signed by C.F. Martin IV and Stan Werbin, includes matching wood guitar stand.			
2012-2013	V	$2,000	$2,500
2013	VS	$2,100	$2,600
000-18 WG Woody Guthrie			
1999. Signed label including artwork and model identification.			
1999		$2,000	$2,500
000-21			
1902-1923 (22 made over that time), 1931(2), 1938-1959, 1965 (1), 1979 (12). Brazilian rosewood back and sides, changed to Indian rosewood in '70, natural.			
1902-1913		$12,000	$15,000
1918-1923		$13,000	$16,300
1931	12-fret	$15,000	$18,800
1938-1939	Early '39, 1.75 neck	$19,000	$23,700
1939	Late '39, 1.68 neck	$15,000	$18,700
1940-1941		$13,000	$16,000
1942-1944		$11,000	$13,800
1945		$10,000	$12,500
1946		$9,600	$11,800
1947-1949		$8,600	$10,600
1950-1954		$6,900	$8,500
1955		$6,800	$8,400
1956		$6,700	$8,300
1957		$6,600	$8,100
1958		$6,500	$8,000
1959		$6,400	$7,900
1965	1 made	$5,100	$6,300
1979	12 made	$2,500	$3,100
000-28			
1902-present. Brazilian rosewood back and sides, changed to Indian rosewood in '70, herringbone purfling through '41, white binding and unbound 'board after '41, no inlays before '01, slotted diamond inlays from '01-'44, dot after, 12 frets until '32, 14 frets '31 on (both 12 and 14 frets were made during '31-'32), natural through '93, sunburst or natural after.			
1902-1927	Gut (standard)	$14,700	$18,200
1925-1927	Steel (mostly)	$26,000	$33,000

MODEL YEAR	FEATURES	EXC. COND. LOW	HIGH
1928	12-fret	$26,000	$33,000
1929	Pyramid bridge, 12-fret	$26,000	$33,000
1930	Belly bridge, 12-fret	$26,000	$33,000
1931-1933	12 fret	$26,000	$33,000
1934	Early '34 long scale	$36,300	$47,000
1934-1937	14-fret	$34,000	$44,000
1938		$31,000	$39,000
1939	Early '39, 1.75 neck	$30,000	$38,000
1939	Late '39, 1.68 neck	$26,000	$33,000
1940-1941		$22,100	$28,000
1942-1944	Scalloped braces	$21,000	$26,000
1944-1946	Herringbone, non-scalloped	$17,500	$23,000
1947-1949	Non herringbone	$12,000	$16,000
1950		$11,000	$14,000
1951		$10,800	$13,500
1952		$10,600	$13,250
1953	Kluson	$10,400	$13,000
1954		$10,200	$12,750
1955		$10,000	$12,500
1956		$9,800	$12,250
1957		$9,700	$12,125
1958	Early '58 Kluson	$9,600	$12,000
1958	Late '58 Grover	$9,500	$11,875
1959		$9,400	$11,750
1960		$6,000	$7,500
1961		$5,800	$7,300
1962		$5,600	$7,100
1964		$5,600	$7,100
1965-1966		$5,400	$6,800
1966-1969	Early '66, Tortoise guard	$5,200	$6,500
1970-1979		$2,400	$3,000
1980-1989		$1,750	$2,150
1990-1999		$1,575	$1,975
2000-2014		$1,575	$1,975

000-28 C
1962-1967. Classical, Brazilian rosewood back and sides, slotted peghead, natural.

| 1962-1967 | | $3,600 | $4,500 |

000-28 EC
1996-present. Eric Clapton specs, sitka spruce top, Indian rosewood back and sides, herringbone trim, sunburst or natural.

| 1996-2014 | Natural | $2,300 | $2,900 |
| 1996-2014 | Sunburst | $2,300 | $2,900 |

000-28 ECB Eric Clapton
2002. Limited edition, EC 000-28 with Brazilian rosewood, certificate of authenticity, label hand-signed by Eric Clapton and Chris Martin.

| 2002 | | $7,000 | $9,000 |

000-28 ECM Eric Clapton
2009. Limited edition, Madagascar rosewood, certificate of authenticity, label hand-signed by Eric Clapton and Chris Martin.

| 2009 | | $4,900 | $6,100 |

000-28 F
1964-1967. Folk, 12-fret, slotted.

| 1964-1967 | | $7,100 | $8,800 |

000-28 G
1937, 1939-1940, 1946-1947, 1949-1950, 1955. Special order classical guitar, very limited production.

1937, 1939		$6,800	$8,500
1940		$6,200	$7,700
1946-1949		$4,800	$6,000
1950, 1955		$4,400	$5,500

000-28 Golden Era
1996 only. Sitka spruce top, rosewood back and sides, scalloped braces, herringbone trim, 12-fret model, natural.

| 1996 | | $3,000 | $3,800 |

000-28 H
2000-present. Herringbone top trim, production model for '00-'01, Custom Shop model made for Elderly Instruments after that (stamped Custom on neck block).

| 2000-2002 | | $1,600 | $2,000 |
| 2003-2014 | Custom Shop | $1,900 | $2,400 |

000-28 HB Brazilian 1937 Reissue
1997. Pre-war specs including scalloped bracing, Brazilian rosewood.

| 1997 | | $5,400 | $6,800 |

000-28 K
1921. Non-catalog special order model, only 2 known to exist, koa top, back and sides.

| 1921 | Rare model | $18,500 | $23,500 |

000-28 K Authentic 1921
2014-present. Slotted, 12-fret, highly figured Koa body.

| 2014-2015 | | $3,500 | $4,600 |

000-28 LSH/LSH Custom
2008. Large sound hole (LSH), style 28 appointments, wild grain East Indian sides and back.

| 2008 | | $2,000 | $2,500 |

000-28 Martin/Mandolin Brothers 25th Anniversary
1997-1998. Limited Edition, 25 made, mandolin 12th fret inlay, signed label.

| 1997-1998 | | $2,500 | $3,125 |

000-28 MEC Eric Clapton Limited Edition
2008-2009. Limited run of 461, Madagascar rosewood back and sides, Carpathian spruce top, 20th fret Eric Clapton signature, natural or sunburst.

| 2008-2009 | | $4,700 | $5,900 |

000-28 Norman Blake
2004-2008. 12-fret neck on 14-fret body, B version is Brazilian rosewood.

| 2004-2008 | Brazilian rosewood | $5,600 | $7,000 |
| 2004-2008 | Indian rosewood | $2,700 | $3,400 |

000-28 NY
1962. 2 made.

| 1962 | | $6,100 | $7,600 |

000-28 Perry Bechtel
2007. East Indian rosewood back and sides, 29 made.

| 2007 | | $3,650 | $4,550 |

1954 Martin 000-28
Garrett Park

Martin 000-28 EC

Martin 000-28 VS

Martin 000-40 S Mark Knopfler

MODEL YEAR	FEATURES	EXC. COND. LOW	HIGH
000-28 S			
1974-1977. Slotted headstock, 12-fret neck.			
1974-1977		$2,200	$2,800
000-28 VS			
1999-present. Vintage Series, spruce top with aging toner, scalloped bracing, rosewood sides and back, slotted diamond markers, herringbone top trim.			
1999-2014		$2,250	$2,800
000-38			
1980. Rosewood back and sides, 3 made.			
1980		$3,000	$3,700
000-40			
1909. Ivoroid bound top and back, snowflake inlay, 1 made.			
1909		$27,000	$34,000
000-40 PR Peter Rowan			
2001. Mahogany back and sides, slotted headstock, 12-fret, phases of the moon inlays.			
2001		$2,600	$3,200
000-40 Q2GN Graham Nash			
2003. Limited edition of 147 guitars, quilted mahagony top/back/sides, flying-heart logo on headstock, Graham Nash signature on frets 18-20.			
2003		$2,900	$3,600
000-41			
1975, 1996. Custom shop style 000-41.			
1975		$3,100	$3,800
1996		$2,900	$3,600
000-42			
1918, 1921-1922, 1925, 1930, 1932, 1934, 1938-1943, 2004-present. Brazilian rosewood back and sides, natural. The 1918-1934 price range is wide due to the variety of specifications.			
1918-1925	Limited production	$32,000	$40,000
1930	1 made	$51,000	$63,000
1932	1 made, 14 fret	$51,000	$63,000
1934	1 made, 14 fret	$61,000	$76,000
1938	27 made	$58,000	$73,000
1939	Early '39, 1.75 neck	$58,000	$73,000
1939	Later '39, 1.68 neck	$52,000	$65,000
1940-1941		$46,000	$57,000
1942-1943	Last pearl border	$44,000	$55,000
2004-2014		$3,400	$4,200
000-42 EC Eric Clapton			
1995. Style 45 pearl-inlaid headplate, ivoroid bindings, Eric Clapton signature, 24.9" scale, flat-top, sunburst top price is $8320 ('95 price), only 461 made; 433 natural, 28 sunburst.			
1995		$6,200	$7,700
000-42 ECB Eric Clapton			
2000-2001. With Brazilian rosewood, 200 made.			
2000-2001		$12,300	$15,400
000-42 M Eric Clapton Limited Edition			
2008-2009. Limited Edition, 250 made, Madagascar rosewood sides and back, Carpathian spruce top.			
2008-2009		$6,000	$7,500
000-42 Marquis			
2007-2009. Indian rosewood.			
2007-2009		$4,200	$5,200

MODEL YEAR	FEATURES	EXC. COND. LOW	HIGH
000-42 SB			
2004. 1935 style with sunburst finish, Indian rosewood back and sides.			
2004		$3,550	$4,400
000-44 Soloist/Olcott-Bickford Artist Model			
1917-1919. Style 44 guitars were made for guitarist Vahdah Olcott-Bickford, rosewood back and sides, 3 made.			
1917-1919		$36,500	$46,000
000-45			
1906, 1911-1914, '17-'19, '22-'29, '34-'42, '70-'94. Brazilian rosewood back and sides, changed to Indian rosewood in '70, 12-fret neck and slotted headstock until '34 (but 7 were made in '70 and 1 in '75), 14-fret neck and solid headstock after '34, natural.			
1906-1919		$48,000	$60,000
1922-1927	Gut	$48,000	$60,000
1926-1929	Steel	$100,000	$125,000
1930-1931	000-45 designated	$100,000	$125,000
1934-1937	14-fret, C.F.M. inlaid	$137,000	$180,000
1938	Early '38	$137,000	$180,000
1938	Late '38	$127,000	$170,000
1940-1942	1.68 neck	$102,000	$128,000
1970-1977		$5,000	$6,250
1980-1989		$4,900	$6,100
1990-1994		$4,800	$5,900
000-45 B			
1985. Brazilian rosewood, 2 made.			
1985		$10,500	$13,000
000-45 JR Jimmie Rodgers			
1997-1998. Adirondack spruce top, Brazilian rosewood back and sides, scalloped high X-braces, abalone trim, natural, 52 made.			
1997-1998		$13,000	$16,500
000-45 S			
1974-1976. 12-fret.			
1974-1976		$5,500	$6,800
000-45 S Stephen Stills			
2005. Only 91 made, Indian rosewood.			
2005		$7,500	$9,500
000C David Gray Custom			
2005-2006. Custom Artist Edition, 000-size cutaway, Italian spruce top, mahogany back and sides, interior label signed by David Gray.			
2005-2006		$1,950	$2,450
000C DB Dion The Wanderer			
2002. Cutaway acoustic/electric, 57 made, scalloped bracing, mahogany sides and back, slotted diamond and square markers, Dion logo on headstock, gloss black finish.			
2002		$3,200	$4,000
000C DG Doug Greth Commemorative Edition			
2011. Nylon string cutaway, slotted headstock, mahogany back and sides, 48 made.			
2011		$1,500	$1,900
000C Steve Miller Pegasus			
2005-2006. Cutaway, mahogany back and sides, Pegasus logo.			
2005-2006		$2,375	$2,925

The *Vintage Guitar Price Guide* shows low to high values for items in all-original excellent condition, and, where applicable, with original case or cover.

MODEL YEAR	FEATURES	EXC. COND. LOW	HIGH

000C-1 E Auditorium
1997-1999. Cutaway, mahogany back and sides, transducer pickup.

1997-1999		$575	$725

000C-16 (T Auditorium)
1990-1998. Cutaway acoustic, mahogany back and sides, diamonds and squares inlay, name changed to 000-C16T Auditorium in '96.

1990-1998		$1,025	$1,275

000C-16 GTE
1999-2003. Cutaway, mahogany.

1999-2003		$925	$1,150

000C-16 RB (Baby Face)
2000-2002. Cutaway acoustic, East Indian rosewood back and sides.

2000-2002		$1,450	$1,825

000C-16 RGTE
2000-2010. Cutaway, rosewood back and sides.

2000-2010		$925	$1,150

000C-16 SGTNE
2003-2006. Classical nylon string, cutaway, mahogany body, 12-fret cedar neck, slotted headstock.

2003-2006		$1,000	$1,250

000C-16 SRNE
2003-2005. Classical cutaway, rosewood body, 12-fret cedar neck, slotted headstock.

2003-2005		$1,000	$1,250

000C-28 Andy Summers
2006. Cutaway, rosewood back and sides, Buddhist Mudra inlays.

2006		$2,900	$3,600

000C-28 SMH Merle Haggard
2001-2002. Cutaway, 12-fret neck, Blue Yodel No. 13 inlay.

2001-2002		$3,200	$4,000

000CME
1999-2002. Laminate back and sides, on-board electronics, satin finish.

1999-2002		$600	$750

000CXE Black
2003-2013. Acoustic-electric, cutaway, laminated body, black finish.

2003-2013		$400	$500

000-ECHF Bellezza Bianca
2005-2006. Eric Clapton and Hiroshi Fujiwara White Beauty model, Engleman spruce top, flamed Pacific big-leaf maple back and sides, model name logo on 20th fret, white finish, all-white case, 410 made. This and the Nera are examples of a 'collectible guitar' that is often found in near mint condition. High-end of price range shown is for near mint, nearly unplayed condition.

2005-2006		$4,200	$5,200

000-ECHF Bellezza Nera
2004-2005. Eric Clapton and Hiroshi Fujiwara Black Beauty Model, 476 made, Italian Alpine spruce top, Indian rosewood back and sides, black finish.

2004-2005		$4,200	$5,200

000-JBP Jimmy Buffett Pollywog
2003. Model name and number on label inside back, 168 made.

2003		$2,500	$3,100

000-M Mahogany Auditorium
2004-2006. Auditorium 000-size, mahogany sides and back.

2004-2006		$500	$625

000RS1
2014-present. Road Series, sapele top, back and sides, Fishman Sonitone electronics.

2014		$500	$625

000X Hippie
2007. Limited Edition of 200, celebrates the 40th Anniversary of the 'Summer of Love'.

2007		$1,175	$1,475

000X1
2000-2010. Mahogany grained HPL (high pressure laminate) back and sides, solid spruce top.

2000-2010		$275	$350

000X1 AE
2010-present. 000X1 with electronics.

2010-2014		$450	$550

000XE Black
2002-2005. Black satin finish.

2002-2005		$350	$435

0000-1
1997-2001. 0000-size, mahogany.

1997-2001		$650	$800

0000-18 Custom/Custom 0000-18 (Gruhn 35th)
2005-2009. 16" lower bout, high X-brace, mahogany back and sides, commissioned for Gruhn Guitars 35th Anniversary and first year models have signed Anniversary labels.

2005-2009		$2,200	$2,750

0000-28 Series
1997-2000. Several models, jumbo-size 0000 cutaway body, models include; H (herringbone trim), Custom (Indian rosewood, sitka spruce top), H-AG (Arlo Guthrie 30th anniversary, Indian rosewood back and sides, only 30 made), H Custom Shop (herringbone).

1997-2000	0000-28 H	$1,800	$2,250
1998	0000-28 Custom	$1,900	$2,400
1999	0000-28 H-AG	$2,600	$3,300

0000-38 (M-38)
1997-1998. Called M-38 in '77-'97 and '07-present (see that listing), 0000-size, Indian rosewood back and sides, multi-bound.

1997-1998		$2,200	$2,800

1/4-28
1973, 1979. 14 made.

1973, 1979		$3,700	$4,500

1-17
1906-1917 (1st version), 1931-1934 (2nd version). First version has spruce top, mahogany back and sides, second version has all mahogany with flat natural finish.

1906-1917		$2,050	$2,550
1931-1934		$2,300	$2,900

1-17 P
1928-1931, 1939. Mahogany back and sides, plectrum neck, 272 made.

1928-1931		$1,300	$1,625
1939	5-string (special)	$1,300	$1,625

Martin 000-45 S Stephen Stills

Martin 000CX1E

To get the most from this book, be sure to read "Using *The Guide*" in the introduction.

1927 Martin 2-17
Tom Siska

1928 Martin 2-17
Folkway Music

MODEL YEAR	FEATURES	EXC. COND. LOW	HIGH

1-18
1899-1903, 1906-1907, 1909-1921, 1923-1927. Brazilian rosewood or mahogany back and sides.

1899-1917	Brazilian rosewood	$3,000	$3,750
1918-1921	Mahogany	$2,300	$2,850
1923-1927	Steel braces, 12-fret	$2,300	$2,850

1-18 H
1918. Hawaiian, only 3 made.

| 1918 | | $2,300 | $2,850 |

1-18 K
1917-1919. Koa.

| 1917-1919 | | $2,900 | $3,600 |

1-18 P
1929. 5-string plectrum, 1 made.

| 1929 | | $1,900 | $2,400 |

1-18 T
1927. Tenor 5-string, only 3 made.

| 1927 | | $1,900 | $2,400 |

1-20
1860s. Parlor guitar, rosewood back and sides.

| 1867 | | $4,500 | $5,700 |

1-21
1860s-1907, 1911, 1913-1921, 1925-1926. Initially offered in size 1 in the 1860s, ornate soundhole rings. A beautiful crack-free instrument is worth twice as much as a worn model with repaired cracks.

1860s-70s		$4,500	$5,700
1890-1897		$3,800	$4,700
1898-1926		$3,500	$4,300

1-21 P
1930. Plectrum.

| 1930 | | $2,300 | $2,800 |

1-22
1850s. Antique market value.

| 1850s | Antique market value | $5,800 | $7,200 |

1-26
1850s-1880s. Rosewood back and sides, ivory-bound top, rope-style purfling, antique market value.

| 1850s-70s | Antique market value | $6,000 | $7,500 |
| 1880s | Antique market value | $5,500 | $7,000 |

1-27
1880s-1907, 1911, 1913-1921, 1925-1926.

| 1880-1889 | | $6,000 | $7,500 |
| 1890-1926 | | $5,800 | $7,200 |

1-28
1880s-1904, 1906-1907, 1909, 1911-1920, 1923. Style 28 appointments including Brazilian rosewood back and sides.

| 1880s-90s | Antique market value | $6,000 | $7,500 |
| 1900-1923 | | $6,000 | $7,500 |

1-28 P
1928-1930. Plectrum.

| 1928-1930 | | $3,900 | $4,800 |

1-30
1860s-1904, 1906-1907, 1911-1914, 1916-1917, 1919. Size 1 Style 30 with pearl soundhole trim, cedar neck.

| 1860s-1919 | Antique market value | $6,600 | $8,300 |

MODEL YEAR	FEATURES	EXC. COND. LOW	HIGH

1-42
1858-1919. Rosewood back and sides, ivory-bound top and 'board.

| 1858-1919 | | $9,000 | $11,200 |

1-45
1904-1905, 1911-1913, 1919. Only 6 made, slotted headstock and Style 45 appointments.

| 1904-1919 | | $18,000 | $22,500 |

2-15
1939-1964. All mahogany body, dot markers.

| 1939 | Special order | $2,100 | $2,800 |
| 1940-1964 | | $1,300 | $1,700 |

2-17
1910, 1922-1934, 1936-1938. 1910 version has spruce top, mahogany back and sides. '22 on, all mahogany body, no body binding after '30.

| 1910 | Gut, 6 made | $2,050 | $2,550 |
| 1922-1938 | Steel | $2,500 | $3,100 |

2-17 H
1927-1929, 1931. Hawaiian, all mahogany, 12 frets clear of body.

| 1927-1929 | | $2,500 | $3,100 |
| 1931 | | $2,500 | $3,100 |

2-17 T
1927-1928. Tenor, 45 made.

| 1927-1928 | | $1,600 | $2,000 |

2-18
1857-1900, 1902-1903, 1907, 1925, 1929, 1934, 1938. Rosewood back and sides, changed to mahogany from 1917, dark outer binding, black back stripe, no dot inlay until 1902.

| 1870s-80s | | $2,500 | $3,100 |

2-18 T
1928-1930. Tenor.

| 1928-1930 | | $1,600 | $2,000 |

2-20
1855-1897. Rare style only offered in size 2.

| 1855-1897 | | $3,500 | $4,400 |

2-21
1850s-1900, 1903-1904, 1909, 1925, 1928-1929. Rosewood back and sides, herringbone soundhole ring.

| 1885-1929 | | $2,800 | $3,500 |

2-21 T
1928. Tenor.

| 1928 | | $2,200 | $2,800 |

2-24
1857-1898. Antique market value.

| 1857-1898 | | $5,000 | $6,200 |

2-27
1857-1880s, 1898-1900, 1907. Brazilian rosewood back and sides, pearl ring, zigzag back stripe, ivory bound ebony 'board and peghead.

| 1857-70s | Antique market value | $6,500 | $8,000 |
| 1880s-1907 | | $5,500 | $6,800 |

2-28
Brazilian rosewood back and sides, slot head.

| 1880 | | $5,700 | $7,000 |

2-28 T
1928-1929. Tenor neck, Brazilian rosewood back and sides, herringbone top purfling.

| 1928-1929 | | $3,700 | $4,500 |

The **Vintage Guitar Price Guide** shows low to high values for items in all-original excellent condition, and, where applicable, with original case or cover.

MODEL YEAR	FEATURES	EXC. COND. LOW	HIGH

2-30
1874, 1902-1904, 1909-1910, 1921. Similar to 2-27, only 7 made.

| 1874 | | $5,700 | $7,000 |
| 1902-1921 | | $5,000 | $6,300 |

2-34
1850s-1898. Similar to 2-30.

| 1850s-1898 | | $6,700 | $8,200 |

2-40
1850s-1898, 1909.

| 1850s-1898 | | $8,000 | $10,000 |

2-42
1858-1900.

| 1874 | | $9,000 | $11,000 |

2-44
1930. Style 44, Olcott-Bickford Soloist custom order, only 4 made.

| 1930 | | $15,000 | $19,500 |

2-45 T
1927-1928. Tenor neck.

| 1927-1928 | | $11,000 | $13,600 |

2 1/2-17
1856-1897, 1909, 1911-1914. The first Style 17s were small size 2 1/2 and 3, these early models use Brazilian rosewood.

1856-1889	Antique market value	$3,000	$3,800
1890-1897	Brazilian/mahogany	$2,500	$3,100
1909-1914		$2,050	$2,550

2 1/2-18
1865-1898, 1901, 1909-1914, 1916-1923. Parlor-size body with Style 18 appointments.

1865-1898	Antique market value	$2,500	$3,100
1901-1917	Brazilian rosewood	$2,500	$3,100
1918-1923	Mahogany	$1,900	$2,400

2 1/2-21
1880s, 1909, 1911-1913, 1917-1921. Brazilian rosewood back and sides.

| 1880s-1921 | | $2,800 | $3,500 |

2 1/2-42
1880s, 1911. Style 42 size 2 1/2 with Brazilian rosewood. Only 1 made 1911.

| 1880s-1911 | | $9,000 | $11,500 |

3-17
1856-1897, 1908 (1 made). The first Style 17s were small size 2 1/2 and 3. The early models use Brazilian rosewood, spruce top, bound back, unbound ebony 'board.

1856-1870s	Brazilian rosewood	$2,300	$2,900
1880s-1897		$1,700	$2,100
1908	1 made	$1,700	$2,100

3-21
1885. Brazilian rosewood.

| 1885 | | $2,800 | $3,500 |

3-24
1860. Brazilian rosewood.

| 1860 | | $5,000 | $6,200 |

3-34
1860. Brazilian rosewood.

| 1860 | | $6,700 | $8,200 |

5-15
2003-2007. Sapele or mahogany body, shorter scale.

| 2003-2007 | | $875 | $1,100 |

5-15 T
1949-1963. Tenor neck, all mahogany, non-gloss finish.

| 1949-1959 | | $1,350 | $1,700 |
| 1960-1963 | | $1,350 | $1,700 |

5-16
1962-1963. Mahogany back and sides, unbound rosewood 'board.

| 1962-1963 | | $1,750 | $2,200 |

5-17
1912-1914, 1916, 1927-1928, 1930-1931, 1933-1943. Special order 1912-'36, standard production '37-'43.

1912-1916		$1,800	$2,200
1927-1928		$2,500	$3,100
1930-1939		$2,300	$2,900
1940-1943		$2,100	$2,600

5-17 T
1927-1949. Tenor neck, all mahogany.

| 1927-1949 | | $1,200 | $1,500 |

5-18
1898-1899, 1912-1914, 1917, 1919-1921, 1923-1924, 1926-1932, 1934-1937, 1940-1941, 1943-1962, 1965, 1968-1977, 1979-1981, 1983-1989. Rosewood back and sides (changed to mahogany from 1917 on), 12 frets, slotted headstock.

1898-1917		$2,750	$3,450
1919-1921	Gut braces	$2,100	$2,625
1923-1937	Steel braces in '23	$3,400	$4,400
1940-1949		$3,300	$4,125
1950-1959		$2,500	$3,150
1960-1962		$2,000	$2,500
1965		$1,875	$2,350
1966-1969		$1,600	$2,000
1970-1979		$1,400	$1,750
1980-1989		$1,300	$1,625

5-18 Marty Robbins
2009-2011. Custom Edition, 12-fret, Adirondack top, mahogany back and sides.

| 2009-2011 | | $1,750 | $2,175 |

5-18 T
1940, 1954, 1960-1961. Tenor, only 1 made each year.

1940		$1,350	$1,700
1954		$800	$1,000
1960-1961		$700	$875

5-21
1890s, 1902, 1912-1914, 1916-1920, 1927, 1977. Rosewood back and sides.

| 1890s-1977 | | $3,100 | $3,900 |

5-21 T
1927-1928. Tenor guitar with 21-styling.

| 1927-1928 | | $2,000 | $2,500 |

5-28
1901-1902, 1904, 1918, 1920-1921, 1923, 1935, 1939, 1969-1970, 1977, 1980-1981, 1988, 2001-2002. Special edition, 1/2-size parlor guitar, rosewood back and sides.

| 1901-1923 | Gut braces | $2,800 | $3,500 |
| 1935-1939 | Steel braces | $4,800 | $6,000 |

Martin 5-15 T
Peter Van Wagner

1952 Martin 5-18
Folkway Music

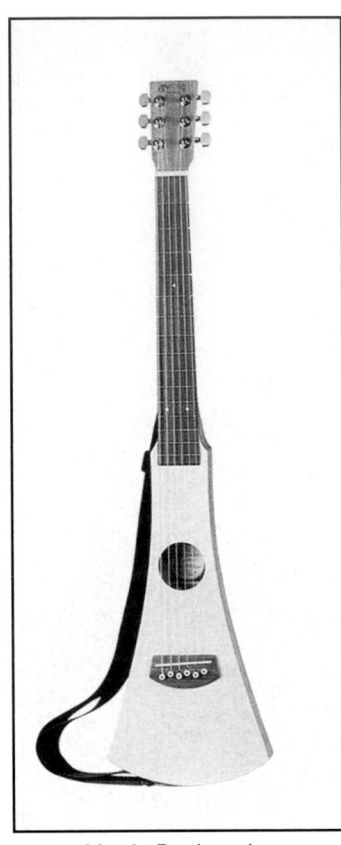

Martin Backpacker

Martin CF-1 American Archtop

MODEL YEAR	FEATURES	EXC. COND. LOW	EXC. COND. HIGH
1969-1970	Brazilian rosewood	$4,900	$6,100
1977	Indian rosewood	$2,400	$3,000
1980-1981		$2,000	$2,500
2001-2002		$1,850	$2,300

7-28
1980-1995, 1997-2002. 7/8-body-size of a D-model, Style 28 appointments.

1980-2002		$1,875	$2,325

7-37 K
1980-1987. 7/8-size baby dreadnought acoustic, koa back and sides, spruce top, oval soundhole.

1980-1987		$1,900	$2,350

Alternative II Resophonic
2004-2007. Textured aluminum top, matching headstock overlay, high pressure laminate sides and back, spun aluminum cone resonator, Fishman pickup.

2004-2007		$550	$700

Alternative X
2001-2013. OO-Grand Concert body shape, textured aluminum top, matching headstock overlay, spun aluminum cone resonator, Fishman pickup.

2001-2013		$550	$700

Alternative X Midi
2003-2004. Roland GK Midi pickup with 13-pin output, additional Fishman Prefix Pro pickup and preamp system, requires Roland GA-20 interface.

2003-2004		$600	$750

Alternative XT
2002-2005. Alternative with DiMarzio humbucker, volume & tone controls, coil tap, Bigsby.

2003-2005		$600	$750

America's Guitar 175th Anniversary
2008. D-style, 14-fret, Adirondack spruce top, Madagascar rosewood sides and back, 175 made, 'America's Guitar' headstock inlay, '175th Anniversary 1833-2008'.

2008		$3,700	$4,600

ASD-41 Australian Series
2005. Tasmanian Blackwood sides and back, Sitka spruce top, Australian theme appointments and label.

2005		$3,400	$4,200

Backpacker
1992-present. Small-bodied travel guitar, nylon called Classic Backpacker.

1992-2014	Steel strings	$110	$140
1994-2014	Nylon strings	$110	$140

C-1
1931-1942. Acoustic archtop, mahogany back and sides, spruce top, round hole until '33, f-holes appear in '32, bound body, sunburst.

1931-1933	Round, 449 made	$2,600	$3,200
1932-1942	F-hole, 786 made	$2,300	$2,900

C-1 P
1931-1933, 1939. Archtop, plectrum.

1931-1933	Round hole	$2,200	$2,800
1939	F-hole	$2,000	$2,500

C-1 R Humphrey
1997-2000. Solid cedar top, laminated rosewood back and sides, satin finish.

1997-2000		$875	$1,150

C-1 T
1931-1934, 1936-1938. Archtop, tenor, round- or f-hole.

1931-1933	Round, 71 made	$2,200	$2,800
1933-1938	F-hole, 83 made	$2,000	$2,500

C-2
1931-1942. Acoustic archtop, Brazilian rosewood back and sides, carved spruce top, round hole until '33, f-holes appear in '32, zigzag back stripe, multi-bound body, slotted-diamond inlay, sunburst.

1931-1933	Round, 269 made	$3,300	$4,100
1932-1942	F-hole, 439 made	$3,100	$3,900

C-2 P
1931. Archtop, plectrum, round hole, 2 made.

1931	Round hole	$3,300	$4,100

C-2 T
1931-1936. Archtop, tenor, round or f-hole.

1931-1934	Round hole	$3,300	$4,100
1934-1936	F-hole	$3,100	$3,900

C-3
1931-1934. Archtop, Brazilian rosewood back and sides, round soundhole until early '33, f-holes after.

1931-1933	Round, 53 made	$5,500	$6,800
1933-1934	F-hole, 58 made	$5,500	$6,800

C-3 T
1933. Archtop, tenor, 1 made.

1933		$5,500	$6,800

Car Talk Special Edition
2008-2010. D-size, East Indian rosewood back and sides, car parts and tools inlay, Car Talk credits on 'guard.

2008-2010		$4,000	$5,000

CEO Series
1997-present. Chief Executive Officer C.F. Martin IV special editions.

1997-2014	Various models	$1,600	$2,000

CF-1 American Archtop
2004-2009. 17", solid maple sides, laminated maple back, ebony 'board, dot markers, 1 pickup, sunburst, natural or black.

2004-2009		$2,075	$2,550

CF-2 American Archtop
2004-2009. CF-1 with 2 humbuckers.

2004-2009		$2,175	$2,650

Concept III
2003. U.S.-made, solid spruce top, solid mahogany back and sides, cutaway, on-board electronics, sparkle-mist finish.

2003		$1,400	$1,750

Cowboy Series
2000-2009. Models include Cowboy X (2000, 250 made), Cowboy II ('01, 500 made), Cowboy III ('03, 750 made), and Cowboy IV ('05-'06, 250 made), Cowboy V ('06-'09, 500 made).

2001-2009		$475	$625

CS-21-11
2011. Limited Edition, 171 made, Madagascar rosewood.

2011		$3,000	$3,700

GUITARS

MODEL YEAR	FEATURES	EXC. COND. LOW	HIGH

CSN (Gerry Tolman Tribute)
2007-2009. CSN logo on headstock, D-style, high-end appointments, East Indian rosewood back and sides. Tolman was CSN's longtime manager and was killed in car wreck in '06.

2007-2009		$2,300	$2,900

C-TSH (Humphrey/Martin)
1997-2002. Designed by classical guitar luthier Thomas Humphrey, based on his Millenium model, arched Englemann spruce top, rosewood back and sides.

1997-2002		$2,100	$2,600

Custom 15
1991-1994. Renamed HD-28V Custom 15 in ca. 2001.

1991-1994		$2,100	$2,600

Custom D Classic Mahogany
2006-2011. D body, spruce top, mahogany back and sides.

2006-2011		$600	$750

Custom D Classic Rosewood
2006-2011. D body, spruce top, rosewood back and sides.

2006-2011		$650	$825

D-1 (D-18)
1931. Name first used for the prototype of the D-18, made in 1931.

1931		$56,000	$73,000

D-1
1992-2005, 2010. Mahogany body, A-frame bracing,

1992-2005		$675	$850
2010	Reintroduced	$675	$850

D12-1
1996-2001. Mahogany, satin finish, 12-string.

1996-2001		$675	$850

D-1 E
1994-1998. Acoustic/electric version.

1994-1998		$725	$900

D-1 GT
2011-2014. Double bound body, gloss finish top, satin back and sides.

2011-2014		$675	$850

D-1 R
1994-2003. D-1 with laminated rosewood back and sides.

1994-2003		$675	$850

D-1 RE
1994-1995, 1998. D-1R with various electronics.

1994-1998		$725	$900

D-2
1931-1932, 1934. Earliest version of the D-28.

1931-1934		$150,000	$195,000

D-2 R
1996-2002. Style 28 appointments, laminated rosewood back and sides, natural satin finish.

1996-2002		$725	$900

D-3 R
1996-2002. Style 35 appointments, laminated rosewood back and sides, natural satin finish.

1996-2002		$775	$950

D-3-18
1991. Sitka spruce top, 3-piece mahogany back, 80-piece limited edition.

1991		$1,600	$1,975

D12 David Crosby
2009-2011. D-size 12-string, quilted mahogany body, Carpathian spruce top.

2009-2011		$3,150	$3,950

D-15/D-15 M
1997-present. Body is all mahogany up to 2002, mahogany or sapele (which is like mahogany) up to '10. Becomes the all-mahogany D-15M in '11.

1997-2010		$700	$875
2011-2014	M	$700	$875

D-15 M Elderly Instruments 40th Anniversary
2012. Only 10 made, solid mahogany body, special appointments, label signed by Elderly president Stan Werbin and Chris Martin.

2012		$1,000	$1,250

D-15 S
2001-2009. Slotted headstock D-15, body is solid sapele or mahogany.

2001-2009		$800	$1,000

D-16 A
1987-1990. North American ash back and sides, scalloped bracing.

1987-1990		$1,300	$1,600

D-16 Adirondack
2009-2013. Adirondack spruce top, mahogany back and sides.

2009-2012		$1,400	$1,750
2013		$1,175	$1,475

D-16 GT
1999-present. D-16 with gloss top.

1999-2014		$950	$1,200

D-16 GTE
1999-present. D-16 GT with Fishman.

1999-2014		$975	$1,225

D-16 H (1991, 1992, 1993)
1990-1994. D-16 with herringbone soundhole ring, replaced by D-16 T in '94

1990-1994		$1,075	$1,350

D-16 K
1986. Koa D-16.

1986		$1,300	$1,600

D-16 Lyptus
2003-2005. Lyptus back and sides.

2003-2005		$950	$1,200

D-16 M
1986-1990. Mahogany back and sides.

1986-1990		$950	$1,200

D-16 O Oak
1999. Red oak or white oak, 4 made.

1999		$950	$1,200

D-16 R/RT
1995-2009. Indian rosewood back and sides.

1995-2009		$950	$1,200

D-16 RGT
1999-present. D-16 T specs with rosewood back and sides, gloss finish.

1999-2014		$875	$1,150

D-16 T
1994-1998. Mahogany back and sides, satin finish.

1994-1998		$950	$1,200

Martin D-15 M

Martin D-16 GT

1946 Martin D-18
Rod Highsmith

1939 Martin D-18
Folkway Music

MODEL YEAR	FEATURES	EXC. COND. LOW	HIGH
D-16 TG			
1995-1997. Gloss.			
1995-1997		$1,000	$1,250
D-16 W Walnut			
1987, 1990. Walnut back and sides.			
1987, 1990		$1,000	$1,250
D-17			
2001-2005. All solid mahogany back, sides and top, natural brown mahogany finish.			
2001-2005		$875	$1,125
DC-17 E			
2002-2003. Cutaway, acoustic/electric version.			
2002-2003		$950	$1,175
D-17 M			
2013-present. Shaded spruce top, solid mahogany back and sides.			
2013-2014		$950	$1,175
D-18			
1931-present. Mahogany back and sides, spruce top, black back stripe, 12-fret neck, changed to 14 frets in '34.			
1931-1934	12-fret	$47,000	$59,000
1934	14-fret, dark top	$39,000	$52,000
1934-1937	14-fret	$39,000	$52,000
1938	Early '38, Advanced X	$36,000	$48,000
1938	Late '38, Rear X	$27,100	$34,000
1939	Early '39, 1.75 neck	$26,100	$32,700
1939	Late '39, 1.68 neck	$23,000	$28,700
1940-1941		$20,000	$25,000
1942-1943	Scalloped braces	$17,600	$22,000
1944	Scalloped braces	$16,100	$20,000
1944-1945	Non-scalloped	$13,800	$17,250
1946-1947		$10,000	$12,500
1948-1949		$6,300	$7,875
1950		$5,500	$6,875
1951		$5,400	$6,750
1952		$5,300	$6,625
1953		$5,200	$6,500
1954		$5,100	$6,375
1955		$5,000	$6,250
1956		$4,900	$6,125
1957		$4,800	$6,000
1958		$4,700	$5,875
1959		$4,600	$5,800
1960-1964		$3,900	$4,900
1965		$3,400	$4,200
1966		$3,200	$4,000
1967		$3,000	$3,750
1968-1969		$2,600	$3,200
1970-1974		$2,300	$2,850
1975-1979		$2,200	$2,750
1980-1989		$1,775	$2,250
1983	50th Ann. 1833-1983	$1,775	$2,250
1990-1999		$1,600	$2,000
2000-2009		$1,600	$2,000
2010-2014		$1,525	$1,900
D12-18			
1973-1995. Mahogany back and sides, 12 strings, 14 frets clear of body, solid headstock.			
1973-1979		$1,550	$1,925

MODEL YEAR	FEATURES	EXC. COND. LOW	HIGH
1980-1989		$1,350	$1,675
1990-1995		$1,250	$1,550
CS-D18-12			
2012. Custom Shop, based on 1929 Ditson 111 (12-string), 75 made, 12-fret mahogany neck, Adirondack spruce top, Madagascar rosewood binding.			
2012		$3,350	$4,200
D-18 75th Anniversary Edition			
2009. '75th Anniversary Edition 1934-2009' noted on label and headstock stencil.			
2009		$2,650	$3,300
D-18 Andy Griffith			
2003. Bear claw spruce top, Andy's script signature on 18th fret.			
2003		$2,100	$2,600
D-18 Authentic 1937			
2006-2012. Authentic pre-war specs, Adirondack spruce, forward X-brace and scalloped Adirondack bracing, 14-fret neck.			
2006-2012		$3,900	$4,800
D-18 Authentic 1939			
2013-present. Adirondack spruce top, mahogany back, sides and neck, ebony 'board, vintage gloss finish.			
2013-2014		$3,900	$4,800
D-18 D			
1975. Frap pickup.			
1975		$2,200	$2,750
D-18 DC David Crosby			
2002. David Crosby signature at 20th fret, Englemann spruce top, quilted mahogany back and sides, 250 made.			
2002		$2,075	$2,600
D-18 Del McCourey 50th Anniversary			
2008. Adirondack spruce top, mahogany sides and back, interior label signed by Del McCourey, 50 made.			
2008		$2,200	$2,800
D-18 E			
1958-1959. D-18 factory built with DeArmond pickups which required ladder bracing (reducing acoustic volume and quality).			
1958-1959		$4,000	$5,500
D-18 E Retro			
2012-present. Sitka spruce top, mahogany back and sides.			
2012-2014		$1,700	$2,100
D-18 GE Golden Era			
1995, 2000-present. 1995 version is a copy of a '37 D-18, 272 made. The current model is based on '34 model.			
1995		$2,300	$2,875
2000-2014	Natural	$2,200	$2,725
2003-2014	Sunburst	$2,200	$2,725
D-18 Golden Era Special Edition 1934			
2005-2008.			
2005-2008		$2,300	$2,875
D-18 LE			
1986-1987. Limited Edition, quilted or flamed mahogany back and sides, scalloped braces, gold tuners with ebony buttons.			
1986-1987		$2,000	$2,500

The *Vintage Guitar Price Guide* shows low to high values for items in all-original excellent condition, and, where applicable, with original case or cover.

MODEL YEAR	FEATURES	EXC. COND. LOW	HIGH

D-18 MB

1990. Limited Edition Guitar of the Month, flame maple binding, Engelmann spruce top signed by shop foremen, X-brace, total of 99 sold.

| 1990 | | $2,000 | $2,500 |

D-18 S

1967-1994. Mahogany back and sides, 12-fret neck, slotted headstock, majority of production before '77, infrequent after that.

1967		$3,600	$4,300
1968-1969		$3,000	$3,700
1970-1979		$2,750	$3,450
1980-1989		$2,050	$2,550
1990-1994		$1,800	$2,275

D-18 Special

1989. Guitar of the Month, 28 made, first Martin to use rosewood for binding, heel cap and endpiece since 1932, scalloped top, mahogany back and sides, slotted-diamond markers.

| 1989 | | $2,000 | $2,500 |

D-18 SS

2009-2012. 24.9" short scale.

| 2009 | | $1,450 | $1,825 |

D-18 V/D-18 Vintage

1985 (V), 1992 (Vintage). Low-profile neck, scalloped braces, bound, total of 218 sold, Guitar of the Month in '85, Vintage Series in '92.

| 1985 | V | $1,850 | $2,300 |
| 1992 | Vintage | $1,850 | $2,300 |

D-18 VE

2004-2007. D-18 V with Fishman Ellipse.

| 2004-2007 | | $1,750 | $2,200 |

D-18 VM/D-18 V

1995-2011. Vintage Series, 14-fret, mahogany (M) back and sides, tortoise binding, V-neck. M dropped from name in '99. Natural finish. 48 sunburst (D-18 VO) made in '95.

1995-1998	D-18VM	$1,700	$2,150
1995	VO sunburst	$1,835	$2,300
1999-2011	D-18V	$1,700	$2,150

D-18 VMS/D-18 VS

1996-2011. Vintage Series, 12-fret version of D-18 VM/V, M dropped from name in '99.

| 1996-1999 | D-18VS | $1,700 | $2,150 |
| 1999-2011 | D-18VMS | $1,700 | $2,150 |

D-19

1977-1988. Deluxe mahogany dreadnought, optional mahogany top, multi-bound but unbound rosewood 'board.

| 1977-1979 | | $2,400 | $3,000 |
| 1980-1988 | | $1,775 | $2,250 |

D12-20

1964-1991. Mahogany back and sides, 12 strings, 12 frets clear of body, slotted headstock.

1964-1969		$1,700	$2,150
1970-1979		$1,550	$1,925
1980-1989		$1,350	$1,675
1990-1991		$1,250	$1,550

D-21

1955-1969. Brazilian rosewood back and sides, rosewood 'board, chrome tuners.

1955		$7,000	$8,700
1956		$6,800	$8,400
1957		$6,700	$8,300
1958		$6,600	$8,100
1959		$6,500	$8,000
1960		$6,000	$7,500
1961		$5,700	$7,200
1962-1964		$5,500	$6,900
1965		$5,400	$6,800
1966-1969		$5,300	$6,700

D-21 JC Jim Croce

1999-2000. Jim Croce signature and 1973 dime inlaid on neck, Indian rosewood back and sides, 73 made.

| 1999-2000 | | $3,800 | $4,800 |

D-21 JCB Jim Croce

1999-2001. Same as above but with Brazilian rosewood back and sides.

| 1999-2001 | | $7,500 | $9,500 |

D-21 LE

1985. Limited Edition, 75 made.

| 1985 | | $1,725 | $2,125 |

D-21 Special/D-21 S

2008-2011. Indian rosewood back and sides, herringbone soundhole.

| 2008-2011 | | $2,000 | $2,500 |

D-25 K

1980-1989. Dreadnought-size, koa back and sides, spruce top.

| 1980-1989 | | $2,100 | $2,600 |

D-25 K2

1980-1989. Same as D-25K, but with koa top and black 'guard.

| 1980-1989 | | $2,100 | $2,600 |

D-28

1931-present. Brazilian rosewood back and sides (changed to Indian rosewood in '70), '36 was the last year for the 12-fret model, '44 was the last year for scalloped bracing, '47 was the last year herringbone trim was offered, natural. Ultra high-end D-28 Martin guitar (pre-'47) valuations are very sensitive to structural and cosmetic condition. Finish wear and body cracks for ultra high-end Martin flat-tops should be evaluated on a case-by-case basis. Small variances within the 'excellent condition' category can lead to notable valuation differences.

1931-1935	12-fret	$140,000	$182,000
1934-1937	14-fret	$89,000	$113,000
1938	Early '38, Advanced X	$89,000	$113,000
1938	Late '38, Rear X	$79,000	$101,000
1939	Early '39, 1.75 neck	$78,000	$97,000
1939	Late '39, 1.68 neck	$69,000	$86,000
1940-1941		$60,000	$75,000
1942	Scalloped	$50,000	$65,000
1943	Scalloped	$45,000	$57,000
1944	Scalloped, herringbone	$45,000	$57,000
1944-1945	Herringbone, non-scalloped	$29,000	$36,000

1957 Martin D-21
Folkway Music

Martin D-25 K
Frank Thoubboron

1972 Martin D-28

Keith Myers

Martin D12-28

MODEL YEAR	FEATURES	EXC. COND. LOW	EXC. COND. HIGH
1946-1947	Herringbone, non-scalloped	$22,000	$27,500
1947-1949	Non-herringbone starting '47	$13,250	$16,650
1950		$11,500	$14,500
1951		$11,300	$14,300
1952		$11,100	$14,100
1953	Klusons	$10,900	$13,900
1954		$10,700	$13,700
1955		$10,500	$13,300
1956		$10,300	$13,100
1957		$10,200	$12,900
1958		$10,100	$12,700
1959	Grover	$10,000	$12,500
1960		$8,000	$10,000
1961		$7,000	$9,000
1962-1964		$6,300	$8,000
1965		$6,100	$7,600
1966	Early '66, Tortoise guard	$6,100	$7,600
1967-1968	Black guard	$5,900	$7,400
1969	Brazilian rosewood	$5,900	$7,400
1970-1979	Indian rosewood	$2,200	$2,750
1980-1989		$1,775	$2,250
1990-1999		$1,600	$2,000
2000-2014		$1,600	$2,000

D12-28
1970-present. Indian rosewood back and sides, 12 strings, 14 frets clear of body, solid headstock.

1970-1979		$1,750	$2,150
1980-1989		$1,500	$1,875
1990-1999		$1,450	$1,800
2000-2014		$1,400	$1,750

D-28 1935 Special
1993. Guitar of the Month, 1935 features, Indian rosewood back and sides, peghead with Brazilian rosewood veneer.

1993		$2,300	$2,900

D-28 1955 CFM IV
2010. Limited Edition, 55 made celebrating Chris Martin IV birthyear 1955, Madagascar rosewood.

2010		$3,300	$4,100

D-28 50th Anniversary
1983. Stamped inside '1833-1983 150th Anniversary', Indian rosewood back and sides.

1983		$1,900	$2,400

D-28 75th Anniversary
2009 only. Limited production celebrating 1934 to 2009, Madagascar rosewood back and sides, Adirondack spruce top.

2009		$4,100	$5,100

D-28 150th Anniversary
1983-1985. Limited production of 268, only '83 vintage have the anniversary stamp, Brazilian rosewood sides and back.

1983	150th stamp	$6,300	$7,800
1984-1985	No stamp	$6,000	$7,500

D-28 Authentic 1937
2007-2009, 2014-present. '37 specs, 50 made of first Brazilian rosewood batch. Reintroduced '14 with Madagascar rosewood and Martin Vintage Tone

MODEL YEAR	FEATURES	EXC. COND. LOW	EXC. COND. HIGH
System (VTS).			
2007-2009	Brazilian	$11,500	$14,500
2014-2015	Madagascar	$4,800	$6,000

D-28 Authentic 1941
2013-present. Adirondack, Madagascar rosewood.

2013-2014		$4,700	$5,900

D-28 Custom
1984. Guitar of the Month Nov. '84, double bound D-body, multi-ring rosette, rosewood back/sides, spruce top, 43 made.

1984		$2,200	$2,800

D-28 CW/CWB Clarence White
2003-2014. CW has Indian rosewood back and sides, the CWB Brazilian, only 150 CWBs were to be built.

2003-2004	CWB	$5,400	$6,800
2003-2014	CW	$2,700	$3,400

D-28 D
1975. Frap pickup.

1975		$2,400	$3,000

D-28 Dan Tyminski
2010-2013. Custom Artist limited edition, Indian rosewood back and sides, Adirondack spruce top, other bracing specs.

2010-2013		$2,275	$2,850

D-28 DM Del McCourey Signature
2003. Limited edition of 115, natural.

2003		$2,500	$3,200

D-28 E
1959-1964. Electric, Brazilian rosewood back and sides, 2 DeArmond pickups, natural.

1959-1964		$5,000	$6,300

D-28 E Retro
2013. Rosewood, Fishman.

2013		$2,100	$2,600

D-28 GE Golden Era
1999-2005. GE Golden Era, Brazilian rosewood, herringbone trim.

1999-2005		$6,700	$8,600

D-28 HW Hank Williams Limited Edition
1998. Replica of Hank Williams' 1944 D-28, Brazilian rosewood sides and back, scalloped braces, herringbone, 150 made.

1998		$6,700	$8,300

D-28 LF Lester Flatt
1998. Limited Edition, 50 made, Brazilian rosewood.

1998		$6,300	$8,000

D-28 Louvin Brothers
2015. Limited run of 50, sitka spruce top, East Indian rosewood back and sides, printed Louvin Brothers artwork from "Satan is Real" album.

2015		$2,600	$3,300

D-28 LSH
1991. Guitar of the Month, Indian rosewood back and sides, herringbone trim, snowflake inlay, zigzag back stripe.

1991		$2,400	$3,000

D-28 LSV
1999-2005. Large soundhole model.

1999-2005		$2,200	$2,900

MODEL YEAR	FEATURES	EXC. COND. LOW	HIGH

D-28 M Elvis Presley Commemorative LE
2009. 175 made, Madagascar rosewood back and sides, Adirondack top, tooled leather guitar cover.

2009		$3,100	$3,900

D-28 M Merle Travis
2008-2010. 100 made, Adirondack top, Madagascar rosewood back and sides, curly maple neck, 6-on-a-side Bigsby-style headstock, heart-diamond-spade-club inlays.

2008-2010		$3,900	$4,900

D-28 M The Mamas and The Papas
2012-2014. 100 made, Madagascar rosewood back and sides.

2012-2014		$2,700	$3,400

D-28 Marquis
2004-present. Golden Era appointments, Adirondack top, Indian rosewood, natural or sunburst.

2004-2014	Natural	$2,700	$3,400
2004-2014	Sunburst	$2,825	$3,525
2007-2009	Madagascar option	$3,150	$3,900

D-28 P
1988-1990, 2011-2012. P indicates low-profile neck, Indian rosewood back and sides. Reintroduced 2011 with high performance neck.

1988-1989		$1,750	$2,150
1990-2012		$1,575	$1,975

D-28 S
1954-1994. Rosewood back and sides, 12-fret neck.

1954	Special order	$12,300	$15,700
1955	Special order	$12,075	$15,300
1956	Special order	$11,800	$15,000
1957	Special order	$11,700	$14,800
1958-1959	Special order	$11,600	$14,600
1960-1961	Special order	$8,050	$10,300
1962-1963	Special order	$7,300	$9,200
1964	Special order	$7,200	$9,100
1965	Special order	$7,000	$8,700
1966	Brazilian	$7,000	$8,700
1967-1969	Brazilian	$6,800	$8,500
1970-1979	Indian	$2,400	$3,000
1980-1989		$2,150	$2,700
1990-1994		$2,100	$2,600

D-28 SW Wurlitzer
1962-1965, 1968. Made for the Wurlitzer Co.

1962-1963		$7,300	$9,200
1964		$7,200	$9,100
1965		$7,000	$8,700
1968		$6,800	$8,500

D-28 V
1983-1985. Limited Edition, Brazilian rosewood back and sides, herringbone trim, slotted diamond inlay.

1983-1985		$5,800	$7,200

D-35
1965-present. Brazilian rosewood sides and 3-piece back, changed to Brazilian wings and Indian center in '70, then all Indian rosewood in '71, natural with sunburst option. For a brief time, on the back side, the center panel was Brazilian and the two side panels were Indian.

1965-1970	Brazilian	$4,600	$6,200
1970	Center panel only Brazilian	$2,400	$3,100

MODEL YEAR	FEATURES	EXC. COND. LOW	HIGH
1970-1979	Indian	$2,100	$2,650
1980-1989		$1,600	$1,975
1983	150th center strip	$1,600	$1,975
1990-1999		$1,500	$1,900
2000-2014		$1,500	$1,900

D12-35
1965-1995. Brazilian rosewood back and sides, changed to Indian rosewood in '70, 12 strings, 12 frets clear of body, slotted headstock.

1965-1969	Brazilian rosewood	$4,500	$5,600
1970-1979	Indian rosewood	$1,750	$2,150
1980-1989		$1,500	$1,875
1990-1995		$1,450	$1,800

D-35 30th Anniversery Limited Edition
1995. D-35 with '1965-1995' inlay on 20th fret, gold hardware, limited edition of 207 instruments.

1995		$2,400	$3,100

D-35 E Retro
2012-present. Sitka spruce top, East Indian rosewood back and sides.

2012-2014		$2,100	$2,600

D-35 Ernest Tubb
2003. Indian rosewood back and sides, special inlays, 90 built.

2003		$2,400	$3,100

D-35 JC Johnny Cash
2006-present. Rosewood back and sides.

2006-2014		$3,100	$3,900

D-35 MP
2011-2012. Madagascar rosewood back and sides, high performance neck.

2011-2012		$1,900	$2,400

D-35 P
1986-1990. P indicates low-profile neck.

1986-1990		$1,750	$2,150

D-35 S
1966-1993. Brazilian rosewood back and sides, changed to Indian rosewood in '70, 12-fret neck, slotted peghead.

1966	Brazilian	$7,000	$8,700
1967-1969	Brazilian	$6,800	$8,500
1970-1979	Indian	$2,400	$3,000
1980-1989		$2,150	$2,700
1990-1993		$2,100	$2,600

D-35 SW Wurlitzer
1966, 1968. Made for the Wurlitzer Co., Brazilian rosewood.

1966, 1968		$6,800	$8,500

D-35 V
1984. Limited Edition, 10 made, Brazilian rosewood back and sides.

1984		$5,000	$6,300

D-37 K
1980-1994. Dreadnought-size, koa back and sides, spruce top.

1980-1994		$2,325	$2,900

D-37 K2
1980-1994. Same as D-37 K, but has a koa top and black 'guard.

1980-1994		$2,325	$2,900

Martin D-28 P

1972 Martin D-35
Billy White Jr.

1973 Martin D-41

Martin D-42

MODEL		EXC. COND.	
YEAR	FEATURES	LOW	HIGH

D-37 W Lucinda Williams
2003. Only 4 made, never put into production, Aztec pearl inlay favored by Lucinda Williams, quilted mahogany sides and back.

2003		$3,450	$4,300

D-40
1997-2005. Indian rosewood back and sides, hexagon inlays.

1997-2005		$1,900	$2,400

D-40 BLE
1990. Limited Edition Guitar of the Month, Brazilian rosewood back and sides, pearl top border except around 'board.

1990		$8,000	$10,000

D-40 DM Don McLean
1998. Only 50 made, Englemann spruce top.

1998		$4,800	$6,000

D-40 FMG
1995-1996. Figured mahogany back and sides, 150 made.

1995-1996		$5,150	$6,450

D-40 FW Limited Edition
1996. Figured claro walnut sides and back, 'Limited Edition D-40 FW' label, 148 made.

1996		$2,200	$2,750

D-40 QM Limited Edition
1996. Limited Edition, 200 made, quilted maple body.

1996		$2,200	$2,750

D-41
1969-present. Brazilian rosewood back and sides for the first ones in '69 then Indian rosewood, bound body, scalloped braces, natural.

1969	Brazilian rosewood	$14,800	$18,500
1970-1979	Indian rosewood	$3,200	$4,000
1980-1989		$2,725	$3,400
1990-1999		$2,500	$3,125
2000-2014		$2,500	$3,125

D-41 BLE
1989. Limited Edition Guitar of the Month, Brazilian rosewood back and sides, pearl top border except around 'board.

1989		$6,000	$7,500

D-41 DF Dan Fogelberg
2001. 141 made, East Indian rosewood back and sides, hexagon 'board inlays, pearl snowflakes inlaid on bridge.

2001		$3,850	$4,800

D-41 E
1971. Indian rosewood.

1971		$3,400	$4,200

D-41 GJ George Jones
2001. Style 41 appointments, limited edition of 100, label signed by the Opossum.

2001		$3,125	$3,900

D-41 K Purple Martin
2013. Limited to 50, labels signed by C.F. Martin IV, highly flamed koa back and sides, purple martin-inspired inlay on 'board, bridge, and 'guard.

2013		$6,500	$8,000

D-41 Porter Wagoner
2008-2011. Custom Artist series, Indian rosewood back and sides.

2008-2011		$2,650	$3,300

D-41 S/SD-41 S
1970-1994. Sunburst, Indian rosewood, 12-fret neck, slotted peghead.

1970-1976		$3,675	$4,600
1980-1989		$3,125	$3,900
1990-1994		$2,875	$3,600

D-41 Special
2004-2011. D-41 with snowflake inlays.

2004-2011		$2,600	$3,250

D-41 A Turbo Mandolin Brothers
2011, 2013. Two Custom Shop models made for Mandolin Bros., Adirondack top. Similar except 10 40th Anniversary models which have abalone and pearl mandolin 12th-fret inlay and label signed by Stan Jay and Chris Martin.

2011	Anniversary model	$3,300	$4,100
2011	Anniversary, signed	$3,500	$4,300

D-42
1996-present. Dreadnought, Indian rosewood back and sides, spruce top, pearl rosette and inlays, snowflake 'board inlays, gold tuners, gloss finish.

1996-1999		$3,100	$4,100
2000-2014		$3,000	$4,000

D-42 E
1996-2008. With Fishman Ellipse VT pickup system.

1996-1999		$3,200	$4,050
2000-2008		$3,200	$4,050

D-42 AR (Amazon Rosewood)
2002-2003. 30 made, Amazon rosewood body which is similar to Brazilian rosewood but a different species and not restricted.

2002-2003		$4,300	$5,400

D-42 JC Johnny Cash
1997. Rosewood back and sides, gloss black lacquer on body and neck, Cash signature inlaid at 19th fret, have label signed by Cash and C.F. Martin IV, 80 sold.

1997		$4,600	$5,750

D-42 K Limited Edition
1998. 150 made, highly flamed koa back and sides, sitka top with aging toner, high X-brace design, 45-style abalone snowflake inlays.

1998		$3,400	$4,300

D-42 K/D-42 K2
1998-2006. K has koa back and sides, the all koa body K2 was discontinued in '05.

1998-1999	D-42 K	$3,200	$4,000
2000-2005	D-42 K2	$3,100	$3,900
2000-2006	D-42 K	$3,100	$3,900

D-42 LE
1988 only. Limited Edition (75 sold), D-42-style, scalloped braces, low profile neck.

1988		$3,125	$3,850

D-42 Peter Frampton
2006-2007. Indian rosewood back and sides, Style 45 features.

2006-2007		$4,300	$5,400

MODEL YEAR	FEATURES	EXC. COND. LOW	HIGH

D-42 SB

2007. Sunburst finish, sitka spruce top, 45-style appointments.

2006-2007		$3,450	$4,300

D-42 V

1985. Vintage Series, 12 made, Brazilian rosewood, scalloped braces.

1985		$6,500	$8,100

D-45

1933-1942 (96 made), 1968-present. Brazilian rosewood back and sides, changed to Indian rosewood during '69. The pre-WW II D-45 is one of the holy grails. A pre-war D-45 should be evaluated on a case-by-case basis. The price ranges are for all-original guitars in excellent condition and are guidance pricing only. These ranges are for a crack-free guitar. Unfortunately, many older acoustics have a crack or two and this can make ultra-expensive acoustics more difficult to evaluate than ultra-expensive solidbody electrics. Technically, a repaired body crack makes a guitar non-original, but the vintage market generally considers a professionally repaired crack to be original. Crack width, length and depth can vary, therefore extra attention is suggested.

1936	2 made	$350,000	$430,000
1937	2 made	$350,000	$430,000
1938	9 made	$310,000	$390,000
1939	Early, wide neck	$310,000	$390,000
1939	Late, thin neck	$280,000	$355,000
1940	19 made	$260,000	$335,000
1941	24 made	$260,000	$335,000
1942	18 made	$260,000	$335,000
1968		$31,000	$39,000
1969	Brazilian rosewood	$31,000	$39,000
1970-1979		$5,000	$6,250
1980-1989		$4,900	$6,100
1990-1999		$4,800	$5,900
2000-2014		$4,800	$5,900

D12-45

1970s-1987. Special order instrument, not a standard catalog item, with D-45 appointments, Indian rosewood.

1970-1979		$4,600	$5,700
1980-1987		$4,500	$5,600

D-45 100th Anniversary LE

1996. Limited Edition, '1896-1996 C.F. Martin Commemorative Anniversary Model' label.

1996		$5,600	$7,000

D-45 150th Anniversary

1983. Brazilian rosewood back and sides, sitka spruce top, '150th' logo stamp.

1983		$10,000	$12,500

D-45 CFM Sr. (200th Anniversary, East Indian)

1996. Commemorating the 200th Anniversary of C.F. Martin Sr. birthday, Indian rosewood back and sides, style 45 pearl bordering, bone nut and saddle, 14-fret neck, gold hardware.

1996		$5,400	$6,800

D-45 Deluxe CFM Sr. (200th Anniversary, Brazilian)

1996. Commemorating the 200th Anniversary of C.F. Martin Sr. birthday, Brazilian rosewood back and sides, style 45 Deluxe pearl bordering, fossilized-ivory nut and saddle, 14-fret neck, gold hardware.

1996		$10,000	$12,500

D-45 (1939 Reissue Mandolin Brothers)

1990. Commissioned by Mandolin Brothers, 5 made, figured Brazilian rosewood. Original name "The Reissue 1939 Martin D-45." Said to be the first reissue of the era and the seed for the '90s Martin Custom Shop.

1990		$10,500	$13,000

D-45 (1939 Reissue)

1992. High-grade spruce top, figured Brazilian rosewood back and sides, high X and scalloped braces, abalone trim, natural, gold tuners.

1992		$10,500	$13,000

D-45 B Brazilian

1994. Brazilian rosewood.

1994		$10,000	$12,500

D-45 Celtic Knot

2004-2005. Brazilian rosewood, Celtic knot 'board inlays, 30 built.

2004-2005		$15,500	$19,500

D-45 Custom Shop

1984, 1991-1992. Various options and models, Indian rosewood back and sides in '84, then Brazilian rosewood.

1984	Indian rosewood	$5,400	$6,800
1991-1992	Brazilian rosewood	$10,500	$13,000

D-45 Deluxe

1993 only. Guitar of the Month, Brazilian rosewood back and sides, figured spruce top, inlay in bridge and 'guard, tree-of-life inlay on 'board, pearl borders and back stripe, gold tuners with large gold buttons, total of 60 sold.

1993		$14,500	$18,500

D-45 E Aura

2010. With Fishman Electronics Ellipse Aura technology.

2010		$5,200	$6,400

D-45 E Retro

2013-present. East Indian rosewood, Fishman.

2014		$5,500	$6,700

D-45 GE Golden Era

2001-2004. 167 made, '37 specs, Brazilian rosewood.

2001-2004		$15,500	$19,500

D-45 Gene Autry

1994 only. Gene Autry inlay (2 options available), natural.

1994	Gene Autry 'board	$14,500	$18,000
1994	Snowflake 'board option	$14,500	$18,000

D-45 KLE

1991. Limited Edition koa, Engelmann, 54 made.

1991		$5,700	$7,000

D-45 Koa

2006-2008. Flamed koa back and sides.

2006-2008		$5,400	$6,700

1942 Martin D-45

Martin D-45

Martin D-45 V

Martin DCPA4 Siris

MODEL YEAR	FEATURES	EXC. COND. LOW	HIGH
D-45 LE			
1987. Limited Edition, 44 made, Guitar of the Month, September '87.			
1987		$13,000	$16,500
D-45 Marquis			
2006-2008. Rosewood back and sides.			
2006-2008		$7,200	$9,000
D-45 Mike Longworth Commemorative Edition			
2005-2006. East Indian rosewood back and sides, Adirondack spruce top, 91 made, label signed by Mike's wife Sue and C.F. Martin IV.			
2005-2006		$5,700	$7,100
D-45 S Deluxe			
1992. Limited Edition, 50 made, Indian rosewood, spruce top, high-end appointments.			
1992		$6,800	$8,500
D-45 S/SD-45 S			
1969-1994. Brazilian rosewood back and sides in '69, Indian rosewood after, 12-fret neck, S means slotted peghead, only 50 made.			
1969	Brazilian	$36,000	$46,000
1970-1979	Indian	$5,750	$7,200
1980-1989	Indian	$5,575	$7,000
1990-1994	Indian	$5,400	$6,800
D-45 SS Steven Stills			
1998. Brazilian rosewood back and sides, 91 made.			
1998		$16,500	$21,000
D-45 V Brazilian			
1983. Brazilian rosewood back and sides, scalloped braces, snowflake inlay, natural.			
1983		$12,500	$16,000
D-45 VR/D-45 V			
1997-present. Vintage specs, Indian rosewood back and sides, vintage aging toner, snowflake inlay. Name changed to D-45 V in '99 (not to be confused with Brazilian rosewood D-45 V of the '80s).			
1997-1998	VR	$5,100	$6,300
1999-2014	V	$5,100	$6,300
D-50 Deluxe/D-50 DX			
2001-2003. Deluxe limited edition, 50 made, one of the most ornate Martin models ever made, Brazilian rosewood back and sides, highly ornate pearl inlay.			
2001-2003		$17,500	$22,000
D-50 Koa Deluxe/D-50 K2 Koa Deluxe			
2003-2006. As D-50 Deluxe with ornate pearl inlay, but with highly flamed koa back and sides (Koa Deluxe, 45 made) or highly flamed koa top, back and sides (K2, 5 made).			
2003-2006	K2 Koa Deluxe	$15,000	$18,500
2003-2006	Koa Deluxe	$15,000	$18,500
D-60			
1989-1995. Birdseye maple back and sides, snowflake inlays, tortoiseshell binding and 'guard.			
1989-1995		$1,850	$2,300
D-62			
1987-1995. Flamed maple back and sides, chrome-plated enclosed Schaller tuners.			
1987-1995		$1,550	$1,900
D-62 LE			
1986. Limited Edition, Guitar of the Month October			

MODEL YEAR	FEATURES	EXC. COND. LOW	HIGH
'86, flamed maple back and sides, spruce top, snowflake inlays, natural.			
1986		$1,700	$2,100
D-76 Bicentennial Limited Edition			
1975-1976. Limited Edition, 200 made in '75 and 1,976 made in '76, Indian rosewood back and sides, 3-piece back, herringbone back stripe, pearl stars on 'board, eagle on peghead.			
1976		$3,000	$3,750
D-93			
1993. Mahogany, spruce, 93 pertains to the year, not a style number.			
1993		$2,000	$2,500
D-100 Deluxe			
2004-present. Limited Edition, guitars have the first 50 sequential serial numbers following the millionth Martin guitar (1,000,001 to 1,000,050), fancy pearl inlay on back, 'guard, headstock, 'board and bridge. Herringbone top and rosette inlay, Adirondack spruce top, Brazilian rosewood back and sides.			
2004-2014		$32,000	$40,000
DC Series			
1980s-present. Cutaway versions, E models have electronics.			
1981-1989	DC-28	$1,825	$2,300
1990-1997	DC-28	$1,700	$2,200
1996-2000	DC-1	$575	$725
1996-2010	DC-1E	$650	$800
1997-2000	DCM	$775	$950
1997-2005	DC-1M	$575	$700
1997-2006	DCME	$800	$1,000
1998	DCXM	$400	$500
1998-2001	DCXME	$425	$525
1998-2010	DC-15E	$825	$1,025
1999-2000	DC-1R	$600	$750
2000	DCRE	$850	$1,050
2000-2013	DCX-1E	$425	$525
2001-2005	DCXE Black	$400	$500
2002-2003	DC-16RE	$775	$975
2003	DC-16E	$1,050	$1,300
2003-2005	DC-16GTE Premium	$1,025	$1,300
2003-2014	DC-16GTE	$925	$1,150
2004-2013	DCX1KE	$425	$525
2004-2013	DCX1RE	$425	$525
2005	DC-16RE Aura	$800	$1,000
2005	DC-16RGTE Aura	$1,050	$1,325
2005-2007	DC-16E Koa	$1,175	$1,475
2005-2008	DC-16RGTE	$1,025	$1,300
2005-2010	DC-Aura	$2,000	$2,500
2006-2010	DC-28E	$1,800	$2,300
2009-2014	DCPA1/ DCPA1 Plus	$1,700	$2,100
2011	DCPA2	$1,275	$1,600
2011	DCPA3	$1,275	$1,600
2011-2014	DCPA4 Rosewood	$850	$1,050
2011-2014	DCPA4 Shaded	$850	$1,050
2013-2014	DCPA5	$500	$625
2013-2014	DCPA5 Black	$475	$600
2013-2014	DCPA5K Koa	$500	$625

MODEL YEAR	FEATURES	EXC. COND. LOW	HIGH

Ditson Dreadnaught 111

2007-2009. Based on 1929 Ditson 111, 12-fret neck, slot head, mahogany back and sides, Brazilian rosewood binding.

| 2007-2009 | | $2,825 | $3,525 |

DM

1996-2009. Solid sitka spruce top, laminated mahogany back and sides, dot markers, natural satin.

| 1996-2009 | | $500 | $625 |

DM-12

1996-2009. 12-string DM.

| 1996-2009 | | $600 | $750 |

DM3 MD Dave Matthews

2000-2001. Englemann top, 3-piece Indian rosewood back, African padauk center wedge, 234 made.

| 2000-2001 | | $3,700 | $4,700 |

Doobie-42 Tom Johnston Signature Edition

2007. D-42 style, 35 made, solid Indian rosewood back and sides, abalone and catseye markers, other special appointments.

| 2007 | | $3,600 | $4,500 |

DR

1997-2008. D-style, rosewood back and sides.

| 1997-2008 | | $500 | $625 |

DRS1 (Road/1 Series)

2011-present. D-size, sapele top, back and sides, satin finish, Fishman.

| 2011-2014 | | $450 | $575 |

DRS2 (Road/1 Series)

2012-present. DRS1 with spruce top.

| 2012-2014 | | $500 | $625 |

DVM Veterans

2002-2008. D-style, spruce top, rosewood back and sides, special veterans ornamentation.

| 2002-2008 | | $1,900 | $2,375 |

DX 175th Anniversary Limited Edition

2008. Rosewood HPL back and sides, founder's picture on top.

| 2008 | | $450 | $550 |

DX Series

1996-present. D-size, high pressure wood laminate (HPL) backs and sides, exterior wood-grain image with gloss finish. M is for mahogany wood-grain, R rosewood and K koa. A 1 indicates a solid spruce top with Series 1 bracing, otherwise top is wood-patterned HPL. C indicates cutaway and E Fishman Presys Plus and AE Fishman Sonitone.

1996-2009	DXM/DMX	$400	$500
1998-2012	DXME	$425	$525
1999-2000	D12XM 12-String	$350	$450
1999-2014	DXMAE	$450	$550
2000-2009	DX1	$400	$500
2000-2014	DX1AE	$450	$550
2001-2009	DX1R	$400	$500
2002-2009	DXK2	$400	$500
2004-2009	DX1K	$425	$525
2008-2010	D12X1 12-String	$350	$450
2010-2014	DX1KAE	$450	$550
2011-2014	D12X1AE 12-String	$475	$575
2013	DX1E	$450	$550

MODEL YEAR	FEATURES	EXC. COND. LOW	HIGH
2014-2015	DXAE Black	$425	$525
2014-2015	DXK2AE	$450	$550
2015	DX1RAE	$450	$550

E-18

1979-1983. Offset double-cut, maple and rosewood laminate solidbody, 2 DiMarzio pickups, phase switch, natural.

| 1979-1983 | | $825 | $1,025 |

E-28

1980-1983. Double-cut electric solidbody, carved top, ebony 'board, 2 humbuckers.

| 1980-1983 | | $1,000 | $1,250 |

EM-18

1979-1983. Offset double-cut, maple and rosewood laminate solidbody, 2 exposed-coil humbucking pickups, coil split switch.

| 1979-1983 | | $825 | $1,025 |

EMP-1

1998-1999. Employee series designed by Martin employee team, cutaway solid spruce top, ovangkol wood back and sides with rosewood middle insert (D-35-style insert), on-board pickup.

| 1998-1999 | | $1,650 | $2,050 |

EMP-2 Limited Edition

1999. D size, tzalam body, flying saucer inlays.

| 1999 | | $1,800 | $2,250 |

F-1

1940-1942. Archtop, mahogany back and sides, carved spruce top, multi-bound, f-holes, sunburst.

| 1940-1942 | 91 made | $1,650 | $2,050 |

F-1-12

1941. F-1 12 string.

| 1941 | | $2,250 | $2,800 |

F-2

1940-1942. Rosewood back and sides, carved spruce top, multi-bound, f-holes.

| 1940-1942 | 46 made | $2,075 | $2,600 |

F-5

1940. 2 made

| 1940 | | $3,600 | $4,500 |

F-7

1935-1942. Brazilian rosewood back and sides, f-holes, carved top, back arched by braces, multi-bound, sunburst top finish.

| 1935-1942 | | $5,600 | $7,000 |

F-9

1935-1942. Highest-end archtop, Brazilian rosewood, Martin inlaid vertically on headstock, 7-ply top binding, 45-style back strip, sunburst.

| 1935-1942 | | $11,250 | $14,000 |

F-50

1961-1965. Single-cut thinline archtop with laminated maple body, 1 pickup.

| 1961-1965 | | $1,100 | $1,400 |

F-55

1961-1965. Single-cut thinline archtop with laminated maple body, 2 pickups.

| 1961-1965 | | $1,500 | $1,900 |

F-65

1961-1965. Electric archtop, double-cut, f-holes, 2 pickups, square-cornered peghead, Bigsby, sunburst.

| 1961-1965 | | $1,500 | $1,900 |

Martin DXMAE

1980 Martin EM-18

2009 Martin Grand J12-40E
Steve Zuckerman

1966 Martin GT-70
Gil Hembree

MODEL YEAR	FEATURES	EXC. COND. LOW	HIGH
Felix The Cat			
2004-2010. Felix the Cat logo art, Don Oriolo logo, red body, Felix gig bag.			
2004	Felix I, 756 made	$425	$525
2005-2006	Felix II, 625 made	$425	$525
2007-2010	Felix III, 1000 made	$425	$525
GCD-16 CP (Guitar Center)			
1998. 15 5/8" Style D.			
1998		$1,725	$2,125
GPC Series			
2010-present. Performing Artist Series, Grand Performance size, cutaway, acoustic/electric, various woods.			
2010-2014	GPCPA1/ Plus Rosewood	$1,700	$2,100
2012-2014	GPCPA5K Koa	$475	$600
2013-2014	GPC12PA4 12-string	$925	$1,150
2013-2014	GPCPA4 Rosewood	$850	$1,050
2013-2014	GPCPA4 Sapele	$850	$1,050
2013-2014	GPCPA5	$475	$600
2013-2014	GPCPA5 Black	$475	$600
Grand J12-40 E Special			
2009-2011. J12-40 with D-TAR Multi-source electronics.			
2009-2011		$2,300	$2,850
Grand J-28 LSE			
2011-2014. Baritone.			
2011-2014		$1,950	$2,450
Grand J-35 E			
2009-2011. Grand jumbo size, rosewood back and sides.			
2009-2011		$2,000	$2,500
GT-70			
1965-1966. Electric archtop, bound body, f-holes, single-cut, 2 pickups, tremolo, burgundy or black finish.			
1965-1966		$2,100	$2,600
GT-75			
1965-1967. Electric archtop, bound body, f-holes, double-cut, 2 pickups, tremolo, burgundy or black finish. There is also a 12-string version.			
1965-1967		$2,100	$2,700
Hawaiian X			
2002-2004. Hawaiian scene painted on top, similar to the Cowboy guitar model, limited edition of 500.			
2002-2004		$575	$725
HD-7 Roger McGuinn			
2005-2008. Rosewood back and sides, herringbone top trim, 7-string with double G.			
2005-2008		$2,450	$3,050
HD-16 R Adirondack			
2008-present. Rosewood back and sides, Adirondack top.			
2010-2014		$1,400	$1,750
HD-16 R LSH			
2007-2013. Indian rosewood (R), large sound hole (LSH).			
2007-2013		$1,400	$1,750
HD-18 JB Jimmy Buffett			
1998. 424 made, solid mahogany back and sides, herringbone trim, palm tree headstock logo, Style 42			

MODEL YEAR	FEATURES	EXC. COND. LOW	HIGH
markers, Buffett pearl signature.			
1998		$4,700	$5,900
HD-18 LE			
1987. Indian rosewood.			
1987		$2,000	$2,500
HD-28 1935 Special			
1993. 'HD-28 1935 Special' model name on label.			
1993		$2,300	$2,900
HD-28 2R			
1991-1997. 2R specification for 2 herringbone soundhole rings, larger soundhole.			
1991-1997		$1,850	$2,300
HD-28 BLE			
1990. Guitar of the Month, 100 made, Brazilian rosewood back and sides, herringbone soundhole ring, low profile neck (LE), chrome tuners, aging toner finish.			
1990		$6,000	$7,500
HD-28 BSE			
1987. Brazilian rosewood, 93 made.			
1987		$6,000	$7,500
HD-28 CTB			
1992. Guitar of the Month, mahogany back and sides, slotted peghead, herringbone back stripe, gold tuners, custom tortoise bound.			
1992		$2,200	$2,800
HD-28 Custom 150th Anniversary			
1983. 150th Anniversary, Martin Custom Shop, Indian rosewood sides and back, '1833-1983 150th Year' stamped on inside backstrip.			
1983		$2,500	$3,100
HD-28 Custom Adirondack			
2013. Elderly Instruments Custom model.			
2013		$2,400	$3,000
HD-28 Custom/Custom HD-28			
1994. Custom Shop model.			
1994-1995		$2,000	$2,500
HD-28 E Retro			
2013-present. Solid sitka spruce top, East Indian rosewood back and sides.			
2013-2014		$2,000	$2,500
HD-28 GM			
1989. Grand Marquis, Guitar of the Month, scalloped braced Sitka spruce top with 1930s-era bracing pattern that replaced the X-brace below the soundhole, herringbone top purfling, soundhole ring and back stripe, gold tuners.			
1989		$3,100	$3,800
HD-28 GM LSH			
1994. Grand Marquis, Guitar of the Month, rosewood back and sides, large soundhole with double herringbone rings, snowflake inlay in bridge, natural (115 made) or sunburst (36 made).			
1994	Natural	$2,800	$3,450
1994	Sunburst	$2,925	$3,575
HD-28 KM Keb Mo Signature Edition			
2001-2002. Hawaiian Koa back and sides, 252 made.			
2001-2002		$2,300	$2,850

*The **Vintage Guitar Price Guide** shows low to high values for items in all-original excellent condition, and, where applicable, with original case or cover.*

MODEL		EXC. COND.	
YEAR	FEATURES	LOW	HIGH

HD-28 LE

1985. Limited Edition, Guitar of the Month, rosewood back and sides, scalloped bracing, herringbone top purfling, diamonds and squares 'board inlay, V-neck.

| 1985 | | $2,600 | $3,200 |

HD-28 LSV

1997-2005. Vintage Series, large Soundhole Vintage, patterned after Clarence White's modified '35 D-28.

| 1997-2005 | | $2,200 | $2,800 |

HD-28 M

1988. Standard profile.

| 1988 | | $1,850 | $2,300 |

HD-28 MP

1990-1991, 2011-2012. Bolivian rosewood back and sides, herringbone top trim, low profile neck. Reissued in 2011 with Madagascar rosewood and modern-style neck.

| 1990-1991 | | $2,300 | $2,900 |
| 2011-2012 | | $2,300 | $2,900 |

HD-28 P

1987-1989. Rosewood back and sides, scalloped braces, herringbone, low profile neck (P), zigzag back stripe.

| 1987-1989 | | $1,800 | $2,300 |

HD-28 PSE

1988. Signature Edition, Guitar of the Month, rosewood back and sides, signed by C.F. Martin IV and foremen, scalloped braces, herringbone top purfling, low profile neck, squared peghead, ebony tuner buttons.

| 1988 | | $2,200 | $2,700 |

HD-28 S Custom

1995. Slotted headstock.

| 1995 | | $2,200 | $2,700 |

HD-28 SE

1986. Signature Edition, Guitar of the Month, rosewood back and sides, signed by Martins and foremen, herringbone top purfling, V-neck, ebony tuner buttons.

| 1986 | | $2,200 | $2,700 |

HD-28 SO Sing Out!

1996. Limited edition, 45 made, Indian rosewood back and sides.

| 1996 | | $2,300 | $2,900 |

HD-28 Standard Series

1976-present. Indian rosewood back and sides, scalloped bracing, herringbone purfling.

1976-1979		$2,400	$3,000
1980-1989		$1,875	$2,350
1990-1999		$1,700	$2,125
2000-2014		$1,700	$2,125

HD-28 V Custom

2007-2012. Indian rosewood back and sides, Adirondack top, wide nut, Elderly Instruments special issue.

| 2007-2012 | | $2,500 | $3,100 |

HD-28 V/HD-28 VR

1996-present. 14-fret, Indian rosewood body, R dropped from name in '99.

| 1996-1999 | HD-28 VR | $2,025 | $2,525 |
| 2000-2014 | HD-28 V | $2,025 | $2,525 |

HD-28 VAW Custom

2007-present. Custom for Elderly Instruments, Indian rosewood back and sides, herringbone trim, diamond and square inlays, aged gloss finish.

| 2007-2014 | | $2,400 | $3,100 |

HD-28 VE

2004-2006. HD-28 V with Fishman Ellipse Blend system.

| 2004-2006 | | $2,075 | $2,575 |

HD-28 VS

1996-present. Slotted headstock, 12-fret, spruce top with aging toner, Indian rosewood sides and back.

| 1996-2014 | | $2,250 | $2,800 |

HD-35

1978-present. Indian rosewood back and sides, herringbone top trim, zipper back stripe.

1978-1979		$2,400	$3,000
1980-1989		$1,950	$2,400
1990-1999		$1,775	$2,200
2000-2014		$1,775	$2,200

HD-35 Custom

2009. Custom Designed on neck block, Adirondack spruce top, East Indian rosewood sides and back.

| 2009 | | $2,200 | $2,700 |

HD-35 Nancy Wilson

2006-2007. Englemann spruce top, 3-piece back with bubinga center wedge, 101 made.

| 2006-2007 | | $2,600 | $3,200 |

HD-35 P

1987-1989. HD-35 with low profile neck.

| 1987-1989 | | $1,750 | $2,150 |

HD-35 SJC Judy Collins

2002. 50 made, Collins signature headstock logo, wildflower headstock inlay, East Indian rosewood, 3 piece back with figured maple center.

| 2002 | | $2,500 | $3,100 |

HD-40 MK Mark Knopfler

2001-2002. Limited Edition of 251 made, Mark Knopfler signature inlay 20th fret, herringbone trim, fancy marquetry soundhole rings.

| 2001-2002 | | $3,200 | $4,000 |

HD-40 MS Marty Stuart

1996. Indian rosewood, 250 made, pearl/abalone inlay.

| 1996 | | $3,200 | $4,000 |

HD-40 Tom Petty SE

2004-2006. Indian rosewood sides and back, high-end appointments, 274 made, inside label with signature.

| 2004-2006 | | $3,800 | $4,800 |

HD-282 R

1992-1996. Large soundhole with 2 herringbone rings, zigzag backstripe.

| 1992-1996 | | $1,950 | $2,450 |

HD Dierks Bentley

2013-2014. Rosewood.

| 2013-2014 | | $2,800 | $3,550 |

HD Elliot Easton Custom Edition

2006-2008. Limited Edition, Adirondack spruce top with aging tone, Fishman Ellipse Aura pickup available on HDE.

| 2006-2008 | | $2,450 | $3,050 |

1966 Martin GT-75
Tom Gingrich

Martin HD-35

Martin J12-16 GT

2004 Martin J-41 Special
Folkway Music

MODEL YEAR	FEATURES	EXC. COND. LOW	HIGH

HDN Negative L.E.
2003. 135 made, unusual appointments include pearloid headstock and black finish, HDN Negative Limited Edition notation on the inside label.

2003		$2,350	$2,950

HDO Grand Ole Opry
1999-2000. 650 made, 'Grand Ole Opry 75th Anniversary' on neck block, WSM microphone headstock logo, off-white Micarta fingerboard, sitka spruce top, East Indian rosewood back and sides.

1999-2000		$1,775	$2,200

HJ-28
1992, 1996-2000. Guitar of the Month in '92, regular production started in '96. Jumbo, non-cut, spruce top, Indian rosewood sides and back, herringbone top purfling, with or without on-board electronics.

1992	69 made	$1,775	$2,200
1996-2000		$1,775	$2,200

HJ-28 M
1994. Mahogany/spruce, herringbone top purfling, Guitar of the Month, 72 made.

1994		$2,500	$3,100

HJ-38 Stefan Grossman
2008-2011. Madagascar rosewood back and sides.

2008-2011		$2,600	$3,250

HM Ben Harper
2008-2009. Special Edition, M-style width, 000-style depth, solid Adirondack spruce top, solid East Indian rosewood sides and back, onboard Fishman Ellipse Matrix Blend.

2008-2009		$2,600	$3,250

HOM-35
1989. Herringbone Orchestra Model, Guitar of the Month, scalloped braces, 3-piece Brazilian rosewood back, bookmatched sides, 14-fret neck, only 60 built.

1989		$3,600	$4,500

HPD-41
1999-2001. Like D-41, but with herringbone rosette, binding.

1999-2001		$2,500	$3,125

HTA Kitty Wells 'Honky Tonk Angel'
2002. D-size with 000-size depth, Indian rosewood back and sides, Queen of Country Music inlay logo on headstock (no Martin headstock logo).

2002		$1,925	$2,400

J-1 Jumbo
1997-2001. Jumbo body with mahogany back and sides.

1997-2001		$800	$1,000

J12-15
2000-2008. 12-string version of J-15.

2000-2008		$825	$1,025

J12-16 GT
2000-2013. 16" jumbo 12-string, satin solid mahogany back and sides, gloss solid spruce top.

2000-2013		$850	$1,050

J12-16 GTE
2014-present. Jumbo 12-string, Fishman.

2014		$850	$1,050

J12-40/J12-40 M
1985-1996. Called J12-40M from '85-'90, rosewood

---

back and sides, 12 strings, 16" jumbo size, 14-fret neck, solid peghead, gold tuners.

1985-1990	J12-40M	$1,800	$2,250
1991-1996	J12-40	$1,700	$2,100

J12-65
1985-1995. Called J12-65M for '84-'90, 12-string, figured maple back and sides.

1985-1995		$1,900	$2,400

J-15
1999-2010. Jumbo 16" narrow-waist body, solid mahogany top, sides, and back, satin finish.

1999-2010		$800	$1,000

J-15 E
2000-2001. Acoustic/electric J-15.

2000-2001		$850	$1,050

J-18/J-18 M
1987-1996. J-size body with Style 18 appointments, natural, called J-18M for '87-'89.

1987-1996	J-18	$1,275	$1,575
1987-1996	J-18M	$1,100	$1,375

J-21 MC
1986. J cutaway, oval soundhole.

1986		$1,725	$2,150

J-21/J-21 M
1985-1996. Called J-21M prior to '90, Indian rosewood back and sides, black binding, rosewood 'board, chrome tuners.

1985-1989	J-21 M	$1,625	$2,025
1990-1996	J-21	$1,625	$2,025

J-40
1990-present. Called J-40 M from '85-'89, Jumbo, Indian rosewood back and sides, triple-bound 'board, hexagonal inlays.

1990-2014		$2,025	$2,525

J-40 BK
1990-1997. Black finish and 'guard, gold hardware.

1990-1997		$1,900	$2,400

J-40 Custom
1993-1996. J-40 with upgrades including abalone top trim and rosette.

1993-1996		$2,050	$2,550

J-40 M/J-40 MBK
1985-1989. Jumbo, Indian rosewood back and sides, triple-bound 'board, hexagonal inlays, MBK ('88-'89) indicates black, name changed to J-40 in '90.

1985-1989	J-40 M	$1,800	$2,250
1988-1989	J-40 MBK	$1,700	$2,150

J-40 MBLE
1987. Brazilian rosewood, Style 45 snowflakes, 17 made.

1987		$4,000	$5,000

J-40 MC
1987-1989. Rounded Venetian cutaway version of J-40 M, oval soundhole, gold-plated enclosed tuners. Becomes JC-40 in '90..

1985-1989		$2,000	$2,500

J-41 Special
2004-2007. East Indian rosewood back and sides, Style 45 snowflake inlays.

2004-2007		$2,000	$2,500

MODEL YEAR FEATURES	EXC. COND. LOW	HIGH

J-45 M Deluxe
1986. Guitar of the Month, East Indian rosewood back and sides, tortoise-colored binding, mother-of-pearl and abalone, gold tuners with ebony buttons.

| 1986 | $3,700 | $4,500 |

J-65 Custom/J-65 FM
1993-1996. White binding, herringbone. Available with MEQ electronics.

| 1993-1996 | $2,100 | $2,600 |
| 1993-1996 With MEQ | $2,200 | $2,700 |

J-65/J-65 E/J-65 M
1985-1995. Jumbo, maple back and sides, gold-plated tuners, scalloped bracing, ebony 'board, tortoise shell-style binding.

| 1985-1995 | $2,000 | $2,500 |

JC Buddy Guy
2006-2007. Only 36 made, rosewood back and sides.

| 2006-2007 | $2,300 | $2,875 |

JC-1 E
1999-2002. Jumbo, mahogany, cutaway, pickup.

| 1999-2002 | $1,000 | $1,250 |

JC-16 GTE
2000-2003. Jumbo, cutaway, mahogany back and sides, gloss top, Fishman.

| 2000-2003 | $1,000 | $1,250 |

JC-16 KWS Kenny Wayne Shepherd Signature
2001-2002. Cutaway, blue lacquer top, back and sides in gloss black, on-board electronics, 198 made.

| 2001-2002 198 made | $1,200 | $1,500 |

JC-16 ME Aura
2006-2009. JC-16 with maple back and sides, Fishman Aura.

| 2006-2009 | $1,550 | $1,950 |

JC-16 RE Aura
2006-2011. Like ME, but with rosewood back and sides.

| 2006-2011 | $1,550 | $1,950 |

JC-16 RGTE Aura
2000-2003. Like RE Aura, but with gloss top.

| 2000-2003 | $1,200 | $1,500 |

JC-16 WE
2002-2003. Jumbo cutaway, solid walnut sides and back, solid sitka spruce top.

| 2002-2003 | $1,000 | $1,250 |

JC-40
1990-1997. Renamed from J-40 MC, cutaway flat-top, oval sound hole.

| 1990-1997 | $2,125 | $2,625 |

LX Elvis Presley
2009. Modified 0-14 fret body size, HPL body, custom leather Elvis Presley style cover.

| 2009 | $320 | $400 |

LX Series
2003-present. The LX series is the Little Martin models, featuring small bodies with high pressure wood laminate (HPL) backs and sides with an exterior wood-grain image with a gloss finish. M is for mahogany wood-grain, R for rosewood and K for koa. They are also offered in all solid-colors. A 1 indicates a HPL spruce top, 2 is HPL koa top. E indicates electronics.

2003-2014 LXM	$210	$260
2004-2014 LX1	$210	$260
2004-2014 LXK2	$235	$290
2009-2014 LX1E	$235	$290
2013-2014 LXME	$320	$400

LX1E Ed Sheeran
2014. HP laminate, Fishman.

| 2014 | $400 | $500 |

M2C-28
1988. Double-cut, Guitar of the Month, 22 made.

| 1988 | $2,000 | $2,500 |

M-3 H Cathy Fink
2005. M 0000-size body, gloss finish, rosewood sides, 3-piece back with flamed koa center panel, torch headstock inlay, herringbone top trim, no Martin logo on headstock.

| 2005 | $2,000 | $2,500 |

M-3 M George Martin
2005-2006. M Model, Style 40 appointments with Style 42 snowflake inlays, 127 made.

| 2005-2006 | $2,800 | $3,500 |

M-3 SC Shawn Colvin
2002-2003. M 0000-size body, 120 made, mahogany sides, 3-piece mahogany/rosewood back, Fishman, Shawn Colvin & C.F.M. III signed label.

| 2002-2003 | $1,750 | $2,175 |

M-18
1984-1988. M size, mahogany.

| 1984-1988 | $1,800 | $2,275 |

M-21
December 1984. Guitar of the Month, low profile neck M-Series, Indian rosewood back and sides, special ornamentation.

| 1984 | $2,000 | $2,500 |

M-21 Steve Earl
2008-2011. East Indian rosewood back and sides, Italian Alpine spruce top.

| 2008-2011 | $2,125 | $2,650 |

M-30 Jorma Kaukonen
2010-2013. M 0000-size body, Style 30 appointments, East Indian rosewood back and sides, Maltese diamond/square inlays, optional electronics.

| 2010-2013 | $3,500 | $4,400 |

M-35/M-36
1978-1997, 2007-present. First 26 labeled as M-35, Indian rosewood back and sides, bound 'board, low profile neck, multi-bound, white-black-white back stripes.

1978 M-35, 26 made	$2,100	$2,650
1978-1979	$2,100	$2,650
1980-1989	$1,600	$1,975
1990-2014	$1,500	$1,900

M-38 (0000-38)
1977-1997, 2007-2011. Called 0000-38 (see that listing) in '97-'98, 0000-size, Indian rosewood back and sides, multi-bound.

1977-1979	$2,500	$3,100
1980-1989	$2,300	$2,700
1990-1997	$2,000	$2,500
2007-2011	$2,000	$2,500

Martin LXME Little Martin

Martin M-30 Jorma Kaukonen

Martin OM-18 V

Martin OM-21

MODEL YEAR	FEATURES	EXC. COND. LOW	HIGH

M-42 David Bromberg
2006. 0000-14 body, rosewood back and sides, snowflakes, 83 made.

| 2006 | | $3,625 | $4,525 |

M-64
1985-1996. Auditorium, flamed maple back and sides, tortoiseshell-style binding.

| 1985-1989 | | $1,600 | $1,975 |
| 1990-1996 | | $1,500 | $1,900 |

MC12-41 Richie Sambora
2006. 12-string version of OMC-41 Richie Sambora, planned 200 made combined models.

| 2006 | | $3,200 | $4,000 |

MC-DSM
2007-2010. Limited Edition of 100, cutaway, designed by District Sales Manager (DSM), spruce top, figured koa back and sides.

| 2007-2010 | | $2,900 | $3,600 |

MC-16 GTE
2002-2004. Acoustic/electric, M-size single cut, gloss top, mahogany sides and back.

| 2002-2004 | | $800 | $1,000 |

MC-28
1981-1996. Rosewood back and sides, single-cut, oval soundhole, scalloped braces.

| 1981-1989 | | $1,825 | $2,300 |
| 1990-1996 | | $1,700 | $2,200 |

MC-37 K
1981-1982, 1987-1994. Cutaway, koa back and sides.

| 1981-1989 | | $2,300 | $2,700 |
| 1990-1994 | | $2,000 | $2,500 |

MC-38 Steve Howe
2009-2011. Indian rosewood back and sides, cutaway, slot headstock.

| 2009-2011 | | $4,325 | $5,400 |

MC-68/MC-68 R/MC-68+
1985-1996. Auditorium-size, single-cut, maple back and sides, scalloped bracing, verticle logo, natural or sunburst. In '85 called the MC-68 R (for adjustable truss-rod), 7 with sunburst shaded top option called MC-68+.

| 1985-1996 | MC-68/MC-68R | $2,250 | $2,800 |
| 1985-1996 | MC-68+ | $2,400 | $3,000 |

Mini-Martin Limited Edition
1999-2009. Size 5 Terz body, solid sitka spruce top, rosewood sides and back, vintage style Martin Geib case with green interior.

| 1999-2009 | | $1,600 | $2,000 |

MMV
2008-2009. D-style, rosewood sides and back, nitro finish.

| 2008-2009 | | $1,175 | $1,475 |

MTV-1 Unplugged Edition
1996. Body is 1/2 rosewood and 1/2 mahogany, scalloped bracing, MTV logo on headstock, gloss (588 sold) or satin (73 sold) finish.

| 1996 | Gloss finish | $1,000 | $1,250 |
| 1996 | Satin finish | $900 | $1,150 |

MTV-2 Unplugged Edition
2003-2004. Body is 1/2 rosewood and 1/2 maple, scalloped bracing, MTV logo on headstock.

| 2003-2004 | | $900 | $1,150 |

MODEL YEAR	FEATURES	EXC. COND. LOW	HIGH

N-10
1968-1993. Classical, mahogany back and sides, fan bracing, wood marquetry soundhole ring, unbound rosewood 'board, 12-fret neck and slotted peghead from '70.

1968-1970	Short-scale	$1,500	$1,875
1970-1979	Long-scale	$1,400	$1,750
1980-1993	Long-scale	$1,200	$1,500

N-20
1968-1992. Classical, Brazilian rosewood back and sides (changed to Indian rosewood in '69), multi-bound, 12-fret neck, solid headstock (changed to slotted in '70), natural.

1968-1969	Brazilian, short-scale	$5,200	$6,400
1970-1979	Indian, long-scale	$2,600	$3,250
1980-1989	Long-scale	$2,200	$2,750
1990-1992	Long-scale	$2,000	$2,500

N-20 B
1985-1986. Brazilian rosewood N-20.

| 1985-1986 | | $4,000 | $5,000 |

OM-18
1930-1934. Orchestra Model, mahogany back and sides, 14-fret neck, solid peghead, banjo tuners (changed to right-angle in '31).

| 1930-1931 | Banjo tuners, small 'guard | $23,000 | $29,000 |
| 1932-1933 | Standard appointments, full 'guard | $15,000 | $18,500 |

OM-18 Authentic 1933
2013-present. Period-correct (1933) appointments, Vintage Tone System, Vintage Gloss finish.

| 2013-2015 | | $3,300 | $4,100 |

OM-18 Golden Era
2003-2009. Mahogany back and sides, Brazilian rosewood purfling and binding.

| 2003-2009 | | $2,200 | $2,725 |

OM-18 P
1930-1931. Plectrum.

| 1930-1931 | | $10,000 | $12,500 |

OM-18 Special
2012. Custom Shop model.

| 2012 | | $2,200 | $2,700 |

OM-18 V
1999-2009. Vintage features.

| 1999-2009 | | $1,700 | $2,150 |

OM-18 VLJ Laurence Juber
2002, 2008-2010. Cutaway.

| 2002-2010 | | $2,700 | $3,400 |

OM-21
1994-present. Indian rosewood back & sides, herringbone back stripe & soundhole ring, 14-fret neck, chrome tuners.

| 1994-2014 | | $1,500 | $1,875 |

OM-21 Special
1991, 2007-2011. Upgrade to ebony 'board, rosewood bindings.

| 1992-2011 | | $2,000 | $2,500 |

OM-21 Special Limited Edition
1991. Custom Shop, prototype to '92 production.

| 1991 | 36 made | $2,000 | $2,500 |

The **Vintage Guitar Price Guide** shows low to high values for items in all-original excellent condition, and, where applicable, with original case or cover.

MODEL		EXC. COND.	
YEAR	FEATURES	LOW	HIGH

OM-28
1929-1933. Brazilian rosewood back and sides, 14-fret neck, solid peghead, banjo tuners (changed to right-angle in '31), reintroduced with Indian rosewood in '90 (see OM-28 Reissue).

1929	Banjo pegs, small 'guard, pyramid end bridge	$73,000	$91,000
1930	Banjo tuners, small 'guard, standard bridge	$65,000	$81,000
1931	Early '31 Banjo tuners, small 'guard, standard	$63,000	$78,000
1931	Late '31 Standard tuners, full-size 'guard	$50,000	$65,000
1931	Mid '31 Banjo tuners, small 'guard, standard bridge	$55,000	$69,000
1932-1933	Standard tuners, full-size 'guard	$50,000	$65,000

OM-28 (Reissue)
1990-1997. Indian rosewood back and sides.

1990-1997		$1,500	$1,875

OM-28 Brazilian
2000		$7,000	$8,700

OM-28 E Retro
2012-present. Sitka top, Indian rosewood back and sides, herringbone binding, Fishman.

2012-2014		$2,100	$2,600

OM-28 Golden Era
2003-2004. Brazilian rosewood back and sides, Adirondack spruce top.

2003-2004		$7,000	$8,700

OM-28 JM John Mayer
2003. Limited Edition, 404 made.

2003		$6,500	$8,100

OM-28 LE
1985. Limited Edition only 40 made, Guitar of the Month, Indian rosewood back and sides, herringbone top binding, V-neck.

1985		$2,600	$3,200

OM-28 M Roseanne Cash
2008. Signature Edition, Madagascar rosewood back and sides, 100 made.

2008		$3,600	$4,500

OM-28 Marquis
2005-present. Pre-war appointments, Adirondack top, East Indian rosewood back, sides and headplate.

2005-2014		$2,700	$3,400

OM-28 Marquis Adirondack
2011-2013. Adirondack spruce top.

2011-2013		$2,700	$3,400

OM-28 Marquis Madagascar
2007-2008. Madagascar rosewood.

2007-2008		$3,150	$3,900

OM-28 PB Perry Bechtel
1993. Guitar of the Month, signed by Perry Bechtel's

widow Ina, Indian rosewood back and sides, zigzag back stripe, chrome tuners, V-neck, 50 made.

1993		$3,800	$4,725

OM-28 SO Sing Out!
1985. For Sing Out! Magazine's 35, label signed by Pete Seeger.

1985		$2,300	$2,900

OM-28 VR/OM-28 V
1984-1990, 1999-2014. VR suffix until '99, then just V (Vintage Series), rosewood back and sides.

1984-1998	VR	$2,025	$2,525
1999-2014	V	$2,025	$2,525

OM-35
2003-2007. 000-size body, Indian rosewood sides and 3-piece back, spruce top, gloss natural finish.

2003-2007		$1,500	$1,875

OM-40 BLE
1990. Limited Edition, 50 made, Brazilian rosewood back and sides.

1990		$6,500	$8,075

OM-40 LE
1994. Limited Edition, Guitar of the Month, Indian rosewood back and sides, double pearl borders, snowflake inlay on 'board, gold tuners, natural (57 sold) or sunburst (29 sold).

1994	Natural	$3,700	$4,625
1994	Sunburst	$4,225	$5,300

OM-40 Rory Block
2004. Limited Edition, 38 made, 000-size, Indian rosewood back and sides, Englemann spruce top, 'the road' inlay markers, vintage-auto inlay on headstock.

2004		$2,500	$3,125

OM-41 Special
2005-2006. Rosewood back and sides, Style 45 snowflake inlays.

2005-2006		$2,600	$3,250

OM-42
1930, 1999-present. Indian rosewood back and sides, Style 45 snowflake inlays, there were 2 guitars labeled OM-42 built in 1930.

1930	2 made	$70,000	$90,000
1999-2014		$3,400	$4,200

OM-42 Flamed Mahogany
2006. Limited Edition, 30 made, flamed mahogany back and sides, vines.

2006		$4,400	$5,500

OM-42 Koa
2005-2008. Koa sides and back.

2006-2008		$3,400	$4,200

OM-42 PS Paul Simon
1997. Bookmatched sitka spruce top, Indian rosewood back and sides, 42- and 45-style features, low profile PS neck, 500 planned but only 223 made.

1997		$3,400	$4,200

OM-45
1930-1933. OM-style, 45 level appointments. Condition is critically important on this or any ultra high-end instrument, minor flaws are critical to value.

1930	Banjo pegs, 19 made	$220,000	$270,000
1931	10 made	$155,000	$195,000

Martin OM-28 E Retro

Martin OM-28 Marquis

Martin OM Jeff Daniels

Martin OMC-16 E

MODEL YEAR	FEATURES	EXC. COND. LOW	HIGH
1932	5 made	$155,000	$195,000
1933	6 made	$155,000	$195,000

OM-45/SOM-45
1977-1994. First batch labeled SOM-45, 2 labeled OM-45 N in '94 that had square tube bar in neck and without scalloped braces.

1977-1979		$5,000	$6,250
1980-1989		$4,900	$6,100
1990-1994		$4,800	$5,900
1994	OM-45 N option	$4,800	$5,900

OM-45 Custom Deluxe
1998-1999. Limited custom shop run of 14, Adirondack spruce and typical Style 45 appointments.

1998-1999		$11,500	$14,500

OM-45 Deluxe
1930. Only 14 made, Brazilian rosewood back and sides, zipper pattern back stripe, pearl inlay in 'guard and bridge. Condition is critically important on this or any ultra high-end instrument, minor flaws are critical to value.

1930		$270,000	$340,000

OM-45 Deluxe (Special)
1999. 4 made on special order, highly figured Brazilian rosewood.

1999		$16,000	$20,000

OM-45 Deluxe Golden Era
1998. Brazilian rosewood.

1998		$15,500	$19,500

OM-45 GE Golden Era
1999, 2001-2005. Red spruce top, Brazilian rosewood.

1999-2005		$15,500	$19,500

OM-45 Marquis
2005-2008. Pre-war appointments based on 1933 OM, spruce top, ebony 'board and bridge, East Indian rosewood back, sides and headplate.

2005-2008		$3,600	$4,500

OM-45 Tasmanian Blackwood
2005. Limited Edition, 29 made, Tasmanian Blackwood (koa-family) back and sides with curly grain, 000-size, OM and 45 style appointments.

2005		$6,000	$7,400

OM-45/OM-45B Roy Rogers
2006. Limited Edition, based on Roy's 1930 OM-45 Deluxe, Indian rosewood (84 made) or Brazilian rosewood (45B, 14 made).

2006	Brazilian rosewood	$15,500	$19,500
2006	Indian rosewood	$7,200	$9,000

OM 1833 Custom Shop Limited Edition
2006. Italian alpine spruce top, flamed claro walnut back and sides, 000-size, low profile 14-fret neck, fancy inlay and appointments, natural gloss finish.

2006		$3,000	$3,700

OMC Aura
2004-2011. OM size, cutaway, rosewood back and sides, Fishman Aura.

2004-2011		$1,800	$2,250

OMC Fingerstyle 1
2005-2008. Cutaway, Spanish cedar back and sides, no inlays.

2005-2008		$1,500	$1,900

OM Chris Hillman
2009-2010. Adirondack top, Indian rosewood back and sides, sunburst.

2009-2010		$2,400	$3,000

OM Jeff Daniels
2012-2013. Based on Daniels 1934 C-2 archtop conversion, Adirondack, Madagascar rosewood back and sides, sunburst.

2012-2013		$2,400	$3,000

OMC Cherry
2008-2013. Sustainable wood program, solid cherry back and sides, solid rescued spruce top, 000 body, cutaway, Fishman.

2008-2013		$1,300	$1,650

OMC Red Birch
2005-2009. Sustainable Series.

2005-2009		$1,675	$2,100

OMC-1 E
2009-2010. Style 28 appointments, cutaway, on-board Fishman.

2009-2010		$650	$800

OMC-15 E
2001-2007. All solid mahogany body.

2001-2007		$750	$1,000

OMC-16 E Koa
2005-2009. Koa back and sides, on-board electronics.

2005-2009		$1,300	$1,650

OMC-16 E Maple
2005-2009. Maple, on-board electronics.

2005-2009		$1,000	$1,250

OMC-16 E/E Premium
2003-2007. Sapele back and sides, on-board electronics.

2003-2007		$1,100	$1,400

OMC-16 RE Aura
2005-2009. East Indian rosewood back and sides, gloss body.

2005-2009		$1,450	$1,825

OMC-16 RE/RE Premium
2003-2005. Solid rosewood back and sides, on-board electronics.

2003-2005		$1,100	$1,400

OMC-16 WE
2002-2003. Walnut back and sides.

2002-2003		$1,125	$1,425

OMC-28
1990. Guitar of the Month, Indian rosewood, low profile neck, label signed by C.F. Martin IV.

1990		$1,800	$2,250

OMC-28 B Laurence Juber
2004. Brazilian rosewood.

2004		$6,100	$7,800

OMC-28 E
2006-2009. OMC-28 with Fishman Ellipse.

2006-2009		$1,850	$2,300

OMC-28 Laurence Juber
2004-2005. OM size, cutaway, Indian rosewood.

2004-2005		$2,300	$2,900

OMC-28 M Laurence Juber
2008-2011. Madagascar rosewood.

2008-2011		$3,100	$3,900

MODEL YEAR	FEATURES	EXC. COND. LOW	HIGH

OMC-41 Richie Sambora
2006-2009. Madagascar rosewood sides and back, combination Style 45 and 41 appointments, 12-string is MC12-41 Richie Sambora, planned 200 made combined models.

2006-2009		$3,600	$4,500

OMC-LJ Pro Laurence Juber
2013. Custom Artist Edition, Adirondack spruce top, flamed maple back and sides.

2013		$2,500	$3,200

OMCPA Series
2010-present. Performing Artist Series, OM size, cutaway, acoustic/electric, various woods.

2010-2014	OMCPA1/ OMCPA1 Plus	$1,700	$2,100
2011	OMCPA2	$1,275	$1,600
2011-2013	OMCPA3	$1,275	$1,600
2011-2014	OMCPA4 Sapele	$850	$1,050
2012-2014	OMCPA4 Rosewood	$850	$1,050
2014	OMCPA4 Black	$475	$600

OMCRE
2008-2009. Carpathian spruce top, East Indian rosewood sides and back, Babicz adjustable neck joint, Fishman, gloss finish.

2008-2009		$1,675	$2,100

OMCXK2E
2006-2009. Hawaiian Koa HPL (high pressure laminate) textured finish.

2006-2009		$500	$625

OMJM John Mayer
2003-present. Indian rosewood sides and back.

2003-2014		$2,000	$2,500

OMM John Renbourne
2011-2013. Madagascar rosewood sides and back.

2011-2013		$2,700	$3,400

OMXAE Black
2014-present. Black HPL back and sides, black Richlite 'board.

2014-2015		$425	$525

POW MIA
2006-2010. POW MIA logo position marker lettering on fretboard, D-style body, dark finish.

2006-2010		$2,300	$2,900

PS2 Paul Simon Signature
2003. Paul Simon signature logo at bottom of fretboard, 200 made.

2003		$2,250	$2,800

R-15
1934. Archtop, Only 2 made, sunburst.

1934		$1,400	$1,750

R-17
1934-1942. All mahogany, arched top and back, 3-segment f-holes (changed to 1-segment in '37).

1934-1942	940 made	$1,400	$1,750

R-18 P
1934-1936. Only 4 made, plectrum neck.

1934-1936		$1,600	$2,000

R-18 S/R-18
1932-1942. Spruce arched top (carved top by 1937), mahogany back and sides, bound top, sunburst.

1932-1942	1,928 made	$2,000	$2,500

R-18 T
1934-1941. Tenor archtop, 14 3/8" lower bout, 2 f-holes, dot markers, sunburst.

1934-1941		$1,600	$2,000

R-21
1938. 000 body archtop, 1 made.

1938		$4,000	$5,000

Schoenberg Soloist by C.F. Martin
1990. Sitka spruce, mahogany.

1990		$4,800	$6,000

Shenandoah Series
1983-1993. Bodies and necks were built in Japan with final assembly and finishing in Nazareth and a Thinline piezo added, styled after U.S. models with a 32 added to the name.

1983-1993	Various models	$800	$1,200

SP000 Series
1996-2002. Special Edition 000-size, spruce top with aging toner, scalloped bracing, rosewood or mahogany body.

1996-2002	16	$1,100	$1,400
1996-2002	16R	$1,100	$1,400
1996-2002	16T	$1,100	$1,400
1996-2002	16TR	$1,100	$1,400
1997	C-16TR	$1,200	$1,500
1997-2002	C-16R	$1,200	$1,500
1999-2002	C-16	$1,200	$1,500
1999-2002	C-16E	$1,250	$1,550
2003	C-16R		
	Custom Shop	$2,000	$2,500

SPD12-16 R
1997-2004. 12-string, solid rosewood body, abalone soundhole ring, Style-45 backstripe.

1999-2000		$1,100	$1,400

SPD-16 Series
1997-2004. D-16 Series Special models.

1996-1999	16TR	$1,100	$1,400
1997-2004	16	$1,100	$1,400
1997-2004	16T	$1,100	$1,400
1999-2001	16B Black	$1,100	$1,400
1999-2002	16M Maple	$1,100	$1,400
1999-2002	16W Walnut	$1,100	$1,400
2000	16E	$1,225	$1,525
2000-2002	16R	$1,100	$1,400
2000-2005	16K	$1,200	$1,500
2000-2005	16K2	$1,200	$1,500

SPDC-16 Series
1997-2001. Cutaway version of SPD-16.

1997-1999	16-TR	$1,200	$1,500
1997-2001	16RE Rosewood	$1,225	$1,525
2000-2002	16R	$1,200	$1,500

SPJC-16 RE
2000-2003. Single-cut, East Indian rosewood body, 000-size, on-board electronics.

2000-2003		$1,225	$1,525

SPOM-16
1999-2001. Mahogany.

1999-2001		$1,100	$1,400

Martin OMCPA4

1937 Martin R-18

Martin SWOMGT

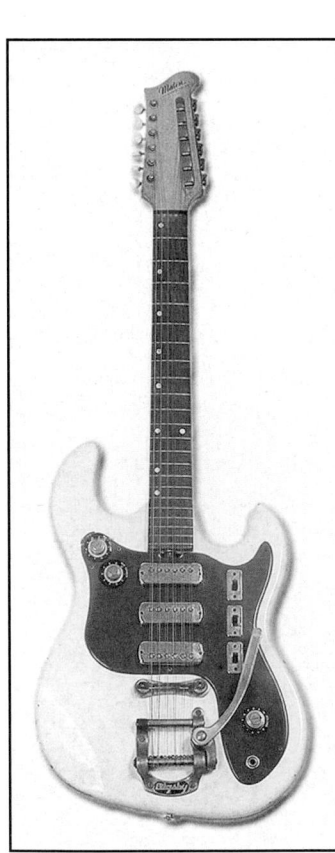

Maton Fyrebird 12
Ben Rogers

MODEL YEAR	FEATURES	EXC. COND. LOW	HIGH

Stauffer
1830s-ca.1850s. One of C.F. Martin's earliest models, distinguished by the scrolled, six-on-a-side headstock, ornamentation varies from guitar to guitar.

1835	Fancy (2nd highest)	$21,000	$26,000
1835	Fancy (highest)	$27,000	$34,000
1835	Mid-level appointments	$17,000	$21,000
1835	Plain (2nd (lowest)	$13,500	$16,500
1835	Plain (lowest)	$8,500	$10,500

Sting Mini
2006. 100 made, Size 5, Western red cedar top, Solomon padauk body.

2005-2006		$1,825	$2,300

Stinger
1980s-1990s. Import copy offset S-style electric solidbody.

1980s-90s		$175	$225

SW00-D8 Machiche
2006-2007. Smartwood Limited Edition, 125 made, rescued solid spruce top, sustainable machiche sides and back.

2006-2007		$1,250	$1,550

SWC
1998. Smartwood 'The Sting Signature Classical Model', machiche wood body.

1998		$1,150	$1,450

SWD
1998-2001. Smartwood D-size, built from wood material certified by the Forest Stewardship Council, sitka top, cherry back and sides, natural satin finish.

1998-2001		$875	$1,100

SWD Red Birch
2003-2005. Red Birch.

2003-2005		$875	$1,100

SWDGT
2001-2005. Gloss top SWD.

2001-2005		$875	$1,100

SWDTG
2000-present. Cherry back and sides, gloss finish.

2000-2007		$875	$1,100

SWMGT
2002-2003. M size, cherry back and sides, gloss finish.

2002-2003		$875	$1,075

SWOM
2000-2001. Sustainable Woods Series.

2000-2001		$875	$1,075

SWOMGT
2001-present. Smartwood OM, rescued solid sitka spruce top, sustainable cherry sides and back, gloss finish.

2001-2014		$875	$1,075

Yuengling 180th Anniversary Custom
2008. Celebrating 180th company anniversary, limited production, large company logo on top of body, fancy D-41 style appointments, certificate.

2008		$2,550	$3,175

MODEL YEAR	FEATURES	EXC. COND. LOW	HIGH

Maruha
1960s-1970s. Japanese-made acoustic, classical, archtop and solidbody guitars, often copies of American brands. Probably not imported into the U.S.

Marvel
1950s-mid-1960s. Brand name used for budget guitars and basses marketed by Peter Sorkin Company in New York, New York. Sorkin manufactured and distributed Premier guitars and amplifiers made by its Multivox subsidiary. Marvel instruments were primarily beginner-grade. Brand disappears by mid-'60s. The name was also used on archtop guitars made by Regal and marketed by the Slingerland drum company in the 1930s to early 1940s.

Electric
1940s-1950s. Various models.

1940s-50s		$225	$600

Marveltone by Regal
1925-1930. Private branded by Regal, Marveltone pearl style logo on headstock.

Guitar
1925-1930. 14" Brazilian.

1925-1930		$3,100	$3,800

Masaki Sakurai
See Kohno brand.

Mason
1936-1939. Henry L. Mason on headstock, wholesale distribution, similar to Gibson/Cromwell, pressed wood back and sides.

Student/Intermediate Student
1936-1939. Various flat-top and archtop student/ budget models.

1936-1939		$325	$800

Mason Bernard
1990-1991. Founded by Bernie Rico (BC Rich founder). During this period BC Rich guitars were licensed and controlled by Randy Waltuch and Class Axe. Most Mason models were designs similar to the BC Rich Assassin, according to Bernie Rico only the very best materials were used, large MB logo on headstock. Around 225 guitars were built bearing this brand.

Maton
1946-present. Intermediate and professional grade, production/custom, acoustic, acoustic/electric, hollowbody and solidbody guitars built in Box Hill, Victoria, Australia. Founded by Bill May and his brother Reg and still run by the family. Only available in USA since '82.

Matsuda Guitars
See listing for Michihiro Matsuda.

MODEL		EXC. COND.	
YEAR	FEATURES	LOW	HIGH

Matsuoka

1970s. Ryoji Matsuoka from Japan built intermediate grade M series classical guitars that often featured solid tops and laminated sides and back.

Matt Pulcinella Guitars

1998-present. Production/custom, professional grade, electric guitars and basses built in Chadds Ford, Pennsylvania by luthier Matt Pulcinella.

Mauel Guitars

Luthier Hank Mauel builds his premium grade, custom, flat-tops in Auburn, California.

Maurer

Late 1880s-1944. Robert Maurer built guitars and mandolins in the late 1880s under the Maurer and Champion brands in his Chicago shop. Carl and August Larson bought the company in 1900 and retained the Maurer name. The Larsons also built under the Prairie State, Euphonon, W. J. Dyer and Wm. C. Stahl brands.

Max B

2000-present. Luthier Sebastien Sulser builds professional grade, production/custom, electric guitars and basses in Kirby, Vermont.

May Bell

1923 1940s. Brand of flat top guitars, some with fake resonators, marketed by the Slingerland Company. Most were made by Regal.

Maya

See El Maya.

McAlister Guitars

1997-present. Premium grade, custom, flat-tops built by luthier Roy McAlister in Watsonville, California.

McCollum Guitars

1994-2009. Luthier Lance McCollum builds his premium grade, custom, flat-top and harp guitars in Colfax, California. McCollum died in 2009.

McCurdy Guitars

1983-present. Premium grade, production/custom, archtops built by luthier Ric McCurdy originally in Santa Barbara, California and, since '91, New York, New York.

McElroy

1995-present. Premium grade, custom, classical and flat-top steel string acoustic guitars built by luthier Brent McElroy in Seattle, Washington.

McGill Guitars

1976-present. Luthier Paul McGill builds his premium grade, production/custom, classical, resonator, and acoustic/electric guitars in Nashville, Tennessee.

McGlincy

Ca. 1974-ca. 1978. Custom flat-tops built by luthier Edward McGlincy in Toms River, New Jersey. Only 12 instruments made and owners included Gordon Lightfoot and David Bromberg. He later offered uke and guitar kits. He also operated Ed's Musical Instruments. McGlincy died in '97.

McGlynn Guitars

2005-2007. Luthier Michael J. McGlynn built his premium and presentation grade, custom, solidbody guitars in Henderson, Nevada. McGlynn died in '07.

McGowan Guitars

Luthier Brian McGowan builds his production/custom, premium grade, steel-string acoustic guitars in Hampton, Virginia.

MCI, Inc

1967-1988. MusiConics International (MCI), of Waco, Texas, introduced the world to the Guitorgan, invented by Bob Murrell. Later, they also offered effects and a steel guitar. In the '80s, a MIDI version was offered. MCI was also involved with the Daion line of guitars in the late '70s and early '80s. MCI also built a double-neck lap steel.

GuitOrgan B-35

1970s (ca. 1976-1978?). Duplicated the sounds of an organ and more. MCI bought double-cut semi-hollow body guitars from others and outfitted them with lots of switches and buttons. Each fret has 6 segments that correspond to an organ tone. There was also a B-300 and B-30 version, and the earlier M-300 and 340.

1970s		$625	$775

McInturff

1996-present. Professional and premium grade, production/custom, solidbody guitars built by luthier Terry C. McInturff originally in Holly Springs, North Carolina, and since '04, in Moncure, North Carolina. McInturff spent 17 years doing guitar repair and custom work before starting his own guitar line.

Glory Standard

1996-2012. Highly figured maple top, double cut solidbody, 2 humbuckers, slash inlay, chrome hardware.

1996-2012		$1,300	$1,625

Glory Custom

1996-2012. Higher figured top than Standard, gold hardware.

1996-2012		$1,700	$2,100

Monarch

2000-2012. Offset double-cut contoured mahogany solidbody, set-neck, single-single-hum pickups, transparent cherry.

2000-2012		$1,200	$1,500

Taurus Custom

2000-2012. Like Standard with Master Grade maple top, bound body.

2000-2012		$1,700	$2,100

McCollum Dreadnaught

McGlincy Acoustic
Norman Peck

McInturff Forum

MODEL		EXC. COND.	
YEAR	FEATURES	LOW	HIGH

Taurus Sportster
Like Standard with mahogany body.
2000s		$1,050	$1,300

Taurus Standard
2000-2014. Single-cut, carved flamed maple top on chambered mahogany body, dual humbucker pickups, gold hardware, sunburst.
2000-2014		$1,300	$1,625

McKnight Guitars
1992-present. Luthier Tim McKnight builds his custom, premium grade, acoustic steel string guitars in Morral, Ohio.

McPherson Guitars
1981-present. Premium grade, production, flat-tops built by luthier Mander McPherson in Sparta, Wisconsin.

Mean Gene
1988-1990. Heavy metal style solidbodies made by Gene Baker, who started Baker U.S.A. guitars in '97, and Eric Zoellner in Santa Maria, California. They built around 30 custom guitars. Baker currently builds b3 guitars.

Megas Guitars
1989-present. Luthier Ted Megas builds his premium grade, custom, archtop and solidbody guitars, originally in San Franciso, and currently in Portland, Oregon.

Melancon
1995-present. Professional and premium grade, custom/production, solid and semi-hollow body guitars and basses built by luthier Gerard Melancon in Thibodaux, Louisiana.

Mello, John F.
1973-present. Premium grade, production/custom, classical and flat-top guitars built by luthier John Mello in Kensington, California.

Melophonic
1960s. Brand built by the Valco Company of Chicago, Illinois.

Resonator Guitar
1965. Valco-made.
1965		$750	$925

Melville Guitars
1988-present. Luthier Christopher Melville builds his premium grade, custom, flat-tops in Milton, Queensland, Australia.

Memphis
One of the many guitar brands built by Japan's Matsumoku company.

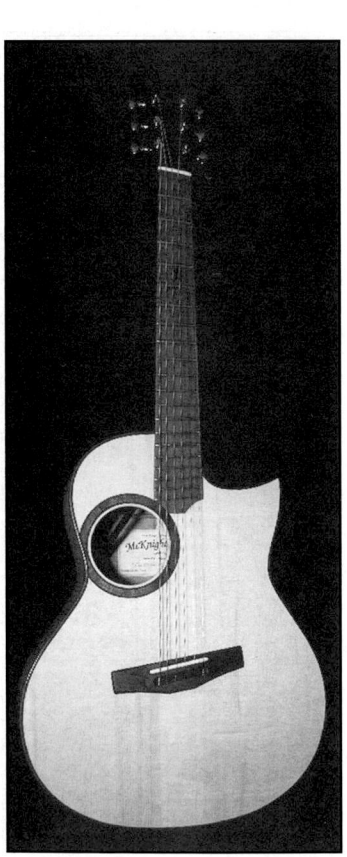

McKnight Soli Deo Gloria

MODEL		EXC. COND.	
YEAR	FEATURES	LOW	HIGH

Mercurio
2002-2005. Luthier Peter Mercurio built his custom/production solidbody guitars, featuring his interchangeable PickupPak system to swap pickups, in Chanhassen, Minnesota.

Mermer Guitars
1983-present. Luthier Richard Mermer builds his premium grade, production/custom, steel-string, nylon-string, and Hawaiian guitars in Sebastian, Florida.

Merrill Brothers
1998-present. Premium grade, production/custom, steel-string and harp guitars built by luthiers Jim and Dave Merrill in Williamsburg, Virginia.

Mesrobian
1995-present. Luthier Carl Mesrobian builds his professional and premium grade, custom, archtop guitars in Salem, Massachusetts.

Messenger
1967-1968. Built by Musicraft, Inc., originally of 156 Montgomery Street, San Francisco, California. The distinguishing feature of the Messengers is a metal alloy neck which extended through the body to the tailblock, plus mono or stereo outputs. Sometime before March '68 the company relocated to Astoria, Oregon. Press touted "improved" magnesium neck, though it's not clear if this constituted a change from '67. Brand disappears after '68. They also made basses.

Electric Hollowbody Archtop
1967-1968. Symmetrical double-cut body shape, metal neck with rosewood 'boards, stereo.
1967-1968	Rojo Red	$2,050	$2,550

Metropolitan
1995-2008. Professional and premium grade, production/custom, retro-styled solidbodies designed by David Wintz reminiscent of the '50s National Res-o-glas and wood body guitars. They featured full-scale set-neck construction and a wood body instead of Res-o-glas. Wintz also made Robin and Alamo brand instruments.

Electric Solidbodies
1995-2008	Various models	$1,225	$1,525

Meyers Custom Guitars
Beginning 2005, professional grade, custom, solidbody electric guitars built by luthier Donald Meyers in Houma, Louisiana.

Miami
1920s. Instruments built by the Oscar Schmidt Co. and possibly others. Most likely a brand made for a distributor.

MODEL		EXC. COND.	
YEAR	FEATURES	LOW	HIGH

Michael Collins Custom Guitars

1975-present. Premium grade, custom/production, classical, flamenco and steel string guitars built in Argyle, New York, by luthier Michael Collins.

Michael Collins Guitars

2002-present. Luthier Michael Collins builds his professional and premium grade, custom, Selmer style, archtop and flat-top guitars in Keswick, Ontario. He also builds mandolins.

Michael Cone

1968-present. Presentation grade, production/custom, classical guitars built previously in California and currently in Kihei Maui, Hawaii by luthier Michael Cone. He also builds ukuleles.

Michael Dunn Guitars

1968-present. Luthier Michael Dunn builds his production/custom Maccaferri-style guitars in New Westminster, British Columbia. He also offers a harp uke and a Weissenborn- or Knutsen-style Hawaiian guitar, and has built archtops.

Michael Kelly

1999-present. Founded by Tracy Hoeft and offering intermediate and professional grade, production, acoustic, solidbody and archtop guitars. The brand was owned by the Hanser Music Group from 2004-'15. They also offer mandolins and basses.

Michael Lewis Instruments

1992-present. Luthier Michael Lewis builds his premium and presentation grade, custom, archtop guitars in Grass Valley, California. He also builds mandolins.

Michael Menkevich

1970-present. Luthier Michael Menkevich builds his professional and premium grade, production/custom, flamenco and classical guitars in Elkins Park, Pennsylvania.

Michael Silvey Custom Guitars

2003-ca. 2007. Solidbody electric guitars built by Michael Silvey in North Canton, Ohio.

Michael Thames

1972-present. Luthier Michael Thames builds his premium grade, custom/production, classical guitars in Taos, New Mexico.

Michael Tuttle

2003-present. Professional and premium grade, custom, solid and hollowbody guitars and basses built by luthier Michael Tuttle in Saugus, California.

Michihiro Matsuda

1997-present. Presentation grade, production/custom, steel and nylon string acoustic guitars built by luthier Michihiro Matsuda in Oakland, California. He also builds harp guitars.

Microfrets

1967-1975, 2004-2005. Professional grade, production, electric guitars built in Myersville, Maryland. They also built basses. Founded by Ralph S. Jones, Sr. in Frederick, Microfrets offered over 20 models of guitars that sported innovative designs and features, with pickups designed by Bill Lawrence. The brand was revived, again in Frederick, by Will Meadors and Paul Rose in '04.

Serial numbers run from about 1000 to about 3800. Not all instruments have serial numbers, particularly ones produced in '75. Serial numbers do not appear to be correlated to a model type, but are sequential by the general date of production.

Instruments can be identified by body styles as follows; Styles 1, 1.5, 2, and 3. An instrument may be described as a Model Name and Style Number (for example, Covington Style 1). Style 1 has a wavey-shaped pickguard with control knobs mounted below the guard and the 2-piece guitar body has a particle board side gasket. Style 1.5 has the same guard and knobs, but no side body gasket. Style 2 has an oblong pickguard with top mounted control knobs and a pancake style seam between the top and lower part of the body. Style 3 has a seamless 2-piece body and a Speedline neck.

Baritone Signature

1971. Baritone version of Signature Guitar, sharply pointed double-cut, with or without f-holes, single- or double-dot inlays.

1971		$900	$1,125

Baritone Stage II

1971-ca. 1975. Double-cut, 2 pickups.

1971-1975		$900	$1,125

Calibra I

1969-1975. Double-cut, 2 pickups, f-hole.

1969-1975		$900	$1,125

Covington

1967-1969. Offset double-cut, 2 pickups, f-hole.

1967-1969		$1,300	$1,625

Golden Comet

1969-1971. Double-cut, 2 pickups, f-hole.

1969-1971		$900	$1,125

Golden Melody

1969-1971, 2004-2005. Offset double-cut, 2 pickups, f-hole, M-shaped metal design behind tailpiece.

1969-1971		$1,300	$1,625

Huntington

1969-1975. Double-cut, 2 pickups.

1969-1975		$1,300	$1,625

Orbiter

1967-1969. Odd triple cutaway body, thumbwheel controls on bottom edge of 'guard.

1967-1969		$1,300	$1,625

Michihiro Matsuda Style Mini

1972 Microfrets Calibra I

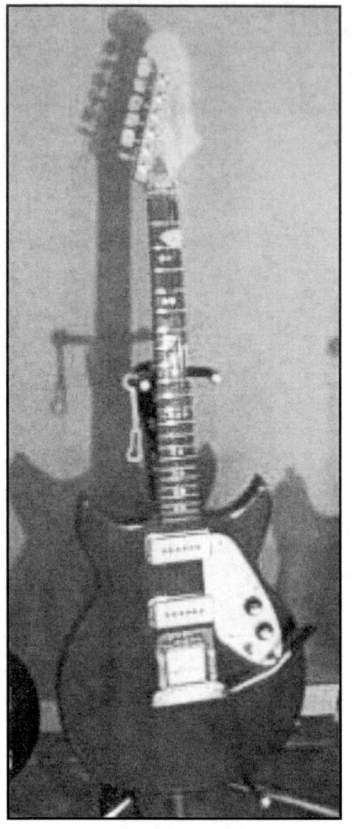

Microfrets Signature
Roland Gonzales

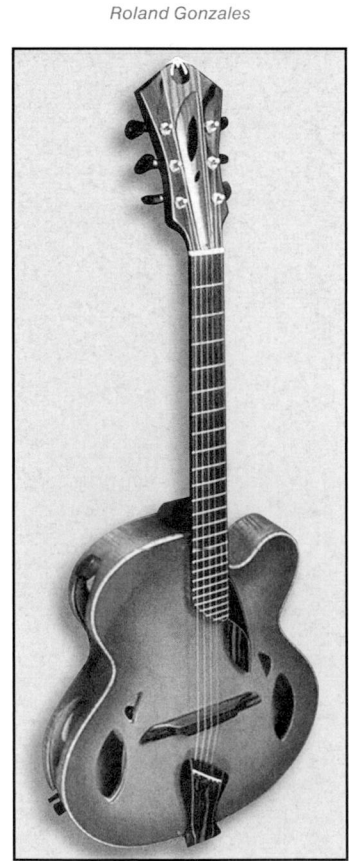

Mirabella Trapdoor

MODEL YEAR	FEATURES	EXC. COND. LOW	HIGH

Plainsman
1967-1969. Offset double-cut, 2 pickups, f-hole, thumbwheel controls on bottom edge of 'guard.

1967-1969		$1,400	$1,725

Signature
1967-1969. Double-cut, 2 pickups.

1967-1969		$1,300	$1,625

Spacetone
1969-1971, 2004-2005. Double-cut semi-hollow body, 2 pickups.

1969-1971		$1,300	$1,625

Stage II
1969-1975. Offset double-cut, 2 pickups.

1969-1975		$1,225	$1,525

Swinger
1971-1975. Offset double-cut, 2 pickups.

1971-1975		$1,300	$1,625

Voyager/The Voyager
1967-1968. Early model, less than a dozen made, Voyager headstock logo (no Microfrets logo), 2 DeArmond-style single-coils, offset double-cut body, FM transmitter on upper bass bout facilitates wireless transmission to Microfrets receiver or FM radio.

1967-1968		$2,300	$2,850

Wanderer
1969. Double-cut, 2 pickups.

1969		$1,100	$1,375

Mike Lull Custom Guitars
1995-present. Professional and premium grade, production/custom, guitars and basses built by luthier Mike Lull in Bellevue, Washington.

Milburn Guitars
1990-present. Luthiers Orville and Robert Milburn build their premium grade, custom, classical guitars in Sweet Home, Oregon.

Miller
1960s. One of the brand names of guitars built for others by Egmond in Holland.

Minarik
Luthier M.E. Minarik builds his professional and premium grade, custom/production, solid and chambered body guitars in Van Nuys, California.

Minerva
1930s. Resonator and archtop guitars sold through catalog stores, likely made by one of the big Chicago builders of the era.

Mirabella
1997-present. Professional and premium grade, custom archtops, flat-tops, hollowbody, and solidbody guitars and basses built by luthier Cristian Mirabella in Babylon, New York. He also builds mandolins and ukes.

Miranda Guitars
2002-present. Owner Phil Green uses components made by various shops in California to assemble and set-up, professional grade, full-size travel/silent-practice guitars in Palo Alto, California.

Mitre
1983-1985. Bolt neck, solidbody guitars and basses made in Aldenville (or East Longmeadow), Massachusetts, featuring pointy body shapes, 2 humbuckers, active or passive electronics.

MJ Guitar Engineering
1993-present. Professional and premium grade, production/custom, hollowbody, chambered and solidbody guitars and basses built by luthier Mark Johnson in Rohnert Park, California.

Mobius Megatar
2000-present. Professional grade, production, hybrid guitars designed for two-handed tapping, built in Mount Shasta, California. Founded by Reg Thompson, Henri Dupont, and Traktor Topaz in '97, they released their first guitars in '00.

Modulus
1978-2013. Founded by Geoff Gould in the San Francisco area, currently built in Novato, California. Modulus currently offers only basses but did build professional grade, production/custom, solidbody electric guitars up to '05.

Genesis 2/2T
1996-2005. Double-cut, long extended bass horn alder body, bolt-on carbon fiber/red cedar neck, hum-single-single pickups, locking vibrato (2T model).

1996-2005		$1,100	$1,375

Moll Custom Instruments
1996-present. Luthier Bill Moll builds his professional and premium grade, archtops in Springfield, Missouri. He has also built violins, violas and cellos.

Monrad, Eric
1993-present. Premium, custom, flamenco and classical guitars built by luthier Eric Monrad in Healdsburg, California.

Monroe Guitars
Luthier Matt Handley builds his custom, professional grade, solidbody electric guitars and basses in State Center, Iowa.

Montalvo
See listing under Casa Montalvo.

Montaya
Late 1970s-1980s. Montaya Hyosung 'America' Inc., Korean acoustic and electric import copies.

MODEL YEAR	FEATURES	EXC. COND. LOW	HIGH

Monteleone

1976-present. Presentation grade, production/custom, archtop guitars built by Luthier John Monteleone in Islip, New York. He also builds mandolins.

Eclipse
1991-2012. 17" electric archtop, natural orange.

1991-2012		$14,500	$18,000

Hot Club
1987. Selmer-style, single-cut acoustic, oval soundhole.

1987		$8,500	$10,500

Radio City
1990s-2014. 18" acoustic archtop cutaway, art deco fretboard inlays, golden blond.

1990s-2014		$33,000	$42,000

Montgomery Ward

The mail-order and retail giant offered a variety of instruments and amps from several different U.S. and overseas manufacturers.

Model 8379/H44 Stratotone
Mid-1950s. Private branded Harmony Stratotone, some without logo but with crown-style stencil/painted logo on headstock, many with gold-copper finish, 1 pickup.

1957		$1,200	$1,500

Monty

1980-present. Luthier Brian Monty builds his professional, premium and presentation grade, production/custom, archtop, semi-hollow, solid-body, and chambered electric guitars originally in Lennoxville, Quebec, and currently in Anne de Prescott, Ontario.

Moog

1964-present. Moog introduced its premium grade, production, Harmonic Control System solid-body guitar in 2008. They also offer guitar effects.

Moon (Japan)

1979-present. Professional and premium grade, production/custom, guitars and basses made in Japan.

Moon (Scotland)

1979-present. Intermediate, professional and premium grade, production/custom, acoustic and electric guitars built by luthier Jimmy Moon in Glasgow, Scotland. They also build mandolin family instruments.

Moonstone

1972-present. Professional, premium, and presentation grade production/custom flat-top, solid and semi-hollow electric guitars, built by luthier Steve Helgeson in Eureka, California. He also builds basses. Higher unit sales in the early-'80s. Some models have an optional graphite composite neck built by Modulus.

Eclipse Standard
1979-1983. Figured wood body, offset double-cut, neck-thru, dot markers, standard maple neck, natural finish.

1979-1983		$1,400	$1,750
1979-1983	XII	$1,400	$1,750

Exploder
1980-1983. Figured wood solidbody, neck-thru, standard maple neck, natural finish.

1980-1983		$1,700	$2,100

Flaming V
1980-1984. Figured wood body, V-shaped, neck-thru, standard maple neck, natural finish.

1980-1984		$1,700	$2,100

M-80
1980-1984. Figured wood double-cut semi-hollow body, standard maple or optional graphite neck, natural finish.

1980s	Optional neck	$2,800	$3,500
1980s	Standard neck	$2,700	$3,400

Vulcan Deluxe
1979-1983. Figured maple carved-top body, offset double-cut, diamond markers, standard maple or optional graphite neck, natural finish.

1979-1983	Optional neck	$2,800	$3,500
1979-1983	Standard neck	$2,700	$3,400

Vulcan Standard
1979-1983. Mahogany carved-top body, offset double-cutaway, dot markers, standard maple or optional graphite neck, natural finish.

1979-1983	Optional neck	$2,400	$3,000
1979-1983	Standard neck	$2,300	$2,900

Morales

Ca.1967-1968. Guitars and basses made in Japan by Zen-On, not heavily imported into the U.S., if at all.

Solidbody Electric

1967-1968	Various models	$130	$225

More Harmony

1930s. Private branded by Dobro for Dailey's More Harmony Music Studio. Private branding for catalog companies, teaching studios, publishers, and music stores was common for the Chicago makers. More Harmony silk-screen logo on the headstock.

Dobro
1930s. 14" wood body with upper bout f-holes and metal resonator, sunburst.

1930s		$975	$1,200

Morgaine Guitars

1994-present. Luthier Jorg Tandler builds his professional and premium grade, production/custom electrics in Germany.

Morgan Monroe

1999-present. Intermediate grade, production, acoustic, acoustic/electric and resonator guitars and basses made in Korea and distributed by SHS International of Indianapolis, Indiana. They also offer mandolins and banjos.

Miranda Travel Guitar

Moll Custom SJ

GUITARS

1961 Mosrite Standard

1966 Mosrite Celebrity 1

Dave Mullikin

MODEL YEAR	FEATURES	EXC. COND. LOW	HIGH

Morris

1967-present. Intermediate, professional and premium grade, production, acoustic guitars imported by Moridaira of Japan. Morris guitars were first imported into the U.S. from the early '70s to around '90. They are again being imported into the U.S. starting in 2001. They also offered mandolins in the '70s.

000 Copy
1970s. Brazilian rosewood laminate body.

1970s		$300	$375

Acoustic-Electric Archtop
1970s. Various models.

1970s		$425	$525

D-45 Copy
1970s. Brazilian laminate body.

1970s		$400	$500

Mortoro Guitars

1992-present. Luthier Gary Mortoro builds his premium grade, custom, archtop guitars in Miami, Florida.

Mosrite

The history of Mosrite has more ups and downs than just about any other guitar company. Founder Semie Moseley had several innovative designs and had his first success in 1954, at age 19, building doubleneck guitars for super picker Joe Maphis and protégé Larry Collins. Next came the Ventures, who launched the brand nationally by playing Mosrites and featuring them on album covers. At its '60s peak, the company was turning out around 1,000 guitars a month. The company ceased production in '69, and Moseley went back to playing gospel concerts and built a few custom instruments during the '70s.

In the early-'80s, Mosrite again set up shop in Jonas Ridge, North Carolina, but the plant burned down in November '83, taking about 300 guitars with it. In early-'92, Mosrite relocated to Booneville, Arkansas, producing a new line of Mosrites, of which 96% were exported to Japan, where the Ventures and Mosrite have always been popular. Semie Moseley died, at age 57, on August 7, '92 and the business carried on until finally closing its doors in '93. The Mosrite line has again been revived, offering intermediate and premium grade, production, reissues.

Throughout much of the history of Mosrite, production numbers were small and model features often changed. As a result, exact production dates are difficult to determine.

Balladeer
1964-1965. Mid-size flat-top, slope shoulder, natural or sunburst.

1964-1965		$1,425	$1,775

MODEL YEAR	FEATURES	EXC. COND. LOW	HIGH

Brass Rail
1970s. Double-cut solidbody, has a brass plate running the length of the 'board.

1970s		$950	$1,175

Celebrity 1
Late-1960s-1970s. Thick hollowbody, 2 pickups, sunburst.

1960s-70s		$950	$1,175

Celebrity 2 Standard
Late-1960s-1970s. Thin hollowbody, 2 pickups, in the '70s, it came in a Standard and a Deluxe version.

1960s-70s		$950	$1,175

Celebrity 3
Late-1960s-1970s. Thin hollowbody, double-cut, 2 pickups, f-holes.

1960s-70s		$950	$1,175

Combo Mark 1
1966-1968. Bound body, 1 f-hole.

1966-1968		$1,625	$2,025

Custom-Built
1952-1962. Pre-production custom instruments hand-built by Semie Moseley, guidance pricing only, each instrument will vary. A wide variety of instruments were made during this period. Some were outstanding, but others, especially those made around '60, could be very basic and of much lower quality. Logos would vary widely and some '60 logos looked especially homemade.

1952-1959	Rare, higher-end	$11,200	$14,000
1960-1962	Common, lower-end	$1,625	$2,025

D-40 Resonator
1960s. Symmetrical double-cut thinline archtop-style body with metal resonator in center of body, 2 pickups, 2 control knobs and toggle switch.

1960s		$1,400	$1,750

D-100 Californian
1960s. Double-cut, resonator guitar with 2 pickups.

1967		$1,400	$1,750

Gospel
1967. Thinline double-cut, f-hole, 2 pickups, vibrato, Gospel logo on headstock.

1967	Sunburst	$1,650	$2,100
1967	White	$2,300	$2,900

Joe Maphis Doubleneck
1963-1968. Limited Edition reissue of the guitar Semie Moseley made for Maphis, with the smaller octave neck, sunburst

1963-1968	Octave 6/\ standard 6	$4,500	$5,600
1963-1968	Standard 6/12	$4,500	$5,600

Joe Maphis Mark 1
1959-1972. Semi-hollow double-cut, 2 single-coils, spruce top, walnut back, rosewood 'board, natural.

1959-1972		$1,900	$2,400

MODEL YEAR	FEATURES	EXC. COND. LOW	HIGH

Joe Maphis Mark XVIII
1960s. 6/12 doubleneck, double-cut, 2 pickups on each neck, Moseley tremolo on 6-string.

1960s		$3,200	$4,000

Mosrite 1988
1988-early-1990s. Has traditional Mosrite body styling, Mosrite pickups and bridge.

1988		$675	$825

Octave Guitar
1963-1965. 14" scale, 1 pickup, Ventures Mosrite body style, single neck pickup, very few made.

1963-1965		$5,600	$7,000

Stereo 350
1974-1975. Single-cut solidbody, 2 outputs, 2 pickups, 4 knobs, slider and toggle, black.

1974-1975		$1,300	$1,650

Ventures Model
1963-1968. Double-cut solidbody, triple-bound body '63, no binding after, Vibramute for '63-'64, Moseley tailpiece '65-'68.

1963	Blue or red, bound	$6,900	$8,250
1963	Sunburst, bound	$5,800	$6,950
1964	Blue or red, Vibramute	$5,200	$6,250
1964	Sunburst, Vibramute	$4,700	$5,650
1965	Moseley (2 screws)	$3,600	$4,350
1965	Vibramute, (3 screws)	$4,600	$5,550
1966	Moseley	$3,400	$4,075
1967	Moseley	$3,200	$3,850
1968	Moseley	$3,100	$3,750

Ventures (Jonas Ridge/Booneville)
1982-1993. Made in Jonas Ridge, NC or Booneville, AR, classic Ventures styling.

1982-1993		$1,400	$1,700

Ventures Mark V
1963-1967. Double-cut solidbody.

1963-1967		$1,500	$1,800

Ventures Mark XII (12-String)
1966-1967. Double-cut solidbody, 12 strings.

1966-1967		$2,900	$3,700

Mossman
1965-present. Professional and premium grade, production/custom, flat-top guitars built in Sulphur Springs, Texas. They have also built acoustic basses. Founded by Stuart L. Mossman in Winfield, Kansas. In '75, fire destroyed one company building, including the complete supply of Brazilian rosewood. They entered into an agreement with C.G. Conn Co. to distribute guitars by '77. 1200 Mossman guitars in a Conn warehouse in Nevada were ruined by being heated during the day and frozen during the night. A disagreement about who was responsible resulted in cash flow problems for Mossman. Production fell to a few guitars per month until the company was sold in '86 to Scott Baxendale. Baxendale sold the company to John Kinsey and Bob Casey in Sulphur Springs in '89.

Flint Hills
1970-mid-1980s. Flat-top acoustic, Indian rosewood back and sides.

1970-1979		$1,500	$1,900

Golden Era
1976-1977. D-style, vine inlay and other high-end appointments, Indian rosewood sides and back.

1976-1977		$2,950	$3,700

Great Plains
1970-mid-1980s. Flat-top, Indian rosewood, herringbone trim.

1970-1979		$1,450	$1,825

Southwind
1976-ca. 1986, mid-1990s-2002. Flat-top, abalone trim top.

1976-1979		$1,775	$2,200

Tennessee
1975-1979. D-style, spruce top, mahogany back and sides, rope marquetry purfling, rope binding.

1975-1979		$1,200	$1,475

Tennessee 12-String

1975-1979		$1,200	$1,475

Timber Creek
1980. D-style, rosewood back and sides, spruce top.

1980		$1,375	$1,700

Winter Wheat
1976-1979, mid-1990s-2000s. Flat-top, abalone trim, natural finish.

1976-1979		$1,800	$2,225

Winter Wheat 12-String
1976-1979. 12-string version of Winter Wheat, natural.

1976-1979		$1,800	$2,225

MotorAve Guitars
2002-present. Luthier Mark Fuqua builds his professional and premium grade, production, electric guitars originally in Los Angeles, California, and currently in Durham, North Carolina.

Mouradian
1983-present. Luthiers Jim and Jon Mouradian build their professional and premium grade, production/custom, electric guitars and basses in Winchester, Massachusetts.

Mozart
1930s. Private brand made by Kay.

Hawaiian (Square Neck)
1930s. Spruce top, solid mahogany sides and back, pealoid overlay on peghead with large Mozart inscribed logo, small jumbo 15 1/2" body.

1935-1939		$825	$1,025

Mozzani
Built in shops of Luigi Mozzani (b. March 9, 1869, Faenza, Italy; d. 1943) who opened lutherie schools in Bologna, Cento and Rovereto in 1890s. By 1926 No. 1 and 2 Original Mozzani Model Mandolin (flat back), No. 3 Mandola (flat back), No. 4 6-String Guitar, No. 5 7-, 8-, and 9-String Guitars, No. 6 Lyre-Guitar.

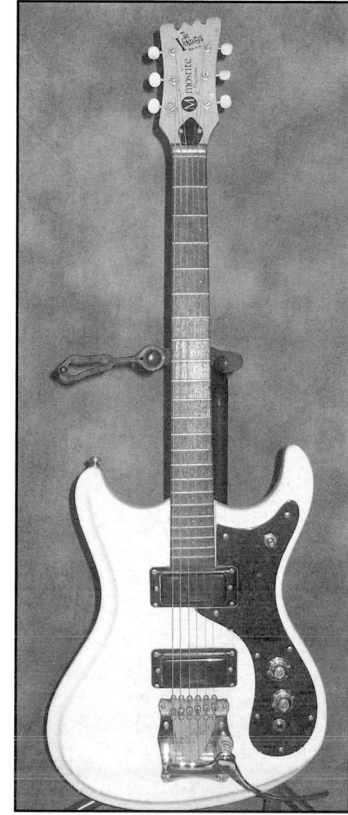

1966 Mosrite Ventures Mark V
James Goode

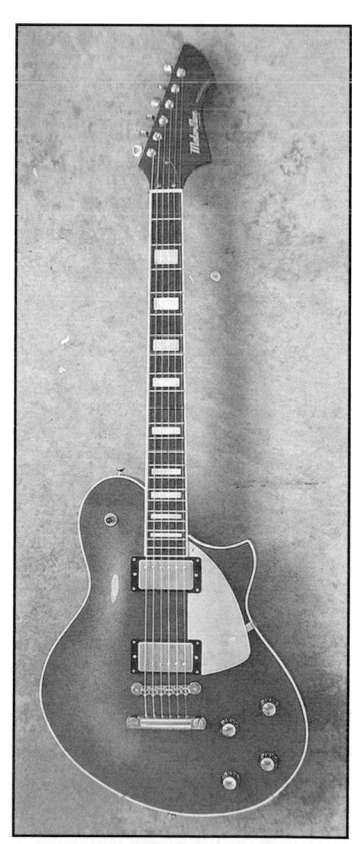

MotorAve Guitars McQueen

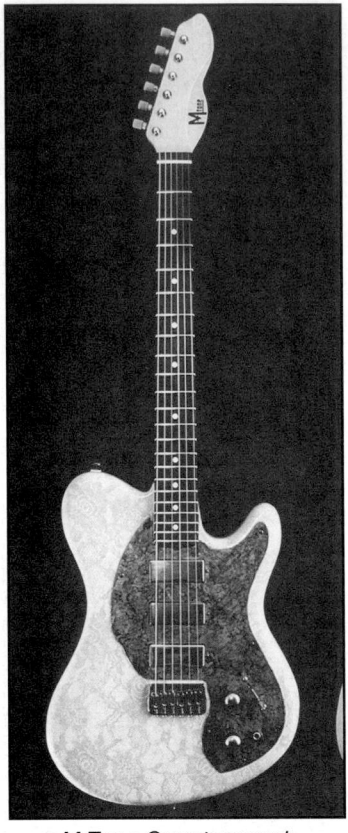

M-Tone Counterpunch

MODEL YEAR	FEATURES	EXC. COND. LOW	HIGH

M-Tone Guitars

2009-present. Professional and premium grade, production/custom, solidbody electric guitars built in Portland, Oregon by luthier Matt Proctor.

Muiderman Guitars

1997-present. Custom, premium grade, steel string and classical guitars built by luthier Kevin Muiderman currently in Grand Forks, North Dakota, and previously in Beverly Hills, Michigan, 1997-2001, and Neenah, Wisconsin, '01-'07. He also builds mandolins.

Murph

1965-1967. Mid-level electric semi-hollow and solidbody guitars built by Pat Murphy in San Fernado, California. Murph logo on headstock. They also offered basses and amps.

Electric Solidbody

1965-1967		$675	$850

Electric XII

1965-1967		$675	$850

Music Man

1972-present. Professional grade, production, solidbody guitars built in San Luis Obispo, California. They also build basses. Founded by ex-Fender executives Forrest White and Tom Walker in Orange County, California. Music Man originally produced guitar and bass amps based on early Fender ideas using many former Fender employees. They contracted with Leo Fender's CLF Research to design and produce a line of solidbody guitars and basses. Leo Fender began G & L Guitars with George Fullerton in '80. In '84, Music Man was purchased by Ernie Ball and production was moved to San Luis Obispo.

Albert Lee Signature

1993-present.

1993-1996	Pinkburst	$1,075	$1,325
1996-2014	Tremolo option	$1,075	$1,325

Axis

1996-present. Offset double-cut solidbody, figured maple top, basswood body, 2 humbucker pickups, Floyd Rose.

1996-2014		$1,075	$1,325

Axis Sport

1996-2002. Two P-90s.

1996-2002		$1,075	$1,325

Axis Super Sport

2003-present. Figured top.

2003-2014		$1,075	$1,325

Edward Van Halen

1991-1995. Basswood solidbody, figured maple top, bolt-on maple neck, maple 'board, binding, 2 humbuckers, named changed to Axis.

1991-1995		$1,750	$2,200

MODEL YEAR	FEATURES	EXC. COND. LOW	HIGH

John Petrucci 6

2008-present. Standard model.

2008-2014		$1,059	$1,325

John Petrucci BFR

2011-present. Ball Family Reserve (BFR).

2011-2014		$1,875	$2,325

S.U.B 1

2004-2006. Offset double-cut solidbody.

2004-2005		$390	$490

Sabre I

1978-1982. Offset double-cut solidbody, maple neck, 2 pickups, Sabre I comes with a flat 'board with jumbo frets.

1978-1979		$1,500	$1,875
1980-1982		$1,400	$1,775

Sabre II

1978-1982. Same as Sabre I, but with an oval 7 1/2" radius 'board.

1978-1979		$1,500	$1,875
1980-1982		$1,400	$1,775

Silhouette

1986-present. Offset double-cut, contoured beveled solidbody, various pickup configurations.

1986-2014		$975	$1,225
2006	20th Anniversary	$975	$1,225

Silhouette 6/12 Double Neck

2009-2014. Alder body, maple or rosewood 'boards, 4 humbuckers.

2009-2014		$2,100	$2,650

Silhouette Special

1995-present. Silhouette with Silent Circuit.

1995-2014		$975	$1,225

Steve Morse

1987-present. Solidbody, 4 pickups, humbuckers in the neck and bridge positions, 2 single-coils in the middle, special pickup switching, 6-bolt neck mounting, maple neck.

1987-2014		$1,300	$1,600

Stingray I

1976-1982. Offset double-cut solidbody, flat 'board radius.

1976-1982		$1,050	$1,300

Stingray II

1976-1982. Offset double-cut solidbody, rounder 'board radius.

1976-1982		$1,150	$1,425

Musicvox

1996-2001, 2011-present. Intermediate grade, production, imported retro-vibe guitars and basses from Matt Eichen of Cherry Hill, New Jersey.

Myka

2003-present. Luthier David Myka builds his professional and premium grade, custom/production, solidbody, semi-hollowbody, hollowbody, archtop, and flat-top guitars in Seattle, Washington. Until '07 he was located in Orchard Park, New York.

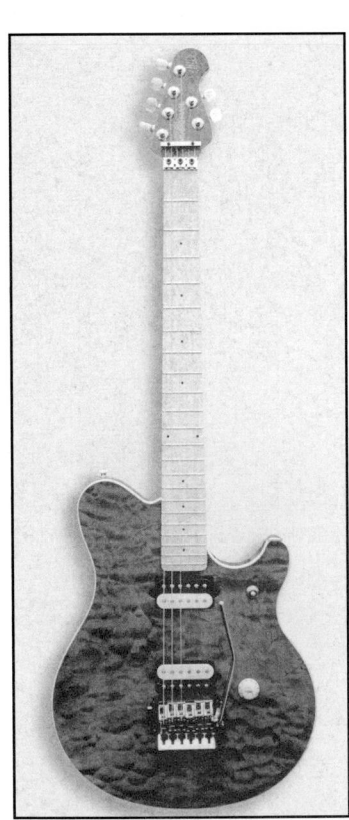

1992 Music Man Edward Van Halen

John DeSilva

The *Vintage Guitar Price Guide* shows low to high values for items in all-original excellent condition, and, where applicable, with original case or cover.

MODEL YEAR	FEATURES	EXC. COND. LOW	HIGH

Nady

1976-present. Wireless sound company Nady Systems offered guitars and basses with built-in wireless systems for 1985-'87. Made by Fernandes in Japan until '86, then by Cort in Korea.

Lightning/Lightning I

1985-1987. Double-cut, neck-thru, solidbody, 24 frets, built-in wireless, labeled as just Lightning until cheaper second version came out in '86.

1985	Fernandes	$500	$600
1986-1987	Cort	$450	$550

Lightning/Lightning II

1986-1987. Cheaper, bolt-neck version of the Lightning I.

1986-1987	Cort	$275	$350

Napolitano Guitars

Luthier Arthur Napolitano began in 1993 to build professional and premium grade, custom, archtop guitars in Allentown, New Jersey.

NashGuitars

2001-present. Luthier Bill Nash builds his professional grade, production/custom, aged solidbody electric guitars and basses in Olympia, Washington.

Nashville Guitar Company

1985-present. Professional and premium grade, custom, flat-top guitars built by luthier Marty Lanham in Nashville, Tennessee. He has also built banjos.

National

Ca. 1927-present. Founded in Los Angeles, California as the National String Instrument Corporation by John Dopyera, George Beauchamp, Ted Kleinmeyer and Paul Barth. In '29 Dopyera left to start the Dobro Manufacturing Company with Rudy and Ed Dopyera and Vic Smith. The Dobro company competed with National until the companies reunited. Beauchamp and Barth then left National to found Ro-Pat-In with Adolph Rickenbacker and C.L. Farr (later becoming Electro String Instrument Corporation, then Rickenbacher). In '32 Dopyera returns to National and National and Dobro start their merger in late-'33, finalizing it by mid-'34. Throughout the '30s, National and Dobro maintained separate production, sales and distribution. National Dobro moved to Chicago, Illinois in '36. In Chicago, archtop and flat-top bodies are built primarily by Regal and Kay; after '37 all National resonator guitar bodies made by Kay. L.A. production is maintained until around '37, although some assembly of Dobros continued in L.A. (primarily for export) until '39 when the L.A. offices are finally closed. By ca. '39 the Dobro brand disappears.

In '42, the company's resonator production ceased and Victor Smith, Al Frost and Louis Dopyera buy the company and change name to Valco Manufacturing Company. Post-war production resumes in '46. Valco is purchased by treasurer Robert Engelhardt in '64. In '67, Valco bought Kay, but in '68 the new Valco/Kay company went out of business. In the Summer of '69 the assets, including brand names, were auctioned off and the National and Supro names were purchased by Chicago-area distributor/importer Strum 'N Drum (Noble, Norma brands). The National brand is used on copies in early- to mid-'70s, and the brand went into hiatus by the '80s.

In '88 National Resophonic Guitars is founded in San Luis Obispo, California, by Don Young, with production of National-style resonator guitars beginning in '89 (see following). In the '90s, the National brand also resurfaces on inexpensive Asian imports.

National Resonator guitars are categorized by materials and decoration (from plain to fancy): Duolian, Triolian, Style 0, Style 1, Style 2, Style 3, Style 4, Don #1, Style 97, Don #2, Don #3, Style 35.

National guitars all have serial numbers which provide clues to date of production. This is a complex issue. This list combines information included in George Gruhn and Walter Carter's Gruhn's Guide to Vintage Guitars, which was originally provided by Bob Brozman and Mike Newton, with new information provided by Mike Newton.

Pre Chicago numbers

A101-A450	1935-1936

Chicago numbers

A prefix (some may not have the prefix)	1936-mid-1997
B prefix	Mid 1937-1938
C prefix	Late-1938-1940
G prefix up to 200	Ea. 1941-ea. 1942
G suffix under 2000	Ea. 1941-ea. 1942
G suffix 2000-3000s (probably old parts)	1943-1945
G suffix 4000s (old parts)	Late 1945-mid-1947
V100-V7500	1947
V7500-V15000	1948
V15000-V25000	1949
V25000-V35000	1950
V35000-V38000	1951
X100-X7000	1951
X7000-X17000	1952
X17000-X30000	1953
X30000-X43000	1954
X43000-X57000	1955
X57000-X71000	1956
X71000-X85000	1957
X85000-X99000	1958
T100-T5000	1958
T5000-T25000	1959
T25000-T50000	1960
T50000-T75000	1961
T75000-T90000	1962
G100-G5000	1962
T90000-T99000	1963
G5000-G15000	1963
G15000-G40000	1964
1 prefix	1965-ea. 1968
2 prefix	Mid-1968

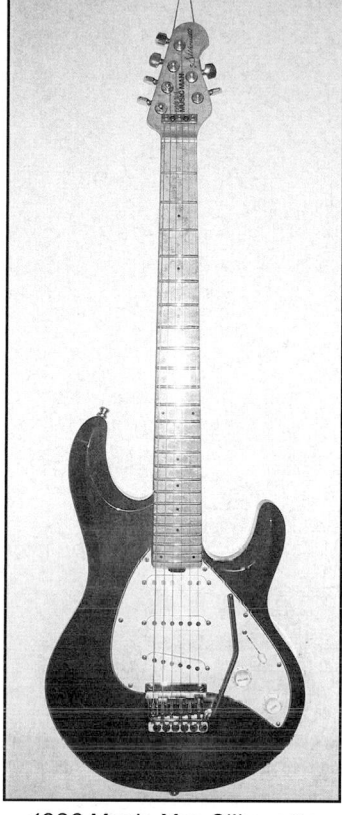

1986 Music Man Silhouette
Greg Gullsacker

Napolitano Primavera

GUITARS

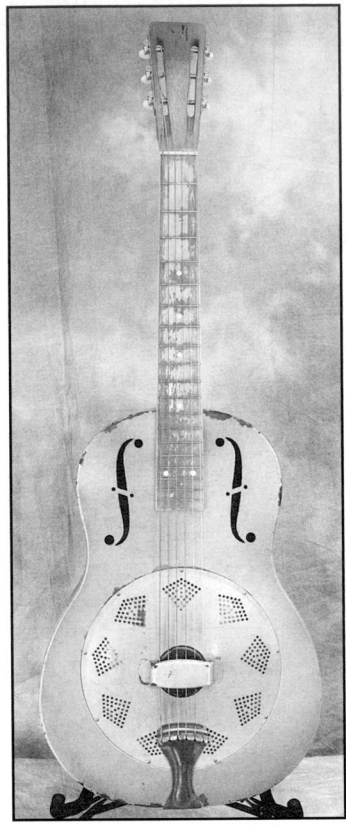

National Duolian

National Glenwood Deluxe

Mike Newton

MODEL YEAR	FEATURES	EXC. COND. LOW	HIGH

Aragon De Luxe
1939-1942. Archtop with resonator (the only archtop resonator offered), spruce top and maple back and sides, light brown.

| 1939-1942 | | $7,000 | $8,600 |

Big Daddy LP-457-2
1970s. Strum & Drum import, single-cut, LP-style, 2 pickups, gold hardware, black.

| 1970s | | $275 | $350 |

Bluegrass 35
1963-1965. Acoustic, non-cut single-cone resonator, Res-O-Glas body in Arctic White.

| 1963-1965 | | $1,500 | $1,875 |

Bobbie Thomas
Ca.1967-1968. Double-cut thinline hollowbody, bat-shaped f-holes, 2 pickups, Bobbie Thomas on 'guard, vibrato.

| 1967-1968 | | $510 | $640 |

Cameo
1957-1958. Renamed from Model 1140 in '57, full-body acoustic archtop with carved top.

| 1957-1958 | | $875 | $1,075 |

Collegian
1942-1943. Metal body resonator similar to Duolian, 14-fret round or square neck, yellow.

| 1942-1943 | | $1,450 | $1,800 |

Don Style 1
1934-1936. Plain body with engraved borders, pearl dot inlay, 14 frets, single-cone, silver (nickel-plated).

| 1934-1936 | | $8,000 | $10,000 |

Don Style 2
1934-1936. Geometric Art Deco body engraving, 14 frets, single-cone, fancy square pearl inlays and pearloid headstock overlay, silver (nickel-plated).

| 1934-1936 | | $9,000 | $11,200 |

Don Style 3
1934-1936. Same as Style 2 but more elaborate floral engravings, fancy pearl diamond inlays, 14 frets, single-cone, silver (nickel-plated), only a very few made.

| 1934-1936 | | $16,000 | $20,000 |

Duolian
1930-1939. Acoustic steel body, frosted paint finish until '36, mahogany-grain paint finish '37-'39, round neck, square neck available in '33, 12-fret neck until '34 then 14-fret.

| 1930-1934 | Round neck, 12 frets | $2,800 | $3,500 |
| 1935-1939 | Round neck, 14 frets | $2,700 | $3,400 |

EG 685 Hollow Body Electric
1970s. Strum & Drum distributed, double-cut hollowbody copy, 2 pickups.

| 1970s | | $300 | $375 |

El Trovador
1933 only. Wood body, 12 frets.

| 1933 | | $2,400 | $3,000 |

Electric Spanish
1935-1938. 15 1/2" archtop with Pat. Appl. For bridge pickup, National crest logo, fancy N-logo 'guard, black and white art deco, sunburst, becomes New Yorker Spanish '39-'58.

| 1935-1938 | | $1,300 | $1,625 |

Estralita
1934-1942. Acoustic with single-cone resonator, f-holes, multi-bound, 14-fret, mahogany top and back, shaded brown.

| 1934-1942 | | $1,000 | $1,225 |

Glenwood 95
1962-1964. Glenwood 98 without third bridge-mount pickup.

| 1962-1964 | Vermillion Red/ Flame Red | $3,100 | $3,900 |

Glenwood 98
1964-1965. USA map-shaped solidbody of molded Res-O-Glas, 2 regular and 1 bridge pickup, vibrato, pearl white finish.

| 1964-1965 | Pearl White | $3,400 | $4,200 |

Glenwood 99
1962-1965. USA map-shaped solidbody of molded Res-O-Glas, 2 regular and 1 bridge pickups, butterfly inlay.

| 1962-1963 | Snow White | $4,200 | $5,200 |
| 1964-1965 | Green/Blue | $6,700 | $8,300 |

Glenwood Deluxe
1959-1961. Renamed from Glenwood 1105, Les Paul-shaped solidbody, wood body, not fiberglass, multi-bound, 2 pickups, factory Bigsby, vibrato, natural.

| 1959-1961 | | $2,100 | $2,650 |

Havana
1938-1942. Natural spruce top, sunburst back and sides.

| 1938-1942 | Round neck | $1,000 | $1,250 |
| 1938-1942 | Square neck | $675 | $850 |

Model 1100 California
1949-1955. Electric hollowbody archtop, multi-bound, f-holes, trapeze tailpiece, 1 pickup, natural.

| 1949-1955 | | $1,100 | $1,400 |

Model 1104 Town and Country
1954-1958. Model just below Glenwood 1105, dots, 2 or 3 pickups, plastic overlay on back, natural finish.

| 1954-1958 | 2 pickups | $1,750 | $2,200 |
| 1954-1958 | 3 pickups | $1,950 | $2,450 |

Model 1105 Glenwood
1954-1958. Les Paul-shaped solidbody, wood body, not fiberglass, single-cut, multi-bound, 2 pickups, natural, renamed Glenwood Deluxe with Bigsby in '59.

| 1954-1958 | | $2,100 | $2,600 |

Model 1106 Val-Trol Baron
1959-1960. Single-cut solidbody, 2 pickups, 1 piezo, block inlays, black.

| 1959-1960 | | $1,700 | $2,100 |

Model 1107 Debonaire
1953-1960. Single rounded-cutaway full-depth 16" electric archtop, single neck pickup, Debonaire logo on 'guard (for most models), large raised National script logo on headstock, sunburst.

| 1953-1960 | | $1,000 | $1,250 |

Model 1109/1198 Bel-Aire
1953-1960. Single pointed cut archtop, 2 (1109) pickups until '57, 3 (1198) after, master tone knob and jack, bound body, sunburst.

| 1953-1957 | 1109, 2 pickups | $1,325 | $1,750 |
| 1958-1960 | 1198, 3 pickups | $1,500 | $1,850 |

MODEL YEAR	FEATURES	EXC. COND. LOW	HIGH

Model 1110/1111 Aristocrat

1941-1954. Electric full body non-cut archtop, 1 pickup, 2 knobs, early model with triple backslash markers, later with block markers, National-crest headstock inlaid logo, natural finish only until model numbers added to name in '48, shaded sunburst finish (1110) and natural (1111).

1941-1948	Natural	$1,100	$1,375
1948-1955	1110, shaded	$1,325	$1,750
1948-1955	1111, natural	$1,400	$1,750

Model 1120 New Yorker

1954-1958. Renamed from New Yorker Spanish, 16.25" electric archtop, 1 pickup on floating 'guard, dot markers, blond.

1954-1958		$1,100	$1,250

Model 1122 Cosmopolitan

1954-1957. Small wood non-cutaway solidbody, dot markers, 1 pickup, 2 knobs on mounted 'guard.

1954-1957		$1,000	$1,250

Model 1122 Val-Trol Junior

1959-1960. Single-cut solidbody, 1 pickup and 1piezo, dot inlays, ivory.

1959-1960		$1,300	$1,600

Model 1123 Bolero

1954-1957. Les Paul-shape, control knobs mounted on 'guard, single pickup, trapeze tailpiece, sunburst.

1954-1957		$1000	$1,250

Model 1124/1124B Avalon

1954-1957. Small wood solidbody, 2 pickups, 4 control knobs and switch on top-mounted 'guard, block markers, short trapeze bridge, sunburst (1124) or blond (1124B).

1954-1957	1124, sunburst	$1,400	$1,750
1954-1957	1124B, blond	$1,500	$1,850

Model 1125 Dynamic

1951-1959. Full body 15.5" acoustic-electric archtop, sunburst version of New Yorker 1120 with some appointments slightly below the New Yorker, dot markers, 1 pickup, sunburst.

1951-1959		$900	$1,125

Model 1135 Acoustic Archtop

1948-1954. 17.25" full body acoustic archtop, carved top, split pearl markers.

1948-1954		$1,175	$1,475

Model 1140 Acoustic Archtop

1948-1957. 15.5" full body acoustic archtop, carved top, dot markers.

1948-1957		$875	$1,100

Model 1150 Flat-Top Auditorium

1951-1958. Auditorium-size flat-top, 14.25" narrowwaist, dot markers.

1951-1958		$875	$1,100

Model 1155 Jumbo

1948-1961. Flat-top acoustic with Gibson Jumbo body, mahogany back and sides, bolt-on neck.

1948-1961	Bolt-on neck	$2,000	$2,500
1948-1961	Set-neck	$3,500	$4,350

Model 1170 Club Combo

1952-1955, 1959-1961. Electric hollowbody archtop, 2 pickups, rounded cutaway.

1952-1961		$1,500	$1,875

N600 Series

1968. Offset double-cut solidbody, 1, 2, and 3 pickup models, with and without vibrato.

1968	N624, 1 pickup	$500	$625
1968	N634, 2 pickups, vibrato	$650	$800
1968	N644, 3 pickups, vibrato	$800	$1,000
1968	N654, 12-string	$650	$800

N700 Series

1968. Flat-top, 700/710 dreadnoughts, 720/730 jumbos.

1968	N700 Western	$625	$800
1968	N710	$325	$425
1968	N720 Western	$400	$500
1968	N730 Deluxe	$575	$725

N800 Series

1968. Double-cut semi-hollow body, various models with or without Bigsby.

1968	No Bigsby	$650	$800
1968	With Bigsby	$750	$900

New Yorker Spanish

1939-1953. Electric archtop, 15.5" body until '47 then 16.25", 1 neck pickup, dot diamond markers, sunburst or natural. Renamed New Yorker 1120 in '54.

1939-1946	15.5"	$1,250	$1,550
1947-1953	16.25"	$1,250	$1,550

Newport 82

1963-1965. Renamed from Val-Pro 82, USA mapshaped Res-O-Glas, 1 pickup, red finish.

1963-1965	Pepper Red	$1,900	$2,350

Newport 84

1963-1965. Renamed from Val-Pro 84, USA mapshaped Res-O Glas, 1 regular and 1 bridge pickup, Sea Foam Green finish.

1963-1965	Sea Foam Green	$2,800	$3,400

Newport 88

1963-1965. Renamed from Val-Pro 88, USA mapshaped Res-O-Glas, 2 regular and 1 bridge pickup, black finish.

1963-1965	Raven Black	$2,400	$2,950

Reso-phonic

1956-1964. Pearloid-covered, single-cut semisolidbody acoustic, single resonator, maroon or white, also a non-cut, square neck version was offered, which is included in these values.

1956-1964	Round neck, common finish	$1,200	$1,500
1956-1964	Round neck, rare finish	$1,600	$2,000
1956-1964	Square neck	$925	$1,150

Rosita

1933-1939. Plywood body by Harmony, plain metal resonator, plain appointments.

1933-1939		$1,000	$1,250

Silvo (Electric Hawaiian)

1937-1941. Nickel-plated metal body flat-top, small upper bout, f-holes, square neck, multiple straight line body art over dark background, Roman numeral parallelogram markers, National badge headstock logo, Silvo name on coverplate.

1937-1941	Silver	$2,800	$3,500

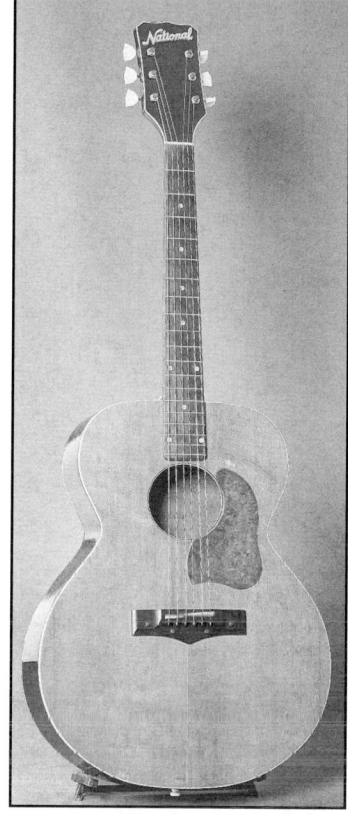

1956 National Model 1150
Folkway Music

1968 National N634

National Style N

1939 National Triolian

MODEL YEAR	FEATURES	EXC. COND. LOW	HIGH

Studio 66
1961-1964. Electric solidbody of Res-O-Glas, single-cut, 1 pickup, renamed Varsity 66 in '65.

| 1961-1962 | Sand Buff, bridge pickup | $1,100 | $1,350 |
| 1963-1964 | Jet Black, neck pickup | $1,100 | $1,350 |

Style O
1930-1942. Acoustic single-cone brass body (early models had a steel body), Hawaiian scene etching, 12-fret neck '30-'34, 14-fret neck '35 on, round (all years) or square ('33 on) neck.

1930-1934	Round neck, 12-fret, common finish	$2,300	$2,900
1930-1934	Round neck, 12-fret, rare finish	$3,600	$4,500
1933-1942	Square, 12-fret, common	$1,300	$1,650
1933-1942	Square, 12-fret, rare	$2,600	$3,300
1935-1942	Round, 14-fret, common	$2,300	$2,900
1935-1942	Round, 14-fret, Knophler	$5,800	$7,300
1935-1942	Round, 14-fret, rare	$3,600	$4,500

Style O Tenor
1929-1930. Tenor, 4 strings, single-cone brass body, Hawaiian scene etching.

| 1929-1930 | | $1,450 | $1,800 |

Style 1 Tricone
1927-1943. German silver body tricone resonator, ebony 'board, mahogany square (Hawaiian) or round (Spanish) neck, plain body, 12-fret neck until '34, 14-fret after.

| 1927-1943 | Round neck | $5,700 | $7,500 |
| 1928-1943 | Square neck | $2,800 | $3,500 |

Style 1 Tricone Plectrum
1928-1935. 26" scale versus the 23" scale of the tenor.

| 1928-1935 | | $1,900 | $2,500 |

Style 1 Tricone Tenor
1928-1935. Tenor, 4 strings, 23" scale, square neck is Hawaiian, round neck is Spanish.

| 1928-1935 | | $1,900 | $2,500 |

Style 1.5 Tricone
1930s. A "1/2" style like the 1.5 represents a different engraving pattern.

| 1930s | Round neck | $8,000 | $10,800 |
| 1930s | Square neck | $3,600 | $4,700 |

Style 2 Tricone
1927-1942. German silver body tricone resonator, wild rose engraving, square (Hawaiian) or round (Spanish) neck, 12-fret neck until '34, 14-fret after.

| 1927-1942 | Round neck | $8,300 | $11,000 |
| 1927-1942 | Square neck | $3,700 | $5,000 |

Style 2 Tricone Plectrum
1928-1935. 26" scale versus the 23" scale of the tenor.

| 1928-1935 | | $2,050 | $2,700 |

Style 2 Tricone Tenor
1928-1935. Tenor.

| 1928-1935 | | $2,050 | $2,700 |

Style 3 Tricone
1928-1941. German silver body tricone resonator, lily-of-the-valley engraving, square (Hawaiian) or round (Spanish) neck, 12-fret neck until '34, 14-fret after, reintroduced with a nickel-plated brass body in '94.

1928-1939	Round neck	$11,800	$15,500
1928-1939	Square neck	$5,600	$7,300
1940-1941	Square neck	$5,700	$7,500

Style 3 Tricone Plectrum
1928-1935. 26" scale versus the 23" scale of the tenor.

| 1928-1935 | | $3,500 | $4,600 |

Style 3 Tricone Tenor
1928-1939. Tenor version.

| 1928-1939 | | $3,500 | $4,600 |

Style 4 Tricone
1928-1940. German silver body tricone resonator, chrysanthemum etching, 12-fret neck until '34, 14-fret after, reissued in '95 with same specs.

| 1928-1940 | Round neck | $16,000 | $20,000 |
| 1928-1940 | Square neck | $6,500 | $8,100 |

Style 35
1936-1942. Brass body tricone resonator, sandblasted minstrel and trees scene, 12 frets, square (Hawaiian) or round (Spanish) neck.

| 1936-1942 | Round neck | $20,000 | $25,000 |
| 1936-1942 | Square neck | $9,000 | $11,000 |

Style 97
1936-1940. Nickel-plated brass body tricone resonator, sandblasted scene of female surfrider and palm trees, 12 frets, slotted peghead.

1930s	Early '30s	$8,500	$10,500
1930s	Late '30s	$6,000	$7,500
1930s	Round neck	$21,000	$26,000

Style N
1930-1931. Nickel-plated brass body single-cone resonator, plain finish, 12 frets.

| 1930-1931 | | $4,500 | $5,500 |

Triolian
1928-1941. Single-cone resonator, wood body replaced by metal body in '29, 12-fret neck and slotted headstock '28-'34, changed to 14-fret neck in '35 and solid headstock in '36, round or square ('33 on) neck available.

| 1928-1936 | Various colors | $2,800 | $3,500 |
| 1936-1937 | Fake rosewood grain finish | $2,600 | $3,300 |

Triolian Tenor
1928-1936. Tenor, metal body.

| 1928-1936 | | $1,000 | $1,250 |

Trojan
1934-1942. Single-cone resonator wood body, f-holes, bound top, 14-fret round neck.

| 1934-1942 | | $1,000 | $1,250 |

Val-Pro 82
1962-1963. USA map-shaped Res-O-Glas, 1 pickup, Vermillion Red finish, renamed Newport 82 in '63.

| 1962-1963 | | $1,650 | $2,050 |

Val-Pro 84
1962-1963. USA map-shaped Res-O-Glas, 1 regular and 1 bridge pickup, snow white finish, renamed Newport 84 in '63.

| 1962-1963 | | $1,750 | $2,200 |

MODEL YEAR	FEATURES	EXC. COND. LOW	HIGH

Val-Pro 88
1962-1963. USA map-shaped Res-O-Glas, 2 regular and 1 bridge pickup, black finish, renamed Newport 88 in '63.

1962-1963		$2,850	$3,500

Varsity 66
1964-1965. Renamed from Studio 66 in '64, molded Res-O-Glas, 1 pickup, 2 knobs, beige finish.

1964-1965		$1,075	$1,350

Westwood 72
1962-1964. USA map-shaped solid hardwood body (not fiberglass), 1 pickup, Cherry Red.

1962-1964		$1,950	$2,450

Westwood 75
1962-1964. USA map-shaped solid hardwood body (not fiberglass), 1 regular and 1 bridge pickup, cherry-to-black sunburst finish.

1962-1964		$2,150	$2,650

Westwood 77
1962-1965. USA map-shaped solid hardwood body (not fiberglass), 2 regular and 1 bridge pickup.

1962-1965	Blond-Ivory	$2,150	$2,650

National Reso-Phonic
1989-present. Professional and premium grade, production/custom, single cone, acoustic-electric, and tricone guitars (all with resonators), built in San Luis Obispo, California. They also build basses, mandolins and ukuleles. McGregor Gaines and Don Young formed the National Reso-Phonic Guitar Company with the objective of building instruments based upon the original National designs. Replicon is the aging process to capture the appearance and sound of a vintage National.

Collegian
2010-present. Thin gauge steel body, 9.5" cone, biscuit bridge, aged ivory finish.

2010-2014		$1,300	$1,600

Delphi
1993-2010. Single cone, steel body.

1993-2010		$1,450	$1,850

Dueco
2012-present. Gold or Silver crystalline finish.

2012-2014		$1,800	$2,300

El Trovador
2010-present. Wood body Dobro-style, single cone, biscuit bridge.

2010-2014		$2,000	$2,500

Estralita Deluxe
2006-present. Single cone, walnut body, figured maple top, koa offered in '03.

2006-2014		$1,650	$2,050

Estralita Harlem Slim
2010. Laminate maple.

2010		$1,150	$1,450

Model 97
2002-2009. Nickel-plated tricone resonator, female surfrider and palm trees scene.

2002-2009		$2,500	$3,100

Model D
2003-2010. Laminate wood body, spruce top, walnut back and sides, spun cone and spider bridge. Replaced by Smith and Young Model 1 (metal body) and Model 11 (wood body).

2003-2010		$1,700	$2,100

Reso Rocket
2005-present. Single-cut steel body, Tricone style grill.

2005-2014		$1,900	$2,400

Reso Rocket N
2009-present. Highly polished nickel-plated finish.

2009-2014		$1,900	$2,400

Resoelectric Jr./Jr. II
2005-2010. Basic model of ResoLectric with painted body, Jr. with P-90, Jr. II with Lollar lipstick-tube. Replaced by the ResoTone.

2005-2010		$750	$925

ResoLectric
1992-present. Single-cut electric resonator, maple (flamed maple since '96), single biscuit, 1 regular pickup (lipstick-tube up to '95, P-90 since) and 1 under-saddle.

1992-1995	Lipstick pickup	$1,550	$1,925
1996-2014	P-90	$1,450	$1,800

Style 1 Tricone
1994-present. Nickel-plated brass body, bound ebony 'board.

1994-2014		$1,900	$2,400

Style M-1/M-2
1990-1994, 2003-2010. Bound mahogany body single-cone, M-1 with ebony 'board, M-2 with bound rosewood 'board.

1990-2010		$1,700	$2,100

Style N
1993-2005. Nickel-plated brass body single-cone resonator, plain mirror finish, 12 fret neck.

1993-2005		$1,800	$2,200

Style O/O Deluxe
1992-present. Nickel plated brass body, Hawaiian palm tree etched. Deluxe has upgrades like figured-maple neck and mother-of-pearl diamond inlays.

1992-2014		$1,800	$2,250
1994-2014	Deluxe	$2,000	$2,500

Triolian 14-Fret
2009-present. Same as above with 14 frets.

2009-2014		$1,450	$1,800

Navarro Custom
1986-present. Professional and premium grade, production/custom, electric guitars and basses built in San Juan, Puerto Rico by luthier Mike Navarro.

Neubauer
1966-1990s. Luthier Helmut Neubauer built his acoustic and electric archtop guitars in Bubenreuth, Germany.

New Era Guitars
See listing under ARK - New Era Guitars.

National Reso-Phonic Collegian

National Reso-Phonic Estralita Deluxe

Normandy Archtop

Nyberg Prairie State

MODEL YEAR	FEATURES	EXC. COND. LOW	HIGH

New Orleans Guitar Company

1992-present. Luthier Vincent Guidroz builds his premium grade, production/custom, solid and semi-hollow body guitars in New Orleans, Louisiana.

Nickerson Guitars

1983-present. Luthier Brad Nickerson builds his professional and premium grade, production/custom, archtop and flat-top guitars in Northampton, Massachusetts.

Nielsen

2004-present. Premium grade, custom/production, archtop guitars built by luthier Dale Nielsen in Duluth, Minnesota.

Nik Huber Guitars

1997-present. Premium grade, production/custom, electric guitars built in Rodgau, Germany by luthier Nik Huber.

Nioma

1932-1952. NIOMA, the National Institute of Music and Arts, was founded in Seattle but soon had schools across the western U.S. and Canada. By '35 they added guitar instruction, offering their own branded Spanish, resonator and lap steel (with matching amps) guitars, made by Regal, Harmony, Dickerson.

Noble

Ca. 1950-ca. 1969. Instruments made by others and distributed by Don Noble and Company of Chicago. Plastic-covered guitars made by EKO debut in '62. Aluminum-necked Wandré guitars added to the line in early-'63. By ca. '65-'66 the brand is owned by Chicago-area importer and distributor Strum 'N Drum and used mainly on Japanese-made solidbodies. Strum 'N Drum bought the National brand name in '69 and imported Japanese copies of American designs under the National brand and Japanese original designs under Norma through the early '70s.

The Noble brand disappears at least by the advent of the Japanese National brand, if not before. They also offered amps.

NoName Guitars

1999-present. Luthier Dan Kugler builds his production/custom, professional and premium grade, acoustic guitars and basses in Conifer, Colorado.

Nordy (Nordstrand Guitars)

2003-present. Professional and premium grade, production/custom, electric guitars and basses built by luthier Carey Nordstrand in Yucaipa, California.

Norma

Ca.1965-1970. Imported from Japan by Strum 'N Drum, Inc. of Chicago (see Noble brand info). Early examples were built by Tombo, most notably sparkle plastic covered guitars and basses.

Electric Solidbody

1965-1970s. Type of finish has affect on value. Various models include; EG-350 (student double-cut, 1 pickup), EG-403 (unique pointy cutaway, 2 pickups), EG-400 (double-cut, 2 pickups), EG-450 (double-cut, 2 split-coil pickups), EG-421 (double-cut, 4 pickups), EG-412-12 (double-cut, 12-string).

MODEL YEAR	FEATURES	EXC. COND. LOW	HIGH
1965-1968	Blue, red, gold sparkle	$350	$450
1965-1970s	Non-sparkle	$200	$250

Norman

1972-present. Intermediate grade, production, acoustic and acoustic/electric guitars built in LaPatrie, Quebec. Norman was the first guitar production venture luthier Robert Godin was involved with. He has since added the Seagull, Godin, and Patrick & Simon brands of instruments.

Normandy Guitars

2008-present. Jim Normandy builds professional grade, production, aluminum archtop and electric guitars and basses in Salem, Oregon.

Northworthy Guitars

1987-present. Professional and premium grade, production/custom, flat-top and electric guitars and basses built by luthier Alan Marshall in Ashbourne, Derbyshire, England. He also builds mandolins.

Norwood

1960s. Budget guitars imported most likely from Japan.

Electric Solidbody

1960s. Offset double-cut body, 3 soapbar-style pickups, Norwood label on headstock.

MODEL YEAR	FEATURES	EXC. COND. LOW	HIGH
1960s		$160	$200

Novax Guitars

1989-present. Luthier Ralph Novak builds his fanned-fret professional and premium grade, production/custom, solidbody and acoustic guitars and basses, originally in San Leandro, California, and since May '06, in Eugene, Oregon.

Noyce

1974-present. Luthier Ian Noyce builds his production/custom, professional and premium grade, acoustic and electric guitars and basses in Ballarat, Victoria, Australia.

Nyberg Instruments

1993-present. Professional grade, custom, flat-top and Maccaferri-style guitars built by luthier Lawrence Nyberg in Hornby Island, British Columbia. He also builds mandolins, mandolas, bouzoukis and citterns.

Oahu

1926-1985, present. The Oahu Publishing Company and Honolulu Conservatory, based in Cleveland, Ohio was active in the sheet music and student instrument business in the '30s. An instrument, set of

MODEL		EXC. COND.	
YEAR	FEATURES	LOW	HIGH

instructional sheet music, and lessons were offered as a complete package. Lessons were often given to large groups of students. Instruments, lessons, and sheet music could also be purchased by mail order. The Oahu Publishing Co. advertised itself as The World's Largest Guitar Dealer. Most '30s Oahu guitars were made by Kay with smaller numbers from the Oscar Schmidt Company.

Guitar Models from the Mid-'30s include: 71K (jumbo square neck), 72K (jumbo roundneck), 68B (jumbo, vine body decoration), 68K (deluxe jumbo square neck), 69K (deluxe jumbo roundneck), 65K and 66K (mahogany, square neck), 64K and 67K (mahogany, roundneck), 65M (standard-size, checker binding, mahogany), 53K (roundneck, mahogany), 51 (black, Hawaiian scene, pearlette 'board), 51K (black, pond scene decoration), 52K (black, Hawaiian scene decoration), 50 and 50K (student guitar, brown). The brand has been revived on a line of tube amps.

Graphic Body
1930s. 13" painted artwork bodies, includes Styles 51 and 52 Hawaiian scene.

1930s	Floral, higher appointments	$325	$400
1930s	Hawaiian scene	$325	$400

Round Neck 14" Flat-Top
1930s. Spruce top, figured maple back and sides, thin logo.

1932		$900	$1,100

Style 50K Student
1930s. Student-size guitar, brown finish.

1935		$225	$275

Style 52K
1930s. 13" with fancy Hawaiian stencil, slotted headstock.

1930s		$300	$375

Style 65M
1933-1935. Standard-size mahogany body, checker binding, natural brown.

1933-1935		$525	$650

Style 68K De Luxe Jumbo
1930s. Hawaiian, 15.5" wide, square neck, Brazilian back and sides, spruce top, fancy pearl vine inlay, abalone trim on top and soundhole, rosewood pyramid bridge, fancy pearl headstock inlay, butterbean tuners, ladder-braced, natural. High-end model made for Oahu by Kay.

1935		$3,000	$3,700

Style 71K Hawaiian
1930s.Hawaiian, gold vine pattern on bound sunburst top, dot inlays.

1930s		$1,000	$1,250

Odessa
1981-1990s. Budget guitars imported by Davitt & Hanser (BC Rich). Mainly acoustics in the '90s, but some electrics early on.

O'Hagan
1979-1983. Designed by clarinetist and importer Jerol O'Hagan in St. Louis Park, Minnesota. Primarily neck-thru construction, most with German-

carved bodies. In '81 became Jemar Corporation and in '83 it was closed by the I.R.S., a victim of recession.

SN=YYM(M)NN (e.g., 80905, September '80, 5th guitar); or MYMNNN (e.g., A34006, April 1983, 6th guitar). Approximately 3000 total instruments were made with the majority being Night-Watches (approx. 200 Twenty Twos, 100-150 Sharks, 100 Lasers; about 25 with birdseye maple bodies).

Electric
1979-1983. Models include; Laser (solidbody, double-cut, maple or walnut body, set-thru neck, 3 single-coil Schaller pickups), Shark (Explorer-looking solidbody) and Twenty Two (V, 2 humbuckers).

1979-1983		$550	$675

Ohio
1959-ca. 1965. Line of electric solidbodies and basses made by France's Jacobacci company, which also built under its own brand. Sparkle finish, bolt-on aluminum necks, strings-thru-body design.

Old Kraftsman
Ca. 1930s-ca. 1960s. Brandname used by the Spiegel catalog company for instruments made by other American manufacturers, including Regal, Kay and even Gibson. The instruments were of mixed quality, but some better grade instruments were comparable to those offered by Wards.

Archtop
1930s-1960s. Various models.

1930s	17", Stauffer-style headstock	$325	$425
1950s-60s		$250	$325

Flat-Top
1930s-1960s. Various models.

1950s	Prairie Ramblers (stencil)	$250	$325

Jazz II K775
1960-1963. Kay 775 with Old Kraftsman logo on large headstock, small double-cut thinline, 2 pickups, Bigsby, natural.

1960-1963		$725	$900

Sizzler K4140
1959. Single-cut, single neck pickup, Sizzler logo on body with other art images.

1959		$400	$500

Thin Twin Jimmy Reed

1952-1958		$1,150	$1,450

Value Leader
1961-1965. Electric single-cut semi-solid, 1 pickup, Kay Value Leader series.

1961-1965		$425	$525

OLP (Officially Licensed Product)
2001-2009. Intermediate grade, production, imported guitars and basses based on higher dollar guitar models officially licensed from the original manufacturer. OLP logo on headstock.

1961 Old Kraftsman

1950s Old Kraftsman Model K1

John Neff

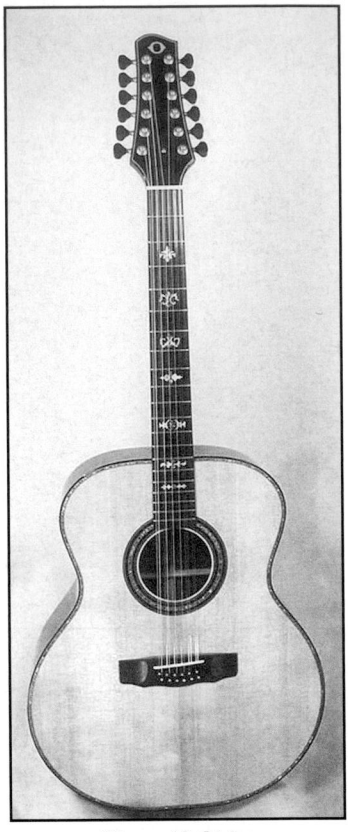

Olson 12-String

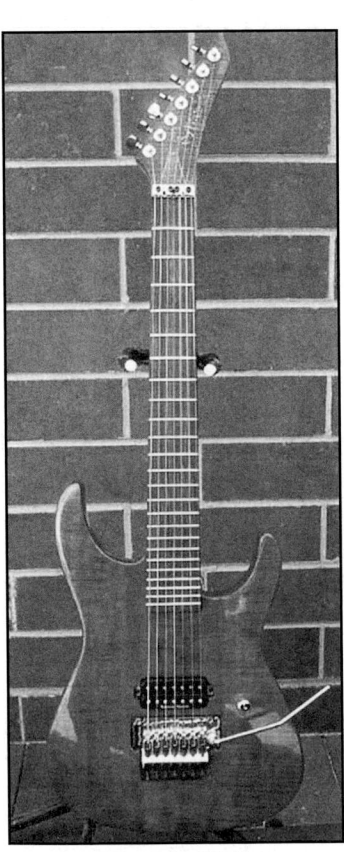

Ormsby SS-7

MODEL YEAR	FEATURES	EXC. COND. LOW	HIGH

Olson Guitars

1977-present. Luthier James A. Olson builds his presentation grade, custom, flat-tops in Circle Pines, Minnesota.

Olympia by Tacoma

1997-2006. Import acoustic guitars and mandolins from Tacoma Guitars.

OD Series
1997-2006	Various models	$75	$300

Omega

1996-2010. Luthier Kevin Gallagher built his premium grade, custom/production acoustic guitars in East Saylorsburg, Pennsylvania. He died in '10.

Oncor Sound

1980-ca. 1981. This Salt Lake City, Utah-based company made both a guitar and a bass synthesizer.

Optek

1980s-present. Intermediate grade, production, imported Fretlight acoustic/electric and electric guitars. Located in Reno, Nevada.

Fretlight
1989-present. Double-cut, 126 LED lights in fretboard controlled by a scale/chord selector.
1989-2014		$300	$400

Opus

1972-Mid 1970s. Acoustic and classical guitars, imported from Japan by Ampeg/Selmer. In '75-'76, Harmony made a line of acoustics with the Opus model name.

Original Senn

2004-present. Luthier Jeff Senn builds his professional and premium grade, production/custom, solidbody electric guitars and basses in Nashville, Tennessee.

Ormsby Guitars

2003-present. Luthier Perry Ormsby builds his custom, professional and premium grade, solid and chambered electric guitars in Perth, Western Australia.

Orpheum

1897-1942, 1944-late 1960s, 2001-2006. Intermediate grade, production, acoustic and resonator guitars. They also offered mandolins. Orpheum originally was a brand of Rettberg and Lange, who made instruments for other companies as well. William Rettberg and William Lange bought the facilities of New York banjo maker James H. Buckbee in 1897. Lange went out on his own in '21 to start the Paramount brand. He apparently continued using the Orpheum brand as well. He went out of business in '42. In '44 the brand was acquired by New York's Maurice Lipsky Music Co. who used it primarily on beginner to medium grade instruments, which were manufactured by Regal, Kay, and United Guitar (and maybe others). In the early '60s Lipsky applied the brand to Japanese and European (by Egmond) imports. Lipsky dropped the name in the early '70s. The brand was revived for '01 to '06 by Tacoma Guitars.

Auditorium Archtop 835/837
1950s. Acoustic archtop, auditorium size, dot markers, Orpheum shell headpiece, white celluloid 'guard, model 835 with spruce top/back/sides, 837 with mahogany.
1950s		$225	$280

Orpheum Special (Regal-made)
1930s. Slot head, Dobro-style wood body, metal resonator, sunburst.
1930s		$825	$1,025

President
1940s. 18" pro-level acoustic archtop, Orpheum block logo and President script logo on headstock, large split-block markers, sunburst.
1940s		$1,500	$1,850

Thin Twin Jimmy Reed 865E
1950s. Model 865E is the Orpheum version of the generically named Thin Twin Jimmy Reed style electric Spanish cutaway thin solidbody, hand engraved shell celluloid Orpheum headpiece, described as #865E Cutaway Thin Electric Guitar in catalog.
1950s		$1,150	$1,450

Ultra Deluxe Professional 899
1950s. 17" cutaway, 2 pickups, 2 knobs, maple back and sides, top material varies, dot markers, finishes as follows: E-C copper, E-G gold, E-G-B gold-black sunburst, E-B blond curly maple, E-S golden orange sunburst.
1950s	All finishes	$1,200	$1,500

Orville

1984-1993. Orville by Gibson and Orville guitars were made by Japan's Fuji Gen Gakki for Gibson. See following listing for details. Guitars listed here state only Orville (no By Gibson) on the headstock.

Electric
1990s	CE Atkins	$725	$900
1990s	ES-335	$1,050	$1,300
1990s	Les Paul Custom	$825	$1,050
1990s	Les Paul Standard	$825	$1,050

Orville by Gibson

1984-1993. Orville by Gibson and Orville guitars were made by Japan's Fuji Gen Gakki for Gibson. Basically the same models except the Orville by Gibson guitars had real Gibson USA PAF '57 Classic pickups and a true nitrocellulose lacquer finish. The Orville models used Japanese electronics and a poly finish. Some Orvilles were made in Korea and are of a lower quality. These Korean guitars had the serial number printed on a sticker. Prices here are for the Orville by Gibson models.

Electric
1984-1993	ES-175	$1,150	$1,450
1984-1993	ES-335	$1,275	$1,650

MODEL YEAR	FEATURES	EXC. COND. LOW	HIGH
1984-1993	Explorer	$1,000	$1,250
1984-1993	Firebird V	$850	$1,050
1984-1993	Firebird VII	$850	$1,050
1984-1993	Flying V	$1,000	$1,250
1984-1993	Les Paul Custom	$1,050	$1,300
1984-1993	Les Paul Jr., double-cut	$500	$625
1984-1993	Les Paul Standard	$1,050	$1,300
1984-1993	Les Paul Studio J.P.	$850	$1,050
1984-1993	MM/Les Paul Jr., single-cut	$425	$525
1984-1993	SG Les Paul Custom	$850	$1,050
1984-1993	SG Les Paul Standard	$700	$900

Osborne Sound Laboratories

Late 1970s. Founded by Ralph Scaffidi and wife guitarist Mary Osborne; originally building guitar amps, they did also offer solidbody guitars.

Oscar Schmidt

1879-1938, 1979-present. Budget and intermediate grade, production, acoustic, acoustic/electric, and electric guitars and basses distributed by U.S. Music Corp. (Washburn, Randall, etc.). They also offer mandolins, banjos, ukuleles and the famous Oscar Schmidt autoharp.

The original Oscar Schmidt Company, Jersey City, New Jersey, offered banjo mandolins, tenor banjos, guitar banjos, ukuleles, mandolins and guitars under their own brand and others (including Sovereign and Stella). By the early 1900s, the company had factories in the U.S. and Europe producing instruments producing instruments under their own brand as well as other brands for mailorder and other distributors. Oscar Schmidt was also an early contributor to innovative mandolin designs and the company participated in the '00-'30 mandolin boom. The company hit hard times during the Depression and was sold to Harmony by the end of the '30s. In '79, Washburn acquired the brand and it is now part of U.S. Music.

Oskar Graf Guitars

1970-present. Premium and presentation grade, custom, archtop, acoustic and classical guitars and basses built in Clarendon, Ontario, by luthier Oskar Graf. He also builds lutes.

Otwin

1950s-1960s. A brand used on electric guitars made by the Musima company of East Germany. Musima also produced guitars under their own brand.

Outbound Instruments

1990-2002. Intermediate grade, production, travel-size acoustics from the Boulder, Colorado-based company.

Ovation

1966-present. Intermediate and professional grade, production, imported acoustic and acoustic/electric guitars. They also build basses and mandolins. Until 2014, they also had U.S. production.

Helicopter manufacturer Kaman Corporation, founded in 1945 by jazz guitarist and aeronautical engineer Charles Huron Kaman in Bloomfield, Connecticut, decided to use their helicopter expertise (working with synthetic materials, spruce, high tolerances) and designed, with the help of employee and violin restorer John Ringso, the first fiberglass-backed (Lyracord) acoustic guitars in '65. Production began in '66 and the music factory moved to New Hartford, Connecticut, in '67. Early input was provided by fingerstyle jazz guitarist Charlie Byrd, who gave Kaman the idea for the name Ovation. Kaman Music purchased Hamer Guitars in '88, and Trace Elliot amplifiers (U.K.) in '90. In '08, Fender acquired Kaman Music Corporation and the Ovation brand and in '14 ceased U.S. production and the brand was sold to Drum Workshop, Inc. DWI reopened the Hartford, CT plant in late '15.

Adamas 1581-KK Kaki King
2011-2014. Deep bowl cutaway, rosewood 'board, 12th-fret crown inlay, OP-Pro preamp, Kaki personally signs the label on each guitar.

2011-2014		$2,400	$2,800

Adamas 1587
1979-1998. Carbon top, walnut, single-cut, bowl back, binding, mini-soundholes.

1979-1998	Black Sparkle	$1,200	$1,500

Adamas 1597
1998-2003. Carbon birch composite top, on-board electronics.

1998-2003	Black	$700	$875

Adamas 1598-MEII Melissa Etheridge
2001-2014. Mid-depth cutaway, ebony 'board, 'ME' maple symbol at 12th fret, OP-Pro preamp, Melissa personally signs the label on each guitar.

2001-2014	12-string	$1,200	$1,400

Adamas 1687
1977-1998. Acoustic/electric, carbon top, non-cut, bowl back, mini-soundholes.

1977-1998	Sunburst	$1,200	$1,500

Adamas CVT W591
2000. Crossweave fiber top, mid-depth body, on-board electronics.

2000		$850	$1,050

Adamas II 1881 NB-2
1993-1998. Acoustic/electric, single-cut, shallow bowl.

1993-1998	Brown	$1,100	$1,400

Adamas Millenium
2000. Limited edition, 75 made, Cobalt Blue, planet inlays.

2000	Cobalt Blue	$1,900	$2,200

Anniversary Electric 1657
1978. Deep bowl, abalone inlays, gold-plated parts, for Ovation's 10th anniversary. They also offered an acoustic Anniversary.

1978		$300	$400

Oskar Graf No. 4/11

1976 Ovation Adamas
Sam Stathakis

GUITARS

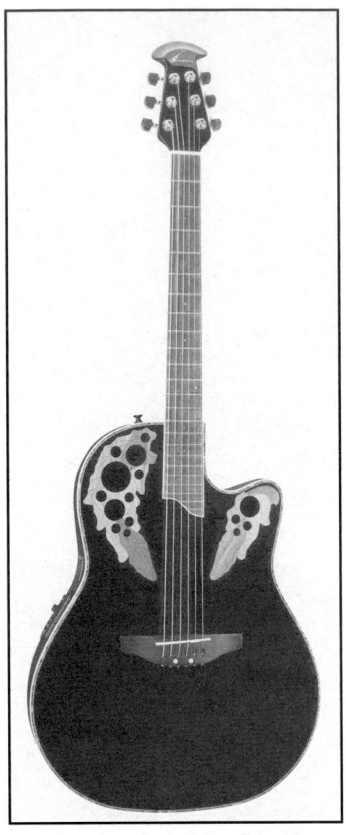

Ovation Celebrity CC-48

1968 Ovation Hurricane 12-String K-1120

MODEL YEAR	FEATURES	EXC. COND. LOW	HIGH
Balladeer 1111			
1968-1983, 1993-2000. Acoustic, non-cut with deep bowl, bound body, natural top, later called the Standard Balladeer.			
1976-1983	Natural	$225	$275
Balladeer Artist 1121			
1968-1990. Acoustic, non-cut with shallow bowl, bound body.			
1968-1969	Early production	$300	$375
1970-1990		$225	$275
Balladeer Classic 1122			
1970s. Classical shallow-bowl version of Concert Classic, nylon strings, slotted headstock.			
1970s		$200	$250
Balladeer Custom 1112			
1976-1990. Acoustic, deep bowl, diamond inlays.			
1976-1990	Natural	$275	$350
Balladeer Custom 12-String Electric 1655/1755			
1982-1994. 12-string version of Balladeer Custom Electric.			
1982-1994	Sunburst	$275	$350
Balladeer Custom Electric 1612/1712			
1976-1990. Acoustic/electric version of Balladeer Custom, deep bowl.			
1976-1990	Natural	$325	$400
Balladeer Standard 1561/1661/1761/1861			
1982-2000. Acoustic/electric, deep bowl, rounded cutaway.			
1982-2000		$350	$425
Balladeer Standard 1771 LX			
2008-2010. Acoustic/electric, mid-depth bowl, rosewood, sitka spruce top.			
2008-2010		$400	$500
Balladeer Standard 12-String 6751 LX			
2008-2010. Acoustic/electric, 12 strings, rosewood, spruce top.			
2008-2010		$475	$575
Breadwinner 1251			
1971-1983. Axe-like shaped single-cut solidbody, 2 pickups, textured finish, black, blue, tan or white.			
1971-1983		$650	$800
Celebrity CC-48			
2007-2013. Acoustic/electric, super shallow, laminated spruce top, white bound rosewood 'board with abalone dot inlays.			
2007-2013		$200	$250
Celebrity CC-57			
1990-1996. Laminated spruce top, shallow bowl, mahogany neck.			
1990-1996		$200	$250
Celebrity CC-63			
1984-1996. Classical, deep bowl, piezo bridge pickup.			
1984-1996		$200	$250
Celebrity CK-057			
2002-2004. Acoustic/electric rounded cutaway, shallow back.			
2002-2004		$260	$320

MODEL YEAR	FEATURES	EXC. COND. LOW	HIGH
Celebrity CS-257			
1992-2005, 2010. Made in Korea, super shallow bowl back body, single-cut, Adamas soundholes, alternating dot and diamond markers.			
1992-2005	Celebrity	$300	$375
2010	Celebrity Deluxe	$350	$450
Classic 1613/1713			
1971-1993. Acoustic/electric, non-cut, deep bowl, no inlay, slotted headstock, gold tuners, natural.			
1971-1993		$325	$410
Classic 1663/1763			
1982-1998. Acoustic/electric, single-cut, deep bowl, cedar top, EQ, no inlay, slotted headstock, gold tuners.			
1982-1998		$400	$500
Classic 1863			
1989-1998. Acoustic/electric, single-cut, shallow bowl, no inlay, cedar top, EQ, slotted headstock, gold tuners.			
1989-1998		$400	$500
Collectors Series			
1982-2008. Limited edition, different model featured each year and production limited to that year only, the year designation is marked at the 12th fret, various colors (each year different).			
1982-2008	Common models	$425	$500
1982-2008	Rare models	$600	$1,200
Concert Classic 1116			
1974-1990. Deep-bowl nylon string classical, slotted headstock.			
1974-1990		$225	$275
Contemporary Folk Classic Electric 1616			
1974-1990. Acoustic/electric, no inlay, slotted headstock, natural or sunburst.			
1974-1990		$200	$300
Country Artist Classic Electric 1624			
1971-1990. Nylon strings, slotted headstock, standard steel-string sized neck to simulate a folk guitar, on-board electronics.			
1971-1990		$350	$400
Country Artist Classic Electric 6773			
1995-2011. Classic electric, soft-cut, solid spruce top, slotted headstock, Ovation pickup system.			
1995-2011		$350	$400
Custom Ballader 1762			
1992. Rounded cutaway, higher-end specs.			
1992		$600	$675
Custom Elite Guitar Center 30th Anniversary			
1994. 50 made.			
1994		$900	$1,250
Custom Legend 1117			
1970s. Non-electrical 2nd generation Ovation, higher-end with abalone inlays and gold hardware, open V-bracing pattern. Model 1117-4, natural.			
1970s		$425	$475
Custom Legend 1569			
1980s. Rounded cutaway acoustic/electric, super shallow bowl, gloss black finish.			
1980s		$475	$600

MODEL YEAR	FEATURES	EXC. COND. LOW	HIGH

Custom Legend 1619/1719
1970s. Acoustic/electric 2nd generation Ovation, electric version of model 1117, higher-end with abalone inlays and gold hardware, open V-bracing pattern.
| 1970s | | $475 | $600 |

Custom Legend 1759
1984-2004. Single-cut acoustic/electric.
| 1984-2004 | | $650 | $775 |

Custom Legend 1769
1982, 1993, 1996-1999. Single-cut acoustic/electric.
| 1982-1999 | | $800 | $900 |

Custom Legend 1869
1994, 2003. Acoustic/electric, cutaway, super shallow bowl.
| 1994, 2003 | | $600 | $750 |

Custom Legend 6759
| 2003 | | $1,200 | $1,500 |

Deacon 1252
1973-1980. Axe-shaped solidbody electric, active electronics, diamond fret markers.
| 1973-1980 | | $850 | $1,000 |

Deacon 12-String 1253
1975. Axe-shaped solidbody, diamond inlay, 2 pickups, only a few made.
| 1975 | | $850 | $1,000 |

Eclipse
1971-1973. Thinline double cut acoustic-electric archtop, 2 pickups.
| 1971-1973 | | $600 | $750 |

Elite 1718
1982-1997. Acoustic/electric, non-cut, deep bowl, solid spruce top, Adamas-type soundhole, volume and tone controls, stereo output.
| 1982-1997 | | $625 | $775 |

Elite 1758
1990-1998. Acoustic/electric, non-cut, deep bowl.
| 1990-1998 | | $625 | $775 |

Elite 1768
1990-1998. Acoustic/electric, cutaway, deep bowl.
| 1990-1998 | | $500 | $625 |

Elite T/TX 1778
2002-present. Acoustic/electric, cutaway, U.S. T replaced by import TX in '08.
| 2002-2008 | T, Original version | $625 | $775 |
| 2008-2014 | TX, Import | $200 | $250 |

Elite 1858 12-String
1993-2004. 12-string acoustic/electric, ebony 'board and bridge.
| 1993-2004 | | $625 | $775 |

Elite 1868
1983-2004. Acoustic/electric, cutaway, shallow bowl.
| 1983-2004 | | $450 | $600 |

Elite 5858
1991. Super shallow bowl, single cutaway, Adamas-style soundhole, gold hardware, on-board factory OP24 pickup.
| 1991 | | $500 | $625 |

Elite Doubleneck
1989-1990s. Six- and 12-string necks, can be ordered with a variety of custom options.
| 1989 | | $650 | $800 |

Elite Standard Cutawy Shallow 6868
1994-1999. Elite Standard with shallow bowl.
| 1994-1999 | | $475 | $600 |

Folklore 1614
1972-1983. Acoustic/electric, 12-fret neck on full-size body, wide neck, on-board electronics.
| 1972-1983 | | $425 | $525 |

GCXT
2008. Acoustic-electric, single-cut, flamed paint graphic, made for Guitar Center.
| 2008 | | $525 | $650 |

Glen Campbell 12-String 1118 (K-1118)
1968-1982. Acoustic, 12 strings, shallow bowl version of Legend, gold tuners, diamond inlay.
| 1968-1982 | | $425 | $525 |

Glen Campbell Artist 1627
2006. Glen Campbell 40th Anniversary model, diamond inlay, gold tuners.
| 2006 | | $850 | $1,050 |

Glen Campbell Artist Balladeer 1127
1968-1990. Acoustic, shallow bowl, diamond inlay, gold tuners, natural.
| 1968-1990 | | $425 | $525 |

Hurricane 12-String K-1120
1968-1969. ES-335-style electric semi-hollowbody, double-cut, 12 strings, f-holes, 2 pickups.
| 1968-1969 | | $575 | $700 |

Josh White 1114
1967-1970, 1972-1983. Wide 12-fret neck, dot markers, classical-style tuners.
| 1967-1970 | | $475 | $575 |
| 1972-1983 | | $400 | $500 |

Legend 1117
1972-1999. Deep bowl acoustic, 5-ply top binding, gold tuners, various colors (most natural).
| 1972-1999 | | $350 | $425 |

Legend 1567/1867
1984-2004. Acoustic/electric, shallow bowl, single-cut, gold tuners.
| 1984-2004 | | $425 | $525 |

Legend 12-String 1866
1989-2007. Acoustic/electric, cutaway, 12 strings, shallow bowl, 5-ply top binding, black.
| 1989-2007 | | $425 | $525 |

Legend 1717
1990-2008. Acoustic/electric, 5-ply top binding, various colors.
| 1990-2008 | | $400 | $500 |

Legend 1767
1990s. Acoustic/electric, deep bowl, single-cut, black.
| 1990s | | $400 | $500 |

Legend Cutaway 1667
1982-1996. Acoustic/electric, cutaway, deep bowl, abalone, gold tuners.
| 1982-1996 | | $450 | $550 |

Legend Electric 1617
1972-1998. Acoustic/electric, deep bowl, abalone, gold tuners, various colors.
| 1972-1998 | | $350 | $435 |

1968 Ovation Josh White 1114
Sam Stathakis

Ovation Legend 1767
James Armstrong

To get the most from this book, be sure to read "Using **The Guide**" in the introduction.

GUITARS

Ovation Tornado
Sam Stathakis

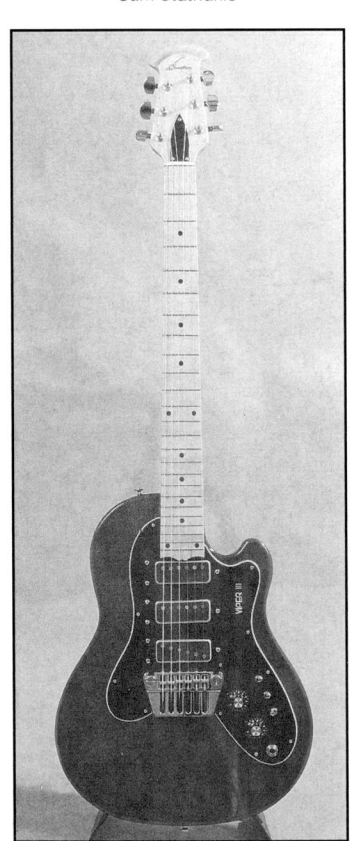

1978 Ovation Viper III 1273

MODEL YEAR	FEATURES	EXC. COND. LOW	HIGH

Pacemaker 12-String 1115/1615
1968-1982. Originally called the K-1115 12-string, Renamed Pacemaker in '72.

1968-1982		$425	$525

Patriot Bicentennial
*1976. Limited run of 1776 guitars, Legend Custom model with drum and flag decal and 1776*1976 decal on lower bout.*

1976		$700	$875

Pinnacle
1990-1992. Spruce or sycamore top, broad leaf pattern rosette, mahogany neck, piezo bridge pickup, sunburst.

1990-1992		$375	$475

Pinnacle Shallow Cutaway
1990-1994. Pinnacle with shallow bowl body and single-cut, sunburst.

1990-1994		$375	$475

Preacher 1281
1975-1982. Solidbody, mahogany body, double-cut, 2 pickups.

1975-1982		$550	$675

Preacher Deluxe 1282
1975-1982. Double-cut solidbody, 2 pickups with series/parallel pickup switch and mid-range control.

1975-1982		$500	$625

Preacher 12-String 1285
1975-1983. Double-cut solidbody, 12 strings, 2 pickups.

1975-1983		$550	$675

Thunderhead 1460
1968-1972. Double-cut, 2 pickups, gold hardware, phase switch, master volume, separate tone controls, pickup balance/blend control, vibrato.

1968-1972	Natural or rare color	$950	$1,175
1968-1972	Sunburst	$800	$975

Tornado 1260
1968-1973. Same as Thunderhead without phase switch, with chrome hardware.

1968-1973		$600	$725

UK II 1291
1980-1982. Single-cut solidbody, 2 pickups, body made of Urelite on aluminum frame, bolt-on neck, gold hardware.

1980-1982		$700	$875

Ultra GS/GP Series
1984. Korean solidbodies and necks assembled in U.S., DiMarzio pickups, offset double-cut (GS) with 1 hum, or hum/single/single or LP style (GP) with 2 humbuckers. There was also a bass.

1984		$325	$400

Ultra Series
1970s-2000s. Various Ultra model acoustic/electrics.

1970-2000s		$175	$600

Viper 1271
1975-1982. Single-cut, 2 single-coil pickups.

1975-1982		$600	$750

Viper EA 68
1994-2008. Thin acoustic/electric, single-cut mahogany body, spruce top over sound chamber with multiple upper bout soundholes, black.

1994-2008		$500	$650

MODEL YEAR	FEATURES	EXC. COND. LOW	HIGH

Viper III 1273
1975-1982. Single-cut, 3 single-coil pickups.

1975-1982		$600	$750

VXT Hybrid
2007-2009. Single-cut solidbody, 2 Seymour Duncan '59 humbuckers, Fishman Power Bridge.

2007-2009		$625	$775

Overture Guitars
2008-present. Luthier Justin Hoffman builds professional to presentation grade, custom/production, solidbody guitars and basses in Morton, Illinois.

P. W. Crump Company
1975-present. Luthier Phil Crump builds his custom flat-top guitars in Arcata, California. He also builds mandolin-family instruments.

Palen
1998-present. Premium grade, production/custom, archtop guitars built by luthier Nelson Palen in Beloit, Kansas.

Palmer
Early 1970s-present. Budget and intermediate grade, production acoustic, acoustic/electric and classical guitars imported from Europe and Asia. They also have offered electrics.

Panache
2004-2008. Budget grade, production, solidbody electric and acoustic guitars imported from China.

PANaramic
1961-1963. Guitars and basses made in Italy by the Crucianelli accordion company and imported by PANaramic accordion. They also offered amps made by Magnatone.

Acoustic-Electric Archtop
1961-1963. Full body cutaway, 2 pickups.

1961-1963		$900	$1,125

Paolo Soprani
Early 1960s. Italian plastic covered guitars with pushbutton controls made by the Polverini Brothers.

Paramount
1921-1942, Late 1940s. The William L. Lange Company began selling Paramount banjos, guitar banjos and mandolin banjos in the early 1920s, and added archtop guitars in '34. The guitars were made by Martin and possibly others. Lange went out of business by '42; Gretsch picked up the Paramount name and used it on acoustics and electrics for a time in the late '40s.

GB
1920s-1930s. Guitar banjo.

1920s		$1,225	$1,550

Style C
1930s. 16" acoustic archtop, maple back and sides.

1930s		$475	$600

MODEL YEAR	FEATURES	EXC. COND. LOW	HIGH

Style L
1930s. Made by Martin, limited to about 36 instruments, small body with resonator, Brazilian rosewood.

1930s	Spanish 6-string	$4,000	$5,000
1930s	Tenor 4-string	$3,750	$4,500

Parker
1992-present. U.S.-made and imported intermediate, professional, and premium grade, production/custom, solidbody guitars featuring a thin skin of carbon and glass fibers bonded to a wooden guitar body. In '05, they added wood body acoustic/electrics. They also build basses. Originally located northwest of Boston, Parker was founded by Ken Parker and Larry Fishman (Fishman Transducers). Korg USA committed money to get the Fly Deluxe model into production in July '93. Parker added a Custom Shop in '03 to produce special build instruments and non-core higher-end models that were no longer available as a standard product offering. In early '04, Parker was acquired by U.S. Music Corp. and moved USA production from the Boston area to Chicago.

Concert
1997 only. Solid sitka spruce top, only piezo system pickup, no magnetic pickups, transparent butterscotch.

1997		$1,150	$1,450

Fly
1993-1994. There are many Parker Fly models, the model simply called Fly is similar to the more common Fly Deluxe, except it does not have the Fishman piezo pickup system.

1993-1994		$1,150	$1,425

Fly Artist
1998-1999. Solid sitka spruce top, vibrato, Deluxe-style electronics, transparent blond finish.

1998-1999		$1,450	$1,800

Fly Classic
1996-1998, 2000-2011. One-piece Honduras mahogany body, basswood neck, electronics same as Fly Deluxe.

1996-2011		$1,350	$1,700

Fly Classic Maple
2000. Classic with maple body (vs. mahogany), transparent butterscotch.

2000		$1,250	$1,550

Fly Deluxe
1993-present. Poplar body, basswood neck, 2 pickups, Fishman bridge transducer, '93-'96 models were offered with or without vibrato, then non-vibrato discontinued. The Deluxe normally came with a gig bag, but also offered with a hardshell case, which would add about $50 to the values listed.

1993-2014		$1,150	$1,425

Fly Supreme
1996-1999. One-piece flame maple body, electronics same as the Fly Deluxe, highly flamed butterscotch, includes hard molded case.

1996-1999		$1,750	$2,200

MaxxFly PDF Series
2013-present. PDF is import line of more traditionally-shaped Maxx solidbodies, various models.

2013	PDF60	$260	$325
2013	PDF70	$325	$400
2013-2014	PDF30	$240	$300

Mojo
2003-2010. Fly either single-cut or double-cut.

2003-2005	Single-cut	$1,200	$1,500
2003-2010	Double-cut	$1,450	$1,850

NiteFly/NiteFly NFV1/NFV3/NFV5
1996-1999. Three single-coil pickup NiteFly, Fishman piezo system, bolt neck, maple body for '96-'98, ash for '99. Called the NiteFly in '96, NiteFly NFV1 ('97-'98), NiteFly NFV3 ('98), NiteFly NFV5 ('99).

1996-1999		$625	$775

NiteFly/NiteFly NFV2/NFV4/NFV6/SA
1996-2009. Two single-coil and 1 humbucker pickup NiteFly, Fishman piezo system, bolt neck, maple body for '96-'98, ash for '99-present. Called the NiteFly in '96, NiteFly NFV2 ('97-'98), NiteFly NFV4 ('98), NiteFly NFV6 ('99), NiteFly SA ('00-present).

1996-2009		$575	$725

P Series
2000-2009. Various models include P-38 (ash body, bolt maple neck, rosewood 'board, vibrato, piezo bridge pickup and active Parker Alnico humbucker and 2 single-coils, gig bag); P-40 (as P-38, but with pickups mounted on body, no 'guard); P-44 (mahogany body, flamed maple top, piezo bridge pickup and 2 special Parker humbuckers).

2000-2009		$250	$450

Tulipwood Limited Edition
1998. Limited build of 35 guitars, standard Deluxe features with tulipwood body.

1998		$1,200	$1,500

Parkwood
2007-present. Intermediate grade, acoustic and acoustic-electric guitars, Parkwood logo on headstock.

Patrick Eggle Guitars
1991-present. Founded by Patrick Eggle and others in Birmingham, England, building solid and semi-solidbody electric guitars and basses. In '95, Eggle left the company to build acoustics.

Patrick James Eggle
2001-present. Eggle co-founded the Patrick Eggle Guitar company in '91 building solidbodies. In '95, he left to do repairs and custom work. In '01 he opened a new workshop in Bedforshire, England, building professional and premium grade, production/custom, archtop and flatop guitars. For a short time he relocated to Hendersonville, North Carolina, but in '05 returned to England and opened a shop in Oswestry.

Paul Berger
1972-present. Acoustic guitars built by luthier Paul Berger in St. Augustine, Florida.

Overture Relic

2011 Parker Dragonfly
Robbie Keene

1995 PRS 10th Anniversary
My Generation Guitars

PRS Artist III
Eric Van Gansen

MODEL YEAR	FEATURES	EXC. COND. LOW	HIGH

Paul H. Jacobson

1974-present. Premium grade, production/custom, classical guitars built by luthier Paul H. Jacobson in Cleveland, Missouri.

Paul Reed Smith

1985-present. Intermediate, professional and premium grade, production/custom, solid, semi-hollow body, and acoustic guitars made in the U.S. and imported. They also build basses. Paul Reed Smith built his first guitar in '75 as an independent study project in college and refined his design over the next 10 years building custom guitars. After building two prototypes and getting several orders from East Coast guitar dealers, Smith was able to secure the support necessary to start PRS in a factory on Virginia Avenue in Annapolis, Maryland. On '95, they moved to their current location on Kent Island in Stevensville. In 2001 PRS introduced the Korean-made SE Series. Acoustics were added in '08.

10th Anniversary

1995. 200 made, mother-of-pearl inlays, abalone purfling, gold pickups, either wide-fat or wide-thin neck, 10th Anniversary logo, price includes Certificate of Authenticity.

1995	With certificate	$4,400	$5,500

305 25th Anniversary

2010. 305 made, 3 single-coilsr wide-fat or wide-thin, 25th Anniversary logo.

2010		$1,450	$1,800

513 Rosewood

Dec.2003-2006. Brazilian rosewood neck, newly developed PRS pickup system with 13 sound settings, hum-single-hum pickups.

2003-2006		$2,200	$2,700

513 Swamp Ash

2010. Figured ash, natural.

2010		$1,500	$1,875

513 25th Anniversary

2010. Carved figured maple top, 25th Anniversary shadow birds inlay.

2010		$2,250	$2,800

Al Di Meola Prism

2008-2014. Curly maple 10 top, 22-fret, prism multicolor finish.

2008-2014		$1,900	$2,400

Artist/Artist I/Artist 24

1991-1994. Carved maple top, offset double-cut, 24-fret neck, bird markers, less than 500 made. A different Custom 24 Artist package was subsequently offered in the 2000s.

1991-1994		$3,300	$4,300

Angelus Cutaway

2009-present. Flat-top, on-board electronics, European spruce top, figured mahogany back and sides, flamed maple binding.

2009-2014		$3,000	$3,800

Artist II/Artist 22

1993-1995. Curly maple top, maple purfling on rosewood 'board, inlaid maple bound headstock, abalone birds, 22 frets, gold hardware, short run of less than 500.

1993-1995		$2,200	$2,800

Artist III

1996-1997. Continuation of the 22-fret neck with some changes in materials and specs, figured maple tops, short run of less than 500 instruments.

1996-1997		$2,500	$3,200

Artist IV

1996. Continuation of the 22-fret neck with some upgrades in materials and specs, short run of less than 70 instruments.

1996		$3,500	$4,400

Artist Limited

1994-1995. Like the Artist II with 14-carat gold bird inlays, abalone purfling on neck, headstock and truss rod cover, Brazilian rosewood 'board, 165 made.

1994-1995		$3,600	$4,500

CE 22

1994-2000, 2005-2008. Double-cut carved alder body (1995), mahogany '96-'00 and '05-'07, back to alder in '08, bolt-on maple neck with rosewood 'board, dot inlays, 2 humbuckers, chrome hardware, translucent colors, options include vibrato and gold hardware and custom colors.

1994-1995	Alder	$1,150	$1,550
1996-2000	Mahogany	$1,150	$1,550
2005-2008	Reintroduced	$1,150	$1,550

CE 22 Maple Top

1994-2008. CE 22 with figured maple top, upgrade options included gold hardware, custom colors or 10 top.

1994-2008		$1,150	$1,550

CE 24 (Classic Electric, CE)

1988-2000, 2005-2008. Double-cut, alder body to '95, mahogany '96-'00 and '05-'07, back to alder in '08, carved top, 24-fret bolt-on maple neck, 2 humbuckers, dot inlays, upgrade options included gold hardware, custom colors or 10 top.

1988-1991	Rosewood 'board	$1,150	$1,550
1992-2000		$1,150	$1,550
2005-2008		$1,150	$1,550

CE 24 Maple Top (CE Maple Top)

1989-2008. CE 24 with figured maple top, upgrade options may include any or all the following: gold hardware, custom colors or 10 top.

1989-2008		$1,150	$1,550

Chris Henderson Signature

2007-2012. Single-cut, 3 exposed humbucker pickups, carved flame maple top on mahogany body, wide flat neck profile, 22 frets.

2007-2012		$1,300	$1,600

Corvette

2005-2006. Custom 22 with Velcity Yellow finish, Standard 22 red finish, Z06 inlays, Corvette logo on body.

2005	Custom 22, yellow	$1,200	$1,500
2006	Standard 22, red	$1,200	$1,500

Custom (Custom 24/PRS Custom)

1985-present. Double-cut solidbody, curly maple top, mahogany back and neck, pearl and abalone moon inlays, 24 frets, 2 humbuckers, tremolo, options include quilted or 10 Top, bird inlays, and gold hardware. 1985 Customs should be evaluated on a case by case basis.

1985	Premium top	$6,000	$10,500

MODEL YEAR	FEATURES	EXC. COND. LOW	HIGH
1985	Pre-standard, low serial	$5,000	$11,000
1985	Pre-standard, low serial, rare color	$6,000	$19,000
1985	Pre-standard, low serial, Vintage Yellow	$19,000	$28,000
1985	Pre-standard, rare color	$5,000	$11,000
1986		$4,600	$6,000
1986	Premium top	$6,000	$10,500
1987		$3,200	$4,000
1987	Premium top	$4,000	$5,000
1988		$2,800	$3,500
1988	Premium top	$3,400	$4,300
1989		$2,300	$2,900
1989	Premium top	$2,500	$3,200
1990-1992		$1,700	$2,150
1992	Premium top	$2,300	$2,900
1993-1995		$1,700	$2,150
1996-2004	Custom 24 Artist	$1,900	$2,350
1996-2014		$1,700	$2,150
2003-2014	Custom 24 Artist	$2,000	$2,500

Custom 22

1993-2009, 2013-present. Custom 22 with flamed or quilted maple top on mahogany body, 22 fret set neck, upgrade option is gold hardware, normally the quilt top is higher than flamed top.

1993-2009		$1,450	$1,800
2000-2009	Custom 22 Artist, bird markers	$1,750	$2,200

Custom 22 (Brazilian)

2003-2004. Limited run of 500 with Brazilian rosewood 'board, figured 10 top, pearl bird inlays.

2003-2004		$3,200	$4,000

Custom 22 20th Anniversary

2005. Abalone 20th Anniversary birds inlay, 20th engraved on truss rod cover.

2005		$2,100	$2,650

Custom 22 Soapbar

1998-2002. 3 Seymour Duncan soapbar single-coils.

1998-2002		$1,750	$2,200

Custom 22/12

December 2003-2009. 12-string version, flame or quilt maple top, hum/single/hum pickups.

2003-2009		$2,500	$3,100

Custom 24 (Brazilian)

2003-2004. Limited run with Brazilian rosewood 'board, figured 10 top, pearl bird inlays.

2003-2004		$3,400	$4,200

Custom 24 (Walnut)

1992. Seamless matched walnut over mahogany, 3 made.

1992		$3,000	$3,800

Custom 24 20th Anniversary

2005. Abalone 20th Anniversary birds inlay, 20th engraved on truss rod cover.

2005		$1,900	$2,400

Custom 24 25th Anniversary

2010. Carved figured maple top, 25th Anniversary shadow birds inlay.

2010		$1,900	$2,400

Dave Navarro Signature

2005-2014. Carved maple top, bird inlays, tremolo, white.

2005-2014		$1,775	$2,225

DC3

2010-2013. Double-cut contoured body, bolt-on neck, 3 special single-coils.

2010-2013		$1,225	$1,550

DGT David Grissom Tremolo

2007-present. Based on the McCarty Tremolo model with an added volume control, a nitro topcoat, vintage colors, large frets designed for .011 gauge strings.

2007-2014		$1,900	$2,350

Dragon I

1992. Fingerboard inlay of a dragon made of 201 pieces of abalone, turquoise and mother-of-pearl, gold hardware, 50 made. The Dragon model collector requires an instrument to be truly mint and pristine with no play wear. The values shown here are for pristine instruments. Any issue whatsoever may dramatically reduce the high-side price shown. Price includes the Certificate of Authenticity.

1992	Amber quilt, amber flame	$25,000	$33,000
1992	Teal black	$23,000	$31,000

Dragon II

1993. Fingerboard inlay of a dragon made of 218 pieces of gold, coral, abalone, malachite, onyx and mother-of-pearl, 100 made.

1993		$15,000	$20,000

Dragon III

1994. Fingerboard inlay of a dragon made of 438 pieces of gold, red and green abalone, mother-of-pearl, mammoth ivory, and stone, 100 made.

1994		$15,000	$20,000

Dragon 2002

2002. Limited edition of 100 guitars, ultra-inlay work depicting dragon head on the guitar body.

2002		$10,000	$13,000

Dragon 25th Anniversary

2009-2010. Multi-material dragon fingerboard inlay, green ripple abalone Modern Eagle headstock, body shape and electronics are modeled after an early company PRS guitar, 60 made.

2009-2010		$11,000	$14,000

Dragon Doubleneck

2005. Limited edition 20th Anniversary model, about 50 made.

2005		$14,000	$18,000

Dragon Millenium/Dragon 2000

1999-2000. Three-D dragon inlay in body versus neck inlay of previous models, limited production of 50 guitars.

1999-2000	Black cherry	$20,000	$25,000
1999-2000	Rare color	$22,000	$29,000

1989 PRS Custom 24
Chris Matthes

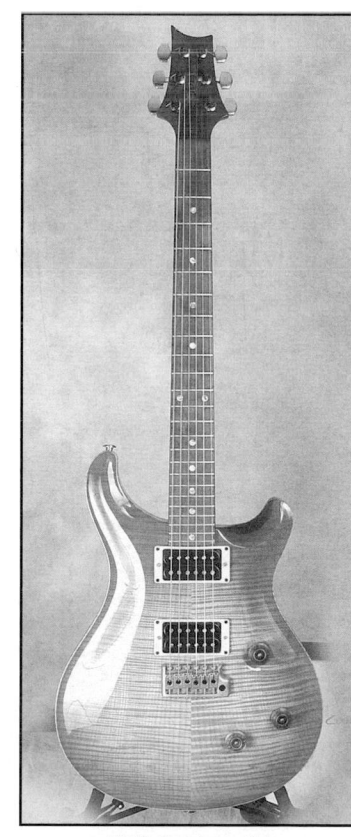

PRS Custom 24

1994 PRS McCarty Model
James Cook

PRS McCarty Archtop II
Eric Van Gansen

MODEL YEAR	FEATURES	EXC. COND. LOW	HIGH
EG II			
1991-1995. Double-cut solidbody, bolt-on neck, 3 single-coils, single-single-hum, or hum-single-hum pickup options, opaque finish.			
1991-1995		$1,000	$1,250
EG II Maple Top			
1991-1995. EG II with flamed maple top, chrome hardware.			
1991-1995		$1,275	$1,600
EG 3			
1990-1991. Double-cut solidbody, bolt-on 22-fret neck, 3 single-coil pickups.			
1990-1991	Flamed 10 top	$1,275	$1,600
1990-1991	Opaque finish	$1,000	$1,250
1990-1991	Plain top, sunburst	$1,000	$1,250
EG 4			
1990-1991. Similar to EG 3 with single-single-hum pickup configuration, opaque finish.			
1990-1991		$1,000	$1,250
Golden Eagle			
1997-1998. Very limited production, eagle head and shoulders carved into lower bouts, varied high-end appointments.			
1997-1998		$14,000	$17,500
Johnny Hiland			
2006-2007. Maple fretboard.			
2006-2007		$1,300	$1,650
KQ-24 Custom 24 (Killer Quilt)			
2009. Limited Edition of 120, quilted maple top over korina body, 24 frets.			
2009		$1,900	$2,400
Limited Edition			
1989-1991, 2000. Double-cut, semi-hollow mahogany body, figured cedar top, gold hardware, less than 300 made. In '00, single-cut, short run of 5 antique white and 5 black offered via Garrett Park Guitars.			
1989-1991	Various colors, tune-o-matic	$3,700	$4,600
2000	Various colors	$3,700	$4,600
Limited Edition Howard Leese Golden Eagle			
2009. Private Stock, curly maple top, old style mother of pearl birds, 100 made.			
2009		$4,400	$5,500
LTD Experience (Limited Experience)			
2007. 200 built to commemorate PRS 2007 Experience Open House, 24 frets, matching headstock, maple top with mahogany body.			
2007		$1,900	$2,400
Mark Tremonti Signature (U.S.A.)			
2001-present. Single-cut, contoured mahogany body, 2 humbuckers.			
2001-2014	Various options	$1,600	$2,000
2004	Tribal finish, about 60 made	$2,000	$2,500
McCarty Model			
1994-2007. Mahogany body with figured maple top, upgrade options may include a 10 top, gold hardware, bird inlays. Replaced by McCarty II.			
1994-1999		$1,500	$1,925
2000-2007	Factory trem	$1,375	$1,700

MODEL YEAR	FEATURES	EXC. COND. LOW	HIGH
McCarty II			
2008-2009. Replaced the McCarty, featured new MVC (Mastering Voice Control) circuitry for switching between a single-coil voice to a heavy-metal voice, opaque finish.			
2008-2009		$1,350	$1,700
McCarty 1957/2008 Limited			
2008. "1957/2008" logo on truss rod cover, 08 serial number series, 150 made.			
2008		$2,500	$3,100
McCarty 58/MC-58			
2009-2011. "MC-58" logo on truss rod cover, similar to other McCarty models except for new neck shape, 57/08 humbucker pickups and V12 finish.			
2009-2011		$2,600	$3,200
McCarty Archtop (Spruce)			
1998-2000. Deep mahogany body, archtop, spruce top, 22-fret set-neck.			
1998-2000		$2,100	$2,600
McCarty Archtop Artist			
1998-2002. Highest grade figured maple top and highest appointments, gold hardware.			
1998-2002		$3,600	$4,500
McCarty Archtop II (Maple)			
1998-2000. Like Archtop but with figured maple top.			
1998-2000	Flamed 10 top	$2,600	$3,200
1998-2000	Quilted 10 top	$2,600	$3,200
McCarty Hollowbody I/Hollowbody I			
1998-2009. Medium deep mahogany hollowbody, maple top, 22-fret set-neck, chrome hardware. McCarty dropped from name in '06.			
1998-2009		$2,300	$3,000
2000-2009	Baggs Piezo option	$2,300	$3,000
McCarty Hollowbody II/Hollowbody II			
1998-present. Like Hollowbody I but with figured maple top and back. McCarty dropped from name in '06.			
1998-2014		$2,300	$3,000
1998-2014	Artist package	$2,600	$3,400
McCarty Hollowbody/Hollowbody Spruce			
2000-2009. Similar to Hollowbody I with less appointmentsm spruce top. McCarty dropped from name in '06.			
2000-2009		$2,000	$2,500
McCarty Model/McCarty Brazilian			
2003-2004. Limited run of 250, Brazilian rosewood 'board, Brazilian is printed on headstock just below the PRS script logo.			
1999		$3,300	$4,200
2003-2004		$3,000	$3,800
McCarty Rosewood			
2004-2005. PRS-22 fret with Indian rosewood neck.			
2004-2005		$2,000	$2,500
McCarty Soapbar (Korina)			
2008-2009. Korina body, 2 Duncan soapbar pickups.			
2008-2009		$1,550	$1,950
McCarty Soapbar (Maple)			
1998-2007. Soapbar with figured maple top option, nickel hardware.			
1998-2007		$1,550	$1,950

MODEL YEAR	FEATURES	EXC. COND. LOW	HIGH

McCarty Soapbar/Soapbar Standard

1998-2009. Solid mahogany body, P-90-style soap-bar pickups, 22-fret set-neck, nickel-plated hardware, upgrade options may include gold hardware and bird inlays.

| 1998-2009 | | $1,350 | $1,700 |

McCarty Standard

1994-2006. McCarty Model with carved mahogany body but without maple top, nickel-plated hardware, upgrade options may include gold hardware and bird inlays.

| 1994-2006 | | $1,350 | $1,700 |

Metal

1985. Solid mahogany body with custom 2-color striped body finish and graphics, 24-fret set-neck, nickel hardware, 2 humbuckers.

| 1985 | | $6,000 | $13,000 |

Metal '85 Reissue (Private Stock)

2008. With certificate of authenticity.

| 2008 | | $4,400 | $5,500 |

Mira

2007-2013. 2 exposed-coil humbuckers, abalone moon inlays, various opaque finishes. Replaced by S2 Mira in '14.

| 2007-2013 | | $875 | $1,100 |

Mira 25th Anniversary

2010. 2 soapbar single-coils, shadow bird inlays.

| 2010 | | $1,050 | $1,300 |

Mira Korina

2007-2009. Korina body and neck version, natural.

| 2007-2009 | | $875 | $1,100 |

Mira Maple Top (MT)

2008-2009. Figured maple, moon or bird inlays.

| 2008-2009 | | $1,100 | $1,400 |

Modern Eagle

2004-2007. Higher-end model based on Private Stock innovations, satin nitrocellulose finish, Brazilian rosewood neck.

| 2004-2007 | | $3,700 | $4,600 |

Modern Eagle II/MEII

2008-2009. Curly maple top, black rosewood neck and 'board.

| 2008-2009 | | $3,100 | $3,900 |

Modern Eagle Quatro/ME Quatro

2010-2012. Updated version of Modern Eagle, 53/10 humbucker pickups, select upgraded woods.

| 2010-2012 | | $2,500 | $3,100 |

Private Stock Program

April 1996-present. Custom instruments based around existing PRS models. Values may be somewhat near regular production equivalent models or higher. The Private Stock option was reintroduced by 2003. That year a standard production offering might retail at about $7,500, but a '03 Santana I Private Stock might retail at over $15,000, so each guitar should be evaluated on a case-by-case basis.

| 1996-2014 | Higher specs | $6,000 | $8,500 |
| 1996-2014 | Normal specs | $4,000 | $6,000 |

PRS Guitar

1975-1985. About 75 to 100 guitars were built by Paul Smith himself or with a team of others, from '75 to '85, before he formed the current PRS company. Each guitar from this era should be evaluated on a case-by-case basis and the values shown are for guidance only. Authentication is highly recommended; these guitars do not have a PRS serial number. Some of these went to celebrity players and, as such, may command values higher than shown here because of that connection.

1975-1983	Mahogany	$10,000	$35,000
1975-1983	Maple	$15,000	$60,000
1984-1985	Preproduction with provenance	$8,000	$35,000
1985-1986	Team-built	$4,000	$12,000

Rosewood Limited

1996. Mahogany body with figured maple top, 1-piece rosewood neck with ultra-deluxe tree-of-life neck inlay, gold hardware.

| 1996 | | $7,400 | $9,700 |

Santana

1995-1998, 2011-present. Limited production special order, figured maple top, 24-fret, symmetric Santana headstock, unique body purfling, chrome and nickel-plated hardware, yellow is most popular color, followed by orange, quality of top will affect price.

| 1995 | 1st 100 signed | $6,500 | $8,300 |
| 1995-1998 | | $4,500 | $5,600 |

Santana II

1998-2007. Three-way toggle replaces former dual mini-switches, special order, Brazilian 'board.

| 1998-2007 | | $4,600 | $5,900 |

Santana III

2001-2006. Less ornate version of Santana II.

| 2001-2006 | | $1,750 | $2,200 |

Santana (Brazilian)

2003. Quilted maple top, Brazilian rosewood neck and fretboard, eagle inlay on headstock, Santana Brazilian logo on back cover plate, 200 made.

| 2003 | | $6,000 | $8,000 |

Santana 25th Anniversary Santana II

2010. Figured maple top, rosewood 'board, eagle inlay on headstock, 25th Anniversary shadow birds.

| 2010 | | $2,600 | $3,200 |

SC 245

2007-2010. Single-cut 22-fret, 2 humbuckers, bird markers, SC 245 logo on truss rod cover.

2007	Sunburst	$1,775	$2,200
2007-2009		$1,500	$1,900
2010	25th Anniversary	$1,775	$2,200

SC 250

2007-2010. Figured maple top, 2 humbuckers, 25" scale and locking tuners.

| 2007-2010 | | $1,500 | $1,900 |

SC-J Thinline

2008. Large full-scale single-cut hollowbody, originally part of Private Stock program until made in limited run of 300, select grade maple top and back over a mahogany middle body section, SC-J logo on truss rod cover.

| 2008 | | $4,400 | $5,500 |

SE Series

2001-present. PRS import line.

| 2001-2014 | Higher-end models | $450 | $800 |
| 2001-2014 | Most models | $250 | $450 |

2008 PRS Mira Maple Top

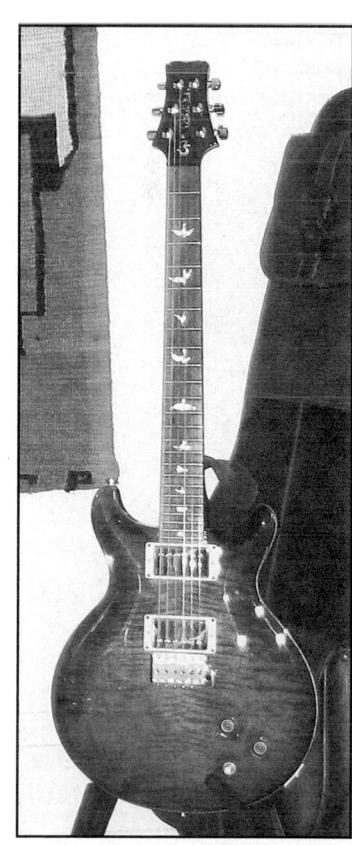

PRS Santana III

GUITARS

PRS Starla X
Luke Single

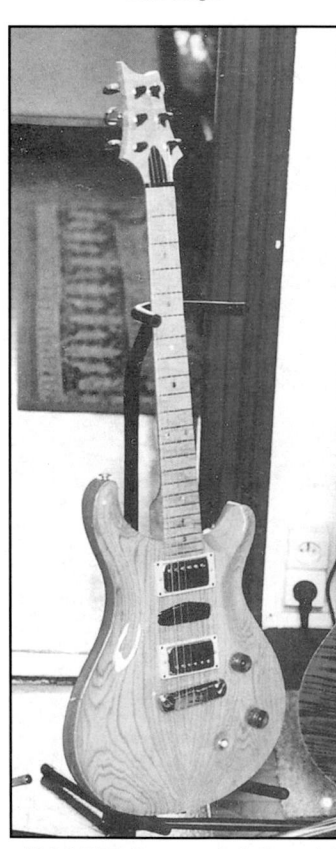

1996 PRS Swamp Ash Special
Eric Van Gansen

MODEL YEAR	FEATURES	EXC. COND. LOW	HIGH
Signature/PRS Signature			

1987-1991. 1,000 made, solid mahogany body, figured maple top, hand-signed signature on headstock, Vintage Yellow is most valuable color and will fetch more, orange is second, quilt top is more valuable than flametop. Each guitar should be evaluated on a case-by-case basis.

MODEL YEAR	FEATURES	EXC. COND. LOW	HIGH
1987		$5,500	$11,000
1988		$4,000	$8,000
1989-1991		$3,000	$6,000
Signature (Private Stock)			

2011. Limited run by Private Stock, 100 made, 408 humbucker pickups (8 tonal configurations), special signature headstock and fretboard inlays.

2011		$6,000	$7,500
Singlecut			

2000-2004, 2005-early 2008. Single-cut mahogany body, maple top, 22-fret 'board, upgrade options include 10 top flamed maple, gold hardware, bird inlays. Replaced by SC 245 and SC 250.

2000-2004	1st edition	$1,500	$1,900
2000-2004	Artist package	$1,650	$2,050
2001	Brazilian neck/'board	$2,700	$3,400
2005-2008	2nd issue	$1,500	$1,900
2005-2008	2nd issue Artist	$1,650	$2,050
2006-2007	Artist 20th Anniv., Brazilian	$2,700	$3,400
2006-2007	Standard 20th Anniv., Indian	$1,500	$1,900
2007-2008	Ltd. Ed., Indian	$1,650	$2,050
Singlecut Hollowbody II CB 25th Anniversary			

2010. Semi-hollow (CB means center block), f-holes, 10 maple top, bird inlays.

2010		$2,200	$2,750
Singlecut Hollowbody Standard			

2008-2009. Mahogany body.

2008-2009		$2,200	$2,700
Singlecut Standard Satin			

2006-2007. Thinner solid mahogany body, thin nitro cellulose finish, humbuckers or soapbars.

2006-2007		$1,275	$1,600
Special			

1987-1990, 1991-1993. Similar to Standard with upgrades, wide-thin neck, 2 HFS humbuckers. From '91-'93, a special option package was offered featuring a wide-thin neck and high output humbuckers.

1987-1990	Solid color finish	$2,400	$3,000
1991-1993	Special order only	$2,700	$3,400
Standard			

1987-1998. Set-neck, solid mahogany body, 24-fret 'board, 2 humbuckers, chrome hardware. Originally called the PRS Guitar from '85-'86 (see that listing), renamed Standard 24 from '98.

1987-1989	Sunburst & optional colors	$3,200	$6,000
1990-1991	Last Brazilian 'board	$2,500	$3,300
1992-1995		$1,300	$1,700
1995-1998	Stevensville	$1,300	$1,700

MODEL YEAR	FEATURES	EXC. COND. LOW	HIGH
Standard 22			

1994-2009. 22-fret Standard.

1994-1995		$1,300	$1,700
1995-1999	Stevensville	$1,300	$1,700
2000-2009		$1,300	$1,700
Standard 24			

1998-2009. Renamed from Standard, solid mahogany body, 24-fret set-neck.

1998-2009		$1,300	$1,700
Starla			

2008-2013. Single-cut solidbody with retro-vibe, glued neck, 2 chrome humbuckers. Replaced by S2 Starla in '14.

2008-2013		$1,300	$1,700
Studio			

1988-1991. Standard model variant, solid mahogany body, 24-fret set-neck, chrome and nickel hardware, single-single-hum pickups, special Studio package offered '91-'96.

1988-1991		$1,750	$2,200
Studio (reintroduced)			

2011-2013. Reissued with 25" scale, 22-fret, 3 pickups, flamed maple top, mahogany back and neck, rosewood 'board.

2011-2013		$1,750	$2,200
Studio Maple Top			

1990-1991. Mahogany solidbody, bird 'board inlays, 2 single-coils and 1 humbucker, tremolo, transparent finish.

1990-1991		$1,750	$2,200
Swamp Ash Special			

1996-2009. Solid swamp ash body, 22-fret bolt-on maple neck, 3 pickups, upgrade options available.

1996-2009		$1,525	$1,900
Swamp Ash Special 25th Anniversary			

2010. Swamp ash body, bolt-on neck, 25th Anniversary shadow bird inlays.

2010		$1,525	$1,900
Tonare Grand			

2009-present. Full-body flat-top, European/German spruce top, rosewood back and sides, optional Adirondack red spruce top or AAAA grade top, onboard Acoustic Pickup System.

2009-2014		$3,000	$3,700
West Street/1980 West Street Limited			

2008. 180 made for US market, 120 made for export market, faithful replica of the model made in the original West Street shop, Sapele top.

2008		$2,500	$3,100

Pawar

1999-2010. Founded by Jay Pawar, Jeff Johnston and Kevin Johnston in Willoughby Hills, Ohio, Pawar built professional and premium grade, production/custom, solidbody guitars.

PBC Guitar Technology

See Bunker Guitars for more info.

Pearl

1971-ca.1974. Acoustic and electric guitars sold by Pearl Musical Instrument Co. (Pearl drums), and built by other Japanese builders.

MODEL YEAR	FEATURES	EXC. COND. LOW	HIGH

Peavey

1965-present. Headquartered in Meridan, Mississippi, Peavey builds budget, intermediate, professional, and premium grade, production/custom, acoustic and electric guitars. They also build basses, amps, PA gear, effects and drums. Hartley Peavey's first products were guitar amps. He added guitars to the mix in '78.

Axcelerator/AX
1994-1998. Offset double-cut swamp ash or poplar body, bolt-on maple neck, dot markers, AX with locking vibrato, various colors.

1994-1998		$325	$400

Cropper Classic
1995-2005. Single-cut solidbody, 1 humbucker and 1 single coil, figured maple top over thin mahogany body, transparent Onion Green.

1995-2005		$325	$400

Defender
1994-1995. Double-cut, solid poplar body, 2 humbuckers and 1 single-coil pickup, locking Floyd Rose tremolo, metallic or pearl finish.

1994-1995		$150	$185

Destiny
1989-1992. Double-cut, mahogany body, maple top, neck-thru-bridge, maple neck, 3 integrated pickups, double locking tremolo.

1989-1992		$240	$300

Destiny Custom
1989-1992. Destiny with figured wood and higher-end appointments, various colors.

1989-1992		$340	$425

Detonator AX
1995-1998. Double-cut, maple neck, rosewood 'board, dot markers, hum/single/hum pickups, black.

1995-1998		$170	$210

EVH Wolfgang
1996-2004. Offset double-cut, arched top, bolt neck, stop tailpiece or Floyd Rose vibrato, quilted or flamed maple top upgrade option.

1996	Pat. pending early production	$2,000	$2,500
1997-1998	Pat. pending	$1,500	$1,900
1999-2004	Flamed maple top	$1,350	$1,700
1999-2004	Standard top	$800	$1,000

EVH Wolfgang Special
1997-2004. Offset double-cut lower-end Wolfgang model, various opaque finishes, flamed top optional.

1996-2004	Standard top, D-Tuna	$750	$925
1997-2004	Flamed maple top	$750	$925
1997-2004	Standard basswood finish	$600	$725

Falcon/Falcon Active/Falcon Custom
1987-1992. Double-cut, 3 pickups, passive or active electronics, Kahler locking vibrato.

1987-1992	Custom color	$300	$350
1987-1992	Standard color	$200	$250

Firenza
1994-1999. Offset double-cut, bolt-on neck, single-coil pickups.

1994-1999		$275	$325

Firenza AX
1994-1999. Upscale Firenza Impact with humbucking pickups.

1994-1999		$300	$375

Generation Custom EX
2006-2008. Single-cut solidbody, 2 humbuckers, 5-way switch.

2006-2008		$125	$175

Generation S-1/S-2/S-3
1988-1994. Single-cut, maple cap on mahogany body, bolt-on maple neck, six-on-a-side tuners, active single/hum pickups, S-2 with locking vibrato system.

1988-1994		$125	$175

Horizon/Horizon II
1983-1985. Extended pointy horns, angled lower bout, maple body, rear routing for electronics, 2 humbucking pickups. Horizon II has added blade pickup.

1983-1985		$145	$180

HP Special USA
2008-2011. Offset cutaway, 2 humbuckers.

2008-2011		$500	$625

Hydra Doubleneck
1985-1989. Available as a custom order, 6/12-string necks each with 2 humbuckers, 3-way pickup select.

1985-1989		$550	$675

Impact 1/Impact 2
1985-1987. Offset double-cut, Impact 1 has higher-end synthetic 'board, Impact 2 with conventional rosewood 'board.

1985-1987		$175	$225

Mantis
1984-1989. Hybrid X-shaped solidbody, 1 humbucking pickup, tremolo, laminated maple neck.

1984-1989		$200	$250

Milestone 12-String
1985-1986. Offset double-cut, 12 strings.

1985-1986		$125	$160

Milestone/Milestone Custom
1983-1986. Offset double-cut solidbody.

1983-1986		$100	$125

Mystic
1983-1989. Double-cut, 2 pickups, stop tailpiece initially, later Power Bend vibrato, maple body and neck.

1983-1989		$150	$225

Nitro I Active
1988-1990. Active electronics.

1988-1990		$200	$250

Nitro I/II/III
1986-1989. Offset double-cut, banana-style headstock, 1 humbucker (I), 2 humbuckers (II), or single/single/hum pickups (III).

1986-1989	Nitro I	$125	$160
1986-1989	Nitro II	$150	$200
1986-1989	Nitro III	$175	$250

Odyssey
1990-1994. Single-cut, figured carved maple top on mahogany body, humbuckers.

1990-1994		$400	$500

Odyssey 25th Anniversary
1990. Single-cut body, limited production.

1990		$525	$650

Peavey Destiny Custom

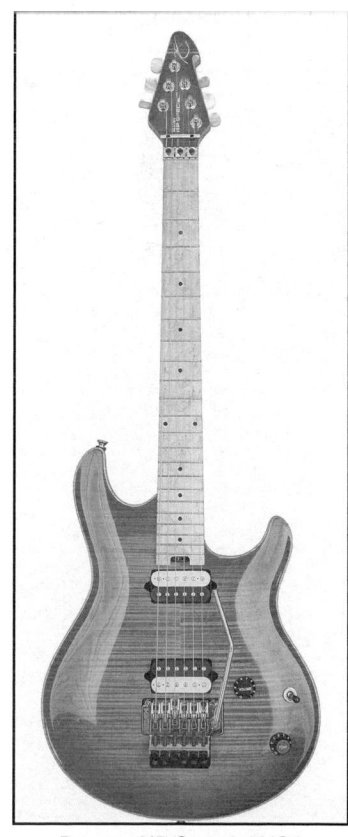

Peavey HP Special USA

1983 Peavey Patriot

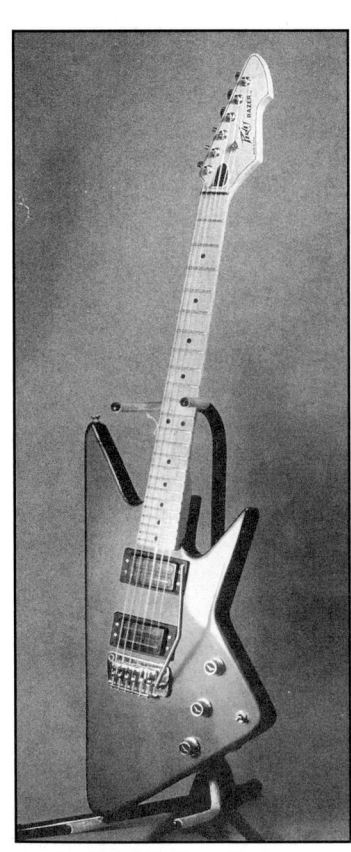

1984 Peavey Razer

MODEL YEAR	FEATURES	EXC. COND. LOW	HIGH

Omniac JD USA

2005-2010. Jerry Donahue-designed single-cut solidbody, 2 single-coils.

2005-2010		$650	$775

Patriot

1983-1987. Double-cut, single bridge humbucker.

1983-1987		$125	$155

Patriot Plus

1983-1987. Double-cut, 2 humbucker pickups, bi-laminated maple neck.

1983-1987		$175	$215

Patriot Tremolo

1986-1990. Double-cut, single bridge humbucker, tremolo, replaced the standard Patriot.

1986-1990		$175	$215

Predator Plus 7ST

2008-2010. 7-string.

2008-2010		$225	$275

Predator Series

1985-1988, 1990-present. Double-cut poplar body, 2 pickups until '87, 3 after, vibrato.

1985-1988		$100	$125
1990-2014		$100	$125

Raptor Series

1997-present. Offset double-cut solidbody, 3 pickups.

1997-2014		$60	$85

Razer

1983-1989. Double-cut with arrowhead point for lower bout, 2 pickups, 1 volume and 2 tone controls, stop tailpiece or vibrato.

1983-1989		$300	$375

Reactor

1993-1999. Classic single-cut style, 2 single-coils.

1993-1999		$260	$325

Rockmaster II Stage Pack

2000s. Student solidbody Rockmaster electric guitar and GT-5 amp pack.

2000		$40	$50

Rotor Series

2004-2010. Classic futuristic body, elongated upper treble bout/lower bass bout, 2 humbuckers.

2004-2008	Rotor EXP	$225	$280
2004-2010	Rotor EX	$195	$240

T-15

1981-1983. Offset double-cut, bolt-on neck, dual ferrite blade single-coil pickups, natural.

1981-1983		$150	$185

T-15 Amp-In-Case

1981-1983. Amplifier built into guitar case and T-15 guitar.

1981-1983		$200	$250

T-25

1979-1985. Synthetic polymer body, 2 pickups, cream 'guard, sunburst finish.

1979-1985		$275	$350

T-25 Special

1979-1985. Same as T-25, but with super high output pickups, phenolic 'board, black/white/black 'guard, ebony black finish.

1979-1985		$275	$350

T-26

1982-1986. Same as T-25, but with 3 single-coil pickups and 5-way switch.

1982-1986		$275	$350

T-27

1981-1983. Offset double-cut, bolt-on neck, dual ferrite blade single-coil pickups.

1981-1983		$300	$375

T-30

1982-1985. Short-scale, 3 single-coil pickups, 5-way select, by '83 amp-in-case available.

1982-1985	Guitar only	$250	$325
1983-1985	Amp-in-case	$325	$425

T-60

1978-1988. Contoured offset double-cut, ash body, six-in-line tuners, 2 humbuckers, thru-body strings, by '87 maple bodies, various finishes.

1978-1988		$450	$600

T-1000 LT

1992-1994. Double-cut, 2 single-coils and humbucker with coil-tap.

1992-1994		$225	$275

Tracer Custom

1989-1990. Tracer with 2 single humbuckers and extras.

1989-1990		$170	$210

Tracer/Tracer II

1987-1994. Offset scooped double-cut with extended pointy horns, poplar body, 1 pickup, Floyd Rose.

1987-1994		$170	$210

Vandenberg Quilt Top

1989-1992. Vandenberg Custom with quilted maple top, 2 humbuckers, glued-in neck, quilted maple top, mahogany body and neck.

1989-1992		$1,000	$1,250

Vandenberg Signature

1988-1992. Double-cut, reverse headstock, bolt-on neck, locking vibrato, various colors.

1988-1992		$475	$600

Vortex I/Vortex II

1986. Streamlined Mantis with 2 pickups, 3-way, Kahler locking vibrato. Vortex II has Randy Rhoads Sharkfin V.

1986		$275	$340

V-Type Series

2004-2007. Offset double-cut solidbody, pointed reverse 6-on-a-side headstock, 2 humbuckers.

2004-2007		$250	$310

Pederson Custom Guitars

2009-present. Luthier Kevin Pederson builds his premium grade, production/custom, hollowbody and solidbody guitars in Forest City, Iowa. From 1997-2009 he produced guitars under the Abyss brand name.

Pedro de Miguel

1991-present. Luthiers Pedro Pérez and Miguel Rodriguez build their professional and premium grade, custom/production, classical guitars in Madrid, Spain. They also offer factory-made instruments built to their specifications.

MODEL		EXC. COND.	
YEAR	FEATURES	LOW	HIGH

Pedulla

1975-present. Known for basses, Pedulla did offer a few solidbody guitar models into the early 1980s.

MVP

1980s. Double-cut solidbody, 2 humbuckers, dot markers, 4 knobs with main toggle and 3 mini-toggle switches, stencil Pedulla logo, MVP serial number series.

1980s		$900	$1,150

Peekamoose

1983-present. Production/custom, premium grade, solidbody, chambered, and archtop electric guitars built in New York City, New York by luthier Paul Schwartz.

Pegasus Guitars and Ukuleles

1977-present. Premium grade, custom steel-string guitars built by luthier Bob Gleason in Kurtistown, Hawaii, who also builds ukulele family instruments.

Penco

Ca. 1974-1978. Generally high quality Japanese-made copies of classic American acoustic, electric and bass guitars. Imported by Philadelphia Music Company of Limerick, Pennsylvania during the copy era. Includes dreadnought acoustics with laminated woods, bolt-neck solidbody electric guitars and basses, mandolins and banjos.

Acoustic Flat-Top

1974-1978. Various models.

1974-1978		$100	$400

Electric

1974-1978. Various copies.

1974-1978	Solidbody	$150	$400
1974-1978	Thinline Archtop	$150	$400

Penn

1950s. Archtop and acoustic guitars built by made by United Guitar Corporation in Jersey City, New Jersey, which also made Premier acoustics. Penn was located in L.A.

Pensa (Pensa-Suhr)

1982-present. Premium grade, production/custom, solidbody guitars and basses built in the U.S. Rudy Pensa, of Rudy's Music Stop, New York City, New York, started building Pensa guitars in '82. In '85 he teamed up with John Suhr to build Pensa-Suhr instruments. Name changed back to Pensa in '96.

Classic

1992-Ca. 1998. Offset double-cut, 3 single-coils, gold hardware.

1992-1998	Various models	$1,750	$2,400

MK 1 (Mark Knopfler)

1985-present. Offset double-cut solidbody, carved flamed maple bound top, 3 pickups, gold hardware, dot markers, bolt-on neck.

1985-2014		$1,750	$2,400

Suhr Custom

1985-1989. Two-piece maple body, bolt-on maple neck with rosewood 'board, custom order basis with a variety of woods and options available.

1985-1989	Various models	$1,750	$2,400

Suhr Standard

1985-1991. Double-cut, single/single/hum pickup configuration, opaque solid finish normally, dot markers.

1985-1991		$1,750	$2,200

Perlman Guitars

1976-present. Luthier Alan Perlman builds his premium grade, custom, steel-string and classical guitars in San Francisco, California.

Perri Ink.

2009-present. Custom, professional grade, solidbody electric guitars built by luthier Nick Perri in Los Angeles, California.

Perry Guitars

1982-present. Premium grade, production/custom, classical guitars built by luthier Daryl Perry in Winnipeg, Manitoba. He also builds lutes.

Petillo Masterpiece Guitars

1965-present. Intermediate, professional and premium grade, custom, steel-string, nylon-string, 12-string, resonator, archtop, and Hawaiian guitars in Ocean, New Jersey, originally by father and son luthiers Phillip J. "Doc" and David Petillo. Doc died in August, 2010.

Petros Guitars

1992-present. Premium grade, production/custom, flat-top, 12-string, and nylon-string guitars built by father and son luthiers Bruce and Matthew Petros in Kaukauna, Wisconsin.

PH Guitars

2006-present. Luthier Paul A. Hartmann builds professional and premium grade, custom, acoustic archtop and electric guitars in Hyde Park, New York.

Phantom Guitar Works

1992-present. Intermediate grade, production/custom, classic Phantom, and Teardrop shaped solid and hollowbody guitars and basses assembled in Clatskanie, Oregon. They also offer the Mando-Guitar. Phantom was established by Jack Charles, former lead guitarist of the band Quarterflash. Some earlier guitars were built overseas.

Pheo

1996-present. Luthier Phil Sylvester builds his unique premium grade, production/custom, electric and acoustic guitars in Portland, Oregon.

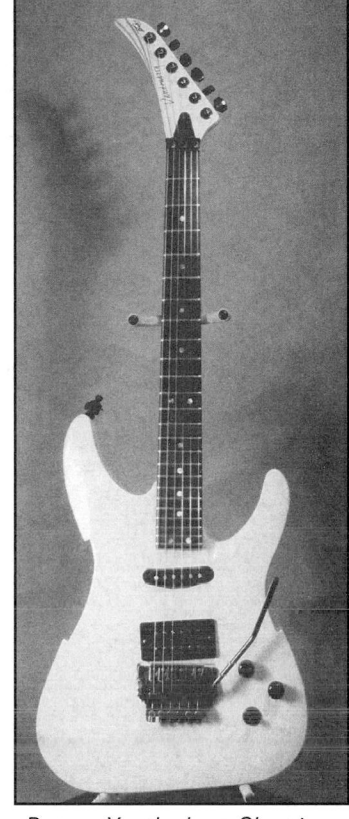

Peavey Vandenberg Signature

Pensa Custom MK 1

Pimentel and Sons Concert Custom Requinto Cutaway

Potvin Mercury

MODEL		EXC. COND.	
YEAR	FEATURES	LOW	HIGH

Phoenix Guitar Company

1994-present. Luthiers George Leach and Diana Huber build their premium grade, production/custom, archtop and classical guitars in Scottsdale, Arizona.

Pieper

Premium grade, custom, solidbody guitars and basses built by luthier Robert Pieper in New Haven, Connecticut starting in 2005.

Pignose

1972-present. The original portable amp company also offers intermediate grade, production, dreadnaught and amplified electric guitars. They also offer effects. Refer to Amps section for more company info.

Pilgrim

1970's-late-1980s, 2010-present. Built in the U.K., luthier Paul Tebbutt introduced the brand back in the '70s and his guitars were available until late '80s. His designs are now used on intermediate grade, production, electric acoustic guitars, built in the Far East and distributed by John Hornby Skewes & Co. Ltd. They also offer mandolins, ukuleles and banjos.

Pimentel and Sons

1951-present. Luthiers Lorenzo Pimentel and sons build their professional, premium and presentation grade, flat-top, jazz, cutaway electric, and classical guitars in Albuquerque, New Mexico.

Player

1984-1985. Player guitars featured interchangable pickup modules that mounted through the back of the guitar. They offered a double-cut solidbody with various options and the pickup modules were sold separately. The company was located in Scarsdale, New York.

Pleasant

Late 1940s-ca.1966. Solidbody electric guitars, obviously others, Japanese manufacturer, probably not imported into the U.S.

Electric Solidbody

1940s-1966. Various models.

1940s-1966		$130	$200

Potvin

2003-present. Production/custom, professional and premium grade, chambered, hollowbody and solidbody electric guitars built by luthier Mike Potvin in Ontario.

Prairie State

1927-ca. 1940. A Larson Brothers brand, basically a derivative of Maurer & Company. The Prairie State models were slightly more expensive than the equivalent Maurer models. They featured a

MODEL		EXC. COND.	
YEAR	FEATURES	LOW	HIGH

patented steel rod mechanism to strengthen the body, which ran from the end block to the neck block. The model usually had Brazilian rosewood back and sides, laminated necks and X-bracing. Some later models were built with figured maple.

Prairiewood

2005-present. Luthier Robert Dixon of Fargo, North Dakota builds professional grade, production/custom, hollowbody archtop and solidbody guitars.

Premier

Ca.1938-ca.1975, 1990s-2010. Brands originally offered by Premier include Premier, Multivox, Marvel, Belltone and Strad-O-Lin. Produced by Peter Sorkin Music Company in Manhattan, New York City, New York, who began in Philadelphia, relocating to NYC in '35. First radio-sized amplifiers and stick-on pickups for acoustic archtops were introduced by '38. After WWII, they set up the Multivox subsidiary to manufacture amplifiers ca. '46. First flat-top with pickup appeared in '46.

Most acoustic instruments made by United Guitar Corporation in Jersey City, New Jersey. Ca. '57 Multivox acquires Strad-O-Lin. Ca.'64-'65 their Custom line guitars are assembled with probably Italian bodies and hardware, Japanese electronics, possibly Egmond necks from Holland. By ca. '74-'75, there were a few Japanese-made guitars, then Premier brand goes into hiatus. The brand reappears on Asian-made budget and intermediate grade, production, solidbody guitars and basses beginning in the '90s.

Bantam Custom

1950s-1960s. Single-cut archtop, dots, earlier with white potted pickups, then metal-covered pickups, and finally Japanese-made pickups (least valued).

1950s-60s		$625	$775

Bantam Deluxe

1950s-1960s. Single-cut archtop, fully bound, sparkle knobs, earlier with white potted pickups, then metal-covered pickups, and finally Japanese-made pickups (least valued), block markers, 1 or 2 pickups (deduct $100 for 1 pickup).

1950s-60s	Blond	$1,250	$1,575
1950s-60s	Sunburst	$1,175	$1,475

Bantam Special

1950s-1960s. Single-cut archtop, dots, early models with white potted pickups, then metal-covered pickups, and finally Japanese-made pickups (least valued), 1 or 2 pickups (deduct $100 for 1 pickup).

1950s-60s		$625	$775

Custom Solidbody

1958-1970. Notable solidbody bass scroll cutaway, various models with various components used, finally import components only.

1958-1970	1 pickup	$425	$525
1958-1970	2 pickups	$500	$625
1958-1970	3 pickups	$650	$825

MODEL YEAR	FEATURES	EXC. COND. LOW	HIGH

Deluxe Archtop

1950s-1960s. Full body 17 1/4" archtop, square block markers, single-cut, early models with white potted pickups, later '60s models with metal pickups.

| 1950s-60s | Blond | $1,250 | $1,550 |
| 1950s-60s | Sunburst | $1,250 | $1,550 |

E-727

1958-1962. E-scroll style solidbody with scroll bass bout, 3 single-coil pickups, Premier headstock logo, made by the Multivox factory in New York.

| 1958-1962 | | $650 | $800 |

Semi-Pro 16" Archtop

1950s-early-1960s. Thinline electric 16" archtop with 2 1/4" deep body, acoustic or electric.

| 1950s-60s | Acoustic | $650 | $800 |
| 1950s-60s | Electric | $750 | $925 |

Semi-Pro Bantam Series

1960s. Thinline electric archtop with 2 3/4" deep body, offered in cutaway and non-cut models.

| 1960s | | $300 | $375 |

Special Archtop

1950s-1960s. Full body 17 1/4" archtop, less fancy than Deluxe, single-cut, early models with white potted pickups, '60s models with metal pickups.

| 1950s-60s | | $825 | $1,025 |

Studio Six Archtop

1950s-early-1960s. 16" wide archtop, single pickup, early pickups white potted, changed later to metal top.

| 1950s-60s | | $475 | $600 |

Prenkert Guitars

1980-present. Premium and presentation grade, production/custom, classical and flamenco guitars built in Sebastopol, California by luthier Richard Prenkert.

Prestige

2003-present. Intermediate, professional, and premium grade, production/custom, acoustic, solidbody and hollowbody guitars and basses from Vancouver, British Columbia.

Queen Shoals Stringed Instruments

1972-ca. 2010. Luthier Larry Cadle builds his production/custom, flat-top, 12-string, and nylon-string guitars in Clendenin, West Virginia.

Queguiner, Alain

1982-present. Custom flat-tops, 12 strings, and nylon strings built by luthier Alain Queguiner in Paris, France.

R.C. Allen

1951-2014. Luthier R. C. "Dick" Allen built professional and premium grade, custom hollowbody and semi-hollowbody guitars in El Monte, California. He has also built solidbody guitars. He passed away in '14.

Rahan

1999-present. Professional grade, production/custom, solidbody guitars built by luthiers Mike Curd and Rick Cantu in Houston, Texas.

Rahbek Guitars

2000-present. Professional and premium grade, production/custom, solidbody electrics built by luthier Peter Rahbek in Copenhagen, Denmark.

Raimundo

1970s-present. Intermediate, professional and premium grade flamenco and classical guitars made in Valencia, Spain, by luthiers Antonio Aparicio and Manual Raimundo.

RainSong

1991-present. Professional grade, production, all-graphite and graphite and wood acoustic guitars built originally in Maui, and currently in Woodinville, Washington. Developed by luthier engineer John Decker with help from luthier Lorenzo Pimentel, engineer Chris Halford, and sailboard builder George Clayton.

RAM Guitars

2007-present. Luthier Ron Mielzynski builds his professional grade, production/custom, solidbody, chambered and archtop electric guitars in Fox River Grove, Illinois.

Rambler

See Strobel Guitars listing.

Ramirez, Jose

1882-present. Professional, premium, and presentation grade, custom/production, classical guitars built in Madrid, Spain. Founded by Jose Ramirez (1858-1923) who was an apprentice at the shop of Francisco Gonzales. Jose opened his own workshop in 1882 working with his younger brother, Manuel. Manuel split with Jose and opened his own, competing workshop. Jose's business was continued by Jose's son Jose Ramirez II (1885-1957), grandson Jose III (1922-1995), and great grandchildren Jose IV (1953-2000) and Amalia Ramirez. In the 1930's a larger body instrument with improved fan bracing was developed to meet the needs for more power and volume. Other refinements were developed and the Ramirez 1A Tradicional was soon introduced which found favor with Andres Segovia. The Ramirez company has produced both student and professional instruments, but in the classical guitar field, like the old-master violin business, a student model is often a very fine instrument that is now valued at $2,000 or more. In the 1980s Ramirez offered the E Series student guitar line that was built for, but not by, Ramirez. In 1991 the company offered the even more affordable R Series which was offered for about $1,300. As is typically the case, Ramirez classical guitars do not have a name-logo on the headstock. The brand is identified by a Ramirez label on the inside back which also may have the model number listed.

Prestige NYS Deluxe MG

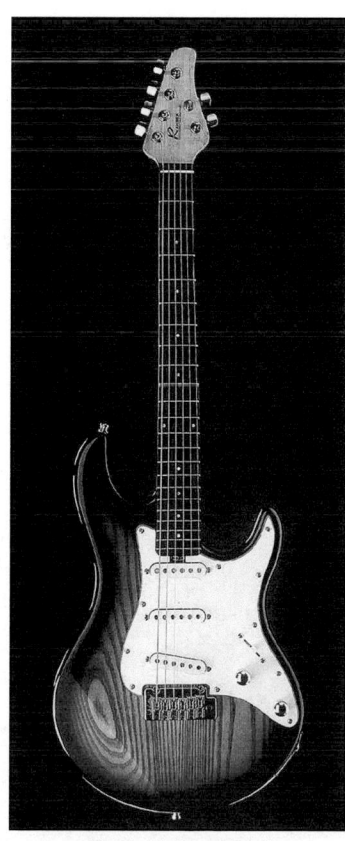

Rahbek Standard

Randy Reynolds Concert Grand

Rayco D-Model

MODEL		EXC. COND.	
YEAR	**FEATURES**	**LOW**	**HIGH**
A/1A			
1960s-2000s. Classical.			
1960s	Brazilian rosewood	$4,500	$7,000
1970-2000s	Indian rosewood	$2,000	$3,000
1970s	Brazilian rosewood	$4,000	$6,500
A/2A			
1970s-80s	Indian rosewood	$2,000	$3,000
AE Estudio			
2004		$1,750	$2,200
De Camera			
1980s. Classical, cedar top, Brazilian rosewood back and sides.			
1980s		$2,800	$3,500
E/1E/Estudio			
1988-1990s. Intermediate level.			
1988-1990s		$1,200	$1,500
E/2E			
1990s-2000s. Red cedar top, Indian rosewood back and sides, Spanish cedar neck, ebony 'board.			
1990-2000s		$1,300	$1,600
E/3E/Estudio			
1990s. Cedar, rosewood.			
1990s		$1,450	$1,850
E/4E/Estudio			
1980s-2000s. Top of the E Series line, solid red cedar top, solid Indian rosewood back and sides.			
1980-2000s		$1,900	$2,500
Flamenco			
1920s-1979. European spruce top, cyprus back and sides.			
1920s-50s		$3,800	$4,900
1960-1969		$2,800	$3,800
1970-1979		$2,700	$3,600
R1			
1991-2014. Red cedar top, mahogany sides and back, Spanish cedar neck, ebony 'board. Replaced by RA series in '14.			
1991-2014		$575	$750
R2			
1991-2014. Red cedar top, Indian rosewood back and sides, cedar neck, ebony 'board. Replaced by RA series in '14.			
1991-2014		$975	$1,350
R3			
1998. Cedar, rosewood.			
1998		$975	$1,350
R4 Classical			
1995-2014. All solid wood, Western red cedar top, rosewood back and sides. Replaced by RB series in '14.			
1995-2014		$1,100	$1,500
S/S1			
2005-2007. Solid German spruce top, African mahogany sides and back, most affordable in Estudio line.			
2005-2007		$625	$775
Segovia			
Cedar, Indian rosewood.			
1974-1978		$3,600	$4,600
SP Series			
2002-present. Semi-professional level designed to be between the company's 'concert/professional' series and 'student' series.			
2002-2014		$4,500	$5,800

MODEL		EXC. COND.	
YEAR	**FEATURES**	**LOW**	**HIGH**

Ramirez, Manuel

1890-1916. Brother of Jose Ramirez, and a respected professional classical guitar builder from Madrid, Spain. His small shop left no heirs so the business was not continued after Manuel's death in 1916. Manuel was generally considered to be more famous during his lifetime than his brother Jose, and while his business did not continue, Manuel trained many well known Spanish classical guitar luthiers who prospered with their own businesses. During Manuel's era his shop produced at least 48 different models, with prices ranging from 10 to 1,000 pesetas, therefore vintage prices can vary widely. Guitars made prior to 1912 have a label with a street address of Arlaban 10, in 1912 the shop moved to Arlaban 11.

Randy Reynolds Guitars

1996-present. Luthier Randy Reynolds builds his premium grade, production/custom classical and flamenco guitars in Colorado Springs, Colorado.

Randy Wood Guitars

1968-present. Premium grade, custom/production, archtop, flat-top, and resonator guitars built by luthier Randy Wood in Bloomingdale, Georgia. He also builds mandolins.

Rarebird Guitars

1978-present. Luthier Bruce Clay builds his professional and premium grade, production/custom, guitars and basses, originally in Arvada, Colorado, and currently in Hoehne, Colorado.

Rat Fink

2002-present. Lace Music Products, the makers of the Lace Sensor pickup, offered the intermediate grade, production, guitars and basses, featuring the artwork of Ed "Big Daddy" Roth until '05. They continue to offer amps.

Rayco

2002-present. Professional and premium grade, custom, resonator and Hawaiian-style acoustic guitars built in British Columbia, by luthiers Mark Thibeault and Jason Friesen.

Recco

1960s. Electric guitar imports made by Teisco, pricing similar to Teisco models, Recco logo on headstock, upscale solidbodies can have four pickups with several knobs and four switches.

Electric Solidbody

1960s	4 pickups	$375	$500

Recording King

1929-1943. Brand name used by Montgomery Ward for instruments made by various American manufacturers, including Kay, Gibson and Gretsch. Generally mid-grade instruments. M Series are Gibson-made archtops.

MODEL YEAR	FEATURES	EXC. COND. LOW	HIGH

Carson Robison/Model K
1933-1940. Flat-top, 14 3/4", mahogany back and sides, renamed Model K in early-'38.

1933-1940		$1,600	$2,000

Kay 17" Flat-Top
1940-1941. Large jumbo, 17" lower bout, pearloid veneer peghead, large Recording King logo.

1940-1941		$750	$925

M-2
1936-1941. Gibson-made archtop with carved top and f-holes, maple back and sides.

1936-1941		$650	$800

M-3
1936-1941. Gibson-made archtop, f-holes, maple back and sides, carved top.

1936-1941		$800	$1,000

M-4
1937-1940. Gibson-made archtop, f-holes, maple back and sides, rope-checkered binding, flying bat wing markers.

1937-1940		$1,000	$1,250

M-5
1936-1941. Gibson-made archtop with f-holes, maple back and sides, trapeze tailpiece, checkered top binding.

1936-1938	16" body	$1,300	$1,600
1939-1941	17" body	$1,400	$1,700

M-6
1938-1939. M-5 with upgraded gold hardware.

1938-1939		$1,400	$1,700

Model 1124
1937. 16" acoustic archtop, body by Gibson, attractive higher-end appointments, block-dot markers, sunburst.

1937		$1,700	$2,100

Ray Whitley
1939-1940. High-quality model made by Gibson, round shoulder flat-top, mahogany (Model 1028) or Brazilian rosewood (Model 1027) back and sides, 5-piece maple neck, Ray Whitley stencil script peghead logo, pearl crown inlay on peghead, fancy inlaid markers.

1939-1940	Brazilian	$19,200	$24,000
1939-1940	Mahogany	$9,500	$12,000

Roy Smeck
1938-1940. 16.25" electric archtop, large Recording King badge logo, Roy Smeck stencil logo, bar pickup, 2 control knobs on upper bass bout, dot markers.

1938-1940		$950	$1,200

Recording King (TML)
2005-present. Budget grade, production, acoustic cowboy stenciled guitars designed by Greg Rich for The Music Link, which also offers Johnson and other brand instruments. They also have banjos and ukes.

Redentore
2007-present. Luthier Mark Piper builds professional and premium grade, production/custom, archtop jazz, acoustic flat-top, carve-top and semi-hollow electric guitars in Columbia, Tennessee.

RedLine Acoustics and RedLine Resophonics
2007-present. Professional and premium grade, production, acoustic and resophonic guitars built in Hendersonville, Tennessee by luthiers Steve Smith, Jason Denton, Christian McAdams and Ryan Futch. They also build mandolins and plan to add lap steels.

Regal
Ca. 1895-1966, 1987-present. Intermediate and professional grade, production, acoustic and wood and metal body resonator guitars and basses. Originally a mass manufacturer founded in Indianapolis, Indiana, the Regal brand was first used by Emil Wulschner & Son. After 1900, new owners changed the company name to The Regal Manufacturing Company. The company was moved to Chicago in '08 and renamed the Regal Musical Instrument Company. Regal made brands for distributors and mass merchandisers as well as marketing its own Regal brand. Regal purchased the Lyon & Healy factory in '28. Regal was licensed to co-manufacture Dobros in '32 and became the sole manufacturer of them in '37 (see Dobro for those instruments). Most Regal instruments were beginner-grade; however, some very fancy archtops were made during the '30s. The company was purchased by Harmony in '54 and absorbed. From '59 to '66, Harmony made acoustics under the Regal name for Fender. In '87 the Regal name was revived on a line of resonator instruments by Saga.

Acoustic Hawaiian
1930s. Student model, small 13" body, square neck, glued or trapeze bridge.

1930s	Faux grain painted finish	$325	$600
1930s	Plain sunburst, birch, trapeze	$200	$375

Concert Folk H6382
1960s. Regal by Harmony, solid spruce top, mahogany back and sides, dot markers, natural.

1960s		$225	$325

Deluxe Dreadnought H6600
1960s. Regal by Harmony, solid spruce top, mahogany back and sides, bound top and back, rosewood 'board, dot markers, natural.

1960s		$225	$325

Dreadnought 12-String H1269
1960s. Regal by Harmony, solid spruce top, 12-string version of Deluxe, natural.

1960s		$225	$325

Esquire
1940s. 15 1/2" acoustic archtop, higher-end appointments, fancy logo art and script pearl Esquire headstock logo and Regal logo, natural.

1940s		$1,025	$1,275

Meteor
1960s. Single-cut acoustic-electric archtop, 2 pickups.

1960s		$800	$975

Redline Rambler Deluxe Resophonic

1939 Regal Domino Big Boy
Larry Krauss

Regal RD-40 NS

Relixx S-Series

MODEL YEAR	FEATURES	EXC. COND. LOW	HIGH

Model 27
1933-1942. Birch wood body, mahogany or maple, 2-tone walnut finish, single-bound top, round or square neck.

1933-1942		$1,000	$1,250

Model 45
1933-1937. Spruce top and mahogany back and sides, bound body, square neck.

1933-1937		$1,600	$2,000

Model 46
1933-1937. Round neck.

1933-1937		$1,600	$2,000

Model 55 Standard
1933-1934. Regal's version of Dobro Model 55 which was discontinued in '33.

1933-1934		$1,000	$1,250

Model 75
1939-1940. Metal body, square neck.

1939-1940		$1,800	$2,200

Model TG 60 Resonator Tenor
1930s. Wood body, large single cone biscuit bridge resonator, 2 upper bout metal ports, 4-string tenor.

1930s		$1,600	$2,000

Parlor
1920s. Small body, slotted headstock, birch sides and back, spruce top.

1920s		$225	$350

Prince
1930s. High-end 18" acoustic archtop, fancy appointments, Prince name inlaid in headstock along with Regal script logo and strolling guitarist art.

1930s		$1,700	$2,100

RD-40 NS
2013-present. Square neck, wood body, hand-spun aluminum cone.

2013-2014		$270	$335

RD-45
1994-2006. Standard style Dobro model with wood body, metal resonator, dual screen holes.

1994-2006		$200	$250

Spirit Of '76
1976. Red-white-blue, flat-top.

1976		$425	$525

Reliance
1920s. Instruments built by the Oscar Schmidt Co. and possibly others. Most likely a brand made for a distributor.

Relixx
2001-2013. Intermediate and professional grade, production/custom, aged vintage-style solidbody guitars built in Sanborn, New York by luthier Nick Hazlett. He discontinued complete guitars in '13 and now offers only vintage parts.

Renaissance
1978-1980. Plexiglass solidbody electric guitars and basses. Founded in Malvern, Pennsylvania, by John Marshall (designer), Phil Goldberg and Daniel Lamb. Original partners gradually leave and John

Dragonetti takes over by late-'79. The line is redesigned with passive electronics on guitars, exotic shapes, but when deal with Sunn amplifiers falls through, company closes. Brandname currently used on a line of guitars and basses made by Rick Turner in Santa Cruz, California.

Fewer than 300 of first series made, plus a few prototypes and several wooden versions; six or so prototypes of second series made. SN=M(M) YYXXXX: month, year, consecutive number.

Electric Plexiglas Solidbody
1978-1980. Models include the SPG ('78-'79, DiMarzio pickups, active electronics), T-200G ('80, Bich-style with 2 passive DiMarzio pickups), and the S-200G ('80, double-cut, 2 DiMarzio pickups, passive electronics).

1978-1980		$650	$800

Renaissance Guitars
1994-present. Professional grade, custom, semi-acoustic flat-top, nylon-string and solidbody guitars and basses built by luthier Rick Turner in Santa Cruz, California. He also builds ukes.

Republic Guitars
2006-present. Intermediate grade, production, reso-phonic and Weissenborn-style guitars imported by American Folklore, Inc. of Austin, Texas. They also offer mandolins and ukes.

Retronix
2013-present. Korean-made solidbody guitars designed and imported by J. Backlund. They also build J. Backlund guitars.

Reuter Guitars
1984-present. Professional and premium grade, custom, flat-top, 12-string, resonator, and Hawaiian guitars built by luthier John Reuter, the Director of Training at the Roberto-Venn School of Luthiery, in Tempe, Arizona.

Reverend
1996-present. Intermediate grade, production, guitars and basses from luthier Joe Naylor, designed and setup by Reverend first in Warren, and since '10 in Livonia, Michigan, and manufactured in South Korea. There were also earlier U.S. production guitars built in Warren. Reverend has built amps and effects in the past. Naylor also founded Naylor Amps, Armor Gold Cables, Stringdog, and Railhammer Pickups.

Rex
1920s-1940s, 1950s-1960s. Generally beginner-grade guitars made by Kay and sold through Fred Gretsch distributors. In the '50s and '60s, the Lamberti Brothers Company in Melbourne, Australia built electrics bearing the Rex brand that were not distributed by Gretsch. They also had built amps.

MODEL		EXC. COND.	
YEAR	FEATURES	LOW	HIGH

Ribbecke Guitars

1973-present. Premium and presentation grade, custom thinline, flat-top, and archtop guitars built by luthier Tom Ribbecke in Healdsburg, California.

Rice Custom Guitars

1998-present. Father and son luthiers, Richard Rice and Christopher Rice, build professional and premium grade, custom, solidbody, semi-hollow and hollowbody electric guitars and basses in Arlington Heights, Illinois.

Rich and Taylor

1993-1996. Custom acoustic and electric guitars, mandolins and banjos from luthiers Greg Rich and Mark Taylor (Crafters of Tennessee).

Richard Schneider

1960s-1997. Luthier Richard Schneider built his acoustic guitars in Washington state. Over the years, he collaborated with Dr. Michael A. Kasha on many guitar designs and innovations. Originally from Michigan, he also was involved in designing guitars for Gretsch and Gibson. He died in early '97.

Richmond

2008-present. Luthiers Robert Godin (Godin Guitars) and Daniel Fiocco build intermediate and professional grade, production, chambered and solidbody electric guitars in Richmond, Quebec.

Richter Mfg.

1930s. One of many Chicago makers of the era, the company allegedly bought already-made guitars from other manufacturers, painted and decorated them to their liking and resold them.

Small 13"

1930s. Typical small 13" lower bout body, slotted headstock, decalmania art over black finish, single dot markers.

1930s		$325	$400

Rick Turner

1979-1981, 1990-present. Rick Turner has a long career as a luthier, electronics designer and innovator. He also makes the Renaissance line of guitars in his shop in Santa Cruz, California. The guitars and basses built in 1979-'81 were numbered sequentially in the order they were completed and shipped with the second part of the serial number indicating the year the instrument was built. Turner estimates that approximately 200 instruments were made during that period.

Rickenbacker

1931-present. Professional and premium grade, production/custom, acoustic and electric guitars built in California. They also build basses. Founded in Los Angeles as Ro-Pat-In by ex-National executives George Beauchamp, Paul Barth and National's resonator cone supplier Adolph Rickenbacher.

Rickenbacher was born in Basel, Switzerland in 1886, emigrated to the U.S. and moved to Los Angeles in 1918, opening a tool and die business in '20. In the mid-'20s, Rickenbacher began providing resonator cones and other metal parts to George Beauchamp and Louis Dopyera of National String Instrument Corporation and became a shareholder in National. Beauchamp, Barth and Harry Watson came up with wooden "frying pan" electric Hawaiian lap steel for National in '31; National was not interested, so Beauchamp and Barth joined with Rickenbacher as Ro-Pat-In (probably for ElectRO-PATent-INstruments) to produce Electro guitars. Cast aluminum frying pans were introduced in '32. Some Spanish guitars (flat-top, F-holes) with Electro pickups were produced beginning in '32. Ro-Pat-In changes their name to Electro String Instrument Corporation in '34, and brand becomes Rickenbacher Electro, soon changed to Rickenbacker, with a "k." Beauchamp retires in '40. There was a production hiatus during World War II. In '53, Electro was purchased by Francis Cary Hall (born 1908), owner of Radio and Television Equipment Company (Radio-Tel) in Santa Ana, California (founded in '20s as Hall's Radio Service, which began distributing Fender instruments in '46). The factory was relocated to Santa Ana in '62 and the sales/distribution company's name is changed from Radio-Tel to Rickenbacker Inc. in '65.

1950s serial numbers have from 4 to 7 letters and numbers, with the number following the letter indicating the '50s year (e.g., NNL8NN would be from '58). From '61 to '86 serial numbers indicate month and year of production with initial letter A-Z for the year (A-1961, Z-1986) followed by letter for the month A-M (A=January) plus numbers as before followed by a number 0-9 for the year (0=1987; 9=1996). To avoid confusion, we have listed all instruments by model number. For example, the Combo 400 is listed as Model 400/Combo 400. OS and NS stands for Old Style and New Style. On the 360, for example, Ric changed the design in 1964 to their New Style with more rounded body horns and rounded top edges and other changes. But they still offered the Old Style with more pointed horns and top binding until the late 1960s. Ric still sometimes uses the two designations on some of their vintage reissues.

Electro ES-16

1964-1971. Double-cut, set neck, solidbody, 3/4 size, 1 pickup. The Electro line was manufactured by Rickenbacker and distributed by Radio-Tel. The Electro logo appears on the headstock.

1964-1971		$900	$1,150

Electro ES-17

1964-1975. Cutaway, set neck, solidbody, 1 pickup.

1964-1975		$1,000	$1,250

Electro Spanish (Model B Spanish)

1935-1943. Small guitar with a lap steel appearance played Spanish-style, hollow black bakelite body augmented with 5 chrome plates (white enamel in

Reverend Warhawk II HB

Rick Turner Model One

1937 Rickenbacker Electro-Spanish Ken Roberts

Ron O'Keefe

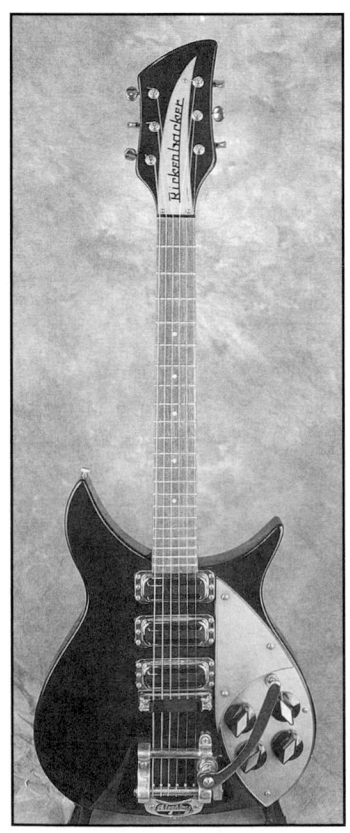

Rickenbacker Model 325V59

Ron O'Keefe

MODEL YEAR	FEATURES	EXC. COND. LOW	HIGH
'40), 1 octagon knob (2 round-ridged in '38), called the Model B ca. '40.			
1935-1937	Chrome, 1 knob	$4,500	$5,600
1935-1937	Tenor 4-string, 1 knob	$4,500	$5,600
1938-1939	Chrome, 2 knobs	$4,300	$5,400
1940-1943	White, 2 knobs	$4,100	$5,100

Electro-Spanish Ken Roberts
1935-1939. Mahogany body, f-holes in lower bout, horseshoe pickup, Kauffman vibrato.

1935-1937		$5,400	$6,800
1938-1939		$5,200	$6,600

Model 220 Hamburg
1992-1997. Solidbody.

1992-1997		$850	$1,050

Model 230 GF Glenn Frey
1992-1997. Glenn Frey Limited Edition, solidbody, 2 high output humbuckers, black hardware, chrome 'guard.

1992-1997		$1,400	$1,750

Model 230 Hamburg
1983-1991. Solidbody, offset double-cut, 2 pickups, dot inlay, rosewood 'board, chrome-plated hardware.

1983-1991		$825	$1,025

Model 250 El Dorado
1983-1991. Deluxe version of Hamburg, gold hardware, white binding.

1983-1991		$700	$875

Model 260 El Dorado
1992-1997. Replaces 250.

1992-1997		$800	$1,000

Model 310
1958-1970, 1981-1985. Two-pickup version of Model 320.

1958-1960	Capri, thick body	$10,000	$12,500
1961-1969	Thinner body	$5,700	$7,100
1981-1985	Reintroduced	$1,500	$1,900

Model 315
1958-1974. Two-pickup version of Model 325.

1958-1960	Capri, thick body	$10,000	$12,500
1960-1969	Thinner body	$5,700	$7,100
1970-1973		$3,400	$4,200
1974		$3,100	$3,800

Model 320
1958-1992. Short-scale hollowbody, 3 pickups, f-holes optional in '61 and standard in '64 and optional again in '79.

1958-1960	Capri, thick body	$12,000	$15,000
1960-1969		$8,500	$10,500
1970-1973		$3,000	$3,800
1974-1979		$2,700	$3,400
1980-1992		$1,800	$2,250

Model 320/12V63
1986. Short run for Japanese market.

1986		$2,500	$3,100

Model 325
1958-1975, 1985-1992. This was a low production model, with some years having no production. In the mid-'60s, the 325 was unofficially known as the John Lennon Model due to his guitar's high exposure on the Ed Sullivan Show and in the Saturday Evening Post.

1958	John Lennon specs, 8 made	$36,000	$45,000

MODEL YEAR	FEATURES	EXC. COND. LOW	HIGH
1959-1960		$18,000	$23,000
1961-1963		$15,000	$19,000
1964-1966	Fireglo or black	$8,900	$11,200
1966	Mapleglo	$8,900	$11,200
1967-1969		$8,900	$11,200
1970-1975		$3,300	$4,100

Model 325 B
1983-1984. Reissue of early '60s model.

1983-1984		$1,900	$2,400

Model 325 JL
1989-1993. John Lennon Limited Edition, 3 vintage Ric pickups, vintage vibrato, maple body; 3/4-size rosewood neck, a 12-string and a full-scale version are also available.

1989-1993		$2,350	$3,000

Model 325 S
1964-1967. F-holes.

1964-1967		$8,900	$11,200

Model 325/12
1984-1985, 1999. Based on John Lennon's one-of-a-kind '64 325/12.

1985-1986		$2,400	$3,000
1999		$2,400	$3,000

Model 325C58
2002-2014. Copy of the '58 model that John Lennon saw in Germany.

2002-2004		$2,950	$3,700
2005-2014	Hamburg	$2,950	$3,700

Model 325C64
2002-present. Copy of the famous '64 model.

2002-2014		$2,450	$3,100

Model 325V59
1984-2001. Reissue of John Lennon's modified '59 325, 3 pickups, short-scale.

1984-2001		$2,750	$3,450

Model 325V63
1984-2001. Reissue of John Lennon's '63 325.

1987-2001		$2,350	$2,950

Model 330
1958-present. Thinline hollowbody, 2 pickups, slash soundhole, natural or sunburst.

1958-1960	Capri, thick body	$8,500	$10,500
1961-1969	Thinner body	$3,900	$4,900
1970-1973		$3,300	$4,200
1974-1979		$3,100	$3,900
1980-1999		$1,550	$1,950
2000-2014		$1,275	$1,600

Model 330 F
1958-1969. F-style.

1958-1960	Thick version	$8,500	$10,500
1961-1969	Thin version	$4,000	$5,000

Model 330/12
1965-present. Thinline, 2 pickups, 12-string version of Model 300.

1964	Only 1 made	$4,000	$5,000
1965-1969	330-style body	$4,000	$5,000
1970-1979		$3,200	$4,000
1980-1989		$1,700	$2,100
1990-1999		$1,350	$1,700
2000-2014		$1,300	$1,625

MODEL YEAR	FEATURES	EXC. COND. LOW	HIGH
Model 330S/12			
1964 (1 made)-1965 (2 made).			
1964-1965		$4,100	$5,100
Model 331 Light Show			

1970-1975. Model 330 with translucent top with lights in body that lit up when played, needed external transformer. The first offering's design, noted as Type 1, had heat problems and a fully original one is difficult to find. The 2nd offering's design, noted as Type 2, was a more stable design and is more highly valued in the market.

1970-1971	Type 1 1st edition	$10,000	$12,500
1972-1975	Type 2 2nd edition	$11,000	$13,800
Model 335			

1961-1977. Thinline, 330-style body, 2 pickups, vibrato, Fireglo. Called the 330VB from '85-'97.

1958-1960	Capri, thick body	$8,500	$10,500
1961-1969	Thinner body	$4,000	$5,000
1970-1973		$3,500	$4,300
1974-1977		$3,200	$4,000
Model 335 F			

1958-1969. F-style.

1958-1961	Thick version	$8,500	$10,500
1961-1969	Thin version	$4,000	$5,000
Model 336/12			

1966-1974. Like 300-12, but with 6-12 converter comb, 330-style body.

1966-1969		$4,000	$5,000
1970-1974		$3,200	$4,000
Model 340			

1958-2014. Thin semi-hollowbody, thru-body maple neck, 2 single-coil pickups, sharp point horns, very limited production '58-'65, with first notable volume of 45 units starting in '66.

1958-1960	Capri, thick body	$8,500	$10,500
1961-1969	Thinner body	$3,800	$4,700
1970-1973		$3,500	$4,300
1974-1979		$3,200	$4,000
1980-1999		$1,700	$2,100
2000-2014		$1,450	$1,800
Model 340 F			

1958-1969. F-style.

1958-1960	Thick version	$8,500	$10,500
1961-1969	Thin version	$3,800	$4,700
Model 340/12			

1980-2014. 12-string version, 330-style body.

1980-1999		$1,800	$2,250
2000-2014		$1,800	$2,250
Model 345			

1961-1974. Thinline 330-345 series, version with 3 pickups and vibrato tailpiece.

1958-1960	Capri, thick body	$8,500	$10,500
1961-1969	Thinner body	$3,800	$4,700
1970-1973		$3,500	$4,400
1974		$3,200	$4,000
Model 345 F			

1958-1969. F-style.

1958-1960	Thick version	$8,500	$10,500
1961-1969	Thin version	$3,800	$4,700
Model 345 Reissue			

2002. Low production, 3 pickups.

2002		$2,000	$2,500

MODEL YEAR	FEATURES	EXC. COND. LOW	HIGH
Model 350 Liverpool			
1983-1997. Thinline, 3 pickups, vibrato, no soundhole.			
1983-1997		$2,200	$2,800
Model 350 SH			
1988-1990. Susanna Hoffs Limited Edition.			
1988-1990		$3,400	$4,200
Model 350/12V63 Liverpool			
1994-2014. Vintage Series, 12-string 350V63.			
1994-2014		$2,100	$2,600
Model 350V59			
1988. Very low production.			
1988		$1,800	$2,250
Model 350V63 Liverpool			
1994-present. Vintage Series, like 355 JL, but without signature.			
1994-2014		$1,900	$2,400
Model 355 JL			
1989-1993. John Lennon model, signature and drawing on 'guard.			
1989-1993		$2,700	$3,400
Model 355/12 JL			
1989-1993. 12-string 355 JL, limited production.			
1989-1993		$2,700	$3,400
Model 360/360 VB			

1958-1991, 2000-present. Deluxe thinline, 2 pickups, slash soundhole, bound body until '64.

1958-1960	Capri, thick body	$8,500	$10,500
1961-1969		$3,300	$4,200
1970-1973	360, no vibrato	$3,300	$4,200
1974-1979	360 VB, vibrato	$3,100	$3,900
1980-1999	360 VB, vibrato	$1,650	$2,100
2000-2014		$1,650	$2,100
Model 360V64			

1991-2003. Reissue of '64 Model 360 old style body without vibrola, has binding with full length inlays.

1991-1999		$2,500	$3,100
2000-2003		$2,300	$2,900
Model 360 CW			

2000. Carl Wilson Limited Edition, 6-string, includes certificate, 500 made.

2000		$2,700	$3,400
Model 360 DCM 75th Anniversary			

2006. 360 with 75th Anniversary dark cherry metallic finish, 75 made.

2006		$2,400	$3,000
Model 360 F			

1959-1972. F-style.

1959-1960	Thick version	$6,800	$8,400
1961-1969	Thin version	$3,700	$4,600
1970-1972	Thin version	$3,100	$3,900
Model 360 SF			

1968-ca. 1972. Slanted frets (SF), standard on some models, an option on others.

1968-1972		$4,200	$5,300
Model 360 Tuxedo			

1987 only. Tuxedo option included white body, white painted fretboard, and black hardware.

1987		$2,000	$2,500

Rickenbacker 350V63
Ron O'Keefe

2007 Rickenbacker Model 360
Ron O'Keefe

GUITARS

1981 Rickenbacker Model 360 WB

Ron O'Keefe

1968 Rickenbacker Model 375

Ron O'Keefe

MODEL YEAR	FEATURES	EXC. COND. LOW	HIGH
Model 360 WB			
1984-1998. Double bound body, 2 pickups, vibrato optional (VB).			
1984-1990		$2,200	$2,700
1991-1998	WB, no vibrato	$2,000	$2,500
1991-1998	WBVB, vibrato	$2,000	$2,500
Model 360/12			
1964-present. Deluxe thinline, 2 pickups, 12-string version of Model 360, Rick-O-Sound stereo.			
1964-1969		$4,500	$5,600
1966	Harrison specs	$9,500	$12,000
1970-1973		$4,000	$5,000
1974-1979		$3,100	$3,900
1980-1999		$1,750	$2,150
2000-2014		$1,700	$2,100
Model 360/12 CW			
2000. Carl Wilson, 12-string version of 360 CW.			
2000		$2,700	$3,400
Model 360/12 Tuxedo			
1987 only. 12-string version of 360 Tuxedo.			
1987		$2,200	$2,700
Model 360/12 VP			
2004. VP is vintage pickup.			
2004		$2,000	$2,500
Model 360/12 WB			
1984-1998. 12-string version of 360 WB.			
1984-1998		$2,200	$2,700
Model 360/12C63			
2004-present. More exact replica of the Harrison model.			
2004-2014		$2,600	$3,200
Model 360/12V64			
1985-2003. Deluxe thinline with '64 features, 2 pickups, 12 strings, slanted plate tailpiece.			
1985-1999		$2,400	$3,000
2000-2003		$2,300	$2,900
Model 362/12			
1975-1992. Doubleneck 6 & 12, 360 features.			
1975-1992		$2,300	$2,900
Model 365			
1958-1974. Deluxe thinline, 2 pickups, vibrato, called Model 360 WBVB from '84-'98.			
1958-1960	Capri, thick body	$8,500	$10,500
1961-1969		$4,000	$5,000
1970-1973		$3,500	$4,300
1974		$3,200	$4,000
Model 365 F			
1959-1972. Thin full-body (F designation), 2 pickups, Deluxe features.			
1959-1960	Thick version	$8,500	$10,500
1961-1969	Thin version	$4,000	$5,000
1970-1972		$3,500	$4,400
Model 366/12 Convertible			
1966-1974. Two pickups, 12 strings, comb-like device that converts it to a 6-string, production only noted in '68, perhaps available on custom order basis.			
1966-1968	OS	$3,800	$4,700
Model 370			
1958-1990, 1994-2007. Deluxe thinline, 3 pickups. Could be considered to be a dealer special order item from '58-'67 with limited production.			
1958-1960	Capri, thick body	$8,500	$10,500

MODEL YEAR	FEATURES	EXC. COND. LOW	HIGH
1961-1969	Thin version	$4,000	$5,000
1970-1973		$3,500	$4,300
1974-1979		$3,200	$4,000
1980-1999		$1,775	$2,200
2000-2007		$1,775	$2,200
Model 370 F			
1959-1972. F-style, 3 pickups, Deluxe features.			
1959-1961	Thick version	$8,500	$10,500
1961-1969	Thin version	$4,000	$5,000
1970-1972		$3,500	$4,300
Model 370 VP			
2006-2007. Limited run with special specs including vintage toaster pickups (VP).			
2006-2007		$2,800	$3,500
Model 370 WB			
1984-1998. Double bound body, 3 pickups, vibrato optional (VB).			
1984-1998		$1,800	$2,250
Model 370/12			
1966-1990, 1994-present. Not regular production until '80, deluxe thinline, 3 pickups, 12 strings. Could be considered to be a dealer special order item in the '60s and '70s with limited production.			
1966		$10,500	$13,000
1967-1999		$1,775	$2,200
2000-2014		$1,775	$2,200
Model 370/12 RM			
1988. Limited Edition Roger McGuinn model, 1000 made, higher-quality appointments.			
1988-1989		$4,500	$5,600
Model 375			
1958-1974. Deluxe thinline, 3 pickups, vibrato, called Model 370 WBVB from '84-'98.			
1958-1960	Capri, thick body	$8,500	$10,500
1961-1969	Thin version	$4,000	$5,000
1970-1973		$3,500	$4,300
1974		$3,200	$4,000
Model 375 F			
1959-1972. F-style, 2 pickups.			
1959-1960	Thick version	$6,800	$8,300
1961-1969	Thin version	$3,900	$4,800
1970-1972		$3,400	$4,200
Model 380 L Laguna			
1996-2005. Semi-hollow, oil-finished walnut body, Maple neck and 'board, 2 humbuckers, PZ saddle pickups optional.			
1996-2005		$1,900	$2,400
1996-2005	PZ option	$1,900	$2,400
Model 381			
1958-1963, 1969-1974. Double-cut archtop, 2 pickups, slash soundhole, solid 'guard, reintroduced in '69 with double split-level 'guard.			
1958-1963	Low production	$8,500	$10,500
1969-1974	Various colors, some rare	$3,300	$4,500
Model 381 JK			
1988-1997. John Kay Limited Edition model, 2 humbucking pickups, active electronics, stereo and mono outputs.			
1988-1997		$2,600	$3,200

MODEL YEAR	FEATURES	EXC. COND. LOW	HIGH

Model 381/12V69

1987-present. Reissue of 381/12, deep double-cut body, sound body cavity, catseye soundhole, triangle inlays, bridge with 12 individual saddles. Finishes include Fireglo, Mapleglo and Jetglo.

1987-1999	Figured top	$3,000	$3,700
2000-2014	Figured top	$3,000	$3,700

Model 381V69

1991-present. Reissue of vintage 381.

1987-1999		$2,900	$3,600
2000-2014		$2,900	$3,600

Model 382

1958-1963, 1969-1974. 381 with vibrato unit. Very light production.

1958-1963	Low production	$8,500	$10,500
1969-1974	Various colors, some rare	$3,200	$4,300

Model 383

1958-1963, 1969-1974. 381 with 3 pickups. Very light production.

1958-1963	Low production	$8,500	$10,500
1969-1974	Various colors, some rare	$3,200	$4,300

Model 384

1958-1963, 1969-1974. 381 with 3 pickups and vibrato unit. Very light production.

1958-1963	Low production	$8,500	$10,500
1969-1974	Various colors, some rare	$3,200	$4,300

Model 400/Combo 400

1956-1958. Double-cut tulip body, neck-thru, 1 pickup, gold anodized 'guard, 21 frets, replaced by Model 425 in '58. Available in black (216 made), blue turquoise (53), Cloverfield Green (53), Montezuma Brown (41), and 4 in other custom colors.

1956-1958	.	$2,700	$3,400

Model 420

1965-1983. Non-vibrato version of Model 425, single pickup.

1965-1968		$1,200	$1,500
1969-1983		$1,100	$1,350

Model 425/Combo 425

1958-1973. Double-cut solidbody, 1 pickup, sunburst.

1958-1959	425 Cresting Wave	$2,700	$3,350
1960		$2,000	$2,500
1961-1964		$1,900	$2,400
1965-1968		$1,400	$1,750
1969-1973		$1,300	$1,600

Model 425/12V63

1999-2000. 136 made.

1999-2000		$1,400	$1,750

Model 425V63

1999-2000. Beatles associated model, 145 JG black made, 116 BG burgundy transparent made, originally custom ordered by Rickenbacker collectors and they were not part of Rickenbacker's sales literature in the late '90s.

1999-2000		$1,400	$1,750

Model 430

1971-1982. Style 200 body, natural.

1971-1982		$750	$950

Model 450/Combo 450

1957-1984. Replaces Combo 450, 2 pickups (3 optional '62-'77), tulip body shape '57-'59, cresting wave body shape after.

1957-1958	450 Tulip body (Combo)	$3,200	$4,000
1958-1959	450 Cresting Wave	$2,800	$3,500
1960	Cresting Wave, flat body	$2,100	$2,600
1961-1966	Cresting Wave, super slim	$2,000	$2,500
1970-1979	Includes rare color	$1,600	$2,000
1980-1984		$1,200	$1,500

Model 450/12

1964-1985. Double-cut solidbody, 12-string version of Model 450, 2 pickups.

1964-1966		$2,000	$2,500
1967-1969		$1,800	$2,200
1970-1979	Includes rare color	$1,600	$2,000
1980-1985		$1,200	$1,500

Model 450V63

1999-2001. Reissue of '63 450.

1999-2001		$1,300	$1,600

Model 456/12 Convertible

1968-1978. Double-cut solidbody, 2 pickups, comb-like device to convert it to 6-string.

1968-1969		$2,500	$3,100
1970-1978		$2,000	$2,500

Model 460

1961-1985. Double-cut solidbody, 2 pickups, neck-thru-body, deluxe trim.

1961-1965		$2,500	$3,100
1966-1969		$2,200	$2,300
1970-1979	Includes rare color	$2,000	$2,500
1980-1985		$1,400	$1,750

Model 480

1973-1984. Double-cut solidbody with long thin bass horn in 4001 bass series style, 2 pickups, cresting wave body and headstock, bolt-on neck.

1973-1979		$2,400	$3,000
1980-1984		$2,100	$2,600

Model 481

1973-1983. Cresting wave body with longer bass horn, 2 humbuckers (3 optional), angled frets.

1973-1979		$2,600	$3,200
1980-1983		$2,100	$2,600

Model 483

1973-1983. Cresting wave body with longer bass horn, 3 humbuckers.

1973-1979		$2,700	$3,350
1980-1983		$2,200	$2,750

Model 600/Combo 600

1954-1958. Modified double-cut, horseshoe pickup.

1954-1957	Blond/white	$3,800	$4,800
1956-1958	OT/Blue Turquoise	$3,800	$4,800

Model 610

1985-1991. Cresting-wave cutaway solidbody, 2 pickups, trapeze R-tailpiece, Jetglo.

1985-1991		$900	$1,125

Model 610/12

1988-1997. 12-string version of Model 610.

1988-1997		$900	$1,125

1968 Rickenbacker 456/12
Ron O'Keefe

Rickenbacker 610

GUITARS

Rickenbacker Model 620-12
Ron O'Keefe

Rickenbacker 1997 RM Reissue
Art Vogue

MODEL YEAR	FEATURES	EXC. COND. LOW	HIGH
Model 615			
1962-1966, 1969-1977. Double-cut solidbody, 2 pickups, vibrato.			
1962-1965		$2,000	$2,500
1966-1969		$1,800	$2,200
1970-1977		$1,600	$2,000
Model 620			
1974-present. Double-cut solidbody, deluxe binding, 2 pickups, neck-thru-body.			
1974-1979		$1,700	$2,100
1980-1989		$1,300	$1,600
1990-1999		$1,175	$1,475
2000-2014		$1,175	$1,475
Model 620/12			
1981-present. Double-cut solidbody, 2 pickups, 12 strings, standard trim.			
1981-1989		$1,400	$1,750
1990-2014		$1,300	$1,600
Model 625			
1962-1977. Double-cut solidbody, deluxe trim, 2 pickups, vibrato.			
1962-1965		$4,000	$5,000
1966-1969		$2,800	$3,500
1970-1977		$2,200	$2,700
Model 650/Combo 650			
1957-1959. Standard color, 1 pickup.			
1957-1959		$3,800	$4,800
Model 650 A Atlantis			
1992-2003. Double cut cresting wave solidbody, maple body wings, neck-thru, 2 pickups, chrome hardware, turquoise.			
1992-2003		$1,000	$1,250
Model 650 C Colorado			
1993-present. Like Atlantis but with balck finish.			
1993-2014		$1,000	$1,250
Model 650 D Dakota			
1993-2013. Like Atlantis but with walnut body wings and oil-satin finish.			
1993-2013		$1,000	$1,250
Model 650 E Excalibur/F Frisco			
1991-2003. Like Atlantis but with brown vermilion body wings and gold hardware. Name changed to Frisco in '95.			
1991-2003		$1,000	$1,250
Model 650 S Sierra			
1993-2013. Like Dakota but with gold hardware.			
1993-2013		$1,000	$1,250
Model 660			
1998-present. Cresting wave maple body, triangle inlays, 2 pickups.			
1998-2014		$1,600	$2,000
Model 660 DCM 75th Anniversary			
2006-2007. 75th 1931-2006 Anniversary pickguard logo.			
2006-2007		$2,100	$2,600
Model 660/12			
1998-present. 12-string 660.			
1998-2014	Fireglo, common color	$1,775	$2,200
1998-2014	Rare color	$2,200	$3,000

MODEL YEAR	FEATURES	EXC. COND. LOW	HIGH
Model 660/12 TP			
1991-1998. Tom Petty model, 12 strings, cresting wave body, 2 pickups, deluxe trim, limited run of 1000.			
1991-1998	With certificate	$3,100	$3,800
Model 800/Combo 800			
1954-1959. Offset double-cut, 1 horseshoe pickup until late-'57, second bar type after.			
1954-1957	Blond/white, 1 pickup	$5,000	$6,200
1954-1957	Blue or green, 1 pickup	$5,000	$6,200
1956-1957	Blue or green, 2 pickups	$5,000	$6,200
1957-1959	Blond/white, 2 pickups	$5,000	$6,200
Model 850/Combo 850			
1957-1959. Extreme double-cut, 1 pickup until '58, 2 after, various colors, called Model 850 in the '60s.			
1957-1959	Various colors	$5,000	$6,200
Model 900			
1957-1980. Double-cut tulip body shape, 3/4 size, 1 pickup. Body changes to cresting wave shape in '69.			
1957-1966		$1,500	$1,900
Model 950/Combo 950			
1957-1980. Like Model 900, but with 2 pickups, 21 frets. Body changes to cresting wave shape in '69.			
1957-1964		$1,800	$2,250
1965-1980		$1,700	$2,100
Model 1000			
1957-1970. Like Model 900, but with 18 frets. Body does not change to cresting wave shape.			
1956-1966		$1,400	$1,750
1967-1970		$1,300	$1,600
Model 1993/12 RM			
1964-1967. Export 'slim-line' 12-string model made for English distributor Rose-Morris of London, built along the lines of the U.S. Model 360/12 but with small differences that are considered important in the vintage guitar market.			
1964	Flat tailpiece	$5,000	$6,200
1965-1967	R tailpiece	$5,000	$6,200
Model 1996 RM			
1964-1967. Rose-Morris import, 3/4 size built similiarly to the U.S. Model 325.			
1964-1967		$9,000	$11,200
Model 1996 RM Reissue			
2006. Reissue of the Rose-Morris version of Model 325, this reissue available on special order in 2006.			
2006		$2,700	$3,400
Model 1997 PT			
1987-1988. Pete Townshend Signature Model, semi-hollowbody, single f-hole, maple neck, 21-fret rosewood 'board, 3 pickups, Firemist finish, limited to 250 total production.			
1987-1988		$3,100	$3,800
Model 1997 RM			
1964-1967. Export 'slim-line' model made for English distributor Rose-Morris of London, built along the lines of the U.S. Model 335, but with small differences that are considered important in the vintage guitar market, 2 pickups, vibrola tailpiece. Rose-Morris			

MODEL YEAR	FEATURES	EXC. COND. LOW	HIGH

export models sent to the USA generally had a red-lined guitar case vs. the USA domestic blue-lined guitar case.

| 1964-1967 | | $4,000 | $5,000 |

Model 1997 RM Reissue

1987-1995. Reissue of '60s Rose-Morris model, but with vibrola (VB) or without.

| 1987-1995 | | $1,800 | $2,250 |

Model 1997 SPC

1993-2002. 3 pickup version of reissue.

| 1993-2002 | | $1,600 | $2,000 |

Model 1998 RM

1964-1967. Export 'slim-line' model made for English distributor Rose-Morris of London, built along the lines of a U.S. Model 345 but with small differences that are considered important in the vintage guitar market, 3 pickups, vibrola tailpiece.

| 1964-1967 | | $4,000 | $5,000 |

Rickenbacker Spanish/Spanish/SP

1946-1949. Block markers.

| 1946-1949 | | $1,900 | $2,400 |

S-59

1940-1942. Arch top body built by Kay, horseshoe magnet pickup.

| 1940-1942 | | $1,800 | $2,300 |

Rigaud Guitars

1978-present. Luthier Robert Rigaud builds his premium grade, custom, parlor to jumbo acoustic guitars in Greensboro, North Carolina. He also builds ukuleles under the New Moon brand.

Ritz

1989. Solidbody electric guitars and basses produced in Calimesa, California, by Wayne Charvel, Eric Galletta and Brad Becnel, many of which featured cracked shell mosiac finishes.

RKS

Professional and premium grade, production/custom, electric hollowbody and solidbody guitars and basses designed by Ravi Sawhney and guitarist Dave Mason and built in Thousand Oaks, California.

Robert Cefalu

1998-present. Luthier Robert Cefalu builds his professional grade, production/custom, acoustic guitars in Buffalo, New York. The guitars have an RC on the headstock.

Robert Guitars

1981-present. Luthier Mikhail Robert builds his premium grade, production/custom, classical guitars in Summerland, British Columbia.

Robertson Guitars

1995-present. Luthier Jeff Robertson builds his premium grade, production/custom flat-top guitars in South New Berlin, New York.

Robin

1982-2010. Professional and premium grade, production/custom, guitars from luthier David Wintz and built in Houston, Texas. Most guitars were Japanese-made until '87; American production began in '88. Most Japanese Robins were pretty consistent in features, but the American ones were often custom-made, so many variations in models exist. They also made Metropolitan ('96-'08) and Alamo ('00-'08) brand guitars.

Avalon Classic

1994-2010. Single-cut, figured maple top, 2 humbuckers.

| 1994-2010 | | $1,125 | $1,400 |

Medley Pro

1990s. Solidbody with 2 extreme cutaway horns, hum-single-single.

| 1990s | U.S.-made | $650 | $800 |

Medley Special

1992-1995. Ash body, maple neck, rosewood 'board, 24 frets, various pickup options.

| 1992-1995 | | $480 | $600 |

Medley Standard

1985-2010. Offset double-cut swamp ash solidbody, bolt neck, originally with hum-single-single pickups, but now also available with 2 humbuckers.

| 1985-1987 | Japan-made | $400 | $500 |
| 1988-2010 | U.S.-made | $650 | $800 |

Octave

1982-1990s. Tuned an octave above standard tuning, full body size with 15 1/2" short scale bolt maple neck. Japanese-made production model until '87, U.S.-made custom shop after.

| 1990s | With original case | $650 | $800 |

Raider I/Raider II/Raider III

1985-1991. Double-cut solidbody, 1 humbucker pickup (Raider I), 2 humbuckers (Raider II), or 3 single-coils (Raider III), maple neck, either maple or rosewood 'board, sunburst.

1985-1991	1 pickup	$400	$500
1985-1991	2 pickups	$425	$525
1985-1991	3 pickups	$450	$560

Ranger

1982. First production model with 2 single-coil pickups in middle and neck position, reverse headstock, dot markers.

| 1982 | | $650 | $800 |

Ranger Custom

1982-1986, 1988-2010. Swamp ash bound body, bolt-on maple neck, rosewood or maple 'board, 2 single coils and 1 humbucker, orange, made in Japan until '86, U.S.-made after.

| 1982-1986 | Japan-made | $400 | $500 |
| 1988-2010 | U.S.-made | $650 | $800 |

RDN-Doubleneck Octave/Six

1982-1985. Six-string standard neck with 3 pickups, 6-string octave neck with 1 pickup, double-cut solidbody.

| 1982-1985 | With original case | $775 | $950 |

Savoy Deluxe/Standard

1995-2010. Semi-hollow thinline single cut archtop, 2 pickups, set neck.

| 1996-2010 | | $1,350 | $1,675 |

Rigaud Acoustic

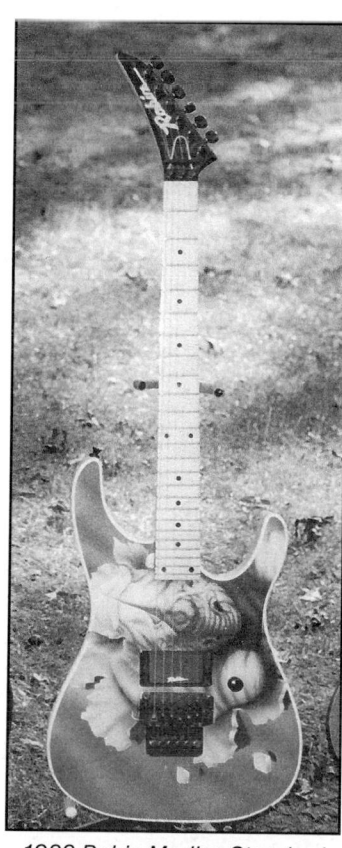

1989 Robin Medley Standard
Bob Reina

To get the most from this book, be sure to read "Using *The Guide*" in the introduction.

1978 Roland GS-500

Rolf Spuler Paradise

MODEL YEAR	FEATURES	EXC. COND. LOW	HIGH

Soloist/Artisan

1982-1986. Mahogany double-cut solidbody, carved bound maple top, set neck, 2 humbuckers. Renamed Artisan in '85. Only about 125 made in Japan.

| 1982-1986 | | $600 | $750 |

Wedge

1985-ca. 1988. Triangle-shaped body, 2 humbuckers, Custom with set neck and triangle inlays, Standard with bolt neck and dots, about 200 made.e.

| 1980s | | $625 | $775 |

Wrangler

1995-2002. Classic '50s single-cut slab body, 3 Rio Grande pickups, opaque finish.

| 1995-2002 | | $600 | $750 |

Robinson Guitars

2002-present. Premium and presentation grade, custom/production, steel string guitars built by luthier Jake Robinson first in Kalamazoo, and since '08 in Hoxeyville, Michigan.

RockBeach Guitars

2005-present. Luthier Greg Bogoshian builds his custom, professional grade, chambered electric guitars and basses in Rochester, New York.

Rockinbetter

2011-2014. Intermediate grade, production electric guitars and basses, copies of Rickenbacker models, made in China.

Rocking F

See listing under Fox.

Rockit Guitar

2006-present. Luthier Rod MacKenzie builds his premium grade, custom, electric guitars and basses in Everett, Washington.

Rogands

Late 1960s. Produced by France's Jacobacci company and named after brothers Roger and Andre. Short-lived brand; the brothers made instruments under several other brands as well.

Roger

Guitars built in Germany by luthier Wenzel Rossmeisl and named for his son Roger. Roger Rossmeisl would go on to work at Rickenbacker and Fender.

Rogue

2001-present. Budget and intermediate grade, production, acoustic, resonator, electric and sitar guitars and basses. They also offer mandolins, banjos, ukuleles, and lap steels. They previously offered effects and amps. Fender offered instruments branded Rogue by Squire for a short period starting in '99.

MODEL YEAR	FEATURES	EXC. COND. LOW	HIGH

Roland

Best known for keyboards, effects, and amps, Roland offered synthesizer-based guitars and basses from 1977 to '86.

GR-707 Synth Guitar

1983-1986. Slab-wedge asymmetrical body, bass bout to headstock support arm, 2 humbucker pickups, multi-controls.

| 1983-1986 | Silver | $900 | $1,125 |

GS-500 Synth Guitar/Module

1977-1986. Snyth functions in a single-cut solidbody guitar. The GS-300 was the same electronics in a classic offset double-cut body.

| 1977-1986 | Sunburst | $750 | $925 |

Rolando

1916-ca. 1919. Private branded instruments made for the Southern California Music Company of Los Angeles, by Martin. There were three models.

00-28K/1500

| 1916-1919 | | $5,500 | $6,800 |

Rolf Spuler

1981-2014. Presentation grade, custom, hybrid electric-acoustic guitars, built by luthier Rolf Spuler in Gebenstorf, Switzerland. He also built basses. He passed away in '14.

Roman & Lipman Guitars

1989-2000. Production/custom, solidbody guitars and basses made in Danbury, Connecticut by Ed Roman Guitars.

Roman Abstract Guitars

1989-present. Professional and premium grade, production/custom, solidbody guitars made by Ed Roman Guitars.

Roman Centurion Guitars

2001-present. Premium and presentation grade, custom guitars made by Ed Roman Guitars.

Roman Pearlcaster Guitars

1999-present. Professional and premium grade, production/custom, solidbody guitars made Ed Roman Guitars.

Roman Quicksilver Guitars

1997-present. Professional and premium grade, production/custom, solid and hollow-body guitars made by Ed Roman Guitars.

Roman Vampire Guitars

2004-present. Professional and premium grade, production/custom, solidbody guitars made by Ed Roman Guitars. Special orders only since about '13.

Rono

In 1967 luthier Ron Oates began building professional and premium grade, production/custom, flattop, jazz, Wiesenborn-style, and resonator guitars and basses in Boulder, Colorado. He also built mandolins..

MODEL		EXC. COND.	
YEAR	FEATURES	LOW	HIGH

Ro-Pat-In
See Rickenbacker.

Rosetti
1950s-1960s. Guitars imported into England by distributor Rosetti, made by Holland's Egmond, maybe others.

Solid 7

1960s. Symmetrical cutaway electric semi-hollow, large 'guard with top-mounted dual pickups, 4 control knobs, value is associated with Paul McCartney's use in '60, value dependent on completely original McCartney specs.

1960s	McCartney model	$1,000	$3,500
1960s	Various other	$450	$600

Roudhloff
1810s-1840s. Luthier Francois Roudhloff built his instruments in France. Labels could state F. Roudhloff-Mauchand or Roudhloff Brothers. Valuation depends strongly on condition and repair. His sons built guitars under the D & A Roudhloff label.

Rowan
Professional and premium grade, production/custom, solidbody and acoustic/electric guitars built by luthier Michael Rowan in Garland, Texas.

Royal
Ca. 1954-ca. 1965. Line of jazz style guitars made by France's Jacobacci company, which also built under its own brand.

Royal (Japan)
1957-1960s. Early budget level instruments made by Tokyo Sound Company and Gakki and exported by Japan's Hoshino (Ibanez).

Royden Guitars
1996-present. Professional grade, production/custom, flat-tops and solidbody electrics built by luthier Royden Moran in Peterborough, Ontario.

RS Guitarworks
1994-present. Professional grade, production/custom, solid and hollowbody guitars built by luthier Roy Bowen in Winchester, Kentucky.

Rubio, German Vasquez
1993-present. Luthier German Vasquez Rubio builds his professional and premium grade, production/custom classical and flamenco guitars in Los Angeles, California.

Ruck, Robert
1966-present. Premium grade, custom classical and flamenco guitars built by luthier Robert Ruck originally in Kalaheo, Hawaii, and currently in Eugene, Oregon.

MODEL		EXC. COND.	
YEAR	FEATURES	LOW	HIGH

Running Dog Guitars
1994-present. Luthier Rick Davis builds his professional and premium grade, custom flat-tops in Seattle, Washington. He was originally located in Richmond, Vermont.

Ruokangas
1995-present. Luthier Juha Ruokangas builds his premium and presentation grade, production/custom, solidbody and semi-acoustic electric guitars in Hyvinkaa, Finland.

Rustler
1993-ca. 1998. Solidbody electrics with hand-tooled leather bound and studded sides and a R branded into the top, built by luthier Charles Caponi in Mason City, Iowa.

RVC Guitars
1999-present. Professional and premium grade, production/custom, solidbody guitars made by Ed Roman Guitars.

RWK
1991-present. Luthier Bob Karger builds his intermediate grade, production/custom, solidbody electrics and travel guitars in Highland Park, Illinois.

Ryder
1963. Made by Rickenbacker, the one guitar with this brand was the same as their solidbody Model 425.

S. Walker Custom Guitars
2002-present. Luthier Scott Walker builds his premium grade, production/custom, solid and semi hollow body electric guitars in Santa Cruz, California.

S. Yairi
Ca. 1960-1980s. Steel string folk guitars and classical nylon string guitars by master Japanese luthier Sadao Yairi, imported by Philadelphia Music Company of Limerick, Pennsylvania. Early sales literature called the brand Syairi. Most steel string models have dreadnought bodies and nylon-string classical guitars are mostly standard grand concert size. All models are handmade. Steel string Jumbos and dreadnoughts have Syairi logo on the headstock, nylon-classical models have no logo. The Model 900 has a solid wood body, others assumed to have laminate bodies.

S.B. Brown Guitars
Custom flat-tops made by luthier Steve Brown in Fullerton, California.

S.B. MacDonald Custom Instruments
1988-present. Professional and premium grade, custom/production, flat-top, resonator, and solidbody guitars built by luthier Scott B. MacDonald in Huntington, New York.

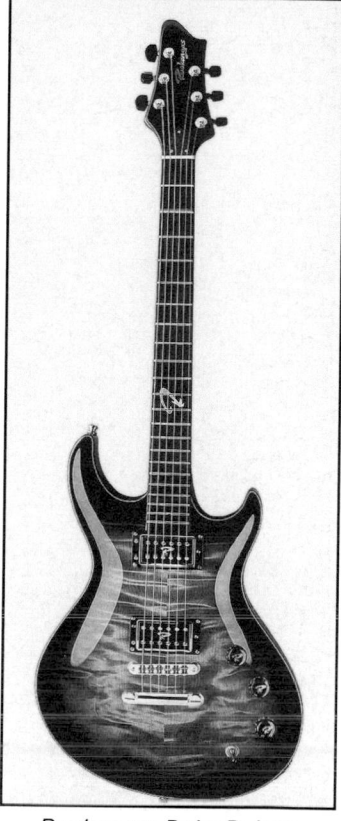

Ruokangas Duke Deluxe

Scott Walker Chimera

GUITARS

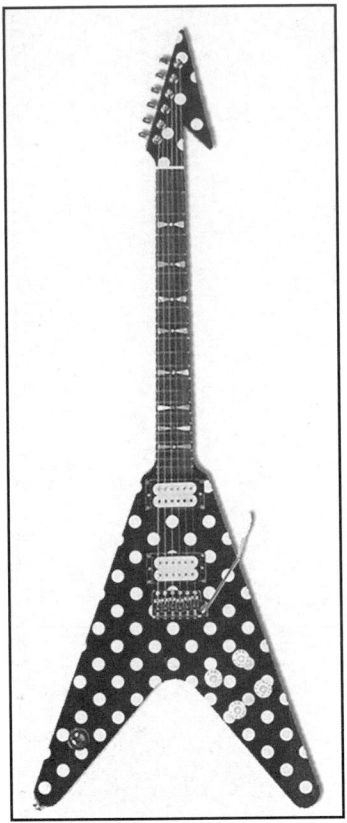

Sandoval Engineering Original Sandoval Dot V

Saga Blueridge BR-140

MODEL		EXC. COND.	
YEAR	FEATURES	LOW	HIGH

S.D. Curlee

1975-1982. Founded in Matteson, Illinois by music store owner Randy Curlee, after an unsuccessful attempt to recruit builder Dan Armstrong. S.D. Curlee guitars were made in Illinois, while S.D. Curlee International instruments were made by Matsumoku in Japan. The guitars featured mostly Watco oil finishes, often with exotic hardwoods, and unique neck-thru-bridge construction on American and Japanese instruments. These were the first production guitars to use a single-coil pickup at the bridge with a humbucker at the neck, and a square brass nut. DiMarzio pickups. Offered in a variety of shapes, later some copies. Approximately 12,000 American-made basses and 3,000 guitars were made, most of which were sold overseas. Two hundred were made in '75-'76; first production guitar numbered 518.

Electric Solidbody

1975-1982. Models include the '75-'81 Standard I, II and III, '76-'81 International C-10 and C-11, '80-'81 Yanke, Liberty, Butcher, Curbeck, Summit, Special, and the '81-'82 Destroyer, Flying V.

1975-1982		$340	$425

S.L. Smith Guitars

Professional grade, production/custom, acoustic guitars built by Steven Smith in Brant Lake, New York.

S.S. Stewart

The original S.S. Stewart Company (1878-1904), of Philadelphia, Pennsylvania is considered to be one of the most important banjo manufacturers of the late 19th century. Samuel Swaim Stewart died in 1988 and his family was out of the company by the early 1900s, and the brand was soon acquired by Bugellsein & Jacobsen of New York. The brand name was used on guitars into the 1960s.

S101

2002-present. Budget and intermediate grade, production, classical, acoustic, resonator, solid and semi-hollow body guitars and basses imported from China by America Sejung Corp. They also offer mandolins, and banjos.

Sadowsky

1980-present. Professional and premium grade, production/custom, solidbody, semi-hollowbody, archtop, and electric nylon-string guitars and basses built by luthier Roger Sadowsky in Brooklyn, New York. He also builds amps. In '96, luthier Yoshi Kikuchi started building Sadowsky Tokyo instruments in Japan.

Saga

Saga Musical Instruments, of San Francisco, California distributes a wide variety of instruments and brands, occasionally including their own line of solidbody guitars called the Saga Gladiator Series (1987-'88, '94-'95). In the 2000s, Saga also offered component kits ($90-$130) that allowed for complete assembly in white wood.

MODEL		EXC. COND.	
YEAR	FEATURES	LOW	HIGH

Sahlin Guitars

1975-present. Luthier Eric Sahlin builds his premium grade, custom, classical and flamenco guitars in Spokane, Washington.

Samick

1958-2001, 2002-present. Budget, intermediate and professional grade, production, imported acoustic and electric guitars and basses. They also offer mandolins, ukes and banjos and distribute Abilene and Silvertone brand instruments.

Samick started out producing pianos, adding guitars in '65 under other brands. In '88 Samick greatly increased their guitar production. The Samick line of 350 models was totally closed out in 2001. A totally new line of 250 models was introduced January 2002 at NAMM. All 2002 models have the new compact smaller headstock and highly styled S logo.

Sammo

1920s. Labels in these instruments state they were made by the Osborne Mfg. Co. with an address of Masonic Temple, Chicago, Illinois. High quality and often with a high degree of ornamentation. They also made ukes and mandolins.

Sand Guitars

1979-present. Luthier Kirk Sand opened the Guitar Shoppe in Laguna Beach, California in 1972 with James Matthews. By '79, he started producing his own line of premium grade, production/custom-made flat-tops.

Sandoval Engineering

1979-present. Luthier Karl Sandoval builds his premium grade, custom, solidbody guitars in Santa Fe Springs, California.

Sano

1944-ca. 1970. Sano was a New Jersey-based accordion company that imported Italian-made solid and semi-hollow body guitars for a few years, starting in 1966; some, if not all, made by Zero Sette. They also built their own amps and reverb units.

Santa Cruz

1976-present. Professional, premium and presentation grade, production/custom, flat-top, 12-string, and archtop guitars from luthier Richard Hoover in Santa Cruz, California. They also build a mandocello and ukuleles. Founded by Hoover, Bruce Ross and William Davis. Hoover became sole owner in '89. Custom ordered instruments with special upgrades may have higher values than the ranges listed here.

00 12-Fret

1997-present. Indian rosewood

1997-2014		$2,600	$3,200

MODEL YEAR	FEATURES	EXC. COND. LOW	HIGH
000 12-Fret			
1994-present. 000 size, 12-fret body, Indian rosewood back and sides, ebony 'board, ivoroid binding.			
1994-2014	Indian rosewood	$2,900	$3,600
2011	Brazilian rosewood	$5,000	$6,200
Archtop			
Early 1980s-2010. Originally the FJZ, by mid-'90s, called the Archtop, offering 16", 17" and 18" cutaway acoustic/electric models, often special order. Curly maple body, ebony 'board, floating pickup, f-holes, sunburst or natural. Many custom options available.			
1980s-90s		$3,800	$4,800
Bob Brozman Baritone			
1998-present. Flat-top acoustic, mahogany body, spruce top.			
1998-2014		$3,500	$4,400
D 12-Fret			
1994-present. 12-fret neck, slotted headstock, round shoulders, mahogany back and sides, notch diamond markers, herringbone trim. Special orders vary in value and could exceed the posted range.			
1994-2014		$2,700	$3,400
D Koa			
1980s-1990s. Style D with koa back and sides.			
1980s-90s		$2,800	$3,500
D/HR			
Style D with Indian rosewood back and sides, Brazilian rosewood headstock overlay.			
2000		$2,700	$3,400
D/PW Pre-War			
2001-present. Pre-war D-style.			
2001-2014		$2,600	$3,200
F			
1979-present. 15 7/8" scale with narrow waist, sitka spruce top, Indian rosewood back and sides, natural.			
1979-2014		$3,500	$4,400
F46R			
1980s. Brazilian rosewood, single-cut.			
1980s		$4,000	$5,000
Firefly			
2009-present. Premium quality travel/parlor guitar, cedar top, flamed maple sides and back.			
2009-2014		$2,600	$3,200
FS (Finger Style)			
1988-present. Single-cut, cedar top, Indian rosewood back and sides, mahogany neck, modified X-bracing.			
1988-2014		$3,300	$4,100
H			
1977-present. Parlor size, originally a 13-fret neck, but soon changed to 14, Indian rosewood back and sides. The H A/E ('92-'04) added electronics and cutaway.			
1977-2014	Indian rosewood	$2,500	$3,100
1994	Flamed koa	$4,000	$5,000
2005	Brazilian rosewood	$4,000	$5,000
H/13			
2004-present. Like H, but with 13-fret neck, mahogany back and sides and slotted headstock.			
2004-2014	Mahogany	$4,000	$5,000
2005	Flamed koa	$4,000	$5,000

MODEL YEAR	FEATURES	EXC. COND. LOW	HIGH
H91			
14 5/8", flamed koa.			
1990s		$4,000	$5,000
Model 1929 00			
2010-present. 00-size, all mahogany, 12-fret neck.			
2010-2014		$2,500	$3,100
OM (Orchestra Model)			
1987-present. Orchestra model acoustic, sitka spruce top, Indian rosewood (Brazilian optional) back and sides, herringbone rosette, scalloped braces.			
1987-2014	Brazilian rosewood	$4,000	$5,000
1987-2014	Indian rosewood	$2,800	$3,500
1995	Koa	$4,000	$5,000
OM/PW Pre-War			
1999-present. Indian rosewood, advanced X and scalloped top bracing.			
1999-2014		$2,300	$2,900
PJ			
1990s-present. Parlor size, Indian rosewood back and sides, 24" scale, 12-fret neck.			
1990s		$2,900	$3,600
Tony Rice			
1976-present. Dreadnought, Indian rosewood body (Brazilian optional until Tony Rice Professional model available), sitka spruce top, solid peghead, zigzag back stripe, pickup optional.			
1976-2014		$2,950	$3,675
Tony Rice Professional			
1997-present. Brazilian rosewood back and sides, carved German spruce top, zigzag back stripe, solid peghead.			
1997-2014		$6,100	$7,600
Vintage Artist			
1992-present. Mahogany body, sitka spruce top, zigzag back stripe, solid peghead, scalloped X-bracing, pickup optional.			
1992-2014		$2,700	$3,400
Vintage Artist Custom			
1992-2004. Martin D-42 style, mahogany body, Indian rosewood back and sides, sitka spruce top, zigzag back stripe, solid peghead, scalloped X-bracing, pickup optional.			
1992-2004		$3,100	$3,900
VJ (Vintage Jumbo)			
2000-present. 16" scale, round shouldered body, sitka spruce, figured mahogany back and sides, natural.			
2000-2014		$2,600	$3,300

Santos Martinez

Ca. 1997-present. Intermediate grade, production, acoustic and electro-acoustic classical guitars, imported from China by John Hornby Skewes & Co. in the U.K.

Sardonyx

1978-1979. Guitars and basses built by luthier Jeff Levin in the back of Matt Umanov's New York City guitar shop, industrial looking design with 2 aluminum outrigger-style tubes extended from the rectangle body. Very limited production.

Santa Cruz H/13

2004 Santa Cruz OM
Folkway Music

To get the most from this book, be sure to read "Using *The Guide*" in the introduction.

Sawchyn SD-85LSH

Schecter Banshee 6 FR Passive

MODEL YEAR	FEATURES	EXC. COND. LOW	HIGH

Saturn

1960s-1970s. Imported, most likely from Japan, solid and semi-hollow body electric guitars and basses. Large S logo with Saturn name inside the S. Many sold through Eaton's in Canada.

Saturn

1960s-1970s. Solidbody, 4 pickups.

1960s		$350	$450
1970s		$325	$400

Sawchyn Guitars

1972-present. Professional and premium grade, production/custom, flat-top and flamenco guitars and mandolins built by luthier Peter Sawchyn in Regina, Saskatchewan.

Schaefer

1997-present. Premium grade, production/custom, flat-top acoustic guitars built by luthier Edward A. Schaefer in Austin, Texas. He previously built archtops, basses and mandolins.

Schecter

1976-present. Intermediate, professional and premium grade, production/custom, acoustic and electric guitars and basses. Guitar component manufacturer founded in California by four partners (David Schecter's name sounded the best), started offering complete instruments in '79. The company was bought out and moved to Dallas, Texas in the early '80s. By '88 the company was back in California and in '89 was purchased by Hisatake Shibuya. Schecter Custom Shop guitars are made in Burbank, California and their intermediate grade Diamond Series is made in South Korea.

Scheerhorn

1989-present. Professional and premium grade, custom, resonator and Hawaiian guitars built by luthier Tim Scheerhorn in Kentwood, Michigan.

Schoenberg

1986-present. Premium grade, production/custom, flat-tops offered by Eric Schoenberg of Tiburon, California. From '86-'94 guitars made to Schoenberg's specifications by Martin. From '86-'90 constructed by Schoenberg's luthier and from '90-'94 assembled by Martin but voiced and inlaid in the Schoenberg shop. Current models made to Schoenberg specs by various smaller shops.

Schon

1986-1991. Designed by guitarist Neal Schon, early production by Charvel/Jackson building about 200 in the San Dimas factory. The final 500 were built by Larrivee in Canada. Leo Knapp also built custom Schon guitars from '85-'87, and '90s custom-made Schon guitars were also available.

Standard (Canadian-made)

1987-1991. Made in Canada on headstock.

1987-1991		$525	$650

Standard (U.S.A.-made)

1986 only. San Dimas/Jackson model, single-cut, pointy headstock shape, Made in U.S.A. on headstock.

1986		$1,100	$1,400

Schramm Guitars

1990-present. Premium grade, production/custom, classical and flamenco guitars built by luthier David Schramm in Clovis, California.

Schroder Guitars

1993-present. Luthier Timothy Schroeder (he drops the first e in his name on the guitars) builds his premium grade, production/custom, archtops in Northbrook, Illinois.

Schulte

1950s-2000. Luthier C. Eric Schulte made solid-body, semi-hollow body, hollow body and acoustic guitars, both original designs and copies, covering a range of prices, in the Philadelphia area.

Custom Copy

1982. Single-cut solidbody, figured maple top.

1982		$750	$925

Schulz

Ca. 1903-1917. Luthier August Schulz built harp guitars and lute-guitars in Nuremberg, Germany.

Harp Guitar

1906		$900	$1,150

Schwartz Guitars

1992-present. Premium grade, custom, flat-top guitars built by luthier Sheldon Schwartz in Concord, Ontario.

ScoGo

Professional and premium grade, production/custom, solidbody guitars built by luthier Scott Gordon in Parkesburg, Pennsylvania.

Scorpion Guitars

1998-2014. Professional and premium grade, custom, solidbody guitars made by Ed Roman Guitars.

Scott French

2004-present. Professional grade, production/custom, electric guitars and basses built by luthier Scott French in Auburn, California. In '12 he discontinued offering custom built.

Scott Walker Custom Guitars

Refer to S. Walker Custom Guitars.

SeaGlass Guitars USA

2011-present. Professional grade, production/custom, electric guitars, built by luthier Roger Mello in Groton, Massachusetts.

MODEL YEAR	FEATURES	EXC. COND. LOW	HIGH

Seagull

1982-present. Intermediate grade, production, acoustic and acoustic/electric guitars built in Canada. Seagull was founded by luthier Robert Godin, who also has the Norman, Godin, and Patrick & Simon brands of instruments.

Sebring

1980s-mid-1990s. Entry level Korean imports distributed by V.M.I. Industries.

Seiwa

Early 1980s. Entry-level to mid-level Japanese electric guitars and basses, logo may indicate Since 1956.

Sekova

Mid-1960s-mid-1970s. Entry level instruments imported by the U.S. Musical Merchandise Corporation of New York.

Selmer

1932-1952. France-based Selmer & Cie was primarily a maker of wind instruments when they asked Mario Maccaferri to design a line of guitars for them. The guitars, with an internal sound chamber for increased volume, were built in Mantes-la-Ville. Both gut and steel string models were offered. Maccaferri left Selmer in '33, but guitar production continued, and the original models are gradually phased out. In '36, only the 14 fret oval model is built. Production is stopped for WWII and resumes in '46, finally stopping in '52. Less than 900 guitars are built in total.

Classique

1942. Solid Rosewood back and sides, no cutaway, solid spruce top, round soundhole, classical guitar size, possibly only 2 built.

1942		$5,700	$7,200

Concert

1932-1933. For gut strings, cutaway, laminated Indian rosewood back and sides, internal resonator, spruce top with D hole, wide walnut neck, ebony 'board, only a few dozen built.

1932		$17,500	$22,000
1933		$18,000	$22,000

Eddie Freeman Special

1933. For steel strings, 4 strings, laminated Indian rosewood back and sides, cutaway, no internal resonator, solid spruce top, D hole, black and white rosette inlays, walnut 12 fret neck, ebony 'board, 640mm scale, approx. 100 made.

1933		$5,900	$7,300

Espagnol

1932. For gut strings, laminated Indian rosewood back and sides, no cutaway, internal resonator, solid spruce top, round soundhole, wide walnut neck, ebony 'board, only a few made.

1932		$9,000	$11,200

Grand Modele 4 Cordes

1932-1933. For steel strings, 4 string model, laminated back and sides, cutaway, internal resonator, solid spruce top, D hole, walnut neck, ebony 'board, 12 fret, 640mm scale, 2 or 3 dozen made.

1932-1933		$12,000	$15,000

Harp Guitar

1933. For gut strings, solid mahogany body, extended horn holding 3 sub bass strings, 3 screw adjustable neck, wide walnut neck, ebony 'board, only about 12 built.

1933		$13,000	$16,000

Hawaienne

1932-1934. For steel strings, 6 or 7 strings, laminated back and sides, no cutaway, internal resonator, solid spruce top, D hole, wide walnut neck, ebony 'board, 2 or 3 dozen built.

1932-1934		$25,000	$31,000

Modele Jazz

1936-1942, 1946-1952. For steel strings, laminated Indian rosewood back and sides (some laminated or solid mahogany), cutaway, solid spruce top, small oval soundhole, walnut neck, ebony 'board (latest ones with rosewood necks), 14 fret to the body, 670mm scale. Production interrupted for WWII.

1936-1952		$32,000	$40,000

Modeles de Transition

1934-1936. Transition models appearing before 14 fret oval hole model, some in solid maple with solid headstock, some with round soundhole and cutaway, some 12 fret models with oval hole.

1934-1936		$19,000	$24,000

Orchestre

1932-1934. For steel strings, laminated back and sides, cutaway, internal resonator, solid spruce top, D hole, walnut neck, ebony 'board, about 100 made.

1932-1934		$34,000	$42,000

Tenor

1932-1933. For steel strings, 4 strings, laminated back and sides, internal resonator, solid spruce top, D hole, walnut neck, ebony 'board, 12 fret, 570mm scale, 2 or 3 dozen built.

1932-1933		$5,500	$6,800

Serenghetti

Late-2007-present. Luthier Ray Patterson builds his professional and premium grade, production/custom, 1-piece and neck-thru guitars and basses in Ocala, Florida.

Serge Guitars

1995-present. Luthier Serge Michaud builds his production/custom, classical, steel-string, resophonic and archtop guitars in Breakeyville, Quebec.

Sexauer Guitars

1967-present. Premium and presentation grade, custom, steel-string, 12-string, nylon-string, and archtop guitars built by luthier Bruce Sexauer in Petaluma, California.

Schoenberg Soloist

SeaGlass Route 6A

GUITARS

Siegmund Outcaster

Sigma DT-4N

MODEL YEAR	FEATURES	EXC. COND. LOW	HIGH

Shadow

1990s. Made in Europe, copy models such as the classic offset double cutaway solidbody, large Shadow logo on headstock, Shadow logo on pickup cover, student to intermediate grade.

Shanti Guitars

1985-present. Premium and presentation grade, custom, steel-string, 12-string, nylon-string and archtop guitars built by luthier Michael Hornick in Avery, California.

Shelley D. Park Guitars

1991-present. Luthier Shelley D. Park builds her professional grade, custom, nylon- and steel-string guitars in Vancouver, British Columbia.

Shelton-Farretta

1967-present. Premium grade, production/custom, flamenco and classical guitars built by luthiers John Shelton and Susan Farretta originally in Portland, Oregon, and since '05 in Alsea, Oregon.

Sheppard Guitars

1993-present. Luthier Gerald Sheppard builds his premium grade, production/custom, steel-string guitars in Kingsport, Tennessee.

Shergold

1968-1992. Founded by Jack Golder and Norman Houlder, Shergold originally made guitars for other brands like Hayman and Barnes and Mullins. In '75, they started building guitars and basses under their own name. By '82, general guitar production was halted but custom orders were filled through '90. In '91, general production was again started but ended in '92 when Golder died.

Sherwood

Late 1940s-early 1950s. Archtop and lap steel guitars made for Montgomery Ward made by Chicago manufacturers such as Kay. There were also Sherwood amps made by Danelectro. Value ranges are about the same as Kay model equivalent.

Shifflett

1990-present. Luthier Charles Shifflett builds his premium grade, production/custom, flat-top, classical, flamenco, resophonic, and harp guitars and basses in High River, Alberta. He also builds banjos.

Sho-Bro

1969-1978. Spanish and Hawaiian style resonator guitars made by Sho-Bud in Nashville, Tennessee and distributed by Gretsch. Designed Shot Jackson and Buddy Emmons.

7-String Dobro

1972-1978		$1,400	$1,750

MODEL YEAR	FEATURES	EXC. COND. LOW	HIGH

Grand Slam

1978. Acoustic, spruce top, mahogany neck, jacaranda sides and back, and mother-of-pearl inlays, abalone soundhole purfling.

1970s		$550	$675

Resonator

1972-1978. Flat-top style guitar with metal resonator with 2 small circular grilled soundholes.

1972-1978		$950	$1,200

Siegmund Guitars & Amplifiers

1993-present. Luthier Chris Siegmund builds his professional, premium, and presentation grade, custom/production, archtop, solidbody, and resonator guitars in Los Angeles, California. He founded the company in Seattle, moving it to Austin, Texas for '95-'97. He also builds effects pedals and amps.

Sierra

2006-present. Budget level imports by Musicorp. There is an unrelated brand of Sierra steels and lap steels.

Sigma

1970-2007. Budget and intermediate grade, production, import acoustic and electric guitars and basses distributed by C.F. Martin Company. They also offered mandolins and banjos. Japanese-made for 1970-'72; lower-end model production moved to Korea in '73; most of remaining Japanese production moved to Korea in '83; most production moved to Taiwan and Indonesia in '96.

CS Series

1970-1990s. Various classical models.

1970-1993		$130	$375

D-10 Anniversary

1980. 10th anniversary model, solid mahogany back and sides, rosewood f'board.

1980		$460	$575

DM Series

1970-2007. Various mahogany dreadnought models.

1987-1988	Various models	$180	$400

DR Series

1970-2007. Various rosewood dreadnought models.

1970-2007		$210	$600

DT Series

1975-1990s. Various tiger-striped maple or chestnut dreadnought models.

1975-1999	Various models	$180	$400

GCS Series

1975-1990s. Various mahogany Grand Concert models.

1975-1994		$180	$400

SB Series

1973-1979. Various solidbody electric guitars and basses.

1973-1979		$180	$400

SE Series

1980-1984. Various acoustic/electric cutaway models.

1980-1984		$180	$400

The Official Vintage Guitar magazine Price Guide 2016 **Sigma** TB Series — **Silvertone** Model 1300/Model 1302 **301**

GUITARS

MODEL YEAR	FEATURES	EXC. COND. LOW	HIGH

TB Series

1990s-2000s. Various 000 Auditorium cutaway models with electronics.

2000s		$180	$400

Signature

2005-present. See listing under Gibson Baldwin.

Signet

1972-Mid 1970s. Acoustic flat-top guitars, imported from Japan by Ampeg/Selmer.

Silber

1992-1998. Solid wood, steel-string guitars designed by Marc Silber, made in Paracho, Mexico, and distributed by K & S Music. Silber continues to offer the same models under the Marc Silber Music brand.

Silver Street

1979-1986. Founded by brothers Bruce and Craig Hardy, production of solidbody electric guitars built in Elkhart, Indiana and later in Shelby, Michigan. Pre-production prototypes were built by luthier Richard Schneider. Suggested list prices ranged from $449 to $889.

Silvertone

1941-ca. 1970, present. Brand of Sears instruments which replaced their Supertone brand in '41. The Silvertone name was used on Sears phonographs, records and radios as early as the 'teens, and on occasional guitar models. When Sears divested itself of the Harmony guitar subsidiary in '40 it turned to other suppliers including Kay. In '40 Kay-made archtops and Hawaiian electric lap steels appeared in the catalog bearing the Silvertone brand, and after '41-'42, all guitars, regardless of manufacturer, were called Silvertone.

Sears offered Danelectro-made solidbodies in the fall of '54. Danelectro hollowbodies appeared in '56. By '65, the Silvertones were Teisco-made guitars from W.M.I., but never sold through the catalog. First imports shown in catalog were in '69.

By '70, most guitars sold by Sears were imports and did not carry the Silvertone name.

Currently, Samick offers a line of acoustic and electric guitars, basses and amps under the Silvertone name.

Special thanks to Brian Conner for providing Silvertone specifications.

Amp-In-Case

1962-1968. The black, sharp double cutaway, 1-pickup 1448, introduced in '62, came with a smaller wattage amp without tremolo. The black, 2-pickup 1449, introduced in '63, came with a higher-watt amp with tremolo and better quality Jensen speaker and was replaced by the red burst 1457 in '64. Gray tolex covered the guitar-amp case. In '66 they were replaced with the black 1451 and 1452 with soft, rounded cutaway horns.

1962-1966	1448, 1 pickup, black	$550	$700
1963-1964	1449, 2 pickups, black	$600	$750
1964-1966	1457, 2 pickups, red burst	$600	$750
1966-1968	1451, 1 pu, round cutaway	$550	$700
1966-1968	1452, 2 pu, round cutaway	$600	$750

Belmont

1958. Single-cut solidbody, 2 pickups, black.

1958		$730	$900

Black Beauty Model 1384L

1956-1958. Called 'The Black Beauty' in Sears catalog, large body acoustic-electric archtop, cutaway, 2 pickups, block markers, white binding, spruce top, mahogany sides and back, black lacquer finish.

1956-1958		$1,360	$1,675

Black Beauty Model 1385

1957. Basically the same as 1384L.

1957		$1,355	$1,675

Espanada

1960s. Bigsby, 2 pickups, black.

1960s		$1,150	$1,450

Estrelita

1960s. Semi-hollowbody archtop, 2 pickups, black, Harmony-made.

1960s		$1,130	$1,400

F-66

1964. Similar to Harmony Rocket III, single-cut, thinline electric, 3 pickups, Bigsby.

1964		$1,030	$1,275

Gene Autry Melody Ranch

1941-1955. 13" Harmony-made acoustic, Gene Autry signature on belly, cowboy roundup stencil, same as earlier Supertone Gene Autry Roundup.

1941-1955		$285	$350

H-1214

1951. Full-size acoustic archtop, script Silvertone headstock logo, dot markers, blond with simulated grain finish.

1951		$365	$450

H-1260 Sovereign Jumbo

1968. Silvertone's version of Harmony's Sovereign jumbo flat-top, dot markers, sunburst.

1968		$520	$645

H-1434 Rocket

1965. Similar to Harmony Rocket H59, sold by Sears, 3 pickups, Bigsby vibrato.

1965		$1,030	$1,275

Meteor

1955. Single-cut, 1 pickup, sunburst.

1955		$520	$650

Model 623

Late-1950s. Large-body acoustic archtop, dot markers, white 'guard, black finish, painted white binding to give a black and white attractive appearance.

1950s		$185	$235

Model 1300/Model 1302

1958-1959. Single-cut, 1 lipstick pickup, dot markers, 3-on-a-side symmetric headstock, bronze (1300) or black (1302).

1958-1959	1300, bronze	$575	$725
1958-1959	1302, black	$575	$725

Silvertone 602
George Cox

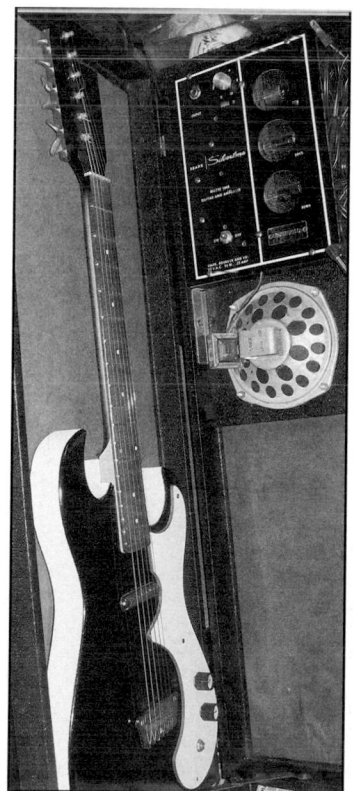

1962 Silvertone Amp-in-Case Model 1448
James Goode

GUITARS

1948 Silvertone 1348
George Cox

Sims Custom Single-cut

MODEL YEAR	FEATURES	EXC. COND. LOW	HIGH

Model 1301/Model 1303
1958-1959. 1300 with 2 lipstick pickups, bronze (1301) or black (1303).

1958-1959	1301, bronze	$775	$975
1958-1959	1303, black	$775	$975

Model 1305
1958-1959. Single-cut, 3 lipstick pickups, dot markers, 3-on-a-side symmetric headstock, white and black finish.

1958-1959		$1,200	$1,475

Model 1317
1957. Single-cut solidbody, 1 lipstick pickup, dot markers, 3-on-a-side symmetric headstock, bronze finish.

1957		$600	$750

Model 1381/Model 1382
1954-1957. Kay-made (many '50s Silvertones were made by Danelectro), slim-style electric similar to Thin Twin/Jimmy Reed, 2 lipstick pickups, 4 knobs, crown-crest logo on 'guard under strings, bolt neck, block markers, sunburst, sold without (Model 1381) and with a case (1382).

1954-1957	1381	$625	$775
1954-1957	1382	$1,150	$1,450

Model 1413
1962-1964. Double-cut slab body, single pickup, 2 control knobs, dot markers.

1962-1964		$240	$300

Model 1415/Model 1417
1960-1962. Single-cut, 1 lipstick pickup, 6-on-a-side dolphin headstock, dot markers, bronze (1415) or black (1417).

1960	1417, black	$550	$700
1961-1962	1415, bronze	$550	$700

Model 1420
1959-1963. Single-cut extra thin solidbody, bolt neck, 2 pickups, natural shaded or black finish.

1959-1963		$460	$575

Model 1423L
1960. Single-cut solidbody, 2 pickups, 5 control knobs with rotator switch, block markers, gleaming gold-color splatter-effect over black finish.

1960		$575	$725

Model 1429L
1962-1963. Harmony-made and similar to Harmony's H-75, single-cut thinline electric, 3 pickups, trapeze tailpiece, 3 toggles, 6 knobs, block marker, sunburst.

1962-1963		$1,000	$1,250

Model 1446
1962-1966. Single-cut thin acoustic archtop, 2 Gibson P-90 pickups, original factory Bigsby tailpiece, black lacquer finish with white 'guard.

1962-1966		$1,350	$1,675

Model 1454
1962-1966. Single-cut thin acoustic archtop, 3 pickups, original factory Bigsby tailpiece, red lacquer finish.

1962-1966		$1,200	$1,500

Model 1476/Model 1477
1964-1966. Offset double-cut solidbody, 2 lipstick pickups, dot markers. 4 control knobs, tremolo, black (1476 or sunburst (1477).

1964-1966	1476, black	$600	$750
1964-1966	1477, sunburst	$600	$750

MODEL YEAR	FEATURES	EXC. COND. LOW	HIGH

Model 1478 Silhouette
1964-1967. Offset double-cut, rectangular pickups, tremolo, bound 'board, block markers.

1964-1967	1 pickup	$260	$325
1964-1967	2 pickups	$365	$450
1964-1967	3 pickups	$390	$480

Model S1353
1955. Full body, single-cut, electric hollowbody, 1 pickup, 2 controls.

1955		$530	$675

Model S1453 Rebel
1968. Two sharp cutaway, single f-hole, 2 pickups, vibrato.

1968		$470	$580

Student-level 13" Flat-Top
1960s. Harmony-made, 13" lower bout.

1960s		$40	$50

Student-level 15.5" Flat-Top
1960s. Harmony-made, 15.5" lower bout.

1960s	Model S621	$155	$190

Ultra Thin Professional
1960s. Harmony-made, thin hollow cutaway, 3 pickups, Bigsby tailpiece.

1960s		$750	$925

Simon & Patrick
1985-present. Intermediate and professional grade, production, acoustic and acoustic/electric guitars built in Canada. Founded by luthier Robert Godin and named after his sons. He also produces the Seagull, Godin, and Norman brands of instruments.

Sims Custom Shop
2007-present. Custom, professional and premium grade, electric guitars built in Chattanooga, Tennessee by luthier Patrick Sims.

Singletouch
Luthier Mark Singleton builds his professional and premium grade, custom/production, solid and semi-hollow body guitars and basses in Phillips Ranch, California.

Skylark
1981. Solidbody guitars made in Japan and distributed by JC Penney. Two set-neck models and one bolt-neck model were offered. Most likely a one-time deal as brand quickly disappeared

Slammer
1998-2009. Budget and intermediate grade, production, guitars and basses imported from Indonesia by Hamer. Not to be confused with Hamer's Korean-made series of guitars from 1990-'97 called Hamer Slammer.
Slammer Series (Import)

1998-2009	Various models	$130	$200

Slingerland
Ca. 1914-present. Henry Slingerland opened a music school in Chicago, Illinois, in 1914 where he

MODEL YEAR	FEATURES	EXC. COND. LOW	HIGH

supplied instruments made by others to students who took his course. That grew into the Slingerland Manufacturing Company, then Slingerland Banjo and Drum Company in '28, selling banjos, guitars and ukes, built by them and others into the '40s. They also marketed the May Bell brand. Many of the guitars were made by other companies, including Regal. Slingerland Drums is now owned by Gibson.

Nitehawk
1930s. 16" archtop, Nitehawk logo on headstock, fancy position neck markers.

1930s		$700	$875

Songster Archtop/Flat-Top

1930s	Archtop	$575	$725
1930s	Flat-Top	$1,000	$1,250

Songster Tenor
1930s. Archtop.

1930s		$475	$600

Smart Musical Instruments
1986-present. Luthier A. Lawrence Smart builds his professional and premium grade, custom, flat-top guitars in McCall, Idaho. He also builds mandolin-family instruments.

Smith, George
1959-present. Custom classical and flamenco guitars built by luthier George Smith in Portland, Oregon.

Smith, Lawrence K.
1989-present. Luthier Lawrence Smith builds his professional and premium grade, production/custom, flat-top, nylon-string, and archtop guitars in Thirrow, New South Wales, Australia. He also builds mandolins.

SMK Music Works
2002-present. Luthier Scott Kenerson builds production/custom, professional grade, solidbody electric guitars and basses in Waterford, Michigan.

Smooth Stone Guitar
2007-present. Luthier R. Dale Humphries builds his professional and premium grade, production/custom, acoustic and electric guitars and basses in Pocatello, Idaho.

Solomon Guitars
1995-present. Luthier Erich Solomon builds his premium and presentation grade, production/custom, archtop, flat-top, classical and electric guitars in Epping, New Hampshire. Prior to '99 he was located in Anchorage, Alaska.

Somervell
Luthier Douglas P. Somervell built premium and presentation grade, production/custom, classical and flamenco guitars in Brasstown, North Carolina.

Somogyi, Ervin
1971-present. Luthier Ervin Somogyi builds his presentation grade, production/custom, flat-top, flamenco, and classical guitars in Oakland, California.

Sonata
1960s. Private brand Harmony-made, Sonata brand logo on headstock and pickguard.

Superior
1965. Grand Auditorium acoustic archtop, block markers, celluloid bound edges, similar to Harmony 1456, Superior logo on headstock.

1965		$380	$475

SonFather Guitars
1994-present. Luthier David A. Cassotta builds his production/custom, flat-top, 12-string, nylon-string and electric guitars in Rocklin, California.

Sorrentino
1930s. Private brand made by Epiphone and distributed by C.M.I. Quality close to similar Epiphone models.

Arcadia
1930s. Lower-end f hole acoustic archtop similar to Epiphone Blackstone.

1930s		$475	$600

Sorrento
1960s. Electric guitar imports made by Teisco, pricing similar to Teisco models, Sorrento logo on headstock, upscale solidbodies can have four pickups with five knobs and four switches.

Electric Solidbody

1960s	4 pickups	$280	$350

Southwell Guitars
1983-present. Premium grade, custom, nylon-string guitars built by luthier Gary Southwell in Nottingham, U.K.

Sovereign
Ca. 1899-1938. Sovereign was originally a brand of The Oscar Schmidt Company of Jersey City, New Jersey, and used on guitars, banjos and mandolins starting in the very late 1800s. In the late '30s, Harmony purchased several trade names from the Schmidt Company, including Sovereign and Stella. Sovereign then ceased as a brand, but Harmony continued using it on a model line of Harmony guitars.

Spaltinstruments
2002-present. Professional and premium grade, production/custom, electric solidbody and hollowbody guitars and basses built by luthier Michael Spalt, originally in Los Angeles, California and since '11 in Vienna, Austria.

Smooth Stone BC Series

Splatinstruments S&S/486

Specimen Maxwell

1966 Standel Custom Deluxe

MODEL YEAR	FEATURES	EXC. COND. LOW	HIGH

Sparrow Guitars

2004-present. Guitars manufactured in China are dismantled and "overhauled" in Vancouver, British Columbia. From these imports, luthier Billy Bones builds his intermediate and professional grade, production/custom solidbody and hollowbody electric guitars.

Specht Guitars

1991-present. Premium grade, production/custom, acoustic, baritone, parlor, jazz and classical guitars and basses built by luthier Oliver Specht in Vancouver, British Columbia.

Specimen Products

1984-present. Luthier Ian Schneller builds his professional and premium grade, production/custom, aluminum and wood body guitars and basses in Chicago, Illinois. He also builds ukes and amps.

Spector/Stuart Spector Design

1975-1990 (Spector), 1991-1998 (SSD), 1998-present (Spector SSD). Known mainly for basses, Spector offered U.S.-made guitars during '75-'90 and '96-'99, and imports for '87-'90 and '96-'99. Since 2003, they again offer U.S.-professional grade, production, solidbody guitars. See Bass Section for more company info.

SPG

2006-2009. Originally professional grade, custom, solidbody and chambered guitars built by luthier Rick Welch in Farmingdale, Maine and Hanson, Massachusetts. He also built lapsteels. Currently brand is used on imported line.

Squier

See models listed under Squier in Fender section.

St. Blues

1980-1989, 2005-present. Intermediate and professional grade, production/custom, solidbody guitars and basses imported and built in Memphis, Tennessee. The original '80s line was designed by Tom Keckler and Charles Lawing at Memphis' Strings & Things.

St. George

Mid to late 1960s. Early Japanese brand imported possibly by Buegeleisen & Jacobson of New York, New York.

Electric Solidbody

1960s. Early Japanese import duplicate of Zim Gar model, top mounted controls, 3 pickups, bolt-on neck.

1960s	Sunburst	$455	$625

St. Moritz

1960s. Guitars and basses imported from Japan by the Manhattan Novelty Corp. Manufacturer unknown, but some appear to be Fuji Gen Gakki products. Generally shorter scale beginner guitars, some with interesting pickup configurations.

Stahl

1900-1941. William C. Stahl, of Milwaukee, Wisconsin, ran a publishing company, taught stringed instrument classes and sold instruments to his students as well as by mail order across America. His label claimed that he was the maker but most of his products were built by the Larson brothers of Maurer & Co. of Chicago, with the balance mostly from Washburn. The most commonly found Larson-built models are the Style 6 and 7 as seen in the ca. 1912 Stahl catalog. Jimi Hendrix was the proud owner of a Style 8. The Style 6 is a moderately trimmed 15" Brazilian rosewood beauty that is much like the highly sought Maurer Style 551. The Style 7 and 8 are pearl trimmed 13 ½" concert size Brazilians comparable to the Maurer Style 562 ½. The 1912 Stahl catalog Styles 4, 5 and 9 were built by Washburn.

Stambaugh

1995-present. Luthier Chris Stambaugh builds his professional grade, custom/production, solidbody guitars basses in Stratham, New Hampshire.

Standel

1952-1974, 1997-present. Amp builder Bob Crooks offered instruments under his Standel brand 3 different times during the '60s. In '61 Semie Moseley, later of Mosrite fame, made 2 guitar models and 1 bass for Standel, in limited numbers. Also in '61, Standel began distributing Sierra steels and Dobro resonators, sometimes under the Standel name. In '65 and '66 Standel offered a guitar and a bass made by Joe Hall, who also made the Hallmark guitars. In '66 Standel connected with Sam Koontz, who designed and produced the most numerous Standel models (but still in relatively small numbers) in Newark, New Jersey. These models hit the market in '67 and were handled by Harptone, which was associated with Koontz. By '70 Standel was out of the guitar biz. See Amp section for more company info.

Custom Deluxe 101/101X

1967-1968. Custom solidbody with better electronics, 101X has no vibrato, sunburst, black, pearl white and metallic red.

1967-1968		$1,050	$1,325

Custom Deluxe 102/102X

1967-1968. Custom thin body with better electronics, 102X has no vibrato, offered in sunburst and 5 solid color options.

1967-1968		$1,050	$1,325

Custom 201/201X

1967-1968. Solidbody, 2 pickups, vibrola, 2 pointed cutaways, headstock similar to that on Fender XII, 201X has no vibrato, sunburst, black, pearl white and metallic red.

1967-1968		$675	$850

MODEL YEAR	FEATURES	EXC. COND. LOW	HIGH
Custom 202/202X			
1967-1968. Thin body, headstock similar to that on Fender XII, 202X has no vibrato, offered in sunburst and 5 solid color options.			
1967-1968		$675	$850
Custom 420S			
1967-1968. Custom thin body with 2 pickups.			
1967-1968		$1,075	$1,350

Star

1957-1960s. Early budget level instruments made by Tokyo Sound Company and Gakki and exported by Japan's Hoshino (translates to Star) company which also has Ibanez.

Starcaster

2000s. Budget brand from Fender that has been used on acoustic, electric and bass guitars, effects, amps and drums and sold through mass retailers such as Costco, Target and others. See Fender listing for guitar values.

Starfield

1992-1993. Solidbody guitars from Hoshino (Ibanez) made in the U.S. and Japan. U.S. guitars are identified as American models; Japanese ones as SJ models. Hoshino also used the Star Field name on a line of Japanese guitars in the late '70s. These Star Fields had nothing to do with the '90s versions and were not sold in the U.S.

Starforce

Ca. 1989. Import copies from Starforce Music/ Starforce USA.

Stars

Intermediate grade, production, solidbody guitars made in Korea.

Status Graphite

Professional grade, production/custom, solidbody guitars and basses built in Colchester, Essex, U.K. Status was the first English company to produce a carbon fiber instrument.

Stauffer

1800s. Old World violin and guitar maker, Georg Stauffer. Valid attributions include signed or labeled by the maker indicating the guitar was actually made by Stauffer, as opposed to attributed to Stauffer or one of his contemporaries. See Martin for listing.

Stefan Sobell Musical Instruments

1982-present. Premium grade, production/custom, flat-top, 12-string, and archtop guitars built by luthier Stefan Sobell in Hetham, Northumberland, England. He also builds mandolins, citterns and bouzoukis.

Steinberger

1979-present. Currently Steinberger offers budget, intermediate, and professional grade, production, electric guitars. They also offer basses. Founded by Ned Steinberger, who started designing NS Models for Stuart Spector in '76. In '79, he designed the L-2 headless bass. In '80, the Steinberger Sound Corp. was founded. Steinberger Sound was purchased by the Gibson Guitar Corp. in '87, and in '92, Steinberger relocated to Nashville, Tennessee.

Headless model codes for '85-'93 are:
First letter is X for bass or G for guitar.
Second letter is for body shape: M is regular offset double-cut guitar body; L is rectangle body; P is mini V shaped body.
Number is pickup designation: 2 = 2 humbuckers, 3 = 3 single coils, 4 = single/single/ humbucker.
Last letter is type of tremolo: S = S-Trem tremolo; T = Trans-Trem which cost more on original retail.

MODEL YEAR	FEATURES	EXC. COND. LOW	HIGH
GL			
1979-1984. Headless, rectangle body, 2 pickups.			
1979-1984		$2,800	$3,400

Steinegger

1976-present. Premium grade, custom steel-string flat-top guitars built by luthier Robert Steinegger in Portland, Oregon.

Stella

Ca. 1899-1974, 2000s. Stella was a brand of the Oscar Schmidt Company which started using the brand on low-mid to mid-level instruments in the very late 1800s. Oscar Schmidt produced all types of stringed instruments and was very successful in the 1920s. Company salesmen reached many rural areas and Stella instruments were available in general stores, furniture stores, and dry goods stores, ending up in the hands of musicians such as Leadbelly and Charlie Patton. Harmony acquired the Stella brand in '39 and built thousands of instruments with that name in the '50s and '60s. Harmony dissolved in '74. The Stella brand was reintroduced in the 2000s by MBT International.

MODEL YEAR	FEATURES	EXC. COND. LOW	HIGH
00 Style			
1900-1930. Oak body flat-top.			
1900-1930		$450	$560
Flat-Top 15" 12-String			
1920s-1930s. Associated with early blues and folk musicians, top of the line for Stella.			
1920s-30s		$6,400	$8,000
Flat-Top by Harmony			
1950s-1960s. The low end of the Harmony-built models, US-made until the end of the '60s, student level, Stella logo on headstock, playing action can often be very high which makes them difficult to play.			
1950s-60s	13"	$55	$125
1950s-60s	14", 12-string	$105	$150
1950s-60s	Sundale (colors)	$410	$510
1950s-60s	Tenor 4-string	$225	$290

1960s Standel Double Cutaway
Landon Furlong

Stella Flat-Top

Stratosphere Doubleneck

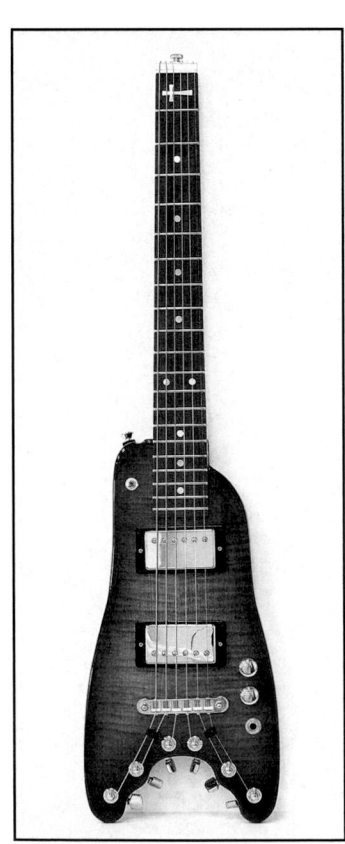

Strobel Rambler Custom

MODEL YEAR	FEATURES	EXC. COND. LOW	HIGH

Harp Guitar
Early-1900s.

1900s		$2,100	$2,600

Singing Cowboy
Late-1990s. Copy of Supertone (black background)/ Silvertone/Harmony Singing Cowboy, import with laminated wood construction and ladder bracing.

1990s	Stencil over black	$40	$55

Stetson
1884-ca. 1924. Stetson was a house brand of William John Dyer's St. Paul, Minnesota, music store. They started advertising this brand as early as 1894, but those built by the Larson brothers of Maurer & Co. date from ca. 1904-c. 1924. Most Stetsons were made by the Larsons. Others were built by Harmony (early ones), Washburn and three are credited to the Martin Co.

Stevenson
1999-present. Professional grade, production/ custom, solidbody electric guitars and basses built by luthier Ted Stevenson in Lachine, Quebec. He also builds amps.

Stiehler
2005-present. Production/custom, professional and premium grade, acoustic electric and electric solidbody guitars built by luthier Bob Stiehler, first in Wellington and since '11 in Carson City, Nevada. He also builds basses.

Stonebridge
1981-present. Czech Republic luthier Frantisek Furch builds professional and premium grade, production/ custom, acoustic guitars. He also builds mandolins.

Stonetree Custom Guitars
1996-present. Luthier Scott Platts builds his professional and premium grade, custom/production, solidbody and chambered electric guitars and basses in Saratoga, Wyoming.

Strad-O-Lin/Stradolin
Ca.1920s-ca.1960s. The Strad-O-Lin company was operated by the Hominic brothers in New York, primarily making mandolins for wholesalers. Around '57 Multivox/Premier bought the company and also used the name on electric and acoustic guitars, basses and amps. Premier also marketed student level guitars under the U.S. Strad brand.

Electric

1960s		$150	$400

Stratosphere
1954-1958. Solidbody electrics made in Springfield, Missouri by brothers Claude and Russ Deaver, some featuring fanned frets. They also made an odd double neck called the Stratosphere Twin with a regular 6-string neck and a 12-string tuned in minor and major thirds. The brothers likely made less than 200 instruments.

MODEL YEAR	FEATURES	EXC. COND. LOW	HIGH

Electric

1954-1958		$825	$1,025

Strobel Guitars
2003-present. Luthier Russ Strobel builds custom, professional grade, electric travel guitars and basses in Boca Raton, Florida. He also offers a production, intermediate grade, travel guitar built first in Korea and since '13 in Asia.

Stromberg
1906-1955, 2001-present. Intermediate and professional grade, production, archtop guitars imported by Larry Davis.

Founded in Boston by master luthier Charles Stromberg, a Swedish immigrant, building banjos and drums. Son Harry joined the company in 1907 and stayed until '27. Son Elmer started in 1910 at age 15. The shop was well known for tenor banjos, but when the banjo's popularity declined, they began building archtop orchestra model guitars. The shop moved to Hanover Street in Boston in '27 and began producing custom order archtop guitars, in particular the 16" G-series and the Deluxe. As styles changed the G-series was increased to 17 3/8" and the 19" Master 400 model was introduced in '37. Stromberg designs radically changed around '40, most likely when Elmer took over guitar production. Both Charles and Elmer died within a few months of each other in '55. Most of the interest in vintage Strombergs comes out of the Boston area.

Larry Davis of WD Music Products revived the Stromberg name and introduced a series of moderately priced jazz guitars in June, 2001. The models are crafted by a small Korean shop with component parts supplied by WD.

Deluxe
1927-1955. Non-cut, 16" body to '34, 17 3/8" body after '35, also sometimes labeled Delux.

1927-1930		$6,800	$8,500
1931-1939		$8,000	$10,000
1940-1955		$8,000	$10,000

G-1
1927-1955. Non-cut, 16" body to '35, 17 3/8" body after '35, sunburst.

1927-1935		$6,800	$8,500
1936-1955		$7,200	$9,000

G-3
Early 1930s. Archtop, 16 3/8", 3 segment F-holes, ladder bracing, gold hardware, engraved tailpiece, 8-ply 'guard, 5-ply body binding, laminate maple back, fancy engraved headstock with Stromberg name, less total refinement than higher-end Stromberg models.

1927-1935		$8,000	$10,000

G-5
1952-1955. 17" cutaway.

1953		$26,000	$33,000

Master 300
1937-1955. 19" non-cut.

1937-1955	Natural	$18,000	$23,000
1937-1955	Sunburst	$15,000	$19,000

MODEL YEAR	FEATURES	EXC. COND. LOW	HIGH

Master 400
1937-1955. 19" top-of-the-line non-cut, the most common of Stromberg's models.

1937-1955	Natural	$26,000	$34,000
1937-1955	Sunburst	$22,000	$28,000

Master 400 Cutaway
1949. Only 7 cutaway Strombergs are known to exist.

1949	Natural	$38,000	$48,000

Stromberg-Voisinet
1921-ca.1932. Marketed Stromberg (not to be confused with Charles Stromberg of Boston) and Kay Kraft brands, plus guitars of other distributors and retailers. Stromberg was the successor to the Groehsl Company (or Groehsel) founded in Chicago, Illinois in 1890; and the predecessor to the Kay Musical Instrument Company. In 1921, the name was changed to Stromberg-Voisinet Company. Henry Kay "Hank" Kuhrmeyer joined the company in '23 and was secretary by '25. By the mid-'20s, the company was making many better Montgomery Ward guitars, banjos and mandolins, often with lots of pearloid.

Joseph Zorzi, Philip Gabriel and John Abbott left Lyon & Healy for S-V in '26 or '27, developing 2-point Venetian shape, which was offered in '27. The first production of electric guitars and amps was introduced with big fanfare in '28; perhaps only 200 or so made. The last Stromberg acoustic instruments were seen in '32. The Kay Kraft brand was introduced by Kuhrmeyer in '31 as the company made its transition to Kay (see Kay).

Archtop Deluxe
1920s-1930s. Venetian cutaways, oval soundhole, decalomania art on top, trapeze tailpiece, light sunburst. Later offered under the Kay-Kraft brand.

1930s		$350	$435

Archtop Standard
1920s-1930s. Venetian cutaways, oval soundhole, no decalomania art, plain top, trapeze tailpiece, light sunburst. Later offered under the Kay-Kraft brand.

1930s		$310	$385

Stroup
2003-present. Luthier Gary D. Stroup builds his intermediate and professional grade, production/custom, archtop and flat-top guitars in Eckley, Colorado.

Stuart Custom Guitars
2004-present. Professional and premium grade, production/custom, solid and semi-hollow body guitars built by luthier Fred Stuart in Riverside, California. Stuart was a Senior Master Builder at Fender. He also builds pickups.

Suhr Guitars
1997-present. Luthier John Suhr builds his professional and premium grade, production/custom, solidbody electrics guitars and basses in

Lake Elsinore, California. He also builds amps. He previously built Pensa-Suhr guitars with Rudy Pensa in New York.

Sunset
2010-present. Luthier Leon White builds professional and premium grade, production/custom, electric solidbody, chambered and hollowbody guitars in Los Angeles, California.

Superior Guitars
1987-present. Intermediate grade, production/custom Hawaiian, flamenco and classical guitars made in Mexico for George Katechis Montalvo of Berkeley Musical Instrument Exchange. They also offer lap steels and mandolin-family instruments.

Supersound
1952-1974. Founded by England's Alan Wootton, building custom amps and radios. In 1958-'59 he worked with Jim Burns to produce about 20 short scale, single-cut solidbodies bearing this name. They also built a bass model. The firm continued to build amps and effects into the early '60s.

Supertone
1914-1941. Brand used by Sears, Roebuck and Company for instruments made by various American manufacturers, including especially its own subsidiary Harmony (which it purchased in 1916). When Sears divested itself of Harmony in '40, instruments began making a transition to the Silvertone brand. By '41 the Supertone name was gone.

Acoustic Flat-Top (High-End Appointments)

1920s	Pearl trim 00-42 likeness	$1,325	$1,650
1920s	Pearl trim, Lindbergh model	$1,325	$1,650

Acoustic Flat-Top 13"

1920s-30s	Non-stencil, plain top	$150	$185
1920s-30s	Stencil top	$200	$250

Gene Autry Roundup
1932-1939. Harmony made acoustic, Gene Autry signature on belly, cowboy roundup stencil, 13" body until '35, then 14".

1932-1939		$310	$385

Lone Ranger
1936-1941. Black with red and silver Lone Ranger and Tonto stencil, silver-painted fretboard, 13 1/2" wide. "Hi-Yo Silver" added in '37, changed to "Hi-Ho Silver" in '38.

1936-1941		$310	$385

Robin Hood
1930s. 13" flat-top similar to Singing Cowboys, but with green and white art showing Robin Hood and his men against a black background.

1933		$325	$400

Suhr Modern
Michael Stover

Sunset Artist

Supro Folk Star

1960 Supro Kingston
Robbie Keene

MODEL		EXC. COND.	
YEAR	FEATURES	LOW	HIGH

Singing Cowboys
1938-1943. Stencil of guitar strumming cowboys around chuck wagon and campfire, branded Silvertone after '41.

1938-1943		$310	$385

Supertone Wedge
1930s. Triangle-shaped wedge body, laminate construction, blue-silver Supertone label inside sound chamber, art decals on body.

1930s		$250	$310

Supro
1935-1968, 2004-present. Budget brand of National Dobro Company and Valco. Some Supro models also sold under the Airline brand for Montgomery Ward. In '42 Victor Smith, Al Frost and Louis Dopyera bought National and changed the name to Valco Manufacturing Company. Valco Manufacturing Company name changed to Valco Guitars, Inc., in '62. Company treasurer Robert Engelhardt bought Valco in '64. In '67 Valco bought Kay and in '68 Valco/Kay went out of business. In the summer of '69, Valco/Kay brands and assets were sold at auction and the Supro and National names purchased by Chicago-area importer and distributor Strum N' Drum (Norma, Noble). In the early-'80s, ownership of the Supro name was transferred to Archer's Music, Fresno, California. Some Supros assembled from new-old-stock parts.

Amp builder Bruce Zinky revived the Supro name for a line of guitars built in the U.S. by luthier John Bolin and others. He also offers amps. In 2013, Absara Audio, LLC acquired the Supro trademark and started releasing amps in July 2014.

Arlington
1967-1967. Jazzmaster-style, wood body, 6 buttons, 4 knobs, vibrato, 2 pickups.

1966-1967	Various colors	$1,150	$1,425

Belmont
1955-1964. For '55-'60, 12" wide, single-cut, 1 neck pickup, 2 knobs treble side in 'guard, reverse-stairs tailpiece, No-Mar plastic maroon-colored covering. For '60, size increased to 13 1/2" wide. For '62-'64, Res-o-glas fiberglass was used for the body, a slight cutaway on bass side, 1 bridge pickup, 2 knobs on opposite sides. Polar White.

1955-1962	Black or white		
	No-Mar	$1,175	$1,450
1961-1964	Polar White		
	Res-o-glas	$1,550	$1,925

Bermuda
1962 only. Slab body (not beveled), double pickups, dot markers, cherry glass-fiber finish.

1962		$1,725	$2,150

Collegian Spanish
1939-1942. Metal body, 12 frets. Moved to National line in '42.

1939-1942		$1,450	$1,825

Coronado/Coronado II
1961-1967. Listed as II in '62 15 1/2" scale, single-cut thinline, 2 pickups, natural blond spruce top. Changed

to slight cutaway on bass side in '62 when renamed II.

1961-1962	Blond, natural		
	spruce top	$2,075	$2,575
1963-1967	Black fiberglass	$2,300	$2,850

Dual-Tone
1954-1966, 2004-2014. The Dual Tone had several body style changes, all instruments had dual pickups. '54, 11 1/4" body, No Mar Arctic White plastic body ('54-'62). '55, 12" body. '58, 13" body. '60, 13 1/2" body. '62, Res-o-glas Ermine White body, light cutaway on bass side.

1954-1961	Arctic White		
	No-Mar	$1,550	$1,925
1962-1964	Ermine White		
	Res-o-glas	$1,725	$2,125

Folk Star/Vagabond
1964-1967. Molded Res-o-glas body, single-cone resonator, dot inlays, Fire Engine Red. Name changed to Vagabond in '66.

1964-1967		$1,250	$1,550

Kingston
1962-1963. Double-cut slab body, bridge pickup, glass-fiber sand finish, similar to same vintage Ozark.

1962-1963		$1,250	$1,550

Lexington
1967. Double-cut, wood body.

1967		$475	$600

Martinique (Val-Trol)
1962-1967. Single-cut, 13 1/2" wide, 2 standard and 1 bridge pickups, block markers, Val-Trol script on 'guard, Bigsby, blue or Ermine White Polyester Glas. Collectors sometimes call this Val-Trol, referring to the 6 mini tone and volume controls. Not to be confused with Silverwood model which also has 6 mini-knobs.

1962-1967		$2,875	$3,550

N800 Thinline Electric
1967-1968. Thin body, symmetrical double-cut, 2 pickups, copy model, similar to National N800 series models.

1967-1968		$625	$775

Ozark
1952-1954, 1958-1967, 2004-2013. Non-cut, 1 pickup, dot inlay, white pearloid body, name reintroduced in '58 as a continuation of model Sixty with single-cut, Dobro tailpiece.

1952-1954	White pearloid	$1,150	$1,425
1958-1961	Red	$1,150	$1,425
1962-1967	Jet Black or		
	Fire Bronze	$1,150	$1,425

Ranchero
1948-1960. Full body electric archtop, neck pickup, dot markers, bound body, sunburst.

1948-1960		$700	$875

Rhythm Master (Val-Trol)
1959. Val-Trol 'guard.

1959		$2,500	$3,150

S710 Flat-Top
1967-1968. Jumbo-style 15.5" flat-top, block markers, asymmetrical headstock, natural.

1967-1968		$380	$475

MODEL YEAR	FEATURES	EXC. COND. LOW	HIGH

Sahara/Sahara 70
1960-1967. 13 1/2" body-style similar to Dual-Tone, single pickup, 2 knobs, Sand-Buff or Wedgewood Blue, Sahara until '63, Sahara 70 after.

| 1960-1967 | | $1,350 | $1,700 |

Silverwood (Val-Trol)
1960-1962. Single-cut, 13 1/2" wide, 2 standard and 1 bridge pickups, block markers, natural blond, Val-Trol script on 'guard, renamed Martinique in '62. Collectors sometimes call this Val-Trol, referring to the guitar's 6 mini tone and volume controls. The Martinique also has the Val-Trol system but the knobs are not in a straight line like on the Silverwood.

| 1960-1962 | | $2,600 | $3,300 |

Sixty
1955-1958. Single-cut, single pickup, white No-Mar, becomes Ozark in '58.

| 1955-1958 | | $950 | $1,175 |

Special 12
1958-1960. Single-cut, replaces Supro Sixty, neck pickup 'guard mounted.

| 1958-1960 | | $950 | $1,175 |

Stratford
1968. ES-335-style double-cut, 3 pickups, 3 switches, 6 knobs, vibrato.

| 1968 | | $700 | $875 |

Strum 'N' Drum Solidbody
1970s. Student-level import, 1 pickup, large Supro logo on headstock.

| 1970s | Higher-end | $475 | $575 |
| 1970s | Lower-end | $375 | $475 |

Super
1958-1964. 12" wide single-cut body style like mid-'50s models, single bridge pickup, short-scale, ivory.

| 1958-1964 | | $700 | $875 |

Super Seven
1965-1967. Offset double-cut solidbody, short scale, middle pickup, Calypso Blue.

| 1965-1967 | | $600 | $750 |

Suprosonic 30
1963-1967. Introduced as Suprosonic, renamed Suprosonic 30 in '64, double-cut, single neck pickup, vibrato tailpiece, more of a student model, Holly Red.

| 1963-1967 | | $675 | $850 |

Tremo-Lectric
1965. Fiberglas hollowbody, 2 pickups, unique built-in electric tremolo (not mechanical), Wedgewood Blue finish, multiple controls associated with electric tremolo.

| 1965 | | $1,775 | $2,250 |

White Holiday/Holiday
1963-1967. Introduced as Holiday, renamed White Holiday in '64, fiberglas double-cut, vibrato tailpiece, single bridge pickup, Dawn White.

| 1963-1967 | | $1,375 | $1,725 |

Suzuki Takeharu
See listing for Takeharu.

SX
See listing for Essex.

Szlag
2000-present. Luthier John J. Slog builds his professional and premium grade, custom carved, guitars and basses in Bethlehem, Pennsylvania.

T.D. Hibbs
Production/custom, professional grade, steel string and classical guitars built in Cambridge, Ontario by luthier Trevor Hibbs.

T.H. Davis
1976-2008. Professional and premium grade, custom, steel string and classical guitars built by luthier Ted Davis in Loudon, Tennessee. He also built mandolins. Davis died in '08.

Tacoma
1995-2009. Intermediate, and professional grade, production, acoustic guitars produced in Tacoma, Washington and New Hartford, Connecticut. They also built acoustic basses and mandolins. In October, '04, Fender acquired Tacoma and in '09 ceased production.

DM-6C Thunderhawk Baritone
2004-2009. Single-cut acoustic baritone

| 2004-2009 | | $900 | $1,105 |

C-1C/C-1CE Chief
1997-2009. Cutaway flat-top with upper bass bout soundhole, solid cedar top, mahogany back and sides, rosewood 'board. Sides laminated until 2000, solid after, CE is acoustic/electric.

| 1997-2009 | | $350 | $450 |
| 1997-2009 | Fishman electronics | $375 | $475 |

DM Series
1997-2006. Dreadnought, solid spruce top, mahogany back and sides, satin finish, natural, C suffix indicates cutaway.

| 1997-2006 | Various models | $250 | $800 |

DR Series
1997-2006. Dreadnought, solid sitka spruce top, rosewood back and sides, natural. Models include DR-20 (non-cut, herringbone trim, abalone rosette), DR-20E (with on-board electronics), DR-8C (cutaway), and DR-38.

| 1997-2006 | Various models | $250 | $800 |

EM Series
1999-2008. Little Jumbo series, spruce top, mahogany back and sides, C suffix indicates cutaway.

| 1999-2008 | Various models | $450 | $575 |

JM Series
1990s-2006. Jumbo series, spruce top, mahogany back and sides.

| 1997-2006 | | $500 | $800 |

JR-14C Jumbo Rosewood
Late-1990s. Jumbo cutaway, 16 5/8" lower bout, gloss spruce top, satin rosewood body.

| 1990s | | $800 | $1,000 |

JR-50CE4 Jumbo Koa
1997-2003. Jumbo cutaway, 17" lower bout, sitka spruce top, figured koa back and sides.

| 1997-2003 | | $800 | $1,000 |

Supro Martinique
Zak Izbinsky

1959 Supro Ranchero

Taylor 110

Taylor 310ce

MODEL YEAR	FEATURES	EXC. COND. LOW	HIGH

P-1/P-2 Papoose
1995-2009. Travel-size mini-flat-top, all solid wood, mahogany back and sides (P-1), with on-board electronics (P-1E) or solid rosewood (P-2), cedar top, natural satin finish.

1995-2000	P-2	$375	$475
1995-2009	P-1	$325	$400
1995-2009	P-1E	$350	$450

Parlor Series
1997-2003. Smaller 14 3/4" body, solid spruce top, various woods for back and sides.

1997-2003	PK-30 Koa	$600	$750
1997-2003	PK-40 Rosewood	$600	$750

PM Series
1997-2003. Full-size, standard soundhole.

1997-2003		$400	$700

Takamine
1962-present. Intermediate and professional grade, production, steel- and nylon-string, acoustic and acoustic/electric guitars and basses. Takamine is named after a mountain near its factory in Sakashita, Japan. Mass Hirade joined Takamine in '68 and revamped the brand's designs and improved quality. In '75, Takamine began exporting to other countries, including U.S. distribution by Kaman Music (Ovation). In '78, Takamine introduced acoustic/electric guitars. They offered solidbody electrics and some archtops for '83-'84.

Acoustic Electric (Laminate)
1980s-1990s. All laminate (plywood) construction, non-cut, standard features, pickup and preamp.

1980s-90s		$210	$400

Acoustic Electric (Solid Top)
1980s-1990s. Solid wood top, sides and back can vary, cutaway, standard features, preamp and pickup.

1980s-90s		$420	$900

Acoustic Electric Cutaway (Laminate)
1980s-1990s. All laminate (plywood) construction, cutaway, standard features, pickup and preamp.

1980s-90s		$210	$400

Classical (Solid Top)
1980s-1990s. Solid wood (often cedar) top, classical, sides and back can vary.

1980s-90s		$400	$600

Collectors (Limited Edition)
1988-present. Each year a different limited edition collector's guitar is issued. '97 - solid top, koa body, cutaway, natural finish, preamp and pickup. '98 - solid top, rosewood body, cutaway, natural finish, preamp and pickup. '99 - solid top, rosewood body, cutaway, natural finish, preamp and pickup. '00 - solid top, rosewood body, cutaway, natural finish, preamp and pickup. '01 - solid top, rosewood body, cutaway, natural finish, preamp and pickup.

1988-2014		$720	$1,100

Solidbody Electric
1983-1984	Various models	$420	$900

MODEL YEAR	FEATURES	EXC. COND. LOW	HIGH

Takeharu (by Suzuki)
Mid-1970s. Classical guitars offered by Suzuki as part of their internationally known teaching method (e.g. Violin Suzuki method), various sized instruments designed to eliminate the confusion of size that has been a problem for classroom guitar programs.

Taku Sakashta Guitars
1994-2010. Premium and presentation grade, production/custom, archtop, flat-top, 12-sting, and nylon-string guitars, built by luthier Taku Sakashta in Sebastopol, California. He died in February, 2010.

Tama
Ca. 1959-1967, 1974-1979. Hoshino's (Ibanez) brand of higher-end acoutic flat-tops made in Japan. Many of the brand's features would be transferred to Ibanez's Artwood acoustics.

Tamura
1970s. Made in Japan by Mitsura Tamura, the line includes intermediate grade solid wood classical guitars.

Tanglewood Guitar Company UK
1991-present. Owners Dirk Kommer and Tony Flatt in Biggin Hill, U.K. import intermediate and professional grade, production, acoustic, classical, resonator and electric guitars and basses from China. They also offer mandolins, banjos, ukuleles and amps.

Taylor
1974-present. Intermediate, professional, premium, and presentation grade, production/custom, steel- and nylon-string, acoustic, acoustic/electric, semi-hollow, and solidbody guitars built in El Cajon, California. They have also built basses. Founded by Bob Taylor, Steve Schemmer and Kurt Listug in Lemon Grove, California, the company was originally named the Westland Music Company, but was soon changed to Taylor (Bob designed the guitars and it fit on the logo). Taylor and Listug bought out Schemmer in '83. Bob Taylor was the first commercially successful guitar maker to harness CAD/CAM CNC technology for acoustic guitars and in '91 introduced the 410 Model, the first all-solid wood American-made guitar with a list price under $1,000. The plain-appointment model using CNC technology was a major innovation combining quality and price. They added semi-hollowbodies in '05 and solidbodies in '07. In '08, they added the Build To Order custom shop.

100/200/300/etc. Series Note:
Several versions of these models may have been offered. The suffix after the model number indicates various features, such as e indicating an electronic version, c for cutaway version, ce cutaway with on-board electronics, and ce-N with nylon strings.

MODEL YEAR	FEATURES	EXC. COND. LOW	HIGH

110 Series
2003-present. Dreadnought, sapele back and sides, sitka spruce top, e and ce begin '08.

| 2003-2014 | | $450 | $550 |

114 Series
2007-present. Grand auditorium, sapele back and sides, sitka spruce top.

| 2007-2014 | 114 | $500 | $625 |
| 2008-2014 | 114ce | $675 | $850 |

214 Series
2004-present. Grand auditorium, sapele or Indian rosewood back and sides, sitka spruce top.

2004-2014	214	$525	$650
2004-2014	214c	$625	$775
2008-2014	214ce	$700	$875
2012-2014	214ce-N	$700	$875
2014	214ce-K DLX (Koa)	$850	$1,050

310 Series
1998-present. Dreadnought, mahogany or sapele back and sides, sitka spruce top. The non-cut 310 discontinued '07-'12, then reappeared in '13 along with 310e version.

| 1998-2006 | 310 | $750 | $950 |
| 1998-2014 | 310ce | $900 | $1,100 |

310ce-L30
2004. Limited Edition 30th Anniversary, myrtle-wood leaf inlays, koa rosette, 30th Anniversary headstock logo.

| 2004 | | $1,000 | $1,250 |

312 Series
1998-present. Grand concert, Venetian cutaway, mahogany or sapele back and sides, sitka spruce top. Non-cut 312 and 312e versions were offered in 2013.

| 1998-2014 | 312ce | $925 | $1,200 |

314 Series
1998-present. Mid-size grand auditorium, mahogany or sapele back and sides, sitka spruce top. Non-cut offered again in '13 along with 314e version.

1998-2006	314	$825	$1,025
1998-2014	314ce	$1,025	$1,275
2000	314ce-K (Koa)	$1,025	$1,275

314ce-LTD
2012. Hawaiian Koa back and sides, Indian rosewood headstock. Also offered with nylon strings (N).

| 2012 | | $1,250 | $1,550 |

315 Series
1998-2011. Jumbo, mahogany or sapele back and sides, sitka spruce top.

| 1998-2011 | 315ce | $1,025 | $1,275 |

316 Series
2012-present. Grand symphony, sitka spruce top, sapele back and sides.

| 2012-2014 | 316ce | $1,250 | $1,550 |
| 2013-2014 | 316/316e | $1,025 | $1,275 |

355 Series
1998-2011. Jumbo 12-string, mahogany or sapele back and sides, sitka spruce top.

| 1998-2006 | 355 | $1,025 | $1,275 |
| 1998-2011 | 355ce | $1,250 | $1,550 |

410 Series
1991-present. Dreadnought, mahogany back and sides until '98, ovangkol after '98, sitka spruce top. Non-cut offered again in '13 along with 410e version.

| 1991-2006 | 410 | $1,050 | $1,300 |
| 1991-2014 | 410cc | $1,250 | $1,550 |

412 Series
1991-present. Grand concert, mahogany back and sides until '98, ovangkol after, sitka spruce top. Cutaway electric version replaced the 412 in '98. Non-cut offered again in '13 along with 412e version.

1991-1998	412	$950	$1,200
1996	412-K (Koa)	$1,050	$1,300
1998-2014	412ce	$1,150	$1,425

414 Series
1998-present. Grand auditorium, ovangkol back and sides, sitka spruce top. Non-cut offered again in '13 along with 414e version.

1998	414-K (Koa)	$1,175	$1,475
1998-2006	414	$1,125	$1,425
1998-2014	414ce	$1,225	$1,525

414ce-LTD
2013. Sitka spruce top, tropical mahogany neck.

| 2013 | | $1,225 | $1,525 |

414-L10
2005. Limited Edition, rosewood sides and back, gloss spruce top, satin finish.

| 2005 | | $1,150 | $1,450 |

414-L30
2004. Limited Edition 30th Anniversary, Hawaiian koa back and sides, Engelmann spruce top, pearl and gold 30th Anniversary inlay.

| 2004 | | $1,325 | $1,650 |

415
1998-2006. Jumbo, ovangkol back and sides, sitka spruce top.

| 1998-2006 | | $1,075 | $1,325 |

418e
2015. Grand orchestra, ovangkol back and sides, sitka spruce top.

| 2015 | | $1,150 | $1,425 |

420
1990-1997. Dreadnought, Indian rosewood back and sides, sitka spruce top.

| 1990-1997 | | $1,100 | $1,350 |

422 Series
1991-1998. Grand concert, solid maple construction.

| 1991-1998 | 422-K (Koa) | $1,100 | $1,350 |
| 1997 | 422-R (Rosewood) | $1,000 | $1,225 |

426ce-LTD
2008. Limited Edition, Tasmanian blackwood top, back and sides.

| 2008 | | $1,600 | $2,000 |

450
1996-1997. Dreadnought 12-string, mahogany back and sides, spruce top.

| 1996-1997 | | $1,000 | $1,275 |

454ce
2004-2011. Grand auditorium 12-string, Ovangkol back and sides, sitka spruce top.

| 2004-2011 | | $1,200 | $1,500 |

Taylor 414ce

Taylor 426ce-LTD

Taylor 510
Emmitt Omar

Taylor 512ce

MODEL YEAR	FEATURES	EXC. COND. LOW	HIGH
455 Series			
2001-2011. Jumbo 12-string, Ovangkol back and sides, sitka spruce top.			
2001-2006	455	$1,200	$1,500
2001-2011	455ce	$1,350	$1,700
455ce-LTD			
2001-2003. Limited Edition, imbuia back and sides.			
2001-2003		$1,450	$1,800
510 Series			
1978-present. Dreadnought, mahogany back and sides, spruce top. Non-cut offered again in '13 along with 510e version.			
1978-2006	510	$1,175	$1,475
1978-2014	510ce	$1,525	$1,900
510ce-AB 25th Anniversary			
1999. D-size, 25th Anniversary on headstock, spruce top, mahogany back, sides and neck.			
1999		$2,000	$2,500
510-LTD			
2002. Mahogany back and sides, sitka spruce top.			
2002		$1,275	$1,575
512 Series			
1978-present. Grand concert, mahogany back and sides, red cedar top. Non-cut offered again in '13 along with 512e version.			
1978-2000	512	$1,200	$1,500
1978-2000	512c	$1,350	$1,700
1978-2014	512ce	$1,600	$1,975
2012-2014	512ce-N	$1,600	$1,975
512ce-L10			
2005. Limited Edition, American mahogany body and neck, abalone soundhole rosette, pearl diamond inlays, gold tuners.			
2005		$1,600	$1,975
512-NG Nanci Griffith			
1996-1997. 512ce with sunburst finish.			
1996-1997		$1,850	$2,325
514 Series			
1990-present. Grand auditorium, mahogany back and sides, Engelmann or sitka spruce top. Western red cedar top on 514c and ce. Non-cut offered again in '13 along with 514e version.			
1990-1998	514	$1,425	$1,775
1996-1998	514c	$1,525	$1,900
1998-2014	514ce	$1,625	$2,025
515-LTD			
1981. Limited Edition, mahogany back and sides, black binding, tortoise 'guard.			
1981		$1,625	$2,000
516 Series			
2008-present. Grand symphony, mahogany back and sides, Engelmann spruce top. Non-cut 516 offered in '13 along with 516e version.			
2008-2014	516ce	$1,700	$2,125
516ce-LTD			
2010. Spring Limited Editions, Tasmanian blackwood back and sides, sitka spruce top.			
2010		$1,900	$2,400
518 Series			
2012-2014. Grand orchestra, tropical mahogany back and sides, sitka spruce top, tortoise 'guard.			
2012-2014	518/518e	$1,750	$2,200

MODEL YEAR	FEATURES	EXC. COND. LOW	HIGH
555 Series			
1978-2006. Jumbo 12-string, mahogany back and sides, sitka spruce top, higher-end appointments.			
1994-2006	555	$1,650	$2,075
1994-2006	555ce	$1,900	$2,375
610 Series			
1978-present. Dreadnought, big leaf maple back and sides, sitka spruce top. Non-cut offered again in '13 along with 610e version.			
1978-1998	610	$1,425	$1,775
1998-2014	610ce	$1,625	$2,025
612 Series			
1984-present. Grand concert, big leaf maple back and sides, sitka spruce top. Non-cut offered again in '13 along with 612e version.			
1984-1998	612	$1,425	$1,775
1998-2014	612ce	$1,625	$2,025
614 Series			
1978-present. Grand auditorium, big leaf maple back and sides, sitka spruce top. Non-cut offered again in '13 along with 614e version.			
1978-1998	614	$1,725	$2,175
1998-2014	614ce	$1,925	$2,425
615 Series			
1981-2011. Jumbo, big leaf maple back and sides, sitka spruce top.			
1981-1998	615	$1,725	$2,175
1998-2011	615ce	$1,925	$2,425
616 Series			
2008-present. Grand symphony, big leaf maple back and sides, sitka spruce top. Non-cut 616 offered in '13 along with 616e version.			
2008-2014	616ce	$2,025	$2,525
618e			
2013-present. Grand orchestra, sitka spruce top, big leaf maple back and sides.			
2013-2014		$1,800	$2,250
654ce			
2004-2011. Grand auditorium 12-string, big leaf maple back and sides, sitka spruce top.			
2004-2011		$2,025	$2,525
655 Series			
1978-1991, 1996-2011. Jumbo 12-string, big leaf maple back and sides, sitka spruce top.			
1978-2006	655	$1,400	$1,750
1998-2011	655ce	$1,550	$1,900
710 Series			
1977-present. Dreadnought, Indian rosewood back and sides, Englemann or sitka spruce top. Non-cut offered again in '13 along with 710e version.			
1977-2006	710	$1,300	$1,650
1990s	710-BR (Brazilian)	$2,700	$3,400
1998-2014	710ce	$1,650	$2,050
710-B 25th Anniversary			
1999. D-size, 25th Anniversary on headstock, spruce top, abalone rosette, Brazilian rosewood sides and back, mahogany neck.			
1999		$2,700	$3,400

MODEL YEAR	FEATURES	EXC. COND. LOW	HIGH

710ce-L30
2004. Limited Edition 30th Anniversary, Englemann top, Indian rosewood body, 30th Anniversary inlay.

2004		$1,700	$2,100

712 Series
1984-present. Grand concert, Indian rosewood back and sides, Englemann or sitka spruce top. Non-cut offered again in '13 along with 712e version.

1984-2006	712	$1,400	$1,750
2000-2014	712ce	$1,750	$2,150

714 Series
1996-present. Grand auditorium, Indian rosewood back and sides, red cedar top. Non-cut offered again in '13 along with 714e version.

1996-2006	714	$1,400	$1,750
1998-2014	714ce	$1,750	$2,150

714ce-L1
2003-2004. Limited Edition, Western red cedar top, grafted walnut sides and back, pearl inlay, Hawaiian koa rosette.

2003-2004		$1,800	$2,200

755
1990-1998. Dreadnought 12-string, rosewood back and sides.

1990-1998		$1,750	$2,150

810 Series
1975-present. Classic dreadnought, Indian rosewood back and sides, sitka spruce top. Non-cut offered again in '13 along with 810e version.

1975-2006	810	$1,575	$1,950
1993-1998	810c	$1,775	$2,175
1996-2014	810ce	$1,975	$2,425
1996-2014	810ce-BR (Brazilian)	$3,000	$3,800

810-L30
2004. Limited Edition 30th Anniversary, maple leaf inlays, soundhole rosette, 30th Anniversary logo.

2004		$1,775	$2,175

810ce-LTD
2010. Limited Edition, Venetian cutaway, Madagascar rosewood back and sides, solid sitka spruce top.

2010		$2,075	$2,550

812 Series
1985, 1993-present. Grand concert, Indian rosewood back and sides, sitka spruce top. Non-cut offered again in '13 along with 812e version.

1985	812	$1,500	$1,900
1993-1998	812c	$1,700	$2,100
1998-2014	812ce	$1,900	$2,400

814 Series
1993-present. Grand auditorium, Indian rosewood back and sides, sitka spruce top. Non-cut offered again in '13 along with 814e version.

1993-1998	814	$1,800	$2,250
1996-1998	814c	$1,900	$2,350
1998-2006	814ce	$2,000	$2,500
2000	814-BE (Brazilian/ Englemann)	$3,100	$3,900

814ce-LTD
2012. Spring Limited Edition, cocobolo back and sides, sitka spruce top.

2012		$2,000	$2,500

815 Series
1970s-2011. Jumbo, Indian rosewood back and sides, sitka spruce top.

1970s-2006	815	$1,750	$2,250
1993-1998	815c	$1,800	$2,300
1997	815c-BR (Brazilian)	$4,000	$5,000
1998-2011	815ce	$1,850	$2,350

816 Series
2008-present. Grand symphony, sitka spruce top, Indian rosewood back and sides.

2008-2014	816ce	$1,850	$2,350
2013-2014	816/816e	$1,750	$2,250

855 Series
1981-2011. Jumbo 12-string, Indian rosewood back and sides, sitka spruce top.

1981-2011		$1,800	$2,250

910 Series
1977-present. Dreadnought, maple back and sides, changed to Brazilian rosewood in '86, wide abalone-style rosette. Non-cut offered again in '13 along with 910e version, Indian rosewood back and sides, sitka spruce top.

1977-1985	910 Maple	$1,800	$2,250
1986-2006	910 Brazilian	$3,000	$3,800
1998-2014	910ce	$2,000	$2,400

912 Series
1993-present. Grand concert, Indian rosewood back and sides, Engelmann spruce top, abalone. Non-cut offered in '13 along with 912e version.

1993-2002	912c	$2,100	$2,600
1993-2014	912ce	$2,250	$2,800

914 Series
1990s-present. Grand concert, Indian rosewood back and sides, Engelmann spruce top. Non-cut offered in '13 along with 914e version.

2002-2014	914ce	$2,600	$3,250

914ce-L1
2003. Fall Limited Edition, Indian rosewood back and sides, Engelmann spruce top, abalone leaf and vine inlays.

2003		$2,700	$3,350

914ce-L7
2004. Sitka spruce top, Brazilian rosewood back and sides, abalone rosette.

2004		$2,900	$3,600

918e
2013-2014. Grand orchestra, sitka spruce top, Indian rosewood back and sides.

2013-2014		$2,500	$3,100

Baby Taylor
1996-present. 3/4-size dreadnought, mahogany laminated back and sides until '99, sapele laminate after, various tops.

1996-2014	BT1, sitka spruce	$175	$250
1998-2014	BT2, mahogany	$175	$250
2000-2003	BT3, maple	$175	$250

Baby Rosewood
2000-2003. Laminated Indian rosewood back and sides Baby.

2000-2003		$175	$250

Taylor 610ce

Taylor 810

To get the most from this book, be sure to read "Using **The Guide**" in the introduction.

Taylor DMSM Dave Matthews Signature

Taylor K22ce

MODEL YEAR	FEATURES	EXC. COND. LOW	HIGH

Baritone 8
2009-2014. Grand symphony size, 8-string baritone, Indian rosewood or mahogany back and sides, sitka spruce top.

2009-2014		$2,200	$2,700

Big Baby BBT
2000-present. 15/16-size dreadnought, sapele laminate back and sides, sitka spruce top.

2000-2014		$250	$325

CPSM Chris Proctor Signature
2001. Limited edition, 100 made, Indian rosewood body, Engelmann spruce top.

2001		$1,600	$2,000

CUJO Model
1997. Dreadnought (CUJO-10) or grand auditorium (CUJO-14), made from 100+ year old black walnut tree appearing in famous Stephen King movie "Cujo" (1983). Robert Taylor purchased the tree when it was dying of old age. The DN has spruce top, GA has cedar, both have elaborate appointments and are signed by Taylor and King. Only 125 made of each.

1997	CUJO-10,		
	CUJO-14	$1,500	$1,875

Custom Shop
2008-present. Custom shop models - some are one-offs, others are series ordered by specific dealers. Previously called Taylor's Build To Order program.

Custom Dreadnought
2008-2014	Rosewood/		
	Adirondack	$2,100	$2,600

Custom Grand Auditorium
2008-2014	Adirondack/		
	mahogany	$2,600	$3,200
2008-2014	Figured koa	$3,800	$4,700
2008-2014	Spruce/maple	$2,600	$3,200

Custom Grand Concert
2008-2014	Rosewood/		
	ovangkol	$2,600	$3,200

Custom T3/BTO T5
2008-2014	Rosewood	$2,100	$2,600

DCSM Dan Crary Signature
1986-2000. Dreadnought, Venetian cutaway, thin spruce top, Indian rosewood back and sides, Crary signature on headstock.

1986-2000		$1,500	$1,900

DDAD Doyle Dykes Signature Anniversary
2005. Indian rosewood back and sides, soft cutaway, on-board transducer.

2005		$2,400	$3,000

DDSM Doyle Dykes Signature
2000-2012. Grand auditorium cutaway acoustic/electric, figured maple body.

2000-2012		$2,400	$3,000

DMSM Dave Matthews Signature
2010-2012. Limited Edition based on 914ce, Taylor Expression pickup system.

2010-2012		$2,600	$3,200

DN Series
2007-2012. Dreadnought Series, various woods.

2007-2012	DN5, mahogany	$1,350	$1,700

MODEL YEAR	FEATURES	EXC. COND. LOW	HIGH

GA Limited Editions
1995. Grand Auditorium Limited Editions. GA-BE has Brazilian rosewood back and sides with Engelmann spruce top, KC has koa/cedar, KS koa/spruce, MC mahogany/cedar, RS Indian rosewood/spruce, and WS walnut/spruce.

1995	GA-BE, 50 made	$4,000	$5,000
1995	GA-KC	$2,600	$3,200
1995	GA-RS, 300 made	$1,750	$2,200
1995	GA-WS	$2,400	$3,000

GA Series
2007-2012. Grand Auditorium Series, various woods.

1995	GA-BE-LTD, Brazilian/ Engelmann	$4,000	$5,000
1995	GA-KC-LTD, koa	$2,600	$3,200
2007-2012	GA3, sapele	$800	$1,000
2007-2012	GA4, ovangkol	$900	$1,100
2007-2012	GA5, mahogany	$1,350	$1,700
2007-2012	GA6, maple	$1,400	$1,750
2007-2012	GA6-12, maple	$1,550	$1,900
2007-2012	GA7, rosewood	$1,250	$1,550
2007-2012	GA8, rosewood	$1,400	$1,750
2008-2012	GA-K-12, koa	$1,750	$2,200

GC Series
2007-2012. Grand Concert Series, various woods.

2007-2012	GC3, sapele	$825	$1,025
2007-2012	GC4, ovangkol	$875	$1,100
2007-2012	GC6, maple	$1,300	$1,625
2007-2012	GC7, rosewood	$1,300	$1,625
2007-2012	GC8, rosewood	$1,300	$1,625
2011	GC-LTD, mahogany	$1,475	$1,850

GS Series
2006-present. Grand Symphony Series, various woods.

2007-2012	GS3, sapele	$725	$925
2007-2012	GS5, mahogany	$1,425	$1,800
2007-2012	GS5-12, 12-string	$1,425	$1,800
2007-2012	GS6, maple	$1,425	$1,800
2007-2012	GS7, cedar	$1,425	$1,800
2007-2012	GS8, rosewood	$1,425	$1,800
2007-2012	GS8-12, 12-string	$1,425	$1,800
2011-2014	GS Mini, sapele	$350	$450

K Series
1983-present. Koa Series, various models with Hawaiian koa.

1983-1992	K20	$2,000	$2,500
1983-2006	K10	$1,625	$2,025
1995-1998	K65, 12-string	$2,500	$3,100
1998-2000	K22	$2,175	$2,750
1998-2002	K14c	$1,750	$2,150
1998-2002	K20c	$2,000	$2,500
1998-2012	K14ce	$2,000	$2,500
2001-2006	K55, 12-string	$2,500	$3,100
2001-2014	K20ce	$2,100	$2,600
2003-2014	K22ce	$2,375	$2,950
2007-2011	K54ce	$2,600	$3,200
2007-2012	K10ce	$2,000	$2,500
2008-2014	K26ce	$2,500	$3,100

The Official Vintage Guitar magazine Price Guide 2016   **Taylor** LKSM-6/12 Leo Kottke Sig. — XXX 30th Ann. Series   **315**

GUITARS

MODEL YEAR	FEATURES	EXC. COND. LOW	HIGH

LKSM-6/12 Leo Kottke Signature

1981-2012. Jumbo 17" body, 6- or 12-string, rounded cutaway, sitka spruce top, mahogany back and sides, gloss finish, Leo Kottke signature.

| 1981-2012 | 12-string | $1,625 | $2,050 |
| 1981-2012 | 6-string | $1,625 | $2,050 |

LTG Liberty Tree L.E.

2002. Limited Edition includes DVD and certificate which are important to instrument's value, solid wood grand concert body, high-end art and appointments. Around 400 made.

| 2002 | | $4,800 | $6,100 |

NS Series

2002-2011. Nylon Strung series, various models and woods, models include NS24e/NS24ce (Indian rosewood/ spruce), NS32ce/NS34ce (mahogany/spruce), NS42ce/ NS44ce (ovangkol), NS52ce/NS54ce (mahogany), NS62ce/NS64ce (maple/Engelmann) and NS72ce/ NS74ce (Indian rosewood/cedar) All models were cutaway electric (ce) by '04, until '10 when NS24e was offered.

2002-2006	NS42ce	$1,025	$1,300
2002-2006	NS44/NS44ce	$1,125	$1,425
2002-2006	NS52ce	$1,125	$1,425
2002-2006	NS54ce	$1,275	$1,600
2002-2011	NS32ce	$950	$1,175
2002-2011	NS62ce	$1,700	$2,125
2002-2011	NS64ce	$1,750	$2,175
2002-2011	NS72ce	$1,825	$2,300
2002-2011	NS74/NS74ce	$1,975	$2,475
2004-2011	NS34ce	$1,025	$1,300
2010-2011	NS24e/NS24ce	$625	$775

Pre-Production Model

1974. Early pre-production custom made (custom order), could be an instrument with the Taylor American Dream label, or may not have a logo or brand.

| 1974 | Fancy | $5,000 | $7,500 |
| 1974 | Standard | $3,000 | $5,000 |

PS Series

1996-present. Presentation Series, various models, Hawaiian koa with Engelmann spruce used early on, followed by Brazilian rosewood, by '07 a variety of woods were offered, values vary depending on specs and appointments.

1996-2003	PS12/PS12c	$4,500	$5,600
1996-2006	PS10	$4,000	$5,000
1996-2006	PS15	$4,500	$5,600

PS14BZ Special Edition

1996. Presentation Series Special Edition, Brazilian rosewood back and sides, Engelmann spruce top, abalone trim.

| 1996 | | $4,500 | $5,600 |

PS14c Special Edition

1998-2000. Presentation Series special edition with spruce top, AAA koa back and sides.

| 1998-2000 | | $4,500 | $5,600 |

PS Limited Edition

2003. Presentation Series Limited Edition, grand concert has quilted maple back and sides with Engelmann spruce top, dreadnought has cocobolo back and sides with sitka spruce top.

| 2003 | | $3,200 | $4,000 |

Solidbody Classic

2008-2014. Single- or double-cut, ash body, 2 humbuckers or single-coils, pearl 'guard.

| 2008-2014 | | $750 | $950 |

Solidbody Custom

2008-2010. Single- or double-cut, koa top with Tasmanian blackwood body in '08 and mahogany after or walnut top with sapele body, 2 humbuckers, diamond inlays, ivoroid binding.

| 2008-2010 | Koa | $1,600 | $2,000 |
| 2008-2010 | Walnut | $1,500 | $1,875 |

Solidbody Standard

2008-2014. Single- or double-cut, Tamo ash top ('08-'09) and maple after, sapele body (08-'10) and mahogany after, 2 exposed coil humbuckers, ivoroid binding.

| 2008-2014 | | $1,050 | $1,325 |

T3 Series

2009-present. Semi-hollow thinline, single-cut, figured maple. T3/B with Bigsby.

| 2009-2014 | T3, T3/B | $1,500 | $1,850 |

T5 Series

2005-present Semi-hollow thinline body, sapele back and sides, spruce, maple, or koa tops, Custom models have gold hardware and Artist inlays, Standard is chrome with micro-dots. Prices will vary depending on type of figured-wood used, figured maple and koa will be more than plain tops.

| 2005-2014 | 12-string | $1,700 | $2,200 |
| 2005-2014 | 6-string | $1,500 | $2,000 |

Walnut Series

1998-2006. Highly figured claro walnut backs and sides with spruce, cedar or walnut tops. Ivoroid, ebony, gold and abalone accents.

1998-2000	W12c	$1,650	$2,050
1998-2006	W10	$1,550	$1,925
2000-2006	W14ce	$1,825	$2,275

WHCM Windham Hill

2003. Commemorative Model, D-size, spruce top, rosewood sides and back, fancy appointments with Windham Hill logo inlay.

| 2003 | | $1,650 | $2,050 |

XX 20th Anniversary Series

1994. Limited Edition, grand auditorium, "XX" solid 18 karat gold inlay, mother-of-pearl inlay, abalone rosette, available either mahogany back and sides with cedar top (XX-MC) or Indian rosewood with spruce (XX-RS).

| 1994 | XX-MC | $2,000 | $2,500 |
| 1994 | XX-RS | $2,100 | $2,650 |

XXV 25th Anniversary

1999-2000. Dreadnought (XXV-DR) and grand auditorium (XXV-GA) models, various woods.

| 1999-2000 | XXV-DR, XXV-GA | $1,550 | $1,925 |

XXX 30th Anniversary Series

2004-2005. Limited Edition, grand concert, "XXX" solid 18 karat gold inlay, fancy appointments, XXX-BE has Brazilian rosewood back and sides with Engelmann spruce top, KE has koa/Engelmann spruce, MS maple/spruce and RS Indian rosewood/spruce.

| 2004-2005 | XXX-BE | $3,400 | $4,300 |

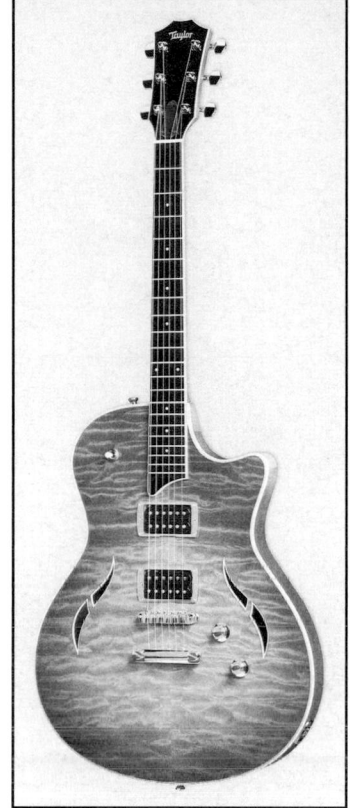

Taylor T3

Taylor T5-C1
Rick Mastry

Teisco EP10
Greg Perrine

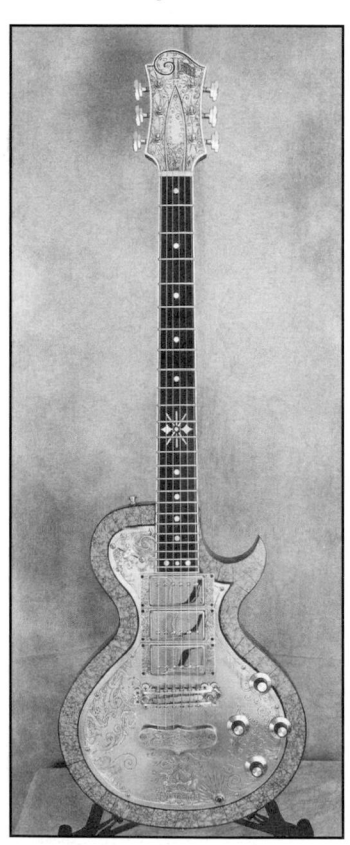

2006 Teye Electric Gypsy

MODEL YEAR	FEATURES	EXC. COND. LOW	HIGH
2004-2005	XXX-KE	$2,100	$2,650
2004-2005	XXX-MS	$2,100	$2,650
2004-2005	XXX-RS	$2,100	$2,650

XXXV 35th Anniversary Series
2009. Limited Edition, various models and woods, "35" between the 11th and 12th frets. Models include DN (Dreadnought), GC (Grand Concert), GS (Grand Symphony), P (Parlor), TF (12-Fret), 9-string, plus more.

2009	XXXV-9, 9-string	$2,100	$2,650

Teisco

1946-1974, 1994-present. Founded in Tokyo, Japan by Hawaiian and Spanish guitarist Atswo Kaneko and electrical engineer Doryu Matsuda, the original company name was Aoi Onpa Kenkyujo; Teisco was the instrument name. Most imported into U.S. by Jack Westheimer beginning ca. '60 and Chicago's W.M.I. Corporation beginning around '64, some early ones for New York's Bugeleisen and Jacobson. Brands made by the company include Teisco, Teisco Del Rey, Kingston, World Teisco, Silvertone, Kent, Kimberly and Heit Deluxe.

In '56, the company's name was changed to Nippon Onpa Kogyo Co., Ltd., and in '64 the name changed again to Teisco Co., Ltd. In January '67, the company was purchased by Kawai. After '73, the brand was converted to Kay in U.S.; Teisco went into hiatus in Japan until being revived in the early-'90s with plexiglass reproductions of the Spectrum 5 (not available in U.S.). Some older Teisco Del Rey stock continued to be sold in U.S. through the '70s.

Electric

1966-1969	1 pickup	$105	$200
1966-1969	2 pickups	$130	$250
1966-1969	3 pickups	$255	$400
1966-1969	4 pickups or special finishes	$360	$500
1966-1969	Spectrum V	$450	$575
1968-1969	May Queen, black	$450	$575
1968-1969	May Queen, red	$500	$625
1968-1969	Phantom	$500	$625

Tele-Star

1965-ca.1972. Imported from Japan by Tele-Star Musical Instrument Corporation of New York, New York. Primarily made by Kawai, many inspired by Burns designs, some in cool sparkle finishes. They also built basses.

Electric

1966-1969	1, 2, or 3 pickups	$105	$400
1966-1969	4 pickups or special finishes	$300	$450
1966-1969	Amp-in-case	$240	$300
1969-1970	Double neck 6/4	$525	$650

Tempo

1950s-1970s. Solid and semi-hollow body electric and acoustic guitars, most likely imported by Merson Musical Products from Japan. They also offered basses and amps.

Tennessee

1970-1993, 1996-present. Luthier Mark Taylor builds his professional and premium grade, production/custom, acoustic guitars in Old Hickory, Tennessee. He also builds mandolins, banjos and the Tut Taylor brand of resophonic guitars. Mark and his father Robert "Tut" Taylor started making the Tennessee brand of acoustic and resophonic guitars, banjos, and mandolins in '71. In '77, Tut left the company and Mark continued on as Crafters of Tennessee. In '93, Mark and Greg Rich started building instruments as Rich and Taylor. In '96, Mark resumed production under the Tennessee brand.

Teuffel

1988-present. Luthier Ulrich Teuffel builds his production/custom, premium and presentation grade electric solidbody guitars in Neu-Ulm, Bavaria, Germany.

Texas

1959-ca. 1965. Line of aluminum neck electric solidbodies and basses made by France's Jacobacci company, which also built under its own brand. One, two, or three pickups.

Teye

2006-present. Luthier Teye Wijterp builds his premium and presentation grade, production/custom, solid and chambered body guitars in Austin, Texas. Some instruments are branded as Electric Gypsy guitars.

Thomas

1960s-1970s. Single, double and triple-neck electrics made by luthier Harvey Thomas in Midway, Washington. Best known for his Maltese cross shaped models, he also offered several other unique shaped designs and one-offs.

Thomas Rein

1972-present. Luthier Thomas Rein builds his premium grade, production/custom, classical guitars in St. Louis, Missouri.

Thompson Guitars

1980-present. Luthier Ted Thompson builds his professional and premium grade, production/custom, flat-top, 12-string, and nylon-string guitars in Vernon, British Columbia.

Thorell Fine Guitars

1994-present. Premium grade, custom/production, archtop, flattop and classical guitars built by luthier Ryan Thorell in Logan, Utah.

Thorn Custom Guitars

2000-present. Professional and premium grade, custom/production, solid and hollowbody electrics built by luthiers Bill Thorn and his sons Bill, Jr. and Ron in Glendale, California. They started Thorn Custom

MODEL YEAR	FEATURES	EXC. COND. LOW	HIGH

Inlay in the early '90s to do custom inlay work for other builders. In '00, they added their own line of guitars.

Thornward

Ca. 1901-ca. 1910. Line of guitars sold by the Montgomery Ward company and built by others including Lyon & Healy. The name is from a combination of last names of company founder Aaron Montgomery Ward and company manager George Thorne.

Threet Guitars

1990-present. Premium grade, production/custom, flat-tops built by luthier Judy Threet in Calgary, Alberta.

Tilton

1850s-late 1800s. Built by William B. Tilton, of New York City, New York. He was quite an innovator and held several guitar-related patents. He also built banjos.

Parlor

1850s-1890s. Parlor guitar with various woods.

1850s-80s	Brazilian, fancy binding	$1,800	$2,300
1890s	Diagonal grain spruce top, Brazilian	$1,400	$1,800
1890s	Pearl trim, Brazilian	$2,700	$3,400
1890s	Standard grain spruce top, Brazilian	$800	$1,000

Tim Reede Custom Guitars

2004-present. Luthier Tim Reede builds his professional and premium grade, production/custom, archtop, flat-top and electric guitars in Minneapolis, Minnesota.

Timeless Instruments

1980-present. Luthier David Freeman builds his professional, premium and presentation grade, custom, flattop, 12-string, nylon-string, and resonator guitars in Tugaske, Saskatchewan. He also builds mandolins and dulcimers.

Timm Guitars

Professional grade, custom, flat-top, resonator and travel guitars built by luthier Jerry Timm in Auburn, Washington.

Timtone Custom Guitars

1993-2006. Luthier Tim Diebert built his premium grade, custom, solidbody, chambered-body and acoustic guitars and basses in Grand Forks, British Columbia. He also built lap steels.

Tippin Guitar Co.

1978-present. Professional, premium and presentation grade, production/custom, flat-top guitars built by luthier Bill Tippin in Marblehead, Massachusetts.

Tobias

1977-present. Known mainly for basses, Tobias did offer guitar models in the '80s. See Bass Section for more company info.

TogaMan GuitarViol

2003-present. Premium grade, production/custom, bow-playable solidbody guitars built by luthier Jonathan Wilson in Sylmar, California.

Tokai

1947-present. Japan's Tokai Company started out making a keyboard harmonica that was widely used in Japanese schools. In '65, they started producing acoustic guitars, followed shortly by electrics. In the late '60s, Tokai hooked up with Tommy Moore, a successful instrument merchandiser from Fort Worth, Texas, and by '70 they were producing private label and OEM guitars, sold in the U.S. under the brands of various importers. By the '70s, the Tokai name was being used on the instruments. Today Tokai continues to offer electrics, acoustics, and electric basses made in Japan and Korea.

ASD-403 Custom Edition

1980s. Strat copy, single-single-hum pickups, locking tremolo.

1980s		$450	$560

AST Series

Early 1980s. Strat copies, maple board (AST-56) or slab rosewood (AST-62), 3 single-coils

1980s	AST-56	$525	$675
1980s	AST-62	$525	$675

ATE Series

Early 1980s. Tele copies, blond (ATE-52) and pink paisley (ATE-67), 2 single-coils.

1980s	ATE-52	$525	$675
1980s	ATE-67	$550	$690

Blazing Fire

1982-1984. Hybrid-shaped solidbody with 2 medium-short pointy horns, cast aluminum body.

1982-1984		$675	$850

Breezy Sound

1977-1984. Copy of '60s rosewood board Tele.

1977-1984		$675	$850

CE-180W Cat's Eyes

Late-1970s-Early-1980s. D-style flat-top, made by Tokai Gakki, Nyatoh sides and back.

1979-1980s		$210	$260

CE-250 Cat's Eyes

Late-1970s-Early-1980s. D-style flat-top.

1979-1980s		$210	$260

CE-300 Cat's Eyes

Late-1970s-Early-1980s. D-style flat-top, made by Tokai Gakki, rosewood sides and back.

1979-1980s		$325	$400

CE-400 Cat's Eyes

Late-1970s-Early-1980s. D-style flat-top, made by Tokai Gakki, rosewood sides and back.

1979-1980s		$450	$560

Tobias
Greg Perrine

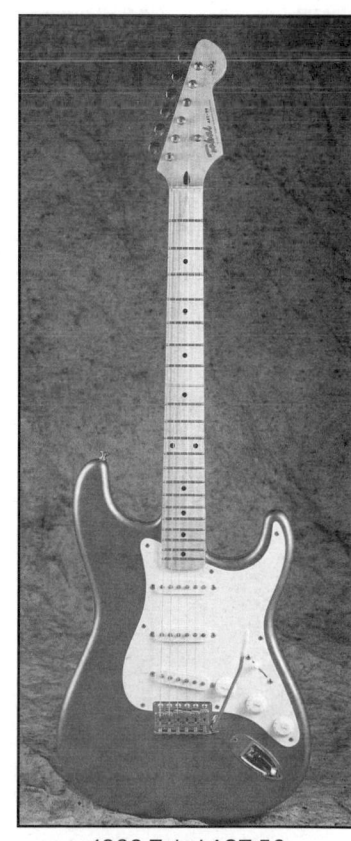

1982 Tokai AST-56
Vintage Series

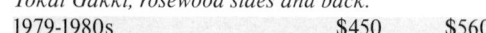

GUITARS

1966 Tom Anderson
Hollow Drop Top Classic
My Generation Guitars

Tony Vines Guitar #100

MODEL YEAR	FEATURES	EXC. COND. LOW	HIGH
CE-600 Cat's Eyes			
1979-1980. D-style flat-top, rosewood sides and back.			
1979-1980		$475	$600
FV48			
1980s. Flying V copy.			
1980s		$460	$570
Goldstar Sound			
1984. Replica that replaced the Springy Sound, new less pointy headstock shape.			
1984		$450	$560
J-200N			
1979-1980. Gibson J-200 natural copy.			
1979-1980		$450	$560
Les Paul Reborn			
1976-1985. LP copy with Gibson-style Tokai headstock logo and Les Paul Reborn script logo instead of Les Paul Model, renamed Reborn Old in '82, becomes Love Rock in mid-'80s.			
1976-1982	Les Paul Reborn	$675	$850
1982-1985	Reborn Old	$675	$850
Love Rock/LS Series			
1980s-2000s. Various LP Std copy models (LC are LP Custom copies), 2 humbuckers, sunburst, gold top, black, figured tops at the high end, Love Rock in script logo on headstock.			
1980s		$675	$850
2003	LS 75 Love Rock	$675	$850
2003	LS 80 Love Rock	$675	$850
SC Series			
Tele copies.			
2000s	SC-1	$325	$400
Silver Star			
1977-1984. Copy of post-CBS large headstock Strat.			
1977-1984		$360	$450
Springy Sound			
1977-1984. Strat copy, original high-end nitro-finish.			
1977-1979	With skunk stripe	$675	$850
1979-1984	No skunk stripe	$675	$850
Vintage Series Electric EX-55			
1980s. Vintage Series Explorer copies, bolt neck, 1 or 2 humbuckers.			
1980s	1 pickup	$450	$560
1980s	2 pickups	$460	$570
Vintage Series TST			
Early-1980s. Copy of maple neck (TST-56) and rosewood slab board (TST-62) Strats, 4-bolt neck plate with serial number.			
1980s	TST-56	$525	$675
1980s	TST-62	$525	$675

Tom Anderson Guitarworks

1984-present. Professional and premium grade, production/custom, solidbody, semi-solidbody and acoustic guitars built by luthier Tom Anderson in Newbury Park, California.

Various Electric Models

1984-2014		$1,500	$3,000

TommyHawk

1993-2005. Acoustic travel guitars built by luthier Tom Barth in Succasunna, New Jersey. They also offered a full-scale acoustic/electric model. Barth died in '05.

Toneline

1950s. Student-level private brand built by Chicago builders (Kay, Harmony). Typical '50s Stella brand specs like birch body with painted binding and rosette, pointed Toneline script logo on headstock.

Tonemaster

1960s. Guitars and basses, made in Italy by the Crucianelli Company, with typical '60s Italian sparkle plastic finish and push-button controls, bolt-on neck. Imported into the U.S. by The Imperial Accordion Company. They also offered guitar amps.

Rhythm Tone

1960-1963. Tonemaster headstock logo, Rhythm Tone logo on 'guard, single neck pickup, 3-in-line control knobs, bolt-on neck, black finish.

1960-1963		$750	$925

ToneSmith

1997-present. Luthier Kevin Smith builds his professional and premium grade, production/custom, semi-hollow body guitars and basses in Rogers, Minnesota. He previously built GLF brand guitars and built the line of Vox USA guitars from '98-'01.

Tony Nobles

Professional and premium grade, custom, acoustic and electric guitars built by luthier Tony Nobles in Wimberley, Texas.

Tony Vines Guitars

1989-present. Luthier Tony Vines builds his premium and presentation grade, custom/production, steel string guitars in Kingsport, Tennessee.

Torres (Antonio de Torres Jurado)

19th Century luthier most often associated with the initial development of the Classical Spanish guitar.

Tosca

1950s. Private economy brand made by Valco, possibly for a jobber, mail-order catalog or local department store.

Bolero 1123

1950s. Small three-quarter size electric similar to National (Valco) model 1123, single-cut, 1 neck pickup, guard mounted controls.

1950s		$600	$800

Toyota

1972-1970s. Imported from Japan by Hershman of New York, New York. At least 1 high-end acoustic designed by T. Kurosawa was ambitiously priced at $650.

MODEL YEAR	FEATURES	EXC. COND. LOW	HIGH

Traphagen, Dake

1972-present. Luthier Dake Traphagen builds his premium grade, custom, classical and steel-string guitars in Bellingham, Washington.

Traugott Guitars

1991-present. Premium grade, production/custom, flat-top and acoustic/electric guitars built by luthier Jeff Traugott in Santa Cruz, California.

Traveler Guitar

1992-present. Intermediate grade, production, travel size electric, acoustic, classical and acoustic/electric guitars and basses made in Redlands, California.

Travis Bean

1974-1979, 1999. Aluminum-necked solidbody electric guitars and basses. The company was founded by motorcycle and metal-sculpture enthusiast Travis Bean and guitar repairman Marc McElwee in Southern California; soon joined by Gary Kramer (see Kramer guitars). Kramer left Travis Bean in '75 and founded Kramer guitars with other partners. Guitar production began in mid-'76. The guitars featured carved aluminum necks with three-and-three heads with a T cutout in the center and wooden 'boards. Some necks had bare aluminum backs, some were painted black. A total of about 3,650 instruments were produced. Travis Bean guitar production was stopped in the summer of '79.

Serial numbers were stamped on headstock and were more-or-less consecutive. Original retail prices were $895 to $1195.

The company announced renewed production in '99 with updated versions of original designs and new models, but it evidently never got going.

TB-500

1975-1976. Aluminum neck, T-slotted headstock, double-cut, 2 single coils mounted in 'guard, 2 controls, dot markers, white.

1975-1976		$4,400	$5,500

TB-1000 Artist

1974-1979. Aluminum neck, T-slotted headstock, double-cut archtop, 2 humbuckers, 4 controls, block inlays.

1974-1979		$4,400	$5,500
1974-1979	Rare colors	$4,800	$6,000

TB-1000 Standard

1974-1979. Similar to TB-1000 Artist, but with dot inlays.

1974-1979		$4,000	$5,000

TB-3000 Wedge

1976-1979. Aluminum neck with T-slotted headstock, triangle-shaped body, 2 humbucking pickups, 4 controls, block markers on 'board.

1976-1979		$4,600	$5,800

Tregan Guitars

2007-present. Solidbody electrics including Bison-style sharp curved horns body style, plus other less traditional styles, student and intermediate grade.

Tremblett Archtops

2006-present. Luthier Mark Tremblett builds his professional grade, custom, archtop guitars in Pouch Cove, Newfoundland.

Tremcaster

2008-present. Luthier John Mosconi, along with Robert Gelley and Jeff Russell, builds professional grade, production/custom, electric and acoustic guitars in Akron, Ohio.

Trenier

1998-present. Premium grade, production/custom, archtop guitars built by luthier Bryant Trenier in Seattle, Washington. From '02 to '04 he was located in Prague, Czech Republic.

Triggs

1992-present. Luthiers Jim Triggs and his son Ryan build their professional and premium grade, production/custom, archtop, flat-top, and solidbody guitars originally in Nashville Tennessee, and, since '98, in Kansas City, Kansas. They also build mandolins.

Acoustic/Electric Archtop

1992-present. Various archtop cutaway models.

1992-2009	Byrdland 17"	$2,100	$2,600
1992-2009	Excel 17"	$3,100	$3,900
1992-2009	Jazzmaster	$1,800	$2,250
1992-2009	New Yorker 18"	$4,500	$5,600
1992-2010	Stromberg		
	Master 400	$4,500	$5,600
2006	San Salvador	$2,600	$3,300

Trinity River

2004-present. Located in Fort Worth, Texas, luthiers Marcus Lawyer and Ross McLeod import their production/custom, budget and intermediate grade, acoustic and resonator guitars and basses from Asia. They also import mandolins and banjos.

True North Guitars

1994-present. Luthier Dennis Scannell builds his premium grade, custom, flat-tops in Waterbury, Vermont.

True Tone

1960s. Guitars, basses and amps retailed by Western Auto, manufactured by Chicago guitar makers like Kay. The brand was most likely gone by '68.

Electric Archtop (K592 Kay)

1960s. Made by Kay and similar to their K592 double-cut thinline acoustic, 2 pickups, Bigsby tailpiece, burgundy red.

1960s		$500	$625

Traphagen Model OO

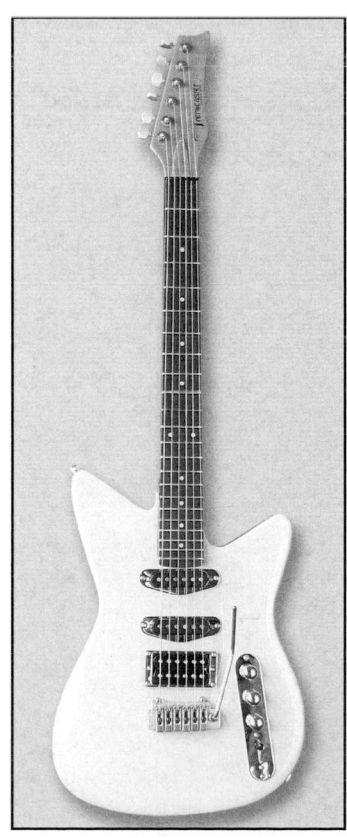

Tremcaster SSH

Tsunami Wild Cherry

Univox Gimme
Greg Perrine

MODEL		EXC. COND.	
YEAR	FEATURES	LOW	HIGH

Fun Time
Early- to mid-1960s. Student 13" flat-top, painted 5-point 'guard, red sunburst finish.
| 1960s | | $55 | $75 |

Imperial Deluxe
Mid-1960s. Harmony-made (Rocket), 3 pickups, trapeze tailpiece, 6 control knobs, block markers, sunburst.
| 1960s | | $700 | $875 |

Jazz King (K573 Kay)
1960s. Kay's K573 Speed Demon, 3 pickups, thinline archtop electric with f-hole, eighth note art on 'guard, sunburst.
| 1960s | | $550 | $675 |

Rock 'n Roll Electric (K100 Kay)
1960s. Kay's K100, slab body, single pickup, but with a bright red multiple lacquer finish.
| 1960s | | $225 | $285 |

Solidbody (K300 Kay)
1960s. Made by Kay and similar to their K300, double-cut, dual pickups and vibrola arm, red.
| 1960s | | $425 | $525 |

Speed Master (K6533 Kay)
1960s. Made by Kay and similar to their K6533 full-body electric archtop Value Leader line, eighth note art 'guard, sunburst.
| 1960s | | $300 | $375 |

Western Spanish Auditorium
Early- to mid-1960s. 15" flat-top, laminate construction, celluloid 'guard, sunburst.
| 1960s | | $150 | $200 |

Tsunami
2009-present. Custom, intermediate grade, one-off solidbody electric guitars built by luthier Paul Brzozowski in Cleveland, Tennessee.

Tucker
Founded by John N. "Jack" Tucker, John Morrall, and David Killingsworth in 2000, Tucker builds professional and premium grade, production/custom, albizzia wood solidbody guitars and basses in Hanalei, Hawaii.

Tuscany Guitars
2008-2013. Intermediate grade, production, classic model electric guitars imported from Asia and finished by luthier Galeazzo Frudua in San Lazzaro di Savena, Italy.

Tut Taylor
Line of professional and premium grade, production/custom, resophonic guitars built by luthier Mark Taylor of Crafters of Tennessee in Old Hickory, Tennessee. Brand named for his father, dobro artist Tut Taylor. Taylor also builds the Tennessee line of guitars, mandolins and banjos and was part of Rich and Taylor guitars for '93-'96.

TV Jones
1993-present. Professional and premium grade, production/custom, hollow, chambered, and solid body guitars built by luthier Thomas Vincent Jones originally in California, now in Poulsbo, Washington. The instruments have either Jones or TV Jones inlaid on the headstock. He also builds pickups.

U. A. C.
1920s. Instruments built by the Oscar Schmidt Co. and possibly others. Most likely a brand made for a distributor.

Unique Guitars
2003-ca. 2007. Professional and premium grade, production/custom, solidbody guitars and basses built by luthier Joey Rico in California. Joey is the son of Bernie Rico, the founder of BC Rich guitars.

Univox
1964-1978. Univox started out as an amp line and added guitars around '68. Guitars were imported from Japan by the Merson Musical Supply Company, later Unicord, Westbury, New York. Many if not all supplied by Arai and Company (Aria, Aria Pro II), some made by Matsumoku. Univox Lucy ('69) first copy of lucite Ampeg Dan Armstrong. Generally mid-level copies of American designs.

Acoustic Flat-Top
1969-1978. Various models.
| 1970s | | $200 | $700 |

Bicentennial
1976. Offset double-cut, heavily carved body, brown stain, 3 humbucker-style pickups.
| 1976 | | $800 | $1,000 |

Deep Body Electric
1960s-1970s. ES-175 style.
| 1960-1970s | | $400 | $500 |

Electric Solidbody
1970s. Includes Flying V, Mosrite and Hofner violin-guitar copies.
1960-1970s	Hi Flier	$650	$800
1960-1970s	Various models	$300	$800
1970s	Effector	$450	$575

Guitorgan FSB C-3000
1970s. Double-cut semi-hollow body, multiple controls, Guitorgan logo on headstock, footpedal.
| 1970s | | $775 | $1,000 |

Thin Line (Coily)
| 1960-1970s | 12-string | $400 | $600 |
| 1960-1970s | 6-string | $400 | $600 |

USA Custom Guitars
1999-present. Professional and premium grade, custom/production, solidbody electric guitars built in Tacoma, Washington. USA also does work for other luthiers.

Vaccaro
1997-2002. Founded by Henry Vaccaro, Sr., one of the founders of Kramer Guitars. They offered intermediate and professional grade, production/custom, aluminum-necked guitars and basses designed by Vaccaro, former Kramer designer Phil Petillo, and Henry Vaccaro, Jr., which were made in Asbury Park, New Jersey.

GUITARS

MODEL YEAR	FEATURES	EXC. COND. LOW	HIGH

Val Dez

Early-1960s-early-1970s. Less expensive guitars built by Landola in Sweden or Finland; they also made the Espana brand.

Valco

1942-1968. Valco, of Chicago, was a big player in the guitar and amplifier business. Their products were private branded for other companies like National, Supro, Airline, Oahu, and Gretsch. In '42, National Dobro ceased operations and Victor Smith, Al Frost and Louis Dopyera bought the company and changed the name to Valco Manufacturing Company. Post-war production resumed in '46. Valco was purchased by treasurer Robert Engelhardt in '64. In '67, Valco bought Kay, but in '68 the new Valco/Kay company went out of business.

Valencia

1985-present. Budget grade, production, classical guitars imported first by Rondo Music of Union, New Jersey and presently distributed by others.

Valley Arts

Ca. 1977-2010. Professional and premium grade, production/custom, semi-hollow and solidbody guitars and basses built in Nashville, Tennessee. Valley Arts originally was a Southern California music store owned by partners Al Carness and Mike McGuire where McGuire taught and did most of the repairs. Around '77, McGuire and Valley Arts started making custom instruments on a large scale. By '83, they opened a separate manufacturing facility to build the guitars. In '92 Samick acquired half of the company with McGuire staying on for a year as a consultant. Samick offered made-in-the-U.S. production and custom models under the Valley Arts name. In '02, Valley Arts became a division of Gibson Guitar Corp., which builds the guitars in Nashville. Founders Carness and McGuire were once again involved with the company. They reintroduced the line in January, '03. The brand has been inactive since '10.

California Pro (U.S.-made)

1983-2002. Double-cut body, six-on-a-side tuners, single/single/hum pickups, 2 knobs and switch, various colors, serial number begins with CAL.

1983-1990		$625	$775
1990-1992	Pre-Samick	$475	$600
1993-1999	Samick owned	$325	$400

Custom Pro (U.S.-made)

1987-2010. Solidbody, maple 'board, ash or alder body, 3 single-coils, several options offered.

1987-2010		$725	$900

Standard Pro (U.S.-made)

1990-1993. Double-cut, six-on-a-side tuners, single/single/hum pickups.

1990-1993		$425	$525

MODEL YEAR	FEATURES	EXC. COND. LOW	HIGH

Vantage

1977-1998. Budget and intermediate grade, production, acoustic and electric guitars and basses from Japan '77-'90 and from Korea '90-'98.

Vega

1889-1980s, 1989-present. Founded in Boston by the Nelson family, Vega was big in the banjo market into the 1930s, before adding guitars to their line. The company was purchased by C.F. Martin in '70 and used on imports. In '80, Martin sold the Vega trademark to Korea's Galaxy Trading Company. The Deering Banjo Company, in Spring Valley, California acquired the brand in '89 and uses it (and the star logo) on a line of banjos.

C Series Archtop

1933-1950s. Carved-top archtops, '30's models are the 14 5/8" mahogany body C-20 and C-40, 16 1/8" maple body C-60, and the C 70 with rosewood body and gold parts, and the figured-maple body C-80 with deluxe appointments. By '40 the line was the 14-16" C-19, -26, -46, and -56, and the 17" Professional Series C-66 Professional, C-71 Soloist, C-76 Artist, and C 86 Deluxe. Optional blond finish available by '40.

1933-1939	C-20	$1,000	$1,250
1933-1939	C-40	$1,000	$1,250
1933-1939	C-60	$1,600	$2,000
1933-1939	C-70	$1,800	$2,300
1933-1939	C-80	$2,000	$2,500
1940-1949	C-19, C-26, C-46	$800	$1,000
1940-1949	C-56	$1,600	$2,000
1940-1949	C-66 Professional	$1,700	$2,200
1940-1949	C-71 Soloist	$1,800	$2,300
1940-1949	C-76 Artist	$1,900	$2,400
1940-1949	C-86 Deluxe	$2,000	$2,500

Duo-Tron Series Electric Archtops

1947-late 1950s. Various mid-level large body cutaway and non-cut carved-top archtops, 1, 2 or 3 (rare) floating pickups, dot or block markers, natural or sunburst.

1947-50s	Higher end models	$1,500	$2,100
1947-50s	Lower end models	$700	$1,100
1947-50s	Mid-range models	$1,100	$1,400

E-201 Electric Archtop

1959. One pickup, sunburst.

1959		$1,600	$2,000

FT-90 Flat-Top

1960s. 15" body with narrow waist, dot markers, Vega logo, natural.

1960s		$350	$450

G-30

1968-ca. 1970. D-style with solid spruce top and solid mahogany sides and back, Vega logo with star on headstock, dot markers, natural finish.

1968-1970		$230	$300

O'Dell

1950s. Full body, single cut, acoustic-electric, 1 pickup, tailpiece controls.

1950s	Sunburst	$1,000	$1,250

Vega Model 66

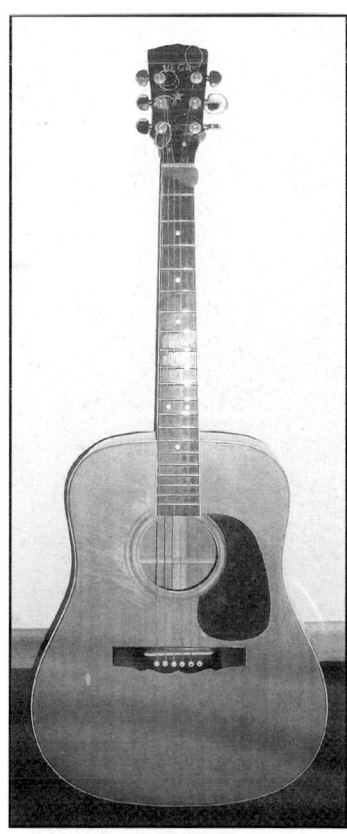

Vega G-30

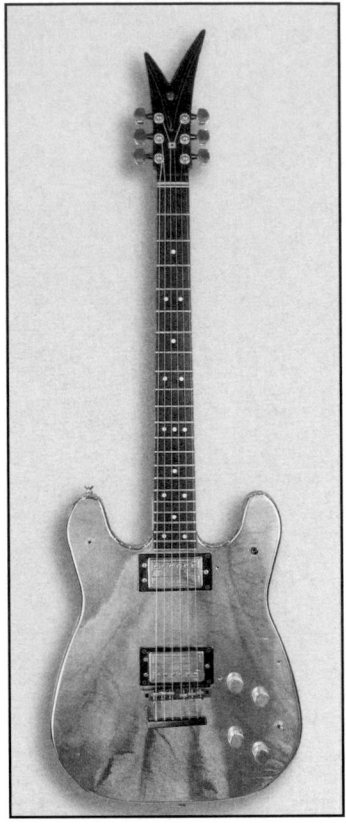

1975 Veleno #115
Barney Roach

Victor Baker Model 14 Custom

MODEL YEAR	FEATURES	EXC. COND. LOW	HIGH

Parlor Guitar

Early-1900s. Small parlor-sized instrument, styles and appointment levels, including binding, purfling and inlays, vary.

| 1900s | Mahogany | $400 | $600 |
| 1910s | Brazilian | $800 | $1,200 |

Profundo Flat-Top

1930s-1950s. Flat-top D-style body, spruce top, mahogany or rosewood back and sides.

| 1930s-50s | Mahogany | $1,300 | $1,625 |
| 1940s-50s | Rosewood | $2,000 | $2,500 |

Solidbody Electric (Import)

1970s-1980s. Solidbody copies of classic designs, Vega script logo on headstock, bolt-on necks.

| 1970s | | $230 | $300 |

Vega Electric Archtop

1939. Full-body electric archtop, figured maple, 1 pickup, 2 control knobs, trapeze bridge, diamond markers, large Vega and star headstock logo, blond.

| 1939 | | $975 | $1,225 |

Vega, Charles

1993-2010. Luthier Charles Vega built his premium, production/custom, nylon-string guitars in Baltimore, Maryland.

Veillette

1991-present. Luthiers Joe Veillette (of Veillette-Citron fame) and Martin Keith build their professional grade, production/custom, acoustic, acoustic/electric, electric 6- and 12-string and baritone guitars and basses in Woodstock, New York. They also build mandolins.

Veillette-Citron

1975-1983. Founded by Joe Veillette and Harvey Citron who met at the New York College School of Architecture in the late '60s. Joe took a guitar building course from Michael Gurian and by the Summer of '76, he and Harvey started producing neck-thru solidbody guitars and basses. Veillette and Citron both are back building instruments.

Velázquez

1948-1972. Manuel Velázquez, New York, New York, gained a reputation as a fine repairman in the late 1940s. He opened his 3rd Avenue guitar building shop in the early 1950s. By the mid-1950s he was considered by some as being the finest American builder of classical guitars. Velázquez left New York in 1972 and moved to Puerto Rico. He continued building guitars for the Japanese market. He returned to the United States in 1982. By the 2000s he built instruments with this son and daughter.

Concert Classical

| 1959 | | $11,500 | $14,500 |

Veleno

1967, 1970-1977, 2003-present. Premium and presentation grade, production/custom, all-aluminum

electric solidbody guitars built by luthier John Veleno in St. Petersburg, Florida. First prototype in '67. Later production begins in late-'70 and lasts until '75 or '76. The guitars were chrome or gold-plated, with various anodized colors. The Traveler Guitar was the idea of B.B. King; only 10 were made. Two Ankh guitars were made for Todd Rundgren in '77. Only one bass was made. Approximately 185 instruments were made up to '77 and are sequentially numbered. In 2003, John Veleno reintroduced his brand.

Original (Aluminum Solidbody)

1973-1976. V-headstock, chrome and aluminum.

| 1973-1976 | Rare color | $7,100 | $9,000 |
| 1973-1976 | Standard | $4,000 | $5,000 |

Traveler Guitar

1973-1976. Limited production of about a dozen instruments, drop-anchor-style metal body.

| 1973-1976 | | $6,500 | $8,100 |

Vengeance Guitars & Graphix

2002-present. Luthier Rick Stewart builds his professional and premium grade, custom/production, solidbody guitars and basses in Arden, North Carolina.

Ventura

1970s. Acoustic and electric guitars imported by C. Bruno Company, mainly copies of classic American models. They also offered basses.

Acoustic Flat-Top

| 1970s | | $125 | $400 |

Guitorgan

1970s. Based on MCI Guitorgan, converts standard electric guitar into a Guitorgan through the addition of electronic organ components, multiple switches, large Barney Kessel sharp-horned acoustic-electric style body.

| 1970s | | $650 | $825 |

Hollowbody Electric

| 1970s | | $175 | $625 |

Solidbody Electric

| 1970s | | $175 | $625 |

Verri

Starting 1992, premium grade, production/custom, archtop guitars built by luthier Henry Verri in Little Falls, New York.

Versoul, LTD

1989-present. Premium grade, production/custom steel-string flat-top, acoustic/electric, nylon-string, resonator, solidbody, and baritone guitars, basses and sitars built by luthier Kari Nieminen in Helsinki, Finland.

VibraWood

2012-present. Luthier John J. Slog builds custom, professional and premium grade, vintage-style guitars and basses in Bethlehem, Pennsylvania.

MODEL YEAR	FEATURES	EXC. COND. LOW	HIGH

Vicente Tatay

1894-late 1930s. Classical guitars built by luthier Vicente Tatay and his sons in Valencia, Spain.

Victor Baker Guitars

1998-present. Professional and premium grade, custom, carved archtop, flat-top and solidbody electric guitars built by luthier Victor Baker in Philadelphia, Pennsylvania. In '10 he relocated to Brooklyn, New York and is currently in Astoria.

Victor Guitars

2002-2008. Luthiers Edward Victor Dick and Greg German built their premium grade, production/custom, flat-top guitars in Denver, Colorado.

Victoria

Ca. 1902-1920s. Brand name for New York distributor Buegeleisen & Jacobson. Instruments built by the Oscar Schmidt Co. and possibly others. Most likely a brand made for a distributor.

Viking Guitars

2003-present. Premium grade, solidbody guitars made by Ed Roman Guitars. Production was '03-'04, custom only since.

Vinetto

2003-present. Luthier Vince Cunetto builds his professional grade, production/custom, solid, chambered and semi-hollow body guitars in St. Louis, Missouri.

Vintage

Ca. 1993-present. Intermediate grade, production, solidbody and semi-hollow acoustic, electro-acoustic and resonator guitars and basses, imported from China, Korea and Vietnam by John Hornby Skewes & Co. in the U.K. They also offer folk instruments.

Vintique

Luthier Jay Monterose built premium grade, custom/production, electric guitars in Suffern, New York. Vintique also manufactured guitar hardware.

Vivi-Tone

1932-1938. Founded in Kalamazoo, Michigan, by former Gibson designer Lloyd Loar, Walter Moon and Lewis Williams, Vivi-Tone built acoustic archtop guitars as well as some of the earliest electric solidbodies. They also built basses and mandolins and offered amps built by Webster Electric. A Vivi-Tone instrument must be all original. Any missing part makes this instrument practically unsellable in the vintage-market.

Guitar

1932-1938. Deep archtop-style body with F-holes on the backside and magnetic bridge pickup.

1932-1938	Rare model	$3,000	$3,800
1932-1938	Standard, sunburst	$2,000	$2,500
1932-1938	Tenor, 4-string	$2,000	$2,500

Vox

1954-present. Name introduced by Jennings Musical Instruments (JMI) of England. First Vox products was a volume pedal, amplifiers were brought to the market in late '57 by Tom Jennings and Dick Denny. Guitars were introduced in '61, with an Echo Unit starting the Vox line of effects in '63.

Guitars and basses bearing the Vox name were offered from '61-'69 (made in England and Italy), '82-'85 (Japan), '85-'88 (Korea), '98-2001 (U.S.), and they introduced a limited edition U.S.-made teardrop guitar in '07 and the semi-hollow Virage guitars in '08. Vox products are currently distributed in the U.S. by Korg USA. Special thanks to Jim Rhoads of Rhoads Music in Elizabethtown, Pennsylvania, for help on production years of these models.

Ace

Late 1960s. Offset double cut solidbody, 2 single-coils, Ace logo.

1967-1968		$550	$700

Apollo

1967-1968. Single sharp cutaway, 1 pickup, distortion, treble and bass booster, available in sunburst or cherry.

1967-1968		$525	$650

Bobcat

1963-1968. Double-cut semi-hollowbody style, block markers, 3 pickups, vibrato, 2 volume and 2 tone controls.

1963-1965	England	$875	$1,100
1966-1968	Italy	$675	$850

Bossman

1967-1968. Single rounded cutaway, 1 pickup, distortion, treble and bass booster, available in sunburst or cherry.

1967-1968		$450	$575

Bulldog

1966. Solidbody double-cut, 3 pickups.

1966		$875	$1,100

Delta

1967-1968. 5-sided Phantom shaped solidbody, 2 pickups, distortion, treble and bass boosters, vibrato, 1 volume and 2 tone controls, available in white only.

1967-1968		$975	$1,225

Folk XII

1966-1969. Dreadnought 12-string flat-top, large 3-point 'guard, block markers, natural.

1966-1969		$325	$400

Guitar-Organ

1966. Standard Phantom with oscillators from a Continental organ installed inside. Plays either organ sounds, guitar sounds, or both. Weighs over 20 pounds.

1966		$1,075	$1,350

Harlem

1965-1967. Offset double-cut solidbody, 2 extended range pickups, sunburst or color option.

1965-1967		$500	$625

1967 Vox Apollo
Dave McDermott

1960s Vox Guitar Organ and Power Supply

GUITARS

Vox Mark VI

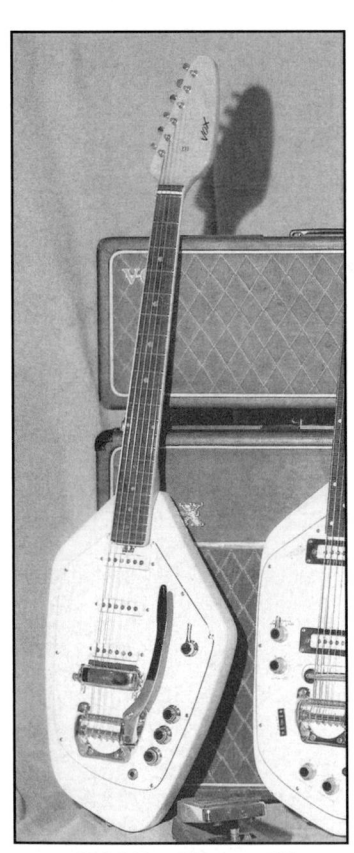

1960 Vox Phantom VI

MODEL YEAR	FEATURES	EXC. COND. LOW	HIGH

Hurricane
1965-1967. Double-cut solidbody, 2 pickups, spring action vibrato, sunburst or color option.

| 1965-1967 | | $500 | $625 |

Invader
1966-1967. Solidbody double-cut, 2 pickups, on-board effects, sunburst.

| 1966-1967 | | $1,775 | $2,225 |

Mando Guitar
1966. Made in Italy, 12-string mandolin thing.

| 1966 | | $1,175 | $1,475 |

Mark III
1998-2001. Teardrop reissue, made in U.S.A., 2 single-coils, fixed bridge or Bigsby. A limited was introduced in '08.

| 1998-2001 | | $725 | $925 |

Mark III 50th Anniversary
2007. Only 100 made, teardrop body, 2 pickups, white finish.

| 2007 | | $700 | $875 |

Mark III/Phantom Mark III
1963-1964. Teardrop body, 2 pickups, 2 controls, Marvin Bigsby, made in England, guitar version of Mark IV bass, while it is called a Phantom Mark III it does not have a Phantom shape.

| 1963-1964 | | $2,525 | $3,125 |

Mark IX
1965-1966. Solidbody teardrop-shaped, 9 strings, 3 pickups, vibrato, 1 volume and 2 tone controls.

| 1965-1966 | | $1,125 | $1,400 |

Mark VI
1965-1967. Teardrop-shaped solidbody, 3 pickups, vibrato, 1 volume and 2 tone controls.

| 1964-1965 | England, white, Brian Jones model | $3,300 | $4,100 |
| 1965-1967 | Italy, sunburst | $1,800 | $2,250 |

Mark VI Reissue
1998-2001. Actually, this is a reissue of the original Phantom VI (Vox couldn't use that name due to trademark reasons), made in U.S.A.

| 1998-2001 | | $675 | $850 |

Mark XII
1965-1967. Teardrop-shaped solidbody, 12 strings, 3 pickups, vibrato, 1 volume and 2 tone controls, sunburst. Reissued for '98-'01.

| 1965-1967 | | $1,125 | $1,400 |

Meteor/Super Meteor
1965-1967. Solidbody double-cut, 1 pickup, Super Meteor with vibrato.

| 1965-1967 | Meteor | $425 | $525 |
| 1965-1967 | Super Meteor | $425 | $525 |

New Orleans
1966. Thin double-cut acoustic electric similar to ES-330, 2 pickups, a scaled down version of the 3-pickup Bobcat model.

| 1966 | | $625 | $775 |

Phantom VI
1962-1967. Five-sided body, 6 strings, 3 pickups, vibrato, 1 volume and 2 tone controls.

| 1962-1964 | English-made | $2,025 | $2,525 |
| 1965-1967 | Italian-made | $1,500 | $1,900 |

Phantom XII
1964-1967. 12 string version of VI.

| 1964 | English-made | $2,025 | $2,525 |
| 1965-1967 | Italian-made | $1,500 | $1,900 |

Phantom XII Stereo
1966. Phantom XII with 3 special offset stereo pickups making 6 pickup conbinations, 3 separate pickup mode selectors, color option.

| 1966 | | $1,500 | $1,900 |

Shadow
1965. Solidbody double-cut, 3 pickups, tremolo tailpiece, sunburst.

| 1965 | English-made | $775 | $975 |

Spitfire
1965-1967. Solidbody double-cut, 3 pickups, vibrato.

| 1965-1967 | | $625 | $800 |

Starstream
1967-1968. Teardrop-shaped hollowbody, 2 pickups, distortion, treble and bass boosters, wah-wah, vibrato, 1 volume and 2 tone controls, 3-way pickup selector, available in cherry or sandburst.

| 1967-1968 | | $1,375 | $1,725 |

Starstream XII
1967-1968. 12 string Starstream.

| 1967-1968 | | $1,225 | $1,525 |

Stroller
1961-1966. Made in England, solidbody, single bridge pickup, Hurricane-style contoured body, dot markers, red.

| 1961-1966 | | $375 | $475 |

Student Prince
1965-1967. Made in Italy, mahogany body thinline archtop electric, 2 knobs, dot markers.

| 1965-1967 | | $290 | $365 |

Super Ace
1963-1965. Solidbody double-cut.

| 1963-1965 | | $525 | $650 |

Super Lynx
1965-1967. Similar to Bobcat but with 2 pickups and no vibrola, double-cut, 2 pickups, adjustable truss rod, 2 bass and 2 volume controls.

| 1965-1967 | | $625 | $800 |

Super Lynx Deluxe
1965-1967. Super Lynx with added vibrato tailpiece.

| 1965-1967 | | $625 | $800 |

Tempest XII
1965-1967. Solidbody double-cut, 12 strings, 3 pickups.

| 1965-1967 | | $625 | $800 |

Thunder Jet
1960s-style with single pickup and vibrato arm.

| 1960s | | $500 | $625 |

Tornado
1965-1967. Thinline archtop, single pickup, dot markers, sunburst.

| 1965-1967 | | $350 | $450 |

Typhoon
1965-1967. Hollowbody single-cut, 2 pickups, 3-piece laminated neck.

| 1965-1967 | | $425 | $525 |

MODEL YEAR	FEATURES	EXC. COND. LOW	HIGH

Ultrasonic
1967-1968. Hollowbody double-cut, 2 pickups, distortion, treble and bass boosters, wah-wah, vibrato, 1 volume and 2 tone controls, 3-way pickup selector, available in sunburst or cherry.

1967-1968	12-string	$1,125	$1,425
1967-1968	6-string	$1,375	$1,725

Viper
1968. Double-cut, thinline archtop electric, built-in distortion.

1968		$1,200	$1,500

Virage/Virage II
2008-2014. Double- and single-cut semi-hollow bodies, 2 triple-coil pickups, made in Japan.

2008-2014		$1,300	$1,625

Wildcat
1965-1967. Single-cut acoustic-electric archtop, 1 pickup, Wildcat and Vox logos on 'guard, dot markers.

1965-1967		$450	$575

W. J. Dyer
See listing under Dyer.

Wabash
1950s. Acoustic and electric guitars distributed by the David Wexler company and made by others, most likely Kay. They also offered lap steels and amps.

Walden Guitars
1996-present. Luthier Jonathan Lee of Portland, Oregon imports production, budget to professional grade, acoustic, acoustic-electric and classical guitars from Lilan, China.

Walker
1994-present. Premium and presentation grade, production/custom, flat-top and archtop guitars built by luthier Kim Walker in North Stonington, Connecticut.

Walker (Kramer)
1981. Kramer came up with idea to offer this brand to produce wood-neck guitars and basses; they didn't want to dilute the Kramer aluminum-neck market they had built up. The idea didn't last long, and few, if any, of these instruments were produced, but prototypes exist.

Wandre (Davoli)
Ca. 1956/57-1969. Solidbody and thinline hollowbody electric guitars and basses created by German-descended Italian motorcycle and guitar enthusiast, artist, and sculptor from Milan, Italy, Wandre Pioli. Brands include Wandre (pronounced Vahn-dray), Davoli, Framez, JMI, Noble, Dallas, Avalon, Avanti I and others. Until '60, they were built by Pioli himself; from '60-'63 built in Milan by Framez; '63-'65 built by Davoli; '66-'69 built in Pioli's own factory.

The guitars originally used Framez pickups, but from '63 on (or earlier) they used Davoli pickups.

Mostly strange shapes characterized by neck-thru-tailpiece aluminum neck with plastic back and rosewood 'board. Often multi-color and sparkle finishes, using unusual materials like linoleum, fiberglass and laminates, metal bindings. Often the instruments will have numerous identifying names but usually somewhere there is a Wandre blob logo.

Distributed early on in the U.K. by Jennings Musical Industries, Ltd. (JMI) and in the U.S. by Don Noble and Company. Model B.B. dedicated to Brigitte Bardot. Among more exotic instruments were the minimalist Krundaal Bikini guitar with a built-in amplifier and attached speaker, and the pogo stick Swedenbass. These guitars are relatively rare and highly collectible. In '05, the brand was revived on a line of imported intermediate grade, production, solidbodies from Eastwood guitars.

Electric

1956-1969	Common models	$2,300	$3,500
1956-1969	Rare models	$3,500	$6,000

Warren
2005-present. Luthier Don Warren builds his professional and premium grade, custom/production, solidbody electric guitars in Latham, New York.

Warrior
1995-present. Professional, premium, and presentation grade, production/custom, acoustic and solidbody electric guitars and basses built by luthier J.D. Lewis in Rossville, Georgia.

Washburn
1962-present. Budget, intermediate, professional, and premium grade, production/custom, acoustic and electric guitars and basses made in the U.S., Japan, and Korea. They also make amps, banjos and mandolins.

Originally a Lyon & Healy brand, the Washburn line was revived on a line of imports in '62 by Roland who sold it to Beckman Musical Instruments in '74/'75. Beckman sold the rights to the Washburn name to Fretted Instruments, Inc. in '76. Guitars originally made in Japan and Korea, but production moved back to U.S. in '91. Currently Washburn is part of U.S. Music.

Washburn (Lyon & Healy)
1880s-ca.1949. Washburn was founded in Chicago as one of the lines for Lyon & Healy to promote high quality stringed instruments, ca. 1880s. The rights to manufacture Washburns were sold to J.R. Stewart Co. in '28, but rights to Washburn name were sold to Tonk Brothers of Chicago. In the Great Depression (about 1930), J.R. Stewart Co. was hit hard and declared bankruptcy. Tonk Brothers bought at auction all Stewart trade names, then sold them to Regal Musical Instrument Co. Regal built Washburns by the mid-'30s. The Tonk Brothers still licensed the name. These Washburn models lasted until ca. '49. In '62 the brand resurfaced on a line of imports from Roland.

Walden CD4041-CERT

Warrior Rick Derringer

Wechter Pathmaker

1925 Weissenborn Style #1
Folkway Music

MODEL YEAR	FEATURES	EXC. COND. LOW	HIGH

Model 1897
1910. High-end appointments, plentiful pearl, 18 frets, slightly larger than parlor size, natural.

| 1910 | | $2,000 | $2,600 |

Model 1915
1928. Brazilian rosewood back and sides.

| 1928 | | $1,400 | $1,800 |

Model 5200 (Tonk Bros by Regal)

| 1934-1935 | | $1,500 | $1,900 |

Model 5249 Flat-Top
1940s. Vertical pearl inlay, Washburn logo and graphic, block markers, round soundhole, sunburst.

| 1940s | | $3,200 | $4,000 |

Model 5257 Solo
1930s. Jumbo size body, rosewood back and sides, natural.

| 1930s | | $3,900 | $4,800 |

Model 5265 Tenor
1920s. Pear-shaped mahogany body, 4-string tenor.

| 1920s | | $510 | $630 |

Parlor Guitar
Early-1900s. Lower-end, small 12"-13" body, plain appointments.

| 1900s | Mahogany | $400 | $600 |

Style 188
1890s. Rosewood back and sides with full pearl 'board inlaid with contrasting colored pearl, pearl on edges and around soundhole.

| 1890s | | $3,000 | $3,800 |

Style A
1920s. Smaller body, rosewood back and sides, top stencil decoration, natural.

| 1920s | | $2,100 | $2,600 |

Washington
Washington was a brand manufactured by Kansas City, Missouri instrument wholesalers J.W. Jenkins & Sons. First introduced in 1895, the brand also offered mandolins.

Waterloo
2015-present. Professional-grade, production, acoustic guitars based on Depression era models, built by Collings Guitars.

Waterstone
2003-present. Intermediate and professional grade, production/custom, electric solid and semi-hollowbody and acoustic guitars and basses imported from Korea by Waterstone Musical Instruments, LLC of Nashville, Tennessee.

Watkins/WEM
1957-present. Watkins Electric Music (WEM) was founded by Charlie Watkins. Their first commercial product was the Watkins Dominator (wedge Gibson stereo amp shape) in '57. They made the Rapier line of guitars and basses from the beginning. Watkins offered guitars and basses up to '82. They currently build accordian amps.

Wayne
1998-present. Professional and premium grade, production/custom, solidbody guitars built by luthiers Wayne and Michael (son) Charvel in Paradise, California. They also build lap steels.

Webber
1988-present. Professional grade, production/custom flat-top guitars built by luthier David Webber in North Vancouver, British Columbia.

Weber
1996-present. Premium grade, production/custom, carved-top acoustic and resonator guitars built by luthier Bruce Weber and his Sound To Earth, Ltd. company, originally in Belgrade, Montana, in '04 moving to Logan, Montana. They also build mandolins. In '12, Two Old Hippies (Breedlove, Bedell) acquired the brand, moving production in '13 to Oregon where Bruce Weber oversees development.

Webster
1940s. Archtop and acoustic guitars, most likely built by Kay or other mass builder.

Model 16C Acoustic Archtop

| 1940s | | $500 | $615 |

Wechter
1984-present. Intermediate, professional and premium grade, production/custom, flat-top, 12-string, resonator and nylon-string guitars and basses from luthier Abe Wechter in Paw Paw, Michigan. The Elite line is built in Paw Paw, the others in Asia. Until '94 he built guitars on a custom basis. In '95, he set up a manufacturing facility in Paw Paw to produce his new line and in '00 he added the Asian guitars. In '04, he added resonators designed by Tim Scheerhorn. Wechter was associated with Gibson Kalamazoo from the mid-'70s to '84. He also offers the Maple Lake brand of acoustics. In '08 he moved his shop to Fort Wayne, Indiana.

Weissenborn
1910s-1937, present. Hermann Weissenborn was well-established as a violin and piano builder in Los Angeles by the early 1910s. Around '20, he added guitars, ukes and steels to his line. Most of his production was in the '20s and '30s until his death in '37. He made tenor, plectrum, parlor, and Spanish guitars, ukuleles, and mandolins, but is best remembered for his koa Hawaiian guitars that caught the popular wave of Hawaiian music. That music captivated America after being introduced to the masses at San Francisco's Panama Pacific International Exposition which was thrown in '15 to celebrate the opening of the Panama Canal and attended by more than 13 million people. He also made instruments for Kona and other brands. The majority of his instruments were most likely sold before the late 1920s. The Weissenborn brand has been revived on a line of reissue style guitars.

MODEL YEAR	FEATURES	EXC. COND. LOW	HIGH

Spanish Acoustic
1920s. High-end Spanish set-up, rope binding, koa top, sides and back, limited production.
| 1920s | | $1,800 | $2,300 |

Style #1 Hawaiian
1920-1930s. Koa, no binding, 3 wood circle soundhole inlays.
| 1920s-30s | | $2,100 | $2,800 |

Style #2 Hawaiian
1920-1930s. Koa, black celluloid body binding, white wood 'board binding, rope soundhole binding.
| 1920s-30s | | $2,300 | $3,000 |

Style #2 Spanish
1920s. Spanish set-up, Style 2 features.
| 1920s | | $1,700 | $2,300 |

Style #3 Hawaiian
1920-1930s. Koa, rope binding on top, 'board, and soundhole.
| 1920s-30s | | $3,000 | $3,900 |

Style #4 Hawaiian
1920-1930s. Koa, rope binding on body, 'board, headstock and soundhole.
| 1920s-30s | | $3,800 | $4,900 |

Teardrop
Late 1920s-1930s. Teardrop/spoon shaped, Style 1 features.
| 1930s | | $750 | $1,000 |

Tenor
| 1920-1927 | | $1,300 | $1,700 |

Welker Custom
Professional and premium grade, production/custom, archtop and flat-top guitars built by luthier Fred Welker in Nashville, Tennessee.

Welson
1960s-1970s. Models made by Quagliardi, an accordion maker in Italy, ranging from acoustics to solidbodies, thinlines, archtops and basses. Some acoustic Welsons were sold in the U.S. by Wurlitzer. By the '70s, they had jumped on the copy-guitar bandwagon.

Electric
| 1960s | Copy models | $260 | $500 |
| 1960s | Plastic cover, original design | $525 | $850 |

Wendler
1999-present. Intermediate and professional grade, production/custom, solidbody, electro-acoustic guitars and basses from luthier Dave Wendler of Ozark Instrument Building in Branson, Missouri. He also builds amps. In '91, Wendler patented a pickup system that became the Taylor ES system.

Westbury-Unicord
1978-ca. 1983. Imported from Japan by Unicord of Westbury, New York. High quality original designs, generally with 2 humbuckers, some with varitone and glued-in necks. They also had basses.

MODEL YEAR	FEATURES	EXC. COND. LOW	HIGH

Westminster
One of the many guitar brands built by Japan's Matsumoku company.

Westone
1970s-1990, 1996-2001. Made by Matsumoku in Matsumoto, Japan and imported by St. Louis Music. Around '81, St. Louis Music purchased an interest in Matsumoku and began to make a transition from its own Electra brand to the Westone brand previously used by Matsumoku. In the beginning of '84, the brand became Electra-Westone with a phoenix bird head surrounded by circular wings and flames. By the end of '84 the Electra name was dropped, leaving only Westone and a squared-off bird with W-shaped wings logo. Electra, Electra-Westone and Westone instruments from this period are virtually identical except for the brand and logo treatment. Many of these guitars and basses were made in very limited runs and are relatively rare.

From '96 to '01, England's FCN Music offered Westone branded electric and acoustic guitars. The electrics were built in England and the acoustics came from Korea. Matsumoku-made guitars feature a serial number in which the first 1 or 2 digits represent the year of manufacture. Electra-Westone guitars should begin with either a 4 or 84.

Weymann
1864-1940s. H.A. Weymann & Sons was a musical instrument distributor located in Philadelphia that marketed various stringed instruments, but mainly known for banjos. Some guitar models made by Regal and Vega, but they also built their own instruments.

Acoustic
| 1930-1945 | Violin-shaped | $3,800 | $4,700 |

Jimmie Rodgers Signature Edition
| 1929 | | $6,500 | $8,000 |

Parlor
1904-ca. 1920. Small 14 5/8" body parlor-style, fancy pearl and abalone trim, fancy fretboard markers, natural.
| 1910 | | $2,500 | $3,100 |

Style 24
1920s. Mid-size body, 12-fret, slotted peghead, made by Vega for Weymann, mahogany sides and back, natural.
| 1920s | | $1,000 | $1,250 |

White Guitars and Woodley White Luthier
1992-present. Premium grade, custom, classical, acoustic and electric guitars, built by luthier Woodley White, first in Portland, Oregon and since 2008 in Naalehu, Hawaii.

Wicked
2004-present. Production/custom, intermediate and professional grade, semi-hollow and electric solidbody guitars and basses built by luthier Nicholas Dijkman in Montreal, Quebec.

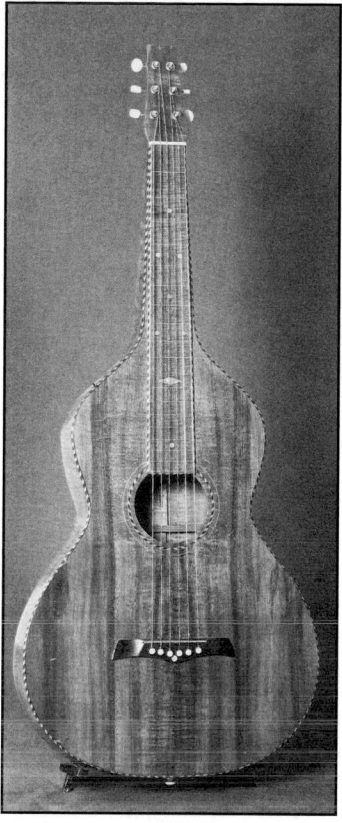

1925 Weissenborn Style #3
Folkway Music

Weissenborn Teardrop

GUITARS

*Widman Custom Electrics
Driftwood T-Master*

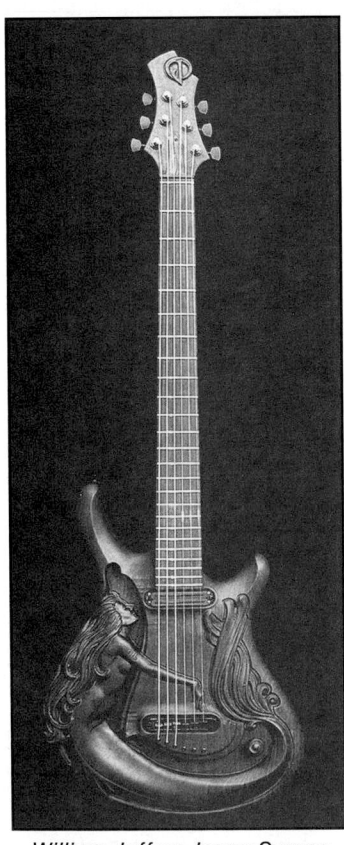

William Jeffrey Jones Syrena

MODEL		EXC. COND.	
YEAR	FEATURES	LOW	HIGH

Widman Custom Electrics

2008-present. Professional and premium grade, custom, electric guitars built in Arden, North Carolina by luthier John Widman.

Wilkanowski

Early-1930s-mid-1940s. W. Wilkanowski primarily built violins. He did make a few dozen guitars which were heavily influenced by violin design concepts and in fact look very similar to a large violin with a guitar neck.

Wilkat Guitars

1998-2013. Professional grade, custom, electric guitars and basses built by luthier Bill Wilkat in Montreal, Quebec. He retired in '13.

Wilkins

1984-present. Custom guitars built by luthier Pat Wilkins in Van Nuys, California. Wilkins also does finish work for individuals and a variety of other builders.

William C. Stahl

See listing under Stahl.

William Hall and Son

William Hall and Son was a New York City based distributor offering guitars built by other luthiers in the mid to late 1800s.

William Jeffrey Jones

2006-present. Luthier William Jeffrey Jones builds his ornately carved, professional and premium grade, production/custom, solidbody and semi-hollow electric guitars in Neosho, Missouri.

Wilson

1960s-1970s. One of the brand names of guitars built in the 1960s for others by Egmond in Holland. Also a brand name used by the U.K.'s Watkins WEM in the 1960s and '70s.

Wilson Brothers Guitars

2004-present. Intermediate and professional grade, production, imported electric and acoustic guitars and basses. Founded by Ventures guitarist Don Wilson. VCM and VSP models made in Japan; VM electrics in Korea; VM acoustic in China.

Windsor

Ca. 1890s-ca. 1914. Brand used by Montgomery Ward for flat-top guitars and mandolins made by various American manufacturers, including Lyon & Healy and, possibly, Harmony. Generally beginner-grade instruments.

Acoustic Flat-Top

1900s		$225	$275

MODEL		EXC. COND.	
YEAR	FEATURES	LOW	HIGH

Winston

Ca. 1963-1967. Imported from Japan by Buegeleisen and Jacobson of New York. Manufacturers unknown, but some are by Guyatone. Generally shorter scale beginner guitars and basses.

Worland

1997-present. Luthier Jim Worland builds professional through presentation grade, production/custom, acoustic flat-top guitars and harp guitars in Rockford, Illinois. He also builds under the Worlatron brand.

Worlatron

2010-present. Professional grade, production/custom, hollowbody electric-acoustic guitars and basses built by luthier Jim Worland in Rockford, Illinois.

WRC Music International

1989-mid-1990s. Guitars by Wayne Richard Charvel, who was the original founder of Charvel Guitars. He now builds Wayne guitars with his son Michael.

Wright Guitar Technology

1993-present. Luthier Rossco Wright builds his unique intermediate and professional grade, production, travel/practice steel-string and nylon-string guitars in Eugene, Oregon. Basses were added in 2009.

Wurlitzer

Wurlitzer had full-line music stores in several major cities and marketed a line of American-made guitars in the 1920s. They also offered American- and foreign-made guitars starting in '65. The American ones were built from '65-'66 by the Holman-Woodell guitar factory in Neodesha, Kansas. In '67, Wurlitzer switched to Italian-made Welson guitars.

00-18

1924		$6,200	$7,900

Model 2077 (Martin 0-K)

1920s. Made by Martin, size 0 with koa top, back and sides, limited production of about 28 instruments.

1920s	Natural	$3,900	$4,800

Model 2090 (Martin 0-28)

1920s. Made by Martin, size 0 with appointments similar to a Martin 0-28 of that era, limited production of about 11 instruments, Wurlitzer branded on the back of the headstock and on the inside back seam, Martin name also branded on inside seam.

1920s	Natural	$5,700	$6,900

Wild One Stereo

1960s. Two pickups, various colors.

1960s		$550	$675

Xaviere

Budget and intermediate grade, production, solid and semi-hollow body guitars from Guitar Fetish, which also has GFS pickups and effects.

MODEL YEAR	FEATURES	EXC. COND. LOW	HIGH

Xotic Guitars

1996-present. Luthier Hiro Miura builds his professional grade, production/custom guitars and basses in San Fernando, California. The Xotic brand is also used on a line of guitar effects.

XOX Audio Tools

2007-present. U.S. debut in '08 of premium grade, production/custom, carbon fiber electric guitars built by luthier Peter Solomon in Europe.

Xtone

2003-2014. Semi-hollow body electric, acoustic and acoustic/electric guitars from ESP. Originally branded Xtone on headstock, in '10 the instruments were marketed as a model series under LTD (ESP's other brand) and stated as such on the headstock.

XXL Guitars

2003-present. Luthier Marc Lupien builds his production/custom, professional grade, chambered electric guitars in Montreal, Quebec.

Yamaha

1946-present. Budget, intermediate, professional, and presentation grade, production/custom, acoustic, acoustic/electric, and electric guitars. They also build basses, amps, and effects. The Japanese instrument maker was founded in 1887. Began classical guitar production around 1946. Solidbody electric production began in '66; steel string acoustics debut sometime after that. They began to export guitars into the U.S. in '69. Production shifted from Japan to Taiwan (Yamaha's special-built plant) in the '80s, though some high-end guitars still made in Japan. Some Korean production began in '90s.

Serialization patterns:

Serial numbers are coded as follows:

H = 1, I = 2, J = 3, etc., Z = 12

To use this pattern, you need to know the decade of production.

Serial numbers are ordered as follows:

Year/Month/Day/Factory Order

Example: NL 29159 represents a N=1987 year, L=5th month or May, 29=29th day (of May), 159=159th guitar made that day (the factory order). This guitar was the 159 guitar made on May 29, 1987.

AE Series
1966-2011. Archtop models.

1966-2011	Higher-end	$800	$1,100
1966-2011	Lower-end	$200	$500
1966-2011	Mid-level	$500	$800

AES Series
1990-2011. Semi-hollowbody models.

1990-2011	Higher-end	$800	$1,100
1990-2011	Lower-end	$350	$500
1990-2011	Mid-level	$500	$800

APX Series
1987-present. Acoustic/electric, various features.

1987-2014	Higher-end	$700	$1,000
1987-2014	Lower-end	$200	$400
1987-2014	Mid-level	$400	$700

CG Series
1984-present. Classical models.

1984-2014	Higher-end	$300	$400
1984-2014	Lower-end	$50	$200
1984-2014	Mid-level	$200	$300

DW Series
1999-2002. Dreadnought flat-top models, sunburst, solid spruce top, higher-end appointments like abalone rosette and top purfling.

1999-2002	Higher-end	$375	$450
1999-2002	Lower-end	$150	$300
1999-2002	Mid-level	$300	$375

EG Series
2000-2009. Electric solidbody models.

2000-2009		$25	$125

Eterna Series
1983-1994. Folk style acoustics, there were 4 models.

1983-1994		$50	$275

FG Series
1970s-present. Economy market flat-top models, laminated sides and back, a 12 suffix indicates 12-string, CE indicates on-board electronics, many models are D-style bodies.

1970-2014	Higher-end	$300	$500
1970-2014	Highest-end	$500	$1,150
1970-2014	Lower-end	$100	$150
1970-2014	Mid-level	$150	$300

G Series
1981-2000. Classical models.

1981-2000		$50	$225

GC Series
1982-present. Classical models, '70s made in Japan, '80s made in Taiwan.

1982-2014	Higher-end	$650	$750
1982-2014	Lower-end	$450	$550
1982-2014	Mid-level	$550	$650

Image Custom
1988-1992. Electric double-cut, Brazilian rosewood 'board, maple top, 2 humbuckers, active circuitry, LED position markers, script Image logo on truss rod cover. The Image was called the MSG in the U.K.

1988-1992		$500	$625

L Series
1984-present. Custom hand-built flat-top models, solid wood.

1984-2014	Higher-end	$800	$1,000
1984-2014	Lower-end	$350	$600
1984-2014	Mid-level	$600	$800

PAC Pacifica Series
1989-present. Offset double-cut with longer horns, dot markers, large script Pacifica logo and small block Yamaha logo on headstock, various models.

1989-2014		$225	$650

RGX Series
1988-2011. Bolt-on neck for the 600 series and neck-thru body designs for 1200 series, various models include 110 (1 hum), 211 (hum-single), 220 (2 hums), 312 (hum-single-single), 603 (3 singles), 612 (hum-

Yamaha APX 7

1970 Yamaha FG-300

1966 Yamaha SA-15

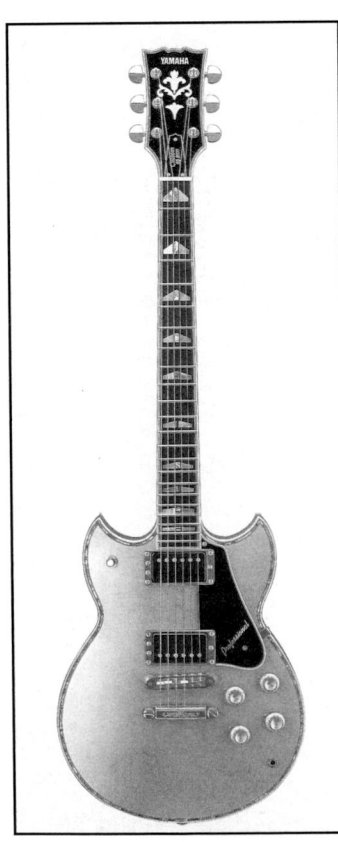

Yamaha SBG-3000

MODEL YEAR	FEATURES	EXC. COND. LOW	HIGH
single-single), 620 (2 hums), 1203S (3 singles), 1212S (hum-single-single), 1220S (2 hums).			
1988-2011	Higher-end	$350	$600
1988-2011	Lower-end	$150	$250
1988-2011	Mid-level	$250	$350

RGZ Series
1989-1994. Double-cut solidbodies, various pickups.

1989-1994	Higher-end	$350	$600
1989-1994	Lower-end	$100	$250
1989-1994	Mid-level	$250	$350

SA Series
1966-1994. Super Axe series, full-size and thinline archtop models.

1966-1994	Higher-end	$800	$1,000
1966-1994	Highest-end	$1,000	$1,400
1966-1994	Lower-end	$450	$600
1966-1994	Mid-level	$600	$800

SBG Series
1983-1992. Solidbody models, set necks, model name logo on truss rod cover.

1983-1992	Higher-end	$1,000	$1,500
1983-1992	Highest-end	$1,500	$2,000
1983-1992	Lower-end	$250	$500
1983-1992	Mid-level	$500	$1,000

SE Series
1986-1992. Solidbody electric models.

1986-1992	Higher-end	$300	$400
1986-1992	Lower-end	$100	$200
1986-1992	Mid-level	$200	$300

SF Super Flighter Series
1977-early 1980s. Double-cut solidbody electrics, 2 humbuckers.

1977-80s		$600	$725

SG-3
1965-1966. Early double-cut solidbody with sharp horns, bolt neck, 3 hum-single pickup layout, large white guard, rotor controls, tremolo.

1965-1966		$825	$975

SG-5/SG-5A
1966-1971. Asymmetrical double-cut solidbody with extended lower horn, bolt neck, 2 pickups, chrome hardware.

1966-1971		$850	$1,000

SG-7/SG-7A
1966-1971. Like SG-5, but with gold hardware.

1966-1971		$950	$1,150

SG-20
1972-1973. Bolt-on neck, slab body, single-cut, 1 pickup.

1972-1973		$275	$375

SG-30/SG-30A
1973-1976. Slab katsura wood (30) or slab maple (30A) solidbody, bolt-on neck, 2 humbuckers, dot inlays.

1973-1976		$300	$400

SG-35/SG-35A
1973-1976. Slab mahogany (35) or slab maple (35A) solidbody, bolt-on neck, 2 humbuckers, parallelogram inlays.

1973-1976		$350	$450

SG-40
1972-1973. Bolt-on neck, carved body, single-cut.

1972-1973		$350	$450

MODEL YEAR	FEATURES	EXC. COND. LOW	HIGH

SG-45
1972-1976. Glued neck, single-cut, bound flat-top.

1972-1976		$400	$500

SG-50
1974-1976. Slab katsura wood solidbody, glued neck, 2 humbuckers, dot inlays, large 'guard.

1974-1976		$400	$500

SG-60
1972 only. Bolt-on neck, carved body, single-cut.

1972		$400	$500

SG-60T
1973 only. SG-60 with large cast vibrato system.

1973		$400	$500

SG-65
1972-1976. Glued neck, single-cut, bound flat-top.

1972-1976		$500	$600

SG-70
1974-1976. Slab maple solidbody, glued neck, 2 humbuckers, dot inlays, large 'guard.

1974-1976		$500	$600

SG-80
1972 only. Bolt-on neck, carved body, single-cut.

1972		$400	$500

SG-80T
1973. SG-60 with large cast vibrato system.

1973		$450	$550

SG-85
1972-1976. Glued neck, single-cut, bound flat-top.

1972-1976		$500	$600

SG-90
1974-1976. Carved top mahogany solidbody, glued neck, elevated 'guard, bound top, dot inlays, chrome hardware.

1974-1976		$600	$725

SG-175
1974-1976. Carved top mahogany solidbody, glued neck, elevated 'guard, abalone bound top, abalone split wing or pyramid inlays, gold hardware.

1974-1976		$675	$825

SG-500
1976-1978. Carved unbound maple top, double pointed cutaways, glued neck, 2 exposed humbuckers, 3-ply bound headstock, bound neck with clay split wing inlays, chrome hardware. Reissued as the SBG-500 (800S in Japan) in '81.

1976-1978		$375	$475

SG-700
1976-1978. Carved unbound maple top, double pointed cutaways, glued neck, 2 humbuckers, 3-ply bound headstock, bound neck with clay split wing inlays, chrome hardware.

1976-1978		$525	$650

SG-700S
1999-2001. Set neck, mahogany body, 2 humbuckers with coil tap.

1999-2001		$525	$650

SG-1000/SBG-1000
1976-1983 ('84 in Japan), 2007-2013. Carved maple top, double pointed cutaways, glued neck, 2 humbuckers, 3-ply bound headstock, unbound body, bound neck with clay split wing inlays, gold hardware. Export

MODEL YEAR	FEATURES	EXC. COND. LOW	HIGH

model name changed to SBG-1000 in '80. SBG-1000 reissued in '07.

| 1976-1979 | SG-1000 | $800 | $1,000 |
| 1980-1983 | SBG-1000 | $800 | $1,000 |

SG-1500

1976-1979. Carved maple top, double pointed cutaways, laminated neck-thru-body neck, laminated mahogany body wings, 2 humbuckers, 5-ply bound headstock and body, bound neck with dot inlays, chrome hardware. Name used on Japan-only model in the '80s.

| 1976-1979 | | $750 | $900 |

SG-2000/SG-2000S

1976-1980 (1988 in Japan). Maple top, double pointed cutaways, neck-thru-body, mahogany body wings, 2 humbuckers, 5-ply bound headstock and body, bound neck with abalone split wing inlays, gold hardware. In '80, the model was changed to the SBG-2000 in the U.S., and the SG-2000S everywhere else except Japan (where it remained the SG-2000). Export model renamed SBG-2100 in '84.

| 1976-1980 | | $775 | $950 |

SG-2100S

1983. Similar to SG-2000 with upgrades such as the pickups.

| 1983 | | $900 | $1,100 |

SG-3000/SBG-3000/Custom Professional

1982-1992. SG-2000 upgrade with higher output pickups and abalone purfling on top

| 1982-1992 | | $1,000 | $1,250 |

SGV-300

2000-2006. 1960s SG model features.

| 2000-2006 | | $300 | $400 |

SHB-400

1981-1985. Solidbody electric, set-in neck, 2 pickups.

| 1981-1985 | | $300 | $400 |

SJ-180

1983-1994. Student Jumbo, entry level Folk Series model, laminated top.

| 1983-1994 | | $100 | $125 |

SJ-400S

1983-1994. Student Jumbo Folk Series model, solid wood top.

| 1983-1994 | | $225 | $275 |

SL Studio Lord Series

1977-1981. LP-style copy models.

| 1977-1981 | | $350 | $450 |

SR SuperRivroller Series

1977-1981. Strat copy models.

| 1977-1981 | | $300 | $400 |

SSC Series

1983-1992. Solidbody electric models.

1983-1992	SSC-400/SC-400	$275	$330
1983-1992	SSC-500	$250	$300
1983-1992	SSC-600/SC-600	$350	$425

Weddington Classic

1989-1992. Electric solidbody, redesigned set-in neck/body joint for increased access to the higher frets.

| 1989-1992 | | $575 | $725 |

Yanuziello Stringed Instruments

1980-present. Production/custom resonator and Hawaiian guitars built by luthier Joseph Yanuziello, in Toronto, Ontario.

Yosco

1900-1930s. Lawrence L. Yosco was a New York City luthier building guitars, round back mandolins and banjos under his own brand and for others.

Zachary

1996-present. Luthier Alex Csiky builds his professional grade, production, solidbody electric guitars and basses in Windsor, Ontario.

Zanini

2007-present. Premium grade, production, electric guitars designed by Luca Zanini of Italy and built by luthier Alex Radovanovic in Switzerland.

Zaukus Guitars

2011-present. Luthier Joseph Zaukus builds his premium grade, production/custom, solidbody electric guitars in Antioch, Tennessee.

Zeiler Guitars

1992-present. Custom flat-top, 12-string, and nylon-string guitars built by luthier Jamonn Zeiler in Aurora, Indiana.

Zemaitis

1960-1999, 2004-present. Professional, premium, and presentation grade, custom/production, electric and acoustic guitars. Tony Zemaitis (born Antanus Casimere Zemaitis) began selling his guitars in 1960. He emphasized simple light-weight construction and was known for hand engraved metal front guitars. The metal front designs were originally engineered to reduce hum, but they became popular as functional art. Each hand-built guitar and bass was a unique instrument. Ron Wood was an early customer and his use of a Zemaitis created a demand for the custom-built guitars. Approximately 6 to 10 instruments were built each year. Tony retired in '99, and passed away in '02 at the age of 67. In '04, Japan's Kanda Shokai Corporation, with the endorsement of Tony Zemaitis, Jr., started building the guitars again. KSC builds the higher priced ones and licenses the lower priced guitars to Greco.

Celebrity association with Zemaitis is not uncommon. Validated celebrity provenance may add 25% to 100% (or more) to a guitar's value. Tony Zemaitis also made so-called student model instruments for customers with average incomes. These had wood tops instead of metal or pearl. Some wood top instruments have been converted to non-Zemaitis metal tops, which are therefore not fully original Zemaitis instruments.

Acoustic instruments are valued more as collectibles and less so for their acoustic sound. Originality

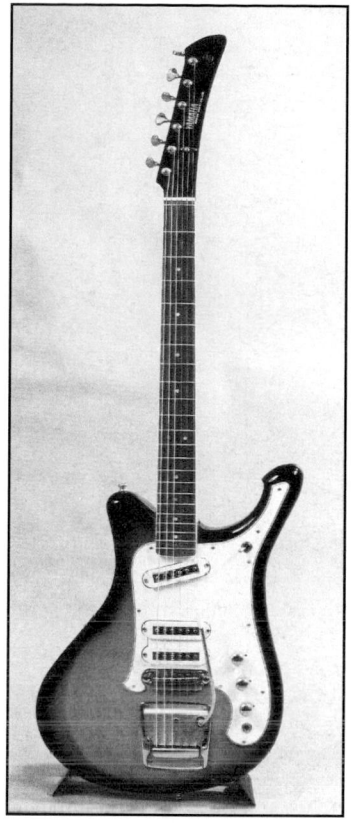

1966 Yamaha SG-5Λ

Zeiler Guitars Georgia Peach

Zerberus Hydra II

Ziegenfuss LR Singlecut

and verifiable, documented provenance is required in the Zemaitis market as fake instruments can be a problem. Prices shown are for fully documented instruments, the best of which is an original letter of authenticity signed by Tony Zemaitis (a copy of a letter is not considered acceptable). Dealers feel 1988 was a cut-off year with post-'88 instruments being valued less and requiring more authentication.

Acoustic Models

MODEL YEAR	FEATURES	EXC. COND. LOW	HIGH
1965	12-string, 1st year	$12,500	$15,500
1970s	6-string	$7,700	$9,600
1980s	12-string, D-hole	$6,200	$7,800
1980s	12-string, heart-hole	$14,000	$17,600
1980s	6-string, D-hole	$6,200	$7,800
1980s	6-string, heart-hole	$12,500	$15,800

Electric Models

MODEL YEAR	FEATURES	EXC. COND. LOW	HIGH
1980s	Disc-front	$17,500	$22,000
1980s	Metal-front	$19,000	$24,000
1980s	Pearl-front	$24,000	$30,000
1980s-90s	Student model, wood top	$8,500	$10,600
1994	"Black Pearl", very few made	$26,000	$33,000
1995	Disc-front 40th Anniversary	$20,000	$25,000

Zen-On

1946-ca.1968. Japanese manufacturer. By '67 using the Morales brand name. Not heavily imported into the U.S., if at all (see Morales).

Acoustic Hollowbody

1946-1968. Various models.

1950s		$180	$225

Electric Solidbody

1960s. Teisco-era and styling.

1960s		$180	$225

Zerberus

2002-present. Professional and premium grade, production/custom, electric guitars built in Speyer, Germany by luthier Frank Scheucher.

Zeta

1982-2010. Zeta made solid, semi-hollow and resonator guitars, many with electronic and MIDI options, in Oakland, California over the years, but mainly offered upright basses, amps and violins.

Ziegenfuss Guitars

2006-present. Luthier Stephen Ziegenfuss builds his professional and premium grade, custom, acoustic and solidbody electric guitars and basses in Jackson, Michigan.

Zim-Gar

1960s. Imported from Japan by Gar-Zim Musical Instrument Corporation of Brooklyn, New York. Manufacturers unknown. Generally shorter scale beginner guitars.

Electric Solidbody

1960s		$180	$225

Zimnicki, Gary

1980-present. Luthier Gary Zimnicki builds his professional and premium grade, custom, flat-top, 12-string, nylon-string, and archtop guitars in Allen Park, Michigan.

Zion

1980-present. Professional and premium grade, production/custom, semi-hollow and solidbody guitars built by luthier Ken Hoover, originally in Greensboro, North Carolina, currently in Raleigh.

Classic

1989-present. Double-cut solidbody, six-on-a-side headstock, opaque finish, various pickup options, dot markers.

1989-2014	Custom quilted top	$560	$700
1989-2014	Opaque finish	$425	$525

Fifty

1994-present. Single-cut ash solidbody, 2 single coils, bolt-on neck.

1994-2014	Custom figured top	$560	$700
1994-2014	Natural, plain top	$425	$525

Graphic

1980s-1994. Double-cut basswood body, custom airbrushed body design, bolt-on neck, Green Frost Marble finish.

1990		$725	$875

Radicaster

1987-present. Double-cut basswood body, graphic finish, bolt-on neck, various pickup configurations, marble/bowling ball finish.

1987-2014		$560	$700

Zolla

1979-present. Professional grade, production/custom, electric guitars and basses built by luthier Bill Zolla in San Diego, California.

Zon

1981-present. Currently luthier Joe Zon only offers basses, but he also built guitars from '85-'91. See Bass Section for more company info.

Zuni

1993-present. Premium grade, custom, solidbody electric guitars built by luthier Michael Blank in Alto Pass, Illinois and Amasa, Michigan.

ZZ Ryder

Solidbody electric guitars and basses from Stenzler Musical Instruments of Ft. Worth, Texas.

BASSES

1962 Airline Pocket Bass

Robbie Keene

Alembic Distillate

Paul J. Allen

| MODEL | | EXC. COND. | |
YEAR	FEATURES	LOW	HIGH

A Basses

1976-2002. Luthier Albey Balgochian built his professional grade, solidbody basses in Waltham, Massachusetts. Sports the A logo on headstock.
Solidbody Bass

| 1976-2002 | | $1,150 | $1,450 |

Acoustic

Ca. 1965-ca. 1987, 2001-2005, 2008-present. Mainly known for solidstate amps, the Acoustic Control Corp. of Los Angeles, did offer guitars and basses from around '69 to late '74. The brand was revived in '01 by Samick for a line of amps.
Black Widow Bass

1969-1970, 1972-1974. The AC600 Black Widow Bass (fretted and fretless) featured a black double-cut body, German carve, Ebonite 'board, 2 pickups with 1 row of adjustable polepieces, and a protective "spider design" pad on back. Also in the AC650 short-scale. The '72-'74 version had the same body design, but with a rosewood 'board and only 1 pickup with 2 rows of adjustable pole pieces (the '72s had a different split-coil pickup with 4 pole pieces, 2 front and 2 back). Acoustic outsourced the production of the basses, possibly to Japan, but at least part of the final production was by Semie Moseley.

| 1969-1970 | | $975 | $1,250 |
| 1972-1974 | | $975 | $1,250 |

Airline

1958-1968, 2004-present. Brand for Montgomery Ward. Built by Kay, Harmony and Valco. In '04, the brand was revived on a line of reissues from Eastwood guitars.
Electric Solidbody Bass

| 1958-1968 | Various models | $400 | $625 |

Pocket 3/4 Bass (Valco/National)

1962-1968. Airline brand of double-cut Pocket Bass, short-scale, 2 pickups, 1 acoustic bridge and 1 neck humbucker, sunburst and other colors.

| 1962-1968 | | $675 | $850 |

Alamo

1947-1982. Founded by Charles Eilenberg, Milton Fink, and Southern Music, San Antonio, Texas. Distributed by Bruno & Sons.
Eldorado Bass (Model 2600)

1965-1966. Solidbody, 1 pickup, angular offset shape, double-cut.

| 1965-1966 | | $350 | $435 |

Titan Bass

1963-1970. Hollowbody, 1 pickup, angular offset shape.

| 1963-1970 | | $350 | $435 |

Alembic

1969-present. Professional, premium, and presentation grade, production/custom, 4-, 5-, and 6-string basses built in Santa Rosa, California. They also build guitars. Established in San Francisco as one of the first handmade bass builders. Alembic basses come with many options concerning woods (examples are maple, bubinga, walnut, vermilion, wenge, zebrawood), finishes, inlays, etc., all of which affect the values listed here. These dollar amounts should be used as a baseline guide to values for Alembic.

Anniversary Bass

1989. 20th Anniversary limited edition, walnut and vermillion with a walnut core, 5-piece body, 5-piece neck-thru, only 200 built.

| 1989 | | $2,300 | $2,850 |

Custom Shop Built Bass

1969-present. Various one-off and/or custom built instruments. Each instrument should be evaluated individually. Prices are somewhat speculative due to the one-off custom characteristics and values can vary greatly.

| 1978 | Dragon Doubleneck | $8,000 | $10,000 |
| 2004 | Dragon 4-string, 4 made | $4,100 | $5,200 |

Distillate Bass

1981-1991. One of Alembic's early lower-cost models, early ones with 1 pickup, 2 pickups by '82, exotic woods, active electronics.

| 1981-1991 | Distillate 4 | $2,075 | $2,600 |
| 1981-1991 | Distillate 5 | $2,175 | $2,700 |

Elan Bass

1985-1996. Available in 4-, 5-, 6- and 8-string models, 3-piece thru-body laminated maple neck, solid maple body, active electronics, solid brass hardware, offered in a variety of hardwood tops and custom finishes.

| 1985-1996 | Elan 4 | $1,800 | $2,250 |
| 1985-1996 | Elan 5 | $1,875 | $2,350 |

Epic Bass

1993-present. Mahogany body with various tops, extra large pointed bass horn, maple/walnut veneer set-neck, available in 4-, 5-, and 6-string versions.

1993-2014	4-string	$1,700	$2,150
1993-2014	5-string	$1,800	$2,250
1993-2014	6-string	$1,900	$2,350

Essence Bass

1991-present. Mahogany body with various tops, extra large pointed bass horn, walnut/maple laminate neck-thru.

1991-2014	Essence 4	$1,800	$2,250
1991-2014	Essence 5	$1,900	$2,350
1991-2014	Essence 6	$2,000	$2,500

Europa Bass

1992-present. Mahogany body with various tops, ebony 'board, available as 4-, 5-, and 6-string.

| 1992-2014 | | $2,600 | $3,250 |

Exploiter Bass

1980s. Figured maple solidbody 4-string, neck-thru, transparent finish.

| 1984-1988 | | $2,000 | $2,500 |

Orion Bass

1996-present. Offset double cut, various figured-wood top solidbody.

| 1996-2014 | | $2,000 | $2,500 |

MODEL YEAR	FEATURES	EXC. COND. LOW	HIGH

Persuader Bass
1983-1991. Offset double-cut solidbody, 4-string, neck-thru.

1983-1991		$2,000	$2,500

Rogue Bass
1996-present. Double-cut solidbody, extreme long pointed bass horn..

1996-2014		$2,000	$2,500

Series I Bass
1971-present. Mahogany body with various tops, maple/purpleheart laminate neck-thru, active electronics, available in 3 scale lengths and with 4, 5 or 6 strings.

1971-1979	Medium- or long-scale	$4,100	$5,100
1971-1979	Short-scale	$4,100	$5,100
1980-1989	Medium- or long-scale	$3,700	$4,600
1980-1989	Short-scale	$3,700	$4,600
1990-2014	All scales, highly figured	$3,700	$4,600

Series II Bass
1971-present. Generally custom-made option, each instrument valued on a case-by-case basis, guidance pricing only.

1971-1979		$4,300	$5,300
1980-2014		$4,100	$5,100

Spoiler Bass
1981-1999. Solid mahogany body, maple neck-thru, 4, 5 or 6 strings, active electronics, various high-end wood options.

1981-1986	6-string	$1,900	$2,400
1981-1989	4-string	$1,900	$2,400
1981-1989	5-string	$2,000	$2,500
1990-1999	4-string	$2,000	$2,500

Stanley Clarke Signature Standard Bass
1990-present. Neck-thru-body, active electronics, 24-fret ebony 'board, mahogany body with maple, bubinga, walnut, vermilion, or zebrawood top, 4-, 5-, and 6-string versions.

1990-2014	All scales	$4,600	$5,800

Alvarez

1965-present. Imported by St. Louis Music, they offered electric basses from '90 to '02 and acoustic basses in the mid-'90s.

Electric Bass (Mid-Level)

1990s	Hollowbody	$310	$400
1990s	Solidbody	$310	$400

American Showster

1986-2004, 2010-2011. Established by Bill Meeker and David Haines, Bayville, New Jersey. They also made guitars.

AS-57-B Bass
1987-1997. Bass version of AS-57 with body styled like a '57 Chevy tail fin.

1987-1997		$2,500	$3,100

Ampeg

1949-present. Ampeg was founded on a vision of an amplified bass peg, which evolved into the Baby

Bass. Ampeg has sold basses on and off throughout its history. In '08 they got back into basses with the reissue of the Dan Armstrong Plexi Bass.

AEB-1 Bass
1966-1967. F-holes through the body, fretted, scroll headstock, pickup in body, sunburst. Reissued as the AEB-2 for '97-'99.

1966-1967		$2,700	$3,350

ASB-1 Devil Bass
1966-1967. Long-horn body, fretted, triangular f-holes through the body, fireburst.

1966-1967		$3,300	$4,100

AUB-1 Bass
1966-1967. Same as AEB-1, but fretless, sunburst. Reissued as the AUB-2 for '97-'99.

1966-1967		$2,700	$3,350

AUSB-1 Devil Bass
1966-1967. Same as ASB-1 Devil Bass, but fretless.

1966-1967		$3,200	$4,000

BB-4 Baby Bass
1962-1971. Electric upright slim-looking bass that is smaller than a cello, available in sunburst, white, red, black, and a few turquoise. Reissued as the ABB-1 Baby Bass for '97-'99.

1962-1971	Solid color	$2,000	$2,500
1962-1971	Sunburst	$1,875	$2,350

BB-5 Baby Bass
1964-1971. Five-string version.

1964-1971	Sunburst	$2,100	$2,600

Dan Armstrong Lucite Bass
1969-1971. Clear solid lucite body, did not have switchable pickups like the Lucite guitar.

1969-1971	Clear	$1,700	$2,100
1969-1971	Smoke	$2,200	$2,750

Dan Armstrong Lucite Reissue/ADA4 Bass
1998-2001, 2008-2009. Lucite body, Dan Armstrong Ampeg block lettering on 'guard. Reissue in '08 as the ADA4.

1998-2001		$750	$950
2008-2009	Reintroduced	$750	$950

GEB-101 Little Stud Bass
1973-1975. Import from Japan, offset double-cut solidbody, two-on-a-side tuners, 1 pickup.

1973-1975		$400	$500

GEB-750 Big Stud Bass
1973-1975. Import from Japan, similar to Little Stud, but with 2 pickups.

1973-1975		$400	$500

Angelica

1967-1975. Student and entry-level basses and guitars imported from Japan.

Electric Solidbody Bass
1970s. Japanese imports.

1970s	Various models	$200	$275

Apollo

Ca. 1967-1972. Entry-level basses imported from Japan by St. Louis Music. They also had guitars and effects.

Ampeg AEB-1

1967 Ampeg Devil Bass
Phil Avelli

BASSES

Aria Pro II SB-Black'n Gold I

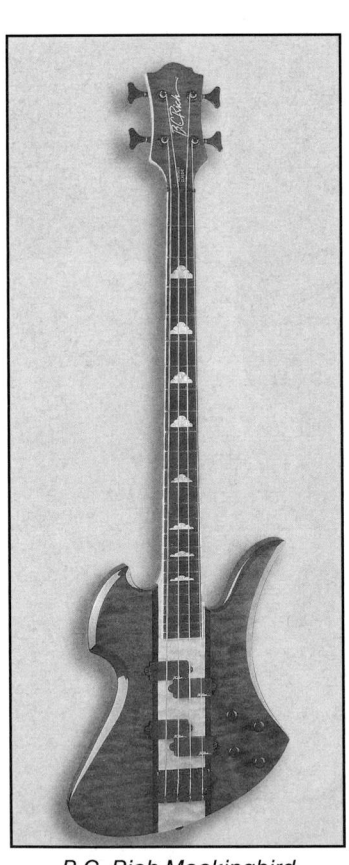

*B.C. Rich Mockingbird
Heritage Classic Bass*

MODEL YEAR	FEATURES	EXC. COND. LOW	HIGH

Electric Hollowbody Bass
1967-1972. Japanese imports.

1967-1972		$175	$325

Arbor
1983-ca. 2013. Budget grade, production, solidbody basses imported by Musicorp (MBT). They also offered guitars.

Electric Bass

1983-2013	Various models	$150	$200

Aria/Aria Pro II
1956-present. Budget and intermediate grade, production, acoustic, acoustic/electric, solidbody, hollowbody and upright basses. They also make guitars, mandolins, and banjos. Originally branded as Aria; renamed Aria Pro II in '75; both names used over the next several year; in '01, the Pro II part of the name was dropped altogether.

Electric Bass

1980s	Various models	$325	$500

Austin Hatchet
Mid-1970s-mid-1980s. Trademark of distributor Targ and Dinner, Chicago, Illinois.

Hatchet Bass

1981	Travel bass	$350	$450

B.C. Rich
1966-present. Budget, intermediate, and premium grade, production/custom, import and U.S.-made basses. They also offer guitars. Many B.C. Rich models came in a variety of colors. For example, in '88 they offered black, Competition Red, metallic red, GlitteRock White, Ultra Violet, and Thunder Blue. Also in '88, other custom colors, graphic features, paint-to-match headstocks, and special inlays were offered.

Bich Bass
1978-1998. Solidbody, neck-thru, 2 pickups.

1978-1979	USA	$1,900	$2,400
1980-1985		$1,450	$1,800
1986-1989		$1,400	$1,750
1989-1993	Class Axe era	$900	$1,125
1994-1998	2nd Rico-era	$750	$950

Bich Supreme 8-String Bass
Late-1970s-early-1980s.

1978-1982		$2,800	$3,500

Eagle Bass (U.S.A. Assembly)
1977-1996. Curved double-cut, solidbody, natural.

1977-1979	Painted wood	$1,800	$2,300
1977-1979	Translucent wood	$2,000	$2,500
1980-1996	Painted wood	$1,700	$2,200
1980-1996	Translucent wood	$1,900	$2,400

Gunslinger Bass
1987-1999. Inverted headstock, 1 humbucker.

1987-1989		$700	$875
1989-1993	Class Axe era	$600	$750
1994-1999		$550	$700

MODEL YEAR	FEATURES	EXC. COND. LOW	HIGH

Ironbird Bass
1984-1998. Kind of star-shaped, neck-thru, solidbody, 2 pickups, active electronics, diamond inlays.

1984-1985		$1,100	$1,350
1986-1989		$1,000	$1,250
1989-1993	Class Axe era	$800	$1,000
1994-1998	2nd Rico era	$700	$900

Mockingbird Bass
1976-2009. US-made, short horn until '78, long horn after.

1976	Painted	$2,000	$2,500
1976	Translucent	$2,200	$2,700
1977-1978	Painted	$1,900	$2,400
1977-1978	Translucent	$2,100	$2,600
1979-1983	Painted	$1,900	$2,400
1979-1983	Translucent	$2,000	$2,500
1984-1985	End 1st Rico-era	$1,800	$2,300
1986-1989	End 1st Rico era	$1,350	$1,750
1994-2009	New Rico-era	$1,250	$1,650

Mockingbird Heritage Classic Bass
2007-present. 4-string, neck-thru, quilted maple top, cloud inlay.

2007-2014		$325	$425

Nighthawk Bass
1979-ca.1980. Bolt-neck.

1978-1982		$700	$875

NJ Series Bass
1983-2006. Various mid-level import models include Beast, Eagle, Innovator, Mockingbird, Virgin and Warlock. Replaced by NT Series.

1983-1984	Early, Japan	$350	$725
1985-1986	Japan	$250	$525
1987-2006		$100	$325

Platinum Series Bass
1986-2006. Lower-priced import versions including Eagle, Mockingbird, Beast, Warlock.

1986-1999		$100	$325

Seagull Bass
1973-1975. Solidbody, single cut, changed to Seagull II in '76.

1973		$2,900	$3,600
1974-1975		$3,000	$4,200

Seagull II Bass
1976-1977. Double-cut version.

1976-1977		$2,300	$2,900

ST-III Bass
1987-1998. Bolt or set neck, black hardware, P-Bass/J-Bass pickup configuration, ebony 'board.

1987-1989	Bolt-on	$500	$650
1987-1989	Neck-thru	$525	$675
1989-1993	Class Axe-era	$500	$650
1994-1998	New Rico-era	$500	$650

Warlock Bass (U.S.A.)
1981-present. Bolt neck, maple body, rosewood 'board, Badass II low profile bridge by '88.

1981-1985		$1,200	$1,500
1986-2014		$1,100	$1,400

Wave Bass

1983		$3,200	$4,100

The **Vintage Guitar Price Guide** shows low to high values for items in all-original excellent condition, and, where applicable, with original case or cover.

MODEL YEAR	FEATURES	EXC. COND. LOW	HIGH

Baldwin

1965-1970. The giant organ company got into guitars and basses in '65 when it bought Burns Guitars of England and sold those models in the U.S. under the Baldwin name.

Baby Bison Bass
1965-1970. Scroll head, 2 pickups, black, red or white finishes.

1965-1966		$800	$1,000
1966-1970	Model 560	$700	$875

Bison Bass
1965-1970. Scroll headstock, 3 pickups, black or white finishes.

1965-1966		$1,125	$1,400
1966-1970	Model 516	$1,075	$1,350

G.B. 66 Bass
1965-1966. Bass equivalent of G.B. 66 guitar, covered bridge tailpiece.

1965-1966		$725	$900

Jazz Split Sound Bass
1965-1970. Offset double-cut solidbody, 2 pickups, red sunburst.

1965-1966	Long scale	$925	$1,150
1966-1970	Short-scale	$775	$975

Nu-Sonic Bass
1965-1966. Bass version of Nu-Sonic.

1965-1966		$725	$900

Shadows/Shadows Signature Bass
1965-1970. Named after Hank Marvin's backup band, solidbody, 3 slanted pickups, white finish.

1965-1966	Shadows	$1,400	$1,750
1966-1970	Shadows Signature	$1,300	$1,600

Vibraslim Bass
1965-1970. Thin body, scroll head, 2 pickups, sunburst

1965-1966		$850	$1,050
1966-1970	Model 549	$775	$975

Barclay

1960s. Generally shorter-scale, student-level imports from Japan. They also made guitars.

Electric Solidbody Bass

1960s	Various models	$180	$225

Bass Collection
1985-1992. Mid-level imports from Japan, distributed by Meisel Music of Springfield, New Jersey. Sam Ash Music, New York, sold the remaining inventory from '92 to '94.

SB300 Series Bass
1985-1992. Offset double-cut, bolt neck, ash or alder body, models include 300, 301 (fretless) and 302 (5-string).

1985-1992		$350	$450

SB400/SB500 Series Bass
1985-1992. Offset double-cut, bolt neck, basswood body, active electronics, models include 401, 402 (fretless), 405 (5-string) and 501 (alder body).

1985-1992		$425	$525

Black Jack

1960s. Entry-level and mid-level imports from Japan. They also offered guitars.

Electric Solidbody Bass

1960s	Various models	$105	$175

Bradford

1960s. House brand of W.T. Grant department store, often imported. They also offered guitars.

Electric Solidbody Bass

1960s	Various models	$130	$180

Brian Moore

1992-present. Brian Moore added basses in '97. Currently they offer professional grade, production, solidbody basses. They also build guitars and mandolins.

i2000 Bass Series
2000-present. Offset double-cut solidbody with extended bass horn, 2 pickups, 4- (i4) or 5-string (i5), options include piezo (p), fretless (-f), Bartolini pickups (B), and 13-pin mid (.13).

2000-2014		$600	$750

Brice

1985-present. Budget grade, production, electric and acoustic basses imported by Rondo Music of Union, New Jersey.

BSX Bass

1990-present. Luthier Dino Fiumara builds his professional and premium grade, production/custom, acoustic, solidbody, semi-solid upright basses in Aliquippa, Pennsylvania.

Burns

1960-1970, 1974-1983, 1992-present. Intermediate and professional grade, production, basses built in England and Korea. They also build guitars.

Nu-Sonic Bass
1964-1965, 2011-present. Offset double-cut solidbody, 2 pickups.

1964-1965		$825	$1,050

Scorpion Bass
Introduced 1979, 2003-2009. Double-cut scorpion-like solidbody.

2003-2009		$325	$425

Cameo

1960s-1970s. Japanese- and Korean-made electric basses. They also offered guitars.

Electric Bass

1960s-70s	EB-2 style	$300	$380

Charvel

1976-present. U.S.-made from '78 to '85 and a combination of imports and U.S.-made post-'85. They also build guitars.

Pre-Pro Bass
1980-1981. Pre-mass production basses, made Nov. '80 to '81. Refer to Charvel guitar section for details.

1980-1981	All models	$2,200	$2,750

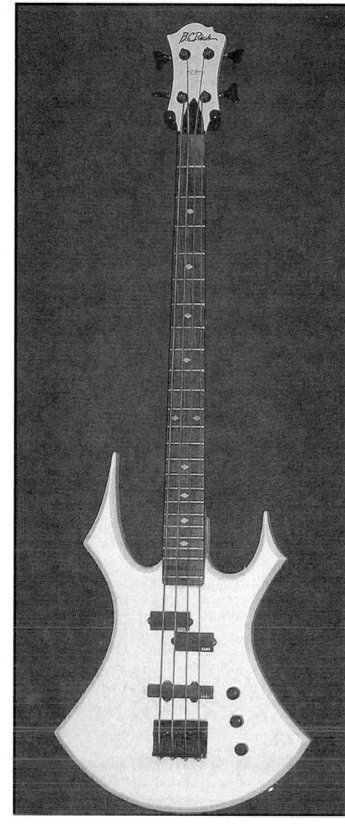

B.C. Rich NJ Series Virgin

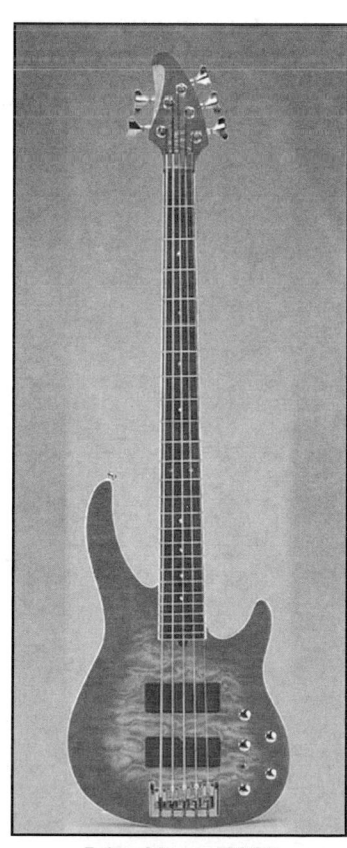

Brian Moore i2000

BASSES

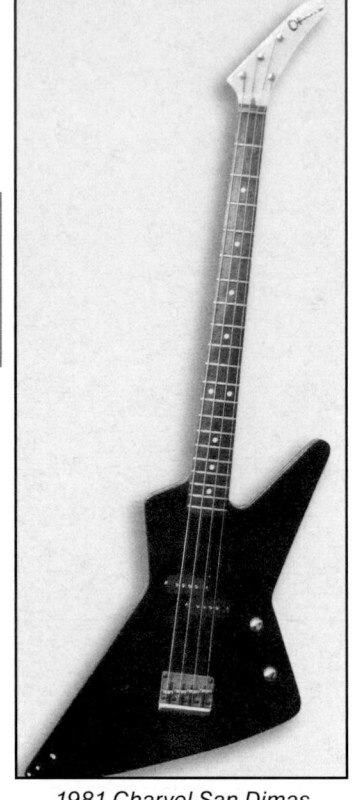

*1981 Charvel San Dimas
Serialized Plated*

John DeSilva

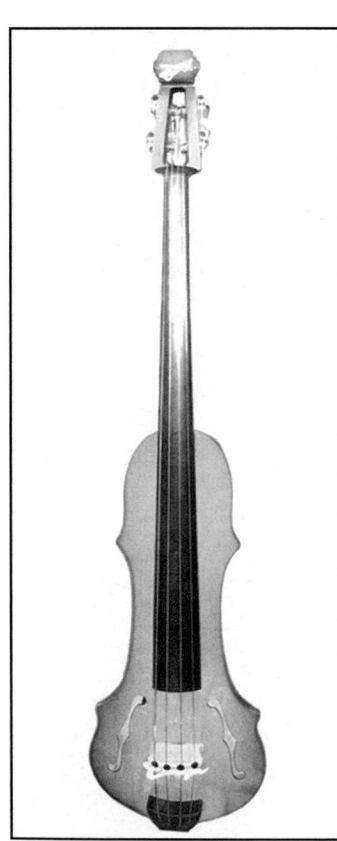

Clevinger Concerto Grande

850 XL Bass
1989. Four-string, neck-thru, active.

MODEL YEAR	FEATURES	EXC. COND. LOW	HIGH
1989		$500	$625

CX-490 Bass
1991-1994. Double-cut, 4-string, bolt neck, red or white.

1991-1994		$250	$315

Eliminator Bass
1990-1991. Offset double-cut, active electronics, bolt neck.

1990-1991		$300	$375

Fusion Bass
1989-1991. 4- and 5-string models, active circuitry.

1989-1991	IV	$300	$375
1989-1991	V	$325	$400

Model 1 Bass
1986-1988. Double-cut, bolt neck, 1 pickup.

1986-1988		$275	$350

Model 2 Bass
1986-1988. Double-cut, bolt neck, 2 pickups.

1986-1988		$275	$350

Model 3 Bass
1986-1988. Neck-thru, 2 single-coils, active, master volume, bass and treble knobs.

1986-1988		$325	$400

Model 4 Bass
1988. Like Model 3, but with bolt neck.

1988		$375	$475

Model 5 Bass
1986-1989. Double-cut, P/J pickups.

1986-1989		$375	$475

San Dimas Serialized Plated Bass
1981-1982. Soft headstock early models.

1981-1982		$2,600	$3,250

SB-4 Bass
1990s. Offset double cut solid, long bass horn, 2 pickups.

1990s		$325	$400

Star Bass
1980-1981. Unique 4-point solidbody, 1 pickup, considered by Charvel collectors to be Charvel's only original early design.

1980-1981		$2,800	$3,450

Surfcaster Bass
1991-1994. Semi-hollow, lipstick tube pickups.

1991-1994		$1,000	$1,300

Cipher
1960s. Student market basses imported from Japan. They also made guitars.

Electric Solidbody Bass
1960s. Japanese imports.

1960s		$175	$225

Clevinger
1982-present. Established by Martin Clevinger, Oakland, California. Mainly specializing in electric upright basses, but has offered bass guitars as well.

College Line
One of many Lyon & Healy brands, made during the era of extreme design experimentation.

Monster (Style 2089) Bass
Early-1900s. 22" lower bout, flat-top guitar/bass, natural.

MODEL YEAR	FEATURES	EXC. COND. LOW	HIGH
1915		$2,700	$3,500

Conrad
Ca.1968-1978. Student and mid-level copy basses imported by David Wexler, Chicago, Illinois. They also offered guitars, mandolins and banjos.

Model 40096 Acoustical Slimline Bass
1970s. 2 pickups.

1970s		$260	$350

Model 40177 Violin-Shaped Bass
1970s. Scroll headstock, 2 pickups.

1970s		$350	$450

Model 40224 Bumper Bass
1970s. Ampeg Dan Armstrong lucite copy.

1970s		$350	$450

Professional Bass
1970s. Offset double-cut.

1970s		$260	$350

Professional Bison Bass
1970s. Solidbody, 2 pickups.

1970s		$260	$350

Coral
1967-1969. In '66 MCA bought Danelectro and in '67 introduced the Coral brand of guitars, basses and amps. The line included several solid and semi-solidbody basses. Special thanks to Brian Conner for his assistance with this brand.

Deluxe Bass D2N4
1967-1969. Offset double-cut, 2 pickups.

1967-1969	Black	$1,225	$1,625
1967-1969	Sunburst	$1,125	$1,525

Fiddle Bass FB2B4
1967-1969. Violin bass hollow body, 2 pickups.

1967-1969		$1,700	$2,200

Firefly Bass F2B4
1968-1969. 335-style semi-hollow, 2 pickups.

1968-1969	Red	$950	$1,250
1968-1969	Sunburst	$900	$1,150

Long Horn Bass
1968-1969. Standard neck (L2B4) or extended neck (L2LB4), 4 strings.

1968	L2LB4	$1,325	$1,775
1968-1969	L2B4	$1,225	$1,625

Wasp Bass
1967-1969. 4-string (2B4) or 6-string (2B6), black, red or sunburst.

1967-1969	2B4, black or red	$1,200	$1,600
1967-1969	2B4, sunburst	$1,000	$1,350
1967-1969	2B6, black or red	$1,400	$1,800
1967-1969	2B6, sunburst	$1,200	$1,600

Crestwood
1970s. Imported by La Playa Distributing Company of Detroit. Product line includes copies of the popular classical guitars, flat-tops, electric solidbodies and basses of the era.

MODEL		EXC. COND.	
YEAR	FEATURES	LOW	HIGH

Electric Bass
1970s. Includes models 2048, 2049, 2079, 2090, 2092, 2093, and 2098.

1970s		$235	$300

Crown
1960s. Violin-shaped hollowbody electrics, solid-body electric guitars and basses, possibly others. Imported from Japan.

Electric Solidbody Bass

1960s	Import	$160	$200

Custom Kraft
Late-1950s-1968. A house brand of St. Louis Music Supply, instruments built by Valco and others. They also offered guitars and amps.

Bone Buzzer Model 12178 Bass
Late 1960s. Symmetrical double-cut thin hollow body, lightning bolt f-holes, 4-on-a-side tuners, 2 pickups, sunburst or emerald sunburst.

1968		$475	$600

D'Agostino
1976-early 1990s. Import company established by Pat D'Agostino. Solidbodies imported from EKO Italy '77-'82, Japan '82-'84, and in Korea for '84 on. Overall, about 60% of guitars and basses were Japanese, 40% Korean.

Electric Solidbody Bass

1970s	Various models	$160	$400

Daion
1978-1984. Higher quality copy basses imported from Japan. Original designs introduced in '80s. They also had guitars.

Electric Bass

1978-1984	Higher-end	$525	$1,000
1978-1984	Lower-end	$325	$400

Danelectro
1946-1969, 1997-present. Danelectro offered basses throughout most of its early history. In '96, the Evets Corporation, of San Clemente, California, introduced a line of Danelectro effects; amps, basses and guitars, many reissues of earlier instruments, soon followed. In early '03, Evets discontinued the guitar, bass and amp lines, but revived the guitar and bass line in '05. Danelectro also built the Coral brand instruments (see Coral). Special thanks to Brian Conner for his assistance with this brand.

Dane A Series Bass
1967. Solidbody, 2 pickups, 4-string.

1967		$900	$1,200

Dane C Series Bass
1967. Semi-solidbody 4- or 6-string, 2 pickups.

1967	4-string	$1,600	$2,000
1967	6-string	$1,800	$2,400

Dane D Series Bass
1967. Solidbody, 2 pickups, 4- or 6-string.

1967	4-string	$1,300	$1,700
1967	6-string	$1,500	$1,900

MODEL		EXC. COND.	
YEAR	FEATURES	LOW	HIGH

Dane E Series Bass
1967. Solidbody, 2 pickups, 4-string.

1967	4-string	$1,100	$1,500

Hawk Bass
1967. Solidbody, 4-string, 1 pickup.

1967		$1,500	$1,850

Model 1444L Bass
Ca.1958-ca.1964. Masonite body, single-cut, 2 pickups, copper finish.

1958-1964		$675	$850

Model 3412 Standard (Shorthorn Bass)
1959-1966. Coke bottle headstock, 4-string, 1 pickup, kidney 'guard through '60, seal 'guard after, copper finish.

1959-1960	Kidney 'guard	$950	$1,175
1961-1962	Seal 'guard	$950	$1,175
1963-1964		$775	$975
1965-1966		$700	$875

Model 3612 Standard (Shorthorn Bass)
1959-1966. 6-string version.

1959-1962	Kidney 'guard	$1,100	$1,400
1961-1962	Seal 'guard	$1,075	$1,350
1963-1964		$1,000	$1,250
1965-1966		$900	$1,125

'58 Shorthorn
1997-2003. Reissues of classic Shorthorn bass.

1997-2003		$255	$325

Longhorn 4-String Bass Model 4423
1959-1966. Coke bottle headstock, 4-string, 2 pickups, tweed case '59, gray tolex after.

1959	Tweed case	$1,250	$1,550
1960-1966	Gray tolex case	$1,150	$1,450

Longhorn 6-String Bass Model 4623
1959-1966. 6-string version.

1959	Tweed case	$1,500	$1,850
1960-1966	Gray tolex case	$1,400	$1,750

'58 Longhorn Reissue/Longhorn Pro Bass
1997-2010. Reissues of classic Longhorn bass.

1997-2010		$255	$325

UB-2 6-String Bass
1957-1958. Single-cut, 2 pickups, black, bronze or ivory.

1957-1958	Black or bronze	$1,500	$1,850
1957-1958	Ivory	$1,500	$1,850

David J King
1987-present. Production/custom, professional and premium grade, electric basses built by luthier David King first in Amherst, Massachusetts and since '92 in Portland, Oregon.

Dean
1976-present. Intermediate and professional grade, production, solidbody, hollowbody, acoustic, and acoustic/electric, basses made overseas. They also offer guitars, banjos, mandolins, and amps.

Baby ML Bass
1982-1986. Downsized version of ML.

1982-1986	Import	$260	$325

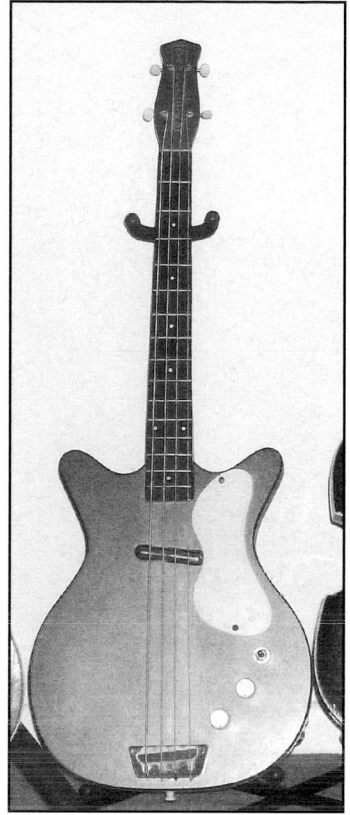

1960 Danelectro 3412

David J King Wesby II

BASSES

1981 Dean ML

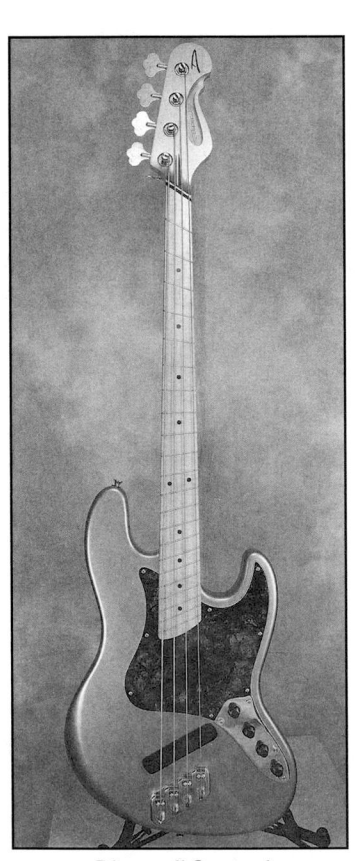

Dingwall Super J

MODEL YEAR	FEATURES	EXC. COND. LOW	HIGH

Mach V Bass
1985-1986. U.S.-made pointed solidbody, 2 pickups, rosewood 'board.

1985-1986	U.S.-made	$1,050	$1,300

ML Bass
1977-1986, 2001-2010. Futuristic body style, fork headstock.

1977-1983	U.S.-made	$1,200	$1,500
1984-1986	Korean import	$365	$450

Rhapsody Series (USA)
2001-2004. Scroll shaped offset double-cut, various models.

2001-2004	12-string	$245	$315
2001-2004	8-string	$220	$275
2001-2004	HFB fretless	$200	$245

DeArmond
1999-2004. Electric basses based on Guild models and imported from Korea by Fender. They also offered guitars.

Electric Bass
1999-2004. Various imported models.

1999-2004	Jet Star, solidbody	$450	$575
1999-2004	Starfire, hollowbody	$525	$650
2001-2002	Pilot Pro, solidbody	$280	$350

Dingwall
1988-present. Luthier Sheldon Dingwall, Saskatoon, Saskatchewan, started out producing guitar bodies and necks, eventually offering complete guitars and basses. Currently Dingwall offers professional to premium grade, production/custom 4-, 5-, and 6-string basses featuring the Novax Fanned-Fret System.

Domino
Ca. 1967-1968. Imported from Japan by Maurice Lipsky Music of New York, mainly copies, but some original designs. They also offered guitars.

Electric Bass
1967-1968. Includes the Beatle Bass and Fireball Bass, a Vox Phantom IV copy.

1967-1968		$250	$400

Dorado
Ca. 1972-1973. Name used briefly by Baldwin/Gretsch on line of Japanese guitar and bass imports.

Electric Solidbody Bass

1970s	Import	$200	$300

Earthwood
1972-1985. Acoustic designs by Ernie Ball with input from George Fullerton and made in Newport Beach, California. One of the first to offer acoustic basses.

Acoustic Bass
1972-1985. Big bodied acoustic bass alternative between Kay double bass and solidbody Fender bass.

1972-1985		$1,125	$1,400

MODEL YEAR	FEATURES	EXC. COND. LOW	HIGH

EKO
1959-1985, 2000-present. Built by the Oliviero Pigini Company, Italy. Original importers included LoDuca Brothers, Milwaukee, Wisconsin. Since about 2000, production, acoustic and electric EKO basses are again available and made in Italy and China. They also make guitars and amps.

Barracuda Bass
1967-1978. Offset double-cut semi-hollow, 2 pickups.

1967-1978		$475	$600

Cobra II Bass
1967-ca.1969. Offset double-cut solidbody, 2 pickups.

1967-1969		$400	$500

Kadett Bass
1967-1978. Red or sunburst.

1967-1978		$475	$600

Model 995/2 Violin Bass
1966-ca.1969.

1966-1969		$650	$825

Model 1100/2 Bass
1961-1966. Jaguar-style plastic covered solidbody, 2 pickups, sparkle finish.

1961-1966		$550	$675

Rocket IV/Rokes Bass
1967-early-1970s. Rocket-shape design, solidbody, says Rokes on the headstock, the Rokes were a popular English band that endorsed EKO guitars. Marketed as the Rocket IV in the U.S. and as the Rokes in Europe. Often called the Rok. Sunburst, 1 pickup.

1967-1971		$650	$825

Electra
1970-1984, 2013-present. Originally basses imported from Japan by St. Louis Music. They also offered guitars. Currently U.S.-made in Tampa, Florida.

Electric Solidbody Bass
1970s. Japanese imports, various models.

1970s		$400	$500

MPC Outlaw Bass
1970s. Symmetric solidbody with large straight horns, 2 separate plug-in modules for different effects, MPC headstock logo, bowtie markers, sunburst.

1970s		$675	$850

Emperador
1966-1992. Student-level basses imported by Westheimer Musical Instruments. Early models appear to be made by either Teisco or Kawai; later models were made by Cort. They also had guitars.

Electric Solidbody Bass
1960s. Japanese imports, various models.

1960s	Beatle violin bass	$300	$375
1960s	Various models	$130	$160

Encore
Mid-1960s-present. Budget grade, production, solidbody basses imported from China and Vietnam by John Hornby Skewes & Co. in the U.K. They also offer guitars.

MODEL YEAR	FEATURES	EXC. COND. LOW	HIGH

Hollowbody Bass
1960s. Copy model, greenburst.

1960s		$275	$340

Engelhardt
Engelhardt specializes in student acoustic basses and cellos and is located in Elk Grove Village, Illinois.

Epiphone
1928-present. Epiphone didn't add basses until 1959, after Gibson acquired the brand. The Gibson Epiphones were American-made until '69, then all imports until into the '80s, when some models were again made in the U.S. Currently Epiphone offers intermediate and professional grade, production, acoustic and electric basses.

B-3 Acoustic Bass Viol
1950s. 3/4-size.

1950s		$1,200	$1,500

B-5 Acoustic Bass Viol
1950s. 3/4-size laminate construction.

1950s		$2,750	$3,400

EA/ET/ES Series (Japan)
1970-1979. Production of the Epiphone brand was moved to Japan in '70. Models included the EA (electric thinline) and ET (electric solidbody).

1970-1975	EA-260, EB-2	$400	$500
1970-1975	ET-280	$400	$500
1970-1975	ET-285		
	Embassy Deluxe	$400	$500

EB-0 Bass
1998-present. SG body style, single pickup, bolt-on neck.

1998-2014		$225	$290

EB-1 Bass
1998-2000. Violin-shaped mahogany body, 1 pickup.

1998-2000		$235	$300

EB-3 Bass
1999-present. SG body style, 2 pickups.

1999-2014		$320	$400

EBM-4 Bass
1991-1998. Alder body, maple neck, split humbucker, white.

1991-1998		$225	$290

Elitist Series Bass
2003-2005. Higher-end appointments such as set-necks and USA pickups.

2003-2005	EB-3	$600	$800

Embassy Deluxe Bass
1963-1969. Solidbody, double-cut, 2 pickups, tune-o-matic bridge, cherry finish.

1963-1964		$3,900	$5,200
1965		$3,500	$4,700
1966-1968		$3,400	$4,500
1969		$3,400	$4,500

Explorer Korina Bass
2000-2001. Made in Korea, Gibson Explorer body style, genuine korina body, set neck, gold hardware.

2000-2001		$350	$450

Genesis Bass
1979-1980. Double-cut solidbody, 2 humbuckers, Made in Taiwan.

1979-1980		$775	$1,050

Jack Cassady Signature Bass
1997-present. Maple body, mahogany neck, rosewood 'board, 1 pickup, metallic gold or ebony finish.

1997-2014		$575	$725

Les Paul Special Bass
1997-2013. LP Jr.-style slab body, single-cut, bolt neck, 2 humbuckers.

1997-2013		$225	$275

Newport EBD Bass
1960-1970. Double-cut solidbody, 1 pickup (2 pickups optional until '63), 2-on-a-side tuners until '63, 4-on-a-side after that, cherry.

1960-1964		$2,000	$2,525
1965		$1,450	$1,800
1966-1969		$1,250	$1,575
1970		$1,050	$1,325

Newport EB-SF Bass
1962-1963. Newport with added built-in fuzz, cherry.

1962-1963		$3,000	$3,750

Rivoli Bass (1 Pickup)
1959-1961, 1964-1970. ES-335-style semi-hollowbody bass, 2-on-a-side tuners, 1 pickup (2 in '70), reissued in '94 as the Rivoli II.

1959-1960	Banjo tuners, natural	$5,400	$6,900
1959-1960	Banjo tuners, sunburst	$4,800	$6,000
1961	Standard tuners, natural	$3,100	$3,900
1961	Standard tuners, sunburst	$2,500	$3,100
1964		$2,400	$3,000
1965		$2,200	$2,700
1966-1969		$2,000	$2,500
1967	Sparkling Burgundy	$2,100	$2,600
1970		$1,850	$2,300

Rivoli Bass (2 Pickups)
1970 only. Double pickup Epiphone version of Gibson EB-2D.

1970		$1,950	$2,400

Rivoli II Reissue
1998. Made in Korea, set neck, blond.

1995-1998		$550	$675

Thunderbird IV (Non-Reverse) Bass
1995-1998. Non-reverse-style mahogany body, 2 pickups, 5-string optional.

1995-1998		$275	$350

Thunderbird IV Bass
1997-present. Reverse-style mahogany body, 2 pickups, sunburst.

1997-2014		$270	$330

Viola Bass
1995-present. Beatle Bass 500/1 copy, sunburst.

1995-2014		$275	$350

1968 Epiphone Rivoli
George Healey

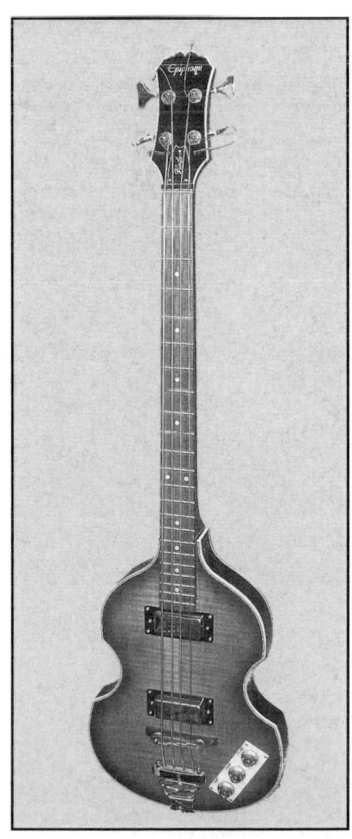

Epiphone Viola

Essex Ursa 2 MN 3TS

1965 Fender Bass VI
Steve Lee

MODEL YEAR	FEATURES	EXC. COND. LOW	HIGH

ESP

1975-present. Intermediate, professional, and premium grade, production/custom, electric basses. Japan's ESP (Electric Sound Products) made inroads in the U.S. market with mainly copy styles in the early '80s, mixing in original designs over the years. In the '90s, ESP opened a California-based Custom Shop. They also build guitars.

B-1 Bass

1990s. Vague DC-style slab solidbody with bolt-on neck, ESP and B-1 on headstock.

1990s		$500	$600

Horizon Bass

1987-1993. Offset double-cut solidbody, 4- and 5-string versions, active electronics, 34" scale.

1987-1993	4-string	$550	$675

Essex (SX)

1985-present. Budget grade, production, electric basses imported by Rondo Music of Union, New Jersey. They also offer guitars.

Electric Solidbody Bass

1990s		$105	$130

Estrada

1960s-1970s. Line of classical, acoustic and electric guitars and basses imported from Japan.

Violin Bass

1960s		$425	$550

Fender

1946-present. Intermediate, professional, and premium grade, production/custom, electric and acoustic basses made in the U.S. and overseas. Leo Fender is the father of the electric bass. The introduction of his Precision Bass in late '51 changed forever how music was performed, recorded and heard. Leo followed with other popular models of basses that continue to make up a large part of Fender's production. Please note that all the variations of the Jazz and Precision Basses are grouped under those general headings.

A custom color is worth more than a standard color. The first Precision Bass standard color was blond but changed to sunburst in the late 1950s. The Jazz Bass standard color is sunburst. To understand a custom color, you need to know what the standard color is. Some custom colors are more rare than others. Below is a list of the custom colors offered in 1960 by Fender. They are sorted in ascending order with the most valuable color, Shell Pink, listed last. In the 1960 list, Black and Blond are the least valuable and Shell Pink is the most valuable. A Fiesta Red is typically worth 12% more than a Black or Blond. In the rare color group a Foam Green is normally worth 8% more than a Shoreline Gold. The two very rare colors are often worth 30% more than a Shoreline Gold. In our pricing information we will list the standard color, then the relative value of a common custom color, and then the value of a rare custom color. Remember that the amount

of fade also affects the price. These prices are for factory original custom colors with slight or no fade in excellent condition. Fade implies a lighter color, but with custom colors a faded example can also be much darker in color. Blue can fade to dark green. White can fade to deep yellow.

The Price Guide lists the standard color, plus the value of a Common Color and the value of a Rare Color. The list below defines which group a color falls into for 1960, and it is in ascending order so, for example, a Daphne Blue should be considered more valuable than a Lake Placid Blue, assuming they are in equal condition.

Common Color: Black, Blond, Candy Apple Red, Olympic White, Lake Placid Blue, Dakota Red, Daphne Blue, Fiesta Red

Rare Color: Shoreline Gold, Inca Silver, Burgundy Mist, Sherwood Green, Sonic Blue, Foam Green

Rare (Very Rare) Color: Surf Green, Shell Pink

Ashbory Bass

2003-2006. Unique-shaped travel bass, Ashbory logo on body, Fender logo on back of headstock, previously sold under Fender's DeArmond brand.

2005-2006		$275	$350

Bass V

1965-1970. Five strings, double-cut, 1 pickup, dot inlay '65-'66, block inlay '66-'70. Please refer to the beginning of the Fender Bass Section for details on Fender color options.

1965	Common color	$4,000	$5,500
1965	Rare color	$5,500	$7,000
1965	Sunburst	$3,500	$4,400
1966-1967	Common color	$3,500	$4,800
1966-1967	Rare color	$4,800	$6,000
1966-1967	Sunburst, block inlay	$2,500	$3,100
1966-1967	Sunburst, dot inlay	$2,600	$3,200
1968-1970	Common color	$3,200	$4,400
1968-1970	Rare color	$4,400	$5,500
1968-1970	Sunburst	$2,200	$2,700

Bass VI

1961-1975. Six strings, Jazzmaster-like body, 3 pickups, dot inlay until '66, block inlay '66-'75. Reintroduced as Japanese-made Collectable model '95-'98. Please refer to the beginning of the Fender Bass Section for details on Fender color options.

1961-1962	Common color	$10,000	$13,800
1961-1962	Rare color	$13,800	$17,200
1961-1962	Sunburst	$7,000	$8,700
1963-1964	Common color	$9,000	$12,400
1963-1964	Rare color	$12,400	$15,500
1963-1964	Sunburst	$6,000	$7,500
1965	Common color	$8,000	$11,000
1965	Rare color	$11,000	$14,000
1965	Sunburst	$5,000	$6,300
1966	Common color	$5,500	$7,500
1966	Rare color	$7,500	$9,500
1966	Sunburst, block inlay	$3,900	$4,800
1966	Sunburst, dot inlay	$4,100	$5,000
1967-1969	Common color	$5,000	$6,900

MODEL YEAR	FEATURES	EXC. COND. LOW	HIGH
1967-1969	Rare color	$6,900	$8,600
1967-1969	Sunburst	$3,800	$4,700
1970-1971	Common color	$4,500	$5,600
1970-1971	Rare color	$5,600	$7,000
1970-1971	Sunburst	$3,300	$4,100
1972-1974	Natural	$2,900	$3,600
1972-1974	Other custom colors	$4,500	$5,600
1972-1974	Sunburst	$3,200	$4,000
1972-1974	Walnut	$3,100	$3,900
1975	Natural	$2,900	$3,600
1975	Olympic White, black, blond	$3,200	$4,000
1975	Sunburst	$3,200	$4,000
1975	Walnut	$3,100	$3,900

Bass VI Reissue (CS)
2006. Custom Shop, 3-tone sunburst, certificate of authenticity.

2006		$1,800	$2,300

Bass VI Reissue (Import)
1995-1998. Import, sunburst.

1995-1998		$1,300	$1,600

Bass VI Reissue (Japan)
2014. JD serial number.

2014		$825	$1,050

Bass VI Pawn Shop
2013-2014. Alder body, maple neck, rosewood 'board, 3-color sunburst.

2013-2014		$450	$575

BG Series Bass
1995-2011. Acoustic flat-top bass, single-cut, two-on-a-side tuners, Fishman on-board controls, black.

1995-2009	BG-29, black	$300	$375
1995-2009	BG-32, natural	$300	$375
1995-2011	BG-31, black	$300	$375

Bullet Bass (B30, B34, B40)
1982-1983. Alder body, 1 pickup, offered in short- and long-scale, red or walnut. U.S.-made, replaced by Japanese-made Squire Bullet Bass.

1982-1983		$650	$800

Bullet Deluxe Bass
1982-1983. Fender logo with Bullet Bass Deluxe on headstock, E-series serial number, small Telecaster-style headstock shape.

1982-1983		$650	$800

Coronado I Bass
1966-1970. Thinline, double-cut, 1 pickup, dot inlay, sunburst and cherry red were the standard colors, but custom colors could be ordered.

1966-1970	Cherry red, sunburst	$1,050	$1,300
1966-1970	Custom colors	$1,125	$1,450

Coronado II Bass
1966-1972. Two pickups, block inlay, sunburst and cherry red standard colors, but custom colors could be ordered. Only Antigua finish offered from '70 on.

1966-1969	Cherry red, sunburst	$1,750	$2,200
1966-1969	Custom colors	$1,750	$2,200
1966-1969	Wildwood option	$2,500	$3,100
1970-1972	Antigua only	$1,950	$2,450

Coronado Bass Reissue

MODEL YEAR	FEATURES	EXC. COND. LOW	HIGH

2014-present. Reissue of the 2 pickup, block inlay, Coronado II.

2014		$400	$500

Dimension Bass
2004-2006. Made in Mexico, 4- or 5-string, P and J pickups.

2004-2006		$400	$500

HM Bass
1989-1991. Japanese-made, 4 strings (IV) or 5 strings (V), basswood body, no 'guard, 3 Jazz Bass pickups, 5-way switch, master volume, master TBX, sunburst.

1989-1991	IV, 4-string	$700	$900
1989-1991	V, 5-string	$700	$900

Jaguar Bass
2006-2010. Made in Japan, Jaguar Bass logo on headstock.

2006-2010		$625	$775

Jaguar Bass Modern Player
2012-present. Made in China, koto body, maple neck and 'board, black.

2012-2014		$265	$325

Jaguar Baritone Custom Bass
2007. Fender Jaguar Baritone Custom logo on headstock, 6-string.

2007		$725	$900

Deluxe Jaguar Bass
2012-2014. Maple neck, rosewood 'board, 2 pickups, 3-color sunburst, Candy Apple Red, Cobalt Blue.

2012-2014		$525	$650

Jazz Bass
The following are variations of the Jazz Bass. The first four listings are for the main U.S.-made models. All others are listed alphabetically after that in the following order:
Jazz Bass
Standard Jazz Bass
American Standard Jazz Bass
American Standard Jazz V Bass
American Series Jazz Bass
American Series Jazz V Bass
50th Anniversary American Standard Jazz Bass
50th Anniversary Jazz Bass Limited Edition
'60s Jazz Bass (Custom Shop)
'60s Jazz Bass (Import)
Road Worn '60s Jazz Bass
60th Anniversary American Jazz Bass
'62 Jazz Bass
'64 Jazz Bass (Custom Shop)
'64 Jazz Bass (American Vintage)
'66 Jazz Bass Special Limited Edition
'74 Jazz Bass (American Vintage)
'75 Jazz Bass (American Vintage)
Aerodyne Jazz Bass
American Deluxe Jazz Bass
American Deluxe Jazz V Bass
American Deluxe FMT Jazz Bass
Contemporary Jazz
Custom Classic Jazz Bass
Deluxe Jazz Bass (Active)

Fender Coronado II
James Goode

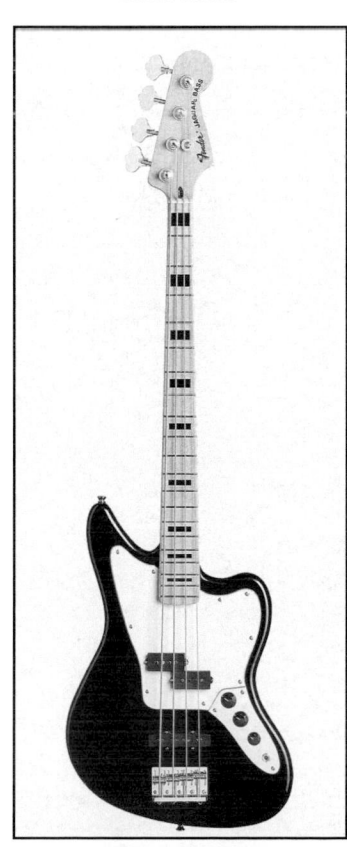

*Fender Jaguar Bass
Modern Player*

BASSES

1965 Fender Jazz

1972 Fender Jazz

Robbie Keene

MODEL YEAR	FEATURES	EXC. COND. LOW	HIGH
	Deluxe Jazz Bass V (Active)		
	Deluxe Power Jazz Bass		
	Foto Flame Jazz Bass		
	FSR Standard Special Edition Jazz Bass		
	Geddy Lee Signature Jazz Bass		
	Gold Jazz Bass		
	Highway One Jazz Bass		
	Jaco Pastorius Jazz Bass		
	Jazz Plus Bass		
	Jazz Plus V Bass		
	Jazz Special Bass (Import)		
	Marcus Miller Signature Jazz Bass		
	Noel Redding Signature Jazz Bass		
	Reggie Hamilton Jazz Bass		
	Roscoe Beck Jazz IV/V Bass		
	Select Jazz Bass		
	Standard Jazz Bass (Import)		
	Standard Jazz Fretless Bass (Import)		
	Standard Jazz V Bass (Import)		
	Ventures Limited Edition Jazz Bass		
	Victor Baily Jazz Bass		

Jazz Bass

1960-1981. Two stack knobs '60-'62, 3 regular controls '62 on. Dot markers '60-'66, block markers from '66 on. Rosewood 'board standard, but maple available from '68 on. With the introduction of vintage reissue models in '81, Fender started calling the American-made version the Standard Jazz Bass. That became the American Standard Jazz Bass in '88 and then became the American Series Jazz Bass in 2000. Renamed back to the American Standard Jazz Bass in '08. Post '71 Jazz Bass values are affected more by condition than color or neck option. The Jazz Bass was fitted with a 3-bolt neck or bullet rod in late-'74. Prices assume a 3-bolt neck starting in '75. Please refer to the beginning of the Fender Bass Section for details on Fender color options.

MODEL YEAR	FEATURES	EXC. COND. LOW	HIGH
1960	Common color	$25,000	$35,000
1960	Rare color	$35,000	$62,000
1960	Sunburst	$19,000	$24,000
1961-1962	Common color, stack knob	$25,000	$35,000
1961-1962	Rare color, stack knob	$35,000	$54,000
1961-1962	Sunburst, stack knob	$18,400	$23,000
1962	Common color, 3 knob, curved	$12,000	$17,000
1962	Common color, 3 knob, slab	$16,000	$22,000
1962	Rare color, 3 knob, curved	$17,000	$25,000
1962	Rare color, 3 knob, slab	$22,000	$35,000
1962	Sunburst, 3 knob, curved	$10,600	$13,400
1962	Sunburst, 3 knob, slab	$11,500	$14,400
1963	Common color	$11,000	$16,000
1963	Rare color	$16,000	$24,000
1963	Sunburst	$9,300	$11,600

MODEL YEAR	FEATURES	EXC. COND. LOW	HIGH
1964	Common color	$10,000	$14,000
1964	Rare color	$14,000	$20,000
1964	Sunburst, early '64	$8,600	$10,700
1964	Sunburst, late '64	$8,100	$10,100
1965	Common color	$8,800	$12,500
1965	Rare color	$12,500	$18,300
1965	Sunburst	$6,550	$8,200
1966	Common color	$8,600	$10,800
1966	Rare color	$10,800	$13,500
1966	Sunburst, blocks	$5,300	$6,600
1966	Sunburst, dots	$5,800	$7,200
1967	Common color	$7,500	$10,000
1967	Rare color	$10,000	$13,500
1967	Sunburst	$5,100	$6,400
1968	Common color	$6,300	$8,500
1968	Rare color	$8,500	$11,500
1968	Sunburst	$4,900	$6,100
1969	Common color	$5,700	$7,800
1969	Rare color	$7,800	$10,400
1969	Sunburst	$4,200	$5,200
1970	Common color	$5,200	$7,000
1970	Rare color	$7,000	$9,600
1970	Sunburst	$3,500	$4,400
1971	Common color	$3,500	$4,700
1971	Rare color	$4,700	$6,500
1971	Sunburst	$3,200	$4,000
1972	Common color	$3,000	$4,100
1972	Natural	$2,800	$3,500
1972	Rare color	$4,100	$5,700
1972	Sunburst	$3,000	$3,700
1973	Common color	$2,900	$3,700
1973	Natural	$2,700	$3,400
1973	Rare color	$3,700	$4,600
1973	Sunburst, walnut	$2,800	$3,500
1974	Custom colors, 3-bolt	$2,700	$3,400
1974	Custom colors, 4-bolt	$2,950	$3,700
1974	Natural, 3-bolt	$2,250	$2,800
1974	Natural, 4-bolt	$2,500	$3,100
1974	Sunburst, 3-bolt, late-'74	$2,250	$2,800
1974	Sunburst, 4-bolt	$2,500	$3,100
1974	Walnut, 3-bolt	$2,250	$2,800
1974	Walnut, 4-bolt	$2,500	$3,100
1975-1977	Black, blond, white, wine, 3-bolt	$2,200	$3,400
1975-1977	Natural, 3-bolt	$2,250	$2,800
1975-1977	Sunburst, 3-bolt	$2,250	$2,800
1975-1977	Walnut, 3-bolt	$2,250	$2,800
1978-1979	Antigua	$2,200	$2,800
1978-1979	Black, blond, white, wine	$2,200	$2,800
1978-1979	Natural	$2,000	$2,500
1978-1979	Sunburst, 3-bolt	$2,000	$2,500
1978-1979	Walnut	$2,000	$2,500
1980	Antigua	$2,200	$2,800
1980	Black, white, wine	$2,200	$2,800

The *Vintage Guitar Price Guide* shows low to high values for items in all-original excellent condition, and, where applicable, with original case or cover.

MODEL YEAR	FEATURES	EXC. COND. LOW	HIGH
1980	Natural	$1,400	$1,800
1980	Sunburst, 3-bolt	$1,700	$2,100
1981	Black & Gold Collector's Edition	$1,500	$1,900
1981	Black, white, wine	$1,500	$1,900
1981	International colors	$2,000	$2,700
1981	Sunburst	$1,500	$1,900

Standard Jazz Bass

1981-1985. Replaced Jazz Bass ('60-'81) and replaced by the American Standard Jazz Bass in '88. Name now used on import version. Please refer to the beginning of the Fender Bass Section for details on Fender color options.

1981-1984		$1,100	$1,450
1985	Japan import	$700	$900

American Standard Jazz Bass

1988-2000, 2008-present. Replaced Standard Jazz Bass ('81-'88) and replaced by the American Series Jazz Bass in '00, back to American Standard in Jan. '08.

1988-2014		$825	$1,025

American Standard Jazz V Bass

1998-2000, 2008-present. 5-string version.

1998-2014		$875	$1,075

American Series Jazz Bass

2000-2007. Replaces American Standard Jazz Bass. Renamed American Standard in '08.

2000-2007		$825	$1,025

American Series Jazz V Bass

2000-2007. 5-string version.

2000-2007		$875	$1,075

50th Anniversary American Standard Jazz Bass

1996. Regular American Standard with gold hardware, 4- or 5-string, gold Fender's 50th Anniversary commemorative neck plate, rosewood 'board, sunburst.

1996	IV	$1,000	$1,250
1996	V	$1,100	$1,350

50th Anniversary Jazz Bass Limited Edition

2010. 50th anniversary of the Jazz Bass, nitro Candy Apple Red with matching headstock, mix of vintage and modern specs, rosewood 'board, block markers, 50th Anniversary neck plate.

2010		$1,750	$2,175

'60s Jazz Bass (Custom Shop)

1994-1998. Early '60s specs, relic for 1996-1998. Replaced by the CS '64 Jazz Bass. Early Relic work was done outside of Fender by Vince Cunetto or his staff.

1994-1995		$1,900	$2,400
1996	Relic (Cunetto)	$2,500	$3,100
1997-1998	Relic (Cunetto staff)	$1,900	$2,400

'60s Jazz Bass (Import)

1991-1994, 2001-present. Classic series, '60s features, rosewood 'board, Japan-made for first years, Mexico after.

1991-1994	Japan	$600	$750
2001-2014	Mexico	$500	$625

Road Worn '60s Jazz Bass

2009-present. Rosewood 'board, aged finish.

2009-2014		$575	$725

60th Anniversary American Jazz Bass

2006. Rosewood 'board, 3-tone sunburst.

2006		$900	$1,125

'62 Jazz Bass

1982-1984, 1986-2012. U.S.A.-made, American Vintage series, reissue of '62 Jazz Bass. Please refer to the beginning of the Fender Bass Section for details on Fender color options.

1982-1984		$2,500	$3,100
1986-1999		$1,200	$1,500
2000-2012		$1,100	$1,400

'64 Jazz Bass (Custom Shop)

1998-2009. Alder body, rosewood 'board, tortoise shell 'guard. From June '95 to June '99 Relic work was done outside of Fender by Vince Cunetto and included a certificate noting model and year built, a bass without the certificate is valued less than shown.

1998-1999	Relic (Cunetto)	$1,900	$2,400
2000-2009	Closet Classic option	$1,900	$2,400
2000-2009	N.O.S option	$1,900	$2,400
2000-2009	Relic option	$2,000	$2,500

'64 Jazz Bass (American Vintage)

2013-present. American Vintage series, dot inlays.

2013-2014		$1,100	$1,400

'66 Jazz Bass Special Limited Edition

2013. Japan, made for retailer Sweetwater, aged Oly White, 132 made for North American distribution.

2013		$700	$875

'74 Jazz Bass (American Vintage)

2013-present. American Vintage series, block inlays.

2013-2014		$1,500	$1,850

'75 Jazz Bass (American Vintage)

1994-2012. American Vintage series, maple neck with black block markers.

1994-2012		$1,050	$1,300

Aerodyne Jazz Bass

2003-present. Bound basswood body, P/J pickups, Deluxe Series.

2003-2014		$600	$750

American Deluxe Jazz Bass

1998-present. U.S., active electronics, alder or ash body. Alder body colors - sunburst or transparent red, ash body colors - white, blond, transparent teal green or transparent purple.

1998-2014	IV	$900	$1,125

American Deluxe Jazz V Bass

1998-present. Five-string model, various colors.

1998-2014		$950	$1,200

American Deluxe FMT Jazz Bass

2001-2006. Flame maple top version (FMT), active EQ, dual J pickups.

2001-2006		$1,150	$1,425

Contemporary Jazz

1987. Made in Japan.

1987		$625	$775

Fender American Vintage '64 Jazz Bass

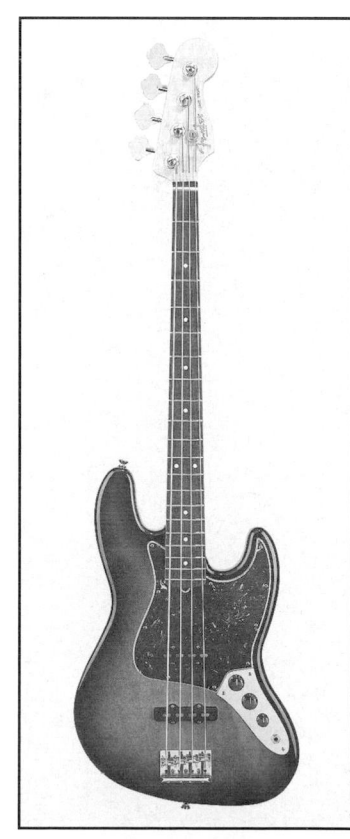

Fender American Standard Jazz

To get the most from this book, be sure to read "Using *The Guide*" in the introduction.

1967 Fender Mustang

1958 Fender Precision
Garrett From Indiana

MODEL YEAR	FEATURES	EXC. COND. LOW	HIGH

Custom Classic Jazz Bass
2001-2009. Custom Shop, slightly slimmer waist, deeper cutaways, maple or rosewood 'board, block inlays, 4 (IV) or 5-string (V).

| 2001-2009 | IV | $1,575 | $1,975 |
| 2001-2009 | V | $1,575 | $1,975 |

Deluxe Jazz Bass (Active)
1995-present. Made in Mexico, active electronics, various colors.

| 1995-2014 | | $375 | $475 |

Deluxe Jazz Bass V (Active)
1995-present. Made in Mexico, various colors.

| 1995-2014 | | $425 | $525 |

Deluxe Power Jazz Bass
2006. Part of Deluxe Series with Fishman piezo power bridge.

| 2006 | | $600 | $750 |

Foto Flame Jazz Bass
1994-1996. Japanese import, alder and basswood body with Foto Flame figured wood image.

| 1994-1996 | | $650 | $800 |

FSR Standard Special Edition Jazz Bass
2007-2009. Made in Mexico, Fender Special Edition logo on back of headstock, ash body with natural finish.

| 2007-2009 | | $325 | $410 |

Geddy Lee Signature Jazz Bass
1998-present. Limited run import in '98, now part of Artist Series, black.

| 1998-2014 | | $675 | $850 |

Gold Jazz Bass
1981-1984. Gold finish and gold-plated hardware.

| 1981-1984 | | $1,300 | $1,600 |

Highway One Jazz Bass
2003-2011. U.S.-made, alder body, satin lacquer finish.

| 2003-2011 | | $600 | $750 |

Jaco Pastorius Jazz Bass
1999-present. Artist Signature Series, standard production model made in Corona, '62 3-color sunburst body without pickup covers.

| 1999-2000 | Fretted | $1,100 | $1,400 |
| 1999-2014 | Fretless | $1,275 | $1,600 |

Jazz Plus Bass
1990-1994. Alder body, 2 Lace Sensors, active electronics, rotary circuit selector, master volume, balance, bass boost, bass cut, treble boost, treble cut, various colors.

| 1990-1994 | | $850 | $1,050 |

Jazz Plus V Bass
1990-1994. Five-string version.

| 1990-1994 | | $900 | $1,125 |

Jazz Special Bass (Import)
1984-1991. Japanese-made, Jazz/Precision hybrid, Precision-shaped basswood body, Jazz neck (fretless available), 2 P/J pickups, offered with active (Power) or passive electronics.

| 1984-1991 | | $350 | $435 |

Marcus Miller Signature Jazz Bass
1998-2014. Artist series.

| 1998-2004 | Import | $825 | $1,025 |
| 2005-2014 | U.S. Custom Shop | $1,400 | $1,750 |

Noel Redding Signature Jazz Bass
1997. Limited Edition import, artist signature on 'guard, sunburst, rosewood 'board.

| 1997 | | $900 | $1,150 |

Reggie Hamilton Jazz Bass
2002-present. Alder body, passive/active switch and pan control.

| 2002-2014 | | $515 | $650 |

Roscoe Beck Jazz IV/V Bass
1997-2009. 5-string version offered '97-'06 , 4-string '09.

| 1997-2009 | 5-string | $1,350 | $1,675 |
| 2004-2009 | 4-string | $1,300 | $1,600 |

Select Jazz Bass
2012-2013. US-made, figured top, rear-headstock 'Fender Select' medallion.

| 2012-2013 | | $1,400 | $1,750 |

Standard Jazz Bass (Import)
1988-present. Standard series, Japan-made into '90, Mexico after. Not to be confused with '81-'88 American-made model with the same name.

1988-1999		$300	$375
2000-2009		$325	$400
2010-2014		$350	$425

Standard Jazz Fretless Bass (Import)
1994-present. Standard series, fretless version.

| 1994-2014 | | $335 | $425 |

Standard Jazz V Bass (Import)
1994-present. Standard series, fretless version.

| 1998-2014 | | $350 | $425 |

Ventures Limited Edition Jazz Bass
1996. Made in Japan, part of Ventures guitar and bass set, dark purple.

| 1996 | | $1,025 | $1,275 |

Victor Baily Jazz Bass
2002-2011. Artist series, koa, rosewood and mahogany body, fretless with white fret markers.

| 2002-2011 | | $1,225 | $1,550 |

JP-90 Bass
1990-1994. Two P/J pickups, rosewood fretboard, poplar body, black or red.

| 1990-1994 | | $350 | $450 |

MB Bass
1994-1995. Made in Japan, offset double-cut, 1 P- and 1 J-style pickup, made in Japan.

| 1994-1995 | 4-String | $325 | $400 |
| 1994-1995 | 5-String | $375 | $475 |

Musicmaster Bass
1970-1983. Shorter scale, solidbody, 1 pickup. various colors.

| 1970-1983 | | $725 | $900 |

Mustang Bass
1966-1982. Shorter scale, solidbody, 1 pickup, offered in standard colors and, for '69-'73, Competition Red, Blue and Orange with racing stripes on the body (with matching headstock for '69-'70).

1966-1969		$1,500	$1,900
1969-1970	Competition	$1,900	$2,400
1970-1979		$1,250	$1,575
1978-1980	Antigua finish	$1,500	$1,900
1980-1982		$925	$1,150

The *Vintage Guitar Price Guide* shows low to high values for items in all-original excellent condition, and, where applicable, with original case or cover.

MODEL YEAR	FEATURES	EXC. COND. LOW	HIGH

Mustang Bass (Japan)
2002-present. Alder body, '60s features.

2002-2014		$575	$725

Performer Bass
1985-1986. Swinger-like body style, active electronics, various colors.

1985-1986		$950	$1,175

Precision Bass

The following are variations of the Precision Bass. The first four listings are for the main U.S.-made models. All others are listed alphabetically after that in the following order:

Precision Bass
Standard Precision Bass
American Standard Precision Bass
American Series Precision Bass
American Series Precision V Bass
40th Anniversary Precision Bass (Custom Shop)
50th Anniversary American Standard Precision
   Bass
50th Anniversary Precision Bass
'50s Precision Bass
Road Worn '50s Precision Bass
'51 Precision Bass
'55 Precision Bass (Custom Shop)
'57 Precision Bass
'57 Precision Bass (Import)
'59 Precision Bass (Custom Shop)
60th Anniversary Precision Bass (Mexico)
60th Anniversary Precision Bass (USA)
'61 Precision Bass (Custom Shop)
'62 Precision Bass
'62 Precision Bass (Import)
'70s Precision Bass (Import)
Adam Clayton Signature Precision Bass
Aerodyne Classic Precision Special Bass
American Deluxe Precision Bass
American Deluxe Precision V Bass
Big Block Precision Bass
California Precision Bass Special
Deluxe Active P-Bass Special
Elite I Precision Bass
Elite II Precision Bass
Foto Flame Precision Bass
Gold Elite I Precision Bass
Gold Elite II Precision Bass
Highway One Precision Bass
Mark Hoppus Signature Precision Bass
Precision Bass Jr.
Precision Bass Lyte
Precision Special Bass (U.S.A.)
Precision Special Bass (Mexico)
Precision U.S. Deluxe/Plus Deluxe Bass
Precision U.S. Plus/Plus Bass
Standard Precision Bass (Import)
Sting Precision Bass
Tony Franklin Precision Bass
Walnut Elite I Precision Bass
Walnut Elite II Precision Bass
Walnut Precision Special Bass

MODEL YEAR	FEATURES	EXC. COND. LOW	HIGH

Precision Bass

1951-1981. Slab body until '54, 1-piece maple neck standard until '59, optional after '69, rosewood 'board standard '59 on (slab until mid-'62, curved after), blond finish standard until '54, sunburst standard after that (2-tone '54-'58, 3-tone after '58). Replaced by the Standard Precision Bass in '81-'85, then the American Standard Precision in '88-'00, and the American Series Precision Bass in '00-'08. Renamed American Standard again in '08. Unlike the Jazz and Telecaster Basses, the Precision was never fitted with a 3-bolt neck or bullet rod. Please refer to the beginning of the Fender Bass Section for details on Fender color options.

YEAR	FEATURES	LOW	HIGH
1951-1954	Blond, slab	$15,000	$19,000
1955	Blond, contour	$13,000	$16,000
1956	Blond, contour	$11,000	$14,000
1956	Sunburst, contour	$10,000	$12,500
1957	Blond	$11,000	$14,000
1957	Blond, anodized guard	$13,000	$16,000
1957	Sunburst	$8,000	$10,000
1957	Sunburst, anodized guard, late '57	$10,000	$12,500
1958	Blond option	$11,000	$14,000
1958	Sunburst, anodized guard	$10,000	$12,500
1959	Blond	$11,000	$14,000
1959	Sunburst, anodized guard	$10,000	$12,500
1959	Sunburst, tortoise guard	$8,000	$10,000
1960	Blond	$11,000	$14,000
1960	Custom color	$20,000	$38,000
1960	Sunburst	$9,500	$12,000
1961	Common color	$20,000	$27,000
1961	Rare color	$27,000	$38,000
1961	Sunburst	$8,000	$10,000
1962	Common color, curved	$9,000	$12,000
1962	Common color, slab	$11,000	$15,000
1962	Rare color, curved	$12,000	$18,000
1962	Rare color, slab	$15,000	$22,000
1962	Sunburst, curved	$6,500	$8,100
1962	Sunburst, slab	$8,000	$10,000
1963	Common color	$9,000	$12,100
1963	Rare color	$12,000	$18,000
1963	Sunburst	$6,700	$8,300
1964	Common color	$9,000	$12,100
1964	Rare color	$12,000	$17,000
1964	Sunburst, early '64	$6,600	$8,200
1964	Sunburst, late '64	$5,900	$7,300
1965	Common color	$8,500	$11,500
1965	Rare color	$11,500	$15,000
1965	Sunburst	$6,500	$8,100
1966	Common color	$7,400	$9,500
1966	Rare color	$9,500	$12,000
1966	Sunburst	$4,650	$5,800
1967	Common color	$6,000	$8,000

1957 Fender Precision

1964 Fender Precision

1971 Fender Precision
Robbie Keene

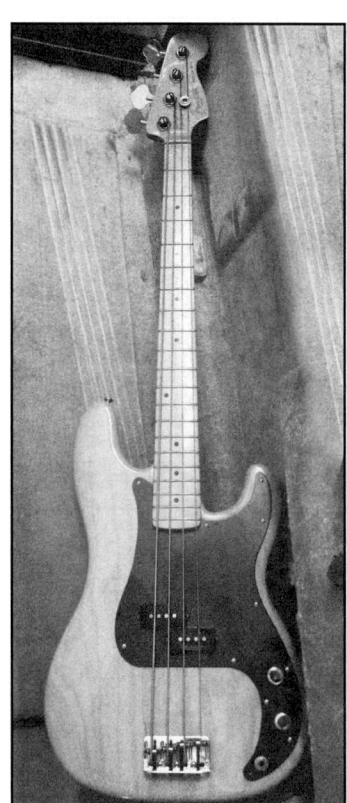

*2001 Fender 50th
Anniversary Precision*
Jonathan Bell

MODEL YEAR	FEATURES	EXC. COND. LOW	HIGH
1967	Rare color	$8,000	$11,000
1967	Sunburst	$4,300	$5,400
1968	Common color	$5,500	$7,300
1968	Rare color	$7,300	$10,000
1968	Sunburst	$4,200	$5,200
1969	Common color	$5,000	$6,600
1969	Rare color	$6,600	$9,000
1969	Sunburst	$3,300	$4,100
1970	Common color	$4,700	$6,300
1970	Rare color	$6,300	$8,500
1970	Sunburst	$2,800	$3,500
1971	Common color	$3,300	$4,300
1971	Rare color	$4,300	$5,700
1971	Sunburst	$2,200	$2,800
1972	Common color	$2,500	$4,000
1972	Rare color	$4,000	$5,000
1972	Sunburst	$2,200	$2,800
1973	Common color	$2,300	$3,100
1973	Natural	$2,000	$2,500
1973	Rare color	$3,100	$4,200
1973	Sunburst	$2,200	$2,800
1973	Walnut	$2,000	$2,500
1974	Black, blond, white	$2,400	$3,000
1974	Natural	$2,000	$2,500
1974	Sunburst	$2,200	$2,800
1974	Walnut	$2,000	$2,500
1975-1977	Black, blond, Olympic White, wine	$2,100	$2,700
1975-1977	Natural, walnut	$1,625	$2,025
1975-1977	Sunburst	$2,100	$2,700
1978-1979	Antigua	$2,100	$2,700
1978-1979	Black, blond, Olympic White, wine	$1,800	$2,300
1978-1979	Natural, walnut	$1,500	$1,900
1978-1979	Sunburst	$1,800	$2,300
1980	Antigua	$2,000	$2,500
1980	Black, Olympic White, wine	$1,700	$2,200
1980	Color with matching headstk, gold hw	$2,000	$2,500
1980	International colors	$2,000	$2,700
1980	Natural	$1,400	$1,800
1980	Sunburst	$1,700	$2,100
1981	Black & gold	$1,500	$1,900
1981	Black, Olympic White, wine	$1,500	$1,900
1981	International colors	$2,000	$2,700
1981	Sunburst	$1,500	$1,900

Standard Precision Bass

1981-1985. Replaces Precision Bass, various colors. Replaced by American Standard Precision '88-'00. The Standard name is used on import Precision model for '88-present.

1981-1984		$1,150	$1,450
1985	Japan import	$675	$850

American Standard Precision Bass

1988-2000, 2008-present. Replaces Standard Precision Bass, replaced by American Series Precision in '00, back to American Standard in Jan. '08.

1988-1989	Blond, gold hardware	$900	$1,125
1988-2000	Various colors	$825	$1,025
2008-2014		$825	$1,025

American Series Precision Bass

2000-2007. Replaces American Standard Precision Bass, various colors. Renamed American Standard in '08.

2000-2007		$825	$1,025

American Series Precision V Bass

2000-2007. 5-string version.

2000-2007		$850	$1,050

40th Anniversary Precision Bass (Custom Shop)

1991. 400 made, quilted amber maple top, gold hardware.

1991		$1,900	$2,400

50th Anniversary American Standard Precision Bass

1996. Regular American Standard with gold hardware, 4- or 5-string, gold 50th Anniversary commemorative neck plate, rosewood 'board, sunburst.

1996		$1,000	$1,250

50th Anniversary Precision Bass

2001. Commemorative certificate with date and serial number, butterscotch finish, ash body, maple neck, black 'guard.

2001	With certificate	$1,000	$1,250

'50s Precision Bass

1992-1996, 2006-present. First run made in Japan, currently in Mexico, 1 split-coil, maple neck.

2006-2014		$500	$625

Road Worn '50s Precision Bass

2009-present. 1 split-coil, maple neck, aged finish.

2009-2014		$575	$725

'51 Precision Bass

1994-1997, 2003-2010. Import from Japan, no pickup or bridge covers, blond or sunburst. Offered in Japan in the '90s.

1994-1997	Japan only	$650	$800
2003-2010		$550	$700

'55 Precision Bass (Custom Shop)

2003-2011. 1955 specs including oversized 'guard, 1-piece maple neck/fretboard, preproduction bridge and pickup covers, single-coil pickup. Offered in N.O.S., Closet Classic or highest-end Relic.

2003-2006	N.O.S.	$1,900	$2,400
2003-2006	Relic	$2,000	$2,500
2003-2011	Closet Classic	$1,900	$2,400

'57 Precision Bass

1982-1984, 1986-2012. U.S.-made reissue, American Vintage series, various colors.

1982-1984		$2,500	$3,100
1986-1989		$1,200	$1,500
1990-1999		$1,200	$1,500
2000-2012		$1,100	$1,400

The ***Vintage Guitar Price Guide*** shows low to high values for items in all-original excellent condition, and, where applicable, with original case or cover.

MODEL YEAR	FEATURES	EXC. COND. LOW	HIGH

'57 Precision Bass (Import)
1984-1986. Foreign-made, black.

1984-1986		$700	$900

'59 Precision Bass (Custom Shop)
2003-2010. Custom Shop built with late-'59 specs, rosewood 'board.

2003-2008	Closet Classic	$1,900	$2,400
2003-2010	N.O.S.	$1,900	$2,400
2003-2010	Relic	$2,000	$2,500

60th Anniversary Precision Bass (Mexico)
2005. Made in Mexico, with 60th Anniversary gig bag.

2005		$300	$375

60th Anniversary Precision Bass (USA)
2011. 1951-2011 Anniversary date label.

2011		$1,050	$1,325

'61 Precision Bass (Custom Shop)
2010-2013. Made for Musician's Friend and Guitar Center.

2010-2013	Closet Classic	$1,900	$2,400
2010-2013	N.O.S.	$1,900	$2,400
2010-2013	Relic	$2,000	$2,500

'62 Precision Bass
1982-1984, 1986-2012. U.S.-made reissue, American Vintage series, alder body. No production in '85.

1982-1984		$2,500	$3,100
1986-1989		$1,200	$1,500
1990	Mary Kaye Blond	$1,650	$2,050
1990-1999		$1,200	$1,500
2000-2012		$1,100	$1,400

'62 Precision Bass (Import)
1984-1986. Foreign-made, black.

1984-1986		$700	$900

'70s Precision Bass (Import)
2011-2013. Classic Series import

2011-2013		$700	$875

Adam Clayton Signature Precision Bass
2011. Custom Shop Limited Edition.

2011		$3,000	$3,700

Aerodyne Classic Precision Special Bass
2006. Made in Japan, labeled Precision and Aerodyne P Bass, figured maple top, matching headstock, P-J pickup.

2006		$600	$750

American Deluxe Precision Bass
1998-present. U.S., active electronics, alder or ash body. Alder body colors - sunburst or transparent red. Ash body colors - white blond, transparent teal green or transparent purple.

1998-2014		$850	$1,075

American Deluxe Precision V Bass
1999-2004. 5-string version.

1999-2004		$900	$1,125

Big Block Precision Bass
2005-2009. Pearloid block markers, black finish with matching headstock, 1 double Jazz Bass humbucker, bass and treble boost and cut controls.

2005-2009		$600	$750

California Precision Bass Special
1997. California Series, assembled and finished in Mexico and California, P/J pickup configuration.

1997		$550	$700

Deluxe Active P-Bass Special
1995-present. Made in Mexico, P/J pickups, Jazz Bass neck.

1995-2014		$375	$475

Elite I Precision Bass
1983-1985. The Elite Series feature active electronics and noise-cancelling pickups, ash body, 1 pickup, various colors.

1983-1985		$1,500	$1,900

Elite II Precision Bass
1983-1985. Ash body, 2 pickups, various colors.

1983-1985		$1,500	$1,900

Foto Flame Precision Bass
1994-1996. Made in Japan, simulated woodgrain finish, natural or sunburst.

1994-1996		$650	$800

Gold Elite I Precision Bass
1983-1985. The Elite Series feature active electronics and noise-cancelling pickups, gold-plated hardware version of the Elite Precision I, 1 pickup.

1983-1985		$1,500	$1,900

Gold Elite II Precision Bass
1983-1985. Two pickup version.

1983-1985		$1,500	$1,900

Highway One Precision Bass
2003-2011. U.S.-made, alder body, satin lacquer finish.

2003-2011		$600	$750

Mark Hoppus Signature Precision Bass
2001. Mark Hoppus engraved on neck plate.

2001		$525	$650

Precision Bass Jr.
2004-2006. 3/4 size.

2004-2006		$300	$375

Precision Bass Lyte
1992-2001. Japanese-made, smaller, lighter basswood body, 2 pickups, sunburst.

1992-2001		$500	$625

Precision Special Bass (U.S.A.)
1980-1982. Gold hardware, matching headstock, active electronics, CA Red, LP Blue, Oly White or walnut (see separate listing).

1980-1982	Common color	$1,100	$1,400
1980-1982	Rare color	$1,400	$2,200

Precision Special Bass (Mexico)
1997-1998. 1 P- and 1 J-pickup. chrome hardware.

1997-1998		$325	$425

Precision U.S. Deluxe/Plus Deluxe Bass
1991-1994. P-style bass with P-bass and Jazz bass pickups, concentric knobs, no 'guard models available, various colors.

1991-1994		$700	$900

Precision U.S. Plus/Plus Bass
1989-1992. P-style bass with P- and J-bass pickup, model variations, black.

1989-1992		$700	$900

Standard Precision Bass (Import)
1988-present. Made in Japan into '90, and Mexico after. Not to be confused with '81-'85 American-made model with the same name.

1988-2014		$300	$375

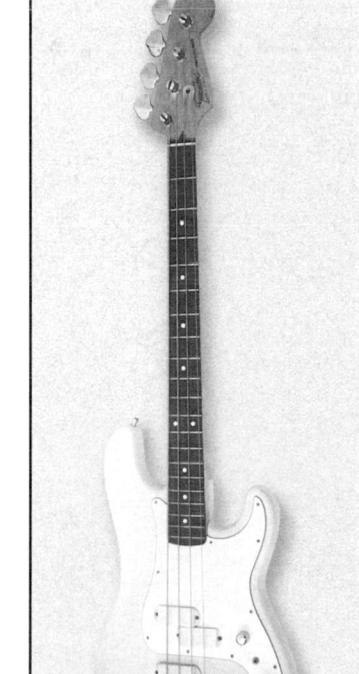

1988 Fender '62 Precision
Jonathan Bell

Fender Elite II Precision

BASSES

BASSES

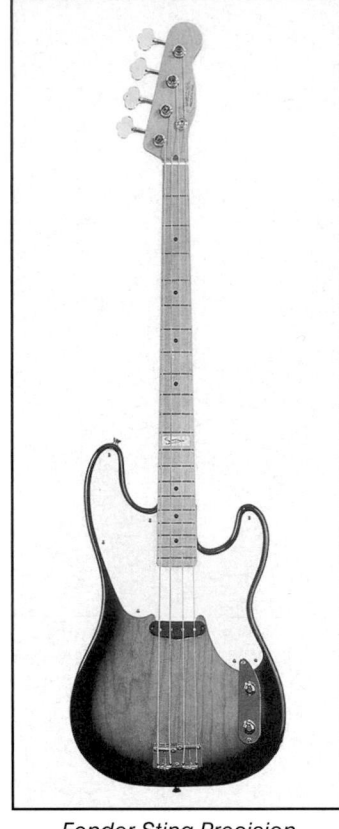

Fender Sting Precision

1960s Framus Sorento 4

MODEL YEAR	FEATURES	EXC. COND. LOW	HIGH
Sting Precision Bass			
2001-2013. Made in Japan, 2-tone sunburst, 1 single-coil, Sting's signature.			
2001-2013		$575	$725
Tony Franklin Precision Bass			
2007-present. P and J pickups, 3-way selector, lacquer finish.			
2007-2014		$1,200	$1,500
Walnut Elite I Precision Bass			
1983-1985. The Elite Series feature active electronics and noise-cancelling pickups. Walnut body, 1 pickup, rosewood 'board, natural.			
1983-1985		$1,500	$1,900
Walnut Elite II Precision Bass			
1983-1985. Two-pickup version.			
1983-1985		$1,500	$1,900
Walnut Precision Special Bass			
1980-1982. Precision Bass Special with a walnut body, natural.			
1980-1982		$1,500	$1,900
Prodigy Active Bass			
1992-1995. U.S.-made, poplar body, 1 J- and 1 P-style pickup, active.			
1992-1995		$575	$725
Rhodes Piano Bass			
1962. Electric keyboard in bass register, Fender-Rhodes sticker, Piano Bass logo, various colors.			
1962		$1,600	$2,200
Squier Affinity Jazz Bass			
1997-present. Affinity is the lower priced series made in China.			
1997-2014		$75	$100
Squier Bronco Bass			
1998-present. The lowest priced Squier bass, single coil plastic cover pickup, 3/4 body.			
1998-2014		$125	$155
Squier Bullet Bass			
1983-2000. Japanese-made, Squier-branded, replaces Bullet Bass, black.			
1983-2000		$250	$310
Squier Classic Vibe '50s Precision Bass			
2009-present. Basswood body, maple neck, 1 pickup, vintage style frets, black dot markers, chrome hardware, various colors.			
2009-2014		$225	$280
Squier HM Bass/HM Bass V			
1989-1993. Korean-made, 5-string also offered.			
1989-1993		$200	$250
Squier Jazz Bass Standard			
1983-2010. Jazz bass import, without cover plates, various colors.			
1983-1984	1st logo	$375	$475
1985-1989	2nd logo	$350	$450
1990-1999		$150	$200
2000-2010		$125	$150
Squier Katana Bass			
1985-1986. Made in Japan, wedge-shaped, arrow headstock.			
1985-1986		$550	$700
Squier Precision Bass Special			
1998-2010. Agathis body, P/J pickups.			
1998-2010		$100	$125

MODEL YEAR	FEATURES	EXC. COND. LOW	HIGH
Squier Precision Bass Standard			
1983-2006.			
1983-1984	1st logo	$375	$475
1985-1989	2nd logo	$350	$450
1990-1999	Some from Mexico	$150	$200
2000-2006	Indonesia	$125	$150
Squier Precision Bass V Special			
2000-2007. 5-string version.			
2000-2007		$100	$125
Squier Vintage Modified Series			
2007-present. Includes Jaguar bass, Jazz and Precision models.			
2007-2014	Various models	$175	$225
Stu Hamm Urge Bass (U.S.A.)			
1992-1999. Contoured Precision-style body with smaller wide treble cutaway, J and P pickups, 32" scale.			
1992-1999		$1,000	$1,250
Stu Hamm Urge II Bass (U.S.A.)			
1999-2009. J and P pickups, 34" scale.			
1999-2009		$1,175	$1,475
Telecaster Bass			
1968-1979. Slab solidbody, 1 pickup, fretless option '70, blond and custom colors available (Pink Paisley or Blue Floral '68-'69). Please refer to the beginning of the Fender Bass Section for details on Fender color options.			
1968	Black, nitro	$3,300	$4,100
1968	Black, poly	$2,800	$3,500
1968	Blond, nitro	$2,800	$3,500
1968	Blond, poly	$2,400	$3,100
1968	Blue Flower	$6,500	$8,000
1968	Lake Placid Blue	$5,100	$6,500
1968	Red (Pink) Paisley	$6,500	$8,000
1969-1972	4-bolt, single-coil	$2,300	$2,850
1973-1974	3-bolt, humbucker	$1,900	$2,375
1973-1974	3-bolt, humbucker, rare color	$2,200	$2,800
1975-1979	3-bolt, humbucker	$1,700	$2,150
Zone Bass American Deluxe			
2001-2006. Smaller lightweight offset double-cut, active humbuckers, exotic tone woods, U.S.-made.			
2001-2006		$1,150	$1,425

Fodera

1983-present. Luthiers Vinnie Fodera and Joseph Lauricella build their professional and premium grade, production/custom, solidbody basses in Brooklyn, New York.

Higher-end Bass

1983-2014	4 strings	$3,500	$6,500
1983-2014	5, 6 strings	$4,000	$7,000

Mid-level Bass

1983-2014	4, 5, 6 strings	$1,000	$1,600

Framus

1946-1975, 1996-present. Professional and premium grade, production/custom, basses made in Germany. They also build guitars and amps.

Atlantic Model 5/140 Bass

1960s. Single-cut thinline with f-holes, 2 pickups, sunburst or blackrose.

1960s		$550	$725

MODEL YEAR	FEATURES	EXC. COND. LOW	HIGH

Atlantic Model 5/143 Bass
1960s. Offset double-cut thinbody with f-holes, 2 pickups, 4-on-a-side keys.

1960s		$550	$725

Atlantic Model 5/144 Bass
1960s. Double-cut thinbody with f-holes, ES-335 body style, 2 pickups. Becomes Model J/144 in '70s.

1960s		$550	$725

Charavelle 4 Model 5/153 Bass
1960s. Double-cut thinline with f-holes, 335-style body, 2 pickups, sunburst, cherry red or Sunset.

1960s		$650	$825

De Luxe 4 Model 5/154 Bass
1960s. Double-cut thinline, sharp horns and f-holes, 2 pickups, mute, sunburst or natural/blond.

1960s		$650	$825

Electric Upright Bass
1950s. Full-scale neck, triangular body, black.

1958		$1,650	$2,100

Star Series (Bill Wyman) Bass
1959-1968. Early flyer says, Bill Wyman of the Rolling Stones prefers the Star Bass. The model name was later changed to Framus Stone Bass. Single-cut semi-hollow body, 5/149 (1 pickup) and 5/150 (2 pickups), sunburst.

1959-1965	Model 5/150	$1,100	$1,400
1960s	Model 5/149	$800	$1,000

Strato De Luxe Star Model 5/165 Bass
Ca. 1964-ca. 1972. Offset double-cut solidbody, 2 pickups, sunburst. There was also a gold hardware version (5/165 gl) and a 6-string (5/166).

1960s		$525	$675

Strato Star Series Bass
Ca. 1963-ca. 1972. Double-cut solidbody, 5/156/50 (1 pickup) or 5/156/52 (2 pickups), beige, cherry or sunburst.

1960s	Model 5/156/50	$525	$675
1960s	Model 5/156/52	$550	$700

T.V. Star Bass
1960s. Offset double-cut thinbody with f-holes, 2 pickups, short-scale, sunburst or cherry red. Most expensive of the '60s Framus basses, although not as popular as the Bill Wyman 5/150 model.

1960s		$550	$725

Triumph Electric Upright Bass
1956-1960. Solidbody bean pole electric bass, small body, long neck, slotted viol peghead, gold or black.

1956-1960		$1,450	$1,825

Fresher
1973-1985. Japanese-made, mainly copies of popular brands and not imported into the U.S., but they do show up at guitar shows. They also made guitars.

Solidbody Electric Bass

1970s		$235	$300

G & L
1980-present. Intermediate and professional grade, production/custom, electric basses made in the U.S. In '03, G & L introduced the Korean-made G & L Tribute Series. A Tribute logo is clearly identified on the headstock. They also build guitars.

MODEL YEAR	FEATURES	EXC. COND. LOW	HIGH

ASAT Bass
1989-present. Single-cut, solidbody, active and passive modes, 2 humbuckers, various colors.

1989-1991	About 400 made	$1,000	$1,250
1992-2014		$750	$950

ASAT Commemorative Bass
1991-1992. About 150 made, 4-string ASAT commemorating Leo Fender's life.

1991-1992		$1,575	$1,950

ASAT Semi-Hollow Bass
2001-present. Semi-hollowbody style on ASAT bass.

2001-2014		$875	$1,100

Climax Bass
1992-1996. Single active humbucker MFD.

1992-1996		$700	$875

El Toro Bass
1983-1989. Double-cut, solidbody, 2 active, smaller, humbuckers, sunburst.

1983-1987		$1,200	$1,500
1988-1989		$1,000	$1,250

Interceptor Bass
1984-1991. Sharp pointed double-cut, solidbody, 2 active, smaller humbuckers, sunburst.

1984-1986		$1,300	$1,600
1988-1991	Body signature	$1,000	$1,250

JB-2 Bass
2001-present. Alder body, 2 Alnico V pickups.

2001-2014		$825	$1,025

L-1000 Bass
1980-1994, 2008. Offset double-cut, solidbody, 1 pickup, various colors. Limited run in '08.

1980-1985	Ash	$1,100	$1,350
1980-1985	Mahogany	$1,100	$1,350
1980-1985	Maple	$900	$1,150
1986-1991	3-bolt	$825	$1,025
1992-1999	3-bolt	$750	$925
2008	4-bolt	$750	$925

L-1500 Bass
1997-present. Offset double-cut solidbody, 1 MFD humbucker.

1997-2014		$700	$875

L-1500 Custom Bass
1997 only.

1997		$700	$875

L-1505 Bass
1998-present. Five-string version, single MFD humbucker.

1998-2014		$700	$875

L-2000 30th Anniversary Bass
2010. Pearl Frost with matching headstock.

2010		$1,200	$1,500

L-2000 Bass
1980-present. Offset double-cut solidbody, 2 pickups, active electronics. Originally, the L-2000 was available with active (L-2000E) or passive (L-2000) electronics.

1980-1985	Ash	$1,100	$1,350
1986		$850	$1,050
1987-1991	Leo signature	$850	$1,050
1992-2014		$775	$950

G & L JB-2 Bass

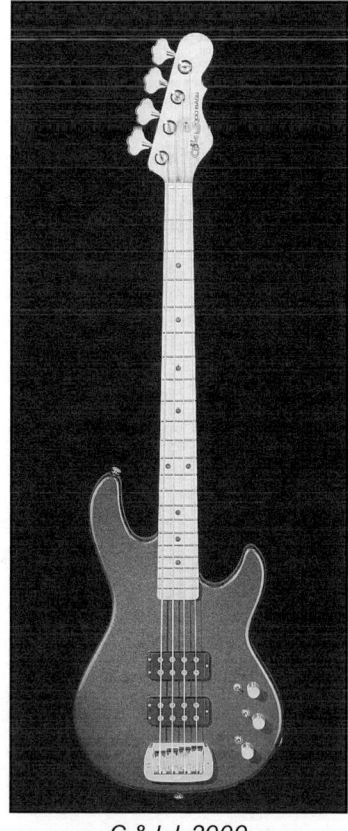

G & L L-2000

G & L SB-2

MODEL YEAR	FEATURES	EXC. COND. LOW	HIGH
L-2000 C.L.F. Centennial			
2009-2010. Swamp ash body, blonde, black hardware, planned run of 50, Certificate of Authenticity.			
2009-2010	COA, CD	$1,550	$1,925
2009-2010	No COA or CD	$1,275	$1,550
L-2000 Custom Bass			
1997. Ash top, wood-grain binding upgrade.			
1997		$850	$1,050
L-2000 Fretless Bass			
1980-1998. Fretless version.			
1980-1982		$1,200	$1,500
L-2000(E) Bass			
1980-1982. Offset double-cut, solidbody, 2 pickups, active electronics. Originally, the L-2000 was available with active (L-2000E) or passive (L-2000) electronics.			
1980-1982		$1,050	$1,300
L-2500 Bass			
1997-present. Five-string, dual MFD humbuckers, figured tops can vary.			
1997-2014		$1,050	$1,300
L-2500 Custom Bass			
1997. Ash top, wood-grain binding upgrade.			
1997		$1,050	$1,300
L-5000 Bass			
1988-1993. Offset double-cut, solidbody, G & L Z-shaped split-humbucker, 5 strings, approximately 400 made.			
1988-1992		$850	$1,050
L-5500 Bass			
1993-1997. Alder body, 5-string.			
1993-1997		$750	$925
L-5500 Custom Bass			
1997. Ash top, wood-grain binding upgrade.			
1997		$775	$950
LB-100 Bass			
1993-2000. Follow-up to earlier Legacy Bass.			
1993-2000		$550	$700
Legacy Bass			
1992-1993. Offset double-cut solidbody, 1 split-coil, renamed LB-100 in '93.			
1992-1993		$650	$825
Lynx Bass			
1984-1991. Offset double-cut, solidbody, 2 single-coils, black.			
1984-1991		$725	$900
SB-1 Bass			
1982-2000, 2014-present. Solidbody, maple neck, body and 'board, split-humbucker, 1 tone and 1 volume control. Reappears in '14.			
1982-2000		$625	$800
SB-2 Bass			
1982-present. Maple neck with tilt adjustment, 1 split-coil humbucker and 1 single-coil.			
1982-1999		$750	$950
2000-2014		$675	$850

Garage by Wicked

2004-2010. A line of basses imported from China by luthier Nicholas Dijkman (Wicked) of Montreal, Quebec.

1959 Gibson EB-2
Robbie Keene

MODEL YEAR	FEATURES	EXC. COND. LOW	HIGH
Gibson			

1890s (1902)-present. Professional grade, production, U.S.-made electric basses. Gibson got into the electric bass market with the introduction of their Gibson Electric Bass in '53 (that model was renamed the EB-1 in '58 and reintroduced under that name in '69). Many more bass models followed. Gibson's custom colors can greatly increase the value of older instruments. Custom colors offered from '63 to '69 are Cardinal Red, Ember Red, Frost Blue, Golden Mist Metallic, Heather Metallic, Inverness Green, Kerry Green, Pelham Blue Metallic, Polaris White, Silver Mist Metallic.

MODEL YEAR	FEATURES	EXC. COND. LOW	HIGH
20/20 Bass			
1987-1988. Designed by Ned Steinberger, slim-wedge Steinberger style solidbody, 2 humbucker pickups, 20/20 logo on headstock, Luna Silver or Ferrari Red finish.			
1987-1988		$1,200	$1,500
Electric Bass (EB-1)			
1953-1958. Introduced as Gibson Electric Bass in '53, but was called the EB-1 by Gibson in its last year of '58, thus, the whole line is commonly called the EB-1 by collectors, reissued in '69 as the EB-1 (see EB-1 ltsttng), brown.			
1953-1958		$4,400	$5,500
EB Bass			
1970 only. Renamed from Melody Maker Bass, SG body, 1 humbucker pickup.			
1970		$1,000	$1,250
EB-0 Bass			
1959-1979. Double-cut slab body with banjo-type tuners in '59 and '60, double-cut SG-type body with conventional tuners from '61 on, 1 pickup. Faded custom colors are of less value.			
1959-1960	Cherry, slab body	$3,500	$4,400
1961	Cherry, SG body	$1,875	$2,350
1962-1964	Cherry	$1,875	$2,350
1965-1966	Cherry	$1,525	$1,900
1965-1966	Pelham Blue	$2,900	$3,600
1967-1968	Cherry	$1,450	$1,800
1967-1968	Pelham Blue	$2,500	$3,100
1968	Black	$1,700	$2,100
1968	Burgundy Metallic	$1,700	$2,100
1969	Cherry, solid head	$1,275	$1,600
1969	Pelham Blue	$2,500	$3,100
1969-1974	Slotted head	$1,100	$1,400
1975-1979		$1,100	$1,400
EB-0 F Bass			
1962-1965. EB-0 with added built-in fuzz, cherry.			
1962-1965		$3,000	$3,700
EB-0 L Bass			
1969-1979. 34.5 inch scale version of the EB-0, various colors.			
1969-1979		$1,150	$1,450
EB-1 Bass			
1969-1972. The Gibson Electric Bass ('53-'58) is often also called the EB-1 (see Electric Bass). Violin-shaped mahogany body, 1 pickup, standard tuners.			
1969-1972		$3,000	$3,800

MODEL YEAR	FEATURES	EXC. COND. LOW	HIGH

EB-2 Bass

1958-1961, 1964-1972. ES-335-type semi-hollowbody, double-cut, 1 pickup, banjo tuners '58-'60 and conventional tuners '60 on.

1958	Sunburst, banjo tuners	$4,900	$6,100
1959	Sunburst, banjo tuners	$4,900	$6,100
1959-1960	Natural, banjo tuners	$5,600	$7,100
1960	Sunburst, banjo tuners	$4,700	$5,900
1961	Sunburst, conventional tuners	$2,500	$3,100
1964	Sunburst	$2,400	$3,000
1965	Sunburst	$2,200	$2,700
1966	Cherry, sunburst	$2,000	$2,500
1967-1969	Cherry, sunburst	$2,000	$2,500
1967-1969	Sparkling Burgundy	$2,100	$2,600
1967-1969	Walnut	$1,850	$2,300
1970-1972	Sunburst	$1,850	$2,300

EB-2 D Bass

1966-1972. Two-pickup version of EB-2, cherry, sunburst, or walnut.

1966	Cherry, sunburst	$2,100	$2,600
1967-1969	Cherry, sunburst	$2,100	$2,600
1967-1969	Sparkling Burgundy	$2,200	$2,750
1967-1969	Walnut	$1,950	$2,400
1970-1972	Cherry, sunburst	$1,950	$2,400

EB-3 Bass

1961-1979. SG-style solidbody, 2 humbuckers, solid peghead '61-'68 and '72-'79, slotted peghead '69-'71, cherry to '71, various colors after.

1961		$4,900	$6,200
1962		$4,700	$5,900
1963-1964		$4,700	$5,900
1965	Early '65, wide control	$4,300	$5,400
1965	Late '65, narrow control	$2,900	$3,700
1965	White (rare)	$4,900	$6,100
1966		$2,600	$3,300
1967		$2,500	$3,100
1968		$2,300	$2,900
1969	Early '69	$1,900	$2,400
1969	Late '69	$1,400	$1,750
1970-1979		$1,175	$1,475

EB-3 L Bass

1969-1972. 34.5" scale version of EB-3, slotted headstock, EB-3L logo on truss rod cover, cherry, natural, or walnut.

1969-1972		$1,200	$1,500

EB-4 L Bass

1972-1979. SG-style, 1 humbucker, 34.5" scale, cherry or walnut.

1972-1979		$1,100	$1,350

EB-6 Bass

1960-1966. Introduced as semi-hollowbody 335-style 6-string with 1 humbucker, changed to SG-style with 2 pickups in '62.

1960	Natural, 335-style	$9,000	$11,200
1960-1961	Sunburst, 335-style	$6,800	$8,500
1962-1964	Cherry, SG-style	$9,500	$12,000
1965	Cherry, SG-style	$7,700	$9,500
1966	Cherry, SG-style	$6,700	$8,400

EB-650 Bass

1991-1993. Semi-acoustic single cut, maple neck, laminated maple body with center block, 2 TB Plus pickups.

1991-1993		$3,100	$3,850

EB-750 Bass

1991-1993. Like EB-650, but with Bartolini pickups and TCT active EQ.

1991-1993		$3,100	$3,850

ES-335 Bass

2013. Sunburst or ebony.

2013		$1,475	$1,825

Explorer Bass

1984-1987, 2011-2012. Alder body, ebony 'board, dot inlays, 2 humbuckers, various colors. Limited run in '11 in sunburst or silverburst.

1984-1987	Standard finish	$1,100	$1,400
1985	Designer series graphics	$1,300	$1,850
2011-2012	Silverburst	$1,000	$1,250

Flying V Bass

1981-1982 only. Solidbody, Flying V body.

1981-1982	Blue stain, ebony	$2,900	$3,600
1981-1982	Silverburst	$3,000	$3,800

Grabber Bass

1974-1982. Double-cut solidbody, 1 pickup, bolt maple neck, maple 'board, various colors.

1974-1982		$1,000	$1,250

Grabber III Bass (G-3)

1975-1982. Double-cut solidbody, 3 pickups, bolt maple neck, maple 'board, nickel-plated hardware, various colors.

1975-1982		$1,200	$1,500

Gibson IV Bass

1986-1988. Mahogany body and neck, double-cut, 2 pickups, black chrome hardware, various colors.

1986-1988		$1,200	$1,500

Gibson V Bass

1986-1988. Double-cut, 5 strings, 2 pickups.

1986-1988		$1,300	$1,600

L9-S Bass

1973. Natural maple or cherry, renamed Ripper Bass in '74.

1973		$1,250	$1,550

Les Paul Bass

1970-1971. Single-cut solidbody, 2 pickups, walnut finish, renamed Les Paul Triumph Bass '71-'79.

1970-1971		$2,100	$2,600

Les Paul Money Bass

2007-2008. Solidbody offset double-cut, 2 humbuckers, dot markers, figured maple top over mahogany body, 400 made.

2007-2008		$1,000	$1,250

Gibson EB-3
Ron Puzzitiello

1978 Gibson Grabber III (G-3)
Robbie Keene

Gibson Les Paul Signature

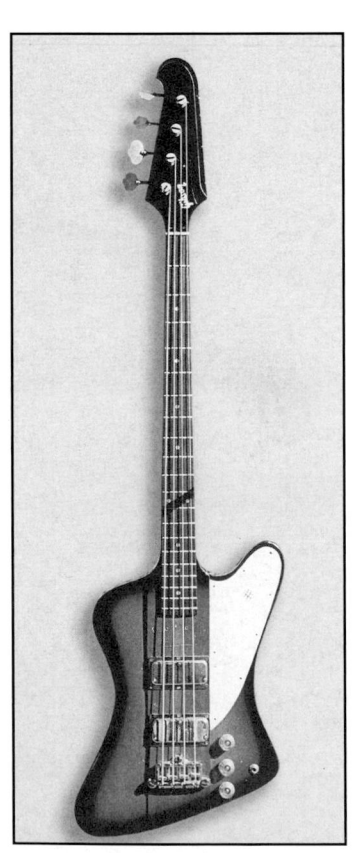

1976 Gibson Thunderbird 76
Ryan Stauffer

MODEL YEAR	FEATURES	EXC. COND. LOW	HIGH

Les Paul Signature Bass
1973-1979. Double-cut, semi-hollowbody, 1 pickup, sunburst or gold (gold only by '76). Name also used on LPB-3 bass in '90s.

| 1973-1975 | Sunburst or gold | $3,200 | $4,200 |

Les Paul Special LPB-1 Bass
1991-1998. 2 TB-Plus pickups, ebony 'board, dots, slab mahogany body, active electronics, also available as 5-string.

| 1991-1998 | | $700 | $875 |

Les Paul Deluxe Plus LPB-2 Bass
1991-1998. Upgraded LPB-1, carved maple top, trapezoid inlays, active eq and Bartolini pickups. Flame maple top Premium version offered '93-'98.

| 1991-1998 | | $1,050 | $1,300 |

Les Paul Smartwood Bass
1998. 2 TB pickups, active electronics, trapezoid inlays.

| 1998 | | $1,300 | $1,625 |

Les Paul Special V Bass
1993-1996. Single-cut slab body, 5-string, 2 pickups, dot markers, black/ebony.

| 1993-1996 | | $750 | $925 |

Les Paul Standard Bass
2000-2008. Maple top, chambered mahogany body, trapezoid inlays, 2 pickups.

| 2000-2008 | Various colors | $1,400 | $2,000 |

Les Paul Standard LPB-3 Bass
1991-1995. Like Les Paul Deluxe LPB-2 Bass, but with TB Plus pickups. Flame maple top Premium version offered '93-'95.

| 1993-1995 | Flamed top | $1,000 | $1,250 |

Les Paul Triumph Bass
1971-1979. Renamed from Les Paul Bass.

| 1971-1979 | Various colors | $1,700 | $2,125 |
| 1973-1974 | Optional white | $1,900 | $2,350 |

Melody Maker Bass
1967-1970. SG body, 1 humbucker pickup.

| 1967-1970 | | $1,000 | $1,250 |

Nikki Sixx Blackbird/Thunderbird Bass
2000-2003, 2009. Blackbird has black finish and hardware, iron cross inlays.'09 Thunderbird was flamed maple.

| 2000-2003 | Blackbird | $1,100 | $1,400 |

Q-80 Bass
1986-1988. Victory Series body shape, 2 pickups, bolt neck, black chrome hardware, renamed Q-90 in '88.

| 1986-1988 | | $400 | $500 |

Q-90 Bass
1988-1992. Renamed from Q-80, mahogany body, 2 active humbuckers, maple neck, ebony 'board.

| 1988-1992 | | $400 | $500 |

RD Artist Bass
1977-1982. Double-cut solid maple body, laminated neck, 2 pickups, active electronics, string-thru-body, block inlays, various colors.

| 1977-1982 | | $1,900 | $2,400 |

RD Artist CMT Bass
1982. Flamed maple top.

| 1982 | | $2,500 | $3,200 |

MODEL YEAR	FEATURES	EXC. COND. LOW	HIGH

RD Artist VI Bass
1980. Only 6 made, 6-string.

| 1980 | | $5,000 | $6,400 |

RD Standard Bass
1977-1979. Double-cut, solid maple body, laminated neck, 2 pickups, regular electronics, string-thru-body, dot inlays, various colors.

| 1977-1979 | | $1,400 | $1,750 |

Ripper Bass
1974-1982. Introduced as L-9 S Bass in '73, double-cut solidbody, glued neck, 2 pickups, string-thru-body, sunburst or natural maple until '76, sunburst only after.

| 1974-1976 | | $1,400 | $1,750 |
| 1977-1982 | | $1,300 | $1,650 |

Ripper II Bass
2009-2011. Solid maple body, 34" scale, 2 pickups, natural nitrocellulose lacquer.

| 2009-2011 | | $1,000 | $1,250 |

SB Series Bass
1971-1978. In '71, had oval pickups, replaced mid-model with rectangular pickups. Includes 300 and 350 (30" scale, 1 and 2 pickups), 350 (30", 2 pickups), 400 (34", 1 pickup), 450 (34", 2 pickups). The 450 was special order only.

1971-1973	SB-300, 400	$850	$1,050
1972-1974	SB-350, 450	$850	$1,050
1975-1978	SB-450 special order	$850	$1,050

SG Reissue/Standard Bass
2005-present. Similar to '60s EB-3, 2 pickups, mahogany body, cherry or ebony, renamed SG Standard Bass in '08.

| 2005-2008 | | $850 | $1,050 |
| 2009-2013 | | $775 | $950 |

SG Standard Faded Bass
2013-present. Solid mahogany body, baked maple 'board, worn cherry or ebony finish.

| 2013 | | $500 | $625 |

SG Supreme Bass
2007-2008. Made in Nashville, SG body with AAA maple top, 2 pickups.

| 2007-2008 | | $1,000 | $1,250 |

Thunderbird II Bass
1963-1969. Reverse solidbody until '65, non-reverse solidbody '65-'69, 1 pickup, custom colors available, reintroduced with reverse body for '83-'84.

1963	Sunburst, reverse	$7,700	$9,700
1964	Pelham Blue, reverse	$11,500	$14,500
1964	Sunburst, reverse	$6,200	$7,800
1965	Cardinal Red, non-reverse	$7,200	$9,000
1965	Inverness Green, non-reverse	$7,200	$9,000
1965	Sunburst, non-reverse	$3,500	$4,300
1965	Sunburst, reverse	$6,000	$7,500
1966	Cardinal Red, non-reverse	$6,300	$7,900
1966	Sunburst, non-reverse	$3,400	$4,300

MODEL YEAR	FEATURES	EXC. COND. LOW	HIGH
1967	Cardinal Red, non-reverse	$6,200	$7,800
1967	Sunburst, non-reverse	$3,300	$4,100
1968	Cardinal Red, non-reverse	$6,200	$7,800
1968	Sunburst, non-reverse	$3,300	$4,100
1969	Sunburst, non-reverse	$3,300	$4,100

Thunderbird IV Bass
1963-1969. Reverse solidbody until '64, non-reverse solidbody '65-'69, 2 pickups, custom colors available, reintroduced with reverse body for '86-present (see Thunderbird IV Bass Reissue).

1963	Sunburst, reverse	$10,500	$13,100
1964	Frost Blue, reverse	$19,300	$24,100
1964	Pelham Blue, reverse	$19,300	$24,100
1964	Sunburst, reverse	$10,500	$13,100
1965	Cardinal Red, non-reverse	$11,500	$14,400
1965	Inverness Green, non-reverse	$11,500	$14,400
1965	Sunburst, reverse	$10,000	$12,500
1965-1966	Sunburst, non-reverse	$6,000	$7,500
1966	White, non-reverse	$9,000	$11,200
1967-1969	Sunburst, non-reverse	$5,500	$6,800

Thunderbird IV Bass (Reissue)
1987-present. Has reverse body and 2 pickups, sunburst.

1987-1989		$1,000	$1,250
1990-2014		$1,000	$1,250
1991-2014	Rare color	$1,200	$1,500

Thunderbird IV Bass Zebra Wood Bass
2007. Guitar of the Week (week 11 of '07), limited run of 400, Zebrawood body.

2007		$1,400	$1,750

Thunderbird 50th Anniversary Bass
2013-present. Mahogany body and neck, rosewood 'board, Bullion Gold finish.

2013		$1,550	$1,950

Thunderbird 76 Bass
1976 only. Reverse solidbody, 2 pickups, rosewood 'board, various colors.

1976		$2,800	$3,500

Thunderbird 79 Bass
1979 only. Reverse solidbody, 2 pickups, sunburst.

1979		$2,600	$3,300

Thunderbird Short Scale Bass
2011-2013. 30.5" scale, 2 pickups, nitro satin ebony finish.

2011-2013		$1,000	$1,250

Thunderbird Studio/IV Studio
2005-2007. 4- or 5-string versions.

2005-2007		$1,000	$1,250

Victory Artist Bass
1981-1985. Double-cut, solidbody, 2 humbuckers and active electronics, various colors.

1981-1985		$750	$925

Victory Custom Bass
1982-1984. Double-cut, solidbody, 2 humbuckers, passive electronics, limited production.

1982-1984		$725	$900

Victory Standard Bass
1981-1986. Double-cut, solidbody, 1 humbucker, active electronics, various colors.

1981-1986		$650	$800

Godin
1987-present. Intermediate and professional grade, production, solidbody electric and acoustic/electric basses from luthier Robert Godin. They also build guitars and mandolins.

A Series Bass
1990s-present. Acoustic/electric, 5-string starts in '00.

1990s-2014	A-4	$475	$600
2000-2014	A-5 SA	$500	$625

Freeway A Series Bass
2005-2012. Double-cut solidbodies, 4- or 5-string, passive or active..

2005-2012	Freeway A-4	$400	$500
2005-2012	Freeway A-5	$425	$525

Godlyke
2006-present. Professional and premium grade, production, solidbody basses from effects distributor Godlyke.

Goya
1955-1996. Originally imports from Sweden, brand later used on Japanese and Korean imports. They also offered basses, mandolins and banjos.

Electric Solidbody Bass

1960s	Various models	$550	$675

Gretsch
1883-present. Intermediate and professional grade, production, solidbody, hollow body, and acoustic/electric basses. Gretsch came late to the electric bass game, introducing their first models in the early '60s. They also build guitars, amps and steels. In 2012 they again offered mandolins, ukes and banjos.

Broadkaster Bass (7605/7606)
1975-1979. Double-cut solidbody, 1 pickup, bolt-on maple neck, natural (7605) or sunburst (7606).

1975-1979		$575	$725

Committee Bass (7629)
1977-1980. Double-cut walnut and maple soldibody, neck-thru, 1 pickup, natural.

1977-1980		$600	$750

G6072 Long Scale Hollow Body Bass
1998-2006. Reissue of the '68 double-cut hollowbody, 2 pickups, sunburst, gold hardware.

1998-2006		$1,000	$1,250

Model 6070/6072 Bass
1963-1971 (1972 for 6070). Originally listed as the PX6070 Cello Bass, large thinline hollowbody double-cut archtop, fake f-holes, 1 pickup (6070) or 2 (6072), gold hardware.

1963-1964	6070, with endpin	$2,050	$2,550

Gibson Victory
Sean Sweeney

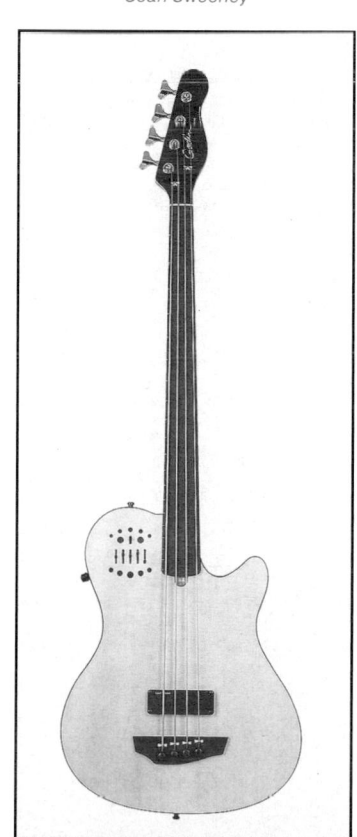

Godin A-4 Fretless

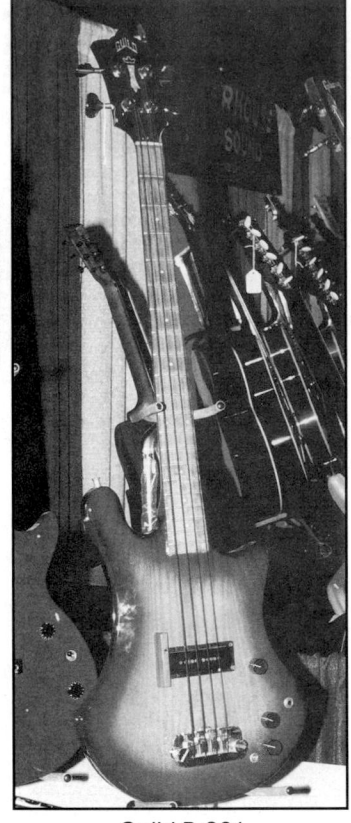

Guild B-301

1980s Guild SB-602 Pilot
Kenny K.

MODEL YEAR	FEATURES	EXC. COND. LOW	HIGH
1965-1972	6070, no endpin, 1 pickup	$1,450	$1,800
1968-1971	6072, 2 pickups	$1,350	$1,700

Model 6071/6073 Bass
1968-1971 (1972 for 6071). Single-cut hollowbody, fake f-holes, 1 pickup (6071) or 2 (6073), padded back, red mahogany.

1968-1971	6073, 2 pickups	$1,650	$2,050
1968-1972	6071, 1 pickup	$1,450	$1,800

Model 7615 Bass
1972-1975. Offset double-cut solidbody, slotted bass horn (monkey grip), large polished rosewood 'guard covering most of the body, 2 pickups, dot markers, brown mahogany finish. Only bass offered in Gretsch catalog for this era.

1972-1975		$750	$950

TK 300 Bass (7626/7627)
1976-1981. Double-cut solidbody, 1 pickup, Autumn Red Stain or natural.

1976-1981		$475	$590

Guild
1952-present. Guild added electric basses in the mid-'60s and offered them until '02.

Ashbory Bass
1986-1988, 2009. 18" scale, total length 30", fretless, silicone rubber strings, active electronics, low-impedance circuitry.

1986-1988		$375	$450
2009	Fender Guild reissue	$150	$200

B-4 E Bass
1993-2000. Acoustic/electric single-cut flat-top, mahogany sides with arched mahogany back, multi-bound, gold hardware until '95, chrome after.

1993-2000		$550	$700

B-30 E Bass
1987-1999. Single-cut flat-top acoustic/electric, mahogany sides, arched mahogany back, multi-bound, fretless optional.

1987-1999		$1,000	$1,250

B-50 Acoustic Bass
1975-1987. Acoustic flat-top, mahogany sides with arched mahogany back, spruce top, multi-bound, renamed B-30 in '87.

1975-1987		$1,150	$1,450

B-301/B-302 Bass
1976-1981. Double-cut solidbody, chrome-plated hardware. Models include B-301 (mahogany, 1 pickup), B-301 A (ash, 1 pickup), B-302 (mahogany, 2 pickups), B-302 A (ash, 2 pickups), and B-302 AF (ash, fretless).

1976-1981	B-301	$800	$1,000
1976-1981	B-302	$850	$1,050
1977-1981	B-301 A	$850	$1,050
1977-1981	B-302 A	$900	$1,125
1977-1981	B-302 AF	$900	$1,125

B-401/B-402 Bass
1980-1983. Model 401 with active circuit, 1 pickup. Model 402 passive and active, 2 pickups. A for ash body.

1980-1981	B-401	$800	$1,000
1980-1982	B-402	$850	$1,050

MODEL YEAR	FEATURES	EXC. COND. LOW	HIGH
1980-1982	B-402 A	$900	$1,125
1980-1983	B-401 A	$850	$1,050

B-500 C Acoustic Bass
1992-1993. Acoustic/electric flat-top, round soundhole, single-cut, solid spruce top, maple back and sides, dark stain, limited production.

1992-1993		$1,200	$1,475

FS-46 Bass
1983. Acoustic-electric flat-top, single-cut, sharp horn fretless.

1983		$650	$800

Jet Star Bass
1964-1970 (limited production '68-'70). Offset double-cut solidbody, short treble horn, 1 pickup, 2-on-a-side tuners '64-'66 and 4 in-line tuners '66-'70.

1964-1966	2-on-side tuners	$1,175	$1,475
1966-1970	4-in-line tuners	$1,175	$1,475

JS I/JS II Bass
1970-1977. Double-cut solidbody, 30" scale, 1 pickup (JS I or 1) or 2 (JS II or 2), carved-top oak leaf design available for '72-'76. 34" long scale (LS) versions offered fretted and fretless for '74-'75.

1970-1975	JS I	$1,075	$1,350
1970-1977	JS II	$1,075	$1,350

M-85 I/M-85 II Bass (Semi-Hollow)
1967-1972. Single-cut semi-hollowbody, 1 pickup (M-85 I) or 2 (M-85 II).

1967-1972	M-85 I	$1,275	$1,625
1967-1972	M-85 II	$1,375	$1,725

M-85 I/M-85 II BluesBird Bass (Solidbody)
1972-1976. Single-cut soldibody archtop, Chesterfield headstock inlay, cherry mahogany, 1 humbucker pickup (I) or 2 (II).

1972-1973	M-85 I	$1,300	$1,650
1972-1976	M-85 II	$1,400	$1,750

MB-801 Bass
1981-1982. Double-cut solidbody, 1 pickup, dot inlays.

1981-1982		$600	$750

SB-201/SB-202/SB-203 Bass
1982-1983. Double-cut solidbody, 1 split coil pickup (201), 1 split coil and 1 single coil (202), or 1 split coil and 2 single coils (203).

1982-1983	SB-201	$725	$900
1982-1983	SB-202	$775	$975
1983	SB-203	$800	$1,000

SB-502 E Bass
1984-1985. Double-cut solidbody, 2 pickups, active electronics.

1984-1985		$800	$1,000

SB-600/Pilot Series Bass
1983-1993. Offset double-cut solidbody, bolt-on neck, poplar body. Models include SB-601 (1 pickup), SB-602 (2 pickups or fretless), SB-602 V (2 pickups, 5-string), SB-604 (2 pickups, offset peghead) and SB-605 (5-string, hipshot low D tuner). Models 604 and 605 are replaced in '93 with Pro4 and Pro5 Pilot.

1983-1989	SB-601	$500	$625
1983-1989	SB-602	$575	$725
1983-1989	SB-602 V	$575	$725

The Vintage Guitar Price Guide shows low to high values for items in all-original excellent condition, and, where applicable, with original case or cover.

MODEL YEAR	FEATURES	EXC. COND. LOW	HIGH
1983-1989	SB-602, fretless	$575	$725
1986-1988	SB-604	$575	$725
1986-1993	SB-605	$600	$750

SB-608 Flying Star Motley Crue Bass

1984-1985. Pointy 4-point star body, 2 pickups, E version had EMG pickups.

1984-1985		$1,000	$1,250

Starfire Bass

1965-1975. Double-cut semi-hollow thinbody, 1 pickup, mahogany neck, chrome-plated hardware, cherry or sunburst.

1965-1969	Single-coil	$2,000	$2,500
1970-1975	Humbucker	$2,000	$2,500

Starfire II Bass

1967-1978. Two-pickup version of Starfire Bass. Single-coils until '69, humbuckers after, sunburst, cherry or very rare black. Starfire II Bass Special had gold hardware.

1967-1969	2 single-coils	$2,400	$3,100
1967-1969	Black	$3,100	$4,000
1970-1978	2 humbuckers	$2,400	$3,100

Starfire II Reissue Bass

1997-2002. Reissue of 2 humbucker version.

1997-2002		$1,250	$1,550

X-701/X-702 Bass

1982-1984. Body with 4 sharp horns with extra long bass horn, 1 pickup (X-701) or 2 (X-702), various metallic finishes.

1982-1984	X-701	$825	$1,050
1982-1984	X-702	$875	$1,075

GW Basses & Luthiery

2004-present. Professional and premium grade, production/custom, basses built by luthier Grandon Westlund in West Lafayette, Indiana.

G'Zan Custom Guitars, LLC

2007-present. Luthier Mark Newsbaum builds his custom, professional and premium grade, electric basses in Columbia, Tennessee. He also builds guitars.

Hagstrom

1921-1983, 2004-present. This Swedish guitar company first offered electric basses in '61.

8-String Bass

1967-1969. Double-cut solidbody, 2 pickups, various colors.

1967-1969		$1,500	$1,850

Coronado IV Bass

1963-1970. Offset double cut, Bi-Sonic pickups.

1963-1964		$1,000	$1,250
1965-1970		$1,000	$1,250

Kent Bass

1963-1964. 2 single-coils, 4 sliders.

1962-1966		$475	$600

Model I B/F-100 B Bass

1965-1973. Offset double-cut solidbody, 2 single-coils, 5 sliders, 30" scale.

1965-1973		$500	$650

Model II B/F-400 Bass

1965-1970. Like Model I, but with 30.75" scale, called F-400 in U.S., II B elsewhere.

1965-1970	Red or black	$550	$700
1965-1970	White or blue	$625	$800

Swede 2000 Bass (With Synth)

1977. Circuitry on this Swede bass connected to the Ampeg Patch 2000 pedal so bass would work with various synths.

1977		$950	$1,200

Swede Bass

1980-1981. Single-cut solidbody, block inlays, bolt neck, 2 humbuckers, 30.75" scale, cherry or black

1971-1976		$900	$1,125

Super Swede Bass

1980-1981. Like Swede, but with neck-thru body, 32" scale, sunburst, mahogany or black.

1980-1981		$900	$1,125

V-IN Bass/Concord Bass

1970s. Bass version of V-IN guitar, 335-style body, 2 pickups, sunburst.

1970s		$900	$1,125

Hamer

1975-2012. Intermediate and professional grade, production/custom, acoustic and electric basses made in the U.S. and imported. Founded in Arlington Heights, Illinois, by Paul Hamer and Jol Dantzig, Hamer was purchased by Kaman in '88. They also built guitars. Fender suspended production of the Hamer brand at the end of 2012.

8-String Short-Scale Bass

1978-1993. Double cut solidbody, 1 or 2 pickups, 30.5" scale.

1978-1993		$1,500	$1,900

12-String Acoustic Bass

1985-2010. Semi-hollow, long scale, single cut, soundhole, 2 pickups. Import XT model added in the 2000s.

1985-2010		$1,500	$1,900

12-String Short-Scale Bass

1978-1996. Four sets of 3 strings - a fundamental and 2 tuned an octave higher, double cut maple and mahogany solidbody, 30.5" scale.

1978-1996		$1,500	$1,900

Blitz Bass

1982-1990. Explorer-style solidbody, 2 pickups, bolt-on neck.

1982-1984	1st edition	$900	$1,125
1984-1990		$700	$875

Chaparral Bass

1986-1995, 2000-2008. Solidbody, 2 pickups, glued-in neck, later basses have bolt-on neck.

1986-1987	Set-neck	$800	$1,000
1987-1995	Bolt-on neck	$700	$875

Chaparral 5-String Bass

1987-1995. Five strings, solidbody, 2 pickups, glued-in neck, later basses have 5-on-a-side reverse peghead.

1987-1995		$550	$675

1968 Guild Starfire II
William Ferguson

Hamer Chaparral 12-String Bass

BASSES

1990s Hamer Cruise Bass
Kenny K.

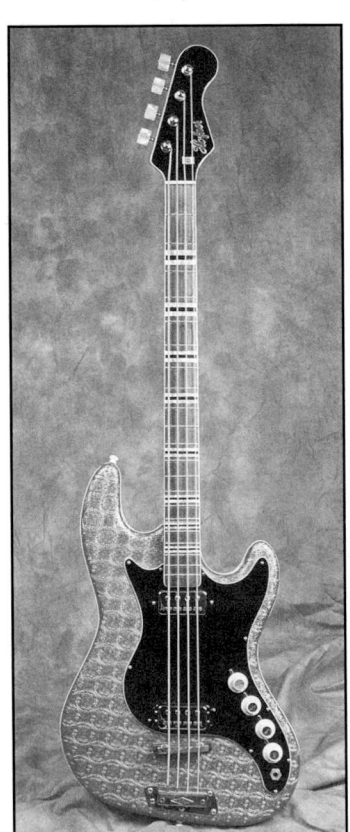

Höfner 185 Bass

MODEL YEAR	FEATURES	EXC. COND. LOW	HIGH

Chaparral 12-String Bass
1992-2012. Long 34" scale 12-string, offset double cut. Import XT model added in '01.

| 1992-2012 | USA | $1,500 | $1,900 |
| 2000-2012 | Import | $300 | $375 |

Chaparral Max Bass
1986-1995. Chaparral Bass with figured maple body, glued-in neck and boomerang inlays.

| 1986-1995 | | $575 | $725 |

Cruise Bass
1982-1990, 1995-1999. J-style solidbody, 2 pickups, glued neck ('82-'90) or bolt-on neck ('95-'99), also available as a 5-string.

| 1982-1990 | Set-neck | $550 | $675 |
| 1995-1999 | Bolt-on neck | $500 | $625 |

Cruise 5 Bass
1982-1989. Five-string version, various colors.

| 1982-1989 | | $550 | $675 |

FBIV Bass
1985-1987. Reverse Firebird shape, 1 P-Bass Slammer and 1 J-Bass Slammer pickup, mahogany body, rosewood 'board, dots.

| 1985-1987 | | $525 | $650 |

Standard Bass
1975-1984, 2001. Explorer-style bound body with 2 humbuckers.

| 1975-1984 | USA | $1,250 | $1,550 |
| 2001 | Import | $300 | $375 |

Velocity 5 Bass
2002-2012. Offset double-cut, long bass horn, active, 1 humbucker.

| 2002-2012 | | $150 | $185 |

Harmony
1892-1976, late 1970s-present. Harmony once was one of the biggest instrument makers in the world, making guitars and basses under their own brand and for others.

H Series Bass
Late-1980s-early-1990s. F-style solidbody copies, 1 or 2 pickups, all models begin H.

| 1980s-90s | | $105 | $130 |

H-22 Bass
1959-1972. Single-cut hollowbody, 2-on-a-side, 1 pickup.

| 1959-1969 | | $650 | $825 |
| 1970-1972 | | $600 | $750 |

H-22 Reissuc Bass
2000s. Imported reissue, 1 pickup.

| 2000s | | $285 | $350 |

H-25 Silhouette Bass
1963-1967. Offset double-cut solidbody.

| 1963-1967 | | $600 | $750 |

H-27 Bass
1968-1972. Double-cut hollowbody, 4-on-a-side, 2 pickups.

| 1968-1972 | | $675 | $850 |

Hartke
Hartke offered a line of wood and aluminum-necked basses from 2000 to '03.

MODEL YEAR	FEATURES	EXC. COND. LOW	HIGH

Heartfield
1989-1994. Distributed by Fender, imported from Japan. They also offered guitars.

Electric Bass
1989-1994. Double-cut solidbody, graphite reinforced neck, 2 single-coils, available in 4-, 5- and 6-string models.

| 1989-1994 | | $325 | $400 |

Heritage
1985-present. Mainly a builder of guitars, Kalamazoo, Michigan's Heritage has offered a few basses in the past.

HB-1 Bass
1987. P-style body, limited production, single-split pickup, 4-on-a-side tuners, figured maple body, bolt-on neck.

| 1987 | | $575 | $725 |

Höfner
1887-present. Professional grade, production, basses. They also offer guitars and bowed instruments. Höfner basses, made famous in the U.S. by one Paul McCartney, are made in Germany.

Icon Series
2007-2011. Chinese versions of classic Höfners, often sold without a case or gigbag.

| 2007-2011 | | $200 | $250 |

Model (G)5000/1 Super Beatle (G500/1) Bass
1968-2011. Bound ebony 'board, gold-plated hardware, natural finish, the version with active circuit is called G500/1 Super Beatle, reissued in '94.

| 1968-2011 | | $1,375 | $1,700 |

Model 172 Series Bass
1968-1970. Offset double-cut, 6-on-a-side tuners, 2 pickups, 2 slide switches, dot markers, 172-S shaded sunburst, 172-R red vinyl covered body, 172-I vinyl covered with white top and black back.

1968-1970	172-I, white	$475	$600
1968-1970	172-R, red	$475	$600
1968-1970	172-S, sunburst	$500	$625

Model 182 Solid Bass
1962-1985. Offset double-cut solidbody, 2 pickups.

| 1962-1965 | | $400 | $500 |

Model 185 Solid Bass
1962-ca. 1970. Classic offset double-cut solidbody, 2 double-coil pickups.

| 1962-1970 | | $450 | $575 |

Model 500/1 Beatle Bass
1956-present. Semi-acoustic, bound body in violin shape, glued-in neck, 2 pickups, sunburst. Listed as 500/1 Vintage '58, '59, '62 and '63 in '90s through 2014. Currently named 500/1 Violin Bass.

1956-1960	Right-handed or lefty	$5,400	$6,700
1960	Lefty, McCartney	$4,700	$5,900
1961	Lefty	$4,700	$5,900
1961	Lefty, McCartney	$5,800	$7,500
1961	Right-handed	$3,800	$4,700
1962	Lefty	$3,800	$4,800

MODEL YEAR	FEATURES	EXC. COND. LOW	HIGH
1962	Right-handed	$3,100	$3,900
1963	Lefty	$3,800	$4,800
1963	Right-handed	$3,100	$3,900
1964	Lefty	$3,800	$4,800
1964	Lefty, McCartney	$4,900	$6,100
1964	Right-handed	$3,100	$3,900
1964	Right-handed, McCartney	$3,400	$4,300
1965	Lefty	$2,400	$3,000
1965	Right-handed	$2,000	$2,500
1966	Lefty	$2,200	$2,800
1966	Right-handed	$1,850	$2,300
1967	Lefty	$2,450	$3,050
1967	Right-handed	$2,050	$2,550
1968-1969	Lefty	$2,000	$2,500
1968-1969	Right-handed	$1,850	$2,300
1970-1973	Lefty	$1,900	$2,400
1970-1973	Right-handed	$1,750	$2,200
1974-1979	Right-handed or lefty	$1,500	$1,900

'58 Model 500/1 Reissue
2008-2013		$1,325	$1,625

'62 Model 500/1 Beatle Bass Reissue
1990s-2014		$1,325	$1,650

'63 Model 500/1 Beatle Bass Reissue
1994-2010. Right- or left-handed.
1994-2010		$1,475	$1,825

Model 500/1 1964-1984 Reissue Bass
1984. '1964-1984' neckplate notation.
1984		$1,525	$1,875

Model 500/1 50th Anniversary Bass
2006. Pickguard logo states '50th Anniversary Höfner Violin Bass 1956-2006', large red Höfner logo also on 'guard, 150 made.
2006		$2,800	$3,500

Model 500/1 Cavern Bass
2005. Limted run of 12, includes certificate.
2005		$1,550	$1,900

Model 500/1 Cavern Bass Music Ground
1993. UK commissioned by Music Ground, said to be one of the first accurate reissues, 40 made.
1993		$1,300	$1,600

Model 500/1 Contemporary
2007-2008. Contemporary Series.
2007-2008		$500	$625

Model 500/2 Bass
1965-1970. Similar to the 500/1, but with 'club' body Höfner made for England's Selmer, sunburst. Club Bass has been reissued.
1965		$1,700	$2,100
1966-1967		$1,350	$1,675
1968-1969		$1,250	$1,550
1970		$1,150	$1,425

Model 500/3 Senator Bass
1962-1964. Single-cut thin body, f-holes, 1 511b pickup, sunburst.
1962-1964		$1,250	$1,550

Model 500/5 Bass
1959-1979. Single-cut body with Beatle Bass-style pickups, sunburst.
1959		$2,800	$3,500
1960-1979		$2,400	$3,000

Model 500/6 Bass
Late-1960s. Introduced in '67, semi-acoustic, thinline, soft double-cut, 2 pickups, 4 control knobs, dot markers, sunburst.
1967		$1,300	$1,625

Model 500/8BZ / B500/8BZ
Late-1960s. Semi-acoustic, thinline, sharp double-cut, multiple-line position markers, built in flip-fuzz and bass boost, sunburst or natural.
1967	500/8BZ, sunburst	$1,400	$1,750
1967	B500/8BZ, natural	$1,500	$1,875

President Bass
Made for England's Selmer, single-cut archtop, 2 pickups, sunburst.
1961-1965		$1,800	$2,250
1966-1969		$1,400	$1,750
1970-1972		$1,350	$1,675

Hondo
1969-1987, 1991-2005. Budget grade, production, imported acoustic and electric solidbody basses. They also offered guitars, banjos and mandolins.

Electric Solidbody Bass
1969-1987, 1991-2005. Various models.
1969-1999	Rare models	$260	$400
1969-1999	Standard models	$80	$125

H 1181 Longhorn Bass
Ca. 1978-1980s. Copy of Danelectro Longhorn Bass, 1 split pickup.
1978-1980s		$400	$500

Hoyer
1874-present. Intermediate grade, production, electric basses. They also build guitars.

Electric Bass
1960s		$400	$500

Ibanez
1932-present. Intermediate and professional grade, production, solidbody basses. They also have guitars, amps, and effects.

AXB Axstar Series Bass
1986-1987. Various models.
1986-1987		$180	$450

BTB Series Bass
1999-present. Various models.
1999-2014		$200	$500

Challenger Bass
1977-1978. Offered as P-bass or J-bass style, and with ash body option.
1977-1978		$325	$400

DB Destroyer II X Series Bass
1984-1986. Futuristic-style body, P- and J-style pickups, dot markers, bolt neck.
1984-1986		$275	$475

DT Destroyer II Series Bass
1980-1985. Futuristic-style body.
1983-1986		$400	$600

1971 Höfner 500/1

Höfner 500/2

BASSES

BASSES

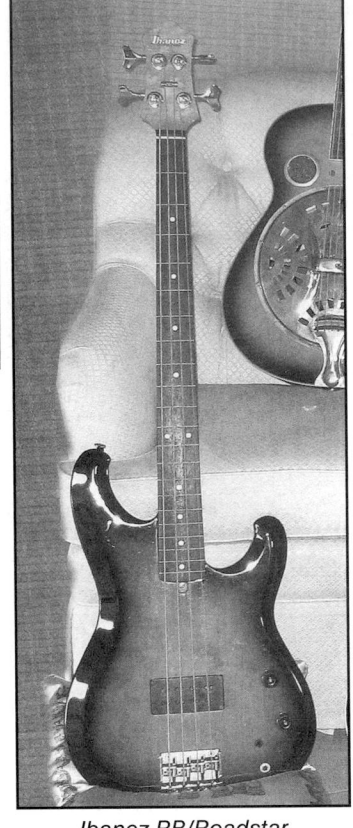

Ibanez RB/Roadstar
David Hinds

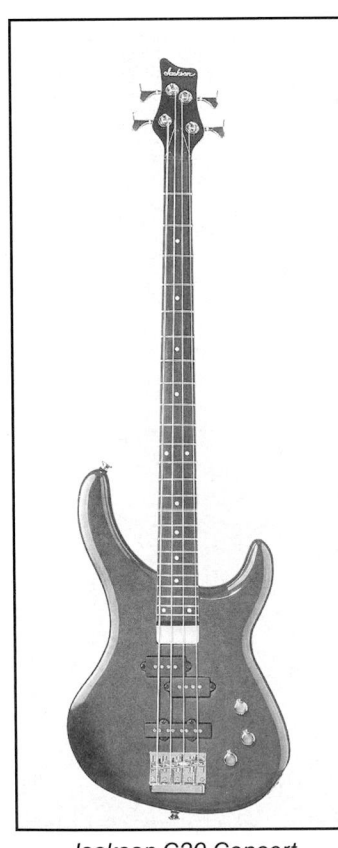

Jackson C20 Concert

MODEL YEAR	FEATURES	EXC. COND. LOW	HIGH
ICB Iceman Bass			
1994-1996, 2011. Iceman body, basswood (300) or *mahogany (500) body. 300 reissued in '11.*			
1994	ICB500, black	$625	$775
1994-1996	ICB300, white	$325	$425
MC Musician Series Bass			
1978-1988. Various models, solidbody, neck-thru.			
1978-1988		$600	$1,200
Model 2030 Bass			
1970-1973. First copy era bass, offset double-cut, *sunburst.*			
1970-1973		$500	$600
Model 2353 Bass			
1974-1976. Copy model, offset double-cut, 1 pickup, black.			
1974-1976		$500	$600
Model 2364B Bass			
1971-1973. Dan Armstrong see-thru Lucite copy with *2 mounted humbucker pickups, clear finish.*			
1971-1973		$700	$850
Model 2365 Bass			
1974-1975. Copy model, Offset double-cut, rosewood *'board, pearloid block markers, sunburst.*			
1974-1975		$500	$600
Model 2366 B/2366 FLB Bass			
1974-1975. Copy model, offset double-cut, 1 split-coil *pickup, sunburst, FLB fretless model.*			
1974-1975		$500	$600
Model 2385 Bass			
1974-1975. Copy model, offset double-cut, 1 pickup, *ash natural finish.*			
1974-1975		$500	$600
Model 2388 B Bass			
1974-1976. Ric 4001 copy.			
1974-1976		$500	$600
Model 2452 Bass			
1975. Ripper copy.			
1975		$500	$600
Model 2459 B Destroyer Bass			
1974-1977. Laminated ash body, copy of Korina *Explorer-style.*			
1974-1977		$1,250	$1,550
Model 2537 DX Bass			
1974-1975. Hofner Beatle copy.			
1974-1975		$500	$600
PL Pro Line Series Bass			
1986-1987. Offset double cut solidbody.			
1986-1987		$225	$450
RB/RS Roadstar Series Bass			
1983-1987. Solidbody basses, various models and colors.			
1983-1987		$250	$500
Rocket Roll Bass			
1974-1976. Korina solidbody, V-shape, natural.			
1974-1976		$1,275	$1,550
S/SB Series Bass			
1990-1992. Various ultra slim solidbody basses.			
1990-1992		$200	$500
SR Sound Gear Series Bass			
1987-present. Sleek, lightweight designs, active *electronics, bolt necks. Model numbers higher than* *1000 are usually arched-top, lower usually flat body.*			
1987-2014		$250	$550

MODEL YEAR	FEATURES	EXC. COND. LOW	HIGH
ST-980 Studio Bass			
1979-1980. Double cut, 8-string, bolt-on neck, *walnut-maple-mahogany body.*			
1979-1980		$400	$500

Imperial

Ca.1963-ca.1970. Imported by the Imperial Accordion Company of Chicago, Illinois. Early guitars and basses made in Italy, but by ca. '66 Japanese-made.

Electric Solidbody Bass			
1960s	Various models	$160	$250
Hollowbody Bass			
1960s. Hollowbody with sharp double-cuts.			
1960s		$200	$280

J.T. Hargreaves Basses & Guitars

1995-present. Luthier Jay Hargreaves builds his premium grade, production/custom, acoustic basses, in Seattle, Washington. He also builds guitars.

Jackson

1980-present. Intermediate, professional, and premium grade, production, solidbody basses. They also offer guitars. Founded by Grover Jackson, who owned Charvel.

Concert C5P 5-String Bass (Import)			
1998-2000. Bolt neck, dot inlay, chrome hardware.			
1998-2000		$125	$155
Concert Custom Bass (U.S.A.)			
1984-1995. Neck-thru Custom Shop bass.			
1984-1985		$900	$1,125
1986-1989		$800	$1,000
1990-1995		$600	$750
Concert EX 4-String Bass (Import)			
1992-1995. Bolt neck, dot inlay, black hardware.			
1992-1995		$225	$280
Concert V 5-String Bass (Import)			
1992-1995. Bound neck, shark tooth inlay.			
1992-1995		$330	$415
Concert XL 4-String Bass (Import)			
1992-1995. Bound neck, shark tooth inlay.			
1992-1995		$275	$340
Kelly Pro Bass			
1994-1995. Pointy-cut bouts, neck-thru solidbody, *shark fin marker inlays.*			
1994-1995		$550	$675
Piezo Bass			
1986. Piezo bridge pickup, neck-thru, shark tooth *inlays. Student model has rosewood 'board, no bind-* *ing. Custom Model has ebony 'board and binding.*			
1986		$1,500	$1,900
Soloist Bass			
1996. Pointy headstock, 4-string.			
1996		$650	$800

Jerry Jones

1981-2011. Intermediate grade, production, semi-hollow body electric basses from luthier Jerry Jones, and built in Nashville, Tennessee. They also build guitars and sitars. Jones retired in 2011.

MODEL YEAR	FEATURES	EXC. COND. LOW	HIGH

Neptune Longhorn 4 Bass
1988-2011. Based on Danelectro longhorn models, 4-string, 2 lipstick-tube pickups, 30" scale.

1988-2011		$900	$1,150

Neptune Longhorn 6 Bass
1988-2011. 6-string version.

1988-2011		$1,150	$1,425

Neptune Shorthorn 4 Bass
1988-2011. Danelectro Coke bottle headstock, short horns double cut, 2 pickups.

1988-2011		$725	$900

Juzek

Violin maker John Juzek was originally located in Prague, Czeckoslavakia, but moved to West Germany due to World War II. Prague instruments considered by most to be more valuable. Many German instruments were mass produced with laminate construction and some equate these German basses with the Kay laminate basses of the same era. Juzek still makes instruments.

Kalamazoo

1933-1942, 1965-1970. Kalamazoo was a brand Gibson used on one of their budget lines. They also used the name on electric basses, guitars and amps from '65 to '67.

Electric Bass

1965-1970	Bolt-on neck	$450	$575

Kapa

Ca. 1962-1970. Kapa was founded by Koob Veneman in Maryland and offered basses and guitars.

Electric Bass

1962-1970	Various models	$200	$575

Kawai

1927-present. Japanese instrument manufacturer Kawai started offering guitars under other brand names around '56. There were few imports carrying the Kawai brand until the late-'70s; best known for high quality basses. Kawai quit offering guitars and basses around 2002.

Electric Bass

1970-2002	Various models	$200	$475

Kay

Ca. 1931-present. Currently, budget and intermediate grade, production, imported solidbody basses. They also make amps, guitars, banjos, mandolins, ukes, and violins. Kay introduced upright acoustic laminate basses and 3/4 viols in '38 and electric basses in '54.

C1 Concert String Bass
1938-1967. Standard (3/4) size student bass, laminated construction, spruce top, figured maple back and sides, shaded light brown.

1938-1949		$1,750	$2,175
1950-1959		$1,650	$2,075
1960-1967		$1,550	$1,950

K-160 Electronic Bass
1955-1956. Same as K-162, but with plain white plastic trim.

1955-1956		$1,425	$1,750

K-162 Electronic Bass
1955-1956. Bass version of K-161Thin Twin "Jimmy Reed," single-cut, 1 tube-style pickup.

1955-1956		$1,425	$1,750

K-5965 Pro Bass
1954-1965. Single-cut, 1 pickup. named K-5965 Pro by 1961.

1954-1965		$1,425	$1,750

K-5970 Jazz Special Electric Bass
1960-1964. Double-cut, pickup, Kelvinator headstock, black or blond.

1960-1964		$2,000	$2,500

M-1 (Maestro) String Bass
1952-late-1960s. Standard (3/4) size bass, laminated construction, spruce top and curly maple back and sides. Model M-3 is the Junior (1/4) size bass, Model M-1 B has a blond finish, other models include the S-51 B Chubby Jackson Five-String Bass and the S-9 Swingmaster.

1952-1959		$1,750	$2,150
1960-1967		$1,550	$1,950

M-5 (Maestro) String Bass
1957-late-1960s. Five strings.

1957-1967		$2,050	$2,575

Semi-hollowbody Bass
1954-1966. Single or double cut, 1 or 2 pickups.

1954-1966	1 pickup	$300	$375
1954-1966	2 pickups	$350	$450

Solidbody Bass
1965-1968. Single or double cut, 1 or 2 pickups.

1965-1968	1 pickup	$450	$550
1965-1968	2 pickups	$475	$625

Ken Smith

See listing under Smith.

Kent

1961-1969. Guitars and basses imported from Japan by Buegeleisen and Jacobson of New York, New York. Manufacturers unknown but many early instruments by Guyatone and Teisco.

Electric Bass
1962-1969. Import models include 628 Newport, 634 Basin Street, 629, and 635.

1961-1969	Common model	$125	$250
1961-1969	Rare model	$250	$325

Kimberly

Late-1960s-early-1970s. Private branded import made in the same Japanese factory as Teisco. They also made guitars.

Violin Bass

1960s		$400	$500

Kingston

Ca. 1958-1967. Imported from Japan by Westheimer Importing Corp. of Chicago. Early examples made by Guyatone and Teisco. They also offered guitars, mandolins and banjos.

1955 Kay K-160

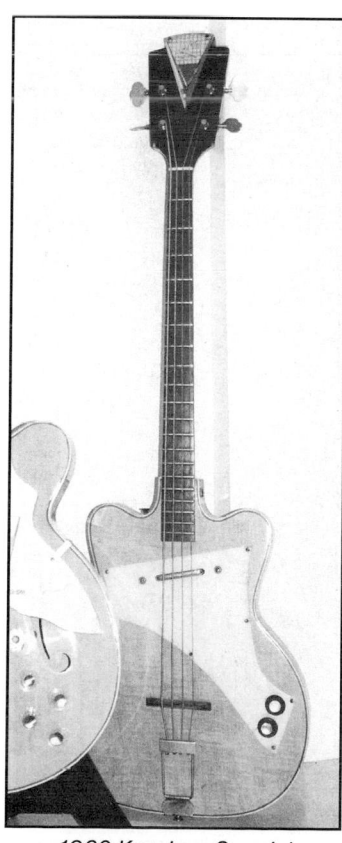

1960 Kay Jazz Special
Dave Linden

Kramer 350-B Standard

Kramer DMZ-4001

MODEL YEAR	FEATURES	EXC. COND. LOW	HIGH

Electric Bass
1960s	Common model	$125	$250
1960s	Rare model	$250	$325

Klira
Founded in 1887 in Schoenbach, Germany, mainly making violins, but added guitars and basses in the 1950s. The instruments of the '50s and '60s were aimed at the budget market, but workmanship improved with the '70s models.

Electric Bass
1960s	Beatle Bass copy	$525	$650
1960s	Common model	$350	$650
1960s	Rare model	$650	$800

Kramer
1976-1990, 1995-present. Budget grade, production, imported solidbody basses. They also offer guitars. Kramer's first guitars and basses featured aluminum necks with wooden inserts on back. Around '80 they started to switch to more economical wood necks and aluminum necks were last produced in '85. Gibson acquired the brand in '97.

250-B Special Bass
1977-1979. Offset double-cut, aluminum neck, Ebonol 'board, zero fret, 1 single-coil, natural.
1977-1979		$575	$725

350-B Standard Bass
1976-1979. Offset double-cut, aluminum neck, Ebonol 'board, tropical woods, 1 single-coil, dots. The 350 and 450 were Kramer's first basses.
1976-1979		$725	$900

450-B Deluxe Bass
1976-1980. As 350-B, but with 2 single-coils and blocks.
1976-1980		$775	$950

650-B Artist Bass
1977-1980. Double-cut, birdseye maple/burled walnut, aluminum neck, zero fret, mother-of-pearl crowns, 2 humbuckers.
1977-1980		$925	$1,150

Deluxe 8 Bass
1980. Multi-piece body, aluminum neck.
1980		$1,000	$1,250

DMB 2000 Bass
1979. Bolt-on aluminum neck, slot headstock.
1979		$575	$725

DMZ 4000 Bass
1978-1982. Bolt-on aluminum neck, slot headstock, double-cut solidbody, active EQ and dual-coil humbucking pickup, dot inlay.
1978-1981		$650	$800
1982	Bill Wyman-type	$675	$850

DMZ 4001 Bass
1979-1980. Aluminum neck, slot headstock, double-cut solidbody, 1 dual-coil humbucker pickup, dot inlay.
1979-1980		$575	$725

DMZ 5000 Bass
1979-1980. Double-cut solidbody, aluminum neck, slotted headstock, 2 pickups, crown inlays.
1979-1980		$725	$900

MODEL YEAR	FEATURES	EXC. COND. LOW	HIGH

DMZ 6000B Bass
1979-1980. Double-cut, aluminum neck, slotted headstock, 2 pickups, crown inlays.
1979-1980		$750	$925

Duke Custom/Standard Bass
1981-1983. Headless, aluminum neck, 1 humbucker.
1981-1983		$340	$425

Duke Special Bass
1982-1985. Headless, aluminum neck, 2 pickups, with frets or fretless.
1982-1985		$380	$475

Ferrington KFB-1/KFB-2 Acoustic Bass
1987-1990. Acoustic/electric, bridge-mounted active pickup, tone and volume control, various colors. KFB-1 has binding and diamond dot inlays; the KFB-2 no binding and dot inlays. Danny Ferrington continued to offer the KFB-1 after Kramer closed in '90.
1987-1990		$225	$275

Focus 7000 Bass
1985-1987. Offset double-cut solidbody, P and double J pickups, Japanese-made.
1985-1987		$200	$250

Focus 8000 Bass
1985-1987. Offset double-cut solidbody, Japanese-made.
1985-1987		$200	$250

Focus K Series Bass
1984-1986. Includes the 1 pickup K 77 and 2 pickup K 88, made in Japan.
1984-1986		$200	$250

Forum Series Bass
1987-1990. Japanese-made double-cut, 2 pickups, neck-thru (I & III) or bolt-neck (II & IV).
1987-1990	Forum I	$400	$500
1987-1990	Forum II	$300	$375
1987-1990	Forum III	$275	$350
1987-1990	Forum IV	$250	$325

Gene Simmons Axe Bass
1980-1981. Axe-shaped bass, slot headstock.
1980-1981		$3,400	$4,300

Hundred Series Bass
1988-1990. Import budget line, 7/8th solidbody.
1988-1990	710	$170	$210
1988-1990	720	$190	$230

Pacer Bass
1982-1984. Offset double-cut solidbody, red.
1982-1984		$525	$650

Pioneer Bass
1981-1986. First wood neck basses, offset double cut, JBX or PBX pickups, dots, '81-'84 models with soft headstocks, later '84 on with banana headstocks.
1981-1986	Double J, 2 JBX	$400	$500
1981-1986	Imperial, JBX & PBX	$375	$475
1981-1986	Special, 1 PBX	$350	$450
1982-1984	Carrera, JBX & PBX	$400	$500

Ripley Four-String Bass
1985-1987. Four-string version.
1985-1987		$700	$875

Ripley Five-String Bass
1984-1987. Offset double-cut, 5 strings, stereo, pan pots for each string, front and back pickups for each

MODEL YEAR	FEATURES	EXC. COND. LOW	HIGH
string, active circuitry.			
1984-1987		$725	$900

Stagemaster Custom Bass (Import)

1982-1985, 1987-1990. First version had an aluminum neck (wood optional). Later version was neck-thru-body, bound neck, either active or passive pickups.

1982-1985	Imperial	$650	$800
1982-1985	Special	$600	$750
1982-1985	Standard	$650	$800

Stagemaster Deluxe Bass (U.S.A.)

1981. Made in USA, 8-string, metal neck.

1981		$850	$1,050

Striker 700 Bass

1985-1989. Offset double-cut, Korean-import, 1 pickup until '87, 2 after. Striker name was again used on a bass in '99.

1985-1987	1 pickup	$200	$250
1988-1989	2 pickups	$250	$310

Vanguard Bass

1981-1983. V-shaped body, Special (aluminum neck) or Standard (wood neck).

1981-1982	Special	$450	$550
1983-1984	Standard	$500	$625

Voyager Bass

1982-1983. X body, headless.

1982-1983		$1,000	$1,250

XKB-10 (Wedge) Bass

1980-1981. Wedge-shaped body, aluminum neck.

1980-1981		$600	$750

XKB-20 Bass

1981. 2nd version, more traditional double cut body.

1981		$550	$675

XL Series Bass

1980-1981. Odd shaped double-cut solidbody, aluminum neck.

1980-1981	XL-9, 4-string	$725	$900
1981	XL-24, 4-string	$825	$1,050
1981	XL-8, 8-string	$925	$1,150

ZX Aero Star Series Bass (Import)

1986-1989. Various models include ZX-70 (offset double-cut solidbody, 1 pickup).

1986-1989		$150	$185

KSD

2003-present. Intermediate grade, production, imported bass line designed by Ken Smith (see Smith listing).

Kubicki

1973-present. Professional and premium grade, production/custom, solidbody basses built by luthier Phil Kubicki in Santa Barbara, California. Kubicki began building acoustic guitars when he was 15. In '64 at age 19, he went to work with Roger Rossmeisl at Fender Musical Instrument's research and development department for acoustic guitars. Nine years later he moved to Santa Barbara, California, and established Philip Kubicki Technology, which is best known for its line of Factor basses and also builds acoustic guitars, custom electric guitars, bodies and necks, and mini-guitars and does custom work, repairs and restorations. Phil Kubicki died in '13.

Ex Factor 4/Factor 4 Bass

1985-present. Solidbody, maple body, bolt-on maple neck, fretless available, 4 strings, 2 pickups, active electronics.

1980s		$975	$1,225

Ex Factor 5/Factor 5 Bass

1985-ca.1990. Solidbody, bolt-on maple neck, fretless available, 5 strings, 2 pickups, active electronics.

1980s		$1,075	$1,325

Kustom

1968-present. Founded by Bud Ross in Chanute, Kansas, and best known for the tuck-and-roll amps, Kustom also offered guitars and basses from '68 to '69.

Electric Hollowbody Bass

1968-1969	Various models	$900	$1,125

La Baye

1967. Short-lived brand out of Green Bay, Wisconsin and built by the Holman-Woodell factory in Neodesha, Kansas. There was also a guitar model.

Model 2x4 II Bass

1967. Very low production, dual pickups, long-scale, small rectangle solidbody, sometimes referred to as the Bass II.

1967		$1,175	$1,450

Model 2x4 Mini-Bass

1967. Short-scale, 1 pickup, small rectangle solidbody.

1967		$1,175	$1,450

Lakland

1994-present. Professional and premium grade, production/custom, solid and hollowbody basses from luthier Dan Lakin in Chicago, Illinois. Lakland basses are built in the U.S. and overseas (Skyline series).

4 - 63 Classic Bass

1994-2002. Offset double-cut alder body, large bass horn, bolt neck.

1994-2002		$1,700	$2,100

4 - 63 Deluxe Bass

1994-2002. Like Classic but with figured maple top on ash body.

1994-2002		$1,900	$2,400

4 - 63 Standard Bass

1994-2002. Like Classic, but with swamp ash body.

1994-2002		$1,700	$2,100

4 - 94/44 - 94 Classic Bass

1994-present. Offset double-cut alder body with maple top, large bass horn, bolt neck. Series now called 44-94.

1994-2014		$1,700	$2,100

4 - 94/44 - 94 Deluxe Bass

1994-present. Like Classic but with flamed maple top on swamp ash body. Series now called 44-94.

1994-2014		$1,900	$2,400

4 - 94/44 - 94 Standard Bass

1994-present. Like Classic, but with quilt maple top. Series now called 44-94.

1994-2014		$1,700	$2,100

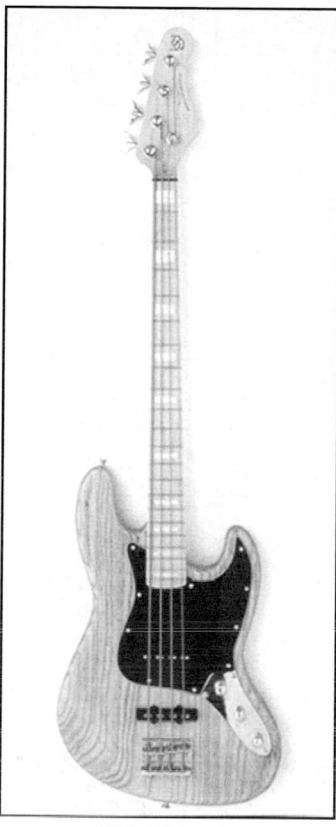

KSD KSD-704

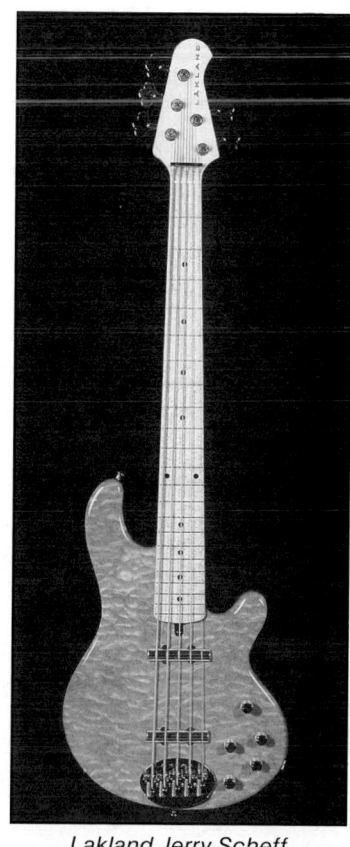

Lakland Jerry Scheff

BASSES

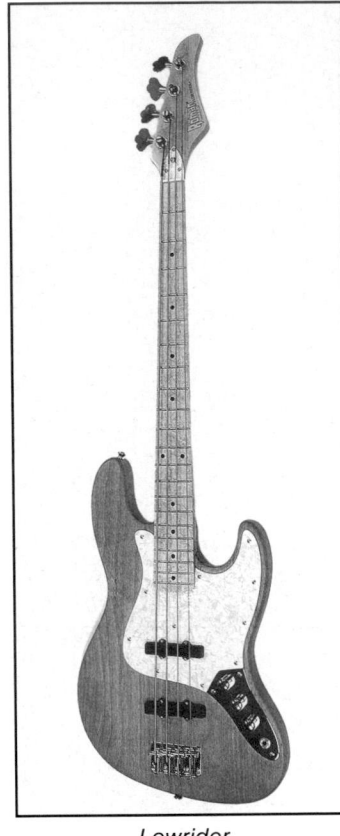

Lowrider

M Basses Mp Elite Series

MODEL YEAR	FEATURES	EXC. COND. LOW	HIGH

Joe Osborn/44-60/55-60 Bass

1998-present. Classic offset double-cut, 4- or 5-string, alder or swamp ash body, 2 pickups, name changed to 44-60 (4-string) and 55-60 (5-string) in '09.

1998-2014		$2,000	$2,500

Skyline Limited Edition

| 2012 | | $1,100 | $1,350 |

Lowrider Basses

2003-present. Professional grade, production/custom, solidbody basses made by Ed Roman Guitars.

M Basses

2001-present. Production/custom, professional and premium grade, solidbody electric basses built in Terryville, Connecticut by luthier Jon Maghini.

Magnatone

Ca. 1937-1971. Founded as Dickerson Brothers, known as Magna Electronics from '47. Produced instruments under own brand and for many others.

Hurricane X-10 Bass

1965-1966. Offset double cut solidbody, 1 single-coil, 4-on-a-side tuners, Magnatone logo on guard and headstock, Hurricane logo on headstock.

| 1965-1966 | | $925 | $1,150 |

Mako

1985-1989. Line of solidbody basses from Kaman (Ovation, Hamer). They also offered guitars and amps.

Electric Solidbody Bass

| 1985-1989 | Student bass | $80 | $230 |

Marco Polo

1960- ca.1964. One of the first inexpensive Japanese brands to be imported into the U.S., they also offered guitars.

Solidbody Bass

| 1960s | Various models | $80 | $230 |

Marleaux

1990-present. Luthier Gerald Marleaux builds his custom, premium grade, electric basses in Clausthal-Zellerfeld, Germany.

Marling

Ca. 1975. Budget line instruments marketed by EKO of Recanati, Italy; probably made by them, although possibly imported. They also had guitars.

Electric Solidbody Bass

Models include the E.495 (copy of LP), E.485 (copy of Tele), and the E.465 (Manta-style).

| 1970s | | $125 | $185 |

Martin

1833-present. Professional grade, production, acoustic basses made in the U.S. In 1978, Martin re-entered the electric market and introduced their solidbody EB-18 and EB-28 Basses. In the '80s they offered Stinger brand electric basses. By the late '80s, they started offering acoustic basses.

00C-16GTAE Bass

2006-2011. Mahogany back and sides, Fishman electronics.

| 2006-2011 | | $850 | $1,050 |

B-1/B-1E Acoustic Bass

2002-2006. Mahogany back and sides, E has Fishman electronics.

| 2002-2006 | | $950 | $1,175 |

B-40 Acoustic Bass

1989-1996. Jumbo, rosewood back and sides, built-in pickup and volume and tone controls. The B-40B had a pickup.

| 1989-1996 | B-40B | $1,350 | $1,675 |
| 1989-1996 | Without pickup | $1,175 | $1,475 |

B-65 Acoustic Bass

1989-1993. Like B-40 but with maple back and sides, built-in pickup and volume and tone controls.

| 1989-1993 | | $1,250 | $1,550 |

BC-15E Acoustic Bass

2000-2006. Single-cut, all mahogany, on-board electronics.

| 2000-2006 | | $1,000 | $1,250 |

BC-16GTE Acoustic Bass

2009-2013. Jumbo, cutaway, mahogany back and sides.

| 2009-2013 | | $1,225 | $1,525 |

BCPA4 Acoustic-Electric Bass

2013-present. Performing Artist series, single-cut, sitka spruce top, sapele back and sides.

| 2013-2014 | | $1,025 | $1,275 |

EB-18 Bass

1979-1982. Electric solidbody, neck-thru, 1 pickup, natural.

| 1979-1982 | | $1,075 | $1,350 |

EB-28 Bass

1980-1982. Electric solidbody.

| 1980-1982 | | $1,175 | $1,450 |

SBL-10 Bass

1980s. Stinger brand solidbody, maple neck, 1 split and 1 bar pickup.

| 1980s | | $180 | $225 |

Marvel

1950s-mid-1960s. Brand used for budget guitars and basses marketed by Peter Sorkin Company in New York, New York.

Electric Solidbody Bass

| 1950s | Various models | $150 | $425 |

Messenger

1967-1968. Built by Musicraft, Inc., Messengers featured a neck-thru metal alloy neck. They also made guitars.

Bass

1967-1968. Metal alloy neck. Messenger mainly made guitars - they offered a bass, but it is unlikely many were built.

| 1967-1968 | | $2,110 | $2,575 |

Messenger Upright

Made by Knutson Luthiery, see that listing.

MODEL YEAR	FEATURES	EXC. COND. LOW	HIGH

Microfrets

1967-1975, 2004-2005. Professional grade, production, electric basses built in Myersville, Maryland. They also built guitars.

Husky Bass
1971-1974/75. Double-cut, 2 pickups, 2-on-a-side tuners.

1971-1975		$775	$950

Rendezvous Bass
1970. One pickup, orange sunburst.

1970		$850	$1,050

Signature Bass
1969-1975. Double-cut, 2 pickups, 2-on-a-side tuners.

1969-1975		$1,125	$1,375

Stage II Bass
1969-1975. Double-cut, 2 pickups, 2-on-a-side tuners.

1969-1975		$1,125	$1,375

Thundermaster Bass
1967-1975. Double-cut, 2 pickups, 2-on-a-side tuners.

1967-1975		$1,125	$1,400

Modulus

1978-2013. Founded by aerospace engineer Geoff Gould, Modulus currently offers professional and premium grade, production/custom, solidbody basses built in California. They also build guitars.

Bassstar SP-24 Active Bass
1981-ca. 1990. EMG J pickups, active bass and treble circuits.

1980s		$1,300	$1,600

Flea 4/Flea Signature Bass
1997-2003. Offset double-cut alder solidbody, also offered as 5-string.

1997-2003		$1,300	$1,600

Genesis Series Bass
1997-1998, 2003-2013. Offset double-cut, 2 pickups, 4- or 5-string.

2003-2013	Various models	$1,300	$1,600

Quantum-4 Series Bass
1982-2013. Offset double-cut, 2 pickups, 35" scale.

1982-2013		$1,900	$2,400

Quantum-5 Series Bass
1982-2013. 5-String version.

1982-2013		$2,000	$2,500

Quantum-6 Series Bass
1982-2013. 6-string version.

1982-2013		$2,100	$2,600

Vintage V Series Bass

2002	VJ-4	$1,500	$1,850

Mollerup Basses

In 1984 luthier Laurence Mollerup began building professional grade, custom/production, electric basses and electric double basses in Vancouver, British Columbia. He has also built guitars.

Moonstone

1972-present. Luthier Steve Helgeson builds his premium grade, production/custom, acoustic and electric basses in Eureka, California. He also builds guitars.

Eclipse Deluxe Bass
1980-1984. Double-cut solidbody.

1980-1984		$1,325	$1,650

Exploder Bass
1980-1983. Figured wood body, Explorer-style neck-thru-body.

1980-1983		$1,600	$1,975

Vulcan Bass
1982-1984. Solidbody, flat-top (Vulcan) or carved top (Vulcan II), maple body, gold hardware.

1982-1984		$1,650	$2,050

Morales

Ca.1967-1968. Guitars and basses made in Japan by Zen-On and not heavily imported into the U.S.

Electric Solidbody Bass

1967-1968	Various models	$130	$200

Mosrite

Semie Moseley's Mosrite offered various bass models throughout the many versions of the Mosrite company.

Brut Bass
Late-1960s. Assymetrical body with small cutaway on upper treble bout.

1960s		$850	$1,050

Celebrity Bass
1965-1969. ES-335-style semi-thick double-cut body with f-holes, 2 pickups.

1965-1966	Custom color	$925	$1,150
1965-1967	Sunburst	$850	$1,050
1968-1969	Red	$775	$950
1969	Sunburst	$775	$950

Combo Bass
1966-1968. Hollowbody, 2 pickups.

1966-1968		$1,650	$2,075

Joe Maphis Bass
1966-1969. Ventures-style body, hollow without f-holes, 2 pickups, natural.

1966-1969		$1,750	$2,200

Ventures Bass
1965-1972. Two pickups, various colors.

1965		$2,250	$2,800
1966		$2,150	$2,675
1967-1968		$1,850	$2,300
1969		$1,750	$2,175
1970-1972		$1,650	$2,075

V-II Bass
1973-1974. Ventures-style, 2 humbuckers, sunburst.

1973-1974		$1,750	$2,200

MTD

1994-present. Intermediate, professional, and premium grade, production/custom, electric basses built by luthier Michael Tobias (who founded Tobias Basses in '77) in Kingston, New York. Since '00, he also imports basses built in Korea to his specifications.

Magnatone Hurricane X-10
Tom Roberts

Modulus Quantum 4

MODEL YEAR	FEATURES	EXC. COND. LOW	HIGH

1976 Music Man Stingray
Craig Brody

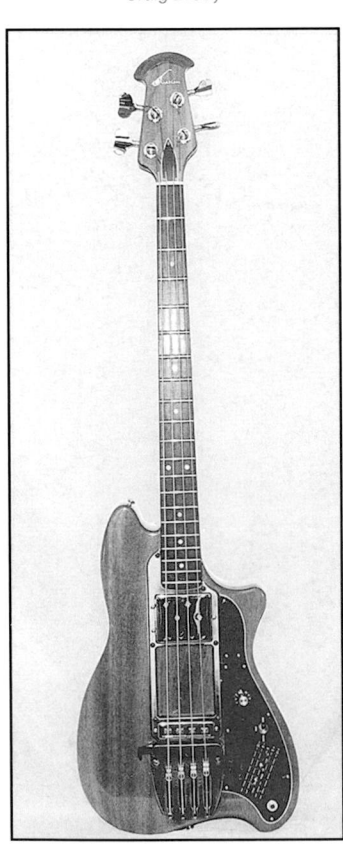

Ovation Magnum II

Murph

1965-1967. Mid-level electric solidbody basses built by Pat Murphy in San Fernado, California. Murph logo on headstock. They also offered guitars and amps.

Solidbody Bass

1965-1967		$700	$875

Music Man

1972-present. Intermediate and professional grade, production, electric basses. They also build guitars.

Bongo Bass

2003-present. Double cut solidbody, squared-off horns, 2 pickups, 4-, 5-, and 6-string.

2003-2014	Bongo 4	$1,000	$1,250
2003-2014	Bongo 5	$1,100	$1,375

Cutlass I/Cutlass II Bass

1982-1987. Ash body, graphite neck, string-thru-body.

1982-1984	CLF era Cutlass I	$1,900	$2,400
1982-1984	CLF era Cutlass II	$2,000	$2,500
1984-1987	Ernie Ball era Cutlass I	$1,500	$1,900
1984-1987	Ernie Ball era Cutlass II	$1,600	$2,000

S.U.B. Series Bass

2003-2007. Offset double-cut, 4- or 5-string, 1 humbucker.

2003-2007	IV Bass	$425	$525
2003-2007	V Bass	$450	$575

Sabre Bass

1978-ca.1991. Double-cut solidbody bass, 3-and-1 tuning keys, 2 humbucking pickups, on-board preamp, natural.

1978-1979	CLF era	$1,900	$2,400
1980-1984	CLF era	$1,500	$1,900
1984-1991	Ernie Ball era	$1,000	$1,250

Sterling Bass

1993-present. Rosewood, 1 pickup, EQ, pearl blue. In '05, additional pickup options available. 5-string introduced in '08.

1993-2014	4-string	$900	$1,125
2008-2014	5-string	$1,000	$1,250

StingRay Bass

1976-present. Offset double-cut solidbody, 1 pickup, 3-and-1 tuners, string-thru until '80, various colors. 5-string introduced in '87. In '05, additional pickup options available.

1976-1979	CLF era	$2,275	$2,850
1980-1984	CLF era	$1,950	$2,400
1984-1989	Ernie Ball era	$1,200	$1,500
1987-2014	5-string	$1,000	$1,250
1990-2014	4-string	$900	$1,125

StingRay 20th Anniversary Bass

1996. 1400 made, flamed maple body.

1996		$1,650	$2,000

StingRay Classic Bass

2010-present. Ash body, birds-eye or flame maple neck, 4- or 5-string.

2010-2014		$1,200	$1,500

National

Ca. 1927-present. National offered electric basses in the '60s when Valco owned the brand.

Beatle (Violin) Bass

1970s. Strum & Drum era import, National script logo on headstock, 2 pickups, shaded brown finish.

1970s		$375	$475

EG 700V-2HB German Style Bass

1970s. Strum & Drum era import, Beatle-style violin body, 2 humbuckers, bolt neck.

1970s		$425	$525

N-850 Bass

1967-1968. Semi-hollow double-cut, art deco f-holes, 2 pickups, block markers, bout control knobs, sunburst.

1967-1968		$600	$750

Val-Pro 85 Bass

1961-1962. Res-O-Glas body shaped like the U.S. map, 2 pickups, snow white, renamed National 85 in '63.

1961-1962		$1,200	$1,500

New York Bass Works

1989-present. Luthier David Segal builds his professional and premium grade, production/custom, electric basses in New York.

Norma

Ca.1965-1970. Guitars and basses imported from Japan by Chicago's Strum and Drum.

Electric Solidbody Bass

1960s	Various models	$125	$200

O'Hagan

1979-1983. Designed by Jerol O'Hagan in St. Louis Park, Minnesota. He also offered guitars.

Electric Solidbody Bass

1979-1983. Models include the Shark Bass, NightWatch Bass, NightWatch Regular Bass, and the Twenty Two Bass.

1979-1983		$460	$575

Old Kraftsman

1930s-1960s. Brand used by the Spiegel Company. Guitars and basses made by other American manufacturers.

Electric Solidbody Bass

1950s	Various models	$350	$450

Orville by Gibson

1984-1993. Orville by Gibson and Orville guitars were made by Japan's Fuji Gen Gakki for Gibson. Basically the same models except the Orville by Gibson guitars had real Gibson USA pickups and a true nitrocellulose lacquer finish. The Orville models used Japanese electronics and a poly finish. Prices here are for the Orville by Gibson models.

Electric Bass

1984-1993	Thunderbird	$850	$1,050

Ovation

1966-present. Intermediate and professional grade, imported, production, acoustic/electric

MODEL YEAR	FEATURES	EXC. COND. LOW	HIGH

basses. Ovation offered electric solidbody basses early on and added acoustic basses in the '90s. They also offer guitars and mandolins.

B768/Elite B768 Bass
1990. Single-cut acoustic-electric bass, Elite body style with upper bout soundholes.

1990		$775	$1,000

Celebrity Series Bass
1990s-2013. Deep bowl back, cutaway, acoustic/electric.

1990s-2013		$250	$315

Magnum Series Bass
1974-1980. Magnum I is odd-shaped mahogany solidbody, 2 pickups, mono/stereo, mute, sunburst, red or natural. Magnum II is with battery-powered preamp and 3-band EQ. Magnum III and IV had a new offset double-cut body.

1974-1978	Magnum I	$800	$1,050
1974-1978	Magnum II	$1,000	$1,200
1978-1980	Magnum III	$800	$1,050
1978-1980	Magnum IV	$1,000	$1,200

NSB778 Elite T Bass Nikki Sixx Limited Edition
2005-2013. Made in USA, acoustic-electric 4-string, 1 pickup, solid spruce top, ebony 'board, custom iron cross inlays, red or gray flame finish.

2005-2013		$1,175	$1,450

Typhoon II/Typhoon III Bass
1968-1971. Ovation necks, but bodies and hardware were German imports. Semi-hollowbody, 2 pickups, red or sunburst. Typhoon II is 335-style and III is fretless.

1968-1971	Typhoon II	$650	$875
1968-1971	Typhoon III	$700	$925

Ultra Bass
1984. Korean solidbodies and necks assembled in U.S., offset double-cut with 1 pickup.

1984		$325	$400

PANaramic
1961-1963. Guitars and basses made in Italy by the Crucianelli accordion company and imported by PANaramic accordion. They also offered amps made by Magnatone.

Electric Bass
1961-1963. Double-cut hollowbody, 2 pickups, dot markers, sunburst.

1961-1963		$875	$1,100

Parker
1992-present. Premium grade, production/custom, solidbody electric basses. They also build guitars.

Fly Bass
2002-2011. Offered in 4- and 5-string models.

2002-2011		$1,100	$1,375

Paul Reed Smith
1985-present. PRS added basses in '86, but by '92 had dropped the models. In 2000 PRS started again offering professional and premium grade, production, solidbody electric basses. Bird inlays can add $100 or more to the values of PRS basses listed here.

Bass-4
1986-1992, 2007. Set neck, 3 single-coil pickups, hum-cancelling coil, active circuitry, 22-fret Brazilian rosewood 'board. Reintroduced (OEB Series) in 2000s.

1986-1987		$2,400	$3,000
1988-1992		$1,700	$2,100
2007		$1,700	$2,100

Bass-5
1986-1992. Five-string, set-neck, rosewood 'board, 3 single-coil pickups, active electronics. Options include custom colors, bird inlays, fretless 'board.

1986-1987		$2,500	$3,100
1988-1992		$1,800	$2,200

CE Bass-4
1986-1991. Solidbody, maple bolt neck, alder body, rosewood 'board, 4-string.

1986-1987		$1,400	$1,800
1988-1991		$1,100	$1,400

CE Bass-5
1986-1991. Five-string solidbody, maple bolt neck, alder body, rosewood 'board.

1986-1987		$1,400	$1,800
1988-1991		$1,100	$1,400

Curly Bass-4
1986-1992. Double-cut solidbody, curly maple top, set maple neck, Brazilian rosewood 'board (ebony on fretless), 3 single-coil and 1 hum-cancelling pickups, various grades of maple tops, moon inlays.

1986-1987		$2,400	$3,000
1988-1992		$2,100	$2,600

Curly Bass-5
1986-1992. Five-string version of Curly Bass-4.

1986-1987		$2,400	$3,000
1988-1992		$2,100	$2,600

Electric Bass
2000-2007. Bolt neck 4-string, offered in regular and maple top versions.

2000-2007	Maple	$1,175	$1,475
2000-2007	Plain	$1,325	$1,650

Private Stock Program
2010-present. Custom instruments based around existing PRS models.

2010-2014	Higher specs	$6,500	$8,000
2010-2014	Normal specs	$5,000	$6,000

Peavey
1965-present. Intermediate and professional grade, production/custom, electric basses. They also build guitars and amps. Hartley Peavey's first products were guitar amps and he added guitars and basses to the mix in '78.

Axcelerator Bass
1994-1998. Offset double-cut, long thin horns, 2 humbuckers, stacked control knobs, bolt neck, dot markers.

1994-1998		$325	$400

Cirrus Series Bass
1998-2012. Offset double-cut, active electronics, in 4-, 5-, 6-string, and custom shop versions.

1998-2009	Cirrus 5	$750	$925
1998-2012	Cirrus 4	$700	$875
1998-2012	Cirrus 6	$800	$975

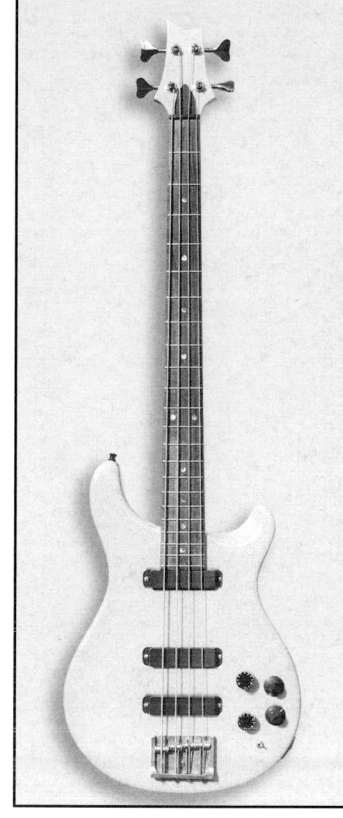

1989 PRS Bass-4

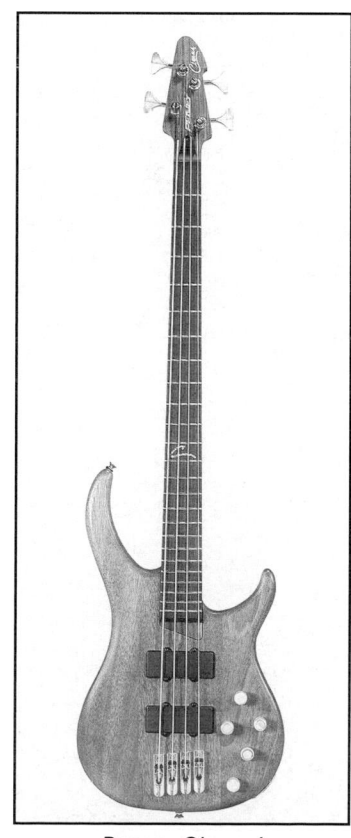

Peavey Cirrus 4

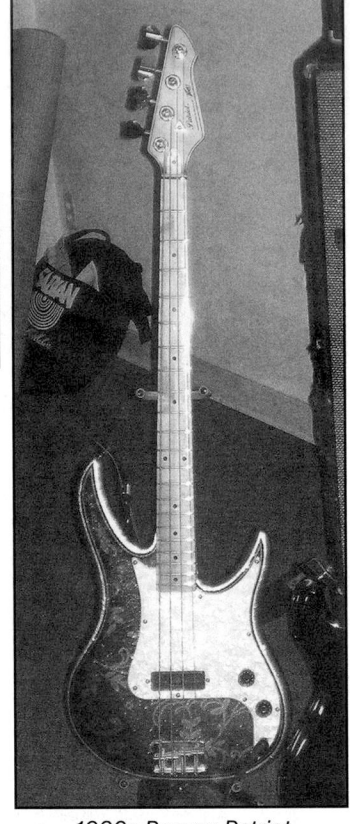

1980s Peavey Patriot
Sean Sweeney

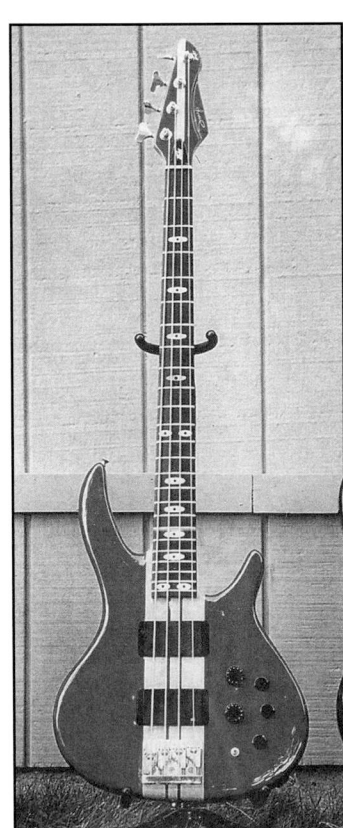

Peavey Rudy Sarzo
Kenny K.

MODEL YEAR	FEATURES	EXC. COND. LOW	HIGH
Dyna-Bass			
1987-1993. Double-cut solidbody, active electronics, 3-band EQ, rosewood 'board, opaque finish.			
1987-1993		$375	$475
Dyna-Bass Limited			
1987-1990. Neck-thru-body, ebony 'board, flamed maple neck/body construction, purple heart strips, mother-of-pearl inlays.			
1987-1990		$475	$600
Forum Bass			
1994-1995. Double-cut solidbody, rosewood 'board, dot inlays, 2 humbuckers.			
1994-1995		$200	$225
Forum Plus Bass			
1994. Forum Bass with added active electronics.			
1994		$225	$250
Foundation Bass			
1984-2002. Double-cut solidbody, 2 pickups, maple neck.			
1984-2002		$200	$225
Foundation S Active Bass			
1987-1991. Similar to Foundation S Bass with added active circuitry, provides low-impedance output, 2 pickups.			
1987-1991		$200	$225
Foundation S Bass			
1986-1991. Two split-coil pickups, maple body, rosewood 'board, black hardware, black painted headstock.			
1986-1991		$200	$225
Fury Bass			
1983-1999. Double-cut solidbody, rosewood 'board, 1 split-coil humbucker.			
1983-1999		$145	$180
Fury Custom Bass			
1986-1993. Fury Bass with black hardware and narrow neck.			
1986-1993		$200	$225
Fury VI Bass			
2001-2003. 6-string, active electronics, quilt top.			
2001-2003		$300	$350
G-Bass V			
1999-2002. Offset double-cut 5-string, humbucker, 3-band EQ.			
1999-2002		$675	$825
Grind Series Bass			
2001-present. Offset double-cut, neck-thru, long bass horn, 2 pickups, 4-, 5-, or 6-string.			
2001-2014	Grind 4	$190	$240
2001-2014	Grind 5, Grind 6	$215	$270
Liberator Series			
2007. 2 humbuckers, black with graphics.			
2007	JT-84	$900	$1,125
Milestone Series Bass			
1994-present. Import offset double cut, Milestone I ('94) replaced by 1 P-style pickup II ('95-'01), split humbucker IV ('99-'04); 2 single-coil III ('99-present) now just called Milestone.			
1994	Milestone I	$75	$95
1995-2001	Milestone II	$75	$95
1999-2004	Milestone IV	$95	$115
1999-2014	Milestone III, Milestone	$95	$115

MODEL YEAR	FEATURES	EXC. COND. LOW	HIGH
Millenium Series Bass			
2001-present. Offset double-cut, agathis bodies, maple tops, in 4- or 5-string.			
2001-2014		$200	$300
Patriot Bass			
1984-1988. General J-Bass styling with larger thinner horns, 1 single-coil, maple neck.			
1984-1988		$125	$155
Patriot Custom Bass			
1986-1988. Patriot with rosewood neck, matching headstock.			
1986-1988		$165	$210
RJ-IV Bass			
1990-1993. Randy Jackson Signature model, neck-thru-body, 2 split-coil active pickups, ebony 'board, mother-of-pearl position markers.			
1990-1993		$325	$400
Rudy Sarzo Signature Bass			
1989-1993. Double-cut solidbody, active EQ, ebony 'board, 2 pickups.			
1989-1993		$475	$600
T-20FL Bass			
1983. Fretless double-cut solidbody, 1 pickup, also available as the fretted T-20 ('82-'83).			
1983		$220	$275
T-40/T-40FL Bass			
1978-1987. Double-cut solidbody, 2 pickups. T-40FL is fretless.			
1978-1987	T-40	$400	$500
1978-1987	T-40FL	$400	$500
T-45 Bass			
1982-1986. T-40 with 1 humbucking pickup, and a mid-frequency rolloff knob.			
1982-1986		$300	$375
TL Series Bass			
1988-1998. Neck-thru-body, gold hardware, active humbuckers, EQ, flamed maple neck and body, 5-string (TL-Five) or 6 (TL-Six).			
1988-1998	TL-Five	$525	$650
1989-1998	TL-Six	$600	$750

Pedulla

1975-present. Professional and premium grade, production/custom, electric basses made in Rockland, Massachusetts. Founded by Michael Pedulla, Pedulla offers various upscale options which affect valuation so each instrument should be evaluated on a case-by-case basis. Unless specifically noted, the following listings have standard to mid-level features. High-end options are specifically noted; if not, these options will have a relatively higher value than those shown here.

MODEL YEAR	FEATURES	EXC. COND. LOW	HIGH
Buzz-4/Buzz-5 Bass			
1980-2008. Double-cut neck-thru solidbody, fretless, long-scale, maple neck and body wings, 2 pickups, preamp, some with other active electronics, various colors, 4-, 5-, 6-, 8-string versions.			
1980-1999		$1,125	$1,425
Interceptor Bass			
1980s. Double-cut, maple/walnut laminated neck-thru.			
1980s		$950	$1,175

MODEL YEAR	FEATURES	EXC. COND. LOW	HIGH

MVP Series Bass

1984-present. Fretted version of Buzz Bass, standard or flame top, 4-, 5-, 6-, 8-string versions, MVP II is bolt-on neck version.

1980s	MVP-6	$1,300	$1,575
1984-1990s	MVP-4 flame top	$1,200	$1,475
1984-1990s	MVP-4 standard top	$1,100	$1,375
1984-1990s	MVP-5	$1,200	$1,475
1990s	MVP II	$800	$1,000

Orsini Wurlitzer 4-String Bass

Mid-1970s. Body style similar to late-'50s Gibson double-cut slab body SG Special, neck-thru, 2 pickups, natural. Sold by Boston's Wurlitzer music store chain.

1970s		$1,250	$1,575

Quilt Limited Bass

Neck-thru-body with curly maple centerstrip, quilted maple body wings, 2 Bartolini pickups, available in fretted or fretless 4- and 5-string models.

1987		$1,250	$1,550

Rapture Series Bass

1995-present. Solidbody with extra long thin bass horn and extra short treble horn, 4- or 5-string, various colors.

1995-2014	Rapture 4	$1,100	$1,400
1995-2014	Rapture 5	$1,200	$1,500

Series II Bass

1987-1992. Bolt neck, rosewood 'board, mother-of-pearl dot inlays, Bartolini pickups.

1987-1992		$775	$950

Thunderbass Series Bass

1993-present. Solidbody with extra long thin bass horn and extra short treble horn, 4-, 5- or 6-string, standard features or triple A top.

1993-1999	4, AAA top	$1,475	$1,800
1993-1999	4, Standard	$1,225	$1,475
1993-1999	5, AAA top	$1,575	$1,900
1993-1999	5, Standard	$1,325	$1,600
1993-1999	6, AAA top	$1,650	$2,000
1993-1999	6, Standard	$1,400	$1,700
2000-2014	4, AAA top	$1,475	$1,800
2000-2014	5, AAA top	$1,575	$1,900
2000-2014	6, AAA top	$1,650	$2,000

Thunderbolt Series Bass

1994-present. Similar to Thunderbass Series but with bolt necks, 4-, 5- or 6-string, standard AA or AAA maple or optional 5A or exotic wood (ET) tops.

1994-2014	Thunderbolt 5	$1,000	$1,250

Penco

Ca. 1974-1978. Generally high quality Japanese-made copies of classic American bass guitars. They also made guitars, mandolins and banjos.

Electric Bass

1974-1978	Various models	$150	$300

Premier

Ca.1938-ca.1975, 1990s-2010. Originally American-made instruments, but by the '60s imported parts were being used. 1990s instruments were Asian imports.

Bantam Bass

1950-1970. Small body, single-cut short-scale archtop electric, torch headstock inlay, sparkle 'guard, sunburst.

1950-1970		$475	$600

Electric Solidbody Bass

1960s	Various models	$325	$400

Renaissance

1978-1980. Plexiglass solidbody electric guitars and basses made in Malvern, Pennsylvania.

Plexiglas Bass

1978-1980. Plexiglas bodies and active electronics, models include the DPB bass (double-cut, 1 pickup, '78-'79), SPB (single-cut, 2 pickups, '78-'79), T-100B (Bich-style, 1 pickup, '80), S-100B (double-cut, 1 pickup, '80), and the S-200B (double-cut, 2 pickups, '80).

1978-1980		$650	$800

Rickenbacker

1931-present. Professional grade, production/custom, electric basses. They also build guitars. Rickenbacker introduced their first electric bass in '57 and has always been a strong player in the bass market.

Electric Upright Bass

1936. Cast aluminum neck and body, horseshoe pickup, extension pole.

1936		$4,000	$5,000

Model 1999 (Rose-Morris) Bass

1964-1967. Export made for English distributor Rose-Morris of London, built along the lines of the U.S. Model 4000 Bass but with small differences that are considered important in the vintage guitar market.

1964-1966		$8,500	$10,500
1967		$7,600	$9,300

Model 2030 Hamburg Bass

1984-1997. Rounded double-cut, 2 pickups, active electronics.

1984-1997		$725	$875

Model 2030GF (Glenn Frey) Bass

1992-1995. Limited Edition, double-cut, 2 humbuckers, Jetglo finish.

1992-1995		$1,500	$1,800

Model 2050 El Dorado Bass

1984-1992. Gold hardware, 2 pickups, active.

1984-1992		$1,125	$1,350

Model 2060 El Dorado Bass

1992-1997. Gold hardware, 2 pickups, active, double-bound body.

1992-1997		$1,225	$1,500

Model 3000 Bass

1975-1984. Rounded double-cut, 30" scale, 1 pickup, brown sunburst.

1975-1984		$1,325	$1,600

Model 3001 Bass

1975-1984. Same as Model 3000 but with longer 33-1/2" scale, Wine Red.

1975-1984		$1,325	$1,600

Model 3261 (Rose-Morris Slim-Line) Bass

1967. Export model made for English distributor Rose-Morris, built along the lines of a U.S. equivalent Model 4005 Bass.

1967		$6,000	$7,500

Pedulla MVP

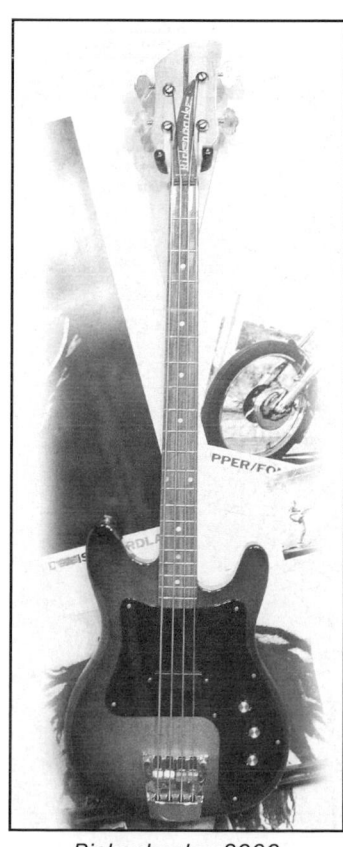

Rickenbacker 3000

Rickenbacker 4001 C64

Ron O'Keefe

Rickenbacker Model 4003

MODEL YEAR	FEATURES	EXC. COND. LOW	HIGH

Model 4000 Bass
1958-1985. Cresting wave body and headstock, 1 horseshoe pickup (changed to regular pickup in '64), neck-thru-body.

1958-1962	Plank style	$13,000	$16,500
1963-1966		$10,000	$12,500
1967-1969		$9,000	$11,200
1970-1972		$3,300	$4,000
1973-1974		$2,100	$3,000
1975-1979		$2,100	$2,600
1980-1985		$1,900	$2,400

Model 4001 Bass
1961-1986. Fancy version of 4000, 1 horseshoe magnet pickup (changed to regular pickup in '64) and 1 bar magnet pickup, triangle inlays, bound neck.

1961-1963	Fireglo	$9,800	$12,200
1963-1966	Mapleglo	$8,300	$10,600
1964-1966	Fireglo	$8,800	$11,200
1967-1969	Various colors	$7,500	$9,400
1970-1972	Various colors	$3,200	$4,100
1973	Big 6 features	$2,525	$3,125
1973	No Big 6 features	$2,025	$2,525
1974-1979	Various colors	$2,025	$2,525
1980-1986	Various colors	$1,775	$2,225

Model 4001 C64S Bass
2001-2014. Recreation of Paul McCartney's 4001 featuring changes he made like a reshaped body and zero-fret 'board.

2001-2014		$2,050	$2,550

Model 4001 CS Bass
1991-1997. Chris Squire signature model.

1991-1997	With certificate	$2,400	$3,000

Model 4001 FL Bass
1968-1986. Fretless version of 4001 Bass, special order in '60s, various colors.

1968-1986		$2,000	$2,500

Model 4001 V63 Bass
1984-2000. Vintage '63 reissue of Model 4001S, horseshoe-magnet pickup, Mapleglo.

1984-2000	Figured top	$3,200	$4,000
1984-2000	Plain top	$2,500	$3,100

Model 4001S Bass
1964-1985. Same as Model 4000, but with 2 pickups, export model.

1980-1985		$1,550	$1,950

Model 4002 Bass
1967-1985. Cresting wave body and headstock, 2 humbuckers, black 'guard, checkerboard binding.

1980-1985		$3,200	$4,000

Model 4003 Bass
1979-present. Similar to Model 4001, split 'guard, deluxe features.

1979-1989		$1,825	$2,300
1990-2014		$1,525	$1,925

Model 4003 FL Bass
1979-2014. Fretless version.

1979-2014		$1,500	$1,850

Model 4003 Shadow Bass
1986. About 60 made for Guitar Center, all black 'board, inlays and hardware, Jetglo finish.

1986		$2,700	$3,400

Model 4003S Bass
1986-2003. Standard feature version of 4003, 4 strings.

1986-2003		$1,525	$1,900

Model 4003S Redneck Bass
1988. Red body, 'board and headstock, black hardware.

1988		$2,600	$3,300

Model 4003S Tuxedo Bass
1987. White body with black 'guard and hardware. 100 made.

1987		$2,600	$3,300

Model 4003S/5 Bass
1986-2003. Model 4003S with 5 strings.

1986-1999		$1,625	$2,000
2000-2003		$1,525	$1,875

Model 4003S/8 Bass
1986-2003. Model 4003S with 8 strings.

1986-1989		$2,750	$3,450
1990-1999		$2,650	$3,350
2000-2003		$2,550	$3,250

Model 4003S/SPC Blackstar Bass
1989. Black version, black finish, 'board, knobs, and hardware. Also offered as 5-string.

1989		$2,200	$2,700

Model 4004C Cheyenne/4004Cii Cheyenne II Bass
1993-present. Cresting wave, maple neck-thru-body with walnut body and head wings, gold hardware, dot inlay. Replaced by maple top 4004Cii Cheyenne II in '00.

1993-1999	Cheyenne	$1,325	$1,650
2000-2014	Cheyenne II	$1,350	$1,650

Model 4004L Laredo Bass
1993-present. Like Cheyenne but without walnut wings.

1993-2014		$1,200	$1,475

Model 4005 Bass
1965-1984. New style double-cut semi-hollowbody, 2 pickups, R tailpiece, cresting wave headstock.

1965-1966	Fireglo	$10,500	$13,000
1965-1966	Jetglo	$8,900	$11,200
1965-1966	Mapleglo	$10,000	$12,500
1967-1969	Fireglo	$9,500	$12,000
1967-1969	Jetglo	$7,900	$10,100
1967-1969	Mapleglo	$8,900	$11,200
1970-1979	Various colors	$6,000	$7,500
1980-1984	Various colors	$5,500	$6,900

Model 4005 L (Lightshow) Bass
1970-1975. Model 4005 with translucent top with lights in body that lit up when played, needed external transformer.

1970-1971	1st edition	$9,100	$11,400
1972-1975	2nd edition	$11,000	$13,600

Model 4005 WB Bass
1966-1983. Old style Model 4005 with white-bound body, Fireglo.

1966		$10,800	$13,400
1967-1969		$9,800	$12,200
1970-1979		$6,000	$7,500
1980-1983		$5,400	$6,800

The *Vintage Guitar Price Guide* shows low to high values for items in all-original excellent condition, and, where applicable, with original case or cover.

MODEL YEAR	FEATURES	EXC. COND. LOW	HIGH

Model 4005-6 Bass
1965-1977. Model 4005 with 6 strings.

1965-1969		$11,200	$14,000
1970-1977		$7,000	$8,700

Model 4005-8 Bass
Late-1960s. Eight-string Model 4005, Fireglo or Mapleglo.

1968-1969		$11,000	$14,000

Model 4008 Bass
1975-1983. Eight-string, cresting wave body and headstock.

1975-1979		$2,000	$2,500
1980-1983		$1,800	$2,300

Model 4080 Doubleneck Bass
1975-1992. Bolt-on 6- and 4-string necks, Jetglo or Mapleglo.

1975-1979		$5,800	$7,200
1980-1992		$5,300	$6,500

Ritter Royal Instruments
Production/custom, solidbody basses built by luthier Jens Ritter in Wachenheim, Germany.

Rob Allen
1997-present. Professional grade, production/custom, lightweight basses made by luthier Robert Allen in Santa Barbara, California.

Robin
1982-2010. Founded by David Wintz and located in Houston, Texas, Robin built basses until 1997. Most basses were Japanese-made until '87; American production began in '88. They also built guitars and also made Metropolitan ('96-'08) and Alamo ('00-'08) brand guitars.

Freedom Bass I
1984-1986. Offset double-cut, active treble and bass EQ controls, 1 pickup.

1984-1986		$525	$650

Freedom Bass I Passive
1986-1989. Non-active version of Freedom Bass, 1 humbucker. Passive dropped from name in '87.

1986-1989		$525	$650

Medley Bass
1984-1997. Offset deep cutaways, 2 pickups, reverse headstock until '89, then split headstock, back to reverse by '94. Japanese-made until '87, U.S. after.

1984-1987	Japan	$400	$500
1988-1997	USA	$650	$800

Ranger Bass
1984-1997. Vintage style body, dot markers, medium scale and 1 pickup from '84 to '88 and long scale with P-style and J-style pickup configuration from '89 to '97.

1984-1987	Japan	$400	$500
1988-1997	USA	$650	$800

Rock Bass
2002-present. Chinese-made, intermediate and professional grade, production, bolt neck solidbody basses from the makers of Warwick basses.

MODEL YEAR	FEATURES	EXC. COND. LOW	HIGH

Roland
Best known for keyboards, effects, and amps, Roland offered synthesizer-based guitars and basses from 1977 to '86.

GR-33B (G-88) Bass Guitar Synthesizer
Early-mid 1980s. Solidbody bass with synthesizer in the guitar case, G-88 deluxe bass.

1983-1985		$750	$935

Roman & Blake Basses
1977-2003. Professional grade, production/custom, solidbody bass guitars made by Ed Roman Guitars.

Roman USA Basses
Professional grade, production/custom, solidbody basses made by Ed Roman Guitars starting in 2000.

Roscoe Guitars
Early 1980s-present. Luthier Keith Roscoe builds his production/custom, professional and premium grade, solidbody electric basses in Greensboro, North Carolina.

S.D. Curlee
1975-1982. S.D. Curlee guitars and basses were made in Illinois; S.D. Curlee International instruments were made in Japan.

Electric Solidbody Bass

1970s	Various models	$350	$435

Serenader
Mainly known for lap steels this Seattle, Washington brand also built a solidbody bass.

Silvertone
1941-ca.1970, present. Brand used by Sears. Instruments were U.S.-made and imported. Currently, Samick offers a line of acoustic and electric guitars, basses and amps under the Silvertone name.

Model 1376L/1373L 6-String Bass
1956-1959. 2 pickups, 6-string.

1956-1959		$1,500	$1,850

Model 1442 Standard Bass
1966-1968. Solidbody 30" standard size, 1 pickup, dot markers, shaded brown.

1966-1968		$575	$725

Model 1443 Extra Long Bass
1966-1968. Solidbody 34" size, 2 pickups, dot markers, red sunburst.

1966-1968		$675	$850

Model 1444 Electric Bass
1959-1965. Bass version of 6-string electric guitar Model 1415 (bronze) and 1416 (black), 4-on-a-side replaces the prior year coke-bottle headstock, 1 pickup on single-cut U-1 style body, black finish.

1959-1965		$650	$800

Simmons
2002-present. Luthier David L. Simmons builds his professional grade, production/custom, 4- and 5-string basses in Hendersonville, North Carolina.

2008 Rickenbacker Model 4004L Laredo
Ron O'Keefe

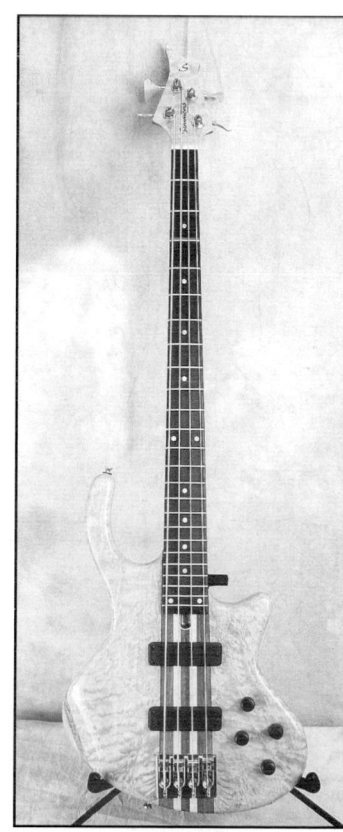

Simmons

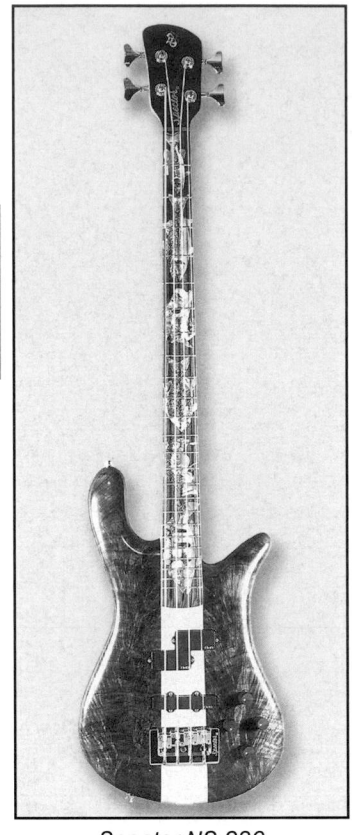

Spector NS-230

Standel 400

MODEL YEAR	FEATURES	EXC. COND. LOW	HIGH

Sinister

2003. A short run of intermediate grade, solid-body basses built for Sinister Guitars by luthier Jon Kammerer.

Smith

1978-present. Professional and premium grade, production/custom, electric basses built by luthier Ken Smith in Perkasie, Pennsylvania. Earlier models had Ken Smith on the headstock, recent models have a large S logo. He also designs the imported KSD line of basses.

American-Made Bass

1978-2014	Various models	$2,200	$2,700

Custom VI Series Bass

1985-2010. Six strings, double-cut, neck-thru-body.

1985-2010		$2,900	$3,600

Imported Bass

1990s	Various models	$525	$650

Soundgear by Ibanez

1987-present. SDGR Soundgear by Ibanez headstock logo, intermediate grade, production, solidbody electric basses, made in Japan, Korea and Indonesia.

Spector/Stuart Spector Design

1975-1990 (Spector), 1991-1998 (SSD), 1998-present (Spector SSD). Intermediate, professional, and premium grade, production/custom, basses made in the U.S., the Czech Republic, Korea, and China. Stuart Spector's first bass was the NS and the company quickly grew to the point where Kramer acquired it in '85. After Kramer went out of business in '90, Spector started building basses with the SSD logo (Stuart Spector Design). In '98 he recovered the Spector trademark.

Bob Series Bass

1996-1999. US-made, offset deep double-cut swamp ash or alder body, bolt neck, various colors, SSD logo on headstock, 4-string (Bob 4) or 5 (Bob 5).

1996-1999	Bob 4	$750	$925
1996-1999	Bob 5	$850	$1,050

NS Series Bass

1979-2010. US-made, offset double-cut solidbody (X body optional), neck-thru, 1 pickup (NS-1, made into '80s) or 2 (NS-2).

1979-1984	NS-1	$1,300	$1,600
1979-1984	NS-2	$1,400	$1,750
1985-1990	NS-1, NS-2, Kramer era	$1,000	$1,250
1990-2010	NS-1, NS-2, SSD era	$1,100	$1,350
2000-2009	NS, USA	$1,025	$1,275
2000-2010	Import	$175	$525
2010	NS, USA	$1,250	$1,275

Squier

See models listed under Squier in Fender section.

Standel

1952-1974, 1997-present. Amp builder Bob Crooks offered instruments under his Standel brand name three different times during the '60s. See Guitar section for production details. See Amp section for more company information.

Custom Deluxe Solidbody 401 Bass

1967-1968. Custom with higher appointments, various colors.

1967-1968		$750	$925

Custom Deluxe Thinbody 402 Bass

1967-1968. Custom with higher appointments, various colors.

1967-1968		$750	$925

Custom Solidbody 501 Bass

1967-1968. Solidbody, 1 pickup, various colors.

1967-1968		$550	$675

Custom Thinbody 502 Bass

1967-1968. Thin solidbody, 2 pickups, various colors.

1967-1968		$600	$750

Steinberger

1979-present. Steinberger offers budget and intermediate grade, production, electric basses. They also offer guitars.

H Series

1980-1982. Reinforced molded plastic wedge-shaped body, headless neck, 1 (H1) or 2 (H2) high impedence pickups, black, red or white.

1980-1982	H1, black	$2,000	$2,500
1980-1982	H1, red or white	$2,100	$2,600
1980-1982	H2, black	$2,000	$2,500
1980-1982	H2, red or white	$2,100	$2,600

L Series

1980-1984. Reinforced molded plastic wedge-shaped body, headless neck, 1 (L1) or 2 (L2) low impedance active pickups, black, red or white. Evolved into XL series.

1980-1984	L1, black	$1,650	$2,050
1980-1984	L1, black, fretless	$1,550	$1,950
1980-1984	L1, red or white	$2,400	$3,000
1980-1984	L2, black	$1,650	$2,050
1980-1984	L2, black, fretless	$1,550	$1,950
1980-1984	L2, red or white	$2,400	$3,000

Q-4 Bass

1990-1991. Composite neck, Double Bass system, headless with traditional-style maple body, low-impedance pickups.

1990-1991		$900	$1,125

Q-5 Bass

1990-1991. Five-string version of Q Bass.

1990-1991		$950	$1,200

XL-2 Bass

1984-1993. Rectangular composite body, 4-string, headless, 2 pickups.

1984-1989	Black	$1,750	$2,150
1990-1993	Red	$1,375	$1,750

XL-2GR Bass

1985-1990. Headless, Roland GR synthesizer controller.

1985-1990		$1,550	$1,950

The *Vintage Guitar Price Guide* shows low to high values for items in all-original excellent condition, and, where applicable, with original case or cover.

MODEL YEAR	FEATURES	EXC. COND. LOW	HIGH

XM-2 Bass
1986-1992. Headless, double-cut maple body, 4-string, 2 low-impedance pickups, optional fretted, lined fretless or unlined fretless, black, red or white.

1986-1992		$1,375	$1,750

XT-2/XZ-2 Spirit Bass
1995-present. Headless, rectangular XL body, import.

1995-2014		$255	$325

Stewart Basses
2000-ca. 2009. Luthier Fred Stewart built his premium grade, custom/production, solidbody basses in Charlton, Maryland. He has also built guitars starting in '94.

Stinger
See Martin listing.

Supro
1935-1968, 2004-present. Supro was a budget brand for the National Dobro Company. Supro offered only two bass models in the '60s. Brand name was revived in '04.

Pocket Bass
1960-1968. Double-cut, neck pickup and bridge mounted pickup, semi-hollow, short-scale, black.

1960-1968		$700	$875

Taurus Bass
1967-1968. Asymmetrical double-cut, neck pickup and bridge mounted pickup.

1967-1968		$475	$600

SX
See listing for Essex.

Szlag
2000-present. Custom carved, professional and premium grade, basses, built by luthier John J. Slog in Bethlehem, Pennsylvania. He also builds guitars.

Tacoma
1995-2009. Professional grade, production, acoustic basses produced in Tacoma, Washington. They also built acoustic guitars and mandolins.

Thunderchief Series Bass
1998-2009. 17 3/4 flat-top, solid spruce top, solid mahogany back, laminated mahogany sides, rounded cutaway, bolt-on neck, dot markers, natural satin finish.

1998-2009	Various models	$800	$1,000

Taylor
1974-present. Professional and premium grade, production, acoustic basses built in El Cajon, California. They presently build guitars.

AB1 Bass
1996-2003. Acoustic/electric, sitka spruce top, imbuia walnut back and sides, designed for 'loose' woody sound.

1996-2003		$1,275	$1,575

AB2 Bass
1996-2003. Acoustic/electric, all imbuia walnut body.

1996-2003		$1,675	$2,100

AB3 Bass
1998-2003. Acoustic/electric, sitka spruce top, maple back and sides.

1998-2003		$1,675	$2,100

Teisco
1946-1974, 1994-present. The Japanese Teisco line started offering basses in '60.

Electric Bass
1968-1969. EB-100 (1 pickup, white 'guard), EB-200 (solidbody), EB-200B (semi-hollowbody) and Violin bass.

1968-1969	EB-100	$100	$150
1968-1969	EB-200	$500	$625
1968-1969	EB-200 B	$500	$625
1968-1969	Violin	$500	$625

Tele-Star
1965-ca.1972. Guitars and basses imported from Japan by Tele-Star Musical Instrument Corporation of New York. Primarily made by Kawai, many inspired by Burns designs, some in cool sparkle finishes.

Electric Solidbody Bass

1960s	Various models	$100	$300

Tobias
1977-present. Founded by Mike Tobias in Orlando, Florida. Moved to San Francisco for '80-'81, then to Costa Mesa, eventually ending up in Hollywood. In '90, he sold the company to Gibson which moved it to Burbank. The first Tobias made under Gibson ownership was serial number 1094. The instruments continued to be made by the pre-Gibson crew until '92, when the company was moved to Nashville. The last LA Tobias/Gibson serial number is 2044. Mike left the company in '92 and started a new business in '94 called MTD where he continues to make electric and acoustic basses. In '99, production of Tobias basses was moved overseas. In late '03, Gibson started again offering U.S.-made Tobias instruments; they are made in Conway, Arkansas, in the former Baldwin grand piano facility. Currently Tobias offers imported and U.S.-made, intermediate and professional grade, production, acoustic and electric basses.

Basic Bass
1984-1999. 30", 32", or 34" scale, neck-thru-body in alder, koa or walnut, 5-piece laminated neck.

1984-1999	Basic B-4	$1,800	$2,250
1984-1999	Basic B-5	$1,900	$2,350

Classic C-4 Bass
1978-1999. One or 2 pickups, active or passive electronics, 2-octave rosewood 'board, available in short-, medium-, and long-scale models.

1978-1999		$2,200	$2,750

Classic C-5 Bass
1985-1999. 30", 32" or 34" scale, alder, koa or walnut body, bookmatched top, ebony or phenolic 'board, hardwood neck.

1985-1999		$2,300	$2,850

Steinberger XM-2

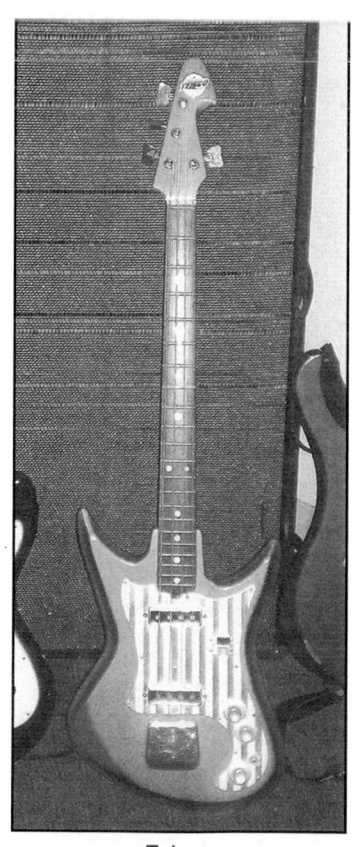

Teisco
Sean Sweeney

Tobias Killer B

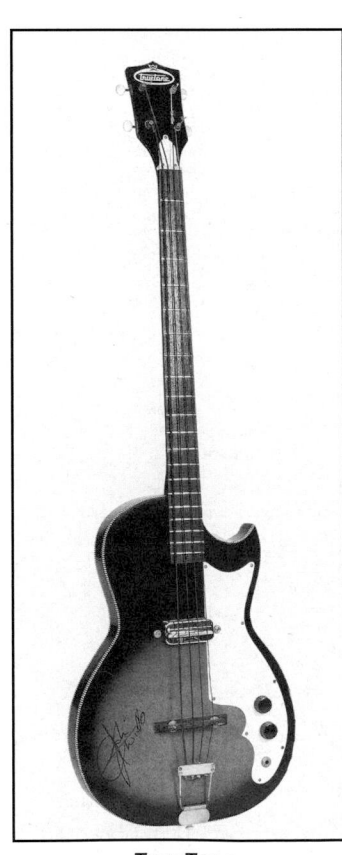

True Tone

MODEL		EXC. COND.	
YEAR	FEATURES	LOW	HIGH

Classic C-6 Bass
Ca. 1986-1999. Flamed maple and padauk neck, alder body, padauk top, ebony 'board, active electronics, 32" or 34" scale.

| 1986-1999 | | $2,400 | $3,000 |

Growler GR-5 Bass
1996-1999. 5-string, offset double-cut, bolt neck, various colors.

| 1996-1999 | | $650 | $825 |

Growler Limited Bass
2009. Natural finish swamp ash body, set-neck.

| 2009 | | $900 | $1,125 |

Killer Bee Bass
1991-1999. Offset double-cut, swamp ash or lacewood body, various colors.

1991-1999	KB-4	$1,025	$1,325
1991-1999	KB-5	$1,125	$1,425
1991-1999	KB-6	$1,225	$1,550

Model T Bass
1989-1991. Line of 4- and 5-string basses, 3-piece maple neck-thru-body, maple body halves, active treble and bass controls. Fretless available.

| 1989-1991 | | $1,100 | $1,400 |

Renegade Bass
1998-2001. Offset double-cut, 1 single-coil and 1 humbucker.

| 1998-2001 | | $1,200 | $1,500 |

Signature S-4 Bass
1978-1999. Available in 4-, 5-, and 6-string models, chrome-plated milled brass bridge.

| 1978-1990 | Tobias-Burbank | $2,800 | $3,500 |
| 1990-1992 | Gibson-Burbank | $2,200 | $2,750 |

Standard ST-4 Bass
1992-1995. Japanese-made, 5-piece maple neck-thru, swamp ash body wings.

| 1992-1995 | | $1,025 | $1,300 |

Toby Deluxe TD-4 Bass
1994-1996. Offset double-cut, bolt neck.

| 1994-1996 | | $425 | $525 |

Toby Deluxe TD-5 Bass
1994-1996. 5-string version.

| 1994-1996 | | $475 | $600 |

Toby Pro 5 Bass
1994-1996. Solidbody 5-string, Toby Pro logo on truss rod cover, neck-thru body.

| 1994-1996 | | $400 | $500 |

Toby Pro 6 Bass
1994-1996. Solidbody 6-string, Toby Pro logo on truss rod cover, neck-thru body.

| 1994-1996 | | $475 | $600 |

Tokai
1947-present. Tokai started making guitars and basses around '70 and by the end of that decade they were being imported into the U.S. Today Tokai offers electrics, acoustics, and electric basses made in Japan and Korea.

Vintage Bass Copies
1970s-1980s. Tokai offered near copies of classic U.S. basses.

| 1970s-80s | | $425 | $800 |

MODEL		EXC. COND.	
YEAR	FEATURES	LOW	HIGH

Tonemaster
1960s. Guitars and basses, imported from Italy, with typical '60s Italian sparkle plastic finish and push-button controls, bolt-on neck.

Electric Bass
| 1960s | Sparkle finish | $550 | $700 |

Traben
2004-present. Intermediate grade, production, solidbody basses imported by Elite Music Brands of Clearwater, Florida.

Travis Bean
1974-1979, 1999. The unique Travis Bean line included a couple of bass models. Travis Bean announced some new instruments in '99, but general production was not resumed.

TB-2000 Bass
1974-1979. Aluminum neck, T-slotted headstock, longer horned, double-cut body, 2 pickups, 4 controls, dot markers, various colors.

| 1974-1979 | | $2,900 | $3,600 |

TB-4000 (Wedge Vee) Bass
1974-1979. Bass version of Bean's Wedge guitar, few made.

| 1974-1979 | | $3,800 | $4,800 |

True Tone
1960s. Western Auto retailed this line of basses, guitars and amps which were manufactured by Chicago builders like Kay. The brand was most likely gone by '68.

Electric Bass
| 1960s | | $225 | $350 |

Univox
1964-1978. Univox started out as an amp line and added guitars and basses around '69. Guitars were imported from Japan by the Merson Musical Supply Company, later Unicord, Westbury, New York. Generally mid-level copies of American designs.

Badazz Bass
1971-ca. 1975. Based on the Guild S-100.

| 1971-1977 | | $400 | $500 |

Bicentennial Bass
1976. Carved eagle in body, matches Bicentennial guitar (see that listing), brown stain, maple 'board.

| 1976 | | $775 | $975 |

Hi Flier Bass
1969-1977. Mosrite Ventures Bass copy, 2 pickups, rosewood 'board.

| 1969-1977 | | $650 | $800 |

'Lectra (Model 1970F) Bass
1969-ca. 1973. Violin bass, walnut.

| 1969-1973 | | $500 | $700 |

Model 3340 Semi-Hollow Bass
1970-1971. Copy of Gibson EB-0 semi-hollow bass.

| 1970-1971 | | $500 | $700 |

Precisely Bass
1971-ca. 1975. Copy of Fender P-Bass.

| 1971-1975 | | $500 | $650 |

MODEL YEAR	FEATURES	EXC. COND. LOW	HIGH

Stereo Bass

1976-1977. Rickenbacker 4001 Bass copy, model U1975B.

| 1976-1977 | | $600 | $775 |

Thin Line Bass

| 1968 | | $500 | $700 |

Ventura

1970s. Import classic bass copies distributed by C. Bruno (Kaman). They also had guitars.

Vintage Electric Bass

| 1970s | Copy models | $225 | $550 |

VibraWood

2012-present. Luthier John J. Slog builds professional and premium grade, custom, vintage-style basses in Bethlehem, Pennsylvania. He also builds guitars.

Vox

1954-present. Guitars and basses bearing the Vox name were offered from 1961-'69 (made in England, Italy), '82-'85 (Japan), '85-'88 (Korea), '98-2001 (U.S.), with a limited edition teardrop bass offered in late '07. Special thanks to Jim Rhoads of Rhoads Music in Elizabethtown, Pennsylvania, for help on production years of these models.

Apollo IV Bass

1967-1969. Single-cut hollowbody, bolt maple neck, 1 pickup, on-board fuzz, booster, sunburst.

| 1967-1969 | | $625 | $775 |

Astro IV Bass

1967-1969. Violin-copy bass, 2 pickups.

| 1967-1969 | | $650 | $825 |

Bassmaster Bass

1961-1965. Offset double-cut, 2 pickups, 2 knobs.

| 1961-1965 | | $650 | $825 |

Clubman Bass

1961-1966. Double-cut 2-pickup solidbody, red.

| 1961-1966 | | $500 | $625 |

Constellation IV Bass

1967-1968. Teardrop-shaped body, 2 pickups, 1 f-hole, 1 set of controls, treble, bass and distortion boosters.

| 1967-1968 | | $1,075 | $1,325 |

Cougar Bass

1963-1967. Double-cut semi-hollow body, 2 f-holes, 2 pickups, 2 sets of controls, sunburst.

| 1963-1967 | | $1,075 | $1,325 |

Delta IV Bass

1967-1968. Five-sided body, 2 pickups, 1 volume and 2 tone controls, distortion, treble and bass boosters.

| 1967-1968 | | $1,075 | $1,325 |

Guitar-Organ Bass

1966. The 4-string bass version of the Guitar-Organ, Phantom-style body, white.

| 1966 | | $1,175 | $1,475 |

Mark IV Bass

1963-1969. Teardrop-shaped body, 2 pickups, 1 set of controls, sunburst.

| 1963-1965 | England, white | $2,300 | $2,900 |
| 1965-1969 | Italy, sunburst | $1,500 | $1,850 |

MODEL YEAR	FEATURES	EXC. COND. LOW	HIGH

Panther Bass

1967-1968. Double-cut solidbody, 1 slanted pickup, rosewood 'board, sunburst.

| 1967-1968 | | $425 | $550 |

Phantom IV Bass

1963-1969. Five-sided body, 2 pickups, 1 set of controls.

| 1963-1964 | England | $2,050 | $2,550 |
| 1965-1969 | Italy | $1,500 | $1,850 |

Saturn IV Bass

1967-1968. Single-cut, 2 f-holes, 1 set of controls, 1 pickup.

| 1967-1968 | | $625 | $775 |

Sidewinder IV Bass (V272)

1967-1968. Double-cut semi-hollow body, 2 f-holes, 2 pickups, 1 set of controls, treble, bass, and distortion boosters.

| 1967-1968 | | $1,100 | $1,400 |

Stinger Bass

1968. Teardrop-shaped, boat oar headstock.

| 1968 | | $750 | $925 |

Violin Bass

1966. Electro-acoustic bass with violin shaped body, 2 extended range pickups, sunburst.

| 1966 | | $775 | $950 |

Wyman Bass

1966. Teardrop-shaped body, 2 pickups, 1 f-hole, 1 set of controls, sunburst.

| 1966 | | $1,300 | $1,625 |

Wal

1976-present. Founded in England by luthier Ian Waller and his partner Peter Stevens, forming the company under the name Electric Wood in '78. Waller died in '88, Stevens enlists help of luthier Paul Herman, and in 2000s Stevens retires and Herman takes over. In the early years, the Mark designation was used generically. Newer contemporary models are named Mk1, Mk2 and Mk3. Prices shown will increase 5% with LED option, or 10% with rare top, but no value difference between fretted and fretless. MIDI electronics does not increase the value.

Custom (IV) Bass

1980s-1990s. 4-string, active, no guard, generally highly figured front and back.

1980	Mark I	$3,200	$4,000
1985	Mark II	$3,700	$4,500
1994	Mark III	$3,700	$4,500

Custom (V) Bass

1980s-1990s. 5-string, active, no guard, generally highly figured front and back.

| 1985 | Mark II | $4,500 | $5,500 |
| 1994 | Mark III | $4,500 | $5,500 |

Custom (VI) Bass

1990s. 6-string, active, no guard, generally highly figured front and back.

| 1994 | Mark III | $4,700 | $5,800 |

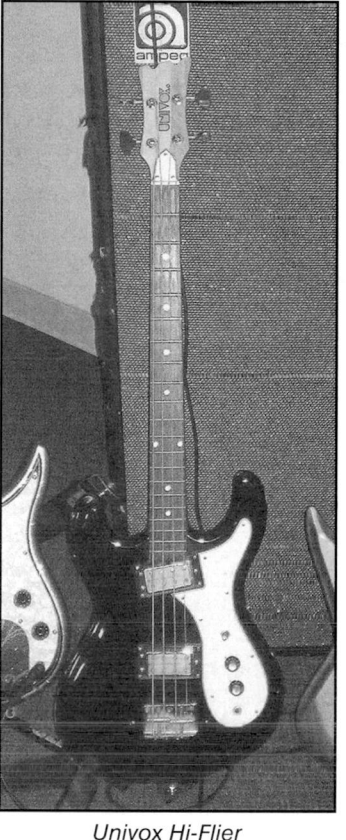

Univox Hi-Flier
Sean Sweeney

Vox Sidewinder IV

BASSES

BASSES

Wal Pro (Mark I)

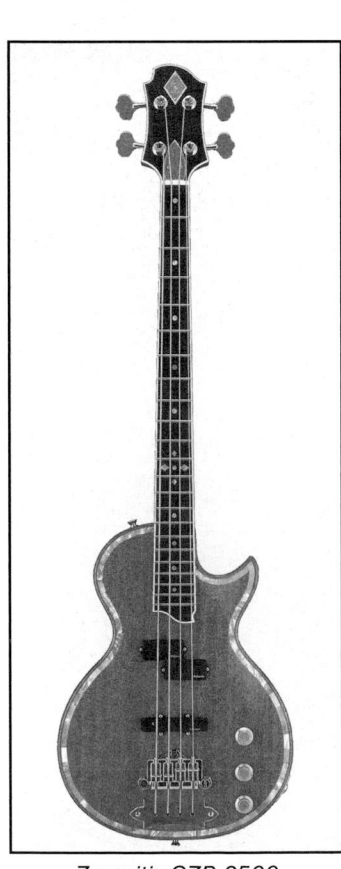

Zemaitis GZB-2500

MODEL YEAR	FEATURES	EXC. COND. LOW	HIGH

JG Bass
1976-1978. 4-string, passive with either tooled leather (34 made), or leather guard.

1976-1978	Non-tooled	$4,300	$5,300
1976-1978	Tooled	$5,300	$6,400

Pro (Mark I) Bass
1978. Passive, black guard.

1978		$2,000	$2,500

Wandre (Davoli)
Ca. 1956/57-1969. Italian-made guitars and basses.

Electric Bass

1956-1969	Common models	$2,000	$3,500
1956-1969	Rare models	$3,500	$10,000

Warwick
1982-present. Professional and premium grade, production/custom, electric and acoustic basses made in Markneukirchen, Germany; founded by Hans Peter Wilfer, whose father started Framus guitars. They also build amps.

Welson
1960s. Italian-made copy model guitars and basses.

Electric Bass

1960s	Copy models	$250	$600

Wurlitzer
Large music retailer Wurlitzer marketed a line of American-made guitars in the 1920s. They also offered American- and foreign-made guitars starting in '65. In '67, Wurlitzer switched to Italian-made Welson guitars.

Hollowbody Electric Bass
1960s. Italian-made.

1967		$450	$600

Yamaha
1946-present. Budget, intermediate, professional and premium grade, production, electric basses. They also build guitars. Yamaha began producing solidbody instruments in '66.

Electric Bass
1960-present. Various models.

1960-2014		$100	$1,200

Zemaitis
1960-1999, 2004-present. Tony Zemaitis began selling his guitars in '60 and he retired in '99. He emphasized simple lightweight construction and his instruments are known for hand engraved metal fronts. Each hand-built custom guitar or bass was a unique instrument. Approximately 10 custom guitars were built each year. In '04, Japan's Kanda Shokai, with the endorsement of Tony Zemaitis, Jr., started building the guitars again.

Electric Bass

1970s	Heart hole (4 made)	$16,000	$20,000
1980s	1/2 metal & spruce	$10,000	$12,500
1980s	Metal-front 4-string	$12,000	$15,000

Zen-On
1946-ca.1968. Japanese-made. By '67 using the Morales brandname. Not heavily imported into the U.S., if at all (see Morales).

Electric Solidbody Bass

1950s	Various models	$150	$300

Zim-Gar
1960s. Japanese guitars and basses imported by Gar-Zim Musical Instrument Corporation of Brooklyn, New York.

Electric Solidbody Bass

1960s	Various models	$150	$300

Zon
1981-present. Luthier Joe Zon builds his professional and premium grade, production/custom, solidbody basses in Redwood City, California. Zon started the brand in Buffalo, New York and relocated to Redwood City in '87. He has also built guitars.

Legacy Elite Bass
1989-present. 34" scale carbon-fiber neck, Bartolini pickups, ZP-2 active electronics.

1989-2014	V, 5-string	$1,000	$1,250
1989-2014	VI, 6-string	$1,100	$1,350

Scepter Bass
1984-1993. Offset body shape, 24 frets, 1 pickup, tremolo.

1984-1993		$900	$1,125

Sonus Custom Bass
1990s-present. Offset swamp ash body, 2 pickups.

1990s-2014		$1,450	$1,800

Zorko
Late-1950s-early-1962. Original maker of the Ampeg Baby Bass (see that listing), sold to Ampeg in 1962, Zorko logo on scroll.

Baby Bass

1950s-1962		$2,100	$2,600

AMPS

Peavey Bandit 65. Photo: VG Archive.

3 Monkeys Sock Monkey

3rd Power British Dream 112

65amps London Pro

3 Monkeys Amps

2007-present. Intermediate and professional grade, production/custom, amps and cabinets built by Greg Howard in Raleigh, North Carolina.

3rd Power

Mid-2009-present. Professional grade, production/custom, guitar amps built in Franklin, Tennessee by Jamie Scott.

65amps

2004-present. Founded by Peter Stroud and Dan Boul, 65amps builds tube guitar head and combo amps and speaker cabs in Valley Village, California.

Ace Tone

Late-1960-1970s. Made by Sakata Shokai Limited of Osaka, Japan, early importer of amps and effects pedals. Later became Roland/Boss.

B-9 Amp
Late-1960s-early-1970s. Solid-state bass amp head.

MODEL YEAR	FEATURES	EXC. COND. LOW	HIGH
1960s-70s		$120	$155

Mighty-5 Amp
Late-1960s-early-1970s. Tubes, 50-watt head.

1960s-70s		$90	$115

Solid A-5 Amp
Late-1960s-early-1970s. Solidstate 2x12 combo with verticle cab, reverb and tremolo, black tolex, silver grille.

1960s-70s		$140	$180

Acoustic

Ca.1965-ca.1987, 2001-2005, 2008-present. The Acoustic Control Corp., of Los Angeles, California, was mostly known for solidstate amplifiers. Heads and cabinets were sold separately with their own model numbers, but were also combined (amp sets) and marketed under a different model number (for example, the 153 amp set was the 150b head with a 2x15" cabinet). The brand was revived by Samick in '01 for a line of amps. In '08 brand back again on line of amps sold through Guitar Center and Musician's Friend.

114 Amp
Ca.1977-mid-1980s. Solidstate, 50 watts, 2x10", reverb, master volume.

1977-1984		$200	$260

115 Amp
1977-1978. Solidstate, 1x12", 50 watts, reverb, master volume.

1977-1978		$200	$260

116 Bass Amp
1978-mid-1980s. Solidstate, 75 watts, 1x15", power boost switch.

1978-1984		$200	$260

120 Amp Head
1977-mid-1980s. Solidstate head, 125 watts.

1977-1984		$160	$210

123 Amp
1977-1984. 1x12" combo.

1977-1984		$160	$210

124 Amp
1977-mid-1980s. Solidstate, 4x10", 5-band EQ, 100 watts, master volume.

1977-1984		$225	$295

125 Amp
1977-mid-1980s. Solidstate, 2x12", 5-band EQ, 100 watts, master volume.

1977-1984		$225	$295

126 Bass Amp
1977-mid-1980s. Solidstate, 100 watts, 1x15", 5-band EQ.

1977-1984		$225	$295

134 Amp
1972-1976. Solidstate, 100-125 watts, 4x10" combo.

1972-1976		$225	$295

135 Amp
1972-1976. Solidstate, 125 watts, 2x12" combo, reverb, tremolo.

1972-1976		$225	$295

136 Amp
1972-1976. Solidstate, 125 watts, 1x15" combo.

1972-1976		$225	$295

140 Bass Amp Head
1972-1976. Solidstate, 125 watts, 2 channels.

1972-1976		$160	$210

150 Amp Head
1960s-1976. Popular selling model, generally many available in the used market. Solidstate, 110 watts until '72, 125 watts after.

1968-1976		$160	$210

150b Bass Amp Head
1960s-1971. Bass amp version of 150 head.

1968-1971		$160	$210

153 Bass Amp Set
1960s-1971. 150b head (bass version of 150) with 2x15" 466 cabinet, 110 watts.

1968-1971		$350	$450

165 Amp
1979-mid-1980s. All tube combo, switchable to 60 or 100 watts, brown tolex.

1979-1984		$270	$350

220 Bass Amp Head
1977-1980s. Solidstate, 5-band EQ, either 125 or 160 watts, later models 170 or 200 watts, black tolex.

1977-1984		$200	$260

230 Amp Head
1977-1980s. Solidstate head, 125/160 watts, 5-band EQ.

1977-1984		$200	$260

260 Amp Head
1960s-1971. Solidstate, 275 watt, stereo/mono.

1968-1971		$325	$425

270 Amp Head
1970s. 400 watts.

1970s		$325	$425

320 Bass Amp Head
1977-1980s. Solidstate, 5-band EQ, 160/300 watts, 2 switchable channels, black tolex.

1977-1984		$350	$450

MODEL YEAR	FEATURES	EXC. COND. LOW	HIGH

360 Bass Amp Head
1960s-1971. One of Acoustic's most popular models, 200 watts. By '72, the 360 is listed as a "preamp only."

1968-1971		$540	$700

370 Bass Amp Head
1972-1977. Solidstate bass head, 365 watts early on, 275 later, Jaco Pastorius associated.

1972-1977	275 or 365 watt	$540	$700

402 Cabinet
1977-1980s. 2x15" bass cab, black tolex, black grille.

1977-1984		$185	$240

404 Cabinet
1970s. 6x10", Jaco Pastorius associated.

1970s		$375	$485

450 Amp Head
1974-1976. 170 watts, 5-band EQ, normal and bright inputs.

1974-1976		$270	$350

455 Amp Set
1974-1977. 170 watt 450 head with 4x12" cabinet, black.

1974-1977		$525	$675

470 Amp Head
1974-1977. 170 watt, dual channel.

1974-1977		$270	$350

AG15 Amp
2008-present. Small combo, 15 watts.

2008-2014		$45	$60

B100 Amp (MK II)
2008-present. Classic style bass combo, 100 watts, 1x15.

2008-2014		$135	$175

B200 Amp (MK II)
2009-present. Bass combo, 200 watts, 1x15.

2009-2014		$215	$275

G20-110 Amp
1981-mid-1980s. Solidstate, 20 watts, 1x10". The G series was a lower-priced combo line.

1981-1985		$110	$145

G20-120 Amp
1981-mid-1980s. Solidstate, 20 watts, 1x12".

1981-1985		$110	$145

G60-112 Amp
1981-mid-1980s. Solidstate, 60 watts, 1x12".

1981-1985		$135	$175

G60-212 Amp
1981-mid-1980s. Solidstate, 60 watts, 2x12".

1981-1985		$160	$210

G60T-112 Amp
1981-1987. Tube, 60 watts, 1x12".

1981-1985		$270	$350

Tube 60 Amp
1986-1987. Combo, 60 watts, 1x12", spring reverb, bright switch, master volume control, effects loop.

1986-1987		$270	$350

ADA
1977-2002. ADA (Analog/Digital Associates) was located in Berkeley, California, and introduced its Flanger and Final Phase in '77. The company later moved to Oakland and made amplifiers, high-tech signal processors, and a reissue of its original Flanger.

Aguilar
1995-present. U.S.-made tube and solidstate amp heads, cabinets, and pre-amps from New York City, New York. They also made effect pedals.

Aiken Amplification
2000-present. Tube amps, combos, and cabinets built by Randall Aiken originally in Buford, Georgia, and since '05 in Pensacola, Florida.

Aims
Ca. 1972-ca. 1976. Aims (American International Music Sales, Inc.) amps were distributed by Randall Instruments in the mid-'70s. They also offered guitars and basses.

Airline
Ca.1958-1968, 2004-present. Brand for Montgomery Ward, built by Danelectro, Valco and others.

Tube Amp 1x6" Speaker
1958-1960s		$215	$270

Tube Amp 1x8" Speaker
1958-1960s		$240	$310

Tube Amp 1x10" Speaker
1958-1960s		$290	$375

Tube Amp 1x12" Speaker
1958-1960s		$450	$585

Tube Amp Higher-End
1958-1960s		$565	$735

Tube Amp Highest-End
1958-1960s		$745	$970

Alamo
1947-1982. Founded by Charles Eilenberg, Milton Fink, and Southern Music, San Antonio, Texas, and distributed by Bruno and Sons. Alamo started producing amps in '49 and the amps were all-tube until '73; solidstate preamp and tube output from '73 to ca. '80; all solidstate for ca. '80 to '82.

Birch "A" Combo Amp
1949-1962. Birch wood cabinets with A-shaped grill cutout, 2 to 5 tubes. Models include the Embassy Amp 3, Jet Amp 4, Challenger Amp 2, Amp 5, and the Montclair.

1949-1962		$270	$350

Bass Tube Amp
1960-1972. Leatherette covered, all tube, 20 to 35 watts, 15" speakers, combo or piggyback, some with Lansing speaker option. Models include the Paragon Special, Paragon Bass, Piggyback Band, Piggyback Bass, Fury Bass, and Paragon Bass (piggyback).

1960-1972		$270	$350

Bass Solidstate Preamp-Tube Output Amp
1973-ca.1979. Solidstate preamp section with tube output section, 35 or 40 watts, 15" speakers, combo or piggyback. Models include the Paragon Bass, Paragon Bass Piggyback, Paragon Country Western Bass, Paragon Super Bass, and the Fury Bass.

1973-1979		$140	$185

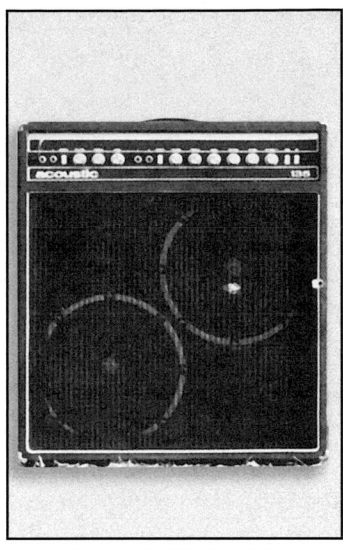
Acoustic Model 135

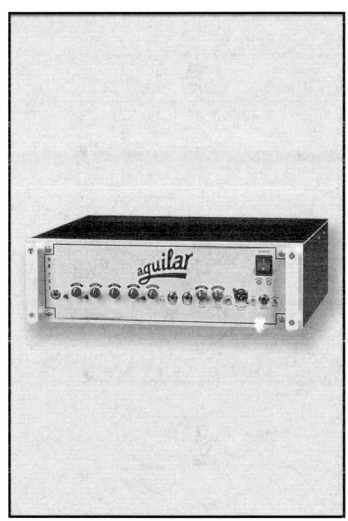
Aguilar DB 751

1962 Alamo Century Twin Ten

AMPS

Alesis Wildfire 60

Allen Brown Sugar

Allen Chihuahua

MODEL YEAR	FEATURES	EXC. COND. LOW	HIGH

Small Tube Amp
1960-1972. Leatherette covered, all tube, 3 to 10 watts, 6" to 10" speakers, some with tremolo. Models include the Jet, Embassy, Challenger, Capri, Fiesta, Dart, and Special.

1960-1972		$240	$315

Mid-Power Tube Amp
1960-1970. Leatherette covered, all tube, 15 to 30 watts, 12" or 15" speakers, some with tremolo and reverb, some with Lansing speaker option. Models include Montclair, Paragon, Paragon Band, Titan, and Futura.

1960-1970		$375	$490

Twin Speaker Tube Amp
1962-1972. Leatherette covered, all tube, up to 45 watts, 8", 10", 12" or 15" speaker configurations, some with tremolo and reverb, some with Lansing speaker option. Models include the Electra Twin Ten, Century Twin Ten, Futuramic Twin Eight, Galaxie Twin Twelve, Galaxie Twin Twelve Piggyback, Piggyback Super Band, Alamo Pro Reverb Piggyback, Futura, Galaxie Twin Ten, Twin-Ten, and Band Piggyback.

1962-1972		$385	$500

Small Solidstate Preamp-Tube Output Amp
1973-ca.1979. Solidstate preamp section with tube output section, 3 to 12 watts, 5" to 12" speaker, some with reverb. Models include the Challenger, Capri, Special, Embassy, Dart, and Jet.

1973-1979		$140	$185

Mid-Power Solidstate Preamp-Tube Output Amp
1973-ca.1979. Solidstate preamp section with tube output section, 25 watts, 12" speaker, with reverb and tremolo. Models include the Montclair.

1973-1979		$140	$185

Twin Speaker Combo (Tube/Hybrid) Amp
1973-ca.1979. Solidstate preamp section with tube output section, 20 or 70 watts, 10", 12" and 15" speaker configurations, some with reverb and tremolo. Models include the 70-watt Paragon Super Reverb Piggybacks, the 45-watt Futura 2x12, and the 20-watt Twin-Ten.

1973-1979		$240	$315

Solidstate Amp
Ca.1980-1982. All solidstate.

1980-1982		$35	$50

Alden
Small budget grade solidstate guitar and bass amps from Muse, Inc. of China.

Alesis
1992-present. Alesis has a wide range of products for the music industry, including digital modeling guitar amps. They also offer guitar effects.

Alessandro
1998-present. Tube amps built by George Alessandro in Huntingdon Valley, Pennsylvania. Founded in '94 as the Hound Dog Corporation, in '98 the company name was changed to Alessandro. The Redbone

('94) and the Bloodhound ('96) were the only models bearing the Hound Dog mark. Serial numbers are consecutive regardless of model (the earliest 20-30 did not have serial numbers). In '98 the company converted to exotic/high-end components and the name changed to Alessandro High-End Products. In '01, he added the Working Dog brand line of amps.

Allen Amplification
1998-present. Tube combo amps, heads and cabinets built by David Allen in Walton, Kentucky. He also offers the amps in kit form and produces replacement and upgrade transformers and a tube overdrive pedal.

Allston Amplifiers
2005-present. Professional and premium grade, custom, amps and cabinets built by Rob Lohr in Allston, Massachusetts.

Aloha
Late-1940s. Electric lap steel and amp Hawaiian outfits made for the Dallas-based Aloha.

Ampeg
1949-present. Ampeg was originally primarily known for their bass amps. In the eastern U.S., Ampeg was Fender's greatest challenger in the '60s and '70s bass amplifier market. Currently offering tube and solidstate heads, combos and speaker cabinets. They also build guitars.

Amp Covering Dates:
Wood veneer 1946-1949, Smooth brown 1949-1952, Dot tweed 1952-1954, Tweed 1954-1955, Rough gray 1957-1958, Rough tan 1957-1958, Cream 1957-1958, Light blue 1958, Navy blue 1958-1962, Blue check 1962-1967, Black pebble 1967, Smooth black 1967-1980, and Rough black 1967-1985.

AC-12 Amp
1970. 20 watts, 1x12", accordion amp that was a market failure and dropped after 1 year.

1970		$300	$400

AX-44 C Amp
1990-1992. AX hybrid amp with solidstate power section and 1 preamp tube, 22 watts, 2x8 combo.

1990-1992		$185	$240

B-2 Bass Amp
1994-2000. Solidstate, 200 watts, 1x15" combo or 4x8" combo, black vinyl, black grille, large A logo.

1994-2000 1x15"		$425	$550

B-2 R Bass Amp Head
1994-2005. 200 watts, rackmount, replaced by 450 watt B2RE.

1994-2005		$215	$280

B-3 Amp
1995-2001. Solidstate head, 150 watts, 1x15".

1995-2001		$375	$490

B-12 N Portaflex Amp
1961-1965. 25 watts, 2x12", 2 6L6 power tubes.

1961-1965		$1,175	$1,525

MODEL		EXC. COND.	
YEAR	FEATURES	LOW	HIGH

B-12 X/B-12 XT Portaflex Amp
1961-1969. Tube, 50 watts, 2x12", reverb, vibrato, 2x7027A power tubes.

| 1961-1969 | Style 1 | $950 | $1,250 |
| 1961-1969 | Style 2 | $1,185 | $1,550 |

B-15 N (NB, NC, NF) Portaflex Amp
1960-1970. Introduced as B-15 using 2 6L6 power tubes, B-15 N in '61, B-15 NB in '62, B-15 NC with rectifier tube in '64, B-15 NF with fixed-bias 2 6L6 power tubes and 30 watts in '67, 1x15".

1960-1965		$1,290	$1,675
1966-1970	1x15"	$1,075	$1,400
1967-1968	2x15"	$1,200	$1,550

B-15 R Portaflex Amp (Reissue)
1997-2007. Reissue of '65 Portaflex 1x15", blue check, 60/100 watts.

| 1997-2007 | | $1,025 | $1,335 |

B-15 S Portaflex Amp
1971-1977. 60 watts, 2x7027A power tubes, 1x12".

| 1971-1977 | | $800 | $1,000 |

B-18 N Portaflex Amp
1964-1969. Bass, 50 watts, 1x18".

| 1964-1965 | | $1,875 | $2,440 |
| 1966-1969 | | $1,650 | $2,150 |

B-25 Amp
1969 only. 55 watts, 2 7027A power tubes, 2x15", no reverb, guitar amp.

| 1969 | | $850 | $1,100 |

B-25 B Bass Amp
1969-1980. Bass amp, 55 watts, 2 7027A power tubes, 2x15".

| 1969-1980 | | $850 | $1,100 |

B-50 R Rocket Bass Amp (Reissue)
1996-2005. 50 watts, 1x12" combo, vintage-style blue check cover.

| 1996-2005 | | $300 | $400 |

B-100 R Rocket Bass Amp (Reissue)
1996-2005. Solidstate, 100 watts, 1x15" combo bass amp, vintage-style blue check cover.

| 1996-2005 | | $300 | $400 |

B-115 Amp
1973-1980. 120 watts, solidstate, 1x15" combo.

| 1973-1980 | | $320 | $415 |

B-410 Bass Amp
1973-1980. Solidstate, 120 watts, 4x10", black vinyl, black grille.

| 1973-1980 | | $375 | $490 |

BA Series Amp
1999-present. Solidstate bass combo amps, model number is speaker configuration.

1999-2014	BA-112, 50w, 1x12	$130	$170
1999-2014	BA-115, 100w, 1x15	$130	$170
2008-2014	BA300/210, 300w, 2x10	$215	$280
2008-2014	BA600/210, 600w, 2x10	$270	$350
2011-2014	BA-108, 25w, 1x8	$25	$35

BT-15 Amp
1966-1968. Ampeg introduced solidstate amps in '66, the same year as Fender. Solidstate, 50 watts, 1x15", generally used as a bass amp. The BT-15D
has 2 1x15" cabinets. The BT-15C is a 2x15" column portaflex cabinet.

| 1966-1968 | | $320 | $415 |

BT-18 Amp
1966-1968. Solidstate, 50 watts, 1x18", generally used as a bass amp. The BT-18D has dual 1x18" cabinets. The BT-18C is a 2x18" column portaflex cabinet.

| 1966-1968 | | $320 | $415 |

Continental I Amp
1956-1959. Single-channel version of Duette, 30 watts, 1x15".

| 1956-1959 | | $550 | $725 |

Dolphin Amp
1956-1960. Smallest combo offered during this era, 15 watts, 1x12", single-channel (I) and dual-channel (II) options.

| 1956-1959 | Dolphin I | $425 | $550 |
| 1956-1960 | Dolphin II | $550 | $700 |

Duette Amp
1956-1958. Dual-channel, 3 combo models offered; Zephyr (20w, 1x15"), Continental (30w, 1x15") and Duette 50 D-50 (50w, 2x12", tremolo).

1956-1958	Continental Duette	$650	$850
1956-1958	Zephyr Duette	$650	$850
1957-1958	Duette 50 D-50	$900	$1,175

ET-1 Echo Twin Amp
1961-1964. Tube, 30 watts, 1x12", stereo reverb.

| 1961-1964 | | $900 | $1,150 |

ET-2 Super Echo Twin Amp
1962-1964. Tube, 2x12", 30 watts, stereo reverb.

| 1962-1964 | | $1,000 | $1,250 |

G-12 Gemini I Amp
1964-1971. Tube, 1x12", 22 watts, reverb.

| 1964-1971 | | $700 | $900 |

G-15 Gemini II Amp
1965-1968. Tube, 30 watts, 1x15", reverb.

| 1965-1968 | | $700 | $900 |

G-18 Amp
1977-1980. Solidstate, 1 channel, 10 watts, 1x8", volume, treble, and bass controls.

| 1977-1980 | | $80 | $105 |

G-20 Gemini 20
1969-1970. Tubes, 35 watts, 2x10".

| 1968-1969 | | $675 | $875 |

G-110 Amp
1978-1980. Solidstate, 20 watts, 1x10", reverb, tremolo.

| 1978-1980 | | $135 | $175 |

G-115 Amp
1979-1980. Solidstate, 175 watts, 1x15" JBL, reverb and tremolo, designed for steel guitar.

| 1979-1980 | | $160 | $210 |

G-212 Amp
1973-1980. Solidstate, 120 watts, 2x12".

| 1973-1980 | | $185 | $240 |

GS-12 Rocket 2 Amp
1965-1968. This name replaced the Reverberocket 2 (II), 15 watts, 1x12".

| 1965-1968 | | $645 | $840 |

GS-12-R Reverberocket 2 Amp
1965-1969. Tube, 1x12", 18 watts, reverb. Called the Reverberocket II in '68 and '69, then Rocket II in '69.

| 1965-1969 | | $700 | $910 |

2005 Ampeg B-50 R Rocket Bass Amp (Reissue)

Ampeg BA300

Ampeg G-15 Gemini II

AMPS

1969 Ampeg GV-22 Gemini 22

*Early-1960s Ampeg
J-12 Jet Amp*

Ampeg Portaflex PF-350

MODEL YEAR	FEATURES	EXC. COND. LOW	HIGH
GS-15-R Gemini VI Amp			
1966-1967. 30 watts, 1x15", single channel, considered to be "the accordion version" of the Gemini II.			
1966-1967		$620	$810
GT-10 Amp			
1971-1980. Solidstate, 15 watts, 1x10", basic practice amp with reverb.			
1971-1980		$135	$175
GV-15 Gemini V			
1968-1971. Unimusic-era tube amp, 30 watts, 1x15" combo, reverb and tremolo.			
1968-1971		$650	$850
GV-22 Gemini 22 Amp			
1969-1972. Tube, 30 watts, 2x12".			
1969-1972		$725	$950
J-12 A Jet Amp			
1964. Jet Amp with 7591A power tubes.			
1964		$425	$550
J-12 D Jet Amp			
1966. Jet Amp with new solidstate rectifier.			
1966		$400	$525
J-12 Jet Amp			
1958-1964, 1967-1972. 20 watts, 1x12", 6V6GT power tubes. Second addition, also known as the Jet II, was like the J-12 D Jet but with 12AX7s.			
1958	Rough tan	$600	$775
1959	Blue	$575	$750
1960-1964	Blue	$425	$550
1967-1972	Model reappears	$325	$425
J-12 R Reverbojet Amp			
1967-1970. Part of Golden Glo Series, nicknamed 'copper front', 18 watts, 1x12" combo, single channel, tremolo and reverb, printed circuit replaces point-to-point wiring.			
1967-1970		$425	$550
J-12 T Jet Amp			
1965, 2006-2008. J-12 A with revised preamp.			
1965		$425	$550
J-20 Jet Amp			
2007-2008. Tubes, 20 watts, 1x12.			
2007-2008		$400	$525
Jet II/J-12 T			
2007-2008. 15 watts, 1x12".			
2007-2008		$275	$360
Jupiter Amp			
1956-1958. Part of Accordiamp Series, similar to Dolphin except preamp voiced for accordion, 15 watts, 1x12".			
1956-1958		$425	$550
M-12 Mercury Amp			
1957-1965. 15 watts, 2 channels, Rocket 1x12".			
1957-1959		$600	$775
1960-1965		$575	$750
M-15 Big M Amp			
1959-1965. 20 watts, 2x6L6 power, 1x15".			
1959		$775	$1,000
1960-1965		$650	$850
Model 815 Bassamp Amp			
1955. 15 watt combo, 1 channel. Ampeg Bassamp logo on control panel.			
1955		$650	$850

MODEL YEAR	FEATURES	EXC. COND. LOW	HIGH
Model 820 Bassamp Amp			
1956-1958. 20 watt combo, 1 channel.			
1956-1958		$700	$900
Model 822 Bassamp Amp			
1957-1958. 2 channel 820.			
1957-1958		$725	$950
Model 830 Bassamp Amp			
1956-1958. 30 watt combo.			
1956-1958		$750	$975
Model 835 Bassamp Amp			
1959-1961. 35 watt 1x15" combo, 2 channels.			
1959-1961		$775	$1,000
New Yorker Amp			
1956-1958. Part of Accordiamp Series, similar to Continental except preamp voiced for accordion, 30 watts, 1x15".			
1956-1958		$550	$725
PB Series Amp			
2002-2008. Portabass Series amps and speaker cabs.			
2002-2004	PB-122H Cab	$250	$325
2002-2008	PB-250 Head	$250	$325
Portaflex (PF) Series Amp			
2011-present. Portaflex (PF) ultra-compact amp heads offered with flip-top cabs, 350 watt or 500 watt head and 115, 210 or 410 cab options.			
2011-2014	PF350	$215	$280
2011-2014	PF500	$225	$290
R-12 Rocket Amp			
1957-1963. 12 watts, 1x12", 1 channel.			
1957-1959		$575	$750
1960-1963		$600	$775
R-12 B Rocket Amp			
1964. 12 watts, 1x12", follow-up to the R-12 Rocket.			
1964		$600	$775
R-12 R Reverberocket Amp			
1961-1963. Rocket with added on-board reverb.			
1961-1963		$700	$900
R-12 R Reverberocket Amp (Reissue)			
1996-2007. 50 watts, 2xEL34 power tubes, 1x12" (R-212R is 2x12").			
1996-2007		$425	$550
R-12 R-B Reverberocket Amp			
1964. 7591A power tubes replace R-12-R 6V6 power tubes.			
1964		$700	$900
R-12 R-T Reverberocket Amp			
1965. 7591A or 7868 power tubes, revised preamp.			
1965		$700	$900
R-15 R Superbreverb (Supereverb) Amp			
1963-1964. 1x15 combo, originally called Supereverb, but Fender had a problem with that name.			
1963-1964		$885	$1,150
R-50H Reverberocket Amp			
1997-2003. 50 watt head usually sold with a 4x12" bottom, blue check covering.			
1997-2003	Head and cab	$550	$725
R-212 R Reverberocket Combo 50 Amp (Reissue)			
1996-2007. 50 watts, 2x12", all tube reissue, vintage-style blue check cover, vintage-style grille.			
1996-2007		$500	$650

MODEL YEAR	FEATURES	EXC. COND. LOW	HIGH

Rhapsody Amp
1956-1958. Part of Accordiamp Series, similar to Zephyr except preamp voiced for accordion, 20 watts, 1x15".

1956-1958		$550	$725

SB-12 Portaflex Amp
1965-1971. 22 watts, 1x12", designed for use with Ampeg's Baby Bass, black.

1965-1971		$700	$900

SBT Amp
1969-1971. 120 watts, 1x15", bass version of SST Amp.

1969-1971		$675	$875

SE-412 Cabinet
1996-1999. 4x12" speakers.

1996-1999		$300	$390

SJ-12 R/RT Super Jet Amp
1996-2007. 50 watts, tube, 1x12", SJ-12 RT has tremolo added.

1996-2007		$310	$400

SS-35 Amp
1987-1992. Solidstate, 35 watts, 1x12", black vinyl, black grille, large A logo.

1987-1992		$160	$210

SS-70 Amp
1987-1990. Solidstate, 70 watts, 1x12".

1987-1990		$190	$250

SS-70 C Amp
1987-1992. Solidstate, 70 watts, 2x10", chorus, black vinyl

1987-1992		$215	$275

SS-140 C Amp
1987-1992. Solidstate, 2x12 combo, chorus and reverb.

1987-1992		$250	$325

SS-150 Amp Head
1987-1992. Solidstate, 150 watts.

1987-1992		$300	$390

SS-412 Cabinet
1987-1992. Matching 4x12 cab for SS series heads.

1987-1992		$300	$390

Super Comboamp/Model 833 Comboamp/Model 950C Super
1956-1960. 30 watts, 3 channels. 950C is 50 watts with 2 15" speakers (very few made).

1956-1957	Super Comboamp	$750	$975
1958	Model 833	$750	$975
1959-1960	Model 950C	$750	$975

SVT Bass Amp Head
1969-1985. 300 watt head only.

1969	Stones World-Tour Assoc.	$2,050	$2,675
1970-1979		$1,750	$2,275
1980-1985		$1,550	$2,025

SVT Bass Cabinets
1969-1985. Two 8x10" cabs only.

1969		$1,500	$1,925
1970-1985		$1,400	$1,825

SVT-II Bass Amp Head
1989-1994. Rackmount, 300 watts, tube.

1989-1994		$1,075	$1,400

SVT-2 Pro Bass Amp Head
1993-2014. 300 watts, rackmount, tube preamp and power section, black metal.

1993-2014		$1,125	$1,450

SVT-III Bass Amp Head
1991-1994. Mosfet, 275/450 watts.

1991-1994		$600	$775

SVT-3 Pro Bass Amp Head
1993-present. Tube preamp and MOS-FET power section, 450 watts, rackmount, black metal.

1993-2014		$550	$725

SVT-4 Pro Bass Amp Head
1997-present. Rackmount, all tube preamp, MOS-FET power section yielding 1600 watts.

1997-2014		$725	$950

SVT-5 Pro Bass Amp Head
2002-2005. Rackmount, all tube preamp, MOS-FET power section yielding 1350 watts.

2002-2005		$725	$950

SVT-6 Pro Bass Amp Head
2005-2009. Rackmount, all tube preamp, MOS-FET power section yielding 1100 watts.

2005-2009		$550	$725

SVT-15 E Bass Cabinet
1994-present. Compact 1x15

1994-2014		$350	$455

SVT-100 T Bass Combo Amp
1990-1992. Solidstate, ultra-compact bass combo, 100 watts, 2x8".

1990-1992		$385	$500

SVT-200 T Amp Head
1987 only. Solidstate, 200 watts to 8 ohms or 320 watts to 4 ohms.

1987		$350	$450

SVT-350 Amp Head
1995-2005. Solidstate head, 350 watts, graphic EQ.

1995-2005		$375	$490

SVT-400 Amp Head
1987-1997. Solidstate, 2 200 watt stereo amps, rack-mountable head with advanced (in '87) technology.

1987-1997		$375	$490

SVT-410 HE Bass Cabinet
1994-present. 4x10, horn/driver.

1994-2014		$350	$450

SVT-450 H Amp Head
2007-present. Solidstate head, 275/450 watts.

2007-2014		$415	$540

SVT-610 HLF Cabinet
2003-present. 6x10, horn/driver.

2003-2014		$515	$675

SVT-810 E Cabinet
1994-present. 8x10.

1994-2014		$565	$735

SVT-AV Anniversary Edition Amp

2001		$800	$1,050

SVT-CL Classic Bass Amp Head
1994-present. Tube, 300 watts.

1994-2014		$950	$1,225

V-2 Amp Cabinet
1971-1980. 4x12" cab, black tolex.

1971-1980		$450	$585

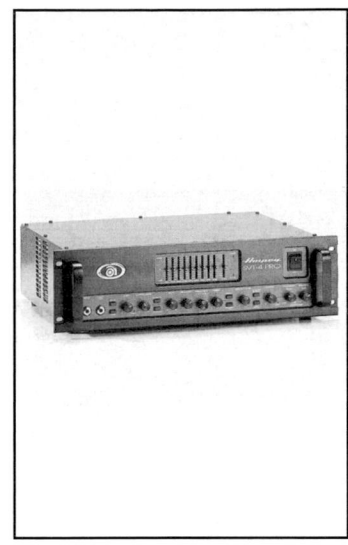

Ampeg SVT-4 Pro

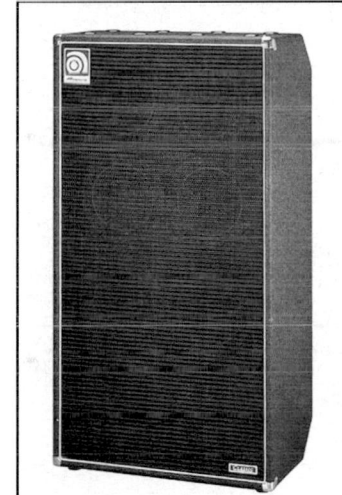

Ampeg SVT-810 E Cabinet

Ampeg SVT-CL Classic Bass Amp Head

To get the most from this book, be sure to read "Using *The Guide*" in the introduction.

AMPS

Andrews Spectraverb

Area 51 Model One

Aria AG-35RX

MODEL YEAR	FEATURES	EXC. COND. LOW	HIGH
V-2 Amp Head			
1971-1980. 60 watt tube head.			
1971-1980	Head only	$550	$715
V-4 B Bass Amp Head			
1972-1980. Bass version of V-4 without reverb.			
1972-1980	Head only	$725	$950
V-4 Cabinet			
1970s. Single 4x12" cabinet only.			
1970-1980		$450	$585
V-7 SC Amp			
1981-1985. Tube, 100 watts, 1x12", master volume, channel switching, reverb.			
1981-1985		$565	$735
VH-70 Amp			
1991-1992. 70 watts, 1x12" combo with channel switching.			
1991-1992		$350	$455
VH-140 C Amp			
1992-1995. Varying Harmonics (VH) with Chorus (C), two 70-watt channel stereo, 2x12".			
1992-1995		$430	$560
VH-150 Amp Head			
1991-1992. 150 watts, channel-switchable, reverb.			
1991-1992		$325	$425
VL-502 Amp			
1991-1995. 50 watts, channel-switchable, all tube.			
1991-1995		$410	$535
VL-1001 Amp Head			
1991-1993. 100 watts, non-switchable channels, all tube.			
1991-1993		$375	$490
VL-1002 Amp Head			
1991-1995. 100 watts, channel-switchable, all tube.			
1991-1995		$400	$525
VT-22 Amp			
1970-1980. 100 watt combo version of V-4, 2x12".			
1970-1980		$650	$850
VT-40 Amp			
1971-1980. 60 watt combo, 4x10".			
1971-1980		$650	$850
VT-60 Amp Head			
1989-1991. Tube head only, 6L6 power, 60 watts.			
1989-1991		$375	$490
VT-60 Combo Amp			
1989-1991. Tube, 6L6 power, 60 watts, 1x12".			
1989-1991		$450	$585
VT-120 Amp Head			
1989-1992. 120 watts, 6L6 tube head.			
1989-1992		$375	$490
VT-120 Combo Amp			
1989-1992. Tube, 6L6 power, 120 watts, 1x12", also offered as head only.			
1989-1992		$450	$585
Zephyr I Amp			
1956-1959. Single-channel, 20 watts, 1x15".			
1956-1959		$550	$725

Anderson Amplifiers

1993-present. Tube amps and combos built by Jack Anderson in Gig Harbor, Washington.

Andrews

2006-present. Professional grade, production/custom, amps and cabinets built by Jeff Andrews in Dunwoody, Georgia.

ARACOM Amplifiers

1997-present. Jeff Aragaki builds his tube amp heads, combos, and cabinets in Morgan Hill, California.

Area 51

2003-present. Guitar amps made in Newaygo, Michigan (made in Texas until early '06), by Dan Albrecht. They also build effects.

Aria/Aria Pro II

1956-present. The Japanese instrument builder offered a range of amps from around '79 to '89.

Ariatone

1962. Another private brand made by Magnatone, sold by private music and accordion studios.

Model 810
1962. 12 watts, 1x8, tremolo, brown cover.

1962		$355	$460

Ark

2005-present. Owners Matt Schellenberg and Bill Compeau build professional and premium grade, production/custom amps in Farmington Hills, Michigan (cabinet shop), with all wiring done in Windsor, Ontario.

Ashdown Amplification

1999-present. Founded in England by Mark Gooday after he spent several years with Trace Elliot, Ashdown offers amps, combos, and cabinets.

Audio Guild

1960s-1974. Audio Guild was already making amps under such brands as Universal and Versatone and others when they launched their own brand in the '60s.

Grand Prix Amp
1969-1974. Tube combo 1x12, reverb and tremolo, dual channel.

1969-1974		$550	$675

Ultraflex Amp
1969-1974. All-tube, higher power combo, 2 speakers, reverb and tremolo.

1969-1974		$925	$1,150

Universal Amp
1960s-1974. Universal was a brand of Audio Guild. Tube combo amp, reverb, tremolo.

1960s-1974		$550	$675

Versatone Pan-O-Flex Amp
1960s-1974. Versatone was a brand of Audio Guild. Mid-power tube amp, 1x12" and 1x8" combo, high and low gain input, volume, bass, treble and pan-o-flex balance control knobs, black cover.

1960s-1974		$925	$1,150

MODEL YEAR	FEATURES	EXC. COND. LOW	HIGH

Audiovox

Ca.1935-ca.1950. Paul Tutmarc's Audiovox Manufacturing, of Seattle, Washington, was a pioneer in electric lap steels, basses, guitars and amps.

Auralux

2000-2011. Founded by Mitchell Omori and David Salzmann, Auralux built effects and tube amps in Highland Park, Illinois.

Austin

1999-present. Budget and intermediate grade, production, guitar and bass amps imported by St. Louis Music. They also offer guitars, basses, mandolins, ukes and banjos.

Bacino

2002-present. Tube combo amps, heads and cabinets built by Mike Bacino in Arlington Heights, Illinois.

Backline Engineering

2004-present. Gary Lee builds his tube amp heads in Camarillo, California. He also builds guitar effects.

Bad Cat Amplifier Company

1999-present. Founded in Corona, California by James and Debbie Heidrich, Bad Cat offers class A combo amps, heads, cabinets and effects. In '09 the company was moved to Anaheim.

Baer Amplification

2009-present. Professional grade, production, bass amps built in Palmdale, California by Roger Baer.

Baldwin

Piano maker Baldwin offered amplifiers from 1965 to '70. The amps were solidstate with organ-like pastel-colored pushbutton switches.

Exterminator Amp

1965-1970. Solidstate, 100 watts, 2x15"/2x12"/2x7", 4' vertical combo cabinet, reverb and tremolo, Supersound switch and slide controls.

1965-1970		$475	$625

Model B1 Bass Amp

1965-1970. Solidstate, 45 watts, 1x15"/1x12", 2 channels.

1965-1970		$245	$320

Model B2 Bass Amp

1965-1970. Solidstate, 35 watts, 1x15", 2 channels.

1965-1970		$225	$300

Model C1 Custom (Professional) Amp

1965-1970. Solidstate, 45 watts, 2x12", reverb and tremolo, Supersound switch and slide controls.

1965-1970		$325	$425

Model C2 Custom Amp

1965-1970. Solidstate, 40 watts, 2x12", reverb and tremolo.

1965-1970		$325	$425

MODEL YEAR	FEATURES	EXC. COND. LOW	HIGH

Professional Deluxe

1965-1970. Supersound, 1x12.

1965-1970		$325	$425

Barcus-Berry

1964-present. Pickup maker Barcus-Berry offered a line of amps from '75 to '79.

Barth

1950s-1960s. Products of Paul Barth's Barth Musical Instrument Company. Barth was also a co-founder of Rickenbacker. He also produced guitars and lap steels.

Studio Deluxe 958 Amp

1950s-1960s. Small practice combo amp.

1950s-60s		$325	$425

Basson

Speaker cabinets for guitar, bass and PA made by Victor Basson in Carlsbad, California, starting in 2001.

BC Audio

2009-present. Bruce Clement builds his production/custom, professional grade, tube amps in San Francisco, California.

Bedrock

1984-1997. Tube amp company founded by Brad Jeter and Ron Pinto in Nashua, New Hampshire. They produced 50 amps carrying the brand name Fred before changing the company name to Bedrock in '86. Around '88, Jay Abend joined the company, eventually becoming President. In '88, Evan Cantor joined the company as an amp designer. In '90, Jeter left Bedrock and, shortly after, Pinto and Abend moved the company to Farmington, Massachusetts. The company closed in '97.

Behringer

1989-present. Founded in Germany by Uli Behringer, offering a full line of professional audio products. In '98 they added tube, solidstate, and modeling amps. They also offer effects and guitars.

Beltone

1950s-1960s. Japan's Teisco made a variety of brands for others, including the Beltone line of amps. There were also guitars sold under this name made from a variety of builders.

Big M

1966-1967, 1975-1976. The Marshall name in Germany was owned by a trumpet maker, so Jim Marshall marketed his amps and cabs there under the Big M Made In England brand name until the issue was resolved. A decade later, in a failed attempt to lower speaker cabinets prices in the U.S., Marshall's American distributor built cabs, with Marshall's permission, on Long Island, mainly for sales with Marshall solidstate lead and bass heads

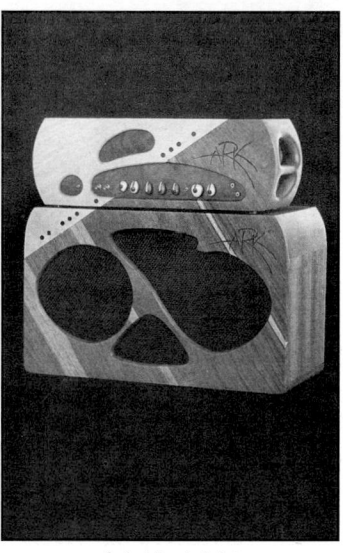

Ark Model A+

Ashdown Peacemaker 60

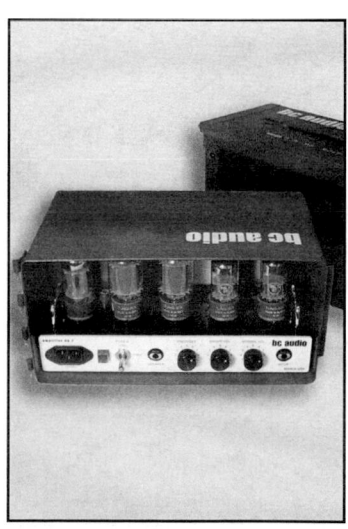

BC Audio

AMPS

Blackstar HT-1RH

Bogen GA5
Gil Hembree

Burriss Toneclassic 112

MODEL YEAR	FEATURES	EXC. COND. LOW	HIGH

of the time, and labeled them Big M. They were loaded with cheaper Eminence speakers, instead of the usual Celestions.

Big M Cabinets

1975-1976. The M2412 with 4x12 for lead and the M2212F 2x12 bass cabs.

1975-1976	2x12	$340	$425
1975-1976	4x12	$675	$850

JTM-45 Amp Head

1966-1967. Branded Big M.

1966-1967		$6,000	$7,500

BigDog Amps

2005-2007. Tube head and combo guitar and bass amps and speaker cabinets built in Galveston, Texas, by Steve Gaines.

Blackstar Amplification

2007-present. Joel Richardson builds his intermediate and professional grade guitar amps and cabinets in Northampton, U.K. He also offers effects pedals.

Blankenship Amplification

2005-present. Roy Blankenship builds his tube head and combo amps and cabinets in Northridge, California. He also built amps under the Point Blank brand.

Bluetone Amplifiers

2002-present. Founded by Alex Cooper in Worcestershire, England, Bluetone offers professional grade, production amps employing their virtual valve technology.

Bogen

1932-present. Founded in New York City by David Bogen, this company has made a wide range of electronic products for consumers and industry including a few small guitar combo tube amps such as the GA-5 and GA-20 and tube PA equipment. The company name (David Bogen, New York) and model number are on the lower back panel. The '50s Bogen tube amps are well respected as tone-generating workhorses. In '56 he sold the company and it was moved to New Jersey, and they continue to offer pro audio PA gear.

Bogner

1988-present. Tube combos, amp heads, and speaker cabinets from builder Reinhold Bogner of North Hollywood, California.

Bolt

2009-present. Professional grade, production, tube amps and cabinets built in Salt Lake City, Utah. They also build the Morpheus brand effects.

Brand X

2004-2007. Small solidstate combo amps from Fender Musical Instruments Corporation.

MODEL YEAR	FEATURES	EXC. COND. LOW	HIGH

Bronson

1930s-1950s. Private brand utilized by Detroit lap steel instruction George Bronson. These amps often sold with a matching lap steel and were made by other companies.

Lap Steel Amp

1930s-50s	Melody King 1x10	$375	$490
1930s-50s	Pearloid	$245	$325
1947	Supreme 1x10, 12w	$485	$630

Bruno (Tony)

1995-present. Tube combos, amp heads, and speaker cabinets from builder Tony Bruno of Cairo, New York.

Budda

1995-present. Amps, combos, and cabinets originally built by Jeff Bober and Scott Sier in San Francisco, California. In '09, Budda was acquired by Peavey and they started building Budda products in their Meridian, Mississippi Custom Shop. They also produce effects pedals.

Bugera

2008-present. Uli Behringer builds his budget and intermediate grade, production, tube amps in China. He also offers the Behringer brand.

Burriss

2001-present. Bob Burriss builds custom and production guitar and bass tube amps, bass preamps and speaker cabinets in Lexington, Kentucky. He also builds effects.

Byers

2001-2010. Tube combo amps built by Trevor Byers, in Corona, California. His initial focus was on small early-Fender era and K & F era models.

Cage

1998-present. Production/custom, professional grade, amp heads and cabinets built in Damascus, Maryland by Pete Cage.

California

2004-present. Student/budget level amps and guitar/amp packs, imported by Eleca International.

Callaham

1989-present. Custom tube amp heads built by Bill Callaham in Winchester, Virginia. He also builds solidbody electric guitars.

Campbell Sound

1999-present. Intermediate and professional grade, production/custom, guitar amps built by Walt Campbell in Roseville, California.

Carl Martin

1993-present. In '05, the Denmark-based guitar effects company added tube combo amps.

MODEL YEAR	FEATURES	EXC. COND. LOW	HIGH

Carlsbro
1959-present. Guitar, bass, and keyboard combo amps, heads and cabinets from Carlsbro Electronics Limited of Nottingham, England. They also offer PA amps and speaker cabinets.

Carol-Ann Custom Amplifiers
2003-present. Premium grade, production/custom, tube guitar amps built by Alan Phillips in North Andover, Massachusetts.

Carr Amplifiers
1998-present. Steve Carr started producing amps in his Chapel Hill, North Carolina amp repair business in '98. The company is now located in Pittsboro, North Carolina, and makes tube combo amps, heads, and cabinets.

Sportsman Amp
2011-present. Available in 1x12 and 1x10 combos and head, 16 watts.

2011-2014	1x10	$1,350	$1,675

Carvin
1946-present. Founded in Los Angeles by Lowell C. Kiesel who sold guitars and amps under the Kiesel name until late-'49, when the Carvin brand was introduced. They added small tube amps to their product line in '47 and today offer a variety of models. They also build guitars, basses and mandolins.

Caswell Amplification
2006-present. Programmable tube amp heads built by Tim Caswell in California.

Chicago Blues Box/Butler Custom Sound
Starting 2001, tube combo amps built by Dan Butler of Butler Custom Sound originally in Elmhurst, then Lombard, Illinois.

Clark Amplification
1995-present. Tweed-era replica tube amplifiers from builder Mike Clark, of Cayce, South Carolina. He also makes effects.

Club Amplifiers
2005-present. Don Anderson builds intermediate to premium grade, custom, vacuum tube guitar amps and cabinets in Felton, California.

CMI
1976-1977. Amps made by Marshall for Cleartone Musical Instruments of Birmingham, England. Mainly PA amps, but two tube heads and one combo amp were offered.

CMI Electronics
Late-1960s-1970s. CMI branded amplifiers designed to replace the Gibson Kalamazoo-made

amps that ceased production in '67 when Gibson moved the electronics lab to Chicago, Illinois.

Sabre Reverb 1 Amp
Late-1960s-early-1970s. Keyboard amp, 1x15" and side-mounted horn, utilized mid- to late-'60s cabinets and grilles, look similar to mid-late '60s Gibson black tolex and Epiphone gray amp series, black or gray tolex and silver grille.

1960s-70s		$140	$185

CMW Amps
2002-present. Chris Winsemius builds his premium grade, production/custom, guitar amps in The Netherlands.

Colby
2012-present. Professional and premium grade, production/custom, tube amp heads, combos and cabinets built by Mitch Colby in City Island, New York.

Comins
1992-present. Archtop luthier Bill Comins, of Willow Grove, Pennsylvania, introduced a Comins combo amp, built in collaboration with George Alessandro, in '03.

Coral
1967-1969. In '66 MCA bought Danelectro and in '67 introduced the Coral brand of guitars, basses and amps. The amp line included tube, solidstate, and hybrid models ranging from small combo amps to the Kilowatt (1000 Watts of Peak Power!), a hybrid head available with two 8x12" cabinets.

Cornell/Plexi
Amps based on the '67 Marshall plexi chassis built by Denis Cornell in the United Kingdom. Large Plexi logo on front.

Cosmosound
Italy's Cosmosound made small amps with Leslie rotating drums in the late '60s and '70s. They also made effects pedals.

Crafter USA
1986-present. Giant Korean guitar and bass manufacturer Crafter also builds an acoustic guitar amp.

Crate
1979-present. Solidstate and tube amplifiers originally distributed by St. Louis Music. In '05 LOUD Technologies acquired SLM and the Crate brand.

CA Series Amps
1995-present. Crate Acoustic series.

1990s	CA-60	$150	$275

Solidstate Amp
1979-1990s. Various student to mid-level amps, up to 150 watts.

1979-90s		$55	$75

Carr Rambler
Rob Bernstein

CMW Amps Plexi Junior

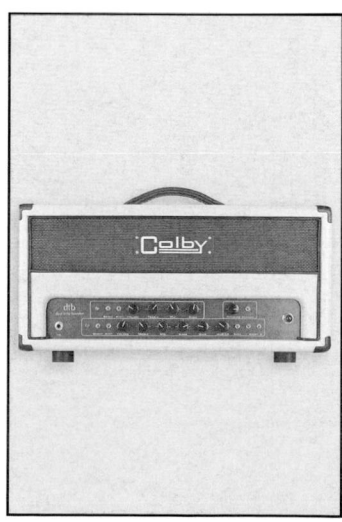
Colby Dual Tone Booster

AMPS

Cruzer CR-15RG

Danelectro Maestro

*Danelectro Model
88 Commando*

MODEL YEAR	FEATURES	EXC. COND. LOW	HIGH
Vintage Club Series Amps			
1994-2001. Various tube amps.			
1994-1997	5310/VC-5310	$320	$415
1994-1999	20	$215	$275
1994-1999	30/VC-2110	$300	$390
1994-1999	30/VC-3112	$320	$415
1994-1999	50/VC-50	$295	$385
1994-1999	60/VC-60	$295	$385
1994-2001	5212/VC-5212	$320	$415

Cruise Audio Systems

1999-2003. Founded by Mark Altekruse, Cruise offered amps, combos, and cabinets built in Cuyahoga Falls, Ohio. It appears the company was out of business by '03.

Cruzer

Solidstate guitar amps built by Korea's Crafter Guitars. They also build guitars, basses and effects under that brand.

Custom Kraft

Late-1950s-1968. A house brand of St. Louis Music Supply, instruments built by others. They also offered basses and guitars.

Import Student Amp
1960s	1x6 or 1x8	$55	$75

Valco-Made Amp
1960s	1x12 or 1x15	$355	$460

Da Vinci

Late-1950s-early-1960s. Another one of several private brands (for example, Unique, Twilighter, Titano, etc.) that Magnatone made for teaching studios and accordion companies.

D60 Custom
1965. 2x12", reverb, vibrato.
1965		$1,150	$1,400

Model 250 Amp
1958-1962. Similar to Magnatone Model 250 with about 20 watts and 1x12".
1958-1962		$900	$1,125

Model 440A/D40 Custom Amp
1964-1966. 1x12", reverb, vibrato.
1964-1966		$1,075	$1,350

Danelectro

1946-1969, 1997-present. Founded in Red Bank, New Jersey, by Nathan I. "Nate" or "Nat" Daniel. His first amps were made for Montgomery Ward in '47, and in '48 he began supplying Silvertone Amps for Sears. His own amps were distributed by Targ and Dinner as Danelectro and S.S. Maxwell brands. In '96, the Evets Corporation, of San Clemente, California, reintroduced the Danelectro brand on effects, amps, basses and guitars. In early '03, Evets discontinued the amp line, but still offers guitars, basses, and effects.

Cadet Amp
1955-1969. A longstanding model name, offered in different era cabinets and coverings but all using the

standard 3-tube 1x6" format. Models 122 and 123 had 6 watts. 1x6", 3 tubes, 1 volume, 1 control, 2 inputs, 16x15x6" 'picture frame' cabinet with light-colored cover, dark grille.
1955-1969	Various models	$205	$255

Challenger Amp
1950s. Compact combo amp, 5 tubes including 2x6L6, 2 channels, bass and treble control, 2 vibrato controls, golden-brown cover, tan woven cloverleaf-shaped grille.
1950s		$385	$475

DM-10 Amp
1965-1967. Combo 'large knobs' cabinet, 10 watts, 1x8", 2 control vibrato, 2 inputs, 1 volume, 1 tone, dark vinyl with light grille, DM-10 logo next to script Danelectro logo right upper front.
1965-1967		$285	$360

DM-25 Amp
1965-1967. Stow-away piggyback, 25 watts, 1x12", reverb, vibrato, 4 inputs, 9 control knobs, dark vinyl cabinet with light grille, DM-25 logo next to script Danelectro logo below control knobs.
1965-1967		$620	$775

DS-50 Amp
1965-1969. 75 watts, 3x10" stow-away piggyback cabinet, reverb and tremolo, suitable for bass accordion.
1965-1969		$1,050	$1,300

DS-100 Amp
1967-1969. 150 watts, stow-away piggyback cabinet, 6x10" Jensens, reverb, tremolo, suitable for bass accordion, 36x22x12" cabinet weighs 79 lbs.
1965-1969		$1,150	$1,425

DTR-40
1965. Solidstate combo, 40 watts, 2x10", vibrato, DTR-40 logo under control knobs.
1965		$360	$450

Model 68 Special Amp
1954-1957. 20 watts, 1x12", light tweed-fabric cover, light grille, leather handle, script Danelectro plexi-plate logo.
1954-1957		$500	$625

Model 72 Centurion Amp
1954-1957. Series D 1x12" combo, blond tweed, rounded front D cabinet.
1954-1957		$525	$650

Model 88 Commando
1954-1957. Series D, 25 watts with 4x6V6 power, suitcase-style amp with 8x8" speaker, light beige cover.
1954-1957		$1,125	$1,400

Model 89 Amp
1954-1957. Series D 1x15" combo, blond tweed, rounded front D cabinet.
1954-1957		$750	$950

Model 98 Twin 12 Amp
1954-ca.1957. Rounded front Series D 2x12", blond tweed-style cover, brown control panel, vibrato speed and strength.
1954-1957		$875	$1,100

MODEL YEAR	FEATURES	EXC. COND. LOW	HIGH

Model 132 Corporal Amp
1962-1964. 2x8", 4 tubes, 3 inputs, 4 control knobs, 19x15x7" picture frame cabinet in light-colored material with dark grille.

1962-1964		$460	$585

Model 142 Viscount Amp
Late-1950s. Combo amp, lower watts, 1x12", light cover, brown grille, vibrato.

1959		$550	$700

Model 143 Viscount Amp
1962-1964. 12 watts, 1x12", 6 tubes, 2 control vibrato, 1 volume, 1 tone, 'picture frame' narrow panel cabinet, light-colored cover with dark grille.

1962-1964		$435	$550

Model 217 Twin-Fifteen Amp
1962-1964. Combo amp, 60 watts, 2x15" Jensen C15P speakers, black cover, white-silver grille, 2 channels with tremolo.

1962-1964		$775	$950

Model 274 Centurion Amp
1961-1962. 15 watts, 1x12", 6 tubes, 2 channels with separate volume, treble, bass controls, Vibravox electronic vibrato, 4 inputs, 20x20x9 weighing 25 lbs., 'picture frame' cabinet with black cover and light grille.

1961-1962		$435	$550

Model 275 Centurion Amp
1963-1964. Reverb added in '63, 15 watts, 1x12", 7 tubes, Vibravox vibrato, 2 channels with separate volume, bass, treble, picture frame cabinet with black cover and light grille.

1963-1964		$565	$700

Model 291 Explorer Amp
1961-1964. 30 watts, 1x15", 7 tubes, 2 channels each with volume, bass, and treble controls, Vibravox vibrato, square picture frame cabinet, black cover and light grille.

1961-1964		$545	$675

Model 300 Twin-Twelve Amp
1962-1964. 30 watts, 2x12", reverb, 8 tubes, 2 channels with separate volume, bass, and treble, Vibravox vibrato, picture frame cabinet with black cover and light grille.

1962-1964		$765	$975

Model 354 Twin-Twelve Amp
Early 1950s. Series C twin 12" combo with diagonal speaker baffle holes, brown cover with light gold grille, Twin Twelve script logo on front as well as script Danelectro logo, diagonally mounted amp chassis, leather handle.

1950s		$900	$1,125

Dean
1976-present. Acoustic, electric, and bass amps made overseas. They also offer guitars, banjos, mandolins, and basses.

Dean Markley
The string and pickup manufacturer added a line of amps in 1983. Distributed by Kaman, they now offer combo guitar and bass amps and PA systems.

K Series Amps
1980s. All solidstate, various models include K-15 (10 watts, 1x6"), K-20/K-20X (10 to 20 watts, 1x8", master volume, overdrive switch), K-50 (25 watts, 1x10", master volume, reverb), K-75 (35 watts, 1x12", master volume, reverb), K-200B (compact 1x12 combo).

1980s	K-15, 20, 20X	$32	$40
1980s	K-200B	$110	$135
1980s	K-50	$36	$45
1980s	K-75	$56	$70

DeArmond
Pickup manufacturer DeArmond starting building tube guitar amps in 1950s. By '63, they were out of the amp business. They also made effects. Fender revived the name for a line of guitars in the late '90s.

R-5T Amp
1950s. Low power, 1 6V6, single speaker combo amp.

1950s		$3,500	$4,400

R-15T Amp
1959-1961. Same amp as Martin 112, low to mid power, 2 6V6 power section, single speaker..

1959-1961		$3,500	$4,400

Decca
Mid-1960s. Small student-level amps made in Japan by Teisco and imported by Decca Records. They also offered guitars and a bass.

Demeter
1980-present. James Demeter founded the company as Innovative Audio and renamed it Demeter Amplification in '90. Originally located in Van Nuys, in '08 they moved to Templeton, California. First products were direct boxes and by '85, amps were added. Currently they build amp heads, combos, and cabinets. They also have pro audio gear and guitar effects.

Devilcat
2012-present. Professional grade, production/custom, tube amps built in Statesboro, Georgia by Chris Mitchell.

Diaz
Early-1980s-2002. Cesar Diaz restored amps for many of rock's biggest names, often working with them to develop desired tones. Along the way he produced his own line of professional and premium grade, high-end custom amps and effects. Diaz died in '02; his family announced plans to resume production of effects in '04.

Dickerson
1937-1947. Dickerson was founded by the Dickerson brothers in 1937, primarily for electric lap steels and small amps. Instruments were also private branded for Cleveland's Oahu company, and for the Gourley brand. By '47, the company changed ownership and was renamed Magna Electronics (Magnatone). Amps were usually sold with a matching lap steel.

Demeter TGA-2.1 Tube Guitar Amplifier

Devilcat Jimmy

Dime Amplification D100C

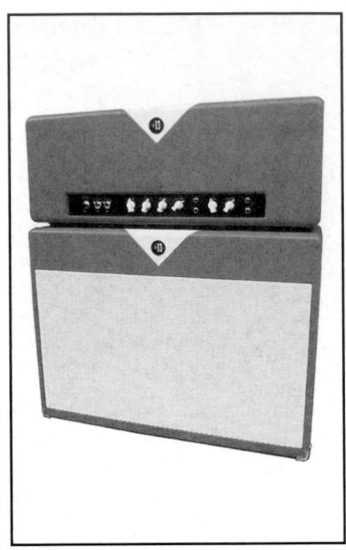

Divided By Thirteen RSA 23

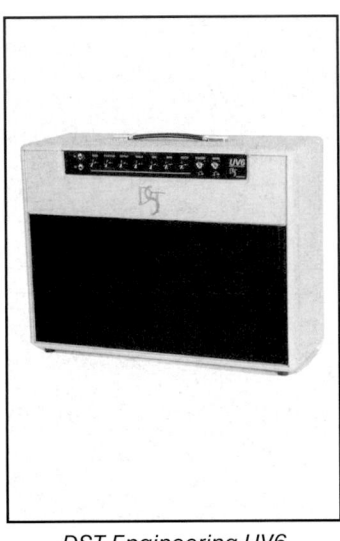

DST Engineering UV6

Dynamo M50X

MODEL YEAR	FEATURES	EXC. COND. LOW	HIGH

Oasis Amp
1940s. Blue pearloid cover, 1x10", low wattage, Dickerson silk-screen logo on grille with Hawaiian background.

1940s		$250	$315

Dime Amplification
2011-ca. 2014. Solidstate combo and head amps and cabinets from Dean Guitars, designed by Gary Sunda and Grady Champion.

Dinosaur
2004-present. Student/budget level amps and guitar/amp packs, imported by Eleca International. They also offer effects.

Divided By Thirteen
Mid-1990s-present. Fred Taccone builds his tube amp heads and cabinets in the Los Angeles, California area. He also builds effects.

Dr. Z
1988-present. Mike Zaite started producing his Dr. Z line of amps in the basement of the Music Manor in Maple Heights, Ohio. The company is now located in its own larger facility in the same city. Dr. Z offers combo amps, heads and cabinets.

Drive
Ca. 2001-ca. 2011. Budget grade, production, import solidstate amps. They also offered guitars.

DST Engineering
2002-2014. Jeff Swanson and Bob Dettorre built their tube amp combos, heads and cabinets in Beverly, Massachusetts. They also built reverb units.

Duca Tone
The Duca Tone brand was distributed by Lo Duca Brothers, Milwaukee, Wisconsin, which also distributed EKO guitars in the U.S.

Tube Amp
1950s. 12 watts, 1x12".

1950s		$500	$625

Dumble
1963-present. Made by Howard Alexander Dumble, an early custom-order amp maker from California. Initial efforts were a few Mosrite amps for Semie Moseley. First shop was in '68 in Santa Cruz, California. Dumble amp values should be considered on a case-by-case basis. Early on, Dumble also modified other brands such as Fender and those Dumble-modified amps are also valuable, based on authenticated provenance.

Overdrive Special Amp and Cabinet
1970s-present. 100 watts, 1x12", known for durability, cabinets vary.

1970s-80s	Original technology	$40,000	$65,000
1990s-2014	New technology	$50,000	$80,000

MODEL YEAR	FEATURES	EXC. COND. LOW	HIGH

Dynamic Amps
2008-present. David Carambula builds production/custom, professional grade, combo amps, heads and cabinets in Kalamazoo, Michigan.

Dynamo
2010-present. Professional and premium grade, production/custom, amps and cabinets built by Ervin Williams in Lake Dallas, Texas.

Earth Sound Research
1970s. Earth Sound was a product of ISC Audio of Farmingdale, New York, and offered a range of amps, cabinets and PA gear starting in the '70s. They also made Plush amps.

2000 G Half-Stack Amp
1970s. 100 watts plus cab.

1970s		$425	$530

Model G-1000 Amp Head

1970s	Reverb	$230	$290

Original 2000 Model 340 Amp
1970s. Black Tolex, 400-watt head and matching 2x15" cab.

1970s		$415	$520

Producer Model 440 Amp
1970s. 700-watt head and matching 2x15" cab.

1970s		$415	$520

Revival Amp
1970s. 2x12" tweed twin copy, with similar back mounted control panel, tweed covering, but with solidstate preamp section and 4x6L6 power.

1970		$415	$520

Super Bass/B-2000 Amp
1970s. Tuck & roll black cover, 2 channels - super and normal, volume, bass, mid range, and treble tone controls, no reverb or tremolo.

1970s	Cabinet	$210	$260
1970s	Head only	$210	$260

Traveler Amp
1970s. Vertical cab solidstate combo amp, 50 watts, 2x12 offset, black tolex.

1977		$310	$390

EBS
1988-present. The EBS Sweden AB company builds professional grade, production bass amps and cabinets in Stockholm, Sweden. They also build effects.

EchoSonic
1950s. Tube combo amps with built-in tape echo built by Ray Butts in Cairo, Illinois, with the first in '53. Used by greats such as Chet Atkins, Scotty Moore and Carl Perkins, probably less than 70 were made. Butts also developed the hum bucking Filter'Tron pickup for Gretsch.

Eden
1976-present. Founded by David Nordschow in Minnesota as a custom builder, Eden now offers a full line of amps, combos, and cabinets for the bass-

AMPS

ist, built in Mundelein, Illinois. In '02, the brand became a division of U.S. Music Corp (Washburn, Randall). They also produce the Nemesis brand of amps.

Egnater

1980-present. Production/custom, intermediate and professional grade, tube amps, combos, preamps and cabinets built in Berkley, Michigan by Bruce Egnater. He also imports some models.

Renegade 65 Amp Head
2009-present. 65 watts, 2 channel head.

2009-2014	$500	$625

Tourmaster 412A/412B Cabinet
2009-present. 4x12", Celestion Vintage 30s, A is slant, B straight.

2009-2014	$385	$480

EKO

1959-1985, 2000-present. In '67 EKO added amps to their product line, offering three piggyback and four combo amps, all with dark covering, dark grille, and the EKO logo. The amp line may have lasted into the early '70s. Since about 2000, EKO Asian-made, solidstate guitar and bass amps are again available. They also make basses and guitars.

El Grande

1951-1953. Tube combo amps built by Chicago's Valco Manufacturing Co., most likely for a retailer, and sold together with lap steels.

Valco Spectator
1952. Same as Supro Spectator, 1x8, 5 watts, volume and tone, red and white two-tone.

1952	$325	$410

Eleca

2004-present. Student level imported combo amps, Eleca logo on bottom of grille. They also offer guitars, effects and mandolins.

Electar

1996-2008. The Gibson owned Electar brand offered tube and solidstate amps, PA gear and wireless systems. Though branded separately, Electar amps were often marketed with other Epiphone products, so see them listed there. Epiphone also had amp models named Electar in the 1930s.

Electro-Harmonix

1968-1981, 1996-present. Electro-Harmonix offered a few amps to go with its line of effects. See Effects section for more company information.

Freedom Brothers Amp
Introduced in 1977. Small AC/DC amp with 2x5 1/2" speakers. E-H has reissued the similar Freedom amp.

1977	$205	$255

Mike Matthews Dirt Road Special Amp
25 watts, 1x12" Celestion, built-in Small Stone phase shifter.

1977	$205	$255

Electromuse

1940s-1950s. Tube amps made by others, like Valco, and usually sold as a package with a lap steel. They also offered guitars.

Amps
Late-1940s. Vertical cabinet with metal handle, Electromuse stencil logo on front of cab.

1948-1949	Lower power	$200	$250

Electrosonic Amplifiers

2002-2009. Intermediate and professional grade, production/custom, tube amps built by Josh Corn in Boonville, Indiana. He also builds effects.

Elk

Late-1960s. Japanese-made by Elk Gakki Co., Ltd. Many were copies of American designs. They also offered guitars and effects.

Custom EL 150L Amp
Late-1960s. Piggyback set, all-tube with head styled after very early Marshall and cab styled after large vertical Fender cab.

1968	$310	$390

Guitar Man EB 105 (Super Reverb) Amp
Late-1960s. All-tube, reverb, copy of blackface Super Reverb.

1968	$260	$325

Twin Amp 60/Twin Amp 50 EB202 Amps
Late-1960s. All-tube, reverb, copy of blackface Dual Showman set (head plus horizontal cab).

1968	$310	$390

Viking 100 VK 100 Amp
Late-1960s. Piggyback set, head styled after very early Marshall and cab styled after very large vertical Fender cab.

1968	$310	$390

Elmwood Amps

1998-present. Jan Alm builds his production/custom, professional and premium grade, guitar tube amps and cabinets in Tanumshede, Sweden.

Elpico

1960s. Made in Europe, PA tube amp heads sometimes used for guitar.

PA Power Tube Amp
1960s. Tubes, 20-watt, metal case, 3 channels, treble and bass control, 2 speaker outs on front panel, Elpico logo on front, small Mexican characterization logo on front.

1960s	$325	$405

Emery Sound

1997-present. Founded by Curt Emery in El Cerrito, California, Emery Sound specializes in custom-made low wattage tube amps.

Emmons

1970s-present. Owned by Lashley, Inc. of Burlington, North Carolina. Amps sold in conjunction with their steel guitars.

Egnater Renegade

Elmwood Bonneville 50

Emery Sound Stagebaby

AMPS

AMPS

*1965 Epiphone EA-
12 RVT Futura*

George Healey

Evans Custom SE200

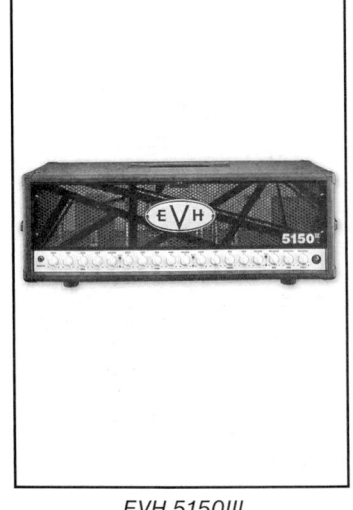

EVH 5150III

MODEL YEAR	FEATURES	EXC. COND. LOW	HIGH

Epiphone

1928-present. Epiphone offered amps into the mid-'70s and reintroduced them in '91 with the EP series. Currently they offer tube and solidstate amps.

Century Amp
1939. Lap steel companion amp, 1x12" combo, lattice wood front with Electar insignia "E" logo.

1939		$400	$500

Cornet Amp
1939. Lap steel companion amp, square shaped wood box, Electar insignia "E" logo.

1939		$345	$425

E-30 B Amp
1972-1975. Solidstate model offered similarly to Gibson G-Series (not GA-Series), 30 watts, 2x10", 4 knobs.

1972-1975		$150	$190

E-60 Amp
1972-1975. Solidstate, 30 watts, 1x10", volume and tone knobs.

1972-1975		$100	$125

E-60 T Amp
1972-1975. E-60 with tremolo, volume, tone, and tremolo knobs.

1972-1975		$105	$130

E-70 T Amp
1971-1975. Solidstate, tremolo, 1x10", 3 knobs.

1971-1975		$110	$135

E-1051 Amp
Ca. 1971-1974. Tube practice amp, 1x10".

1971-1974		$150	$185

EA-12 RVT Futura Amp
1962-1967. 50 watts, originally 4x8" but 4x10" by at least '65, '60s gray tolex, light grille.

1962-1967		$475	$600

EA-14 RVT Ensign Amp
1965-1969. Gray tolex, silver-gray grille, 50 watts, 2x10", split C logo.

1965-1969		$450	$550

EA-15 RVT Zephyr Amp
1961-1965. 14 or 20 watts, 1x15", gray tolex, light grille, split C logo on panel, tremolo and reverb, script Epiphone logo lower right grille.

1961-1965		$475	$575

EA-16 RVT Regent Amp
1965-1969. 25 watts, 1x12", gray vinyl, gray grille, tremolo, reverb. Called the Lancer in first year.

1965-1969		$350	$425

EA-22 RVT Mighty Mite Amp
1964-1967. 1x12", mid-level power, stereo, reverb, vibrato, old style rear mounted control panel.

1964-1967		$800	$1,000

EA-26 RVT Electra Amp
1965-1969. Gray tolex, reverb, tremolo, footswitch, 1x12".

1965-1969		$350	$450

EA-28 RVT Pathfinder Amp
Mid-1960s. Similar to Gibson's GA-19 RVT, medium power, 1x12, reverb and tremolo.

1964-1966		$400	$500

EA-30 Triumph Amp
1959-1961. Low-power, limited production, 1x12, light colored cover, 3 knobs.

1959-1961		$650	$800

EA-32 RVT Comet Amp
1965-1967. 1x10", tremolo, reverb.

1965-1967		$300	$375

EA-33 RVT Galaxie Amp
1963-1964. Gray tolex, gray grille, 1x10".

1963-1964		$350	$450

EA-35 Devon Amp
1961-1963. 1x10" until '62, 1x12" with tremolo in '63.

1961-1963		$350	$450

EA-35 T Devon Amp
1963. Tremolo, 6 knobs.

1963		$350	$450

EA-50 Pacemaker Amp
1961-1969. 1x8" until '62, 1x10" after. EA-50T with tremolo added in '63. Non-tremolo version dropped around '67.

1961-1964	1x8"	$325	$400
1965-1966	1x8" or 1x10"	$250	$300
1967-1969	1x10"	$200	$250

EA-300 RVT Embassy Amp
1965-1969. 90 watts, 2x12", gray vinyl, gray grille, tremolo, reverb.

1965-1969		$500	$625

EA-500T Panorama Amp
1963-1967. 65 watts, head and large cabinet, tremolo, 1x15" and 1x10" until '64, 1x15" and 2x10" after.

1964-1967		$425	$525

EA-600 RVT Maxima Amp
1966-1969. Solidstate Epiphone version of Gibson GSS-100, gray vinyl, gray grille, two 2x10" cabs and hi-fi stereo-style amp head.

1966-1969		$275	$350

Electar Amp
1935-1939. All models have large "E" insignia logo on front, first model Electar in rectangular box with 1x8" speaker, 3 models introduced in '36 (Model C, Model M, and Super AC-DC), the Special AC-DC was introduced in '37, later models were 1x12" combos. Old Electar amps are rarely found in excellent working condition and prices shown are for those rare examples.

1935	Electar	$425	$540
1936-1939	Model C	$550	$700
1936-1939	Model M	$550	$700
1936-1939	Super AC-DC	$700	$875
1937-1939	Special AC-DC	$650	$825

Electar Tube 10 Amp
1997-2004. These modern Electar amps were branded as Electar, not Epiphone, but since they were often marketed with other Epi products, they are included here. 10 watt combo, all tube, 8" speaker.

1997-2004		$80	$150

Electar Tube 30 Amp
1997-2004. 30 watt combo, all tube, 10" speaker, reverb added in 2002.

1997-2004		$55	$125

MODEL YEAR	FEATURES	EXC. COND. LOW	HIGH

Model 100 Amp

1960s. Made in Kalamazoo, label with serial number, Model 100 logo on small 10" speaker, blue cover, 3 tubes, 3 knobs.

1960s		$225	$280

Zephyr Amp

1939-1957. Maple veneer cabinet, 30 watts with 2x6L6 power, 1x12" until '54, 1x15" after, made by Danelectro using their typical designs, Dano D-style blond covering, large split "E" logo on front, brown grille cloth, large block Zephyr logo on back panel.

1939-1953	1x12"	$650	$800
1953-1957	1x15"	$675	$850

Zephyr Dreadnaught Amp

1939. Similar to Zephyr amp but higher power and added microphone input.

1939		$650	$800

Esteban

2005-2007. Imported brand from China, student budget level compact amps.

Compact Amp

2005-2007		$25	$50

Evans Custom Amplifiers

1994-present. Professional grade, production, solidstate head and combo amps built by Scot Buffington in Burlington, North Carolina.

EVH

2007-present. Eddie Van Halen's line of professional and premium grade, production, tube amp heads and cabinets built by Fender. They also build guitars.

Evil Robot

2010-2014. Produced by David Brass and Fretted Americana, made in the U.S.A., initial product produced in limited quantities is based on the '59 Tonemaster (Magnatone) Troubadour amp. Production ceased in '14.

Excelsior

The Excelsior Company started offering accordions in 1924 and had a large factory in Italy by the late '40s. They started offering guitars and amps, uaually built by others including Valco and possibly Sano, around '62. By the early '70s they were out of the guitar business.

Americana Stereophonic High Fidelity Amp

Late 1960s. 50 watts, 1x15", 2x8", 2x3x9" ovals, 2xEL34 power, tube rectifier, large Excelsior logo and small Excelsior The House of Music logo, guitar and accordion inputs, stereo reverb and vibrato.

1968-1969		$800	$1,000

Citation C-15 Amp

1962. Made by Sano, mid power with 2x6V6 power tubes, single speaker combo amp, large Citation by Excelsior logo on front panel.

1962		$540	$675

Fargen

1999-present. Benjamin Fargen builds his professional and premium grade, production/custom, guitar and bass tube amps in Sacramento, California. He also builds guitar effects.

Fender

1946-present. Leo Fender developed many groundbreaking instruments, but Leo's primary passion was amplifiers, and of all his important contributions to musicians, none exceed those he made to the electric tube amplifier.

Tweed Fender amp circuits are highly valued because they defined the tones of rock and roll. Blackface models remained basically the same until mid-'67. Some silverface circuits remained the same as the blackface circuits, while others were changed in the name of reliability. Price Guide values are for all original, excellent condition amps. Small differences in an amp's condition can generate larger differences in selling prices. Non-original speakers will significantly reduce a pre-'68 amp's value. Reconed speakers will reduce the value, but a reconed speaker is preferable to a replacement speaker. Multi-speaker amps generally have matching speaker codes. Different speaker codes require explanation. Fender leather handles are often broken and replaced. A replacement handle drops the value of an amp. Grille cloths should have no tears and a single tear can drop the value of an amp. Each Tweed amp should be evaluated on a case-by-case basis, and it is not unusual for a Tweed amp to have a wide range of values. Alnico speaker replacement is more significant than ceramic speaker replacement. Fender converted to ceramic about '62. Speaker replacement is of less concern in post-'70 Fender amps.

From 1953 to '67, Fender stamped a two-letter date code on the paper tube chart glued inside the cabinet. The first letter was the year (C='53, D='54, etc.) with the second the month (A=January, etc.).

The speaker code found on the frame of an original speaker will identify the manufacturer, and the week and year that the speaker was assembled. The speaker code is typically six (sometimes seven) digits. The first three digits represent the Electronics Industries Association (E.I.A.) source code which identifies the manufacturer. For example, a speaker code 220402 indicates a Jensen speaker (220), made in '54 (4) during the second week (02) of that year. This sample speaker also has another code stamped on the frame. ST654 P15N C4964 indicates the model of the speaker, in this case it is a P15N 15" speaker. The sample speaker also had a code stamped on the speaker cone, 4965 1, which indicates the cone number. All of these codes help identify the originality of the speaker. The value ranges provided in the Guide are for amps with the original speaker and original speaker cone.

Most Fender speakers from the '50s will be Jensens (code 220). By the late-'50s other suppliers were used. The supplier codes are: Oxford (465), C.T.S.

Evil Robot Custom 214

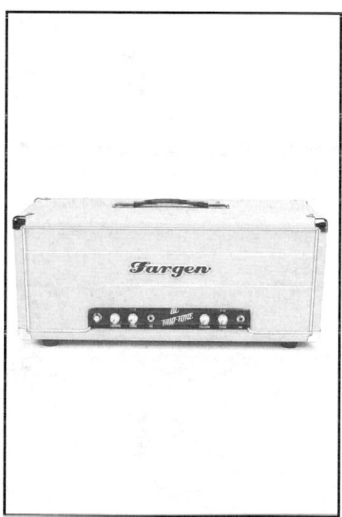

Fargen AC Duo-Tone

Fender Acoustasonic 100 Combo Amp

AMPS

Late-1950s Fender Bandmaster

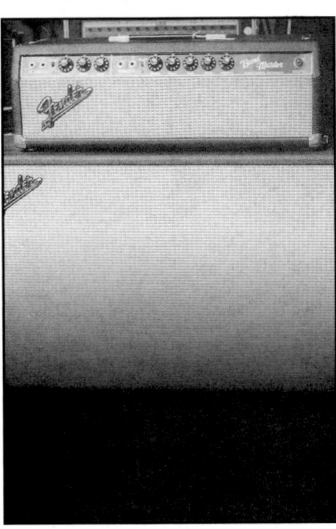

1965 Fender Bandmaster
My Generation Guitars

'58 Fender Bassman

(137), Utah (328). JBL speakers were first used in the late-'50s Vibrasonic, and then in the Showman series, but JBL did not normally have a E.I.A. source code. An amp's speaker code should be reconciled with other dating info when the amp's original status is being verified.

Piggyback amps from '68-'79 utilize rather heavy, bulky cabinets, which can be difficult and expensive to ship. Therefore a standalone amp head from this period is worth significantly more than a standalone cabinet.

General Production Eras:
Diagonal tweed era, Brown tolex era, Blackface era, Silverface era with raised Fender logo with underlining tail, Silverface era with raised Fender logo without underlining tail, and Silverface era with raised Fender logo with small MADE IN USA designation.

Nameplate and Logo Attribution:
Fender nameplate with city but without model name (tweed era), Fender nameplate without city or model name (tweed era), Fender nameplate with model name noted (tweed era), Fender flat logo (brown era), and Fender script raised logo (blackface era).

30 Amp
1980-1981. Tube combo amp, 30 watts, 2x10" or 1x12".

MODEL YEAR	FEATURES	EXC. COND. LOW	HIGH
1980-1981	1x12"	$450	$560
1980-1981	2x10"	$475	$595

75 Amp
1980-1982. Tube, 75 watts, offered as a 1x15" or 1x12" combo, or as head and 4x10" or 2x12" cab.

1980-1982	1x15"	$475	$595
1980-1982	2x12"	$500	$630
1980-1982	4x10"	$550	$685

85 Amp
1988-1992. Solidstate, 85 watt 1x12" combo, black cover, silver grille.

1988-1992		$230	$285

800 Pro Bass Amp Head
2004-2008. Rack-mount, 800 watts, 5-band EQ.

2004-2008		$380	$475

Acoustasonic 100 Combo Amp
2012-2013. 100 watts, 1x8", horn.

2012-2013		$290	$360

Acoustasonic 150 Combo Amp
2012-present. 150 (2x75 stereo) watts, 2x8", piezo horn.

2012-2014		$325	$400

Acoustasonic 30/30 DSP Amp
2000-2011. Small combo, brown tolex, wheat grille. Upgrade model includes DSP (Digital Signal Processor) effects.

2000-2005	30	$230	$285
2000-2011	30 DSP	$245	$310

Acoustasonic Junior/Junior DSP Amp
1998-2011. 2x40 watts, 2x8", Piezo horn.

1998-2011		$250	$310

Acoustasonic SFX/SFX II Amp
1998-2011. SFX technology, 32 stereo digital presents, 2x80 watts, SFX is taller combo with one 10", a sideways mounted 8", and a horn. SFX II is shorter cab with 8", sideways 6".

MODEL YEAR	FEATURES	EXC. COND. LOW	HIGH
1998-2003	SFX, tall cab	$350	$450
2003-2011	SFX II, short cab	$350	$450

Acoustasonic Ultralight Amp
2006-2009. Small 2x125-watt 2 channel head with 2x8 w/tweeters stereo cab.

2006-2009		$525	$650

AmpCan Amp
1997-2008. Cylindrical can-shaped battery powered portable amp.

1997-2008		$160	$200

Automatic SE Amp
1998-2000. Solidstate 25-watt, 1x10" (12" in 2000) combo, blackface cosmetics.

1998-2000		$90	$115

Bandmaster Amp
1953-1974. Wide-panel 1x15" combo '53-'54, narrow-panel 3x10" combo '55-'60, tolex '60, brownface with 1x12" piggyback speaker cabinet '61, 2x12" '62, blackface '62-'67, silverface '68-'74.

The Fender tweed 4x10" Bassman and tweed 3x10" Bandmaster amps are highly sensitive to condition. Because there are so few that are truly excellent, the price ranges listed may be misleading. Most Bassman amps are at best very good minus (VG-) because their tweed is so damaged and stained. It is also rare to find the original speakers, and if the frames are original, they have often been reconed. 4x10" Bassman and 3x10" Bandmasters that are excellent plus plus (Exc++) may have price ranges that are much higher than the values listed. It is estimated that 90% of the vintage 4x10" Bassman are really only VG or less. Because of the extreme condition factor for these tweed amps, the prices below include amps in very good (VG) condition. Therefore the condition for these listed amps is VG to Exc. Exc+ will be more than the values listed here. As per other high-end collectible, each amp should be taken on a case by case basis.

Fender piggyback amps include a head and separate cabinet. The prices shown are for a factory-original matching set. A factory-original set is worth 25% more than the combined value of a head and cabinet that were not originally sold together when new. Heads are worth more than cabinets. The value of a separate head is 40% of the value shown here, and the value of a separate cabinet is 35% of the value shown. In summary, the math is as follows: 40% head + 35% cabinet + 25% premium = 100% value of factory-original set.

1953-1954	Tweed, 1x15"	$3,525	$4,400
1955-1958	Tweed, 3x10"	$7,500	$9,500
1959-1960	Old style cab, pink-brown tolex	$8,000	$10,000
1959-1960	Tweed, 3x10"	$8,000	$10,000
1960	Brown tolex, 3x10"	$3,500	$4,500
1960	Brown tolex, 3x10", reverse controls	$6,300	$8,000
1961	Rough white/ oxblood, 1x12"	$2,500	$3,100

AMPS

MODEL YEAR	FEATURES	EXC. COND. LOW	HIGH
1961-1962	Rough white/ oxblood, 2x12"	$2,100	$2,600
1963-1964	Smooth white/ gold, 2x12"	$2,100	$2,600
1964-1967	Black tolex, 2x12"	$1,250	$1,550
1967-1968	Black, 2x12"	$875	$1,100
1967-1969	Silverface, 2x12"	$725	$900
1970-1974	Silverface, 2x12"	$575	$725

Bandmaster Reverb Amp
1968-1980. 45 watt silverface head with 2x12" cabinet.

1968-1972		$1,025	$1,275
1973-1980		$975	$1,215

Band-Master VM Amp Set
2009-2012. Vintage Modified, 40 watts, piggyback, DSP reverb and effects.

2009-2012		$525	$650

Bantam Bass Amp
1969-1971. 50 watts, large unusual 1x10" Yamaha speaker.

1969-1971	Original speaker	$535	$670

Bassman Amp
1952-1971. Tweed TV front combo, 1x15" in '52, wide-panel '53-'54, narrow-panel and 4x10" '54-'60, tolex brownface with 1x12" in piggyback cabinet '61, 2x12" cabinet '61-'62, blackface '63-'67, silverface '67-'71, 2x15" cabinet '68-'71. Renamed the Bassman 50 in '72.

The Fender tweed 4x10" Bassman and tweed 3x10" Bandmaster amps are highly sensitive to condition. Because there are so few that are truly excellent, the price ranges listed may be misleading. Most Bassman amps are at best very good minus (VG-) because their tweed is so damaged and stained. It is also rare to find the original speakers, and if the frames are original, they have often been reconed. 4x10" Bassmans and 3x10" Bandmasters that are excellent plus plus (Exc++) may have price ranges that are much higher than the values listed. It is estimated that 90% of the vintage 4x10" Bassman are really only VG or less. Because of the extreme condition factor for these tweed amps, the prices below include amps in very good (VG) condition. Therefore the condition for these listed amps is VG to Exc. Exc+ will be more than the values listed here. As per other high-end collectibles, each amp should be taken on a case by case basis.

Fender piggyback amps include a head and separate cabinet. The prices shown are for a factory-original matching set. A factory-original set is worth 25% more than the combined value of a head and cabinet that were not originally sold together when new. Heads are worth more than cabinets. The value of a separate head is 40% of the value shown here, and the value of a separate cabinet is 35% of the value shown. In summary, the math is as follows: 40% head + 35% cabinet + 25% premium = 100% value of factory-original set.

1952	TV front, 1x15"	$2,400	$3,000
1953-1954	Wide panel, 1x15"	$2,500	$3,100
1955-1957	Tweed, 4x10", 2 inputs	$7,500	$9,500
1957-1958	Tweed, 4x10", 4 inputs	$7,500	$9,500

MODEL YEAR	FEATURES	EXC. COND. LOW	HIGH
1959-1960	Old style cab, pink-brown tolex	$8,000	$10,000
1959-1960	Tweed, 4x10", 4 inputs	$8,000	$10,000
1961	White 1x12", 6G6, tube rectifier	$3,200	$4,000
1962	Late '62, white 2x12	$2,300	$2,900
1962	White 1x12", 6G6A, s.s. rectifier	$2,700	$3,350
1963-1964	Smooth white 2x12", 6G6A/B	$2,300	$2,900
1964	Transition, black, white knobs	$1,475	$1,850
1965-1966	AA165/AB165, black knobs	$1,325	$1,650
1967-1969	Silverface, vertical 2x15"	$725	$900
1970-1971	Silverface, 2x15"	$575	$725

'59 Bassman Reissue Amp
1990-2004. Tube, 45 watts, 4x10", tweed covering.

1990-2004		$800	$1,000

Bassman LTD/'59 Limited Edition Amp
2004-2009. Limited edition with solid pine finger-jointed cabinet, tube rectifier, 45 watts, 4x10", vintage laquered tweed (for original look).

2004-2009		$890	$1,100

Bassman 10 Amp
1972-1982. 4x10" combo, silverface and 50 watts for '72-'80, blackface and 70 watts after.

1972-1980	50w	$625	$775
1981-1982	70w	$650	$800

Bassman 20 Amp
1982-1985. Tubes, 20 watts, 1x15".

1982-1985		$500	$625

Bassman 25 Amp
2000-2005. Wedge shape, 1x10", 25 watts, 3-band EQ.

2000-2005		$75	$95

Bassman 50 Amp
1972-1977. 50 watts, with 2x12" cab.

1972-1977		$550	$700

Bassman 60 Amp
1972-1976. 60 watts, 1x12".

1972-1976		$550	$700

Bassman 60 Amp (later version)
2000-2005. Solidstate, 60 watts, 1x12".

2000-2005	Combo	$105	$130

Bassman 70 Amp
1977-1979. 70 watts, 2x15" cab.

1977-1979		$725	$900

Bassman 100 Amp
1972-1977, 2000-2009. Tube, 100 watts, 4x12", name reused on solidstate combo amp.

1972-1977	4x12"	$725	$900
2000-2009	1x15" combo	$210	$260

Bassman 100 T Amp
2012-present. 100-watt head, master volume, '65 blackface cosmetics. Usually paired with Bassman NEO cabs.

2012-2014	Head only	$960	$1,210

1961 Fender Bassman

1962 Fender Bassman

Fender Bassman 100 T

AMPS

Fender Blues Deville Reissue

1995 Fender Blues Junior
Denny Harmison

1966 Fender Champ
David Green

MODEL YEAR	FEATURES	EXC. COND. LOW	HIGH
Bassman 135 Amp			
1978-1983. Tube, 135 watts, 4x10".			
1978-1983		$660	$825
Bassman 150 Combo Amp			
2005-2009. Solidstate 1x12" combo, 150 watts.			
2005-2009		$225	$280
Bassman 250 Combo Amp			
2006. Import from Indonesia, 250 watts, 2x10".			
2006		$235	$295
Bassman 300 Pro Amp Head			
2002-2012. All tube, 300 watts, 6x6550, black cover, black metal grille.			
2002-2012		$850	$1,075
Bassman 400 Amp			
2000-2004. Solidstate, 350 watts with 2x10" plus horn, combo, black cover, black metal grille.			
2000-2004	Combo	$310	$385
2000-2004	Head	$255	$315
Bassman Bassbreaker (Custom Shop) Amp			
1998-2003. Classic Bassman 4x10" configuration. Not offered by 2004 when the '59 Bassman LTD was introduced.			
1998-2003	2x12"	$860	$1,075
1998-2003	4x10"	$860	$1,075
Bassman NEO Cabinet			
2012-present. Cabinets used with Bassman 100 T head and Super Bassman head, standard '65 black-face cosmetics.			
2012-2014	410	$535	$675
2012-2014	610	$575	$725
2012-2014	810	$950	$1,200
Bassman Solidstate Amp			
1968-1971. Small head, piggyback cab. The whole late 1960s Solidstate series were unreliable and prone to overheating, more of a historical novelty than a musical instrument.			
1968-1971		$375	$475
B-Dec 30 Amp			
2006-2009. Bass version of the G-Dec, 30 watts, 1x10.			
2006-2009		$175	$220
Blues Deluxe Amp			
1993-2005. All tube, 40 watts, reverb, 1x12", tweed covering (blond tolex optional '95 only).			
1993-2005		$450	$575
Blues Deluxe Reissue Amp			
2006-present. All tube, tweed, 40 watts, reverb, 1x12".			
2006-2014		$450	$575
Blues DeVille Amp			
1993-1996. All tube Tweed Series, 60 watts, 4x10" (optional 2x12" in '94), reverb, high-gain channel, tweed cover (blond tolex optional '95 only).			
1993-1996		$600	$750
Blues DeVille Reissue Amp			
2006-present. 60 watts, 4x10, tweed.			
2006-2014		$600	$750
Blues Junior Amp (III)			
1995-present. All tube, 15 watts, 1x12", spring reverb, tweed in '95, black tolex with silver grille standard			

MODEL YEAR	FEATURES	EXC. COND. LOW	HIGH
'96 on. Tweed available again '04-'05 and '08-'10, blond 2000-'09, brown '08, surf green '09. III update new in '10.			
1995-2014	Various colors	$350	$435
2008-2010	Lacquer tweed	$400	$500
Blues Junior III Limited Amp			
2010, 2012-2013. Limited Edition models with unique colors, '10 is red tolex/wheat grille, 150 made, sold exclusively at ProGuitarShop, others include "After the Gold Rush" (570 made, gold vinyl/wheat grille), "Red Nova Two-Tone" (482 made, 2-tone red and black vinyl/black grille), "Chocolate Tweed" (262 made, 2-tone dark chocolate vinyl and tweed/oxblood grille), "Creamy Wine Two-Tone" (600 made, 2-tone wine red and dark vanilla cream vinyl/wheat grille), "Navy Blues" (100 made, navy blue vinyl/silver grille).			
2010-2012	Various colors	$350	$435
Blues Junior III Western Amp			
2011. Tooled vinyl, wheat grille.			
2011		$350	$435
Blues Junior Woody Amp			
2002-2003. Custom Shop exotic hardwood version of Blues Jr.			
2002-2003		$600	$750
Bronco 40 Bass Amp			
2012-present. 40 watts, 1x10", 12 effects.			
2012-2014		$150	$185
Bronco Amp			
1968-1974, 1993-2001. 1x 8" speaker, all tube, 5 watts until '72, 6 watts for '72-'74, ('90s issue is 15 watts), solidstate, tweed covering (blond tolex was optional for '95 only).			
1968-1974	tubes	$400	$500
1993-2001	15w, no reverb	$100	$120
Bullet/Bullet Reverb Amp			
1994-2005. Solidstate, 15 watts, 1x8", with or without reverb.			
1994-2005		$25	$65
BXR Series Bass Amp			
1987-2000. Various models.			
1987-2000		$45	$175
Capricorn Amp			
1970-1972. Solidstate, 105 watts, 3x12".			
1970-1972		$500	$625
Champ Amp			
1953-1982. Renamed from the Champion 600. Tweed until '64, black tolex after, 3 watts in '53, 4 watts '54-'64, 5 watts '65-'71, 6 watts '72-'82, 1x6" until '57, 1x8" after.			
1953-1954	Wide panel, 1x6"	$1,175	$1,450
1955-1956	Narrow panel, 1x6"	$1,175	$1,450
1956-1964	Narrow panel, 1x8"	$1,450	$1,800
1964	Old cab, black, 1x8", last F51	$1,100	$1,350
1964-1967	New cab, black tolex, 1x8", AA764	$550	$700
1968-1980	Silverface, 1x8"	$430	$530
1981-1982	Blackface	$430	$530
Champ II Amp			
1982-1985. 18 watts, 1x10".			
1982-1985		$460	$575

The *Vintage Guitar Price Guide* shows low to high values for items in all-original excellent condition, and, where applicable, with original case or cover.

MODEL YEAR	FEATURES	EXC. COND. LOW	HIGH

'57 Champ Reissue Amp
2009-2011. Custom Series reissue with tweed and leather handle, handwired.

2009-2011		$800	$1,000

Champ 12 Amp
1986-1992. Tube, 12 watts, overdrive, reverb, 1x12".

1986-1992	Black	$275	$345
1986-1992	Red, white, gray or snakeskin	$300	$375

Champ 25 SE Amp
1992-1993. Hybrid solidstate and tube combo, 25 watts, 1x12".

1992-1993		$190	$240

Champion 30/30 DSP Amp
1999-2003. Small solidstate combo, 30 watts, 1x8", reverb.

1999-2003		$80	$100

Champion 40 Amp
2014-present. Solidstate, 40 watts, 1x12".

2014-2015		$100	$125

Champion 110 Amp
1993-2000. Solidstate, 25 watts, 1x10", 2 channels, black tolex, silver grille

1993-2000		$90	$115

Champion 300 Amp
2004-2007. 30 watt solidstate combo, Dyna-Touch Series, DSP effects.

2004-2007		$150	$185

Champion 600 Amp
1949-1953. Replaced the Champion 800, 3 watts, 1x6", 2-tone tolex, TV front. Replaced by the Champ.

1949-1953		$1,000	$1,250

Champion 600 Amp (later version)
2007-2012. Small 5 watt combo.

2007-2012		$120	$150

Champion 800 Amp
1948. About 100 made, TV front, luggage tweed cover, 1x8, 3 tubes, becomes Champion 600 in '49.

1948		$1,100	$1,350

Concert Amp
1960-1965. Introduced with 40 watts and 4x10", brown tolex until '63, blackface '63-'65. In '62 white tolex was ordered by Webbs Music (CA) instead of the standard brown tolex. A wide range is noted for the rare white tolex, and each amp should be valued on a case-by-case basis. In '60, the very first brown tolex had a pink tint but only on the first year amps.

1960	Brown (pink) tolex	$2,450	$3,050
1960	Brown (pink), tweed grille	$2,650	$3,300
1961-1963	Brown tolex	$2,350	$2,925
1962	White tolex (Webb Music)	$2,450	$3,050
1963-1965	Blackface	$2,200	$2,800

Concert (Pro Tube Series) Amp
1993-1995. Tube combo, 60 watts, 1x12, blackface.

1993-1995		$600	$750

Concert Reverb (Pro Tube Series) Amp
2002-2005. 4x10" combo, reverb, tremolo, overdrive.

2002-2005		$625	$775

Concert 112 Amp
1982-1985. Tube, 60 watts, 1x12", smaller Concert logo (not similar to '60s style logo).

1982-1985		$850	$1,050

Concert 210 Amp
1982-1985. Tube, 60 watts, 2x10".

1982-1985		$850	$1,050

Concert 410 Amp
1982-1985. Tube, 60 watts, 4x10".

1982-1985		$875	$1,075

Concert II Amp Head
1982-1987. 60 watts, 2 channels.

1982-1987		$750	$950

Cyber Champ Amp
2004-2005. 65 watts, 1x12", Cyber features, 21 presets.

2004-2005		$200	$250

Cyber Deluxe Amp
2002-2005. 65 watts, 1x12", Cyber features, 64 presets.

2002-2005		$360	$450

Cyber-Twin (SE) Amp
2001-2011. Hybrid tube/solidstate modeling amp, 2x65 watts, head or 2x12" combo, becomes the SE in '05.

2001-2003	Head only	$400	$500
2001-2004	Combo	$440	$550
2005-2011	2nd Edition SE	$440	$550

Deco-Tone (Custom Shop) Amp
2000. Art-deco styling, 165 made, all tube, 15 watts, 1x12", round speaker baffle opening, uses 6BQ5/ES84 power tubes.

2000		$700	$875

Deluxe Amp
1948-1966. Name changed from Model 26 ('46-'48) 10 watts (15 by '54 and 20 by '63), 1x12", TV front with tweed '48-'53, wide-panel '53-'55, narrow-panel '55-'60, brown tolex with brownface '61-'63, black tolex with blackface '63-'66.

1948-1952	Tweed, TV front	$3,000	$3,800
1953-1954	Wide panel	$3,000	$3,800
1955	Narrow panel, small cab	$4,600	$5,800
1956-1960	Narrow panel, large cab	$4,300	$5,400
1961-1963	Brown tolex	$2,550	$3,200
1964-1966	Black tolex	$2,550	$3,200

Deluxe Reverb Amp
1963-1981. 1x12", 20 watts, blackface '63-'67, silverface '68-'80, blackface with silver grille option introduced in mid-'80. Replaced by Deluxe Reverb II. Reissued as Deluxe Reverb '65 Reissue.

1963-1967	Blackface	$2,600	$3,250
1967-1968	Silverface	$2,000	$2,500
1969-1970	Silverface	$1,625	$2,025
1971-1972	Silverface	$1,200	$1,500
1973-1980	Silverface	$1,200	$1,500
1980-1981	Blackface	$1,200	$1,500

Deluxe Reverb Solidstate Amp
1966-1969. Part of Fender's early solidstate series.

1966-1969		$400	$500

1967 Fender Deluxe
David Daviee

1970s Fender Deluxe

1965 Fender Deluxe Reverb
Rob Bernstein

AMPS

Fender '65 Deluxe Reverb Reissue Amp

Fender Dual Showman Reverb

Fender Frontman 25R

MODEL YEAR	FEATURES	EXC. COND. LOW	HIGH

'57 Deluxe Reissue Amp
2007-2011. Custom Series reissue, handwired, tweed, 12 watts, 1x12".

2007-2011		$1,000	$1,250

'65 Deluxe Reverb Reissue Amp
1993-present. Blackface reissue, 22 watts, 1x12".

1993-2014	Various colors	$675	$850

Deluxe Reverb II Amp
1982-1986. Updated Deluxe Reverb with 2 6V6 power tubes, all tube preamp section, black tolex, blackface, 20 watts, 1x12".

1982-1986		$850	$1,060

Deluxe 85 Amp
1988-1993. Solidstate, 65 watts, 1x12", black tolex, silver grille, Red Knob Series.

1988-1993		$260	$325

Deluxe 90 Amp
1999-2003. Solidstate, 90 watts, 1x12" combo, DSP added in '02.

1999-2002		$185	$230
2002-2003	DSP option	$210	$265

Deluxe 112 Amp
1992-1995. Solidstate, 65 watts, 1x12", black tolex with silver grille.

1992-1995		$165	$210

Deluxe 112 Plus Amp
1995-2000. 90 watts, 1x12", channel switching.

1995-2000		$185	$230

Deluxe 900 Amp
2004-2006. Solidstate, 90 watts, 1x12" combo, DSP effects.

2004-2006		$225	$285

Deluxe VM Amp
2009-2013. Vintage Modified Series, 40 watts, 1x12", black.

2009-2013		$490	$610

Dual Professional Amp
1994-2002. Custom Shop amp, all tube, point-to-point wiring, 100 watts, 2x12" Celestion Vintage 30s, fat switch, reverb, tremolo, white tolex, oxblood grille.

1994-2002		$1,250	$1,560

Dual Professional/Super Amp
1947. V-front, early-'47 small metal name tag "Fender/Dual Professional/Fullerton California" tacked on front of cab, 2x10 Jensen PM10-C each with transformer attached to speaker frame, tube chart on inside of cab, late-'47 renamed Super and new metal badge "Fender/Fullerton California".

1947		$4,800	$6,000

Dual Showman Amp
1962-1969. Called the Double Showman for the first year. White tolex (black available from '64), 2x15", 85 watts. Reintroduced '87-'94 as solidstate, 100 watts, optional speaker cabs.

Fender piggyback amps include a head and separate cabinet. The prices shown are for a factory-original matching set. A factory-original set is worth 25% more than the combined value of a head and cabinet that were not originally sold together when new. Heads are worth more than cabinets. The value of a separate head is 40% of the value shown here,

and the value of a separate cabinet is 35% of the value shown. In summary, the math is as follows: 40% head + 35% cabinet + 25% premium = 100% value of factory-original set.

1962	Rough blond/oxblood	$3,800	$4,800
1963	Smooth blond/wheat	$2,900	$3,600
1964-1967	Black tolex, horizontal cab	$2,000	$2,500
1968	Blackface, large vertical cab	$1,100	$1,400
1968-1969	Silverface	$840	$1,050

Dual Showman Reverb Amp
1968-1981. Black tolex with silver grille, silverface, 100 watts, 2x15".

1968-1972		$1,100	$1,400
1973-1981		$975	$1,225

Fender '57 Amp
2007. Only 300 made, limited edition combo, handwired, 1x12", retro styling.

2007		$1,100	$1,375

FM Series Amp
2003-2010. Lower-priced solidstate amps, heads and combos.

2003-2006	FM-212R, 2x12	$200	$250
2003-2010	FM-100 Head/Cab	$225	$285

Frontman Series Amp
1997-present. Student combo amps, models include 10G (10 watts, 1x6"), 15/15B/15G/15R (15 watts, 1x8"), 25R (25 watts, 1x10", reverb), 212R (100 watts, 2x12", reverb).

1997-2004	15DSP w/15 FX selections	$70	$90
1997-2004	25DSP	$110	$140
1997-2006	65DSP	$150	$185
1997-2011	15/15B/15G/15R	$50	$70
1997-2011	65R	$125	$160
1997-2013	25R	$75	$95
2007-2013	212R	$200	$250

G-Dec Amp
2005-2012. Digital, amp and effects presets.

2005-2009	G-Dec (small cab)	$125	$155
2006-2009	G-Dec 30 (large cab)	$175	$220
2007-2008	G-Dec Exec, maple cab	$230	$285
2011-2012	G-Dec Jr, Champ cab	$70	$90

H.O.T. Amp
1990-1996. Solidstate, 25 watts, 1x10", gray carpet cover (black by '92), black grille.

1990-1996		$80	$100

Harvard Solidstate Amp
1980-1983. Reintroduced from tube model, black tolex with blackface, 20 watts, 1x10".

1980-1983		$120	$150

Harvard Tube Amp
1956-1961. Tweed, 10 watts, 1x10", 2 knobs volume and roll-off tone, some were issued with 1x8". Reintroduced as a solidstate model in '80.

1956-1961		$2,400	$3,000

MODEL YEAR	FEATURES	EXC. COND. LOW	HIGH

Harvard Reverb Amp
1981-1982. Solidstate, 20 watts, 1x10", reverb, replaced by Harvard Reverb II in '83.

1981-1982		$120	$150

Harvard Reverb II Amp
1983-1985. Solidstate, black tolex with blackface, 20 watts, 1x10", reverb.

1983-1985		$120	$150

Hot Rod Blues Junior Limited Amp
2000s. Compact tube combo, rough blond tolex, dark tolex sides, wheat grille.

2000s		$350	$435

Hot Rod Deluxe III Limited Edition "Chocolate Tweed" Amp
2012. 253 made, 2-tone chocolate vinyl and tweed, classic wheat grille.

2012		$475	$600

Hot Rod Deluxe III Limited Edition "Emerald Isle" Amp
2012. 550 made, emerald green vinyl, classic wheat grille.

2012		$475	$600

Hot Rod Deluxe III Limited Edition "Silver Noir Two-Tone" Amp
2012-2013. 197 made, 2-tone black and silver vinyl, black grille.

2012-2013		$475	$600

Hot Rod Deluxe/Deluxe III Amp
1996-present. Updated Blues Deluxe, tube, 40 watts, 1x12", black tolex. Various covering optional by '98, also a wood cab In 2003. III added to name in '11.

1996-2014	Various colors	$475	$600

Hot Rod DeVille 212 Amp
1996-2011. Updated Blues DeVille, tube, 60 watts, black tolex, 2x12".

1996-2000		$550	$700
2001-2011	Black tolex	$550	$700

Hot Rod DeVille 410/DeVille 410 III Amp
1996-present. Tube, 60 watts, black tolex, 4x10". III added to name in '11.

1996-2000		$600	$750
2001-2006	Ltd. Ed. brown tolex	$600	$750
2001-2014	Black tolex	$600	$750

Hot Rod Pro Junior III Amp
2010-present. 15 watts, 1x10", black textured vinyl covering with blackface-style black/silver grille cloth.

2011	Red October Ltd. Ed.	$285	$360
2011-2014	Black	$285	$360

J.A.M. Amp
1990-1996. Solidstate, 25 watts, 1x12", 4 preprogrammed sounds, gray carpet cover (black by '92).

1990-1996		$67	$84

Jazz King Amp
2005-2008. 140 watt solidstate 1x15" combo.

2005-2008		$475	$600

KXR Series Amp
1995-2002. Keyboard combo amps, 50 to 200 watts, solidstate, 1x12" or 15".

1995-2002		$75	$125

Libra Amp
1970-1972. Solidstate, 105 watts, 4x12" JBL speakers, black tolex.

1970-1972		$500	$625

London 185 Amp
1988-1992. Solidstate, 160 watts, black tolex.

1988-1992	Head only	$225	$280

London Reverb 112 Amp
1983-1985. Solidstate, 100 watts, black tolex, 1x12".

1983-1985		$295	$375

London Reverb 210 Amp
1983-1985. Solidstate, 100 watts, black tolex, 2x10".

1983-1985		$315	$400

London Reverb Amp Head
1983-1985. Solidstate head, 100 watts.

1983-1985		$240	$300

M-80 Amp
1989-1994. Solidstate, 90 watts, 1x12". The M-80 series were also offered as head only amp.

1989-1993		$175	$215

M-80 Bass Amp
1991-1994. Solidstate, bass and keyboard amp, 160 watts, 1x15".

1991-1994		$175	$215

M-80 Chorus Amp
1990-1994. Solidstate, stereo chorus, 2 65-watt channels, 2x12", 90 watts.

1990-1994		$220	$275

M-80 Pro Amp
1992. Rackmount version of M-80, 90 watts.

1992		$175	$215

Model 26 Amp
1946-1947. Tube, 10 watts, 1x10", hardwood cabinet. Sometimes called Deluxe Model 26, renamed Deluxe in '48.

1946-1947		$1,700	$2,100

Montreux Amp
1983-1985. Solidstate, 100 watts, 1x12", black tolex with silver grille.

1983-1985		$300	$380

Musicmaster Bass Amp
1970-1983. Tube, 12 watts, 1x12", black tolex.

1970-1980	Silverface	$425	$525
1981-1983	Blackface	$425	$525

Mustang Series Amp
2010-present. Mustang I thru V, modeling amp effects, small combo up to a half-stack.

2010-2014	I, 20w, 1x8	$50	$70
2010-2014	II, 40w, 1x12	$115	$145
2011-2014	III, 100w, 1x12	$150	$190
2011-2014	IV, 150w, 2x12	$260	$325
2011-2014	V, 150w, 4x12	$275	$355

PA-100 Amp Head
Early to mid-1970s. All tube head, 100 watts, 4 channels with standard guitar inputs, master volume.

1970s		$360	$450

PA-135 Amp Head
Later 1970s. All tube head, 135 watts, 4 channels, master volume.

1970s		$450	$560

Fender G-Dec 30

2012 Fender Hot Rod Deluxe III Limited Edition "Emerald Isle" Amp

Fender Mustang I

AMPS

Fender Pawn Shop Special Excelsior

Fender Pawn Shop Special Vaporizer

1963 Fender Princeton
Roger Myers

MODEL YEAR	FEATURES	EXC. COND. LOW	HIGH

Pawn Shop Special Excelsior/Excelsior Pro Amp
2012-2013. Retro late-'40s vertical combo slate-grille cab, 13-watt 1x15" combo tube amp, tremolo, brown textured vinyl covering.

2012-2013		$200	$250

Pawn Shop Special Ramparte Amp
2014. Tube amp, 9 watts, 1x12", 2-tone chocolate and copper grille cloth with wheat.

2014		$200	$250

Pawn Shop Special Vaporizer Amp
2014. Tube amp, 12 watts, 2x10", Rocket Red, Slate Blue or Surf Green dimpled vinyl covering with silver grille cloth.

2014		$240	$300

Performer 650 Amp
1993-1995. Solidstate hybrid amp with single tube, 70 watts, 1x12".

1993-1995		$180	$225

Performer 1000 Amp
1993-1995. Solidstate hybrid amp with a single tube, 100 watts, 1x12".

1993-1995		$195	$245

Princeton Amp
1948-1979. Tube, 4.5 watts (12 watts by '61), 1x8" (1x10" by '61), tweed '48-'61, brown '61-'63, black with blackface '63-'69, silverface '69-'79.

1948	Tweed, TV front	$1,300	$1,600
1949-1953	Tweed, TV front	$1,300	$1,600
1953-1954	Wide panel	$1,300	$1,600
1955-1956	Narrow panel, small cab	$1,700	$2,100
1956-1961	Narrow panel, large cab	$1,700	$2,100
1961-1963	Brown, 6G2	$1,700	$2,100
1963-1964	Black, 6G2	$1,700	$2,100
1964-1966	Black, AA964, no grille logo	$1,200	$1,500
1966-1967	Black, AA964, raised grille logo	$1,200	$1,500
1968-1969	Silverface, alum. grille trim	$800	$1,000
1969-1970	Silverface, no grille trim	$800	$1,000
1971-1979	Silverface, AB1270	$800	$1,000
1973-1975	Fender logo-tail	$800	$1,000
1975-1978	No Fender logo-tail	$800	$1,000
1978-1979	With boost pull-knob	$800	$1,000

Princeton Reverb Amp
1964-1981. Tube, black tolex, blackface until '67, silverface after until blackface again in '80.

1964-1967	Blackface	$1,825	$2,300
1968-1972	Silverface, Fender logo-tail	$975	$1,225
1973-1979	Silverface, no Fender logo-tail	$900	$1,125
1980-1981	Blackface	$900	$1,125

Princeton Reverb II Amp
1982-1985. Tube amp, 20 watts, 1x12", black tolex, silver grille, distortion feature.

1982-1985		$750	$935

MODEL YEAR	FEATURES	EXC. COND. LOW	HIGH

'65 Princeton Reverb Reissue Amp
2009-present. Vintage Reissue series.

2009-2014	Various colors	$615	$775

Princeton Chorus Amp
1988-1996. Solidstate, 2x10", 2 channels at 25 watts each, black tolex. Replaced by Princeton Stereo Chorus in '96.

1988-1996		$180	$225

Princeton 65 Amp
1999-2003. Combo 1x2", reverb, blackface, DSP added in '02.

1999-2001		$155	$190
2002-2003	With DSP	$165	$205

Princeton 112/112 Plus Amp
1993-1997. Solidstate, 40 watts (112) or 60 watts (112 Plus), 1x12", black tolex.

1993-1994	40 watt	$155	$190
1995-1997	60 watt	$155	$190

Princeton 650 Amp
2004-2006. Solidstate 65 watt 1x12" combo, DSP effects, black tolex.

2004-2006		$155	$190

Princeton Recording Amp
2007-2009. Based on classic '65 Princeton Reverb, 15 watts, 1x10" combo, 2 on-board effects (overdrive/compression), 4-button footswitch, blackface cosmetics.

2007-2009		$525	$650

Pro Amp
1946-1965. Called Professional '46-'48. 15 watts (26 by '54 and 25 by '60), 1x15", tweed TV front '48-'53, wide-panel '53-'54, narrow-panel '55-'60, brown tolex and brownface '60-'63, black and blackface '63-'65.

1946-1953	Tweed, TV front	$2,900	$3,600
1953-1954	Wide panel	$3,100	$3,900
1955	Narrow panel (old chassis)	$3,900	$4,850
1955-1959	Narrow panel (new chassis)	$4,100	$5,100
1960	Pink/brown, tweed-era cover	$2,400	$3,000
1961-1962	Brown tolex	$2,400	$3,000
1963-1965	Black tolex	$2,200	$2,800

Pro Reverb Amp
1965-1982. Tube, black tolex, 40 watts (45 watts by '72, 70 watts by '81), 2x12", blackface '65-'69 and '81-'83, silverface '69-'81.

1965-1967	Blackface	$2,200	$2,700
1968	Silverface	$1,525	$1,900
1969-1970		$1,450	$1,800
1971-1972		$1,050	$1,325
1973-1980	Silverface	$1,050	$1,325
1981-1982	Blackface	$1,050	$1,325

Pro Reverb Solidstate Amp
1967-1969. Fender's first attempt at solidstate design, the attempt was unsuccessful and many of these models will overheat and are known to be unreliable. 50 watts, 2x12", upright vertical combo cabinet.

1967-1969		$400	$500

Pro Reverb Reissue (Pro Series) Amp
2002-2005. 50 watts, 1x12", 2 modern designed channels - clean and high gain.

2002-2005		$625	$775

The *Vintage Guitar Price Guide* shows low to high values for items in all-original excellent condition, and, where applicable, with original case or cover.

MODEL YEAR	FEATURES	EXC. COND. LOW	HIGH

Pro 185 Amp
1989-1991. Solidstate, 160 watts, 2x12", black tolex.

1989-1991		$265	$330

Pro Junior Amp
1995-2009. All tube, 2xEL84 tubes, 15 watts, 1x10" Alnico Blue speaker, tweed or blond in '95, black tolex '96 on.

1995	Blond	$350	$435
1995	Tweed	$500	$625
1996-2009	Black tolex	$285	$360

Pro Junior 60th Anniversary Woody Amp
2006. Recreation of original Fender model (1946-2006), 15 watts, 1x10, lacquered wood cab.

2006		$535	$675

Pro Junior Masterbuilt Custom Shop Amp
Late 1990s. Transparent white-blond wood finish.

1990s		$535	$675

Prosonic Amp
1996-2001. Custom Shop 2x10" combo or head/4x12" cab, 60 watts, 2 channels, 3-way rectifier switch, tube reverb, black, red or green.

1996-2001	Cab	$300	$375
1996-2001	Combo	$660	$825
1996-2001	Head	$585	$730

Quad Reverb Amp
1971-1978. Black tolex, silverface, 4x12", tube, 100 watts. Large Fender combo amps built in the '70s are not often in excellent condition. Any grille stain or tear to the grille can mean an amp is not in excellent condition and can significantly reduce the values shown.

1971-1978		$740	$925

R.A.D. Amp
1990-1996. Solidstate, 20 watts, 1x8", gray carpet cover until '92, black after.

1990-1996		$60	$75

R.A.D. Bass Amp
1992-1994. Solidstate, 25 watts, 1x10", renamed BXR 25.

1992-1994		$60	$75

Roc-Pro 1000 Amp
1997-2001. Hybrid tube combo or head, 100 watts, 1x12", spring reverb, 1000 logo on front panel.

1997-2001	Combo	$180	$225
1997-2001	Half stack, head & cab	$300	$375

Rumble Bass Amp
1994-1998. Custom Shop tube amp, 300 watts, 4x10" cabs, blond tolex, oxblood grille.

1994-1998	Cab	$425	$525
1994-1998	Head	$1,050	$1,325

Rumble Series Amp
2003-present. Solidstate bass amps, include Rumble 15 (15w, 1x8"), 25 (25w, 1x10"), 30 (30w, 1x10"), 40 (40w, 1x10"), 60 (60w, 1x12"), 75 (75w, 1x12"), 100 (100w, 1x15" or 2x10"), 150 (150w, 1x15") and 350 (350w, 2x10"). Some models discontinued '09 then restarted in '14.

2003-2009	Rumble 60	$150	$185
2003-2013	Rumble 150	$175	$215
2003-2013	Rumble 150 Head	$130	$160
2003-2013	Rumble 30	$110	$135

MODEL YEAR	FEATURES	EXC. COND. LOW	HIGH
2003-2013	Rumble 350	$275	$340
2003-2013	Rumble 350 Head	$185	$230
2003-2013	Rumble 75	$150	$185
2003-2014	Rumble 100	$175	$215
2003-2014	Rumble 15	$55	$70
2003-2014	Rumble 25	$70	$87
2003-2014	Rumble 40	$125	$155

Scorpio Amp
1970-1972. Solidstate, 56 watts, 2x12", black tolex.

1970-1972		$500	$625

SFX Keyboard 200 Amp
1998-1999. Keyboard combo amp, digital effects, black tolex.

1998-1999		$250	$310

SFX Satellite Amp
1997-2001. Hybrid tube combo or head, 100 watts, 1x12", spring reverb.

1998-2000		$300	$375

Showman 12 Amp
1960-1966. Piggyback cabinet with 1x12", 85 watts, blond tolex (changed to black in '64), maroon grille '61-'63, gold grille '63-'64, silver grille '64-'67.

1960-1962	Rough blond/oxblood	$3,500	$4,400
1963-1964	Smooth blond/gold	$3,000	$3,775
1964-1966	Black	$1,750	$2,200

Showman 15 Amp
1960-1968. Piggyback cabinet with 1x15", 85 watts, blond tolex (changed to black in '64), maroon grille '61-'63, gold grille '63-'64, silver grille '64-'67.

1960-1962	Rough blond/oxblood	$3,300	$4,100
1963-1964	Smooth blond/gold	$2,800	$3,500
1964-1967	Blackface	$1,750	$2,200
1967-1968	Silverface	$725	$900

Showman 112 Amp
1983-1987. Solidstate, 2 channels, 200 watts, reverb, 4 button footswitch, 5-band EQ, effects loop, 1x12".

1983-1987		$400	$500

Showman 115 Amp
1983-1987. Solidstate, 1x15", 2 channels, reverb, EQ, effects loop, 200 watts, black tolex.

1983-1987		$400	$500

Showman 2 10 Amp
1983-1987. Solidstate, 2 channels, reverb, EQ, effects loop, 2x10", 200 watts, black tolex.

1983-1987		$400	$500

Showman 212 Amp
1983-1987. Solidstate, 2 channels, reverb, EQ, effects loop, 2x12", 200 watts, black tolex.

1983-1987		$425	$525

Sidekick 10 Amp
1983-1985. Small solidstate Japanese or Mexican import, 10 watts, 1x8".

1983-1985		$50	$62

Sidekick Bass 30 Amp
1983-1985. Combo, 30 watts, 1x12".

1983-1985		$60	$75

Sidekick Reverb 15 Amp
1983-1985. Small solidstate import, reverb, 15 watts.

1983-1985		$70	$87

1966 Fender Princeton Reverb
Roger Myers

Fender Pro Reverb
Frank Salvato

Fender Rumble 100

AMPS

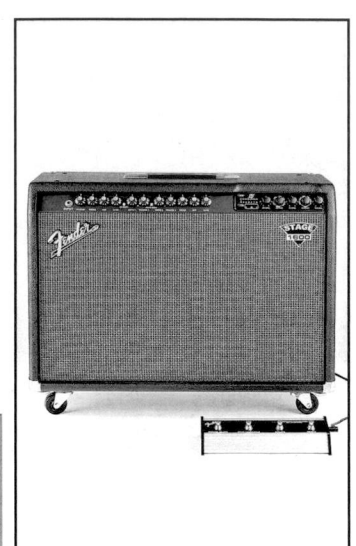

Fender Stage 1600

Fender Super Bassman Head

1967 Fender Super Reverb

MODEL YEAR	FEATURES	EXC. COND. LOW	HIGH
Sidekick Reverb 20 Amp			
1983-1985. Small solidstate Japanese or Mexican import, 20 watts, reverb, 1x10".			
1983-1985		$75	$93
Sidekick Reverb 30 Amp			
1983-1985. Small solidstate Japanese or Mexican import, 30 watts, 1x12", reverb.			
1983-1985		$80	$100
Sidekick Reverb 65 Amp			
1986-1988. Small solidstate Japanese or Mexican import, 65 watts, 1x12".			
1986-1988		$100	$125
Sidekick 100 Bass Amp Head			
1986-1993. 100 watt bass head.			
1986-1993		$75	$93
Squier Champ 15 Amp			
2000s		$45	$57
Squier SKX Series Amp			
1990-1992. Solidstate, 15 watts, 1x8", model 15R with reverb. Model 25R is 25 watts, 1x10, reverb.			
1990-1992	15, non-reverb	$32	$40
1990-1992	15R, reverb	$36	$45
1990-1992	25R, reverb	$45	$57
Squier SP10 Amp			
2003-2012. 10 watt solidstate, usually sold as part of a Guitar Pack.			
2003-2012		$32	$40
Stage 100/Stage 1000 Amp			
1999-2006. Solidstate, 1x12", combo or head only options, 100 watts, blackface. Head available until 2004.			
1999-2004	Head only	$205	$255
1999-2006	Combo	$265	$325
1999-2006	Combo stack, 2 cabs	$340	$425
Stage 1600 DSP Amp			
2004-2006. Solidstate, 160 watts, 2x12" combo, 16 digital effects (DSP).			
2004-2006 .		$265	$325
Stage Lead/Lead II Amp			
1983-1985. Solidstate, 100 watts, 1x12", reverb, channel switching, black tolex. Stage Lead II has 2x12".			
1983-1985	1x12"	$215	$265
1983-1985	2x12"	$240	$295
Starcaster by Fender 15G Amp			
2000s. Student economy pac amp, sold with a guitar, strap and stand, Starcaster by Fender logo. Sold in Costco and other discounters.			
2000s		$20	$25
Steel-King Amp			
2004-2009. Designed for pedal steel, 200 watts, solidstate, 1x15".			
2004-2009		$535	$675
Studio 85 Amp			
1988. Studio 85 logo on upper right front of grille, solidstate, 1x12" combo, 65 watts, red knobs.			
1988		$125	$155
Studio Bass Amp			
1977-1980. Uses Super Twin design, tube, 200 watt combo, 5-band eq, 1x15".			
1977-1980		$375	$475

MODEL YEAR	FEATURES	EXC. COND. LOW	HIGH
Studio Lead Amp			
1983-1986. Solidstate, 50 watts, 1x12", black tolex.			
1983-1986		$200	$250
Super Amp			
1947-1963, 1992-1997. Introduced as Dual Professional in 1946, renamed Super '47, 2x10" speakers, 20 watts (30 watts by '60 with 45 watts in '62), tweed TV front '47-'53, wide-panel '53-'54, narrow-panel '55-'60, brown tolex '60-'64. Reintroduced '92-'97 with 4x10", 60 watts, black tolex.			
1947-1952	V-front	$4,700	$5,800
1953-1954	Tweed, wide panel	$4,000	$5,000
1955	Tweed, narrow panel, 6L6	$5,600	$7,100
1956-1957	Tweed, narrow panel, 5E4, 6V6	$4,400	$5,600
1957-1960	Tweed, narrow panel, 6L6	$6,100	$7,700
1960	Pink, tweed-era grille	$2,500	$3,100
1960	Pink/brown metal knobs	$2,650	$3,300
1960	Pink/brown reverse knobs	$2,650	$3,300
1960-1962	Brown, oxblood grille, 6G4	$2,400	$3,000
1962-1963	Brown, tan/wheat grille, 6G4	$2,400	$3,000
Super 60 Amp			
1989-1993. Red Knob series, 1x12", 60 watts, earlier versions with red knobs, later models with black knobs, offered in optional covers such as red, white, gray or snakeskin.			
1989-1993	Combo	$325	$405
1989-1993	Head	$225	$280
Super 112 Amp			
1990-1993. Red Knob series, 1x12", 60 watts, earlier versions with red knobs, later models with black knobs, originally designed to replace the Super60 but the Super60 remained until '93.			
1990-1993		$325	$405
Super 210 Amp			
1990-1993. Red Knob series, 2x10", 60 watts, earlier versions with red knobs, later models with black knobs.			
1990-1993		$345	$430
Super 410 Amp			
1992-1997. 60 watts, 4x10", black tolex, silver grille, blackface control panel.			
1992-1997		$600	$750
Super Bassman Amp Head			
2012-present. 300-watt head, 6x6550 power tubes, master volume, standard '65 blackface cosmetics.			
2012-2014		$1,025	$1,300
Super Champ Amp			
1982-1986. Black tolex, 18 watts, blackface, 1x10".			
1982-1986		$825	$1,025
Super Champ Deluxe Amp			
1982-1986. Solid oak cabinet, 18 watts, upgrade 10" Electro-Voice speaker, see-thru brown grille cloth.			
1982-1986		$1,300	$1,650

The ***Vintage Guitar Price Guide*** shows low to high values for items in all-original excellent condition, and, where applicable, with original case or cover.

MODEL YEAR	FEATURES	EXC. COND. LOW	HIGH

Super Champ XD Amp

2008-2011. Tube amp with extra preamp voicing, 1x10" combo, blackface cosmetics. Replaced by X2 version.

2008-2011		$210	$260

Super Reverb Amp

1963-1982. 4x10" speakers, blackface until '67 and '80-'82, silverface '68-'80. Large Fender combo amps built in the '70s are not often in excellent condition. Any grille stain or tear to the grille can mean an amp is not in excellent condition and can significantly reduce the values shown.

1963-1967	Blackface	$2,300	$2,850
1968	Silverface, AB763	$1,600	$2,000
1969-1970	Silverface	$1,450	$1,800
1970-1972	Silverface, AA270	$1,275	$1,600
1973-1980	Silverface, no MV	$1,050	$1,300
1981-1982	Blackface	$1,050	$1,300

Super Reverb Solidstate Amp

1967-1970. 50 watts, 4x10".

1967-1970		$400	$500

'65 Super Reverb Reissue Amp

2001-present. 45 watts, all tube, 4x10", blackface cosmetics.

2001-2014		$785	$975

Super Six Reverb Amp

1970-1979. Large combo amp based on the Twin Reverb chassis, 100 watts, 6x10", black tolex. Large Fender combo amps built in the '70s are not often in excellent condition. Any grille stain or tear to the grille can mean an amp is not in excellent condition and can significantly reduce the values shown.

1970-1979		$1,050	$1,300

Super Twin Amp

1975-1980. 180 watts (6 6L6 power tubes), 2x12", distinctive dark grille.

1975-1976	Non-reverb	$800	$1,000
1976-1980	Reverb	$850	$1,075

Super-Sonic Amp

2006-present. All tube, various options, 1x12 combo or 2x12 piggyback, blond and oxblood.

2006-2013	1x12" combo, blond/oxblood	$675	$850
2006-2014	1x12" combo, blackface	$675	$850
2006-2014	2x12" piggyback, blond	$825	$1,050

Super-Sonic 22 Combo Limited Edition "Black Gold" FSR Amp

2012-2013. 150 made, 1x12, 2-tone gold and black vinyl with white piping, black grille.

2012-2014		$675	$850

Taurus Amp

1970-1972. Solidstate, 42 watts, 2x10" JBL, black tolex, silver grille, JBL badge.

1970-1972		$400	$500

Tonemaster Amp Set

1993-2002. Custom Shop, hand-wired head with Tonemaster 2x12" or 4x12" cabinet, blond or oxblood.

1993-2002		$1,400	$1,750

Tremolux Amp

1955-1966. Tube, tweed, 1x12" '55-'60, white tolex with piggyback 1x10" cabinet '61-'62, 2x10" '62-'64, black tolex '64-'66.

1955-1960	Tweed, 1x12", narrow panel	$3,500	$4,400
1961	Rough white/ oxblood, 1x10"	$2,550	$3,150
1961-1962	Rough white/ oxblood, 2x10"	$2,450	$3,050
1962-1963	Rough white/ wheat, 2x10"	$2,250	$2,800
1963-1964	Smooth white/gold, 2x10"	$2,250	$2,800
1964-1966	Black tolex, 2x10"	$1,800	$2,250

Twin Amp

1952-1963, 1996-2010. Tube, 2x12"; 15 watts, tweed wide-panel '52-'55; narrow-panel '55-'60; 50 watts '55-'57; 80 watts '58; brown tolex '60; white tolex '61-'63. Reintroduced in '96 with black tolex, spring reverb and output control for 100 watts or 25 watts.

1952-1954	Tweed, wide panel	$6,900	$8,525
1955-1957	Tweed, 50 watts	$10,000	$12,550
1958-1959	Tweed, 80 watts	$14,000	$17,550
1960	Brown tolex, 80 watts	$10,000	$12,550
1960-1962	Rough white/ oxblood	$7,000	$8,700
1963	Smooth white/gold	$6,000	$7,500

'57 Twin Reissue Amp

2004-2011. Custom Shop '57 tweed, low power dual rectifier model, 40 watts, 2x12", authentic tweed lacquering.

2004-2011		$1,450	$1,825

Twin Reverb Amp

1963-1982. Black tolex, 85 watts (changed to 135 watts in '81), 2x12", blackface '63-'67 and '81-'82, silverface '68-'81, blackface optional in '80-'81 and standard in '82. Large Fender combo amps built in the '70s are not often in excellent condition. Any grille stain or tear to the grille can mean an amp is not in excellent condition and can significantly reduce the values shown.

1963-1967	Blackface	$2,250	$2,850
1968	Silverface, no master vol.	$1,600	$2,000
1969-1970	Silverface, no master vol.	$1,450	$1,800
1971-1972	Silverface, no master vol.	$1,275	$1,600
1973-1975	Silverface, master vol.	$1,050	$1,300
1976-1980	Silverface, push/pull	$1,050	$1,300
1980-1982	Blackface	$1,050	$1,300

Twin Reverb Solidstate Amp

1966-1969. 100 watts, 2x12", black tolex.

1966-1969		$400	$500

'65 Twin Reverb Reissue Amp

1992-present. Black tolex, 2x12", 85 watts.

1992-2014		$775	$950

Fender Super Reverb

AMPS

Fender Super-Sonic

Fender '65 Twin Reverb Reissue

1965 Fender Vibro Champ
Steve Lee

1965 Fender Vibrolux Reverb
Rob Bernstein

1963 Fender Vibroverb

MODEL YEAR	FEATURES	EXC. COND. LOW	HIGH

'65 Twin Reverb Custom 15 Amp
2009-2014. 85 watt Twin Reverb with 1x15".

2009-2014		$800	$975

Twin Reverb II Amp
1983-1985. Black tolex, 2x12", 105 watts, channel switching, effects loop, blackface panel, silver grille.

1983-1985		$900	$1,125

Twin "The Twin"/"Evil Twin" Amp
1987-1992. 100 watts, 2x12", red knobs, most black tolex, but white, red and snakeskin covers offered.

1987-1992		$700	$875

Two-Tone (Custom Shop) Amp
2001-2003. Limited production, modern styling, slanted grille, 15 watts, 1x10" and 1x12", 2-tone blond cab, based on modified Blues Deluxe circuit, Two Tone on name plate.

2001-2003		$775	$975

Ultimate Chorus DSP Amp
1995-2001. Solidstate, 2x65 watts, 2x12", 32 built-in effect variations, blackface cosmetics.

1995-2001		$200	$250

Ultra Chorus Amp
1992-1994. Solidstate, 2x65 watts, 2x12", standard control panel with chorus.

1992-1994		$185	$235

Vibrasonic Amp
1959-1963. First amp to receive the new brown tolex and JBL, 1x15", 25 watts.

1959-1963		$2,400	$3,000

Vibrasonic Custom Amp
1995-1997. Custom Shop designed for steel guitar and guitar, blackface, 1x15", 100 watts.

1995-1997		$700	$875

Vibrasonic Reverb Amp
1972-1981. Black tolex, 100 watts, 1x15", silverface.

1972-1981		$775	$975

Vibro-Champ Amp
1964-1982. Black tolex, 4 watts, (5 watts '69-'71, 6 watts '72-'80), 1x8", blackface '64-'68 and '82, silverface '69-'81.

1964-1967	Blackface, AA764	$750	$925
1968-1981	Silverface	$500	$625
1982	Blackface	$500	$625

Vibro-Champ XD Amp
2008-2011. Made in China, 5 watts, 1x8.

2008-2011		$150	$185

Vibro-King Custom Amp
1993-2012. Custom Shop combo, blond tolex, 60 watts, 3x10", vintage reverb, tremolo, single channel, all tube, blond or black.

1993-2012		$1,575	$1,975

Vibro-King 212 Amp Cabinet
1993-2012. Custom Shop extension cab, blond tolex, 2x12" Celestion GK80.

1993-2012		$440	$550

Vibro-King Custom Limited Edition "Chocolate Crème Two-Tone"
2012. 25 made, 2-tone chocolate and crème vinyl, classic wheat grille..

2012		$1,950	$2,475

MODEL YEAR	FEATURES	EXC. COND. LOW	HIGH

Vibro-King Limited Edition "Tequila Sunrise" Amp
2013. 3-color sunburst on figured birdseye maple cab, oxblood grille..

2013		$2,500	$3,100

Vibrolux Amp
1956-1964. Narrow-panel, 10 watts, tweed with 1x10" '56-'61, brown tolex and brownface with 1x12" and 30 watts '61-'62, black tolex and blackface '63-'64.

1956-1961	Tweed, 1x10"	$3,100	$3,800
1961-1962	Brown tolex, 1x12", 2x6L6	$2,700	$3,400
1963-1964	Black tolex, 1x12"	$2,400	$3,000

Vibrolux Reverb Amp
1964-1982. Black tolex, 2x10", blackface '64-'67 and '81-'82, silverface '70-'80. Reissued in '96 with blackface and 40 watts.

1964-1967	Blackface	$2,600	$3,500
1968	Silverface	$2,000	$2,600
1969-1970	Silverface	$1,625	$2,100
1971-1980	Silverface	$1,200	$1,500
1981-1982	Blackface	$1,200	$1,500

Vibrolux Reverb Solidstate Amp
1967-1969. Fender CBS solidstate, 35 watts, 2x10", black tolex.

1967-1969		$400	$500

Custom Vibrolux Reverb Amp
1995-2013. Part of Professional Series, Custom Shop designed, standard factory built, 40 watts, 2x10", tube, white knobs, blond tolex and tan grill for '95 only, black tolex, silver grille after. Does not say Custom on face plate.

1995-2013		$700	$875

Vibroverb Amp
1963-1964. Brown tolex with 35 watts, 2x10" and brownface '63, black tolex with 1x15" and blackface late '63-'64.

1963	Brown tolex, 2x10"	$6,400	$8,000
1963-1964	Black tolex, 1x15"	$4,000	$5,000

'63 Vibroverb Reissue Amp
1990-1995. Reissue of 1963 Vibroverb, 40 watts, 2x10", reverb, vibrato, brown tolex.

1990-1995		$750	$950

'64 Vibroverb Custom Shop Amp
2003-2008. Reissue of 1964 Vibroverb with 1x15" blackface specs.

2003-2008		$1,400	$1,750

Yale Reverb Amp
1983-1985. Solidstate, black tolex, 50 watts, 1x12", silverface.

1983-1985		$285	$350

FireBelly Amps
2008-present. Production/custom, professional and premium grade, vintage tube amps built by Steven Cohen in Santa Monica, California.

Fishman
2003-present. Larry Fishman offers professional grade, production, amps that are designed and engineered in Andover, Massachusetts and assembled in China. They also build effects.

MODEL		EXC. COND.	
YEAR	FEATURES	LOW	HIGH

Loudbox 100 Amp
2006-2013. 100 watts, 1x8" with dome.

2006-2013		$375	$475

Loudbox Artist Pro-LBX-600 Amp
2006-present. 120 watts,

2006-2014		$425	$525

Loudbox Mini Pro-LBX-500 Amp
2006-present. 60 watts.

2006-2014		$225	$275

Loudbox Performer Pro-LBX-700 Amp
2006-present. 180 watts.

2006-2014		$550	$675

FJA Mods

2002-present. In 2007, Jerry Pinnelli began building his professional grade, production, guitar amps in Central Square, New York. He also builds effects.

Flot-A-Tone

Ca.1946-early 1960s. Flot-A-Tone was located in Milwaukee, Wisconsin, and made a variety of tube guitar and accordion amps. Most were distrubuted by the Lo Duca Brothers.

Large Amp
1960s. Four speakers.

1960s		$590	$740

Small Amp
1960s. 1x8" speaker.

1960s		$310	$390

Fortune

1978-1979. Created by Jim Kelley just prior to branding Jim Kelley Amplifiers in 1980, Fortune Amplifiers logo on front panel, specifications and performance similar to early Jim Kelley amplifiers, difficult to find in original condition, professional grade, designed and manufactured by Active Guitar Electronics company.

Fox Amps

2007-present. Marc Vos builds professional grade, production/custom, guitar amps and cabinets in Budel, Netherlands.

Framus

1946-1977, 1996-present. Tube guitar amp heads, combos and cabinets made in Markneukirchen, Germany. They also build guitars, basses, mandolins and banjos. Begun as an acoustic instrument manufacturer, Framus added electrics in the mid-'50s. In the '60s, Framus instruments were imported into the U.S. by Philadelphia Music Company. The brand was revived in '96 by Hans Peter Wilfer, the president of Warwick, with production in Warwick's factory in Germany. Distributed in the U.S. by Dana B. Goods.

Fred

1984-1986. Before settling on the name Bedrock, company founders Brad Jeter and Ron Pinto produced 50 amps carrying the brand name Fred in Nashua, New Hampshire.

Frenzel

1952-present. Jim Frenzel built his first amp in '52 and began using his brand in '01. He offers intermediate and professional grade, production/custom, hand-wired, vintage tube, guitar and bass amps built in Mabank, Texas.

Frudua Guitar Works

1988-present. Intermediate grade, production, guitar and bass amps built by guitar luthier Galeazzo Frudua in Calusco d'Adda, Italy. He also builds guitars and basses.

Fryette

2009-present. Professional and premium grade amps, combos, and cabinets built by Steven M. Fryette, who also founded VHT amps. At the beginning of '09 AXL guitars acquired the VHT name to build their own product. Fryette continues to manufacture the VHT amp models under the Fryette brand in Burbank, California.

Fuchs Audio Technology

2000-present. Andy Fuchs started the company in '99 to rebuild and modify tube amps. In 2000 he started production of his own brand of amps, offering combos and heads from 10 to 150 watts. They also custom build audiophile and studio tube electronics. Originally located in Bloomfield, New Jersey, since '07 in Clifton, New Jersey.

Fulton-Webb

1997-present. Steve Fulton and Bill Webb build their tube amp heads, combos and cabinets in Austin, Texas.

Gabriel Sound Garage

2004-2014. Gabriel Bucataru built his tube amp heads and combos in Arlington Heights, Illinois.

Gallien-Krueger

1969-present. Gallien-Krueger has offered a variety of bass and guitar amps, combos and cabinets and is located in San Jose, California.

Garcia

Tube amp heads and speaker cabinets built by Matthew Garcia in Myrtle Beach, South Carolina, starting in 2004. He also built effects.

Garnet

Mid 1960s-1989. In the mid '60s, "Gar" Gillies started the Garnet Amplifier Company with his two sons, Russell and Garnet, after he started making PA systems in his Canadian radio and TV repair shop. The first PA from the new company was for Chad Allen & the Expressions (later known as The Guess Who). A wide variety of tube amps were offered and all were designed by Gar, Sr. The company also produced the all-tube effects The Herzog, H-zog, and two stand-alone reverb units designed

Fryette Memphis

Gallien-Krueger 800 RB

1970s Garnet Revolution II
Sean McLean Carrie

AMPS

George Dennis Blue 60 Combo

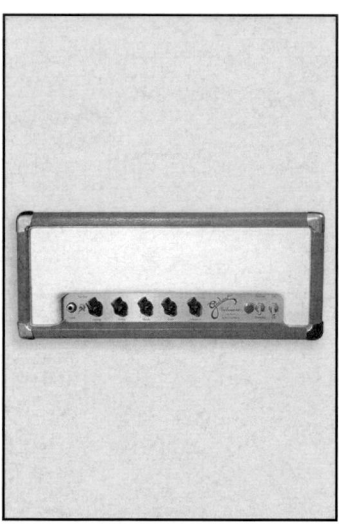

Gerhart Gilmore

1948 Gibson BR-9
David Stuckey

MODEL YEAR	FEATURES	EXC. COND. LOW	HIGH

by Gar in the late '60s and early '70s. The company closed in '89, due to financial reasons caused largely by a too rapid expansion. Gar repaired and designed custom amps up to his death in early 2007.

GDS Amplification

1998-present. Tube amps, combos and speaker cabinets from builder Graydon D. Stuckey of Fenton, Michigan. GDS also offers amp kits. In January, '09, GDS bought the assets of Guytron Amplification.

Genesis

Genesis was a 1980s line of student amps from Gibson.

B40 Amp

1984-late-1980s. Bass combo with 40 watts.

1984-1989		$115	$145

G Series Amps

1984-late-1980s. Small combo amps.

1984-1989	G10, 10w	$65	$80
1984-1989	G25, 25w	$85	$105
1984-1989	G40R, 40w, reverb	$130	$165

Genz Benz

1984-present. Founded by Jeff and Cathy Genzler and located in Scottsdale, Arizona, the company offers guitar, bass, and PA amps and speaker cabinets. In late 2003, Genz Benz was acquired by Kaman (Ovation, Hamer, Takamine). On January 1, '08, Fender acquired Kaman Music Corporation and the Genz Benz brand.

George Dennis

1991-present. Founded by George Burgerstein, original products were a line of effects pedals. In '96 they added a line of tube amps. The company is located in Prague, Czech Republic.

Gerhart

2000-present. Production/custom, intermediate and professional grade, amps and cabinets from builder Gary Gerhart of West Hills, California. He also offers an amp in kit form.

Germino

2002-present. Intermediate to professional grade tube amps, combos and cabinets built by Greg Germino in Graham, North Carolina.

Gibson

1890s (1902)-present. Gibson has offered a variety of amps since the mid-'30s to the present under the Gibson brandname and others. The price ranges listed are for excellent condition, all original amps though tubes may be replaced without affecting value. Many Gibson amps have missing or broken logos. The prices listed are for amps with fully intact logos. A broken or missing logo can diminish the value of the amp. Amps with a changed handle, power cord, and especially a broken logo should be

MODEL YEAR	FEATURES	EXC. COND. LOW	HIGH

taken on a case-by-case basis.

Vintage amplifiers are rarely found in original, excellent condition. Many vintage amps have notable wear and have a non-original speaker. The prices shown are for fully original (except tubes and caps) amplifiers that are pleasing clean, and contain no significant wear, blemishes, grille stains, or damage.

Atlas IV Amp

1963-1967. Piggyback head and cab, introduced with trapezoid shape, changed to rectangular cabs in '65-'66 with black cover, simple circuit with 4 knobs, no reverb or tremolo, mid-power with 2 6L6, 1x15".

1963-1965	Brown	$525	$650
1966-1967	Black	$525	$650

Atlas Medalist Amp

1964-1967. Combo version with 1x15".

1964-1967		$500	$625

B-40 Amp

1972-1975. Solidstate, 40 watts, 1x12".

1972-1975		$220	$275

BR-1 Amp

1946-1948. 15 watts, 1x12" field-coil speaker, brown leatherette cover, rectangular metal grille with large G.

1946-1948		$650	$825

BR-3 Amp

1946. 12 watts, 1x12" Utah field-coil speaker (most BR models used Jensen speakers).

1946		$650	$825

BR-4 Amp

1946-1947. 14 watts, 1x12" Utah field-coil speaker (most BR models used Jensen speakers).

1946-1947		$550	$700

BR-6 Amp

1946-1954. 10 to 12 watts, 1x10", brown leatherette, speaker opening split by cross panel with G logo, bottom mounted chassis with single on-off volume pointer knob.

1946-1947	Verticle cab	$550	$700
1948-1954	Horizontal cab	$550	$700

BR-9 Amp

1948-1954. Cream leatherette, 10 watts, 1x8". Originally sold with the BR-9 lap steel. Renamed GA-9 in '54.

1948-1954		$400	$500

Duo Metalist Amp

1968-early 1970s. Upright vertical combo cab, tubes, faux wood grain panel, mid-power, 1x12".

1968-1970s		$425	$525

EH-100 Amp

1936-1942. Electric-Hawaiian companion amp, 1x10". AC/DC version called EH-110.

1936-1942		$575	$725

EH-125 Amp

1941-1942. 1x12", rounded shoulder cab, brown cover in '41 and dark green in '42, leather handle.

1941-1942		$650	$825

EH-126 Amp

1941. Experimental model, 6-volt variant of EH-125, about 5 made.

1941		$1,075	$1,350

MODEL		EXC. COND.	
YEAR	FEATURES	LOW	HIGH

EH-135 Amp

1941. Experimental model, alternating and direct current switchable, about 7 made.

1941		$1,075	$1,350

EH-150 Amp

1935-1942. Electric-Hawaiian companion amp, 1x12" ('35-'37) or 1x10" ('38-'42). AC/DC version called EH-160.

1935	13 3/4" square cab	$1,075	$1,350
1936-1937	14 3/4" square cab	$1,075	$1,350
1937-1942	15 3/8" round cab	$1,075	$1,350

EH-185 Amp

1939-1942. 1x12", tweed cover, black and orange vertical stripes, marketed as companion amp to the EH-185 Lap Steel. AC/DC version called EH-195.

1939-1942		$1,500	$1,900

EH-195 Amp

1939-1942. EH-185 variant with vibrato.

1939-1942		$1,500	$1,900

EH-250 Amp

1940. Upgraded natural maple cabinet using EH-185 chassis, only 2 made, evolved into EH-275.

1940		$1,900	$2,400

EH-275 Amp

1940-1942. Similar to EH-185 but with maple cab and celluloid binding, about 30 made.

1940-1942		$1,800	$2,250

Epoch Series

2000s. Solidstate student practice amps.

2000s	G-10	$20	$30

Falcon III F-3 Amp

Early 1970s. Solidstate, 1x12" combo, 65 watts, made in Chicago by CMI after Gibson ceased amp production in Kalamazoo ('67), black tolex, dark grille.

1970		$240	$300

Falcon Medalist (Hybrid) Amp

1967. Transitional tube 1x12" combo amp from GA-19 tube Falcon to the solidstate Falcon, Falcon logo and Gibson logo on front panel, brown control panel, dark cover and dark grille, vertical combo cabinet.

1967		$275	$350

Falcon Medalist (Solidstate) Amp

1968-1969. Solidstate combo, 15 watts, 1x12".

1968-1969		$275	$350

G-10 Amp

1972-1975. Solidstate, 10 watts, 1x10", no tremolo or reverb.

1972-1975		$80	$100

G-20 Amp

1972-1975. Solidstate with tremolo, 1x10", 10 watts.

1972-1975		$100	$125

G-25 Amp

1972-1975. 25 watts, 1x10".

1972-1975		$145	$180

G-35 Amp

1975. Solidstate, 30 watts, 1x12".

1975		$165	$210

G-40/G-40 R Amp

1972-1974. Solidstate with tremolo and reverb, 40 watts, 1x12" (G-40) and 2x10" (G-40 R).

1972-1974		$220	$275

G-50/G-50 A/G-50 B Amp

1972, 1975. Solidstate with tremolo and reverb, models G-50 and 50 A are 1x12", 40 watts, model 50 B is a bass 1x15", 50 watts.

1972-1975		$235	$295

G-55 Amp

1975. 50 watts, 1x12".

1975		$250	$315

G-60 Amp

1972-1973. Solidstate with tremolo and reverb, 1x15", 60 watts.

1972-1973		$275	$340

G-70 Amp

1972-1973. Solidstate with tremolo and reverb, 2x12", 60 watts.

1972-1973		$290	$365

G-80 Amp

1972-1973. Solidstate with tremolo and reverb, 4x10", 60 watts.

1972-1973		$340	$425

G-100 A/G-100 B Amp

1975. 100 watts, model 100 A is 2x12" and 100 B is 2x15".

1975		$350	$435

G-105 Amp

1974-1975. Solidstate, 100 watts, 2x12", reverb.

1974-1975		$350	$435

G-115 Amp

1975. 100 watts, 4x10".

1974-1975		$375	$475

GA-5 Les Paul Jr. Amp

1954-1957. Tan fabric cover (Mottled Brown by '57), 7" oval speaker, 4 watts. Renamed Skylark in '58.

1954-1957		$525	$650

GA-5 Les Paul Jr. Amp (Reissue)

2004-2008. Goldtone Series, class A, 5 watts, 1x8".

2004-2008		$275	$350

GA-5 Skylark Amp

1957-1968. Gold cover (brown by '63 and black by '66), 1x8" (1x10" from '64 on), 4.5 watts (10 watts from '64 on), tremolo. Often sold with the Skylark Lap Steel.

1957-1959	Gold, 4.5w, 1x8"	$400	$500
1960	Gold, 4.5w, 1x8"	$375	$475
1961-1962	Gold, 4.5w, 1x8"	$325	$400
1963	Brown, 4.5w, 1x8"	$325	$400
1964	Brown, 10w, 1x10"	$325	$400
1965-1967	Black, 10w, 1x10"	$250	$300
1968	Skylark, last version	$200	$250

GA-5 T Skylark Amp

1960-1968. Tremolo, 4.5 watts early, 10 later, gold covering and 1x8" until '63, brown '63-'64, black and 1x10" after.

1961-1962	Gold, 4.5w, 1x8"	$350	$425
1963	Brown, 4.5w, 1x8"	$275	$350
1964	Brown, 10w, 1x10"	$275	$350
1965-1967	Kalamazoo, black, 10w, 1x10"	$275	$350
1968	Norlin, vertical cab, 10w, 1x10, tubes	$180	$230

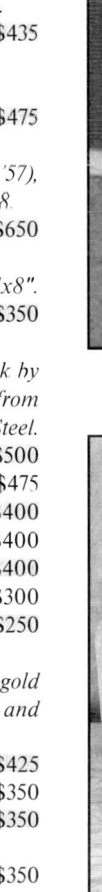

Gibson EH-150

Rich E. Hall

1959 Gibson GA-5

David Stuckey

Gibson GA-5 Les Paul Junior

AMPS

1960 Gibson GA-8 T Discoverer

David Stuckey

Gibson GA-20 RVT

Gibson GA-30

MODEL YEAR	FEATURES	EXC. COND. LOW	HIGH

GA-5 W Amp
Late-1960s. Norlin-era, post-Kalamazoo production, 15 watts, small speaker, volume and tone controls.

1969		$75	$95

GA-6 Amp
1956-1959. Replaced the BR-6, 8 to 12 watts, 1x12", has Gibson 6 above the grille. Renamed GA-6 Lancer in '60.

1956-1959		$525	$675

GA-6 Lancer Amp
1960-1961. Renamed from GA-6, 1x12", tweed cover, 3 knobs, 14 watts.

1960-1961		$600	$775

GA-7 Les Paul TV Model Amp
1954-1956. Basic old style GA-5 with different graphics, 4 watts, small speaker.

1954-1956		$425	$525

GA-8 Discoverer Amp
1962-1964. Renamed from GA-8 Gibsonette, gold fabric cover, 1x12", 10 watts.

1962-1964		$425	$525

GA-8 Gibsonette Amp
1955-1962. Tan fabric cover (gold by '58), 1x10", 8 watts (9 watts by '58). See Gibsonette for 1952-'54. Name changed to GA-8 Discoverer in '62.

1955	Gibsonette logo on front, square hole	$450	$575
1956-1957	Gibsonette logo on front	$450	$575
1958-1959	Gibson logo on front	$450	$575
1960-1962	Gibson logo upper right front	$450	$575

GA-8 T Discoverer Amp
1960-1966. Gold fabric cover, 1x10", 9 watts (tan cover, 1x12" and 15 watts by '63), tremolo.

1960-1962	Tweed, 9w, 1x10"	$450	$575
1963-1964	Brown, 15w, 1x12"	$350	$450
1965-1966	Black, 15w, 1x12"	$350	$450

GA-9 Amp
1954-1959. Renamed from BR-9, tan fabric cover, 8 watts, 1x10". Often sold with the BR-9 Lap Steel.

1954-1957	Gibson 9 logo	$425	$525
1958-1959	Tweed, 6V6s	$425	$525

GA-14 Titan Amp
1959-1961. About 15 watts using 2x6V6 power tubes, 1x10", tweed cover.

1959-1961		$475	$600

GA-15 RV Goldtone Amp
1999-2004. 15 watts, Class A, 1x12", spring reverb.

1999-2004		$425	$530

GA-15 RVT Explorer Amp
1965-1967. Tube, 1x10", tremolo, reverb, black vinyl.

1965-1967		$350	$450

GA-17 RVT Scout Amp
1963-1967. Low power, 1x10", reverb and tremolo.

1963	Smooth brown	$450	$550
1964-1965	Textured brown	$400	$500
1966-1967	Black	$350	$450

GA-18 Explorer Amp
1959. Tweed, tube, 14 watts, 1x10". Replaced in '60 by the GA-18 T Explorer.

1959		$725	$900

GA-18 T Explorer Amp
1960-1963. Tweed, 14 watts, 1x10", tremolo.

1960-1962	Tweed	$725	$900
1963	Brown	$375	$475

GA-19 RVT Falcon Amp
1961-1967. One of Gibson's best selling amps. Initially tweed covered, followed by smooth brown, textured brown, and black. Each amp has a different tone. One 12" Jensen with deep-sounding reverb and tremolo.

1961-1962	Tweed, 6V6	$950	$1,200
1962-1963	Smooth brown	$550	$675
1964	Textured brown	$450	$550
1965-1967	Black	$400	$500

GA-20 Amp
1950-1962. Brown leatherette (2-tone by '55 and tweed by '60), tube, 12 watts early, 14 watts later, 1x12". Renamed Crest in '60.

1950-1954	Brown, single G logo on front	$675	$850
1955-1958	2-tone salt/maroon	$800	$1,000
1959	2-tone blue/blond	$800	$1,000

GA-20 Crest Amp
1960-1961. Tweed, tube, 14 watts, 1x12".

1960-1961		$875	$1,100

GA-20 RVT Amp
2004-2007. 15 watts, 1x12", reverb, tremolo.

2004-2007		$550	$675

GA-20 RVT Minuteman Amp
1965-1967. Black, 14 watts, 1x12", tube, reverb, tremolo.

1965-1967		$325	$400

GA-20 T Amp
1956-1959. Tube, 16 watts, tremolo, 1x12", 2-tone. Renamed Ranger in '60.

1956-1958	2-tone	$850	$1,050
1959	New 2-tone	$850	$1,050

GA-20 T Ranger Amp
1960-1961. Tube, 16 watts, tremolo, 1x12", tweed.

1960-1962	Tweed	$925	$1,150

GA-25 Amp
1947-1948. Brown, 1x12" and 1x8", 15 watts. Replaced by GA-30 in '48.

1947-1948		$650	$800

GA-25 RVT Hawk Amp
1963-1968. Reverb, tremolo, 1x15".

1963	Smooth brown	$550	$700
1964	Rough brown	$450	$550
1965-1967	Black	$400	$500
1968	Last version	$300	$375

GA-30 Amp (Invader)
1948-1961. Brown until '54, 2-tone after, tweed in '60, 1x12" and 1x8", 14 watts. Renamed GA-30 Invader in '60.

1948-1954	Brown	$725	$900
1955-1959	2-tone salt/maroon	$875	$1,100
1960-1961	Invader, tweed	$875	$1,100

GA-30 RV Invader Amp
1961. Tweed, 1x12" and 1x8", 14-16 watts, reverb but no tremolo.

1961		$950	$1,200

MODEL YEAR	FEATURES	EXC. COND. LOW	HIGH

GA-30 RVH Goldtone Amp Head
1999-2004. 30 watts, Class A head, reverb.

1999-2004		$700	$875

GA-30 RVS (Stereo) Goldtone Amp
1999-2004. 15 watts per channel, Class A stereo, 2x12", reverb.

1999-2004		$825	$1,025

GA-30 RVT Invader Amp
1962-1967. Updated model with reverb and tremolo, 25 watts, 1x12" and 1x10" speakers, first issue in tweed.

1962	Tweed	$1,150	$1,450
1963	Smooth brown	$650	$825
1964	Rough brown	$525	$650
1965-1967	Black	$450	$550

GA-35 RVT Lancer Amp
1966-1967. Black, 1x12", tremolo, reverb.

1966-1967		$400	$500

GA-40 Les Paul Amp
1952-1960. Introduced with the Les Paul Model guitar, 1x12" Jensen speaker, 14 watts early and 16 later, recessed leather handle using spring mounting (the handle is easily broken and replacement handle is more common than not). Two-tone leatherette covering, '50s checkerboard grille ('52-early-'55), Les Paul script logo on front of the amp ('52-'55), plastic grille insert with LP monogram, gold Gibson logo above grille. Cosmetics changed dramatically in early/mid-'55. Renamed GA-40 T Les Paul in '60.

1952-1955	Brown 2-tone, LP grille	$1,200	$1,500
1955-1957	2-tone salt/maroon	$1,200	$1,500
1958-1959	2-tone blue/blond	$1,200	$1,500

GA-40 RVT Limited Edition Amp
2008-2011. GA-40RVT Limited Edition logo, 2-tone brown/tan, front control panel, 30/15 switchable watts.

2008-2011		$450	$550

GA-40 T Les Paul Amp
1960-1962. Renamed from GA-40 Les Paul, 1x12", 16 watts, tremolo. Renamed Mariner in '62-'67.

1960-1961	Tweed	$1,625	$2,025
1962	Smooth brown	$500	$625

GA-40 T Mariner Amp
1962-1967. 1x12" combo, 25 watts, tremolo.

1962-1963	Smooth brown	$475	$600
1964	Rough brown	$375	$450
1965-1967	Black	$375	$450

GA-45 RVT Saturn Amp
1965-1967. 2x10", mid power, tremolo, reverb.

1965-1967		$450	$550

GA-50/GA-50 T Amp
1948-1955. Brown leatherette, 25 watts, 1x12" and 1x8", T had tremolo.

1948-1955	GA-50	$1,525	$1,900
1948-1955	GA-50 T	$1,600	$2,000

GA-55 RVT Ranger Amp
1965-1967. Black cover, 4x10", tremolo, reverb.

1965-1967		$475	$600

GA-55/GA-55 V Amp
1954-1958. 2x12", 20 watts, GA-55 V with vibrato.

1954-1958	GA-55	$2,000	$2,500
1954-1958	GA-55 V	$2,000	$2,500

GA-60 Hercules Amp
1962-1963. 25 watts, 1x15, no-frills 1-channel amp, no reverb, no tremolo.

1962-1963		$525	$650

GA-60 RV Goldtone Amp
1999-2004. 60 watts, A/B circuit, 2x12", spring reverb, earliest production in England.

1999-2004		$875	$1,075

GA-70 Country and Western Amp
1955-1958. 25 watts, 1x15", 2-tone, longhorn cattle western logo on front, advertised to have extra bright sound.

1955-1958		$1,675	$2,100

GA-75 Amp
1950-1955. Mottled Brown leatherette, 1x15", 25 watts.

1950-1955		$1,275	$1,600

GA-75 L Recording Amp
1964-1967. 1x15" Lansing speaker, no reverb or tremolo, 2 channels, dark cover, gray grille.

1964-1967		$450	$575

GA-75 Recording Amp
1964-1967. 2x10" speakers, no reverb or tremolo, 2 channels, dark cover, gray grille.

1964-1967		$450	$575

GA-77 Amp
1954-1959. 1x15" JBL, 25-30 watts, 2x6L6 power tubes, 2-tone covering, near top-of-the-line for the mid-'50s.

1954-1957	2-tone salt/maroon, leather handle	$1,050	$1,300
1958-1959	2-tone blue/blond, metal handle	$1,050	$1,300

GA-77 RET Vanguard Amp
1964-1967. Mid-power, 2x10", tremolo, reverb, echo.

1964	Rough brown	$550	$700
1965-1967	Black	$450	$575

GA-77 RETL Vanguard Amp
1964-1967. GA-77 RET with 1x15" Lansing speaker option (L).

1964-1967		$550	$700

GA-77 RVTL Vanguard Amp
1962-1967. 50 watts, 1x15", Lansing speaker option (L), tremolo, reverb, smooth brown.

1962-1967		$550	$700

GA-77 Vanguard Amp
1960-1961. 1x15" JBL, 25-30 watts, 2 6L6 power tubes, tweed cover, first use of Vanguard model name.

1960-1961		$1,250	$1,550

GA-78 Bell Stereo Amp
1960. Gibson-branded amp made by Bell, same as GA-79 series, Bell 30 logo on front, 30 watts, 2x10" wedge cab.

1960		$1,675	$2,100

GA-79 RV Amp
1960-1962. Stereo-reverb, 2x10", 30 watts.

1960-1961	Tweed	$1,925	$2,400
1962	Gray tolex	$1,650	$2,050

Gibson GA-40 RVT Limited Edition

2008 Gibson GA-42 RVT

1961 Gibson GA-79 RV

Ginelle El Toro Pequeno

Gnome White Stallion Head

Goodsell Custom 33

MODEL YEAR	FEATURES	EXC. COND. LOW	HIGH

GA-79 RVT Multi-Stereo Amp
1961-1967. Introduced as GA-79 RVT, Multi-Stereo was added to name in '61. Stereo-reverb and tremolo, 2x10", tweed (black and brown also available), 30 watts.

1961	Tweed	$1,925	$2,400
1961-1962	Gray sparkle	$1,650	$2,050
1963-1964	Textured brown	$1,650	$2,050
1965-1967	Black	$1,550	$1,950

GA-80/GA-80 T/Vari-Tone Amp
1959-1961. 25 watts, 1x15", 2 channels, described as "6-in-1 amplifier with improved tremolo," 6 Vari-Tone pushbottons which give "six distinctively separate sounds," 7 tubes, tweed cover.

1959-1961		$1,350	$1,700

GA-83 S Stereo-Vibe Amp
1959-1961. Interesting stereo amp with front baffle mounted 1x12" and 4x8" side-mounted speakers (2 on each side), 35 watts, Gibson logo on upper right corner of the grille, tweed cover, brown grille (late '50s Fender-style), 3 pointer knobs and 3 round knobs, 4 inputs.

1959-1961		$2,125	$2,650

GA-85 Bass Reflex Amp
1957-1958. Removable head, 25 watts, 1x12", very limited production.

1957-1958		$950	$1,200

GA-86 Ensemble Amp
1960. 25 watt head plus 1x12" cab, tweed.

1960		$1,350	$1,700

GA-88S Stereo Twin Amp
1960. Control panel and 2 separate 1x12" speaker cabs, 35 watts, 8 tubes, tweed.

1960		$3,200	$4,000

GA-90 High Fidelity Amp
1953-1960. 25 watts, 6x8", 2 channels, advertised for guitar, bass, accordion, or hi-fi.

1953-1960		$1,150	$1,425

GA-95 RVT Apollo Amp
1965-1967. 90 watts, 2x12", black vinyl, black grille, tremolo, reverb.

1965-1967		$525	$650

GA-100 Bass Amp
1960-1963. 35 watts, 1x12" cabinet, for '60-'61 tweed and tripod included for separate head, for '62-'63 brown covering and Crestline Tuck-A-Way head.

1960-1961	Tweed	$950	$1,200
1962-1963	Smooth brown	$475	$600

GA-200 Rhythm King Amp
1957-1961. Introduced as GA-200, renamed Rhythm King in '60, 2-channel version of GA-400. Bass amp, 60 watts, 2x12".

1957-1959	2-tone	$1,700	$2,100
1960-1961	Tweed	$1,700	$2,100
1961	Smooth brown, no trem or reverb	$1,500	$1,875

GA-300 RVT Super 300 Amp
1962-1963. 60 watts, 2x12" combo, reverb, tremolo, smooth brown.

1962-1963		$1,500	$1,875

GA-400 Super 400 Amp
1956-1961. 60 watts, 2x12", 3 channels, same size as GA-200 cab, 1 more tube than GA-200.

1956-1959	2-tone	$1,900	$2,350
1960-1961	Tweed	$1,900	$2,350
1961	Smooth brown, no trem or reverb	$1,600	$2,000

GA-CB Custom-Built Amp
1949-1953. 25-30 watts, 1x15", the top model in Gibson's '51 line of amps, described as having sound quality found only in the finest public address broadcasting systems, about 47 made, this high-end amp was replaced by the GA-77 and a completely different GA-90.

1949-1953		$1,600	$2,000

Gibsonette Amp
1952-1954. Gibsonette logo on front, round hole. See GA-8 Gibsonette for later models.

1952-1954		$450	$575

GM05 Amp
2009-2012. Small 5 watt solidstate amp usually sold with Maestro guitar pack.

2009-2012		$15	$25

GSS-50 Amp
1966-1967. Solidstate, 50 watts, 2x10" combo, reverb and tremolo, black vinyl cover, silver grille, no grille logo.

1966-1967		$300	$375

GSS-100 Amp
1966-1967, 1970. Solidstate, 100 watts, two 24"x12" 2x10" sealed cabs, black vinyl cover, silver grille, 8 black knobs and 3 red knobs, slanted raised Gibson logo. Speakers prone to distortion. Reissued in '70 in 3 variations.

1966-1967		$275	$350

Lancer
1968-1969. CMI-Chicago produced, small combo, black upright cab, dark grille, post-McCarty era Gibson logo.

1968-1969		$55	$80

LP-1/LP-2 Amp Set
1970. Les Paul model, piggyback amp and cab set, LP-1 head and LP-2 4x12" plus 2 horns cab, large vertical speaker cabinet, rather small compact 190 watt solidstate amp head.

1970		$350	$440

Medalist 2/12 Amp
1968-1970. Vertical cabinet, 2x12", reverb and temolo.

1968-1970		$400	$500

Medalist 4/10 Amp
1968-1970. Vertical cabinet, 4x10", reverb and tremolo.

1968-1970		$400	$500

Mercury I Amp
1963-1965. Piggyback trapezoid-shaped head with 2x12" trapezoid cabinet, tremolo, brown.

1963-1965		$475	$600

Mercury II Amp
1963-1967. Mercury I with 1x15" and 1x10", initially trapezoid cabinets then changed to rectangular.

1963-1964	Brown trapezoid cabs	$550	$700

MODEL YEAR	FEATURES	EXC. COND. LOW	HIGH
1965-1967	Black rectangular cabs	$475	$600

Plus-50 Amp

1966-1967. 50 watts, powered extension amplifier. Similar to GSS-100 cabinet of the same era, 2x10" cab, black vinyl cover, silver grille, slant Gibson logo.

1966-1967		$450	$560

Super Thor Bass Amp

1970-1974. Solidstate, part of the new G-Series (not GA-Series), 65 watts, 2x15", black tolex, black grille, upright vertical cab with front control, single channel.

1970-1974		$360	$450

Thor Bass Amp

1970-1974. Solidstate, smaller 2x10" 50 watt version of Super Thor.

1970-1974		$320	$400

Titan I Amp

1963-1965. Piggyback trapezoid-shaped head and 2x12" trapezoid-shaped cabinet, tremolo.

1963-1965		$475	$600

Titan III Amp

1963-1967. Piggyback trapezoid-shaped head and 1x15" + 2x10" trapezoid-shaped cabinet, tremolo.

1963-1964	Brown	$525	$650
1965-1967	Black	$525	$650

Titan Medalist Amp

1964-1967. Combo version of Titan Series with 1x15" and 1x10", tremolo only, no reverb, black.

1964-1967		$550	$675

Titan V Amp

1963-1967. Piggyback trapezoid-shaped tube head and 2x15" trapezoid-shaped cabinet, tremolo.

1963-1964	Brown	$550	$675
1965-1967	Black	$550	$675

TR-1000 T/TR-1000 RVT Starfire Amp

1962-1967. Solidstate, 1x12" combo, 40 watts, tremolo, RVT with reverb.

1962-1967		$275	$350

Ginelle

Rick Emery builds his tube combo amps in Ardmore, Pennsylvania starting in 1996.

Giulietti

1962. Amps made by Magnatone for the Giulietti Accordion Company, New York. Models closely approximate the Magnatone equivalent and model numbers are often similar to the copied Magnatone model.

S-9 Amp (Magnatone 460)

1962. 35 watts, 2x12 plus 2 tweeters, true vibrato combo, black sparkle.

1962		$1,290	$1,610

Gnome Amplifiers

2008-present. Dan Munro builds professional grade, production, guitar amps and cabinets in Olympia, Washington. He also builds effects.

Gomez Amplification

2005-present. Tube combo amps built by Dario G. Gomez in Rancho Santa Margarita, California.

Goodsell

2004-present. Tube head and combo amps built by Richard Goodsell in Atlanta, Georgia.

Gorilla

1980s-2009. Small solidstate entry-level amps, distributed by Pignose, Las Vegas, Nevada.

Compact Practice Student Amp

1980s-2009. Solidstate, 10 to 30 watts, compact design.

1980s-2009		$25	$50

Goya

1955-1996. Goya was mainly known for acoustics, but offered a few amps in the '60s. The brand was purchased by Avnet/Guild in '66 and by Martin in the late '70s.

Grammatico Amps

2009-present. Production/custom, professional and premium grade, hand-wired, guitar and bass amps built by John Grammatico in Austin, Texas.

Green

1993-present. Amp model line made in England by Matamp (see that brand for listing), bright green covering, large Green logo on the front.

Greer Amplification

1999-present. Tube guitar amps and speaker cabinets built by Nick Greer in Athens, Georgia. He also builds effects.

Gregory

1950s-1960s. Private branded amps sold via music wholesalers, by late '60s solidstate models made by Harmony including the 007, C.I.A., Mark Six, Mark Eight, Saturn 80, most models were combo amps with Gregory logo.

Solidstate Amps

1960s		$135	$170

Gretsch

1883-present. In '05, Gretsch again starting offering amps after previously selling them from the 1950s to '73. Initially private branded for them by Valco (look for the Valco oval or rectangular serialized label on the back). Early-'50s amps were covered in the requisite tweed, but evolved into the Gretsch charcoal gray covering. The mid-'50s to early-'60s amps were part of the Electromatic group of amps. The mid-'50s to '62 amps often sported wrap-around and slanted grilles. In '62, the more traditional box style was introduced. In '66, the large amps went piggyback. Baldwin-Gretsch began to phase out amps effective '65, but solidstate amps continued being offered for a period of time. The '73 Gretsch product line only offered Sonax amps, made in Canada and Sho-Bud amps made in the U.S. In '05, they introduced a line of tube combo amps made in U.S. by Victoria Amp Company.

Grammatico Kingsville

Green Electric

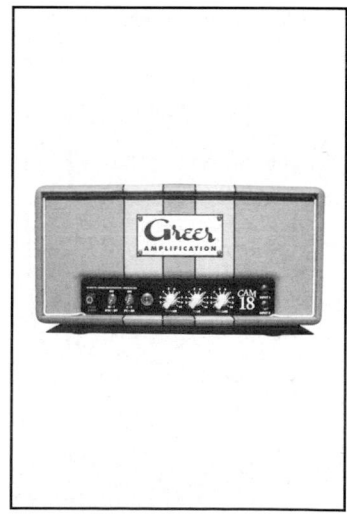

Greer Cam 18

AMPS

Gretsch Model 6156 Playboy

*Gretsch Model 6161
Dual Twin Tremolo*

Paul Moser III

*1964 Gretsch Model
6164 Variety Amp*

MODEL YEAR	FEATURES	EXC. COND. LOW	HIGH

Artist Amp

1946. Early post-war Gretsch amp made before Valco began to make their amps. Appears to be made by Operadio Mfg. Co., St. Charles, Illinois. Low power small combo amp, Gretsch Artist script logo on grille, round speaker baffle hole.

1946		$250	$325

Broadkaster Mini Lead 50 Amp

Late 1960s. Solidstate compact verticle combo amp.

1969		$225	$290

Carousel Amp

1960s. Solidstate,1x10" and 1x3" speakers, tremolo speed and depth knobs, brown cover.

1960s		$575	$750

Electromatic Amp

1947-1949. Valco-made with era-typical styling, 3 slat speaker baffle openings, leather handle, two-tone leatherette, 3 tubes with small speaker, single volume knob.

1947-1949		$550	$715

Electromatic Artist Amp (6155)

1950s. Small amp, 2x6V6 power, 1x10", volume and tone knobs.

1950s		$550	$725

Electromatic Deluxe Amp (6163)

1950s. 1x12", 2x6L6, brown tweed grille. Also offered in Western Finish.

1950s		$825	$1,075

Model 6150 Compact Amp

Late-1950s-1960s. Early amps in tweed, '60s amps in gray covering, no tremolo, single volume knob, no treble or bass knob, 1x8".

1950s	Brown tweed	$425	$550
1960s	Gray	$425	$550

Model 6151 Electromatic Standard/ Compact Tremolo Amp

Late-1940s-late-1960s. 1x8", various covers.

1940s-60s		$425	$550

Model 6152 Compact Tremolo Reverb Amp

Ca.1964-late-1960s. Five watts, 11"x6" elliptical speaker early on, 1x12" later.

1964-1966	Elliptical speaker	$550	$725
1966-1969	Round speaker	$550	$725

Model 6153T White Princess Amp

1962. Compact combo, 6x9" oval speaker, higher priced than the typical small amp because it is relatively rare and associated with the White Princess guitar - making it valuable in a set, condition is very important, an amp with any issues will be worth much less.

1962		$750	$975

Model 6154 Super-Bass Amp

Early-1960s-mid-1960s. Gray covering, 2x12", 70 watts, tube.

1960s		$675	$875

Model 6156 Playboy Amp

Early-1950s-1966. Tube amp, 17 watts, 1x10" until '61 when converted to 1x12", tweed, then gray, then finally black covered.

1950s-1960	Tweed, 1x10"	$550	$725
1961-1962	Tweed, 1x12"	$550	$725
1963-1966	Black or gray, 1x12"	$550	$725

Model 6157 Super Bass (Piggyback) Amp

Mid-late-1960s. 35 watts, 2x15" cabinet, single channel.

1960s		$500	$650

Model 6159 Dual Bass Amp

Mid-late-1960s. 35 watts, tube, 2x12" cabinet, dual channel, black covering. Replaced by 6163 Chet Atkins Piggyback Amp.

1965		$675	$875

Model 6160 Chet Atkins Country Gentleman Amp

Early-late-1960s. Combo tube amp, 35 watts, 2x12" cabinet, 2 channels. Replaced by 6163 Chet Atkins Piggyback amp with tremolo but no reverb.

1960s		$700	$925

Model 6161 Dual Twin Tremolo Amp

Ca.1962-late-1960s. 19 watts (later 17 watts), 2x10" with 5" tweeter, tremolo.

1962-1967		$725	$950

Model 6161 Electromatic Twin Amp

Ca.1953-ca.1960. Gray Silverflake covering, two 11x6" speakers, 14 watts, tremolo, wraparound grille '55 and after.

1953-1960		$825	$1,075

Model 6162 Dual Twin Tremolo/Reverb Amp

Ca.1964-late-1960s. 17 watts, 2x10", reverb, tremolo. Vertical combo amp style introduced in '68.

1964-1967	Horizontal combo style	$725	$950
1968-1969	Vertical combo style	$500	$650

Model 6163 Chet Atkins (Piggyback) Amp

Mid-late-1960s. 70 watts, 1x12" and 1x15", black covering, tremolo, reverb.

1960s		$625	$825

Model 6163 Executive Amp

1959. 1x15, gray cover.

1959		$1,300	$1,700

Model 6164 Variety Amp

Early-mid-1960s. 35 watts, tube, 2x12".

1960s		$700	$925

Model 6165 Variety Plus Amp

Early-mid-1960s. Tube amp, 35 watts, 2x12", reverb and tremolo, separate controls for both channels.

1960s		$775	$1,000

Model 6166 Fury (Combo) Amp

Mid-1960s. Tube combo stereo amp, 70 watts, 2x12", separate controls for both channels, large metal handle, reverb.

1960s		$775	$1,000

Model 6169 Electromatic Twin Western Finish Amp

Ca.1953-ca.1960. Western finish, 14 watts, 2-11x6" speakers, tremolo, wraparound grill '55 and after.

1953-1960		$5,400	$7,000

Model 6169 Fury (Piggyback) Amp

Late-1960s. Tube amp, 70 watts, 2x12", separate controls for both channels.

1960s		$750	$975

Model 6170 Pro Bass Amp

1966-late-1960s. 25 or 35 watts, depending on model, 1x15", vertical cabinet style (vs. box cabinet).

1966-1969		$500	$650

MODEL YEAR FEATURES	EXC. COND. LOW HIGH

Model 7154 Nashville Amp
Introduced in 1969. Solidstate combo amp, 4' tall, 75 watts, 2x15", reverb, tremolo, magic echo.

1969-1970s	$465	$605

Model 7155 Tornado PA System Amp
Introduced in 1969. Solidstate piggyback head and cab, 150 watts, 2 column speaker cabs, reverb, tremolo, magic echo.

1969-1970s 2x2x15"	$425	$550
1969-1970s 2x4x15"	$490	$635

Model 7517 Rogue Amp
1970s. Solidstate, 40 watts, 2x12", tall vertical cabinet, front control panel.

1970s	$235	$305

Model G6156 Playboy Amp
2005-2007. 15 watts, 1x12" combo amp with retro Gretsch styling, made by Victoria.

2005-2007	$1,000	$1,300

Model G6163 Executive Amp
2005-2007. Boutique quality made by Victoria for FMIC Gretsch, 20 watts, 1x15", cabinet Uses to the modern retro early '60s Supro Supreme modified-triangle front grille pattern, maroon baffle with white grille, tremolo and reverb.

2005-2007	$1,025	$1,330

Rex Royal Amp Model M-197-3V
1950s. Small student compact amp, low power, 1x8", Rex Royal logo on grille, Fred Gretsch logo on back panel, single on-off volume knob.

1951	$350	$450

Gries
2004-present. Dave Gries builds his intermediate and professional grade, production/custom, amps and cabinets in Mattapoisett, Massachusetts.

Groove Tubes
1979-present. Started by Aspen Pittman in his garage in Sylmar, California, Groove Tubes is now located in San Fernando. GT manufactures and distributes a full line of tubes. In '86 they added amp production and in '91 tube microphones. Aspen is also the author of the Tube Amp Book. The Groove Tubes brand was purchased by Fender in June, '08.

Guild
1952-present. Guild offered amps from the '60s into the '80s. Some of the early models were built by Hagstrom.

Double Twin Amp
1953-1955. 35 watts, 2x12" plus 2 tweeters, 2-tone leatherette covered cab.

1953-1955	$700	$925

G-1000 Stereo Amp
1992-1994. Stereo acoustic combo amp with cushioned seat on top, 4x6 and 1x10 speakers.

1992-1994	$600	$775

Master Amp
Ca. 1957- Ca. 1959. Combo 2x6L6 power, tremolo, 2-tone tweed and leatherette.

1957-1959	$450	$575

MODEL YEAR FEATURES	EXC. COND. LOW HIGH

Maverick Amp
Late-1960s-early-1970s. Dual speaker combo, 6 tubes, verticle cab, tremolo, reverb, red/pink control panel, 2-tone black and silver grille.

1960s-70s	$385	$500

Model One Amp
Mid-1970s-1977. Solidstate 1x12" vertical cab combo, 30 watts, reverb and tremolo.

1970s	$175	$225

Model Two Amp
Mid-1970s-1977. Solidstate 2x10" vertical cab combo, 50 watts, reverb and tremolo.

1977-1978	$225	$300

Model Three Amp
Mid-1970s-1977. Solidstate 1x15" vertical cab bass combo, 60 watts, organ and guitar.

1977-1978	$210	$275

Model Four Amp
Early-1980s. Solidstate, 6 watts.

1980s	$125	$165

Model Five Amp
Early-1980s. Solidstate, 10 watts, 6.25" speaker.

1980s	$140	$185

Model Six Amp
Early-1980s. Same as Model Five but with reverb.

1980s	$175	$225

Model Seven Amp
Early-1980s. Solidstate, 12 watts, small amp for guitar, bass and keyboard.

1980s	$200	$260

Model 50-J Amp
Early-1960s. 14 watts, 1x12", tremolo, blue/gray vinyl.

1962-1963	$430	$560

Model 66 Amp
1953-1955. 15 watts, 1x12", tremolo, 2-tone leatherette.

1953-1955	$440	$575

Model 66-J Amp
1962-1963. 20 watts, 1x12", tremolo, blue/gray vinyl.

1962-1963	$465	$605

Model 98-RT Amp
1962-1963. The only stand-alone reverb amp from Guild in the early '60s, 30 watts, 1x12", blue/gray vinyl.

1962-1963	$620	$805

Model 99 Amp
1953-1955. 30 watts, 1x12", tremolo, 2-tone leatherette.

1953-1955	$465	$605

Model 99-J Amp
Early-1960s. 30 watts, 1x12", tremolo, blue/gray vinyl.

1962-1963	$475	$625

Model 99-U Ultra Amp
Early-1960s. Piggyback 30-watt head with optional 1x12" or 1x15" cab, cab and head lock together, tremolo, blue/gray vinyl.

1962-1963	$490	$635

Model 100-J Amp
Early-1960s. 35 watts, 1x15", blue/gray vinyl.

1962-1963	$490	$635

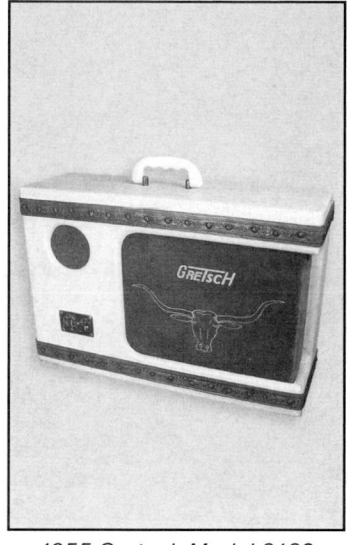

1955 Gretsch Model 6169 Electromatic Twin

Groove Tubes Soul-O

1971 Guild Maverick

AMPS

Guild Thunder 1 (11RVT)
Greg Gagliono

Harmony Model H-303A

Headstrong Lil' King

MODEL YEAR	FEATURES	EXC. COND. LOW	HIGH

Model 200-S Stereo Combo Amp
Early-1960s. 25 watts per channel, total 50 watts stereo, 2x12", tremolo, blue/gray vinyl, wheat grille.

1962-1963		$745	$975

Model RC-30 Reverb Converter Amp
Early-1960s. Similar to Gibson GA-1 converter, attaches with 2 wires clipped to originating amp's speaker, 8 watts, 1x10", blue/gray vinyl.

1962-1963		$475	$625

Superbird Amp
1968. Piggyback tube amp with 2x12 cab.

1968		$575	$750

SuperStar Amp
Ca.1972-ca.1974. 50 watts, all tubes, 1x15" Jensen speakers, vertical combo, reverb, tremolo, black vinyl cover, 2-tone black/silver grille.

1972-1974		$425	$550

Thunder 1 Amp
1965-1972. Combo with single speaker, no reverb, light tan cover, 2-tone tan grille.

1965-1972	1x10"	$260	$340
1965-1972	1x12"	$285	$375

Thunder 1 (Model 11RVT)/T1 Amp
1965-1972. Combo with dual speakers and reverb, light tan cover, 2-tone tan grille.

1965-1972		$475	$625

ThunderBass Amp
1965-1972. Piggyback combo, 2x15".

1965-1972	100 watt	$525	$685
1965-1972	200 watt	$550	$725

ThunderBird Amp
1965-1972. 50 watts, tube, 2x12", reverb, tremolo, with or without TD-1 dolly, black vinyl, black/silver grille.

1965-1972		$475	$625

ThunderStar Bass Amp
1965-1972. Piggyback bass tube head or combo, 50 watts.

1965-1972	Full stack, 2x1x15"	$600	$775
1965-1972	Half stack, 1x1x15"	$525	$685

ThunderStar Guitar Amp
1965-1972. Combo, 50 watts, 1x12".

1965-1972		$475	$625

Guyatone
1933-present. Started offering amps by at least the late '40s with their Guya lap steels. In '51 the Guyatone brand is first used on guitars and most likely amps. Guyatone also made the Marco Polo, Winston, Kingston, Kent, LaFayette and Bradford brands.

Guytron
1995-present. Tube amp heads and speaker cabinets built by Guy Hedrick in Columbiaville, Michigan. In January, '09, GDS Amplification bought the assets of Guytron Amplification.

Hagstrom
1921-1983, 2004-present. The Swedish guitar maker built a variety of tube and solidstate amps from ca. 1961 into the '70s. They also supplied amps to Guild.

Hanburt
1940-ca. 1950. Harvey M. Hansen built electric Hawaiian guitars in Seattle, Washington, some sold as a set with a small amp. The wooden amps have a large HB in the speaker cutout. He also built at least one mandolin.

Harmony
1892-1976, late-1970s-present. Harmony was one of the biggest producers of guitars, and offered amps as well. MBT International offered Harmony amps for 2000-'02.

H Series Amps
1940s-1960s. Harmony model numbers begin with H, such as H-304, all H series models shown are tube amps unless otherwise noted as solidstate.

1940-1950s	H-190/H-191	$415	$520
1940-1950s	H-200	$415	$520
1950s	H-204, 18w, 1x12"	$415	$520
1960s	H-303A, 8w, 1x8"	$225	$280
1960s	H-304, low pwr, small spkr	$225	$280
1960s	H-305A, low pwr, small spkr	$225	$280
1960s	H-306A, combo 1x12"	$325	$405
1960s	H306C, piggyback 2x12"	$410	$515
1960s	H-400, 8w, 1x8", vol	$195	$245
1960s	H-400A, 8w, 1x8", vol/tone	$225	$280
1960s	H-410A, 10w, 1x10"	$385	$480
1960s	H-415, 18w, 2x12"	$625	$780
1960s	H-420, 20w, 1x12"	$410	$515
1960s	H-430, 30w, 2x10"	$625	$780
1960s	H-440, 2x12", trem & verb	$650	$825

Solidstate Amps
1970s. Dark covering, dark grille.

1970s	Large amp	$125	$165
1970s	Small amp	$25	$32

Harry Joyce
1993-2011, 2015-present. Hand-wired British tube amps, combos, and cabinets from builder/designer Harry Joyce. Joyce was contracted to build Hiwatt amps in England during the '70s. Joyce died in 2002, and the brand was carried on by Charles Bertonazzi and George Scholz until 2011. Brand brought back by Kevin Wood and Scholz through Harry Joyce USA with new versions of the classic models.

Hartke
1984-present. Guitar and bass amps, combos and cabinets made in the U.S. Founded by Larry Hartke, since the mid-'80s, Hartke has been distributed by Samson Technologies. Hartke also offered basses in the past.

Haynes
Haynes guitar amps were built by the Amplifier Corporation of America (ACA) of Westbury, New York. ACA also made an early distortion

MODEL YEAR	FEATURES	EXC. COND. LOW	HIGH

device powered by batteries. Unicord purchased the company in around 1964, and used the factory to produce its Univox line of amps, most likely discontinuing the Haynes brand at the same time.

Jazz King II Amp
1960s. Solidstate, stereo console-style, 2x12", Haynes logo upper left side.

1960s		$310	$390

Headstrong
2003-present. Tube combo amps and cabinets built by Wayne Jones in Asheville, North Carolina.

Henriksen JazzAmp
2006-present. Professional grade, production, solidstate amps voiced for jazz guitar built by Peter Henriksen in Golden, Colorado.

Heritage
2004-present. Founded by Malcolm MacDonald and Lane Zastrow who was formerly involved with Holland amps. Located in the former Holland facility in Brentwood, Tennessee, they built tube combo and piggyback amps.

Hilgen
1960s. Mid-level amplifiers from Hilgen Manufacturing, Hillside, New Jersey. Dark tolex covering and swiggle-lined light color grille cloth. Examples have been found with original Jensen speakers.

Basso B-2501 Amp
1960s. 25 watts, 1x15" combo, swirl grille, Hilgen crest logo, compact size.

1965		$375	$470

Basso B-2502 Amp
1960s. 25 watts, 1x15" combo, swirl grille, Hilgen crest logo, large cab.

1965		$410	$515

Basso Grande B-2503 Amp
1960s. Brown sparkle cover, piggyback, 2x12".

1965		$540	$675

Basso Profondo B-2502 Amp
1965. Combo 1x15"

1965		$375	$470

Champion R-2523 Amp
Mid-1960s. Highest offering in their amp line, piggyback with 2x12" cab, tremolo, reverb, swirl grille cloth.

1965		$540	$675

Galaxie T-2513 Amp
1960s. 25 watts, 2x12" piggyback cab, tremolo.

1965		$540	$675

Metero T-2511 Amp
Mid-1960s. Compact 1x12" combo, tremolo.

1965		$410	$515

Pacesetter R-2521 Amp
Mid-1960s. 1x12" combo, tremolo, reverb, swirl grille cloth.

1965		$410	$515

Star T-2512 Amp
1960s. 25 watts, 1x12" combo, tremolo.

1965		$410	$515

Troubadour T-1506 Amp
Mid-1960s. Small practice amp.

1965		$295	$370

Victor R-2522 Amp
Mid-1960s. 1x12" combo, larger cab, reverb, tremolo.

1965		$540	$675

HiWatt
1963-1984, ca.1990-present. Amp builder Dave Reeves started his Hylight Electronics in a garage in England in the early 1960s, doing amp and other electronic repairs. By 1964 he had produced the first amps bearing the Hiwatt brand. By the early '70s, Hiwatt's reputation was growing and production was moved to a factory in Kingston-upon-Thames, expanding the amp line and adding PA gear. In '81, Reeves suffered a fatal fall, and ownership of Hiwatt was taken over by Biacrown Ltd, a company made up of Hiwatt employees. Biacrown struggled and closed up in '84. From ca.1990 to ca.1994, a line of American-made Hiwatts, designed by Frank Levi, were available. By the mid-'90s, amps with the Hiwatt brand were again being built in England and, separately, imported from Asia by Fernandes.

Bass 100 Amp Head

1980s	100w, England	$1,300	$1,600

Bulldog SA112 Amp
1980s, 1994-present. 50 watts, combo, 1x12".

1980s		$1,200	$1,500
1994-2014		$1,100	$1,400

Bulldog SA112FL Amp
1980s-1990s. 100 watts, combo, 1x12".

1980s		$1,200	$1,500
1990s		$1,100	$1,400

Custom 100 Amp Head

2007	100w	$1,175	$1,525

DR-103 Custom 100 Amp Head
1970-late-1980s, 2005-present. Tube head, 100 watts, custom Hiwatt 100 logo on front.

1970-1980s		$2,200	$2,750

DR-201 Hiwatt 200 Amp Head
1970s. 200-watt amp head, Hiwatt 200 logo on front.

1970s		$2,200	$2,750

DR-405 Hiwatt 400 Amp Head
1970s. 400-watt amp head.

1970s		$2,200	$2,750

DR-504 Custom 50 Amp Head
1970-late-1980s, 1995-1999. Tube head, 50 watts.

1970-1980s		$2,200	$2,750

Lead 20 (SG-20) Amp Head
1980s. Tube amp head, 30 watts, black cover, rectangular HiWatt plate logo.

1980s		$550	$700

Lead 50R Combo Amp
1980s. Combo tube amp, 50 watts, 1x12", reverb, dark cover, dark grille, HiWatt rectangular plate logo.

1980s		$800	$1,000

OL-103 Lead 100 Amp Head

1982	100w, England	$1,200	$1,500

Henriksen JazzAmp

HiWatt Bulldog SA112

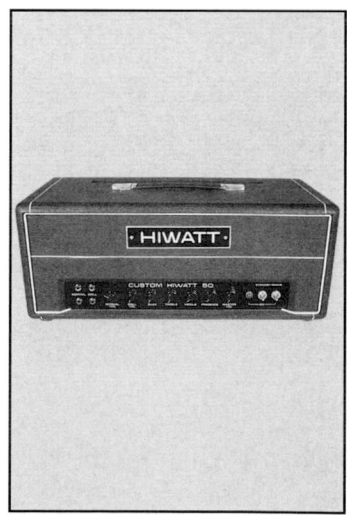
HiWatt DR-504 Custom 50

Hottie Super Chef

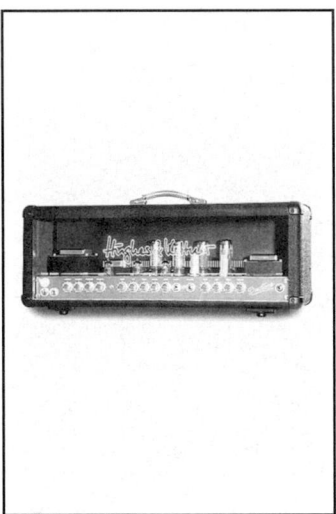

Hughes & Kettner Duotone

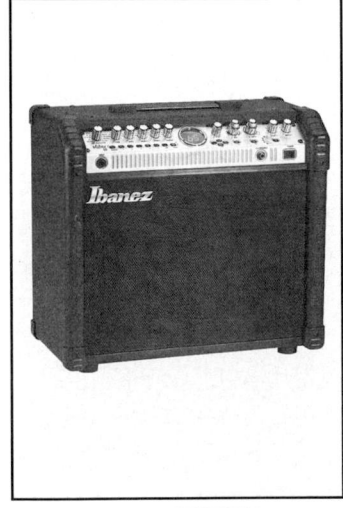

Ibanez MIMX65

MODEL YEAR	FEATURES	EXC. COND. LOW	HIGH
PW-50 Tube Amp			
1989-1993. Stereo tube amp, 50 watts per channel.			
1989-1993		$800	$1,000
S50L Amp Head			
1989-1993. Lead guitar head, 50 watts, gain, master volume, EQ.			
1989-1993		$700	$875
SA 112 Combo Amp			
1970s	50w, 1x12"	$2,500	$3,100
SA 212 Combo Amp			
1970s	50w, 2x12"	$2,700	$3,350
SA 412 Combo Amp			
1970s	50w, 4x12"	$3,300	$4,100
SE 2150 Speaker Cabinet			
1970s	2x15" vertical	$1,700	$2,150
SE 4121 Speaker Cabinet			
1970s	4x12", half stack	$1,800	$2,250
SE 4122 (Lead) Speaker Cabinet			
1971- mid-1980s. 4x12", Fane speakers, 300 watts.			
1971-1980s	4x12", half stack	$1,800	$2,250
SE 4123 (Bass) Speaker Cabinet			
1970s. Bass version of SE, often used with DR103 head, straight-front cab and stackable, black tolex with gray grille, Hiwatt logo plate in center of grille.			
1970s		$1,800	$2,250
SE 4129 (Bass) Speaker Cabinet			
1970s. SE series for bass, 4x12", often used with DR 201 head.			
1970s		$1,800	$2,250
SE 4151 Speaker Cabinet			
1970s. SE series with 4x15".			
1970s		$1,800	$2,300

Hoagland

Professional grade, production, guitar amps built by Dan Hoagland in Land O Lakes, Florida starting in 2008.

Hoffman

1993-present. Tube amps, combos, reverb units, and cabinets built by Doug Hoffman from 1993 to '99, in Sarasota, Florida. Hoffman no longer builds amps, concentrating on selling tube amp building supplies, and since 2001 has been located in Pisgah Forest, North Carolina.

Hoffmann

1983-present. Tube amp heads for guitar and other musical instruments built by Kim Hoffmann in Hawthorne, California.

Hohner

1857-present. Matthias Hohner, a clockmaker in Trossingen, Germany, founded Hohner in 1857, making harmonicas. Hohner has been offering guitars and amps at least since the early '70s.

Panther Series Amps

1980s. Smaller combo amps, master volume, gain, EQ.

1980s	P-12, 12w	$77	$97
1980s	P-20, 20w	$83	$103

MODEL YEAR	FEATURES	EXC. COND. LOW	HIGH
1980s	P-25R, 25w	$83	$103
1980s	PBK-20 bass/keyboard, 25w	$88	$110
Sound Producer Series Amps			
1980s. Master volume, normal and overdrive, reverb, headphone jack.			
1980s	BA 130 bass	$83	$103
1980s	SP 35	$88	$110
1980s	SP 55	$93	$115
1980s	SP 75	$110	$135

Holland

1992-2004. Tube combo amps from builder Mike Holland, originally in Virginia Beach, Virginia, and since 2000 in Brentwood, Tennessee. In 2000, Holland took Lane Zastrow as a partner, forming L&M Amplifiers to build the Holland line. The company closed in '04.

Holmes

1970-late 1980s. Founded by Harrison Holmes. Holmes amplifiers were manufactured in Mississippi and their product line included guitar and bass amps, PA systems, and mixing boards. In the early '80s, Harrsion Holmes sold the company to On-Site Music which called the firm The Holmes Corp. Products manufactured by Harrison have an all-caps HOLMES logo and the serial number plate says The Holmes Company.

Performer PB-115 Bass Amp

60 watts, 1x15", black tolex.

1982		$110	$140

Pro Compact 210S Amp

60 watts, 2x10", 2 channels, active EQ, black tolex.

1982		$110	$140

Pro Compact 212S Amp

2x12" version of Pro.

1982		$135	$170

Rebel RB-112 Bass Amp

35 watts, 1x12", black tolex.

1982		$85	$105

Hondo

1969-1987, 1991-2005. Hondo has offered imported amps over the years. 1990s models ranged from the H20 Practice Amp to the H160SRC with 160 watts (peak) and 2x10" speakers.

Amps

1970s-1990s. Various models.

1970s-90s	Mid-size	$45	$70
1970s-90s	Small	$20	$30

Hottie

2005-present. Jean-Claude Escudie and Mike Bernards build their budget and intermediate grade, production/custom, solid state "toaster" amps in Portland, Oregon. They also offer guitars.

Hound Dog

1994-1998. Founded by George Alessandro as the Hound Dog Corporation. Name was changed to Alessandro in 1998 (see that brand for more information).

MODEL YEAR	FEATURES	EXC. COND. LOW	HIGH

Hughes & Kettner

1985-present. Hughes & Kettner offers a line of solidstate and tube guitar and bass amps, combos, cabinets and effects, all made in Germany.

Humphrey

2010-present. Custom, professional and premium grade, tube amps built in Chanhassen, Minnesota by Gerry Humphrey. He also builds preamps and reverb units.

Hurricane

Tube guitar and harmonica combo amps built by Gary Drouin in Sarasota, Florida. Drouin started the company in 1998 with harp master Rock Bottom, who died in September, 2001.

Hy Lo

1960s-1970s. Budget grade, small compact amps made in Japan, Hy Lo logo on grille.

Ibanez

1932-present. Ibanez added solidstate amps to their product line in '98. They also build guitars, basses and effects.

Idol

Late-1960s. Made in Japan. Dark tolex cover, dark grille, Hobby Series with large Idol logo on front.

Hobby Series Amps

1968	Hobby 10	$80	$105
1968	Hobby 100	$165	$215
1968	Hobby 20	$100	$130
1968	Hobby 45	$155	$200

Impact

1963-early 1970s. Based in London, England, tube amps made by Don Mackrill and Laurie Naiff for Pan Musical Instrument Company and their music stores. About a dozen different models of combos, piggyback half-stacks and PAs were offered.

Imperial

Ca.1963-ca.1970. The Imperial Accordion Company of Chicago, Illinois offered one or two imported small amps in the '60s.

Jack Daniel's

2004-present. Tube guitar amp built by Peavey for the Jack Daniel Distillery, offered until about '10. They still offer guitars.

Jackson

1980-present. The Jackson-Charvel Company offered budget to intermediate grade amps and cabinets in the late '80s and the '90s.

Jackson Ampworks

2001-present. Brad Jackson builds his tube amp heads and speaker cabinets in Bedford, Texas.

Jackson-Guldan

1920s-1960s. The Jackson-Guldan Violin Company, of Columbus, Ohio, offered lap steels and small tube amps early on. They also built acoustic guitars.

Jay Turser

1997-present. Smaller, inexpensive imported solidstate guitar and bass amps. They also offer basses and guitars.

JCA Circuits

Tube guitar combo amps built by Jason C. Arthur in Pottstown, Pennsylvania, starting in 1995.

Jennings

Late 1960s. Tom Jennings formed another company after resigning from Vox. Large block letter Jennings logo on front panel, Jennings Amplifier logo on back control plate with model number and serial number.

Jet City Amplification

2009-present. Budget to professional grade, production/custom, guitar amps and cabinets designed in Seattle, Washington by Doug White, Dan Gallagher, Michael Soldano and built in Asia.

Jim Kelley

1979-1985. Channel-switching tube amps, compact combos and heads, hardwood cabinets available, made by Jim Kelley at his Active Guitar Electronics in Tustin, California. He produced about 100 amps a year. In 1978 and early '79 he produced a few amps under the Fortune brand name for Fortune Guitars.

JMI (Jennings Musical Industries)

2004-present. Jennings built the Vox amps of the 1960s. They are back with tube amp heads and cabinets based on some of their classic models.

Johnson

Mid-1990s-present. Line of solidstate amps imported by Music Link, Brisbane, California. Johnson also offers guitars, basses, mandolins and effects.

Johnson Amplification

1997-present. Intermediate and professional grade, production, modeling amps and effects designed by John Johnson, of Sandy, Utah. The company is part of Harman International. In 2002, they quit building amps, but continue the effects line.

JoMama

1994-present. Tube amps and combos under the JoMama and Kelemen brands built by Joe Kelemen in Santa Fe, New Mexico.

Jackson Ampworks Britain

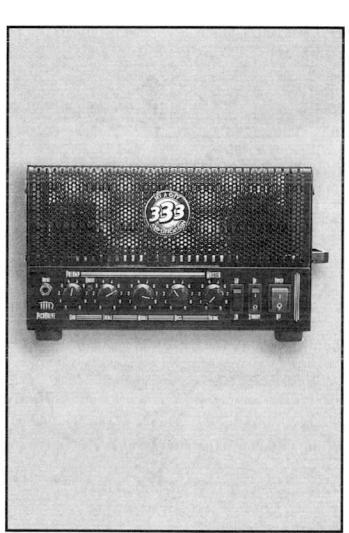

Jet City PicoValve

Johnson Barn Burner

Kafel S150 Head

1964 Kay 405
Steve Lee

Kingsley ToneBaron

Jordan

1966-early 1970s. Jordan Electronics, of Alhambra, California, built a range of electronics, including, starting around 1966, solid state guitar amps and effects.

Juke

1989-present. Tube guitar and harmonica amps built by G.R. Croteau in Troy, New Hampshire. He also built the Warbler line of amps.

Kafel

Jack Kafel built his tube amp heads in Chicago, Illinois, starting in 2004.

Kalamazoo

1933-1942, 1965-1970. Kalamazoo was a brand Gibson used on one of their budget lines. They used the name on amps from '65 to '67.

Bass Amp
1965-1967. Enclosed back, 2x10", flip-out control panel, not a commonly found model as compared to numerous Model 1 and 2 student amps.

1965-1967		$410	$535

Bass 30 Amp
Late 1960s-early 1970s. Tube combo, verticle cabinet, 2x10".

1970		$285	$370

KEA Amp
1948-1952. Small compact amp, round speaker baffle grille, slant Kalamazoo logo on front, oxblood leatherette.

1948-1952		$387	$500

Lap Steel Amp
1940s. Kalamazoo logo on front lower right, low power with 1-6V6, round speaker grille opening, red/brown leatherette.

1940s		$335	$435

Model 1 Amp
1965-1967. No tremolo, 1x10", front control panel, black.

1965-1967		$180	$235

Model 2 Amp
1965-1967. Same as Model 1 with tremolo, black.

1965-1967	Black panel	$230	$300
1967	Silver panel	$180	$235

Model 3 Amp
Late 1960s-early 1970s. Made by CMI Electronics in Chicago, post Gibson Kalamazoo era, student compact solidstate combo, Kalamazoo 3 logo on front panel, Kalamazoo Model 3 logo on label on speaker magnet.

1960s-70s		$85	$110

Model 4 Amp
Late 1960s-early 1970s. Made by CMI Electronics in Chicago, post Gibson Kalamazoo era, student compact solidstate combo, 3 control knobs, tone, tremolo, volume, Kalamazoo 4 logo on front panel, Kalamazoo Model 4 logo on label on speaker magnet.

1960s-70s		$85	$110

Reverb 12 Amp
1965-1967. Black vinyl cover, 1x12", reverb, tremolo.

1965-1967		$415	$540

Kay

Ca.1931-present. Kay originally offered amps up to around '68 when the brand changed hands. Currently they offer a couple small solidstate imported amps. They also make basses, guitars, banjos, mandolins, ukes, and violins.

K506 Vibrato 12" Amp
1960s. 12 watts, 1x12", swirl grille, metal handle.

1960s		$385	$500

K507 Twin Ten Special Amp
1960s. 20 watts, 2x10", swirl grille, metal handle.

1960s		$425	$550

K700 Series Amp
Introduced in 1965. Value Leader/Vanguard/Galazie models, transistorized amps promoted as eliminates tube-changing annoyance and reliable performance, combo amps with tapered cabinets, rear slant control panel, rich brown and tan vinyl cover, brown grille cloth.

1965	700, 1x8"	$115	$150
1965	703, 1x8"	$115	$150
1965	704, 1x8"	$115	$150
1965	705, 1x10"	$125	$165
1965	706, 1x15"	$135	$175
1965	707, 1x12"	$135	$175
1965	708, 1x12"	$135	$175
1965	720 bass, 1x15"	$135	$175
1966	760, 1x12"	$135	$175

Model 703 Amp
1962-1964. Tube student amp, small speaker, 3 tubes, 1 volume, 1 tone, 2-tone white front with brown back cabinet, metal handle, model number noted on back panel, Kay logo and model number badge lower front right.

1962-1964		$190	$250

Model 803 Amp
1962-1964. Student amp, 1x8", 3 tubes, 1 volume, 1 tone, metal handle, 14.75x11.75x6.75" cabinet with dark gray cover.

1962-1964		$190	$250

Model 805 Amp
1965. Solidstate, 35 watts, 1x10", 4 control knobs, 2-tone cabinet.

1965		$115	$150

Small Tube Amp
1940s	Wood cabinet	$285	$375
1950s	Various models	$285	$375
1960s	Models K503, K504, K505	$335	$435

Kelemen

1994-present. Tube amps and combos under the JoMama and Kelemen brands built by Joe Kelemen in Santa Fe, New Mexico.

Kendrick

1989-present. Founded by Gerald Weber in Austin, Texas and currently located in Kempfner, Texas. Mainly known for their intermediate to professional grade, tube amps, Kendrick also offers guitars, speakers, and effects.

AMPS

MODEL YEAR	FEATURES	EXC. COND. LOW	HIGH

Kent

Ca.1962-1969. Imported budget line of guitars and amps.

Guitar and Bass Amps

1960s. Various models.

YEAR	FEATURES	LOW	HIGH
1966	1475, 3 tubes, brown	$55	$75
1966	2198, 3 tubes, brown	$55	$75
1966	5999, 3 tubes, brown	$75	$100
1966	6104, piggyback, 12w	$115	$150
1969	6610, solidstate, small	$35	$45

Kiesel

See Carvin.

King Amplification

2005-present. Tube combo amps, head and cabinets built by Val King in San Jose, California.

Kingsley

1998-present. Production/custom, professional grade, tube amps and cabinets built by Simon Jarrett in Vancouver, British Columbia.

Kingston

1958-1967. Economy solidstate amps imported by Westheimer Importing, Chicago, Illinois.

Cat Amps

Mid-1960s. Solidstate Cat Series amps have dark vinyl, dark grilles.

YEAR	FEATURES	LOW	HIGH
1960s	P-1 3w, P-2 5w	$50	$65
1960s	P-3 8w, P-8 20w	$55	$70

Cougar BA-21 Bass Piggyback Amp

Mid-1960s. Solidstate, 60 watts, 2x12" cab, dark vinyl, light silver grille.

1960s		$110	$145

Cougar PB-5 Bass Combo Amp

Mid-1960s. Solidstate, 15 watts, 1x8".

1960s		$55	$75

Lion 2000 Piggyback Amp

Mid-1960s. Solidstate, 90 watts, 2x12" cab.

1960s		$135	$175

Lion 3000 Piggyback Amp

Mid-1960s. Solidstate, 250 watts, 4x12" cab.

1960s		$160	$210

Lion AP-281 R Piggyback Amp

Mid-1960s. Solidstate, 30 watts, 2x8" cab, dark vinyl cover, light silver grille.

1960s		$90	$125

Lion AP-281 R10 Piggyback Amp

Mid-1960s. Solidstate, 30 watts, 2x10" cab.

1960s		$115	$150

Kinsman

2012-present. Budget and intermediate grade, production, guitar amps and cabinets built in China and distributed worldwide by John Hornby Skewes & Co. Ltd. in England. They also use the brand on a line of guitar effects.

Kitchen-Marshall

1965-1966. Private branded for Kitchen Music by Marshall, primarily PA units with block logos. Limited production.

JTM 45 MKII 45-Watt Amp Head

1965-1966. Private branded for Kitchen Music, JTM 45 Marshall with Kitchen logo plate, 45 watts.

1965-1966		$5,700	$7,100

Slant 4x12 1960 Cabinet

1965-1966. Slant front 4x12" 1960-style cab with gray bluesbreaker grille, very limited production.

1965-1966	Black on green vinyl	$3,000	$3,800

KJL

1995-present. Founded by Kenny Lannes, MSEE, a professor of Electrical Engineering at the University of New Orleans. KJL makes budget to intermediate grade, tube combo amps, heads and an ABY box.

KMD (Kaman)

1986-ca.1990. Distributed by Kaman (Ovation, Hamer, etc.) in the late '80s, KMD offered a variety of amps and effects.

Koch

All-tube combo amps, heads, effects and cabinets built in The Netherlands.

Komet

1999-present. Intermediate to professional grade, tube amp heads built in Baton Rouge, Louisanna, by Holger Notzel and Michael Kennedy with circuits designed by Ken Fischer of Trainwreck fame. They also build a power attenuator.

Kona Guitar Company

2001-present. Budget solidstate amps made in Asia. They also offer guitars, basses, mandolins, ukes and banjos.

Krank

1996-2013, 2015-present. Founded by Tony Dow and offering tube amp heads, combos and speaker cabinets built in Tempe, Arizona. They also build effects.

Kustom

1965-present. Kustom, a division of Hanser Holdings, offers guitar and bass combo amps and PA equipment. Founded by Bud Ross in Chanute, Kansas, who offered tuck-and-roll amps as early as '58, but began using the Kustom brand name in '65. From '69 to '75 Ross gradually sold interest in the company (in the late '70s, Ross introduced the line of Ross effects stomp boxes). The brand changed hands a few times, and by the mid-'80s it was no longer in use. In '89 Kustom was in bankruptcy court and was purchased by Hanser Holdings Incorporated of Cincinnati, Ohio (Davitt & Hanser) and by '94, they had a new line of amps available.

Kinsman K50

AMPS

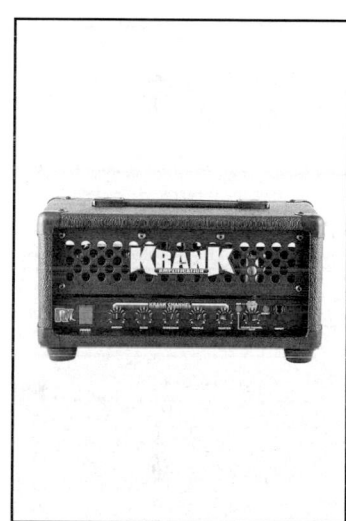

Krank Rev Jr. Standard

Early-1970s Kustom Challenger

Kustom 36

1972 Kustom K50-2 SC
Randy Bacus

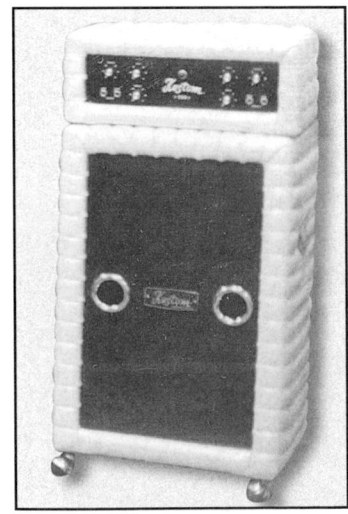

Kustom K100

Prices are for excellent condition amps with no tears in the tuck-and-roll cover and no grille tears. A tear in the tuck-and-roll will reduce the value, sometimes significantly.

Kustom model identification can be frustrating as they used series numbers, catalog numbers (the numbers in the catalogs and price lists), and model numbers (the number often found next to the serial number on the amp's back panel). Most of the discussion that follows is by series number (100, 200, 300, etc.) and catalog number. Unfortunately, vintage amp dealers use the serial number and model number, so the best way is to cross-check speaker and amplifier attributes. Model numbers were used primarily for repair purposes and were found in the repair manuals. In many, but not all cases, the model number is the last digit of the catalog number; for example the catalog lists a 100 series Model 1-15J-1, where the last digit 1 signifies a Model 1 amplifier chassis which is a basic amp without reverb or tremolo. A Model 1-15J-2 signifies a Model 2 amp chassis that has reverb and tremolo. In this example, Kustom uses a different model number on the back of the amp head. For the 1-15J-2, the model number on the back panel of the amp head would be K100-2, indicating a series 100 (50 watts) amp with reverb and tremolo (amp chassis Model 2).

Model numbers relate to the amplifier's schematic and electronics, while catalog numbers describe the amp's relative power rating and speaker configuration.

Amp Chasis Model Numbers ('68-'72)
Model 1 Amp (basic)
Model 2 Amp with reverb
Model 3 Amp with Harmonic Clip and Boost
Model 4 Amp with reverb, tremolo, vibrato,
    Harmonic Clip and Selective Boost
Model 5 PA with reverb
Model 6 Amp (basic) with Selectone
Model 7 Amp with reverb, tremolo, vibrato,
    boost (different parts)
Model 8 Amp with reverb, tremolo, vibrato,
    boost (different parts)

Naugahyde Tuck-&-Roll 200 ('65-'67)
The very first Kustoms did not have the model series on the front control panel. The early logo stipulated Kustom by Ross, Inc. The name was then updated to Kustom Electronics, Inc. 1965-'67 amp heads have a high profile/tall "forehead" area (the area on top of the controls) and these have been nicknamed "Frankenstein models." The '65-'67 catalog numbers were often 4 or 5 digits, for example J695. The first digit represents the speaker type (J = Jensen, etc.), other examples are L995, L1195, L795RV, etc. Some '67 catalog numbers changed to 2 digits followed by 3 digits, like 4-D 140f, or 3-15C (3 CTS speakers), etc. Others sported 5 characters like 4-15J-1, where 4 = 4 speakers, 15 = 15" speakers, J = Jensen, and 1 = basic amp chassis with no effects. The fifth digit indicated amp chassis model number as described above.

Naugahyde Tuck-&-Roll 100/200/400 ('68-'71)
Starting in '68, the Kustom logo also included the

model series. A K100, for example, would have 100 displayed below the Kustom name. The model series generally is twice the relative output wattage, for example, the 100 Series is a 50-watt amp. Keep in mind, solidstate ratings are often higher than tube-amp ratings, so use the ratings as relative measurements. Most '68-'70 Kustom catalog numbers are x-xxx-x, for example 1-15L-1. First digit represents the number of speakers, the 2nd and 3rd represent the speaker size, the fourth represents the speaker type (A = Altec Lansing, L = J.B.L., J = Jensen, C = C.T.S. Bass), the fifth digit represents the amp chassis number. The power units were interchangeable in production, so amps could have similar front-ends but different power units (more power and different effect options) and visa versa. Some '68 bass amp catalog numbers were 4 digits, for example 2-12C, meaning two 12" CTS speakers. Again, there were several different numbers used. Kustom also introduced the 200 and 400 amp series and the logo included the series number. The catalog numbers were similar to the 100 series, but they had a higher power rating of 100 equivalent watts (200 series), or 200 equivalent watts (400 series). Kustom U.S. Naugahyde (tuck-&-roll) covers came in 7 colors: black (the most common), Cascade (blue/green), silver (white-silver), gold (light gold), red, blue, and Charcoal (gray). The market historically shows color options fetching more. The market has not noticeably distinguished power and features options. Condition and color seem to be the most important. Gold and Cascade may be the rarest seen colors.

Naugahyde Tuck-&-Roll 150/250/300/500/600 (c.'71-c.'75)
The amp heads changed with a slightly slanted control panel and the Kustom logo moved to the right/upper-right portion of the front panel. They continued to be tuck-&-roll offered in the same variety of colors. The sales literature indicated a 150 series had 150 watts, 250 had 250 watts, etc.

Naugahyde Tuck-&-Roll SC (Self Contained) Series
Most SC combo amps were rated at 150 watts, with the 1-12SC listed at 50 watts. They were offered in 7 colors of tuck-and-roll. Again the model numbers indicate the features as follows: 4-10 SC is a 4 x 10", 2-10 SC is a 2x10", etc.

Super Sound Tuck-and-Roll Combo Series
The last tuck-and-roll combo amps with slightly smaller tucks. Amp control panel is noticeably smaller and the Kustom logo is in the right side of the control panel.

Black Vinyl ('75-c.'78)
By '75 ownership changes were complete and the colorful tuck-and-roll was dropped in favor of more traditional black vinyl. The products had a slant Kustom logo spelled-out and placed in a position on the grille similar to a Fender blackface baffle. Models included the I, II, III, and IV Lead amps. Heads with half- and full-stacks were available. Bass amps included the Kustom 1, Bass I, II, III, IV, and IV SRO.

Black Vinyl K logo ('78-'83)
This era is easily recognized by the prominent capital K logo.

MODEL YEAR	FEATURES	EXC. COND. LOW	HIGH

Bass V Amp

1990s. Large Kustom Bass V logo upper right side of amp, 35 watts, 1x12", black vinyl.

1990s		$85	$110

Challenger Combo Amp

1973-1975. 1x12" speaker.

1973-1975	Black	$260	$340
1973-1975	Color option	$385	$500

Hustler Combo Amp

1973-1975. Solidstate, 4x10", tremolo, tuck-and-roll.

1973-1975	Black	$285	$375
1973-1975	Color option	$410	$535

K25/K25 C-2 SC Amp

1960s. SC (self-contained) Series, small combo tuck-and-roll, 1x12", solidstate, reverb, black control panel.

1971-1973	Black	$260	$340
1971-1973	Color option	$385	$500

K50-2 SC Amp

1971-1973. Self-contained (SC) small combo tuck-and-roll, 1x12", reverb and tremolo.

1971-1973	Black	$260	$340
1971-1973	Color option	$385	$500

K100-1 1-15C Bass Amp Set

1968-1972. The K100-1 with 1-15C speaker option with matching 1x15" cab, black tuck-and-roll standard, but several sparkle colors offered, C.T.S. bass reflex speaker.

1968-1972	Black	$260	$340
1968-1972	Color option	$550	$725

K100-1 1-15L-1/1-15A-1/1-15J-1 Amp Set

1968-1972. K100-1 with matching 1x15" cab, black tuck-and-roll standard, but several colors offered, speaker options are JBL, Altec Lansing or Jensen.

1968-1972	Black	$260	$340
1968-1972	Color option	$550	$725

K100-1 1-D140F Bass Amp

1968-1972. K100-1 with matching 1x15" JBL D-140F cab, black tuck-and-roll standard, but several sparkle colors offered.

1968-1972	Black	$260	$340
1968-1972	Color option	$550	$725

K100-1 2-12C Bass Amp Set

1968-1972. K100-1 with matching 2x12" cab, black tuck-and-roll standard, but several sparkle colors offered, C.T.S. bass reflex speakers.

1968-1972	Black	$310	$400
1968-1972	Color option	$725	$950

K100-2 1-15L-2/1-15A-2/1-15J-2 Amp Set

1968-1972. K100-2 head and matching 1x15" cab, black tuck-and-roll standard, but several sparkle colors offered.

1968-1972	Black	$260	$340
1968-1972	Color option	$550	$725

K100-2 2-12A-2/2-12J-2 Amp Set

1968-1972. K100-2 head with matching 2x12" cab, black tuck-and-roll standard, but several sparkle colors offered.

1968-1972	Black	$310	$400
1968-1972	Color option	$725	$950

K100-5 PA Amp Head

1968-1972. 50 watts, 2 channels with 8 control knobs per channel, reverb.

1968-1972	Black	$370	$480

K100-6 SC Amp

1970-1972. Basic combo amp with selectone, no reverb.

1970-1972	Black	$230	$300

K100-7 SC Amp

1970-1972. Combo amp with reverb, tremolo, vibrato and boost.

1970-1972	Black	$260	$340
1970-1972	Color option	$385	$500

K100-8 SC Amp

1970-1972. Combo amp with reverb, tremolo, vibrato and boost.

1970-1972	Black	$260	$340
1970-1972	Color option	$385	$500

K100C-6 Combo Amp

1968-1970. Kustom 100 logo middle of the front control panel, 1x15" combo, selectone option.

1968-1970	Black	$260	$340
1968-1970	Color option	$385	$500

K100C-8 Combo Amp

1968-1970. Kustom 100 logo middle of the front control panel, 4x10" combo, reverb, tremolo, vibrato.

1968-1970	Black	$370	$480

K150-1 Amp Set

1972-1975. Piggyback, 150 watts, 2x12", no reverb, logo in upper right corner of amp head, tuck-and-roll, black or color option.

1972-1975	Color option	$385	$500

K150-2 Amp Set

1972-1975. K150 with added reverb and tremolo, piggyback, 2x12", tuck-and-roll, black or color option.

1972-1975	Color option	$500	$650

K150-5 PA Amp Set

1972-1975. PA head plus 2 PA cabs.

1972-1975		$335	$435

K150/150C Combo Amp

1972-1975. Combo, 2x10".

1972-1975	Black	$260	$340

K200-1/K200B Bass Amp Set

1966-1972. K200 head with 2x15" cab.

1966-1972	Black	$415	$540
1966-1972	Color option	$600	$775

K200-2 Reverb/Tremolo Amp Set

1966-1972. K200-2 head with 2x15" or 3x12" cab, available with JBL D-140F speakers, Altec Lansing (A) speakers, C.T.S. (C), or Jensen (J).

1966-1972	Black	$415	$540
1966-1972	Color option	$600	$775

K250 Amp Set

1971-1975. K250 head with 2x15" cab, tuck-and-roll cover.

1971-1975	Black	$335	$435
1971-1975	Color option	$625	$800

K300 PA Amp and Speaker Set

1971-1975. Includes 302 PA, 303 PA, 304 PA, 305 PA, head and 2 cabs.

1971-1975	Color option	$600	$775

Late-1960s Kustom K200-2 Reverb/Tremolo Set

Randy Bacus

Kustom K150C

Randy Bacus

Kustom K250-2-15

AMPS

AMPS

Kustom K400-2

Laboga Caiman Series

Lace 20 watt

MODEL YEAR	FEATURES	EXC. COND. LOW	HIGH

K400-2 Reverb/Tremolo Amp Set

1968-1972. 200 relative watts, reverb, tremolo, with 6x12" or 8x12" cab, available with JBL D-140F speakers, Altec Lansing (A), C.T.S. (C), or Jensen (J). The K400 was offered with no effects (suffix 1), with reverb and tremolo (suffix 2), with Harmonic Clipper & Boost (suffix 3), and Reverb/Trem/Clipper/Boost (suffix 4). The 400 heads came with a separate chrome amp head stand.

1968-1972	Black	$335	$435
1968-1972	Color option	$625	$800

KBA-10 Combo Amp

Late-1980s-1990s. Compact solidstate bass amp, 10 watts, 1x8".

1990s		$30	$40

KBA-20 Combo Amp

Late-1980s-early-1990s. KBA series were compact solidstate bass amps with built-in limiter, 20 watts, 1x8".

1989-1990		$30	$40

KBA-30 Combo Amp

Late-1980s-early-1990s. 30 watts, 1x10".

1989-1990		$30	$40

KBA-40 Combo Amp

Late-1980s-early-1990s. 40 watts, 1x12".

1989-1990		$55	$70

KBA-80 Combo Amp

Late-1980s-early-1990s. 80 watts, 1x15".

1989-1990		$80	$100

KBA-160 Combo Amp

Late-1980s-early-1990s. Solidstate bass amp with built-in limiter, 160 watts, 1x15".

1989-1990		$110	$145

KGA-10 VC Amp

1999-2006. 10 watts, 1x6.5" speaker, switchable overdrive.

1999-2006		$30	$40

KLA-15 Combo Amp

Late-1980s-early-1990s. Solidstate, overdrive, 15 watts, 1x8".

1989-1990		$55	$70

KLA-20 Amp

Mid-1980s-late-1980s. 1x10", MOS-FET, gain, EQ, reverb, headphone jack.

1986		$55	$70

KLA-25 Combo Amp

Late-1980s-early-1990s. Solidstate, overdrive, reverb, 25 watts, 1x10".

1989-1990		$55	$70

KLA-50 Combo Amp

Late-1980s-early-1990s. Solidstate, overdrive, reverb, 50 watts, 1x12".

1989-1990		$80	$100

KLA-75 Amp

Mid-1980s-late-1980s. 75 watts, reverb, footswitching.

1987		$110	$145

KLA-100 Combo Amp

Late-1980s-early-1990s. Solidstate, reverb, 100-watt dual channel, 1x12".

1989-1990		$110	$145

MODEL YEAR	FEATURES	EXC. COND. LOW	HIGH

KLA-185 Combo Amp

Late-1980s-early-1990s. Solidstate, reverb, 185-watt dual channel, 1x12".

1989-1990		$130	$170

KPB-200 Bass Combo Amp

1994-1997. 200 watts, 1x15".

1994-1997		$210	$275

SC 1-12 SC Amp

1971-1973. 50 watts, 1x12" Jensen speaker.

1971-1973	Black	$260	$340
1971-1973	Color option	$465	$600

SC 1-15 SC Amp

1971-1973. 150 watts, 1x15" C.T.S. speaker.

1971-1973	Black	$260	$340
1971-1973	Color option	$465	$600

SC 1-15AB SC Amp

1971-1973. 150 watts, 1x15" Altec Lansing speaker.

1971-1973	Black	$260	$340
1971-1973	Color option	$465	$600

SC 2-12A SC Amp

1971-1973. 150 watts, 2x12" Altec Lansing speakers.

1971-1973	Black	$285	$375
1971-1973	Color option	$500	$650

SC 2-12J SC Amp

1971-1973. 150 watts, 2x12" Jensen speakers.

1971-1973	Black	$285	$375
1971-1973	Color option	$500	$650

SC 4-10 SC Amp

1971-1973. 150 watts, 4x10" Jensen speakers.

1971-1973	Black	$285	$375
1971-1973	Color option	$500	$650

Lab Series

1977-1980s. Five models of Lab Series amps, ranging in price from $600 to $3,700, were introduced at the '77 NAMM show by Norlin (then owner of Gibson). Two more were added later. The '80s models were Lab Series 2 amps and had a Gibson logo on the upper-left front.

B120 Bass Amp Combo

Ca.1984. 120 watts, 2 channels, 1x15".

1984		$360	$450

G120 R-10 Amp Combo

Ca.1984. 120 watts, 3-band EQ, channel switching, reverb, 4x10".

1984		$440	$550

G120 R-12 Amp Combo

Ca.1984. 120 watts, 3-band EQ, channel switching, reverb, 2x12".

1984		$440	$550

L2 Amp Head

1977-ca.1983. 100 watts, black covering.

1977-1983		$260	$325

L3 Amp Combo

1977-ca.1983. 60-watt 1x12".

1977-1983		$335	$420

L4 Amp Head

1977-ca.1983. Solidstate, 200 watts, black cover, dark grille, large L4 logo on front panel.

1977-1983		$260	$325

The *Vintage Guitar Price Guide* shows low to high values for items in all-original excellent condition, and, where applicable, with original case or cover.

MODEL YEAR	FEATURES	EXC. COND. LOW	HIGH

L5 Amp Combo
1977-ca.1983. Solidstate, 100 watts, 2x12" combo.

| 1977-1983 | | $440 | $550 |

L5 Amp Set
1977-ca.1983. Solidstate, 100 watts, 2x12" piggyback.

| 1977-1983 | | $440 | $550 |

L7 Amp Set
1977-ca.1983. Solidstate, 100 watts, 4x10" piggyback.

| 1977-1983 | | $440 | $550 |

L9 Amp Combo
1977-ca.1983. Solidstate, 100 watts, 1x15".

| 1977-1983 | | $360 | $450 |

L11 Amp Set
1977-ca.1983. 200 watts, 8x12" piggyback.

| 1977-1983 | | $525 | $650 |

Laboga
1973-present. Adam Laboga builds intermediate and professional grade, production, tube guitar amps and cabinets in Wroclaw, Poland.

Lace Music Products
1979-present. Lace Music Products, founded by pickup innovator Don Lace Sr., offered amplifiers for a while starting in '96. They also offered amps under the Rat Fink and Mooneyes brands.

Lafayette
Ca.1963-1967. Japanese-made guitars and amps sold through the Lafayette Electronics catalogs.

Tube Amp
1960s. Japanese-made tube, gray speckle 1x12" with art deco design or black 2x12".

| 1960s | Larger, 2 speakers | $185 | $230 |
| 1960s | Small, 1 speaker | $140 | $175 |

Landry
2008-present. Production, professional grade, amps and cabinets built by Bill Landry in St. Louis, Missouri.

Laney
1968-present. Founded by Lyndon Laney and Bob Thomas in Birmingham, England. Laney offered tube amps exclusively into the '80s. Currently they offer intermediate and professional grade, tube and solidstate amp heads and combos and cabinets.

100-Watt Amp Head
1968-1969. Similar to short head Plexi Marshall amp cab, large Laney with underlined "y" logo plate on upper left front corner, black vinyl cover, grayish grille.

| 1968-1969 | | $1,600 | $2,000 |

Lectrolab
1950s-1960s. Budget house brand for music stores, made by Sound Projects Company of Cicero, Illinois. Similar to Valco, Oahu, and Danelectro student amps of the '50s, cabinets were generally made from inexpensive material. The Lectrolab logo can generally be found somewhere on the amp.

MODEL YEAR	FEATURES	EXC. COND. LOW	HIGH

Tube Amp

| 1950s-60s | Larger | $300 | $375 |
| 1950s-60s | Small | $225 | $280 |

Legend
1978-1984. From Legend Musical Instruments of East Syracuse, New York, these amps featured cool wood cabinets. They offered heads, combos with a 1x12" or 2x12" configuration, and cabinets with 1x12", 2x12" or 4x12".

A-30 Amp
1978-1984. Natural wood cabinet, 30 watts, 1x12".

| 1978-1984 | | $385 | $480 |

A-60 Amp
1978-1984. Natural wood cabinet, transtube design dual tube preamp with solidstate power section.

| 1978-1984 | | $465 | $580 |

Rock & Roll 50 Amp Set
1978-1983. Tube preamp section and solidstate power supply.

| 1978-1983 | Half stack matching | $565 | $700 |

Rock & Roll 50 Combo Amp
1978-1983. Mesa-Boogie-style wood compact combo, either 1x15" or 2x12" options, tube preamp section and solidstate power supply.

| 1978-1979 | 2x12" option | $515 | $645 |
| 1978-1983 | 1x15" option | $385 | $480 |

Super Lead 50 Amp
1978-1983. Rock & Roll 50-watt model with added bass boost and reverb, 1x12", hybrid tube and solidstate.

| 1978-1983 | | $385 | $480 |

Super Lead 100 Amp
1978-1983. 100-watt version, 2x12".

| 1978-1983 | | $515 | $645 |

Lenahan
Starting in 1983, professional grade, production/custom, vintage-style amps and cabinets built by James T. Lenahan presently in Fort Smith, Arkansas and prior to '91 in Hollywood, California. He also builds guitar effects.

Leslie
Most often seen with Hammond organs, the cool Leslie rotating speakers have been adopted by many guitarists. Many guitar effects have tried to duplicate their sound. And they are still making them.

122 Amp/122RV Amp
A Hammond-only model, considered the official Hammond B-3 Leslie.

| 1960s | | $675 | $845 |

125 Amp
Late-1960s. All tube amp with 2-speed rotating 1x12" speaker, bottom rotor only, less features.

| 1960s | | $440 | $550 |

142 Amp
A Hammond-only model, smaller cabinet than 122 Amp.

| 1960s | | $575 | $725 |

Landry LS100

Laney VH100R

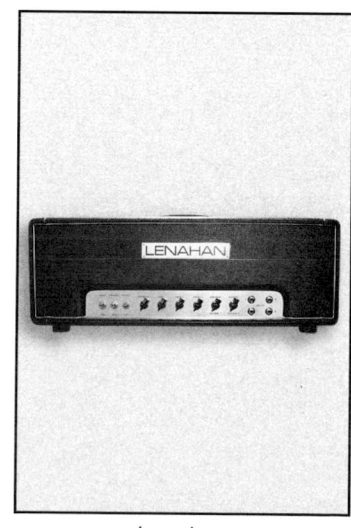

Lenahan

AMPS

Little Walter Vintage 30W Combo

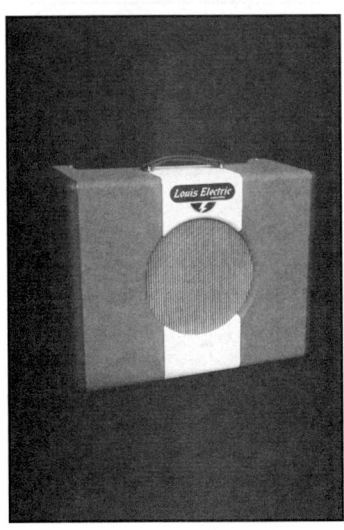

Louis Electric Ferrari

Mack Heatseeker HS-18

MODEL YEAR	FEATURES	EXC. COND. LOW	HIGH

145 Amp
Similar to 147 Amp, but smaller and easier to move.

1960s		$575	$725

147 Amp/147RV Amp
A universal-use model, "7" denotes "universal" useage. RV has added reverb.

1960s		$575	$725

Lickliter Amplification
Starting in 2009, professional and premium grade, custom, guitar amps built in Punta Gorda, Florida by Michael Lickliter.

Line 6
1996-present. Founded by Marcus Ryle and Michel Doidic and specializing in digital signal processing in both effects and amps. They also produce tube amps. Purchased by Yamaha in 2014.

Little Lanilei
1997-present. Small hand-made, intermediate grade, production/custom, amps made by Mahaffay Amplifiers (formerly Songworks Systems & Products) of Aliso Viejo, California. They also build a reverb unit and a rotary effect.

Little Walter
2008-present. Phil Bradbury builds his professional grade, production, amp heads and cabinets in West End, North Carolina.

London City
Late 1960s-early 1970s. Intermediate to professional grade amps and cabinets made in Netherlands, London City logo.

Louis Electric Amplifier Co.
1993-present. Founded by Louis Rosano in Bergenfield, New Jersey. Louis produces custom-built tweeds and various combo amps from 35 to 80 watts.

Luker
2006-present. Professional grade, production/custom, guitar and bass amps and cabinets built in Eugene, Oregon by Ken Luker.

Luna Guitars
2005-present. Located in Tampa, Florida, Yvonne de Villiers imports her budget to professional grade, production, acoustic and electric guitars from Japan, Korea and China. She also imports guitars, basses and ukes.

Mack
2005-present. Made in Toronto, Ontario by builder Don Mackrill, the company offers intermediate and professional grade, production, tube amps.

MODEL YEAR	FEATURES	EXC. COND. LOW	HIGH

Mad Professor
2002-present. Bjorn Juhl and Jukka Monkkonen build their premium grade, production/custom, tube amps in Tampere, Finland. They also offer effects pedals.

Maestro
Maestro amps are associated with Gibson and were included in the Gibson catalogs. For example, in the '62-'63 orange cover Gibson catalog, tweed Maestro amps were displayed in their own section. Tweed Maestro amps are very similar to Gibson tweed amps. Maestro amps were often associated with accordions in the early-'60s but the amps featured standard guitar inputs. Gibson also used the Maestro name on effects in the '60s and '70s and in 01, Gibson revived the name for a line of effects, banjos, and mandolins and added guitars and amps in '09.

The price ranges listed are for excellent condition, all original amps though tubes may be replaced without affecting value. The prices listed are for amps with fully intact logos. A broken or missing logo may diminish the value of the amp. Amps with a changed handle, power cord, and especially a broken logo, should be taken on a case-by-case basis.

Amp models in '58 include the Super Maestro and Maestro, in '60 the Stereo Maestro Accordion GA-87, Super Maestro Accordion GA-46 T, Standard Accordion GA-45 T, Viscount Accordion GA-16 T, in '62 the Reverb-Echo GA-1 RT, Reverb-Echo GA-2 RT, 30 Stereo Accordion Amp, Stereo Accordion GA-78 RV.

GA-1 RT Reverb-Echo Amp
1961. Tweed, 1x8".

1961		$500	$625

GA-2 RT Deluxe Reverb-Echo Amp
1961. Deluxe more powerful version of GA-1 RT, 1x12", tweed.

1961		$800	$1,000

GA-15 RV/Bell 15 RV Amp
1961. 15 watts, 1x12", gray sparkle.

1961		$575	$725

GA-16 T Viscount Amp
1959-1961. 14 watts, 1x10", white cab with brown grille.

1959-1961		$450	$575

GA-45 Maestro Amp
1955-1961. 14-16 watts, 4x8", 2-tone.

1955-1961		$800	$1,000

GA-45 RV Standard Amp
1961. 16 watts, 4x8", reverb.

1961		$1,000	$1,250

GA-45 T Standard Accordion Amp
1961. 16 watts, 4x8", tremolo.

1961		$800	$1,000

GA-46 T Super Maestro Accordion and Bass Amp
1957-1961. Based on the Gibson GA-200 and advertised to be designed especially for amplified accordions, 60 watts, 2x12", vibrato, 2-tone cover, large Maestro Super logo on top center of grille.

1957-1961		$1,600	$2,000

AMPS

MODEL YEAR	FEATURES	EXC. COND. LOW	HIGH

GA-78 Maestro Series Amps
1960-1961. Wedge stereo cab, 2x10", reverb and tremolo.

1960-1961	GA-78 RV		
	Maestro 30	$1,675	$2,100
1960-1961	GA-78 RVS	$1,675	$2,100
1960-1961	GA-78 RVT	$1,675	$2,100

Magnatone

Ca.1937-1971, 2013-present. Magnatone made a huge variety of amps sold under their own name and under brands like Dickerson, Oahu (see separate listings), and Bronson. They also private branded amps for several accordion companies or accordion teaching studios. Brands used for them include Da Vinci, PAC - AMP, PANaramic, Titano, Tonemaster, Twilighter, and Unique (see separate listings for those brands). In 2013, Ted Kornblum revived the Magnatone name on a line of tube amps based on the earlier models and built in St. Louis, Missouri.

Model 108 Varsity Amp
1948-1954. Gray pearloid cover, small student amp or lap steel companion amp.

1948-1954		$490	$615

Model 109 Melodier Amp
1950s. 10 watts, 2 speakers.

1950s		$570	$715

Model 110 Melodier Amp
1953-1954. 12 watts, 1x10", brown leatherette cover, light grille.

1953-1954		$540	$675

Model 111 Student Amp
1955-1959. 1x8", 2-3 watts, brown leatherette, brown grille.

1955-1959		$490	$615

Model 112/113 Troubadour Amp
1955-1959. 18 watts, 1x12", brown leatherette, brown grille, slant back rear control panel.

1955-1959		$775	$975

Model 118 Amp
1960. Compact, tubes, low power, volume and tone knobs, brown tolex era, Model 118 logo on rear-mounted control panel.

1960		$400	$500

Model 120B Cougar Bass Amp
1967-1968. Initial Magnatone entry into the solidstate market, superseded by Brute Series in '68, 120 watts, 2x12" solidstate bass piggyback amp, naugahyde vinyl cover with polyester rosewood side panels.

1967-1968		$260	$325

Model 120R Sting Ray Reverb Bass Amp
1967-1968. Initial Magnatone entry into the solidstate market, superseded by Brute Series in '68, 150 watts, 4x10" solidstate combo amp, naugahyde vinyl cover with polyester rosewood side panels.

1967-1968		$260	$325

Model 130V Custom Amp
1969-1971. Solidstate 1x12" combo amp.

1969-1971		$185	$230

Model 150R Firestar Reverb Amp
1967-1968. Initial Magnatone entry into the solidstate market, superseded by Brute Series in '68, 120 watts, 2x12" solidstate combo amp, naugahyde vinyl cover with polyester rosewood side panels.

1967-1968		$185	$230

Model 180 Triplex Amp
Mid-to-late-1950s. Mid-level power using 2 6L6 power tubes, 1x15" and 1x8" speakers.

1950s		$800	$1,000

Model 192-5-S Troubadour Amp
Early-1950s. 18 watts, 1x12" Jensen Concert speaker, brown alligator covering, lower back control panel, 3 chicken-head knobs, Magnatone script logo on front, Troubadour script logo on back control panel.

1950s		$570	$715

Model 194 Lyric Amp
1947-mid-1950s. 1x12" speaker, old-style tweed vertical cab typical of '40s.

1940s		$570	$715

Model 195 Melodier Amp
1951-1954. Vertical cab with 1x10" speaker, pearloid with flowing grille slats.

1951-1954		$570	$715

Model 196 Amp
1947-mid-1950s. 1x12", 5-10 watts, scroll grille design, snakeskin leatherette cover.

1940s		$570	$715

Model 197-V Varsity Amp
1948-1952. Small compact student amp, 1x8", tubes, Varsity model logo and model number on back panel, old style layout with back bottom-mounted chasis, curved cross-bars on front baffle, brown lizard leatherette, leather handle.

1948-1952		$490	$615

Model 198 Varsity Amp
1948-1954. 1x8", tubes.

1948-1954		$490	$615

Model 199 Student Amp
1950s. About 6 to 10 watts, 1x8", snakeskin leatherette cover, metal handle, slant grille design.

1950s		$490	$615

Model 210 Deluxe Student Amp
1958-1960. 5 watts, 1x8", vibrato, brown leatherette, V logo lower right front on grille.

1958-1960		$490	$615

Model 213 Troubadour Amp
1957-1958. 10 watts, 1x12", vibrato, brown leatherette cover, V logo lower right of grille.

1957-1958		$950	$1,175

Model 240 SV Magna-Chordion Amp
1967-1968. Initial Magnatone entry into the solidstate market, superseded by Brute Series in '68, 240 watts, 2x12" solidstate stereo accordion or organ amp, naugahyde vinyl cover, polyester rosewood side panels, input jacks suitable for guitar, reverb and vibrato, lateral combo cab, rear mounted controls.

1967-1968		$290	$365

Model 250 Professional Amp
1958-1960. 20 watts, 1x12", vibrato, brown leatherette with V logo lower right front of grille.

1958-1960		$950	$1,200

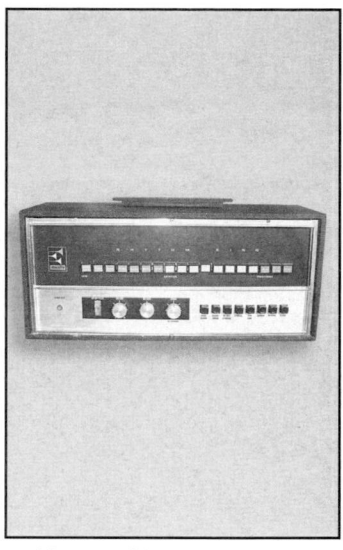

Maestro Rhythm King MkII

Magnatone Varsity Reverb 12

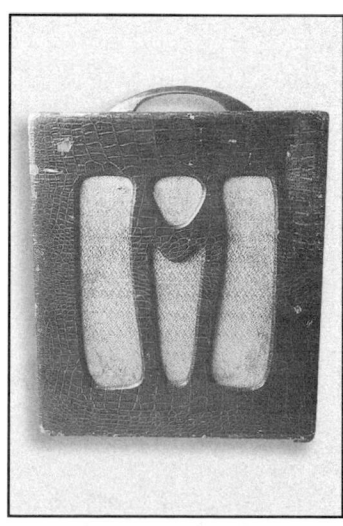

Magnatone Model 112/113 Troubadour

Magnatone 280

Magnatone 401-A

Magnatone 480 Venus

AMPS

MODEL YEAR	FEATURES	EXC. COND. LOW	HIGH

Model 260 Amp
1957-1958. 35 watts, 2x12", brown leatherette, vibrato, V logo lower right front corner of grille.

1957-1958		$1,400	$1,750

Model 262 Jupiter/Custom Pro Amp
1961-1963. 35 watts, 2x12", vibrato, brown leatherette.

1961-1963		$1,025	$1,275

Model 280/Custom 280 Amp
1957-1958. 50 watts, brown leatherette covering, brown-yellow tweed grille, 2x12" plus 2x5" speakers, double V logo.

1957-1958		$1,400	$1,750

Model 280A Amp
1958-1960. 50 watts, brown leatherette covering, brown-yellow tweed grille, 2x12" plus 2x5" speakers, V logo lower right front.

1958-1960		$1,400	$1,750

Model 410 Diana Amp
1961-1963. Five watts, 1x12", advertised as a 'studio' low power professional amp, brown leatherette cover, vibrato.

1961-1963		$570	$715

Model 412 Amp
1960s. Estey era compact student amp, low power, 1x8", tubes.

1960s		$215	$270

Model 413 Centaur Amp
1961-1963. 18 watts, 1x12", brown leatherette cover, vibrato.

1961-1963		$875	$1,100

Model 415 Clio Bass Amp
1961-1963. 25 watts, 4x8", bass or accordion amp, brown leatherette cover.

1961-1963		$925	$1,150

Model 422 Amp
1966-1967. Low power 1x12", 3 inputs, black vinyl, light swirl grille.

1966-1967		$490	$615

Model 432 Amp
Mid-1960s. Compact student model, wavey-squiggle art deco-style grille, black cover, vibrato and reverb.

1960s		$570	$715

Model 435 Athene Bass Amp
1961-1963. 55 watts, 4x10", piggyback head and cab, brown leatherette.

1961-1963		$1,150	$1,450

Model 440 Mercury Amp
1961-1963. 18 watts, 1x12", vibrato, brown leatherette.

1961-1963		$950	$1,190

Model 450 Juno/Twin Hi-Fi Amp
1961-1963. 25 watts, 1x12" and 1 oval 5"x7" speakers, reverb, vibrato, brown leatherette.

1961-1963		$1,150	$1,450
1961-1963	Extension cab only	$515	$645

Model 460 Victory Amp
1961-1963. 35 watts, 2x12" and 2 oval 5"x7" speakers, early-'60s next to the top-of-the-line, reverb and vibrato, brown leatherette.

1961-1963		$1,200	$1,500

Model 480 Venus Amp
1961-1963. 50 watts, 2x12" and 2 oval 5"x7" speakers, early-'60s top-of-the-line, reverb and stereo vibrato, brown leatherette.

1961-1963		$1,200	$1,500

Model M6 Amp
1964 (not seen in '65 catalog). 25 watts, 1x12", black molded plastic suitcase amp.

1964		$575	$725

Model M7 Bass Amp
1964-1966. 38 watts, 1x15" bass amp, black molded plastic suitcase amp.

1964-1966		$575	$725

Model M8 Amp
1964-1966. 27 watts, 1x12", reverb and tremolo, black molded plastic suitcase amp.

1964-1966		$675	$850

Model M9 Amp
1964-1966. 38 watts, 1x15", tremolo, no reverb, black molded plastic suitcase amp.

1964-1966		$650	$800

Model M10/M10A Amp
1964-1966. 38 watts, 1x15", tone boost, tremolo, transistorized reverb section, black molded plastic suitcase amp.

1964-1966		$650	$800

Model M12 Bass Amp
1964-1966. 80 watts, 1x15" or 2x12", mid-'60s top-of-the-line bass amp, black molded plastic suitcase amp.

1964-1966		$650	$800

Model M14 Amp
1964-1966. Stereo, 75 watts, 2x12" plus 2 tweeters, stereo vibrato, no reverb, black molded plastic suitcase amp.

1964-1966		$800	$1,000

Model M15 Amp
1964-1966. Stereo 75 watts, 2x12" plus 2 tweeters, stereo vibrato, transistorized reverb, black molded plastic suitcase amp.

1964-1966		$850	$1,050

Model M27 Bad Boy Bass Amp
1968-1971. 150 watts, 2x15" (1 passive), reverb, vibrato, solidstate, vertical profile bass amp, part of Brute Series.

1968-1971		$250	$315

Model M30 Fang Amp
1968-1971. 150 watts, 2x15" (1 passive), 1 exponential horn, solidstate, vibrato, reverb, vertical profile amp.

1968-1971		$250	$315

Model M32 Big Henry Bass Amp
1968-1971. 300 watts, 2x15" solidstate vertical profile bass amp.

1968-1971		$250	$315

Model M35 The Killer Amp
1968-1971. 300 watts, 2x15" and 2 horns, solidstate, vibrato, vertical profile amp.

1968-1971		$250	$315

Model MP-1 (Magna Power I) Amp
1966-1967. 30 watts, 1x12", dark vinyl, light grille, Magnatone-Estey logo on upper right of grille.

1966-1967		$575	$725

The *Vintage Guitar Price Guide* shows low to high values for items in all-original excellent condition, and, where applicable, with original case or cover.

MODEL YEAR	FEATURES	EXC. COND. LOW	HIGH

Model MP-3 (Magna Power 3) Amp
1966-1967. Mid-power, 2x12", reverb, dark vinyl, light grille, Magnatone-Estey logo on upper right of grille.

| 1966-1967 | | $650 | $815 |

Model MP-5 (Magna Power) Amp
1966-1967. Mid-power, piggyback 2x12", Magnatone-Estey logo on upper right of grille.

| 1966-1967 | | $725 | $900 |

Model PS150 Amp
1968-1971. Powered slave speaker cabinets, 150 watts, 2x15" linkable cabinets.

| 1968-1971 | | $185 | $230 |

Model PS300 Amp
1968-1971. Powered slave speaker cabinets, 300 watts, 2x15" (1 passive) linkable cabinets.

| 1968-1971 | | $185 | $230 |

Small Pearloid Amp
1947-1955. Pearloid (MOTS) covered low- and mid-power amps generally associated with pearloid lap steel sets.

| 1947-1955 | Fancy grille | $360 | $450 |
| 1947-1955 | Plain grille | $250 | $315 |

Starlet Amp
1951-1952. Student model, 1x8", pearloid cover early, leatherette later, low power, single on-off volume control, Starlet logo on back panel, Magnatone logo plate upper left front of grille.

| 1951-1954 | Pearloid | $300 | $375 |
| 1955-1959 | Leatherette | $300 | $375 |

Starlite Model 401 Amp
Magnatone produced the mid-'60s Starlite amplifier line for the budget minded musician. Each Starlite model prominently notes the Magnatone name. The grilles show art deco wavy circles. Magnatone 1960-'63 standard amps offer models starting with 12" speakers. Starlite models offer 10" and below. Model 401 has 15 watts, 1x8" and 3 tubes.

| 1960s | | $300 | $375 |

Starlite Model 411 Amp
Mid-1960s. 15 watts, 1x8", 5 tubes, tremolo (not advertised as vibrato), art deco wavy grille.

| 1960s | | $300 | $375 |

Starlite Model 441A Bass Amp
Early-mid-1960s. Lower power with less than 25 watts, 1x15", tube amp.

| 1960s | | $465 | $580 |

Starlite Model Custom 421 Amp
Early-mid-1960s. Tube amp, 25 watts, 1x10".

| 1960s | | $465 | $580 |

Starlite Model Custom 431 Amp
Early-mid-1960s. Tube amp, 30 watts, 1x10", vibrato and reverb.

| 1960s | | $515 | $645 |

Mahaffay Amplifiers
2009-present. See Little Lanilei.

Mako
1985-1989. Line of solidstate amps from Kaman (Ovation, Hamer). They also offered guitars and basses.

Marlboro Sound Works
1970-1980s. Economy solidstate amps imported by Musical Instruments Corp., Syosset, New York. Initially, Marlboro targeted the economy compact amp market, but quickly added larger amps and PAs.

GA-2 Amp
1970-1980s. 3 watts, 1x8".

| 1970s-80s | | $15 | $20 |

GA-3 Amp
1970-1980s. 3 watts, 1x8", tremolo.

| 1970s-80s | | $20 | $30 |

GA-20B Amp
1970-1980s. Bass/keyboard amp, 25 watts, 1x12".

| 1970s-80s | | $30 | $70 |

GA-20R Amp
1970-1980s. 25 watts, 1x12", tremolo, reverb.

| 1970s-80s | | $30 | $70 |

GA-40R Amp
1970-1980s. 30 watts, 1x12", tremolo, reverb.

| 1970s-80s | | $75 | $125 |

Model 520B Amp
1970-1980s. 25 watts, 1x15", bass/keyboard amp.

| 1970s-80s | | $75 | $125 |

Model 560A Amp
1970-1980s. 45 watts, 2x10".

| 1970s-80s | | $75 | $125 |

Model 760A Amp
1970-1980s. Guitar/bass/keyboard, 60 watts, 1x15".

| 1970s-80s | | $75 | $125 |

Model 1200R Amp Head
1970-1980s. 60 watts, reverb.

| 1970s-80s | | $75 | $125 |

Model 1500B Bass Amp Head
1970-1980s. 60 watts.

| 1970s-80s | | $75 | $125 |

Model 2000 Bass Amp Set
1970-1980s. 1500B head and 1x12" cab.

| 1970s-80s | | $75 | $125 |

Marshall
1962-present. Drummer Jim Marshall (1923-2012) started building bass speaker and PA cabinets in his garage in 1960. He opened a retail drum shop for his students and others and soon added guitars and amps. When Ken Bran joined the business as service manager in '62, the two decided to build their own amps. By '63 they had expanded the shop to house a small manufacturing space and by late that year they were offering the amps to other retailers. Marshall also made amps under the Park, CMI, Narb, Big M, and Kitchen-Marshall brands.

Mark I, II, III and Ivs are generally '60s and '70s and also are generally part of a larger series (for example JTM), or have a model number that is a more specific identifier. Describing an amp only as Mark II can be misleading. The most important identifier is the Model Number, which Marshall often called the Stock Number. To help avoid confusion we have added the Model number as often as possible. In addition, when appropriate,

Magnatone Model 3802

Mahaffay The Little Lanilei 3350LT

Mako MAK2

Marshall SL-5

Marshall AVT-50

Marshall Haze MHZ40C

AMPS

we have included the wattage, number of channels, master or no-master info in the title. This should help the reader more quickly find a specific amp. Check the model's description for such things as two inputs or four inputs, because this will help with identification. Vintage Marshall amps do not always have the Model/Stock number on the front or back panel, so the additional identifiers should help. The JMP logo on the front is common and really does not help with specific identification. For example, a JMP Mark II Super Lead 100 Watt description is less helpful than the actual model/stock number. Unfortunately, many people are not familiar with specific model/stock numbers. VG has tried to include as much information in the title as space will allow.

Marshall amps are sorted as follows:
AVT Series - Advanced Valvestate Technology
Club and Country Series (Rose-Morris)-introduced in '78
JCM 800 Series - basically the '80s
JCM 900 Series - basically the '90s
JCM 2000 Series - basically the '00s
JTM Series
Micro Stack Group
Model Number/Stock Number (no specific series, basically the '60s, '70s) - including Artist and Valvestate models (Valvestate refers to specific Model numbers in 8000 Series)
Silver Jubilee Series

Acoustic Soloist AS Series Amps
1994-present. Acoustic guitar amps, models include AS50R and D (50 watts, 2 channels, 2x8"), AS80R (40 watt x2 stereo, 3 channels, 2x10"), AS100D (50 watt x2 stereo, 4 channels, 2x8").

Year	Features	Low	High
1994-2000	AS80R, 80w	$265	$330
1999-2006	AS50R, 50w	$225	$285
2000-2014	AS100D, 100w	$285	$355
2007-2014	AS50D, 50w	$225	$285

AVT 20 Combo Amp
2001-2011. Solidstate, 20 watts, 12AX7 preamp tube, 1x10", Advanced Valvestate Technology (AVT) models have black covering and grille, and gold panel.

		Low	High
2001-2011		$175	$225

AVT 50/50H Amp
2001-2011. Solidstate, 50 watts, 4x12".

Year	Features	Low	High
2001-2011	Combo	$240	$300
2001-2011	Head & cab	$400	$500

AVT 100 Combo Amp
2001-2011. Solidstate, 100 watts, tube preamp, 1x12".

		Low	High
2001-2011		$275	$350

AVT 150 Amp
2001-2011. Solidstate, 150 watts, 1x12".

Year	Features	Low	High
2001-2011	Combo	$300	$375
2001-2011	Half-stack	$400	$500

AVT 275 Combo Amp
2001-2007. Solidstate DFX stereo, 75 watts per side, 2x12".

		Low	High
2001-2007		$375	$475

Class 5 Combo Amp
2009-2014. 5 watts, 1x10" tube combo.

Year	Features	Low	High
2009-2014	Head	$325	$400
2009-2014	Head/cab set	$360	$450

Club and Country Model 4140 Amp
1978-1982. Tubes, 100 watts, 2x12" combo, Rose-Morris era, designed for the country music market, hence the name, brown vinyl cover, straw grille.

		Low	High
1978-1982		$775	$965

Club and Country Model 4145 Amp
1978-1982. Tubes, 100 watts, 4x10" combo, Rose-Morris era, designed for the country music market, hence the name, brown vinyl, straw grille.

		Low	High
1978-1982		$775	$965

Club and Country Model 4150 Bass Amp
1978-1982. Tubes, 100 watts, 4x10" bass combo, Rose-Morris era, designed for the country music market, hence the name, brown vinyl cover, straw grille.

		Low	High
1978-1982		$775	$965

Haze (MHZ) Series Amp
2009-2014. All tube, multi-functional amp, 15-watt head, 40-watt combo.

Year	Features	Low	High
2009-2014	MHZ15	$650	$825
2009-2014	MHZ40C	$375	$475

JCM 600 Series
1997-2000. All tube, 60 watt models with modern features, includes the JCM600 head, JCM601 1x12" combo and JCM602 2x12" combo.

Year	Features	Low	High
1997-2000	JCM600	$375	$475
1997-2000	JCM601	$400	$500
1997-2000	JCM602	$475	$600

JCM 800 Model 1959 Amp Head
1981-1991. 100 watts.

		Low	High
1981-1991		$1,250	$1,550

JCM 800 Model 1987 Amp Head
1981-1991. 50 watts.

		Low	High
1981-1991		$1,250	$1,550

JCM 800 Model 1992 Bass Amp Head
1981-1986. Active tone circuit.

		Low	High
1981-1986		$1,250	$1,550

JCM 800 Model 2000 Amp Head
1981-1982. 200 watts.

		Low	High
1981-1982		$1,250	$1,550

JCM 800 Model 2001 Amp Head
1981-1982. Bass head, 300 watts.

		Low	High
1981-1982		$1,250	$1,550

JCM 800 Model 2004 Amp Head
1981-1990. 50 watts, master.

		Low	High
1981-1990		$1,250	$1,550

JCM 800 Model 2004S Amp Head
1986-1987. 50 watts, short head.

		Low	High
1986-1987		$1,250	$1,550

JCM 800 Model 2005 Amp Head
1983-1990. 50 watts, split channel.

		Low	High
1983-1990		$1,250	$1,550

JCM 800 Model 2005 Full Stack Amp
1983-1990. Limited Edition, 2005 head with 2 2x12 cabs.

		Low	High
1983-1990		$1,850	$2,300

MODEL YEAR	FEATURES	EXC. COND. LOW	HIGH

JCM 800 Model 2203 20th Anniversary Half Stack Amp
1982. 20th Anniversary plate in lower right corner of matching 1960A cab, matching white tolex cover.

| 1982 | | $2,200 | $2,700 |

JCM 800 Model 2203 Amp Head
1981-1990, 2002-present. 100 watts, master volume, reissued '02 in Vintage Series.

| 1981-1990 | | $1,400 | $1,750 |
| 2002-2014 | Reissue | $900 | $1,100 |

JCM 800 Model 2203KK Kerry King Signature Amp
2008-2012. King Signature logo, 100 watts, 3-band EQ.

| 2008-2012 | | $1,200 | $1,500 |

JCM 800 Model 2203ZW Zack Wylde Signature Amp
2002. About 600 amp heads and 60 half-stacks made.

| 2002 | Half-stack | $2,650 | $3,300 |
| 2002 | Head only | $1,450 | $1,800 |

JCM 800 Model 2204 Amp Head
1981-1990. 50 watts, 1 channel, 2 inputs, master volume, front panel says JCM 800 Lead Series, back panel says Master Model 50w Mk 2.

| 1981-1990 | | $1,250 | $1,550 |

JCM 800 Model 2204S Amp Head
1986-1987. Short head, 50 watts.

| 1986-1987 | | $1,250 | $1,550 |

JCM 800 Model 2205 Amp
1983-1990. 50 watts, split channel (1 clean and 1 distortion), switchable, both channels with reverb, 4x12" cabinet, front panel reads JCM 800 Lead Series.

| 1983-1990 | 4x12 cab | $550 | $700 |
| 1983-1990 | Head only | $1,250 | $1,550 |

JCM 800 Model 2210 Amp Head
1983-1990. 100 watts.

| 1983-1990 | | $1,250 | $1,550 |

JCM 800 Model 4010 Combo Amp
1981-1990. 50 watts, 1x12", non-reverb ('80), reverb begins '81, single channel master volume.

| 1981-1990 | | $1,300 | $1,600 |

JCM 800 Model 4103 Combo Amp
1981-1990. Lead combo amp, 100 watts, 2x12".

| 1981-1990 | | $1,350 | $1,675 |

JCM 800 Model 4104 Combo Amp
1980-1990. Tube lead amp, 50 watts, 2x12".

| 1980-1990 | Black | $1,350 | $1,675 |
| 1980-1990 | White option | $1,350 | $1,675 |

JCM 800 Model 4210 Combo Amp
1982-1990. 50 watts, 1x12" tube combo, split-channel, single input, master volume.

| 1982-1990 | | $1,200 | $1,500 |

JCM 800 Model 4211 Combo Amp
1983-1990. Lead combo amp, 100 watts, 2x12".

| 1983-1990 | | $1,200 | $1,500 |

JCM 800 Model 4212 Combo Amp
1983-1990. 2x12" 50-watt combo.

| 1983-1990 | | $1,200 | $1,500 |

JCM 800 Model 5005 Combo Amp
1983-1990. Solidstate combo amp, 12 watts, master volume, 1x10".

| 1983-1990 | | $325 | $400 |

JCM 800 Model 5010 Combo Amp
1983-1990. Solidstate combo amp, 30 watts, master volume, 1x12".

| 1983-1990 | | $350 | $430 |

JCM 800 Model 5150 Combo Amp
1987-1991. Solidstate combo amp, 150 watts, specially designed 12" Celestion speaker, split channel design, separate clean and distortion channels, presence and effects-mix master controls.

| 1987-1991 | | $475 | $600 |

JCM 800 Model 5212 Combo Amp
1986-1991. Solidstate 2x12" split channel reverb combo.

| 1986-1991 | | $500 | $625 |

JCM 800 Model 5213 Combo Amp
1986-1991. MOS-FET solidstate combo, 2x12", channel-switching, effects loop, direct output, remote footswitch.

| 1986-1991 | | $300 | $375 |

JCM 800 Model 5215 Combo Amp
1986-1991. MOS-FET solidstate, 1x15", Accutronics reverb, effects loop.

| 1986-1991 | | $300 | $375 |

JCM 900 Model 2100 Mark III Amp Head
1990-1993. FX loop, 100/50-watt selectable lead head.

| 1990-1993 | | $750 | $950 |

JCM 900 Model 2100 SL-X Amp Head
1992-1998. Hi-gain 100 watt head amp, additional 12AX7 preamp tube.

| 1992-1998 | | $750 | $950 |

JCM 900 Model 2500 SL-X Amp Head
1990-2000. 50 watt version of SL-X.

| 1992-1998 | | $750 | $950 |

JCM 900 Model 4100 Dual Reverb Amp
1990-present. Vintage Series, 100/50 switchable head, JCM 900 on front panel, 4x10 or 2x12 matching cab, black with black front.

| 1990-2014 | 4x10 or 2x12 | $475 | $600 |
| 1990-2014 | Head only | $650 | $825 |

JCM 900 Model 4101 Combo Amp
1990-2000. All tube, 100 watts, 1x12" combo.

| 1990-2000 | | $700 | $875 |

JCM 900 Model 4102 Combo Amp
1990-2000. Combo amp, 100/50 watts switchable, 2x12".

| 1990-2000 | | $750 | $925 |

JCM 900 Model 4500 Amp Head
1990-2000. All tube, 2 channels, 50/25 watts, EL34 powered, reverb, effects loop, compensated recording out, master volume, black.

| 1990-2000 | | $650 | $800 |

JCM 900 Model 4501 Dual Reverb Combo Amp
1990-2000. 50/25 switchable, 1x12".

| 1990-2000 | | $750 | $950 |

JCM 900 Model 4502 Combo Amp
1990-2000. 50/25 switchable, 2x12".

| 1990-2000 | | $800 | $1,000 |

JCM 2000 DSL Series Amp
1998-present. DSL is Dual Super Lead, 2 independent channels labelled classic and ultra, JCM 2000 and DSL logos both on front panel.

| 1998-2014 | Half-stacks/combos | $500 | $1,000 |

Mid-1980s Marshall JCM 800 Model 2204

Tony Romagna

Marshall JCM 800 2203KK Kerry King Signature

Marshall, JCM 800 Model 4010

Stephan Brown

To get the most from this book, be sure to read "Using *The Guide*" in the introduction.

Marshall JCM 2000 TSL 100

Marshall JTM 45
Model 1961 MKIV

Pang Leo

Marshall JTM 45/100
Limited Edition

JCM 2000 TSL Series Amp

1998-2013. TSL is Triple Super Lead, 3 independent channels labelled clean, crunch and lead, 8 tubes, JCM 2000 and TSL logos both on front panel.

MODEL YEAR	FEATURES	LOW	HIGH
1998-2013	Full stacks	$1,250	$1,850
1998-2013	Half-stacks/combos	$650	$1,250

JCM Slash Signature Model 2555SL Amp Set

1996. Based on JCM 800 with higher gain, matching amp and cab set, JCM Slash Signature logo on front panel, single channel, Slash Signature 1960AV 4x12" slant cab, black.

1996	4x12 cab	$700	$875
1996	Head only	$1,700	$2,100

JTM 30 Series Amp

1995-1997. Tube combo, reverb, 30 watts, effects loops, 5881 output sections, footswitchable high-gain modes. Available as 1x15", 1x12", 2x12" or 3x10" combo or as 4x10" half-stack.

1995-1997	Combo 1x12	$450	$575
1995-1997	Combo 2x10	$475	$600
1995-1997	Combo 2x12	$500	$625
1995-1997	Combo 3x10	$500	$625

JTM 45 Amp Head

1962-1964. Amp head, 45 watts. The original Marshall amp. Became the Model 1987 45-watt for '65-'66.

1962		$10,000	$12,500
1963-1964		$8,800	$11,000

JTM 45 Model 1961 MK IV 4x10 Combo Amp

1965-1966. 45 watts, 4x10", tremolo, JTM 45 MK IV on panel, Bluesbreaker association.

1965-1966		$8,400	$10,500

JTM 45 Model 1962 MK IV 2x12 Combo Amp

1965-1966. 45 watts, 2x12", tremolo, JTM 45 MK IV on panel, Bluesbreaker association.

1965-1966		$8,700	$10,900

JTM 45 Model 1987 Amp Head Reissue

1988-1999. Black/green tolex.

1988-1999		$1,000	$1,250

JTM 45 Model 1987 Mark II Lead Amp Head

1965-1966. Replaced JTM 45 Amp ('62-'64), but was subsequently replaced by the Model 1987 50-watt Head during '66.

1965-1966		$6,000	$7,500

JTM 45 Offset Limited Edition Amp Set Reissue

Introduced in 2000. Limited run of 300 units, old style cosmetics, 45-watt head and offset 2x12" cab, dark vinyl cover, light gray grille, rectangular logo plate on front of amp and cab, Limited Edition plate on rear of cab, serial number xxx of 300.

2000		$2,600	$3,300

JTM 50 Model 1961 MK IV 4x10 Amp

1965-1972. 50 watts, 4x10", Bluesbreaker association, tremolo, JTM 50 MK IV on front panel to '68, plain front panel without model description '68-'72.

1966-1967		$7,600	$9,500
1968		$7,100	$8,800
1969		$6,500	$8,000

MODEL YEAR	FEATURES	LOW	HIGH
1970		$5,500	$6,900
1971-1972		$4,500	$5,700

JTM 50 Model 1962 Bluesbreaker Amp Reissue

1989-1999. 50 watts, 2x12", Model 1962 reissue Bluesbreaker.

1989-1999		$1,300	$1,650

JTM 50 Model 1962 MK IV 2x12 Amp

1966-1972. 50 watts, 2x12", tremolo, Bluesbreaker association, JTM 50 MK IV on front panel to '68, plain front panel without model description '68-'72.

1966-1967		$9,300	$11,500
1968		$8,600	$10,700
1969		$7,100	$8,800
1970		$6,600	$8,200
1971-1972		$5,600	$6,900

JTM 50 Model 1963 PA Amp Head

1965-1966. MK II PA head, block logo.

1965-1966		$2,400	$3,000

JTM 60 Series Amp

1995-1997. Tube, 60 watts, 1x12", 1x15", 2x12" or 3x10" combo or as 4x10" half-stack.

1995-1997	Combo 1x12	$500	$625
1995-1997	Combo 2x12	$525	$650
1995-1997	Half-stack 4x10	$525	$650

JTM 310 Amp

1995-1997. JTM 30 with 2x10".

1995-1997		$475	$600

JTM 612 Combo Amp

1995-1997. Tube combo amp, 60 watts, 1x12", EQ, reverb, effects loop.

1995-1997		$475	$600

JVM2/JVM4 Series

2000s-present. Models include 205H/205C (50-watt head/combo 2x12), 210H/210C (100-watt head/combo 2x12), 410H/410C (100-watt head/combo 2x12, 4-channel).

2000-2014	JVM205H	$725	$900
2000-2014	JVM210C	$1,000	$1,250
2000-2014	JVM210H	$800	$1,000
2000-2014	JVM410C	$900	$1,125

MA Series Amp

2009-2013. Models include 50C (50 watts, 1x12"), 50H (50-watt head), 100C (100 watts, 2x12"), 100H (100-watt head) and 412 (4x12" slant cabinet).

2009-2013	MA100C	$390	$490
2009-2013	MA100H	$345	$440
2009-2013	MA412	$185	$235
2009-2013	MA50C	$345	$430
2009-2013	MA50H	$315	$400

MB Series Amp

2006-2012. Bass Combo Series, models include 30C (30watts, 1x10").

2006-2012	MB30C	$120	$150

MG Series Amp

1999-present. Models include 10KK (10 watts, 1x6"), 15CD, 15RCD or CDR (15 watts, 1x8"), 15MS (15 watts, micro stack, 1x8" slant and straight cabs), 15MSII, (in '02, 10" speakers), 15MSZW (15 watts, 2x1x10"), 50DFX (50 watts, 1x12"), 100DFX (100 watts, combo), 100HDFX (100-watt head), 100RCD (Valvestate

MODEL YEAR	FEATURES	EXC. COND. LOW	HIGH

Series, 100-watt), 102FX (100 watts, 2x12"), 250DFX (250 watts, combo), 412A (4x12" cabinet).

| 1999-2014 | Various models | $50 | $650 |

Micro Stack 3005 Amp

1986-1991. Solidstate head, 12 watts, 2 1x10" stackable cabs (one slant, one straight). Standard model is black, but was also offered in white, green, red, or the silver Silver Jubilee version with Jubilee 25/50 logo.

1986-1991	Black	$275	$350
1986-1991	Green or red	$375	$475
1986-1991	White	$350	$440
1987-1989	Silver Jubilee/silver	$475	$600

Mini-Stack 3210 MOS-FET Amp Head with 2x4x10"

1984-1991. Model 3210 MOS-FET head with 2 4x10" cabs, designed as affordable stack.

| 1984-1991 | | $325 | $410 |

Model 1710 Bass Cabinet

1990s. 1x15" speaker.

| 1990s | | $275 | $340 |

Model 1912 Cabinet

1989-1998, 2013-present. 1x12", 150 watts.

| 2013-2014 | | $275 | $340 |

Model 1917 PA-20 Amp Head

1967-1973. PA head with 20 watts, but often used for guitar, matching cabinet.

1967-1968	Matching cab	$1,075	$1,375
1967-1968	Plexi head	$2,500	$3,200
1969-1973	Aluminum head	$1,875	$2,400
1969-1973	Matching cab	$900	$1,150

Model 1922 Amp Cabinet

1989-present. 2x12" extension cab for JCM 800 Series amps.

| 1989-2014 | | $225 | $280 |

Model 1930 Popular Combo Amp

1969-1973. 10 watts, 1x12", tremolo.

| 1969-1972 | | $2,150 | $2,650 |
| 1973 | | $1,950 | $2,400 |

Model 1933 Amp Cabinet

1981-1991. 1x12" extension cab for JCM 800 Series amps.

| 1981-1991 | | $275 | $340 |

Model 1935/1935A/1935B Bass Cabinet

1967-1990s. Models 1935, 4x12", black, A slant front, B straight front.

1967-1970	75w	$2,300	$2,825
1971-1972	Black, weave	$1,200	$1,500
1973-1975	Black, checkerboard	$1,000	$1,250
1976-1979	Black	$900	$1,125
1979-1983	260w	$525	$655
1983-1986	280w	$460	$575
1990s		$360	$450

Model 1936 Amp Cabinet

1981-2011. Extension straight-front cab for JCM 800/900 Series amps, 2x12" speakers, black.

| 1981-2011 | | $300 | $375 |

Model 1937 Bass Cabinet

1981-1986. 4x12", 140 watts.

| 1981-1986 | | $440 | $550 |

Model 1958 18-Watt Lead Amp

1965-1968. 18 watts, 2x10" combo, Bluesbreaker cosmetics.

| 1965-1968 | | $5,300 | $6,700 |

Model 1958 20-Watt Lead Amp

1968-1972. 20 watts, 2x10" combo, tremolo.

1968		$4,700	$6,000
1969		$4,200	$5,200
1970		$4,000	$5,000
1971-1972		$3,600	$4,500

Model 1959 Super Lead Amp

1966-1981. Two channels, 100 watts, 4 inputs, no master volume. Plexiglas control panels until mid-'69, aluminum after. See Model T1959 for tremolo version. Early custom color versions are rare and more valuable.

1966-1969	Black, plexi	$4,400	$5,500
1966-1969	Custom color, plexi	$6,400	$8,000
1969-1970	Black, aluminum	$2,500	$3,200
1969-1970	Custom color, aluminum	$5,200	$6,500
1971-1972	Black, hand-wired, small box	$2,000	$2,500
1971-1972	Custom color, hand-wired	$2,800	$3,500
1973-1975	Black, printed C.B., large box	$1,800	$2,250
1973-1975	Custom color, printed C.B.	$2,500	$3,100
1976-1979	Black	$1,500	$1,900
1976-1979	Custom color	$1,800	$2,200
1980-1981	Black	$1,300	$1,600
1980-1981	Custom color	$1,500	$1,900

Model T1959 Super Lead (Tremolo) Amp Head

1966-1973. Head amp, 100 watts, plexi until mid-'69, aluminum after. Tremolo version of the Model 1959 Amp.

1966-1969	Black, plexi	$4,600	$5,700
1966-1969	Custom color, plexi	$6,900	$8,500
1969-1970	Black, aluminum	$2,800	$3,500
1969-1970	Custom color, aluminum	$5,300	$6,600
1971-1973	Black, hand-wired, small box	$2,200	$2,700
1971-1973	Custom color, hand-wired	$2,900	$3,600

35th Anniversary Marshall Limited Edition Set

1997. Limited Edition 1997 logo, includes matching Super Lead MKII 100-watt head, PB100 power brake and MKII 1960A slant cab, all in white covering.

| 1997 | | $2,350 | $2,950 |

Model 1959 SLP Reissue Amp Head

1992-present. Vintage Series, Super Lead Plexi (SLP).

1992-1999	Black vinyl	$1,200	$1,500
1992-1999	Purple vinyl	$1,300	$1,625
1992-1999	White ltd. ed.	$1,300	$1,625
2000-2014	Black vinyl	$1,400	$1,750

Marshall JTM 50
1962 Bluesbreaker

Marshall JTM 60
Stephan Brown

1976 Marshall 1959 Super Lead

To get the most from this book, be sure to read "Using *The Guide*" in the introduction.

1971 Marshall Model 1959 Super Lead
William Bethurem

Marshall Model 1962 Bluesbreaker Combo

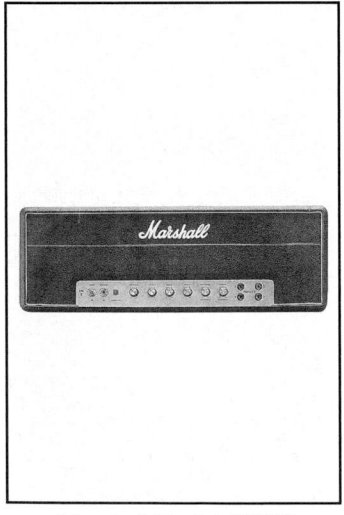

Marshall Model 1987X

MODEL YEAR	FEATURES	EXC. COND. LOW	HIGH
Model 1959 SLP Reissue Amp Set			
1992-2013. Vintage Series, 100 watt Super Lead head and matching 4x12" slant cab.			
1992-2014	4x12 Cab	$550	$675
Model 1959HW Amp			
2005-present. Hand-wired, 100 watts, 4x12" slant front cab.			
2005-2014	Cab	$550	$675
2005-2014	Head only	$1,350	$1,675
Model 1959RR Ltd. Ed. Randy Rhoads Amp			
2008-2013. Randy Rhoads Tribute, full stack, 100 watts.			
2008-2013		$2,350	$2,950
Model 1960 4x12 Speaker Cabinet			
1964-1979. Both straight and slant front. The original Marshall 4x12" cab designed for compact size with 4x12" speakers. First issue in '64/'65 is 60-watt cab, from '65-'70 75 watts, from '70-'79 100 watts. After '79, model numbers contained an alpha suffix: A for slant front, B straight.			
1966-1970	Black, weave	$2,500	$3,100
1966-1970	Custom color, weave	$3,700	$4,600
1971-1972	Black, weave	$1,500	$1,900
1971-1972	Custom color, weave	$2,100	$2,600
1973-1975	Black, checkerboard	$925	$1,150
1973-1975	Custom color, checkerboard	$1,400	$1,800
1976-1979	Black	$875	$1,100
1976-1979	Custom color	$1,450	$1,800
Model 1960A/1960B 4x12 Speaker Cabinet			
1980-1983 (260 watts), '84-'86 (280 watts, JCM 800 era), '86-'90 (300 watts, JCM 800 era), '90-present (300 watts, JCM 900 era, stereo-mono switching). A for slant front, B straight.			
1980-1983	Black	$525	$650
1980-1983	Custom color	$775	$950
1984-1986	Black	$450	$575
1984-1986	Custom color	$675	$850
1984-1986	Rare color	$900	$1,125
1987-1990	Black	$425	$525
1987-1990	Custom color	$550	$700
1987-1990	Rare color	$800	$1,000
2000-2007	Black	$465	$575
Model 1960AC/1960BC Classic Speaker Cabinet			
2005-2013. 100 watts, 4x12" Celestion G-12M-25 green-back speakers, black, AC slant front, BC straight front.			
2005-2013		$650	$825
Model 1960AHW 4x12 Slant Cabinet			
2005-2008. Half stack slant front cab for HW series.			
2005-2008		$685	$850
Model 1960AV 4x12 Slant Cabinet			
1990-2012. JCM 900 updated, stereo/mono switching, AV slant, BV straight front.			
1990-1999	Red vinyl, tan grille	$465	$575
1990-2012	Black vinyl, black grille	$430	$535

MODEL YEAR	FEATURES	EXC. COND. LOW	HIGH
Model 1960AX/1960BX 4x12 Cabinet			
1990-2012. Cab for Model 1987X and 1959X reissue heads, AX slant, BX straight.			
1990-2012	AX	$500	$625
1990-2012	BX	$500	$625
Model 1960BV 4x12 Straight Cabinet			
1990-2012. JCM 900 updated, stereo/mono switching, AV slant, BV straight front.			
1990-2012	Various colors	$425	$525
Model 1960TV 4x12 Slant Cabinet			
1990-2012. Extra tall for JTM 45, mono, 100 watts.			
1990-2012	Various colors	$525	$650
Model 1962 Bluesbreaker Combo Amp			
1999-present. Vintage Series, similar to JTM 45 but with 2 reissue 'Greenback' 25-watt 2x12" speakers and addition of footswitchable tremolo effect.			
1999-2014		$1,300	$1,650
Model 1964 Lead/Bass 50-Watt Amp Head			
1973-1976. Head with 50 watts, designed for lead or bass.			
1973-1976		$875	$1,090
Model 1965A/1965B Cabinet			
1984-1991. 140 watt 4x10" slant front (A) or straight front (B) cab.			
1984-1991		$360	$450
Model 1966 Cabinet			
1985-1991. 150 watt 2x12" cab.			
1985-1991		$360	$450
Model 1967 Major 200-Watt Amp Head			
1968-1974. 200 watts, the original Marshall 200 Pig was not popular and revised into the 200 'Major'. The new Major 200 was similar to the other large amps and included 2 channels, 4 inputs, but a larger amp cab.			
1968	Plexi	$2,600	$3,300
1969-1970	Aluminum	$2,400	$3,100
1971-1972	Small box	$1,300	$1,625
1973-1974	Large box	$1,200	$1,500
Model 1967 Pig 200-Watt Amp Head			
1967-early-1968 only. Head with 200 watts. The control panel was short and stubby and nicknamed the Pig, the 200-watt circuit was dissimilar (and un-popular) to the 50-watt and 100-watt circuits.			
1967-1968		$2,600	$3,300
Model 1968 100-Watt Super PA Amp Head			
1966-1975. PA head with 100 watts, 2 sets of 4 inputs (identifies PA configuration), often used for guitar, matching cabinet.			
1966-1969	Matching cab	$1,375	$1,700
1966-1969	Plexi	$3,200	$4,000
1969-1972	Aluminum	$2,400	$3,000
1969-1975	Matching cab	$1,000	$1,250
Model 1973 Amp			
1965-1968. Tube combo, 18 watts, 2x12".			
1965		$7,700	$9,700
1966		$7,300	$9,200
1967		$6,000	$7,500
1968		$5,300	$6,600

MODEL YEAR	FEATURES	EXC. COND. LOW	HIGH

Model 1973 JMP Lead/Bass 20 Amp
1973 only. Front panel: JMP, back panel: Lead & Bass 20, 20 watts, 1x12" straight front checkered grille cab, head and cab black vinyl.

1973		$2,100	$2,600

Model 1974 Amp
1965-1968. Tube combo, 18 watts, 1x12".

1965		$4,700	$5,900
1966		$4,500	$5,600
1967		$4,100	$5,100
1968		$3,800	$4,700

Model 1974X Amp
2004-present. Handwired Series, reissue of 18-watt, 1x12" combo, extension cabinet available.

2004-2014	1974CX cab	$500	$625
2004-2014	Combo	$1,450	$1,825

Model 1982 Cabinet
1970-1980. 100-watt, 4x12".

1970-1980		$1,000	$1,250

Model 1986 50-Watt Bass Amp Head
1966-1981. Bass version of 1987, 50-watt.

1966-1969	Black, plexi	$3,000	$3,800
1969-1970	Black, aluminum	$2,000	$2,500
1971-1972	Black, hand-wired, small box	$1,700	$2,100
1973-1975	Black, printed C.B., large box	$1,700	$2,100
1976-1979	Black	$1,400	$1,775
1980-1981	Black	$1,200	$1,500

Model 1987 50-Watt Amp Head
1966-1981. Head amp, 50 watts, plexiglas panel until mid-'69, aluminum panel after.

1966-1969	Black, plexi	$3,000	$3,800
1966-1969	Custom color, plexi	$4,800	$6,000
1969-1970	Black, aluminum	$2,000	$2,500
1969-1970	Custom color, aluminum	$4,000	$5,000
1971-1972	Black, hand-wired, small box	$1,700	$2,100
1971-1972	Custom color, hand-wired	$2,400	$3,000
1973-1975	Black, printed C.B., large box	$1,700	$2,100
1973-1975	Custom color, printed C.B.	$2,000	$2,500
1976-1979	Black	$1,400	$1,775
1976-1979	Custom color	$1,700	$2,100
1980-1981	Black	$1,200	$1,500
1980-1981	Custom color	$1,400	$1,775

Model 1987X Amp Head
1992-present. Vintage Series amp, all tube, 50 watts, 4 inputs, plexi.

1992-2014		$1,150	$1,450

Model 1992 Super Bass Amp Head
1966-1981. 100 watts, plexi panel until mid-'69 when replaced by aluminum front panel, 2 channels, 4 inputs.

1966-1969	Black, plexi	$4,200	$5,300
1966-1969	Custom color, plexi	$6,100	$7,600
1969-1970	Black, aluminum	$2,500	$3,200

MODEL YEAR	FEATURES	EXC. COND. LOW	HIGH
1969-1970	Custom color, aluminum	$4,900	$6,100
1971-1972	Black, hand-wired, small box	$2,000	$2,500
1971-1972	Custom color, hand-wired	$2,800	$3,500
1973-1975	Black, printed C.B., large box	$1,800	$2,250
1973-1975	Custom color, printed C.B.	$2,500	$3,100
1976-1979	Black	$1,200	$1,500
1976-1979	Custom color	$1,800	$2,200
1980-1981	Black	$1,100	$1,400
1980-1981	Custom color	$1,500	$1,900

Model 1992LEM Lemmy Signature Super Bass Amp
2008-2013. Lemmy Kilmister specs, matching 100-watt head with 4x12" and 4x15" stacked cabinets.

2008-2013	Full stack	$3,450	$4,300

Model 2040 Artist 50-Watt Combo Amp
1971-1978. 50 watts, 2x12" Artist/Artiste combo model with a different (less popular?) circuit.

1971-1978		$1,800	$2,250

Model 2041 Artist Head/Cabinet Set
1971-1978. 50 watts, 2x12" half stack Artist/Artiste cab with a different (less popular?) circuit.

1971-1978		$2,050	$2,550

Model 2046 Specialist 25-Watt Combo Amp
1972-1973. 25 watts, 1x15" speaker, limited production due to design flaw (amp overheats).

1972-1973		$725	$900

Model 2060 Mercury Combo Amp
1972-1973. Combo amp, 5 watts, 1x12", available in red or orange covering.

1972-1973		$1,000	$1,250

Model 2061 20-Watt Lead/Bass Amp Head
1968-1973. Lead/bass head, 20 watts, plexi until '69, aluminum after. Reissued in '04 as the Model 2061X.

1968-1969	Black, plexi	$3,600	$4,500
1969-1970	Black, aluminum	$2,500	$3,100
1971-1972	Black, aluminum	$2,000	$2,500
1973	Black, aluminum	$1,800	$2,250

Model 2061X 20-Watt Lead/Bass Amp Head Reissue
2004-present. Handwired Series, reissue of 2061 amp head, 20 watts.

2004-2014	1x12 cab	$365	$455
2004-2014	2x12 cab	$425	$535
2004-2014	Head only	$925	$1,150

Model 2078 Combo Amp
1973-1978. Solidstate, 100 watts, 4x12" combo, gold front panel, dark cover, gray grille.

1973-1978		$725	$900

Model 2103 100-Watt 1-Channel Master Combo Amp
1975-1981. One channel, 2 inputs, 100 watts, 2x12", first master volume design, combo version of 2203 head.

1975-1981		$1,075	$1,325

Marshall 1992LEM Lemmy Super Bass

1971 Marshall Model 2060 Mercury

Steve Lee

Marshall 2061X

AMPS

1981 Marshall Model 2203
Stephan Brown

Marshall Model 2203X JCM 800

*2007 Marshall Model
2466 Vintage/Modern*
Joseph Bradshaw Jr.

MODEL YEAR	FEATURES	EXC. COND. LOW	HIGH

Model 2104 50-Watt 1-Channel Master Combo Amp
1975-1981. One channel, 2 inputs, 50 watts, 2x12", first master volume design, combo version of 2204 head.

1975-1981		$1,025	$1,275

Model 2144 Master Reverb Combo Amp
1978 only. Master volume similar to 2104 but with reverb and boost, 50 watts, 2x12".

1978		$1,325	$1,650

Model 2150 100-Watt 1x12 Combo Amp
1978. Tubes.

1978		$750	$925

Model 2159 100-Watt 2-Channel Combo Amp
1977-1981. 100 watts, 2 channels, 4 inputs, 2x12" combo version of Model 1959 Super Lead head.

1977-1981		$1,100	$1,350

Model 2199 Amp
1979. Solidstate 2x12" combo.

1979		$475	$600

Model 2200 100-Watt Lead Combo Amp
1977-1981. 100 watts, 2x12" combo, early solidstate, includes boost section, no reverb.

1977-1981		$525	$650

Model 2203 Lead Amp Head
1975-1981. Head amp, 100 watts, 2 inputs, first master volume model design, often seen with Mark II logo.

1975-1981	Black	$1,250	$1,550
1975-1981	Fawn Beige	$1,450	$1,800

Model 2203X JCM800 Reissue Amp Head
2002-2010. 100 watts

2002-2010		$1,350	$1,675

Model 2204 50-Watt Amp Head
1975-1981. Head only, 50 watts with master volume.

1975-1981		$1,350	$1,675

Model 2266 50-Watt Combo Amp
2007-2013. Vintage Modern series, 2x12".

2007-2013		$690	$865

Model 2466 100-Watt Amp Head
2007-2013. Vintage Modern series.

2007-2013		$675	$850

Model 3203 Artist Amp Head
1986-1991. Tube head version of earlier '84 Model 3210 MOS-FET, designed as affordable alternative, 30 watts, standard short cab, 2 inputs separated by 3 control knobs, Artist 3203 logo on front panel, black.

1986-1991		$400	$500

Model 3210 MOS-FET Amp Head
1984-1991. MOS-FET solidstate head, refer Mini-Stack listing for 3210 with 4x10" stacked cabinets. Early-'80s front panel: Lead 100 MOS-FET.

1984-1991		$275	$340

Model 3310 100-Watt Lead Amp
1988-1991. Solidstate, 100 watts, lead head with channel switching and reverb.

1988-1991		$450	$565

Model 4001 Studio 15 Amp
1985-1992. 15 watts using 6V6 (only model to do this up to this time), 1x12" Celestion Vintage 30 speakers.

1985-1992		$750	$950

MODEL YEAR	FEATURES	EXC. COND. LOW	HIGH

Model 4104 50-Watt Combo Amp
1981-1990. Combo version of 2204 head, 50 watts, 2x12", master volume.

1981-1990		$1,350	$1,700

Model 4203 Artist 30 Combo Amp
1986-1991. 30-watt tube hybrid combo, 1x12", channel switching.

1986-1991		$500	$625

Model 5002 Combo Amp
1984-1991. Solidstate combo amp, 20 watts, 1x10", master volume.

1984-1991		$175	$220

Model 5005 Combo Amp
1984-1991. Solidstate, 12 watts, 1x10", practice amp with master volume, headphones and line-out.

1984-1991		$150	$190

Model 5302 Keyboard Amp
1984-1988. Solidstate, 20 watts, 1x10", marketed for keyboard application.

1984-1988		$175	$220

Model 5502 Bass Amp
1984-ca.1992. Solidstate bass combo amp, 20 watts, 1x10" Celestion.

1984-1992		$175	$220

Model 6100 30th Anniversary Amp
1992-1998. Head with 100/50/25 switchable watts and 4x12" cabinet (matching colors), first year and into early '93 was blue tolex, black afterwards.

1992-1998	4x12 cab	$500	$625
1992-1998	Head only	$850	$1,050

Model 6101 30th Anniversary Combo Amp
1992-1998. 1x12" combo version of 6100 amp, first year and into early '93 was blue tolex, black afterwards.

1992-1998		$1,000	$1,250

Model 8008 Valvestate Rackmount Amp
1991-2001. Valvestate solidstate rack mount power amp with dual 40-watt channels.

1991-2001		$155	$196

Model 8010 Valvestate VS15 Combo Amp
1991-1997. Valvestate solidstate, 10 watts, 1x8", compact size, black vinyl, black grille.

1991-1997		$130	$160

Model 8040 Valvestate 40V Combo Amp
1991-1997. Valvestate solidstate with tube preamp, 40 watts, 1x12", compact size, black vinyl, black grille.

1991-1997		$155	$196

Model 8080 Valvestate 80V Combo Amp
1991-1997. Valvestate solidstate with tube 12AX7 preamp, 80 watts, 1x12", compact size, black vinyl, black grille.

1991-1997		$155	$196

Model 8100 100-Watt Valvestate VS100H Amp Head
1991-2001. Valvestate solidstate head, 100 watts.

1991-2001		$175	$220

Model 8200 200-Watt Valvestate Amp Head
1993-1998. Valvestate solidstate reverb head, 2x100-watt channels.

1993-1998		$200	$250

The *Vintage Guitar Price Guide* shows low to high values for items in all-original excellent condition, and, where applicable, with original case or cover.

MODEL YEAR	FEATURES	EXC. COND. LOW	HIGH

Model 8222 Valvestate Cabinet
1993-1998. 200 watts, 2x12 extention cab, designed for 8200 head.

1993-1998		$155	$196

Model 8240 Valvestate Stereo Chorus Amp
1992-1996. Valvestate, 80 watts (2x40 watts stereo), 2x12" combo, reverb, chorus.

1992-1996		$225	$280

Model 8280 2x80-Watt Valvestate Combo Amp
1993-1996. Valvestate solidstate, 2x80 watts, 2x12".

1993-1996		$250	$315

Model 8412 Valvestate Cabinet
1991-2001. 140 watts, 4x12 extention cab, designed for 8100 head.

1991-2001		$200	$250

MS-2/R/C Amp
1990-present. Microamp series, 1 watt, battery operated, miniature black half-stack amp and cab. Red MS-2R and checkered speaker grille and gold logo MS-2C added in '93.

1990-2014		$25	$35

MS-4 Amp
1998-present. Full-stack version of MS-2, black.

1998-2014		$35	$45

Silver Jubilee Model 2550 50/25 (Tall) Amp Head
1987-1989. 50/25 switchable tall box head for full Jubilee stack, silver vinyl and chrome control panel.

1987-1989		$2,000	$2,500

Silver Jubilee Model 2551 4x12 Cabinet
1987-1989. Matching silver 4x12" cabs for Jubilee 2550 head, various models, silver vinyl.

1987-1989	2551A, slant	$750	$950
1987-1989	2551AV, Vintage 30	$750	$950
1987-1989	2551B, straight	$750	$950
1987-1989	2551BV, Vintage 30	$750	$950

Silver Jubilee Model 2553 50/25 (Short) Amp Head
1987-1988. 50/25 switchable small box head for mini-short stack, silver vinyl and chrome control panel.

1987-1988		$2,000	$2,500

Silver Jubilee Model 2554 1x12 Combo Amp
1987-1989. 50/25 watts, 1x12" combo using 2550 chassis, silver vinyl and chrome control panel.

1987-1989		$2,000	$2,500

Silver Jubilee Model 2555 Amp Head
1987-1989. 100/50 version of 2550 head, silver vinyl and chrome control panel.

1987-1989		$2,000	$2,500

Silver Jubilee Model 2556 2x12 Cabinet
1987-1989. Matching silver 2x12" cabs for Jubilee heads, various models, silver vinyl.

1987-1989	2556A, slant	$525	$660
1987-1989	2556AV, Vintage 30	$525	$660
1987-1989	2556B, straight	$525	$660
1987-1989	2556BV, Vintage 30	$525	$660

Silver Jubilee Model 2558 2x12 Combo Amp
1987-1989. 50/25 watts, 2x12" combo using 2550 chassis, silver vinyl and chrome control panel.

1987-1989		$2,000	$2,500

Silver Jubilee Model 3560 600 Amp Head
1987. Rackmount 2x300 watts.

1987		$350	$435

Super 100 40th Anniversary JTM45 MK II Full Stack
2005. 100 watts, 2 4x12 cabs, 250 made.

2005		$4,200	$5,200

Martin
Martin has dabbled in amps a few times, under both the Martin and Stinger brand names. The first batch were amps made by other introduced with their electric acoustics in 1959.

Model 112 Amp
1959-1961. Branded C.F. Martin inside label, made by Rowe-DeArmond, 1x12 combo, limited production, 2x6V6 power tubes, 2x12AX7 preamp tubes, with tube rectifier. 4 inputs, 3 control knobs.

1959-1961		$3,300	$4,125

SS140 Amp

1965-1966		$725	$900

Stinger FX-1 Amp
1988-1990. 10 watts, EQ, switchable solidstate tube-synth circuit, line out and footswitch jacks.

1988		$125	$155

Stinger FX-1R Amp
1988-1990. Mini-stack amp, 2x10", 15 watts, dual-stage circuitry.

1989		$155	$195

Stinger FX-6B Amp
1989-1990. Combo bass amp, 60 watts, 1x15".

1989		$155	$195

Masco
1940s-1950s. The Mark Alan Sampson Company, Long Island, New York, produced a variety of electronic products including tube PA amps and small combo instrument amps. The PA heads are also popular with harp players.

Massie
1940s. Ray Massie worked in Leo Fender's repair shop in the 1940s and also built tube amps. He later worked at the Fender company.

Matamp
1966-present. Tube amps, combos and cabinets built in Huddersfield, England, bearing names like Red, Green, White, Black, and Blue. German-born Mat Mathias started building amps in England in '58 and designed his first Matamp in '66. From '69 to '73, Mathias also made Orange amps. In '89, Mathias died at age 66 and his family later sold the factory to Jeff Lewis.

1x15" Cabinet

1970s		$750	$940

Marshall MS-2

Masco Map-15

Massie

AMPS

1995 Matchless Chieftain
Steve Lee

Matchless HC-30 Head

Matchless Nighthawk

MODEL YEAR	FEATURES	EXC. COND. LOW	HIGH
GT-120 Amp Head			
1971		$2,100	$2,625
GT-120 Green Stack Amp			
1990s. 120 watt GT head with 4x12" straight front cab.			
1993-1999		$1,475	$1,850

Matchless

1989-1999, 2001-present. Founded by Mark Sampson and Rick Perrotta in California. Circuits based on Vox AC-30 with special attention to transformers. A new Matchless company was reorganized in 2001 by Phil Jamison, former head of production for the original company.

MODEL YEAR	FEATURES	EXC. COND. LOW	HIGH
Avalon 35 Amp Head			
2009-2010. 35 watts head, reverb.			
2009-2010		$1,350	$1,700
Brave 40 112 Amp			
1997-1999. 40 watts class A, 1x12", footswitchable between high and low inputs.			
1997-1999		$1,300	$1,625
Brave 40 212 Amp			
1997-1999. 2x12" version of Brave.			
1997-1999		$1,400	$1,750
Chief Amp Head			
1995-1999. 100 watts class A, head.			
1995-1999		$2,200	$2,750
Chief 212 Amp			
1995-1999. 100 watts class A, 2x12", reverb.			
1995-1999		$2,300	$2,875
Chief 410 Amp			
1995-1999. 100 watts class A, 4x10", reverb.			
1995-1999		$2,375	$2,975
Chieftan Amp Head			
1995-1999. 40 watts class A head, reverb, chicken-head knobs.			
1995-1999		$1,450	$1,800
Chieftan 112 Amp			
1995-1999, 2001. 40 watts class A, 1x12", reverb.			
1995-1999		$1,900	$2,375
2001	Jamison era	$1,900	$2,375
Chieftan 210 Amp			
1995-1999. 40 watts class A, 2x10", reverb.			
1995-1999		$2,000	$2,500
Chieftan 212 Amp			
1995-1999, 2001-present. 40 watts class A, 2x12", reverb.			
1995-1999		$2,025	$2,525
2001-2014	Jamison era	$2,025	$2,525
Chieftan 410 Amp			
1995-1999. 40 watts class A, 4x10", reverb.			
1995-1999		$2,200	$2,750
Clipper 15 112 Amp			
1998-1999. 15 watts, single channel, 1x12".			
1998-1999		$900	$1,125
Clipper 15 210 Amp			
1998-1999. 15 watts, single channel, 2x10".			
1998-1999		$975	$1,225
Clubman 35 Amp Head			
1993-1999. 35 watts class A head.			
1993-1999		$1,600	$2,000

MODEL YEAR	FEATURES	EXC. COND. LOW	HIGH
DC-30 Standard Cabinet			
1991-1999. 30 watts, 2x12", with or without reverb.			
1991-1999		$2,525	$3,150
DC-30 Exotic Wood Cabinet Option			
1995-1999. 30 watts, 2x12", gold plating, limited production.			
1995-1999		$4,125	$5,150
ES/EB Cabinet			
ES = speaker cabinets and EB = bass speaker cabinets.			
1991-1999	1x12	$370	$460
1993-1999	2x10	$465	$580
1993-1999	2x10+2x12	$580	$725
1993-1999	2x12	$490	$610
1993-1999	4x12	$620	$775
1997-1999	1x15	$385	$480
1997-1999	4x10	$540	$675
HC-30 Amp Head			
1991-1999, 2003. The first model offered by Matchless, 30 watts class A head.			
1991-1999		$1,800	$2,250
2003	Jamison era	$1,800	$2,250
HC-85 Amp Head			
1992. Only 25 made, similar to HC-30 but more flexible using various tube substitutions.			
1992		$1,900	$2,375
Hurricane Amp Head			
1997. 15 watts class A head.			
1997		$1,075	$1,350
Hurricane 112 Amp			
1994-1997. 15 watts class A, 1x12".			
1994-1997		$1,075	$1,350
Hurricane 210 Amp			
1996-1997. 15 watts class A, 2x10".			
1996-1997		$1,300	$1,600
Independence 35 Amp Head			
2005-present. 35 watts, with or without reverb.			
2005-2014		$1,625	$2,025
JJ-30 112 John Jorgensen Amp			
1997-1999. 30 watts, DC-30 chasis with reverb and tremolo, 1x12" Celestion 30, offered in white, blue, gray sparkle tolex or black.			
1997-1999		$3,275	$4,100
Lightning 15 Amp Head			
1994-1997, 2005-present. 15 watts class A head.			
1994-1997		$1,175	$1,475
Lightning 15 112 Amp			
1994-1999, 2001-present. 15 watts class A, 1x12".			
1994-1999		$1,650	$2,075
2001-2014	Jamison era	$1,650	$2,075
Lightning 15 210 Amp			
1996-1997, 2001-2006. 15 watts class A, 2x10".			
1996-1997		$1,750	$2,175
2001-2006	Jamison era	$1,750	$2,175
Lightning 15 212 Amp			
1998, 2001-present. 15 watts class A, 2x12".			
1998		$1,800	$2,250
2001-2014	Jamison era	$1,800	$2,250
Little Monster Amp			
2007-2009. 9 watts, offered as head, and 1x12" or 2x12" combo.			
2007-2009		$1,150	$1,450

MODEL YEAR	FEATURES	EXC. COND. LOW	HIGH
Nighthawk Amp			
2003-present. 15 watts, offered as head, and 1x12", 2x10" or 2x12" combo.			
2003-2014	1x12	$1,000	$1,250
2003-2014	2x10	$1,075	$1,350
2003-2014	2x12	$1,125	$1,400
Phoenix 35 (PH-35) Amp Head			
2003-present. 35-watt head, red.			
2003-2014		$1,600	$2,000
SC-30 Standard Cabinet Amp			
1991-1999. 30 watts class A, 1x12".			
1991-1999		$2,375	$2,950
2001-2006	Jamison era	$2,200	$2,750
SC-30 Exotic Wood Cabinet Amp			
1995-1999. 30 watts class A, 1x12", gold plating, limited production.			
1995-1999		$3,875	$4,850
Skyliner Reverb 15 112 Amp			
1998-1999. 15 watts, 2 channels, 1x12".			
1998-1999		$800	$1,000
Skyliner Reverb 15 210 Amp			
1998-1999. 15 watts, 2 channels, 2x10".			
1998-1999		$900	$1,125
Spitfire 15 Amp Head			
1997. 15 watts, head.			
1997		$1,050	$1,325
Spitfire 15 112 Amp			
1994-1997. 15 watts, 1x12".			
1994-1997		$1,200	$1,500
Spitfire 15 210 Amp			
1996-1997. 15 watts, 2x10".			
1996-1997		$1,300	$1,625
Starliner 40 212 Amp			
1999. 40 watts, 2x12".			
1999		$1,350	$1,700
Superchief 120 Amp Head			
1994-1999. 120 watts, class A head.			
1994-1999		$2,150	$2,675
TC-30 Standard Cabinet Amp			
1991-1999. 30 watts, 2x10" class A, low production numbers makes value approximate with DC-30.			
1991-1999		$2,325	$2,900
TC-30 Exotic Wood Cabinet Amp			
1991-1999. 30 watts, 2x10" class A, limited production.			
1991-1999		$2,950	$3,675
Thunderchief Bass Amp Head			
1994-1999. 200 watts, class A bass head.			
1994-1999		$1,650	$2,050
Thunderman 100 Bass Combo Amp			
1997-1998. 100 watts, 1x15" in portaflex-style flip-top cab.			
1997-1998		$2,300	$2,875
Tornado 15 112 Amp			
1994-1995. Compact, 15 watts, 1x12", 2-tone covering, simple controls--volume, tone, tremolo speed, tremolo depth.			
1994-1995		$775	$975

Maven Peal

1999-present. Amps, combos and cabinets built by David Zimmerman in Plainfield, Vermont. Serial number format is by amp wattage and sequential build; for example, 15-watt amp 15-001.

Mega Amplifiers

Budget and intermediate grade, production, solidstate and tube amps from Guitar Jones, Inc. of Pomona, California.

Merlin

Rack mount bass heads built in Germany by Musician Sound Design. They also offer the MSD guitar effects.

Mesa-Boogie

1971-present. Founded by Randall Smith in San Francisco, California. Circuits styled on high-gain Fender-based chassis designs, ushering in the compact high-gain amp market. The following serial number information and specs courtesy of Mesa Engineering.

MODEL YEAR	FEATURES	EXC. COND. LOW	HIGH
.50 Caliber/.50 Caliber+ Amp Head			
Jan. 1987-Dec. 1988, 1992-1993. Serial numbers: SS3100 - SS11,499. Mesa Engineering calls it Caliber .50. Tube head amp, 50 watts, 5-band EQ, effects loop. Called the .50 Caliber Plus in '92 and '93.			
1987-1988	Caliber	$550	$700
1992-1993	Caliber+	$550	$700
.50 Caliber+ Combo Amp			
Dec. 1988-Oct. 1993. Serial numbers FP11,550 - FP29,080. 50 watts, 1x12" combo amp.			
1988-1993		$600	$750
20/20 Amp			
Jun. 1995-2010. Serial numbers: TT-01. 20-22 watts per channel.			
1995-2010		$600	$750
50/50 (Fifty/Fifty) Amp			
May 1989-2001. Serial numbers: FF001-. 100 watts total power, 50 watts per channel, front panel reads Fifty/Fifty, contains 4 6L6 power tubes.			
1989-2001		$575	$725
395 Amp			
Feb. 1991-Apr. 1992. Serial numbers: S2572 - S3237.			
1991-1992		$800	$1,000
Bass 400/Bass 400+ Amp Head			
Aug. 1989-Aug. 1990. Serial numbers: B001-B1200. About 500 watts using 12 5881 power tubes. Replaced by 400+ Aug.1990-present, serial numbers: B1200- . Update change to 7-band EQ at serial number B1677.			
1989-1990	Bass 400	$1,025	$1,275
1990-1999	Bass 400+	$1,075	$1,350
Big Block Series Amp			
2004-2014. Rackmount bass amps, models 750 and Titan V-12.			
2004-2014	750 Bass Head, 750w	$1,025	$1,275
2006-2010	Titan V-12, 650-1200w	$1,025	$1,275

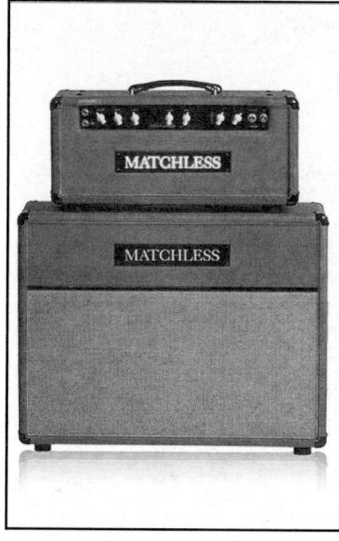

Matchless Phoenix 35

Maven Peal Naked Zeeta 1->50

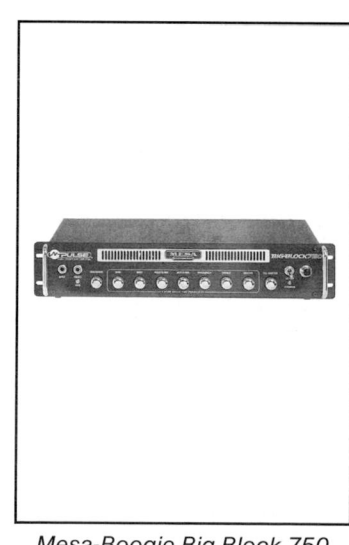

Mesa-Boogie Big Block 750

Mesa-Boogie Electra Dyne

1977 Mesa-Boogie Mark I

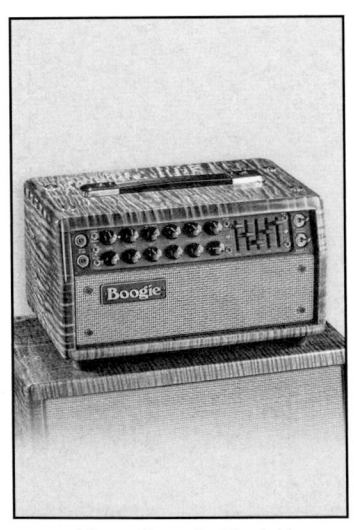

Mesa-Boogie Mark V

MODEL YEAR	FEATURES	EXC. COND. LOW	HIGH

Blue Angel Series Amp
Jun. 1994-2004. Serial numbers BA01-. Switchable between 15, 33 or 38 watts, offered as head, 1x12" combo or 4x10" combo, blue cover.

1994-2004	Combo 1x12"	$800	$1,000
1994-2004	Combo 4x10"	$925	$1,150

Buster Bass Amp Head
Dec. 1997-Jan. 2001. Serial numbers: BS-1-999. 200 watts via 6 6L6 power tubes.

1997-2001	$575	$725

Buster Bass Combo Amp
1999-2001. 200 watts, 2x10", wedge cabinet, black vinyl, metal grille.

1999-2001	$575	$725

Coliseum 300 Amp
Oct. 1997-2000. Serial numbers: COL-01 - COL-132. 200 watts/channel, 12 6L6 power tubes, rack mount.

1997-2000	$1,115	$1,400

D-180 Amp Head
Jul. 1982-Dec. 1985. Serial numbers: D001-D681. All tube head amp, 200 watts, preamp, switchable.

1982-1985	$850	$1,075

DC-3 Amp
Sep. 1994-Jan. 1999. Serial numbers: DC3-001 - DC3-4523. 35 watts, 1x12".

1994-1999	Combo 1x12"	$675	$850
1994-1999	Head only	$650	$825

DC-5 Amp
Oct. 1993-Jan. 1999. Serial numbers: DC1024 - DC31,941. 50-watt head, 1x12" combo.

1993-1999	Combo 1x12"	$700	$875
1993-1999	Head only	$700	$875

DC-10 Amp
May 1996-Jan. 1999. Serial numbers: DCX-001 - DCX-999. Dirty/Clean (DC), 100 watts (6L6s), 2x12".

1993-1996	Combo 2x12"	$800	$1,000
1996-1999	Head only	$725	$900

Electra Dyne Amp Head
2009-2013. 45/90 watts, Black Taurus/black grille or British Tan Bronco/tan grille.

2009-2013	$925	$1,150

Express Series Amp
2007-present. Compact combo tube amps with power switching.

2007-2014	5:25, 1x10" or 1x12", 5-25w	$725	$900
2007-2014	5:50, 1x12", 5-50w	$800	$1,000
2007-2014	5:50, 2x12", 5-50w	$850	$1,075
2008	5:25, short head, 25w	$650	$825

Extension Cabinet
1980s-present. Mesa-Boogie offered 'extension cabinets' which could be mixed and matched with amp heads, using different configurations with correct impedance. Other manufacturers often consider an extension cab as an extra cab, but Mesa Engineering considers it to be the main cab (not an extra). Most cabs are listed here. The company has generic cabs as well as cabs associated with specific models, but both generic and model-specific fall into similar price ranges. Some other variances include; vertical or horizontal, open back or closed, slant or straight front, grille could be metal or

MODEL YEAR	FEATURES	EXC. COND. LOW	HIGH

cloth, and some cabs are designated for bass guitar. Specialized cabinets may be more than values shown.

1980s-2014	1x12"	$335	$425
1980s-2014	1x15"	$375	$475
1980s-2014	2x10", Powerhouse Bass	$415	$525
1980s-2014	2x12"	$440	$550
1980s-2014	2x15"	$465	$575
1980s-2014	4x10", Powerhouse Bass	$465	$575
1980s-2014	4x12"	$540	$675
1980s-2014	6x10"	$575	$725
1980s-2014	8x10"	$675	$850

F-30 Amp
2002-Feb. 2007. Combo, 30 watts, 1x12".

2002-2007	$600	$750

F-50 Amp
2002-Feb. 2007. Combo, 50 watts, 1x12", AB 2 6L6 power.

2002-2007		$625	$775
2002-2007	Head only	$575	$725

F-100 Amp
2002-Feb. 2007. Combo, 100 watts, 2x12".

2002-2007	Combo 2x12"	$775	$975
2002-2007	Head only	$675	$850

Formula Preamp
Jul. 1998-2002. Serial numbers: F-01. Used 5 12AX7 tubes, 3 channels.

1998-2002	$375	$475

Heartbreaker Amp Head
1996-2001. Head only, 100 watts.

1996-2001	$850	$1,075

Heartbreaker Combo Amp
Jun. 1996-2001. Serial numbers: HRT-01. 60 to 100 watts switchable, 2x12" combo, designed to switch-out 6L6s, EL34s or the lower powered 6V6s in the power section, switchable solidstate or tube rectifier.

1996-2001	$950	$1,175

Lone Star Series Amp
2004-present. Designed by founder Randall Smith and Doug West with focus on boutique-type amp. Class A (EL84) or AB (4 6L6) circuits, long or short head, 1x12" combo, 2x12" combo, and short head 4x10" cab, and long head 4x12" cab.

2004-2014	Combo 1x12"	$1,125	$1,400
2004-2014	Combo 1x12", hardwood	$1,650	$2,050
2004-2014	Combo 2x12"	$1,235	$1,550
2004-2014	Combo 4x10", blue	$1,275	$1,600
2004-2014	Head, class A or AB	$1,025	$1,275

Lone Star Special Amp
2005-present. Smaller lighter version using EL84 power tubes, 5/15/30 watts, long or short head amp or 1x12", 2x12" or 4x10" combo.

2005-2014	Combo 1x12"	$1,225	$1,525

M-180 Amp
Apr. 1982-Jan. 1986. Serial numbers: M001-M275. Rack mount tube power amp.

1982-1986	$625	$775

MODEL YEAR	FEATURES	EXC. COND. LOW	HIGH

M-190 Amp
1980s. Rack mount tube power amp.

1980s		$465	$575

M-2000 Amp
Jun. 1995-2003. Serial numbers: B2K-01.

1995-2003		$675	$850

M6 Carbine Bass Amp Head
2011-present. 600-watt head, also offered in 2x12 combo.

2011-2014		$650	$800

Mark I Amp Head
1990. 60/100 watts, tweed cover.

1990		$1,350	$1,675

Mark I Combo (Model A) Amp
1971-1978. The original Boogie amp, not called the Mark I until the Mark II was issued, 60 or 100 watts, 1x12", Model A serial numbers: 1-2999, very early serial numbers 1-299 had 1x15".

1971-1978	1x12" or 1x15"	$1,350	$1,675

Mark I Reissue Amp
Nov. 1989-Sept. 2007. Serial numbers: H001-. 100 watts, 1x12", reissue features include figured maple cab and wicker grille.

2000-2007	Hardwood cab	$1,350	$1,675
2000-2007	Standard cab	$1,025	$1,275

Mark II B Amp Head
1981-1983. Head only.

1981-1983		$750	$950

Mark II B Combo Amp
1980-1983. Effective Aug. '80 1x12" models, serial numbers 5575-110000. May '83 1x15" models, serial numbers 560-11000. The 300 series serial numbers K1-K336.

1981-1983	1x12" or 1x15", tolex	$900	$1,125
1981-1983	Custom hardwood cab	$1,225	$1,525

Mark II C/Mark II C+ Amp
May 1983-Mar. 1985. Serial numbers 11001-14999 for 60 watts, 1x15", offered with optional white tolex cover. 300 series serial numbers after C+ are in the series K337-K422.

1983-1985		$2,375	$2,975
1985	Hardwood	$2,875	$3,600

Mark II C+ Amp Head
1983-1985. 60-watt head.

1983-1985	Hardwood	$2,875	$3,600
1983-1985	Standard	$2,025	$2,525

Mark II Combo Amp
1978-1980. Late-'78 1x12", serial numbers: 3000-5574. Effective Aug.'80 1x15", serial numbers: 300-559 until Mark II B replaced.

1978-1980	1x12" or 1x15"	$900	$1,125

Mark III Amp Head
1985-1999. 100 watts, black vinyl.

1985-1990		$900	$1,125
1985-1990	Custom hardwood	$1,525	$1,900
1990-1999	Graphic EQ model	$1,075	$1,350

Mark III Combo Amp
Mar. 1985-Feb. 1999. Serial numbers: 15,000 - 28,384. 300 series serialization K500-. Graphic equalizer only Mark III since Aug.'90, 100 watts,

1x12" combo. Custom cover or exotic hardwood cab will bring more than standard vinyl cover cab. There is also a Simul-Class Mark III which can run in 25, 60 or 85 watts.

1985-1990	Black	$975	$1,225
1985-1990	Custom color	$1,050	$1,325
1985-1999	Custom hardwood	$1,600	$2,000
1990-1999	Graphic EQ, standard cab	$1,150	$1,425

Mark IV (Rack Mount) Amp Head
1990-May 2008. Rack mount version.

1990-2008		$1,125	$1,400

Mark IV Amp Head
1990-May 2008. Clean rhythm, crunch rhythm and lead modes, 85 watts, EQ, 3-spring reverb, dual effects loops, digital footswitching. Also available in custom hardwood cab with wicker grille.

1990-2008	Custom hardwood	$1,750	$2,200
1990-2008	Short head, tolex	$1,275	$1,600

Mark IV/Mark IV B Combo Amp
May 1990-May 2008. Changed to Model IV B Feb.'95, serial numbers: IV001. Clean rhythm, crunch rhythm and lead modes, 40 watts, EQ, 3-spring reverb, dual effects loops, digital footswitching.

1991-1999		$1,175	$1,475
1991-1999	Custom hardwood	$1,700	$2,125
2000-2008		$1,175	$1,475
2000-2008	Custom hardwood	$1,700	$2,125

Mark V Amp
2010-present. 3 channels, 10/45/90 watts, also in 1x12" combo.

2010-2014	Combo 1x12"	$1,750	$2,200
2010-2014	Head	$1,600	$2,000

Maverick Dual Rectifier Amp Head
1994-Feb. 2005. 35 watts, Dual Rectifier head, white/blond vinyl cover.

1994-2005		$750	$950

Maverick Dual Rectifier Combo Amp
1997-Feb. 2005. Dual channels, 4 EL84s, 35 watts, 1x12", 2x12" or 4x10" combo amp, 5AR4 tube rectifier, cream vinyl covering. Serial number: MAV. Also available as head.

1997-2005	1x12"	$825	$1,025
1997-2005	2x12"	$925	$1,150
2005	4x10"	$950	$1,200

Mini Rectifier Twenty-Five Amp Head
2012-present. Ultra compact design, 10/25 watts, 2 channels.

2012-2014		$675	$850

M-Pulse 360 Amp
Jul. 2001-2005. Serial numbers: MP3-01-. Rack mount, silver panel.

2001-2003		$650	$800

M-Pulse 600 Amp
Apr. 2001-2011. Serial numbers: MP6-01- . Rack mount bass with 600 watts, tube preamp.

2001-2011		$725	$900

Nomad 45 Amp Head
1999-Feb. 2005. 45 watts, dark vinyl cover, dark grille.

1999-2005		$500	$625

Mesa-Boogie Mark V

Mesa-Boogie Mini Rectifier Twenty-Five

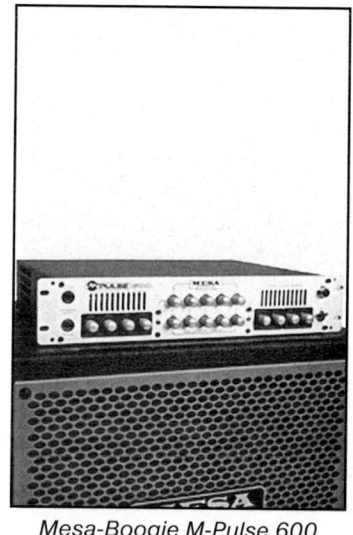

Mesa-Boogie M-Pulse 600

AMPS

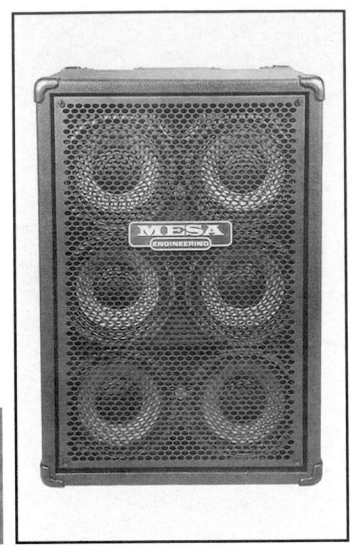

Mesa-Boogie Powerhouse Series Bass Cabinet

Mesa-Boogie Roadster

Mesa-Boogie TransAtlantic TA-15

AMPS

MODEL YEAR	FEATURES	EXC. COND. LOW	HIGH

Nomad 45 Combo Amp
Jul. 1999-Feb. 2005. Serial numbers: NM45-01. 45 watts, 1x12, 2x12" or 4x10" combo, dark vinyl cover, dark grille.

1999-2005	1x12"	$525	$650
1999-2005	2x12"	$600	$750
1999-2005	4x10"	$650	$800

Nomad 55 Amp Head
1999-2004. 55 watt head only.

1999-2004		$550	$675

Nomad 55 Combo Amp
Jul. 1999-2004. Serial numbers: NM55-01. 55 watts, 1x12", 2x12" or 4x10" combo.

1999-2004	1x12"	$575	$725
1999-2004	2x12"	$675	$850

Nomad 100 Amp Head
Jul. 1999-Feb. 2005. 100 watts, black cover, black grille.

1999-2005		$650	$800

Nomad 100 Combo Amp
Jul. 1999-Feb. 2005. 100 watts, 1x12" or 2x12" combo, black cover, black grille.

1999-2005	1x12"	$675	$850
1999-2005	2x12"	$800	$1,000

Princeton Boost Fender Conversion Amp
1970. Fender Princeton modified by Randall Smith, Boogie badge logo instead of the Fender blackface logo on upper left corner of the grille. About 300 amps were modified and were one of the early mods that became Mesa-Boogie.

1970		$2,275	$2,850

Quad Preamp
Sep. 1987-1992. Serial numbers: Q001-Q2857. Optional Quad with FU2-A footswitch Aug.'90-Jan.'92, serial numbers: Q2022-Q2857.

1990-1992	With footswitch	$600	$750

Recto Recording Preamp
2004-present. Rack mount preamp.

2004-2014		$750	$950

Rect-O-Verb Combo Amp
Dec. 1998-2001. Serial numbers R50-. 50 watts, 1x12", black vinyl cover, black grille.

1998-2001		$800	$1,000

Rect-O-Verb I Amp Head
Dec. 1998-2001. Serial numbers: R50-. 50 watts, head with 2 6L6 power tubes, upgraded Apr.'01 to II Series.

1998-2001		$750	$950

Rect-O-Verb II Amp Head
Apr. 2001-2010. Upgrade, serial number R5H-750.

2001-2010		$750	$950

Rect-O-Verb II Combo Amp
April 2001-2010. Upgrade R5H-750, 50 watts, AB, 2 6L6, spring reverb.

2001-2010		$825	$1,025

Road King Dual Rectifier Amp Head
2002-present. Tube head, various power tube selections based upon a chasis which uses 2 EL34s and 4 6L6, 2 5U4 dual rectifier tubes or silicon diode rectifiers, 50, 100 or 120 watts. Series II upgrades start in '06.

2002-2011		$1,825	$2,275
2006-2014	Series II	$1,825	$2,275

MODEL YEAR	FEATURES	EXC. COND. LOW	HIGH

Road King Dual Rectifier Combo Amp
2002-present. 2x12" combo version, Series II upgrades start in '06.

2002-2005	Select watts	$1,925	$2,400
2006-2014	Series II	$1,925	$2,400

Roadster Dual Rectifier Amp
2006-present. 50/100 watts, head only, 1x12" or 2x12" combo.

2006-2014	Combo 1x12	$1,550	$1,950
2006-2014	Combo 2x12	$1,650	$2,050
2006-2014	Head	$1,525	$1,900

Rocket 44 Amp
2011. 45 watts, 1x12" combo, spring reverb, FX loop.

2011		$415	$520

Rocket 440 Amp
Mar. 1999-Aug. 2000. Serial numbers: R440-R44-1159. 45 watts, 4x10".

1999-2000		$700	$875

Satellite/Satellite 60 Amp
Aug. 1990-1999. Serial numbers: ST001-ST841. Uses either 6L6s for 100 watts or EL34s for 60 watts, dark vinyl, dark grille.

1990-1999		$600	$750

Solo 50 Rectifier Series I Amp Head
Nov. 1998-Apr. 2001. Serial numbers: R50. 50-watt head.

1998-2001		$675	$850

Solo 50 Rectifier Series II Amp Head
Apr. 2001-2011. Upgrade, serial numbers: S50-S1709. Upgrades preamp section, head with 50 watts.

2001-2011		$675	$850

Solo Dual Rectifier Amp
1997-2011. Dual Rectifier Solo logo on front panel, 3x5U4, 150 watts.

1997-2011		$1,200	$1,500

Solo Triple Rectifier Amp
1997-2011. Triple Rectifier Solo logo on front panel, 3x5U4, 150 watts.

1997-2011		$1,250	$1,550

Son Of Boogie Amp
May 1982-Dec. 1985. Serial numbers: S100-S2390. 60 watts, 1x12", considered the first reissue of the original Mark I.

1982-1985		$550	$675

Stereo 290 (Simul 2-Ninety) Amp
Jun. 1992-present. Serial numbers: R0001-. Dual 90-watt stereo channels, rack mount.

1992-2014		$750	$950

Stereo 295 Amp
Mar. 1987-May 1991. Serial numbers: S001-S2673. Dual 95-watt class A/B stereo channels, rack mount. Selectable 30 watts Class A (EL34 power tubes) power.

1987-1991		$500	$625

Stilleto Ace Series Amp
2007-2011.

2007-2011	Combo 1x12"	$875	$1,100
2007-2011	Combo 2x12"	$1,000	$1,250
2007-2011	Head only	$825	$1,025

MODEL YEAR	FEATURES	EXC. COND. LOW	HIGH

Stilleto Series Amp Head
2004-2011. Series includes the Deuce (50 or 100 watts, 4 EL-34s) and Trident (50 or 150 watts, 6 EL-34s).

2004-2011	Deuce	$1,075	$1,350
2004-2011	Trident	$1,125	$1,400

Strategy 400 Amp
Mar. 1987-May 1991. Serial numbers: S001-S2627. 400 to 500 watts, power amplifier with 12 6L6 power tubes.

1987-1991		$725	$900

Strategy 500 Amp
Jun. 1991-Apr. 1992. S2,552- . Rack mount, 500 watts, 4 6550 power tubes.

1991-1992		$975	$1,225

Studio .22/Studio .22+ Amp
Nov. 1985-1988. Serial numbers: SS000-SS11499, black vinyl, black grille, 22 watts, 1x12". Replaced by .22+ Dec. '88-Aug. '93. Serial numbers: FP11,500-FP28,582. 22 watts.

1985-1988	.22	$450	$575
1988-1993	.22+	$450	$575

Studio Caliber DC-2 Amp
Apr. 1994-Jan. 1999. Serial numbers: DC2-01 - DC2-4247 (formerly called DC-2). 20 watts, 1x12" combo, dark vinyl, dark grille.

1994-1999		$450	$575

Studio Preamp
Aug. 1988-Dec. 1993. Serial numbers: SP000-SP7890. Tube preamp, EQ, reverb, effects loop.

1988-1993		$450	$575

Subway Reverb Rocket Amp
Jun. 1998-Aug. 2001. Serial numbers: RR1000-RR2461. 20 watts, 1x10".

1998-2001		$575	$725

Subway Rocket (Non-Reverb) Amp
Jan. 1996-Jul. 1998. Serial numbers: SR001-SR2825. No reverb, 20 watts, 1x10".

1996-1998		$575	$725

Subway/Subway Blues Amp
Sep. 1994-Aug. 2000. Serial numbers: SB001-SB2515. 20 watts, 1x10".

1994-2000		$475	$600

TA-15 Amp Head
2010-present. TransAtlantic series, lunchbox-sized tube head, 2 channels, 5/15/25 watts.

2010-2014		$650	$800

TA-30 Combo Amp
2012-present. TransAtlantic series, 15/30/40 watts, 1x12" or 2x12" combo, 2 channels.

2012-2014		$900	$1,125

Trem-O-Verb Dual Rectifier Amp Head
Jun. 1993-Jan. 2001. 100-watt head version.

1993-2001		$975	$1,225
1993-2001	Rackmount version	$975	$1,225

Trem-O-Verb Dual Rectifier Combo Amp
Jun.1993-Jan.2001. Serial numbers: R- to about R-21210. 100 watts, 2x12" Celestion Vintage 30.

1993-2001		$975	$1,225

Triaxis Programmable Preamp
Oct. 1991-present. Serial numbers:T0001-. 5 12AX7 tube preamp, rack mount.

1991-2014		$975	$1,225

MODEL YEAR	FEATURES	EXC. COND. LOW	HIGH

Venture Bass (M-Pulse) Amp

2007-2009		$875	$1,100

V-Twin Rackmount Amp
May 1995-Jun. 1998. Serial numbers: V2R-001 to V2R-2258.

1995-1998		$475	$600

WalkAbout M-Pulse Bass Amp Head
Sep. 2001-present. Serial numbers: WK-01-. Light-weight 13 pounds, 2 12AX7s + 300 MOS-FET.

2001-2014		$625	$775

WalkAbout Scout Convertible Combo Amp
2001-present. Head and 1x12 combo.

2001-2014		$750	$950

Meteoro
1986-present. Guitar, bass, harp and keyboard combo amps, heads, and cabinets built in Brazil. They also build effects.

Metropoulos Amplification
2004-present. George Metropoulos builds his professional and premium grade amps in Flint, Michigan.

MG
2004-present. Tube combo guitar amps built by Marcelo Giangrande in São Paulo, Brazil. He also builds effects.

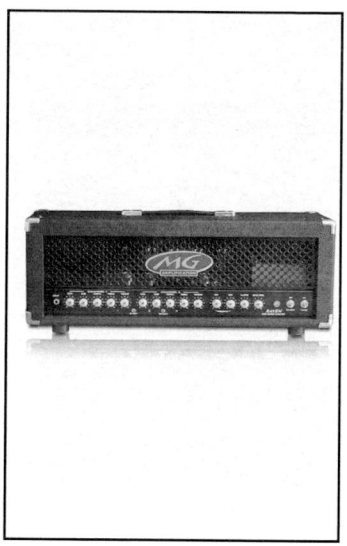
MG Raven

Mighty Moe Ampstraps
Peter Bellak built his guitar amp straps in Sacramento, California, starting in 2007. He also offered an amp strap for ukulele.

Milbert Amplifiers
2009-present. Professional and premium grade, production/custom, amps for guitars and cars, built in Gaithersburg, Maryland by Michael Milbert.

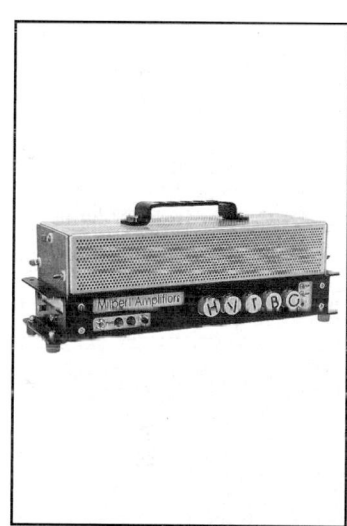
Milbert GAGA D-90

Mission Amps
1996-present. Bruce Collins' Mission Amps, located in Arvada, Colorado, produces a line of custom-made combo amps, heads, and cabinets.

Mojave Amp Works
2002-present. Tube amp heads and speaker cabinets by Victor Mason in Apple Valley, California.

Montgomery Ward
Amps for this large retailer were sometimes branded as Montgomery Ward, but usually as Airline (see that listing).

1x12" Combo Amp
1950s. 1x12", about 2 6L6 power tubes, includes Model 8439 and brown covered Maestro C Series with cloverleaf grille.

1950s		$400	$550

Model 55 JDR 8437 Amp
1950s. 4x8" speakers in 'suitcase' amp cabinet, brown control panel.

1950s		$540	$675

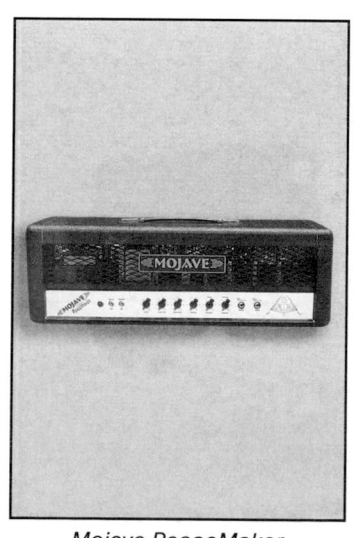
Mojave PeaceMaker

AMPS

Mosrite 400 Fuzzrite
Dennis Carden

Music Man 210 Sixty Five
KC Cormack

Music Man 410 Sixty Five Amp

MODEL YEAR	FEATURES	EXC. COND. LOW	HIGH

Mooneyes

Budget solid state amp line from Lace Music Products. They also offered amps under the Rat Fink and Lace brands. Lace had a Mooneyes guitar model line.

Morley

Late-1960s-present. The effects company offered an amp in the late '70s. See Effects section for more company information.

Bigfoot Amp

1979-ca.1981. Looks like Morley's '70s effects pedals, produced 25 watts and pedal controlled volume. Amp only, speakers were sold separately.

1979-1981		$200	$250

Mosrite

1968-1969. Mosrite jumped into the amp business during the last stages of the company history, the company was founded as a guitar company in 1954 and attained national fame in the '60s but by the time the company entered the amp business, the guitar boom began to fade, forcing the original Mosrite out of business in '69.

Model 400 Fuzzrite Amp

1968-1969. Solidstate, 1x15 combo, black tolex with silver grille, reverb and tremolo.

1968-1969		$600	$750

Model SS-550 The Gospel Amp

1968. Solidstate, 1 speaker combo, 2 channels normal and tremolo, reverb, black tolex.

1968		$575	$725

Mountain

Mountain builds a 9-volt amp in a wood cabinet. Originally built in California, then Nevada; currently being made in Vancouver, British Columbia.

Multivox

Ca.1946-ca.1984. Multivox was started as a subsidiary of Premier to manufacture amps, and later, effects. Generally student grade to low intermediate grade amps.

Murph

1965-1967. Amps marketed by Murph Guitars of San Fernado, California. At first they were custom-made tube amps, but most were later solidstate production models made by another manufacturer.

Music Man

1972-present. Music Man made amps from '73 to '83. The number preceding the amp model indicates the speaker configuration. The last number in model name usually referred to the watts. RD indicated Reverb Distortion. RP indicated Reverb Phase. Many models were available in head-only versions and as combos with various speaker combinations.

Sixty Five Amp

1973-1981. Head amp, 65 watts, reverb, tremolo.

1973-1981		$450	$550

Seventy Five Reverb/75 Reverb Amp

1973-1981. Head amp, 75 watts, reverb.

1973-1981		$500	$625

110 RD Fifty Amp

1980-1983. 50 watts, 1x10", reverb, distortion.

1980-1983		$600	$750

112 B Bass Amp

1983. 50 watts, 1x12".

1983		$600	$750

112 RD Fifty Amp

1980-1983. 50 watts, 1x12", reverb, distortion.

1980-1983		$625	$775

112 RD Sixty Five Amp

1978-1983. 65 watts, 1x12", reverb, distortion.

1978-1983		$625	$775

112 RD One Hundred Amp

1978-1983. 100 watts, 1x12", reverb, distortion, EVM option for heavy duty 12" Electro-Voice speakers.

1978-1983		$650	$800
1978-1983	EVM option	$650	$800

112 RP Sixty Five Amp

1978-1983. 65 watts, 1x12", reverb, built-in phaser.

1978-1983		$625	$775

112 RP One Hundred Amp

1978-1983. Combo amp, 100 watts, 1x12", reverb, built-in phaser.

1978-1983		$625	$775

112 Sixty Five Amp

1973-1981. Combo amp, 65 watts, 1x12", reverb, tremolo.

1973-1977		$625	$775
1978-1981		$625	$775

115 Sixty Five Amp

1973-1981. Combo amp, 65 watts, 1x15", reverb, tremolo.

1973-1981		$625	$775

210 HD130 Amp

1973-1981. 130 watts, 2x10", reverb, tremolo.

1973-1981		$675	$850

210 Sixty Five Amp

1973-1981. 65 watts, 2x10", reverb, tremolo.

1973-1981		$675	$850

212 HD130 Amp

1973-1981. 130 watts, 2x12", reverb, tremolo.

1973-1981		$700	$875

212 Sixty Five Amp

1973-1981. 65 watts, 2x12", reverb, tremolo.

1973-1981		$700	$875

410 Sixty Five Amp

1973-1981. 65 watts, 4x10", reverb, tremolo.

1973-1981		$700	$875

410 Seventy Five Amp

1982-1983. 75 watts, 4x10", reverb, tremolo.

1982-1983		$700	$875

HD-130 Amp

1973-1981. Head amp, 130 watts, reverb, tremolo.

1973-1981	Head only	$500	$625

HD-150 Amp

1973-1981. Head amp, 75/100 watts.

1973-1981	Head only	$500	$625

MODEL YEAR	FEATURES	EXC. COND. LOW	HIGH
RD Fifty Amp			
1980-1983. Head amp, 50 watts, reverb, distortion.			
1980-1983	Head only	$500	$625

Nady

1976-present. Wireless sound company Nady Systems started offering tube combo and amp heads in '06.

NARB

1973. Briefly made by Ken Bran and Jim Marshall, about 24 made, all were Marshall 100-watt tremolo half-stack, NARB logo on amp and cabinet.

100 Watt Half-Stack
1973. 100 watts, 4x12".

1973		$3,500	$4,375

National

Ca.1927-present. National/Valco amps date back to the late-'30s. National introduced a modern group of amps about the same time they introduced their new Res-O-Glas space-age guitar models in '62. In '64, the amp line was partially redesigned and renamed. By '68, the Res-O-Glas models were gone and National introduced many large vertical and horizontal piggyback models which lasted until National's assets were assigned during bankruptcy in '69. The National name went to Chicago importer Strum N' Drum. Initially, Strum N' Drum had one amp, the National GA 950 P Tremolo/Reverb piggyback.

Aztec Amp
1950s. Combo, early '50s version with 3 Rola 7x11" speakers using 3 speaker baffle openings, about 20 watts using 2x6L6 power tubes, 2-tone brown leatherette and tweed cover. By '56, amp has one 15" speaker and does not have segmented grill.

1950s	3 Rola 7x11	$825	$1,025
1956	1x15	$775	$975

Bass 70/Bass 75 Amp
1962-1967. 35 watts (per channel), 2x12" (often Jensen) speakers, large knobs, Raven Black tolex with silver and white grille, designed for bass. New model name in '64 with nearly identical features but listed as total of 70 watts, in '62 called Bass 70 but renamed Bass 75 in '64.

1962-1963	Bass 70	$725	$900
1964-1967	Bass 75 N6475B	$725	$900

Chicagoan Model 1220 Amp
1950s. 17 watts, 1x10", tube, says "Valco Chicago 51" on control panel.

1950s		$625	$775

Dynamic 20 Amp
1962-1963. 17 watts, 2x8" (often Jensen) speakers, 2 large knobs, Raven Black tolex with silver and white grille, compact student-intermediate amp.

1962-1963		$675	$850

Glenwood 90 Amp
1962-1967. 35 watts, 2x12" (often Jensen) speakers, large knobs, reverb, tremolo, Raven Black tolex with silver and white grille, top of the line, becomes the nearly identical N6490TR in '64.

1962-1963		$1,125	$1,400
1964-1967	Model N6490TR	$1,025	$1,275

Glenwood Vibrato Amp
Two 12" speakers, reverb, tremolo.

1964-1967	Model N6499VR	$1,125	$1,400

Model 75 Amp
1940s. Vertical tweed combo cabinet, volume and tone knobs, 3 inputs.

1940s		$490	$615

Model 100 Amp
1940. Tube amp, 40 watts, 1x12".

1940		$575	$725

Model 1202 Twin Amp
1954. 18 watts, 2x8" Jensen speaker, 2 channels (Instrument and microphone), horizontal flying bird logo on grille.

1954		$775	$975

Model 1210 High Fidelity Amp
1954. 20 watts, 1x15" Jensen speaker, 4 input jacks, 2 channels (instrument and microphone), 20x24x10" combo, metal handle.

1954		$725	$900

Model 1212 Amp
1954. 12 watts, 1x12", 5 tubes, 3 inputs, 15x18x8" combo, diving flying bird logo on grille, plastic handle.

1954		$675	$850

Model 1275 Amp
1953. Combo 1x10", 12 watts, 5 tubes, light tan weave cover, deep brown grille cloth.

1953		$625	$775

Model GA 950-P Tremolo/Reverb Piggyback Amp
1970s. Strum N' Drum/National model, solidstate, 50 watts, 2-channel 2x12" and 1x7" in 32" tall vertical cabinet, black.

1970s		$240	$300

Model N6800 - N6899 Piggyback Amps
1968-1969. National introduced a new line of tube amps in '68 and most of them were piggybacks. The N6895 was sized like a Fender piggyback Tremolux, the N6875 and N6878 bass amps were sized like a '68 Fender large cab piggyback with a 26" tall vertical cab, the N6898 and N6899 were the large piggyback guitar amps. These amps feature the standard Jensen speakers or the upgrade JBL speakers, the largest model was the N6800 for PA or guitar, which sported 3x70-watt channels and 2 column speakers using a bass 2x12" + 1x3" horn cab and a voice-guitar 4x10" + 1x3" horn cab.

1968-1969		$515	$650

Model N6816 (Model 16) Amp
1968-1969. Valco-made tube amp, 6 watts, 1x10" Jensen speaker, 17" vertical cab, tremolo, no reverb, black vinyl cover and Coppertone grille.

1968-1969		$385	$475

Model N6820 Thunderball Bass Amp
1968-1969. Valco-made tube amp, about 35 watts, 1x15" Jensen speaker, 19" vertical cab, black vinyl cover and Coppertone grille.

1968-1969		$445	$550

Model N6822 (Model 22) Amp
1968-1969. Valco-made, 6 watts tube (4 tubes) amp, 1x12" Jensen speaker, 19" vertical cab, tremolo and reverb, black vinyl cover and Coppertone grille.

1968-1969		$415	$525

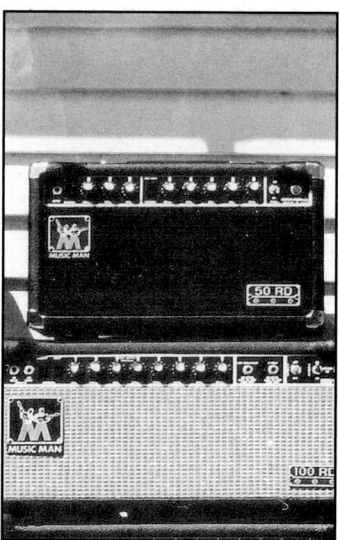
Music Man RD Fifty
Terry Loose

National Glenwood 90

National Stagestar

444 National National Dobro — Norma GA-725 B

Naylor Electra-Verb 60 Head

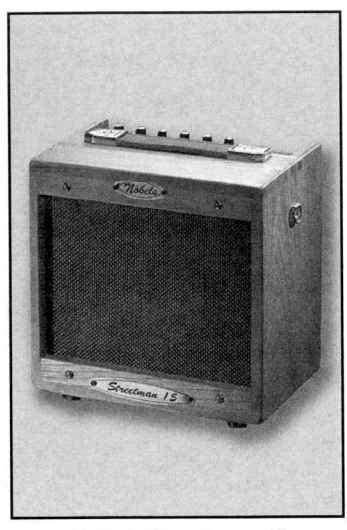

Nobels Streetman 15

1960 Oahu Holiday

MODEL YEAR	FEATURES	EXC. COND. LOW	HIGH

National Dobro Amp
1930s. Sold by the National Dobro Corp. when the company was still in Los Angeles (they later moved to Chicago). National Dobro plate on rear back panel, suitcase style case that flips open to reveal the speaker and amp, National logo on outside of suitcase. The noted price is for an all-original amp in excellent condition (this would be a rare find), there are other 1930s models included in the price range below.

1930s	Early metal baffle	$575	$725
1930s	Later standard baffle	$475	$600
1930s	Suitcase style	$575	$725

Newport 40 Amp
1964-1967. 17 watts, 2x10", tremolo only.
| 1964-1967 | Model N6440T | $675 | $850 |

Newport 50 Amp
1964-1967. 17 watts, 2x10", tremolo and reverb.
| 1964-1967 | Model N6450TR | $675 | $850 |

Newport 97 Amp
1964-1967. 35 watts, 1x15", rear mounted chasis, tremolo.
| 1964-1967 | Model N6497T | $700 | $875 |

Sportsman Amp
1950s. Tweed combo with brown leatherette speaker surround, 1x10".
| 1950s | | $625 | $775 |

Student Practice Amp
1970s. Strum N' Drum era, small solidstate, single control.
| 1970s | | $35 | $45 |

Studio 10 Amp
1962-1967. Five watts, 1x8", 3 tubes, 1 channel, 1 volume control, no tone control, no reverb or tremolo.
| 1962-1963 | | $475 | $600 |
| 1964-1967 | Model N6410 | $475 | $600 |

Tremo-Tone Model 1224 Amp
1956-1959. Small combo, tremolo, dual Rola oval 6x11" speakers, tweed, by Valco, flying bird pattern on lower front grille.
| 1956-1959 | | $850 | $1,075 |

Val-Pro 80 Amp
1962-1963. 35 watts, 2x12" (often Jensen) speakers, 8 tubes, large control knobs, tremolo, black cover with white and silver trim, replaced by Glenwood 90 in '64 with added reverb.
| 1962-1963 | | $1,075 | $1,350 |

Val-Trem 40 Amp
1962-1963. 17 watts, 2x10" (often Jensen) speakers, large knobs, Val-Trem logo on back panel, Clear-Wave tremolo, Raven Black tolex with silver and white grille, open back combo amp, becomes Newport 40 in '64.
| 1962-1963 | | $875 | $1,100 |

Val-Verb 60 Amp
1962-1963. 17 watts, 2x10" (often Jensen) speakers, large knobs, Val-Verb logo on back panel, reverb, no tremolo, Raven Black tolex with silver and white grille, open back combo amp.
| 1962-1963 | | $1,025 | $1,275 |

Westwood 16 Amp
1964-1967. Five watts using 1 6V6 power, 2 12AX7 preamp, 1 5Y3GT rectifier, tremolo, 2x8", dark vinyl cover, silver grille.
| 1964-1967 | Model N6416T | $700 | $875 |

MODEL YEAR	FEATURES	EXC. COND. LOW	HIGH

Westwood 22 Amp
1964-1967. 5 watts, 2x8", reverb and tremolo, 1 channel, 6 tubes.
| 1964-1967 | Model N6422TR | $775 | $975 |

Naylor Engineering
1994-present. Joe Naylor and Kyle Kurtz founded the company in East Pointe, Michigan, in the early '90s, selling J.F. Naylor speakers. In '94 they started producing amps. In '96, Naylor sold his interest in the business to Kurtz and left to form Reverend Guitars. In '99 David King bought the company and moved it to Los Angeles, California, then to Dallas, Texas. Currently Naylor builds tube amps, combos, speakers, and cabinets.

Nemesis
From the makers of Eden amps, Nemesis is a line of made-in-the-U.S., FET powered bass combos and extension cabinets. The brand is a division of U.S. Music Corp.

Newcomb
1950s. Newcomb Audio Products, Hollywood, California, Newcomb script logo on back panel along with model number, they offered instrument amplifiers that could also be used as small PA.
Model G 12
1953. 1x12" (Rolla) combo amp, 2 controls (volume and tone), large metal handle, oxblood-brown leatherette.
| 1953 | | $320 | $400 |

Nobels
1997-present. Effects manufacturer Nobels Electronics of Hamburg, Germany also offers a line of small practice and portable amps.

Noble
Ca. 1950-ca. 1969. From Don Noble and Company, of Chicago, Illinois, owned by Strum N' Drum by mid-'60s. They also offered guitars and amps.
Model 381/Custom 381 Amp
1950s. 2x12" and 2x5".
| 1958-1960 | | $900 | $1,125 |

Norma
1965-1970. Economy line imported and distributed by Strum N' Drum, Wheeling (Chicago), Illinois. As noted in the National section, Strum N' Drum acquired the National brand in the '70s. Some early amps were tube, but the majority were solidstate.
GA-93 Amp
1969-1970. 6 watts, 1x6".
| 1969-1970 | | $55 | $70 |
GA-97 T Amp
1969-1970. 13 watts, 1x8", tremolo.
| 1969-1970 | | $60 | $75 |
GA-725 B Amp
1969-1970. Bass amp, 38 watts, 1x10".
| 1969-1970 | | $60 | $75 |

MODEL YEAR	FEATURES	EXC. COND. LOW	HIGH

Model 1213 100W Reverb Combo Amp
Late 1960s-early 1970s. 100 watts, 2x12", reverb, tube.

| 1960s-70s | | $1,750 | $2,175 |

Model 1228 50-Watt Lead Amp Head
Late 1970s-1982. 50 watts, based upon Marshall 50-watt made during same era.

| 1970s-82 | | $1,650 | $2,075 |

Model 1229 100W Lead Amp Head
Late 1970s-1982. 100 watts, tube.

| 1970s-82 | | $1,650 | $2,075 |

Model 1231 Vintage 20 LE Combo Amp
Late 1970s-1980s. 20 watts, 1x12".

| 1970s-80s | | $1,650 | $2,075 |

Model 1239 50W Master Volume Reverb Combo Amp
Late 1970s-1982. 50 watts, 1x12".

| 1970s-82 | | $1,650 | $2,075 |

Paul Reed Smith
1985-present. In the late '80s, PRS offered two amp models. Only 350 amp units shipped. Includes HG-70 Head and HG-212 Combo. HG stands for Harmonic Generator, effectively a non-tube, solid-state amp. In '09, PRS introduced tube combo and head amps and cabinets designed by Doug Sewell.

Paul Ruby Amplifiers
2000-present. Professional grade, custom, tube amps built by Paul Ruby in Folsom, California.

Peavey
1965-present. Hartley Peavey's first products were guitar amps. He added guitars to the mix in '78. Headquartered in Meridan, Mississippi, Peavey continues to offer a huge variety of guitars, amps, and PAs. TransTube redesign of amps occurs in '95.

3120 Amp Head
2009-present. Tubes, 120 watts, 3 foot-switchable channels.

| 2009-2014 | | $350 | $450 |

5150 212 Combo Amp
1995-2004. Combo version of 5150 head, 60 watts, 2x12", large 5150 logo on front panel, small Peavey logo on lower right of grille.

| 1995-2004 | | $450 | $550 |

5150 EVH Head/Cabinet Amp Set
1995-2008. Half stack 5150 head and 4x12" cab, large 5150 logo on front of amp.

1995-2004	Cab only	$360	$450
1995-2004	Head & cab	$1,025	$1,280
1995-2008	Head only	$670	$840

5150 II Amp
2004. Has 5051 II logo on front, look for 'II' designation.

| 2004 | Head & cab | $1,025 | $1,280 |

6505 Series Amp
2008-present.

| 2008-2014 | 2x12 combo, 60w | $525 | $650 |
| 2008-2014 | 6505+ head, 120w | $525 | $650 |

Alphabass Amp
1988-1990. Rack mount all tube, 160 watts, EQ, includes 2x15" Black Widow or 2x12" Scorpion cabinet.

| 1988-1990 | | $225 | $280 |

Artist Amp
Introduced in 1975 as 120 watts, 1x12", bright and normal channels, EQ, reverb, master volume.

| 1970s | | $250 | $310 |

Artist 110 Amp
1990s. TransTubes, 10 watts.

| 1990s | | $110 | $140 |

Artist 240 Amp
1975-1980s. 120 watt combo, 1x12".

| 1975-80s | | $175 | $225 |

Artist 250 Amp
1990s. 100 watts, 1x12", solidstate preamp, 4 6L6 power tubes.

| 1990s | | $190 | $235 |

Artist VT Amp
1990s. Combo amp, 120 watts, 1x12".

| 1990s | | $250 | $310 |

Audition 20 Amp
1980s-1990s. 20 watts, single speaker combo.

| 1980-1990s | | $40 | $50 |

Audition 30 Amp
1980s-1990s. 30 watts, 1x12" combo amp, channel switching.

| 1980-1990s | | $45 | $55 |

Audition 110 Amp
1990s. 25 watts, 1x10" combo, 2 channels.

| 1990s | | $55 | $70 |

Audition Chorus Amp
1980s. 2x10-watt channels, 2x6", channel switching, post gain and normal gain controls.

| 1980s | | $80 | $100 |

Audition Plus Amp
1980s. Solidstate, 20 watts, 1x10".

| 1980s | | $50 | $65 |

Backstage Amp
1977-mid-1980s. Master gain control, 18 watts, 1x10", 3-band EQ. Name reused in 2000s on small 6.5" speaker, 10 watt amp.

| 1977-1984 | | $40 | $50 |

Backstage 30 Amp
1980s. 30 watts, 1x8".

| 1980s | | $40 | $50 |

Backstage 110 Amp
Repackaged and revoiced in 1988, 65 watts, 1x10", Peavey SuperSat preamp circuitry, new power sections.

| 1980s | | $55 | $70 |

Backstage Chorus 208 Amp
1990s. 150 watts, 2x8", reverb, channel switching.

| 1990s | | $100 | $125 |

Backstage Plus Amp
1980s. 35 watts, 1x10" combo, reverb, saturation effect.

| 1980s | | $55 | $70 |

Bandit/65/75 Amp
1981-1989. 1x12" combo, originally 50 watts, upped to 65 watts in '85 and 75 in '87, renamed Bandit 112 in '90.

1981-1984	Bandit	$105	$130
1985-1986	Bandit 65	$105	$130
1987-1989	Bandit 75	$105	$130

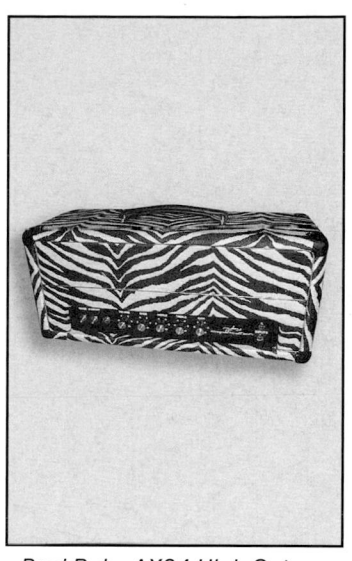
Paul Ruby AX84 High Octane

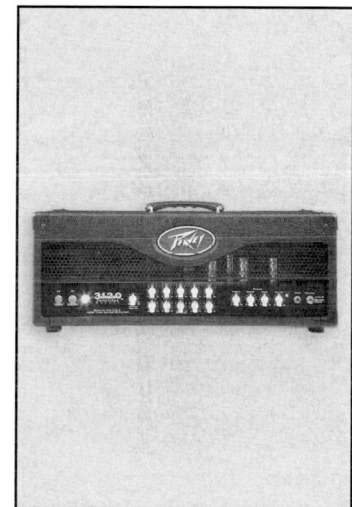
Peavey 3120

Peavey 5150 2x12"

AMPS

To get the most from this book, be sure to read "Using *The Guide*" in the introduction.

Peavey Delta Blues

Peavey Ecoustic E110

Peavey Envoy 110

MODEL YEAR	FEATURES	EXC. COND. LOW	HIGH
Bandit 112/Bandit II 112 Amp			
1990-present. 80 watts (II is 100), 1x12", active EQ circuit for lead channel, active controls. TransTube in '95.			
1990-1994		$130	$160
1994-2014	TransTube	$180	$225
Basic 40 Amp			
1980s. 40 watts, 1x12".			
1980s		$85	$105
Basic 60 Amp			
1988-1995. Solidstate combo amp, 50-60 watts, 1x12", 4-band EQ, gain controls, black.			
1988-1995		$130	$160
Basic 112 Bass Amp			
1996-2006. 75 watts, 1x12" bass combo, 2000-era red border control panel.			
1996-2006		$130	$160
Blazer 158 Amp			
1995-2005. 15 watts, 1x8", clean and distortion, later called the TransTube Blazer III.			
1995-2005		$70	$90
Bluesman Amp			
1992. Tweed, 1x12" or 1x15".			
1992		$235	$300
Bravo 112 Amp			
1988-1994. All tube reverb, 25 watts, 1x12", 3-band EQ, 2 independent input channels.			
1988-1994		$180	$225
Butcher Amp Head			
1985-1987, 2010-present. All tube head, 120 watts. Current version is all tube, 100 watts with half power switch			
1985-1987		$335	$425
Classic 20 Amp			
1990s. Small tube amp with 2xEL84 power tubes, 1x10" narrow panel combo, tweed cover.			
1990s		$225	$280
Classic 30/112 Amp			
1994-present. Tweed combo, 30 watts, 1x12", EL84 tubes.			
1994-2014	Narrow panel combo	$310	$390
2008-2014	Badge front	$360	$450
2008-2014	Head	$285	$355
Classic 50/212 Amp			
1990-present. Combo, 50 watt, 2x12", 4 EL84s, 3 12AX7s, reverb, high-gain section.			
1990-2014		$435	$550
Classic 50/410 Amp			
1990-present. Combo amp, 4x10", EL84 power, reverb, footswitchable high-gain mode.			
1990-2014		$435	$550
Classic 120 Amp			
1988-ca.1990. Tube, 120 watts.			
1988-1990		$300	$375
Combo 300 Amp			
1982-1993. 1x15" bass combo, 300 watts.			
11982-1993		$155	$195
DECA/750 Amp			
1989-ca.1990. Digital, 2 channels, 350 watts per channel, distortion, reverb, exciter, pitch shift, multi-EQ.			
1989-1990		$205	$255

MODEL YEAR	FEATURES	EXC. COND. LOW	HIGH
Decade Amp			
1970s. Practice amp, 10 watts, 1x8", runs on 12 volt or AC.			
1970s		$75	$95
Delta Blues Amp			
1995-present. 30 watts, tube combo, 4 EL84 tubes, 1x15" or 2x10", tremolo, large-panel-style cab, blond tweed.			
1995-2014		$390	$485
Deuce Amp			
1972-1980s. 120 watts, tube amp, 2x12" or 4x10".			
1972-1980s		$175	$215
Deuce Amp Head			
1972-1980s. Tube head, 120 watts.			
1972-1980s		$130	$165
Ecoustic Series Amp			
1996-present. Acoustic combo amps, 110 (1x10) and 112 (1x12, offered until '10) at 100 watts, digital effects (EFX, later E) added in '03. E20 and E208 added in '11.			
1996-2010	112	$125	$155
2003-2014	E110	$125	$155
Encore 65 Amp			
1983. Tube combo, 65 watts.			
1983		$230	$290
Envoy 110 Amp			
1988-present. Solidstate, 40 watts, 1x10", Trans-Tubes.			
1988-2014		$85	$105
Heritage VTX Amp			
1980s. 130 watts, 4 6L6s, solidstate preamp, 2x12" combo.			
1980s		$155	$195
Jazz Classic Amp			
1980s. Solidstate, 210 watts, 1x15", electronic channel switching, 6-spring reverb.			
1980s		$155	$195
JSX (Joe Satriani) Amp			
2004-2010. Joe Satriani signature, 120 watt tube head. Also offered were JSX 50 (50 watts, '09-'10), JSX 212 Combo ('05-'10) and 5-watt JSX Mini Colossal ('07-'10).			
2004-2010	120w head	$515	$650
KB Series Amp			
1980s. Keyboard amp, models include KB-60 (60 watts, 1x12", reverb), KB-100 (100w, 1x15"), and KB-300 (300w, 1x15" with horn).			
1980s	KB-100	$155	$195
1980s	KB-300	$225	$280
1980s	KB-60	$130	$165
LTD Amp			
1975-1980s. Solidstate, 200 watts, 1x12" Altec or 1x15" JBL.			
1975-1982		$155	$195
Mace Amp Head			
1976-1980s. Tube, 180 watts.			
1976-1980s		$235	$295
Mark III Bass Amp Head			
1978-1983. 300 watts, 2 channels, graphic EQ.			
1978-1983		$165	$205

MODEL YEAR	FEATURES	EXC. COND. LOW	HIGH

MegaBass Amp
1986-ca. 1992. Rack mount preamp/power amp, 200 watts per 2 channels, solidstate, EQ, effects loop, chorus.

1986-1992		$185	$230

Microbass Amp
1988-2005. 20 watts, 1x8" practice amp, made in China.

1988-2005		$40	$50

Minx 110 Bass Amp
1987-2005. Solidstate, 35 watts RMS, 1x10" heavy-duty speaker.

1987-2005		$90	$110

Musician Amp Head
Introduced in 1965 as 120 watt head, upped to 210 watts in '72.

1965-1970s		$125	$155

Nashville 112 Steel Guitar Amp
2008-present. Compact size, 1x12", 80 watts.

2008-2014		$380	$475

Nashville 400 Steel Guitar Amp
1982-2000. 210 watts, 1x15" solidstate steel guitar combo amp.

1982-2000		$380	$475

Nashville 1000 Steel Guitar Amp
1998-2008. 1x15" speaker, solidstate steel guitar combo amp.

1998-2008		$380	$475

Pacer Amp
1974-1985. Master volume, 45 watts, 1x12", 3-band EQ.

1974-1985		$70	$90

Penta Amp Head/Gary Rossington Signature Penta
2005-present. Tubes, 140 watts, 4x12", 5 selectable preamp settings. Becomes the Gary Rossington Signature Penta in 2009.

2005-2014	Cab	$240	$300
2005-2014	Head	$290	$350

ProBass 1000 Amp
1980s. Rack mount, effects loops, preamp, EQ, crossover, headphone output.

1980s		$130	$165

Rage/Rage 158 Amp
1988-2008. Compact practice amp, 15 watts, 1x8". 158 starts '95. Replaced by 25 watt Rage 258.

1988-2008		$35	$45

Reno 400 Amp
1984-late 1980s. Solidstate, 200 watts, 1x15" with horn, 4-band EQ.

1980s		$130	$165

Renown 112 Amp
1989-1994. Crunch and lead SuperSat, 160 watts, 1x12", master volume, digital reverb, EQ.

1989-1994		$130	$165

Renown 212 Amp
1989-1994. Crunch and lead SuperSat, 160 watts, 2x12", master volume, digital reverb, EQ.

1989-1994		$155	$195

Renown 400 Amp
1981-late 1980s. Combo, 200 watts, 2x12", channel switching, Hammond reverb, pre- and post-gain controls.

1980s		$205	$255

Revolution 112 Amp
1992-2002. 100 watts, 1x12" combo, black vinyl, black grille.

1992-2002		$175	$220

Session 400 Amp
1974-ca. 1999. 200 watts, 1x15 or early on as 2x12, steel amp, available in the smaller box LTD, offered as a head in '76, available in wedge-shaped enclosure in '88.

1974-1999		$400	$500

Session 500 Amp
1979-1980s. 250 watts, 1x15", steel amp.

1979-1985		$400	$500

Special 112 Amp
1981-1994. 160 watts, 1x12". In 1988, available in wedge-shaped enclosure.

1981-1994		$150	$186

Special 130 Amp
1980s. 1x12", 130 watts.

1980s		$150	$186

Special 212 Amp
1995-2005. 160 watts, 2x12", transtube, solidstate series.

1995-2005		$175	$220

Studio Pro 50 Amp
1986-late 1980s. 50 watts, 1x12".

1980s		$105	$130

Studio Pro 112 Amp
1980s. Repackaged and revoiced in 1988. Solidstate, 65 watts, 1x12", Peavey SuperSat preamp circuitry, new power sections.

1980s		$115	$145

TKO Series Bass Amp
1978-2011. Solidstate, 1x15, original TKO was 40 watts, followed by TKO 65 (65 watts) for '82-'87, TKO 75 for '88-'90, and TKO 80 for '91-'92. Renamed TKO 115 in '93 with 75, 80 or 100 watts until '09 when jumping to 400 watts.

1982-1987	TKO 65	$105	$130
1988-1990	TKO 75	$140	$175
1991-1992	TKO 80	$175	$225

TNT Series Bass Amp
1974-2009. Solidstate, 1x15, original TNT was 45 watts, upped to 50 for '79-'81, followed by TNT 130 (130 watts) for '82-'87, TNT 150 for '88-'90, and TNT 160 for '91-'92. Renamed TNT 115 in '93 with 150, 160 or 200 watts until '09 when jumping to 600 watts (Tour TNT 115 - see Tour Series).

1982-1987	TNT 130	$185	$230
1988-1990	TNT 150	$185	$230
1991-1992	TNT 160	$230	$290

Tour Series
2004-present. Imported bass heads and cabinets, various models.

2004-2014	Various models	$260	$325

Peavey Nashville 112

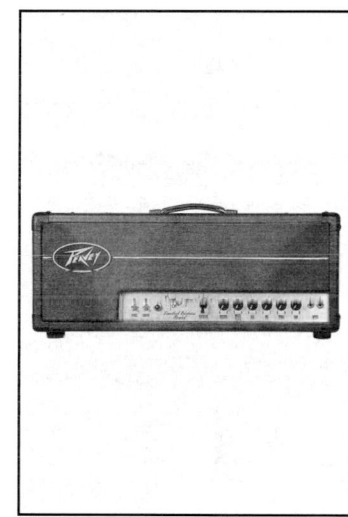

*Peavey Penta Amp Head/
Gary Rossington Sign*

1978 Peavey TNT Series

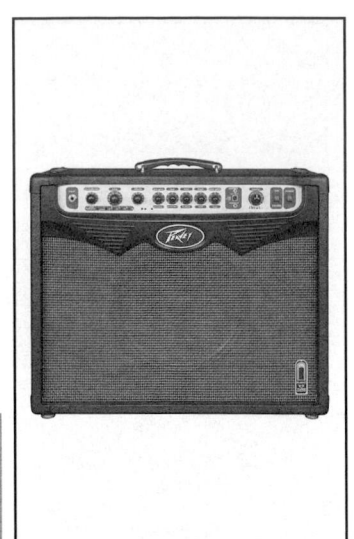

Peavey Vypyr Tube 60

Penn Pennalizer 35

Pignose Hog

MODEL YEAR	FEATURES	EXC. COND. LOW	HIGH
Transchorus 210 Amp			
1999-2000. 50 watts, 2x10 combo, stereo chorus, channel switching, reverb.			
1999-2000		$230	$290
Triple XXX Series Amp			
2001-2009. Made in USA.			
2001-2009	Head, 120w	$490	$615
2001-2009	Super 40, 40w, 1x12	$440	$550
Triumph 60 Combo Amp			
1980s. Tube head, effects loop, reverb, 60 watts, 1x12", multi-stage gain.			
1980s		$150	$190
Triumph 120 Amp			
1989-1990. Tube, 120 watts, 1x12", 3 gain blocks in preamp, low-level post-effects loop, built-in reverb.			
1989-1990		$180	$225
Ultra 60 Amp Head			
1991-1994. 60 watts, all tube, 2 6L6 power, black, black grille.			
1991-1994		$230	$290
Ultra 112 Amp			
1998-2002. 60 watts, 1x12", all tube, 2 6L6 power, black, black grille.			
1998-2002		$225	$280
Ultra 212 Amp			
1998-2002. 60 watts, 2x12".			
1998-2002		$275	$350
Ultra 410 Amp			
1998-2002. 60 watts, 4x10".			
1998-2002		$275	$350
Ultra Plus 120 Amp Head			
1998-2002. 120 watts, all tube.			
1998-2002		$325	$400
ValveKing Series Amp			
2005-present. Tube head, combos and cabs.			
2005-2014	VK100, 100w head	$200	$250
2005-2014	VK112, 50w, 1x12	$225	$280
2005-2014	VK212, 100w, 2x12	$250	$315
Vegas 400 Amp			
1984-late 1980s. 210 watts, 1x15, some prefer as a steel guitar amp.			
1980s		$335	$425
VTM Series Amp			
1987-1993. Vintage Tube Modified series, tube heads, 60 or 120 watts.			
1987-1993	VTM120, 120w	$300	$375
1987-1993	VTM60, 60w	$275	$350
Vypyr Series Amp			
2008-2014. Modeling amp heads and combos, 60 and 120-watt tube and 15, 30, 75 and 100-watt solidstate models. Changes to Vypyr VIP in late '14.			
2008-2014	15w, combo	$60	$75
2008-2014	30w, 1x12 combo	$130	$165
2010	75w, combo	$175	$225
Wiggy 212 Amp			
2001-2008. 100-watt head in mono (2x75-watt in stereo) with matching 2x12" cab, 2 EQ, 5-band sliders, rounded amp head.			
2001-2008		$400	$500

MODEL YEAR	FEATURES	EXC. COND. LOW	HIGH

Penn

1994-present. Tube amps, combos, and cabinets built by Billy Penn, originally in Colts Neck, New Jersey, currently in Long Branch, New Jersey.

Pignose

1972-present. Made in Las Vegas, Nevada. Pignose Industries was started by people associated with the band Chicago, including guitarist Terry Kath, with help from designers Wayne Kimball and Richard Erlund. In '74, it was sold to Chicago's band accountant, who ran it until '82, when ownership passed to the company that made its sturdy, wood cabinets. They also offer guitars and effects.

MODEL YEAR	FEATURES	EXC. COND. LOW	HIGH
7-100 Practice Amp			
1972-present. The original Pignose, 7"x5"x3" battery-powered portable amplifier, 1x5".			
1972-2014		$45	$65
30/60 Amp			
1978-ca.1987. Solidstate, 30 watts, 1x10", master volume.			
1978-1987		$55	$95
60R Studio Reverb Amp			
Solidstate, 30 watts.			
1980		$90	$125
G40V Amp			
2000s. Tubes, 1x10", 40 watts.			
2000s		$150	$185
G60VR Amp			
2000s. Tubes, 1x12", 60 watts.			
2000s		$160	$200
Hog Amps			
2000-present. Battery powered, Hog 20 (20 watts, 6.5" speaker) and Hog 30 (30 watts, 8").			
2000-2014	Hog 20	$45	$65
2000-2014	Hog 30	$50	$70

Plush

Late 1960s-early 1970s. Tuck and roll covered tube amps made by the same company that made Earth Sound Research amps in Farmingdale, New York.

MODEL YEAR	FEATURES	EXC. COND. LOW	HIGH
Tube Amplifiers			
Early 1970s. All tube heads and combos including the 450 Super 2x12" combo, 1000/P1000S head, and 1060S Royal Bass combo.			
1971-1972		$475	$600

Point Blank

2002-2004. Tube amps built by Roy Blankenship in Orlando, Florida before he started his Blankenship brand.

Polytone

1960s-present. Made in North Hollywood, California, Polytone offers compact combo amps, heads, and cabinets and a pickup system for acoustic bass.

MODEL YEAR	FEATURES	EXC. COND. LOW	HIGH
Guitar or Bass Amps			
1980s-present. Various models.			
1980-2014		$250	$425

MODEL		EXC. COND.	
YEAR	FEATURES	LOW	HIGH

Port City

2005-present. Daniel Klein builds his amp heads, combos, and cabinets in Rocky Point, North Carolina.

Premier

Ca.1938-ca.1975, 1990s-2010. Produced by Peter Sorkin Music Company in Manhattan. First radio-sized amplifiers introduced by '38. After World War II, established Multivox subsidiary to manufacture amplifiers ca.'46. By mid-'50s at least, the amps featured lyre grilles. Dark brown/light tan amp covering by '60. By '64 amps covered in brown woodgrain and light tan. Multivox amps were made until around '84.

B-160 Club Bass Amp
1963-1968. 15 to 20 watts, 1x12" Jensen speaker, '60s 2-tone brown styling, 6V6 tubes.

1963-1968		$575	$725

Model 50 Amp
1940s-1960s In '62 this was their entry-level amp, 4 to 5 watts, 1x8" similar to Fender Champ circuit with more of a vertical suitcase-style cab.

1940s-60s		$350	$435

Model 71 Amp
1961-1962. Combo with 1x12" (woofer) and 2 small tweeters, 24 watts. '61 styling with circular speaker baffle protected with metal X frame, 2 tweeter ports on upper baffle, 2-tone light tan and brown, 8 tubes, tremolo. The '62 styling changed to baffle with a slight V at the top, and 2-tone cover.

1961	Round baffle	$800	$1,000
1962	V-baffle	$800	$1,000

Model 76 Amp
1950s-1960s. Suitcase latchable cabinet that opens out into 2 wedges, 2-tone brown, lyre grille, 1x12".

1950s-60s		$800	$1,000

Model 88 Multivox Amp
1962. Multi-purpose combo amp, organ-stop control panel, 1x15" woofer with 2 tweeters, vertical suitcase cab, 2-tone cover, classic circular speaker baffle with X brace, 10 tubes, top-of-the-line in '62 catalog.

1962		$800	$1,000

Model 88N Amp
1950s-1961. Rectangular suitcase cabinet, 2-tone tan and brown, Premier and lyre logo, 25 watts, 1x12".

1950s-1961		$800	$1,000

Model 100R Amp
1960s. Combo amp, 1x12", reverb and tremolo.

1960s		$800	$1,000

Model 110 Amp
1962. 12-watt 1x10 student combo, lyre grille logo, 2-tone cab.

1962		$515	$650

Model 120 Amp
1958-1963. 12-watt 1x12" combo, tremolo, 2-tone brown cab.

1958-1963		$575	$725

Model 200 Rhythm Bass Amp
1962. 1x15" combo bass amp.

1962		$575	$725

MODEL		EXC. COND.	
YEAR	FEATURES	LOW	HIGH

T-8 Twin-8 Amp
1950s, 1964-1966. 20 watts, 2x8", tremolo, reverb.

1950s		$1,000	$1,250
1964-1966		$900	$1,150

T-12 Twin-12 Amp
1958-1962. Early reverb amp with tremolo, 2x12", rectangular cabinet typical of twin 12 amps (Dano and Fender), brown cover.

1958-1959		$1,100	$1,375
1960-1962		$1,000	$1,250

Pritchard Amps

2004-present. Professional grade, production/custom, single and two-channel amps and cabinets built by Eric Pritchard in Berkeley Springs, West Virginia.

Pyramid Car Audio

2008-present. Inexpensive student models, imported.

Quantum

1980s. Economy amps distributed by DME, Indianapolis, Indiana.

Q Terminator Economy Amps

1980s. Economy solidstate amps ranging from 12 to 25 watts and 1x6" to 1x12".

1980s		$25	$30

Quidley Guitar Amplifiers

Intermediate and professional grade, production/custom, tube guitar amp heads, combos and cabinets built by Ed Quidley in Wilmington, North Carolina, starting in 2006.

Quilter

2011-present. Patrick Quilter builds his intermediate and professional grade, production, portable guitar amps in Costa Mesa, California.

Quinn

2005-present. Professional and premium grade, production/custom, amps and cabinets built by Shadwell J. Damron III in Vancouver, Washington.

Randall

1960s-present. Randall Instruments was originally out of California and is now a division of U.S. Music Corp. They have offered a range of tube and solidstate combo amps, heads and cabinets over the years.

Guitar and Bass Amps
1980s-present. Mostly solidstate amps.

1980s-2014	Intermediate-grade	$260	$325
1980s-2014	Student-grade	$100	$130

Rastop Designs

2002-present. Professional grade, custom amps built by Alexander Rastopchin in Long Island City, New York. He also builds effects.

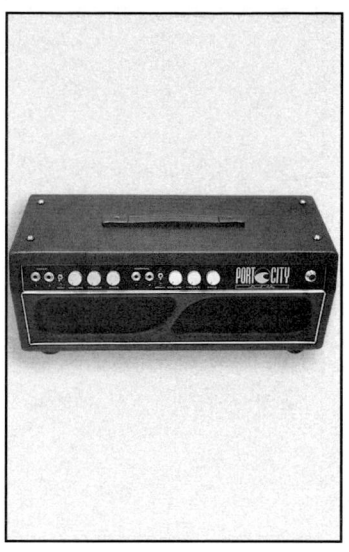

Port City Dual Fifty

Quilter Open Twelve

Randall Hammett LTD 2008

AMPS

Reason SM25

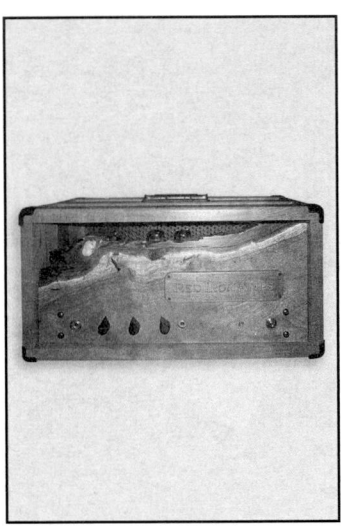

Red Iron Mil Spec

Reinhardt Titan Combo
Rob Bernstein

MODEL YEAR	FEATURES	EXC. COND. LOW	HIGH

Rat Fink

Early 2000s. Solidstate amp line from Lace Music Products. They also sold guitars and basses under this brand and offered amps under the Mooneyes and Lace brands.

Realistic

Radio Shack offered a couple made-in-the-U.S. combo tube amps in the '60s, including the Entertainer 34 with a flip down record turntable in the back! Their radio and stereo gear were also branded Realistic.

Reason

2007-present. Professional grade, production/custom, amps and cabinets built by Obeid Khan and Anthony Bonadio in St. Louis, Missouri.

Red Bear

1994-1997. Tube amps designed by Sergei Novikov and built in St. Petersburg, Russia. Red Bear amps were distributed in the U.S. under a joint project between Gibson and Novik, Ltd. Novik stills builds amps under other brands.

MK 60 Lead Tube Amp
1994-1997. Head with 4x12" half stack, Red Bear logo on amp and cab.

1994-1997		$625	$775

MK 100 Full Stack
1994-1997. 100 watts, 2x4x12".

1994-1997		$900	$1,125

Red Iron Amps

2001-present. Paul Sanchez builds his tube amp heads in Lockhart, Texas.

RedPlate Amps

2006-present. Professional and premium grade, production/custom, guitar amplifiers built in Phoenix, Arizona by Henry Heistand.

Reeves Amplification

2002-present. Started by Bill Jansen, Reeves builds tube amps, combos, and cabinets in Cincinnati, Ohio, based on the classic British designs of Dan Reeves.

Regal

Ca.1895-1966, 1987-present. The original Regal company distributed instruments built by them and others.

Gibson EH Amp
1936. Rare private-branded Gibson EH amp, 1x10", single control, alligator tweed.

1936		$515	$650

Reinhardt

2004-2012. Bob Reinhardt builds his professional grade, production/custom, guitar and bass amps and cabinets in Lynchburg, Virginia. He also builds effects pedals.

Resonant Amplifiers

2007-present. Owners Wes Kuhnley and Peter Bregman build their professional grade, vacuum tube guitar and hi-fi amps in Minneapolis, Minnesota. They also build the Field Effects.

Retro-King Amplifier Company

2004-present. Tube combo and head amps built by Chuck Dean in Marcellus, New York.

Revenge Amps

1996-present. Greg Perrine builds intermediate grade, production/custom, guitar amplifiers and attenuators in Conway, Arkansas. He also imports a line of amps.

Reverend

1996-present. Joe Naylor started building amps under the Naylor brand in '94. In '96 he left Naylor to build guitars under the Reverend brand. From '01 to '05, Reverend offered tube amps, combos, and cabinets built in Warren, Michigan, that Naylor co-designed with Dennis Kager.

Rex

1950s-1960s. Tube amps built by the Lamberti Bros. Co. in Melbourne, Australia. They also built guitars. In the 1920s-1940s, Gretsch has an unrelated line of guitars with that brand.

Reynolds Valveart

1997-present. Professional and premium grade, production/custom, amps and cabinets built by Peter Reynolds in Windsor, Australia.

Rickenbacker

1931-present. Rickenbacker made amps from the beginning of the company up to the late '80s. Rickenbacker had many different models, from the small early models that were usually sold as a guitar/amp set, to the large, very cool, Transonic.

E-12 Amp
1963. 1x12" combo with tremolo depth and speed, volume, and on-off tone knobs.

1963		$490	$615

Electro-Student Amp
Late-1940s. Typical late-'40s vertical combo cabinet, 1x12" speaker, lower power using 5 tubes, bottom mounted chassis, dark gray leatherette cover.

1948-1949		$465	$580

Hi Fi Model 98
1956. Tube amp, long horizontal cab with 3 speakers, Rickenbacker Hi Fi and Model 98 logo on back panel, blond cover, wheat grille cloth.

1956		$1,075	$1,350

Model B-9E Amp
1960s. 1x12" combo, 4 knobs, gray.

1960s		$575	$725

Model M-8 Amp
1950s-1960s. Gray, 1x8".

1950s-60s		$430	$540

The *Vintage Guitar Price Guide* shows low to high values for items in all-original excellent condition, and, where applicable, with original case or cover.

MODEL YEAR	FEATURES	EXC. COND. LOW	HIGH

Model M-11 Amp
1950s. 12-15 watts, 1x12", 2x6V6 power. There was a different M-11 offered in the 1930s.

1950s		$625	$775

Model M-12 Amp
1950s. 12-15 watts, 1x12", M-12 logo on back panel, brown leatherette. There was a different M-12 offered in the 1930s.

1950s		$675	$850

Model M-14A Amp
Late 1950s-early 1960s. 1x12 combo, mid-power 2x6V6, dual channel with vibrato, rough-brown tolex cover.

1950s-60s		$675	$850

Model M-15 Amp
1950s-Early 1960s. 1x15" combo, 35 watts, 2 x 6L6 power tubes, model name on top panel.

1950s-60s		$700	$875

Model M-30 EK-O-Sound Amp
1961. Recording echo chamber and amp in 1x12 combo format, 11 tubes, gray grille and cover, very limited production.

1961		$3,300	$4,125

Professional Model 200-A Amp
1938. 15 watts, was sold with the Vibrola Spanish guitar.

1938		$475	$600

RB30 Amp
1986. Bass combo amp, 30 watts, tilted control panel, 1x12".

1986		$205	$255

RB60 Amp
1986. Bass combo amp, 60 watts, tilted control panel, 1x15".

1986		$230	$290

RB120 Amp
1986. Bass combo amp, 120 watts, tilted control panel, 1x15".

1986		$260	$325

Supersonic Model B-16 Amp
1960s. 4x10" speakers, gray cover.

1960s		$725	$900

Supersonic Model B-22 Amp Head
1960s. Tube head, gray cover.

1960s		$570	$715

TR7 Amp
1978-1982. Solidstate, 7 watts, 1x10", tremolo.

1978-1982		$125	$160

TR14 Amp
1978-ca.1982. Solidstate, 1x10", reverb, distortion.

1978-1982		$125	$160

TR25 Amp
1979-1982. Solidstate, 1x12" combo, reverb, tremolo, distortion.

1979-1982		$300	$375

TR35B Bass Amp
1978-ca.1982. Solidstate, mid-power, 1x15".

1978-1982		$300	$375

TR75G Amp
1978-ca.1982. 75 watts, 2x12", 2 channels.

1978-1982		$325	$400

TR75SG Amp
1978-ca.1983. 1x10" and 1x15" speakers.

1978-1982		$325	$400

TR100G Amp
1978-ca.1982. Solidstate, 100 watts with 4x12", 2 channels.

1978-1982		$350	$435

Transonic TS100 Amp
1967-1973. Trapezoid shaped 2x12" combo, solidstate, 100 watts, Rick-O-Select

1967-1973		$1,225	$1,550

Risson
1970-1984, 2012-present. Bob Rissi builds his intermediate, professional and premium grade, production/custom, guitar and bass amplifiers in Placentia, California. From 1970-84 they were built in Santa Ana.

Rivera
1985-present. Amp designer and builder Paul Rivera modded and designed amps for other companies before starting his own line in California. He offers heads, combos, and cabinets. He also builds guitar pedals.

Chubster 40 Amp
2000-present. 40 watts, 1x12" combo, burgundy tolex, light grille.

2000-2014		$700	$875

Clubster 25 Amp
2005-present. 25 watts, 1x10", 6V6.

2005-2014		$550	$675

Clubster 45 Amp
2005-present. 45 watts, 1x12" combo.

2005-2014		$700	$875

Fandango 112 Combo Amp
2001-present. 55 watts, 2xEL34, 1x12".

2001-2014		$700	$875

Fandango 212 Combo Amp
2001-present. 55 or 100 watts, 2x12" tube amp.

2001-2014		$800	$1,000

Jake Studio Combo Amp
1997. 55 watts, 1x12", reverb and effects loop.

1997		$700	$875

Knucklehead 55 Amp
1994-2002. 55-watt amp head, replaced by reverb model.

1994-2002		$575	$725

Knucklehead 100 Amp
1994-2002. 100-watt amp head, replaced by reverb model.

1994-2002		$625	$775

Knucklehead Reverb 112 Amp
2003-2007. 55 watts, 1x12" amp combo, reverb.

2003-2007		$800	$1,000

Los Lobottom/Sub 1 Amp
1999-2004. 1x12" cabinet with 300-watt powered 12" subwoofer.

1999-2004		$400	$500

M-60 Amp Head
1990-2009. 60 watts.

1990-2009		$500	$625

Reverend Goblin 5-15

Rickenbacker Model M-11

Rivera Clubster 45

AMPS

To get the most from this book, be sure to read "Using *The Guide*" in the introduction.

Rivera Suprema R-55 112

Rocktron V50D

Roland AC-100

MODEL YEAR	FEATURES	EXC. COND. LOW	HIGH
M-60 112 Combo Amp			
1989-2009. 60 watts, 1x12".			
1989-2009		$575	$725
M-100 Amp Head			
1990-2009. 100 watts.			
1990-2009		$550	$675
M-100 212 Combo Amp			
1990-2009. 100 watts, 2x12" combo.			
1990-2009		$650	$800
Pubster 25 Amp			
2005-present. 25 watts, 1x10".			
2013		$375	$475
Pubster 45 Amp			
2005-present. 45 watts, 1x12".			
2005-2014 .		$400	$500
Quiana Combo Amp			
2000-2014. Combo, 55 watts.			
2000-2014	1x12	$850	$1,050
2000-2014	2x12	$950	$1,175
2000-2014	4x10	$950	$1,200
R-30 112 Combo Amp			
1993-2007. 30 watts, 1x12", compact cab, black tolex cover, gray-black grille.			
1993-2007		$650	$825
R-100 212 Combo Amp			
1993-2007. 100 watts, 2x12".			
1993-2007		$750	$950
Sedona 55 Combo Amp			
1997-present. For electric and acoustic guitars, 55 watts, 1x12".			
1997-2014		$875	$1,100
Suprema R-55 112/115 Combo Amp			
2000-present. Tube amp, 55 watts, 1x12" (still available) or 1x15" ('00-'01).			
2000-2014	1x12 or 1x15	$725	$900
TBR-1 Amp			
1985-1999. First Rivera production model, rack mount, 60 watts.			
1985-1999		$650	$825
Venus Series			
2007-present. Series includes the 7/15-watt Venus 3 combo (1x10 or 1x12), and the 15-watt Venus 5 and 35-watt Venus 6, both offered as combos (1x12, 2x12) and heads with cabs (1x12, 2x12).			
2007-2014	Venus 3, 1x10	$750	$950
2007-2014	Venus 5, 1x12	$800	$1,000
2007-2014	Venus 6, 1x12	$850	$1,075
2007-2014	Venus 6, 2x12	$950	$1,200

Roccaforte Amps

1993-present. Tube amps, combos, and cabinets built by Doug Roccaforte in San Clemente, California.

Rocktron

1980s-present. Tube and solidstate amp heads, combos and cabinets. Rocktron is a division of GHS Strings and also offers stomp boxes and preamps.

MODEL YEAR	FEATURES	EXC. COND. LOW	HIGH
Rogue			

2001-present. They offered student-level solid-state import (Korea) compact amps up to around '06. They also offer guitars, basses, lap steels, mandolins, banjos, ukuleles and effects.

MODEL YEAR	FEATURES	EXC. COND. LOW	HIGH
Small Solidstate Amps			
2001-2006. Various models.			
2001-2006		$35	$100

Roland

Japan's Roland Corporation's products include amplifiers and keyboards and, under the Boss brand, effects.

MODEL YEAR	FEATURES	EXC. COND. LOW	HIGH
Acoustic Chorus Series Amp			
1995-present. Number in model indicates wattage (i.e. AC-60 = 60 watts).			
1995-2009	AC-100, 1x12", 2x5"	$375	$475
1995-2014	AC-60, 2x6"	$375	$475
1995-2014	AC-90, 2x8"	$375	$475
Bolt 60 Amp			
Early 1980s. Solidstate/tube, 1x12".			
1980s		$235	$295
Cube Series Amp			
1978-present. Number in model indicates wattage (i.e. Cube-15X = 15 watts).			
1978-1982	100, 1x12"	$200	$250
1978-1982	20, 1x8"	$125	$155
1978-1983	40, 1x10"	$150	$185
1978-1983	60, 1x12"	$200	$250
1978-1983	60B, 1x12"	$200	$250
2000-2009	30 Bass, 1x10"	$150	$185
2000s	80GX, 1x12	$300	$375
2000s	80XL, 1x12	$250	$315
2000s	BC30	$150	$185
2006-2010	30X, 1x10"	$150	$185
2006-2013	15X, 1x8"	$125	$155
2006-2013	20X, 1x8"	$125	$155
2008-2013	80X, 1x12"	$175	$200
Jazz Chorus Series Amp			
1975-present. Includes the JC-50 (50 watts, 1x12"), JC-55 (50 watts, 2x8"), JC-77 (80 watts, 2x10"), JC-90 (90 watts, 2x10") and JC-120 (120 watts, 2x12" and 4x12").			
1975-2014	JC-120, 2x12"	$465	$580
1980s	JC-50, 1x12"	$260	$325
1987-1994	JC-55, 2x8"	$285	$355
1987-1994	JC-77, 2x10"	$310	$390
1990s	JC-120, 4x12"	$540	$675
1990s	JC-90, 2x10"	$335	$420
Micro Cube Amp			
2000-present. Compact AC power or battery, 2 watts, 1x5".			
2000-2014		$85	$105
Spirit Series Amp			
1982-1989. Compact, model number indicates wattage.			
1982-1989	Spirit 30, 1x12	$105	$130
1982-1989	Spirit 40A, combo	$105	$130
1982-1989	Spirit 50, combo	$130	$165
Studio Bass Amp			
1979		$205	$255

MODEL YEAR	FEATURES	EXC. COND. LOW	HIGH

VGA3 V-Guitar Amp
2003-2009. GK digital modeling amp, 50 watts, 1x12" combo.

2003-2009		$260	$325

VGA5 V-Guitar Amp
2001-2004. GK digital modeling amp, 65 watts, 1x12".

2001-2004		$285	$355

VGA7 V-Guitar Amp
2000-2009. 65 + 65 watts, 2x12", digital modeling with analog-style controls.

2000-2009		$310	$390

S.S. Maxwell
See info under Danelectro.

Sadowsky
1980-present. From '05 to '07, luthier Roger Sadowsky built a bass tube amp head in Brooklyn, New York. He also builds basses and guitars.

Sam Ash
1960s 1970s. Sam Ash Music was founded by Sam Ash (formerly Ashkynase) in Brooklyn, New York, in 1924, and by '66 there were about four Ash stores. During the '60s they private branded their own amp line, was built by Jess Oliver of Oliver Amps and based upon Oliver's Ampeg designs.

Sam Ash Mark II Pro Combo Amp
1960s. 2x12" with reverb combo amp.

1960s		$570	$715

SamAmp
2004-present. Intermediate and professional grade, boutique amps built by Sam Timberlake in Vestavia Hills, Alabama.

Sano
1951-ca. 1980. Combos, heads and cabinets made in three factories around New Jersey. Founded by Joseph Zonfrilli, Louis Iorio, and Nick Sano, initially offering accordion pickups, amplifiers, and all-electric accordions. Sano patented his accordion pickup in '44 and also developed a highly acclaimed stereophonic pickup accordion and matching amp. By '66 the Sano Corporation augmented their all-tube accordion amps with new solidstate circuitry models. In the mid-'60s they offered a new line of amps specifically designed for the guitar and bass market. Sano amps are generally low-gain, low power amplifiers. They also marketed reverb units and guitars.

Compact Combo Amp

1960s	160R, 15w, 1x12"	$415	$520
1960s	Sano-ette	$335	$420

Satellite Amplifiers
2004-present. Professional and premium grade, production/custom, tube amps, preamps and cabinets built by Adam Grimm in San Diego, California. He also builds effects.

Savage
1994-present. Tube combos, amp heads and cabinets built by Jeff Krumm at Savage Audio, in Savage, Minnesota.

Sceptre
1960s. Canadian-made. Sceptre script logo on upper left side of grille ('60s Fender-style and placement).

Signet Amp
1960s. Low power, 1x10", Class-A 6V6 power.

1960s		$250	$310

Schaller
1945-present. The German guitar accessory company's main products in the late '50s were tube amps and they had solid-state amps in the '60s.

Schertler
Made in Switzerland, model logo (e.g. David model) on front, intermediate to professional grade, modern designs for modern applications.

SDG Vintage
2003-present. Intermediate and professional grade, production/custom, tube amps, combos and heads built by Steven Gupta in Bristow, Virginia.

Selmer
1930s-late 1970s. The Selmer UK distributor offered mid- to high-level amps starting as early as 1935 and by the '50s was one of the strongest European brands of amps.

Constellation 14 Amp
1965. Single speaker combo, 14 watts, gray snakeskin tolex-type cover.

1965		$1,750	$2,200

Futurama Corvette Amp
1960s. Class A low power 1x8", 4 tubes, volume and tone controls, plus amplitude and speed tremolo controls, large script Futurama logo on front of amp, Futurama Corvette and Selmer logo on top panel.

1960s		$775	$975

Mark 2 Treble and Bass Amp Head
1960s. About 30 watts (2xEL34s), requires power line transformer for U.S. use, large Selmer logo on grille.

1960s		$1,025	$1,275

Thunderbird Twin 30 Amp
1960s. 30 watts, 2x12".

1962-1963		$4,125	$5,150
1965		$3,300	$4,125

Thunderbird Twin 50 Amp
1960s. 50 watts, 2x12".

1964		$4,125	$5,150
1968		$2,475	$3,100

Truvoice Amp
1961. Truvoice and Selectortone logo on top-mounted chasis, 30-watt combo, 1x15 Goodmans speaker, 2xEL34 power tubes, tremolo, 6 push button Selectortone Automatic.

1961		$2,075	$2,600

SamAmp VAC 40 Series

Satellite Niveus

SDG Vintage Tweed Twin High Power

AMPS

Shaw Retro-Mod 15

Sherlock Angry Ant

Siegmund Diamond

MODEL YEAR	FEATURES	EXC. COND. LOW	HIGH

Zodiac Twin 30 Amp
1964-1971. Combo amp, gray snakeskin tolex cover.

1964-1971		$2,900	$3,625

Sewell
1998-2008. Doug Sewell built his tube combo and head amps in Texas. He currently is the senior amp designer for Paul Reed Smith.

Seymour Duncan
Pickup maker Seymour Duncan, located in Santa Barbara, California, offered a line of amps from around 1984 to '95.

84-40/84-50 Amp
1989-1995. Tube combo, 2 switchable channels, 1x12", includes the 84-40 ('89-'91, 40 watts) and the 84-50 ('91-'95, 50 watts).

1989-1995	84-40 or 84-50	$235	$295

Bass 300 x 2 Amp
1986-1987. Solidstate, 2 channels (300 or 600 watts), EQ, contour boost switches, effects loop.

1986-1987		$235	$295

Bass 400 Amp
1986-1987. Solidstate, 400 watts, EQ, contour boost, balanced line output, effects loop.

1986-1987		$205	$255

Convertible Amp
1986-1995. 60-watt; dual-channel; effects loop; Accutronics spring reverb; 3-band EQ.

1986-1987	Head only	$285	$355
1988-1995	Combo	$335	$425

KTG-2075 Stereo Amp
1989-1993. Part of the King Tone Generator Series, 2 channels with 75 watts per channel.

1989-1993		$205	$255

SG Systems
1970s. A Division of the Chicago Musical Instrument Company (CMI), who also owned Gibson Guitars. Gibson outsourced amplifier production from Kalamazoo to CMI in '67 and CMI (Chicago) continued for a year or two with Gibson-branded amplifiers. In the early '70s CMI introduced the SG Systems brand of hybrid amplifiers, which had a tube power section and a solidstate preamp section. CMI was trying to stay modern with SG Systems by introducing futuristic features like the Notch Shift which would quickly switch between popular rock sounds and mellow jazz delivery. SG amps have a large SG logo on the front baffle and were built with metal corners. Amplifiers have similar power specs; for example, the models issued in '73 all were rated with 100-watt RMS with 200-watts peak music power, so models were based on different speaker configurations.

SG Series Amp

1970s	SG-115, 1x15"	$300	$375
1970s	SG-212, 2x12"	$330	$415
1970s	SG-215 Bass, 2x15"	$330	$415
1970s	SG-410, 4x10"	$330	$415
1970s	SG-610, 6x10"	$360	$450
1970s	SG-812 PA	$265	$330

MODEL YEAR	FEATURES	EXC. COND. LOW	HIGH

Shaw
2008-present. Custom/production, intermediate and professional grade, guitar amp heads and cabinets built by Kevin Shaw in Lebanon, Tennessee.

Sherlock Amplifiers
1990-present. Dale Sherlock builds his intermediate to premium grade, production/custom, tube guitar amps and cabinets in Melbourne Victoria, Australia.

Sherwood
Late 1940s-early 1950s. Amps made by Danelectro for Montgomery Ward. There are also Sherwood guitars and lap steels made by Kay.

Sho-Bud
Introduced and manufactured by the Baldwin/Gretsch factory in 1970. Distributed by Kustom/Gretsch in the '80s. Models include D-15 Model 7838, S-15 Model 7836, Twin Tube Model 7834, and Twin Trans Model 7832.

Compactra 100 Amp
1960s. Hybrid tube, 45 watts, 1x12".

1960s		$500	$625

D15 Double Amp
Introduced in 1970. Solidstate, 100 watts. 2 channels 1x15" JBL speaker.

1970s		$450	$575

S15 Single Amp
Introduced in 1972. Like D15, but with single channel.

1970s		$325	$400

Sho-Bass Amp
Introduced in 1972. 100 watts, 1x15", solidstate combo, black grille, black vinyl cover.

1970s		$325	$400

Twin Trans Amp
Introduced in 1972. 100 watts, solidstate combo, 2x12", reverb, black vinyl cover, dark grille, Sho-Bud script logo front upper right.

1970s		$450	$575

Twin Tube Amp
Introduced in 1972. 100 watt tube combo, 4 6L6s, 2x12", reverb, black vinyl cover, dark grille.

1970s		$575	$725

Siegmund Guitars & Amplifiers
1993-present. Chris Siegmund builds his tube amp heads, combos and cabinets in Los Angeles, California. He founded the company in Seattle, moving it to Austin, Texas for '95-'97. He also builds effects pedals and guitars.

Silvertone
1941-ca.1970, present. Brand used by Sears. All Silvertone amps were supplied by American companies up to around '66.

Special thanks to Brian Conner for his assistance with Silvertone amplifier identification.

MODEL YEAR	FEATURES	EXC. COND. LOW	HIGH

Model 1300 Amp
1948. Vertical combo cab, treble-clef logo on grille, 2-tone, 3 inputs, 2 controls.

| 1948 | | $465 | $580 |

Model 1304 Amp
1949-1951. 18 watts, 1x12, 2x6L6 power tubes, 2-tone leatherette cover, round speaker baffle hole, volume, treble, bass and tremolo control knobs, becomes Model 1344.

| 1949-1951 | | $440 | $550 |

Model 1330 Amp
1954-1957. Introduced in Sears Fall '54 catalog, 3 tubes (with rectifier), 1x6", wide-panel 13x13.75x7.5" cab in tan artificial leather, 9 lbs., replaced Model 1339 at the same price but with new wide-panel style, small Silvertone logo above the grille, replaced in '58 by Model 1390 Silvertone Meteor.

| 1954-1957 | | $185 | $230 |

Model 1331 Amp
1954-1957. Made by Danelectro, 14 lbs., 1x8" student combo, 3 tubes (with rectifier), 1 volume, 1 tone, 2 inputs, tan tweed-effect cover with brown alligator trim, large-thread wheat-gold grille, brown metal control panel.

| 1954-1957 | | $205 | $256 |

Model 1333 Amp
1954-1957. Made by Danelectro, 23 lbs., 1x12" combo, 2x6V6 power, 5 tubes (with rectifier), 2 volumes, 1 tone, 3 inputs, 2-control vibrato, tan tweed-effect cover with brown alligator trim, large-thread wheat-gold grille, brown metal control panel.

| 1954-1957 | | $465 | $580 |

Model 1334 Amp
1954-1957. Made by Danelectro, 29 lbs., heavy-duty 1x12" combo, 6 tubes (with rectifier), 2 volumes, 2 tones, 3 inputs, 2-control vibrato, tan tweed-effect cover with brown alligator trim, large-thread wheat-gold grille, brown metal control panel.

| 1954-1957 | | $515 | $645 |

Model 1335 Amp
1954-1957. Made by Danelectro, 99 lbs., heavy-duty 1x15" combo, 6 tubes (with rectifier), 2 volumes, 2 tones, 4 inputs, 2-control vibrato, tan tweed-effect cover with brown alligator trim, large-thread wheat-gold grille, brown metal control panel.

| 1954-1957 | | $565 | $705 |

Model 1336 (Twin Twelve) Amp
1954-1957. Made by Danelectro, 26.75x17.5x9.25" cab, 45 lbs., 2x12" combo, 4x6L6 powe tubes, 3 volumes, 2 tones, 4 inputs, 2-control vibrato, tan tweed-effect cover with brown alligator trim, large-thread wheat-gold grille, brown metal control panel.

| 1954-1957 | | $620 | $775 |

Model 1337 "Wide Range Eight Speaker" Amp
1956. Odd-looking suitcase cab that opens into 2 separate speaker baffles each containing 4x8" speakers, 2 preamps, 2 channels with separate controls for volume, bass and treble, 2-control vibrato, 42 lbs.

| 1956 | | $515 | $645 |

Model 1339 Amp
Ca.1952-1954. Sears lowest-priced amp, 3 tubes (with rectifier), 1x6", 1 input, 1 knob, maroon artificial leather cover over 10.5x8x5" verticle cab, script Silvertone logo on low right grille, 7 lbs.

| 1952-1954 | | $180 | $225 |

Model 1340 Amp
Ca.1952-1954. Sears second lowest-priced amp, 3 tubes (with rectifier), 1x6", 2 inputs, 1 knob, brown and white imitation leather cover over 15x12x8.5" verticle cab, script Silvertone logo on low right grille, 14 lbs.

| 1952-1954 | | $205 | $255 |

Model 1342 Streamlined Amp
Ca.1952-1954. Sears third lowest-priced amp, 4 tubes (with rectifier), 1x12", 3 inputs, 2 knobs, green and beige imitation leather cover over 16x19x7.25" slanted-side cab, script Silvertone logo on low right grille, 23 lbs.

| 1952-1954 | | $410 | $515 |

Model 1344 Amp
1950-1954. Retro-styled vertical 22.5x15.5x9.5" cab with round speaker baffle hole, 1x12" combo, first Silvertone built-in vibrato, 6 tubes (with rectifier), 3 inputs, 3 controls (treble, bass, volume) plus vibrato control, maroon imitation leather cover with sports-stripe around the bottom, 33 lbs., script Silvertone logo low right side of cab.

| 1952-1954 | | $465 | $580 |

Model 1346 (Twin Twelve) Amp
Ca.1952-1954. Danelectro-made, brown control panel, 2x12", 4 6L6s, vibrato, leather handle, tan smooth leatherette cover, 2 speaker baffle openings.

| 1952-1954 | | $620 | $775 |

Model 1390 Meteor Amp
1958-1959. Renamed from Model 1330, Meteor logo on front panel, 1x6" practice amp, 3 tubes (with rectifier), tan simulated leather cover, in '60 renamed Model 1430 (but no longer a Meteor).

| 1958-1959 | | $205 | $255 |

Model 1391 Amp
1958-1959. Modern-style cab, 3 tubes (with rectifier), 5 watts, 1x8".

| 1958-1959 | | $285 | $355 |

Model 1392 Amp
1958-1959. Modern-style cab, 6 tubes (with rectifier), 10 watts, 1x12", vibrato.

| 1958-1959 | | $410 | $515 |

Model 1393 Amp
1958-1959. Modern-style cab, 7 tubes (with rectifier), 15 watts, heavy-duty 1x12", vibrato.

| 1958-1959 | | $410 | $515 |

Model 1396 Two-Twelve Amp
1958-1959. Script Two-Twelve logo on lower left front and Silvertone logo on lower right front, 50 watts, 2x12", 4x6L6 power tubes, 9 tubes (with rectifier), vibrato, 26.75x17.5x9.25" with gray and metallic fleck cover, white grille, 45 lbs.

| 1958-1959 | | $620 | $775 |

Model 1420 Amp
1968. Tube-powered, 5 watts, 1x8" student combo.

| 1968 | | $155 | $195 |

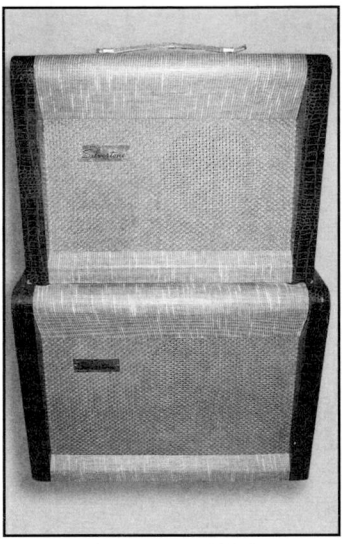

Silvertone 1331

Silvertone 1392

Silvertone 1464
Dave McDermott

AMPS

Silvertone 1481
Luke Single

Silvertone Model 1482

Simms-Watts Super PA-200

MODEL YEAR	FEATURES	EXC. COND. LOW	HIGH

Model 1421 Amp
1968. Tube-powered, 10 watts, 1x8" combo, covered in dark olive vinyl.

1968		$180	$230

Model 1422 Amp
1968. Tube-powered, 40 watts, 1x12" combo, covered in dark olive vinyl.

1968		$335	$420

Model 1423 Amp
1968. Solidstate, 125 watts, 2x12" cab, 55 lbs., dark olive.

1968		$360	$450

Model 1425 Amp
1968. Solidstate, 200 watts, 6x10" cab, 86 lbs., dark olive.

1968		$360	$450

Model 1426 Amp
1968. Solidstate, 250 watts, 6x15" cab, slide switches instead of control knobs, automatic E-tone for tuning, casters for 149 lb. head and cab.

1968		$360	$450

Model 1428 Amp
1968. Solidstate, 60 watts, 1x15" cab, 36 lbs., dark olive.

1968		$310	$390

Model 1430 Amp
1959-1966. Silvertone's lowest-price model, 3 tubes, 1x6", previously called Model 1390 Meteor, and prior to that named Model 1330, retro cab basically unchanged since first introduced in '54.

1959-1966		$205	$255

Model 1431 Amp
1959-1961. 5 watts, 1x8", overhanging-top wrap-around grille cab, 3 tubes (with rectifier), light gray cover with white grille.

1959-1961		$205	$255

Model 1431 Bass Amp
1968. Solidstate, 200 watts, 6x12" cab, 91 lbs., dark olive.

1968		$465	$580

Model 1432 Amp
1959-1961. 10 watts, 1x12", vibrato, overhanging-top wrap-around grille cab, 6 tubes (with rectifier), dark gray tweed-effect cover with white grille.

1959-1961		$415	$520

Model 1433 Amp
1959-1961. 15 watts, 1x15", vibrato, overhanging-top wrap-around grille cab, 7 tubes (with rectifier), gray with metallic fleck cover with white grille.

1959-1961		$465	$580

Model 1434 Twin Twelve Amp
1959-1961. 50 watts using 4x6L6 power, 2x12" combo, vibrato, 2 channels each with volume, bass and treble controls, black cover with gold-colored trim.

1959-1961		$620	$775

Model 1459 Amp
1960s. Student tube amp, 3 watts, 1x8", black vinyl, square cab, 1 tone, 1 volume, 1 channel, 2 inputs.

1967-1968		$205	$255

Model 1463 Bass Amp
1967-1968. Solidstate, 1x15", piggyback, 60 lbs., reverb, tremolo.

1967-1968		$310	$390

MODEL YEAR	FEATURES	EXC. COND. LOW	HIGH

Model 1464 Amp
1967-1968. Solidstate, 100 watts, 2x12", piggyback, 60 lbs., reverb, tremolo, gray vinyl cover.

1967-1968		$375	$470

Model 1465 Amp
1966-1968. Solidstate, piggyback, 150 watts, 6x10", reverb, tremolo, gray vinyl cover, replaces Model 1485.

1966-1968		$465	$580

Model 1466 Bass Amp
1966-1968. Solidstate, 150 watts, 6x10", gray vinyl cover.

1966-1968		$465	$580

Model 1471 Amp
1961-1963. 5 watts, 1x8", 3 tubes, 1 volume, 1 tone, 2 inputs, black leathette cover with white grille.

1961-1963		$310	$390

Model 1472 Amp
1960s. 10 watts, 2 6V6s provide mid-level power, 1x12", front controls mounted vertically on front right side, black cover with silver grille, large stationary handle, tremolo.

1961-1963		$465	$580

Model 1473 Bass Amp
1961-1963. Designed for bass or accordion, 25 watts, 1x15" combo, 6 tubes (with rectifier), 2 channels, 4 inputs, 19x29x9" cab, 43 lbs., black leatherette with white grille.

1961-1963		$620	$775

Model 1474 Twin Twelve Amp
1961-1963. Silvertone's first reverb amp, 50 watts, 4x6L6 power, 10 tubes (with rectifier), 2x12" combo, 2 control vibrato with dual remote footswitch, 2 channels each with bass, treble, and volume, 4 inputs, ground switch, standby switch, 19x29x9" combo cab, 54 lbs., black leatherette with silver grille.

1961-1963		$825	$1,030

Model 1481 Amp
1963-1968. Compact student amp, 5 watts, 1x8", 3 tubes (with rectifier), volume and tone controls, gray leatherette cover with white grille, replaces Model 1471.

1963-1968		$325	$400

Model 1482 Amp
1960s. 15 watts, 1x12", 6 tubes, control panel mounted on right side vertically, tremolo, gray leatherette.

1963-1968		$490	$615

Model 1483 Bass Amp
1963-1966. 23 watts, 1x15" piggyback tube amp, gray tolex and gray grille.

1963-1966		$575	$725

Model 1484 Twin Twelve Amp
1963-1966. 60 watts, 2x12" piggyback tube amp, tremolo and reverb, gray cover with light grille.

1963-1966		$825	$1,030

Model 1485 Amp
1963-1965. 120 watts, 6x10" (Jensen C-10Q) piggyback, 10 tubes with 5 silicon rectifiers, 2 channels, reverb, tremolo, charcoal-gray tolex-style cover, white grille, replaced in '66 by solidstate Model 1465.

1963-1965		$1,210	$1,525

MODEL		EXC. COND.	
YEAR	FEATURES	LOW	HIGH

Model 4707 Organ Amp
1960s. Interesting '60s family room style cabinet with legs, 45-watt tube amp with vibrato, 1x12", front controls, could be used for organ, stereo, or record player turntable.

1960s		$385	$480

Simms-Watts
Late 1960s-1970s. Tube amp heads, combos, PA heads and cabinets made in London, England. Similar to Marshall and HiWatt offerings of the era.

Skip Simmons
1990-present. Custom and production tube combo amps built by Skip Simmons in Loma Rica, California.

Skrydstrup R&D
1997-present. Production/custom, premium grade, amps and cabinets built by Steen Skrydstrup in Denmark. He also builds effects.

Sligo Amps
2004-present. Intermediate and professional grade, production/custom, amps built by Steven Clark in Leesburg, Virginia.

SMF
Mid-1970s. Amp head and cabinets from Dallas Music Industries, Ltd., of Mahwah, New Jersey. Offered the Tour Series which featured a 150 watt head and 4x12" bottoms with metal speaker grilles and metal corners.

Tour MK 2 Amp Head
1970s. 150-watt head, high- and low-gain inputs, master volume, 8xEL34 power tubes, black.

1970s		$850	$1,075

SMF (Sonic Machine Factory)
2002-2009. Tube amps and cabinets designed by Mark Sampson (Matchless, Bad Cat, Star) and Rick Hamel (SIB effects) and built in California.

Smicz Amplification
Tube combos and extension cabinets built by Bob Smicz in Bristol, Connecticut.

Smith Custom Amplifiers
All tube combo amps, heads and speaker cabinets built by Sam Smith in Montgomery, Alabama starting in 2002.

Smokey
1997-present. Mini amps often packaged in cigarette packs made by Bruce Zinky in Flagstaff, Arizona. He also builds Zinky amps and effects and has revived the Supro brand on a guitar and amp.

Snider
1999-present. Jeff Snider has been building various combo tube amps in San Diego, California, since '95. In '99 he started branding them with his last name.

MODEL		EXC. COND.	
YEAR	FEATURES	LOW	HIGH

Soldano
1987-present. Made in Seattle, Washington by amp builder Mike Soldano, the company offers a range of all-tube combo amps, heads and cabinets. They also offer a reverb unit.

Astroverb 16 Combo Amp
1997-present. Atomic with added reverb.

1997-2014		$700	$876

Atomic 16 Combo Amp
1996-2001. Combo, 20 watts, 1x12".

1996-2001		$600	$750

Avenger Amp Head
2004-present. Single channel, 4 preamp tubes, 100-watt with 4 power tubes, or 50-watt with 2.

2004-2014		$1,100	$1,350

Decatone Combo Amp
1998-present. 2x12" 100-watt combo, rear mounted controls, still available as a head.

1998-2008	2x12 combo	$1,650	$2,100
2009-2014	Head only	$1,300	$1,650

HR 50/Hot Rod 50 Amp Head
1992-2012. 50-watt single channel head.

1992-2012		$900	$1,125

HR 100/Hot Rod 100 Amp Head
1994-2001. 100-watt single channel head.

1994-2001		$1,000	$1,250

Lucky 13 Combo Amp
2000-present. 100 watts (50 also available), 2x12" combo.

2000-2014		$1,250	$1,550

Reverb-O-Sonic Combo Amp
1990s-present. 50 watts, 2 channels, 2x12" combo, reverb.

1990s-2014		$1,050	$1,350

SLO-100 Super Cabinet
1988-present. 4x12" slant-front or straight-front cabinet, prices shown are for slant, deduct $100 for straight.

1988-1989		$775	$975
1990-2014		$725	$900

SLO-100 Super Lead Overdrive 100-Watt Amp
1988-present. First production model, 100-watt amp head, snakeskin cover, 4x12" cabinet.

1988-1989		$2,500	$3,100
1990-2009		$2,400	$3,000
2010-2014		$2,300	$2,900

Sommatone
1998-present. Jim Somma builds his tube combo and head amps and cabinets in Somerville, New Jersey.

Sonax
Introduced in 1972. Budget line of solidstate amps offered by Gretsch/Baldwin, made by Yorkville Sound (Traynor) in Toronto. Introduced with dark grille and dark cover.

530-B Bass Amp
1970s. Solidstate, 30 watts, 1x12".

1970s		$130	$165

Snider Chicago Combo

Soldano Lucky 13

2008 Sommatone Roaring 40

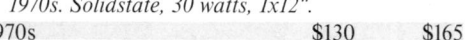

Sonny Jr. Super Cruncher

Southbay Ampworks

Specimen Horn

MODEL YEAR FEATURES	EXC. COND. LOW	HIGH
550-B Bass Amp		
1970s. Solidstate, 50 watts, 1x15".		
1970s	$155	$195
720-G Amp		
1970s. Solidstate student amp, 20 watts, 2x8", reverb.		
1970s	$155	$195
730-G Amp		
1970s. Solidstate, 30 watts, 2x10", reverb and tremolo.		
1970s	$215	$270
750-G Amp		
1970s. Solidstate, 50 watts, 2x12", reverb and tremolo.		
1970s	$235	$295
770-G Amp		
1970s. Solidstate, 75 watts, 4x10", reverb and tremolo.		
1970s	$270	$340

Songworks Systems

See listing under Little Lanilei.

Sonny Jr.

1996-present. Harmonica amplifiers built by harmonica player Sonny Jr. in conjunction with Cotton Amps in Tolland, Connecticut.

Sonola

Tube combo amps made for the Sonola Accordian company of Chicago in the 1950s and '60s, possibly built by Guild or Ampeg. There are also Sonola tube amp heads from the '70s made by MHB Amplifiers in Adelaide, South Australia.

Sound City

Made in England from 1966-'67 to the late-'70s, the tube Sound City amps were Marshall-looking heads and separate cabinets. They were imported, for a time, into the U.S. by Gretsch.

50 PA Plus Amp		
Late-1960s-late-1970s. Similar to 50 Plus but with 4 channels.		
1970s	$675	$850
50 Plus/50R Amp Head		
Late-1960s-late-1970s. Amp head, labeled 50 Plus or 50 R.		
1960s-70s	$850	$1,075
120 Energizer Slave Unit Amp		
1970s. 120-watt power amp only, no preamp, Energizer Slave Unit logo on front panel.		
1970s	$575	$725
120/120R Amp Head		
Early-late-1970s. The 120-watt head replaced the late-1960s 100-watt model.		
1970s 120 no reverb	$925	$1,150
1970s With reverb	$975	$1,225
200 Plus Amp Head		
1970s	$1,025	$1,275
Concord Combo Amp		
80 watts, 2x12" Fane speakers, cream, basketweave grille.		
1968	$1,025	$1,275

MODEL YEAR FEATURES	EXC. COND. LOW	HIGH
L-80 Cabinet		
1970s. 4x10" speaker cabinet.		
1970s	$515	$645
L-412 Cabinet		
1970s. 4x12" speaker cabinet.		
1970s	$575	$725
X-60 Cabinet		
1970s. 2x12" speaker cabinet.		
1970s	$525	$650

Sound Electronics

Sound Electronics Corporation introduced a line of amplifiers in 1965 that were manufactured in Long Island. Six models were initially offered, with solidstate rectifiers and tube preamp and power sections. Their catalog did not list power wattages but did list features and speaker configurations. The initial models had dark vinyl-style covers and sparkling silver grille cloth. The amps were combos with the large models having vertical cabinets, silver script Sound logo on upper left of grille. The larger models used JBL D120F and D130F speakers. Stand alone extension speakers were also available.

Various Model Amps		
Mid-1960s. Includes X-101, X-101R, X-202 Bass/Organ, X-404 Bass and Organ, X-505R amps, hi-fi chassis often using 7868 power tubes.		
1960s	$400	$650

Southbay Ampworks/ Scumback Amps

2002-present. Tube combo amps and speaker cabinets built by Jim Seavall in Whittier, California. He also builds Scumback Speakers. In '14, name changed to Scumback Amps.

Sovtek

1992-1996. Sovtek amps were products of Mike Matthews of Electro-Harmonix fame and his New Sensor Corporation. The guitar and bass amps and cabinets were made in Russia.

Mig 30 Amp Head		
1994-1996. Tube head, 30 watts.		
1994-1996	$450	$550
Mig 50 Amp Head		
1992-1996. Tube head, 50 watts.		
1992-1996	$450	$550
Mig 60 Amp Head		
1994-1996. Tube head, 60 watts, point-to-point wiring.		
1994-1996	$476	$600
Mig 100 Amp Head		
1992-1996. Tube head, 100 watts.		
1992-1996	$450	$550
Mig 100B Amp Head		
1996. Bass tube head, 100 watts.		
1996	$476	$600
Mig Cabinet		
1992-1996 2x12"	$300	$375

MODEL		EXC. COND.	
YEAR	FEATURES	LOW	HIGH

Space Tone
See Swart Amplifiers.

Specimen Products
1984-present. Luthier Ian Schneller added tube amps and speaker cabinets in '93. He also builds guitars, basses and ukes in Chicago, Illinois.

Speedster
1995-2000, 2003-2007. Founded by Lynn Ellsworth, offering tube amps and combos designed by Bishop Cochran with looks inspired by dashboards of classic autos. In '03, Joe Valosay and Jevco International purchased the company and revived the brand with help from former owner Cory Wilds. Amps were originally built by Soldono, but later ones built by Speedster in Gig Harbor, Washington. They also built effects pedals.

Splawn
2004-present. Production, professional grade, tube amps and cabinets built by Scott Splawn in Dallas, North Carolina.

St. George
1960s. There were Japanese guitars bearing this brand, but these amps may have been built in California.
Mid-Size Tube Amp
1965. Low power, 1x10" Jensen, 2 5065 and 2 12AX7 tubes.

1960s		$190	$240

Standel
1952-1974, 1997-present. Bob Crooks started custom building amps part time in '52, going into full time standard model production in '58 in Temple City, California. In '61 Standel started distributing guitars under their own brand and others. By late '63 or '64, Standel had introduced solidstate amps, two years before Fender and Ampeg introduced their solidstate models. In '67 Standel moved to a new, larger facility in El Monte, California. In '73 Chicago Musical Instruments (CMI), which owned Gibson at the time, bought the company and built amps in El Monte until '74. In '97 the Standel name was revived by Danny McKinney who, with the help of original Standel founder Bob Crooks and Frank Garlock (PR man for first Standel), set about building reissues of some of the early models in Ventura, California.
A-30 B Artist 30 Bass Amp
1964-early-1970s. Artist Series, the original Standel solidstate series, 80 watts, 2x15".

1964-1969		$300	$375

A-30 G Artist 30 Guitar Amp
1964-early-1970s. Solidstate, 80 watts, 2x15".

1964-1974		$325	$400

A-48 G Artist 48 Guitar Amp
1964-early-1970s. Solidstate, 80 watts, 4x12".

1964-1974		$375	$475

A-60 B Artist 60 Bass Amp
1964-early-1970s. Solidstate, 160 watts, 4x15".

1964-1974		$375	$475

A-60 G Artist 60 Guitar Amp
1964-early-1970s. Solidstate, 160 watts, 4x15".

1964-1974		$375	$475

A-96 G Artist 96 Guitar Amp
1964-early-1970s. Solidstate, 160 watts, 8x12".

1964-1974		$425	$525

C-24 Custom 24 Amp
Late-1960s-1970s. Custom Slim Line Series, solidstate, 100 watts, 2x12", dark vinyl, dark grille.

1960s-70s		$325	$400

I-30 B Imperial 30 Bass Amp
1964-early-1970s. Imperial Series, the original Standel solidstate series, 100 watts, 2x15".

1964-1974		$350	$450

I-30 G Imperial 30 Guitar Amp
1964-early-1970s. Imperial Series, the original Standel solidstate series, 100 watts, 2x15".

1964-1974		$375	$475

S-10 Studio 10 Amp
Late-1960s-1970s. Studio Slim Line Series, solidstate, 30 watts, 1x10", dark vinyl, dark grille.

1970s		$250	$325

S-24 G Amp
1970s. Solidstate, 2x12".

1970s		$325	$400

S-50 Studio 50 Amp
Late-1963 or early-1964-late-1960s. Not listed in '69 Standel catalog, 60 watts, gray tolex, gray grille, piggyback.

1964		$325	$400

SM-60 Power Magnifier Amp
1970. Tall, verticle combo solidstate amp, 100 watts, 6x10".

1970		$300	$375

Tube Amp
1953-1958. Early custom made tube amps made by Bob Crooks in his garage, padded naugahyde cabinet with varying options and colors. There are a limited number of these amps, and brand knowledge is also limited, therefore there is a wide value range. Legend has it that the early Standel amps made Leo Fender re-think and introduce even more powerful amps.

1953-1958	Various models	$2,500	$5,000

Star
Starting in 2004, tube amps, combos and speaker cabinets built by Mark Sampson in the Los Angeles, California area. Sampson has also been involved with Matchless, Bad Cat, and SMF amps.

Starcaster
See listing under Fender.

Starlite
Starlite was a budget brand made and sold by Magnatone. See Magnatone for listings.

Splawn Supersport

Standel 100 UL15

Star Gain Star

Stephenson Standard

Straub Twisted Triode

Suhr Badger
Rob Bernstein

MODEL YEAR	FEATURES	EXC. COND. LOW	HIGH

Stella Vee
1999-2005. Jason Lockwood built his combo amps, heads, and cabinets in Lexington, Kentucky.

Stephenson
1997-present. Mark Stephenson builds his intermediate to premium grade, production/custom, tube amps and cabinets in Regina, Saskatchewan 1997-'99, in Hope, British Columbia 2000-'06, and since in Parksville, British Columbia. He also offers effects.

Stevenson
1999-present. Luthier Ted Stevenson, of Lachine, Quebec, added amps to his product line in '05. He also builds basses and guitars.

Stimer
Brothers Yves and Jean Guen started building guitar pickups in France in 1946. By the late '40s they had added their Stimer line of amps to sell with the pickups. Early amp models were the M.6, M.10 and M.12 (6, 10 and 12 watts, respectively). An early user of Guen products was Django Reinhardt.

Stinger
1980s-1990s. Stinger was a budget line of guitars and solidstate amps imported by Martin.

Strad-O-Lin/Stradolin
Ca.1920s-ca.1960s. The Strad-O-Lin company primarily made mandolins for wholesalers but around '57 Multivox/Premier bought the company and used the name on guitars and amps.

Compact Solidstate Amp
1960s. Made in U.S.A., logo on control panel and grille, black grille and cover.

1960s		$90	$115

Stramp
1970s. Stramp, of Hamburg, Germany, offered audio mixers, amps and compact powered speaker units, all in aluminum flight cases.

Solidstate Amp
1970s. Solidstate amp head in metal suitcase with separate Stramp logo cabinet.

1970s		$375	$500

Straub Amps
2003-present. Harry Straub builds his professional grade, production/custom, amps in St. Paul, Minnesota.

Suhr
1997-present. John Suhr builds his production/custom amps in Lake Elsinore, California. He also builds guitars and basses.

Sundown
1983-1988. Combo amps, heads and cabinets designed and built by Dennis Kager of Ampeg fame. By '88, he had sold out his interest in the company.

Sunn
1965-2002. Started in Oregon by brothers Conrad and Norm Sundhold (Norm was the bass player for the Kingsman). Sunn introduced powerful amps and extra heavy duty bottoms and was soon popular with many major rock acts. Norm sold his interest to Conrad in '69. Conrad sold the company to the Hartzell Corporation of Minnesota around '72. Fender Musical Instruments acquired the brand in '85 shortly after parting ways with CBS and used the brand until '89. They resurrected the brand again in '98, but quit offering the name in '02.

100S Amp and Cabinet Set
1965-1970s. 60 watts, 1x15" JBL D130F and 1 LE 100S JBL Driver and Horn, piggyback, 5 tubes (with rectifier).

1965-1969		$1,150	$1,450

190L Amp and Cabinet Set
1970s. Solidstate, 80 watts, 2 speakers.

1970s		$600	$750

200S/215B Amp and Cabinet Set
1966-1970s. 60 watts, 2x6550s, large vertical cab with 1x15" or 2x15" speakers.

1966-1969	1x15"	$1,150	$1,450
1966-1969	2x15"	$1,150	$1,450

601-L Cabinet
1980s. 6x10" plus 2 tweeters cab.

1980s		$385	$480

2000S Amp
1968-1970s. 4x6550 power tubes, 120 watts.

1968-1970s	Head & cab	$1,325	$1,650

Alpha 112 Amp
1980s. Solidstate, MOS-FET preamp section, 1x12" combo, reverb, overdrive, black.

1980s		$175	$225

Alpha 115 Amp
1980s. Solidstate, MOS-FET preamp section, 1x15", clean and overdrive.

1980s		$235	$300

Alpha 212 R Amp
1980s. Solidstate, MOS-FET preamp section, 2x12", reverb.

1980s		$270	$340

Beta Bass Amp
1978-1980s. Solidstate 100-watt head and combos, large Beta Bass logo on front panel.

1978-1980s	4x12"	$570	$715
1978-1980s	6x10"	$570	$715
1978-1980s	Combo 1x15"	$570	$715
1978-1980s	Combo 2x12"	$570	$715
1978-1980s	Combo 4x10"	$570	$715

Coliseum 300 Bass Amp
1970s. Solidstate, Colisium-300 logo on front.

1970s	Head & cab	$675	$845

Coliseum Lead Amp
1970s. Solidstate, Coliseum Lead logo on front.

1970s	Head & cab	$675	$845

Coliseum Lead Full Stack Amp
1970s. Coliseum Lead logo on amp head, two 4x12" cabs.

1970s		$1,025	$1,275

The *Vintage Guitar Price Guide* shows low to high values for items in all-original excellent condition, and, where applicable, with original case or cover.

MODEL YEAR	FEATURES	EXC. COND. LOW	HIGH

Concert 215S Bass Amp Set
1970s. Solidstate head, 200 watts, Model 215S tall vertical cabinet with 2x12" Sunn label speakers, dark vinyl cover, silver sparkle grille.

1970s		$650	$815

Concert Lead 610S Amp Set
1970s. Solidstate, 200 watts, 6x10" piggyback, reverb and built-in distortion.

1970s		$775	$975

Enforcer Amp
1980s. Tube, 60/100 watt 2x12" or 100 watt head.

1980s	Combo	$800	$1,000
1980s	Head & cab	$850	$1,075

Fuse 200S Amp
1970s. Sunn Fuse logo and model number on front panel, 140 watts.

1970s		$850	$1,075

Model T Amp Head
Early-1970s. 100 watts.

1970s		$2,150	$2,700

Model T Amp Reissue
1998-2002. Reissue of '70s Model T, 100 watts, with 4x12" cab.

1998-2002	Head & cab	$1,275	$1,600

SB-160 Bass Amp
1985. Combo, 60 watts.

1985		$360	$450

SB-200 Amp
1985. 200 watts, 1x15", 4-band EQ, master volume, compressor.

1985		$385	$480

Sceptre Amp
1968-1972. 60 watts, 6550 power tubes, tremolo, reverb.

1968-1972	Head & cab	$1,050	$1,325

Sentura Amp
1967-1970s. Rectifier and power tubes, I and II versions.

1967-1969	I, 1x15" set	$950	$1,175
1967-1969	II, 2x15" set	$1,000	$1,250

SL 250 Amp
1980s. 60 watts, 2x12" combo, SL 250 logo.

1980s		$515	$650

SL 260 Amp
1982-ca.1985. 60 watts, 2x12" combo with reverb, SL 260 logo.

1982-1985		$575	$725

Solarus Amp
1967-1970s. Tube amp (EL34s), reverb, tremolo, 2x12" 40 watt combo to '68; 60 watt head with 2x12" cab for '69 on.

1967-1968	Combo	$600	$750
1969-1970s	Piggyback	$675	$850

Solo II Amp
Early-1970s. Solo II logo on front panel, 120 watts, 2x12" combo, black tolex.

1970s		$600	$750

Sonaro Amp
Early-1970s. 60 watts, 2x6550s.

1970s		$650	$825

Sonic 1-40 Amp
1967-1969. Tube head, 1x15" bass amp, 40 watts.

1967-1969	Head & cab	$950	$1,200

Sonic I Amp
1967-1969. 125 watts, 1x15" JBL D130F in short cabinet, 5 tubes (with rectifier), piggyback, dark tolex.

1967-1969	Head & cab	$950	$1,200

Sonic II Amp
1967-1969. 250 watts, 2x15" JBL D130F in folding horn large cabinet, 5 tubes (with rectifier), piggyback, dark tolex.

1967-1969	Head & cab	$1,000	$1,250

Sorado Amp
1970s. 50 watts, tubes, 2x15" matching cab.

1970s	Head & cab	$875	$1,100

Spectrum I Amp
1967-1969. 125 watts, 1x15" JBL D130F large cabinet, 5 tubes (with rectifier), piggyback, dark tolex cover.

1967-1969	Head & cab	$925	$1,150

Spectrum II Amp
1967-1969. 250 watts, 2x12", piggyback, 5 tubes (with rectifier), Spectrum II logo on front panel.

1967-1969	Head & cab	$975	$1,225

SPL 7250 Amp
Dual channels, 250 watts per channel, forced air cooling, switch-selectable peak compressor with LEDs.

1989	Head & cab	$525	$650

Stagemaster
1980s. 120 watts, 2x12".

1980s	Combo	$465	$575
1980s	Head & cab	$540	$675

T50C
1998-2002. Combo 1x12", 50 watts.

1998-2002		$575	$725

Supersound
1952-1974. Founded by England's Alan Wootton, building custom amps and radios, the firm continued to build amps and effects into the early '60s. They also built guitars and basses.

Supertone
1914-1941. Supertone was a brand used by Sears for their musical instruments. In the '40s Sears started using the Silvertone name on those products. Amps were made by other companies.

Amp

1930s		$300	$375

Supro
1935-1968, 2004-present. Supro was a budget brand of the National Dobro Company, made by Valco in Chicago, Illinois. Amp builder Bruce Zinky revived the Supro name in '04 for a line of guitars and amps. In '13, Absara Audio, LLC acquired the Supro trademark and started releasing amps in July '14.

Accordion 1615T Amp
1957-1959. Compact combo, 1x15", 24 watts, 2x6L6 power, 5V4, 3x12AX7, 2 channels, tremolo, 3 control knobs, Accordion (model) logo upper left corner of grille, Supro logo lower right, Rhino-Hide gray with white sides.

1957-1959		$775	$975

Sundown

1975 Sunn Model T
Stephan Brown

1972 Sunn Solarus
Ken Schultz

AMPS

1967 Supro Corsica

Peter Daniels

Supro Golden Holiday

Supro Supreme Twin Speaker

MODEL YEAR	FEATURES	EXC. COND. LOW	HIGH

Bantam Amp

1961-1966. Petite, 4 watts, 3 tubes, 1x 8" Jensen, gold weave Saran Wrap grille, Spanish Ivory fabric cover, red in '64, gray in '66. Also sold as matching set, for example in '64 with student-level red and white lap steel, add 65% to price for matching guitar and amp set.

1961-1963	1611S, Spanish ivory	$310	$390
1964-1965	S6411, red cover	$310	$390
1966	Gray cover	$310	$390

Bass Combo Amp

Early 1960s. 35 watts, 2x12", 2 channels (bass and standard), 7 tubes, tremolo, woven embossed black and white tolex that appears grey. The '61 model 1688T has a narrow panel body style somewhat similar to the Fender narrow panel cab style of the late '50s, in '62 the cab panel was removed and the 'no panel' style became the 1688TA model, the new cab was less expensive to build and Supro offered a price reduction on applicable models in '62.

1961	1688T, narrow panel	$675	$850
1962-1963	1688TA, no panel	$675	$850

Big Star Reverb S6451TR Amp

1964. 35 watts, 2x12", reverb and tremolo, 'no panel' cab.

1964		$925	$1,150

Brentwood 1650T Amp

Mid-1950s. Advertised as Supro's "finest amplifier", model 1650T described as the "professional twin speaker luxury amplifier", 2 channels including high-gain, tremolo with speed control.

1956		$925	$1,150

Combo Amp

1961-1964. 24 watts, 6 tubes, 1x15" Jensen, Rhino-Hide covering in black and white, light grille, tremolo.

1961	1696T, narrow panel	$675	$850
1962-1963	1696TA, no panel	$675	$850

Combo Tremolo S6497T Amp

1964. 35 watts, 1x15", standard 'no panel' cab, tremolo.

1964		$725	$900

Comet 1610B Amp

1957-1959. Gray Rhino-Hide, 1x10".

1957-1959		$625	$775

Comet 1610E Amp

Mid-1950s. Supro's only 1x10" amp from the mid-'50s, 3 input jacks, 2 control knobs, woven tweed and leatherette 2-tone covering.

1956		$625	$775

Coronado Amp

1960-1963. 24 watts, 2x10", tremolo, 2 channels, 6 tubes, Supro logo upper right above grille, black and white mixed tolex appears gray, described as tremolo twin-speaker pro amp, '61 has 'narrow panel' body style, new body style in '62 becomes 1690TA model with grille only and no panel.

1960-1961	1690T, narrow panel	$725	$900
1962-1963	1690TA, no panel	$725	$900

Corsica Amp

Mid-1960s. Redesigned vertical combo amp, reverb, tremolo, blue control panel, black tolex, silver grille.

1965-1967		$515	$650

MODEL YEAR	FEATURES	EXC. COND. LOW	HIGH

Dual-Tone Amp

1961-1965. 17 watts, 6 tubes, 1x12" Jensen, organ tone tremolo, restyled in '64, Trinidad Blue vinyl fabric cover, light color grille.

1961	1624T, narrow panel	$725	$900
1962-1963	1624TA, no panel	$725	$900
1964-1965	S6424T, no panel	$725	$900

Galaxy Tremolo S6488 Amp

1965. 35 watts, 2x12" (often Jensen), 7 tubes, tremolo, multi-purpose for guitar, bass and accordion.

1965		$750	$950

Galaxy Tremolo S6688 Amp

1966-1967. 35 watts, 2x12" (often Jensen), turquoise front control panel with Supro logo (not on grille), model name/number also on front control panel.

1966-1967		$625	$775

Golden Holiday 1665T Amp

Mid-1950s. Supro's model for the 'semi-professional', 2 oval 11x6" speakers, 14 watts, 6 tubes, tremolo, 2 control knobs, black and tweed cover.

1956		$775	$975

Model 24 Amp

1965. 18 watts, 1x12 combo, 2 channels each with bass and treble inputs, tremolo, Model 24 logo on top panel, Calypso Blue vinyl cover.

1965		$625	$775

Reverb 1650R Amp

1963. 17 watts, 1x10", 'no panel' grille front style cab, reverb.

1963		$625	$775

Royal Reverb 1650TR Amp

1963-1965. 17 watts, 15 tubes, 2x10" Jensens, catalog says "authentic tremolo and magic-reverberation."

1963-1965		$850	$1,075

Royal Reverb S6650 Amp

1965-1967. Updated cabinet with turquoise-blue front control panel, 2x10" combo, 2 channels (standard and reverb-tremolo).

1965-1967		$550	$675

Special 1633E Amp

Mid-1950s. Supro's entry level student amp, 1x8", 3 tubes, large Supro stencil logo on grille, 2-tone red and white fabric cover, leather handle, available with matching Special Lap Steel covered in wine-maroon plastic.

1956		$415	$525

Spectator 1614E Amp

Mid-1950s. 1x8", 3 tubes, 2 control knobs, white front with red and black body.

1956		$515	$650

Sportsman S6689 Amp

1966. Piggyback, twin speakers.

1966		$800	$1,000

Statesman S6699 Amp

1966. Piggyback with blue-green control panel, 4x6L6 power, horizontal 2x12" cab, reverb, tremolo, script Statesman logo with model number on upper left front of chasis.

1966		$675	$850

*The **Vintage Guitar Price Guide** shows low to high values for items in all-original excellent condition, and, where applicable, with original case or cover.*

MODEL YEAR	FEATURES	EXC. COND. LOW	HIGH

Studio 1644E Amp

Mid-1950s. Supro's student model for teaching studios, 2 input jacks for student and instructor or guitar and lap steel guitar, 3 tubes, advertised for "true Hawaiian tone reproduction", covered in royal blue leatherette (in '56), available with a matching Studio Lap Steel covered in blue plastic.

1956-1957	Blue leatherette	$515	$650

Super 1606E Amp

Mid-1950s. Supro advertising states "with features important to women", oval 11x6" Rola speaker, 3 tubes, 1 control knob, 2 inputs, white (front) and grey sides, elliptical baffle soundhole with Supro logo, model number with E suffix common for '50s Supro's.

1956	White front & grey	$515	$650

Super Amp

1961-1963. 4.5 watts, 3 tubes, 1x8", 1606S has contrasting black and white covering with old narrow panel cab, in '63 new 1606B has 'no panel' style cab with lighter (gray) covering.

1961-1962	1606S	$350	$440
1963	1606B	$350	$440

Super Six S6406 Amp

1964-1965. Student practice amp, 4.5 watts, 1x8", blue vinyl cover.

1964-1965		$350	$440

Super SIx S6606 Amp

1966. Updated version of student compact amp.

1966		$275	$350

Supreme Amp

1961-1963. 17 watts, 1x10", designed for use with Model 600 Reverb Accessory Unit, value shown does not include the Model 600 (see Effects Section for reverb unit). The initial 1600R model was designed with a triangle-like shaped soundhole, in '62 the more typical Supro no panel cab was introduced which Supro called the new slope front design.

1961	1600R	$925	$1,150
1962-1963	1600S, no panel	$925	$1,150

Supreme 17 S6400 Amp

1964-1965. 17 watts, 1x10", cab larger than prior models of this type.

1964-1965		$650	$800

Supreme Twin Speaker 1600E Amp

Mid-1950s. 2 oval 11x6" speakers, 5 tubes, 3 input jacks, 2 control knobs, grille logo states "Twin Speaker" but unlike most Supro amps of this era the Supro logo does not appear on the front.

1956		$625	$775

Thunderbolt S6420(B) Bass Amp

1964-1967. 35 watts, 1x15" Jensen, introduced in the '64 catalog as a no frills - no fancy extra circuits amp. Sometimes referred to as the "Jimmy Page amp" based on his use of this amp in his early career.

1964-1967		$1,240	$1,550

Thunderbolt S6920 Amp

1967-1968. Redesign circuit replaced S6420B, 35 watts, 1x12".

1967-1968		$650	$825

Tremo-Verb S6422TR Amp

1964-1965. Lower power using 4 12AX7s, 1 5Y3GT, and 1 6V6, 1x10", tremolo and reverb, Persian Red vinyl cover.

1964-1965		$925	$1,150

Trojan Tremolo Amp

1961-1966. 5 watts, 4 tubes, 1 11"x6" oval (generally Rolla) speaker, '61-'64 black and white fabric cover and Saran Wrap grille, '64-'66 new larger cab with vinyl cover and light grille.

1961	1616T, narrow panel	$410	$515
1962-1963	1616TA, no panel	$385	$480
1964-1966	S6461, blue vinyl cover	$385	$480

Vibra-Verb S6498VR Amp

1964-1965. Billed as Supro's finest amplifier, 2x35-watt channels, 1x15" and 1x10" Jensens, vibrato and reverb.

1964-1965		$1,225	$1,525

Surreal Amplification

2007-present. Production/custom, professional grade amp heads, combos and cabinets built in Westminster, California by Jerry Dyer.

Swampdonkey

2006-present. Professional and premium grade, production/custom, guitar amp heads, combos and speaker cabinets built in Rural Rocky View, Alberta by Chris Czech.

Swanpro Amps

2004-present. Robert Swanson builds his tube combo and head amps and cabinets in Denver, Colorado.

Swart Amplifier Co. (Space Tone)

2003-present. Michael J. Swart builds tube combo and head amps and cabinets under the Swart and Space Tone brand names in Wilmington, North Carolina. He also builds effects.

SWR Sound

1984-present. Founded by Steve W. Rabe in '84, with an initial product focus on bass amplifiers. Fender Musical Instruments Corp. acquired SWR in June, 2003.

Baby Blue Studio Bass System

1990-2003. Combo, all tube preamp, 150 watts solidstate power amp, 2x8", 1x5" cone tweeter, gain, master volume, EQ, effects-blend.

1990-2003		$450	$560

Basic Black Amp

1992-1999. Solidstate, 100 watts, 1x12", basic black block logo on front, black tolex, black metal grille.

1992-1999		$300	$375

California Blonde Amp

2000s. Vertical upright combo, 100 watts, 1x12" plus high-end tweeters, blond cover, thin black metal grille.

2003		$300	$375

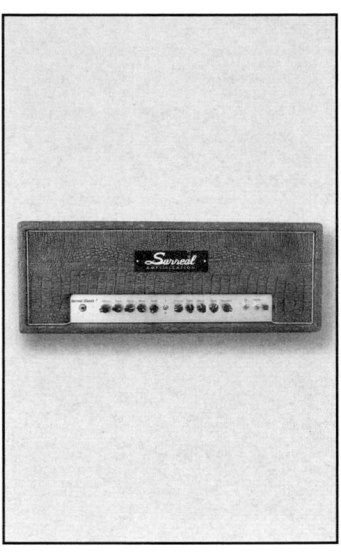

Surreal Classic

AMPS

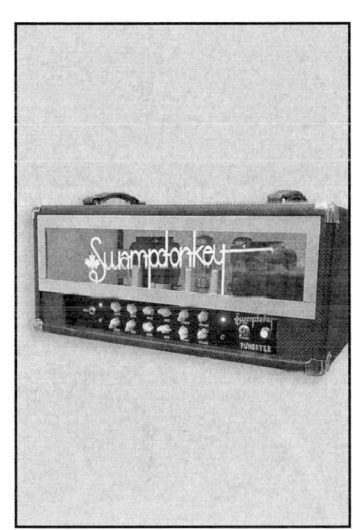

Swampdonkey Punkster

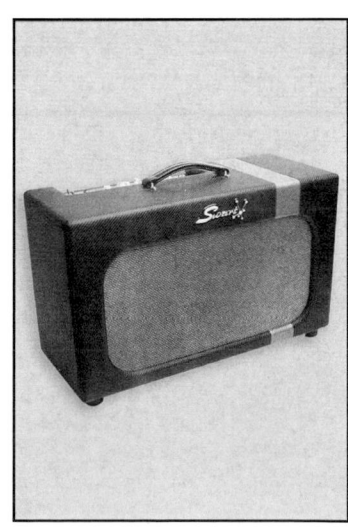

Swart Amps Mod

Synaptic Catalyst

The Valve 105 Bimbo

TomasZewicZ 70W Stack

MODEL YEAR	FEATURES	EXC. COND. LOW	HIGH
Goliath III Cabinet			
1996-2008. Black tolex, black metal grille, includes the Goliath III Jr. (2x10") and the Goliath III (4x10").			
1996-2008	2x10"	$250	$310
1996-2008	4x10"	$300	$375
Strawberry Blonde Amp			
1998-2011. 80 watts, 1x10" acoustic instrument amp.			
1998-2011		$300	$375
Strawberry Blonde II Amp			
2007-2011. 90 watts, 1x10" acoustic instrument amp.			
2007-2011		$300	$375
Studio 220 Bass Amp			
1988-1995. 220 watt solidstate head, tube preamp			
1988-1995		$200	$250
Workingman's Series Amp			
1995-2004. Introduced in '95, replaced by WorkingPro in '05.			
1995-2004	10, 200w, 2x10"	$225	$275
1995-2004	12, 100w, 1x12"	$225	$275
1995-2004	15 Bass, 1x15"	$225	$275

Symphony

1950s. Probably a brand from an teaching studio, large Symphony script red letter logo on front.

Small Tube Amp
1950s. Two guitar inputs, 1x6" speaker, alligator tweed suitcase.

1950		$250	$315

Synaptic Amplification

2007-present. Intermediate to premium grade, production/custom, amps built in Brunswick, Maine by Steven O'Connor.

Takt

Late-1960s. Made in Japan, tube and solidstate models.

GA Series Amps
1968. GA-9 (2 inputs and 5 controls, 3 tubes), GA-10, GA-11, GA-12, GA-14, GA-15.

1968	GA-14/GA-15	$55	$70
1968	GA-9 thru GA-12	$35	$45

Talos

2004-present. Doug Weisbrod and Bill Thalmann build their tube amp heads, combo amps, and speaker cabinets in Springfield, Virginia. They started building and testing prototypes in '01.

Tanglewood Guitar Company UK

1991-present. Intermediate and professional grade, production, acoustic amps imported from China by Dirk Kommer and Tony Flatt in United Kingdom. They also import guitars, basses, mandolins, banjos and ukes.

Tech 21

1989-present. Long known for their SansAmp tube amplifier emulator, Tech 21 added solidstate combo amps, heads and cabinets in '96.

Teisco

1946-1974, 1994-present. Japanese brand first imported into the U.S. around '63. Teisco offered both tube and solidstate amps.

Checkmate CM-10 Amp
1960s. Tubes or solidstate, 10 watts.

1960s	Solidstate	$40	$50
1960s	Tubes	$165	$205

Checkmate CM-15 Amp
Late-1960s. Tubes, 15 watts.

1960s		$180	$225

Checkmate CM-16 Amp
1960s. Tubes or solidstate, 15 watts.

1960s	Solidstate	$50	$65
1960s	Tubes	$180	$225

Checkmate CM-17 Amp
1960s. Tubes, 1x10", reverb, tremolo.

1960s		$285	$355

Checkmate CM-20 Amp
Late-1960s. Tubes, 20 watts.

1960s		$285	$355

Checkmate CM-25 Amp
Late-1960s. Tubes, 25 watts.

1960s		$285	$355

Checkmate CM-50 Amp
Late-1950s-early-1960s. Tubes, 2 6L6s, 50 watts, 2x12" open back, reverb, tremolo, piggyback, gray tolex cover, light gray grille.

1960s		$385	$485

Checkmate CM-60 Amp
Late-1960s. Tubes, 60 watts, piggyback amp and cab with wheels.

1960s		$230	$290

Checkmate CM-66 Amp
Late-1960s. Solidstate, dual speaker combo, Check Mate 66 logo on front panel.

1960s		$60	$75

Checkmate CM-88 Amp
1960s. Solidstate, 10 watts, 2x8".

1960s		$60	$75

Checkmate CM-100 Amp
Late-1960s. Tubes, 4x6L6 power, 100 watts, piggyback with Vox-style trolley stand.

1960s		$235	$300

King 1800 Amp
Late-1960s. Tubes, 180 watts, piggyback with 2 cabinets, large Teisco logo on cabinets, King logo on lower right side of one cabinet.

1960s		$375	$475

Teisco 8 Amp
Late-1960s. Solidstate, 5 watts.

1960s		$60	$75

Teisco 10 Amp
Late-1960s. Solidstate, 5 watts.

1960s		$60	$75

Teisco 88 Amp
Late-1960s. Solidstate, 8 watts.

1960s		$85	$105

MODEL		EXC. COND.	
YEAR	FEATURES	LOW	HIGH

Tempo

1950s-1970s. Tube (early on) and solidstate amps, most likely imported from Japan by Merson Musical Products. They also offered basses and guitars.

Model 39

1950s. Compact amp, vertical cab, tweed, 3 tubes, single control knob for on-off volume.

1953		$325	$400

Teneyck

1960s. Solidstate amp heads and speaker cabinets built by Bob Teneyck, who had previously done design work for Ampeg.

THD

1987-present. Tube amps and cabinets built in Seattle, Washington, founded by Andy Marshall.

The Valve

2000-present. Guitar luthier Galeazzo Frudua also builds a line of professional grade, production/custom, amps in San Lazzaro di Savena, Italy.

ThroBak Electronics

2004-present. Jonathan Gundry builds his tube combo guitar amps in Grand Rapids, Michigan. He also builds guitar effects and pickups.

Titano (Magnatone)

1961-1963. Private branded by Magnatone, often for an accordion company or accordion studio, uses standard guitar input jacks.

Model 262 R Custom Amp

1961-1963. 35 watts, 2x12" + 2x5", reverb and vibrato make this one of the top-of-the-line models, black vinyl, light silver grille.

1961-1963		$1,025	$1,275

Model 313 Amp

1961-1963. Like Magnatone 213 Troubadour, 10 watts, 1x12" combo, vibrato, brown tolex, brownish grille.

1961-1963		$775	$975

Model 415 Bass Amp

1961-1963. 25 watts, 4x8", bass or accordion amp, black cover, darkish grille.

1961-1963		$925	$1,150

TomasZewicZ Amplifiers

2008-present. Intermediate and professional grade, production/custom, tube guitar amp heads and combos built by John Tomaszewicz in Coral Springs, Florida. He also builds effects.

Tombo

This Japanese harmonica manufacturer introduced a solidbody electric ukulele and a Silvertone-esque case with onboard amplifier in the mid-1960s.

Tone Americana

2011-2014. David and Caroline Brass built intermediate and professional grade, production/ custom, amp heads, combos and cabinets in Calabasas, California. They also offered an amp combo built in Asia.

Tone King

1993-present. Tube amps, combos, and cabinets built by Mark Bartel in Baltimore, Maryland. The company started in New York and moved to Baltimore in '94.

Tonemaster (Magnatone)

Late-1950s-early-1960s. Magnatone amps private branded for Imperial Accordion Company. Prominent block-style capital TONEMASTER logo on front panel, generally something nearly equal to Magnatone equivalent. This is just one of many private branded Magnatones. Covers range from brown to black leatherette and brown to light silver grilles. They also offered guitars.

Model 214 (V logo) Amp

1959-1960. Ten watts, 1x12", vibrato, brown leatherette, V logo lower right corner front, large TONEMASTER logo.

1959-1960		$775	$975

Model 260 Amp

1961-1963. About 30 watts, 2x12", vibrato, brown leatherette and brown grille, large TONEMASTER logo on front.

1961-1963		$1,400	$1,750

Model 261 Custom Amp

1961-1963. Tonemaster Custom 261 High Fidelity logo on back chasis panel, Tonemaster logo on front panel, 35 watts, 2x12" combo, 2 channels, vibrato.

1961-1963		$1,400	$1,750

Model 380 Amp

1961-1963. 50 watts, 2x12" and 2 oval 5"x7" speakers, vibrato, no reverb.

1961-1963		$1,400	$1,750

Model 381 Custom Amp

1961-1963. Tonemaster Custom 381 High Fidelity logo on back chasis panel, Tonemaster logo on front panel, 2x12", 1x5".

1961-1963		$1,400	$1,750

Small Combo Amp

1950s-1960s. 1x8", tremolo, light tan.

1950s-60s		$475	$600

ToneTron Amps

2006-present. Professional grade, custom, guitar and bass tube amps and cabinets built in Minneapolis, Minnesota by Jeffrey Falla.

ToneVille Amps

2013-present. Matthew Lucci and Phil Jung build their professional grade, production, amps and cabinets in Colorado Springs, Colorado.

Tonic Amps

2003-present. Darin Ellingson builds professional and premium grade, production/custom, amps and cabinets in Redwood City, California.

Tone King Imperial MK II

ToneVille Sunset Strip

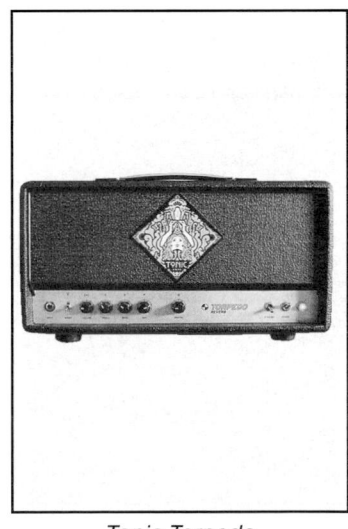

Tonic Torpedo

AMPS

MODEL YEAR	FEATURES	EXC. COND. LOW	HIGH

Top Hat Amplification

1994-present. Mostly Class A guitar amps built by Brian Gerhard, previously in La Habra, California, and Apex, North Carolina, and currently in Fuquay-Varina, North Carolina. He also makes effects.

Ambassador 100 TH-A100 Amp Head

Jan.1999-2013. 100 watts, Class AB, 4 6L6s, reverb, dark green vinyl cover, white chicken-head knobs.

1999-2013		$1,125	$1,400

Ambassador T-35C 212 Amp

1999-2013. 35 watts, 2x12" combo, reverb, master volume, blond cover, tweed-style fabric grille.

1999-2013		$1,175	$1,475

Club Deluxe Amp

1998-2009. 20 watts, 6V6 power tubes, 1x12".

1998-2009		$1,100	$1,375

Club Royale TC-R1 Amp

Jan.1998-present. Class A using EL84s, 20 watts, 1x12".

1998-2014		$750	$950

Club Royale TC-R2 Amp

Jan.1999-2014. Class A using EL84s, 20 watts, 2x12".

1999-2014		$1,125	$1,400

Emplexador 50 TH-E50 Amp Head

Jan.1997-present. 50 watts, Class AB vint/high-gain head.

1997-2014		$1,250	$1,575

King Royale Amp

1996-present. 35 watts, Class A using 4 EL84s, 2x12".

1996-2014		$1,250	$1,575

Portly Cadet TC-PC Amp

Jan.1999-2004. Five watts, 6V6 power, 1x8", dark gray, light gray grille.

1999-2004		$500	$625

Prince Royale TC-PR Amp

Jan.2000-2002. Five watts using EL84 power, 1x8", deep red, light grille.

2000-2002		$500	$625

Super Deluxe TC-SD2 Amp

Jan.2000-2012. 30 watts, Class A, 7591 power tubes, 2x12".

2000-2012		$1,175	$1,475

Torres Engineering

Founded by Dan Torres, the company builds tube amps, combos, cabinets and amp kits originally in San Mateo, California, then San Carlos and since '11 in Milton, Washington. Dan wrote monthly columns for *Vintage Guitar* Magazine for many years and authored the book *Inside Tube Amps.*

Trace Elliot

1978-present. Founded in Essex, England. U.S. distribution picked up by Kaman (Ovation) in '88 which bought Trace Elliot in '92. In '98 Gibson acquired the brand and in early '02 closed the factory and moved what production was left to the U.S. In '05 Peavey bought the brand name, hiring back many of the old key people, and currently offers

professional grade, production, tube and solidstate, acoustic guitar and bass amp heads, combos, and cabinets, with product built in England and the U.S.

Trainwreck

1983-2006. High-end tube guitar amp heads built by Ken Fischer in Colonia, New Jersey. Limited production, custom-made amps that are generally grouped by model. Models include the Rocket, Liverpool and Express, plus variations on those themes. Instead of using serial numbers, he gave each amp a woman's name. Due to illness, Fischer didn't make many amps after the mid '90s, but he continued to design amps for other builders. His total production is estimated at less than 100. Each amp's value should be evaluated on a case-by-case basis. Ken wrote many amp articles for *Vintage Guitar.* Fischer died in late 2006.

Custom Built Amp

1980s	High-end model	$21,500	$26,800

Traynor

1963-present. Started by Pete Traynor and Jack Long in the back of Long & McQuade Music in Toronto, Canada where Traynor was a repairman. Currently offering tube and solidstate amp heads, combos and cabinets made by parent company Yorkville Sound, in Pickering, Ontario.

YBA1 Bass Master Amp Head

1963-1979. 45 watts, called Dynabass for 1963-'64, this was Pete Traynor's first amp design.

1963-1979		$475	$600

YBA1A Mark II Bass Master Amp Head

1968-1976. Like YBA1, but with 90 watts and cooling fan.

1968-1976		$475	$600

YBA3 Custom Special Bass Amp Set

1967-1972. Tube head with 130 watts and 8x10" large vertical matching cab, dark vinyl cover, light grille.

1967-1972		$825	$1,025

YBA4 Bass Master Amp

1967-1972. 45-watt 1x15" combo.

1967-1972		$725	$900

YCV80 Custom Valve Amp

2003-2009. Tube, 80 watts, 4x10" combo.

2003-2009		$410	$515

YGA1 Amp Head

1966-1967. 45 watts guitar amp, tremolo.

1966-1967		$475	$600

YGL3 Mark III Amp

1971-1979. All tube, 80 watts, 2x12" combo, reverb, tremolo.

1971-1979		$625	$775

YGM3 Guitar Mate Reverb Amp

1969-1979. Tubes, 25 watts, 1x12", black tolex, gray grille until '74, black after.

1969-1979		$625	$775

YGM3 Guitar Mate Reverb Reissue Amp

2011-2013. 1x12" combo, 'flying wing' Traynor badge.

2011-2013		$465	$580

Top Hat Club Royale TC-R1

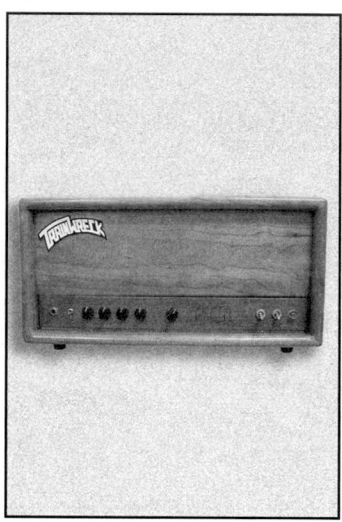

Trainwreck Express

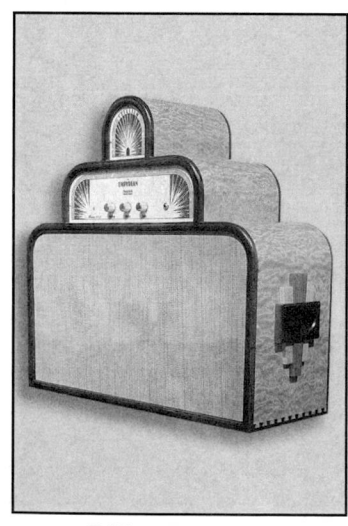

Trillium Empyrean

MODEL YEAR	FEATURES	EXC. COND. LOW	HIGH

YRM1 Reverb Master Amp Head
1973-1979. 45 watt tube amp, reverb, tremolo.

1973-1979		$425	$525

YRM1SC Reverb Master Amp
1973-1979. YRM1 as a 4x10" combo.

1973-1979		$600	$750

YSR1 Custom Reverb Amp Head
1968-1973. 45 watt tube amp, reverb, tremolo.

1968-1973		$425	$525

YVM Series PA Amp Head
1967-1980. Public address heads, models include tube YVM-1 Voice Master, and solidstate YVM-2 and 3 Voice Mate and YVM-4, all with 4 inputs.

1967-1972	1, tubes	$360	$450
1969-1975	2, solidstate	$155	$195
1970-1980	3, solidstate, reverb	$210	$265
1972-1977	4, solidstate, reverb	$210	$265

Trillium Amplifier Company
2007-present. Brothers Stephen and Scott Campbell build their professional and premium grade, production/custom tube amps in Indianapolis, Indiana.

Trinity Amps
2003-present. Stephen Cohrs builds his production/custom, professional grade, tube amps and cabinets in Toronto, Ontario.

True Tone
1960s. Guitars and amps retailed by Western Auto, manufactured by Chicago guitar makers like Kay.

Hi-Fi 4 (K503 Hot-Line Special) Amp
1960s. Similar to K503, 4 watts from 3 tubes, gray cabinet, gray grille, metal handle.

1960s		$310	$390

Model 5 (K503A) Amp
1960s. 4 tubes, 1x8".

1960s		$335	$420

Vibrato 704 Amp
1960s. Solidstate, 10 watts, 1x8", white sides and gray back, gray grille.

1960s		$115	$145

Vibrato 706 Amp
1960s. Solidstate, 15 watts, 1x15", white sides and gray back, brown grille.

1960s		$135	$170

Tube Works
1987-2004. Founded by B.K. Butler in Denver, Tube Works became a division of Genz Benz Enclosures of Scottsdale, Arizona in 1997. Tube Works' first products were tube guitar effects and in '91 they added tube/solidstate amps, cabinets, and DI boxes to the product mix. In '04, Genz Benz dropped the brand.

Twilighter (Magnatone)
Late-1950s-early-1960s. Magnatone amps private branded for LoDuca Brothers. Prominent block-style capital TWILIGHTER logo on front panel,

generally something nearly equal to Magnatone equivalent. This is just one of many private branded Magnatones. Covers range from brown to black leatherette, and brown to light silver grilles.

Model 213 Amp
1961-1963. About 20 watts, 1x12", vibrato, brown leatherette and brown grille.

1961-1963		$725	$900

Model 260R Amp
1961-1963. About 18 to 25 watts, 1x12", vibrato, brown leatherette cover.

1961-1963		$950	$1,175

Model 280A Amp
Late-1950s-early-1960s. About 35 watts, 2x12", vibrato, brown leatherette cover.

1961-1963		$1,175	$1,475

Two-Rock
1999-present. Tube guitar amp heads, combos and cabinets built by Joe Mloganoski and Bill Krinard (K&M Analog Designs) originally in Cotati, California, currently in Rohnert Park. They also build speakers.

Ugly Amps
2003-present. Steve O'Boyle builds his tube head and combo amps and cabinets in Burbank, California and Reading, Pennsylvania.

UltraSound
A division of UJC Electronics, UltraSound builds acoustically transparent amps, designed by Greg Farres for the acoustic guitarist, in Adel, Iowa.

Unique (Magnatone)
1961-1963. Private branded, typically for an accordion company or accordion studio, uses standard guitar input jacks.

Model 260R Amp
1961-1963. Based on Magnatone 260 Series amp, 35 watts, 2x12" but with reverb, black vinyl-style cover with distinctive black diamond-check pattern running through the top and sides.

1961-1963		$1,400	$1,750

Model 460 Amp
1961-1963. 35 watts, 2x12" and oval 5"x7" speakers, reverb and vibrato make it one of the top models, black vinyl, black grille.

1961-1963		$1,200	$1,500

Universal (Audio Guild)
See Audio Guild amps.

Univox
1964-ca.1978. From '64 to early-'68, these were American-made tube amps with Jensen speakers. By '68, they were using Japanese components in American cabinets, still with Jensen speakers. Electronics were a combination of tube and transistors during this time; this type lasted until the mid-'70s. Around '71, Univox introduced a line of all solidstate amps, as well.

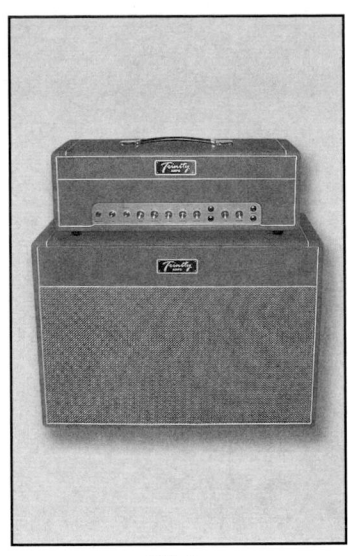

Trinity

Two-Rock Studio Pro 35

UltraSound DS4

AMPS

1950s Valco Ampro
Folkway Music

VHT Standard 12

Victoria 518

MODEL YEAR FEATURES	EXC. COND. LOW	HIGH
Lead Model Tube Amp		
1960s. Tube amp, 2x10" or 2x12".		
1965-1969	$600	$750
Model U45B Bass Amp		
1965-1968. 1x12" combo tube bass amp, 10 watts.		
1965-1968	$310	$390
Model U60A Amp		
1965-1968. 1x12" tube combo.		
1965-1968	$335	$420
Model U65R Amp		
1965-1968. 20 watts, 1x12" tube combo.		
1965-1968	$385	$480
Model U65RD Lead 65 Amp		
1976-1978. Solidstate, 65 watts, reverb, 1x12" or 2x12" in a vertical cab.		
1976-1978	$55	$70
Model U102 Amp		
1965-1968. 1x12" tube combo.		
1965-1968	$385	$480
Model U130B Bass Amp		
1976-1978. Solidstate, 130 watts, 1x15".		
1976-1978	$150	$190
Model U130L Lead Amp		
1976-1978. Solidstate, 130 watts.		
1976-1978	$150	$190
Model U155R Amp		
1965-1968. 20 watts, 1x12" tube combo.		
1965-1968	$500	$625
Model U202R Amp		
1965-1968. 1x12" tube combo.		
1965-1968	$500	$625
Model U305R Amp		
1965-1968. 30 watts, 1x15" tube combo.		
1965-1968	$575	$725
Model U1011 Lead Amp Head		
1976-1978. Solidstate, 100 watts, reverb, tremolo. Name also used on earlier tube head.		
1976-1978	$225	$280
Model U1061 Bass Amp Head		
1976-1978. Solidstate.		
1976-1978	$225	$280
Model U1220 Amp		
1968-1971. Tubes or tube-hybrid, piggyback, 2x12".		
1968-1971	$350	$435
Model U1226 Amp Head		
1971-1972. 60-watt tube amp head.		
1971-1972	$500	$625
Model U1246B Bass Amp Head		
1976-1978. Solidstate, 60 watts.		
1976-1978	$210	$265
Model U1246L Lead Amp Head		
1976-1978. Solidstate.		
1976-1978	$210	$265

Valco

Valco, from Chicago, Illinois, was a big player in the guitar and amplifier business. Their products were private branded for other companies like National, Supro, Airline, Oahu, El Grande and Gretsch.

MODEL YEAR FEATURES	EXC. COND. LOW	HIGH

Valvetech

1997-present. Production/custom, professional grade, amps built by Rob Pierce in Ossian, Indiana.

Valvetrain Amplification

2005-present. Tube combos, amp heads, and speaker cabinets built by Rick Gessner in Sorrento, Florida. He also builds reverb units.

Vamp

1970s. Tube and solidstate amps and speaker cabinets built at Triumph Electronics in England.

Bass Master Amp Head

1970s	100 watts	$1,125	$1,400

VanAmps

1999-present. Tim Van Tassel builds professional, production/custom, amps and cabinets in Golden Valley, Minnesota. He also builds effects.

Vega

1903-present. The original Boston-based company was purchased by C.F. Martin in '70. In '80, the Vega trademark was sold to a Korean company.

A-49 Amp
1960s. Tubes, 6 watts, 1x8", tan cover.

1960s		$250	$310

Director Combo Amp
1950s. Small to mid-size tube amp, 2-tone cover, 2 volume and 1 tone controls, rear mounted control chassis similar to Fender or Gibson from the '50s.

1950s		$425	$525

Lap Steel Amp
1930s-1940s. Various models.

1936	1x12, dark cover	$425	$525
1940s	1x10, tweed	$425	$525

Super Amp
Early 1950s. 1 6L6, 1x10", vertical combo amp typical of the era.

1950s		$425	$525

Triumphal Amp
Late 1940s. 6L6 power, 1x12".

1940s		$425	$525

Versatone (Audio Guild)

See Audio Guild amps.

Vesta Fire

1980s. Japanese imports by Shiino Musical Instruments Corp.; later by Midco International. Mainly known for effects pedals.

VHT

1989-present. Founded by Steven M. Fryette, VHT built amps, combos, and cabinets in Burbank, California. At the beginning of '09 AXL guitars acquired the VHT name and manufactures their own product under that brand. Fryette continues to build the VHT amp models under Fryette Amplification.

MODEL		EXC. COND.	
YEAR	FEATURES	LOW	HIGH

Vibe Amplification

2008-2013. Intermediate grade, production, tube amps, imported from Asia by Lorenzo Brogi in Bologna, Italy.

Victor

Late-1960s. Made in Japan.

Victoria

1994-present. Tube amps, combos, and reverb units built by Mark Baier in Naperville, Illinois. In '08, they changed the logo from the original script Victoria Amp Co. to the current stylized lightning bolt Victoria logo.

Cherry Bomb Amp

2011-present. Tube tremolo, 40 watts, 1x15", alligator/cream tolex.

| 2011-2014 | | $1,450 | $1,850 |

Double Deluxe Amp

1994-present. 35 watts, 2x12".

| 1994-2014 | | $1,500 | $1,875 |

Electro King Amp

2008-present. 1957 GA-40 type circuit, tubes, 15 watts, 1x12".

| 2008-2014 | | $1,350 | $1,700 |

Golden Melody Amp

2008-present. Tubes, reverb, 50 watts, 2x12", alligator/brown tolex.

| 2008-2014 | | $1,500 | $1,900 |

Ivy League Amp

2010-present. Tweed Harvard specs, 14 watts, 1x10".

| 2011-2014 | | $900 | $1,125 |

Model 518 Amp

1994-present. Tweed, 1x8".

| 1994-2014 | | $600 | $750 |

Model 5112-T Amp

2001-present. Tweed, 5 watts, 5F1 circuit, 1x12".

| 2001-2014 | | $675 | $850 |

Model 20112 Amp

1994-present. Tweed, 20 watts, 1x12", tweed.

| 1994-2014 | | $1,100 | $1,250 |

Model 35115 Amp

1994-present. Tweed combo, 28 watts, 1x15".

| 1994-2014 | | $1,400 | $1,750 |

Model 35210 Amp

1994-present. Tweed, 28 watts, 2x10", tweed.

| 1994-2014 | | $1,400 | $1,750 |

Model 35212-T Amp

1990s. Tweed, 35 watts, 2x12".

| 1990s | | $1,550 | $1,925 |

Model 35310-T Amp

1994-present. Tweed, 28 watts, 3x10".

| 1994-2014 | | $1,550 | $1,925 |

Model 45115-T Amp

2008-2009. Tweed, 45 watts, 1x15".

| 2008-2009 | | $1,400 | $1,750 |

Model 45410-T Amp

1994-present. Tweed, 45 watts, 4x10" combo, tweed.

| 1994-2014 | | $1,550 | $1,925 |

Model 50212-T Amp

2002-present. Tweed, 50 watts, 2x12" combo.

| 2002-2014 | | $1,600 | $2,000 |

Model 80212 Amp

1994-present. Tweed, 80 watts, 2x12", tweed.

| 1994-2014 | | $1,700 | $2,100 |

Regal Amp

2004-2006. Class A with 1 x 6L6, 15 watts, 1x15", brown tolex cover, rear mount controls.

| 2004-2006 | | $1,400 | $1,750 |

Regal II/Regal Amp

2006-present. Class A, 35 watts, 1x15", tweed or vanilla tolex, rear mount controls. The II removed from name about '13.

| 2006-2014 | | $1,400 | $1,750 |

Silver Sonic Amp

2011-present. Tube reverb, 20 watts, 1x12", 2-tone black/cream cab with Sonic Blue or black tolex.

| 2011-2014 | | $1,725 | $2,150 |

Trem D'La Trem

2007-present. Tweed design,14 watts, 1x15".

| 2007-2014 | | $1,375 | $1,700 |

Victoriette Amp

2001-present. 20 watts, 1x12" or 2x10", reverb, tremolo in '01.

| 2001-2014 | 2x10 | $1,400 | $1,750 |

Victorilux Amp

2001-present. 15 watts, 2x12", 3x10" or 1x15", EL84s, reverb, tremolo.

| 2001-2014 | 3x10 | $1,550 | $1,925 |

Vintage47

2010-present. Founder/builder David Barnes, of California, builds retro-inspired compact amps that reflect old-school Valco values, handwired, intermediate and professional grade.

Vivi-Tone

1932-1938. Founded in Kalamazoo, Michigan, by former Gibson designer Lloyd Loar and others, Vivi-Tone sold small amps built by Webster Electric to accompany their early electric solidbody guitars.

V-M (Voice of Music) Corp.

1944-1977. Started out building record changers in Benton Harbor, Michigan. By the early '50s had added amplified phonographs, consoles, and tape recorders as well as OEM products for others. Their portable PA systems can be used for musical instruments. Products sport the VM logo.

Small Portable Amp

1950s. Standard phono input for instrument, phono and microphone controls, wood combo cabinet, 1x10" or 1x12" Jensen.

| 1950s | | $280 | $350 |

Voltmaster

Trapezoid-shaped combo amps and reverb units made in Plano, Texas, in the late 1990s.

Voodoo

1998-present. Tube amp heads and speaker cabinets built in Lansing, New York by Trace Davis, Anthony Cacciotti, and Mike Foster.

Victoria Regal

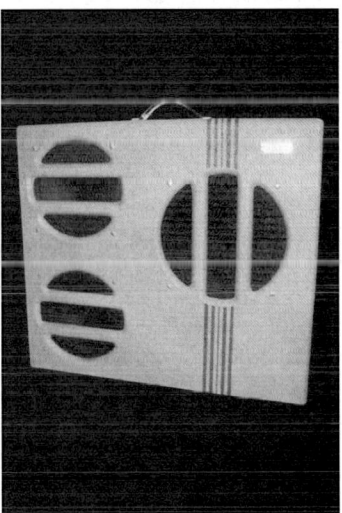

Vintage47

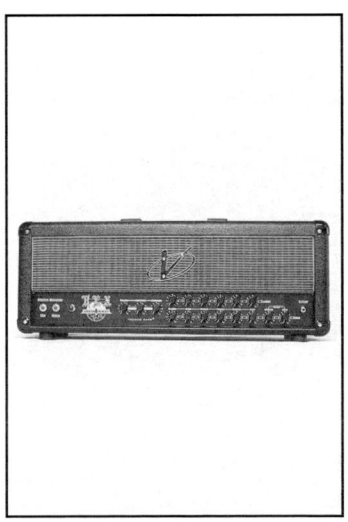

Voodoo Hex

To get the most from this book, be sure to read "Using *The Guide*" in the introduction.

Vox AC-4 TV Mini

1965 Vox AC-4
Steve Lee

Vox AC-15CC

Vox

1954-present. Tom Jennings and Dick Denney combined forces in '57 to produce the first Vox amp, the 15-watt AC-15. The period between '57-'68 is considered to be the Vox heyday. Vox produced tube amps in England and also the U.S. from '64 to '65. English-made tube amps were standardized between '60 and '65. U.S.-made Vox amps in '66 were solidstate. In the mid-'60s, similar model names were sometimes used for tube and solidstate amps. In '93 Korg bought the Vox name and current products are built by Marshall. Those amps that originally came with a trolley or stand are priced including the original trolley or stand, and an amp without one will be worth less than the amount shown. Smaller amps were not originally equipped with a trolley or stand (if a speaker cabinet mounts to it and it tilts, it is called a trolley; otherwise referred to as a stand).

4120 Bass Amp
1966-1967. Hybrid solidstate and tube bass amp.

MODEL YEAR	FEATURES	EXC. COND. LOW	HIGH
1966-1967		$525	$655

7120 Guitar Amp
1966-1967. Hybrid solidstate and tube amp, 120 watts.

1966-1967		$525	$655

AC-4 Amp
1961-1965. Made in England, early Vox tube design, 3.5 watts, 1x8", tremolo.

1961-1965		$1,155	$1,450

AC-4TV Amp
2009-present. Tube, 4 watts, in 1x10 (AC-4TV8 is 1x8) combo or amp head with 1x12 cab, EL84 power tube, 12AX7 powered preamp. AC-4TVmini combo has 6.5 inch speaker.

2009-2013	1x12	$110	$140
2009-2013	1x8	$115	$145
2009-2013	Head only	$130	$165
2009-2014	1x10	$130	$165

AC-10 Amp
1958-1965. Made in England, 12 watts, 1x10", tremolo, this tube version not made in U.S. ('64-'65).

1958-1965		$2,075	$2,600

AC-10 Twin Amp
1962-1965. Made in England, also made in U.S. '64-'65, 12 watts (2xEL84s), 2x10".

1962-1965		$2,750	$3,400

AC-15 Amp
1958-1965. 15 watts, 1x12", TV front changed to split front in fall '60.

1958	TV front	$4,250	$5,250
1958-1965	Split front	$3,650	$4,550

AC-15 Twin Amp
1961-1965. Tube, 2x12", 18 watts.

1961-1965	Standard colors	$3,850	$4,750
1962-1965	Custom colors	$4,050	$5,050

AC-15 50th Anniversary Amp
2007. 50th Anniversary 1957-2007 plaque on lower left front of grille, hand wired, white tolex.

2007		$735	$920

AC-15H1TV Amp
2008-2009. Part of Heritage Collection, limited edition, 200 made, hand wired, oiled mahogany cabinet.

MODEL YEAR	FEATURES	EXC. COND. LOW	HIGH
2008-2009		$950	$1,190

AC-15TBX Amp
1996-2000. 15 watts, top boost, 1x12" Celestion (lower cost Eminence available).

1996-2000		$840	$1,050

AC-15C1 Amp
2010-2013. China, 15 watts, 1x12", tube, reverb and tremolo.

2010-2014		$450	$575

AC-15CC Custom Classic Amp
2006-2012. Made in China, 15 watts, 1x12" tube combo, master volume, reverb, tremolo, 2-button footswitch.

2006-2012		$450	$575

AC-30 Reissue Model Amp
1980s-1990s-2000s. Standard reissue and limited edition models with identification plate on back of the amp. Models include the AC-30 Reissue and Reissue custom color (1980s-1990s), AC-30 25th Anniv. (1985-1986), AC-30 30th Anniv. (1991), AC-30 Collector Model (1990s, mahogany cabinet) and the AC-30HW Hand Wired (1990s).

1980s	Reissue	$1,365	$1,700
1985-1986	25th Anniv.	$1,365	$1,700
1990s	Collector Model	$1,900	$2,375
1990s	Custom colors	$1,475	$1,850
1990s	Hand wired	$1,900	$2,375
1990s	Reissue	$1,155	$1,450
1991	30th Anniv.	$1,625	$2,025
2000s	Reissue	$1,150	$1,450

AC-30 Super Twin Amp Set
1960-1965. Piggyback head and 2x12" pressure cabinet with amp trolley.

1960-1965		$5,450	$6,825

AC-30 Twin/AC-30 Twin Top Boost Amp
1960-1972. Made in England, tube, 30-watt head, 36 watts 2x12", Top Boost includes additional treble and bass, custom colors available in '60-'63.

1960-1963	Custom colors	$4,300	$5,375
1960-1965		$3,750	$4,650
1966		$3,050	$3,800
1967-1972		$2,800	$3,500

AC-30BM Brian May Limited Edition Amp
2007. 30 watts, 2x12" combo.

2007		$1,475	$1,850

AC-30CC Custom Classic Amp
2006. Made in China, 30 watts, 2x12", tubes, 2-button footswitch.

2006		$760	$950

AC-30VR Valve Reactor Amp
2010-present. 2x12" combo, digital reverb, 30 watts.

2010-2014		$340	$425

AC-50 Amp Head
1963-1975. Made in England, 50-watt head, U.S. production '64-'65 tube version is Westminster Bass, U.S. post-'66 is solidstate.

1963-1975		$1,775	$2,225

MODEL YEAR	FEATURES	EXC. COND. LOW	HIGH
AC-50 Cabinet			
1963-1975	Black	$735	$925

AC-100 MK I Amp

1963-1965. All tube 100-watt with 4x12 cab, due to reliability concerns it was transitioned to AC-100 Super De Luxe MK II in '65.

1963-1965		$4,200	$5,250

AC-100 Super De Luxe MK II Amp

1965. Solidstate 100-watt head with 4x12 cab on speaker trolley.

1965		$2,300	$2,875

Berkeley II V108 (Tube) Amp

1964-1966. U.S.-made tube amp, revised '66-'69 to U.S.-made solidstate model V1081, 18 watts, 2x10" piggyback.

1964-1966		$1,025	$1,275

Berkeley II V1081 (Solidstate) Amp

1966-1967. U.S.-made solidstate model V1081, 35 watts, 2x10" piggyback, includes trolley stand.

1966-1967		$735	$925

Berkeley III (Solidstate) Amp

1968. Berkeley III logo on top panel of amp.

1968		$850	$1,065

Buckingham Amp

1966-1969. Solidstate, 70 watts, 2x12" piggyback, includes trolley stand.

1966-1968		$850	$1,065

Cambridge 15 Amp

1999-2001. 15 watts, 1x8", tremolo.

1999-2001		$135	$170

Cambridge 30 Reverb Amp

1999-2002. 30 watts, 1x10", tremolo and reverb.

1999-2002		$160	$200

Cambridge 30 Reverb Twin 210 Amp

1999-2002. 30 watts hybrid circuit, 2x10", reverb.

1999-2002		$195	$245

Cambridge Reverb V1031/V1032 (Solidstate) Amp

1966-1968. Solidstate, 35 watts, 1x10", model V1031 replaced tube version V103.

1966-1968		$575	$725

Cambridge Reverb V3/V103 (Tube) Amp

1965-1966. U.S-made tube version, 18 watts, 1x10", a Pacemaker with reverb, superceded by solidstate Model V1031 by '67.

1965-1966		$950	$1,200

Churchill PA V119 Amp Head and V1091 Cabinet Set

Late-1960s. PA head with multiple inputs and 2 column speakers.

1960s	Head & cabs	$800	$1,000
1960s	PA head only	$425	$530

Climax V-125/V-125 Lead Combo Amp

1970-1991. Solidstate, 125 watts, 2x12" combo, 5-band EQ, master volume.

1970-1991		$525	$655

DA Series Amp

2006-2013. Small digital modeling amps, AC/DC power, solidstate.

2006-2013	DA5, 5w, 1x6.5	$80	$100
2007-2009	DA10, 10w, 2x6	$100	$125
2007-2009	DA20, 20w, 2x8	$110	$140
2010	DA15, 15w, 1x8	$75	$95

Defiant Amp

1966-1970. Made in England, 50 watts, 2x12" + Midax horn cabinet.

1966-1970		$1,625	$2,030

Escort Amp

Late 1960s-1983. 2.5 watt battery-powered portable amp.

1968-1986		$375	$475

Essex V1042 Bass Amp

1966-1968. U.S.-made solidstate, 35 watts, 2x12". Also called Essex Bass Deluxe.

1966-1968		$525	$655

Foundation Bass Amp

1966-1970. Tube in '66, solidstate after, 50 watts, 1x18", made in England only.

1966	Tubes	$1,550	$1,940
1967-1970	Solidstate	$685	$855

Kensington V1241 Bass Amp

1966-1968. U.S.-made solidstate bass amp, 22 watts, 1x15", G-tuner, called Kensington Bass Deluxe in '67.

1966-1968		$630	$790

Night Train 15 Amp Head

2009-2013. Small tube head, mirror-finish chrome body, 15 watts.

2009-2013		$290	$365

Pacemaker V1021 (Solidstate) Amp

1966-1968. U.S.-made solidstate amp, 35 watts, 1x10", replaced Pacemaker model V102.

1966-1968		$420	$525

Pacemaker V2/V102 (Tube) Amp

1965-1966. U.S.-made tube amp, 18 watts, 1x10", replaced by solidstate Pacemaker model V1021.

1965-1966		$865	$1,080

Pathfinder (Import) Amp

1998-present. Compact amps with 1960s cosmetics.

1998-2013	15, 15w, 1x8"	$70	$90
2002-2014	10, 10w, 6.5"	$60	$75

Pathfinder V1/V101 (Tube) Amp

1965-1966. U.S.-made tube amp, 4 watts, 1x8", '66-'69 became U.S.-made solidstate V1011.

1965-1966		$865	$1,080

Pathfinder V1011 (Solidstate) Amp

1966-1968. U.S.-made solidstate, 25 watts peak power, 1x8".

1966-1968		$400	$500

Royal Guardsman V1131/V1132 Amp

1966-1968. U.S.-made solidstate, 50 watts piggyback, 2x12" + 1 horn, the model below the Super Beatle V1141/V1142.

1966-1968		$1,285	$1,600

Scorpion (Solidstate) Amp

1968. Solidstate, 120 watts, 4x10" Vox Oxford speaker.

1968		$550	$690

Super Beatle Reissue Amp Cabinet

2011-2012. 2x15" cab only.

2011-2012		$340	$425

1960 Vox AC-30 Twin

1970 Vox Escort
Steve Lee

Vox Pathfinder 10

Vox Valvetronix VT15

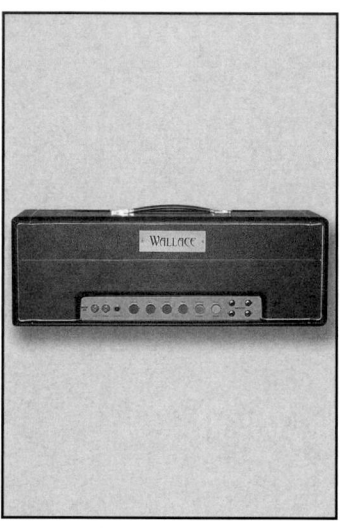

Wallace BKW 45/100

Warwick LWA 1000

MODEL YEAR	FEATURES	EXC. COND. LOW	HIGH

Super Beatle V1141/V1142 Amp
1965-1966. U.S.-made 120 watt solidstate, 4x12" + 2 horns, with distortion pedal (V1141), or without (V1142).

1965-1966		$3,650	$4,550

T-60 Amp
1962-1966. Solidstate bass head, around 40 watts, sold with 2x15" or 1x12" and 1x15" cabinet.

1962-1966		$685	$855

VBM1 Brian May Special Amp
2010. Compact 10-watt, 1x6" speaker, also called VBM1 Brian May Recording Amp, white cover, includes headphone/recording line out, Brian May logo on lower right grille.

2010		$130	$165

Viscount V1151/V1152 Amp
1966-1968. U.S.-made solidstate, 70 watts, 2x12" combo, 1151, 1153, and 1154 with distortion.

1966-1968		$735	$925

VT Valvetronix Series Amps
2008-present. Line of digital modeling combo amps, ranging from the 15 watt, 1x8" VT15 ('08-'11) to the 120 watt, 2x12" VT120.

2008-2011 VT15		$125	$155
2012-2014 VT20+		$140	$175

Westminster V118 Bass Amp
1966. Solidstate, 120 watts, 1x18".

1966		$600	$750

V-Series
See Crate.

Wabash
1950s. Private branded amps, made by others, distributed by the David Wexler company. They also offered lap steels and guitars.

Model 1158 Amp
1955. Danelectro-made, 1x15", 2x6L6 power tubes, tweed.

1955		$440	$550

Small Amp
1940s	3 tubes	$215	$270

Wallace Amplification
2000-present. Production/custom, professional grade, amps built by Brian Wallace in Livonia, Michigan. (Not affiliated with a 1970's amp company from the United Kingdom also called Wallace that has since gone out of business.)

Warbler
See listing under Juke amps.

Warwick
1982-present. Combos, amp heads and cabinets from Warwick Basses of Markneukirchen, Germany.

Washburn
1962-present. Imported guitar and bass amps. Washburn also offers guitars, banjos, mandolins, and basses.

MODEL YEAR	FEATURES	EXC. COND. LOW	HIGH

Watkins
1957-present. England's Watkins Electric Music (WEM) was founded by Charlie Watkins. Their first commercial product was the Watkins Dominator (wedge Gibson stereo amp shape) in '57, followed by the Copicat Echo in '58. They currently build accordion amps.

Clubman Amp
1960s. Small combo amp with typical Watkins styling, blue cover, white grille.

1960s		$600	$750

Dominator MK Series Amp
1970s. Similar circuit to '50s tube amps except solidstate rectifier, 25 watts, different speaker used for different applications.

1970s	MK I, bass, 1x15	$475	$600
1970s	MK II, organ, 1x12	$475	$600
1970s	MK III, guitar, 1x12	$600	$750

Dominator V-Front Amp
Late-1950s-1960s, 2004. 18 watts, 2x10", wedge cabinet similar to Gibson GA-79 stereo amp, tortoise and light beige cab, light grille, requires 220V step-up transformer. Was again offered in '04.

1959-1962		$2,200	$2,775

Scout Amp
1960s. 17 watts, 1x10 combo, 6 tubes.

1960		$600	$750

Westminster Tremolo Amp
1959-1962. 10-watt 1x10" combo, Westminster Tremolo logo on top panel, 3 control knobs, blue and white cover.

1959-1962		$600	$750

Webcor
1940s-1950s. The Webster-Chicago Company built recording and audio equipment including portable amplifiers suitable for record turntables, PAs, or general utility. Low power with one or two small speakers.

Small Amp
1950s	1 or 2 speakers	$220	$275

West Laboratories
1965-1970s, 2005-. Founded by David W. West in Flint, Michigan, moved to Lansing in '68. The '71 catalog included three tube and two solidstate amps, speaker cabinets, as well as Vocal Units and Mini Series combo amps. Amps were available as heads, piggyback half-stacks and full-stacks, with the exception of the combo Mini Series. The Fillmore tube amp head was the most popular model. West equipment has a West logo on the front and the cabinets also have a model number logo on the grille. David West reestablished his company in 2005, located in Okemos, Michigan, with models offered on a custom order basis, concentrating on lower power EL84 designs.

Avalon Amp Head
1970s. 50 watts, 2 6CA7 output tubes.

1970s		$565	$700

MODEL YEAR	FEATURES	EXC. COND. LOW	HIGH

Fillmore Amp Head
1970s. 200 watts, 4 KT88 output tubes.

1970s		$2,125	$2,650

Grande Amp Head
1970s. 100 watts, 2 KT88 output tubes.

1970s		$860	$1,075

Mini IR Amp
1970s. 50 watts, 1x12 tube combo with reverb, black tolex, large West logo and model name Mini IR on front panel.

1970s		$760	$950

White

1955-1960. The White brand, named after plant manager Forrest White, was established by Fender to provide steel and small amp sets to teaching studios that were not Fender-authorized dealers. The amps were sold with the matching steel guitar. See Steel section for pricing.

White (Matamp)

See Matamp listing.

Winfield Amplification

2001-present. Intermediate and professional grade, production, vacuum tube amps built by Winfield N. Thomas first in Greensboro, Vermont and presently in Cochise, Arizona.

Wizard

1988-present. Professional and premium grade, production/custom, guitar and bass, amps and cabinets built by Rick St Pierre in Cornwall, Ontario.

Woodson

Early 1970s. Obscure builder from Bolivar, Missouri. Woodson logo on front panel and Woodson Model and Serial Number plate on back panel, solidstate circuit, student level pricing.

Working Dog

2001-present. Lower cost tube amps and combos built by Alessandro High-End Products (Alessandro, Hound Dog) in Huntingdon Valley, Pennsylvania.

Wright Amplification

2004-present. Aaron C. Wright builds his professional grade, production/custom, amps and cabinets in Lincoln, Nebraska.

Yamaha

1946-present. Yamaha started building amps in the '60s and offered a variety of guitar and bass amps over the years. The current models are solidstate bass amps. They also build guitars, basses, effects, sound gear and other instruments.

Budokan HY-10G II Amp
1987-1992. Portable, 10 watts, distortion control, EQ.

1987-1992		$80	$100

G30-112 Amp
1983-1992. Solidstate combo, 30 watts, 1x12".

1983-1992		$200	$250

G50-112 Amp
1983-1992. 50 watts, 1x12".

1983-1992		$225	$275

G100-112 Amp
1983-1992. 100 watts, 1x12" combo, black cover, striped grille.

1983-1992		$250	$300

G100-212 Amp
1983-1992. 100, 2x12" combo, black cover, striped grille.

1983-1992		$275	$350

JX30B Amp
1983-1992. Bass amp, 30 watts.

1983-1992		$170	$210

TA-20 Amp
1968-1972. Upright wedge shape with controls facing upwards, solidstate.

1968-1972		$150	$185

TA-25 Amp
1968-1972. Upright wedge shape with controls facing upwards, 40 watts, 1x12", solidstate, black or red cover.

1968-1972		$175	$220

TA-30 Amp
1968-1972. Upright wedge shape, solidstate.

1968-1972		$200	$250

TA-50 Amp
1971-1972. Solidstate combo, 80 watts, 2x12", includes built-in cart with wheels, black cover.

1971-1972		$225	$280

TA-60 Amp
1968-1972. Upright wedge shape, solidstate, most expensive of wedge-shape amps.

1968-1972		$230	$285

VR3000 Amp
1988-1992. Combo 1x12", 2 channels, identical control sections for each channel, settings are completely independent.

1988-1992		$180	$225

VR4000 Amp
1988-1992. 50-watt stereo, 2 channels, EQ, stereo chorus, reverb and dual effects loops.

1988-1992		$275	$340

VR6000 Amp
1988-1992. 100-watt stereo, 2 channels which can also be combined, EQ, chorus, reverb and dual effects loops.

1988-1992		$365	$455

VX-15 Amp
1988-1992. 15 watts.

1988-1992		$135	$170

VX-65D Bass Amp
1984-1992. 80 watts, 2 speakers.

1984-1992		$175	$220

YBA-65 Bass Amp
1972-1976. Solidstate combo, 60 watts, 1x15".

1972-1976		$175	$220

Early-1970s Watkins WEM Dominator MkIII

Wizard Vintage Classic

Yamaha VR4000

To get the most from this book, be sure to read "Using *The Guide*" in the introduction.

Z.Vex Nano Head

*Zeppelin Design
Labs Percolator*

Zinky Blue Velvet

MODEL YEAR	FEATURES	EXC. COND. LOW	HIGH
YTA-25 Amp			
1972-1976. Solidstate combo, 25 watts, 1x12".			
1972-1976		$175	$220
YTA-45 Amp			
1972-1976. Solidstate combo, 45 watts, 1x12".			
1972-1976		$175	$220
YTA-95 Amp			
1972-1976. Solidstate combo, 90 watts, 1x12".			
1972-1976		$175	$220
YTA-100 Amp			
1972-1976. Solidstate piggyback, 100 watts, 2x12".			
1972-1976		$225	$280
YTA-110 Amp			
1972-1976. Solidstate piggyback, 100 watts, 2x12" in extra large cab.			
1972-1976		$225	$280
YTA-200 Amp			
1972-1976. Solidstate piggyback, 200 watts, 4x12".			
1972-1976		$270	$335
YTA-300 Amp			
1972-1976. Solidstate piggyback, 200 watts, dual cabs with 2x12" and 4x12".			
1972-1976		$390	$485
YTA-400 Amp			
1972-1976. Solidstate piggyback, 200 watts, dual 4x12".			
1972-1976		$390	$485

Z.Vex Amps

2002-present. Intermediate grade, production amps built by Zachary Vex in Minneapolis, Minnesota with some subassembly work done in Michigan. He also builds effects.

MODEL YEAR	FEATURES	EXC. COND. LOW	HIGH

Zapp

Ca.1978-early-1980s. Zapp amps were distributed by Red Tree Music, Inc., of Mamaroneck, New York.

Z-10 Amp			
1978-1980s. Small student amp, 8 watts.			
1979-1982		$40	$60
Z-50 Amp			
1978-1980s. Small student amp, 10 watts, reverb, tremelo.			
1978-1982		$45	$65

Zeppelin Design Labs

2014-present. Brach Siemens and Glen van Alkemade build budget and intermediate grade amps and cabinets in Chicago, Illinois. They also offer their products as DIY kits.

Zeta

1982-2010. Solid state amps with MIDI options, made in Oakland, California. They also made upright basses and violins.

Zinky

1999-present. Tube head and combo amps and cabinets built by Bruce Zinky in Flagstaff, Arizona. He also builds the mini Smokey amps (since '97), effects, and has revived the Supro brand on a guitar and amp.

ZT Amplifiers

2009-present. Ken Kantor of Berkeley, California imports intermediate grade, production, solid state compact amps from China. He also offers effects.

EFFECTS

ADA Flanger ca. 1970s

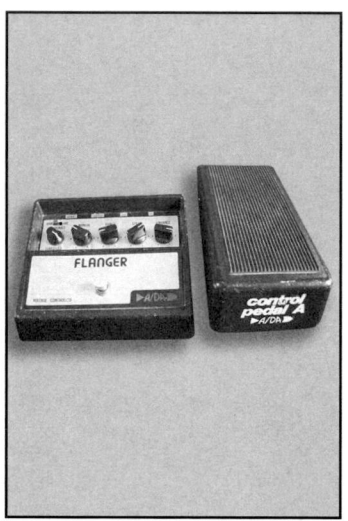

ADA Flanger with Control Pedal

Jim Schreck

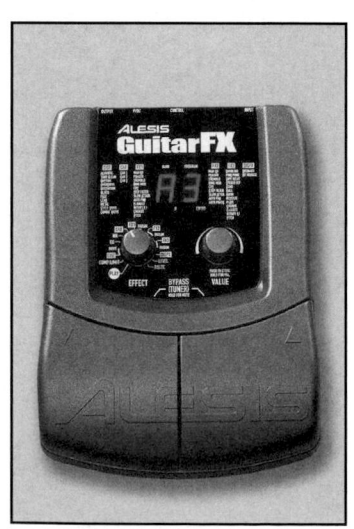

Alesis GuitarFX

Ace-Tone

1968-1972. Effects from Ace Electronic Industry, which was a part of Sakata Shokai Limited of Osaka, Japan, which also made organs, amps, pioneering Rhythm Ace FR-1 and FR-2 drum machines, etc. Their Ace-Tone effects line was the predecessor to Roland and Boss.

Echo Chamber EC-10
1968-1972. Solidstate tape echo.

1968-1972	$200	$400

Expander EXP-4
1968-1972. "Expander" effect.

1968-1972	$175	$200

Fuzz Master FM-1
1968-1972. Distortion and overdrive.

1968-1972	$250	$350

Fuzz Master FM-2
1968-1972. Fuzz. Black housing. 2 Control knobs.

1968-1972	$175	$250

Fuzz Master FM-3
1968-1972. Distortion and clean boost.

1968-1972	$450	$600

Stereo Phasor LH-100
1968-1972. Phaser.

1968-1972	$275	$340

Wah Master WM-1
1968-1972. Filter wah.

1968-1972	$75	$150

Acoustyx

1977-1982. Made by the Highland Corporation of North Springfield, Vermont.

Image Synthesizer IS-1
1977-ca.1982. Synthesizer effects.

1977-1982	$50	$60

Phase Five
1977-ca.1982. Used 6 C cell batteries!

1977-1982	$50	$60

ADA

1975-2002. Analog/Digital Associates was located in Berkeley, California, and introduced its Flanger and Final Phase in '77. The company later moved to Oakland and made amplifiers, high-tech signal processors, and a reissue of its original Flanger.

Final Phase
1977-1979. Reissued in '97.

1977-1979	$375	$450

Flanger
1977-1983, 1996-2002. Reissued in '96.

1977-1979	With control pedal	$375	$450
1977-1979	Without control pedal	$325	$400
1980-1983		$225	$300
1996-2002		$75	$100

MP-1
1987-1995. Tube preamp with chorus and effects loop, MIDI.

1987-1995	With optional foot controller	$200	$250
1987-1995	Without optional foot controller	$150	$200

MP-2
Ca.1988-1995. Tube preamp with chorus, 9-band EQ and effects loop, MIDI.

1988-1995	$225	$275

Pitchtraq
1987. Programmable pitch transposer including octave shifts.

1987	$150	$200

Stereo Tapped Delay STD-1
Introduced in 1981.

1980s	$150	$200

TFX4 Time Effects
Introduced in 1982, includes flanger, chorus, doubler, echo.

1980s	$150	$200

Aguilar

1995-present. The New York, New York amp builder also offers a line of tube and solidstate pre-amps.

Akai

1984-present. In '99, Akai added guitar effects to their line of electronic samplers and sequencers for musicians.

Alamo

1947-1982. Founded by Charles Eilenberg, Milton Fink, and Southern Music, San Antonio, Texas. Distributed by Bruno & Sons. Mainly known for guitars and amps, Alamo did offer a reverb unit.

Reverb Unit
1965-ca.1979. Has a Hammond reverb system, balance and intensity controls. By '73 the unit had 3 controls - mixer, contour, and intensity.

1965-1970	$300	$375

Alesis

1992-present. Alesis has a wide range of products for the music industry, including digital processors and amps for guitars.

Allen Amplification

1998-present. David Allen's company, located in Richwood, Kentucky, mainly produces amps, but they also offer a tube overdrive pedal.

Altair Corp.

1977-1980s. Company was located in Ann Arbor, Michigan.

Power Attenuator PW-5
1977-1980. Goes between amp and speaker to dampen volume.

1977-1980	$90	$120

Amdek

Mid-1980s. Amdek offered many electronic products over the years, including drum machines and guitar effects. Most of these were sold in kit form so quality of construction can vary.

EFFECTS

MODEL YEAR	FEATURES	EXC. COND. LOW	HIGH

Delay Machine DMK-200
1983. Variable delay times.

1983		$85	$115

Octaver OCK-100
1983. Produces tone 1 or 2 octaves below the note played.

1983		$75	$100

Phaser PHK-100

1983		$75	$100

Ampeg
Ampeg entered the effects market in the late-1960s. Their offerings in the early-'60s were really amplifier-outboard reverb units similar to the ones offered by Gibson (GA-1). Ampeg offered a line of imported effects in '82-'83, known as the A-series (A-1 through A-9), and reintroduced effects to their product line in '05.

Analog Delay A-8
1982-1983. Made in Japan.

1982-1983		$75	$125

Chorus A-6
1982-1983. Made in Japan.

1982-1983		$50	$75

Compressor A-2
1982-1983. Made in Japan.

1982-1983		$50	$75

Distortion A-1
1982-1983. Made in Japan.

1982-1983		$50	$75

Echo Jet Reverb EJ-12
1963-1965. Outboard, alligator clip reverb unit with 12" speaker, 12 watts, technically a reverb unit. When used as a stand-alone amp, the reverb is off. Named EJ-12A in '65.

1963-1965		$550	$650

Echo Satellite ES-1
1961-1963. Outboard reverb unit with amplifier and speaker alligator clip.

1961-1963		$550	$650

Flanger A-5
1982-1983. Made in Japan.

1982-1983		$50	$75

Multi-Octaver A-7
1982-1983. Made in Japan.

1982-1983		$50	$100

Over Drive A-3
1982-1983. Made in Japan.

1982-1983		$50	$75

Parametric Equalizer A-9
1982-1983. Made in Japan.

1982-1983		$45	$70

Phaser A-4
1982-1983. Made in Japan.

1982-1983		$50	$75

Phazzer

1975-1977		$50	$75

Scrambler Fuzz
1969. Distortion pedal, black housing. 2 Control knobs. Reissued in '05.

1969		$150	$200

Amplifier Corporation of America
Late '60s company that made amps for Univox and also marketed effects under their own name.

Amptweaker
2010-present. James Brown, an amp design engineer previously employed by Peavey, then for Kustom amps, now designs and builds effects in Batavia, Ohio.

amukaT Gadgets
2006-present. Guitar effects built by Takuma Kanaiwa in New York, New York.

Analog Man
1994-present. Founded by Mike Piera in '94 with full-time production by 2000. Located in Danbury, Connecticut (until '07 in Bethel), producing chorus, compressor, fuzz, and boost pedals by '03.

Aphex Systems
1975-present. Founded in Massachusetts by Marvin Caesar and Curt Knoppel, to build their Aural Exciter and other pro sound gear. Currently located in Sun Valley, California, and building a variety of gear for the pro audio broadcast, pro music and home-recording markets.

Apollo
Ca.1967-1972. Imported from Japan by St. Louis Music, includes Fuzz Treble Boost Box, Crier Wa-Wa, Deluxe Fuzz. They also offered basses and guitars.

Crier Wa-Wa
Ca.1967-1972.

1967-1972		$125	$200

Fuzz/Deluxe Fuzz
Ca.1967-1972. Includes the Fuzz Treble Boost Box and the Deluxe Fuzz.

1967-1972		$125	$200

Surf Tornado Wah Wah
Ca.1967-1972.

1967-1972		$175	$250

Arbiter
Ivor Arbiter and Arbiter Music, London, began making the circular Fuzz Face stompbox in 1966. Other products included the Fuzz Wah and Fuzz Wah Face. In '68 the company went public as Arbiter and Western, later transitioning to Dallas-Arbiter. Refer to Dallas-Arbiter for listings.

Area 51
2003-present. Guitar effects made in Newaygo, Michigan (made in Texas until early '06), by Dan Albrecht. They also build amps.

Aria/Aria Pro II
1956-present. Aria provided a line of effects, made by Maxon, in the mid-'80s.

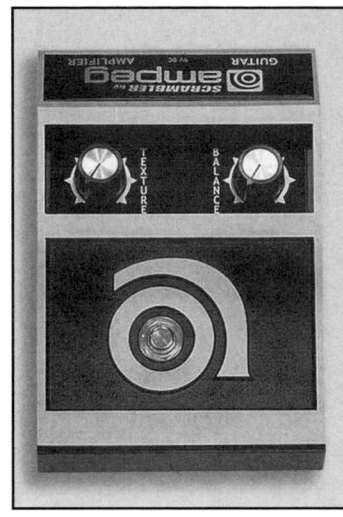
Ampeg Scrambler Fuzz

amukaT Gadgets Optical Expression Device

Analog Man Sun Face
Keith Myers

EFFECTS

To get the most from this book, be sure to read "Using *The Guide*" in the introduction.

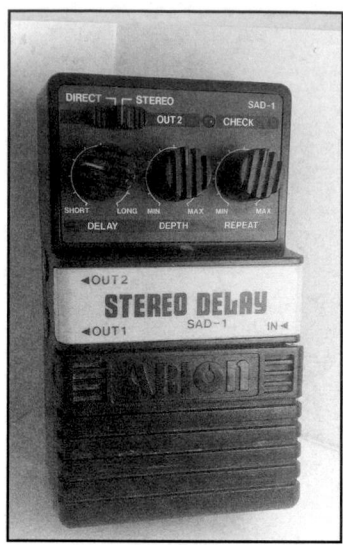

Arion Delay SAD-1
Keith Myers

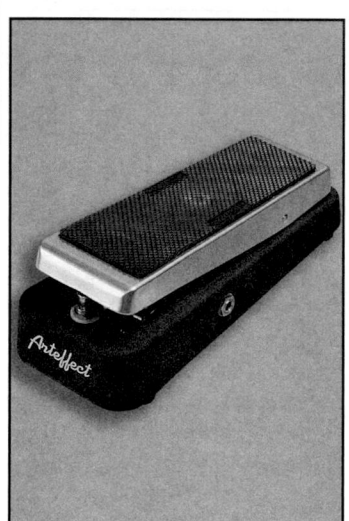

Arteffect Bonnie Wah

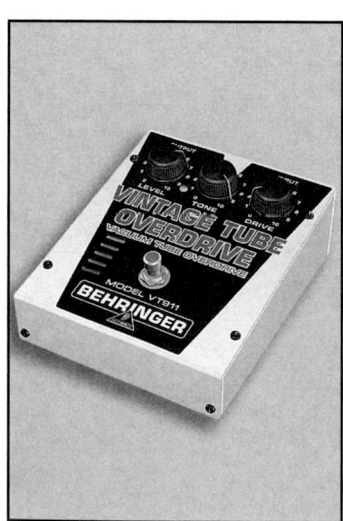

Behringer Vintage Tube Overdrive VT911

MODEL YEAR FEATURES	EXC. COND. LOW	HIGH
Analog Delay AD-10		
1983-1985. Dual-stage stereo.		
1983-1985	$65	$75
Chorus ACH-1		
1986-1987. Stereo.		
1986-1987	$40	$50
Chorus CH-10		
1983-1985. Dual-stage stereo.		
1983-1985	$40	$50
Chorus CH-5		
1985-1987	$40	$50
Compressor CO-10		
1983-1985	$40	$50
Digital Delay ADD-100		
1984-1986. Delay, flanging, chorus, doubling, hold.		
1984-1986	$65	$75
Digital Delay DD-X10		
1985-1987	$65	$75
Distortion DT-5		
1985-1987	$40	$50
Distortion DT-10		
1983-1985. Dual-stage.		
1983-1985	$40	$50
Flanger AFL-1		
1986. Stereo.		
1986	$50	$60
Flanger FL-10		
1983-1985. Dual-stage stereo.		
1983-1985	$50	$60
Flanger FL-5		
1985-1987	$50	$60
Metal Pedal MP-5		
1985-1987	$40	$50
Noise Gate NG-10		
1983-1985	$30	$40
Over Drive OD-10		
1983-1985. Dual-stage.		
1983-1985	$40	$50
Parametric Equalizer EQ-10		
1983-1985	$40	$50
Phase Shifter PS-10		
1983-1984. Dual-stage.		
1983-1984	$50	$60
Programmable Effects Pedal APE-1		
1984-1986. Compression, distortion, delay, chorus.		
1984-1986	$50	$60

Arion

1984-present. Arion offers a wide variety of budget imported effects.

Guitar and Bass Effects

1984-2014	$15	$45

Arteffect

2006-present. Tom Kochawi and Dan Orr build analog effects in Haifa and Natanya, Israel.

Asama

1970s-1980s. This Japanese company offered solidbody guitars with built-in effects as well as stand-alone units. They also offered basses, drum machines and other music products.

Astrotone

Late 1960s. By Universal Amp, which also made the Sam Ash Fuzzz Boxx.

Fuzz

1966. Introduced in '66, same as Sam Ash Fuzzz Boxx.

1966	$175	$275

ATD

Mid-1960s-early 1980s. Made by the All-Test Devices corporation of Long Beach, New York. In the mid-'60s, Richard Minz and an associate started making effects part-time, selling them through Manny's Music in New York. They formed All-Test and started making Maestro effects and transducer pickups for CMI, which owned Gibson at the time. By '75, All-Test was marketing effects under their own brand. All-Test is still making products for other industries, but by the early to mid-'80s they were no longer making products for the guitar.

PB-1 Power Booster

1976-ca.1980.

1979-1980	$50	$60

Volume Pedal EV-1

1979-ca.1980.

1979-1980	$30	$40

Wah-Wah/Volume Pedal WV-1

1979-ca.1981.

1979-1981	$50	$60

Audio Matrix

1979-1984. Effects built by B.K Butler in Escondido, California. He later designed the Tube Driver and founded Tube Works in 1987. He nows operates Butler Audio, making home and auto hybrid tube stereo amps.

Mini Boogee B81

1981. Four-stage, all-tube preamp, overdrive, distortion.

1981	$100	$135

Audioworks

1980s. Company was located in Niles, Illinois.

F.E.T. Distortion

1980s	$40	$55

Auralux

2000-2011. Founded by Mitchell Omori and David Salzmann, Auralux built effects and tube amps in Highland Park, Illinois.

Austone Electronics

1997-2009. Founded by Jon Bessent and Randy Larkin, Austone offered a range of stomp boxes, all made in Austin, Texas. Bessent passed away in '09.

Overdrive and Fuzz Pedals

1997-2009. Various overdrive and fuzz boxes.

1997-2009	$125	$175

MODEL YEAR	FEATURES	EXC. COND. LOW	HIGH

Automagic

1998-present. Wah pedals and distortion boxes made in Germany by Musician Sound Design.

Avalanche

Late 1980s. Effects built by Brian Langer in Toronto, Ontario.

Brianizer

Late-1980s. Leslie effect, dual rotor, adjustable speed and rates.

1980s		$75	$90

Axe

1980s. Early '80s line of Japanese effects, possibly made by Maxon.

B & M

1970s. A private brand made by Sola/Colorsound for Barns and Mullens, a U.K. distributor.

Fuzz Unit

1970s. Long thin orange case, volume, sustain, tone knobs, on-off stomp switch.

1970s		$275	$325

Backline Engineering

2004-present. Guitar multi-effects built by Gary Lee in Camarillo, California. In '07, they added tube amps.

Bad Cat Amplifier Company

2000-present. Amp company Bad Cat, originally of Corona, California, also offers guitar effects. In '09 the company was moved to Anaheim.

Baldwin

1965-1970. The piano maker got into the guitar market when it acquired Burns of London in '65, and sold the guitars in the U.S. under the Baldwin name. They also marketed a couple of effects at the same time.

Banzai

2000-present. Effects built by Olaf Nobis in Berlin, Germany.

Bartolini

The pickup manufacturer offered a few effects from around 1982 to '87.

Tube-It

1982-ca.1987. Marshall tube amplification simulator with bass, treble, sustain controls.

1982-1987	Red case	$80	$90

Basic Systems' Side Effects

1980s. This company was located in Tulsa, Oklahoma.

Audio Delay

1986-ca.1987. Variable delay speeds.

1986-1987		$75	$100

Triple Fuzz

1986-ca.1987. Selectable distortion types.

1986-1987		$50	$60

BBE

1985-present. BBE, owner of G & L Guitars and located in California, manufactures rack-mount effects and added a new line of stomp boxes in '05.

Behringer

1989-present. The German professional audio products company added modeling effects in '01 and guitar stomp boxes in '05. They also offer guitars and amps.

Beigel Sound Lab

1980, 2013-present. Music product designer Mike Beigel helped form Musitronics Corp, where he made the Mu-Tron III. In 1978 he started Beigel Sound Lab to provide product design in Warwick, New York, where in '80 he made 50 rack-mount Enveloped Controlled Filters under this brand name. As of 2013, Mike Beigel's Beigel Sound Lab has started making a Mu-FX Tru-Tron 3X and Octave Divider.

Bell Electrolabs

1970s. This English company offered a line of effects in the '70s.

Vibrato

1970s		$150	$200

Bennett Music Labs

Effects built in Chatanooga, Tennessee by Bruce Bennett.

Bigsby

1948-1966. Paul Bigsby made steel guitars, pedal steels, and electric guitars and mandolins, as well as developing the Bigsby vibrato tailpiece and other components.

Foot Volume and Tone Control

1950s-1960s. Beautifully crafted pedal in a cast-aluminum housing featuring a side-to-side tone sweep.

1950s-60s		$400	$650

Binson

Late 1950s-1982. Binson, of Milan, Italy, made several models of the Echorec, using tubes or transistors. They also made units for Guild, Sound City and EKO.

Echorec

Ca.1960-1979. Four knob models with 12 echo selections, 1 head, complex multitap effects, settings for record level, playback and regeneration. Includes B1, B2, Echomaster1, T5 (has 6 knobs), T5E, and Baby. Used a magnetic disk instead of tape. Guild later offered the Guild Echorec by Binson which is a different stripped-down version.

1960s	Tube	$2,500	$3,250
1970s	Solidstate	$700	$800

Bixonic

1995-2007. The round silver distortion pedals were originally distributed by SoundBarrier Music, later by Godlyke, Inc.

Banzai Cold Fusion Overdrive

Bigsby Foot Volume and Tone Control
Monte Klein

Bixonic Expandora EXP-2001
Keith Myers

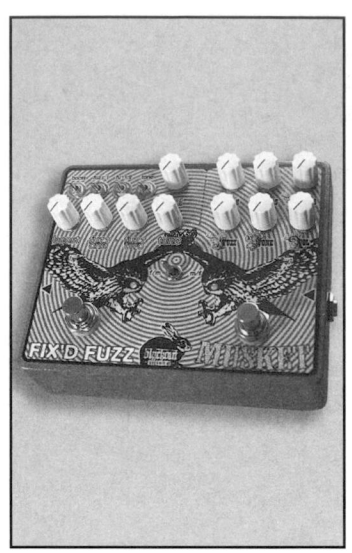

Blackout Effectors Dual Fix'd Fuzz & Musket Fuzz

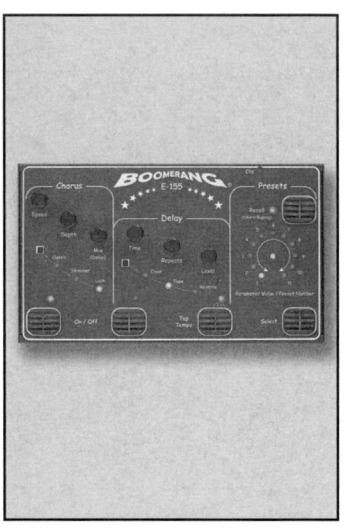

Boomerang Chorus Delay E-155

Boss Blues Driver BD-2

EFFECTS

MODEL YEAR	FEATURES	EXC. COND. LOW	HIGH
Expandora EXP-2000	*1995-2000. Analog distortion, round silver case, internal DIP switches.*		
1995-2000		$175	$200

Black Cat Pedals

1993-2007, 2009-present. Founded by Fred Bonte and located in Texas until late 2007 when production was discontinued. In '09, using Bonte's same designs, new owner Tom Hughes restarted production in Foxon, Connecticut.

Blackbox Music Electronics

2000-2009. Founded by Loren Stafford and located in Minneapolis, Minnesota, Blackbox offered a line of effects for guitar and bass. The Blackbox models are now made under the Ooh La La brand.

Blackout Effectors

2007-present. Kyle Tompkins began building effects pedals in Vancouver, British Columbia and now builds them in Asheville, North Carolina.

Blackstar Amplification

2007-present. Guitar effects pedals built by Joel Richardson in Northampton, U.K. He also builds amps.

Blackstone Appliances

1999-present. Distortion effects crafted by Jon Blackstone in New York, New York.

Bon, Mfg

Bon was located in Escondido, California.
Tube Driver 204
   1979-ca.1981.

MODEL YEAR	FEATURES	EXC. COND. LOW	HIGH
1979-1981		$100	$150

Boomerang

1995-present. Effects pedals built in Grapevine, Texas by Boomerang Musical Products, Ltd.

Boss

1976-present. Japan's Roland Corporation first launched effect pedals in '74. A year or two later the subsidiary company, Boss, debuted its own line. They were marketed concurrently at first but gradually Boss became reserved for effects and drum machines while the Roland name was used on amplifiers and keyboards. Boss still offers a wide line of pedals.

MODEL YEAR	FEATURES	EXC. COND. LOW	HIGH
Acoustic Simulator AC-2	*1997-2007. Four modes that emulate various acoustic tones.*		
1997-2007		$50	$60
Auto Wah AW-2			
1991-1999		$40	$50
Bass Chorus CE-2B			
1987-1995		$40	$50
Bass Equalizer GE-7B	*1987-1995. Seven-band, name changed to GEB-7 in '95.*		
1987-1995		$40	$50

MODEL YEAR	FEATURES	EXC. COND. LOW	HIGH
Bass Flanger BF-2B			
1987-1994		$40	$50
Bass Limiter LM-2B			
1990-1994		$35	$40
Bass Overdrive ODB-3	*1994-present. Yellow case.*		
1994-2014		$40	$50
Blues Driver BD-2	*1995-present. Blue case.*		
1995-2014		$40	$50
Chorus Ensemble CE-1	*1976-1984. Vibrato and chorus.*		
1976-1984		$145	$245
Chorus Ensemble CE-2			
1979-1982		$45	$95
Chorus Ensemble CE-3			
1982-1992		$45	$95
Chorus Ensemble CE-5	*1991-present. Pale blue case.*		
1991-2014		$45	$95
Compressor Sustainer CS-1			
1978-1982		$70	$95
Compressor Sustainer CS-2			
1981-1986		$70	$95
Compressor Sustainer CS-3	*1986-present. Blue case.*		
1986-2014		$70	$95
Delay DM-2	*1981-1984. Analog, hot pink case.*		
1981-1984		$170	$245
Delay DM-3			
1984-1988		$145	$195
Digital Delay DD-2			
1983-1986		$120	$170
Digital Delay DD-3	*1986-present. Up to 800 ms of delay, white case.*		
1986-1989		$120	$170
1990-2014		$95	$145
Digital Delay DD-5	*1995-2005. Up to 2 seconds of delay.*		
1995-2005		$95	$145
Digital Delay DD-6	*2003-2007. Up to 5 seconds of delay.*		
2003-2007		$55	$70
Digital Dimension C DC-2	*1985-1989. Two chorus effects and tremolo.*		
1985-1989		$135	$145
Digital Metalizer MZ-2			
1987-1992		$80	$90
Digital Reverb RV-2			
1987-1990		$95	$145
Digital Reverb RV-5	*2003-present. Dual imput and dual output, four control knobs, silver case.*		
2003-2014		$60	$95
Digital Reverb/Delay RV-3			
1994-2004		$95	$120
Digital Sampler/Delay DSD-2			
1985-1986		$120	$170

MODEL YEAR	FEATURES	EXC. COND. LOW	HIGH
Digital Space-D DC-3/Digital Dimension DC-3			
1988-1993. Originally called the Digital Space-D, later changed to Digital Dimension. Chorus with EQ.			
1988-1993		$130	$180
Digital Stereo Reverb RV-70			
1994-1995. Rack mount, MIDI control, reverb/delay, 199 presets.			
1994-1995		$130	$180
Distortion DS-1			
1978-1989, 1990s-present. Orange case.			
1978-1989		$50	$60
1990-1999		$30	$50
2000-2014		$20	$25
Dr. Rhythm DR-55			
1979-1989. Drum machine.			
1979-1989		$145	$195
Dual Over Drive SD-2			
1993-1998		$45	$55
Dynamic Filter FT-2			
1986-1988. Auto wah.			
1986-1988		$70	$95
Dynamic Wah AW-3			
2000-present. Auto wah with humanizer, for guitar or bass.			
2000-2014		$50	$60
Enhancer EH-2			
1990-1998		$35	$45
Flanger BF-1			
1977 1980		$55	$70
Flanger BF-2			
1980-1989		$55	$70
1990-2005		$40	$55
Foot Wah FW-3			
1992-1996		$45	$55
Graphic Equalizer GE-6			
1978-1981. Six bands.			
1978-1981		$45	$70
Graphic Equalizer GE-7			
1981-present. Seven bands, white case.			
1982-1989		$70	$95
1990-2014		$45	$65
Graphic Equalizer GE-10			
1976-1985. 10-band EQ for guitar or bass.			
1976-1985		$95	$120
Harmonist HR-2			
1994-1999. Pitch shifter.			
1994-1999		$70	$95
Heavy Metal HM-2			
1983-1991. Distortion.			
1983-1991		$30	$40
Hyper Fuzz FZ-2			
1993-1997		$45	$70
Hyper Metal HM-3			
1993-1998		$35	$45
Limiter LM-2			
1987-1992		$25	$35
Line Selector LS-2			
1991-present. Select between 2 effects loops, white case.			
1991-2014 With adapter		$45	$70
Mega Distortion MD-2			
2003-present. Red case.			
2003-2014		$45	$55

MODEL YEAR	FEATURES	EXC. COND. LOW	HIGH
Metal Zone MT-2			
1991-present. Distortion and 3-band EQ, grey case.			
1991-2014		$45	$70
Multi Effects ME-5			
1988-1991. Floor unit.			
1988-1991		$70	$120
Multi Effects ME-6			
1992-1997		$70	$120
Multi Effects ME-8			
1996-1997		$70	$120
Multi Effects ME-30			
1998-2002		$70	$120
Multi Effects ME-50			
2003-2009. Floor unit.			
2003-2009		$170	$195
Noise Gate NF-1			
1979-1988		$40	$50
Noise Suppressor NS-2			
1987-present. White case.			
1987-2014		$40	$50
Octaver OC-2/Octave OC-2			
1982-2003. Originally called the Octaver.			
1982-2003		$55	$70
Overdrive OD-1			
1977-1979		$95	$170
1980-1985		$70	$145
Overdrive OD-3			
1997-present. Yellow case.			
1997-2014		$45	$70
Parametric Equalizer PQ-4			
1991-1997		$45	$70
Phaser PH-1			
1977-1981		$70	$95
Phaser PH-1R			
1982-1985. Resonance control added to PH-1.			
1982-1985		$70	$120
Pitch Sifter/Delay PS-2			
1987-1993		$95	$120
Reverb Box RX-100			
1981-mid-1980s.			
1981-1985		$70	$95
Rocker Distortion PD-1			
1980-mid-1980s. Variable pedal using magnetic field.			
1980-1985		$45	$70
Rocker Volume PV-1			
1981-mid-1980s.			
1980-1985		$45	$55
Rocker Wah PW-1			
1980-mid-1980s. Magnetic field variable pedal.			
1980-1985		$55	$65
Slow Gear SG-1			
1979-1982. Violin swell effect, automatically adjusts volume.			
1979-1982		$325	$375
Spectrum SP-1			
1977-1981. Single-band parametric EQ.			
1977-1981		$325	$375
Super Chorus CH-1			
1989-present. Blue case.			
1989-2014		$45	$70

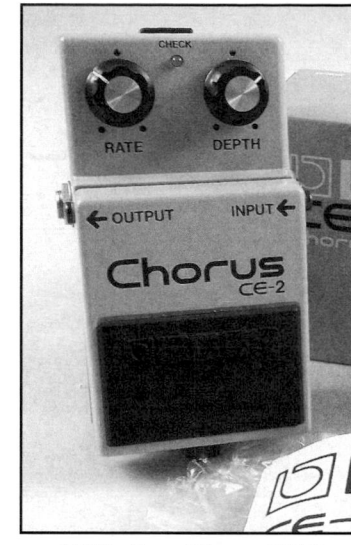

1990s Boss Chorus CE-2
Keith Myers

Boss Flanger BF-1
Keith Myers

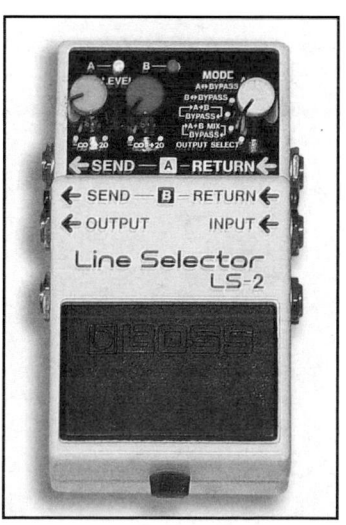

Boss Line Selector LS-2

EFFECTS

EFFECTS

Boss Super Overdrive SD-1

Boss Turbo Distortion DS-2

Budda Budwah

MODEL YEAR	FEATURES	EXC. COND. LOW	HIGH
Super Distortion & Feedbacker DF-2			
1984-1994. Also labeled as the Super Feedbacker & Distortion.			
1984-1994		$95	$120
Super Over Drive SD-1			
1981-present. Yellow case.			
1981-1989		$45	$85
1990-2014		$30	$50
Super Phaser PH-2			
1984-1989		$45	$85
1990-2001		$30	$50
Super Shifter PS-5			
1999-2013. Pitch shifter/harmonizer, aqua case.			
1999-2013		$95	$120
Touch Wah TW-1/T Wah TW-1			
1978-1987. Auto wah, early models were labeled as Touch Wah.			
1978-1987		$95	$120
Tremolo TR-2			
1997-present. Aqua case.			
1997-2014		$65	$75
Tremolo/Pan PN-2			
1990-1995		$120	$145
Turbo Distortion DS-2			
1987-present. Orange case.			
1987-2014		$70	$120
Turbo Overdrive OD-2			
1985-1994. Called OD-2R after '94, due to added remote on/off jack.			
1985-1994		$70	$120
Vibrato VB-2			
1982-1986. True pitch-changing vibrato, warm analog tone, 'rise time' control allows for slow attach, 4 knobs, aqua-blue case.			
1982-1986		$400	$550
Volume FV-50H			
1987-1997. High impedance, stereo volume pedal with inputs and outputs.			
1987-1997		$45	$55
Volume FV-50L			
1987-1997. Low impedance version of FV-50.			
1987-1997		$35	$45
Volume Pedal FV-100			
Late-1980s-1991. Guitar volume pedal.			
1987-1991		$35	$45

Brimstone Audio

2011-present. Shad Sundberg builds his guitar effects in California.

Browntone Electronics

2006-2012. Guitar effects built in Lincolnton, North Carolina by Tim Brown.

Bruno

Music distributor Bruno and Sons had a line of Japanese-made effects in the early '70s.

Budda

1995-present. Wahs and distortion pedals originally built by Jeff Bober and Scott Sier in San Francisco, California. In '09, Budda was acquired by Peavey Electronics. They also build amps.

Build Your Own Clone

2005-present. Build it yourself kits based on vintage effects produced by Keith Vonderhulls in Othello, Washington. Assembled kits are offered by their Canadian distributor.

Burriss

2001-present. Guitar effects from Bob Burriss of Lexington, Kentucky. He also builds amps.

Carl Martin

1993-present. Line of effects from Søren Jongberg and East Sound Research of Denmark. In '06 they added their Chinese-made Vintage Series. They also build amps.

Carlsbro

1959-present. English amp company Carlsbro Electronics Limited offered a line of effects from '77 to '81.

Carrotron

Late-1970s-mid-1980s. Carrotron was out of California and offered a line of effects.

MODEL YEAR	FEATURES	EXC. COND. LOW	HIGH
Noise Fader C900B1			
1981-ca.1982.			
1981-1982		$50	$60
Preamp C821B			
1981-ca.1982.			
1981-1982		$55	$65

Carvin

1946-present. Carvin introduced its line of Ground Effects in '02 and discontinued them in '03.

Castle Instruments

Early 1980s. Castle was located in Madison, New Jersey, and made rack-mount and floor phaser units.

MODEL YEAR	FEATURES	EXC. COND. LOW	HIGH
Phaser III			
1980-1982. Offered mode switching for various levels of phase.			
1980-1982		$100	$175

Catalinbread

2003-present. Nicholas Harris founded Catalinbread Specialized Mechanisms of Music in Seattle, Washington, in '02 to do mods and in '03 added his own line of guitar effects.

Cat's Eye

Dean Solorzano and Lisa Kroeker began building their analog guitar effects in Oceanside, California in 2001.

Cause & Effect Pedals

2009-present. Guitar effects pedals built in Ontario by Mark Roberts and Brian Alexson.

Celmo

2008-present. The Celmo Sardine Can Compressor is made by Kezako Productions in Montcaret, France.

Chandler

1984-present. Located in California, Chandler Musical Instruments offers instruments, pickups, and pickguards, as well as effects.

Digital Echo
1992-2000. Rackmount, 1 second delay, stereo.

Model Year	Features	Low	High
1992-2000		$350	$425

Tube Driver
1986-1991. Uses a 12AX7 tube. Not to be confused with the Tube Works Tube Driver.

Model Year	Features	Low	High
1980s	Large Box	$175	$330
1980s	Rackmount	$100	$175
1990s	Rackmount	$90	$150

Chapman

1970-present. From Emmett Chapman, maker of the Stick.

Patch of Shades
1981, 1989. Wah, with pressure sensitive pad instead of pedal. 2 production runs.

Model Year	Features	Low	High
1980s		$50	$75

Chicago Iron

1998-present. Faithful reproductions of classic effects built by Kurt Steir in Chicago, Illinois.

Chunk Systems

1996-present. Guitar and bass effects pedals built by Richard Cartwright in Sydney, Australia.

Clark

1960s. Built in Clark, New Jersey, same unit as the Orpheum Fuzz and the Mannys Music Fuzz.

SS-600 Fuzz
1960s. Chrome-plated, volume and tone knobs, toggle switch.

Model Year	Features	Low	High
1960s		$150	$200

Clark Amplification

1995-present. Amplifier builder Mike Clark, of Cayce, South Carolina, offers a reverb unit and started building guitar effects as well, in '98.

ClinchFX

2006-present. Hand made pedals by Peter Clinch in Brisbane, Queensland, Australia.

Coffin

Case manufacturer Coffin Case added U.S.-made guitar effects pedals to their product line in 2006.

Colorsound

1967-2010. Colorsound effects were produced by England's Sola Sound, beginning with fuzz pedals. In the late-'60s, wah and fuzz-wah pedals were added, and by the end of the '70s, Colorsound of-fered 18 different effects, an amp, and accessories. Few early Colorsound products were imported into the U.S., so today they're scarce. Except for the Wah-Wah pedal, Colorsound's production stopped by the early '80s, but in '96 most of their early line was reissued by Dick Denny of Vox fame. Denny died in 2001. Since then, Anthony and Steve Macari build Colorsound effects in London.

Mutronics offered a licensed rack mount combination of 4 classic Colorsound effects for a short time in the early 2000s.

Flanger

Model Year	Features	Low	High
1970s		$110	$210

Fuzz Phazer
Introduced in 1973.

Model Year	Features	Low	High
1970s		$160	$235

Jumbo Tone-Bender
1974-early 1980s. Replaced the Tone-Bender fuzz, with wider case and light blue lettering.

Model Year	Features	Low	High
1974-1980s		$275	$335

Octivider
Introduced in 1973.

Model Year	Features	Low	High
1970s		$160	$235

Overdriver
Introduced in 1972. Controls for drive, treble and bass.

Model Year	Features	Low	High
1970s		$160	$235

Phazer
Introduced in 1973. Magenta/purple-pink case, slanted block Phazer logo on front.

Model Year	Features	Low	High
1970s		$160	$235

Ring Modulator
Introduced in 1973. Purple case, Ring Modulator name with atom orbit slanted block logo on case.

Model Year	Features	Low	High
1970s		$260	$285

Supa Tone-Bender Fuzz
1977-early 1980s. Sustain and volume knobs, tone control and toggle. Same white case as Jumbo Tone-Bender, but with new circuit.

Model Year	Features	Low	High
1970s		$250	$300

Supa Wah-Swell
1970s. Supa Wah-Swell in slanted block letters on the end of the pedal, silver case.

Model Year	Features	Low	High
1970s		$160	$235

Supaphase

Model Year	Features	Low	High
1970s		$160	$235

Supasustain

Model Year	Features	Low	High
1960s		$135	$210

Tremolo

Model Year	Features	Low	High
1970s		$160	$210

Tremolo Reissue
1996-2009. Purple case.

Model Year	Features	Low	High
1996-2009		$110	$135

Wah Fuzz Straight
Introduced in 1973. Aqua-blue case, Wah-Fuzz-Straight in capital block letters on end of wah pedal.

Model Year	Features	Low	High
1970s		$185	$260

Wah Fuzz Swell
Introduced in 1973. Yellow case, block letter Wah Fuzz Swell logo on front, three control knobs and toggle.

Model Year	Features	Low	High
1970s		$260	$360

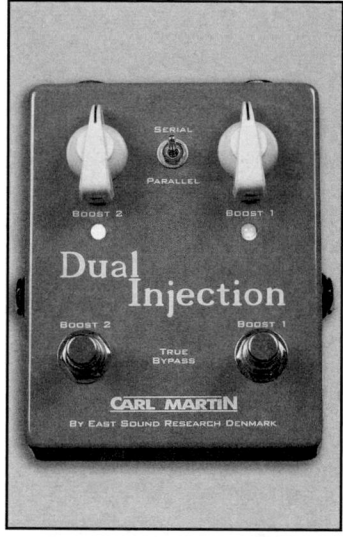

Carl Martin Dual Injection

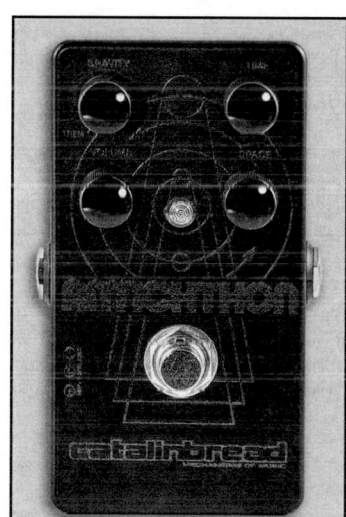

Catalinbread Antichthon

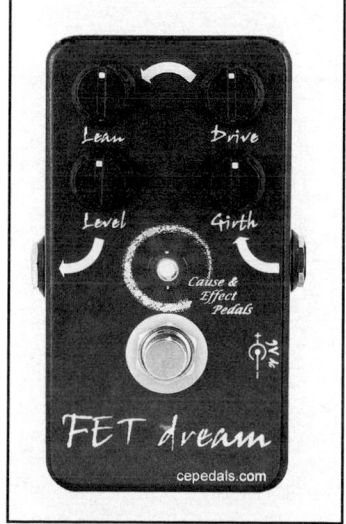

Cause & Effect FET Dream

EFFECTS

Coopersonic The Tubecleaner

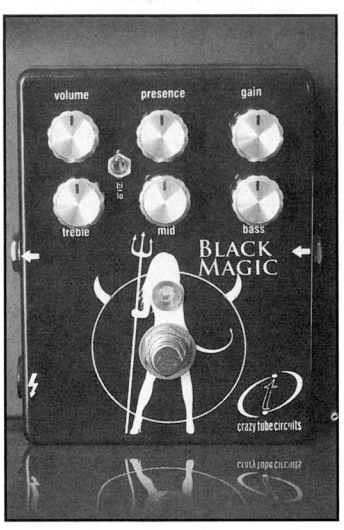

*Crazy Tube Circuits
Black Magic*

Creation Audio Labs Holy Fire 9

MODEL YEAR	FEATURES	EXC. COND. LOW	HIGH

Wah Swell
1970s. Light purple case, block letter Wah-Swell logo on front.

1970s		$235	$285

Wah Wah
1970s. Dark gray case, Wah-Wah in capital block letters on end of wah pedal.

1975		$310	$360

Wah Wah Reissue
1996-2005. Red case, large Colorsound letter logo and small Wah Wah lettering on end of pedal.

1996-2005		$85	$150

Wah Wah Supremo
1970s. Silver/chrome metal case, Wah-Wah Supremo in block letters on end of wah pedal.

1975		$435	$485

Companion
1970s. Private branded by Shinei of Japan, which made effects for others as well.

Tape Echo
1960-1970		$400	$600

Wah Pedal
1970s		$150	$225

Conn
Ca.1968-ca.1978. Band instrument manufacturer and distributor Conn/Continental Music Company, of Elkhart, Indiana, imported guitars and effects from Japan.

Strobe Tuner
Brown or later, grey, case.

1960s	ST-4	$50	$100
1960s	ST-6	$75	$100
1960s	ST-8	$75	$125
1968	ST-2	$50	$100
1970s	Strobotuner ST-11	$75	$100
1970s	Strobotuner ST-12	$75	$100

Coopersonic
2006-present. Martin Cooper builds his guitar effects in Nottingham, UK.

Coron
1970s-1980s. Japanese-made effects, early ones close copies of MXR pedals.

Cosmosound
Italy's Cosmosound made small amps with Leslie drums and effects pedals in the late '60s and '70s. Cosmosound logo is on top of pedals.

Wah Fuzz CSE-3
1970s. Volume and distortion knobs, wah and distortion on-off buttons, silver case.

1970s		$275	$350

Wild Sound
1970s		$175	$195

Crazy Tube Circuits
2004-present. Guitar effects designed and built by Chris Ntaifotis in Athens, Greece.

MODEL YEAR	FEATURES	EXC. COND. LOW	HIGH

Creation Audio Labs
2005-present. Guitar and bass boost pedal and re-amplifying gear built in Nashville, Tennessee.

Crowther Audio
1976-present. Guitar effects built by Paul Crowther, who was the original drummer of the band Split Enz, in Auckland, New Zealand. His first effect was the Hot Cake.

Crucial Audio
Effects made by Steve Kollander in Santa Rosa, California, including the tube-driven Time Warp and Echo-Nugget analog delays.

Cruzer
Effects made by Korea's Crafter Guitars. They also build guitars, basses and amps under that brand.

Crybaby
See listing under Vox for early models, and Dunlop for recent versions.

CSL
Sola Sound made a line of effects for C. Summerfield Ltd., an English music company.

Cusack Music
2003-present. Effects built in Holland, Michigan by Jon Cusack.

Dallas/Dallas Arbiter
Dallas Arbiter, Ltd. was based in London and it appeared in the late-1960s as a division of a Dallas group of companies headed by Ivor Arbiter. Early products identified with Dallas logo with the company noted as John E. Dallas & Sons Ltd., Dallas Building, Clifton Street, London, E.C.2. They also manufactured Sound City amplifiers and made Vox amps from '72 to '78. The Fuzz Face is still available from Jim Dunlop.

Fuzz Face
1966-1975, 1977-1981, 1986-1987, 1993-present. Late '70s and '80s version was built for Dallas Arbiter by Crest Audio of New Jersey. The current reissue is built by Jim Dunlop USA (see that listing).

1968-1969	Red	$925	$1,250
1970	Red	$925	$1,150
1970-1975	Blue	$750	$1,100
1977-1980	Blue	$650	$850
1981	Grey, reissue	$450	$550

Fuzz Wah Face
1970s	Black	$550	$650
1990s	Reissue copy	$65	$80

Rangemaster Treble Booster
1966. 2000s. Grey housing. 1 Control knob. On-off slider switch. Old-style round-barrel 9-volt battery powered; many converted to later rectangular battery. Various current reissues built by JMI and other firms.

1966		$1,675	$2,500
2000s	JMI reissue	$175	$225

MODEL YEAR	FEATURES	EXC. COND. LOW	HIGH
Sustain			
1970s		$400	$500
Treble and Bass Face			
1960s		$500	$600
Trem Face			
Ca.1970-ca.1975. Reissued in '80s, round red case, depth and speed control knobs, Dallas-Arbiter England logo plate.			
1970-1975		$500	$600
Wah Baby			
1970s. Gray speckle case, Wah Baby logo caps and small letters on end of pedal.			
1970s		$500	$600

Damage Control
2005-present. Guitar effects pedals and digital multi-effects built in Moorpark, California.

Dan Armstrong
1976-1981, 1991-present. In '76, Musitronics, based in Rosemont, New Jersey, introduced 6 inexpensive plug-in effects designed by Dan Armstrong. Perhaps under the influence of John D. MacDonald's Travis McGee novels, each effect name incorporated a color, like Purple Peaker. Shipping box labeled Dan Armstrong by Musitronics. They disappeared a few years later but were reissued by WD Products from '91 to '02 (See WD for those models). From '03 to '06, Vintage Tone Project offered the Dan Armstrong Orange Crusher. Since '06, a licensed line of Dan Armstrong effects that plug directly into the output of a guitar or bass (since '07 some also as stomp boxes) has been offered by Grafton Electronics of Grafton, Vermont. Dan Armstrong died in '04.

MODEL YEAR	FEATURES	EXC. COND. LOW	HIGH
Blue Clipper			
1976-1981. Fuzz, blue-green case.			
1976-1981		$100	$170
Green Ringer			
1976-1981. Ring Modulator/Fuzz, green case.			
1976-1981		$95	$110
Orange Squeezer			
1976-1981.			
1976-1981		$100	$150
Purple Peaker			
1976-1981. Frequency Booster, light purple case.			
1976-1981		$100	$160
Red Ranger			
1976-1981. Bass/Treble Booster, light red case.			
1976-1981		$85	$100
Yellow Humper			
1976-1981. Yellow case.			
1976-1981		$85	$100

Danelectro
1946-1969, 1996-present. The Danelectro brand was revived in '96 with a line of effects pedals. They have also offered the Wasabi line of effects. Prices do not include AC adapter, add $10 for the Zero-Hum adapter.

MODEL YEAR	FEATURES	EXC. COND. LOW	HIGH
Chicken Salad Vibrato			
2000-2009. Orange case.			
2000-2009		$20	$25

MODEL YEAR	FEATURES	EXC. COND. LOW	HIGH
Cool Cat Chorus			
1996-2014. Blue case.			
1996-2014		$20	$25
Corned Beef Reverb			
2000-2009. Blue-black case.			
2000-2009		$15	$20
Daddy-O Overdrive			
1996-2009. White case.			
1996-2009		$30	$40
Dan Echo			
1998-2009. Lavender case.			
1998-2009		$40	$45
Fab Tone Distortion			
1996-2014. Red case.			
1996-2014		$30	$40
Reverb Unit Model 9100			
1965. Tube-driven reverb. Grey housing.			
1965		$195	$300

Daredevil
2012-present. Guitar effects pedals built in Chicago, Illinois by Johnny Wator.

Davoli
1960s-1970. Davoli was an Italian pickup and guitar builder and is often associated with Wandre guitars.

MODEL YEAR	FEATURES	EXC. COND. LOW	HIGH
TRD			
1970s. Solidstate tremolo, reverb, distortion unit.			
1970s		$175	$225

DDyna Music
2008-present. Dan Simon builds his guitar effects pedals in Bothell, Washington.

Dean Markley
The string and pickup manufacturer offered a line of effects from 1976 to the early-'90s.

MODEL YEAR	FEATURES	EXC. COND. LOW	HIGH
Overlord Classic Overdrive Model III			
1990-1991. Battery-powered version of Overlord pedal. Black case with red letters.			
1990-1991		$40	$70
Overlord Classic Tube Overdrive			
1988-1991. Uses a 12AX7A tube, AC powered.			
1988-1991		$60	$80
Voice Box 50 (Watt Model)			
1976-1979		$75	$125
Voice Box 100 (Watt Model)			
1976-1979, 1982-ca.1985.			
1976-1979		$75	$125
Voice Box 200 (Watt Model)			
1976-1979		$75	$125

DeArmond
In 1946, DeArmond may have introduced the first actual signal-processing effect pedal, the Tremolo Control. They made a variety of effects into the '70s, but only one caught on - their classic volume pedal. DeArmond is primarily noted for pickups.

Cusak Tap-A-Whirl
Keith Myers

1981 Dallas Fuzz Face
Keith Myers

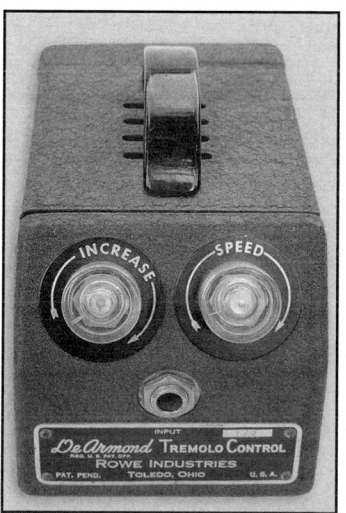

DeArmond Tremolo Control

EFFECTS

DeArmond Volume Pedal Model 602

Keith Myers

Death By Audio Echo Dream 2

DigiTech Whammy Pedal

Jim Schreck

MODEL YEAR	FEATURES	EXC. COND. LOW	HIGH
Pedal Phaser Model 1900			
1974-ca.1979.			
1974-1979		$75	$125
Square Wave Distortion Generator			
1977-ca.1979.			
1977-1979		$100	$150
Thunderbolt B166			
1977-ca.1979. Five octave wah.			
1977-1979		$50	$100
Tone/Volume Pedal 610			
1978-ca.1979.			
1978-1979		$75	$125
Tornado Phase Shifter			
1977-ca.1979.			
1977-1979		$100	$125
Tremolo Control Model 60A/60B			
The Model 60 Tremolo Control dates from ca. 1941 to the early-1950s. Model 60A dates from mid- to late-'50s. Model 60B (plastic housing), early-'60s. Also labeled as the Trem-Trol or 601.			
1950s	60A	$350	$525
1960s	60B	$175	$275
1960s	800 Trem-Trol	$100	$250
Twister 1930			
1980. Phase shifter.			
1980		$100	$125
Volume Pedal Model 602			
1960s		$40	$70
Volume Pedal Model 1602			
1978-ca. 1980s.			
1970s		$40	$95
Volume Pedal Model 1630			
1978-1980s. Optoelectric.			
1970s		$35	$65
Weeper Wah Model 1802			
1970s. Weeper logo on foot pedal.			
1970s		$100	$125

Death By Audio

2001-present. Oliver Ackermann builds production and custom guitar effects in Brooklyn, New York.

DeltaLab Research

Late 1970s-early 1980s. DeltaLab, which was located in Chelmsford, Massachusetts, was an early builder of rackmount gear.

MODEL YEAR	FEATURES	EXC. COND. LOW	HIGH
DL-2 Acousticomputer			
1980s. Delay.			
1980s		$75	$125
DL-4 Time Line			
1980s. Delay.			
1980s		$75	$125
DL-5			
1980s. Various digital processing effects, blue case, rackmount.			
1980s		$175	$225
DLB-1 Delay Control Pedal			
1980s. Controls other DeltaLab pedals, chrome, Morley-looking pedal.			
1980s		$50	$75

MODEL YEAR	FEATURES	EXC. COND. LOW	HIGH
Electron I ADM/II ADM			
1980s. Blue case, rackmount effects. Models include the Electron I ADM, and the Electron II ADM.			
1980s	Electron I ADM	$50	$75
1980s	Electron II ADM	$75	$125

Demeter

1980-present. Amp builder James Demeter and company, located in Van Nuys, California, also build guitar effects.

Denio

Line of Japanese-made Boss lookalikes sold in Asia and Australia.

Devi Ever : Fx

2009-present. Devi Ever builds his guitar effects in Portland, Oregon. Prior to '09 he built the Effector 13 effects.

Diamond Pedals

2004-present. Designed by Michael Knappe and Tim Fifield, these effects are built in Bedford, Nova Scotia.

Diaz

Line of effects that Cesar Diaz introduced in the '80s. Diaz died in '02; in '04, his family announced plans to resume production.

MODEL YEAR	FEATURES	EXC. COND. LOW	HIGH
Texas Ranger			
1980s-2002. Treble booster. 2 control knobs. Variety of colorful housings.			
1980s-02		$115	$150
Texas Square Face			
1980s-2002. Fuzz pedal. 2 control knobs. Variety of colorful housings.			
1980s-02		$230	$375
Tremodillo			
1980s-2002. Tremolo pedal. 2 control knobs. Variety of colorful housings.			
1980s-02		$125	$225

DigiTech

The DigiTech/DOD company is in Utah and the effects are made in the U.S.A. The DigiTech name started as a line under the DOD brand in the early 1980s; later spinning off into its own brand. They also produce vocal products and studio processors and are now part of Harman International Industries.

MODEL YEAR	FEATURES	EXC. COND. LOW	HIGH
Digital Delay and Sampler PDS 2000			
1985-1991. 2 second delay.			
1985-1991		$125	$175
Digital Delay PDS 1000			
1985-ca.1989. One second delay.			
1985-1989		$100	$150
Digital Delay PDS 2700 Double Play			
1989-1991. Delay and chorus			
1989-1991		$125	$175
Digital Stereo Chorus/Flanger PDS 1700			
1986-1991.			
1986-1991		$100	$150

MODEL YEAR FEATURES	EXC. COND. LOW	HIGH
Echo Plus 8 Second Delay PDS 8000		
1985-1991	$175	$200
Guitar Effects Processor RP 1		
1992-1996. Floor unit, 150 presets.		
1992-1996	$100	$150
Guitar Effects Processor RP 3		
1998-2003. Floor unit.		
1998-2003	$110	$150
Guitar Effects Processor RP 5		
1994-1996. Floor unit, 80 presets.		
1994-1996	$120	$175
Guitar Effects Processor RP 6		
1996-1997. Floor unit.		
1996-1997	$125	$200
Guitar Effects Processor RP 7		
1996-1997. Floor unit.		
1996-1997	$125	$175
Guitar Effects Processor RP 10		
1994-1996. Floor unit, 200 presets.		
1994-1996	$125	$175
Guitar Effects Processor RP 14D		
1999. Floor unit with expression pedal, 1x12AX7 tube, 100 presets.		
1999	$300	$350
Guitar Effects Processor RP 100		
2000-2006	$100	$125
Guitar Effects Processor RP 200		
2001-2006. 140 presets, drum machine, Expression pedal.		
2001-2006	$100	$125
Hot Box PDS 2730		
1989-1991. Delay and distortion		
1989-1991	$100	$125
Modulator Pedal XP 200		
1996-2002. Floor unit, 61 presets.		
1996-2002	$100	$125
Multi Play PDS 20/20		
1987-1991. Multi-function digital delay.		
1987-1991	$125	$150
Pedalverb Digital Reverb Pedal PDS 3000		
1987-1991	$100	$125
Programmable Distortion PDS 1550		
1986-1991 Yellow case	$50	$75
Programmable Distortion PDS 1650		
1989-1991 Red case	$50	$75
Rock Box PDS 2715		
1989-1991. Chorus and distortion.		
1989-1991	$50	$75
Two Second Digital Delay PDS 1002		
1987-1991	$100	$125
Whammy Pedal Reissue		
2000-present. Reissue version of classic WP-1 with added dive bomb and MIDI features.		
2000-2014	$125	$150
Whammy Pedal WP I		
1990-1993. Original Whammy Pedal, red case, reissued as WP IV in '00.		
1990-1993	$375	$475
Whammy Pedal WP II		
1994-1997. Can switch between 2 presets, black case.		
1994-1997	$200	$275

MODEL YEAR FEATURES	EXC. COND. LOW	HIGH
DiMarzio		

The pickup maker offered a couple of effects in the late-1980s to the mid-'90s.

MODEL YEAR FEATURES	EXC. COND. LOW	HIGH
Metal Pedal		
1987-1989	$50	$75
Very Metal Fuzz		
Ca.1989-1995. Distortion/overdrive pedal.		
1989-1995	$50	$75

Dino's

1995-present. A social co-op founded by Alessio Casati and Andy Bagnasco, in Albisola, Italy. It builds a line of boutique analog pedals as well as guitars.

Dinosaur

2004-present. Guitar effects pedals imported by Eleca International. They also offer amps.

Divided By Thirteen

Mid-1990s-present. Fred Taccone builds his stomp box guitar effects in the Los Angeles, California area. He also builds amps.

DLS Effects

1999-present. Guitar effects pedals built by Dave Sestito in Fairport, New York.

DNA Analogic

2006-present. Line of Japanese-built guitar effects distributed first by Godlyke and presently Pedals Plus+ Effects Warehouse.

DOD

DOD Electronics started in Salt Lake City, Utah in 1974. Today, they're a major effects manufacturer with dozens of pedals made in the U.S. They also market effects under the name DigiTech and are now part of Harman International Industries.

MODEL YEAR FEATURES	EXC. COND. LOW	HIGH
6 Band Equalizer EQ601		
1977-1982	$45	$65
AB Box 270		
1978-1982	$25	$30
American Metal FX56		
1985-1991	$35	$45
Analog Delay 680		
1979-ca. 1982		
1979-1982	$120	$145
Attacker FX54		
1992-1994. Distortion and compressor.		
1992-1994	$35	$45
Bass Compressor FX82		
1987-ca.1989.		
1987-1989	$35	$45
Bass EQ FX42B		
1987-1996	$35	$45
Bass Grunge FX92		
1995-1996	$35	$45
Bass Overdrive FX91		
1998-2012. Yellow case.		
1998-2012	$35	$45

Divided By Thirteen Joyride

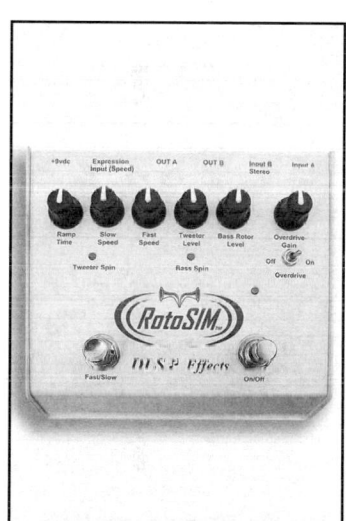

DLS Effects RotoSIM

DNA Analogic Bass Dragger

EFFECTS

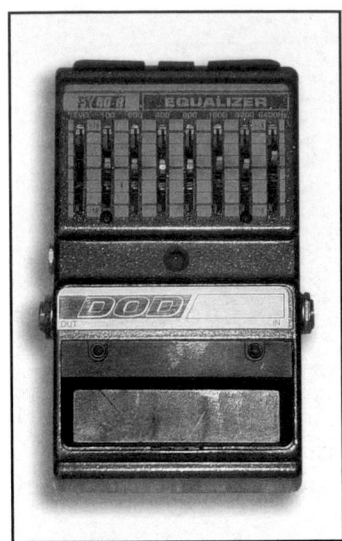

DOD Equalizer FX40B

DOD Mystic Blues Overdrive FX102

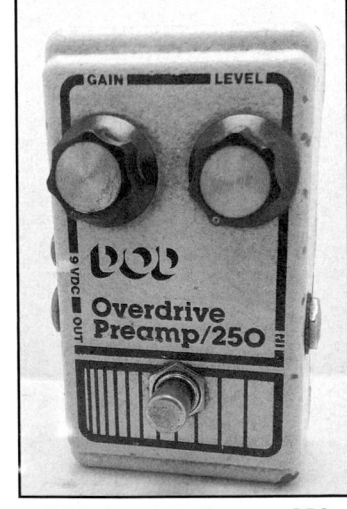

DOD Overdrive Preamp 250
Keith Myers

MODEL YEAR	FEATURES	EXC. COND. LOW	HIGH
Bass Stereo Chorus Flanger FX72			
1987-1997		$45	$55
Bass Stereo Chorus FX62			
1987-1996		$45	$55
Bi-FET Preamp FX10			
1982-1996		$25	$35
Buzz Box FX33			
1994-1996. Grunge distortion.			
1994-1996		$40	$55
Chorus 690			
1980-ca.1982. Dual speed chorus.			
1980-1982		$70	$95
Classic Fuzz FX52			
1990-1997		$30	$40
Classic Tube FX53			
1990-1997		$40	$50
Compressor 280			
1978-ca.1982.			
1978-1982		$40	$50
Compressor FX80			
1982-1985		$40	$50
Compressor Sustainer FX80B			
1986-1996		$40	$50
Death Metal FX86			
1994-2009. Distortion.			
1994-2009		$30	$45
Delay FX90			
1984-ca.1987.			
1984-1987		$70	$95
Digital Delay DFX9			
1989-ca.1990.			
1989-1990		$60	$85
Digital Delay Sampler DFX94			
1995-1997		$70	$95
Distortion FX55			
1982-1986. Red case.			
1982-1986		$30	$40
Edge Pedal FX87			
1988-1989		$20	$40
Envelope Filter 440			
1981-1982		$60	$70
Envelope Filter FX25			
1982-1997. Replaced by FX25B.			
1982-1997		$40	$60
Envelope Filter FX25B			
1981-2013. Light aqua case.			
1998-2013		$40	$60
Equalizer FX40			
1982-1986		$35	$50
Equalizer FX40B			
1987-2010. Eight bands for bass.			
1987-2010		$35	$50
Fet Preamp 210			
1981-ca.1982.			
1981-1982		$35	$50
Flanger 670			
1981-1982		$70	$95
Gate Loop FX30			
1980s		$25	$35

MODEL YEAR	FEATURES	EXC. COND. LOW	HIGH
Graphic Equalizer EQ-610			
1980-ca.1982. Ten bands.			
1980-1982		$45	$60
Graphic Equalizer EQ-660			
1980-ca.1982. Six bands.			
1980-1982		$35	$50
Grunge FX69			
1993-2009. Distortion.			
1993-2009		$30	$45
Hard Rock Distortion FX57			
1987-1994. With built-in delay.			
1987-1994		$30	$45
Harmonic Enhancer FX85			
1986-ca.1989.			
1986-1989		$30	$45
I. T. FX100			
1997. Intergrated Tube distortion, produces harmonics.			
1997		$45	$55
IceBox FX64			
1996-2008. Chorus, high EQ.			
1996-2008		$20	$30
Juice Box FX51			
1996-1997		$25	$35
Master Switch 225			
1988-ca.1989. A/B switch and loop selector.			
1988-1989		$25	$35
Meat Box FX32			
1994-1996		$35	$45
Metal Maniac FX58			
1990-1996		$35	$45
Metal Triple Play Guitar Effects System TR3M			
1994		$35	$45
Metal X FX70			
1993-1996		$35	$45
Milk Box FX84			
1994-2012. Compressor/expander, white case.			
1994-2012		$35	$45
Mini-Chorus 460			
1981-ca.1982.			
1981-1982		$45	$70
Mixer 240			
1978-ca.1982.			
1978-1982		$20	$30
Momentary Footswitch			
Introduced in 1987. Temporally engages other boxes.			
1980s		$20	$30
Mystic Blues Overdrive FX102			
1998-2012. Medium gain overdrive, purple case.			
1998-2012		$20	$25
Noise Gate 230			
1978-1982		$25	$35
Noise Gate FX30			
1982-ca.1987.			
1982-1987		$25	$35
Octoplus FX35			
1987-1996. Octaves.			
1987-1996		$35	$40
Overdrive Plus FX50B			
1986-1997		$30	$40

The *Vintage Guitar Price Guide* shows low to high values for items in all-original excellent condition, and, where applicable, with original case or cover.

MODEL YEAR	FEATURES	EXC. COND. LOW	HIGH
Overdrive Preamp 250			
1978-1982, 1995-present. Reissued in '95, yellow case.			
1978-1982		$75	$230
1995-2014		$25	$40
Overdrive Preamp FX50			
1982-1985		$30	$40
Performer Compressor Limiter 525			
1981-1984		$50	$55
Performer Delay 585			
1982-1985		$55	$70
Performer Distortion 555			
1981-1984		$35	$45
Performer Flanger 575			
1981-1985		$35	$45
Performer Phasor 595			
1981-1984		$40	$50
Performer Stereo Chorus 565			
1981-1985. FET switching.			
1981-1985		$55	$70
Performer Wah Filter 545			
1981-1984		$45	$70
Phasor 201			
1981-ca.1982. Reissued in '95.			
1981-1982		$65	$95
Phasor 401			
1978-1981		$65	$95
Phasor 490			
1980-ca.1982.			
1980-1982		$65	$95
Phasor FX20			
1982-1985		$35	$45
Psychoacoustic Processor FX87			
1988-1989		$35	$45
Punkifier FX76			
1997		$35	$45
Resistance Mixer 240			
1978-ca.1982.			
1978-1982		$25	$30
Silencer FX27			
1988-ca.1989. Noise reducer.			
1988-1989		$30	$40
Stereo Chorus FX60			
1982-1986		$35	$45
Stereo Chorus FX65			
1986-1996. Light blue case.			
1986-1996		$35	$45
Stereo Flanger FX70			
1982-ca.1985.			
1982-1985		$35	$45
Stereo Flanger FX75			
1986-1987. Silver case with blue trim.			
1986-1987		$40	$50
Stereo Flanger FX75B			
1987-1997		$40	$50
Stereo Phasor FX20B			
1986-1999		$40	$50
Stereo Turbo Chorus FX67			
1988-1991		$35	$45
Super American Metal FX56B			
1992-1996		$30	$40

MODEL YEAR	FEATURES	EXC. COND. LOW	HIGH
Super Stereo Chorus FX68			
1992-1996		$35	$45
Supra Distortion FX55			
1986-2012. Red case.			
1986-2012		$25	$35
Thrash Master FX59			
1990-1996		$25	$35
Votec Vocal Effects Processor and Mic Preamp			
1998-2001		$55	$60
Wah-Volume FX-17 (pedal)			
1987-2000		$40	$50

Dredge-Tone

Located in Berkeley, California, Dredge-Tone offers effects and electronic kits.

DST Engineering

2001-2014. Jeff Swanson and Bob Dettorre built reverb units in Beverly, Massachusetts. They also built amps.

Dunlop

Jim Dunlop, USA offers the Crybaby, MXR (see MXR), Rockman, High Gain, Heil Sound (see Heil), Tremolo, Jimi Hendrix, Rotovibe, Uni-Vibe and Way Huge brand effects.

MODEL YEAR	FEATURES	EXC. COND. LOW	HIGH
Crybaby Bass			
1985-present. Bass wah.			
1985-2014		$75	$100
Crybaby Multi-Wah 535/535Q			
1995-present. Multi-range pedal with an external boost control.			
1995-2014		$70	$90
Crybaby Wah-Wah GCB-95			
1982-present. Dunlop began manufacturing the Crybaby in '82.			
1982-1989		$55	$75
1990-1999		$45	$70
2000-2014		$40	$50
Fuzz Face			
1993-present. Reissue of the classic Dallas Arbiter effect (see that listing for earlier versions).			
1993-2014	Red, reissue	$100	$125
High Gain Volume + Boost Pedal			
1983-1996		$35	$45
High Gain Volume Pedal GCB-80			
1983-2010		$40	$50
Jimi Hendrix Fuzz JH-2 (Round)			
1987-1993. Round face fuzz, JH-2S is the square box version.			
1987-1993		$50	$75
Rotovibe JH-4S Standard			
1989-1998. Standard is finished in bright red enamel with chrome top.			
1989-1998		$125	$150
Tremolo Volume Plus TVP-1			
1995-1998. Pedal.			
1995-1998		$125	$140

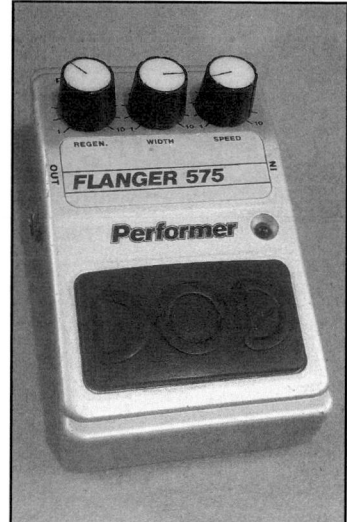

DOD Flanger 575
Keith Myers

EFFECTS

DOD Stereo Flanger FX75

Dunlop Jimi Hendrix Fuzz JH-2
Jesse Isselbacher

Durham Crazy Horse

EBS Valve Drive

Effectrode Helios

MODEL YEAR	FEATURES	EXC. COND. LOW	HIGH
Uni-Vibe UV-1			
1995-2012. Rotating speaker effect.			
1995-1999		$225	$335
2000-2012		$175	$225

Durham Electronics

2001-present. Alan Durham builds his line of guitar effects in Austin, Texas.

Dutch Kazoo

2013-present. Guitar effects pedals built in Parker Ford, Pennsylvania by Corinne Mandell.

Dynacord

1950-present. Dynacord is a German company that makes audio and pro sound amps, as well as other electronic equipment and is now owned by TELEX/EVI Audio (an U.S. company), which also owns the Electro-Voice brand. In the '60s they offered tape echo machines and guitars. In '94 a line of multi-effects processors were introduced under the Electro-Voice/Dynacord name, but by the following year they were just listed as Electro-Voice.

EchoCord

Introduced in 1959. Tape echo unit.

1959-1960s		$275	$400

Dyno

See Dytronics.

Dytronics

Mid-1970s-early 1980s. The Japanese Dytronics company made a chorus rackmount unit for electric piano called the Dyno My Piano with flying piano keys or a lightning bolt on the front. Another version was called the Tri-Stereo Chorus and a third, called the Songbird, had a bird's head on the front.

E Bow

See Heet Sound Products.

E.W.S. (Engineering Work Store)

2007-present. Guitar effects pedals built in Tokyo, Japan for Prosound Communications in Van Nuys, California.

EarthQuaker Devices

2006-present. Guitar effects pedals built by Jamie Stillman in Akron, Ohio.

EBS

1992-present. Bass and guitar effects built in Stockholm, Sweden by the EBS Sweden AB company. They also build bass amps.

Ecco-Fonic

1959-1968. The Ecco-Fonic was designed by Ray Stolle and sold from his radio and TV repair shop in Los Angeles. Theis first Ecco Ecco-Fonic was distributed by Fender in 1958-'59. Stolle sold the company to E.S. "Eddie" Tubin in late 1959-'60, who sold the company in 1961 to Milton Brucker. Starting in 1963, Fender offered a solidstate Ecco-Fonic designed by new-owner Bob Marks and Russ Allee and labeled as the Fender Echo.

Model 109

1959-1960. Tube-driven tape-echo unit, 2 control knobs, revised to 3 knobs, 1-piece top, gold housing.

1959	Brown case	$900	$1,500

Model 109-B

1960-1962. Tube-driven tape echo unit, 4 Control knobs, 2-piece top, gold housing.

1960-1962	Brown or black case	$500	$1,200

Model 109-C

1961-1962. Tube-driven tape echo unit, multiple playback heads, black housing.

1961-1962	Black case	$500	$1,000

Echoplex

The Echoplex tape echo unit was invented around 1959 in Akron, Ohio, by Don Dixon and Mike Battle, who originally produced it in small numbers. Production was soon moved to Market Electronics in Cleveland, and those units were sold under the Maestro brand (see listings under Maestro). After Maestro dropped the Echoplex, it was marketed under the Market Electronics name from the late-'70s to the late-'80s (see listing under Market Electronics for '80s models). In '94, Gibson's Oberheim division introduced a rackmount unit called the Echoplex. In '01, it was relabeled as Gibson.

Echoplex

1959. Dixon- and Battle-built pre-Maestro production tube-driven tape echo. Black case.

1959		$900	$1,200

Eden Analog

2004-present. Guitar effects pedals built by Chris Sheppard and Robert Hafley in Pelham, Alabama.

Effector 13

2002-2008. Guitar effects built by Devi Ever in Minneapolis, Minnesota. Located in Austin, Texas until mid-'04. Name changed to Devi Ever : Fx in '09.

Effectrode

1996-present. Effects pedals built in Corvallis, Oregon by Phil Taylor.

EFX

1980s. Brand name of the Los Angeles-based EFX Center; they also offered a direct box and a powered pedal box/board.

Switch Box B287

1984. Dual effects loop selector.

1984		$25	$35

EKO

1959-1985, 2000-present. In the '60s and '70s EKO offered effects made by EME and JEN Elettronica, which also made Vox effects.

Eleca

2004-present. Guitar effects pedals imported by Eleca International. They also offer guitars, mandolins and amps.

Electra

1970-1984, 2013-present. Guitar importer St. Louis Music offered Electra effects in the late '70s.

Chorus 504CH
Ca.1975-ca.1980.

1975-1980	$55	$75

Compressor 502C/602C
Ca.1975-ca.1980.

1975-1980	$45	$55

Distortion 500D
Ca.1976-ca.1980.

1976-1980	$55	$75

Flanger (stereo) 605F
Ca.1975-ca.1980.

1975-1980	$55	$75

Fuzz Wah
Ca.1975-ca.1980.

1975-1980	$75	$150

Pedal Drive 515AC
Ca.1976-ca.1980. Overdrive.

1976-1980	$40	$50

Phaser Model 501P
Ca.1976-ca.1980.

1976-1980	$50	$60

Phaser Model 875
Ca.1975-ca.1980.

1975-1980	$50	$60

Roto Phase I
1975-ca.1980. Small pocket phaser.

1975-1980	$70	$85

Roto Phase II
1975-ca.1980. Pedal phasor.

1975-1980	$80	$95

Electro-Harmonix

1968-1984, 1996-present. Founded by Mike Matthews in New York City, the company initially produced small plug-in boosters such as the LPB-1. In '71, they unveiled the awe-inspiring Big Muff Pi fuzz and dozens of innovative pedals followed. After years of disputes, the nonunion E-H factory became the target of union organizers and a '81 union campaign, combining picketing and harrying of E-H employees, brought production to a halt. Matthews' financier then cut his funding, and in early '82, E.H. filed for bankruptcy. Later that year, Matthews was able to reopen and continue through '84. In '96, he again began producing reissues of many of his classic effects as well as new designs.

10 Band Graphic Equalizer
1977-1981. Includes footswitch.

1977-1981	$60	$70

16-Second Digital Delay
Early-1980s, 2004-2008. An updated version was reissued in '04.

1980s	With foot controller	$675	$850
1980s	Without foot controller	$500	$625
1990s		$325	$500
2004-2008		$275	$375

3 Phase Liner

1981	$50	$60

5X Junction Mixer

1977-1981	$30	$40

Attack Equalizer
1975-1981. Active EQ, a.k.a. "Knock Out."

1975-1981	$150	$200

Attack/Decay
1980-1981. Tape reverse simulator.

1980-1981	$200	$225

Bad Stone Phase Shifter
1975-1981.

1975-1981	Three knobs	$200	$250
1975-1981	Two knobs, color switch	$175	$225

Bass Micro-Synthesizer
1981-1984, 1999-present. Analog synthesizer sounds.

1981-1984	$225	$300
1999-2014	$150	$175

Bassballs
1978-1984, 1998-present. Bass envelope filter/distortion.

1978-1984	$200	$225

Big Muff Pi
1971-1984. Sustain, floor unit, issued in 3 different looks, as described below.

1970s	Earlier black graphics, knobs in triangle pattern	$325	$450
1970s	Later red/black graphics, 1/2" letters	$250	$400
1980s	Red/black graphics, logo in 1" letters	$150	$250

Big Muff Pi (reissue)
1996-present. Originally made in Russia, but currently both Russian- and U.S.-made versions are available.

1996-2014	Russian-made	$40	$45

Big Muff Sovtek
2000s. Big Muff Pi, Electro Harmonix, and Sovtek logos on an olive green case. Sold in a wooden box.

2000s	With wooden box	$150	$300

Black Finger Compressor Sustainer
1977, 2003-present. Original has 3 knobs in triangle pattern.

1977	$125	$225
2003-2014	$75	$100

Clap Track
1980-1984. Drum effect.

1980-1984	$40	$60

Clone Theory
1977-1981. Chorus effect, The Clone Theory logo.

1977-1981	$150	$175

Eleca Chorus

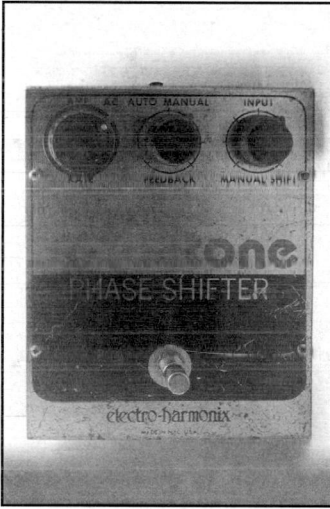

E-H Bad Stone Phase Shifter
Keith Myers

Early-'70s E-H Big Muff Pi
Andrea Scarfone

EFFECTS

1977 E-H Doctor Q
Keith Myers

EFFECTS

E-H Electric Mistress
Jim Schreck

E-H Muff Fuzz
Keith Myers

MODEL YEAR	FEATURES	EXC. COND. LOW	HIGH
Crash Pad			
1980-1984. Percussion synth.			
1980-1984		$40	$60
Crying Tone Pedal			
1976-1978. Wah-wah.			
1976-1978		$175	$225
Deluxe Big Muff Pi			
1978-1981. Sustain, AC version of Big Muff Pi, includes a complete Soul Preacher unit.			
1978-1981	Red graphics	$125	$200
Deluxe Electric Mistress Flanger			
1977-1983, 1996-present. AC.			
1977-1979		$150	$250
1980-1983		$125	$175
Deluxe Memory Man			
1977-1983, 1996-present. Echo and delay, featured 4 knobs '77-'78, from '79-'83 it has 5 knobs and added vibrato and chorus.			
1977-1978	Four knobs	$225	$300
1979-1983	Five knobs	$200	$275
1996-2014		$150	$165
Deluxe Octave Multiplexer			
1977-1981		$200	$250
Digital Delay/Chorus			
1981-1984. With digital chorus.			
1981-1984		$250	$300
Digital Rhythm Matrix DRM-15			
1981-1984		$225	$250
Digital Rhythm Matrix DRM-16			
1979-1983		$225	$250
Digital Rhythm Matrix DRM-32			
1981-1984		$225	$250
Doctor Q Envelope Follower			
1976-1983, 2001-present. For bass or guitar.			
1976-1983		$150	$200
2001-2014		$30	$35
Domino Theory			
1981. Sound sensitive light tube.			
1981		$50	$100
Echo 600			
1981		$175	$225
Echoflanger			
1977-1982. Flange, slapback, chorus, filter.			
1977-1982		$200	$250
Electric Mistress Flanger			
1976-1979		$225	$275
1980-1984		$175	$225
Electronic Metronome			
1978-1980		$25	$30
Frequency Analyzer			
1977-1984, 2001-present. Ring modulator.			
1977-1984		$200	$250
Full Double Tracking Effect			
1978-1981. Doubling, slapback.			
1978-1981		$100	$150
Fuzz Wah			
Introduced around 1974.			
1970s		$175	$225
Golden Throat			
1977-1984		$600	$800

MODEL YEAR	FEATURES	EXC. COND. LOW	HIGH
Golden Throat Deluxe			
1977-1979. Deluxe has a built-in monitor amp.			
1977-1979		$600	$800
Golden Throat II			
1978-1981		$150	$300
Guitar Synthesizer			
1981. Sold for $1,495 in May '81.			
1981		$225	$300
Hog's Foot Bass Booster			
1977-1980		$70	$90
Holy Grail			
2002-present. Digital reverb.			
2002-2014		$80	$90
Hot Foot			
1977-1978. Rocker pedal turns knob of other E-H effects.			
1977-1978	Gold case, red graphics	$75	$100
Hot Tubes			
1978-1984, 2001-2007. Tube distortion.			
1978-1984		$125	$200
Linear Power Booster LPB-1			
1968-1983.			
1976-1979		$55	$80
1980-1983		$45	$75
Linear Power Booster LPB-2			
Ca.1968-1983.			
1968-1983		$90	$100
Little Big Muff Pi			
1976-1980, 2006-present. Sustain, 1-knob floor unit.			
1976-1980		$150	$175
Memory Man/Stereo Memory Man			
1976-1984, 1999-present. Analog delay, newer version in stereo.			
1976-1979		$200	$250
1980-1984		$125	$155
Micro Synthesizer			
1978-1984, 1998-present. Mini keyboard phaser.			
1978-1979		$225	$250
1978-1984		$225	$250
1998-2014		$150	$170
Mini Q-Tron/Micro Q-Tron			
2002-present. Battery-operated smaller version of Q-Tron envelope follower, changed to identical effect in smaller box Micro in '06.			
2002-2014		$40	$45
Mini-Mixer			
1978-1981. Mini mic mixer, reissued in '01.			
1978-1981		$30	$40
MiniSynthesizer			
1981-1983. Mini keyboard with phaser.			
1981-1983		$300	$400
MiniSynthesizer With Echo			
1981		$375	$500
Mole Bass Booster			
1968-1978.			
1968-1969		$60	$80
1970-1978		$40	$60
Muff Fuzz			
1976-1983. Fuzz and line boost, silver case with orange lettering.			
1976-1983		$85	$100

MODEL YEAR FEATURES	EXC. COND. LOW	HIGH
Muff Fuzz Crying Tone		
1977-1978. Fuzz, wah.		
1977-1978	$150	$250
Octave Multiplexer Floor Unit		
1976-1980	$175	$275
Octave Multiplexer Pedal		
1976-1977, 2001-present.		
1976-1977	$150	$250
2001-2014	$40	$45
Panic Button		
1981. Siren sounds for drum.		
1981	$30	$40
Poly Chorus/Stereo Polychorus		
1981, 1999-present. Same as Echoflanger.		
1981	$175	$200
1999-2014	$125	$150
Polyphase		
1979-1981. With envelope.		
1979-1981	$175	$225
Pulsar/Stereo Plusar		
2004-present. Variable wave form tremolo.		
2004-2014	$45	$55
Pulse Modulator		
Ca.1968 -ca.1972. Triple tremolo.		
1968-1969	$250	$325
1970-1972	$200	$250
Q Tron		
1997-present. Envelope controlled filter.		
1997-2014	$125	$175
Q-Tron +		
1999-present. With added effects loop and Attack Response switch.		
1999-2014	$70	$80
Queen Triggered Wah		
1976-1978. Wah/Envelope Filter.		
1976-1978	$125	$150
Random Tone Generator RTG		
1981	$40	$60
Rhythm 12 (Rhythm Machine)		
1978	$75	$125
Rolling Thunder		
1980-1981. Percussion synth.		
1980-1981	$40	$50
Screaming Bird Treble Booster		
Ca.1968-1980. In-line unit.		
1968-1980	$75	$100
Screaming Tree Treble Booster		
1977-1981. Floor unit.		
1977-1981	$100	$150
Sequencer Drum		
1981. Drum effect.		
1981	$40	$50
Slapback Echo		
1977-1978. Stereo.		
1977-1978	$150	$200
Small Clone		
1983-1984, 1999-present. Analog chorus, depth and rate controls, purple face plate, white logo.		
1983-1984	$150	$200
1999-2014	$35	$40

MODEL YEAR FEATURES	EXC. COND. LOW	HIGH
Small Stone Phase Shifter		
1975-1984, 1996-present. Both Russian and U.S. reissues were made.		
1975-1979	$175	$225
1980-1984	$125	$175
Soul Preacher		
1977-1983, 2007-present. Compressor sustainer. Nano version for present.		
1977-1983	$100	$150
Space Drum/Super Space Drum		
1980-1981. Percussion synthesizer.		
1980-1981	$125	$175
Switch Blade		
1977-1983. A-B Box.		
1977-1983	$45	$55
Talking Pedal		
1977-1978. Creates vowel sounds.		
1977-1978	$350	$550
The Silencer		
1976-1981. Noise elimination.		
1976-1981	$60	$80
The Wiggler		
2002-present. All-tube modulator including pitch vibrato and volume tremolo.		
2002-2014	$100	$110
The Worm		
2002-present. Wah/Phaser.		
2002-2014	$55	$65
Tube Zipper		
2001-present. Tube (2x12AX7) envelope follower.		
2001-2014	$100	$120
Vocoder		
1978-1981. Modulates voice with instrument.		
1978-1981 Rackmount	$425	$525
Volume Pedal		
1978-1981	$45	$65
Y-Triggered Filter		
1976-1977	$140	$160
Zipper Envelope Follower		
1976-1978. The Tube Zipper was introduced in '01.		
1976-1978	$200	$300

Electrosonic Amplifiers

2002-2010. Amp builder Josh Corn also offers a preamp pedal, built in Boonville, Indiana.

Elk

Late-1960s. Japanese company Elk Gakki Co., Ltd. mainly made guitars and amps, but did offer effects as well.

Elka

In the late '60s or early '70s, Italian organ and synthesizer company Elka-Orla (later just Elka) offered a few effects, likely made by JEN Elettronica (Vox, others).

EMMA Electronic

Line of guitar effects built in Denmark and distributed by Godlyke.

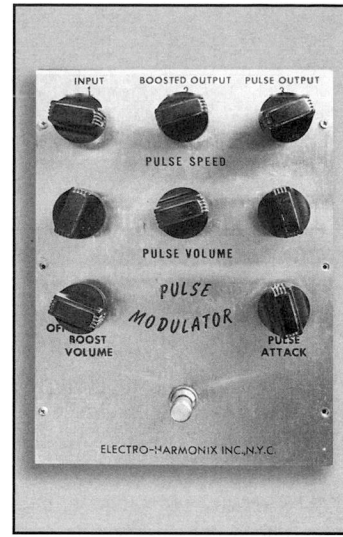

E-H Pulse Modulator
Jim Schreck

E-H Small Stone

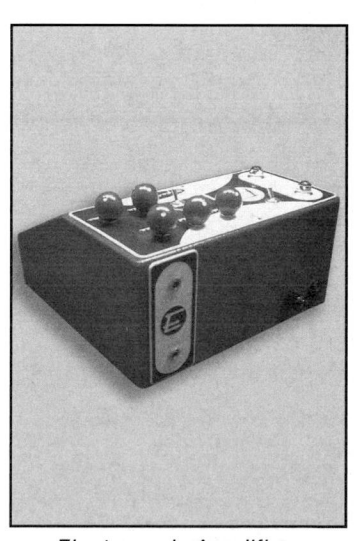

Electrosonic Amplifiers EF86 Preamp

EFFECTS

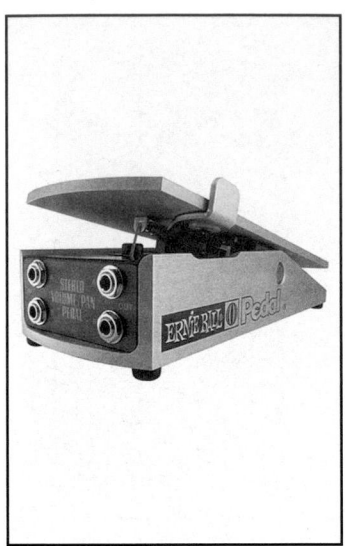

Ernie Ball 500K Stereo Volume/Pan

Fender Blender
Wade Jones

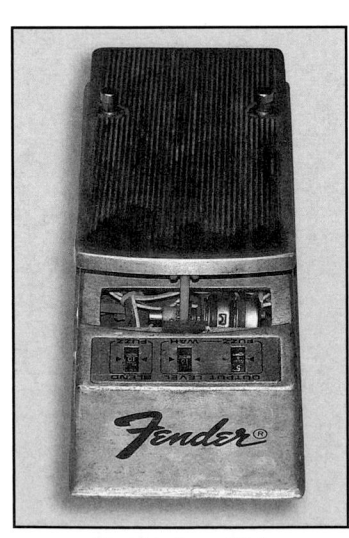

Fender Fuzz-Wah

MODEL YEAR	FEATURES	EXC. COND. LOW	HIGH

ReezaFRATzitz RF-1/ReezaFRATzitz II
2004-present. Overdrive and distortion, red case.

2004-2014		$80	$95

Empress Effects
2005-present. Guitar effects pedals built by Steve Bragg and Jason Fee in Ottawa, Ontario.

EMS
1969-1979. Peter Zinnovieff's English synth company (Electronic Music Studios) also offered a guitar synthesizer. The company has reopened to work on original EMS gear.

eowave
2002-present. Effects built first in Paris and now in Burgundy, France by Marc Sirguy.

Epiphone
Epiphone pedals are labeled G.A.S Guitar Audio System and were offered from around 1988 to '91.
Pedals
Various models with years available.

1988-1989	Chorus EP-CH-70	$35	$45
1988-1989	Delay EP-DE-80	$45	$60
1988-1991	Compressor EP-CO-20	$35	$40
1988-1991	Distortion EP-DI-10	$35	$45
1988-1991	Flanger EP-FL-60	$40	$55
1988-1991	Overdrive EP-OD-30	$35	$45

Ernie Ball
1972-present. The Ernie Ball company also builds Music Man instruments.
Volume Pedals
1977-present. Aluminum housing.

1977-2014		$35	$65

Euthymia Electronics
Line of guitar effects built by Erik Miller in Alameda, California.

Eventide
1971-present. This New Jersey electronics manufacturer has offered studio and rackmount effects since the late '70s. In '08 they added guitar effects pedals.

EXR
The EXR Corporation was located in Brighton, Michigan.
Projector
1983-ca.1984. Psychoacoustic enhancer pedal.

1983-1984		$65	$75

Projector SP III
1983-ca.1984. Psychoacoustic enhancer pedal, volume pedal/sound boost.

1983-1984		$65	$70

Farfisa
The organ company offered effects pedals in the 1960s. Their products were manufactured in Italy by the Italian Accordion Company and distributed by Chicago Musical Instruments.
Model VIP 345 Organ
Mid-1960s. Portable organ with Synthslalom used in the rock and roll venue.

1960s		$500	$600

Repeater

1969		$100	$150

Sferasound
1960s. Vibrato pedal for a Farfisa Organ but it works well with the guitar, gray case.

1960s		$275	$375

Wah/Volume

1969		$100	$150

Fargen
1999-present. Guitar effects built in Sacramento, California by Benjamin Fargen. He also builds amps.

Fender
1946-present. Although Fender has flirted with effects since the 1950s (the volume/volume-tone pedal and the Ecco-Fonic), the company concentrated mainly on guitars and amps. Fender effects ranged from the sublime to the ridiculous, from the tube Reverb to the Dimension IV. In 2013 Fender added a line of pedals.
'63 Tube Reverb
1994-present. Reissue spring/tube Reverb Units with various era cosmetics as listed below. Currently offered in brown or, since '09, in lacquered tweed.

1994	White (limited run)	$375	$425
1994-1997	Black	$350	$400
1994-1997	Blond	$375	$450
1994-1997	Tweed	$375	$425
1994-2008	Brown	$350	$400
2009-2014	Lacquered Tweed	$300	$375

Blender
1968-1977, 2005-2010. Battery-operated unit with fuzz, sustain, and octave controls.

1968-1969		$290	$400
1970-1977		$275	$350
2005-2010	Reissue	$125	$175

Contempo Organ
1967-1968. Portable organ, all solidstate, 61 keys including a 17-key bass section, catalog shows with red cover material.

1967-1968		$525	$550

Dimension IV
1968-1970. Multi-effects unit using an oil-filled drum.

1968-1970		$195	$300

Echo and Electronic Echo Chamber
1963-1968. Solidstate tape echo built by Ecco-Fonic, up to 400 ms of delay, rectangle box with 2 controls '63-'67, slanted front '67-'68.

1963-1967		$300	$500
1967-1968		$225	$350

Echo-Reverb
1966-1970. Solidstate, echo-reverb effect produced by rotating metal disk, black tolex, silver grille.

1966-1970		$300	$350

Fuzz-Wah

1968-1984, 2007-2011. Has Fuzz and Wah switches on sides of pedal '68-'73, has 3 switches above the pedal '74-'84. Newer version ('07-'11) has switches on sides.

1968-1973	Switches on side	$150	$225
1974-1984	Switches above	$100	$200
2007-2011	Switches on side	$80	$90

Phaser

1975-1977, 2007-2011. AC powered, reissued in '07.

1975-1977	$95	$175
2007-2011	$60	$80

Reverb Unit

1961-1966, 1975-1978. Fender used a wide variety of tolex coverings in the early-'60s as the coverings matched those on the amps. Initially, Fender used rough blond tolex, then rough brown tolex, followed by smooth white or black tolex.

1961	Blond tolex, Oxblood grille	$1,000	$1,200
1961	Brown tolex	$1,000	$1,200
1962	Blond tolex, Oxblood grille	$1,000	$1,200
1962	Brown tolex, Wheat grille	$800	$1,100
1963	Brown tolex	$800	$1,100
1963	Rough blond tolex	$800	$1,200
1963	Smooth white tolex	$800	$1,200
1964	Black tolex	$800	$1,200
1964	Brown tolex, gold grille	$800	$1,100
1964	Smooth white tolex	$800	$1,100
1965-1966	Black tolex	$775	$1,000
1966	Solidstate, flat cabinet	$150	$225
1975-1978	Tube reverb reinstated	$500	$600

Vibratone

1967-1972. Fender's parent company at the time, CBS, bought Leslie in 1965, and Fender began offering a Leslie-type rotating-speaker-emulator as the Vibratone in 1967. Based on the Leslie Model 16 cabinet and made specifically for the guitar, it featured a single fixed 4-ohm 10-inch speaker fronted by a rotating drum. Designed to be powered by an external amp. 2-speed motor. Black tolex.

1967-1968	Fender cast logo in upper left corner	$600	$850
1968-1972	Fender logo plate through the center	$500	$850

Volume-Tone Pedal

1954-1984, 2007-present. Swivel foot controller.

1954-1984	$90	$100
2007-2014	$35	$40

Field Effects by Resonant Electronic Design

2010-present. Guitar effects pedals built in Minneapolis, Minnesota by Wes Kuhnley and Peter Bregman. They also build the Resonant brand amps.

Fishman

2003-present. Larry Fishman of Andover, Massachusetts offers a line of acoustic guitar effects pedals. He also builds amps.

FJA Mods

2002-present. Jerry Pinnelli builds amp effects and guitar pedals in Central Square, New York. In 2007 he also began building amps.

FlexiSound

FlexiSound products were made in Lancaster, Pennsylvania.

F. S. Clipper

1975-ca.1976. Distortion, plugged directly into guitar jack.

1975-1976	$55	$65

The Beefer

1975. Power booster, plugged directly into guitar jack.

1975	$40	$50

Flip

Line of tube effects by Guyatone and distributed in the U.S. by Godlyke Distributing.

Tube Echo (TD-X)

2004-present. Hybrid tube power delay pedal.

2004-2014	$90	$100

FM Acoustics

FM Acoustics pedals were made in Switzerland.

E-1 Pedal

1975. Volume, distortion, filter pedal.

1975	$70	$80

Foxx

Foxx pedals are readily identifiable by their fur-like covering. They slunk onto the scene in 1971 and were extinct by '78. Made by Hollywood's Ridinger Associates, their most notable product was the Tone Machine fuzz. Foxx-made pedals also have appeared under various brands such as G & G, Guild, Yamaha and Sears Roebuck, generally without fur. Since 2005, reissues of some of the classic Foxx pedals are being built in Provo, Utah.

Clean Machine

1974-1978	$250	$275

Down Machine

1971-1977. Bass wah.

1971-1977	Blue case	$225	$275

Foot Phaser

1975-1977, 2006-present.

1975-1977	$450	$650

Fuzz and Wa and Volume

1974-1978, 2006-present. Currently called Fuzz Wah Volume.

1974-1978	$225	$350

Guitar Synthesizer I

1975	$300	$350

Field Effects by Resonant Electronic Design Acceleron Fuzz

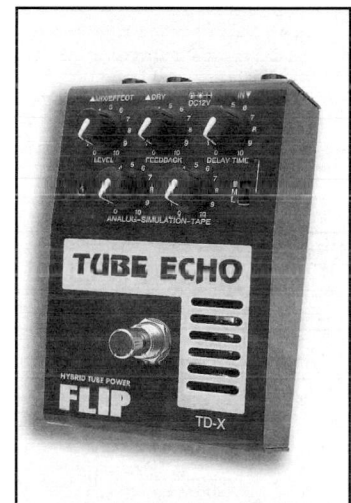

Flip Tube Echo TD-X

Foxx Wah and Volume

Keith Myers

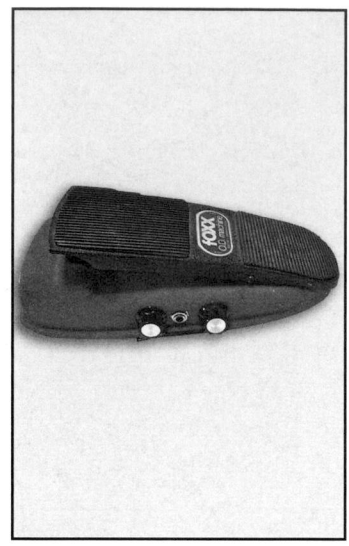

Foxx O.D. Machine
Rich Kislia

G2D Custom Overdrive

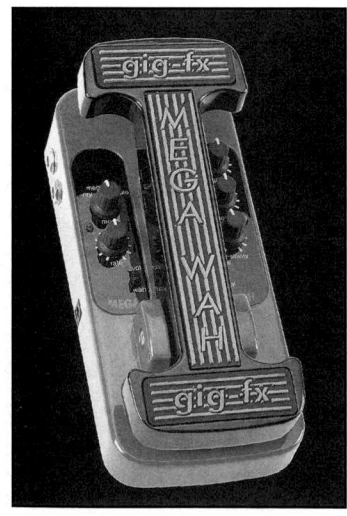

Gig-FX Mega Wah

MODEL YEAR	FEATURES	EXC. COND. LOW	HIGH
Loud Machine	*1970s. Volume pedal.*		
1970s		$25	$40
O.D. Machine	*1972-ca.1975.*		
1972-1975		$150	$200
Phase III			
1975-1978		$100	$150
Tone Machine	*1971-1978, 2005-present. Fuzz with Octave, blue or black housing.*		
1971-1978		$400	$600
Wa and Volume			
1971-1978		$200	$225
Wa Machine	*1971-ca.1978.*		
1971-1978		$150	$200

Framptone

2000-present. Founded by Peter Frampton, Framptone offers hand-made guitar effects.

3 Banger
2000-present. Three-way amp switch box, white housing.

2000-2014		$200	$240

Amp Switcher
2000-present. A-B switch box, white housing.

2000-2014		$80	$100

Talk Box
2000-present. Talk box, white housing, no control knobs, on-off footswitch.

2000-2014		$160	$250

Frantone

1994-present. Effects and accessories hand built in New York City.

Fulltone

1991-present. Effects based on some of the classics of the past and built in Los Angeles, California, by Michael Fuller.

DejàVibe
1991-2004. Uni-Vibe-type pedal, later models have a Vintage/Modern switch. Stereo version also available.

1991-1993	Mono, gold housing	$175	$200
1993-2004	Mono, black housing	$150	$175

DejàVibe 2
1997-2013. Like DejàVibe but with built-in speed control. Stereo version also available.

1997-2013	Mono	$200	$225

Distortion Pro
2002-2008. Red case, volume and distortion knobs with four voicing controls.

2002-2008		$125	$150

Fat Boost
2001-2007. Clean boost, silver-sparkle case, volume and drive knobs.

2001-2007		$125	$135

Full-Drive 2
1995-present. Blue case, four control knobs.

1995-2014		$120	$145

MODEL YEAR	FEATURES	EXC. COND. LOW	HIGH
Mini-DejàVibe	*2004-present. Uni-Vibe-type pedal, white housing, 3 Control knobs, stereo version also available.*		
2004-2014	Mono	$125	$150
Octafuzz	*1996-present. Copy of the Tycobrahe Octavia.*		
1996-2014		$100	$135
Soul Bender	*1994-present. Volume, tone and dirt knobs.*		
1994-2014		$100	$125
Supa-Trem	*1995-present. Black case, white Supa-Trem logo, rate and mix controls.*		
1995-2014		$100	$150
Supa-Trem2	*2000s. Yellow housing, 3 control knobs.*		
2000s		$150	$200
Tube Tape Echo	*2000s. Echo-Plex-style echo unit, white case.*		
2000s		$675	$800

Furman Sound

1993-present. Located in Petaluma, California, Furman makes audio and video signal processors and AC power conditioning products for music and other markets.

LC-2 Limiter Compressor
1990s. Rackmount unit with a black suitcase and red knobs.

1990s		$40	$50

PQ3 Parametric EQ
1990s. Rackmount preamp and equalizer.

1998-1999		$110	$150

PQ6 Parametric Stereo

1990s		$135	$175

RV1 Reverb Rackmount

1990s		$110	$150

Fxdoctor

2003-present. Joshua Zalegowski originally built his effects in Amherst, Massachusetts, and in 2005 moved to Boston.

Fxengineering

2002-present. Production and custom guitar effects built by Montez Aldridge in Raleigh, North Carolina.

G2D

1999-present. David Manning and Grant Wills build their guitar effects pedals in Auckland, New Zealand.

Garcia

Guitar effects built by Matthew Garcia in Myrtle Beach, South Carolina, starting in 2004. He also built amps.

Geek MacDaddy

See listing under The Original Geek.

MODEL		EXC. COND.	
YEAR	FEATURES	LOW	HIGH

George Dennis

1991-present. Founded by George Burgerstein, original products were a line of effects pedals. In '96 they added a line of tube amps. The company is located in Prague, Czech Republic.

Gibson

Gibson did offer a few effects bearing their own name, but most were sold under the Maestro name (see that listing).

Echoplex Digital Pro Plus

1994-2010. Rackmount unit with digital recording, sampling and digital delay. Labeled as just Echoplex until '01 when Gibson name added.

1994-2010		$425	$650

GA-3RV Reverb Unit

1964-1967. Small, compact, spring reverb unit, black tolex, gray grille.

1964-1967		$325	$400

GA-4RE Reverb-Echo Unit

1964-1967. Small, compact, lightweight accessory reverb-echo unit that produces complete reverberation and authentic echo, utilizes Gibson's "electronic memory" system for both reverb and echo, black tolex, gray grille.

1964-1967		$425	$550

Gig-FX

2004-present. Founder Jeff Purchon of Waltham, Massachusetts, imports guitar effects pedals built at his company-owned factory in Shenzhen, China.

Gizmo, Inc.

Ca.1980. Short-lived company that grew out of the ashes of Musitronics' attempt to make the Gizomotron. See Mu-Tron.

Gizmoaudio

2009-present. Guitar effects built by Charles Luke in Cumming, Georgia.

Gnome Amplifiers

2008-present. Guitar effects pedals built by Dan Munro in Olympia, Washington. He also builds amps.

Godbout

Godbout sold a variety of effects do-it-yourself kits in the 1970s, which are difficult to value because quality depends on skills of builder.

Effects Kits

1970s		$20	$30

Godley Crème

1978-1980. Kevin Godley and Lol Crème, members of the band 10cc, developed the Gizmotron, which mounted on the face of a bass or guitar and continously strummed the strings to give a bowed-string effect. The device was built by Musitronics of New Jersey, which built the MuTron III and other effects.

Gizmotron

1978-1980. A "ultimate sustain" mechanical add-on to guitar or bass bridges with rotating plectrums.

1978-1980		$300	$500

Goodrich Sound

1970s-present. Originally located in Michigan, and currently in Dublin, Georgia, Goodrich currently offers volume pedals and a line boost.

Match Box Line Boost

Early-1980s-2011. Small rectangular line buffer/driver.

1980s-2011		$45	$55

Volume Pedal 6122

Late 1970s-1980s. Uses a potentiometer.

1970s		$45	$55

Volume Pedal 6400ST

Late 1970s-1980s. Stereo pedal, using photocells.

1970s		$45	$55

Volume Pedal 6402

Late 1970s-1980s. Uses photocell.

1970s		$45	$55

Goran Custom Guitars

1998-present. Luthier Goran Djuric from Belgrade, Serbia also offers guitar pedals.

Greer Amplification

1999-present. Guitar stomp box effects built by Nick Greer in Athens, Georgia. He also builds amps.

Gretsch

Gretsch has offered a limited line of effects from time to time.

Controfuzz

Mid-1970s. Distortion.

1970s		$150	$225

Deluxe Reverb Unit Model 6149

1963-1969. Similar to Gibson's GA-1 introduced around the same time.

1963-1969		$475	$700

Expandafuzz

Mid-1970s. Distortion.

1970s		$200	$375

Reverb Unit Model 6144 Preamp Reverb

1963-1967. Approximately 17 watts, preamp functionality, no speaker.

1963-1967		$450	$600

Tremofect

Mid-1970s. Tremolo effect, 3-band EQ, speed, effect, bass, total, and treble knobs.

1970s		$225	$300

Guild

Guild marketed effects made by Binson, Electro-Harmonix, Foxx, WEM and Applied in the 1960s and '70s.

Copicat

1960s-1979. Echo.

1970s		$300	$400

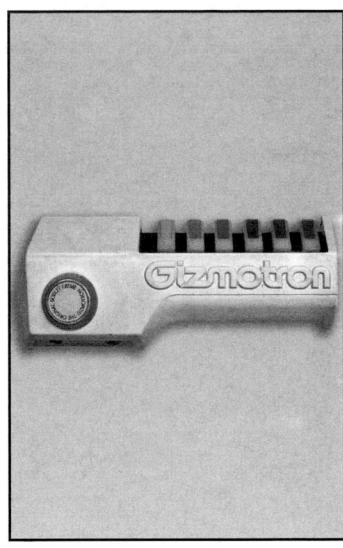

Gizmo, Inc. Gizmotron
Aaron Klpness.

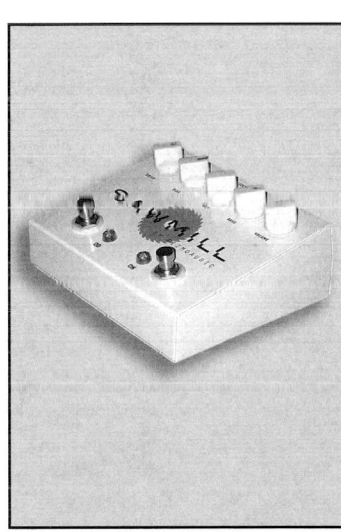

Gizmoaudio Sawmill

Goran Fat Boy Drive

EFFECTS

Guild Foxey Lady
Jim Schreck

HomeBrew Electronics Psilocybe
Keith Myers

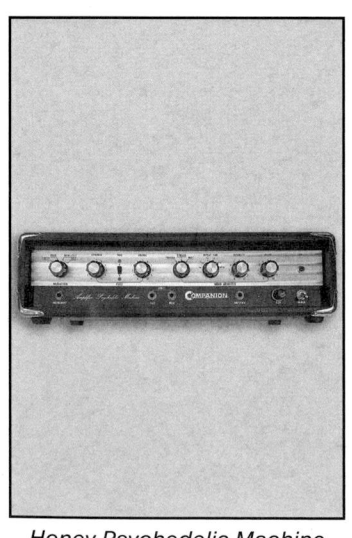

Honey Psychedelic Machine
Ash Sandler

MODEL YEAR	FEATURES	EXC. COND. LOW	HIGH

DE-20 Auto-Rhythm Unit
1971-1974. 50 watt rhythm accompaniment unit. Included 20 rhythms and a separate instrument channel with its own volume control. 1x12" plus tweeter.

1971-1974		$200	$300

Echorec (by Binson)
Ca.1960-1979. Stripped-down version of the Binson Echorec.

1960s		$675	$825

Foxey Lady Fuzz
1968-1977. Distortion, sustain.

1968-1975	2 knobs, made by E-H	$200	$450
1976-1977	3 knobs in row, same as Big Muff	$250	$550

Fuzz Wah FW-3
1975-ca.1979. Distortion, volume, wah, made by Foxx.

1970s		$150	$175

HH Echo Unit
1976-ca.1979.

1970s		$200	$300

VW-1
1975-ca.1979. Volume, wah, made by Foxx.

1970s		$200	$250

Guyatone
1998-present. Imported stomp boxes, tape echo units and outboard reverb units distributed by Godlyke Distributing.

HAO
2000-present. Line of guitar effects built in Japan by J.E.S. International, distributed in the U.S. by Godlyke.

Harden Engineering
2006-present. Distortion/boost guitar effects pedals built by William Harden in Chicago, Illinois. He also builds guitars.

Heathkit
1960s. These were sold as do-it-yourself kits and are difficult to value because quality depends on skills of builder.

TA-28 Distortion Booster
1960s. Fuzz assembly kit, heavy '60s super fuzz, case-by-case quality depending on the builder.

1960s		$140	$150

Heavy Metal Products
Mid-1970s. From Alto Loma, California, products for the heavy metal guitarist.

Raunchbox Fuzz

1975-1976		$75	$100

Switchbox
1975-1976. A/B box.

1975-1976		$25	$35

Heet Sound Products
1974-present. The E Bow concept goes back to '67, but a hand-held model wasn't available until '74. Made in Los Angeles, California.

E Bow
1974-1979, 1985-1987, 1994-present. The Energy Bow, hand-held electro-magnetic string driver.

1974-1979		$50	$60

E Bow for Pedal Steels
1979. Hand-held electro-magnetic string driver.

1979		$35	$55

Heil Sound
1960-present. Founded by Bob Heil, Marissa, Illinois. Created the talk box technology as popularized by Joe Walsh and Peter Frampton. In the '60s and '70s Heil was dedicated to innovative products for the music industry. In the late-'70s, innovative creations were more in the amateur radio market, and by the '90s Heil's focus was on the home theater market. The Heil Sound Talkbox was reissued by Jim Dunlop USA in '89.

Talk Box
1976-ca.1980, 1989-present. Reissued by Dunlop.

1976-1980		$100	$150
1989-1999		$60	$85
2000-2014		$60	$80

Henretta Engineering
2009-present. Analog guitar effects built by Kevin Henretta first in Chicago, Illinois and presently Saint Paul, Minnesota.

Hermida Audio
2003-present. Alfonso Hermida builds his guitar effects in Miramar, Florida.

High Gain
See listing under Dunlop.

Hohner
Hohner offered effects in the late-1970s.

Dirty Booster
1977-ca.1978. Distortion.

1977-1978		$55	$65

Dirty Wah Wah'er
1977-ca.1978. Adds distortion.

1977-1978		$65	$75

Fuzz Wah
1970s. Morley-like volume pedal with volume knob and fuzz knob, switch for soft or hard fuzz, gray box with black foot pedal.

1970s		$65	$75

Multi-Exciter
1977-ca.1978. Volume, wah, surf, tornado, siren.

1977-1978		$60	$70

Tape Echo/Echo Plus
1970s. Black alligator suitcase.

1970s		$200	$275

Tri-Booster
1977-ca.1978. Distortion, sustain.

1977-1978		$55	$65

MODEL YEAR	FEATURES	EXC. COND. LOW	HIGH
Vari-Phaser			
1977-ca.1978.			
1977-1978		$55	$65
Vol-Kicker Volume Pedal			
1977-ca.1978.			
1977-1978		$30	$40
Wah-Wah'er			
1977-ca.1978. Wah, volume.			
1977-1978		$55	$65

HomeBrew Electronics

2001-present. Stomp box effects hand made by Joel and Andrea Weaver in Glendale, Arizona.

Honey

1967-1969. Formed by ex-Teisco workers after that firm was acquired by Kawai. Honey launched several effects designed by engineer Fumio Mieda, before going bankrupt in March, '69. The company was reborn as Shin-ei and many of its designs continued production in various forms; see Shin-ei for more.

MODEL YEAR	FEATURES	EXC. COND. LOW	HIGH
Psychedelic Machine			
1967-1969. Amp head-sized effect with numerous controls.			
1967-1969		$750	$1,000

Hughes & Kettner

1985-present. Hughes & Kettner builds a line of tube-driven guitar effects made in Germany. They also build amps and cabinets.

Ibanez

1932-present. Ibanez effects were introduced ca. 1974, and were manufactured by Japan's Maxon Electronics. Although results were mixed at first, a more uniform and modern product line, including the now legendary Tube Screamer, built Ibanez's reputation for quality. They continue to produce a wide range of effects.

MODEL YEAR	FEATURES	EXC. COND. LOW	HIGH
60s Fuzz FZ5 (SoundTank)			
1991-1992, 1996-1998. Fuzz with level, tone and distortion controls, black plastic case, green label.			
1990s		$25	$30
7th Heaven SH7 (Tone-Lok)			
2000-2004. Lo, high, drive and level controls, gray-silver case, blue-green label.			
2000-2004		$20	$30
Acoustic Effects PT4			
1993-1998. Acoustic guitar multi-effect with compressor/limiter, tone shaper, stereo chorus, digital reverb, with power supply.			
1993-1998		$75	$100
Analog Delay AD9			
1982-1984. 3 control analog delay, Hot Pink metal case.			
1982-1984		$200	$275
Analog Delay AD80			
1980-1981. Pink case.			
1980-1981		$225	$300

MODEL YEAR	FEATURES	EXC. COND. LOW	HIGH
Analog Delay AD99			
1996-1998. Reissue, 3 control knobs and on/off switch, winged-hand logo, black case.			
1996-1998		$125	$150
Analog Delay AD100 (Table Unit)			
1981-1983. Stand-alone table/studio unit (not rack mount) with power cord.			
1981-1983		$200	$250
Analog Delay 202 (Rack Mount)			
1981-1983. Rack mount with delay, doubling, flanger, stereo chorus, dual inputs with tone and level.			
1981-1983		$200	$250
Auto Filter AF9			
1982-1984. Replaces AF201 model.			
1982-1984		$150	$200
Auto Filter AF201			
1981. Two min-max sliders, 3 mode toggle switches, orange metal case.			
1981		$175	$200
Auto Wah AW5 (SoundTank)			
1994-1999. Plastic case SoundTank series.			
1994-1999		$30	$40
Auto Wah AW7 (Tone-Lok)			
2000-2010. Silver case.			
2000-2010		$20	$30
Bass Compressor BP10			
1986-1991		$70	$80
Bi-Mode Chorus BC9			
1984. Dual channel for 2 independent speed and width settings.			
1984		$75	$100
Chorus CS-505			
1980-1981. Speed and depth controls, gray-blue case, stereo or mono input, battery or external power option.			
1980-1981		$200	$250
Chorus Flanger CF7 (Tone-Lok)			
1999-2010. Speed, depth, delay, regeneration controls, mode and crazy switches.			
1999-2010		$35	$40
Classic Flange FL99			
1997-1999. Analog reissue, silver metal case, winged-hand artwork, 4 controls, 2 footswitch buttons.			
1997-1999		$90	$110
Classic Phase PH99			
1995-1999. Analog reissue, silver metal case, winged-hand artwork, speed, depth, feedback, effect level controls, intense and bypass footswitches.			
1995-1999		$90	$110
Compressor CP5 (SoundTank)			
1991-1998		$20	$30
Compressor CP10			
1986-1992		$75	$80
Compressor CP830			
1975-1979		$100	$125
Compressor II CP835			
1980-1981		$100	$125
Compressor Limiter CP9			
1982-1984		$100	$125
Delay Champ CD10			
1986-1989. Red case, 3 knobs.			
1986-1989		$125	$150

Hughes & Kettner Tube Rotosphere MKII

Ibanez Analog Delay AD9

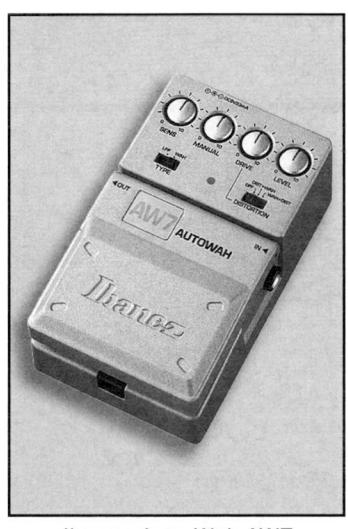

Ibanez Auto Wah AW7 (Tone-Lok)

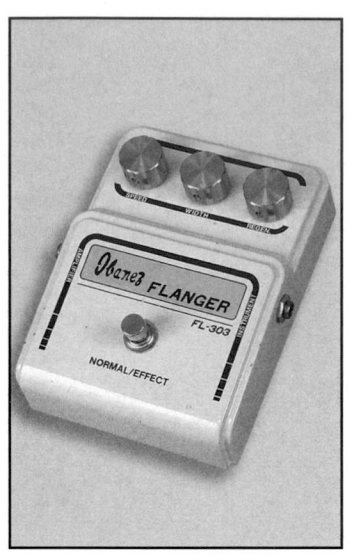

1978 Ibanez Flanger FL-303

Ibanez LA Metal LM7

Ibanez Metal Charger MS10
Keith Myers

MODEL YEAR	FEATURES	EXC. COND. LOW	HIGH
Delay Echo DE7 (Tone-Lok)	*1999-2010. Stereo delay/echo.*		
1999-2010		$40	$50
Delay Harmonizer DM1000	*1983-1984. Rack mount, with chorus, 9 control knobs.*		
1983-1984		$175	$225
Delay III DDL20 Digital Delay	*1988-1989. Filtering, doubling, slap back, echo S, echo M, echo L, Seafoam Green coloring on pedal.*		
1988-1989		$100	$125
Delay PDD1 (DPC Series)	*1988-1989. Programmable Digital Delay (PDD) with display screen.*		
1988-1989		$125	$150
Digital Chorus DSC10	*1990-1992. 3 control knobs and slider selection toggle.*		
1990-1992		$75	$100
Digital Delay DL5 (SoundTank)			
1991-1998		$35	$45
Digital Delay DL10	*1989-1992. Digital Delay made in Japan, blue case, 3 green control knobs, stompbox.*		
1989-1992		$100	$125
Distortion Charger DS10			
1986-1989		$70	$90
Distortion DS7 (Tone-Lok)	*2000-2010. Drive, tone, and level controls.*		
2000-2010		$40	$45
Echo Machine EM5 (SoundTank)	*1996-1998. Simulates tape echo.*		
1996-1998		$45	$55
Fat Cat Distortion FC10	*1987-1989. 3-knob pedal with distortion, tone, and level controls.*		
1987-1989		$50	$75
Flanger FFL5 (Master Series)	*1984-1985. Speed, regeneration, width, D-time controls, battery or adapter option.*		
1984-1985		$70	$90
Flanger FL5 (SoundTank)			
1991-1998		$25	$35
Flanger FL9	*1982-1984. Yellow case.*		
1982-1984		$100	$150
Flanger FL301	*1979 1982. Mini flanger, 3 knobs, called the FL-301 DX in late '81-'82.*		
1979-1982		$100	$125
Flanger FL305	*1976-1979. Five knobs.*		
1976-1979		$100	$125
Flying Pan FP777	*1976-1979. Auto pan/phase shifter, 4 control knobs, phase on/off button, pan on/off button, silver metal case with blue trim and Flying Pan winged-hand logo.*		
1976-1979		$575	$725
Flying Pan FP777 Reissue			
2007	777 made	$275	$350

MODEL YEAR	FEATURES	EXC. COND. LOW	HIGH
Fuzz FZ7 (Tone-Lok)	*2000-2010. Drive, tone and level controls, gray-silver case, blue-green FZ7 label.*		
2000-2010		$45	$50
Graphic Bass EQ BE10	*1986-1992. Later labeled as the BEQ10.*		
1986-1992		$60	$80
Graphic EQ GE9	*1982-1984. Six EQ sliders, 1 overall volume slider, turquoise blue case.*		
1982-1984		$60	$80
Graphic EQ GE10	*1986-1992. Eight sliders.*		
1986-1992		$60	$80
Graphic Equalizer GE601 (808 Series)	*1980-1981. 7-slider EQ, aqua blue metal case.*		
1980-1981		$75	$100
Guitar Multi-Processor PT5	*1993-1997. Floor unit, programmable with 25 presets and 25 user presets, effects include distortion, chorus, flanger, etc, green case.*		
1993-1997		$100	$125
LA Metal LM7	*1988-1989. Silver case.*		
1988-1989		$55	$65
LoFi LF7 (Tone-Lok)	*2000-2010. Filter, 4 knobs.*		
2000-2010		$20	$30
Metal Charger MS10	*1986-1992. Distortion, level, attack, punch and edge control knobs, green case.*		
1986-1992		$45	$55
Metal Screamer MSL	*1985. 3 control knobs.*		
1985		$55	$65
Modern Fusion MF5 (SoundTank)	*1990-1991. Level, tone and distortion controls.*		
1990-1991		$45	$50
Modulation Delay DM500	*1983-1984. Rack mount.*		
1983-1984		$75	$100
Modulation Delay DM1000	*1983-1984. Rack mount with delay, reverb, modulation.*		
1983-1984		$100	$125
Modulation Delay PDM1	*1988-1989. Programmable Digital Modulation pedal.*		
1988-1989		$100	$125
Mostortion MT10	*1990-1992. Mos-FET circuit distortion pedal, 5 control knobs, green case.*		
1990-1992		$50	$60
Multi-Effect PUE5/PUE5 Tube (Floor Unit)	*1990-1993. Yellow version has tube, blue one does not. Also available in PUE5B bass version.*		
1990-1993	Tube	$350	$450
Multi-Effect UE300 (Floor Unit)	*1983-1984. Floor unit, 4 footswitches for super metal, digital delay, digital stereo chorus, and master power, 3 delay modes.*		
1983-1984		$275	$350

MODEL		EXC. COND.	
YEAR	FEATURES	LOW	HIGH

Multi-Effect UE300B (Floor Unit)
1983-1984. Floor unit for bass.

1983-1984		$275	$350

Multi-Effect UE400 (Rackmount)
1980-1984. Rack mount with foot switch.

1980-1984		$300	$375

Multi-Effect UE405 (Rackmount)
1981-1984. Rack mount with analog delay, parametric EQ, compressor/limiter, stereo chorus and loop.

1981-1984		$300	$375

Noise Buster NB10
1988-1989. Eliminates 60-cycle hum and other outside signals, metal case.

1988-1989		$70	$75

Overdrive OD850

1975-1979		$275	$400

Overdrive II OD855
1977-1979. Distortion, tone, and level controls, yellow/green case, large Overdrive II logo.

1977-1979		$300	$400

Pan Delay DPL10
1990-1992. Royal Blue case, 3 green control knobs.

1990-1992		$100	$125

Parametric EQ PQ9

1982-1984		$125	$175

Parametric EQ PQ401
1981. 3 sliders, dial-in knob, light aqua blue case.

1981		$125	$175

Phase Tone PT909
1979-1982. Blue box, 3 knobs, early models with flat case (logo at bottom or later in the middle) or later wedge case

1979-1982		$140	$150

Phase Tone PT999
1975-1979. Script logo, 1 knob, round footswitch, becomes PT-909.

1975-1979		$125	$150

Phase Tone PT1000
1974-1975. Morley-style pedal phase, light blue case, early model of Phase Tone.

1974-1975		$200	$300

Phase Tone II PT707
1976-1979. Blue box, script logo for first 2 years.

1976-1979		$100	$130

Phaser PH5 (SoundTank)

1991-1998		$20	$30

Phaser PH7 (Tone-Lok)
1999-2010. Speed, depth, feedback and level controls.

1999-2010		$35	$40

Phaser PT9
1982-1984. Three control knobs, red case.

1982-1984		$75	$100

Powerlead PL5 (SoundTank)
1991-1998. Metal case '91, plastic case '91-'98.

1991	Metal	$25	$40
1991-1998	Plastic	$15	$20

Renometer
1976-1979. 5-band equalizer with preamp.

1976-1979		$75	$100

MODEL		EXC. COND.	
YEAR	FEATURES	LOW	HIGH

Rotary Chorus RC99
1996-1999. Black or silver cases available, requires power pack and does not use a battery.

1996-1999	Black case	$100	$125

Session Man SS10
1988-1989. Distortion, chorus.

1988-1989		$70	$80

Session Man II SS20
1988-1989. 4 controls plus toggle, light pink-purple case.

1988-1989		$70	$80

Slam Punk SP5 (SoundTank)

1996-1999		$35	$40

Smash Box SM7 (Tone-Lok)

2000-2010		$30	$35

Sonic Distortion SD9

1982-1984		$75	$100

Standard Fuzz (No. 59)
1974-1979. Two buttons (fuzz on/off and tone change).

1974-1979		$175	$200

Stereo Box ST800
1975-1979. One input, 2 outputs for panning, small yellow case.

1975-1979		$175	$225

Stereo Chorus CS9

1982-1984		$75	$100

Stereo Chorus CSL (Master Series)

1985-1986		$70	$90

Super Chorus CS5 (SoundTank)

1991-1998		$20	$30

Super Metal SM9
1984. Distortion.

1984		$75	$95

Super Stereo Chorus SC10

1986-1992		$75	$100

Super Tube Screamer ST9
1984-1985. 4 knobs, light green metal case.

1984-1985		$225	$300

Super Tube STL

1985		$75	$95

Swell Flanger SF10
1986-1992. Speed, regeneration, width and time controls, yellow case.

1986-1992		$55	$100

Trashmetal TM5 (SoundTank)
1990-1998. Tone and distortion pedal, 3 editions (1st edition, 2nd edition metal case, 2nd edition plastic case).

1990-1998		$15	$20

Tremolo Pedal TL5 (SoundTank)

1995-1998		$45	$95

Tube King TK999
1994-1995. Has a 12AX7 tube and 3-band equalizer.

1994-1995	Includes power pack	$150	$200

Tube King TK999US
1996-1998. Has a 12AX7 tube and 3-band equalizer, does not have the noise switch of original TK999. Made in the U.S.

1996-1998	Includes power pack	$150	$200

1977 Ibanez Phase Tone II PT707
Keith Myers

Ibanez Phaser PH7 (Tone-Lok)

Ibanez Tube King TK999US
Keith Myers

EFFECTS

EFFECTS

Ibanez Turbo Tube Screamer TS9DX

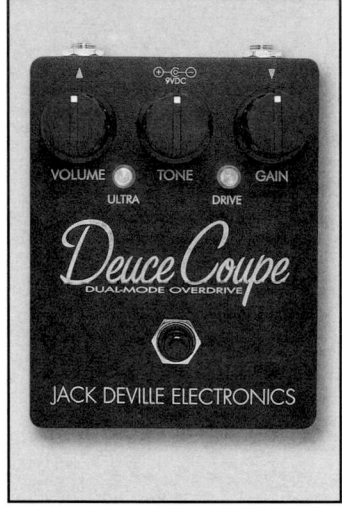

Jack Deville Deuce Coupe Overdrive

Jax Fuzz
Jim Schreck

MODEL YEAR	FEATURES	EXC. COND. LOW	HIGH
Tube Screamer TS5 (SoundTank)			
1991-1998		$20	$25
Tube Screamer TS7 (Tone-Lok)			
1999-2010. 3 control knobs.			
1999-2010		$30	$35
Tube Screamer TS9			
1982-1984, 1993-present. Reissued in '93.			
1982-1984		$300	$450
1993-2013		$75	$125
Tube Screamer Classic TS10			
1986-1993		$175	$225
Tube Screamer TS808			
1980-1982, 2004-present. Reissued in '04.			
1980-1982	Original	$350	$500
2004-2014	Reissue	$75	$100
Turbo Tube Screamer TS9DX			
1998-present. Tube Screamer circuit with added 3 settings for low-end.			
1998-2014		$70	$85
Twin Cam Chorus TC10			
1986-1989. Four control knobs, light blue case.			
1986-1989		$75	$100
Virtual Amp VA3 (floor unit)			
1995-1998. Digital effects processor.			
1995-1998		$55	$75
VL10			
1987-1997. Stereo volume pedal.			
1987-1997		$50	$75
Wah Fuzz Standard (Model 58)			
1974-1981. Fuzz tone change toggle, fuzz on toggle, fuzz depth control, balance control, wah volume pedal with circular friction pads on footpedal.			
1974-1981		$225	$300
Wah WH10			
1988-1997		$50	$75

Ilitch Electronics

2003-present. Ilitch Chiliachki builds his effects in Camarillo, California.

Indy Guitarist

See listing under Wampler Pedals.

Intersound

1970s-1980s. Intersound, Inc. was located in Boulder, Colorado and was a division of Electro-Voice.

Reverb-Equalizer R100F
1977-1979. Reverb and 4-band EQ, fader.

1977-1979		$75	$100

J. Everman

2000-present. Analog guitar effects built by Justin J. Everman in Richardson, Texas.

Jack Deville Electronics

2008-present. Production/custom, guitar effects built in Portland, Oregon by Jack Deville.

Jacques

One-of-a-kind handmade stomp boxes and production models made in France.

MODEL YEAR	FEATURES	EXC. COND. LOW	HIGH

JangleBox

2004-present. Stephen Lasko and Elizabeth Lasko build their guitar effects in Springfield, Virginia and Dracut, Massachusetts.

Jan-Mar Industries

Jan-Mar was located in Hillsdale, New Jersey.

The Talker
1976. 30 watts.

1976		$75	$125

The Talker Pro
1976. 75 watts.

1976		$100	$150

Jax

1960s-1970. Japanese imports made by Shin-ei.

Fuzz Master

1960s		$350	$425

Vibrachorus
1969. Rotating-speaker simulator, with control pedal. Variant of Uni-Vibe.

1969		$575	$750

Wah-Wah

1960s		$400	$500

Jen

Italy's Jen Elettronica company made a variety of guitar effects pedals in the 1960s and '70s for other brands such as Vox and Gretsch name. They also offered many of them, including the Cry Baby, under their own name.

Jersey Girl

1991-present. Line of guitar effects pedals made in Japan. They also build guitars.

Jet Sounds LTD

1977. Jet was located in Jackson, Mississippi.

Hoze Talk Box
1977. Large wood box, 30 watts.

1977		$90	$125

Jetter Gear

2005-present. Brad Jeter builds his effects pedals in Marietta, Georgia.

JHD Audio

1974-1990. Hunt Dabney founded JHD in Costa Mesa, California, to provide effects that the user installed in their amp. Dabney is still involved in electronics and builds the BiasProbe tool for tubes.

SuperCube/SuperCube II
1974-late 1980s. Plug-in sustain mod for Fender amps with reverb, second version for amps after '78.

1974-1980s		$50	$75

JHS Pedals

2007-present. Located in Mississippi 2007-08, Josh Scott presently builds his guitar and bass effects in Kansas City, Missouri.

MODEL YEAR	FEATURES	EXC. COND. LOW	HIGH

Jimi Hendrix

See listing under Dunlop.

John Hornby Skewes & Co.

Mid-1960s-present. Large English distributor of musical products, which has also self-branded products from others, over the years. The early Zonk Machines, Shatterbox and pre-amp boosts were designed and built by engineer Charlie Ramskirr of Wilsic Electronics, until his death in '68. Later effects were brought in from manufacturers in Italy and the Far East.

Bass Boost BB1

1966-1968. Pre-amp.

1966-1968		$250	$400

Fuzz FZIII

1970s. Fuzz pedal, 2 control knobs, 1 footswitch.

1970s		$150	$200

Phaser PZ111

1970s. Phaser pedal, 2 control knobs, 1 footswitch.

1970s		$150	$200

Selectatone TB2

1966-1968. Pre-amp combining treble and bass boost.

1966-1968		$250	$650

Treble Boost TB1

1966-1968. Pre-amp.

1966-1968		$250	$750

Zonk Machine I

1965-1968. Fuzz pedal, gray-blue housing, 2 control knobs, 1 footswitch, 3 germanium transistors.

1965-1968		$1,500	$2,000

Zonk Machine II

1966-1968. Fuzz pedal, gray-blue housing, 2 control knobs, 1 footswitch, 3 silicon transistors.

1966-1968		$1,000	$1,500

Zonk Machine reissue

2000s. Reissued by JMI starting in 2013, reissues also made by the British Pedal Company, 2 control knobs, 1 footswitch.

2000s		$150	$200

Zonk Shatterbox

1966-1968. Combined the Zonk Machine II fuzz circuit with the Treble Boost, 2 control knobs, gold housing, 2 foot switches.

1966-1968		$1,500	$2,000

Zonk Shatterbox reissue

2000s. Reissues made by the British Pedal Company, gold housing, 2 foot switches.

2000s		$150	$200

Zoom Spring Reverb Unit

1967-1968		$500	$700

Johnson

Mid-1990s-present. Budget line of effects imported by Music Link, Brisbane, California. Johnson also offers guitars, amps, mandolins and basses.

Johnson Amplification

1997-present. Modeling amps and effects designed by John Johnson, of Sandy, Utah. The company is part of Harman International. In '02, they quit building amps, but continue the effects line.

Jordan

1966-early 1970s. Jordan Electronics - originally of Alhambra, California, later in Pasadena - built a range of electronics, including, starting around 1966, solid state guitar amps and effects. Sho-Bud of Nashville, Tennessee, licensed the Boss Tone and sold it as the Sho-Sound Boss Tone. Mahoney later reissued the Boss Tone as the Buzz Tone.

Boss Tone Fuzz

1967-1970s. Tiny effect plugged into guitar's output jack, 2 control knobs, black plastic housing, extremely delicate wiring.

1967-70s		$100	$225

Compressor J-700

1967-70s		$75	$100

Creator Volume Sustainer

1967-70s		$125	$175

Gig Wa-Wa Volume

1967-70s		$125	$150

Phaser

1967-1970s. Black case, yellow knobs.

1967-70s	Black case	$125	$150

Kay

1931-present. Kay was once one of the largest instrument producers in the world, offering just about everything for the guitarist, including effects.

Effects Pedals

1970s. Includes the Wah, Graphic Equalizer GE-5000, Rhythmer, and Tremolo.

1970s		$50	$75

Keeley

2001-present. Line of guitar effects designed and built by Robert Keeley in Edmond, Oklahoma. Keeley Electronics also offers a range of custom modifications for other effects.

Kendrick

1989-present. Texas' Kendrick offers guitars, amps, and effects.

ABC Amp Switcher

1990s		$100	$140

Buffalo Pfuz

1990s		$70	$100

Model 1000 Reverb

1991-2003. Vintage style, 3 knobs: dwell, tone, and mix, brown cover, wheat grille with art deco shape.

1991-2003		$400	$450

Powerglide Attenuator

1998-present. Allows you to cut the output before it hits the amp's speakers, rack mount, metal cab.

1998-2014		$180	$200

Kent

1961-1969. This import guitar brand also offered a few effects.

1978 Jen Cry Baby
Ritchie Hayden

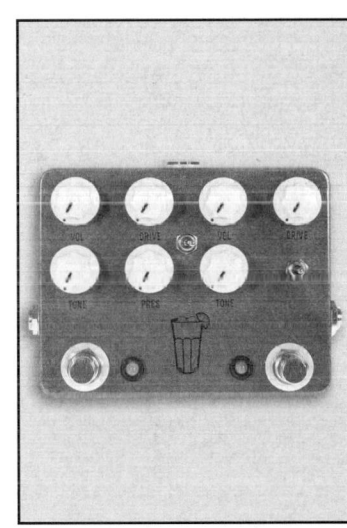

JHS Pedals Sweet Tea

Kay Rhythmer R-12
Keith Myers

EFFECTS

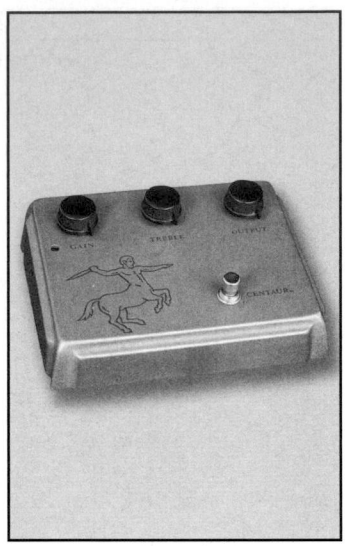

1997 Klon Centaur Overdrive
Folkway Music

KR Musical Mega Vibe
Keith Myers

Krank Distortus Maximus

MODEL		EXC. COND.	
YEAR	FEATURES	LOW	HIGH

Kern Engineering

Located in Kenosha, Wisconsin, Kern offers pre-amps and wah pedals.

Kinsman

2012-present. Guitar effects pedals built in China and distributed by John Hornby Skewes & Co. Ltd.

Klon

1994-present. Originally located in Brookline, Massachusetts, and now located in Cambridge, Massachusetts, Klon was started by Bill Finnegan after working with two circuit design partners on the Centaur Professional Overdrive.

Centaur

2010. Smaller overdrive unit with burnished silver case.

2010		$700	$900

Centaur Professional Overdrive

1994-2009. Standard size with gold case. A smaller unit was introduced in '10.

1994-2009		$1,050	$1,300

KMD (Kaman)

1986-ca. 1990. Distributed by Kaman (Ovation, Hamer, etc.) in the late '80s.

Effects Pedals

1986-1990	Analog Delay	$65	$90
1986-1990	Overdrive	$30	$45
1987-1990	Distortion	$30	$45
1987-1990	Flanger	$30	$50
1987-1990	Phaser	$30	$50
1987-1990	Stereo Chorus	$30	$50

Korg

Most of the Korg effects listed below are modular effects. The PME-40X Professional Modular Effects System holds four of them and allows the user to select several variations of effects. The modular effects cannot be used alone. This system was sold for a few years starting in 1983. Korg currently offers the Toneworks line of effects.

PEQ-1 Parametric EQ

1980s. Dial-in equalizer with gain knob, band-width knob, and frequency knob, black case.

1980s		$40	$50

PME-40X Modular Effects

1983-1986	KAD-301 Delay	$60	$70
1983-1986	KCH-301 Chorus	$25	$35
1983-1986	KCO-101 Compressor	$45	$55
1983-1986	KDI-101 Distortion	$45	$55
1983-1986	KDL-301 Echo	$90	$110
1983-1986	KFL-401 Flanger	$40	$50
1983-1986	KGE-201 Graphic EQ	$25	$35
1983-1986	KNG-101 Noise Gate	$25	$35
1983-1986	KOD-101 Over Drive	$45	$55
1983-1986	KPH-401 Phaser	$45	$55
1983-1986	OCT-1 Octaver	$70	$80

PME-40X Professional Modular Effects System

1983-ca.1986. Board holds up to 4 of the modular effects listed below.

1983-1986		$125	$150

MODEL		EXC. COND.	
YEAR	FEATURES	LOW	HIGH

SSD 3000 Digital Delay

1980s. Rack mount, SDD-3000 logo on top of unit.

1980s		$775	$925

KR Musical Products

2003-present. Kevin Randall presently builds his vintage style, guitar effects in White Marsh, Virginia.

Krank

1996-2013, 2015-present. Tempe, Arizona, amp builder Tony Krank also builds effects pedals.

Kustom

1965-present. Founded in '64 by Charles "Bud" Ross in his Chanute, Kansas, garage to build amps for his band. While Fender, Rickenbacker, and others tried and failed with solid-state amps, Ross' Kustom creations were a big hit. Kustom likely only ever made one foray into effects, producing The Bag, designed by Doug Forbes.

The Bag

1969-1971. Pioneering "talk box" effect housed in a "bota" wineskin-type bag worn over the player's shoulder. Covered in multiple styles of mod fabrics.

1969-1971		$900	$1,500

Lafayette Radio Electronics

1960s-1970s. Effects that claimed to be made in the U.S., but were most likely built by Shin-ei of Japan.

Deluxe AC Super Fuzz

1969-1970s. Made by Shin-ei, AC power.

1969-70s		$300	$500

Echo Verb/Echo Verb II

1970s. Solid-state echo/reverb. Likely made by Shin-ei.

1970s	2 instrument inputs	$200	$300
1970s	Instrument & mic inputs	$150	$250

Fuzz Sound

1970s. Likely made by Shin-ei.

1970s		$150	$250

Roto-Vibe

1969-1970s. Rotating-speaker simulator, with control pedal. Variant of Uni-Vibe made by Shin-ei.

1969-70s		$575	$750

Super Fuzz

1969-1970s. Made by Shin-ei.

1969-70s		$300	$500
1969-70s	Battery power	$300	$500

Laney

1968-present. Founded by Lyndon Laney and Bob Thomas in Birmingham, U.K., this amp builder also offered a reverb unit.

Reverberation Unit

1968-1969. Sleek reverb unit, plexi-style front panel, black vinyl cover.

1968-1969		$300	$400

EFFECTS

MODEL		EXC. COND.	
YEAR	FEATURES	LOW	HIGH

Larry Alan Guitars

2003-present. Luthier Larry Alan Daft offers effects pedals built in Lansing, Michigan. He also builds guitars and basses.

Lehle

2001-present. Loop switches from Burkhard Georg Lehle of Lehle Gitarrentechnik in Voerde, Germany.

D.Loop Signal Router

2004		$150	$175

Lenahan

Amp builder James Lenahan also offers a line of guitar pedals, built in Fort Smith, Arkansas.

Leslie

1966-1970s. In 1941, Donald Leslie began building speakers for Hammond organs to emulate pipe-organ sounds. Using a rotating baffle in front of a stationary speaker, he replicated the tremolo sound. He sold his company to CBS in 1965, and Fender launched its Vibratone based on Leslie technology in 1967. Leslie also offered its Model 16 and 18 speakers for guitarists. The Leslie 16/18 were also sold by Selmer as the Selmer-Leslie.

Model 16

1966-1970s. Rotating-speaker emulator, single fixed 4-ohm 10-inch speaker fronted by a rotating drum. Designed to be powered by an external amp. Black covering, cast Leslie badge in upper left corner.

1966-70s		$600	$750

Model 18

1966-1970s. Rotating-speaker emulator, single fixed 4-ohm 12-inch speaker fronted by a rotating drum. Designed to be powered by an external amp. Black covering, cast Leslie badge in upper left corner.

1966-70s		$500	$700

Line 6

1996-present. Founded by Marcus Ryle and Michel Doidic. Purchased by Yamaha in 2014. They also produce amps and guitars. All prices include Line 6 power pack if applicable.

DL-4 Delay Modeler

1999-present. Green case.

1999-2014		$175	$225

DM-4 Distortion Modeler

1999-present. Yellow case.

1999-2014		$100	$125

FM-4 Filter Modeler

2001-present. Purple case.

2001-2014		$175	$225

MM-4 Modulation Modeler

1999-present. Aqua blue case.

1999-2014		$150	$185

POD 2.0

2001-2014. Updated version of the original Amp Modeler.

2001-2014		$150	$200

Little Lanilei

1997-present. Effects made by Mahaffay Amplifiers (formerly Songworks Systems & Products) of Aliso Viejo, California. They also build amps.

Lizard Leg Effects

2007-present. Steve Miller builds a line of effects pedals in Gonzales, Louisiana.

Lock & Rock

2003-present. Line of floor pedal guitar and microphone effects produced by Brannon Electronics, Inc. of Houston, Texas.

Loco Box

1982-1983. Loco Box was a brand of effects distributed by Aria Pro II for a short period starting in '82. It appears that Aria switched the effects to their own brand in '83.

Effects

1982-1983	Analog Delay AD-01	$35	$45
1982-1983	Chorus CH-01	$55	$65
1982-1983	Compressor CM-01	$35	$45
1982-1983	Distortion DS-01	$40	$55
1982-1983	Flanger FL-01	$35	$45
1982-1983	Graphic Equalizer GE-06	$25	$35
1982-1983	Overdrive OD-01	$40	$50
1982-1983	Phaser PH-01	$45	$55

Lotus Pedal Designs

2009-present. Guitar effects pedals built in Duluth, Minnesota by Sean Erspamer.

Lovepedal

2000-present. Sean Michael builds his preamps and guitar stomp boxes in Detroit, Michigan.

Lovetone

1995-present. Hand-made analog effects from Oxfordshire, U.K.

Ludwig

For some reason, drum builder Ludwig offered a guitar synth in the 1970s.

Phase II Guitar Synth

1970-1971. Oversized synth, mushroom-shaped footswitches, vertical silver case.

1970-1971		$650	$800

M.B. Electronics

Made in San Francisco, California.

Ultra-Metal UM-10

1985. Distortion.

1985		$35	$40

Mad Professor

2002-present. Guitar effects pedals built by Bjorn Juhl and Jukka Monkkonen in Tampere, Finland. They also build amps.

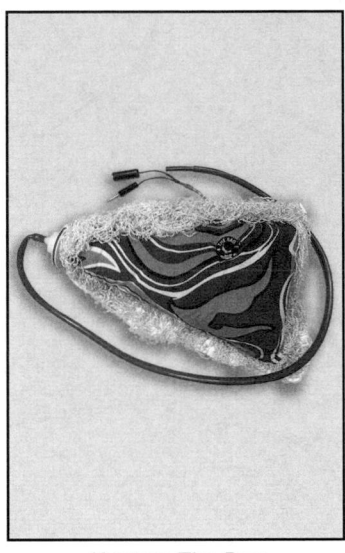

Kustom The Bag
The Bag Man

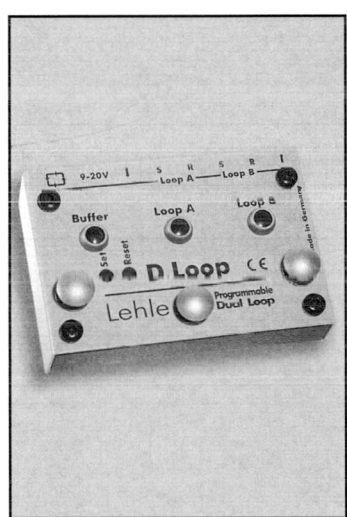

Lehle D.Loop Signal Router

Lizard Leg Effect
Draconis Dual Boost

EFFECTS

Maestro Fuzz Tone FZ-1B
Bob Cain

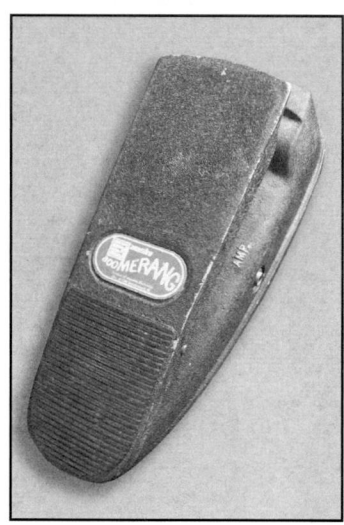
Maestro Boomerang Wah
Jim Schreck

Maestro Stage Phaser MPP-1
Jim Schreck

MODEL		EXC. COND.	
YEAR	FEATURES	LOW	HIGH

Maestro

1950s-1970s, 2001-present. Maestro was a Gibson subsidiary; the name appeared on 1950s accordian amplifiers. The first Maestro effects were the Echoplex tape echo and the FZ-1 Fuzz-Tone, introduced in the early-'60s. Maestro products were manufactured by various entities such as Market Electronics, All-Test Devices, Lowrey and Moog Electronics. In the late-'60s and early-'70s, they unleashed a plethora of pedals; some were beautiful, others had great personality. The last Maestro effects were the Silver and Black MFZ series of the late-'70s. In 2001, Gibson revived the name for a line of effects, banjos and mandolins, adding guitars and amps in '09.

Bass Brassmaster BB-1
1971-ca.1974. Added brass to your bass.

1971-1974		$775	$1,100

Boomerang
Ca.1969-ca.1972. Wah pedal made by All-Test Devices.

1969-1972		$175	$200

Boomerang BG-2
1972-ca.1976. Wah pedal made by All-Test Devices.

1972-1976		$200	$225

Echoplex EM-1 Groupmaster
Ca.1970-ca.1977. Two input Echoplex, solidstate.

1970-1977	Without stand	$900	$1,400

Echoplex EP-1
1959-mid-1960s. Original model, smaller green box, tube-driven tape echo, separate controls for echo volume and instrument volume, made by Market Electronics. Though not labeled as such, it is often referred to as the EP-1 by collectors.

1959-60s	Earlier small box	$900	$1,200

Echoplex EP-2
Mid-1960s-ca.1970. Larger gray or green box than original, tube-driven tape echo, single echo/instrument volume control, made by Market Electronics. Around '70, the EP-2 added a Sound-On-Sound feature. Limited-edition EP6T reissue made by Market in 1980s (see Market Electronics listing).

1960s	Larger box	$600	$1,200

Echoplex EP-3
Ca.1970-1977. Solidstate, made by Market Electronics, black box.

1970-1977		$500	$800

Echoplex EP-4 (IV)
1977-1978. Solidstate, last version introduced by Maestro. See Market Electronics and Echoplex brands for later models.

1977-1978		$500	$750

Echoplex Sireko ES-1
Ca.1971-mid-1970s. A budget solidstate version of the Echoplex, made by Market.

1971-1975		$250	$350

Envelope Modifier ME-1
1971-ca.1976. Tape reverse/string simulator, made by All-Test.

1971-1976		$150	$225

MODEL		EXC. COND.	
YEAR	FEATURES	LOW	HIGH

Filter Sample and Hold FSH-1
1975-ca.1976.

1975-1976		$475	$700

Full Range Boost FRB-1
1971-ca.1975. Frequency boost with fuzz, made by All-Test.

1971-1975		$150	$200

Fuzz MFZ-1
1976-1979. Made by Moog.

1976-1979		$150	$200

Fuzz Phazzer FP-1
1971-1974.

1971-1974		$200	$300

Fuzztain MFZT-1
1976-1978. Fuzz, sustain, made by Moog.

1976-1978		$200	$250

Fuzz-Tone FZ-1
1962-1963. Brown housing, uses 2 AA batteries.

1962-1963		$400	$650

Fuzz-Tone FZ-1A
1965-1967. Brown housing, uses 1 AA battery. With "Kalamazoo, Michigan" on front.

1965-1967		$275	$500

Fuzz-Tone FZ-1A (reissue)
2001-2009. Reissue. With "Nashville, Tennessee" on front.

2001-2009		$755	$125

Fuzz-Tone FZ-1B
Late-1960s-early-1970s. Black housing, uses 9-volt battery.

1970s		$275	$325

Mini-Phase Shifter MPS-2
1976. Volume, speed, slow and fast controls.

1976		$110	$125

Octave Box OB-1
1971-ca.1975. Made by All-Test Devices.

1971-1975		$225	$300

Parametric Filter MPF-1
1976-1978. Made by Moog.

1976-1978		$350	$450

Phase Shifter PS-1
1971-1975. With or without 3-button footswitch, made by Oberheim.

1971-1975	With footswitch	$275	$325
1971-1975	Without footswitch	$175	$225

Phase Shifter PS-1A
1976.

1976		$150	$250

Phase Shifter PS-1B
1970s.

1970s		$150	$250

Phaser MP-1
1976-1978. Made by Moog.

1976-1978		$250	$325

Repeat Pedal RP-1
1970s.

1970s		$200	$300

Rhythm King MRK-2
1971-ca.1974. Early drum machine.

1971-1974		$400	$500

Rhythm Queen MRQ-1
Early 1970s. Early rhythm machine.

1970s		$125	$150

Rhythm'n Sound G-2
Ca.1969-1970s. Multi-effect unit.

1969-1975		$600	$750

MODEL YEAR	FEATURES	EXC. COND. LOW	HIGH

Ring Modulator RM-1
| 1971-1975 | With MP-1
control pedal | $650 | $700 |
| 1971-1975 | Without
control pedal | $550 | $600 |

Rover Rotating Speaker
1971-ca.1973. Rotating Leslie effect that mounted on a large tripod.
| 1971-1973 | RO-1 model | $1,200 | $1,500 |

Sound System for Woodwinds W-1
1960s-1970s. Designed for clarinet or saxaphone input, gives a variety of synthesizer-type sounds with voices for various woodwinds, uses Barrel Joint and integrated microphone.
| 1960-1970s | | $350 | $400 |

Stage Phaser MPP-1
1976-1978. Has slow, fast and variable settings, made by Moog.
| 1976-1978 | | $175 | $225 |

Super Fuzz-Tone FZ-1S
| 1971-1975 | | $200 | $300 |

Sustainer SS-2
1971-ca.1975. Made by All-Test Devices.
| 1971-1975 | | $100 | $150 |

Theramin TH-1
1971-mid-1970s. Device with 2 antennae, made horror film sound effects. A reissue Theremin is available from Theremaniacs in Milwaukee, Wisconsin.
| 1971-1975 | | $825 | $975 |

Wah-Wah/Volume WW-1
1970s. Wah-Wah Volume logo on end of pedal, green foot pad.
| 1971-1975 | | $150 | $250 |

Magnatone
Ca.1937-1971, 2013-present. Magnatone built very competitive amps from '57 to '66. In the early-'60s, they offered the RVB-1 Reverb Unit. The majority of Magnatone amps pre-'66 did not have on-board reverb.

Model RVB-1 Reverb Unit
1961-1966. Typical brown leatherette cover, square box-type cabinet. From '64-'66, battery operated, solidstate version of RVB-1, low flat cabinet.
| 1961-1963 | | $275 | $400 |
| 1964-1966 | Battery and
solidstate | $200 | $300 |

Mahoney
2000s. Reissues of the Jordan Boss Tone.
Buzz Tone
2000s. Similar black-plastic housing to the original Boss Tone. 2 Control knobs.
| 2000s | | $40 | $75 |

Manny's Music
Issued by the New York-based retailer.
Fuzz
1960s. Same unit as the Orpheum Fuzz and Clark Fuzz.
| 1960s | | $225 | $325 |

Market Electronics
Market, from Ohio, made the famous Echoplex line. See Echoplex and Maestro sections for earlier models.
Echoplex EP 6T
1980-ca.1988. Limited-edition all-tube reissue of the Echoplex EP-2.
| 1980-1988 | | $400 | $500 |

Marshall
1962-present. The fuzz and wah boom of the '60s led many established manufacturers, like Marshall, to introduce variations on the theme. They got back into stomp boxes in '89 with the Gov'nor distortion, and currently produce several distortion/overdrive units.
Blues Breaker
1992-1999. Replaced by Blues Breaker II in 2000.
| 1992-1999 | | $100 | $130 |
Blues Breaker II Overdrive
2000-present. Overdrive pedal, 4 knobs.
| 2000-2013 | | $50 | $65 |
Drive Master
| 1992-1999 | | $70 | $75 |
Guv'nor
1989-1991. Distortion, Guv'nor Plus introduced in '99.
| 1989-1991 | | $75 | $100 |
Jackhammer
1999-present. Distortion pedal.
| 1999-2014 | | $55 | $65 |
PB-100 Power Brake
1993-1995. Speaker attenuator for tube amps.
| 1993-1995 | | $190 | $230 |
Shred Master
| 1992-1999 | | $75 | $100 |
Supa Fuzz
Late-1960s. Made by Sola Sound (Colorsound).
| 1967 | | $550 | $850 |
Supa Wah
Late-1960s. Made by Sola Sound (Colorsound).
| 1969 | | $300 | $425 |
Vibratrem VT-1
1999-present. Vibrato and tremolo.
| 1999-2014 | | $75 | $85 |

Matchless
1989-1999, 2001-present. Matchless amplifiers offered effects in the '90s.
AB Box
1990s. Split box for C-30 series amps (DC 30, SC 30, etc.).
| 1990s | | $175 | $300 |
Coolbox
1997-1999. Tube preamp pedal.
| 1997-1999 | | $275 | $350 |
Dirtbox
1997-1999. Tube-driven overdrive pedal.
| 1997-1999 | | $300 | $500 |

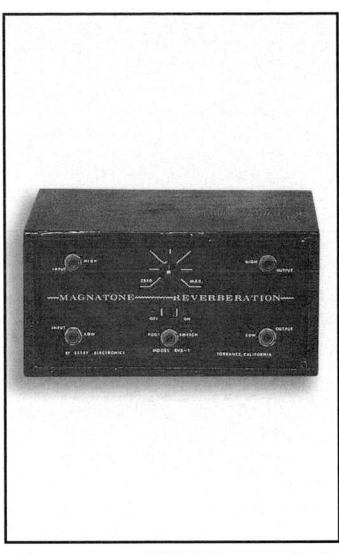
Magnatone RVB-1 Reverb Unit

Marshall Guv'nor
Keith Myers

Marshall Shred Master

EFFECTS

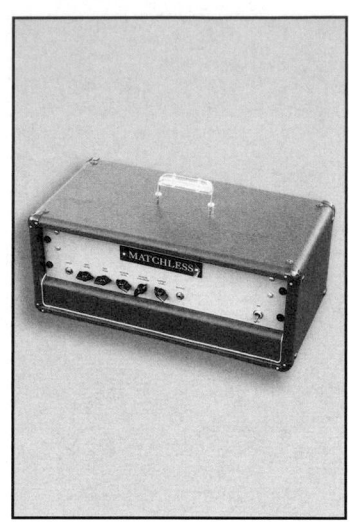

Matchless Reverb RV-1

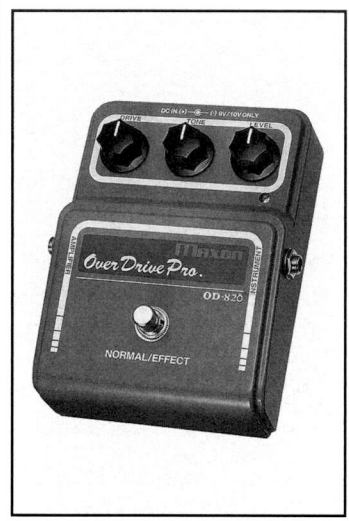

Maxon OD820 Over Drive Pro

Metal Pedals Demon Drive

MODEL YEAR	FEATURES	EXC. COND. LOW	HIGH

Echo Box
1997-1999. Limited production because of malfunctioning design which included cassette tape. Black case, 8 white chickenhead control knobs.

| 1990s | Original unreliable status | $300 | $400 |
| 1990s | Updated working order | $700 | $850 |

Hotbox/Hotbox II
1995-1999. Higher-end tube-driven preamp pedal.

| 1995-1999 | | $395 | $565 |

Mix Box
1997-1999. 4-input tube mixer pedal.

| 1997-1999 | | $375 | $425 |

Reverb RV-1
1993-1999. 5 controls, tube-driven spring-reverb tank, various colors.

| 1993-1999 | | $1,400 | $1,675 |

Reverb RV-2
2000s. 5 controls, tube-driven spring-reverb tank, various colors.

| 2000s | | $900 | $1,000 |

Split Box
1990s. Tube AB box.

| 1997 | Standard AB | $275 | $325 |

Tremolo/Vibrato TV-1
1993-1995. Tube unit.

| 1993-1995 | | $350 | $480 |

Maxon
1970s-present. Maxon was the original manufacturer of the Ibanez line of effects. Currently offering retro '70s era stomp boxes distributed in the U.S. by Godlyke.

AD-9 Analog Delay
2001-present. Purple case.

| 2001-2014 | | $225 | $275 |

CS-550 Stereo Chorus
2001-present. Light blue case.

| 2001-2014 | | $100 | $130 |

DS-830 Distortion Master
2001-present. Light blue-green case.

| 2001-2014 | | $100 | $125 |

OD-820 Over Drive Pro
2001-present. Green case.

| 2001-2014 | | $140 | $175 |

McQuackin FX Co.
Rich McCracken II began building his analog guitar effects in 1997, first in Nashville, Tennessee, then Augusta, Georgia.

Mesa-Boogie
1971-present. Mesa added pre-amps in the mid '90s, then pedals in 2013.

V-Twin Bottle Rocket
| 2000-2004 | | $100 | $150 |

V-Twin Preamp Pedal
Dec. 1993-2004. Serial number series: V011-. 100 watts, all tube preamp, floor unit, silver case.

| 1993-1999 | | $225 | $275 |

MODEL YEAR	FEATURES	EXC. COND. LOW	HIGH
2000-2004	Updated tone adj.	$275	$325

Metal Pedals
2006-present. Brothers Dave and Mike Pantaleone build their guitar effects in New Jersey.

Meteoro
1986-present. Guitar effects built in Brazil. They also build guitar and bass amps.

MG
2004-present. Guitar effects built by Marcelo Giangrande in São Paulo, Brazil. He also builds amps.

Mica
Early 1970s. These Japanese-made effects were also sold under the Bruno and Marlboro brand names.

Tone Fuzz
1970s. Silver case, black knobs.

| 1970s | | $200 | $250 |

Tone Surf Wah Siren
1970s. Wah pedal.

| 1970s | | $150 | $195 |

Wailer Fuzz
| 1970 | | $75 | $100 |

Wau Wau Fuzz
1970s. Wau Wau Fuzz logo on end of pedal, black.

| 1970s | | $150 | $175 |

Mooer
2012-present. A line of guitar pedals built by Mooer Audio in China. Dana B Goods distributes this brand in the USA.

Moog/Moogerfooger
1964-present. Robert Moog, of synth fame, introduced his line of Moogerfooger analog effects in 1998. They also offer guitars.

Misc. Effects
2004-present.

| 2004-2010 | MF-105 MuRF | $250 | $400 |
| 2004-2010 | Theremin | $250 | $400 |

Moonrock
2002-present. Fuzz/distortion unit built by Glenn Wylie and distributed by Tonefrenzy.

Morley
Late-1960s-present. Founded by brothers Raymond and Marvin Lubow, Morley has produced a wide variety of pedals and effects over the years, changing with the trends. In '89, the brothers sold the company to Accutronics (later changed to Sound Enhancements, Inc.) of Cary, Illinois.

ABY Switch Box
1981-ca.1985. Box.

| 1981-1985 | | $25 | $35 |

Auto Wah PWA
1976-ca.1985.

| 1976-1985 | | $25 | $35 |

EFFECTS

MODEL YEAR	FEATURES	EXC. COND. LOW	HIGH
Bad Horsie Steve Vai Signature Wah			
1997-present.			
1997-2014		$65	$70
Black Gold Stereo Volume BSV			
1985-1991		$25	$35
Black Gold Stereo Volume Pan BSP			
1985-1989		$30	$40
Black Gold Volume BVO			
1985-1991		$25	$35
Black Gold Wah BWA			
1985-1991		$30	$40
Black Gold Wah Volume BWV			
1985-1989		$30	$40
Chrystal Chorus CCB			
1996-1999. Stereo output.			
1996-1999		$25	$30
Deluxe Distortion DDB			
1981-1991. Box, no pedal.			
1981-1991		$40	$60
Deluxe Flanger FLB			
1981-1991. Box, no pedal.			
1981-1991		$55	$65
Deluxe Phaser DFB			
1981-1991. Box, no pedal.			
1981-1991		$40	$60
Distortion One DIB			
1981-1991. Box, no pedal.			
1981-1991		$35	$45
Echo Chorus Vibrato ECV			
1982-ca.1985.			
1982-1985		$150	$225
Echo/Volume EVO-1			
1974-ca.1982.			
1974-1982		$150	$225
Electro-Pik-a-Wah PKW			
1979-ca.1982.			
1979-1982		$55	$65
Emerald Echo EEB			
1996-1999. 300 ms delay.			
1996-1999	Green case	$40	$50
Jerry Donahue JD-10			
1995-1997. Multi-effect, distortion, overdrive.			
1995-1997		$80	$90
Power Wah PWA/PWA II			
1992-2006. Wah with boost. Changed to II in '98.			
1992-2006		$40	$50
Power Wah PWO			
Ca.1969-1984, 2006-present. Reissued in '06.			
1969-1984		$60	$100
Power Wah/Boost PWB			
Introduced in 1973, doubles as a volume pedal.			
1970s		$80	$150
Power Wah/Fuzz PWF			
Ca.1969-ca.1984.			
1969-1984		$125	$275
Pro Compressor PCB			
1978-1984. Stomp box without pedal, compress-sustain knob and output knob.			
1978-1984		$45	$55
Pro Flanger PFL			
1978-1984		$100	$125

MODEL YEAR	FEATURES	EXC. COND. LOW	HIGH
Pro Phaser PFA			
1975-1984		$100	$125
Rotating Sound Power Wah Model RWV			
1971-1982		$325	$400
Select-Effect Pedal SEL			
1980s. Lets you control up to 5 other pedals.			
1980s		$20	$30
Slimline Echo Volume 600			
1983-1985. 20 to 600 ms delay.			
1983-1985		$45	$55
Slimline Echo Volume SLEV			
1983-1985. 20 to 300 ms delay.			
1983-1985		$50	$60
Slimline Variable Taper Stereo Volume SLSV			
1982-1986		$70	$100
Slimline Variable Taper Volume SLVO			
1982-1986		$35	$50
Slimline Wah SLWA			
1982-1986. Battery operated electro-optical.			
1982-1986		$55	$75
Slimline Wah Volume SLWV			
1982-ca.1986. Battery operated electro-optical.			
1982-1986		$55	$75
Stereo Chorus Flanger CFL			
1980-ca. 1986. Box, no pedal.			
1980-1986		$60	$70
Stereo Chorus Vibrato SCV			
1980-1991. Box, no pedal.			
1980-1991		$80	$100
Stereo Volume CSV			
1980-ca. 1986. Box, no pedal.			
1980-1986		$30	$45
Volume Compressor VCO			
1979-1984		$30	$45
Volume Phaser PFV			
1977-1984. With volume pedal.			
1977-1984		$125	$150
Volume VOL			
1975-ca.1984.			
1975-1979		$30	$45
1980-1984		$25	$40
Volume XVO			
1985-1988		$25	$40
Volume/Boost VBO			
1974-1984		$50	$60
Wah Volume CWV			
1987-1991. Box, no pedal.			
1987-1991		$65	$80
Wah Volume XWV			
1985-ca.1989.			
1985-1989		$65	$90
Wah/Volume WVO			
1977-ca.1984.			
1977-1984		$80	$100

Morpheus

2009-present. Guitar effects pedals manufactured in Salt Lake City, Utah by the same builders of the Bolt brand amps.

Mica Wau-Wau SG-150
Jim Schreck

1973 Morley Power Wah/Boost PWB
Lou Allard

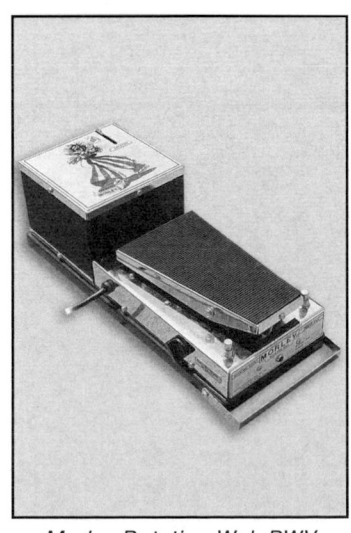

Morley Rotating Wah RWV
Nate Westgor

EFFECTS

Mosferatu

EFFECTS

1970s Multivox Little David LD-2

MXR Analog Delay

Mosferatu
Line of guitar effects pedals built by Hermida Audio Technology.

Mosrite
Semie Moseley's Mosrite company dipped into effects in the 1960s.

Fuzzrite
1960s-1970s, 1999. Silver housing as well as some painted housings, 2 front-mounted control knobs. Sanner reissued in '99.

MODEL YEAR	FEATURES	EXC. COND. LOW	HIGH
1960s-70s	Mosrite logo	$225	$500
1999	Reissue, Sanner logo	$100	$225

Mu-FX
See Beigel Sound Lab.

Multivox
New York-based Multivox offered a variety of effects in the 1970s and '80s.

Big Jam Effects
Multivox offered the Big Jam line of effects from 1980 to ca. '83.

1980-1983	Analog Echo/Reverb	$100	$125
1980-1983	Bi-Phase 2, Flanger, Jazz Flanger	$50	$60
1980-1983	Chorus	$45	$55
1980-1983	Compressor, Phaser, 6-Band EQ, Spit-Wah	$40	$50
1980-1983	Distortion	$70	$80
1980-1983	Octave Box	$40	$55
1981-1983	Noise Gate, Parametric EQ	$35	$45
1981-1983	Space Driver, Delay	$60	$70
1982-1983	Volume Pedal	$30	$35

Full Rotor MX-2
1978-ca.1982. Leslie effect.

1978-1982		$300	$350

Little David LD-2
1970s. Rotary sound effector in mini Leslie-type case.

1970s	With pedal	$375	$450
1970s	Without pedal	$325	$375

Multi Echo MX-201
1970s. Tape echo unit, reverb.

1970s		$200	$250

Multi Echo MX-312
1970s. Tape echo unit, reverb.

1970s		$225	$300

Rhythm Ace FR6M
1970s. 27 basic rhythms.

1970s		$60	$80

Mu-Tron
1972-ca.1980. Made by Musitronics, founded by Mike Beigel and Aaron Newman in Rosemont, New Jersey, these rugged and unique-sounding effects were a high point of the '70s. The Mu-Tron III appeared in '72 and more products followed, about 10 in all. Musitronics also made the U.S. models of the Dan Armstrong effects. In '78 ARP synthesizers bought Musitronics and sold Mutron products to around '80. In '78, Musitronics also joined with Lol Creme and Kevin Godley of 10cc to attempt production of the Gizmotron, which quickly failed (see listing under Godley Crème). A reissue of the Mu-Tron III was made available in '95 by NYC Music Products and distributed by Matthews and Ryan Musical Products. As of 2013, Mike Beigel's Beigel Sound Lab has started making a hot-rodded Tru-Tron III.

Bi-Phase
1975-ca.1980. Add $50-$75 for Opti-Pot pedal.

MODEL YEAR	FEATURES	EXC. COND. LOW	HIGH
1971-1980	Optical pedal option	$800	$1,200
1975-1980	2-button footswitch	$800	$1,200

C-100 OptiPot Control Pedal

1975-1980	Blue case	$550	$700

C-200 Volume-Wah

1970s		$300	$400

Flanger
1977-ca.1980.

1977-1980		$800	$1,000

III Envelope Filter
1972-ca.1980. Envelope Filter.

1972-1980		$600	$800

Micro V
Ca.1975-ca.1977. Envelope Filter.

1970s		$200	$250

Octave Divider
1977-ca.1980.

1977-1980		$550	$700

Phasor
Ca.1974-ca.1976. Two knobs.

1974-1976		$300	$470

Phasor II
1976-ca.1980. Three knobs.

1976-1980		$250	$325

Muza
2006-present. Digital guitar effects made in China by Hong Kong's Medeli Electronics Co., Ltd. They also build digital drums.

MXR
1972-present. MXR Innovations launched its line of pedals in '72. Around '77, the Rochester, New York, company changed lettering on the effects from script to block, and added new models. MXR survived into the mid-'80s. In '87, production was picked up by Jim Dunlop. Reissues of block logo boxes can be differentiated from originals as they have an LED above the switch and the finish is slightly rough; the originals are smooth.

6 Band EQ
1975-1982. Equalizer.

1975-1979		$70	$85
1980-1982		$60	$70

6 Band EQ M-109 (Reissue)
1987-present. Reissued by Jim Dunlop.

1987-2014		$30	$40

10 Band EQ M-108
1975-1981, 2004-present. Graphic equalizer.

1975-1981	With AC power cord	$80	$100

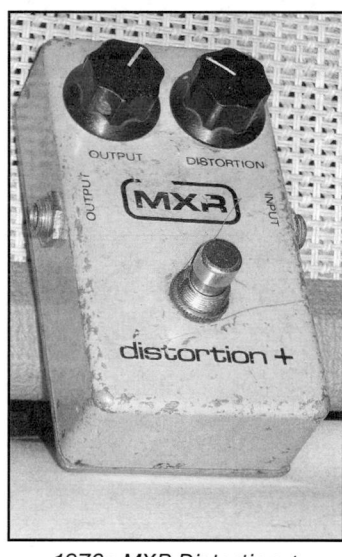

1970s MXR Distortion +
Dan Melanson

MXR Dyna Comp M-102
Keith Myers

MXR Super Comp M-132

Analog Delay
1975-1981. Green case, power cord.

Year	Features	Low	High
1975-1979	Earlier 2-jack model	$300	$325
1980-1981	Later 3-jack model	$150	$200

Blue Box
1972-ca.1978. Octave pedal, M-103.

Year	Features	Low	High
1970s	Earlier script logo	$350	$400
1970s	Later block logo	$225	$250

Blue Box M-103 (Reissue)
1995-present. Reissued by Jim Dunlop, blue case. Produces 1 octave above or 2 octaves below.

Year	Features	Low	High
1995-2014		$40	$45

Carbon Copy M169
1987-present. Analog delay. 3 Control knobs. I Toggle switch. Green housing.

Year	Features	Low	High
1987-2014		$90	$105

Commande Effects
1981-1983. The Commande series featured plastic housings and electronic switching.

Year	Features	Low	High
1981-1983	Overdrive	$40	$50
1981-1983	Phaser	$100	$110
1981-1983	Preamp	$40	$50
1981-1983	Stereo Chorus	$60	$70
1981-1983	Sustain	$60	$70
1981-1983	Time Delay	$70	$80
1982-1983	Stereo Flanger	$70	$80

Distortion +
1972-1982.

Year	Features	Low	High
1970s	Earlier script logo	$185	$225
1970s	Later block logo	$85	$110
1980s	Block logo	$80	$95

Distortion + (Series 2000)

Year	Features	Low	High
1983-1985		$60	$70

Distortion + M-104 (Reissue)
1987-present. Reissued by Jim Dunlop, yellow case.

Year	Features	Low	High
1987-1990		$55	$65
1991-2014		$45	$55

Distortion II

Year	Features	Low	High
1981-1983	With AC power cord	$140	$150

Distortion III M115
1987-present. 3 Control knobs. Red housing.

Year	Features	Low	High
1987-2014		$25	$60

Double Shot Distortion M-151
2003-2005. 2 channels.

Year	Features	Low	High
2003-2005		$65	$75

Dyna Comp
1972-1982. Compressor.

Year	Features	Low	High
1970s	Earlier script logo, battery	$175	$200
1970s	Later block logo, battery	$90	$120
1980s	Block logo, battery	$65	$80

Dyna Comp (Series 2000)

Year	Features	Low	High
1982-1985		$65	$75

Dyna Comp M-102 (Reissue)
1987-present. Reissued by Jim Dunlop, red case.

Year	Features	Low	High
1987-2014		$35	$40

Envelope Filter

Year	Features	Low	High
1976-1983		$125	$225

Flanger
1976-1983, 1997-present. Analog, reissued by Dunlop in '97.

Year	Features	Low	High
1976-1979	AC power cord, 2 inputs	$175	$225
1980-1983	AC power cord	$100	$150
1997-2014	M-117R reissue	$60	$70

Flanger/Doubler

Year	Features	Low	High
1979	Rack mount	$150	$175

Fullbore Metal M116
1987-present. 6 Control knobs. Bare metal housing.

Year	Features	Low	High
1987-2014		$35	$100

Limiter
1980-1982. AC, 4 knobs.

Year	Features	Low	High
1980-1982	AC power cord	$125	$200

Loop Selector
1980-1982. A/B switch for 2 effects loops.

Year	Features	Low	High
1980-1982		$50	$60

Micro Amp
1978-1983, 1995-present. Variable booster, creme case, reissued in '95.

Year	Features	Low	High
1978-1983		$75	$100
1995-2014	M-133 reissue	$40	$45

Micro Chorus
1980-1983. Yellow case.

Year	Features	Low	High
1980-1983		$125	$175

Micro Flanger

Year	Features	Low	High
1981-1982		$100	$150

Noise Gate Line Driver
1974-1983.

Year	Features	Low	High
1970s	Script logo	$75	$125
1980s	Block logo	$75	$100

Omni
1980s. Rack unit with floor controller, compressor, 3-band EQ, distortion, delay, chorus/flanger.

Year	Features	Low	High
1980s		$425	$475

Phase 45
Ca.1976-1982.

Year	Features	Low	High
1970s	Script logo, battery	$125	$175
1980s	Block logo, battery	$75	$125

Phase 90
1972-1982.

Year	Features	Low	High
1970s	Earlier script logo	$325	$400
1970s	Later block logo	$175	$275
1980s	Block logo	$150	$200

Phase 90 M-101 (Reissue)
1987-present. Reissued by Jim Dunlop, orange case.

Year	Features	Low	High
1987-1989	Block logo	$60	$85
1990-2014	Block or script logo	$50	$75

Phase 100
1974-1982.

Year	Features	Low	High
1970s	Earlier script logo	$250	$325
1970s	Later block logo, battery	$175	$275

Phaser (Series 2000)
1982-1985. Series 2000 introduced cost cutting die-cast cases.

Year	Features	Low	High
1982-1985		$60	$85

Pitch Transposer

Year	Features	Low	High
1980s		$400	$475

Power Converter

Year	Features	Low	High
1980s		$45	$60

EFFECTS

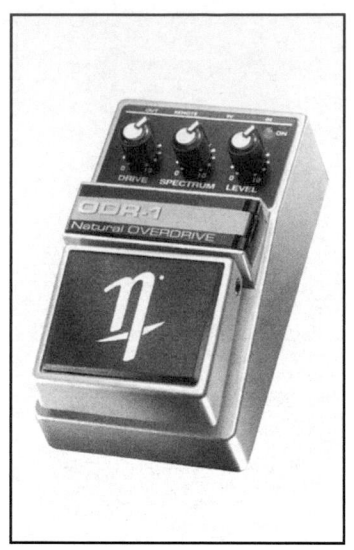

Nobels ODR-1 Natural Overdrive

Option 5 Destination Bump

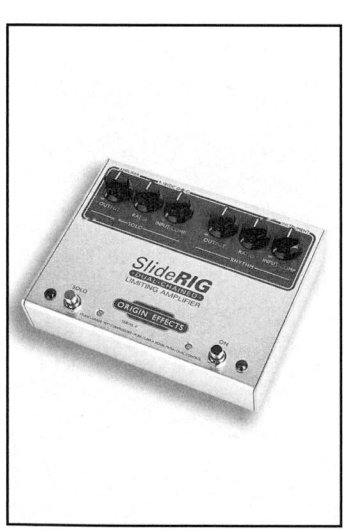

Origin Effects SlideRig

MODEL YEAR	FEATURES	EXC. COND. LOW	HIGH

Smart Gate M-135
2002-present. Noise-gate, single control, battery powered, gray case.

| 2002-2014 | | $60 | $70 |

Stereo Chorus
1978-1985. With AC power cord.

| 1978-1979 | | $175 | $275 |
| 1980-1985 | | $150 | $200 |

Stereo Chorus (Series 2000)
1983-1985. Series 2000 introduced cost cutting die-cast cases.

| 1983-1985 | | $55 | $75 |

Stereo Flanger (Series 2000)
1983-1985. Series 2000 introduced cost cutting die-cast cases, black with blue lettering.

| 1983-1985 | | $60 | $80 |

Super Comp M-132
2002-present. 3 knobs, black case.

| 2002-2013 | | $40 | $55 |

Nobels
1997-present. Effects pedals from Nobels Electronics of Hamburg, Germany. They also make amps.

ODR-1 Natural Overdrive
1997-present. Classic overdrive, green case.

| 1997-2014 | | $30 | $40 |

TR-X Vintage Tremolo
1997-present. Tremolo effect using modern technology, purple case.

| 1997-2014 | | $30 | $40 |

Nomad
1960s. Effects that claimed to be made in the U.S., but most likely built by Shinei of Japan. Models include the Verberola and the Fuzz wah, both of which were sold under other brands such as Applied, Jax USA, and Companion.

Fuzz wah
1960s. Fuzz wah pedal similar to Morley pedals of the era with depth and volume controls and fuzz switch, silver and black.

| 1960s | | $75 | $125 |

Oddfellow Effects
2013-present. Jon Meleika builds his guitar effects pedals in Riverside, California.

Olson
Olson Electronics was based in Akron, Ohio.

Reverberation Amplifier RA-844
1967. Solidstate, battery-operated, reverb unit, depth and volume controls, made in Japan.

| 1967 | | $100 | $150 |

Ooh La La Manufacturing
2007-present. Hand-made guitar effects built in St. Louis Park, Minnesota, including the models formerly offered under the Blackbox brand.

MODEL YEAR	FEATURES	EXC. COND. LOW	HIGH

Option 5
2002-present. Jay Woods builds his guitar effects pedals in Mishwaka, Indiana.

Origin Effects
2012-present. Custom-built and production guitar effects made in Oxfordshire, U.K. by Simon Keats.

Ovation
Ovation ventured into the solidstate amp and effects market in the early '70s.

K-6001 Guitar Preamp
1970s. Preamp with reverb, boost, tremolo, fuzz, and a tuner, looks something like a Maestro effect from the '70s, reliability may be an issue.

| 1970s | | $100 | $125 |

PAIA
1967-present. Founded by John Paia Simonton in Edmond, Oklahoma, specializing in synthesizer and effects kits. PAIA did make a few complete products but they are better known for the various electronic kit projects they sold. Values on kit projects are difficult as it depends on the skills of the person who built it.

Roctave Divider 5760
1970s. Kit to build analog octave divider.

| 1970s | | $70 | $85 |

Pan*Damn*ic
2007-2012. Guitar effects pedals made by PLH Professional Audio in West Chester, Pennsylvania.

Park
1965-1982, 1992-2000. Sola/Colorsound made a couple of effects for Marshall and their sister brand, Park. In the '90s, Marshall revived the name for use on small solidstate amps.

Pax
1970s. Imported Maestro copies.

Fuzz Tone Copy

| 1970s | | $125 | $150 |

Octave Box Copy
1970s. Dual push-buttons (normal and octave), 2 knobs (octave volume and sensitivity), green and black case.

| 1970s | | $125 | $150 |

Pearl
Pearl, located in Nashville, Tennessee, and better known for drums, offered a line of guitar effects in the 1980s.

Analog Delay AD-08
1983-1985. Four knobs.

| 1983-1985 | | $100 | $150 |

Analog Delay AD-33
1982-1984. Six knobs.

| 1982-1984 | | $175 | $225 |

MODEL YEAR	FEATURES	EXC. COND. LOW	HIGH
Chorus CH-02			
1981-1984. Four knobs.			
1981-1984		$75	$100
Chorus Ensemble CE-22			
1982-1984. Stereo chorus with toggling between chorus and vibrato, 6 knobs.			
1982-1984		$125	$175
Compressor CO-04			
1981-1984		$50	$75
Distortion DS-06			
1982-1986		$40	$60
Flanger FG-01			
1981-1986. Clock pulse generator, ultra-low frequency oscillator.			
1981-1986		$75	$100
Graphic EQ GE-09			
1983-1985		$40	$55
Octaver OC-07			
1982-1986		$100	$250
Overdrive OD-05			
1981-1986		$75	$100
Parametric EQ PE-10			
1983-1984		$45	$60
Phaser PH-03			
1981-1984. Four knobs.			
1981-1984		$75	$100
Phaser PH-44			
1982-1984. Six knobs.			
1982-1984		$150	$175
Stereo Chorus CH-22			
1982-1984. Blue case.			
1982-1984		$75	$125
Thriller TH-20			
1984-1986. Exciter, 4 knobs, black case.			
1984-1986		$175	$225

Peavey

1965-present. Peavey made stomp boxes from '87 to around '90. They offered rack mount gear after that.

MODEL YEAR	FEATURES	EXC. COND. LOW	HIGH
Accelerator Overdrive AOD-2			
1980s		$30	$35
Biampable Bass Chorus BAC-2			
1980s		$30	$35
Companded Chorus CMC-1			
1980s		$25	$30
Compressor/Sustainer CSR-2			
1980s		$35	$40
Digital Delay DDL-3			
1980s		$30	$35
Digital Stereo Reverb SRP-16			
1980s		$50	$55
Dual Clock Stereo Chorus DSC-4			
1980s		$30	$35
Hotfoot Distortion HFD-2			
1980s		$25	$30

PedalDoctor FX

1996-present. Tim Creek builds his production and custom guitar effects in Nashville, Tennessee.

Pedalworx

2001-present. Bob McBroom and George Blekas build their guitar effects in Manorville, New York and Huntsville, Alabama. They also do modifications to wahs.

Pharaoh Amplifiers

1998-2010. Builder Matt Farrow builds his effects in Raleigh, North Carolina.

Pignose

1972-present. Guitar stomp boxes offered by the amp builder in Las Vegas, Nevada. They also offer guitars.

Pigtronix

2003-present. Dave Koltai builds his custom guitar effects originally in Brooklyn, and currently in Yonkers, New York and also offers models built in China.

Plum Crazy FX

2005-present. Guitar effects built by Kaare Festovog in Apple Valley, Minnesota.

Premier

Ca.1938-ca.1975, 1990-2010. Premier offered a reverb unit in the '60s.

MODEL YEAR	FEATURES	EXC. COND. LOW	HIGH
Reverb Unit			
1961-late-1960s. Tube, footswitch, 2-tone brown.			
1960s		$250	$350

Prescription Electronics

1994-present. Located in Portland, Oregon, Jack Brossart offers a variety of hand-made effects.

MODEL YEAR	FEATURES	EXC. COND. LOW	HIGH
Dual-Tone			
1998-2009. Overdrive and distortion.			
1998-2009		$165	$175
Throb			
1996-present. Tremolo.			
1996-2014		$165	$175
Yardbox			
1994-present. Patterned after the original Sola Sound Tonebender.			
1994-2014		$90	$125

Pro Tone Pedals

2004-present. Guitar effects pedals built by Dennis Mollan in Dallas, Texas until early-2011, and presently in Summerville, South Carolina.

ProCo

1974-present. Located in Kalamazoo, Michigan and founded by Charlie Wicks, ProCo produces effects, cables and audio products.

MODEL YEAR	FEATURES	EXC. COND. LOW	HIGH
Rat			
1979-1987. Fuzztone, large box until '84. The second version was 1/3 smaller than original box. The small box version became the Rat 2. The current Vintage Rat is a reissue of the original large box.			
1979-1984	Large box	$200	$250
1984-1987	Compact box	$100	$150

Peavey Companded Chorus CMC-1

Pedalworx McFuzz

Pro Tone DBH Tremolo

EFFECTS

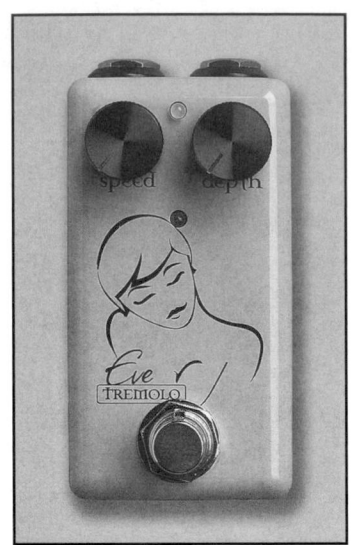

Red Witch Eve Tremolo

Retro-Sonic Distortion

Rocktron Rampage Distortion

MODEL YEAR	FEATURES	EXC. COND. LOW	HIGH
Rat 2			
1987-present. Classic distortion.			
1987-1999		$50	$75
2000-2014		$40	$50
Turbo Rat			
1989-present. Fuzztone with higher output gain, slope-front case.			
1989-2014		$40	$50
Vintage Rat			
1992-2005. Reissue of early-'80s Rat.			
1992-2005		$40	$50

Pro-Sound

The effects listed here date from 1987, and were, most likely, around for a short time.

MODEL YEAR	FEATURES	EXC. COND. LOW	HIGH
Chorus CR-1			
1980s		$25	$40
Delay DL-1			
1980s. Analog.			
1980s		$35	$55
Distortion DS-1			
1980s		$20	$35
Octaver OT-1			
1980s		$25	$40
Power and Master Switch PMS-1			
1980s		$15	$25
Super Overdrive SD-1			
1980s		$20	$35

Providence

1996-present. Guitar effects pedals built in Japan for Pacifix Ltd. and distributed in the U.S. by Godlyke Distributing, Inc.

Radial Engineering

1994-present. Radial makes a variety of products in Port Coquitlam, British Columbia, including direct boxes, snakes, cables, splitters, and, since '99, the Tonebone line of guitar effects.

Rapco

The Jackson, Missouri based cable company offers a line of switch, connection and D.I. Boxes.

MODEL YEAR	FEATURES	EXC. COND. LOW	HIGH
The Connection AB-100			
1988-present. A/B box.			
1988-2014		$25	$35

Rastop Designs

2002-present. Alexander Rastopchin builds his effects in Long Island City, New York. He also builds amps.

Real McCoy Custom

1993-present. Wahs and effects by Geoffrey Teese. His first wah was advertised as the Real McCoy, by Teese. He now offers his custom wah pedals under the Real McCoy Custom brand. He also used the Teese brand on a line of stomp boxes, starting in '96. The Teese stomp boxes are no longer being made. In '08 he moved to Coos Bay, Oregon.

Recycled Sound

2009-present. Greg Perrine designs attenuators in Conway, Arkansas, which are then built in China.

Red Witch

2003-present. Analog guitar effects, designed by Ben Fulton, and made in Paekakariki, New Zealand.

Reinhardt

2004-2012. Amp builder Bob Reinhardt of Lynchburg, Virginia also offers a line of effects pedals.

Retro FX Pedals

2006-ca. 2010. Guitar effects pedals built by John Jones in St. Louis, Missouri.

Retroman

2002-present. Joe Wolf builds his retro effects pedals in Janesville, Wisconsin.

Retro-Sonic

2002-present. Tim Larwill builds effects in Ottawa, Ontario.

Reverend

1996-present. Reverend offered its Drivetrain effects from '00 to '04. They also build guitars.

RGW Electronics

2003-present. Guitar effects built by Robbie Wallace in Lubbock, Texas.

Rivera

1985-present. Amp builder Paul Rivera also offers a line of guitar pedals built in California.

Rocco

Introduced in 1937, the Rocco Tonexpressor was a volume pedal designed by New York City steel-guitarist Anthony Rocco and built and distributed by Epiphone. Generally credited with being the first guitar effect pedal.

Rockman

See listings under Scholz Research and Dunlop.

Rocktek

1986-2009. Imports formerly distributed by Matthews and Ryan of Brooklyn, New York; and later by D'Andrea USA.

Effects

MODEL YEAR	FEATURES	EXC. COND. LOW	HIGH
1986-2009	Delay, Super Delay	$30	$40
1986-2009	Distortion, 6 Band EQ, Bass EQ, Chorus, Compressor	$15	$25
1986-2009	Overdrive, Flanger, Metal Worker, Phaser, Vibrator Tremolo	$15	$20

MODEL YEAR FEATURES	EXC. COND. LOW	HIGH

Rocktron

1980s-present. Rocktron is a division of GHS Strings and offers a line of amps, controllers, stomp boxes, and preamps.

Austin Gold Overdrive
1997-2011. Light overdrive.

1997-2011	$25	$35

Banshee Talk Box
1997-present. Includes power supply.

1997-2014	$65	$80

Hush Rack Mount
1980s-present.

2000-2014	$50	$100

Hush The Pedal
1996-present. Pedal version of rackmount Hush.

1996-2014	$25	$35

Rampage Distortion
1996-2013. Sustain, high-gain and distortion.

1996-2013	$25	$35

Surf Tremolo

1997-2000	$60	$80

Tsunami Chorus
1996-2000. Battery or optional AC adaptor.

1996-2009 Battery power	$40	$50
1996-2009 With power supply	$50	$60

Vertigo Vibe
2003-2006. Rotating Leslie speaker effect.

2003-2006 Battery power	$50	$60
2003-2006 With power supply	$60	$70

XDC
1980s. Rack mount stereo preamp, distortion.

1980s	$100	$150

Roger Linn Design

2001-present. Effects built in Berkeley, California by Roger Linn.

Roger Mayer Electronics

1964-present. Roger Mayer started making guitar effects in the U.K. in '64 for guitarists like Jimmy Page and Jeff Beck. He moved to the U.S. in '69 to start a company making studio gear and effects. Until about 1980, the effects were built one at a time in small numbers and not available to the general public. In the '80s he started producing larger quantities of pedals, introducing his rocket-shaped enclosure. He returned to the U.K. in '89.

Axis Fuzz
1987-present.

1987-2014	$125	$150

Classic Fuzz
1987-present. The Fuzz Face.

1987-2014	$175	$200

Metal Fuzz
Early 1980s-1994.

1987-1994	$125	$150

Mongoose Fuzz
1987-present.

1987-2014	$175	$200

MODEL YEAR FEATURES	EXC. COND. LOW	HIGH

Octavia
1981-present. Famous rocket-shaped box.

1981-2014	$150	$200

Voodoo-1
Ca.1990-present.

1990-2014	$175	$300

Rogue

2001-present. Budget imported guitar effects. They also offer guitars, basses, lap steels, mandolins, banjos, ukuleles and amps.

Roland

Japan's Roland Corporation first launched effect pedals in 1974; a year or two later the subsidiary company, Boss, debuted its own line. They were marketed concurrently at first, but gradually Boss became reserved for compact effects while the Roland name was used on amplifiers, keyboards, synths and larger processors.

Analog Synth SPV
1970s. Multi-effect synth, rack mount.

1970s	$750	$900

Bee Baa AF-100
1975-ca.1980. Fuzz and treble boost.

1975-1980	$300	$550

Bee Gee AF-60
1975-ca.1980. Sustain, distortion.

1975-1980	$75	$125

Double Beat AD-50
1975-ca.1980. Fuzz wah.

1975-1980	$175	$200

Expression Pedal EV-5

1970s	$50	$75

Expression Pedal EV-5 Reissue
2000. Black pedal, blue foot pad.

2000	$25	$30

Guitar Synth Pedal GR-33 and Pickup GK-2A
2000-2005. Requires optional GK-2A pickup, blue case.

2000-2005	$475	$550

Human Rhythm Composer R-8
1980s. Drum machine, key pad entry.

1980s	$175	$250

Human Rhythm Composer R-8 MK II
2000s. Black case.

2000s	$300	$400

Jet Phaser AP-7
1975-ca.1978. Phase and distortion.

1975-1978	$525	$650

Phase Five AP-5
1975-ca.1978.

1975-1978	$200	$225

Phase II AP-2
1975-ca.1980. Brown case.

1975-1980	$125	$175

Space Echo Unit
1974-ca. 1980. Tape echo and reverb, various models.

1970s RE-101 Space Echo	$350	$500

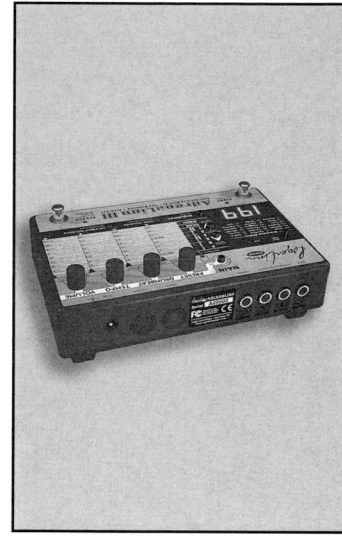

*Roger Linn Design
Adrenalinn III*

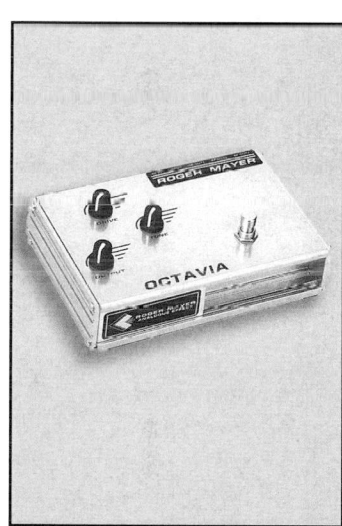

*Roger Mayer Electronics
Octavia*

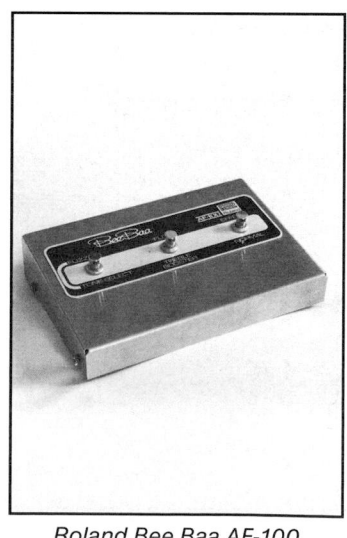

*Roland Bee Baa AF-100
Niclas Löfgren*

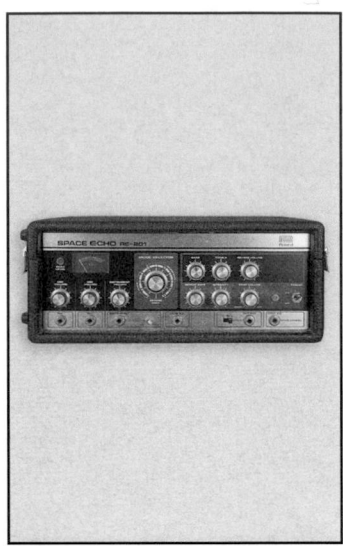

Roland Space Echo

Ross Compressor
Stephan Brown

Sam Ash Fuzzz Boxx

MODEL YEAR	FEATURES	EXC. COND. LOW	HIGH
1970s	RE-150 Space Echo	$350	$550
1970s	RE-200 Space Echo	$500	$750
1970s	RE-201 Space Echo with spring reverb	$700	$1,200
1970s	RE-301 Chorus Echo	$700	$950
1970s	RE-501 Chorus Echo	$700	$1,000
1970s	SRE-555 Chorus Echo	$950	$1,100

Vocoder SVC-350
Late-1970s-1980s. Vocal synthesis (vocoder) for voice or guitar, rack mount version of VP-330.

1980		$550	$700

Vocoder VP-330 Plus
Late-1970s-1980s. Analog vocal synthesis (vocoder) for voice or guitar, includes 2 1/2 octaves keyboard.

1978-1982		$750	$900

Wah Beat AW-10
1975-ca.1980.

1975-1980		$100	$125

Rosac Electronics

1969-1970s. Founded by Ralph Scaffidi and former Mosrite engineer Ed Sanner with backing from Morris Rosenberg and Ben Sacco in Bakersfield, California. Made the Nu-Fuzz which was a clone of Mosrite's Fuzzrite and the Nu-Wah. Closed in mid- to late- '70s and Scaffidi went on to co-found Osborne Sound Laboratories.

Ross

Founded by Bud Ross, who also established Kustom, in Chanute, Kansas, in the 1970s. Ross produced primarily amplifiers. In about '78, they introduced a line of U.S.-made effects. Later production switched to Asia.

10 Band Graphic Equalizer

1970s		$80	$100

Compressor
1970s. Gray or black case.

1970s		$350	$450

Distortion
1978-ca.1980. Brown.

1979-1980		$75	$125

Flanger
1977-ca.1980. Red.

1977-1980		$100	$150

Phase Distortion R1
1979. Purple.

1979		$100	$125

Phaser
1978-ca.1980. Orange.

1978-1980		$80	$100

Stereo Delay
1978-ca.1980.

1978-1980		$125	$175

Rotovibe

See listing under Dunlop.

S. Hawk Ltd.

1970s. Various effect pedals, no model names on case, only company name and logo.

Hawk I Fuzz
1970s. Linear pre-amp, fuzz, headphone amp, 1 slider.

1970s		$300	$400

Sam Ash

1960s-1970s, 2013-present. Sam Ash Music was founded by Sam Ash (nee Askynase), in '24, in Brooklyn, and by '66, there were about four Ash stores. During this time, Ash Music private branded their own amps and effects. In 2013, Sam Ash reissued the Fuzzz Boxx.

Fuzzz Boxx
1966-1967, 2013. Red, made by Universal Amplifier Company, same as Astrotone Fuzz. There is also a Fuzzola II. Fuzzz reissued in '13.

1967		$200	$225

Volume Wah
1970s. Italian-made.

1970s		$175	$200

Sanner

1999. Reissue from Eddie Sanner, who was the engineer behind the 1960s Mosrite Fuzzrite, using the identical circuitry as the original. Issued as a limited edition.

Sano

1944-ca. 1970. Sano was a New Jersey-based accordion company that built their own amps and a reverb unit. They also imported guitars for a few years, starting in '66.

Satellite Amplifiers

2004-present. Analog effects pedals made in San Diego, California by amp builder Adam Grimm.

Schaller

1945-present. The German guitar accessories company offered guitar effects off and on since the '60s and currently has reissue versions of its volume pedal and tremolo.

Scholz Research

1982-1995. Started by Tom Scholz of the band Boston. In '95, Jim Dunlop picked up the Rockman line (see Dunlop).

Power Soak

1980s		$100	$160

Rockman

1980s		$70	$130

Rockman X100
1980s. Professional studio processor.

1980s		$100	$150

Soloist
1980s. Personal guitar processor.

1980s		$50	$80

MODEL YEAR	FEATURES	EXC. COND. LOW	HIGH

Seamoon

1973-1977, 1997-2002. Seamoon made effects until '77, when Dave Tarnowski bought up the remaining inventory and started Analog Digital Associates (ADA). He reissued the brand in '97.

Fresh Fuzz
1975-1977. Recently reissued by ADA.

1975-1977		$150	$200

Funk Machine
1974-1977. Envelope filter. Recently reissued by ADA.

1974-1977		$175	$225

Studio Phase
1975-1977. Phase shifter.

1975-1977		$75	$125

Sekova

Mid-1960s-mid-1970s. Entry level instruments imported by the U.S. Musical Merchandise Corporation of New York.

Seymour Duncan

In late 2003, pickup maker Seymour Duncan, located in Santa Barbara, California, added a line of stomp box guitar effects.

Shin-ei

1969-1970s. When the Honey company went bankrupt in March, '69, it was reborn as Shin-ei and many Honey designs continued in production in various forms. Their chief engineer was Fumio Mieda who later did design work for Korg. Shin-ei also made effects for Univox (including the Uni-Fuzz, Super-Fuzz and Uni-Vibe), Companion, Applied, Apollo, Jax, Nomad, Shaftsbury, Pax, Crown, Royal, Mica, Kent, Marlboro, Memphis, Bruno, Boomer, Alex, Ace Tone, Aria, Goya, Kimbara, Lord, National, Northland, Tele Star, Tempo, and probably others.

Fuzz Wah

1970s		$400	$500

FY-2 Fuzz Box
1969-1970s. 2 transistors.

1969-1970s		$750	$1,000

FY-6 Super Fuzz
1969-1970s. Built from fuzz circuitry of Psychedelic Machine, 6 transistors.

1969-1970s		$750	$1,000

Psychedelic Machine
1969. Amp head-sized effect with numerous controls.

1969		$750	$1,000

Resly (Repeat Time) Machine
1970s. Black case, 3 speeds.

1970s		$400	$500

Sho-Bud

1956-1980. This pedal steel company offered volume pedals as well.

Sho-Sound Boss Tone
1970s-1980. Licensed version of the Jordan Boss Tone, 2 control knobs, similar black plastic housing.

1970s-80		$65	$150

Volume Pedal

1965		$90	$95

SIB

Effects pedals from Rick Hamel, who helped design SMF amps.

Siegmund Guitars & Amplifiers

1993-present. Los Angeles, California amp and guitar builder Chris Siegmund added effects to his product line in '99.

Sitori Sonics

2006-present. Emanual Ellinas builds his guitar effects in Birmingham, Alabama.

Skrydstrup R&D

1997-present. Effects pedals built by Steen Skrydstrup in Denmark. He also builds amps.

Skull Crusher

2009-present. Partners John Kasha and Shawn Crosby of Tone Box Effects, build their guitar effects in Simi Valley, California.

Snarling Dogs

1997-present. Started by Charlie Stringer of Stringer Industries, Warren, New Jersey in '97. Stringer died in May '99. The brand is now carried by D'Andrea USA.

Sobbat

1995-present. Line of effects from Kinko Music Company of Kyoto, Japan.

Sola/Colorsound

1962-2010. Sola was founded by London's Macari's Musical Exchange in '62, which was launched by former Vox associate Larry Macari and his brother Joe. The first product was the Tone-Bender fuzz box, designed by Gary Stewart Hurst and modeled in part on the Maestro Fuzz-Tone FZ-1. The first readily available fuzz in Britain, it was an instant success. Sola soon began making effects for Vox, Marshall, Park, and B & M and later under their own Colorsound brand. Refer to Colorsound for further listings and more company info.

Tone Bender Mk 1.5
1966-late 1960s.

1966-1969		$1,000	$2,000

Tone Bender Mk I

1965-1966		$1,500	$2,400

Tone Bender Professional Mk II
Late 1960s.

1960s		$900	$2,000

Soldano

1987-present. Seattle, Washington amp builder Soldano also built a reverb unit.

Sekova 2011 Bass Booster
Bill Cherensky

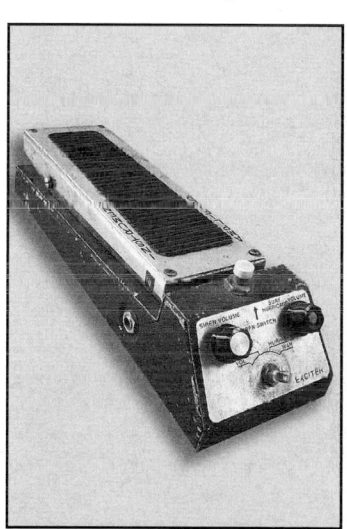

1970s Shin-ei Fuzz Wah
Keith Myers

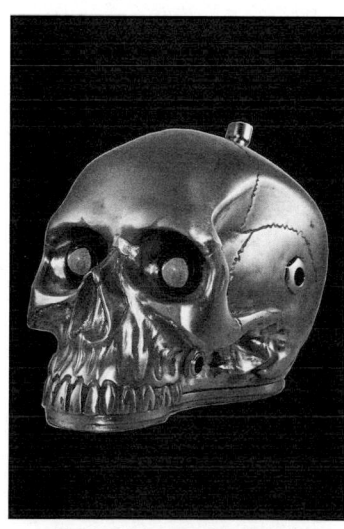

Skull Crusher Gun Metal

EFFECTS

EFFECTS

Sonic Edge J and J

Strymon Deco

*Sweet Sound
Fillmore West Fuzz*

MODEL YEAR	FEATURES	EXC. COND. LOW	HIGH

Space Box
1987-2009. Tube-driven spring reverb.

1987-2009		$800	$900

Songbird
See Dytronics.

Sonic Edge
Guitar and bass effects pedals built by Ben Fargen in Sacramento, California starting in 2010. He also builds the Fargen amps.

Sonuus
2009-present. Guitar effects built in China and imported by owners James Clark and John McAuliffe in the U.K.

Speedster
1995-2000, 2003-2007. Amp builder Speedster added guitar effects pedals to their product line in '04, built in Gig Harbor, Washington.

StarTouch
2001-present. Tony Chostner builds production/custom, effects pedals in Salem, Oregon.

Stephenson
1997-present. Amp builder Mark Stephenson in Parksville, British Columbia also offers a line of guitar pedals.

Stinger
Stinger effects were distributed by the Martin Guitar Company from 1989 to '90.
Effects

1989-1990	CH-70 Stereo Chorus	$25	$55
1989-1990	CO-20 Compressor	$35	$55
1989-1990	DD-90 Digital Delay	$45	$65
1989-1990	DE-80 Analog Delay	$50	$70
1989-1990	DI-10 Distortion	$40	$65
1989-1990	FL-60 Flanger	$40	$65
1989-1990	OD-30 Overdrive	$40	$65
1989-1990	TS-5 Tube Stack	$45	$65

Strymon
2008-present. Owners Gregg Stock, Pete Celi and Dave Fruehling offer a line of guitar pedals built in Chatsworth, California.

Studio Electronics
1989-present. Synth and midi developer Greg St. Regis' Studio Electronics added guitar pedal effects to their line in '03.

Subdecay Studios
2003-present. Brian Marshall builds his guitar effects in Woodinville, Washington.

Supersound
1952-1974. Founded by England's Alan Wootton, this firm built echo units in the 1960s. They also built amps, guitars and basses.

Supro
1935-1968, 2004-present. Supro offered a few reverb units in the '60s. Brand name was revived in '04.
500 R Standard Reverb Unit
1962-1963. Outboard reverb unit.

1962-1963		$250	$500

600 Reverb Power Unit
1961-1962. Independent reverb unit amp combination to be used with Supro Model 1600R amp or other amps, 3 tubes, 1x8" speaker.

1961-1962		$500	$1,100

Swart Amplifier
2003-present. Effects pedals built by Michael J. Swart in Wilmington, North Carolina. He also builds amps.

Sweet Sound
1994-present. Line of effects from Bob Sweet, originally made in Trenton, Michigan, and then in Coral Springs, Florida. Bob died in 2008. Currently built by his brother Gerald.

Swell Pedal Company
1997-2012. Mike Olienechak builds his line of tube pedals for guitar and bass in Nashville, Tennessee.

SynapticGroove
2013-present. Benjamin Harrison and Chrystal Gilles build their guitar effects in Edmond, Oklahoma.

Systech (Systems & Technology in Music, Inc)
1975-late-1970s. Systech was located in Kalamazoo, Michigan.
Effects

1975-1979	Envelope & Repeater	$75	$125
1975-1979	Envelope Follower	$75	$125
1975-1979	Flanger	$75	$125
1975-1979	Harmonic Energizer	$150	$225
1975-1979	Overdrive Model 1300	$75	$125
1975-1979	Phase Shifter Model 1200	$75	$125

T.C. Jauernig Electronics
2004-present. Tim Jauernig, of Rothschild, Wisconsin, built effects for several years before launching his T.C. Jauernig brand in '04.

TC Electronic
1976-present. Brothers Kim and John Rishøj founded TC Electronic in Risskov, Denmark, and made guitar effects pedals for several years before moving into rack-mounted gear. Currently they offer a wide range of pro audio gear and rack and floor guitar effects.
Booster + Distortion

1980s		$325	$400

MODEL YEAR	FEATURES	EXC. COND. LOW	HIGH
Dual Parametric Equalizer			
1980s		$275	$350
Stereo Chorus/Flanger			
Introduced in 1982, and reissued in '91.			
1980s		$175	$225
Sustain + Equalizer			
1980s		$225	$300

Tech 21

1989-present. Tech 21 builds their SansAmp and other effects in New York City. They also build amps.

Sansamp

1989-present. Offers a variety of tube amp tones.

1989	1st year	$125	$175
1990-2014		$100	$125

XXL Pedal

1995-2000, 2005-2012. Distortion, fuzz.

1995-2012		$50	$75

Teese

Geoffrey Teese's first wah was advertised as the Real McCoy, by Teese. He now offers his custom wah pedals under the Real McCoy Custom brand. The Teese brand was used on his line of stomp boxes, starting in '96. The Teese stomp boxes are no longer being made.

TEN

2013-present. Guitar effects built in Spokane, Washington by Ryan Dunn and Doug Harrison. From 2001-'13 they used the ToadWorks brand.

The Original Geek

Jeff Rubin began building guitar effects pedals in Los Angeles, California under the Geek MacDaddy brand in 2004. After a breakup with his business partner in '09 he began using The Original Geek brand.

Thomas Organ

The Thomas Organ Company was heavily involved with Vox from 1964 to '72, importing their instruments into the U.S. and designing and assembling products, including the wah-wah pedal. Both Thomas Organ and JMI, Vox's European distributor, wanted to offer the new effect. The problem was solved by labeling the Thomas Organ wah the Crybaby. The Crybaby is now offered by Dunlop. Refer to Vox listing for Crybaby Stereo Fuzz Wah, Crybaby Wah, and Wah Wah.

ThroBak Electronics

2004-present. Jonathan Gundry builds his guitar effects in Grand Rapids, Michigan. He also builds guitar amps and pickups.

ToadWorks

See listing for TEN.

MODEL YEAR	FEATURES	EXC. COND. LOW	HIGH

TomasZewicZ or TZZ

2008-present. Guitar effects pedals built by John Tomaszewicz in Coral Springs, Florida, which he labels TZZ. He also builds amps.

Tone Box Effects

See listing for Skull Crusher.

Tonebone

See Radial Engineering listing.

ToneCandy

2007-present. Mike Marino builds his guitar effects pedals in Santa Rosa, California.

Top Gear

1960s-1970s. Top Gear was a London music store. Their effects were made by other manufacturers.

Rotator

1970s. Leslie effect.

1970s		$100	$175

Top Hat Amplification

1994-present. Brian Gerhard builds his amps and effects in Fuquay-Varina, North Carolina. He previously built them in La Habra, California and Apex, North Carolina.

Traynor

1963-present. Amp and PA builder Traynor also built two spring reverb units, one tube and one solidstate, in Canada from 1966-'72 and a 7 band EQ from '73-'78.

Tremolo

See listing under Dunlop.

T-Rex

2003-present. Made in Denmark and imported by European Musical Imports.

TSVG

2011-present. Owner Mike Klein builds his guitar effects in his shop located in Philadelphia, Pennsylvania.

Tube Works

1987-2004. Founded by B.K. Butler (see Audio Matrix) in Denver, Colorado, Tube Works became a division of Genz Benz Enclosures of Scottsdale, Arizona in 1997 which dropped the brand in 2004. They also offered tube/solidstate amps, cabinets, and DI boxes.

Blue Tube

1989-2004. Overdrive bass driver with 12AX7A tube.

1989-2004		$100	$150

Real Tube

Ca.1987-2004. Overdrive with 12AX7A tube.

1987-1999		$100	$150

Tube Driver

1987-2004. With tube.

1987-2004		$100	$150

Tech 21 XXL

T-Rex Duck Tail Dynamic Delay

Tube Works Real Tube
Keith Myers

MODEL YEAR	FEATURES	EXC. COND. LOW	HIGH

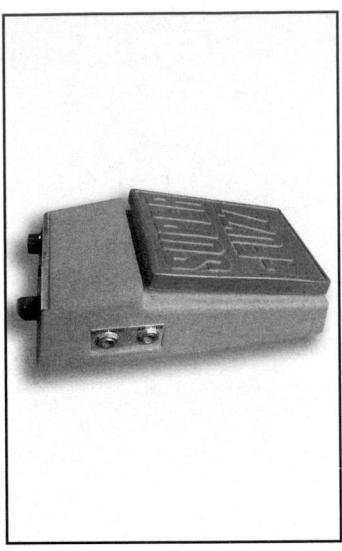

Univox Super-Fuzz

Jim Schreck

TWA (Totally Wycked Audio)

2009-present. Boutique analog effect pedals made in the U.S. and offered by Godlyke, Inc.

Tycobrahe

The Tycobrahe story was over almost before it began. Doing business in 1976-1977, they produced only three pedals and a direct box, one the fabled Octavia. The company, located in Hermosa Beach, California, made high-quality, original devices, but they didn't catch on. Now, they are very collectible. Reissues were made by Chicago Iron.

Octavia
1976-1977, 2000s. Octave doubler.

1976-1977		$1,100	$1,900
2000s	Octavia and Octavian reissue	$260	$300

Parapedal
1976-1977, 2000s. Wah.

1976-1977		$700	$1,350
2000s	Reissue, light blue housing.	$200	$300

Pedalflanger
1976-1977. Blue pedal-controlled flanger.

1976-1977		$1,100	$1,350

Uni-Vibe

See listings under Univox and Dunlop.

Univox

Univox was a brand owned by Merson (later Unicord), of Westbury, New York. It marketed guitars and amps, and added effects in the late-'60s. Most Univox effects were made by Shin-ei, of Japan. They vanished in about '81.

EC-80 A Echo
Early-1970s-ca.1977. Tape echo, sometimes shown as The Brat Echo Chamber.

1970s	$75	$100

EC-100 Echo
1970s. Tape, sound-on-sound.

1970s	$75	$150

Echo-Tech EM-200
1970s. Disc recording echo unit.

1970s	$130	$170

Fuzz FY-2

1970s	$185	$300

Micro 41 FCM41 4 channel mixer

1970s	$35	$50

Micro Fazer
1970s. Phase shifter.

1970s	$75	$100

Noise-Clamp EX110

1970s	$45	$55

Phaser PHZ1
1970s. AC powered.

1970s	$50	$75

Pro Verb
1970s. Reverb (spring) unit, black tolex, slider controls for 2 inputs, 1 output plus remote output.

1970s	$80	$100

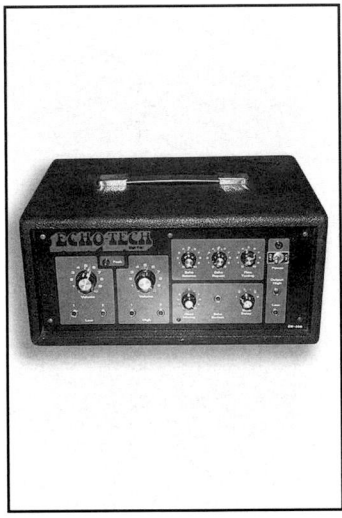

Univox Echo-Tech EM-200

Voodoo Lab Tremolo

Square Wave SQ150
Introduced in 1976. Distortion, orange case.

1970s	$75	$125

Super-Fuzz
1968-1973. Made by Shin-ei and similar to the FY-6 Super Fuzz, built from fuzz circuitry of Honey/Shin-ei Psychedelic Machine, 6 transistors, battery powered.

1968-1973	Gray box, normal bypass switch	$500	$900
1968-1973	Unicord, various colors, blue bypass pedal	$400	$500

Surf Siren
1970s. Wah pedal.

1970s	$90	$150

Uni-Comp
1970s. Compression limiter.

1970s	$50	$100

Uni-Drive

1970s	$150	$200

Uni-Fuzz
1969-1973. Fuzz tone in blue case, 2 black knobs and slider switch. Made by Shin-ei, AC-powered version of Super-Fuzz, built from fuzz circuitry of Honey/Shin-ei Psychedelic Machine.

1969-1973	$300	$500

Uni-Tron 5
1975. A.k.a. Funky Filter, envelope filter.

1975	$200	$525

Uni-Vibe
Introduced ca. 1969-1970s. Rotating-speaker simulator, with control pedal. Made by Shin-ei, built from circuitry of Honey/Shin-ei Psychedelic Machine.

1960s	$1,100	$2,000
1970s	$800	$1,500

Uni-Wah Wah/Volume

1970s	$100	$125

VanAmps

1999-present. Amp builder Tim Van Tassel of Golden Valley, Minnesota, also offers a line of reverb effects pedals.

Vesta Fire

Ca.1981-ca.1988. Brand of Japan's Shiino Musical Instrument Corp.

Effects

1981-1988	Chorus/Flange FLCH	$35	$50
1981-1988	Distortion DST	$35	$50
1981-1988	Flanger	$35	$50
1981-1988	Noise Gate	$25	$40
1981-1988	Stereo Chorus SCH	$35	$50

Vintage Tone Project

2003-present. Line of guitar effects made by Robert Rush and company in Delmar, New York. They also built reissues of Dan Armstrong's '70s effects from '03 to '06.

VintageFX

2003-present. Effects based on vintage pedals from the '60s and '70s built by Dave Archer in Grand Island, New York.

Visual Sound

1995-present. Effects pedals designed by Bob Weil and R.G. Keen in Spring Hill, Tennessee and built in China.

VooDoo Lab

1994-present. Line of effects made by Digital Music Corp. in California.

Analog Chorus
1997-2012. Based on '76 CE-1.

Model Year	Features	Low	High
1997-2012		$100	$120

Bosstone
1994-1999. Based on '60s Jordan Electronics Fuzz.

1994-1999		$70	$75

Microvibe
1996-present. Uni-Vibe rotating-speaker simulator.

1996-2014		$55	$65

Overdrive
1994-2002. Based on '70s overdrive.

1994-2002		$55	$65

Superfuzz
1999-present.

1999-2014		$75	$90

Tremolo
1995-present.

1995-2014		$55	$75

Vox

1954-present. The first Vox product was a volume pedal. Ca. '66, they released the Tone Bender, one of the classic fuzzboxes of all time. A year or so later, they delivered their greatest contribution to the effects world, the first wah-wah pedal. The American arm of Vox (then under Thomas Organ) succumbed in '72. In the U.K., the company was on-again/off-again.

Clyde McCoy Wah-Wah Pedal
Introduced in 1967, reissued in 2001-2008. Clyde's picture on bottom cover.

Year	Features	Low	High
1967	Clyde's picture	$800	$1,000
1968	No picture	$600	$800
2001-2008	Model V-848	$150	$175

Crybaby Wah
Introduced in 1968. The Thomas Organ Company was heavily involved with Vox from '64 to '72, importing their instruments into the U.S. and designing and assembling products. One product developed in conjunction with Vox was the wah-wah pedal. Both Thomas Organ and JMI, Vox's European distributor, wanted to offer the new effect. The problem was solved by labeling the Thomas Organ wah the Crybaby. The original wahs were built by Jen in Italy, but Thomas later made them in their Chicago, Illinois and Sepulveda, California plants. Thomas Organ retained the marketing rights to Vox until '79, but was not very active with the brand after '72. The Crybaby brand is now offered by Dunlop.

1960s	Jen-made	$200	$250
1970	Sepulveda-made	$125	$175

Double Sound
1970s. Jen-made, Double Sound model name on bottom of pedal, double sound derived from fuzz and wah ability.

1970s		$200	$250

Flanger

1970s		$200	$250

King Wah
1970s. Chrome top, Italian-made.

1970s		$200	$250

Repeat Percussion
Late-1960s. Plug-in module with on-off switch and rate adjustment.

1968		$100	$125

Stereo Fuzz Wah
Stereo Fuzz Wah

1970s		$150	$200

Tone Bender V-828
1966-1970s. Fuzz box, reissued as the V-829 in '93.

Year	Features	Low	High
1966-1968	Mark I, gray housing	$550	$700
1969	Mark II, black housing	$475	$625
1970s	Mark III	$475	$600

ToneLab Valvetronix
2003-present. Multi-effect modeling processor (ToneLab EX or ToneLab ST), 12AX7 tube preamp.

2003-2014		$400	$425

V-807 Echo-Reverb Unit
1967. Solidstate, disc echo.

1967		$275	$375

V-837 Echo Deluxe Tape Echo
1967. Solidstate, multiple heads.

1967		$350	$450

V-846 Wah
1969-1970s. Chrome top, Italian-made.

Year	Features	Low	High
1969	Transitional Clyde McCoy	$500	$650
1970s		$300	$400

V-847 Wah-Wah
1992-present. Reissue of the original V-846 Wah.

1992-2014		$65	$80

Volume Pedal
1954-late 1960s. Reissued as the V850.

1960s		$50	$100

Wampler Pedals

2004-present. Brian Wampler began building effects under the brand Indy Guitarist in 2004, and changed the name to Wampler Pedals in 2007. They are built in Greenwood, Indiana.

Warmenfat

2004-present. Pre-amps and guitar effects built in Sacramento, California, by Rainbow Electronics.

Wasabi

2003-2008. Line of guitar effect pedals from Danelectro.

Vox Tone Bender MKII
Niclas Löfgren

Vox V847 Union Jack

Wampler Hot Wired

EFFECTS

WMD Super Fatman

Xotic SP Compressor

Z.Vex Fuzz Factory
Keith Myers

MODEL YEAR	FEATURES	EXC. COND. LOW	HIGH

Washburn

Washburn offered a line of effects from around 1983 to ca. '89.

Effects

1980s	Analog Delay AX:9	$30	$35
1980s	Flanger FX:4	$35	$40
1980s	Phaser PX:8	$40	$45
1980s	Stack in a Box SX:3	$30	$35

Watkins/WEM

1957-present. Watkins Electric Music (WEM) was founded by Charlie Watkins. Their first commercial product was the Watkins Dominator amp in '57, followed by the Copicat Echo in '58.

Copicat Tape Echo

1958-1970s, 1985-present. The Copicat went through several detail changes, subsequently known as the Marks I, II, III, and IV versions. It has been reissued in various forms by Watkins.

1958-1970s	Solidstate	$525	$1,000
1958-1970s	Tube	$850	$1,100

Way Huge Electronics

1995-1998, 2008-present Way Huge offered a variety of stomp boxes, made in Sherman Oaks, California. Jim Dunlop revived the brand in '08.

WD Music

Since 1978, WD Music has offered a wide line of aftermarket products for guitar players. From '91 to '02, they offered a line of effects that were copies of the original Dan Armstrong color series (refer to Dan Armstrong listing).

Blue Clipper

1991-2002. Fuzz.

1991-2002	$30	$45

Orange Squeezer

1991-2002. Signal compressor.

1991-2002 Light Orange case	$40	$50

Purple Peaker

1991-2002. Mini EQ.

1991-2002	$40	$50

Westbury

1978-ca.1983. Brand imported by Unicord.

Tube Overdrive

1978-1983. 12AX7.

1978-1983	$150	$200

Whirlwind

1976-present. Effects from Michael Laiacona, who helped found MXR, originally made in Rochester, New York. Currently the company offers guitar effects, DI boxes and other music devices built in Greece, New York.

Commander

1980s. Boost and effects loop selector.

1980s	$75	$100

Wilson Effects

2007-present. Guitar effects built by Kevin Wilson in Guilford, Indiana.

WMD (William Mathewson Devices)

2008-present. William Mathewson builds his instrument effects in Denver, Colorado.

Wurlitzer

Wurlitzer offered the Fuzzer Buzzer in the 1960s, which was the same as the Clark Fuzz.

Xotic Effects

2001-present. Hand-wired effects made in Los Angeles, California, and distributed by Prosound Communications.

Yamaha

1946-present. Yamaha has offered effects since at least the early '80s. They also build guitars, basses, amps, and other musical instruments.

Analog Delay E1005

1980s. Free-standing, double-space rack mount-sized, short to long range delays, gray case.

1980s	$160	$180

Yubro

Yubro, of Bellaire, Texas, offered a line of nine effects in the mid- to late-'80s.

Analog Delay AD-800

1980s	300 ms.	$75	$125

Stereo Chorus CH-600

1980s	$50	$75

Z.Vex Effects

1995-present. Zachary Vex builds his effects in Minneapolis, Minnesota, with some subassembly work done in Michigan. Painters on staff create stock and custom versions of many pedals, which often bring higher prices. Vexter pedals are silk-screened pedals made in Taiwan. U.S. Vexters are manufactured in Taiwan, but engraved in Minnesota. California Mini models are manufactured in California. In 2000-2002, Vex built the solidbody Drip Guitar with an onboard Wah. In 2002, Vex also began building amps.

Basstortion

2011-present. Bass distortion, bright/dark switch.

2011-2014	$95	$130

Box of Metal

2007-present. High-gain distortion, switchable noise gate.

2007-2014	$120	$150

Box of Rock

2005-present. 2-in-1 pedal. Tube amp-type distortion pedal and clean post-gain boost.

2005-2014	$100	$150

Channel 2

2014-present. Mini boost pedal, master volume.

2014	$70	$90

Distortion

2009-present. Tube amp-style distortion, sub contour and gain switches.

2009-2014	$60	$75

MODEL YEAR	FEATURES	EXC. COND. LOW	HIGH

Double Rock
2012-present. Dual switchable distortion/boost pedal.

| 2012-2014 | | $175 | $200 |

Fat Fuzz Factory
2011-present. Fuzz Factory with additional 3-position mini toggle to select frequency range.

| 2011-2014 | | $175 | $200 |

Fuzz Factory
1995-present. Powerful, tweaky, and unique germanium fuzz pedal, with idiosyncratic hand-painted housings. Also available as Vexter and US Vexter models.

| 1995-2014 | | $120 | $145 |
| 1995-2014 | Unique hand-painted versions | $140 | $200 |

Fuzz Factory 7
2013-present. Limited edition Fuzz Factory with footswitchable EQ and 9-position rotary frequency selector.

| 2013-2014 | | $300 | $375 |

Fuzz Probe
2000-present. Theremin-controlled Fuzz Factory.

| 2000-2014 | | $100 | $175 |

Fuzzolo
2014-present. Mini footprint 2-knob silicon fuzz for guitar and bass.

| 2014 | | $80 | $100 |

Instant Lo-Fi Junky
2011-present. Filter, compression, and wave shapeable vibrato and blend for chorus effect.

| 2011-2014 | | $150 | $175 |

Inventobox
2010-present. Dual pedal chasis for DIY builders or for use with Z.Vex modules.

| 2010-2014 | | $150 | $200 |

Jonny Octave
2005-present. Octave pedal.

| 2005-2014 | | $140 | $185 |

Lo-Fi Loop Junky
2002-present. Sampler, single 20-second sample with vibrato.

| 2002-2014 | | $150 | $200 |

Loop Gate
2012-present. Audio looping mixer with foot switchable noise gate.

| 2012-2014 | | $100 | $130 |

Machine
1996-present. Crossover distortion generator.

| 1996-2014 | | $150 | $200 |

Mastrotron
2009-present. Silicon fuzz with mini toggle sub contour.

| 2009-2014 | | $70 | $95 |

Octane I, II, and III
1995-present. Ring modulator fuzz.

| 1995-2014 | | $85 | $125 |

Ooh Wah I and II
2003-2013. 8-step sequencer using wah filters with random sequencing.

| 2003-2013 | | $90 | $115 |

Ringtone and Ringtone TT
2006-2013. 8-step sequencer using ring modulator.

| 2006-2013 | | $175 | $190 |

Seek Trem I and II
2006-2013. 8-step sequencer using volume.

| 1999-2013 | | $135 | $175 |

Seek Wah I and II
2006-2013. 8-step sequencer using wah filters.

| 2006-2013 | | $140 | $180 |

Sonar Tremolo and Stutter
2012-present. Tremolo with wave shaping, distortion circuit, tap tempo, and auto tempo ramping.

| 2012-2014 | | $175 | $190 |

Super Duper 2-in-1
2001-present. Dual boost with master volume on 2nd channel.

| 2001-2014 | | $120 | $170 |

Super Hard On
1996-present. Sparkly clean boost.

| 1996-2014 | | $110 | $170 |

Super Ringtone
2013-present. 16-step sequencer using ring modulator with MIDI sync, tap tempo, tap tempo sync, and glissando.

| 2013-2014 | | $150 | $225 |

Super Seek Trem
2013-present. 16-step sequencer using volume with MIDI sync, tap tempo, tap tempo sync, and glissando.

| 2013-2014 | | $150 | $195 |

Super Seek Wah
2013-present. 16-step sequencer using wah filters with MIDI sync, tap tempo, tap tempo sync, and glissando.

| 2013-2014 | | $150 | $195 |

Trem Probe
2000-present. Theremin-controlled volume.

| 2000-2014 | | $100 | $175 |

Tremorama
2004-2013. 8-step sequencer using volume with random sequencing.

| 2004-2014 | | $195 | $230 |

Volume Probe
2000-2002. Theremin-controlled volume using coiled cable for antenna.

| 2000-2002 | | $100 | $175 |

Wah Probe
2000-present. Theremin-controlled wah.

| 2000-2014 | | $100 | $175 |

Woolly Mammoth
1999-present. Silicon fuzz for guitar and bass.

| 1999-2014 | | $200 | $290 |

Zinky
1999-present. Guitar effects built by Bruce Zinky in Flagstaff, Arizona. He also builds amps and has revived the Supro brand on a guitar and amp.

Zoom
Effects line from Samson Technologies Corp. of Syosset, New York.

Z.Vex Woolly Mammoth

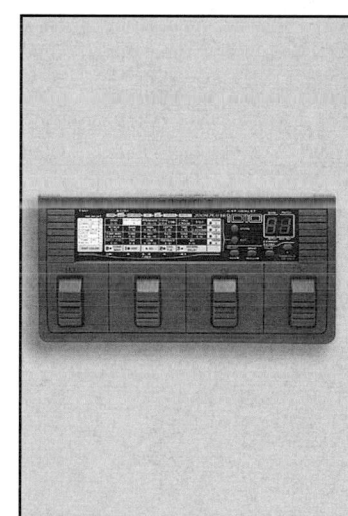

Zoom 1010 Player

Zinky True Grit Overdrive

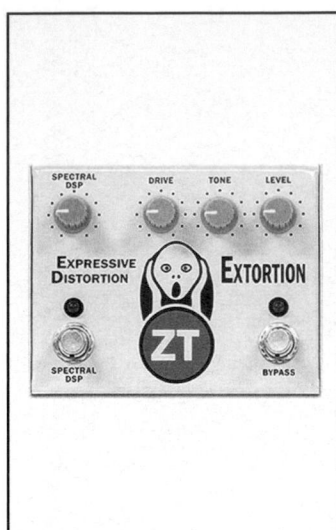

ZT Extortion (Expressive Distortion)

MODEL YEAR	FEATURES	EXC. COND. LOW	HIGH
503 Amp Simulator			
1998-2000		$25	$40
504 Acoustic Pedal			
	1997-2000. Compact multi-effects pedal, 24 effects, tuner, replaced by II version.		
1997-2000		$25	$40
505 Guitar Pedal			
	1996-2000. Compact multi-effects pedal, 24 effects, tuner, replaced by II version.		
1996-2000		$30	$40
506 Bass Pedal			
	1997-2000. Compact multi-effects bass pedal, 24 effects, tuner, black box, orange panel. Replaced by II version.		
1997-2000		$35	$45

MODEL YEAR	FEATURES	EXC. COND. LOW	HIGH
507 Reverb			
1997-2000		$25	$40
1010 Player			
	1996-1999. Compact multi-effects pedal board, 16 distortions, 25 effects.		
1996-1999		$40	$75

ZT Amplifiers

2009-present. Effects pedals built in China and offered by Ken Kantor in Berkeley, California. He also imports amps.

STEELS & LAP STEELS

STEELS & LAPS

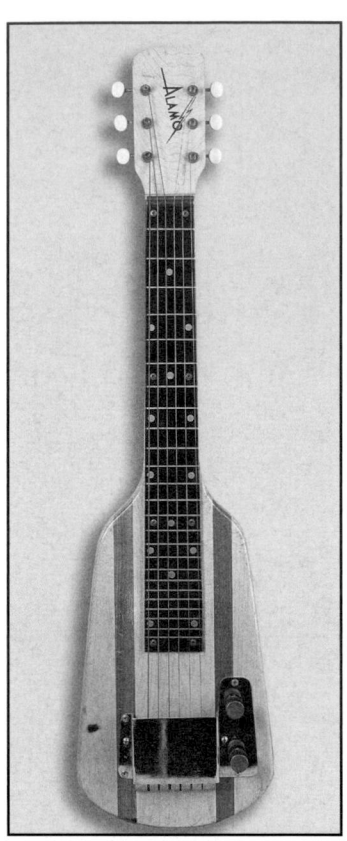

Alamo Embassy No. 2943

1948 Aloha
Dan Bishop

MODEL YEAR	FEATURES	EXC. COND. LOW	HIGH

Airline
Ca. 1958-1968. Name used by Montgomery Ward for instruments built by Kay, Harmony and Valco.
Lap Steel

| 1960s | Res-O-Glas/plastic | $450 | $550 |
| 1960s | Wood | $275 | $350 |

Rocket 6-String Steel
1960s. Black and white, 3 legs, Valco-made.

| 1960s | | $325 | $400 |

Student 6 Steel

| 1950s | Black | $225 | $275 |

Alamo
1947-1982. The first musical instruments built by Alamo, of San Antonio, Texas, were lap steel and amp combos with early models sold with small birch amps.
Hawaiian Lap Steels
1947-ca. 1967. Models include the '50s Challenger and Futuramic Dual Eight, the '50s and early-'60s Embassy (pear-shape) and Jet (triangular), the early-'60s Futuramic Eight and Futuramic Six, and the late-'60s Embassy (triangular Jet).

| 1950s | | $225 | $275 |

Alkire
1939-1950s. Founded by musician and teacher Eddie Alkire, with instruments like his E-Harp Steel built by Epiphone and maybe others (see Epiphone for values).

Aloha
1935-1960s. Private branded by Aloha Publishing and Musical Instruments Company, Chicago, Illinois. Made by others. There was also the Aloha Manufacturing Company of Honolulu which made musical instruments from around 1911 to the late '20s.

Alvarez
1965-present. Imported by St. Louis Music from mid-'60s. They also offered guitars, banjos and mandolins.
Model 5010 Koa D Steel-String

| 1960s | | $200 | $250 |

Aria/Aria Pro II
1956-present. Aria offered Japanese-made steels and lap steels in the '60s.
Lap Steel

| 1960s | | $225 | $275 |

Asher
1982-present. Intermediate, professional and premium grade, production/custom, solidbody, semi-hollow body and acoustic lap steels built by luthier Bill Asher in Venice, California. He also builds guitars.

Audiovox
Ca. 1935-ca. 1950. Paul Tutmarc's Audiovox Manufacturing, of Seattle, Washington, was a pioneer in electric lap steels, basses, guitars and amps.
Lap Steel

| 1940s | | $700 | $875 |

Bel-Tone
1950s. Private branded by Magnatone, Bel-Tone oval logo on headstock.
Lap Steel

| 1950s | Pearloid cover | $225 | $275 |

Bigsby
1947-1965, 2002-present. All handmade by Paul Arthur Bigsby, in Downey, California. Bigsby was a pioneer in developing pedal steels and they were generally special order or custom-made and not mass produced. The original instruments were made until '65 and should be valued on a case-by-case basis. Models include the Single Neck pedal steel, Double 8 pedal steel, 8/10 Doubleneck pedal steel, Triple 8 pedal steel (all ca. '47-'65), and the '57-'58 Magnatone G-70 lap steel. A solidbody guitar and a pedal steel based upon the original Paul Bigsby designs were introduced January, 2002.
Triple 8-String Neck Steel
1947-1965. Bigsby steel were generally special order or custom-made and not mass produced. Instruments should be valued on a case-by-case basis.

| 1947-1959 | Natural | $5,500 | $6,800 |

Blue Star
1984-present. Intermediate grade, production/custom, lap steels built by luthier Bruce Herron in Fennville, Michigan. He also builds guitars, mandolins, dulcimers, and ukes.

Breedlove
1990-present. Founded by Larry Breedlove and Steve Henderson. Professional and premium grade, custom, Weissenborn-style lap steels made in Bend, Oregon. They also offer guitars, basses, mandolins and ukes. In 2010 they became part of Bedell Guitars.

Bronson
Ca. 1934-early 1960s. George Bronson was a steel guitar instructor in the Detroit area from the 1930s to the early '60s and sold instruments under his own brand. Most instruments and amps were made by Rickenbacker, Dickerson or Valco.
Leilani Lap Steel and Amp Set
1940s. Pearloid lap steel and small matching amp.

| 1940s | | $400 | $500 |

Melody King Model 52 Lap Steel
1950s. Brown bakelite body with 5 gold cavity covers on the top, made by Rickenbacker.

| 1950s | | $800 | $975 |

Model B Style
1948-1952. Rickenbacker-made.

| 1948-1952 | | $950 | $1,175 |

MODEL YEAR	FEATURES	EXC. COND. LOW	HIGH

Singing Electric
1950s. Round body, Valco-made.

1950s		$400	$500

Streamliner Lap Steel
1950s. Guitar-shape body, 1 pickup, 1 knob, red-orange pearloid cover.

1950s		$225	$275

Carvin
1946-present. Founded by Lowell C. Kiesel who produced lapsteels under the Kiesel brand for 1947-'50. In late '49, he renamed the instrument line Carvin after sons Carson and Galvin. Until '77, they offered lap, console, and pedal steels with up to 4 necks.

Double 6 Steel With Legs

1960s		$725	$900

Double 8 Steel With Legs

1960s	Sunburst	$800	$975

Electric Hawaiian Lap Steel

1950s		$250	$300

Single 8 With Legs
1960s. Large block position markers, 1 pickup, 2 knobs, blond finish.

1960s		$500	$625

Chandler
1984-present. Intermediate grade, production/custom, solidbody Weissenborn-shaped electric lap steels built by luthiers Paul and Adrian Chandler in Chico, California. They also build guitars, basses and effects.

Coppock
1930s-1959. Lap and console steels built by luthier John Lee Coppock in the Los Angeles area and in Peshastin, Washington. Coppock played Hawaiian music professionally in the 1920s and '30s and had a music studio where he started building his brand of steels around 1932. He moved to Washington in '44.

Cromwell
1935-1939. Budget model brand built by Gibson and distributed by various mail-order businesses.

Lap Steel
1939. Charlie Christian bar pickup.

1939	Sunburst	$300	$375

Danelectro
1946-1969, 1997-present. Known mainly for guitars and amps, Danelectro did offer a few lap steels in the mid-'50s.

Hawaiian Guitar
1958-1961. Three-tiered poplar solidbody lap steel, 1 lipstick tube pickup.

1958-1961		$1,100	$1,400

Deckly
1970s-1980s. Intermediate and professional grade pedal steel models, Deckly logo on front side of body.

Denley
1960s. Pedal steels built by Nigel Dennis and Gordon Huntley in England. They also made steels for Jim Burns' Ormston brand in the '60s.

Dickerson
1937-1948. Founded by the Dickerson brothers in '37, primarily for electric lap steels and small amps. Besides their own brand, Dickerson made instruments for Cleveland's Oahu Company, Varsity, Southern California Music, Bronson, Roland Ball, and Gourley. The lap steels were often sold with matching amps, both covered in pearloid mother-of-toilet-seat (MOTS). By '48, the company changed ownership and was renamed Magna Electronics (Magnatone).

Lap Steel
1940s. Dickerson appears to have offered 3 Hawaiian guitars. The Student was pear-shaped with a volume control; the Standard with had a volume and tone; both have decal 'boards and gray pearloid. The De Luxe is rare and came in tan pearloid and had sparkle plastic inlays and trim. Pre-War Dickersons have a heavier cast tailpiece; Post-War models have a metal rod and thru-body grommets. These were usually sold with a matching amp.

1940	Student or Standard	$250	$300

Dobro
1929-1942, ca.1954-present. Dobro offered lap steels from '33 to '42. Gibson now owns the brand and recently offered a lap steel.

E-45 Lap Steel
Late 1970s-1986. Reproduction of '37-'41 wood body Hawaiian lap steel, offered as 6-, 7-, 8-, or 10-string.

1980s	6-string	$675	$825
1980s	8-string	$700	$875

Hawaiian Lap Steel
1937-1941. Bell-shaped wood body Hawaiian.

1937-1941		$650	$800

Lap Steel Guitar and Amp Set
1930s-1940s. Typical pearloid covered student 6 string lap steel and small matching amp (with 3 tubes and 1 control knob).

1933-1942		$700	$875

Metal Body Lap Steel
1936. All metal body, Dobro logo on body.

1936		$800	$1,000

Dwight
1950s. Private branded instruments made by National-Supro. Epiphone made a Dwight brand guitar in the '60s which was not related to the lap-steels.

Lap Steel
1950s. Pearloid, 6 strings.

1950s		$400	$500

Electro
1964-1975. The Electro line was manufactured by Electro String Instruments and distributed

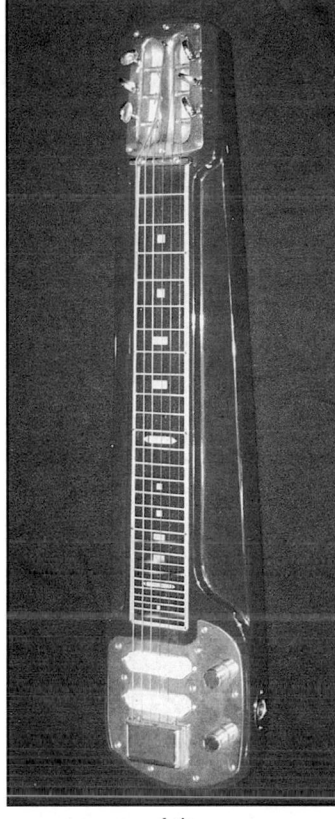

Aria

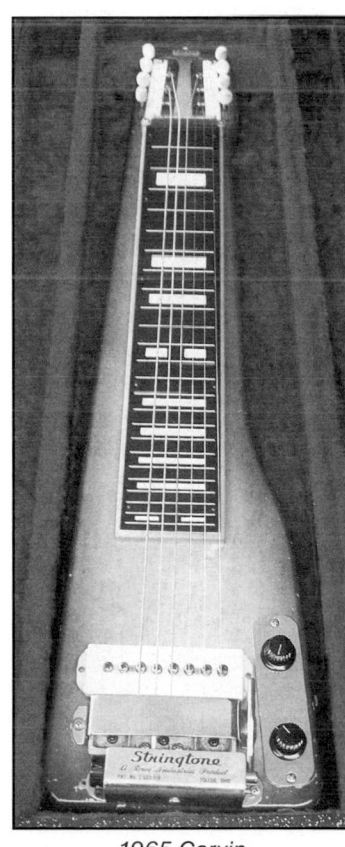

1965 Carvin
Backwoods Guitar LLC

STEELS & LAPS

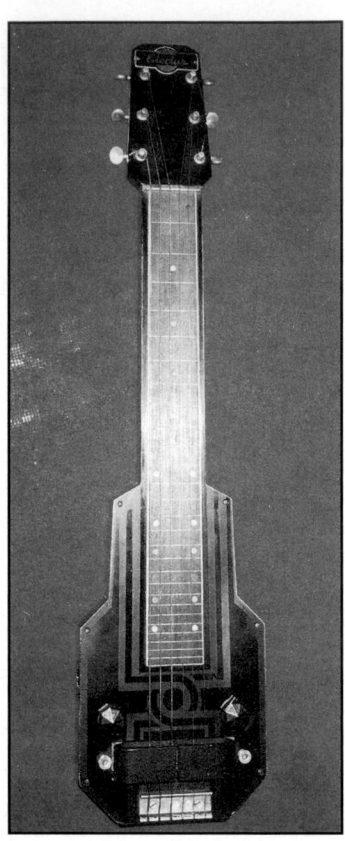

Epiphone Electar Model M

STEELS & LAPS

1952 Fender Deluxe 6

Ahmad Hasan

MODEL		EXC. COND.	
YEAR	FEATURES	LOW	HIGH

by Radio-Tel. The Electro logo appeared on the headstock rather than Rickenbacker. Refer to the Rickenbacker section for models.

Electromuse
1940s-1950s. Mainly offered lap steel and tube amp packages but they also offered acoustic and electric hollowbody guitars.
Lap Steel

1940s		$275	$350

Ellis
2008-present. Professional and premium grade, production/custom, lap steel guitars built by Andrew Ellis in Perth, Western Australia. He also builds guitars.

Emmons
1970s-present. Professional and premium grade, production/custom, pedal steels built by Lashley, Inc. of Burlington, North Carolina.
Double 10 Steel
1970-1982. Push/pull pedal steel.

1970-1982		$2,700	$3,300

Lashley LeGrande III Steel
2001-present. Double-neck, 8 pedals, 4 knee levers, 25th Anniversary.

2001-2014		$2,500	$3,100

S-10 Pedal Steel
1970-1982. Single 10-string neck pedal steel.

1970-1982		$1,900	$2,400

Student, 3-Pedal Steel
1970s. Single neck.

1970s		$600	$750

English Electronics
1960s. Norman English had a teaching studio in Lansing, Michigan, where he gave guitar and steel lessons. He had his own private-branded instruments made by Valco in Chicago.
Tonemaster Lap Steel
1960s. Cream pearloid, 6 strings, 3 legs, Valco-made.

1960s		$450	$550
1960s	Stringtone pitch changer	$600	$750

Epiphone
1928-present. The then Epiphone Banjo Company was established in '28. Best known for its guitars, the company offered steels from '35 to '58 when Gibson purchased the brand.
Century Lap Steel
1939-1957. Rocket-shaped maple body, 1 pickup, metal 'board, 6, 7 or 8 strings, black finish.

1939-1957		$475	$575

Eddie Alkire E-Harp
1939-1950s. 10-string, similar to Epiphone lap steel with Epi-style logo, offered in lap steel or console.

1939-1950s		$900	$1,100

MODEL		EXC. COND.	
YEAR	FEATURES	LOW	HIGH

Electar Hawaiian Lap Steel
1935-1937. Wood teardrop-shaped body, bakelite top, black, horseshoe pickup, 6 string.

1935-1937		$575	$700

Electar Model M Hawaiian Lap Steel
1936-1939. Metal top, stair-step body, art deco, black ('36-'37) or gray ('38-'39), 6, 7 or 8 strings.

1936-1939		$700	$875

Kent Hawaiian Lap Steel
1949-1953. Guitar-shaped maple body, 6 strings, lower-end of Epiphone Hawaiian line, Electar script logo below bottom of fretboard.

1949-1953		$325	$400

Solo Console Steel
1939-1954. Maple with white mahogany laminated body, black binding, black metal 'board, 6, 7 or 8 strings.

1939-1954		$575	$700

Triple-Neck Console Steel
1954-1957. neck version of Solo, sunburst or natural finish.

1954-1957		$1,250	$1,550

Zephyr Hawaiian Lap Steel
1939-1957. Maple stair-step body, metal 'board, 6, 7 or 8 strings.

1939-1949	Black, with white top	$625	$775
1950-1957	Sunburst	$600	$750

Ernie Ball
Best known for their strings and Music Man guitars, Ernie Ball offered a steel guitar under their own name for 1974-1979, building a very small quantity.
Black Eagle S-10 Pedal Steel
1974-1979. 3 pedals, 3 levers.

1974-1979		$1,200	$1,500

Fender
1946-present. Fender offered lap and pedal steels from '46 to '80. In 2005 they introduced a new lap steel model under their Folk Music series, which lasted until 2009.
400 Pedal Steel
1958-1976. One 8-string neck with 4 to 10 pedals.

1958-1976		$900	$1,125

800 Pedal Steel
1964-1976. One 10-string neck, 6 to 10 pedals.

1964-1976		$950	$1,175

1000 Pedal Steel
1957-1976. Two 8-string necks, 8 or 10 pedals, sunburst or natural.

1957-1976		$1,000	$1,250

2000 Pedal Steel
1964-1976. Two 10-string necks, 10 or 11 pedals, sunburst.

1964-1976		$1,200	$1,500

Artist Dual 10 Pedal Steel
1976-1981. Two 10-string necks, 8 pedals, 4 knee levers, black or mahogany.

1976-1981		$900	$1,125

MODEL YEAR	FEATURES	EXC. COND. LOW	HIGH
Champ Lap Steel			
1955-1980. Replaced Champion Lap Steel, tan.			
1955-1959		$725	$900
1960-1969		$625	$750
1970-1980		$525	$650
Champion Lap Steel			
1949-1955. Covered in what collectors call mother-of-toilet-seat (MOTS) finish, also known as pearloid. Replaced by Champ Lap Steel.			
1949-1955	Tan	$850	$1,075
1949-1955	White or yellow pearloid	$850	$1,075
Deluxe 6/Stringmaster Single Steel			
1950-1981. Renamed from the Deluxe, 6 strings, 3 legs.			
1950-1969	Blond or walnut	$825	$1,025
1970-1981	Black or white	$825	$1,025
Deluxe 8/Stringmaster Single Steel			
1950-1981. Renamed from the Deluxe, 8 strings, 3 legs.			
1950-1969	Blond or walnut	$825	$1,025
1970-1981	Black or white	$825	$1,025
Deluxe Steel			
1949-1950. Strings-thru-pickup, Roman numeral markers, became the Deluxe 6 or Deluxe 8 Lap Steel in '50.			
1946	Wax	$825	$1,025
1947-1950	Blond or walnut	$825	$1,025
Dual 6 Professional Steel			
1952-1981. Two 6-string necks, 3 legs optional, blond or walnut.			
1952-1969	Blond or walnut	$1,100	$1,350
1970-1981	Blond or walnut	$1,100	$1,350
Dual 8 Professional Steel			
1946-1957. Two 8-string necks, 3 legs optional, blond or walnut.			
1946-1957	Blond or walnut	$1,100	$1,350
FS-52 Lap Steel			
2008-2009. Two-piece ash body, 22.5" scale, chrome hardware, white blonde gloss finish.			
2008-2009		$265	$325
K & F Steel			
1945-1946. Made by Doc Kauffman and Leo Fender, strings-thru-pickup.			
1945-1946	Black	$1,600	$1,975
Organ Button Steel			
1946-1947. Strings-thru-pickup, Roman numerals, red pushbutton for organ effect, most have a wax-like, non-lacquered finish.			
1946-1947	Wax	$850	$1,050
Princeton Steel			
1946-1948. Strings-thru-pickup, Roman numeral markers.			
1946-1948	Wax	$950	$1,150
Stringmaster Steel (Two-Neck)			
1953-1981. The Stringmaster came in 3 versions, having 2, 3 or 4 8-string necks (6-string necks optional).			
1953-1954	Blond, 26" scale	$1,300	$1,600
1953-1954	Walnut, 26" scale	$1,200	$1,500
1955-1959	Blond, 24.5" scale	$1,300	$1,600
1955-1959	Walnut, 24.5" scale	$1,200	$1,500

MODEL YEAR	FEATURES	EXC. COND. LOW	HIGH
1960-1969	Blond	$1,200	$1,500
1960-1969	Walnut	$1,100	$1,375
1970-1981	Blond or walnut	$1,100	$1,375
Stringmaster Steel (Three-Neck)			
1953-1981.			
1953-1954	Blond, 26" scale	$1,650	$2,075
1953-1954	Walnut, 26" scale	$1,400	$1,750
1955-1959	Blond, 24.5" scale	$1,650	$2,075
1955-1959	Walnut, 24.5" scale	$1,400	$1,750
1960-1969	Blond	$1,400	$1,750
1960-1969	Walnut	$1,300	$1,600
1970-1981	Blond or walnut	$1,300	$1,600
Stringmaster Steel (Four-Neck)			
1953-1968.			
1953-1954	Blond, 26" scale	$1,650	$2,075
1953-1954	Walnut, 26" scale	$1,400	$1,750
1955-1959	Blond, 24.5" scale	$1,650	$2,075
1955-1959	Walnut, 24.5" scale	$1,400	$1,750
1960-1968	Blond	$1,400	$1,750
1960-1968	Walnut	$1,400	$1,750
Studio Deluxe Lap Steel			
1956-1981. One pickup, 3 legs.			
1956-1981	Blond	$850	$1,050

Framus

1946-1977, 1996-present. Imported into the U.S. by Philadelphia Music Company in the '60s. The brand was revived in '96 by Hans Peter Wilfer, the president of Warwick.

Deluxe Table Steel 0/7

1970s	White	$325	$400

Student Hawaiian Model 0/4

1970s	Red	$165	$200

G.L. Stiles

1960-1994. Gilbert Lee Stiles made a variety of instruments, mainly in the Miami, Florida area.

Doubleneck Pedal Steel

1970s		$500	$625

GFI

1989-present. Professional and premium grade, production/custom, pedal steel guitars built by luthier Gene Fields, in Arlington, Texas from '89-2008 and since in Marshfield, Missouri.

Gibson

1890s (1902)-present. Gibson offered steels from '35-'68.

BR-3 Lap Steel

1946-1947. Guitar-shaped, 1 P-90, 2 knobs, sunburst, mahogany. Replaced by BR-4 in '47.

1946-1947		$700	$875

BR-4 Lap Steel

1947. Guitar-shaped of solid mahogany, round neck, 1 pickup, varied binding.

1947	Sunburst	$700	$875

BR-6 Lap Steel

1947-1960. Guitar-shaped solid mahogany body, square neck (round by '48).

1947-1960		$600	$750

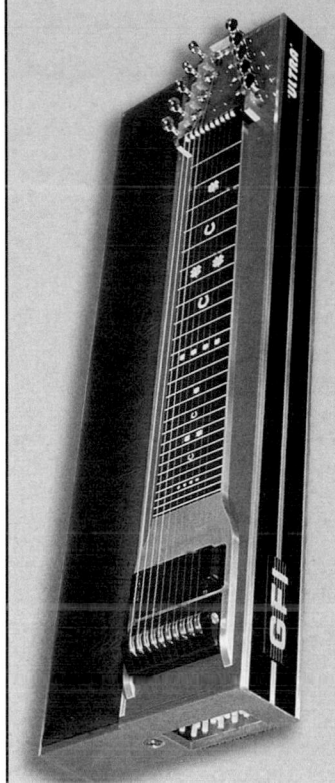

GFI Ultra S-10

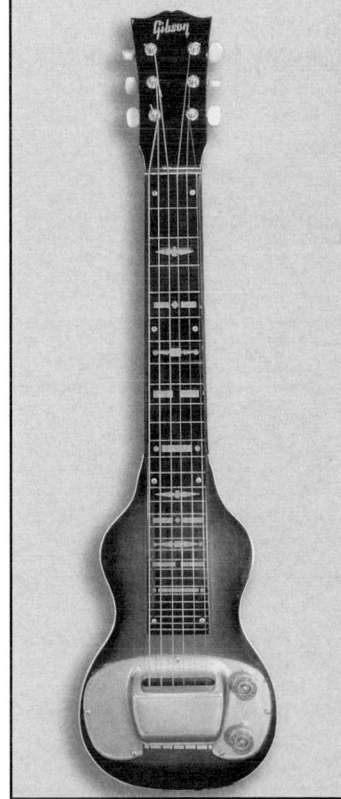

1954 Gibson BR-4
Fuller's Guitar

STEELS & LAPS

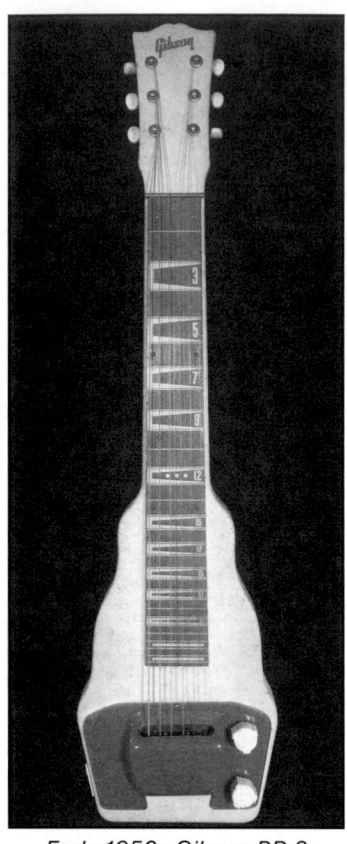

Early-1950s Gibson BR-9
Player Built Guitars

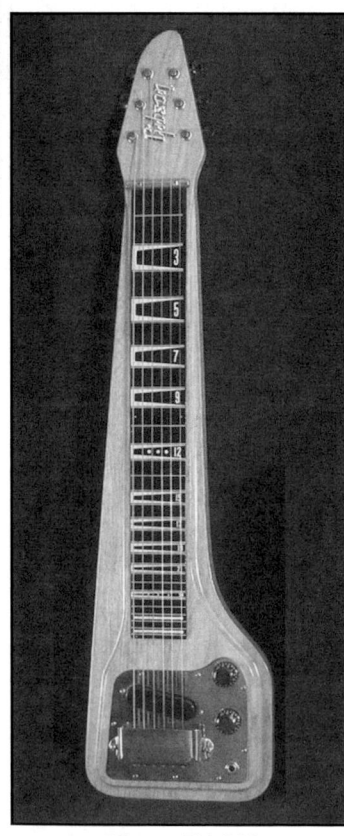

Gibson EH-500

MODEL YEAR	FEATURES	EXC. COND. LOW	HIGH
BR-9 Lap Steel			
1947-1959. Solidbody, 1 pickup, tan.			
1947-1949	Non-adj. poles	$425	$525
1950-1959	Adj. poles	$500	$625
Century Lap Steel			
1947-1968. Solid maple body, 6 or 10 ('48-'55) strings, 1 pickup, silver 'board.			
1947-1968		$825	$1,025
Console Grand Steel			
1938-1942, 1948-1967. Hollowbody, 2 necks, triple-bound body, standard 7- and 8-string combination until '42, double 8-string necks standard for '48 and after, by '61 becomes CG-620.			
1938	String-mute	$2,025	$2,525
1939-1942		$2,025	$2,525
1948-1954		$2,025	$2,525
1955-1967	CG-520	$2,025	$2,525
1961-1967	CG-530	$2,025	$2,525
Console Grand Triple Neck (CGT)			
1951-1956. Three 8-string necks, sunburst or natural, 4 legs.			
1951-1956		$2,425	$3,025
Console Steel (C-530)			
1957-1966. Replaced Consolette during '56-'57, double 8-string necks, 4 legs optional.			
1957-1966	With legs	$1,125	$1,400
Consolette Table Steel			
1952-1957. Rectangular korina body, 2 8-string necks, 4 legs, replaced by maple-body Console in '57.			
1952-1955	P-90	$900	$1,125
1955-1957	Humbucking	$1,075	$1,350
EH-100 Lap Steel			
1936-1949. Hollow guitar-shaped body, bound top, 6 or 7 strings.			
1936-1939		$725	$900
EH-125 Lap Steel			
1939-1942. Hollow guitar-shaped mahogany body, single-bound body, metal 'board, sunburst.			
1939-1942		$725	$925
EH-150 Doubleneck Electric Hawaiian Steel			
1937-1939. Doubleneck EH-150 with 7- and 8-string necks.			
1937-1939		$2,250	$2,800
EH-150 Lap Steel			
1936-1943. Hollow guitar-shaped body, 6 to 10 strings available, bound body.			
1936	1st offering, metal body	$1,500	$1,900
1937-1939	Sunburst	$925	$1,150
1940-1943	Sunburst	$900	$1,125
EH-185 Lap Steel			
1939-1942. Hollow guitar-shaped curly maple body, triple-bound body, 6, 7, 8 or 10 strings.			
1939-1942	Sunburst	$1,500	$1,850
EH-500 Skylark Deluxe Lap Steel			
1958-1959. Like Skylark, but with dot markers.			
1958-1959		$625	$800
EH-500 Skylark Lap Steel			
1956-1968. Solid korina body, 8-string available by '58, block markers with numbers.			
1956-1968	Natural	$625	$800

MODEL YEAR	FEATURES	EXC. COND. LOW	HIGH
EH-610 Lap Steel			
1957-1966. Six strings, 4 pedals.			
1957-1966		$1,050	$1,300
EH-620 Lap Steel			
1955-1967. Eight strings, 6 pedals.			
1955-1967	Natural	$1,050	$1,300
EH-630 Electraharp Steel			
1941-1967. Eight strings, 8 pedals (4 in '49-'67). Called just EH-630 from '56-'67.			
1941-1967	Sunburst	$900	$1,125
EH-820 Lap Steel			
1960-1966. Two necks, 8 pedals, Vari-Tone selector.			
1960-1966	Cherry	$1,000	$1,250
Multiharp Steel			
1956-1965. Three necks, 6 pedals, humbuckers.			
1956-1965		$1,100	$1,400
Royaltone Lap Steel			
1950-1952, 1956-1957. Volume and tone knobs on treble side of pickup, Gibson silk-screen logo, brown pickup bridge cover.			
1950-1952	Symmetrical body	$625	$775
1956-1957	Guitar-shaped body	$550	$675
Ultratone Lap Steel			
1948-1959. Solid maple body, plastic 'board, 6 strings.			
1948-1959		$850	$1,100

Gilet Guitars

1976-present. Production/custom, premium grade, lap steels built in Botany, Sydney, New South Wales, Australia by luthier Gerard Gilet. He also builds guitars.

Gold Tone

1993-present. Wayne and Robyn Rogers build their intermediate grade, production/custom lap steels in Titusville, Florida. They also build guitars, basses, mandolins, ukuleles, banjos and banjitars.

Golden Hawaiian

1920s-1930s. Private branded lap guitar most likely made by one of the many Chicago makers for a small retailer, publisher, cataloger, or teaching studio.

Hawaiian Lap Acoustic

1930s. Small body, acoustic flat-top for Hawaiian lap-style playing, Golden Hawaiian logo on headstock.

1930s		$325	$425

Gourley

See Dickerson listing.

Gretsch

1883-present. Gretsch offered a variety of steels from 1940-'63. Gretsch actually only made 1 model; the rest were built by Valco. Currently they offer 2 lap steel models.

Electromatic (5700/5715) Lap Steel

2005-present. Made in China, designed like the original Jet Mainliner (6147) steel, tobacco sunburst (5700) or black sparkle (5715).

2005-2014		$150	$175

STEELS & LAPS

MODEL		EXC. COND.	
YEAR	FEATURES	LOW	HIGH

Electromatic Console (6158) Twin Neck Steel

1949-1955. Two 6-string necks with six-on-a-side tuners, Electromatic script logo on end cover plates, 3 knobs, metal control panels and knobs, pearloid covered.

1949-1955		$600	$750

Electromatic Hawaiian Lap Steel

1940-1942. Guitar shaped mahogany body, wooden pickup cover.

1940-1942		$600	$750

Electromatic Standard (6156) Lap Steel

1949-1955. Brown pearloid.

1949-1955		$350	$425

Electromatic Student (6152) Lap Steel

1949-1955. Square bottom, brown pearloid, pearloid cover.

1949-1955		$375	$475

Jet Mainliner (6147) Steel

1955-1963. Single-neck version of Jet Twin.

1955-1963		$525	$650

Jet Twin Console (6148) Steel

1955-1963. Valco-made, 2 6-string necks, six-on-a-side tuners, Jet Black.

1955-1963		$850	$1,050

Guyatone

1933-present. Large Japanese maker. Brands also include Marco Polo, Winston, Kingston, Kent, LaFayette and Bradford. They offered lap steels under various brands from the '30s to the '60s.

Lap Steels

1960s		$275	$350

Table Steels

1960s. Three legs, 2 pickups.

1960s		$450	$550

Hanburt

1940-ca. 1950. Harvey M. Hansen built his electric Hawaiian guitars in Seattle, Washington that were sold through his wife's music instruction studio. His designs were influenced by Seattle's Audiovox guitars. He also built amps and at least one mandolin.

Harlin Brothers

1930s-1960s. Harlin Brothers, of Indianapolis, Indiana, were one of the early designers of pedal steel applications. Prices can vary because some instruments have a reputation of being hard to keep in tune.

Multi-Kord Pedal Steel

1950s	Single neck	$500	$625

Harmony

1982-1976, late 1970s-present. Founded by Wilhelm Schultz and purchased by Sears in 1916. The company evolved into the largest producer of stringed instruments in the U.S. in the '30s. They offered electric lap steels by '36.

Consolectric Steel

1953. Combo unit that combines steel guitar neck and built-in amp, 3 legs, Harmony Consolectric script logo on end of case, luggage tweed cover.

1953		$575	$700

Lap Steels

1936-1959	Various models	$275	$400
1960s	Painted body	$275	$400
1960s	Pearloid body	$275	$400

Hilo

1920s-1930s. Weissenborn-style guitars most likely made by New Jersey's Oscar Schmitt Company, Hilo orange label inside back.

Hawaiian Steel Guitar

1930s. Guitar shaped body, round sound hole, acoustic steel.

1930s		$1,300	$1,650

Hollingworth Guitars

1995-present. Premium grade, production/custom, lap steels built by luthier Graham Hollingworth in Mermaid Beach, Gold Coast, Queensland, Australia. He also builds guitars.

Jackson-Guldan

1920s-1960s. The Jackson-Guldan Violin Company, of Columbus, Ohio, offered lap steels and small tube amps early on. They also built acoustic guitars.

Jim Dyson

1972-present. Production/custom, intermediate, professional and premium grade lap steels built in Torquay, Southern Victoria, Australia by luthier Jim Dyson. He also builds guitars and basses.

K & F (Kaufman & Fender)

See listing under Fender.

Kalamazoo

1933-1942, 1946-1947, 1965-1970. Budget brand produced by Gibson in Kalamazoo, Michigan. They offered lap steels in the '30s and '40s.

Lap Steel

1938-1942, 1946-1947.

1938-1942		$400	$550
1946-1947		$350	$500

Kamico

Late-1940s. Private branded by Kay for student lap steel market, Kamico logo on lap steels and amplifiers. They also made guitars.

Lap Steel and Amp Set

1948. Symmetrical 6-string lap steel with small, single-knob 1x8" amp, both with matching sunburst finish.

1948		$325	$400

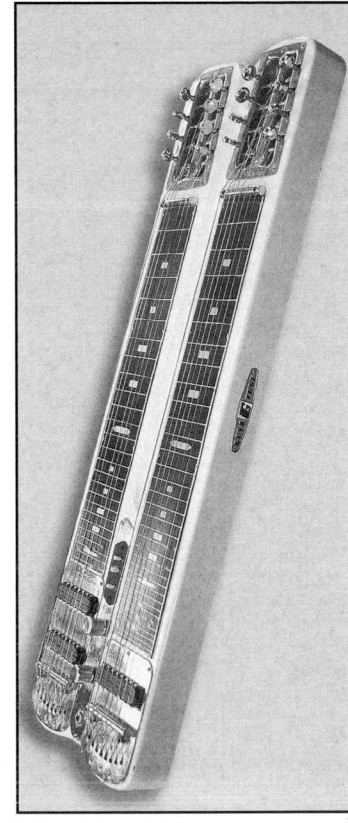

1969 Guyatone Double 8-String
Robbie Keene

Harmony-built (no brand)
Tim Kummer

STEELS & LAPS

Lapdancer Aero Commander XII

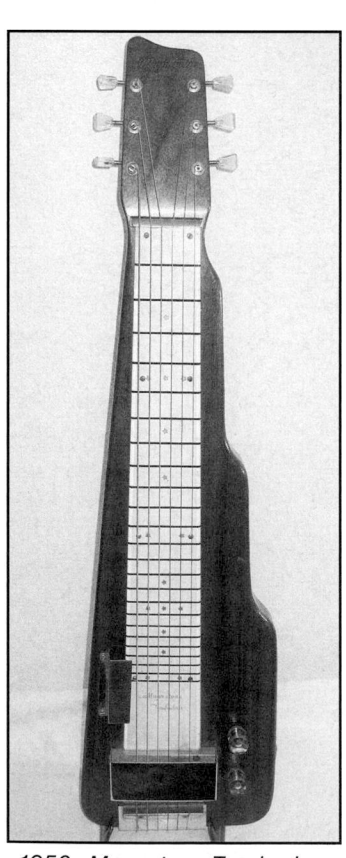

1950s Magnatone Troubadour
Dan Bishop

MODEL YEAR	FEATURES	EXC. COND. LOW	HIGH

Kay

Ca. 1931-present. Huge Chicago manufacturer Kay offered steels from '36 to '60 under their own brand and others.

Lap Steel

1936-1960		$275	$375

Lap Steel With Matching Amp

1940s	Dark mahogany	$500	$625
1950s	Green	$500	$625

Kiesel

1946-1949, 2015-present. Founded by Lowell Kiesel as L.C. Kiesel Co., Los Angeles, California, but renamed Carvin in '49. Kiesel logo on the headstock. Kiesel brand name revived by Carvin in '15 for use on their guitars.

Bakelite Lap Steel

1946. Small guitar-shaped bakelite body, 1 pickup, 2 knobs, diamond markers.

1946		$350	$425

Knutson Luthiery

1981-present. Professional grade, custom, electric lap steels built by luthier John Knutson in Forestville, California. He also builds guitars, basses and mandolins.

Lapdancer

2001-present. Intermediate and professional grade, custom/production, lap steels built by luthier Loni Specter in West Hills, California.

Lockola

1950s. Private brand lap and amp sets made by Valco for Lockola of Salt Lake City, Utah.

Lap Steel

1950s	Pearloid	$300	$375

Maestro

A budget brand made by Gibson.

Lap Steel

1940s-1950s. Pearloid, 1 pickup, 6 strings.

1940s-50s		$300	$375

Magnatone

Ca.1937-1971, 2013-present. Magnatone offered lap steels from '37 to '58. Besides their own brand, they also produced models under the Dickerson, Oahu, Gourley, and Natural Music Guild brands.

Lyric Doubleneck Lap Steel

Ca.1951-1958. Model G-1745-D-W, 8 strings per neck, hardwood body, 3 legs included.

1951-1958		$950	$1,150

Maestro Tripleneck Steel

Ca.1951-1958. Model G-2495-W-W, maple and walnut, 8 strings per neck, legs.

1951-1958		$1,050	$1,300

Pearloid (MOTS) Lap Steel

1950s. These were often sold with a matching amp; price here is for lap steel only.

1950s	Common	$250	$350
1950s	Less common	$500	$650

Pearloid Steel Guitar

1950s. Six-string non-pedal steel, 3 legs, 2 knobs, 8 push buttons, star position markers, pearloid cover, Magnatone script logo at lower end of fretboard.

1950s		$525	$650

Troubadour Lap Steel

1955. Wood body, 2 knobs, single metal pickup, Magnatone script logo on headstock and body.

1955		$475	$575

Marvel

1950-mid 1960s. Budget brand marketed by the Peter Sorkin Company of New York.

Electric Hawaiian Lap Steel

1950s		$160	$200

Mastertone

Late 1920s-early 1940s. Mastertone was a budget brand made by Gibson and was used on lap steel, Hawaiian and archtop guitars.

Special Lap Steel

1920s-40s	Brown crinkle	$475	$600

May Bell

See listing under Slingerland.

McKinney

1950s. Private branded for McKinney Guitars by Supro, blue McKinney Guitar logo on headstock.

Lap Steel

1950s. Similar to Supro Comet.

1950s	White pearloid	$325	$400

Melobar

1967-present. Designed by Walt Smith, of Smith Family Music, Melobar instruments feature a guitar body with a tilted neck, allowing the guitarist to play lap steel standing up. The instrument was developed and first made in Ed and Rudy Dopyera's Dobro factory. Most were available in 6-, 8-, and 10-string versions. Ted Smith took over operations from his father. Ted retired in late 2002. Production ceased in '06, pending a sale of the company, but resumed in '07 under new owners Jim and Carrie Frost.

Electric Steel or Power-Slide Guitar

1970s-2006. Various 6-, 8-, and 10-string models.

1970s-2006		$500	$625

MSA

1963-1983, 2001-present. Professional and premium grade, production/custom, pedal and lap steel guitars built in Dallas, Texas by Maurice Anderson. The company was dissolved in '83, and reorganized in '01.

S-12 Pedal Steel

1980s. 12-string.

1980s		$1,400	$1,725

Sidekick 3/1 Steel

1970s-1980s. 10-string, 3 pedals, 1 lever.

1970s-80s		$800	$1,000

STEELS & LAPS

MODEL YEAR	FEATURES	EXC. COND. LOW	HIGH

National

Ca. 1927-present. Founded in Los Angeles as the National String Instrument Corporation in '27, the brand has gone through many ownership changes over the years. National offered lap steels from '35 to '68.

Chicagoan Lap Steel
1948-1960. Gray pearloid, metal hand rest.

1948-1960		$400	$500

Clipper Model 1026 Lap Steel
1952-1955. Guitar-shaped wood body, celluloid bound, 1 pickup, volume, tone, 'visual octaves' position markers on neck, shaded brown finish.

1952-1955		$525	$650

Console (Dual 8) Steel
1939-1942. Two 8-string necks, parallelogram markers, black top with white sides.

1939-1941		$775	$950

Dynamic Lap Steel
1941-1968. New Yorker-style body, 6 strings, 3 detachable screw-in legs added by '56.

1941-1965	Lap	$650	$800
1956-1968	With legs	$650	$800

Electric Hawaiian Lap Steel
1935-1937. Cast aluminum round body, 1 pickup, square neck, 6 or 7 strings.

1935-1937		$775	$950

Grand Console Steel
1947-1967. Double (1050) or triple (1052) 8-string necks, Totem Pole 'board markers, came with or without legs, black and white finish, National's answer to Fender Stringmaster Series.

1947-1959	Model 1052		
	3 necks	$1,025	$1,275
1947-1967	Model 1050, 2 necks	$850	$1,075

New Yorker Lap Steel
1939-1967. Introduced as Electric Hawaiian model in '35, square end body with stair-step sides, 7 or 8 strings, black and white finish.

1939-1949		$750	$925
1950-1967		$600	$750

Princess Lap Steel
1941-1947. Strings-thru-pickup, parallelogram markers, white pearloid.

1941-1947		$400	$500

Rocket One Ten Lap Steel
1956-1957. Rocket-shaped, black and white finish.

1956-1957		$475	$600

Studio 76 N476 Lap Steel
1964. Half and half stair-step inlay design, 3-on-a-side tuners with open-book shaped headstock, 1 pickup, 2 knobs, onyx black pearloid, soft shoulders.

1964		$350	$450

Trailblazer Steel
1948-1949. Square end, numbered markers, black.

1948-1949		$325	$400

Triplex 1088 Chord Changer Lap Steel
1944-1958. Maple and walnut body, 2 knobs, natural.

1944-1958		$750	$925

Nioma

1932-1952. NIOMA was a music and arts school founded in Seattle. By '35 they added guitar instruction, offering their own branded lap steels (with matching amps), made by Dickerson. They also offered guitars.

Lap Steel

1930s	Pearloid	$250	$325

Oahu

1926-1985. The Oahu Publishing Company and Honolulu Conservatory, based in Cleveland, published a very popular guitar study course. They sold instruments to go with the lessons, starting with acoustic Hawaiian and Spanish guitars, selling large quantities in the '30s. As electric models became popular, Oahu responded with guitar-amp sets. Lap steel and matching amp sets were generally the same color; for example, yellow guitar and yellow amp, or white pearloid guitar and white amp. These sets were originally sold to students who would take private or group lessons. The instruments were made by Oahu, Valco, Harmony, Dickerson, and Rickenbacker and were offered into the '50s and '60s.

Dianna Lap Steel
1950s. Oahu and Diana logos on headstock, Oahu logo on fretboard, fancy bridge, pleasant unusual sunburst finish.

1950s		$325	$425

Hawaiian Lap Steel

1930s	Sunburst, student-grade	$250	$325
1930s	Tonemaster with decal art	$300	$375
1930s-40s	Rare style, higher-end	$375	$850
1930s-40s	Rare style, student-grade	$300	$375
1940s	Pearloid, Supro-made	$300	$375
1950s	Pearloid or painted	$300	$375
1950s	Tonemaster	$300	$375

Iolana
1941-1951, Late-1950s. Gold hardware, 2 6-string necks. Early model is lap steel, later version a console.

1941-1951	Lap	$500	$625
1950s	Console	$750	$925

K-71 Acoustic Lap Steel
1930s. Flat-top, round sound hole, decals on lower bouts.

1930s		$375	$475

Triplex 1088 Chord Changer Lap Steel
1940s. National-built 6-string lap steel with 'tuning change mechanism.'

1940s		$750	$925

Ormston

1966-1968. Pedal steels built in England by Denley and marketed by James Ormston Burns between his stints with Burns London, which was bought by America's Baldwin Company in '65, and the Dallas Arbiter Hayman brand.

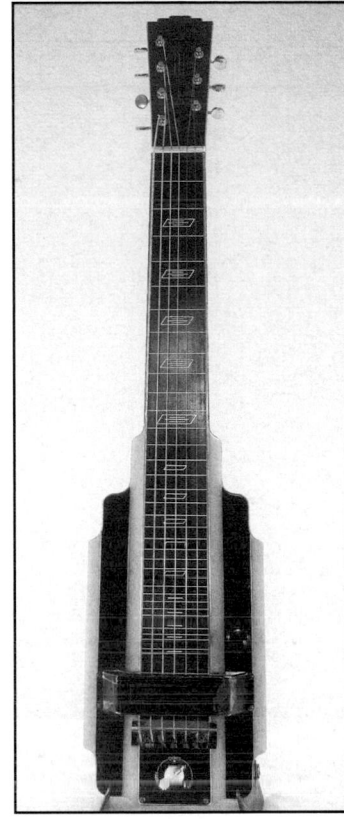

1939 National New Yorker
Dan Bishop

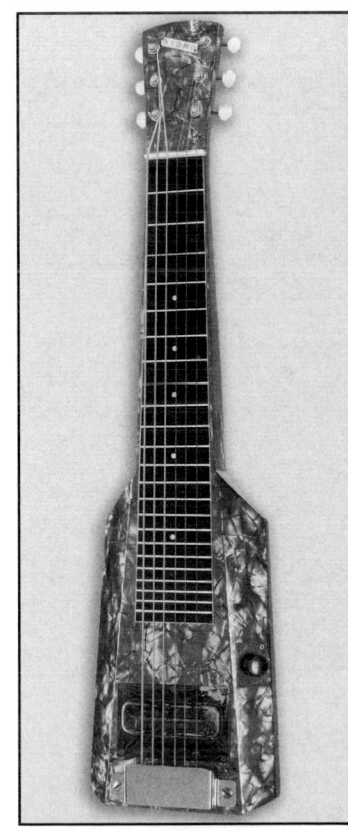

1930s Nioma Lap Steel
Lynn Wheelwright

1938 Recording King Roy Smeck Model AB104

Player Built Guitars

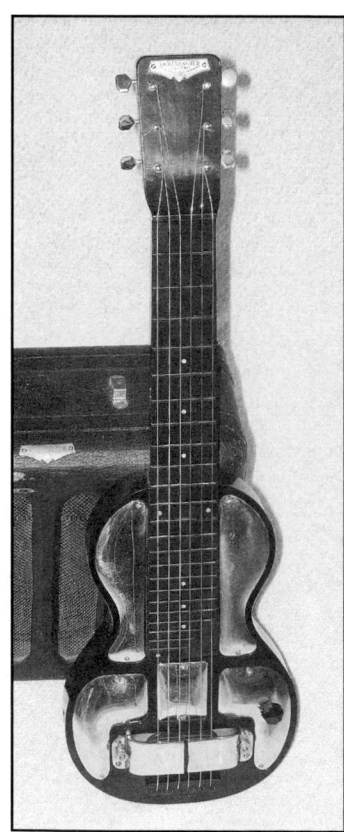

1936 Rickenbacker

Tim Kummer

MODEL		EXC. COND.	
YEAR	FEATURES	LOW	HIGH

Premier
Ca.1938-ca.1975, 1990s-2010. Premier made a variety of instruments, including lap steels, under several brands.

Recording King
Ca. 1930-1943. Brand used by Montgomery Ward for instruments made by Gibson, Regal, Kay, and Gretsch.

Electric Hawaiian Lap Steel

1930s		$375	$475

Roy Smeck Model AB104 Steel
1938-1941. Pear-shaped body, 1 pickup.

1938-1941		$650	$800

Regal
Ca. 1895-1966, 1987-present. Regal offered their own brand and made instruments for distributors and mass-merchandisers. The company sold out to Harmony in '54. See guitars for more company info.

Electric Hawaiian Lap Steel

1940s		$325	$400
1940s	With matching amp	$550	$675

Reso-phonic Steel
1930s. Dobro-style resonator and spider assembly, round neck, adjustable nut.

1930s		$775	$950

Rickenbacker
1931-present. Rickenbacker produced steels from '32 to '70.

Academy Lap Steel
1946-1947. Bakelite student model, horseshoe pickup, replaced by the Ace.

1946-1947		$425	$525

Ace Lap Steel
1948-1953. Bakelite body, 1 pickup.

1948-1953		$425	$525

Console 208 Steel
1955-1970. Two 8-string necks.

1955-1970		$1,250	$1,550

Console 518 Triple Neck Steel
1955-1970. 22.5" scale, 3 8-string necks.

1955-1970		$1,350	$1,700

Console 758 Triple Neck Steel
1957-1970. 25" scale, 3 8-string necks.

1957-1970		$1,350	$1,700

CW Steel
1957-1970. Single neck on wood body, several neck options, 3 attachable legs.

1957-1970		$725	$875

DC-16 Steel
1950-1952. Metal, double 8-string necks.

1950-1952		$800	$1,000

Electro Lap Steel
1940s, 1960s. Large Rickenbacker logo and smaller Electro logo on headstock ('40s), then on side ('60s).

1940s	Headstock logo	$750	$950
1960s	Side logo	$750	$950

Electro Doubleneck Steel
1940-1953. Two bakelite 8-string necks.

1940-1953		$1,300	$1,600

MODEL		EXC. COND.	
YEAR	FEATURES	LOW	HIGH

Electro Tripleneck Steel
1940-1953. Three bakelite 8-string necks.

1940-1953		$1,500	$1,900

Electro EH-3 Lap Steel
1970s. 6-string neck, legs.

1971		$525	$650

JB (Jerry Byrd) Model Steel
1961-1970. Single neck on large wood body, 6-, 7-, 8-, or 10-string neck, 3 attachable legs, Jerry Byrd Model logo on top plate.

1961-1970		$900	$1,100

Model 59 Lap Steel
1937-1943. Sheet steel body, baked-enamel light-colored crinkle finish, 1 pickup.

1937-1943		$725	$900

Model 100 Lap Steel
1956-1970. Wood body, 6 strings, block markers, light or silver gray finish.

1956-1970		$475	$575

Model 102 Lap Steel
1960s. Wood body, 6 strings, slot head, block markers, natural finish.

1960		$450	$550

Model A-22 Frying Pan Steel
1932-1936. Originally called the Electro-Hawaiian Guitar, small round body lap steel, offered as 6- or 7-string, 22.5" scale (the A-25 25" scale also available).

1932-1936		$2,800	$3,500

Model B Steel
1935-1955. Bakelite body and neck, 1 pickup, strings-thru-body, decorative metal plates, 6 or 8 strings, black.

1935-1955	6-string	$1,500	$1,900
1935-1955	8-string	$1,600	$2,000

Model B-10 Steel
1935-1955. Model B with slot head and 12 strings.

1935-1955		$1,100	$1,350

Model BD Steel
1949-1970. Bakelite body, 6 strings, deluxe version of Model B, black.

1949-1960		$800	$1,000

Model CW-6 Steel
1957-1961. Wood body, grille cloth on front, 6 strings, 3 legs, walnut finish, renamed JB (Jerry Byrd) model in '61.

1957-1961		$800	$1,000

Model DW Steel
1955-1961. Wood body, double 6- or 8-string necks, optional 3 legs.

1955-1961		$1,000	$1,250

Model G Lap Steel
Ca.1948-1957. Chrome-plated ornate version of Silver Hawaiian, gold hardware and trim, 6 or 8 strings.

1948-1957		$900	$1,100

Model S/NS (New Style) Steel
1946-early-1950s. Sheet steel body, 1 pickup, gray, gray sparkle or grayburst, also available as a doubleneck.

1946-1949		$850	$1,050

STEELS & LAPS

MODEL YEAR	FEATURES	EXC. COND. LOW	HIGH

Model SD Steel

1949-1953. Deluxe NS, sheet steel body, 6, 7 or 8 strings, Copper Crinkle finish.

| 1949-1953 | | $750 | $950 |

Model SW

1956-1962. Straight body style, 6 or 8 strings, block markers, dark or blond finish.

| 1956-1962 | 8 strings | $1,100 | $1,350 |
| 1956-1962 | 8 strings with legs | $1,400 | $1,750 |

Silver Hawaiian Lap Steel

1937-1943. Chrome-plated sheet steel body, 1 horseshoe pickup, 6 strings.

| 1937-1943 | | $1,350 | $1,650 |

Rogue

2001-present. Budget grade, production, lap steels. They also offer guitars, basses, mandolins, banjos, and ukuleles.

Roland Ball

See Dickerson listing.

Scantic River Guitar Co.

2008-present. Luthiers Thomas Ford, Steve Collin and Dennis Moore build their premium grade, custom, lap steel guitars in Durham, Maine.

Serenader

Built by the Bud Electro Manufacturing Company which was founded in Seattle, Washington in the late 1940s by Paul "Bud" Tutmarc, Jr., whose father built Audiovox instruments. He built mainly lap steels but also offered a solidbody bass.

Sherwood

Late 1940s-early 1950s. Lap steel guitars made for Montgomery Ward made by Chicago manufacturers such as Kay. They also had archtop guitars and amps under that brand.

Deluxe Lap Steel

1950s. Symmetrical body, bar pickup, volume and tone controls, wood body, sunburst, relatively ornate headstock with script Sherwood logo, vertical Deluxe logo, and lightning bolt art.

| 1950s | | $175 | $225 |

Sho-Bud

1956-1981. Founded by Shot Jackson in Nashville. Distributed by Gretsch. They also had guitar models. Baldwin bought the company and closed the factory in '81.

Crossover Twin Neck Steel

1967-1971. Sho-Bud Baldwin double neck, Sho-Bud logo.

| 1967-1971 | | $1,900 | $2,400 |

Maverick Pedal Steel

Ca. 1970-1981. Beginner model, burl elm cover, 3 pedals.

| 1970-1981 | | $875 | $1,100 |

MODEL YEAR	FEATURES	EXC. COND. LOW	HIGH

Pro I

1970-1981. Three pedals, natural.

| 1970-1975 | Round front | $1,650 | $2,050 |
| 1976-1981 | Square front | $1,750 | $2,150 |

Pro II

1973-1981. Birdseye maple, double 10-string necks, natural.

| 1973-1975 | Round front | $1,850 | $2,250 |
| 1976-1981 | Square front | $1,950 | $2,400 |

Pro III

1975-1981. Metal necks.

| 1975 | Round front | $1,950 | $2,400 |
| 1976-1981 | Square front | $2,050 | $2,550 |

Super Pro

1977-1980. Doubleneck 10 strings, 8 floor pedals, 6 knee levers, Jet Black.

| 1977-1980 | | $2,300 | $2,850 |

Sierra

1960-present. Originally designed and built by Chuck Wright in California and Oregon until '74, then by Don Christensen in Gresham and Portland, Oregon. In 2003, Ed W. Littlefield Jr. took ownership, with professional and premium grade, production, lap and pedal steel guitars built by luthiers Tom Baker and Rob Girdis in Molalla, Oregon. Girdis died in '09. There is an unrelated Sierra brand of guitars.

Silvertone

1940-1970, present. Brand name for instruments sold by Sears.

Amp-In-Case Lap Steel

Early 1940s. Lap steel and amp set, amp cabinet doubles as lap case with the lap stored above the amp, amp is in a long vertical cabinet with brown tweed covering, manufacturer appears to be the same as used by Gibson in the late '30s, low to mid power, 1x10" speaker.

| 1941-1942 | | $700 | $875 |

Six-String Lap Steel

1940s-1960s. Includes Valco-made, standard or pearloid finish.

| 1940s-60s | Various models | $325 | $575 |

Slingerland

Ca. 1914-present. Offered by Slingerland Banjos and Drums. They also sold the May Bell brand. Instruments were also made by others and sold by Slingerland in the '30s and '40s.

May Bell Lap Steel

1930s. Guitar-shaped lap steel with May Bell logo. This brand also had '30s Hawaiian and Spanish guitars.

| 1930s | | $250 | $300 |

Songster Lap Steel

1930s. Slingerland logo headstock, Songster logo near nut, guitar-shaped body, sunburst maple top, some with figured maple back, 1 pickup, 2 bakelite brown knobs, dot markers.

| 1930s | | $700 | $875 |

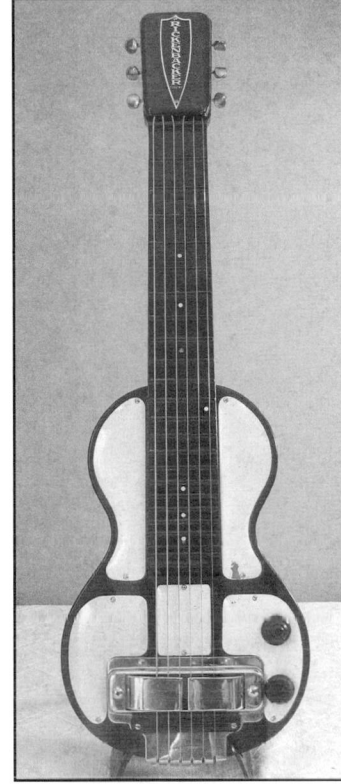

Early-1950s Rickenbacker Model BD

Dan Bishop

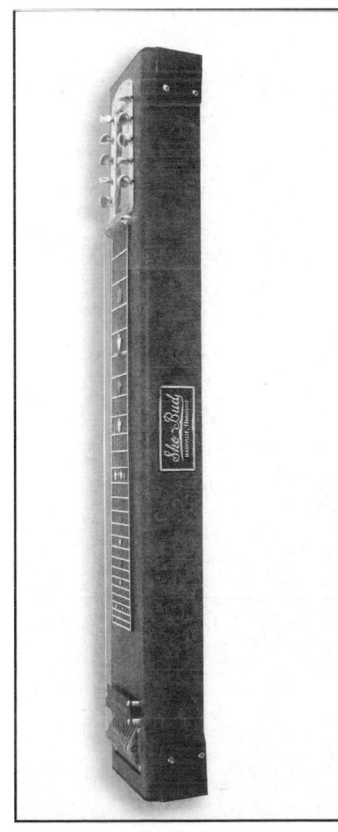

Sho-Bud Maverick

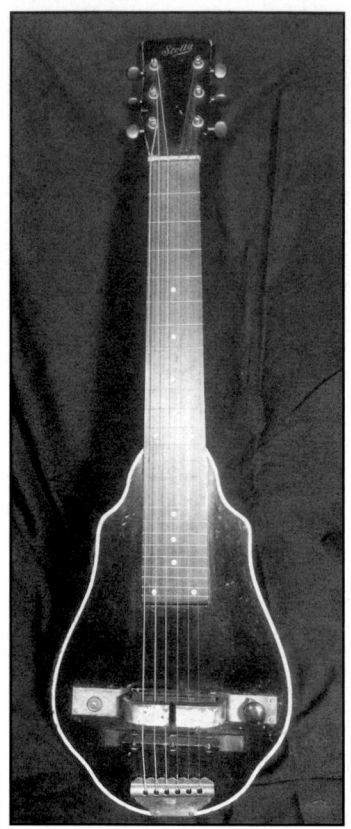

1938 Stella
James Clements

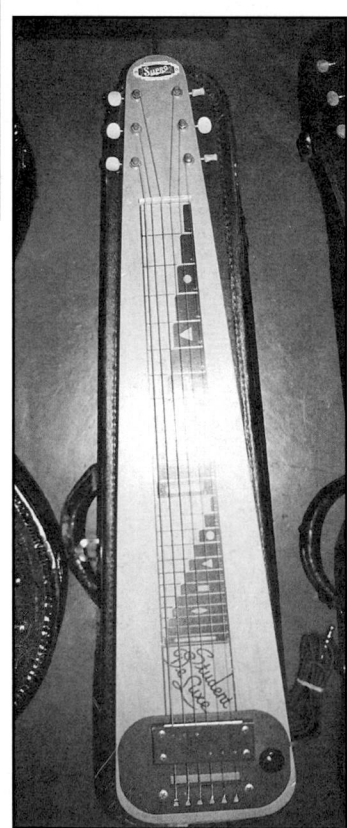

1950s Supro Student De Luxe

MODEL YEAR	FEATURES	EXC. COND. LOW	HIGH

SPG

2006-2009. Intermediate grade, custom, solid-body lapsteels originally built by luthier Rick Welch in Farmingdale, Maine and Hanson, Massachusetts; more recently by luthier Eric C. Brown in Farmingdale, Maine.

Stella

Ca. 1899-1974, 2000s. Stella was a brand of the Oscar Schmidt Company. Harmony acquired the brand in '39. The Stella brand was reintroduced in the 2000s by MBT International.

Electric Hawaiian Lap Steel

1937		$475	$600

Supertone

1914-1941. Brand name for Sears which was replaced by Silvertone. Instruments made by Harmony and others.

Electric Hawaiian Lap Steel

1930s	Various models	$250	$325

Supro

1935-1968, 2004-present. Budget brand of the National Dobro Company. Brand name was revived in '04.

Airline

1952-1962. Asymmetrical body with straight left side and contoured right (treble) side, black pearloid with small white pearloid on right (treble) side, 2 knobs, available with optional set of 3 legs, later versions available with 6 or 8 strings, described in catalog as "Supro's finest". Renamed Jet Airliner in '64.

1952-1962	6-string	$450	$575
1952-1962	8-string	$500	$625
1952-1962	With optional legs	$525	$675

Clipper Lap Steel

1941-1943. One pickup, bound rosewood 'board, dot inlay, brown pearloid.

1941-1943		$325	$425

Comet Lap Steel

1947-1966. One pickup, attached cord, painted-on 'board, pearloid.

1947-1949	Gray pearloid	$325	$425
1950-1966	White pearloid	$325	$425

Comet Steel (With Legs)

1950s-1960s. Three-leg 6-string steel version of the lap steel, 2 knobs, Supro logo on cover plate, 1 pickup.

1960s	Black & white	$475	$600

Console 8 Steel

1958-1960. Eight strings, 3 legs, black and white.

1958-1960		$575	$700

Irene Lap Steel

1940s. Complete ivory pearloid cover including headstock, fretboard and body, Roman numeral markers, 1 pickup, 2 control knobs, hard-wired output cord.

1940s		$325	$425

Jet Airliner Steel

1964-1968. Renamed from Airline, described in catalog as "Supro's finest", 1 pickup, totem pole markings, 6 or 8 strings, pearloid, National-made.

1964-1968	6-string	$500	$600
1964-1968	8-string	$525	$650
1964-1968	With optional legs	$575	$700

Professional Steel

1950s. Light brown pearloid.

1950s		$325	$425

Special Steel

1955-1962. Pearloid lap steel, student model, large script Special logo near pickup on early models, red until '57, white after.

1955-1957	Red pearloid	$325	$425
1957-1962	White pearloid	$325	$425

Spectator Steel

1952-1954. Wood body, 1 pickup, painted-on 'board, natural.

1952-1954		$250	$325

Student De Luxe Lap Steel

1952-1955. One pickup, pearloid, large script Student De Luxe logo located near pickup, replaced by Special in '55.

1952-1955	Black & white, or red pearloid	$325	$425
1952-1955	Natural or white paint	$250	$325

Studio

1955-1964. Symmetrical body, 2 knobs, priced in original catalog below the Comet, but above the Special, issued in '55 with blue plastic covered body.

1955-1964		$325	$425

MODEL YEAR	FEATURES	EXC. COND. LOW	HIGH

Supreme Lap Steel
1947-1960. One pickup, painted-on 'board, brown pearloid until ca.'55, then red until ca.'58, Tulip Yellow after that.

1947-1960		$400	$500

Supro 60 Lap Steel and Amp-in-Case
Late 1930s-early '40s. Supro 60 logo near the single volume knob, long horizontal guitar case which houses a small tube amp and speaker, the case cover folds out to allow ventilation for the tubes, white pearloid, black amp case, the amp was made by National Dobro of Chicago.

1939-1941		$700	$875

Twin Lap Steel
1948-1955. Two 6-string necks, pearloid covering, renamed Console Steel in '55.

1948-1955		$525	$650

Teisco
1946-1974. The Japanese guitar-maker offered many steel models from '55 to around '67. Models offered '55-'61: EG-7L, -K, -R, -NT, -Z, -A, -S, -P, -8L, -NW, and -M. During '61-'67: EG-TW, -O, -U, -L, -6N, -8N, -DB, -DB2, -DT, H-39, H-905, TRH-l, Harp-8 and H-850.

Hawaiian Lap Steel

1955-1967		$250	$375

Timtone Custom Guitars
1993 2006. Luthier Tim Diebert built his professional grade, custom, lap steel guitars in Grand Forks, British Columbia. He also built guitars and basses.

True Tone
1960s. Brand name sold by Western Auto (hey, everybody was in the guitar biz back then). Probably made by Kay or Harmony.

Lap Steel
1960s. Guitar-shaped, single-cut, 1 pickup.

1960s		$250	$325

Varsity
See Dickerson listing.

Vega
1889-present. The original Boston-based company was purchased by C.F. Martin in '70. In '80, the Vega trademark was sold to a Korean company. The company was one of the first to enter the electric market by offering products in '36 and offered lap steels into the early '60s. The Deering Banjo Company acquired the brand in '89 and uses it on a line of banjos.

DG-DB Steel
1950s. Two necks, 8 strings.

1950s		$850	$1,050

Odell Lap Steel
1950s. White pearloid.

1950s		$325	$400

Other Lap Steels

1930s	Rare models	$500	$1,200
1930s-40s	Common models	$350	$450
1940s	Art deco-style	$450	$550

Wabash
1950s. Lap steels distributed by the David Wexler company and made by others. They also offered guitars and amps.

Lap Steel (Hawaiian Scene Tallpiece)
1950s. Natural, 12 frets.

1950s		$225	$300

Wayne
1998-present. Luthiers Wayne and Michael Charvel, of Paradise, California, added intermediate grade, production, lap steel guitars to their line in '04. They also build guitars.

White
1955-1960. The White brand, named after plant manager Forrest White, was established by Fender to provide steel and small amp sets to teaching studios that were not Fender-authorized dealers. A standard guitar was planned, but never produced.

6-String Steel
1955-1956. White finish, block markers, 2 knobs, 3 legs. The 6 String Steel was usually sold with the matching white amp Model 80. Possibly only 1 batch of these was made by Fender in October/November '55.

1955-1956		$1,300	$1,600

Matching Steel and Amp Set

1955-1956		$2,300	$2,900

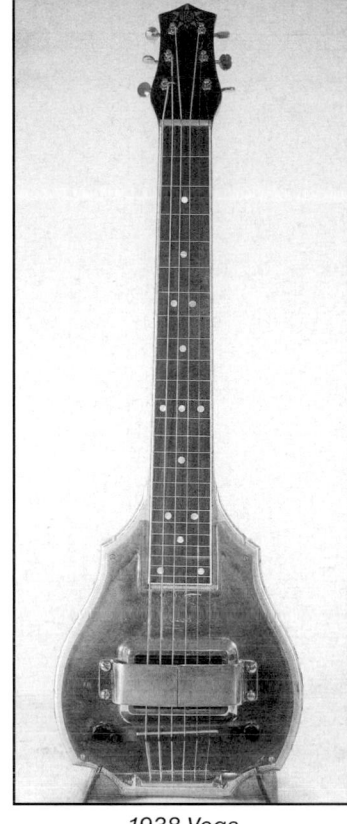

1938 Vega
Dan Bishop

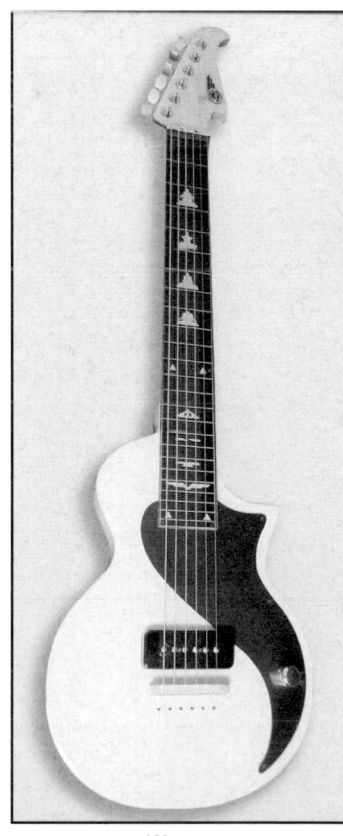

Wayne

STEELS & LAPS

MANDOLINS

MODEL YEAR	FEATURES	EXC. COND. LOW	HIGH

Alvarez A800

Airline

Ca. 1958-1968. Brand for Montgomery Ward. Instruments were built by Kay, Harmony and Valco.

Electric Mandolin (Kay K390)

Early-1960s. In '62 the K390 was advertised as the Kay Professional Electric Mandolin. Venetian shape with sunburst spruce top, curly maple back and sides, tube-style pickup, white 'guard, rope-style celluloid binding.

1962		$400	$500

Mandolin (Lower-End)

1960s. Acoustic, plain features.

1960s		$225	$275

Allen

1982-present. Premium grade, production resonators, steel-string flat-tops, and mandolins built by Luthier Randy Allen, Colfax, California.

Alvarez

1965-present. An import brand for St. Louis Music, Alvarez currently offers intermediate grade, production, mandolins. They also offer guitars, lap steels and banjos.

Mandolins

1970s-2000s. Classic style mandolin features, round soundhole or f-holes.

1970s	A style	$425	$525
1970s	F style	$475	$575

American Conservatory (Lyon & Healy)

Late-1800s-early-1900s. Mainly catalog sales of guitars and mandolins from the Chicago maker. Marketed as a less expensive alternative to the Lyon & Healy Washburn product line.

Arched Back Mandolin

1910s. Flat back with a mild arch, standard appointments, nothing fancy.

1910s		$375	$475

Bowl Back Mandolin

1917. Bowl back style, 14 ribs, Brazilian.

1917		$275	$350

Bowl Back Mandolin Style G2603

Early-1900s. Bowl back-style, 28 rosewood ribs (generally more ribs and use of rosewood ribs versus mahogany indicates higher quality), color corded soundhole and edge inlay, inlaid tortoise shell celluloid guard plate underneath strings and below the soundhole, bent top, butterfly headstock inlay.

1917		$450	$550

Bowl Back Mandolin Style G2604

Early-1900s. Bowl back-style, 42 rosewood ribs (generally more ribs indicated higher quality), extra fancy color corded soundhole and edge inlay around, extra fancy inlaid tortoise shell celluloid guard plate underneath strings and below the soundhole, bent top, butterfly headstock inlay.

1917		$550	$675

Apitius Rosine

MODEL YEAR	FEATURES	EXC. COND. LOW	HIGH

Andersen Stringed Instruments

1978-present. Luthier Steve Andersen builds his premium grade, production/custom mandolins in Seattle, Washington. He also builds guitars.

Andy Powers Musical Instrument Co.

1996-2010. Luthier Andy Powers, built his premium grade, custom, mandolins in Oceanside, California. He also built guitars and ukes.

Apitius

1976-present. Luthier Oliver Apitius builds his premium and presentation grade, production/custom, mandolins in Shelburne, Ontario.

Applause

1994-present. Applause offered intermediate grade, production, Ovation-styled, imported mandolins.

Mandolin

1990s		$115	$200

Aria/Aria Pro II

1956-present. Intermediate grade, production, acoustic and electric mandolins from Aria/Aria Pro II, which added Japanese and Korean mandolins to their line in '76.

AM200 Mandolin

1994-2012. Pear-shaped A body, plywood.

1994-2012		$175	$225

AM400 Mandolin

1994-2012. F-style, plywood.

1994-2012		$275	$350

AM600 Mandolin

1994-2008. F-style, solid wood.

1994-2008		$325	$400

PM750 Mandolin

1976-ca. 1982. F-style Loar copy, maple plywood body, sunburst.

1976-1982		$425	$525

Armstrong, Rob

1971-present. Custom mandolins made in Coventry, England, by luthier Rob Armstrong. He also builds basses, flat-tops, and parlor guitars.

Atkin Guitars

1993-present. Luthier Alister Atkin builds his production/custom mandolins in Canterbury, England. He also builds flat-top guitars.

Austin

1999-present. Budget and intermediate grade, production, mandolins imported by St. Louis Music. They also offer guitars, basses, amps, ukes and banjos.

MODEL YEAR	FEATURES	EXC. COND. LOW	HIGH

Bacon & Day

Established in 1921 by David Day and Paul Bacon, primarily known for fine quality tenor and plectrum banjos in the '20s and '30s.

Mandolin Banjo Orchestra
1920s. Mandolin neck and banjo body with open back, headstock with Bacon logo.

1920s		$375	$450

Professional Mandolin
1920s. Figured birch back and sides, spruce top, oval sound hole, 2-point flat back.

1920s		$1,400	$1,750

Senorita Banjo Mandolin

1930s		$725	$875

Silverbell #1 Banjo Mandolin
1920s. Fancy appointments, closed-back resonator.

1920s		$900	$1,125

Bauer (George)

1894-1911. Luthier George Bauer built guitars and mandolins in Philadelphia, Pennsylvania. He also built instruments with Samuel S. Stewart (S.S. Stewart).

Acme Professional Bowl Mandolin
1894-1911. Bowl back, 29 ribs, Brazilian.

1894-1911	Fancy	$475	$600
1894-1911	Mid-level	$325	$400
1894-1911	Plain	$250	$300

Beltona

1990-present. Production metal body resonator mandolins made in New Zealand by Steve Evans and Bill Johnson. They also build guitars and ukes.

Beltone

1920s-1930s. Acoustic and resonator mandolins and banjo-mandolins made by others for New York City distributor Perlberg & Halpin. Martin did make a small number of instruments for Beltone, but most were student-grade models most likely made by one of the big Chicago builders. They also made guitars.

Resonator Mandolin
1930s. F-hole top, banjo-style resonator back.

1930s		$400	$500

Bertoncini Stringed Instruments

In 1995 Luthier Dave Bertoncini mainly began building flat-top guitars in Olympia, Washington, but has also built mandolins.

Bigsby

Ca. 1947-present. Guitar builder Paul Arthur Bigsby also built 6 electric mandolins.

Blindworm Guitars

2008-present. Premium and presentation grade, production/custom, acoustic and electric mandolins built in Colorado Springs, Colorado by luthiers Andrew J. Scott and Steven Sells. They also build guitars, basses and banjos.

Blue Star

1984-present. Luthier Bruce Herron builds his intermediate grade, production/custom, electric solidbody mandolins in Fennville, Michigan. He also builds guitars, lap steels, dulcimers, and ukes.

Bohmann

1878-ca.1926. Established by Czechoslavakian-born Joseph Bohmann in Chicago, Illinois.

Bowl Mandolin
1890-1900. Spruce top, marquetry trimmed, inlay, pearl.

1890-1900	Fancy	$700	$1,600
1890-1900	Mid-level	$425	$600
1890-1900	Plain	$350	$425

Brandt

Early 1900s. John Brandt started making mandolin-family instruments in Chicago, Illinois around 1898.

Mandola
1900s. Spruce top, rosewood body, scroll headstock, pearl and abalone fretboard binding.

1900s		$1,150	$1,400

Presentation Mandolin
1900s. Spruce top, tortoise shell-bound.

1900s		$850	$1,050

Breedlove

1990-present. Founded by Larry Breedlove and Steve Henderson. Professional and premium grade, production/custom, mandolins made in Bend, Oregon. They also produce guitars, basses, laps and ukes. In 2010 they were acquired by Bedell Guitars.

Alpine Mandolin
2000s-2013. Master Class series, O-style body, spruce/maple.

2000s-2013		$1,800	$2,200

K-5 Mandolin
1990s. Asymmetric carved top, maple body.

1990s		$1,500	$1,850

Olympic Mandolin
1990s. Solid spruce top, teardrop-shaped, oval soundhole, highly flamed maple back, sunburst.

1990s		$1,200	$1,500

Quartz OF/OO Mandolin
2000s. Basic A-style body with f-holes.

2000s		$850	$1,050

Brian Moore

1992-present. Brian Moore offered premium grade, production/custom, semi-hollow electric mandolins. They also build guitars and basses.

Bruno and Sons

Established in 1834 by Charles Bruno, primarily as a distributor, Bruno and Sons marketed a variety of brands, including their own. In the '60s or '70s, a Japanese-made solidbody electric mandolin was sold under the Bruno name.

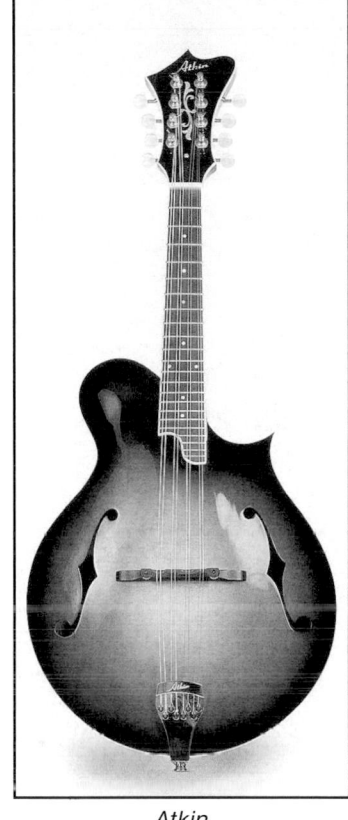

Atkin

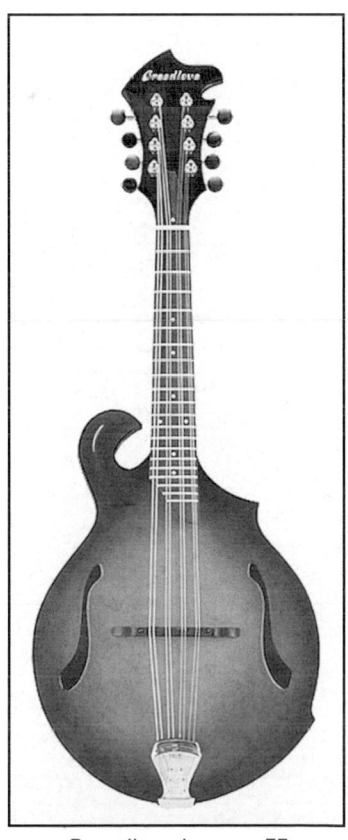

Breedlove Legacy FF

MANDOLINS

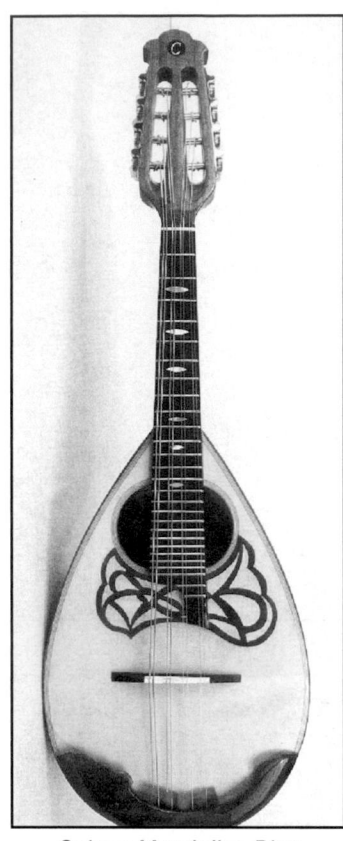

Calace Mandolino Ripa

Collings MF O

MANDOLINS

MODEL		EXC. COND.	
YEAR	FEATURES	LOW	HIGH

Banjo Mandolin
1920s. Open back, 10" model.

| 1920s | | $325 | $400 |

Bowl Back Mandolin
1890s-1920s. Brazilian rosewood, spruce, rosewood ribs.

| 1920s | Less fancy | $325 | $400 |
| 1920s | More fancy | $400 | $650 |

Calace
1825-present. Nicola Calace started The Calace Liuteria lute-making workshop in 1825 on the island of Procida, which is near Naples. The business is now in Naples and still in the family.

Lyre/Harp-Style Mandolin
Late-1800s-early-1900s. Lyre/harp-style, 8 strings, round soundhole, slightly bent top. Condition is important for these older instruments and the price noted is for a fully functional, original or pro-restored example.

| 1900 | | $1,200 | $1,500 |

Carvin
1946-present. Carvin offered solidbody electric mandolins from around '56 to the late '60s, when they switched to a traditional pear-shaped electric/acoustic. They also offer guitars, basses and amps.

MB Mandolin
1956-1968. Solidbody, 1 pickup, single-cut Les Paul shape until '64, double-cut Jazzmaster/Strat shape after. Models include the #1-MB and the #2-MB, with different pickups.

| 1950s | | $1,400 | $1,700 |

Clifford
Clifford mandolins were manufactured by Kansas City, Missouri instrument wholesalers J.W. Jenkins & Sons. First introduced in 1895, the brand also offered guitars.

Cole
1890-1919. After leaving Fairbanks & Cole in 1890, W.A. Cole started his own line. He also made guitars and banjos.

Imperial G Bowl Back Mandolin
1905-1910. 27 ribs.

| 1905-1910 | | $900 | $1,150 |

Collings
1986-present. Professional and premium grade, production/custom, mandolins built in Austin, Texas. Collings added mandolins to their line in '99. They also build guitars and ukuleles.

MF Mandolin
1999-present. F-style, carved top and back.

| 1999-2014 | | $3,100 | $3,900 |

MF-5 Deluxe Mandolin
2005. Limited production, varnish finish, hand engraved nickel tailpiece unique to each instrument.

| 2005 | | $10,100 | $12,600 |

MODEL		EXC. COND.	
YEAR	FEATURES	LOW	HIGH

MF-5V Mandolin
2007. Carved Adirondack spruce top, highly flamed maple body.

| 2007 | | $6,100 | $7,600 |

MT Mandolin
1999-present. A-style, 2 f-holes, carved top and back, matte finish, tortoise-bound top.

| 1999-2014 | | $1,725 | $2,150 |

MT-2 Mandolin
1999-present. MT with high gloss finish, ivoroid body, neck and headstock binding.

| 1999-2014 | | $2,700 | $3,400 |

MT-2V Mandolin
2009-present. Like MT-2, but with oil-based varnish finish and ivoroid-bound ebony 'guard.

| 2009-2014 | | $3,000 | $3,800 |

Comins
1992-present. Luthier Bill Comins builds premium and presentation grade, custom mandolins in Willow Grove, Pennsylvania. He also builds guitars and offers an amp.

Conrad
Ca. 1968-1977. Imported from Japan by David Wexler and Company, Chicago, Illinois. Mid- to better-quality copy guitars, mandolins and banjos.

Crafter
1986-present. Intermediate grade, production, solidbody basses made in Korea. They also build guitars and mandolins.

Crestwood
1970s. Copy models imported by La Playa Distributing Company of Detroit.

Mandolin
1970s. Includes models 3039 (electric A-style), 3041 (bowl back-style, flower 'guard), 3043 (bowl back-style, plain 'guard), 71820 (A-style), and 71821 (F-style).

| 1970s | | $160 | $200 |

Cromwell
1935-1939. Private branded instruments made by Gibson at their Parsons Street factory in Kalamazoo, Michigan. Distributed by a variety of mail order companies such as Continental, Grossman, and Richter & Phillips.

GM-2 Mandolin
1935-1939. Spruce top, mahogany back and sides, similar to KM-11.

| 1935-1939 | | $600 | $750 |

GM-4 Mandolin
1935-1939. Style A, f-holes, solid wood arched top, mahogany back and sides, block capital letter Cromwell headstock logo, dot markers, elevated 'guard, sunburst.

| 1935-1939 | | $675 | $850 |

Dan Kellaway
1976-present. Luthier Dan Kellaway builds his production/custom, premium grade, mandolins in Singleton NSW, Australia. He also builds guitars.

MODEL YEAR	FEATURES	EXC. COND. LOW	HIGH

D'Angelico

1932-1964. Handcrafted by John D'Angelico. Models include Excel, Teardrop, and Scroll. Appointments can vary from standard to higher-end so each mandolin should be evaluated on a case-by-case basis.

D'Aquisto

1965-1995. James D'Aquisto apprenticed under D'Angelico. He started his own production in '65.

Dayton

1910-late 1930s. Mandolins built by luthier Charles B. Rauch in Dayton, Ohio. He also built banjos, violins, guitars and banjo-ukuleles.

Style B Mandolin

1911		$1,400	$1,750

Dean

1976-present. Intermediate grade, production, acoustic and acoustic/electric mandolins made overseas. They also offer guitars, banjos, basses, and amps.

Dearstone

1993-present. Luthier Ray Dearstone builds his professional and premium grade, custom, mandolin-family instruments in Blountville, Tennessee. He also builds guitars and violins.

DeCava Guitars

1983-present. Premium grade, production/custom, mandolins built by luthier Jim DeCava in Stratford, Connecticut. He also builds guitars, ukes, and banjos.

DeGennaro

2003-present. Professional and premium grade, custom/production, acoustic and electric mandolins built by luthier William DeGennaro in Grand Rapids, Michigan. He also builds guitars and basses.

Delgado

1928-present. Luthier Manuel A. Delgado builds premium grade, custom, classical mandolins in Nashville, Tennessee. He also builds guitars, basses, ukuleles and banjos.

DeLucia, Vincenzo

1910s-1920s. Luthier Vincenzo DeLucia built mandolins in Philadelphia, Pennsylvania.

Mandolin

Early-1900s. High quality material, rosewood body, fine ornamentation.

1910s		$950	$1,200

Dennis Hill Guitars

Premium grade, production/custom, mandolins built by luthier Dennis Hill in Panama City, Florida. He has also built dulcimers, guitars, and violins.

Dillion

1996-present. Dillion, of Cary, North Carolina, offers intermediate grade, production, semi-hollow electric mandolins made in Korea and Vietnam. They also have guitars and basses.

Ditson

Mandolins made for the Oliver Ditson Company of Boston, an instrument dealer and music publisher. Turn of the century and early-1900s models were bowl back-style with the Ditson label. The '20s Ditson Style A flat back mandolins were made by Martin. Models were also made by Lyon & Healy of Boston, often with a Ditson Empire label.

Mandola

1920. Bowl back.

1920		$900	$1,150

Style A Mandolin

1920s. Style A flat back made by Martin, mahogany sides and back, plain ornamentation.

1920s		$900	$1,150

Victory Mandolin

1890s. Brazilian rib bowl back with fancy inlays.

1890s		$725	$900

Dobro

1929-1942, 1954-present. Dobro offered mandolins throughout their early era and from the '60s to the mid-'90s.

Mandolin

1930s-1960s. Resonator on wood body.

1930s-60s		$950	$1,200

Dudenbostel

1989-present. Luthier Lynn Dudenbostel builds his limited production, premium and presentation grade, custom, mandolins in Knoxville, Tennessee. He started with guitars and added mandolins in '96.

F-5 Mandolin

1996-2005. Loar-style, about 30 made.

1996-2005		$18,000	$22,500

Duff Mandolins

1982-present. Premium and presentation grade, custom/production, mandolin family instruments built by luthier Paul Duff in Palmyra, Western Australia.

F-5 (Loar) Mandolin

1999	Adirondack	$5,200	$6,600

Dyer

1902-1939. House brand for the W. J. Dyer store in St. Paul, Minnesota. The Larson brothers of Chicago built mandolin family instruments for the store from around 1906 to 1920. Other companies also built instruments for them.

Eastman

1992-present. Intermediate and professional grade, production, mandolins built in China. Eastman added mandolins in '04. They also build guitars, violins, and cellos.

1937 D'Angelico Scroll
Laurence Wexer

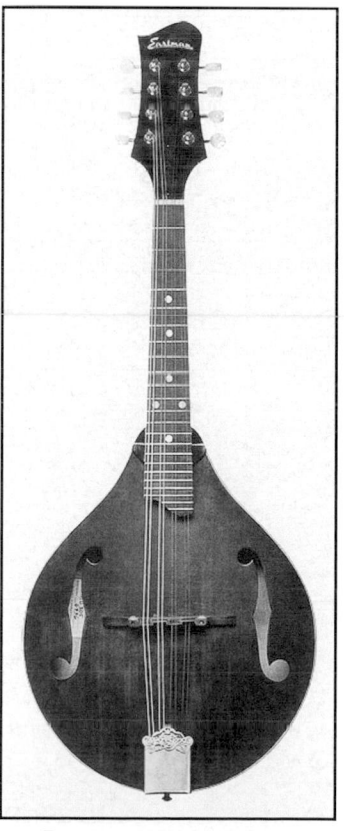

Eastman MD305 A-Style

MANDOLINS

Eastwood Mandocaster

Epiphone MM-50

MODEL YEAR	FEATURES	EXC. COND. LOW	HIGH

Eastwood

1997-present. Intermediate grade, production, solidbody electric mandolins. They also offer basses and guitars.

EKO

1961-1985, 2000-present. The Italian-made EKOs were imported by LoDuca Brothers of Milwaukee. The brand was revived around 2000, but does not currently include mandolins.

Baritone Mandolin

1960s. Baritone mandolin with ornate inlays.

1960s		$400	$500

Octave Mandolin

1960s. Octave mandolin with ornate inlays.

1960s		$400	$500

Eleca

2004-present. Student/budget level, production, acoustic and electric mandolins, imported by Eleca International. They also offer guitars, amps and effects.

Elijah Jewel

2009-present. Professional grade, production/custom, acoustic mandolins built by luthier Michael Kerry in Mineola, Texas. He also builds guitars.

Epiphone

1928-present. Intermediate grade, production, acoustic mandolins. Epiphone has offered several mandolin-family models over the years. Those from the '30s to the '60s were U.S.-made, the later models imported.

Adelphi Mandolin

1932-1948. A-style body, maple back and sides, f-holes, single-bound top and back.

1932-1948		$900	$1,100

Mandobird VIII Mandolin

2004-2012. Reverse Firebird-style body with mandolin neck, electric, various colors.

2004-2012		$170	$210

MM Series Mandolin

1979-present. Imported A and F styles.

2005-2013	MM20, A-style	$100	$125
1980-2015	MM30, A-style	$125	$150
1979-1913	MM50, F-style	$325	$400
1979-1985	MM70, F style	$425	$550

Strand Mandolin

1932-1958. Walnut back and sides, f-holes, multibound, sunburst.

1944-1947		$950	$1,175

Venetian Electric Mandolin

1961-1970. Gibson-made, pear-shaped body, 4 pole P-90 'dog-ear' mounted pickup, volume and tone knobs, dot markers, sunburst finish.

1961-1964		$1,350	$1,675
1965-1970		$1,350	$1,675

Windsor Special Mandolin

1936-1949. Scroll body, f-holes, slot-block inlays.

1940s		$12,000	$15,000

MODEL YEAR	FEATURES	EXC. COND. LOW	HIGH

Zephyr Mandolin

1939-1958. A-style, electric, f-holes, maple body, 1 pickup, slotted block inlay.

1950s		$600	$750

Esquire

1930s. Student level instruments with painted Esquire logo and painted wood grain.

Mandolin

1930s. Laminate A-style wood body, sunburst.

1930s		$250	$310

Euphonon

1930-1944. Euphonon was a brand of the Larson Brothers of Chicago, introduced so Larson could compete in the guitar market with the new larger body 14-fret guitar models. Production also included mandolins, and most models were A-style, with teardrop body and flat backs.

Everett Guitars

1977-present. Luthier Kent Everett, of Atlanta, Georgia, mainly builds guitars, but has also built mandolins.

Evergreen Mountain

1971-present. Professional grade, custom, mandolins built by luthier Jerry Nolte in Cove, Oregon. He also builds guitars and basses.

Fairbanks

1875-1922. Primarily known for banjos, Fairbanks also offered banjo mandolins when owned by Vega.

Little Wonder Banjo Mandolin

1920s. Banjo body, mando neck, dot inlays.

1921		$450	$550

Style K Banjo Mandolin

1920s. Banjo body, mando neck, dot inlays.

1920		$400	$500

Fairbuilt Guitar Co.

2000-present. Professional grade, custom/production, mandolins built by luthiers Martin Fair and Stuart Orser in Loudoun County, Virginia. They also build guitars.

Falk

1989-present. Luthier Dave Falk builds professional and premium grade, production/custom mandolins, in Amarillo, Texas. He also builds guitars and dulcimers.

Fender

1946-present. Intermediate grade, production, acoustic and acoustic/electric mandolins. Fender also offered an electric mandolin for 20 years.

FM Series Mandolin

2001-present. Made in Korea, acoustic and acoustic-electric, models include 52E (acou-elec, A-style), 53S (acoustic, A-style), 60E (5 string, 2 pu) and 61SE (8-string, 1 pu) (both acou-elec, double-cut, block-

MODEL YEAR	FEATURES	EXC. COND. LOW	HIGH

end 'board), 62SE (acou-elec, double-cut, extended 'board), 63S (acoustic, F-style), 63SE (acou-elec, F-style), 100 (acoustic, A-style).

2001-2002	FM-60E/61SE	$300	$375
2001-2007	FM-62SE/62SCE	$300	$375
2001-2014	FM-52E	$110	$135
2001-2014	FM-53S	$135	$165
2001-2014	FM-63S	$250	$310
2011-2014	FM-63SE/63SCE	$285	$360
2013-2014	FM-100	$70	$85

Mandolin
1956-1976. Electric solidbody, often referred to as the Mandocaster by collectors.

1956-1957	Blond	$2,600	$3,300
1958-1959	Sunburst	$2,100	$2,700
1960-1965	Sunburst	$1,800	$2,300
1966-1976	Sunburst	$1,700	$2,200

Fine Resophonic
1988-present. Professional grade, production/custom, wood and metal-bodied resophonic mandolins built by luthiers Mike Lewis and Pierre Avocat in Vitry Sur Seine, France. They also build guitars and ukes.

Flatiron
1977-2003, 2006-2009. Gibson purchased Flatiron in 1987. Production was in Bozeman, Montana until the end of '96, when Gibson closed the Flatiron mandolin workshop and moved mandolin assembly to Nashville, Tennessee. General production tapered off after the move and Flatirons were available on a special order basis for a time. The brand was revived in '06 on an import model sold through Epiphone.

A Style Mandolins
Includes A style Performer series (1990-'95, maple back & sides, mahogany neck, ebony board, top binding, sunburst) and Festival series (1988-'95, same, in cherry finish and with no binding).

1988-1995	Festival	$1,000	$1,250
1990-1995	Performer	$1,100	$1,350

A-2 Mandolin
1977-1987	Early, no truss rod	$2,600	$3,200

A-5 Mandolin
Teardrop shape, f-holes, figured maple body and neck, carved spruce top, X-bracing, unbound ebony 'board, nickel hardware, fleur-de-lis headstock inlay.

1987-1994	Gibson Montana	$1,300	$1,600
1996-2003		$1,300	$1,600

A-5 1 Mandolin
Carved top and back, bound body, dot inlays, The Flatiron headstock inlay.

1983-1985	Pre-Gibson	$2,600	$3,200

A-5 2 Mandolin
Carved top and back, bound body, neck, headstock and pickguard, dot inlays, modified fern headstock inlay.

1983-1985	Pre-Gibson	$3,200	$3,950

A-5 Artist Mandolin
A-5 with highly figured maple body and neck, bound ebony headstock, gold hardware, fern headstock inlay.

1987-1990	Gibson Montana	$2,400	$3,000
1996-2003		$1,900	$2,400

A-5 Junior Mandolin
As A-5 but with tone bar bracing, mahogany neck, The Flatiron headstock inlay.

1987-1990	Gibson Montana	$950	$1,150
1996-2003		$950	$1,150

Cadet Mandolin
Flat-top, teardrop body, spruce top, maple body, rosewood 'board, nickel hardware.

1990-1996		$500	$625

F Style Mandolin
Includes F style Performer series (1990-'95, maple back & sides and neck, ebony board, fern/banner headstock inlay, top and back of body and headstock bound, sunburst top) and Festival series (1988-'95, same, but without headstock or back binding).

1988-1995	Festival	$2,400	$2,975
1990-1995	Performer	$2,500	$3,100
2001	Festival, Gibson Montana	$2,400	$2,975

F-2 Mandolin
1977-1987	Early, no truss rod	$5,200	$6,400

F-5 Mandolin
F-style body, f-holes, flamed maple body and neck, carved spruce top, tone bar bracing, bound ebony 'board and headstock, nickel hardware, flower pot headstock inlay, cherry finish.

1987-1990	Gibson Montana	$3,300	$4,100

F-5 Artist Mandolin
F-5 but with X-braces, bound ebony 'board, gold hardware, fern headstock inlay, and sunburst.

1984-1985	Pre-Gibson	$4,500	$5,600
1987-1990	Gibson Montana	$3,400	$4,300
1994-1995		$3,400	$4,300
1996-2003	Modified fern	$3,400	$4,300

Model 1 Mandola
Model 1 features.

1977-1987	Pre-Gibson	$750	$925
1983-1995	Gibson Montana	$575	$700

Model 1 Mandolin
Oval shape, spruce top, maple body, rosewood 'board, walnut headstock veneer.

1977-1987	Pre-Gibson	$725	$900
1988-1995	Gibson Montana	$575	$700

Model 2 Mandola
Model 2 features, birdseye maple (MB) or curly maple (MC) body.

1977-1987	Pre-Gibson	$850	$1,050
1988-1995	Gibson Montana	$750	$950

Model 2 Mandolin
Like Model 1, but with curly maple (MC) or birdseye maple (MB) back and sides, ebony 'board, rosewood headstock veneer.

1977-1987	Pre-Gibson	$725	$900
1977-1995	Flamed koa back/sides	$775	$950
1988-1995	Gibson Montana	$625	$775

1957 Fender Mandolin

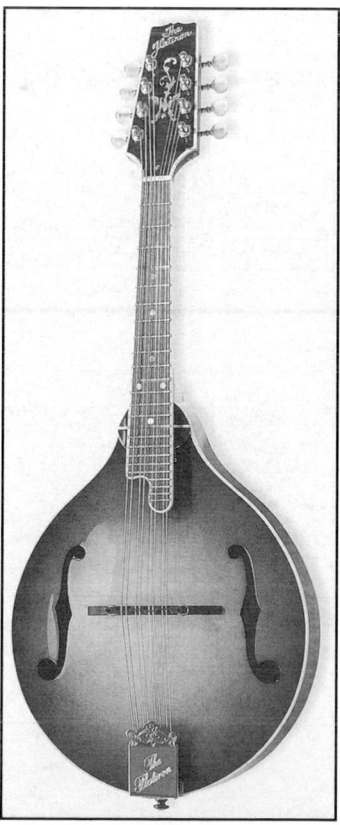

Flatiron A-5

MANDOLINS

1908 Gibson A-4
Scott J. Newman

1950 Gibson A-40

MANDOLINS

MODEL YEAR	FEATURES	EXC. COND. LOW	HIGH

Model 3 Octave Mandolin
Model 2 features, birdseye maple (MB) or curly maple (MC) body.

1977-1987	Pre-Gibson	$850	$1,050
1988-1995	Gibson Montana	$750	$950

Fletcher Brock Stringed Instruments
1992-present. Custom mandolin-family instruments made by luthier Fletcher Brock originally in Ketchum, Idaho, and currently in Seattle, Washington. He also builds guitars.

Fox Hollow Guitars
2004-present. Professional and premium grade, custom, acoustic and electric mandolins built by luthier Don Greenough in Eugene, Oregon. He also builds guitars.

Framus
1946-1977, 1996-present. Founded in Erlangen, Germany by Fred Wilfer. In the '60s, Framus instruments were imported into the U.S. by Philadelphia Music Company. They offered acoustic and electric mandolins. The brand was revived in '96.

12-String Mandolin

1960s		$425	$550

Freshwater
1992-2011. Luthier Dave Freshwater and family built mandolin family instruments in Beauly, Inverness, Scotland. They also built bouzoukis, dulcimers and harps.

Furch
See listing for Stonebridge.

Fylde
1973-present. Luthier Roger Bucknall builds his intermediate and professional, production/custom mandolins and mandolas in Penrith, Cumbria, United Kingdom. He also builds guitars and basses, bouzoukis, and citterns.

G.L. Stiles
1960-1994. Built by Gilbert Lee Stiles in Florida. He also built acoustics, solidbodies, basses, steels, and banjos.

Galiano/A. Galiano
New Yorkers Antonio Cerrito and Raphael Ciani offered instruments built by them and others under the Galiano brand during the early 1900s.

Mandolin
Bowl back, some fancy appointments.

1920s		$375	$475

Galveston
Budget and intermediate grade, production, imported mandolins. They also offer basses and guitars.

MODEL YEAR	FEATURES	EXC. COND. LOW	HIGH

Gaylord
1940s. Private brand made by Harmony, painted Gaylord logo on headstock.

Artistic A Mandolin

1940s	Painted logo	$200	$250

Giannini
1900-present. Acoustic mandolins built in Salto, SP, Brazil near Sao Paolo. They also build guitars, violas, and cavaquinhos.

Gibson
1890s (1902)-present. Orville Gibson created the violin-based mandolin body-style that replaced the bowl back-type. Currently Gibson offers professional, premium and presentation grade, production/custom, mandolins.

Special Designations:
Snakehead headstock: 1922-1927 with production possible for a few months plus or minus.
Lloyd Loar era: Mid-1922-late 1924 with production possible for a few months plus or minus.

Mandolin (Orville Gibson)
1890s-1902. Mandolin models built during Orville Gibson era, before he sold out to others in 1902, covering a range of features and levels of appointments.

1890s-1902	Less rare, plain	$4,000	$6,000
1980s-1902	Rare, fancy	$20,000	$25,000

A Mandolin
1902-1933. Oval soundhole, snakehead headstock '22-27, Loar era mid-'22-late-'24.

1902-1918	Orange	$1,400	$1,775
1918-1921	Brown	$1,400	$1,775
1922-1924	Loar era	$2,650	$3,300
1925-1933		$2,450	$3,100

A-0 Mandolin
1927-1933. Replaces A Jr., oval soundhole, dot inlay, brown finish.

1927-1933		$1,450	$1,800

A-00 Mandolin
1933-1943. Oval soundhole, dot inlay, carved bound top.

1933-1943	Sunburst	$1,450	$1,800

A-1 Mandolin
1902-1918, 1922-1927, 1933-1943. Snakehead headstock '23-'27.

1902-1918	Orange	$1,550	$1,950
1922-1924	Loar era	$3,000	$3,800
1925-1927	Black	$2,300	$2,900
1927	Not snaked	$2,300	$2,900
1927	Snaked	$2,300	$2,900
1929		$2,300	$2,900
1932	Re-intro., oval	$2,300	$2,900
1933-1943	Sunburst, f-holes	$1,500	$1,875

A-2/A-2Z Mandolin
1902-1908, 1918-1922. A-2Z '22-'27. Renamed A-2 '27-'28. Snakehead headstock '23-'27. Lloyd Loar era mid-'22-late-'24.

1902-1908	Orange	$1,650	$2,050
1918-1921	Brown	$1,650	$2,050

MODEL YEAR	FEATURES	EXC. COND. LOW	HIGH
1922-1924	Loar Era	$5,000	$6,200
1923-1924	Loar era, extra binding	$5,000	$6,200
1925-1928		$2,100	$2,600

A-3 Mandolin

1902-1922. Oval soundhole, single-bound body, dot inlay.

1902-1917	Orange	$2,000	$2,500
1918-1922	Ivory	$2,200	$2,750

A-4 Mandolin

1902-1935. Oval soundhole, single-bound body, dot inlay, snakehead '23-'27.

1902-1917	Various colors	$2,300	$2,900
1918-1921	Dark mahogany	$2,300	$2,900
1922-1924	Loar era	$5,400	$6,700
1925-1935	Various colors	$2,800	$3,500

A-5 Mandolin

1957-1979. Oval soundhole, maple back and sides, dot inlay, scroll headstock, sunburst. Name now used on extended neck version.

1957-1969		$1,900	$2,400
1970-1979		$1,300	$1,650

A-5G Mandolin

1988-1996. Less ornate version of the A-5 L, abalone fleur-de-lis headstock inlay.

1988-1996		$1,575	$1,975

A-5L/A-5 Mandolin

1988-2013. Extended neck, raised 'board, flowerpot headstock inlay, curly maple and spruce, sunburst, based on custom-made 1923 Loar A-5. L has been dropped from name.

1988-2013		$2,150	$2,675

A-9 Mandolin

2002-2013. Spruce top, maple back and sides, black bound top, satin brown finish.

2002-2013		$1,200	$1,500

A-12 Mandolin

1970-1979. F-holes, long neck, dot inlay, fleur-de-lis inlay, sunburst.

1970-1979		$1,100	$1,400

A-40 Mandolin

1948-1970. F-holes, bound top, dot inlay, natural or sunburst.

1948-1949		$1,175	$1,450
1950-1959		$1,100	$1,350
1960-1964		$900	$1,125
1965-1970		$950	$1,175

A-50 Mandolin

1933-1971. A-style oval bound body, f-holes, sunburst.

1933	Oval soundhole	$1,550	$1,925
1934-1937	Larger 11.25" body	$1,550	$1,925
1938-1941		$1,550	$1,925
1942-1949	Smaller 10" body	$1,150	$1,425
1950-1959		$1,100	$1,375
1960-1964		$1,000	$1,250
1965-1971		$950	$1,175

A-75 Mandolin

1934-1936. F-holes, raised fingerboard, bound top and back.

1934-1936		$2,100	$2,600

A-C Century Mandolin

1933-1934, 1936-1937. A body, built to commemorate the 1933-1934 Century of Progress Exhibition in Chicago, pearloid 'board.

1933-1937		$3,500	$4,500

A-Junior Mandolin

1920-1927. The Junior was the entry level mandolin for Gibson, but like most entry level Gibsons (re: Les Paul Junior), they were an excellent product. Oval soundhole, dot markers, plain tuner buttons. Becomes A-0 in '27.

1920-1927	Sheraton Brown	$1,450	$1,800

AN-Custom (Army-Navy) Mandolin

Mid-1990s. Made in Bozeman, Montana, round teardrop shape, flat spruce top, flat maple back, maple rims, Gibson script logo on headstock.

1995		$1,000	$1,250

Army and Navy Special Style DY/Army-Navy Mandolin

1918-1922. Lower-end, flat top and back, round soundhole, no logo, round label with model name, brown stain. Reintroduced as Army-Navy (AN Custom) '88-'96.

1918-1922		$700	$875

C-1 Mandolin

1932. Flat top, mahogany back and sides, oval soundhole, natural, painted on guard, a '32 version of the Army and Navy Special. This model was private branded for Kel Kroydon in the early-'30s.

1932		$700	$875

CB-3 Mando-Cello (Cello Banjo)

1930s. TB-3 Mastertone rim, 4 strings.

1930s		$3,200	$4,000

D "The Alrite" Mandolin

1917. Round body style, round soundhole, The Alrite on inside label, colored wood on top binding and around center hole.

1917		$1,000	$1,250

EM-100/EM-125 Mandolin

1938-1943. Initially called EM-100, renamed EM-125 in '41-'43. Style A (pear-shape) archtop body, 1 blade pickup, 2 knobs on either side of bridge, dot markers, tortoise 'guard, sunburst.

1938-1940	EM-100	$1,450	$1,825
1941-1943	EM-125	$1,450	$1,825

EM-150 Mandolin

1936-1971. Electric, A-00 body, 1 Charlie Christian pickup early on, 1 P-90 later, bound body, sunburst.

1936-1940	Charlie Christian pickup	$2,400	$3,000
1941-1949	Rectangular pickup	$1,350	$1,700
1949-1965	P-90 pickup	$1,350	$1,675
1966-1971	P-90 pickup	$1,350	$1,675

EM-200/Florentine Mandolin

1954-1971. Electric solidbody, 1 pickup, gold-plated hardware, 2 control knobs, dot markers, sunburst. Called the EM-200 in '60 and '61.

1954-1960	Florentine	$3,000	$3,800
1960-1961	Renamed EM-200	$3,000	$3,800

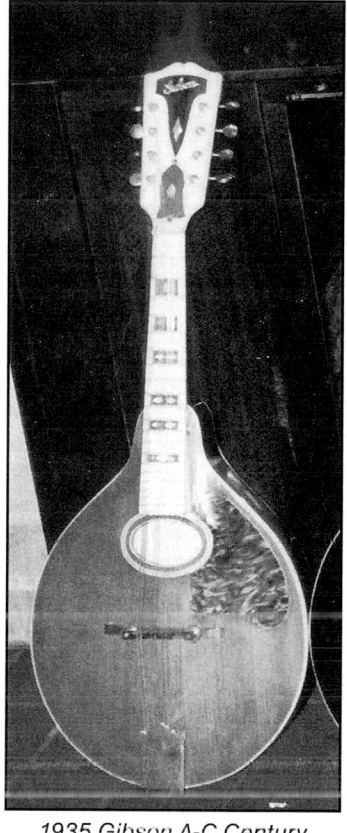

1935 Gibson A-C Century
John C. Ellig

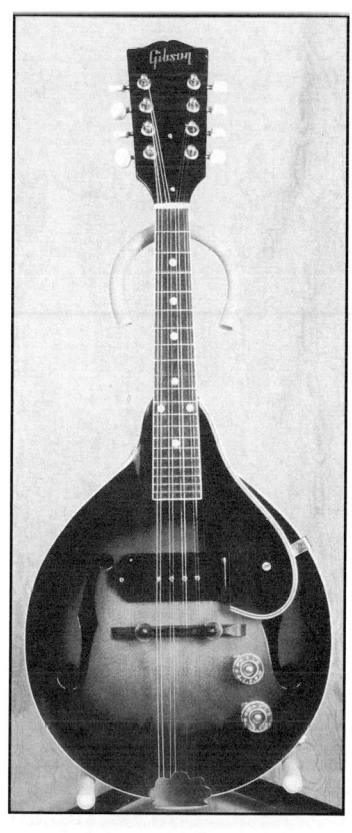

1954 Gibson EM-150
Tom Smiley

To get the most from this book, be sure to read "Using *The Guide*" in the introduction.

1904 Gibson F-2

Scott J. Newman

1918 Gibson F-4

MODEL YEAR	FEATURES	EXC. COND. LOW	HIGH
1962-1965	Renamed Florentine	$3,000	$3,800
1966-1969	Florentine	$2,500	$3,100
1970-1971	Florentine	$2,500	$3,100

F Mandolin

1900-1903. 1900 model has O.H. Gibson Kalamazoo label, 3-point unbound body, early Gibson F-style, historically important design, inlaid star and crescent headstock. 1903 model is 3-point F-style, bound top rope-style, fancy inlay below-the-string guard, inlaid star and crescent headstock, large dot markers, black finish. Early F-style mandolin ornamentation can vary and values will vary accordingly.

1900	1900, signed by Orville	$4,000	$25,000
1900	1900, unsigned	$3,000	$20,000
1901-1902		$2,000	$13,000
1903		$1,800	$12,000

Bill Monroe Model F Mandolin

1992-1995. Limited run of 200, sunburst.

1991-1995	Lacquer	$10,000	$12,500
1991-1995	Varnish	$10,000	$12,500

Doyle Lawson F Mandolin

2003-present. Artist Series, F-5 style, carved spruce top, figured maple sides and back, sunburst finish.

2003-2014		$5,400	$6,600

F-2 Mandolin

1902-1934. Oval soundhole, pearl inlay, star and crescent inlay on peghead.

1902-1909	3-point	$3,300	$4,100
1910-1921	2-point	$3,300	$4,100
1922-1924	Loar era	$5,000	$6,300
1925-1934		$4,000	$5,000

F-3 Mandolin

1902-1908. Three-point body, oval soundhole, scroll peghead, pearl inlayed 'guard, limited production model, black top with red back and sides.

1902-1908		$4,000	$5,000

F-4 Mandolin

1902-1943. Oval soundhole, rope pattern binding, various colors.

1902-1909	3-point	$5,600	$7,000
1910-1921	2-point	$5,600	$7,000
1922-1924	Loar era	$5,900	$7,500
1925-1943		$5,100	$6,500

F-5 Mandolin

1922-1943; 1949-1980. F-holes, triple-bound body and 'guard. The '20s Lloyd Loar era F-5s are extremely valuable. Reintroduced in '49 with single-bound body, redesigned in '70. The Loar era F-5 market is very specialized to the point that individual instrument valuations can vary based upon the actual sound of the particular instrument. Valuations should be considered on a case-by-case basis.

1922	Loar no virzi	$136,000	$178,000
1923	Loar July 9, 1923, side bound	$140,000	$185,000
1923	Loar non-side bound	$136,000	$178,000
1924	Late-1924, unsigned	$95,000	$125,000

MODEL YEAR	FEATURES	EXC. COND. LOW	HIGH
1924	Loar Feb. 18, 1924	$140,000	$185,000
1924	Loar March 31, 1924	$135,000	$180,000
1924	Loar no virzi	$135,000	$180,000
1924	Loar with virzi	$120,000	$160,000
1925-1928	Fern, Master Model	$69,000	$90,000
1928-1929	Fern, not Master Model	$53,000	$70,000
1930-1931	Fern peghead inlay	$45,000	$60,000
1932-1935	Fern peghead inlay	$41,000	$54,000
1936-1937	Fern peghead inlay	$29,000	$38,000
1938-1940		$29,000	$38,000
1940-1943	Fleur-de-lis peghead inlay	$25,000	$33,000
1949	Flower pot, mahogany neck	$8,500	$11,000
1950-1953	Flower pot, maple neck	$6,500	$8,600
1954	Flower pot peghead inlay	$6,500	$8,600
1955-1956	Flower pot peghead inlay	$6,300	$8,200
1957-1959	Flower pot peghead inlay	$5,200	$6,800
1960-1965		$4,700	$6,200
1966-1969	Sunburst	$3,800	$5,000
1970-1980	Sunburst	$3,300	$4,200

F-5 Custom Mandolin

1993. Custom Shop model.

1993		$7,500	$9,500

F-5 Fern Mandolin

2003-2010. Custom Shop model.

2003-2010		$5,300	$6,600

F-5 Master Model Mandolin

2003-present. F-holes, triple-bound body and guard, red spruce top, maple back and sides, flowerpot inlay.

2003-2004	Derrington signed	$10,000	$13,700
2003-2009	F-5 Distressed	$12,000	$16,000
2003-2013	Ricky Skaggs Distressed	$13,700	$18,000
2003-2014		$9,500	$12,700

F-5G/F-5G Deluxe Mandolin

1997-present. Two point style F, Deluxe has a slightly wider neck profile.

1997-2014		$3,000	$3,700

F-5L/F-5L "The Fern" Mandolin

1978-present. Reissue of Loar F-5, gold hardware, fern headstock inlay (flowerpot inlay with silver hardware also offered for '88-'91), sunburst.

1978-1984	Kalamazoo-made	$4,800	$6,300
1984-1999		$5,800	$7,600
2000-2014		$5,000	$6,500

F-5V Mandolin

1990s-2000s. Based on Lloyd Loar's original F-5s of 1922-24, varnish Cremona Brown sunburst finish.

1990-2000s		$6,800	$8,200

The *Vintage Guitar Price Guide* shows low to high values for items in all-original excellent condition, and, where applicable, with original case or cover.

MODEL		EXC. COND.	
YEAR	FEATURES	LOW	HIGH

F-5X Mandolin

1996. F-5 Fern model, X-braced.

1996		$4,800	$6,000

Bella Voce F-5 Mandolin

1989. Custom Shop master-built model, high-end materials and construction, engraved tailpiece with Bella Voce F-5, sunburst.

1989		$6,600	$8,200

Sam Bush Signature F-5 Mandolin

2000-present. Artist Series model, carved spruce top, gold hardware, built at Opry Mill plant in Nashville.

2000-2014		$5,000	$6,300

Wayne Benson Signature F-5 Mandolin

2003-2006. Limited edition of 50, solid spruce top, figured maple back, sides and neck, gold hardware, vintage red satin.

2003-2006		$5,300	$6,500

F-7 Mandolin

1934-1940 F-holes, single-bound body, neck and 'guard, short neck, fleur-de-lis peghead inlay, sunburst.

1934-1937		$7,900	$10,000

F-9 Mandolin

2002-present. F-5 style, carved spruce top, no inlays, black bound body.

2002-2014		$1,750	$2,150

F-10 Mandolin

1934-1936. Slight upgrade of the '34 F-7 with extended 'board and upgraded inlay, black finish.

1934-1936		$12,000	$15,000

F-12 Mandolin

1934-1937, 1948-1980. F-holes, bound body and neck, scroll inlay, raised 'board until '37, 'board flush with top '48-on, sunburst.

1934-1937		$10,100	$12,500
1948-1959		$3,300	$4,100
1960-1964		$3,300	$4,100
1965-1969		$2,700	$3,300
1970-1980		$2,600	$3,200

H-1 Mandola

1902-1936. Has same features as A-1 mandolin, but without snakehead headstock.

1902-1908	Orange	$1,600	$2,100
1918-1921	Brown	$2,000	$2,700
1922-1924	Loar era	$3,000	$3,900
1925-1928		$2,700	$3,500

H-1E Mandola

Late-1930s. Limited number built, electric with built-in adjustable bar pickup, sunburst.

1938		$3,500	$4,300

H-2 Mandola

1902-1922. Has same features as A-4 mandolin.

1902-1917	Various colors	$2,700	$3,400
1918-1921	Dark Mahogany	$3,300	$4,100

H-4 Mandola

1910-1940. Same features as F-4 mandolin.

1910-1921		$6,500	$8,200
1922-1924	Loar era	$8,000	$10,000
1925-1940		$7,000	$8,500

H-5 Mandola

1923-1929 (available by special order 1929-1936), 1990-1991. Same features as the high-end F-5 Mandolin. This is a very specialized market and instruments should be evaluated on a case-by-case basis.

1923-1924	Loar era	$75,000	$92,000
1990-1991	Limited production	$4,800	$5,900

J Mando Bass

1912-1931. Large 24" wide A-style body, 4 strings, extension endpin for upright bass-style playing, optional colors available.

1912-1917	Sunburst	$5,000	$6,300
1918-1922	Brown	$5,000	$6,300
1923-1931	Black	$5,000	$6,300

K-1 Mandocello

1902-1943. Same features as H-1 mandola, off & on production, special order available.

1902-1908	Orange	$3,300	$4,100
1918-1921	Brown	$3,300	$4,100
1922-1924	Loar era	$4,000	$5,000
1925-1943		$3,500	$4,300

K-2 Mandocello

1902-1922. Same features as A-4 mandolin.

1902-1917	Black or red	$3,800	$4,700
1918-1922		$3,800	$4,700

K-4 Mandocello

1912-1929 (offered as special order post-1929). Same features as F-4 mandolin, sunburst.

1912-1921		$7,300	$9,200
1922-1924	Loar era	$13,000	$16,000
1925-1929		$7,600	$9,500

M-6 (Octave Guitar)

2002-2006. A-style mandolin body, short-scale 6-string guitar neck.

2002-2006		$1,125	$1,400

MB-1 Mandolin Banjo

1922-1923, 1925-1937.

1922-1937		$875	$1,100

MB-2 Mandolin Banjo

1920-1923, 1926-1937.

1920-1937		$1,025	$1,275

MB-3 Mandolin Banjo

1923-1939.

1923-1939		$1,300	$1,700

MB-4 Mandolin Banjo

1923-1932. Fleur-de-lis inlay.

1923-1932		$875	$1,100

MB-11 Mandolin Banjo

1931-1942.

1941	Pearloid headstock	$2,900	$3,700

MB-Junior Mandolin Banjo

1924-1925. Open back, budget level.

1924-1925		$650	$800

SPF-5 Mandolin

1938. F-style, single bar pickup with volume and tone controls, very limited production, natural.

1938		$21,000	$27,000

Gibson Sam Bush Signature

1923 Gibson H-4 Mandola
Vintage Instruments.

MANDOLINS

MODEL YEAR	FEATURES	EXC. COND. LOW	HIGH

Gold Tone GM-110

Gretsch G9350 Park Avenue F-Mandolin AE

Gilchrist

1978-present. Premium and presentation grade, custom, mandolins made by luthier Steve Gilchrist of Warrnambool, Australia. Custom ordered but were also initially distributed through Gruhn Guitars, Nashville, Tennessee and then exclusively by Carmel Music Company. Designs are based upon Gibson mandolins built between 1910 and '25.

Mandola
1999. Classical styling.

1999		$18,000	$23,000

Model 1 Mandolin
Model A Jr. style.

2000		$6,100	$7,500

Model 4 Junior Mandolin
Model F style.

2012		$9,500	$12,000

Model 4 Mandolin
F style, scroll body, oval hole.

1978-2006		$12,500	$15,500

Model 5 Mandolin
1978-present. Based on the Gibson '22-'24 Loar-era F-5 mandolin, Gilchrist slant logo, spruce top, flamed maple back, sides, and neck, ebony 'board, multiple binding, sunburst.

1978-2014		$18,000	$23,000

Model 5C Classical Mandolin

1993	Blond	$18,000	$23,000

Givens

1962-1992. Luthier R. L. (Bob) Givens handcrafted about 800 mandolins and another 700 in a production shop.

A Mandolin
1962-1975. Early production A-style.

1962-1975		$2,900	$3,700

A-3 Mandolin
Mid-1970s-mid-1980s. Distinguished by use of decal (the only model with Givens decal).

1975-1988		$2,900	$3,700

A-4 Mandolin
1988-1993. No 'board binding, simple block-like multiple-line RL Givens inlay, nicer maple.

1988-1993		$2,900	$3,700

A-5 Mandolin
1988-1993. Bound 'board, pearl headstock inlay.

1988-1993		$2,900	$3,700

A-6 (Torch) Mandolin
1988-1992. Torch inlay (the only A model with this), gold hardware, snowflake markers.

1988-1992		$3,700	$4,700

A-6 Custom Mandolin
1991-1992. Elaborate customized A-6 model.

1991-1992		$4,500	$5,500

A-6 Legacy Mandolin
2007.

2007		$1,700	$2,200

F-5 (Fern) Mandolin
1973-1985. Givens' own version with fern ornamentation.

1973-1985		$6,000	$7,600

F-5 (Loar) Mandolin
1962-1972. Givens' own version based upon the Loar model F-5.

1962-1972		$6,000	$7,600

F-5 (Torch) Mandolin
1988-1992. Givens F-5 with torch inlay (the only F model with this).

1988-1992		$8,000	$10,000

F-5 (Wheat Straw) Mandolin
1986-1988. Givens F-5-style with wheat straw ornamentation.

1986-1988		$6,500	$8,100

Godin

1987-present. Intermediate grade, production, acoustic/electric mandolins from luthier Robert Godin. They also build basses and guitars.

A-8 Mandolin
2000-present. Single-cut chambered body, acoustic/electric.

2000-2014		$450	$565

Gold Tone

1993-present. Intermediate grade, production/custom mandolins built by Wayne and Robyn Rogers in Titusville, Florida. They also offer guitars, basses, lap steels, ukuleles, banjos and banjitars.

Goodman Guitars

1975-present. Premium grade, custom/production, mandolins built by luthier Brad Goodman in Brewster, New York. He also builds guitars.

Goya

1955-1996. Originally made in Sweden, by the late '70s from Japan, then from Korea.

Mandolin

1960s	Japan/Korea	$225	$300
1960s	Sweden built	$350	$500
1970s	Sweden built	$350	$500

Gretsch

1883-present. Gretsch started offering mandolins by the early 1900s, then stopped after the late '50s. In 2012 they again offered mandolins.

New Yorker Mandolin
Late 1940s-late 1950s. Teardrop shape, f-holes, arched top and back, spruce top, maple back, sides, and neck, rosewood 'board.

1940s-50s		$475	$600

G Series Mandolins
2012-present. Part of the Roots Collection, spruce top, mahogany body, rosewood 'board, includes G9300 New Yorker Standard and acoustic/electric G9320 New Yorker Deluxe.

2012-2014	New Yorker Standard	$75	$100

G Series Mandolins
2012-present. Part of the Roots Collection, spruce top, mahogany body, rosewood 'board, includes G9300 New Yorker Standard and acoustic/electric G9320 New Yorker Deluxe.

2012-2014	New Yorker Deluxe	$100	$125

MODEL YEAR	FEATURES	EXC. COND. LOW	HIGH

GTR

1974-1978. GTR (for George Gruhn, Tut Taylor, Randy Wood) was the original name for Gruhn Guitars in Nashville, Tennessee (it was changed in '76). GTR imported mandolins and banjos from Japan. An A-style (similar to a current Gibson A-5 L) and an F-style (similar to mid- to late-'20s F-5 with fern pattern) were offered. The instruments were made at the Moridaira factory in Matsumoto, Japan by factory foreman Sadamasa Tokaida. Quality was relatively high but quantities were limited.

A-Style Mandolin
1974-1978. A5-L copy with GTR logo on headstock.

1974-1978		$1,050	$1,300

F-Style Mandolin
1974-1978. F-5 Fern copy with slant GTR logo on headstock, sunburst, handmade in Japan.

1974-1978		$1,900	$2,400

Guitar Company of America

1971-present. Luthier Dixie Michell builds professional grade, production mandolins in Tulsa, Oklahoma. She also builds guitars.

Haight

1989-present. Luthier Norman Haight builds his production/custom, premium and presentation grade, acoustic mandolins in Scottsdale, Arizona. He also builds guitars.

Harmony

1892-1976, late 1970s-present. Founded by Wilhelm Schultz in 1892, and purchased by Sears in 1916. The company evolved into one of the largest producers of stringed instruments in the U.S. in the '30s.

Baroque H35/H835 Electric Mandolin
Late 1960s-early 1970s. Electric version of Baroque H425 with single pickup and two controls.

1969-1970	H35	$335	$425
1971-1976	H835	$335	$425

Baroque H425/H8025 Mandolin
F-style arched body, extreme bass bout pointy horn, close grained spruce top, sunburst.

1969-1970	H425	$300	$375
1971-1976	H8025	$300	$375

Lute H331/H8031 Mandolin
1960s-1970s. A-style, flat top and back, student level.

1960s	H331	$250	$315
1970s	H8031	$250	$315

M-100 Mandolin
1980s. A-style, sunburst.

1980s		$150	$190

Monterey H410/H417/H8017 Mandolin
1950s-1970s. A-style arched body with f-holes, sunburst.

1950s-70s	All models	$150	$190

Heiden Stringed Instruments

1974-present. Luthier Michael Heiden builds his premium grade, production/custom mandolins in Chilliwack, British Columbia. He also builds guitars.

Heritage

1985-present. Started by former Gibson employees in Gibson's Kalamazoo, Michigan plant, Heritage offered mandolins for a number of years.

H-5 Mandolin
1986-1990s. F-style scroll body, f-holes.

1986-1990s		$2,800	$3,500

Höfner

1887-present. Höfner has offered a wide variety of instruments, including mandolins, over the years. They currently again offer mandolins.

Model 545/E545 Mandolin
1960s. Pear-shaped A-style with catseye f-holes, 545 (acoustic), E545 (acoustic-electric), block-style markers, engraved headstock, Genuine Höfner Original and Made in Germany on back of headstock, transparent brown.

1968-1969	545	$375	$475
1968-1969	E545	$450	$575

Hohner

1857-present. Intermediate grade, production, acoustic and acoustic/electric mandolins. They also offer guitars, basses, banjos and ukuleles.

Holst

1984-present. Premium grade, custom, mandolins built in Creswell, Oregon by luthier Stephen Holst. He also builds guitars.

Hondo

1969-1987, 1991-2005. Budget grade, production, imported mandolins. They also offered banjos, basses and guitars. Hondo also offered mandolins from around '74 to '87.

Mandolin
1974-1987. Hondo offered F-style, A-style, and bowl back mandolin models.

1974-1987	Acoustic	$100	$135
1974-1987	Acoustic-electric	$150	$200
1974-1987	Style F	$225	$275

Hopf

1906-present. Professional grade, production/custom, mandolins made in Germany. They also make basses, guitars and flutes.

Howe-Orme

1897-ca. 1910. Elias Howe patented a guitar-shaped mandolin on November 14, 1893 and later partnered with George Orme to build a variety of mandolin family instruments and guitars in Boston.

Mandola
1897-early-1900s. Guitar body-style with narrow waist, not the common mandolin F- or S-style body, pressed (not carved) spruce top, mahogany back and sides, flat-top guitar-type trapeze bridge, decalomania near bridge.

1890s		$1,400	$1,750

Gretsch New Yorker

Heiden F Artist

MANDOLINS

Ibanez M522S

J.L. Smith Deluxe 5-String

MODEL		EXC. COND.	
YEAR	FEATURES	LOW	HIGH

Mandolinetto
1890s. Guitar body, mandolin neck and tuning, 'guard below oval soundhole, slightly arched top, Brazilian rosewood sides and back, dot/diamond/oval markers.

1890s		$1,700	$2,100

Style 4 Mandolin
1900. Guitar-shaped, Brazilian rosewood.

1900		$1,700	$2,100

Ianuario Mandolins
1990-2009. Professional and premium grade, custom, mandolins built by luthier R. Anthony Ianuario in Jefferson, Georgia. He also built banjos and violins. Tony and his wife Ann died in an auto accident in '09.

Ibanez
1932-present. Ibanez offered mandolins from '65 to '83. In '04 they again added mandolins to the product line.

Model 511 Mandolin
1974-1980. A-style, f-holes, dot markers, sunburst.

1974-1980		$275	$350

Model 513 Mandolin
1974-1979. A-5 copy with double cutaways, oval sound hole, dot markers, sunburst.

1974-1979		$325	$400

Model 514 Mandolin
1974-1979. Arched back, spruce, rosewood, dot inlays, sunburst.

1974-1979		$325	$400

Model 522 Mandolin
1974-1978. Symmetrical double point.

1974-1978		$350	$450

Model 524 Artist Mandolin
1974-1978. F-5 Loar copy, solid wood carved top and solid wood carved top and solid wood back, sunburst.

1974-1978		$800	$1,000

Model 526 (Electric) Mandolin
1974-1978. A-style body, single pickup, two control knobs, sunburst.

1974-1978		$375	$475

Model 529 Artist Mandolin
1982-1983. F-5 Loar era copy, solid wood carved top and solid wood spruce top and solid maple sides and back, sunburst.

1982-1983		$1,000	$1,250

Model M500 Series Mandolins
2004-present. F-Style and A-Style bodies, acoustic and acoustic-electric option, various finishes.

2004-2014		$50	$160

Imperial
1890-1922. Imperial mandolins were made by the William A. Cole Company of Boston, Massachusetts.

Bowl Back Mandolin

1890s		$275	$350

J.B. Player
1980s-present. Budget grade, production, imported mandolins. They also offer basses, banjos and guitars.

J.L. Smith
2008-present. Custom, intermediate and professional grade, mandolins built by luthier John L. Smith first in Myrtle Beach, South Carolina, and presently in Sebastian, Florida.

J.R. Zeidler Guitars
1977-2002. Luthier John Zeidler built premium grade, custom, mandolins in Wallingford, Pennsylvania. He also built guitars.

John Le Voi Guitars
1970-present. Production/custom, mandolin family instruments built by luthier John Le Voi in Lincolnshire, United Kingdom. He also builds guitars.

Johnson
Mid-1990s-present. Budget and intermediate grade, production, mandolins imported by Music Link, Brisbane, California. Johnson also offers guitars, amps, basses and effects.

MA Series A-Style Mandolins
Mid-1990s-2013. Import, A-style copy. Several levels offered; the range shown is for all value levels.

1990s-2013		$100	$150

MF Series F-Style Mandolins
Mid-1990s-2006. Import, F-style copy. Several levels offered; the range shown is for all value levels.

1990s-2006		$100	$225

K & S
1992-1998. Mandolins and mandolas distributed by George Katechis and Marc Silber and handmade in Paracho, Mexico. They also offered guitars and ukes.

Kalamazoo
1933-1942, 1946-1947, 1965-1970. Budget brand produced by Gibson in Kalamazoo, Michigan. They offered mandolins until '42.

Kalamazoo/Oriole A-Style Mandolin
1930s. Kalamazoo and Oriole on the headstock, KM/A-style.

1930s		$650	$800

KK-31 Mandocello
1936-1938. Archtop, f-hole body, sunburst.

1936-1938		$3,400	$4,200

KM-11 Mandolin
1935-1941. Gibson-made, A-style, flat top and back, round soundhole, dot inlay, sunburst.

1935-1941		$500	$625

KM-12N Mandolin
1935-1941. A-style with f-holes, spruce top, flamed maple sides and back, bound top and bottom, natural finish.

1935-1941		$600	$750

The *Vintage Guitar Price Guide* shows low to high values for items in all-original excellent condition, and, where applicable, with original case or cover.

MODEL		EXC. COND.	
YEAR	FEATURES	LOW	HIGH

KM-21 Mandolin

1936-1940. Gibson-made, A-style, f-holes, arched bound spruce top and mahogany back, sunburst.

| 1936-1940 | | $700 | $875 |

KM-22 Mandolin

1939-1942. Same as KM-21 with bound top and back.

| 1939-1942 | | $750 | $925 |

KMB Mandolin/Banjo

1930s. Banjo-mandolin with resonator.

| 1930s | | $450 | $550 |

Kay

1931-present. Located in Chicago, Illinois, the Kay company made an incredible amount of instruments under a variety of brands, including the Kay name. From the beginning, Kay offered several types of electric and acoustic mandolins. In '69, the factory closed, marking the end of American-made Kays. The brand survives today on imported instruments.

K68/K465 Concert Mandolin

1952-1968. Pear-shape, spruce top, mahogany back and sides, natural. Renamed the K465 in '66. Kay also offered a Venetian-style mandolin called the K68 in '37-'42.

| 1952-1968 | | $300 | $375 |

K70 Mandolin

1939-1966. Venetian-style, bound top and back, f-holes.

| 1939-1940s | | $675 | $850 |

K73 Mandolin

1939-1952. Solid spruce top, maple back and sides, A-style body, f-holes, cherry sunburst.

| 1939-1952 | | $225 | $275 |

K390/K395 Professional Electric Mandolin

1960-1968. Modified Venetian-style archtop, 1 pickup, f-hole, spruce top, curly maple back and sides, sunburst finish. Renamed K395 in '66.

| 1960-1968 | | $450 | $550 |

K494/K495 Electric Mandolin

1960-1968. A-style archtop, single metal-covered (no poles) pickup, volume and tone control knobs, sunburst. The K494 was originally about 60% of the price of the K390 model (see above) in '65. Renamed K495 in '66.

| 1960-1968 | | $350 | $450 |

Kay Kraft

1931-1937. First brand name of the newly formed Kay Company. Brand replaced by Kay in '37.

Mandocello

| 1935 | | $1,100 | $1,400 |

Mandola

| 1937 | | $750 | $925 |

Mandolin

1931-1937. Kay Kraft offered Venetian- and tear-drop-shaped mandolins.

| 1931-1937 | | $325 | $400 |

Style C Mandolin

1928-1935. Deluxe Venetian, rosewood back and sides.

| 1928-1935 | | $1,500 | $1,850 |

KB

1989-present. Luthier Ken Bebensee builds his premium grade, production/custom, mandolins in North San Juan, California. He also builds guitars and basses.

Kel Kroydon (by Gibson)

1930-1933. Private branded budget level instruments made by Gibson. They also had guitars and banjos.

KK-20 (Style C-1) Mandolin

1930-1933. Flat top, near oval-shaped body, oval soundhole, natural finish, dark finish mahogany back and sides.

| 1930-1933 | | $800 | $1,000 |

Kent

1961-1969. Japanese-made instruments. Kent offered teardrop, A style, and bowlback acoustic mandolins up to '68.

Acoustic Mandolin

1961-1968. Kent offered teardrop, A-style, and bowlback acoustic mandolins up to '68.

| 1961-1968 | | $150 | $190 |

Electric Mandolin

1964-1969. Available from '64-'66 as a solidbody electric (in left- and right-hand models) and from '67-'69 an electric hollowbody Venetian-style with f-holes (they called it violin-shaped).

| 1964-1969 | | $175 | $225 |

Kentucky (Saga M.I.)

1977-present. Brand name of Saga Musical Instruments currently offering budget, intermediate, and professional grade, production, A- and F-style mandolins. Early models made in Japan, then Korea (roughly the '90s), currently made in China.

KM Series Mandolin

1980s-present.

1980s	KM-1000 F-style	$900	$1,150
1980s	KM-180 A-style	$250	$300
1980s	KM-650 F-style	$500	$600
1980s	KM-700 F-style	$500	$600
1980s	KM-800 F-style	$500	$600
1988-2009	KM-850 F-style	$1,075	$1,350
1990-2000s	KM-250S A-style	$300	$375
1990s	KM-200S A-style	$275	$350
1990s	KM-500S A-style	$500	$625
1990s	KM-620 F-style	$500	$600
1990s	KM-675, Korea	$450	$550
2000-2014	KM-1000 F-style	$900	$1,150
2000-2014	KM-140 A-style	$100	$125
2000-2014	KM-150 A-style	$150	$185
2000-2014	KM-675	$500	$625
2000-2014	KM-700 F-style	$350	$400
2000s	KM-380S	$225	$275

Kay K73
Larry Briggs

Kentucky KM-900

MANDOLINS

Larson Brothers Harp Mandola

Lewis F5 Series

MODEL YEAR	FEATURES	EXC. COND. LOW	HIGH
2000s	KM-620 F-style	$300	$375
2000s	KM-630 F-style	$350	$425
2000s	KM-750 F-style	$485	$585
2000s	KM-800 F-style	$350	$400
2010-2014	KM-1500 F-5 style	$1,600	$2,000
2010s	KM-615 F-style	$375	$450
2011	KM-171 A-style	$185	$230
2011-2014	KM-900 A-style	$650	$800

Kimble
2000-present. Luthier Will Kimble builds his premium grade, custom/production, mandolins, mandocellos, and mandolas in Cincinnati, Ohio.

Kingston
Ca. 1958-1967. Mandolins imported from Japan by Jack Westheimer and Westheimer Importing Corporation of Chicago, Illinois. They also offered guitars, basses and banjos.
Acoustic Mandolin
1960s		$150	$190

EM1 Electric Mandolin
1964-1967. Double-cut solidbody electric, 15.75" scale, 1 pickup.
1960s		$175	$225

Knutsen
1890s-1920s. Luthier Chris J. Knutsen of Tacoma and Seattle, Washington, and Los Angeles, California after around 1916, was known for his Hawaiian and harp guitar models. He also made mandolins.

Knutson Luthiery
1981-present. Professional and premium grade, custom, acoustic and electric mandolins built by luthier John Knutson in Forestville, California. He also builds guitars, basses and lap steels.

Kona Guitar Company
2001-present. Budget grade, production, acoustic mandolins made in Asia. They also offer guitars, basses, banjos, ukes and amps.

La Scala
Ca. 1920s-1930s. A brand of the Oscar Schmidt Company of New Jersey, used on guitars, banjos, and mandolins. These were often the fanciest of the Schmidt instruments.

Lakeside (Lyon & Healy)
1890-early-1900s. Mainly catalog sales of guitars and mandolins from the Chicago maker. Marketed as a less expensive alternative to the Lyon & Healy Washburn product line.
Style G2016 12-String Mandolin
1890-early-1900s. 12-string, 18 mahogany ribs with white inlay between, celluloid guard plate, advertised as "an inexpensive instrument, possessing a good tone, correct scale, and durable construction."
1890-1900s		$350	$425

Lakewood
1986-present. Luthier Martin Seeliger built his professional grade, production/custom, mandolins in Giessen, Germany up to '07. He continues to build guitars.

Larson Brothers
1900-1944. Luthiers Carl and August Larson built and marketed instruments under a variety of brands including Stetson, Maurer, Prairie State, Euphonon, Dyer, Stahl and others, but never under the Larson name.

Laurie Williams Guitars
1983-present. Luthier Laurie Williams builds his premium grade, custom/production, acoustic mandolins on the North Island of New Zealand. He also builds guitars.

Levin
1900-1973. Acoustic mandolins built in Sweden. Levin was best known for their classical guitars, which they also built for other brands, most notably Goya. They also built ukes.

Lewis
1981-present. Luthier Michael Lewis builds his premium and presentation grade, custom/production, mandolin family instruments in Grass Valley, California. He also builds guitars.

Loar (The)
2005-present. Intermediate and professional grade, production, imported mandolins designed by Greg Rich for The Music Link, which also has Johnson and other brands of instruments.

Lotus
Late-1970s-2004. Acoustic mandolins imported by Musicorp. They also offered banjos and guitars.

Lyle
Ca. 1969-1980. Instruments imported by distributor L.D. Heater of Portland, Oregon. Generally Japanese-made copies of American designs. They also had basses and guitars.
TM-200 Mandolin
1970s	A-style	$165	$200

Lyon & Healy
1864-present. Lyon & Healy was an early large musical instrument builder and marketer, and produced instruments under many different brands.
Style A Mandocello
1910s-1920s. Scroll peghead, symmetrical 2-point body, natural.
1910s-20s		$5,000	$6,300

Style A Professional Mandolin
1918-1920s. Violin scroll peghead, natural.
1918-1920s	Basic options	$5,000	$6,300
1918-1920s	Fancy options	$6,300	$8,000

MANDOLINS

MODEL YEAR	FEATURES	EXC. COND. LOW	HIGH

Style B Mandolin
1920s. Maple back and sides, 2-point body, natural.

| 1920s | | $1,825 | $2,300 |

Style C Mandolin
1920s. Like Style A teardrop Gibson body style, oval soundhole, carved spruce top, carved maple back, natural.

| 1920s | | $2,000 | $2,500 |

Lyra
1920s-1930s. Private brand made by Regal, Lyra name plate on headstock.

Style A (Scroll) Mandolin
1920s-1930s. Scroll on upper bass bout.

| 1925-1935 | | $450 | $575 |

Maccaferri
1923-1990. Mario Maccaferri made a variety of instruments over his career. He produced award-winning models in Italy and France until he fled to the U.S. due to WW II. He applied the new plastic to a highly successful line of instruments after the war. A mandolin was about the only stringed instument they didn't offer in plastic. His Europe-era instruments are very rare.

Mandolins/Mandolas made by Maccaferri 1928-ca. '31: No. 1 Mandolone, No. 2 Mandoloncello, No. 3 Mandola Baritono, No. 4 Mandola Tenore, No. 5 Mandolu Soprano, No. 6 Mandolino, No. 7 Quartino.

Mann Mandolins
2002-present. Luthier Jonathan Mann builds his professional grade, production/custom, acoustic and electric mandolins in Joelton, Tennessee.

Manuel & Patterson
1993-present. Professional and premium grade, production/custom, carved top mandolins built by luthiers Joe Manuel and Phil Patterson in Abita Springs, Louisiana. They also build guitars.

Martin
1833-present. Martin got into the mandolin market in 1895 starting with the typical bowl back designs. By 1914, Gibson's hot selling, innovative, violin-based mandolin pushed Martin into a flat back, bent top hybrid design. By '29, Martin offered a carved top and carved back mandolin. Most models were discontinued in '41, partially because of World War II. Production resumed and standard models are offered up to 1993. From '94 to '02 mandolins are available on a custom order basis only.

Martin offered a Backpacker mandolin up to '06.

Backpacker Mandolin
1999-2006. Bell-shaped body.

| 1999-2006 | | $120 | $150 |

Style 0 Mandolin
1905-1925. Bowl back-style, 18 rosewood ribs, solid peghead.

| 1905-1925 | | $750 | $925 |

Style 00 Mandolin
1908-1925. Bowl back-style, 9 rosewood ribs (14 ribs by '24), solid peghead.

| 1908-1925 | | $675 | $850 |

Style 000 Mandolin
1914 only. Bowl back, solid peghead, dot inlay, 9 mahogany ribs.

| 1914 | | $675 | $850 |

Style 1 Mandolin
1898-1924. Bowl back, German silver tuners, 18 ribs.

| 1898-1924 | | $800 | $1,000 |

Style 2 Mandolin
1898-1924. Bowl back, 26 rosewood ribs, higher appointments than Style 1.

| 1898-1924 | | $1,000 | $1,250 |

Style 2-15 Mandolin
1936-1964. Carved spruce top, maple back and sides, f-hole, single-bound back, solid headstock.

| 1936-1964 | | $1,100 | $1,350 |

Style 2-20 Mandolin
1936-1941. Carved spruce triple-bound top and bound maple back and sides, f-hole, dot inlay.

| 1936-1942 | | $2,800 | $3,500 |

Style 2-30 Mandolin
1937-1941. Carved spruce top and maple back and sides, multi-bound, f-holes, diamond and square inlays.

| 1937-1941 | | $3,200 | $4,000 |

Style 4 Mandolin
1898-1921. Bowl back, 34 rosewood ribs.

| 1898-1921 | | $1,800 | $2,250 |

Style 5 Mandolin
1898-1920. Bowl back, vine inlay, abalone top trim.

| 1898-1920 | | $1,900 | $2,350 |

Style 6 Mandolin
1898-1921. Bowl back, top bound with ivory and abalone, vine or snowflake inlay.

| 1898-1921 | | $2,000 | $2,500 |

Style 20 Mandolin
1929-1942. Symmetrical 2-point body, carved top and back with oval soundhole, dot markers.

| 1929-1942 | | $2,200 | $2,800 |

Style A Mandolin
1914-1995. Flat back, oval soundhole, dot inlay, solid headstock.

| 1914-1949 | | $750 | $925 |
| 1950-1995 | | $700 | $875 |

Style AA Mandola
1915-1931, 1935, 1941. Mandola version of Style A mandolin.

| 1915-1941 | | $1,550 | $1,950 |

Style AK Mandolin
1920-1937. Koa wood version of Style A, flat back.

| 1920-1937 | | $1,200 | $1,500 |

Style A Bitting Special Mandolin
1917. Private branded, small number produced, Martin and model impressed on back of headstock.

| 1917 | | $950 | $1,200 |

The Loar LM-700-VS

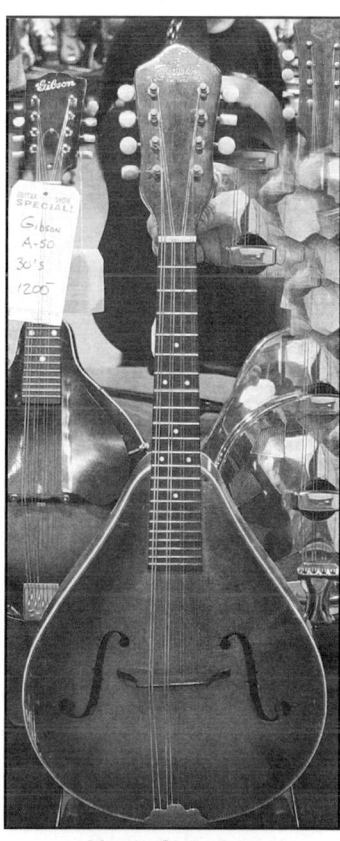

Martin Style 2-15

MANDOLINS

Mirabella Model 5

Monteleone Grand Artist
Laurence Wexer

MODEL		EXC. COND.	
YEAR	FEATURES	LOW	HIGH

Style B Mandolin
1914-1946, 1981-1987. Flat back with bent top, spruce top and rosewood back and sides, herringbone back stripe, multi-bound.
1914-1939		$1,200	$1,500
1940-1946		$1,100	$1,375
1981-1987		$825	$1,025

Style BB Mandola
1917-1921, 1932-1939. Brazilian rosewood, herringbone trim, features like Style B mandolin. This is the only Mandola offered.
| 1917-1939 | | $2,000 | $2,500 |

Style C Mandolin
1914-1934. Flat back.
| 1914-1916 | | $1,700 | $2,100 |
| 1917-1934 | | $2,100 | $2,600 |

Style D Mandolin
1914-1916. Flat back.
| 1914-1916 | | $2,600 | $3,300 |

Style E Mandolin
1915-1937. Flat back, rosewood back and sides, bent spruce top, Style 45 snowflake fretboard inlay and other high-end appointments. Highest model cataloged.
| 1915-1919 | | $5,100 | $6,300 |
| 1920-1937 | | $6,300 | $7,800 |

Maurer
Late 1880s-1944. Started by Robert Maurer in Chicago, and continued by Carl and August Larson after 1900. Earlier models were bowl-backs with flat-backs being offered by 1912. Models ranged from plain to presentation-style. Maurer Mandolins from the 1930s include Style 30 Flat Model, Style 40, Octave Mandola Style 45, Mandocello Style 50, and Mandola Tenor.

May Flower
Ca. 1901-1910. H. J. Flower's Chicago-based May Flower Music Company offered bowl back mandolins that he may or may not have built. There were also May Flower harp guitars built by others.
Bowl Back Mandolin
1901-1910. Mid-level bowl back-style with 19 rosewood ribs and mid-level appointments.
| 1901-1910 | Fancy | $1,250 | $1,550 |
| 1901-1910 | Plain | $950 | $1,200 |

Menzenhauer & Schmidt
1894-1904. Founded by Frederick Menzenhauer and Oscar Schmidt International. Menzenhauer created the guitar-zither in the U.S. He had several patents including one issued in September 1899 for a mandolin-guitar-zither. Control of operations quickly went to Oscar Schmidt.
12-String Mandolin
1890s. Bowl back mandolin with 3 strings per course that were tuned in octaves, designed during an experimental era for mandolin-related instruments, 13 rosewood ribs, spruce top, inlays.
| 1890s | | $300 | $375 |

MODEL		EXC. COND.	
YEAR	FEATURES	LOW	HIGH

Michael Collins Guitars
2002-present. Luthier Michael Collins builds his professional and premium grade, production/custom, mandolins in Keswick, Ontario. He also builds guitars.

Michael Kelly
1999-present. Intermediate and professional grade, production, imported, acoustic and acoustic/electric mandolins. They also offer guitars and basses.

Michael Lewis Instruments
1992-present. Luthier Michael Lewis builds his premium grade, custom, mandolins in Grass Valley, California. He also builds guitars.

Mid-Missouri/The Big Muddy Mandolin Company
1995-present. Intermediate grade, production, acoustic and electric mandolins and mandolas built by luthier Michael Dulak in Columbia, Missouri. In late '06, they changed their name to The Big Muddy Mandolin Company.
M Series Mandolin
1995-present. Teardrop A-style body, solid spruce top, solid maple, mahogany or rosewood back and sides.
1995-1999	M-0	$300	$375
1995-1999	M-1	$300	$375
1995-2014	M-2	$350	$425
1995-2014	M-3	$375	$475
1995-2014	M-4	$450	$550
M Series Mandolin
1995-present. Teardrop A-style body, solid spruce top, solid maple, mahogany or rosewood back and sides.
| 1995-2014 | M-15 Mandola | $575 | $700 |

Mirabella
1997-present. Professional and premium grade, custom, mandolins built by luthier Cristian Mirabella in Babylon, New York. He also builds guitars, basses and ukes.

Mix
2007-present. Carbon fiber mandolins built by Peter Mix, Will Kimball, and Matt Durham of New Millennium Acoustic Design (NewMAD) in Waterville, Vermont.

Monteleone
1971-present. Primarily a guitar maker, luthier John Monteleone also builds presentation grade, custom, mandolins in West Islip, New York.
Grand Artist Mandola
1979-2013. 15 7/8" scale until '90, then 17".
| 1977-1989 | | $18,000 | $22,000 |
Grand Artist Mandolin
1977-2013. Style F body, spruce top, curly maple back and sides, dot markers, currently offered in a Standard and Deluxe model.
| 1990-1995 | | $18,000 | $22,000 |
| 1996-2013 | | $22,000 | $27,000 |

MODEL YEAR	FEATURES	EXC. COND. LOW	HIGH

Radio Flyer Mandolin
1996-2012. Style F body, currently offered in a Standard and Deluxe model.

1996-2012		$21,000	$26,000

Style B Mandolin
1982-1990s. Long A body style with long f-holes, flamed curly maple back and sides, elongated fretboard over body, sunburst.

1982-1990		$15,000	$18,500

Moon (Scotland)
1979-present. Intermediate and professional grade, production/custom, acoustics and acoustic/electric mandolins and mandolas built by luthier Jimmy Moon in Glasgow, Scotland. They also build guitars.

Morales
Ca.1967-1968. Japanese-made, not heavily imported into the U.S.

Electric Mandolin

1967-1968		$375	$450

Morgan Monroe
1999-present. Intermediate and professional grade, production, acoustic mandolins made in Korea and distributed by SHS International of Indianapolis, Indiana. They also offer guitars, basses, banjos, and fiddles.

Morris
1967-present. Imported by Moridaira of Japan, Morris offered copy-era mandolins during the 1970s, including the popular F-5 style copy. They also build guitars.

Mozzani
Late-1800s-early-1900s. Founder Luigi Mozzani was an Italian (Bologna) master luthier and renowned composer and musician. There are original Mozzani-built mandolins and also factory-built instruments made later at various workshops.

Mandolin
1920s. Factory-built bowl back model.

1920s		$350	$450

Original Bowl Back Mandolin
Late-1800s-early-1900s. Handcrafted by Luigi Mozzani, about 24 ribs, soundhole ornamentation, snowflake-like markers.

1800-1900s		$1,100	$1,400

Muiderman Guitars
1997-present. Custom, premium grade, mandolins built by luthier Kevin Muiderman currently in Grand Forks, North Dakota, and previously in Beverly Hills, Michigan, 1997-2001, and Neenah, Wisconsin, '01-'07. He also builds guitars.

National
Ca.1927-present. The National brand has gone through many ownership changes and offered resonator mandolins from around 1927 to '41.

MODEL YEAR	FEATURES	EXC. COND. LOW	HIGH

Style O Mandolin
1931-early-1940s. Metal body with Hawaiian scenes, single-cone resonator.

1930s		$2,400	$3,000

Style 1 Mandolin
1928-1936. Plain metal body, tri-cone resonator.

1928-1936	Single cone	$2,100	$2,600
1928-1936	Tricone version	$2,800	$3,500

Style 2 Mandolin
1928-1936. Metal body with rose engraving, tri-cone resonator.

1928-1936	Single cone	$3,100	$3,800
1928-1936	Tricone version	$4,200	$5,200

Style 3 Mandolin

1930s	Single cone	$4,100	$5,000
1930s	Tricone version	$4,700	$5,800

Style 97 Mandolin
1936-1940. Metal body, tri-cone resonator.

1936-1940		$5,100	$6,300

Triolian Mandolin
1928-1940. Metal body with palm trees, single-cone resonator.

1928-1940	Single cone	$2,600	$3,200

National Reso-Phonic
1988-present. Successors to the National name, with the designs and patented amplifying resonator assemblies of the original National models, they offer professional grade, production, mandolins from their shop in San Luis Obispo, California. They also build guitars, basses and ukuleles.

Northworthy
1987-present. Professional and premium grade, production/custom, mandolin-family instruments built by luthier Alan Marshall in Ashbourne, Derbyshire, England. He also builds guitars.

Nouveau (Gibson)
1986-1989. Mandolin bodies and necks made in Japan, assembled and finished in U.S. Became Nouveau (by Epiphone) in '88 and the brand was discontinued in '89. They also made guitars.

C7 Mandolin
1986-1987. F-style, white wood body and neck.

1986-1987		$1,600	$2,000

Nugget
1970s-present. Luthier Mike Kemnitzer builds his premium grade mandolins in Central Lake, Michigan.

Nyberg Instruments
1993-present. Professional grade, custom, mandolins and mandolas built by luthier Lawrence Nyberg in Hornby Island, British Columbia. He also builds guitars, bouzoukis and citterns.

O'Dell, Doug
See listing under Old Town.

Monteleone Radio Flyer

Nugget Deluxe F

MANDOLINS

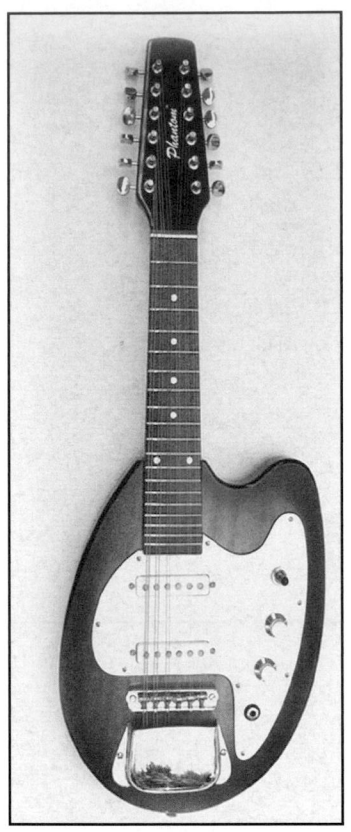

Phantom MandoGuitar

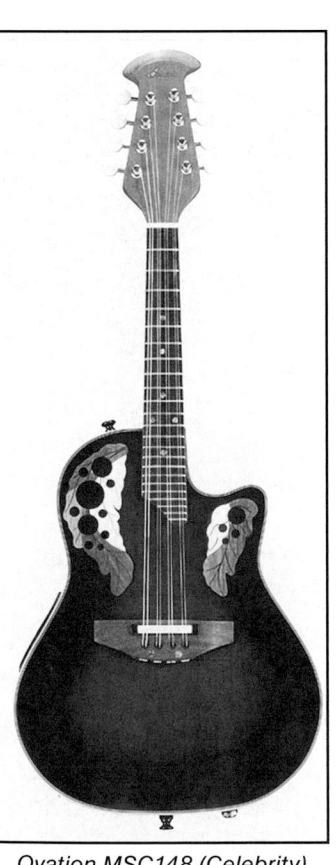

Ovation MSC148 (Celebrity)

MODEL YEAR	FEATURES	EXC. COND. LOW	HIGH

Old Hickory
2005-2010. Budget grade, production, imported F- and A-style acoustic mandolins from Musician's Wholesale America, Nashville, Tennessee. They also offer banjos.

Style A Mandolin

2005-2010	AC-100 mid-level	$45	$75
2005-2010	FC-100 highest level	$75	$130
2005-2010	M-1 lowest level	$35	$45

Old Kraftsman
1930s-1960s. Brand name used by the Siegel Company on instruments made by Kay and others (even Gibson). Quality was mixed, but some better-grade instruments were offered.

Mandolin

1950s		$260	$325

Old Town
1974-2007. Luthier Doug O'Dell built his professional and premium grade, production/custom acoustic and electric mandolins in Ohio.

EM-10 Electric Mandolin
1980s-2006. Double-cut, flamed maple top, 1 pickup, 2 control knobs.

1980s-2006		$1,600	$2,000

Old Wave
1990-present. Luthier Bill Bussmann builds his professional and premium grade, production/custom, mandolins and mandolas in Caballo, New Mexico. He has also built guitars and basses.

Orpheum
1897-1942, 1944-early 1970s, 2001-2006. Intermediate grade, production, mandolins. They also offered guitars. An old brand often associated with banjos, 1930s branded guitars sold by Bruno and Sons. 1950s branded guitars and mandolins sold by Maurice Lipsky Music, New York, New York. The brand was revived for '01 to '06 by Tacoma Guitars.

Electric Mandolin Model 730 E
1950s. Private branded for Maurice Lipsky as a student model, A-style body, 1 bar pickup, 2 side-mounted knobs, maple back and sides, dots, sunburst.

1950s		$600	$750

Mandolin-Banjo
1910-1930. Mandolin neck on small banjo body, fancy headstock and fretboard inlay, carved heel.

1910-1930	Model No. 1	$625	$775
1910-1930	Model No. 2	$725	$900
1910-1930	Model No. 3	$825	$1,025

Style A Mandolin

1950s		$425	$525

Oscar Schmidt
1879-ca. 1939, 1979-present. Currently offering budget and intermediate grade, production, mandolins. They also offer guitars, basses, banjos, ukuleles and the famous Oscar Schmidt autoharp. The original Schmidt company offered innovative mandolin designs during the 1900-'30 mandolin boom.

Mandolin Harp Style B
1890s. More zither-autoharp than mandolin, flat autoharp body with soundhole.

1890s		$200	$250

Sovereign Mandolin
1920s. Bowl back, bent top, rope-style binding, mahogany ribs, dot inlay, plain headstock, natural.

1920s	Basic	$275	$350
1920s	Fancy	$750	$950

Ovation
1966-present. Ovation added mandolins in '94 and currently offers intermediate and professional grade, production, mandolins. They also offer guitars and basses.

MCS148 (Celebrity) Mandolin
1994-present. Single-cut, small Ovation body, Ovation headstock, red sunburst.

1994-2014		$275	$350

P. W. Crump Company
1975-present. Luthier Phil Crump builds his custom mandolin-family instruments in Arcata, California. He also builds guitars.

Paris Swing
2005-2008. Intermediate grade, production, imported acoustic mandolins from The Music Link, which also offers instruments under Johnson and other brands.

Penco
Ca. 1974-1978. Japanese-made copies of classic American mandolins. They also made guitars, basses and banjos.

Phantom Guitar Works
1992-present. Intermediate grade, production, solidbody MandoGuitars assembled in Clatskanie, Oregon. They also build guitars and basses.

Phoenix
1990-present. Premium grade, production/custom, mandolins built by luthier Rolfe Gerhardt (formerly builder of Unicorn Mandolins in the '70s) in South Thomaston, Maine. Gerhardt's Phoenix company specializes in a 2-point Style A (double-cut) body style.

Pilgrim
1970s-late-1980s, 2010-present. Brand dates back to '70s with luthier Paul Tebbutt and is presently owned by John Hornby Skewes & Co. Ltd. In the United Kingdom. Used on guitars, mandolins, banjos and ukes, all built in the Far East.

Premier
Ca.1938-ca.1975, 1990s-2010. Brand produced by Peter Sorkin Music Company in New York City. Around '57 the company acquired Strad-O-Lin and many of their mandolins were offered under that brand. By '75, the Premier brand went into hiatus.

MODEL		EXC. COND.	
YEAR	FEATURES	LOW	HIGH

By the '90s, the Premier brand re-appears on Asian-made solidbody guitars and basses.

Ramsey
1990s. Built by luthier John Ramsey of Colorado Springs, Colorado.

Randy Wood Guitars
1968-present. Premium and presentation grade, custom/production, mandolins, mandolas, and mandocellos built by luthier Randy Woods in Bloomingdale, Georgia. He also builds guitars.

Ratliff
1982-present. Professional and premium grade, production/custom, mandolin family instruments built by luthier Audey Ratliff in Church Hill, Tennessee.

R Series Mandolin
1990s-present. R-5 is an F-style mando, R-4 is round-hole version of 5.

1995-2014	R-4	$1,600	$2,000
1995-2014	R-5	$2,200	$2,700

Silver Eagle Mandolin
1998	A-style	$1,250	$1,500

Recording King
1929-1943. Montgomery Ward house brand. Suppliers include Gibson, Kay, Regal, and Gretsch. Brand name revived by The Music Link in '05.

Style A Mandolin
1929-1943. Gibson-made, plain appointments, sunburst.

1929-1943		$500	$625

Red Diamond
Early 1980s-present. Luthier Don MacRostie builds his premium grade, production/custom, mandolins in Athens, Ohio.

RedLine Acoustics and RedLine Resophonics
2007-present. Luthiers Steve Smith, Jason Denton, Christian McAdams and Ryan Futch build their intermediate to premium grade, production, flat-top and carved A-style mandolins in Hendersonville, Tennessee. They also build guitars.

Regal
Ca. 1895-1966, 1987-present. Large Chicago-based manufacturer which made their own brand name and others for distributors and mass merchandisers. Absorbed by the Harmony Company in 1954.

Bicentennial 76 Mandolin
1976. A-style body, flat back, oval soundhole, '76 logo on 'guard, white body, red peghead, blue stars on front and back.

1976		$350	$425

Mandolin
1920s	A-style	$450	$550
1930s	Standard	$450	$550
1930s	Ultra Grand Deluxe	$700	$875

Octofone
1920s-1930s. It had 8 strings, but Regal's marketing department named this the Octo because it was "eight instruments in one" as it could be tuned as a mandolin, tenor banjo, tenor guitar and other instruments, long body with double points, round soundhole.

1920s-30s		$375	$475

Resonator Mandolin
1937	Model 250	$1,000	$1,250
1950s		$600	$750

Rich and Taylor
1993-1996. Custom mandolins from luthiers Greg Rich and Mark Taylor (Crafters of Tennessee). They also built guitars and banjos.

Rickenbacker
1931-present. Rickenbacker had the Electro Mandolin in the late '30s and introduced 4-, 5- and 8-string electric models in 1958 and currently offers one model.

Model 5002V58 Mandolin
1997-present. 8 strings, maple front, walnut back, rosewood 'board.

1997-2014		$1,300	$1,650

Rigel
1990-2006. Professional and premium grade, production/custom mandolins and mandolas built by luthier Pete Langdell in Hyde Park, Vermont.

A-Plus Series Mandolin
1990s-2006. A-style body, carved spruce top, maple back and sides, dot markers.

1990-2006	F-holes	$950	$1,200
1990s	Oval soundhole	$875	$1,100

Classic S Mandolin
2000s. Double cutaway, f-holes.

2000s		$1,300	$1,600

Model G-110 Mandolin
1990-2006. Maple neck, back and sides, red spruce top, f-holes, sunburst.

1990-2006		$1,750	$2,200

Roberts
1980s. Built by luthier Jay Roberts of California.

Tiny Moore Jazz 5 Mandolin
1980s. Based on Bigsby design of the early-1950s as used by Tiny Moore, five-string electric, sunburst.

1985		$1,550	$1,950

Rogue
2001-present. Budget grade, production, imported mandolins. They also offer guitars, basses, ukes, and banjos.

Rono
In 1967 luthier Ron Oates began building professional grade, production/custom, electric mandolins in Boulder, Colorado. He also built guitars and basses.

RedLine Traveler

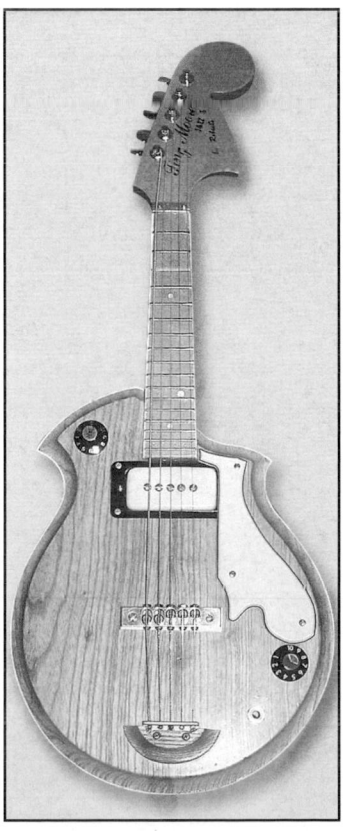

Roberts Tiny Moore J5

MANDOLINS

MODEL		EXC. COND.	
YEAR	FEATURES	LOW	HIGH

Sawchyn A2

Stelling S-5

Ryder

1992-present. Luthier Steve Ryder builds his professional and premium grade, production/custom solid and semi-hollowbody electric mandolins, mandola and octave mandolins in South Portland, Maine.

S. S. Stewart

1878-1904. S.S. Stewart of Philadelphia was primarily known for banjos. Legend has it that Stewart was one of the first to demonstrate the mass production assembly of stringed instruments.

Mandolin Banjo

Early-1900s. Mandolin neck and a very small open back banjo body, star inlay in headstock.

1900s		$375	$475

S101

2002-present. Budget and intermediate grade, production, mandolins imported from China. They also offer guitars, basses, and banjos.

Samick

1958-2001, 2002-present. Budget and intermediate grade, production, imported acoustic and acoustic/electric mandolins. They also offer guitars, basses, ukes and banjos.

Sammo

1920s. Labels in these instruments state they were made by the Osborne Mfg. Co. with an address of Masonic Temple, Chicago, Illinois. High quality and often with a high degree of ornamentation. They also made ukes and guitars.

Sawchyn

1972-present. Intermediate and professional grade, production/custom, mandolins built by luthier Peter Sawchyn in Regina, Saskatchewan. He also builds flat-top and flamenco guitars.

Schaefer

1997-present. Premium grade, production, electric mandolins built in Austin, Texas by luthier Edward A. Schaefer. He also builds guitars and basses.

Sekova

Mid-1960s-mid-1970s. Entry level, imported by the U.S. Musical Merchandise.

Electric Mandolin

Mid-1960s-mid-1970s. Kay-Kraft-style hollowbody with f-holes, 1 pickup and Sekova logo on the headstock.

1960s-70s		$325	$425

Sigma

1970-2007. Budget and intermediate grade, production, import mandolins distributed by C.F. Martin Company. They also offered guitars, basses and banjos.

SM6 Mandolin

1970-2007. Made in Korea.

1970-2007		$250	$300

Silvertone

1941-ca.1970, present. Brand name used by Sears on their musical instruments.

Mandolin

1941-ca.1970. Arched top and back, sunburst.

1940s-50s		$225	$350

Smart Musical Instruments

1986-present. Premium and presentation grade, custom, mandolin family instruments built by luthier A. Lawrence Smart in McCall, Idaho. He also builds guitars.

Smith, Lawrence K.

1989-present. Luthier Lawrence Smith builds his premium grade, production/custom, mandolins in Australia. He also builds guitars.

Sovereign

Ca. 1899-ca. 1938. Sovereign was originally a brand of the Oscar Schmidt company of New Jersey. In the late '30s, Harmony purchased several trade names from the Schmidt Company, including Sovereign. Sovereign then ceased as a brand, but Harmony continued using it on a model line of Harmony guitars.

Mandolin

1920s-1930s. Old-style bent top.

1920s-30s		$225	$350

Stahl

The William C. Stahl music publishing company claimed their instruments were made in Milwaukee, Wisconsin, in the early-1900s, but the Larson Brothers of Chicago built mandolin family instruments for them. Models included Style 4 (22 ribs) to Style 12 Presentation Artist Special. The more expensive models were generally 44-rib construction.

Stanley Mandolins

2003-present. Luthier Chris Stanley builds his premium grade, production/custom, A-style and F-style mandolins in Rhinelander, Wisconsin.

Stathopoulo

1903-1916. Original design instruments, some patented, by Epiphone company founder A. Stathopoulo.

A-Style Mandolin

1903-1916. A-style with higher-end appointments, bent-style spruce top, figured maple back and sides.

1912		$1,000	$1,250

Stefan Sobell Musical Instruments

1982-present. Luthier Stefan Sobell builds his premium grade, production/custom, mandolins in Hetham, Northumberland, England. He also builds guitars, citterns and bouzoukis.

MODEL		EXC. COND.	
YEAR	FEATURES	LOW	HIGH

Stella

Ca. 1899-1974, 2000s. Stella was a brand of the Oscar Schmidt Company which was an early contributor to innovative mandolin designs and participated in the 1900-'30 mandolin boom. Pre-World War II Stella instruments were low-mid to mid-level instruments. In '39, Harmony purchased the Stella name and '50s and '60s Stella instruments were student grade, low-end instruments. The Stella brand was reintroduced in the 2000s by MBT International.

Banjo-Mandolin
1920s. One of several innovative designs that attempted to create a new market, 8-string mandolin neck with a banjo body, Stella logo normally impressed on the banjo rim or the side of the neck.

1920s		$250	$300

Bowl Back Mandolin
1920s. Typical bowl back, bent top-style mandolin with models decalomania, about 10 (wide) maple ribs, dot markers.

1920s		$200	$250

Pear-Shape Mandolin
1940s-1960s. Harmony-made lower-end mandolins, pear-shaped (Style A) flat back, oval soundhole.

1940s-60s		$225	$500

Stelling

1974-present. Mainly known for banjos, Stelling also builds premium grade, production/custom mandolins in Afton, Virginia.

Sterling

Early-1900s. Distributed by wholesalers The Davitt & Hanser Music Co.

Stetson

1884-ca. 1924. Stetson was another house brand of the W. J. Dyer store in St. Paul, Minnesota. Starting around 1904, the Larson brothers built a few student grade Stetson mandolins under this brand.

Stiver

1971-present. Premium grade, custom/production, mandolins built by luthier Louis Stiver in Polk, Pennsylvania.

A Model Mandolin
1982-2014		$2,600	$3,300

F-5 Mandolin
1982-2014		$3,600	$4,500

Stonebridge

1981-present. Luthier Frantisek Furch builds his production/custom, professional and premium grade, acoustic mandolins in the Czech Republic. He also builds guitars.

Strad-O-Lin/Stradolin

Ca.1920s-ca.1960s. The Strad-O-Lin company was operated by the Hominic brothers in New York, primarily making mandolins for wholesalers. In the

late '50s, Multivox/Premier bought the company and used the name on mandolins, guitars and amps.

Baldwin Electric Mandolin
1950s-1960s. A-Style, single pickup, tone and volume knobs, spruce top, maple back and sides, Baldwin logo on headstock, natural.

1950s-60s	Various models	$175	$400

Junior A Mandolin
1950s-1960s. A-Style, Stradolin Jr. logo on headstock, dot markers, sunburst.

1950s-60s		$150	$190

Style A Mandolin
1920s-1950s. A-style body with f-holes, dot markers.

1920s-30s		$425	$525
1940s-50s		$425	$525

Stromberg-Voisinet

1921-ca.1932. Marketed Stromberg (not to be confused with Charles Stromberg of Boston) and Kay Kraft brands, plus instruments of other distributors and retailers. Became the Kay Musical Instrument Company. By the mid-'20s, the company was making many better Montgomery Ward guitars, banjos and mandolins, often with lots of pearloid. The last Stromberg acoustic instruments were seen in '32.

Summit

1990-present. Professional and premium grade, production/custom mandolins built by luthier Paul Schneider in Hartsville, Tennessee. He was originally located in Mulvane, Kansas.

Superior

1987-present. Intermediate grade, production/custom mandolin-family instruments made in Mexico for George Katechis Montalvo of Berkeley Musical Instrument Exchange. They also offer guitars.

Supertone

1914-1941. Brand used by Sears before they switched to Silvertone. Instruments made by other companies.

Mandolin
Spruce top, mahogany back and sides, some with decalomania vine pattern on top.

1920s-30s	Fancy	$450	$575
1920s-30s	Standard	$300	$375

Supro

1935-1968, 2004-present. Budget line from the National Dobro Company. Brand name was revived in '04.

T30 Electric Mandolin
1950s		$600	$750

T.H. Davis

1976-present. Premium grade, custom, mandolins built by luthier Ted Davis in Loudon, Tennessee. He also builds guitars.

Stiver F Model

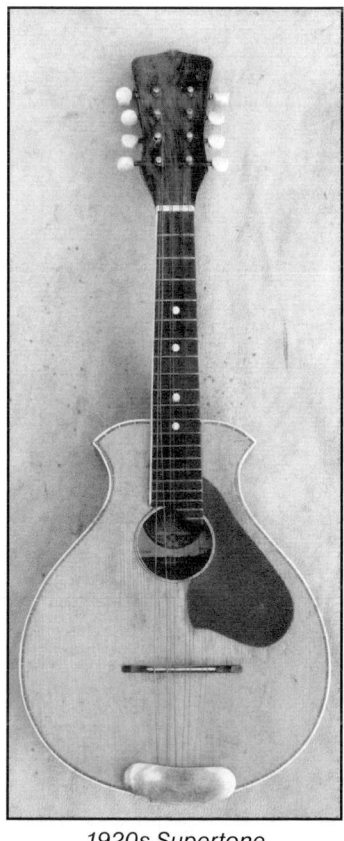

1920s Supertone

MANDOLINS

Tacoma M-1

Triggs Satin Fern F5

MODEL YEAR	FEATURES	EXC. COND. LOW	HIGH

Tacoma
1995-2009. Tacoma offered intermediate, professional and premium grade, production, electric and acoustic mandolins up to '06. They also built guitars and basses.

M Series Mandolin
1999-2006. Solid spruce top, typical Tacoma body-style with upper bass bout soundhole, E (i.e. M-1E) indicates acoustic/electric.

1999-2006	M1, mahogany	$425	$525
1999-2006	M1E, mahogany	$450	$575

M Series Mandolin
1999-2006. Solid spruce top, typical Tacoma body-style with upper bass bout soundhole, E (i.e. M-1E) indicates acoustic/electric.

1999-2004	M2, rosewood	$500	$625
1999-2006	M3/M3E, maple	$650	$800

Tanglewood Guitar Company UK
1991-present. Dirk Kommer and Tony Flatt in United Kingdom import intermediate grade, production, mandolins from China. They also import guitars, basses, amps, banjos and ukes.

Tennessee
1970-1993, 1996-present. Luthier Mark Taylor builds his professional and premium grade, production/custom, mandolins in Old Hickory, Tennessee. He also builds guitars, banjos and the Tut Taylor brand of resophonic guitars.

Timeless Instruments
1980-present. Luthier David Freeman builds his intermediate grade, mandolins in Tugaske, Saskatchewan. He also builds guitars and dulcimers.

Triggs
1992-present. Luthiers Jim Triggs and his son Ryan build their professional and premium grade, production/custom, mandolins in Kansas City, Kansas. They also build guitars. They were located in Nashville, Tennessee until '98.

Trinity River
2004-present. Production/custom, budget and intermediate grade, mandolins imported from Asia by luthiers Marcus Lawyer and Ross McLeod in Fort Worth, Texas. They also import guitars, basses and banjos.

Unicorn
1970s-late 1980s. Luthier Rolfe Gerhardt (currently luthier for Phoenix Mandolins) founded Unicorn in the mid-'70s. Gerhardt built 149 mandolins before selling Unicorn to Dave Sinko in '80. Sinko closed Unicorn in the late-'80s.

Vega
1889-present. The original Boston-based company was purchased by C.F. Martin in '70.

MODEL YEAR	FEATURES	EXC. COND. LOW	HIGH

10-String Lute Mandola
1915. 15" scale, few made.

1915		$2,200	$2,800

Lansing Special Bowl Mandolin
1890s. Spruce top, abalone, vine inlay.

1890s		$400	$500

Little Wonder Mandolin Banjo
1920s. Maple neck, resonator.

1920s		$425	$525

Mando Bass Mandolin
1910s-1920s. Large upright bass-sized instrument with bass tuners, body-style similar to dual-point A-style, scroll headstock.

1910s-20s		$3,000	$3,700

Mandolin Cittern
1910s. 10-string (five double strings tuned in 5ths), vague A-style with oval soundhole and cylinder back, natural.

1910s		$2,000	$2,500

Style 202 Lute Mandolin
Early-1900s. Basic A-style with small horns, natural spruce top, mahogany sides and cylinder back, dot markers.

1910s		$2,000	$2,500

Style 205 Cylinder Back Mandolin
1910s-1920s. Rounded tube cylinder shape runs the length of the back.

1910s		$1,550	$1,975
1920s		$1,325	$1,675

Style A Mandolin

1910s		$500	$625

Style D 100 Electric Hollowbody Mandolin

1940		$550	$700

Style F Mandolin
1910s. Scroll upper bass bout, oval soundhole, Vega and torch inlay in headstock.

1910s		$750	$950

Style K Mandolin Banjo

1910s-30s		$310	$380

Style L Banjo Mandolin/Whyte Laydie
1910s-1920s. Open back banjo body and mandolin 8-string neck.

1910s-20s		$1,050	$1,300

Style S Mandolin Banjo

1915		$600	$800

Super Deluxe Mandolin

1910s	Sunburst	$800	$1,000

Tubaphone Style X Mandolin Banjo

1922-1923		$800	$1,000

Veillette
1991-present. Luthiers Joe Veillette and Martin Keith build their professional grade, production/custom, mandolins in Woodstock, New York. They also build basses and guitars.

Vinaccia
Italian-made by Pasquale Vinaccia, luthier.

Bowl Back Mandolin
1900-1920s. High-end appointments and 'guard, 30 rosewood ribs.

1900-1920s		$1,725	$2,150

Vintage

Ca. 1993-present. Intermediate grade, production, mandolins, imported from China, Korea and Vietnam by John Hornby Skewes & Co. in the U.K. They also offer guitars, basses and ukuleles.

Vivi-Tone

1933-ca. 1936. Lloyd Loar's pioneering guitar company also built early electric mandolins and mandocellos in Kalamazoo, Michigan.

Electric Mandocello
1933-1935. Traditonal guitar-arch body, Vivi-Tone silkscreen logo on headstock.

1933-1935	$4,600	$5,700

Electric Mandola
1933-1935. Traditonal European teardrop/pear-shaped top, Vivi-Tone silkscreen logo on headstock.

1933-1935	$3,800	$4,800

Electric Mandolin
1933-1935. Vivi-Tone silkscreen logo on headstock

1933-1935	$3,300	$4,200

Waldo

1891- early 1900s. Mandolin family instruments built in Saginaw, Michigan.

Bowl Back Mandolin
1890s. Alternating rosewood and maple ribs, some with script Waldo logo on pickguard.

1890s	$180	$225

Washburn

1962-present. Currently, Washburn offers imported intermediate and professional grade, production, mandolins.

Mandolin/Mandolin Family
1974-present. Various models plywood to carved.

1974-2014	$75	$350

Washburn (Lyon & Healy)

1880s-ca.1949. Washburn was founded in Chicago as one of the lines for Lyon & Healy to promote high quality stringed instruments, ca. 1880s. The rights to Washburn were sold to Regal which built Washburns by the mid-'30s until until ca. '49. In '74 the brand resurfaced.

Bowl Back Mandolin
1890s-1900s. Lyon and Healy sold a wide variety of bowl back mandolins, Brazilian ribs with fancy inlays and bindings.

1890-1900s	Fancy	$650	$1,500
1890-1900s	Plain	$300	$375
1900s	Standard appointments	$390	$490

Style A Mandolin
1920s. Professional quality.

1920s	$3,000	$3,700

Style E Mandolin
1915-1923. Brazilian rosewood.

1915-1923	$650	$800

Washington

Washington mandolins were manufactured by Kansas City, Missouri instrument wholesalers J.W. Jenkins & Sons. First introduced in 1895, the brand also offered guitars.

Weber

1996-present. Intermediate, professional, and premium grade, production/custom, mandolins, mandolas, and mandocellos. Many former Flatiron employees, including Bruce Weber, formed Sound To Earth, Ltd., to build Weber instruments when Gibson moved Flatiron from Montana, to Nashville. Originally in Belgrade, Montana, and after '04, in Logan, Montana. They also build guitars. In '12, Two Old Hippies (Breedlove, Bedell) acquired the brand, moving production in '13 to Oregon where Bruce Weber oversees development.

Absaroka Mandolin
2000s. A style body, white binding, diamond inlays.

2002	$1,750	$2,200

Alder #1 Mandola
Celtic A style body, black binding, diamond inlays.

1997	$1,000	$1,250

Alder #2 Mandola
2000-2012. Teardrop body, X-braced, spruce top, maple back and sides.

2000-2012	$1,000	$1,250

Aspen #1 Mandolin
1997-2011. Teardrop A-style, solid spruce top, maple sides and back, mahogany neck.

1997-2011	$800	$1,000

Aspen #2 Mandolin
1997-2011. Like #1, but with maple neck.

1997-2011	$850	$1,050

Beartooth Mandolin
1997-2009. Teardrop A-style, solid spruce top, curly maple sides, back, and neck.

1997-2009	$1,475	$1,825

Big Sky Mandolin
F-style.

1999	$2,800	$3,500

Bighorn Mandolin
2006-2008. A-style, oval, double Venetian.

2006-2008	$2,400	$3,000

Bitterroot Mandolin
2005-present. F-style.

2005-2014	$1,950	$2,400

Bridger Mandolin
2000-present. A-style, long neck.

2003	A-Celtic style	$1,850	$2,250

Custom Vintage Mandolin
2007-present.

2007-2014	A-style	$2,400	$3,000
2007-2014	F-style	$3,400	$4,300

Fern Mandolin
1997-present. Top of the product line.

1997-2014	A-style	$3,700	$4,700
1997-2014	F-style	$4,000	$5,000

Vintage Pilgrim Redwood

Weber Fern

MANDOLINS

1920s Wurlitzer Mandolin Banjo
Folkway Music

MODEL YEAR	FEATURES	EXC. COND. LOW	HIGH
Gallatin Mandolin			
1999-present.			
1999-2014	A-style	$1,000	$1,250
1999-2014	F-style	$1,375	$1,700
Octar Mandolin			
2008. Octave mando, 15" archtop body.			
2008		$2,000	$2,500
Sage #1 Octave Mandolin			
2000s. Octave mando, diamond inlays.			
2006		$1,150	$1,425
Sweet Pea Mandolin			
2000s. Travel mando.			
2009-2012		$220	$275
Y2K Mandolin			
2000. Celtic-style teardrop body, satin natural finish.			
2000		$600	$750
Yellowstone Mandolin			
1997-present. A-style and F-style available, solid spruce top, curly maple sides, back, and neck, sunburst.			
1997-2014	A-style	$1,600	$2,000
1997-2014	F-style	$2,400	$3,000
2010	Octave	$2,000	$2,500

Weymann

1864-1940s. H.A. Weymann & Sons was a musical instrument distributor located in Philadelphia. They also built their own instruments.

MODEL YEAR	FEATURES	EXC. COND. LOW	HIGH
Keystone State Banjo Mandolin			
1910s. Maple rim and back, ebony fretboard.			
1910s		$360	$450
Mandolin Banjo			
1920s. Mandolin neck on a open banjo body.			
1920s	Various models	$360	$450

MODEL YEAR	FEATURES	EXC. COND. LOW	HIGH
Mando-Lute			
1920s. Lute-style body, spruce top, flamed maple sides and back, rope binding, deluxe rosette, natural.			
1920s	Various models	$400	$725

Wurlitzer

The old Wurlitzer company would have been considered a mega-store by today's standards. They sold a wide variety of instruments, gave music lessons, and operated manufacturing facilities.

MODEL YEAR	FEATURES	EXC. COND. LOW	HIGH
Banjolin			
1920s. Mandolin neck on banjo body.			
1920s		$525	$650
Mandolin			
1920s. Various woods and appointments.			
1920s		$350	$500
Mandolin Banjo			
1900-1910. Mandolin neck on open back banjo body, plain-style.			
1900-1910		$260	$325

Yosco

1900-1930s. Lawrence L. Yosco was a New York City luthier building guitars, round back mandolins and banjos under his own brand and for others.

Zeta

1982-2010. Zeta has made professional grade, acoustic/electric mandolins in Oakland, California over the years, but currently only offer upright basses, amps and violins.

UKULELES

Nicola Turturro Turnover Ukulele. Photo: Randy Klimpert.

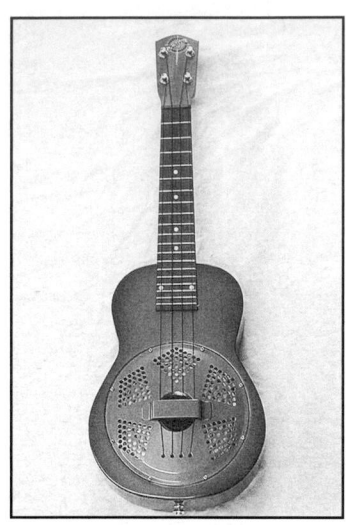

Beltona Blue Uke

DeCava Maui Creek

Ditson Style 1
Randy Klimpert

MODEL YEAR	FEATURES	EXC. COND. LOW	HIGH

Aero Uke

1920s. Never branded, but almost certainly produced by Chicago's Stromberg-Voisenet Company, the precursor of Kay, the Aero Uke is an instrument quite unlike any other. With its spruce-capped body resembling an old-timey airplane wing and a neck and headstock that approximate a plane's fuselage, this clever '20s offering cashed in on the Lindbergh craze (like the Harmony Johnny Marvin model with its airplane-shaped bridge), and must have been a big hit at parties.

Aero Ukulele
Airplane body.

1927	Black deco on wing	$2,500	$2,800
1927	Gold deco on wing	$2,700	$3,000

Aloha

1935-1960s. The Aloha brand turns up on numerous vastly different ukes. In fact, the variety of features exhibited by Aloha ukuleles leads the modern observer to believe that the ukes that bear this headstock decal were made by as many as a dozen different manufacturers, each with access to the same logo. Many were undoubtedly Island-made, with all koa bodies and some with fancy rope binding; others bear unmistakable mainland traits. Some of these have a more traditional look and are stamped Akai inside the soundhole, while still others, strongly resembling mainland C.F. Martins in design, typically sport a decal of the Sam F. Chang curio shop on the reverse of the headstock.

Akai Soprano Ukulele
Koa construction.

1930s		$600	$800

Soprano Ukulele
Koa body, plain.

1950s		$600	$800

Andy Powers Musical Instrument Co.

1996-2010. Luthier Andy Powers, built his professional grade, custom, ukuleles in Oceanside, California. He also built guitars and mandolins.

Applause

1976-present. DW, Inc.'s entry-level Ovation-styled import brand offers budget grade, production, ukuleles.

Austin

1999-present. Budget and intermediate grade, production, ukuleles imported by St. Louis Music. They also offer guitars, basses, amps, mandolins and banjos.

Bear Creek Guitars

1995-present. Intermediate and professional grade ukuleles built by luthier Bill Hardin in Kula, Hawaii. He also builds guitars.

MODEL YEAR	FEATURES	EXC. COND. LOW	HIGH

Beltona

1990-present. Production metal body resonator ukuleles made in New Zealand by Steve Evans and Bill Johnson. They also build guitars and mandolins.

Beneteau

1974-present. Professional grade, custom, ukuleles built by luthier Marc Beneteau in St. Thomas, Ontario. He also builds guitars.

Bertoncini Stringed Instruments

Luthier Dave Bertoncini mainly builds flat-top guitars in Olympia, Washington, but has also built ukuleles and mandolins. He began in 1995.

Blackbird

2006-present. At the 2010 NAMM Show, luthier Joe Luttwak introduced the first ever carbon fiber ukulele, built in San Francisco, California. He also builds guitars.

Blue Star

1984-present. Intermediate grade, production/custom, acoustic and electric ukuleles built by luthier Bruce Herron in Fennville, Michigan. He also builds guitars, mandolins, dulcimers and lap steels.

Bluebird Guitars

2011-present. Intermediate and professional grade, custom, ukuleles built by luthiers Rob Bluebird and Gian Maria Camponeschi in Rome, Italy. They also build guitars and basses.

Boulder Creek

2007-present. Imported, intermediate and professional grade, production, acoustic ukuleles distributed by Morgan Hill Music of Morgan Hill, California. They also offer guitars and basses.

Breedlove

1990-present. Founded by Larry Breedlove and Steve Henderson. Professional and premium grade, production/custom, ukuleles made in Bend, Oregon. They also build guitars, basses, laps and mandolins.

Bruno

This New York distributor certainly subcontracted all of its ukulele production to other manufacturers, and as a result you'd be hard pressed to find two identical Bruno ukes.

Soprano Ukulele

1920s	Koa, rope soundhole	$300	$400
1930s	Koa, rope bound body	$400	$500

Chantus

1984-present. Professional grade, production/custom, ukuleles built in Austin, Texas, by luthier William King. He also builds guitars.

UKULELES

MODEL YEAR	FEATURES	EXC. COND. LOW	HIGH

Char

1985-present. Luthier Kerry Char builds his professional grade, custom, ukuleles in Portland, Oregon. He also builds guitars and harpguitars.

Collings

1986-present. The Austin, Texas, based guitar builder added ukuleles in the summer of '09.

DeCava Guitars

1983-present. Professional grade, production/custom, ukuleles built by luthier Jim DeCava in Stratford, Connecticut. He also builds guitars, banjos, and mandolins.

Del Vecchio Dimonaco

With a design patterned after the pioneering work of Dobro and National, this Brazilian company produced a full line of resonator instruments, all constructed of native Brazilian rosewood, from the 1950s onward.

Resonator Ukulele
Brazilian rosewood.

1950s		$900	$1,200

Delgado

1928-present. Custom, premium grade, classical ukuleles built by luthier Manuel A. Delgado in Nashville, Tennessee. He also builds guitars, basses, mandolins and banjos.

Ditson

1915-1926. Don't be fooled. While some of the ukes that were commissioned by this East Coast music publisher and chain store were actually manufactured by C.F. Martin, Martin was by no means the sole supplier. The Martin-made instruments often bear a Martin brand as well as a Ditson one, or, barring that, at least demonstrate an overall similarity to the rest of the ukes in the regular Martin line, both inside and out. The most telling and desirable feature of these Martin-made Ditsons is a dreadnaught-style wide waisted body design.

Dreadnaught Soprano Ukulele

1919	as Martin Style 1 M	$1,300	$1,700
1921	as Martin Style 1 K	$2,500	$3,200
1922	as Martin Style O	$1,300	$1,600
1923	as Martin Style 2 M	$1,500	$1,800
1923	as Martin Style 5 K	$10,000	$15,000
1926	as Martin Style 3 M	$3,200	$4,000

Dreadnaught Taropatch

1916	as Martin Style 1	$1,500	$2,500
1927	as Martin Style 2	$1,500	$2,500
1927	as Martin Style 3	$3,200	$4,000

Standard Soprano Ukulele

1917	as Martin Style 1 M	$700	$900
1922	as Martin Style 2 M	$800	$1,000
1922	as Martin Style O	$600	$800
1925	as Martin Style 3 M	$2,000	$2,500

Dobro

1929-1942, ca. 1954-present. The ukulele version of the popular amplifying resonator instruments first produced in California, the Dobro uke was offered in 2 sizes (soprano and tenor), 2 styles (f-holes and screen holes), and 2 colors (brown and black). Models with Dobro headstock decals are often outwardly indistinguishable from others bearing either a Regal badge or no logo at all, but a peek inside often reveals the presence of a sound well in the belly of the former, making them the more desirable of the two.

Resonator Ukulele
Wood body.

1930s	F-holes, Regal-made	$300	$500
1930s	Screen holes	$600	$900
1935	Tenor, cyclops screen	$1,300	$1,700

Douglas Ching

1976-present. Luthier Douglas J. Ching builds his professional grade, production/custom, ukuleles currently in Chester, Virginia, and previously in Hawaii ('76-'89) and Michigan ('90-'93). He also builds guitars, lutes and violins.

Earnest Kaai

Hawaiian Earnest Kaai was many things (teacher, songbook publisher, importer/exporter) during the early part of the 20th century, but ukulele manufacturer was certainly one job that he couldn't add to his resume. Still, scads of ukes proudly bear his name, in a variety of different styles and variations. Even more puzzling is the fact that while some appear to actually have been island-made, an equal number bear the telltale signs of mainland manufacture. Some Kaai labeled ukes may have been made by the Larson Brothers of Chicago.

Soprano Ukulele
Koa body.

1925	No binding, decal on headstock	$600	$700
1930	No binding, rope inlaid soundhole	$700	$800
1935	Pearl inlaid top & soundhole	$1,200	$1,500
1935	Rope binding on top/back only	$800	$900

Epiphone

Ca. 1873-present. Epiphone made banjo ukes in the 1920s and '30s and recently got back into the market with koa and mahogany models.

Favilla

1890-1973. The small New York City family-owned factory that produced primarily guitars also managed to offer some surprisingly high quality ukes, the best of which rival Martin and Gibson for craftsmanship and tone. As a result, Favilla ukuleles are a real value for the money.

Char Spalted Koa Concert

Delgado Custom Koa Concert Ukulele

Epiphone Les Paul Acoustic/Electric

UKULELES

Fine Resophonic Model 2

Late-1930s Gibson Uke-1
Randy Klimpert

Gibson Uke-2 (with rare inlay)

MODEL YEAR	FEATURES	EXC. COND. LOW	HIGH
Baritone Ukulele			
1950s	Plain mahogany	$300	$500
Soprano Ukulele			
1925	Wimbrola, unbound teardrop, flat sides	$500	$700
1950s	Mahogany, triple bound	$500	$600
1950s	Plain mahogany	$300	$500
1950s	Teardrop-shaped, birch	$300	$500
1950s	Teardrop-shaped, stained blue	$300	$500

Fender

1946-present. Fender offered Regal-made ukuleles in the 1960s, including the R-275 Baritone Ukulele. In '09 they again started offering ukes. Starting in '09 Fender offered budget and intermediate grade, production ukes.

Fin-der

1950s. The pitch of this short-lived plastic ukulele was apparently the ease of learning, since the included instructional brochure helped you to "find" your chords with the added help of rainbow color-coded nylon strings.

MODEL YEAR	FEATURES	EXC. COND. LOW	HIGH
Diamond Head Ukulele			
Styrene plastic, in original box.			
1950s		$100	$150

Fine Resophonic

1988-present. Intermediate and professional grade, production/custom, wood and metal-bodied resophonic ukuleles built by luthiers Mike Lewis and Pierre Avocat in Vitry Sur Seine, France. They also build guitars and mandolins.

Flamingo

1950s. If swanky designs hot-foil stamped into the surface of these '50s swirly injection molded polystyrene ukes didn't grab you, certainly the built-in functional pitch pipe across the top of the headstock would. And I ask you, who can resist a ukulele with a built-in tuner?

MODEL YEAR	FEATURES	EXC. COND. LOW	HIGH
Soprano Ukulele			
1955	Brown top, white 'board	$100	$150
1955	White top, brown 'board	$100	$150

Gibson

1890s (1902)-present. A relative late-comer to the uke market, Gibson didn't get a line off the ground until 1927, fully nine years after Martin had already been in production. Even then they only produced three soprano styles and one tenor version. Worse still, they never made any ukes in koa, sticking to the easier-to-obtain mahogany.

Nonetheless, Gibson ukuleles exhibit more unintentional variety than any other major maker, with

enough construction, inlay, binding, and cosmetic variations to keep collectors buzzing for many a year to come. In general, the earliest examples feature a Gibson logo in script, later shortened to just Gibson. Post-war examples adopted the more square-ish logo of the rest of the Gibson line, and, at some point in the late '50s, began sporting ink-stamped serial numbers on the back of the headstock like their guitar and mandolin brethren.

MODEL YEAR	FEATURES	EXC. COND. LOW	HIGH
ETU-1 Ukulele			
Electric tenor, unbound body, square black pickup, 88 made.			
1949		$3,500	$5,000
ETU-3 Ukulele			
Electric tenor, triple bound body, rectangle pickup, rare.			
1953		$5,000	$8,000
Poinsettia Ukulele			
Fancy inlays and 'board, painted body.			
1930		$9,000	$12,000
TU-1 Ukulele			
Tenor, called the TU until 1 added in 1949, mahogany body, sunburst finish.			
1930s		$1,100	$1,500
Uke-1 Ukulele			
Soprano, plain mahogany body.			
1927		$600	$800
1966	Red SG guitar-like finish	$500	$700
Uke-2 Ukulele			
Soprano, mahogany body.			
1934	Triple bound	$800	$1,000
Uke-3 Ukulele			
Soprano, dark finish.			
1933	Diamonds & squares inlay	$1,000	$1,500
1935	Diamond inlay, short 'board	$1,000	$1,500
1935	Rare curved designs inlay	$2,500	$3,000

Gold Tone

1993-present. Wayne and Robyn Rogers build their intermediate grade, production/custom ukuleles in Titusville, Florida. They also offer guitars, basses, lap steels, mandolins, banjos and banjitars.

Graziano

1969-present. Luthier Tony Graziano has been building ukuleles almost exclusively since '95 in his Santa Cruz shop. Like many, he sees the uke as the instrument of the new millennium, and his entirely handmade, custom orders can be had in a variety of shapes, sizes, and woods.

Gretsch

1883-present. The first (and most desirable) ukuleles by this New York manufacturer were actually stamped with the name Gretsch American or with interior brass nameplates. Subsequent pieces, largely inexpensive laminate-bodied catalog offer-

UKULELES

MODEL YEAR	FEATURES	EXC. COND. LOW	HIGH

ings, are distinguished by small round Gretsch headstock decals, and a lack of any kerfed linings inside the bodies. They stopped making ukes in the late '50s, then in 2012 began offering them again.

Plain Soprano Ukulele
Natural mahogany body, no binding.

1950s		$100	$200

Round Ukulele
Round body, blue to green sunburst.

1940		$100	$200

Soprano Ukulele

1935	Bound koa, 'board as Martin 5K	$1,700	$2,000
1940s	Koa, fancy 'board inlay	$900	$1,100
1940s	Mahogany, fancy 'board inlay	$900	$1,000
1940s	Unbound, engraved rose peghead	$1,000	$1,200
1950s	Darker finish, dark binding border	$350	$500

Guild
1952 present. By rights this fine East Coast shop should have produced a full line of ukes to complement its impressive flat and carved-top guitar offerings. Alas, a lone baritone model was all that they could manage. And it's a darned shame, too.

B-11 Baritone Ukulele
1963-1976. Mahogany body, rosewood 'board.

1960s		$1,000	$1,200

Harmony
1892-1976, late 1970s-present. This manufacturer surely produced more ukuleles than all other makers put together. Their extensive line ran the gamut from artist endorsed models and ukes in unusual shapes and materials, to inexpensive but flashy creations adorned with eye-catching decals and silk screening. The earliest examples have a small paper label on the back of the headstock, and a branded logo inside the body. This was replaced by a succession of logo decals applied to the front of the headstock, first gold and black, later green, white, and black. By the '60s Harmony had become so synonymous with ukulele production that they were known around their Chicago locale as simply "the ukulele factory," as in, "Ma couldn't come to the bar-b-que on-a-counta she got a job at the ukulele factory."

Baritone Ukulele
Bound mahogany body.

1960s		$200	$300

Concert Ukulele
Mahogany body, bound, concert-sized.

1935		$200	$300

Harold Teen Ukulele
Carl Ed cartoon decals on front.

1930	Gray-blue	$600	$800
1930	Red	$600	$800
1930	Yellow	$600	$800

Johnny Marvin Tenor Ukulele
Sports an airplane bridge.

1930s	Flamed koa	$1,200	$1,500
1930s	Sunburst mahogany	$500	$700

Roy Smeck Concert Ukulele
Concert-sized, sunburst spruce top.

1935		$500	$700

Roy Smeck Ukulele
Mahogany body.

1955	Plastic 'board	$100	$150
1955	Wood 'board	$300	$400

Roy Smeck Vita Ukulele
Pear-shaped body, seal-shaped f-holes.

1926		$600	$800

Tiple Ukulele
Multicolored binding, 10 steel strings.

1935		$500	$700

Ukulele

1930	Koa, unbound	$200	$300
1935	Plain mahogany, unbound	$150	$250

Hilo Bay Ukuleles
2003-present. Intermediate grade, production, tenor ukuleles made in Cebu City, Philippines for Hilo Guitars and Ukuleles of Hilo, Hawaii.

Hohner
1857-present. They currently offer budget grade, tenor, baritone, standard, pineapple, and concert ukuleles. They also have guitars, basses, banjos, and mandolins.

Johnson
Mid-1990s-present. Budget ukuleles imported by Music Link of Brisbane, California. They also offer guitars, amps, mandolins and effects. Most notable of the Johnson ukes are the National metal-bodied uke copies, which come surprisingly close to the look and feel of the originals, at an unfathomably low price.

K & S
1992-1998. Ukes distributed by George Katechis and Marc Silber and handmade in Paracho, Mexico. They also offered guitars. In '98, Silber started marketing the ukes under the Marc Silber Guitar Company brand and Katechis continued to offer instruments under the Casa Montalvo brand. The Mexican-made 'Frisco Uke' takes its inspiration from the inimitable '20s Roy Smeck Vita Uke (see Harmony), but with none of the whimsy of the original.

Kala
2005-present. Mike Upton's Petaluma, California company offers budget and intermediate grade, production, ukuleles.

Graziano Concert

Gretsch Fancy Koa

1930s Harmony Johnny Marvin Tenor
Tim Fleck

UKULELES

1960s Kamaka
Randy Klimpert

1970 Kamaka Tenor

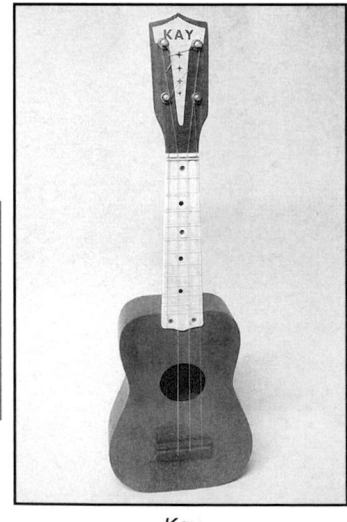

Kay

UKULELES

MODEL YEAR	FEATURES	EXC. COND. LOW	HIGH

Kamaka

Part of the second wave of ukulele builders on the Hawaiian islands (after Nunes, Dias, and Santos) Kamaka distinguished itself first with ukes of extremely high quality, subsequently with the most enduring non-guitar-derived designs, the Pineapple Uke, patented in 1928. Kamaka is the only maker which has been in continuous production for nearly a hundred years, offering Hawaiian-made products from native woods in virtually every size and ornamentation. In the early '70s, Kamaka began rubber stamping the full date of manufacture on the end of the neck block of each uke, visible right through the sound hole. Now don't you wish that every manufacturer did that?

Concert Ukulele
Koa body, extended rosewood 'board.

1975		$700	$900

Lili'u Ukulele
Concert-sized koa body.

1965	8 strings	$900	$1,000
1985	6 strings	$900	$1,000

Pineapple Ukulele

1928	Full 'painted' pineapple decal top or back	$1,500	$2,000
1928	Pearl inlay on top and/or 'board	$3,000	$3,500
1930	Monkeypod wood, plain, unbound	$1,200	$1,500
1930	Rope bound top only, koa	$1,500	$2,000
1935	Rope bound soundhole only	$1,200	$1,500
1960	Koa, unbound, 2 Ks logo	$800	$1,000
1970	Koa, extended rosewood 'board	$700	$900

Soprano Ukulele
Traditional uke shape, plain koa body.

1920		$700	$900

Tenor Ukulele
Koa body, extended rosewood 'board.

1955		$800	$1,000

Kanile'a Ukulele

1998-present. Joseph and Kristen Souza build their intermediate, professional and premium grade, production/custom, ukuleles in Kaneohe, Hawaii.

Kay

1931-present. Kay offered banjo ukuleles in the 1920s and again in the late '50s; they offered ukuleles from '66-'68 and currently offer budget grade, production, imported ukuleles. They also make amps, guitars, banjos, mandolins, basses, and violins.

Kent

1961-1969. Large, student quality ukes of laminated construction were offered by this Japanese concern throughout the '60s.

MODEL YEAR	FEATURES	EXC. COND. LOW	HIGH

Baritone Ukulele
Mahogany body, bound top, bound back.

1960s		$100	$150

Knutsen

1890s-1920s. While Christopher Knutsen was the inventor of flat-topped harp instruments featuring an integral sound chamber on the bass side of the body, he almost certainly left the manufacturing to others. Striking in both concept and design, Knutsen products nonetheless suffer from compromised construction techniques.

Harp Taro Patch Ukulele
Koa body, large horn chamber, 8 strings, unbound.

1915		$3,000	$4,000

Harp Ukulele
Koa body, large horn chamber.

1915	Bound	$2,500	$3,000
1915	Unbound	$2,000	$2,500

Kona Guitar Company

2001-present. Budget grade, production, acoustic ukuleles made in Asia. They also offer guitars, basses, amps, mandolins and banjos.

Kumalae

Along with Kamaka, Kumalae was also of the second wave of Hawaiian uke makers. Jonah Kumalae's company quickly snagged the prestigious Gold Award at the Pan Pacific Exhibition in 1915, and the headstock decals and paper labels aren't about to let you forget it, either. Many assume that these all date from exactly that year, when in fact Kumalaes were offered right up through the late 1930s.

Soprano Ukulele
Figured koa body.

1919	Bound top/back/ 'board	$700	$900
1920	Rope bound top/back	$600	$800
1927	As 1919 but with fiddle-shaped peghead	$2,000	$3,000
1930	Unbound body	$600	$800
1933	Rope bound soundhole only	$600	$800

Tenor Ukulele
Koa body, unbound top and back.

1930s		$1,500	$1,700

Laka

2010-present. Budget and intermediate grade, production ukuleles built in the Far East and distributed worldwide by John Hornby Skewes & Co. Ltd. from the United Kingdom.

Lanikai

2000-present. Line of budget and intermediate grade, production, koa or nato wood, acoustic and acoustic/electric, ukuleles distributed by Hohner.

MODEL YEAR	FEATURES	EXC. COND. LOW	HIGH

Larrivee

1968-present. This mainstream guitar manufacturer has an on-again off-again relationship with the ukulele, having occasionally produced some superb examples in various sizes, woods and degrees of ornamentation. They introduced three ukulele models in '00. They also build guitars.

Le Domino

This line of striking ukuleles turned the popularity of domino playing into a clever visual motif, displaying not only tumbling dominos on their soundboards and around their soundholes, but 'board markers represented in decal domino denominations (3, 5, 7, 10, 12, etc.). The ukuleles were, in fact, produced by at least two different companies - Stewart and Regal - but you can scarcely tell them apart.

Concert Ukukele
Concert size, black-finish, white bound, dominos.

1932		$1,200	$1,500

Soprano Ukukele
Domino decals.

1930	Black finish, white bound	$500	$700
1940	Natural finish, unbound	$150	$200

Leonardo Nunes

Leonardo was the son of Manuel, the self professed inventor of the ukulele. Whether actually the originator or not, Dad was certainly on the ship that brought the inventor to the islands in 1879. Leonardo, instead of joining up and making it Manuel & Son, set out on his own to produce ukes that are virtually indistinguishable from Pop's. All constructed entirely of koa, some exhibit considerable figure and rope binding finery, making them as highly desirable to collectors as Manuel's.

Radio Tenor Ukulele
Koa body, bound top, back and neck.

1935		$1,500	$1,700

Soprano Ukulele
Figured koa body.

1919	Bound top/back/'board	$800	$1,000
1920	Rope bound top/back	$800	$1,000
1927	Bound body/'board/head	$1,200	$1,500
1930	Unbound	$700	$900
1933	Rope bound soundhole only	$700	$900

Taro Patch Fiddle
Koa body, unbound top and back.

1930		$1,500	$1,700

Tenor Ukulele
Koa body, unbound top and back.

1930		$1,200	$1,500

Levin

1900-1973. Ukuleles built in Sweden. Levin was best known for their classical guitars, which they also built for other brands, most notably Goya. They also built mandolins.

Loprinzi

1972-present. Intermediate and professional grade, production/custom, ukuleles built in Clearwater, Florida. They also build guitars.

Luna Guitars

2005-present. Budget and intermediate grade, production, ukes imported from Japan, Korea and China by Yvonne de Villiers in Tampa, Florida. She also imports guitars, basses and amps.

Lyon & Healy

1880s-ca.1949. During different periods several different makers constructed ukes bearing this stamp - often with an additional Washburn tag as well. After initial production by Lyon & Healy, instrument manufacture then apparently bounced between Regal, Stewart, and Tonk Brothers all within a span of only a few short years. Adding to the confusion, ukes surface from time to time bearing no maker's mark that can be reasonably attributed to Lyon & Healy. Suffice it to say that the best of these ukes, those displaying the highest degrees of quality and ornamentation, rival Gibson and Martin for collectability and tone and beauty.

Bell-Shaped Ukulele
Mahogany body.

1927		$3,000	$3,500

Camp Ukulele
Round nissa wood body, black binding.

1935		$200	$300

Concert Ukulele
Mahogany body, bound top and back.

1930		$1,500	$2,000

Shrine Ukulele
Triangular body.

1927	Koa, abalone body inlay	$3,000	$4,000
1930	Mahogany, green binding	$3,000	$3,500
1933	Koa, green binding	$2,500	$3,500

Soprano Ukulele (Koa)

1927	Bound top, pearl rosette	$3,500	$4,000
1934	Bound top/back	$1,000	$1,200
1935	Pearl bound top/back	$9,000	$11,000

Soprano Ukulele (Mahogany)

1930	Unbound	$700	$1,000
1932	Bound top/back	$700	$1,000

Tenor Ukulele (Koa)

1935	Pearl bound top/back	$10,000	$12,000

Tenor Ukulele (Mahogany)

1933	Bound top/back	$1,500	$2,000

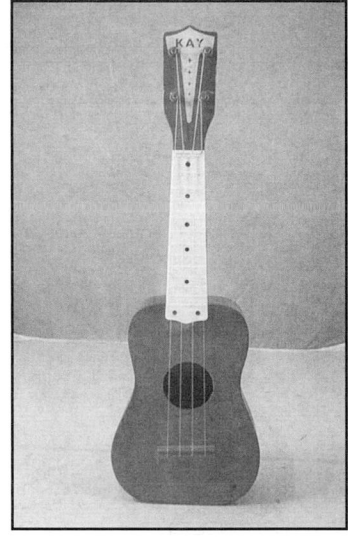

1950s Kay Soprano
Keith Myers

Kumalae

Lanikai CMTU-S Curly Mango Soprano Tuna Uke

UKULELES

Maccaferri Islander
Bill Ruxton

Mainland

1917 Martin Style 2

Maccaferri

1923-1990. Between the time he designed the Selmer guitar that became instantly synonymous with Django's gypsy jazz and his invention of the plastic clothespin, guitar design genius and manufacturing impresario Mario Maccaferri created a line of stringed instruments revolutionary for their complete plastic construction. The ukuleles were by far the greatest success, and most bore the tiny Maccaferri coat of arms on their tiny headstock.

Islander Baritone Ukulele
Large polystyrene cutaway body.

MODEL YEAR	FEATURES	EXC. COND. LOW	HIGH
1959		$200	$250

Islander Ukulele
Polystyrene plastic body, crest in peghead.

1953		$150	$200

Maestro Baritone Electric Ululele
Large polystyrene cutaway body, pickup.

1960		$400	$500

Playtune Ukulele
Polystyrene body.

1956		$100	$150

TV Pal Deluxe Ukulele
Extended 'board.

1960		$100	$150

TV Pal Ukulele
Polystyrene plastic body.

1955		$100	$150

Magic Fluke Company

1999-present. Budget grade, production, ukuleles made in New Hartford, Connecticut. With a clever design, exceptional quality, dozens of catchy finishes, and surprisingly affordable prices, it's little wonder that these little wonders have caught on. Riding – if not almost single-handedly driving – the coming third wave of uke popularity (the '20s and '50s were the first and second), Dale and Phyllis Webb of the Magic Fluke, along with Phyllis' brother, author Jumpin' Jim Beloff, are downright ukulele evangelists. The Fluke is the first new uke that you're not afraid to let the kids monkey with.

Mainland Ukes

2008-present. Mike Hater imports parts built in China to set-up his budget and intermediate grade, production/custom, solid wood ukes and banjo-ukes in Nashville, Indiana.

Manuel Nunes

The self-professed father of the ukulele was at least one of the first makers to produce them in any quantity. Beginning after 1879, when he and the first boat load of Portuguese settlers landed in Hawaii, until at least the 1930s, Manuel and his son Leonardo (see Leonardo Nunes section) produced some of the most beautiful and superbly crafted ukes offered by any Island maker.

Soprano Ukulele
Koa body.

MODEL YEAR	FEATURES	EXC. COND. LOW	HIGH
1919	Figured koa, bound top/back/ 'board	$1,000	$1,300
1920	Rope bound top/back	$600	$800
1927	Bound body/ 'board/head	$1,500	$2,000
1930	Unbound	$600	$800
1933	Rope bound soundhole only	$600	$800

Taro Patch Fiddle
Koa body.

1930	Rope bound top/back	$2,500	$3,000
1930	Unbound top/back	$2,000	$2,500

Tenor Ukulele
Koa body, unbound top and back.

1930		$1,000	$1,500

Marc Silber Guitar Company

1998-present. Mexican-made ukes from designer Marc Silber of Berkley, California. He also offers guitars. His Frisco Uke takes its inspiration from the inimitable Roy Smeck Vita Uke (see Harmony), but without the whimsy of the original.

Martin

1833-present. The C.F. Martin Company knew they wanted in on the uke craze, and toyed with some prototypes as early as 1907 or so, but didn't get around to actually getting serious until '16. The first of these were characterized by rather more primitive craftsmanship (by stringent Martin standards), bar frets, and an impressed logo in the back of the headstock. By '20, koa became available as a pricey option, and by the early '30s, regular frets and the familiar Martin headstock decal had prevailed. Martin single-handedly created the archetype of the mainland uke and the standard by which all competitors are measured.

Martin has recently re-entered the ukulele market with its budget Mexican-made model S-0, the Backpacker Uke, as well as a limited edition of the ornate, and pricey, 5K, 5M and 3K ukes.

Style 0 Ukulele
Unbound mahogany body.

1920	Wood pegs	$800	$900
1953	Patent pegs	$800	$900

Style 0-C Concert Ukulele
Mahogany body, bound top.

1931		$1,500	$1,700

Style 1 Ukulele
Mahogany body.

1917	Bound top only	$800	$900
1950	Tortoise bound top only	$800	$900
1967	Tortoise bound top only	$800	$900

UKULELES

MODEL YEAR	FEATURES	EXC. COND. LOW	HIGH
Style 1-C Concert Ukulele			
Mahogany body, bound top.			
1947		$1,200	$1,500
Style 1-T Tenor Ukulele			
Mahogany body, bound top only.			
1940		$1,500	$1,800
Style 1-K Ukulele			
Koa body, rosewood bound top.			
1928	Wood pegs	$1,000	$1,500
1939	Patent pegs	$1,500	$2,000
Style 1-C K Concert Ukulele			
Koa body, bound top.			
1928		$2,500	$3,500
Style 1 Taro Patch Ukulele			
Mahogany body, 8 strings, rosewood bound.			
1917		$1,200	$1,500
Style 1-K Taro Patch Ukulele			
Style 1 with koa body.			
1922		$1,500	$2,000
Style 2 Ukulele			
Mahogany body, ivoroid bound top and back.			
1922		$1,000	$1,200
1935		$1,000	$1,200
1961		$1,000	$1,200
Style 2-K Ukulele			
Figured koa body, bound top and back.			
1923		$2,000	$2,500
1939	Patent pegs	$2,000	$2,500
Style 2-C K Concert Ukulele			
Same specs as 2-K, but in concert size.			
1927		$5,000	$6,000
Style 2 Taro Patch Ukulele			
Mahogany body, 8 strings, ivoroid bound.			
1925		$1,500	$2,000
Style 2-K Taro Patch Ukulele			
Style 2 with koa body.			
1924		$1,700	$2,500
Style 3 Ukulele			
Mahogany body.			
1925	Kite inlay in headstock	$2,700	$3,200
1937	B/W lines in ebony 'board	$2,500	$3,000
1950	Extended 'board, dots	$2,200	$2,700
Style 3-K Ukulele			
Figured koa body.			
1920	Bow-tie 'board inlay	$3,500	$5,000
1931	B/W lines, diamonds, squares	$3,000	$4,000
1939	B/W lines and dot inlay	$3,000	$4,000
Style 3-C K Concert Ukulele			
Same specs as 3-K, but in concert size.			
1928		$10,000	$15,000
Style 3 Taro Patch Ukulele			
Mahogany body, 8 strings, multiple bound.			
1923		$2,500	$3,500
Style 3-K Taro Patch Ukulele			
Style 3 with koa body.			
1929		$3,000	$4,000

MODEL YEAR	FEATURES	EXC. COND. LOW	HIGH
Style 5 Ukulele			
Highly flamed mahogany body, all pearl trimmed, extremely rare.			
1941		$25,000	$30,000
Style 5-K Ukulele			
Highly figured koa body, all pearl trimmed.			
1926		$7,500	$10,000
Style 5-C K Concert Ukulele			
Same specs as 5-K, but in concert size.			
1926		$12,000	$15,000
Style 5-T K Tenor Ukulele			
Same specs as 5-K, but in tenor size.			
1929		$12,000	$15,000
Style 51 Baritone Ukulele			
Mahogany body, bound top and back.			
1966		$1,000	$1,300
Style T-15 Tiple Ukulele			
Mahogany body, 10 metal strings, unbound.			
1971		$800	$1,000
Style T-17 Tiple Ukulele			
Mahogany body, 10 strings, unbound top and back.			
1940		$1,000	$1,200
Style T-18 Tiple Ukulele			
Mahogany body, 10 strings, spruce top.			
1925		$1,000	$1,200
Style T-28 Tiple Ukulele			
Rosewood body, 10 strings, bound top and back.			
1950		$3,000	$4,000

Maurer

The Larson brothers of Maurer & Co., Chicago, built a few ukes and at least one taro patch under this brand from 1915 into the 1930s. Their small tops and backs are built-under-tension in the Larson tradition. A few of them have surfaced with the Hawaiian teacher/player's Earnest Kaai label and were probably sold through Stahl's Milwaukee store.

Miami

Apparently endorsed by the not-so-famous "Ukulele Hughes" - whose smiling mug graces the inside labels - these ukes' actual origins are unknown, but were distributed by the Stadlmair company of New York, also the east coast distributor of Weissenborn instruments during the 1920s.

Miami "Baby"
Smaller mahogany body, unbound.
1925 $400 $500

Soprano Ukulele
Plain mahogany body, unbound.
1925 $400 $500

Michael Cone

1968-present. Luthier Michael Cone builds his professional and premium grade, production/custom, ukuleles in Kihei Maui, Hawaii. He also builds guitars.

Michael Dunn Guitars

1968-present. Luthier Michael Dunn builds a Knutsen-style harp uke in New Westminster, British Columbia. He also builds guitars.

1930s Martin Style 2K
Randy Klimpert

1924 Martin 3K 4 String Taro Patch (one of 3 made)

Martin Style 5-K

UKULELES

1934 National Silver Ukulele Style 2

Oscar Schmidt

Pegasus Curly Koa Concert

UKULELES

Mirabella

1997-present. Professional grade, custom ukuleles built by luthier Cristian Mirabella in Babylon, New York. He also builds guitars, basses and mandolins.

National

Ca. 1927-present. To capitalize on the success of their amplifying guitars, the Dopyera brothers introduced metal-bodied ukuleles and mandolins as well. Large, heavy, and ungainly by today's standards, these early offerings nonetheless have their charms. Their subsequent switch to a smaller body shape produced an elegant and sweet-sounding resonator uke that soon became much sought after.

Style O Ukulele
Metal body, soprano size, sandblasted scenes.

MODEL YEAR	FEATURES	EXC. COND. LOW	HIGH
1931		$2,000	$3,000

Style 1 Ukulele
Nickel body.

1928	Tenor, 6" resonator	$2,000	$2,500
1933	Soprano	$2,000	$2,500

Style 2 Ukulele
Nickel body, engraved roses.

1928	Tenor	$2,500	$3,000
1931	Soprano	$1,500	$2,000

Style 3 Ukulele
Nickel body, lilies-of-the-valley.

1929	Tenor	$3,000	$4,000
1933	Soprano	$3,500	$4,500

Triolian Ukulele

1928	Tenor, sunburst painted body	$1,500	$2,000
1930	Soprano, sunburst painted body	$1,500	$2,000
1934	Soprano, wood-grained metal body	$2,000	$3,000

National Reso-Phonic

1988-present. Successors to the National name, with the designs and patented amplifying resonator assemblies of the original National models, they offer professional grade, production, single cone ukuleles from their shop in San Luis Obispo, California. They also build guitars, basses and mandolins.

New Moon Ukulele

1978-present. Professional and premium grade, custom, acoustic ukuleles built in Greensboro, North Carolina by luthier Robert Rigaud. He also builds guitars under the Rigaud brand.

Oscar Schmidt

1879-1938, 1979-present. The same New Jersey outfit responsible for Leadbelly's 12-string guitar offered ukes as well during the same period. Many of these were odd amalgams of materials, often combining koa, mahogany, and spruce in the same instrument. Since 1979, when the name was acquired by the U.S. Music Corp. (Washburn,

Randall, etc.), they have offered a line of budget grade, production, Asian-made ukes. They also offer guitars, basses, mandolins, and banjos.

Soprano Ukulele
Spruce top, bound mahogany body.

1930		$200	$300

Pegasus Guitars and Ukuleles

1977-present. Professional grade, custom, ukulele family instruments built by luthier Bob Gleason in Kurtistown, Hawaii, who also builds steel-string guitars.

Pilgrim

1970s-late-1980s, 2010-present. Brand dates back to '70s with luthier Paul Tebbutt and is presently owned by the U.K.'s John Hornby Skewes & Co. Ltd and used on guitars, mandolins, banjos and ukes, all built in the Far East.

Polk-a-lay-lee

1960s. These inexplicably shaped oddities were produced by Petersen Products of Chicago ca. the mid-'60s, and anecdotal Midwestern lore has it that their intent was to be offered as giveaways for the Polk Brothers, a local appliance chain. This may be how they ended up, although the gargantuan original packaging makes no reference to any such promotion. The box does call out what the optional colors were.

Many have noted the striking resemblance to the similarly named wares of the Swaggerty company (see Swaggerty) of California, who also offered brightly colored plywood-bodied ukes in comically oversized incarnations, but who was copying whom has yet to be determined.

Ukulele
Long boat oar body, uke scale, brown, natural, red, black or fruitwood.

1965	Brown or natural	$300	$400
1965	Red, black, fruitwood	$400	$500

Recording King (TML)

2005-present. The Music Link added budget grade, production, stenciled ukuleles designed by Greg Rich. They also have banjos and guitars.

Regal

Ca. 1895-1966, 1987-present. Like the other large 1930s Chicago makers, Harmony and Lyon & Healy, the good ukes are very, very good, and the cheap ukes are very, very cheap. Unlike its pals, however, Regal seems to have produced more ukuleles in imaginative themes, striking color schemes, and in more degrees of fancy trim, making them the quintessential wall-hangers. And lucky for you, there's a vintage Regal uke to suit every décor.

Carson Robison Ukulele
Top sports painted signature, cowboy scene.

1935		$500	$700

MODEL YEAR	FEATURES	EXC. COND. LOW	HIGH
Jungle Ukulele			
Birch body, covered in leopard skin fabric.			
1950		$1,000	$1,200
Resonator Ukulele			
Black body, f-holes, see Dobro uke.			
1934		$200	$400
Soprano Ukulele (Birch)			
Birch body.			
1931	Brown sunburst	$100	$200
1931	Nautical themes, various colors	$100	$200
1945	Painted body, victory themes	$1,000	$1,200
Soprano Ukulele (Koa)			
Koa body, multicolored rope bound top.			
1930		$300	$500
Soprano Ukulele (Mahogany)			
Mahogany body.			
1930	Multiple bound top	$500	$800
1935	Spruce top, inlays	$300	$500
1940	Extended 'board	$200	$300
Tiple Ukulele			
1930	Birch body stained dark, black binding	$300	$500
1935	Spruce top, mahogany, fancy binding	$400	$600
Wendall Hall Red Head Ukulele			
Koa body, celebrity decal on headstock.			
1935		$500	$800

Renaissance Guitars

1994-present. In '05 luthier Rick Turner added a line of acoustic and acoustic/electric ukuleles built in Santa Cruz, California. He also builds guitars and basses.

Rogue

2001-present. Budget grade, production, imported ukuleles. They also offer guitars, basses, lap steels, mandolins, banjos, effects and amps.

S. S. Stewart

Not much is known about the ukuleles of this Philadelphia firm, except that they were most certainly sub-contracted from another maker or makers.

Soprano Ukulele
Mahogany body, bound top and back.

1927		$200	$300

Samick

1958-2001, 2002-present. Budget grade, production, imported ukuleles. They also offer guitars, basses, mandolins and banjos.

Sammo

Flashy internal paper labels trumpet that these ukes (mandolins and guitars, too) were products of the Osborne Mfg. Co. Masonic Temple, Chicago-Illinois and what the heck any of that means is still open to modern speculation. Your guess is as good as mine. Still, the high quality and often opulent degree of ornamentation that the instruments exhibit, coupled with even the vaguest implication that they were made by guys wearing fezzes and/or men who ride around in tiny cars at parades is all the reason we need to buy every one we see.

Soprano Ukulele

1925	Bound koa, fancy headstock shape	$600	$800
1925	Figured maple, 5-ply top, back binding	$300	$500
1925	Unbound koa, fancy headstock shape	$400	$600

Santa Cruz

1976-present. Professional grade, production, ukuleles from luthier Richard Hoover in Santa Cruz, California. They also build guitars.

Silvertone

1941-ca. 1970, present. Silvertone was the house brand of Sears & Roebuck and most (if not all) of its ukes were manufactured for them by Harmony.

Soprano Ukulele
Mahogany body, Harmony-made.

1950	Sunburst	$200	$300
1950	Unbound	$200	$300
1955	Bound	$200	$300
1960	Green	$200	$300

Slingerland

Slingerland started marketing ukes around 1916. Banjo ukuleles bearing this brand (see Slingerland Banjo uke section below) were certainly made by the popular drum company (banjos being little more than drums with necks, after all). Slingerland standard ukuleles, on the other hand, bear an uncanny resemblance to the work of the Oscar Schmidt company.

Soprano Ukulele
Koa body, rope bound top and soundhole.

1920		$200	$300

Specimen Products

1984-present. Luthier Ian Schneller builds his professional grade, production/custom, ukuleles in Chicago, Illinois. He also builds guitars, basses, amps and speaker cabs. Schneller has built some of the most offbeat, endearing - and high quality - custom ukuleles available.

Sterling

The miniscule reference buried deep within the headstock decal to a T.B. Co. can only mean that the Sterling ukulele somehow fits into the mind-numbing Tonk Bros./Lyon & Healy/Regal/S.S. Stewart manufacturing puzzle. Nonetheless, the brand must have been reserved for the cream of the crop, since the Sterling ukes that surface tend to be of the drop-dead-gorgeous variety.

Sammo

Specimen Electric

Sterling

UKULELES

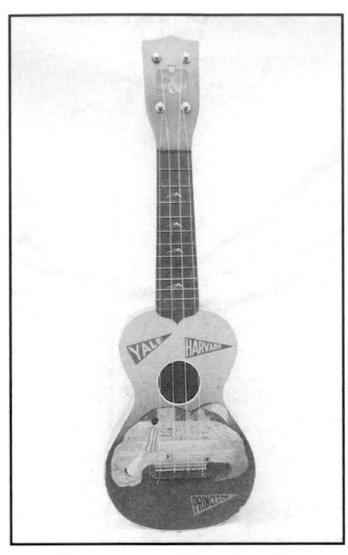

Supertone Cheerleader

Nicola Turturro Ukulele

Washburn Fancy Pearl-Trimmed

MODEL YEAR	FEATURES	EXC. COND. LOW	HIGH

Soprano Ukulele
Flamed koa, multiple fancy binding all over.

1935		$2,000	$3,000

Stetson

Popular misconception – to say nothing of wishful thinking and greed – has it that all instruments labeled with the Stetson brand were the work of the Larson Brothers of Chicago. While a few Stetson guitars and a very few mandolins may be genuine Larson product, the ukuleles surely were made elsewhere.

Soprano Ukulele
Mahogany body, single bound top and back.

1930		$200	$300

Supertone

1914-1940s. For whatever reason, Supertone was the name attached to Sears' musical instruments before the line became Silvertone (see above). These, too, were all Harmony-made.

Soprano Ukulele (Koa)
Koa body, Harmony-made.

1935	Rope bound	$300	$500
1943	Unbound	$300	$500

Soprano Ukulele (Mahogany)
Mahogany body, Harmony-made.

1930	Unbound	$200	$300
1940	Bound	$200	$300

Swaggerty

Not enough is known of this West Coast company, except that their product line of unusually shaped 4-stringed novelty instruments oddly mirrors those made by Petersen Products in Chicago at the same time (see Polk-a-lay-lee). The two companies even seem to have shared plastic parts, such as 'boards and tuners. Go figure.

Kook-a-Lay-Lee Ukulele
Green plywood body, twin necks.

1965		$300	$500

Singing Treholipee
Orange plywood body, long horn.

1965		$300	$500

Surf-a-Lay-Lee Ukulele
Plywood body, long horn, green, yellow, or orange.

1965		$300	$500

Tabu

The Tabu brand on either the back of a ukulele's headstock or inside its soundhole was never an indication of its original maker. Rather, it was intended to assure the purchaser that the uke was, indeed of bona fide Hawaiian origin. So rampant was the practice of mainland makers claiming Island manufacture of their wares that in the late 'teens Hawaii launched a campaign to set the record straight, and – lucky for you – a nifty little brand was the result. The Tabu mark actually was used to mark the ukes of several different makers.

MODEL YEAR	FEATURES	EXC. COND. LOW	HIGH

Soprano Ukulele
Figured koa body.

1915	Rope bound	$800	$1,000
1915	Unbound	$500	$700

Tanglewood Guitar Company UK

1991-present. Production, intermediate grade, ukuleles imported from China by Dirk Kommer and Tony Flatt in United Kingdom. They also import guitars, basses, mandolins, banjos and amps.

Tombo

This venerable Japanese harmonica manufacturer jumped on two bandwagons at once with its mid-'60s introduction of a solid body electric ukulele. The Tombo Ukulet shares a tenor scale length and single coil pickup with Gibson's ETU electric tenor ukes, but the Tombo's thin, solidbody design is decidedly more Fender than jumping flea. Completing the imitation-is-the-sincerest-form-of-flattery theme is a snazzy Silvertone-esque case with onboard amplifier.

Ukulet
Solid body, amp-in-case, red sunburst, white or blue finish.

1967	Red sunburst	$800	$1,000
1968	White or blue	$1,200	$1,500

Tonk Brothers

The Tonk Brothers Company was a huge Chicago-based distributor of musical merchandise, founded in 1893. They carried many of the popular brands of the day and also offered a line of ukuleles under their own brand name.

Soprano Ukulele
Plain mahogany body, celluloid bound.

1930		$300	$500

Turturro

Unlike manufacturers like Regal and Harmony who were content to produce novelty ukes by merely spray painting or applying decals with eye-catching motifs, New York manufacturer Nicola Turturro issued novelty ukuleles from his own patented designs. The most well-known is the Turnover Uke, a playable two-sided contraption strung as a 4-string uke on one side, and an 8-string mandolin on the other.

Concert Ukulele
Concert size, plain mahogany body.

1930		$400	$600

Peanut Ukulele
Ribbed peanut shaped body.

1928		$1,000	$1,500

Turnover Ukulele
Two-sided uke and mandolin.

1926		$1,000	$1,500
1926	Spruce topped mandolin	$1,200	$1,700

MODEL YEAR	FEATURES	EXC. COND. LOW	HIGH

Vega

Famous for their banjos, the Vega name was applied to a sole baritone uke, tied with the endorsement of 1950s TV crooner Arthur Godfrey.

Arthur Godfrey Baritone Ukulele
Mahogany body, unbound.

1955		$300	$500

Vintage

Ca. 1993-present. Budget and intermediate grade, production, ukuleles, imported from China, Korea and Vietnam by John Hornby Skewes & Co. in the U.K. They also offer guitars, basses and mandolins.

Washburn

See Lyon & Healy.

Weissenborn

1910s-1937, present. The mainland maker famous for their hollow-necked Hawaiian guitars was responsible for several uke offerings over the course of its 20-or-so-year run. Like their 6-stringed big brothers, they were the closest thing to Island design and detail to come from the mainland. The Weissenborn brand has been revived on a line of reissue style guitars.

Soprano Ukulele
Figured koa body.

1920	Rope bound	$1,500	$2,000
1920	Unbound	$1,500	$1,700

Weymann

Renowned for fine tenor banjos, Weyman affixed their name to a full line of soprano ukes of varying degrees of decoration, quite certainly none of which were made under the same roof as the banjos. Most were C.F. Martin knock-offs.

Soprano Ukulele

1925	Mahogany, unbound	$800	$1,000
1930	Koa, fancy pearl vine 'board inlay	$1,000	$1,200

Wm. Smith Co.

1920s. Like Ditson, the Wm. Smith Co. was a company for which C.F. Martin moonlighted without getting much outward credit. The South American cousin of the uke, the tiple, with its 10 metal strings and tenor uke sized body, was first produced exclusively for Smith by Martin starting around 1920, before being assumed into the regular Martin line with appropriate Martin branding.

Tiple Ukulele
Mahogany body, spruce top, ebony bridge.

1920		$1,200	$1,500

Banjo Ukuleles
Bacon

This legendary Connecticut banjo maker just couldn't resist the temptation to extend their line with uke versions of their popular banjos. As with Gibson, Ludwig, Slingerland, and Weyman, the banjo ukuleles tended to mimic the already proven construction techniques and decorative motifs of their regular banjo counterparts. In materials, finish, and hardware, most banjo ukes share many more similarities with full sized banjos than differences. The banjo ukes were simply included as smaller, plainer, variations of banjos, much as concert, tenor, and baritone options fleshed out standard ukulele lines.

Banjo Ukulele
Walnut rim.

1927	Fancy 'board inlays	$1,200	$1,500
1927	Plain 'board inlays	$700	$1,000

Silver Bell Banjo Ukulele
Engraved pearloid 'board and headstock.

1927		$1,800	$2,500

Dixie

With chrome plated all-metal design, there's only one word for these banjo ukes - shiny. Their bodies, necks, and frets are die cast together in zinc (think Hot Wheels cars and screen door handles), the Dixie must have made the perfect indestructible instrument for Junior's birthday back in the 1960s. Similar to one made by Werko.

Banjo Ukulele
One-piece, all-metal construction.

1960		$100	$200

Gibson
BU-1 Banjo Ukulele
Small 6" head, flat panel resonator.

1928		$500	$700

BU-2 Banjo Ukulele
8" head, dot inlay.

1930		$700	$900

BU-3 Banjo Ukulele
8" head, diamond and square inlay.

1935		$1,200	$1,500

BU-4 Banjo Ukulele
8" head, resonator and flange.

1932		$1,500	$2,000

BU-5 Banjo Ukulele
8" head, resonator and flange, gold parts.

1937		$3,500	$5,000

Le Domino
Banjo Ukulele
Resonator, decorated as Le Domino uke.

1933		$350	$500

Ludwig

The Ludwig was then, and is today, the Cadillac of banjo ukes. British banjo uke icon George Formby's preference for Ludwig continues assuring their desirability, while the fact that they were available in only a couple of models, for a few short years, and in relatively small production numbers only adds to the mystique.

Weissenborn Soprano

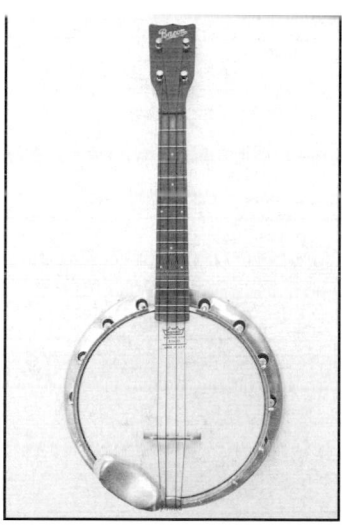
1926 Bacon 1A Banjo Uke

Ludwig Banjo Uke

UKULELES

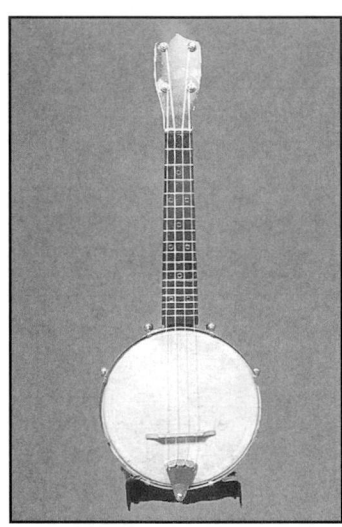

Richter Banjo Uke

Werko Banjo Uke

MODEL YEAR	FEATURES	EXC. COND. LOW	HIGH
Banjo Ukulele			
Flange with crown holes.			
1927	Gold-plated parts	$4,000	$5,000
1928	Nickel-plated parts	$3,000	$4,000
1928	Silver-plated parts	$3,500	$4,500
1930	Ivoroid headstock overlay w/ art deco detail	$4,000	$5,000
Wendell Hall Professional Banjo Ukulele			
Walnut resonator, flange with oval holes.			
1927		$1,500	$2,000

Lyon & Healy
Banjo Ukulele
Walnut neck and resonator, fancy pearl inlay.

1935		$800	$1,200

Paramount
1920s-1942, Late 1940s. The William L. Lange Company began selling Paramount banjos, guitar banjos and mandolin banjos in the early 1920s. Gretsch picked up the Paramount name and used it on guitars for a time in the late '40s.

Banner Blue Banjo Ukulele
Brass hearts 'board inlay, walnut neck.

1933		$800	$1,000

Regal
Banjo Ukulele
Mahogany rim, resonator, fancy rope bound.

1933		$300	$500

MODEL YEAR	FEATURES	EXC. COND. LOW	HIGH

Richter
Allegedly, this Chicago company bought the already-made guitars, ukes, and mandolins of other manufacturers, painted and decorated them to their liking and resold them. True or not, they certainly were cranked out in a bevy of swanky colors.

Banjo Ukulele
Chrome-plated body, 2 f-holes in back.

1930		$100	$200
1930	Entire body/ neck painted	$100	$200

Slingerland
May Bell Banjo Ukulele
Walnut resonator with multicolored rope.

1935		$100	$200

Werko
These Chicago-made banjo ukuleles had construction similar to the Dixie brand, and except for the addition of a swank layer of blue sparkle drum binding on the rim, you would be hard pressed to tell them apart.

Banjo Ukulele
Chrome-plated metal body and neck.

1960		$150	$200

Weymann
Banjo Ukulele
Maple rim, open back, ebony 'board.

1926		$1,200	$1,400

UKULELES

BANJOS

MASTERTONE

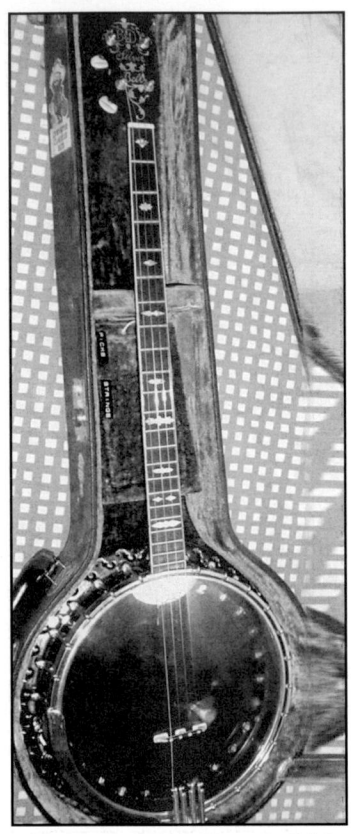

Bacon and Day Silver Bell #1

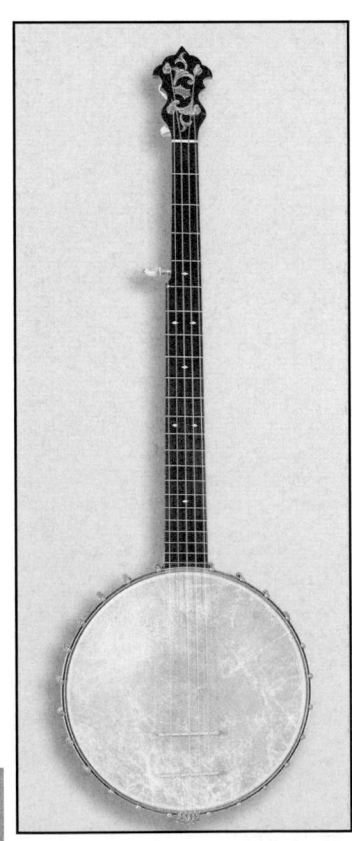

1913 Cole Eclipse Pro Special

MODEL YEAR	FEATURES	EXC. COND. LOW	HIGH

Banjo collectors, hobbyists, and dealers often think nothing of changing the neck on a banjo; a banjo may have a true vintage neck or a new replacement neck. So, our all original parts concept that applies to the rest of this Price Guide doesn't always apply to vintage banjos.

The banjo market operates somewhat differently than many of the other markets that are covered in the Guide. The prices shown are guidance prices only and each instrument should be evaluated on a case by case basis.

Acme

1893-early 1900s. Banjos made for Sears by S.S. Stewart, and later George Bauer, both of Philadelphia.

The Pearl
1908. Open back, 5-string, pearl fretboard.

1908		$950	$1,200

Alvarez

1965-present. An import brand for St. Louis Music, Alvarez currently offers intermediate grade, production, banjos. They also offer guitars, lap steels and mandolins.

Aria/Aria Pro II

1956-present. Aria offered banjos from time to time under both the Aria and Aria Pro II brand names. They also make guitars, basses, and mandolins.

Resonator 5-String
1976-1978. 5-string resonator back, Aria Pro II brand, models PB450, PB550 and PB650.

1976-1978		$550	$700

Austin

1999-present. Budget and intermediate grade, production, banjos imported by St. Louis Music. They also offer guitars, basses, amps and mandolins.

Bacon

1906-1920. Frederick Bacon was a well-known banjo player when he started selling banjos under his name before partnering with David Day in Bacon and Day. At least the earliest Bacon banjos were built by other companies.

FF Professional No. 3

1906-1907	5-string	$13,000	$16,000

Special

1914	5-string	$2,800	$3,500

Style C

1920	Tenor	$525	$650

Bacon & Day

1920-1967. David Day left Vega to join up with Fred Bacon in '21. Gretsch purchased Bacon & Day in '40, and ran the Bacon line until '67.

Blue Bell

1922-1939	Tenor	$1,000	$1,250

MODEL YEAR	FEATURES	EXC. COND. LOW	HIGH
Blue Ribbon 17			
1933-1939	Tenor	$700	$875
Blue Ribbon Deluxe Tenor			
1933-1939		$1,700	$2,100
Blue Ribbon Orchestra Tenor			
1933-1939		$1,050	$1,325
FF Professional No. 2			
1921	5-string	$1,650	$2,050
FF Professional No. 3			
1921-1922	Tenor	$775	$975
Ne Plus Ultra			
1920s	#5, plectrum	$7,800	$9,800
1920s	#5, tenor	$7,500	$9,400
1920s	#6, plectrum	$9,300	$11,500
1920s	#6, tenor	$8,900	$11,100
1920s	#7, plectrum	$14,000	$17,400
1920s	#7, tenor	$13,400	$16,600
1920s	#8, plectrum	$22,000	$27,300
1920s	#8, tenor	$21,000	$26,100
1920s	#9, plectrum	$22,200	$27,300
1920s	#9, tenor	$21,000	$26,100
1930s	Tenor	$8,900	$11,100
1940s	Plectrum	$3,300	$4,100
1950s	Tenor	$2,250	$2,800
1960s	Tenor	$2,250	$2,800
Roy Smeck			
1930s. Silver Bell #1, tenor.			
1930s		$2,050	$2,550
Senorita			
1930s	Plectrum, pearloid, resonator	$775	$975
1950s	4-string	$575	$725
Silver Bell Series			
1920-1933	#1, tenor/plectrum	$1,300	$1,650
1920-1933	#2, tenor	$1,600	$2,000
1920-1933	#3 Montana, tenor	$2,550	$3,200
1920-1933	#3, tenor	$2,050	$2,550
1920-1939	#1, 5-string	$2,450	$3,100
1920s	#5, 5-string	$4,500	$5,600
1927	#6 Montana, tenor	$6,400	$8,000
1928	#4 Montana, tenor	$3,500	$4,400
1931	#3 Sultana, tenor	$2,550	$3,200
1933-1939	#1 Montana, tenor	$1,300	$1,650
1933-1939	#1 Serenader, tenor	$1,300	$1,650
1933-1939	#1 Symphonie, tenor	$2,150	$2,700
1933-1939	#3 Montana, plectrum	$3,100	$3,900
Super			
1920-1925	Tenor, non-carved neck	$900	$1,125
1926-1927	5-string, carved neck	$2,775	$3,500
1926-1927	5-string, non-carved neck	$2,475	$3,100
1926-1927	Tenor, non-carved neck	$1,125	$1,400
Symphonie Silver Bell			
1960. By Gretsch, script Symphonie logo on headstock, fancy ornamentation, gold-plated hardware.			
1960	5-string	$1,950	$2,450

BANJOS

MODEL YEAR	FEATURES	EXC. COND. LOW	HIGH

Baldwin

1966-1976. Baldwin was one of the largest piano retailers in the Midwest and in 1965, they got into the guitar market. In '66 they bought the ODE Banjo company. From '66 to '71 the banjos were labeled as Baldwin; after that ODE was added below the Baldwin banner. In '76 Gretsch took over ODE production.

Ode 2R

| 1968 | Plectrum, 4-string | $1,025 | $1,275 |

Ode Style C

| 1968 | Bluegrass, 5-string | $1,475 | $1,825 |

Style D

| 1968-1969 | 5-string | $2,700 | $3,400 |

Barratt

1890s. Made by George Barratt in Brooklyn, New York.

Style D 5-String

| 1890s | Victorian era | $375 | $475 |

Benary and Sons

1890-1899. Manufactured by the James H. Buckbee Co. for music instrument wholesaler Robert Benary.

Celebrated Benary

1890-1899. 5-string, open back, plain appointments.

| 1890-1899 | | $625 | $775 |

Bishline

1985-present. Professional and premium grade, production/custom, banjos built by luthier Robert Bishline in Tulsa, Oklahoma.

Blindworm Guitars

2008-present. Premium grade, production/custom, banjos built in Colorado Springs, Colorado by luthiers Andrew J. Scott and Steven Sells. They also build guitars, basses and mandolins.

Boucher

1830s-1850s. William Boucher's operation in Baltimore is considered to be one of the very first banjo shops. Boucher and the Civil War era banjos are rare. The price range listed is informational guidance pricing only. The wide range reflects conservative opinions. 150 year old banjos should be evaluated per their own merits.

Double Tack

| 1840s | | $11,500 | $14,000 |

Single Tack

| 1840s | | $10,500 | $13,000 |

Bruno and Sons

Established in 1834 by Charles Bruno, primarily as a distributor, Bruno and Sons marketed a variety of brands, including their own.

Royal Artist Tenor

| 1920s | Figured resonator | $650 | $800 |

Buckbee

1863-1897. James H. Buckbee Co. of New York was the city's largest builder. The company did considerable private branding for companies such as Benery, Dobson, and Farland.

5-String

1890-1897. 5-string, open back, plain appointments.

1890-1897	High-level models	$1,600	$2,000
1890-1897	Low-level models	$625	$800
1890-1897	Mid-level models	$1,350	$1,650

Charles Shifflett Acoustic Guitars

1990-present. Luthier Charles Shifflett builds his premium grade, custom, banjos in High River, Alberta. He also builds guitars and basses.

Christy

1960s. Banjos built by luthier Art Christianson in Colorado.

5-String Long Neck Folk Banjo

| 1965 | Rare models | $675 | $850 |
| 1965 | Standard models | $450 | $575 |

Cole

1890-1919. W.A. Cole, after leaving Fairbanks & Cole, started his own line in 1890. He died in 1909 but the company continued until 1919. He also made guitars and mandolins.

Eclipse

1890-1919	Dot diamond inlays	$1,900	$2,350
1890-1919	Flower inlays	$2,200	$2,700
1890-1919	Man-in-the moon inlays	$2,500	$3,100

Dean

1976-present. Intermediate grade, production, acoustic and acoustic/electric banjos made overseas. They also offer guitars, basses, mandolins and amps.

DeCava Guitars

1983-present. Premium grade, production/custom, banjos built by luthier Jim DeCava in Stratford, Connecticut. He also builds guitars, ukes, and mandolins.

Deering

1975-present. Greg and Janet Deering build their banjos in Spring Valley, California. In 1978 they introduced their basic and intermediate banjos. They also offer banjos under the Goodtime and Vega brands.

B6

1986-2002. Mahogany neck and resonator, ebony 'board, 6 strings, satin finish.

| 1986-2002 | | $1,000 | $1,250 |

Basic

1979-1982. Resonator back, 5 strings.

| 1979-1982 | | $750 | $950 |

Dean Backwoods 2

Deering Maple Blossom

BANJOS

Delgado

Fairbanks Whyte Laydie 1906

MODEL YEAR	FEATURES	EXC. COND. LOW	HIGH
Black Diamond			
1998-present. Black head, mahogany neck, 5 strings, ebony 'board, diamond inlays.			
1998-2014		$1,200	$1,500
Boston			
1998-present. Mahogany resonator and neck, 5 or 6 strings, ebony 'board, seed and vine inlays.			
1998-2014	5-string	$850	$1,075
1998-2014	6-string	$1,000	$1,250
Calico			
1998-present. Curly maple resonator and neck, 5 strings, ebony 'board, plectrum and tenor available.			
1998-2014		$2,400	$3,000
Calico Custom			
1997-2007	5-string	$3,000	$3,800
Crossfire			
1998-present. Alder body, maple neck, 5 strings, ebony 'board, diamond inlays. Available in tenor.			
1998-2014		$1,850	$2,300
Deluxe			
1995-present. Mahogany resonator, mahogany or maple neck, ebony 'board, white and gold inlays on 6-string. Available 5-, 6- or 12-string, plectrum 4-string, 17- or 19-fret tenor 4-string.			
1995-2014	5- or 6-string	$1,500	$1,850
2001-2014	Plectrum 4-string	$1,450	$1,800
Eagle II			
2010-present. Resonator back, available as 5-string, 6-string, openback 5-string and 19-fret tenor.			
2010-2014	5-string	$1,300	$1,650
G.D.L. Greg Deering Limited Edition			
2001-2010. Figured walnut neck, burl walnut resonator, abalone and mother-of-pearl inlays, ebony 'board, 5 strings.			
2001-2010		$3,200	$4,000
Golden Era			
1995-present. Deeper resonator sound chamber, curly maple, 5 strings, ebony 'board, Cremona Sunburst stain finish.			
1995-2014		$2,100	$2,700
Golden Wreath			
2006-present. Deep resonator, 5 strings, mahogany neck, ebony 'board, mother of pearl wreath inlay.			
2006-2014		$2,100	$2,600
Goodtime Grand Ole Opry			
2005. Limited Edition for Opry's 80th anniversary, hand signed by Greg and Janet Deering, only 80 produced.			
2005	5-string	$3,600	$4,500
Goodtime Special			
2001-present. Maple neck, rim and resonator, black inlays and binding. Available 4-string plectrum and 19-fret tenor, or 5-string openback.			
2001-2014		$375	$600
Maple Blossom			
1983-present. Dark walnut stained maple neck, 4, 5, or 6 strings, fancy inlays, high gloss finish. Originally called the Advanced ('78-'82).			
1983-2014		$1,800	$2,250
1983-2014	Tenor	$1,700	$2,150

MODEL YEAR	FEATURES	EXC. COND. LOW	HIGH
Sierra			
1998-present. Mahogany or maple neck and resonator, maple rim, ebony 'board, 4- or 5-string, electric/acoustic or openback.			
1998-2014		$1,300	$1,650
Tenbrooks Saratoga Star			
Curly maple neck and deep resonator, 5-string, ebony 'board.			
2010		$3,100	$3,900
Texas Calico			
1986. Limited run of 150, Texas and 1836-1986 logo on fretboard, engraved gold-plated metal hardware, 5 strings.			
1986		$8,000	$10,000
Vega No. 2 Tubaphone			
2011-present. Curly maple 5-string neck, ebony 'board.			
2011-2014		$2,200	$2,700

Delgado
1928-present. Premium grade, custom, classical banjos built by luthier Manuel A. Delgado in Nashville, Tennessee. He also builds guitars, basses, mandolins and ukuleles.

Ditson
1916-1930. The Oliver Ditson Company of Boston offered a variety of musical instruments.

MODEL YEAR	FEATURES	EXC. COND. LOW	HIGH
Tenor			
1920. 4-string, resonator with typical appointments.			
1920		$550	$700

Dobson, George
1870-1890. Marketed by George C. Dobson of Boston, Massachusetts. Brothers Henry, George, and Edgar Dobson were banjo teachers and performers. They designed banjos that were built for them by manufactures such as Buckbee of New York.

MODEL YEAR	FEATURES	EXC. COND. LOW	HIGH
Matchless			
1880s	5-string	$800	$1,000

Dobson, H.C.
1860s-early 1900s. Henry C. Dobson was a successful musical instrument distributor out of New York. Most, if not all, banjos made by others.

MODEL YEAR	FEATURES	EXC. COND. LOW	HIGH
Silver Chime 5-String			
1890	Fancy	$1,400	$1,800
1890	Plain	$675	$850

E.L. Bashore Guitars
2011-present. Premium grade, custom, banjos built in Danville, Pennsylvania by luthier Eric L. Bashore. He also builds guitars and basses.

Epiphone
1873-present. Epiphone introduced banjos in the early 1920s, if not sooner, offering them up to WW II. After Gibson bought the company in '57, they reintroduced banjos to the line, which they still offer.

MODEL YEAR	FEATURES	EXC. COND. LOW	HIGH
Black Beauty Tenor			
1920		$500	$625

The Vintage Guitar Price Guide shows low to high values for items in all-original excellent condition, and, where applicable, with original case or cover.

MODEL YEAR	FEATURES	EXC. COND. LOW	HIGH
EB-44 Campus			
1962-1970. Long neck, open back, folk-era 5-string.			
1962-1970		$950	$1,200
EB-88 Minstrel			
1961-1969. Flat head, standard neck, 5 strings.			
1961-1969		$1,600	$2,000
EB-99 5-String			
1970s. Import, higher-end.			
1970s		$575	$725
EB-188 Plantation			
1962-1968. Long neck, open back, 5 strings.			
1962-1968		$1,450	$1,800
Electar (Electric)			
1930s	Tenor	$950	$1,200
MB-200			
1998-present. Mahogany neck and body, rosewood 'board, 5 strings.			
1998-2014		$290	$360
MB-250			
1998-2013. Mahogany resonator body and neck, rosewood 'board, 5 strings.			
1998-2013		$400	$500
Peerless Plectrum			
1920-1925. Fancy headstock.			
1920-1925		$525	$650
Recording A			
Ca. 1925-ca. 1935. Epiphone Recording logo on headstock, flamed maple neck and resonator, fancy pearl inlay markers.			
1920s	Tenor	$1,400	$1,750
Recording B			
Ca. 1925-ca. 1935.			
1930s	Tenor	$1,900	$2,400
Recording Concert C Special			
1930s. Tenor, maple body, fancy appointments, resonator.			
1930s		$2,800	$3,500
TB-100			
Mid 1960s.			
1960s	Tenor	$750	$925
White Beauty Tenor			
1920. Closed-back resonator, large dot markers, White Beauty headstock logo.			
1920		$500	$625

Excelsior

Ca.1885-ca. 1990. Brand name of guitars and banjos marketed by Boston's John C. Haynes & Company. Instruments were more basic without tone rings. Brand most likely faded out in very early 1890s when Haynes started their more refined line of Bay State instruments.

MODEL YEAR	FEATURES	EXC. COND. LOW	HIGH
Model 218			
1889		$1,600	$2,000

Fairbanks/Vega Fairbanks/ A.C. Fairbanks

1875-1922. From 1875 to 1880, A. C. Fairbanks built his own designs in Boston. In 1880, W. A. Cole joined the company, starting Fairbanks & Cole, but left in 1890 to start his own line. The company went by Fairbanks Co. until it was purchased by Vega in 1904. The banjos were then branded Vega Fairbanks (see Vega listings) until 1922.

MODEL YEAR	FEATURES	EXC. COND. LOW	HIGH
Acme (F & C)			
1880-1890. 5 string, open back, fancy markers.			
1880-1890		$800	$1,000
Electric 5-String Series			
1890s	F & C	$4,200	$5,300
1890s	Imperial	$2,500	$3,200
1890s	No. 3	$4,400	$5,500
1890s	No. 6	$6,700	$8,500
1901	Special	$2,900	$3,700
Electric Banjeaurine			
1890s	5-string	$2,600	$3,250
Imperial			
1888. Open back, 5-string.			
1888		$3,400	$4,200
Regent			
1900-1904	5-string	$2,600	$3,200
Senator No. 1/Fairbanks 3			
1900-1904	5-string	$1,000	$1,250
Special #0			
1890-1904		$800	$1,000
Special #2			
1890-1904	5-string	$900	$1,125
Special #4			
1900-1904	5-string	$1,175	$1,450
Whyte Laydie #2			
1901-1904	5-string	$3,700	$4,600
Whyte Laydie #7			
1901	1st year	$6,500	$8,100
1902-1904		$5,600	$7,000

Farland

Ca. 1890-1920s. Buckbee and others made instruments for New York banjo teacher and performer A. A. Farland.

MODEL YEAR	FEATURES	EXC. COND. LOW	HIGH
Concert Grand			
1900-1920	5-string	$1,000	$1,250
Grand Artist No. 2			
1890s-1910. Ornate floral markers, open back, 5-string.			
1890s-1910		$2,000	$2,500

Fender

1946-present. Fender added banjos to their product mix in the late 1960s, and continues to offer them.

MODEL YEAR	FEATURES	EXC. COND. LOW	HIGH
Allegro			
Late 1960s-1970s.			
1960s-70s	Tenor or 5-string	$925	$1,150
Artist			
1960s-70s	5-string	$1,400	$1,750
FB-54			
1998-present. Mahogany resonator and neck, 27.4" scale, aluminum rim, rosewood 'board, pearloid inlay.			
1998-2014	5-string	$225	$280

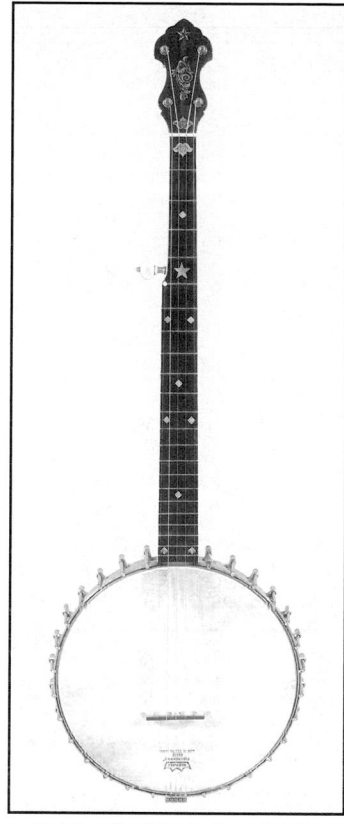

Fairbanks Whyte Laydie #2

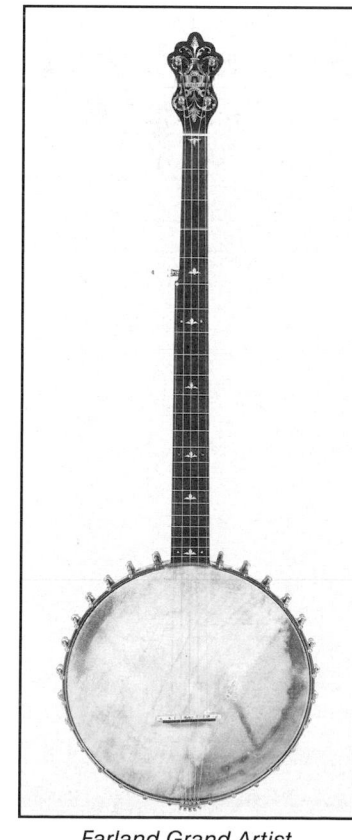

Farland Grand Artist

BANJOS

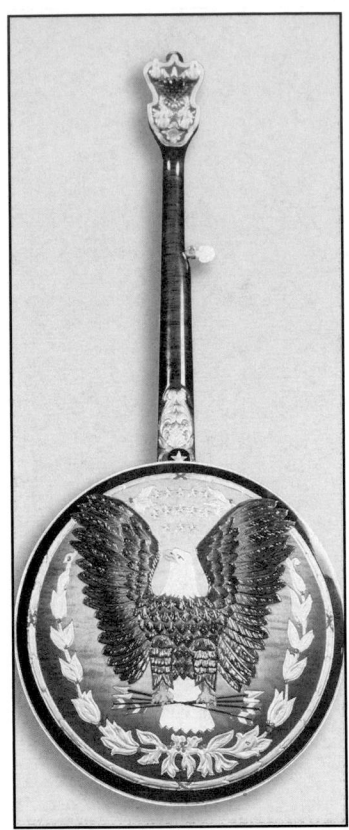

Gibson All American

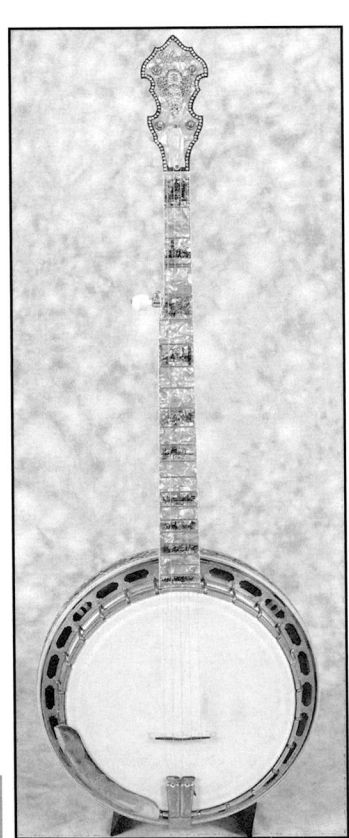

Gibson Florentine Conversion

MODEL YEAR	FEATURES	EXC. COND. LOW	HIGH

FB-55
1998-present. Mahogany resonator and neck, 26.4" scale, laminated maple rim, rosewood 'board, snowflake inlay.

| 1998-2014 | 5-string | $300 | $375 |

FB-58
1999-present. Flame maple resonator and neck, 26.4" scale, laminated maple rim, rosewood 'board, pearloid inlay.

| 1999-2014 | 5-string | $400 | $500 |

FB-59
2004-present. Walnut resonator, walnut with maple strip neck, 26.4" scale, maple rim, rosewood 'board, deluxe flower mother-of-pearl inlay.

| 2004-2014 | 5-string | $550 | $675 |

Leo Deluxe
1980-1988. Fancy inlay, Japanese-made.

| 1980-1988 | | $725 | $900 |

Framus
1946-1977, 1996-present. The new Framus company, located in Markneukirchen, Germany, continues to offer banjos.

Various Models

| 1960s | | $225 | $285 |
| 1970s | | $125 | $155 |

Gibson
1890s (1902)-present. Gibson started making banjos in 1918. Vega and Gibson were the only major manufacturing companies that offered banjos in their product catalog in the '50s.

RB prefix = regular banjo (5-string)
TB prefix = tenor banjo (4-string, tenor tuning)
PB prefix = plectrum banjo (4-string, plectrum tuning)

The prices shown are guidance prices only and each instrument should be evaluated on a case by case basis.

All American
1930-1937, 1970-1986. Tenor banjo, fancy appointments, historic art, gold hardware. Reissue offered in RB, TB, or PB.

| 1930-1937 | | $32,000 | $40,000 |
| 1975-1980 | 5-string | $5,600 | $7,000 |

Bella Voce
1927-1931. Tenor or plectrum, fancy appointments, flower-pattern art, gold hardware.

| 1927-1931 | Plectrum | $24,000 | $30,000 |
| 1927-1931 | Tenor | $23,000 | $29,000 |

Earl Scruggs '49 Classic
1992-2008. Figured maple resonator and neck, rosewood 'board, multiple bindings.

| 1998-2008 | | $3,100 | $3,850 |

Earl Scruggs Golden Deluxe
1991-2013. Satin gold hardware, hearts and flowers inlay.

| 1991-2013 | | $4,100 | $5,100 |

Earl Scruggs Standard
1984-2013. 5-string, high-end appointments, Standard added to model name in '92.

| 1984-1989 | | $3,100 | $3,850 |
| 1990-2013 | | $2,900 | $3,600 |

ETB Electric Tenor
1938-1941. Electric Tenor Banjo, Charlie Christian pickup.

| 1938-1941 | | $2,250 | $2,800 |

Flint Hill Special
2005-2006. Earl Scruggs style, 5-string.

| 2005-2006 | | $3,600 | $4,500 |

Florentine Plectrum

| 1925-1930 | 2-piece flange | $15,000 | $19,000 |

Florentine Tenor
1927-1937. High-end appointments, gold hardware.

| 1927-1937 | 40-hole | $14,000 | $17,500 |

GB-1
1922-1940. Guitar-banjo, style 1 appointments, 6-string neck, walnut.

1922-1924	Trap-door	$1,150	$1,450
1925-1930	Diamond flange, resonator	$1,600	$2,000
1931-1940	1-piece flange, resonator	$2,300	$2,900

GB-3
1918-1937. Guitar-banjo, style 3 appointments, mahogany.

1918-1924	Trap-door	$1,000	$1,300
1925-1926	2-piece flange, ball bearing arch-top tone ring	$2,600	$3,500
1926-1929	2-piece flange, cast arch-top tone ring	$2,600	$3,500
1928-1937	40-hole tone ring	$2,600	$3,500

GB-4
1918-1931. Guitar-banjo, style 4 appointments, maple. Very early models were called GB without -4 suffix.

1918-1924	GB/GB-4, trap-door	$2,200	$3,900
1925-1926	2-piece flange, ball bearing arch-top tone ring	$3,200	$4,200
1926-1929	2-piece flange, cast arch-top tone ring	$3,200	$4,200
1928-1931	40-hole tone ring	$3,200	$4,200

GB-5
1924. Rare, gold plated, trap-door.

| 1924 | | $5,200 | $6,600 |

GB-6/GB-6 Custom
1922-1934. Guitar-banjo, style 6 appointments, special order availability.

1922-1924	Trap-door	$3,000	$3,800
1925-1926	2-piece flange, ball bearing arch-top tone ring	$4,600	$5,800
1928-1934	40-hole tone ring	$4,600	$5,800

Granada FE
2004. Flying eagle inlay.

| 2004 | | $3,900 | $4,850 |

Granada RB
1925-1939. 5-string banjo with either a 2-piece flange (1925-1930), or a 1-piece flange (1933-1939).

1925-1926	Ball bearing	$17,800	$22,200
1927-1930	40 hole arched	$27,900	$35,100
1933-1939	Flat head	$164,000	$202,000

MODEL YEAR	FEATURES	EXC. COND. LOW	HIGH
Granada RB (Reissue)			
1986-2006. Resonator back, 5-string.			
1986-2006		$3,500	$4,700
Granada RB Pot and Reneck			
1933-1939. Original pot and replacement neck.			
1933-1939	Flat head	$42,000	$53,000
Granada TB			
1925-1939. Tenor banjo with either a 2-piece flange (1925-1930), or a 1-piece flange (1933-1939).			
1925-1926	Ball bearing	$7,200	$9,000
1927-1930	40 hole arched	$11,000	$14,000
1933-1939	Flat head	$103,000	$127,000
PB-1			
1926-1930s. PB stands for Plectrum Banjo.			
1926-1930s	Bracket-shoe	$800	$1,000
PB-2			
1920s	Bracket-shoe	$800	$1,000
1930s	1-piece flange	$3,150	$3,900
PB-3			
1923-1937. Laminated maple resonator Mastertone model, plectrum neck and tuning.			
1925-1927	2-piece flange, tube & plate	$2,000	$2,500
PB-4			
1925-1940. Plectrum with either a 2-piece flange ('25-'32), or 1-piece ('33-'40).			
1925-1927	Ball bearing	$2,500	$3,000
1928-1932	Archtop	$3,100	$3,900
1933-1940	Archtop	$8,000	$10,000
1933-1940	Flat head	$48,000	$60,000
PB-11			
1931-1942. Plectrum, pearloid 'board, headstock and resonator cover.			
1931-1942	1-piece flange	$3,150	$3,900
PB-100			
1948-1979. Plectrum with either a 1-piece flange ('48-'68), or 2-piece ('69-'79).			
1948-1979		$850	$1,050
RB Jr.			
1924-1925. Budget line, 5-string, open back.			
1924-1925		$1,200	$1,425
RB-00			
1932-1942. Maple resonator, 1-piece flange.			
1932-1942		$3,700	$4,600
RB-1			
1922-1940. RB stands for resonator banjo.			
1922-1930	Early specs	$3,600	$4,500
1930-1932	1-piece flange	$3,600	$4,500
1933-1940	Diamond flange	$3,600	$4,500
RB-1 Reissue			
1990-1993. Fleur-de-lis, brass tone ring.			
1990-1993		$1,600	$2,000
RB-2			
1933-1939		$6,200	$7,800
RB-3			
1923-1937. Dot inlay.			
1923-1937	5-string	$14,600	$18,400
RB-3 Reissue			
1988-2013. Currently called the RB-3 Wreath.			
1988-2013		$2,600	$3,200

MODEL YEAR	FEATURES	EXC. COND. LOW	HIGH
RB-4			
1922-1937. 5-string with either a 2-piece flange ('25-'31), or 1-piece ('33-'37). Trap or non-trap door on earlier models ('22-'24).			
1922-1924	Trap or non-trap door	$2,700	$3,300
1925-1931	Archtop, resonator	$13,000	$16,000
1933-1937	Archtop	$28,000	$35,000
1933-1937	Flat head	$80,000	$100,000
RB-4/R-4/Retro 4			
1991-2006. Flying eagle inlay, multi-bound.			
1991-2006		$3,000	$3,800
RB-5			
1995-2008			
1995-2008		$5,600	$7,000
RB-6 New Century Style 6 Gold Sparkle			
1995-2008. Figured-maple, gold sparkle binding.			
1995-2008	5-string	$5,600	$7,000
RB-7 Top Tension			
1994-2008. Maple, bow-tie inlay.			
2003		$3,100	$3,900
RB-11			
1931-1942. Pearloid covered fingerboard, headstock and resonator.			
1931-1942		$6,200	$7,800
RB-75 J.D. Crowe			
1997-2006. Based on Crowe's instrument.			
1997-2006		$2,700	$3,400
RB-100			
1948-1979. Maple resonator.			
1948-1965		$1,600	$2,000
1966-1979		$1,250	$1,550
RB-150			
1948-1959. Laminated mahogany resonator, bow tie inlay.			
1948-1959		$1,800	$2,250
RB-170			
1960-1973. No resonator, 5-string, dot markers, decal logo, multi-ply maple rim.			
1960-1965		$925	$1,175
1966-1973		$750	$950
RB-175			
1962-1973. 2000s. Open back, long neck typical of banjos of the '60s. Models include the RB-175, RB-175 Long Neck, RB-175 Folk.			
1962	RB-175	$1,375	$1,700
1962-1964	Long Neck	$1,375	$1,700
1965-1969	Folk	$1,375	$1,700
1970-1973	RB-175	$1,375	$1,700
RB-250			
1954-2013. Mahogany, 2-piece flange until '88, 1 after.			
1954-1965		$2,800	$3,500
1966-1969	Flat head	$2,400	$3,000
1970-1989	Mastertone	$2,000	$2,500
1990-1999		$2,000	$2,500
2002-2013	Reissue	$2,000	$2,500
RB-800			
1964-1971, 1979-1986. Maple resonator, 1-piece flange until '69, 2 after.			
1964-1986		$2,900	$3,600

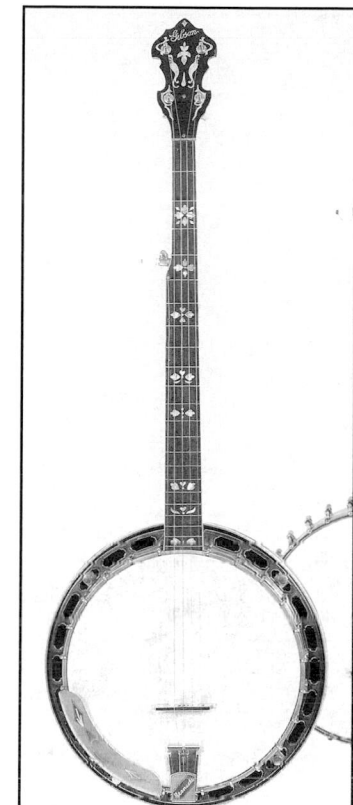

1933 Gibson Granada Flat Head

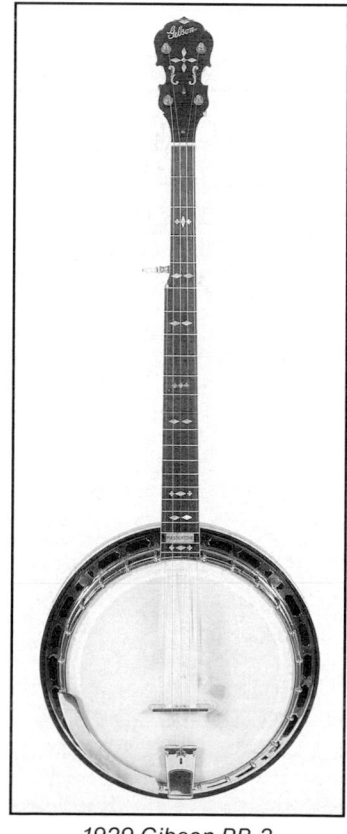

1929 Gibson RB-3

BANJOS

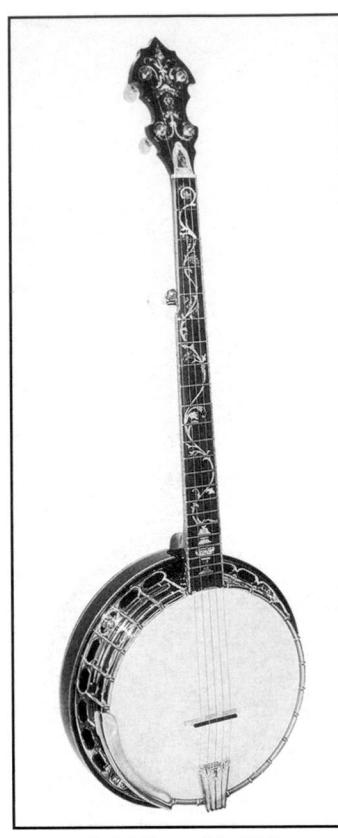

Gold Tone OB-300

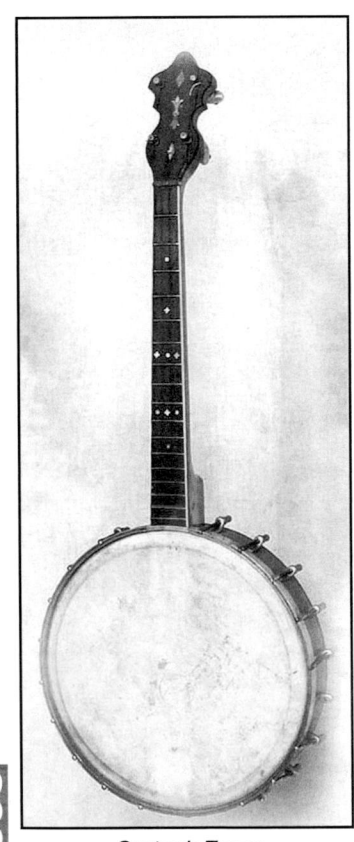

Gretsch Tenor

MODEL YEAR	FEATURES	EXC. COND. LOW	HIGH
TB			
1918-1923. Renamed TB-4.			
1918-1923		$1,100	$1,400
TB-00			
1932-1942. Maple resonator, 1-piece flange.			
1932-1942		$1,600	$2,000
TB-1			
1922-1939. Tenor banjo with a 1-piece flange.			
1922-1924	Trap door	$650	$800
1925	No resonator	$650	$800
1926	Maple resonator, shoe-plate	$800	$1,000
1933-1939	Simple hoop tone ring	$2,600	$3,200
TB-2			
1920-1937.			
1920-1928	Wavy flange	$750	$950
1933-1937	Pearloid board	$2,700	$3,400
TB-3			
1925-1939. Tenor banjo with either a 2-piece flange ('25-'31), or a 1-piece flange ('33-'39).			
1925-1926	Ball-bearing	$2,100	$2,600
1927-1931	40 or no hole ring	$3,700	$4,600
1933-1939	40 or no hole ring	$8,900	$11,000
1933-1939	Archtop	$8,600	$10,700
1933-1939	Flat head	$62,000	$78,000
TB-4			
1923-1937. Dot inlay.			
1923-1924	Trap door	$800	$1,050
1925-1926	Ball-bearing	$4,000	$5,000
1927-1931	40 or no hole ring	$4,000	$5,000
1933-1937	40 or no hole ring	$6,800	$8,500
TB-5			
1923-1929.			
1923-1924	Trap door	$1,150	$1,450
1925-1926	2-piece flange, ball bearing	$7,500	$9,500
1927-1929	40 or no hole ring	$10,000	$12,500
TB-6			
1927-1940.			
1927-1940	40 or no hole ring	$11,000	$13,500
1933-1940	Flat head	$29,000	$36,000
TB-12			
1937-1939. Produced in limited quantities, 1-piece flange, flat head tone ring, double bound walnut resonator, price levels include both original and conversion instruments, conversions with original flat head tone rings are somewhat common in the vintage banjo market.			
1937-1939	Top tension pot assembly	$47,000	$58,000
TB-18			
1937. Rare model.			
1937	Flat head top tension	$60,000	$75,000
TB-100			
1948-1979.			
1948-1959		$1,000	$1,250
1960-1979		$900	$1,125

MODEL YEAR	FEATURES	EXC. COND. LOW	HIGH
TB-250			
1954-1996.			
1954-1965		$1,600	$2,000
1966-1996	Mastertone	$1,600	$2,000
TB-800			
1975	Flying eagle markers	$2,400	$3,000
Trujo Plectrum			
1928-1934		$2,600	$3,200

Gold Star

1970s-present. A brand name of Saga Musical Instruments offering professional and premium grade, production banjos.

5-String

1970s-present. Various 5-string models.

1970s	G-11HF	$1,150	$1,450
1980s-2014	GF-85	$1,150	$1,450
2000-2014	GF-200	$1,050	$1,300

Gold Tone

1993-present. Professional and premium grade, production/custom banjos and banjitars built by Wayne and Robyn Rogers in Titusville, Florida. They also offer guitars, basses, lap steels, mandolins and ukuleles.

BG-250F Bluegrass Special

2000-present. Bell brass tone ring, 3-Ply Canadian maple rim, 5-string.

2000-2014		$525	$650

CC-100 Cripple Creek

1993-present. Entry level, 5 strings, maple neck and rim.

1993-2014		$450	$550

IT-250R Irish Tenor

2011. Irish Tenor series, imported.

2011		$625	$800

OB-250AT Orange Blossom

2000-present. Archtop, 40-hole sand cast bell brass tone ring, 5-string.

2000-2014		$800	$1,000

OT-800 Old Tone

2008-present. Tubaphone-style tone ring, 5-string.

2008-2014		$550	$675

TB-250 Travel Banjo

2010-present. Short scale neck, 5 strings.

2010-2014		$575	$700

WL-250 White Ladye

2010-present. Open back, 5 strings.

2010-2014		$525	$650

Goya

1952-1996. Martin offered Goya banjos while they owned the brand name in the '70s.

Student 5-String

1976-1996. Goya-Martin era.

1976-1996		$175	$250

Gretsch

1883-present. Gretsch offered banjos in the '20s and again in the '50s and '60s. In 2012 they again started building them.

MODEL YEAR	FEATURES	EXC. COND. LOW	HIGH
5-String			
1977		$325	$400
Broadkaster			
1920s-1939. Tenor or 5-string banjo with pearloid head and board.			
1920s	Tenor	$450	$550
1932-1939	5-string	$925	$1,150
1932-1939	Tenor	$325	$400
Model 6536 Folk			
1960s. Open-back, 5-string, long-neck style.			
1964		$400	$500
New Yorker			
1930s-1960s. New Yorker logo on headstock, 5-string or tenor.			
1930s-60s		$250	$350
Orchestella			
1925-1929. Tenor or 5-string banjo with gold engravings.			
1925-1929	5-string	$1,600	$2,000
1925-1929	Tenor	$400	$500
Tenor Short-Scale			
1925-1929	Plain styling	$250	$315
1950s	Plain styling	$250	$315

GTR

1974-1978. GTR (for George Gruhn, Tut Taylor, Randy Wood) was the original name for Gruhn Guitars in Nashville, and they imported mandolins and banjos from Japan.

MODEL YEAR	FEATURES	EXC. COND. LOW	HIGH
5-String Copy			
1974-1978		$925	$1,150

Harmony

1892-1976, late 1970s-present. Huge, Chicago-based manufacturer of fretted instruments, mainly budget models under the Harmony name or for many other American brands and mass marketers.

MODEL YEAR	FEATURES	EXC. COND. LOW	HIGH
Bicentennial			
1976. Red, white and blue, '76 logo, 5-string.			
1976		$575	$725
Electro			
1950s. Electric banjo, 5-string, wood body, 1 pickup.			
1950s		$600	$750
Holiday Folk			
1960s. Long neck, 5-string.			
1960s		$200	$250
Reso-Tone Tenor			
1960s		$200	$250
Roy Smeck Student Tenor			
1963		$225	$285
Sovereign Tenor			
1960s		$200	$250

Hohner

1857-present. They currently offer budget grade, open back, resonator style or travel size banjos. They also have guitars, basses, mandolins and ukuleles.

Hondo

1969-1987, 1991-2005. Budget grade, production, imported banjos. They also offer guitars, basses and mandolins.

Howard

Howard is a brand name of Cincinnati's Wurlitzer Co. used in the 1920s on banjos built by The Fred Gretsch Manufacturing Co. The brand name was also appeared on guitars in the mid-'30s by Epiphone.

MODEL YEAR	FEATURES	EXC. COND. LOW	HIGH
Tenor			
1920s	Open back	$200	$250
1920s	Resonator	$450	$565

Huber

1999-present. Premium grade, production, 5-string banjos built by luthier Steve Huber in Hendersonville, Tennessee.

Ianuario Mandolins

1990-2009. Professional and premium grade, custom, banjos built by Luthier R. Anthony Ianuario in Jefferson, Georgia. He also built mandolins and violins.

Ibanez

1932-present. Ibanez introduced their Artist line of banjos in 1978 in a deal with Earl Scruggs, but they were dropped by '84.

MODEL YEAR	FEATURES	EXC. COND. LOW	HIGH
Model 591			
1978-1984. Flat head, 5-string.			
1978-1984		$900	$1,125
Model 593			
1977. Vine inlay, 5-string.			
1978-1984		$1,200	$1,500

J.B. Player

1980s-present. Budget grade, production, imported banjos. They also offer basses, mandolins and guitars.

John Wesley

Introduced in 1895 by Kansas City, Missouri instrument wholesalers J.W. Jenkins & Sons, founded by cello builder John Wesley Jenkins. May have been built by Jenkins until circa 1905, but work was later contracted out to others.

Kalamazoo

1933-1942, 1965-1970. Budget brand built by Gibson. Made flat-tops, solidbodies, mandolins, lap steels, banjos and amps.

MODEL YEAR	FEATURES	EXC. COND. LOW	HIGH
Banjo			
1933-1940	KPB, plectrum	$400	$500
1935-1942	KRB, 5-string	$600	$900

Kay

Ca. 1931 (1890)-present. Kay was a huge manufacturer and built instruments under their name and for a large number of other retailers, jobbers, and brand names.

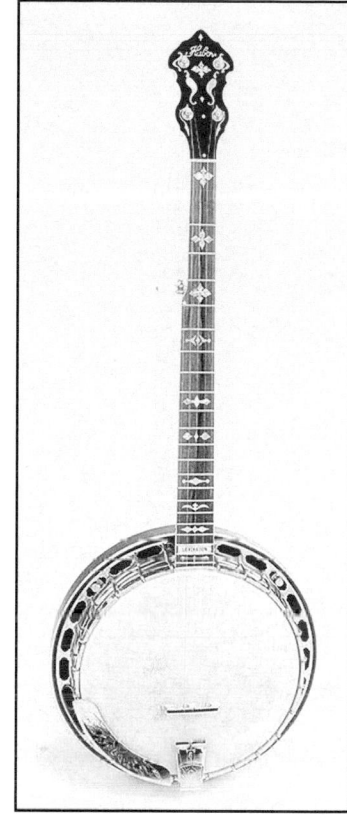

Huber Lexington

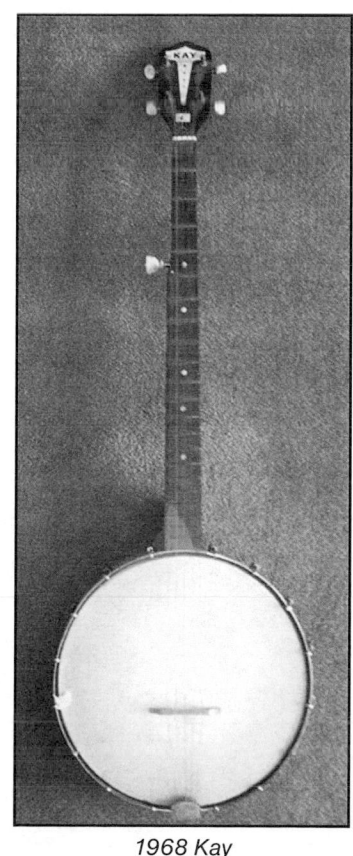

1968 Kay

BANJOS

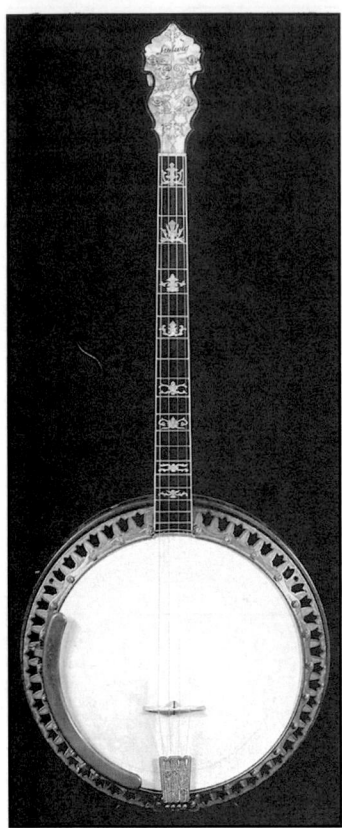

Ludwig Standard Art Tenor

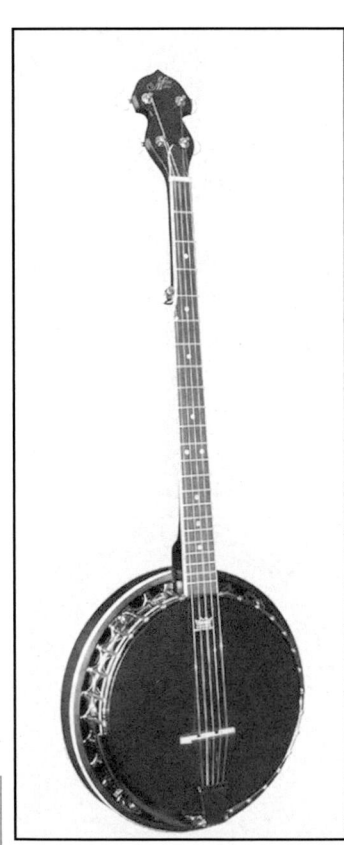

Morgan Monroe MB-75BK 30

MODEL YEAR	FEATURES	EXC. COND. LOW	HIGH

Silva
1950s. Top of the line 5-string, Silva verticle logo along with Kay logo on headstock, block markers.

1950s		$675	$825

Student Tenor

1950s		$165	$210

Kel Kroydon
1930-1933. Private branded budget level instruments made by Gibson. They also had guitars and banjos. The name has been revived on a line of banjos by Tom Mirisola and made in Nashville.

KK-11 Tenor

1933-1937		$3,000	$3,800

Kingston
Ca. 1958-1967. Imported from Japan by Westheimer Importing Corp. of Chicago. They also offered guitars, basses and mandolins.

Student Tenor

1965		$45	$60

Kona Guitar Company
2001-present. Budget grade, production, banjos made in Asia. They also offer guitars, basses, mandolins, ukes and amps.

Lange
1920s-1942, Late 1940s. The William L. Lange Company began selling Paramount banjos, guitar banjos and mandolin banjos in the early 1920s. Gretsch picked up the Paramount name and used it on acoustics and electrics for a time in the late '40s. See Paramount for more listings.

Tourraine Deluxe

1920s	Tenor	$575	$725

Leedy
1889-1930. Founded in Indianapolis by U. G. Leedy, the company started making banjos in 1924. Leedy was bought out by C. G. Conn in '30.

Arcadian

1925	Plectrum	$475	$600

Olympian

1930	Tenor	$500	$625

Solotone

1924-1930	A Tenor	$1,000	$1,200
1924-1930	B Tenor	$1,200	$1,450
1924-1930	C Tenor	$1,400	$1,600
1924-1930	D Tenor	$1,500	$1,800

Libby Bros.
1890s. Made in Gorham, Maine, rarity suggests limited production.

Open Back
1890-1895. Fancy position markers, 5-string.

1890-1895		$1,300	$1,600

Ludwig
The Ludwig Drum Company was founded in 1909. They saw a good business opportunity and

MODEL YEAR	FEATURES	EXC. COND. LOW	HIGH

entered the banjo market in '21. When demand for banjos tanked in the '30s, Ludwig dropped the line and concentrated on its core business.

Ambassador

1920s-1932	Tenor	$975	$1,200

Bellevue
1920s. Tenor, closed-back banjo with fancy appointments.

1920s		$750	$900

Big Chief
1930. Carved and engraved plectrum banjo.

1930		$6,300	$7,800

Capitol

1920s		$600	$750

Columbia

1920s	Tenor, student-level	$400	$500

Commodore
1930s. Tenor or plectrum, with gold hardware and fancy appointments.

1930s	Tenor, Ambassador	$1,250	$1,550
1932	Plectrum	$1,500	$1,900

Deluxe
1930s. Engraved tenor, with gold hardware.

1930s		$2,000	$2,500

Dixie

1930s	Tenor	$350	$435

Kenmore Plectrum

1920s	Open back	$600	$750

Kingston

1924-1930	Tenor	$450	$550

Standard Art Tenor
1924-1930. Tenor banjo with fancy appointments.

1924-1930		$2,800	$3,500

The Ace
1920s. Tenor banjo, resonator and nickel appointments.

1920s		$1,000	$1,200

Luscomb
1888-1898. John F. Luscomb was a well-known banjo player who designed a line of instruments for Thompson & Odell of Boston.

Open Back 5-String

1890s		$700	$875

Matao
1967-1983. Japanese copies of American brands, offered guitars, basses, banjos and ukes.

Bluegrass

1970s	5-string	$280	$350

Mitchell (P.J.)
1850s. Early gut 5-string banjo maker from New York City.

Gut 5-String

1850s		$3,900	$4,700

Morgan Monroe
1999-present. Intermediate and professional grade, production, banjos made in Korea and distributed by SHS International of Indianapolis, Indiana. They also offer guitars, basses, mandolins, and fiddles.

MODEL YEAR	FEATURES	EXC. COND. LOW	HIGH

Morrison

Ca. 1870-ca. 1915. Marketed by New Yorker James Morrison, made by Morrison or possibly others like Buckbee. After 1875, his instruments sported the patented Morrison tone ring.

5-String

1885-1890		$650	$825

ODE/Muse

1961-1980. Founded by Charles Ogsbury in Boulder, Colorado, purchased by Baldwin in '66 and moved to Nashville. Until '71 the banjos were branded as Baldwin; afterwards as Baldwin ODE. Gretsch took over production in '76. Muse was a retail store brand of banjos produced by ODE from '61 to '66. In '71, Ogsbury started the OME Banjo Company in Colorado.

Model C

1976-1980. 5-string banjo, resonator and fancy markers.

1976-1980		$1,500	$1,850

Model D

1976-1980. 5-string banjo, resonator and gold engravings.

1976-1980		$2,200	$2,700

Old Hickory

2005-2010. Budget grade, production, imported banjos from Musician's Wholesale America, Nashville, Tennessee. They also offer mandolins.

OME

1971-present. Charles Ogsbury started OME outside Boulder, Colorado after he sold his first banjo company, ODE, to Baldwin.

Bright Angel

2012-2014	5-string	$2,200	$2,800

Columbine

2012-2014	Tenor	$2,900	$3,600

Grubstake

1972-1980	5-string	$800	$1,000

Juggernaut

1973-1979	5-string	$1,800	$2,250

Juggernaut II

1974	5-string	$2,300	$2,850

Mogul

1973-2014	5-string, silver	$2,400	$3,000
1973-2014	Plectrum, black	$2,200	$2,800
1973-2014	Plectrum, silver	$2,200	$2,800
1974-2014	5-string, gold	$3,100	$3,900

Primrose

2013-2014	5-string	$2,500	$3,100

X 5-String

1971		$1,000	$1,250

XX 5-String

1971		$1,100	$1,350
1972	Extra Long Neck	$1,000	$1,250
1975		$1,000	$1,250

XX Tenor

1973		$1,000	$1,250

XXX 5-String

1971		$1,400	$1,750

MODEL YEAR	FEATURES	EXC. COND. LOW	HIGH

Orpheum

1897-1922. Lange and Rettberg purchased the J.H. Buckbee banjo factory in 1897 and started making banjos under the Orpheum label. William Lange took control in 1922 and changed the name to Paramount.

Model #1

1910s-20s	Tenor	$650	$800
1914-1916	5-string, open back	$1,825	$2,275
1920-1922	Plectrum	$750	$950

Model #2

1920-1922	5-string	$1,350	$1,700
1920-1922	Tenor	$775	$975

Model #3

1900-1910s	5-string	$2,400	$3,000
1910s	Plectrum, fancy	$1,875	$2,350
1910s	Tenor, fancy	$1,075	$1,350

Oscar Schmidt

1879-ca. 1939, 1979-present. Currently offering budget and intermediate grade, production, banjos. They also offer guitars, basses, mandolins, ukuleles and the famous Oscar Schmidt autoharp.

Paramount

1921-1935. William Lange and his Paramount company are generally accredited with commercializing the first modern flange and resonator in 1921.

Aristocrat

1921-1935	Plectrum	$1,650	$2,000
1921-1935	Tenor	$1,350	$1,675

Aristocrat Special

1921-1935. Plectrum or tenor with fancy appointments.

1921-1935	Plectrum	$2,500	$3,000
1921-1935	Tenor	$2,000	$2,500

Artists Supreme

1930s. High-end appointments, 19-fret tenor, engraved gold-plated hardware.

1930s	Tenor	$4,300	$5,300

Junior

1921-1935	Plectrum	$800	$1,000
1921-1935	Tenor	$700	$900

Leader

1921-1935	Plectrum	$1,300	$1,575
1921-1935	Tenor	$1,200	$1,450

Style 1

1921-1935	Plectrum	$800	$975
1921-1935	Tenor	$600	$750

Style 2

1921-1935. Tenor banjo, resonator and plain appointments.

1921-1935		$600	$750

Style A

1921-1935. Models include the Style A Tenor, Plectrum, and the 5-string (with resonator and fancy appointments).

1921-1935	5-string	$1,800	$2,250
1921-1935	Plectrum	$1,275	$1,600
1921-1935	Tenor	$1,025	$1,275

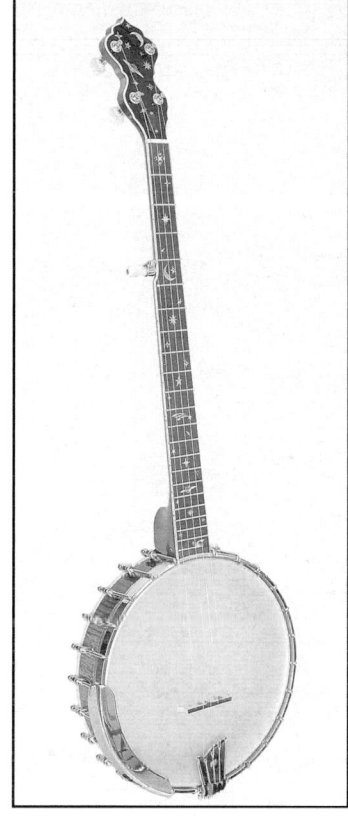

OME Bright Angel

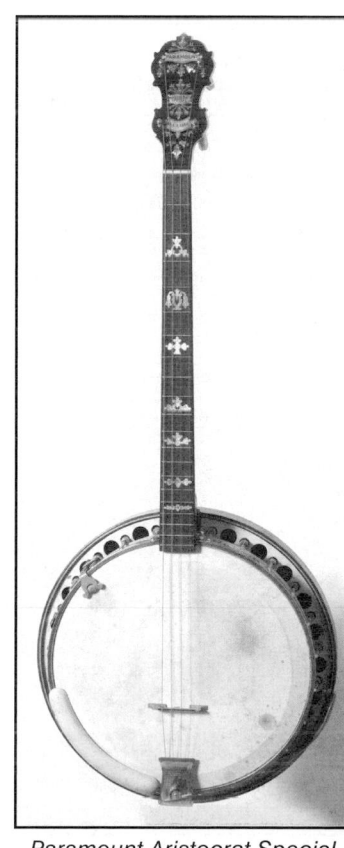

Paramount Aristocrat Special

BANJOS

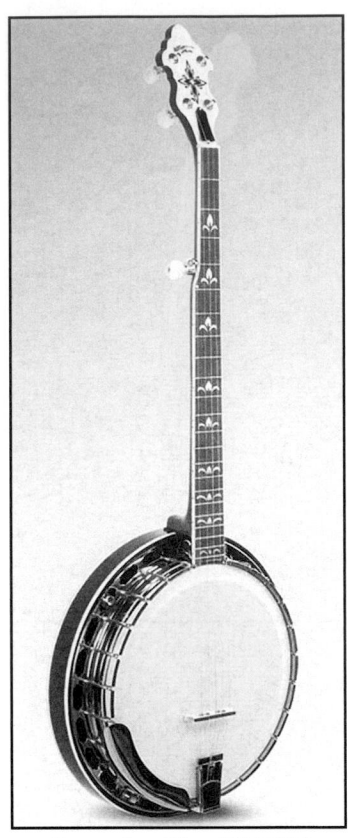

Recording King RK-R60A

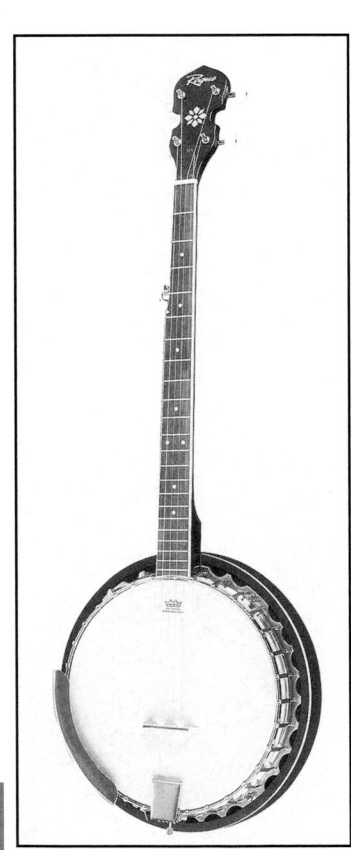

Rogue B30

MODEL YEAR	FEATURES	EXC. COND. LOW	HIGH
Style B			
1921-1935. Models include the Style B Tenor, and the Plectrum (with resonator and fancy appointments).			
1921-1935	Plectrum	$1,300	$1,600
1921-1935	Tenor	$1,100	$1,400
Style C			
1921-1935. Models include the Style C Tenor, Plectrum, and the 5-string (with resonator and fancy appointments).			
1921-1935	5-string	$3,800	$4,800
1921-1935	Plectrum	$1,300	$1,650
1921-1935	Tenor	$1,200	$1,500
Style D			
1921-1935	Plectrum	$1,900	$2,350
1921-1935	Tenor	$1,700	$2,100
Style E			
1921-1935	Plectrum	$2,400	$3,000
1921-1935	Tenor	$2,200	$2,750
Style F			
1921-1935	Plectrum	$3,300	$4,100
1921-1935	Tenor	$3,100	$3,900
Super/Super Paramount			
1929-1935	Plectrum	$3,600	$4,400
1929-1935	Tenor	$3,300	$4,100
Tenor Harp II			
1924		$1,000	$1,250
Trooper			
1921-1935	Plectrum	$650	$800
1921-1935	Tenor	$550	$700

Penco

Ca. 1974-1978. Japanese-made banjos imported into Philadelphia. They also offered guitars, basses and mandolins.

Deluxe Tenor

1970s	Japan	$200	$250

Pilgrim

1970s-late-1980s, 2010-present. Brand dates back to '70s with luthier Paul Tebbutt and is presently owned by John Hornby Skewes & Co. Ltd. in the United Kingdom. Used on guitars, mandolins, banjos and ukes, all built in the Far East.

Recording King

1929-1932, 1936-1941. Brand name used by Montgomery Ward for instruments made by various American manufacturers, including Kay, Gibson and Gretsch.

Studio King Tenor

1929-1932. Gibson-made, 40 hole archtop.

1929-1932		$3,200	$4,000

Recording King (TML)

2005-present. Intermediate and professional grade, production, banjos imported by The Music Link, which also offers Johnson and other brand instruments. They also have guitars and ukes.

Regal

Ca. 1895-1966, 1987-present. Mass manufacturer Regal made brands for others as well as marketing its own brand. In '87 the Regal name was revived by Saga.

Bicentennial '76

1976. Part of a series of Regal instruments with Bicentennial model logo on headstock (similar to the '76 Regal guitar model), blue finish on neck and headstock, large '76 on banjo head, American-Eagle USA art on back of resonator. Another style with red finish neck and fife and drum art on back of the resonator.

1976	5-string	$375	$450

Rogue

2001-present. Budget grade, production, imported banjos. They also offer guitars, basses, lap steels, mandolins, and ukuleles.

S.S. Stewart

1878-1904. S.S. Stewart of Philadelphia is considered to be one of the most important and prolific banjo manufacturers of the late 19th century. It's estimated that approximately 25,000 banjos were made by this company. The brand name was used on guitars into the 1960s.

20th Century

1890s		$1,000	$1,250

American Princess

1890s. 5-string, 10" rim.

1890s		$950	$1,150

Banjeaurine

1890. 5-string banjo, 10" head with an open back.

1890	Plain appointments	$1,000	$1,250

Champion

1895. Open back, 5-string.

1895	Plain appointments	$1,000	$1,250

Orchestra #1

1890s	5-string	$1,250	$1,500

Piccolo

1880s. 5-string, 7" rim.

1880s	Plain appointments	$1,000	$1,200

Special Thoroughbred

1890s-1900s. Open back, 5-string, carved heel.

1890-1900s	Plain appointments	$1,200	$1,500

Universal Favorite

1892. 11" head.

1892	Plain appointments	$1,000	$1,250

Wonder Tone Tenor

1920s	Plain appointments	$575	$700

S101

2002-present. Budget and intermediate grade, production, banjos imported from China. They also offer guitars, basses, and mandolins.

Samick

1958-2001, 2002-present. Budget and intermediate grade, production, imported banjos. They also offer guitars, basses, ukes and mandolins.

Shifflett

1990-present. Luthier Charles Shifflett builds his premium grade, custom, banjos in High River, Alberta. He also guitars and basses.

Silvertone

1941-ca. 1970, present. Brand of Sears instruments which replaced their Supertone brand in '41. Currently, Samick offers a line of amps under the Silvertone name.

5-String Copy

1960s	$200	$350

Slingerland

Ca. 1914-present. The parent company was Slingerland Banjo and Drums, Chicago, Illinois. The company offered other stringed instruments into the '40s. Slingerland Drums is now owned by Gibson.

Deluxe

1920s	Tenor, higher-end	$1,325	$1,650

May Bell

1920s-30s	Various styles	$250	$1,100

Student/Economy

1930s	Tenor	$200	$300

Stathopoulo

1917-1928. House of Stathopoulo evolved from the A. Stathopoulo brand in 1917, and in 1929 became the Epiphone Banjo Corporation which later became Epiphone, the well known guitar brand.

Super Wonder XX Tenor

1920s	$800	$975

Stelling

1974-present. Founded by Geoff Stelling, building premium and presentation grade, production/custom banjos in Afton, Virginia. They also build mandolins.

5-string Banjos

1974-present. Various models.

1970s	Bellflower	$2,200	$2,800
1980s	Golden Cross	$2,900	$3,600
1980s	Hartford	$2,300	$2,900
1980s	Master Flower	$2,900	$3,600
1990s	Masterpiece	$4,600	$5,700
1970s-80s	Staghorn	$3,700	$4,700
2000s	Sunflower	$2,900	$3,600
2010s	Swallowtail	$2,900	$3,600
1970s	Whitestar	$1,900	$2,400

Stetson, J.F.

1880s-1900s. J. F. Stetson branded banjos were distributed by W.J. Dyer & Bros. of St. Paul, Minnesota and others.

Presentation

1890s. Highest-end style, by Fairbanks, open back, 5-string.

1890s	$11,500	$14,500

Studio King

1930s. Banjos made by Gibson, most likely for a mail-order house or a jobber.

Studio King

1933-1937	TB-3 Tenor	$9,000	$11,200

Superb

1920s. Private brand made by House of Stathopoulo, Inc., the company name of Epiphone from 1917 to 1928. The brand was also used on banjo ukuleles.

Mayfair Tenor

1920s	Resonator	$400	$500

Supertone

1914-1941. Brand used by Sears, Roebuck and Company for instruments made by various American manufacturers, including its own Harmony subsidiary Harmony. In '40, Sears began making a transition to the Silvertone brand.

Prairie Wonder

1925. 5-string, open back banjo.

1925	$435	$550

Tanglewood Guitar Company UK

1991-present. Intermediate grade, production, banjos imported from China by Dirk Kommer and Tony Flatt in United Kingdom. They also offer guitars, basses, mandolins, amps and ukes.

Tennessee

1970-1993, 1996-present. Luthier Mark Taylor builds his professional and premium grade, production/custom, banjos in Old Hickory, Tennessee. He also builds guitars, mandolins and the Tut Taylor brand of resophonic guitars.

Thompson & Odell

1875-1898. Boston instrument importers Thompson & Odell started building banjos in the 1880s. They sold the company to Vega in 1898.

Artist

1880s	Various models	$775	$1,100

Tilton

1850s-late 1800s. Built by William B. Tilton, of New York City. He was quite an innovator and held several instrument-related patents. He also built guitars.

Toneking

1927. Private brand of the NY Band Instruments Company, Toneking logo on headstock.

Tenor

1927		$325	$400

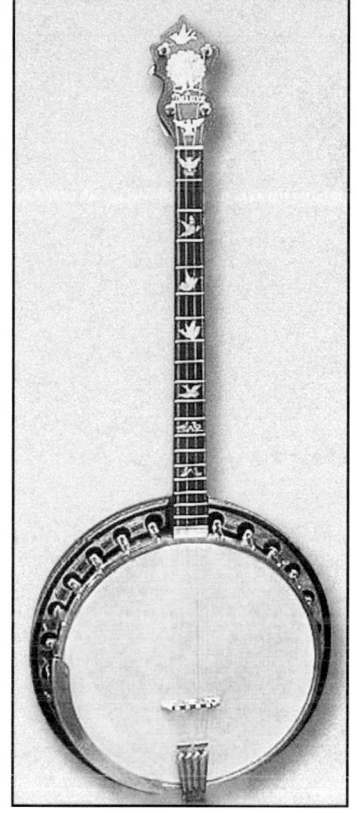

Slingerland May Bell

Tanglewood Union Series TWB 18 M5

BANJOS

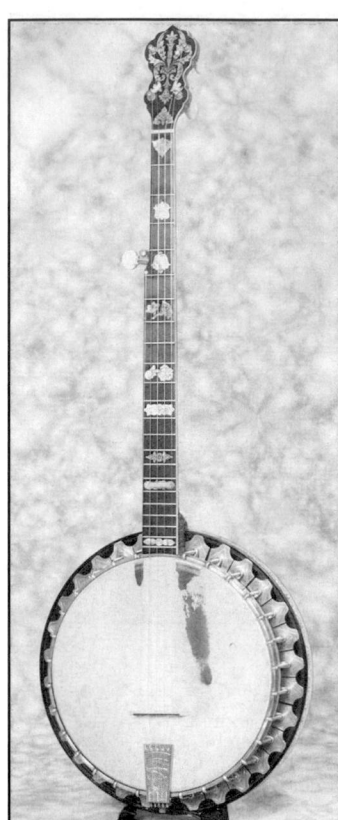

Vega Vegaphone De-Luxe

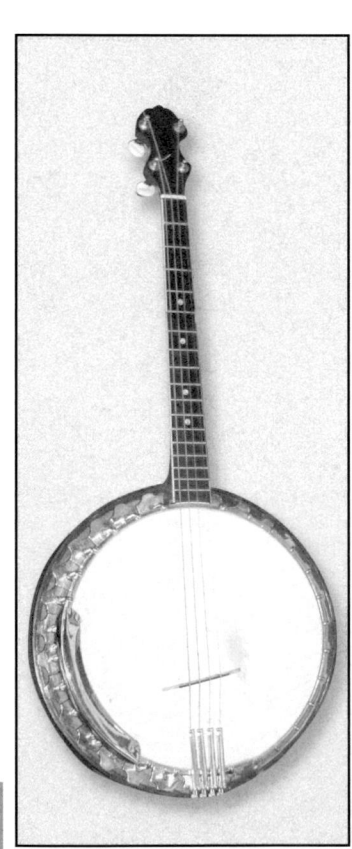

Vega Little Wonder

MODEL YEAR	FEATURES	EXC. COND. LOW	HIGH

Trinity River

2004-present. Luthiers Marcus Lawyer and Ross McLeod from Fort Worth, Texas import their intermediate grade, production/custom, banjos from Asia. They also import guitars, basses and mandolins.

Univox

1964-1978. Instruments imported from Japan by the Merson Musical Supply Company, later Unicord, Westbury, New York.

Tenor

1970s	Import	$225	$375

Van Eps

1920s. Designed by virtuoso banjo artist Fred Van Eps and sold through Lyon & Healy.

Recording 5-String

1920s		$1,300	$1,600

Vega

1889-1980s, 1989-present. Vega of Boston got into the banjo business in 1904 when it purchased Fairbanks. Vega and Gibson were the only major manufacturing companies that offered banjos in their product catalog in the 1950s. The Deering Banjo Company acquired the brand in '89 and uses it on a line of banjos.

Artist
1927-1929	Tenor	$1,900	$2,400

Artist Deluxe
1931	Tenor	$2,000	$2,500

Artist Professional #9
1923-1929	Tenor	$2,100	$2,600

Earl Scruggs STII
1969	5-string, resonator	$1,500	$1,900

Folk Ranger FR-5
1960s	5-string, open back	$575	$700

Folk Wonder
1960s	5-string	$675	$825

Folklore SS-5
1966. Open back, long neck folk banjo.
1963-1966	5-string	$1,150	$1,450

Imperial Electric
1918-1921	5-string	$2,000	$2,500

Little Wonder
1910s-1950s.
1910s-20s	Guitar banjo	$900	$1,125
1920s	Plectrum	$600	$750
1920s-30s	Tenor	$525	$650
1950s	5-string	$900	$1,100

Moderne Tenor
1931		$1,600	$2,000

Pete Seeger
1958-1970. 5-string, long neck banjo.
1958-1961	Dowel-stick	$3,900	$4,875
1962-1970	Folk era	$3,400	$4,250

Professional
1960. 5-string banjo with a Tubaphone tone ring.
1960	Pro II, slits	$1,300	$1,600
1960	Professional, holes	$1,400	$1,750

Ranger
1960s. Standard appointments, dot markers.
1966	5-string	$500	$625

Regent
1920s. Open back and dot markers.
1920s	5-string	$1,550	$1,950

Soloist
1920s. Oettinger tailpiece.
1920s	5-string	$4,900	$6,100

Style M
1920-1929. Tenor banjo, models include the Style M and the Style M Tubaphone.
1920-1929	With Tubaphone TR	$950	$1,200

Style N
1910s-20s	Tenor	$400	$500

Style X No. 9
1922-1930. Tenor with fancy appointments.
1922-1930		$1,850	$2,275

Tubaphone #3
1910-1919		$4,000	$5,000
1918-1929	5-string	$2,900	$3,700
1923-1929	Plectrum	$2,600	$3,300
1923-1929	Tenor	$2,300	$2,900

Tubaphone #9
1921-1929	5-string	$7,400	$9,200

Tubaphone Deluxe
1920s. Higher-end appointments, carved heel, Deluxe logo on tailpiece.
1923	5-string	$10,000	$12,500

V.I.P. Tenor
1970s. 4-string, open back, fancy engraved pearl markers, on-board electronics.
1970		$1,225	$1,525

V-45
1970. Plectrum banjo, flat head tone ring, fancy appointments.
1970s		$2,700	$3,300

Vega Lady's Banjo
1913		$800	$1,000

Vegaphone De-Luxe
1929	Plectrum	$3,000	$3,700

Vegaphone Professional
1920s	Plectrum	$1,100	$1,350
1920s-30s	Tenor	$1,000	$1,250
1960s	5-string	$850	$1,050

Vegavox I 5-String
1960s		$1,500	$1,900

Vegavox I Plectrum
1956-1959		$1,500	$1,850

Vegavox I Tenor
1930s-1969. Vox-style deep resonator, alternating block/dot markers.
1930s		$1,900	$2,400
1956-1959		$1,500	$1,850
1960-1969		$1,400	$1,750

BANJOS

MODEL YEAR	FEATURES	EXC. COND. LOW	HIGH
Vegavox IV			
1956-1975. IV logo on truss rod cover, high-end appointments, 4-string plectrum neck.			
1956-1975	Plectrum or tenor	$3,700	$4,700
Whyte Laydie			
1975	5-string	$2,000	$2,400
Whyte Laydie #2			
1919	Vega Fairbanks	$2,200	$2,700
1923-1928	5-string	$2,200	$2,700
Whyte Laydie #7			
1905	5-string	$6,500	$8,000
1909		$6,000	$7,500
1921		$6,000	$7,500
1927-1928		$6,000	$7,500
Whyte Laydie Style R			
1920s-1930s. Tenor banjo with closed back.			
1920s-30s		$1,000	$1,250
Wonder Tenor			
1973. Made by C.F. Martin (brand owner in the '70s), closed back resonator style.			
1973		$525	$650

Vega/Deering

1989-present. Deering purchased the Vega brand in '89. They also make banjos under the Deering brand.

Kingston Trio			
1990s-present. Folk-style banjo similar to '50s and '60s Vega Long Neck, 5-string.			
1990s-2014		$2,700	$3,300
Old Tyme Wonder			
2012-present. Maple neck, ebony 'board, 5 strings, brown stained satin finish.			
2012-2014		$925	$1,150
Senator			
2009-present. Open back, 5-string.			
2009-2014		$950	$1,150
Tubaphone #2			
2005. Open back, 5-string.			
2005		$2,200	$2,800

Washburn

1962-present. Currently, Washburn offers imported intermediate and professional grade, production, banjos.

Washburn (Lyon & Healy)

1880s-ca.1949. Washburn was the brand name of Lyon & Healy of Chicago. They made banjos from 1880-1929.

5-String			
1896	Old 1890s style	$800	$1,000
Irene			
1920s	5-string	$700	$875
Model 1535			
1917	5-string, open back	$1,475	$1,850

MODEL YEAR	FEATURES	EXC. COND. LOW	HIGH
Weymann			
1864-1940s. The Weymann company was founded in 1864 and got seriously into the banjo manufacturing business in 1917. They manufactured banjos until around 1930.			
Keystone State Style 2			
1920s		$800	$1,000
Plectrum			
1924-1928	Style A	$675	$825
1928	Style #2	$1,550	$1,950
Tenor			
1924-1928	Style #1	$1,100	$1,400
1924-1928	Style #2	$1,300	$1,650
1924-1928	Style #4	$2,400	$3,000
1924-1928	Style #50	$475	$600
1924-1928	Style #6	$3,800	$4,700
1924-1928	Style A, low pro model	$650	$825

Wildwood Banjos

1973-present. Traditional and bluegrass banjos made originally in Arcata, California, and since 2008, in Bend, Oregon.

Minstrel			
1990s-present. Maple neck, ebony 'board, tuba phone-style tone ring, 5 strings.			
1990s-2014		$1,000	$1,250
Paragon			
1990s-present. Curly maple or Claro black walnut neck, ebony 'board, mother-of-pearl inlay, 5 strings.			
1990s-2014		$1,450	$1,800
Troubador			
1973-present. Curly maple neck, ebony 'board, tubaphone-style tone ring, 5 strings.			
1973-2014		$1,150	$1,450

Wilson Brothers

1915-1928. Brand name, possibly made by Lyon & Healy, for the Wilson Brothers Manufacturing Company, of Chicago, which was better known as a builder of drums.

Tenor			
1915-1928	Resonator	$350	$450

Yosco

1900-1930s. Lawrence L. Yosco was a New York City luthier building guitars, round back mandolins and banjos under his own brand and for others.

Style 3			
1920s	Tenor	$950	$1,200

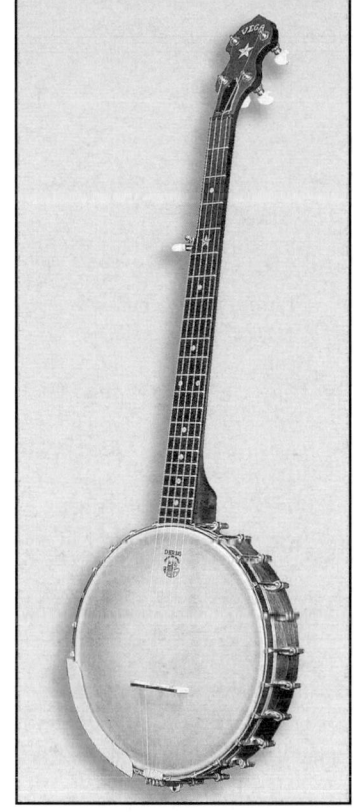

*Vega/Deering Senator
5-String Banjo*

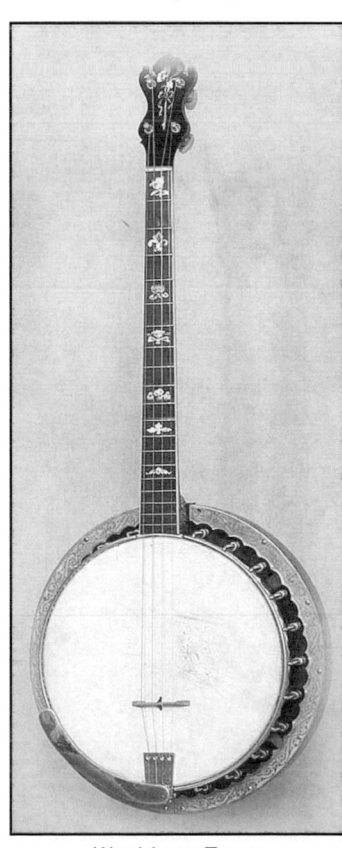

Washburn Tenor

BANJOS

BIBLIOGRAPHY

By Ken Achard: *The Peavey Revolution*, 2005, Backbeat.

By Tony Bacon: *60 Years of Fender*, 2010; *50 Years of Gretsch Electrics*, 2005; *Six Decades of the Fender Telecaster*, 2005; *Squier Electrics*, 2012, all Backbeat Books.

By Tony Bacon & Paul Day: *The Bass Book*, 1994; *The Gretsch Book*, 1996; *The Rickenbacker Book*, 1994, all Balafon Books/GPI Books; *The Ultimate Guitar Book*, 1991, Alfred A. Knopf.

By Paul Bechtoldt: *G&L: Leo's Legacy*, 1994, Woof Associates.

By J.W. Black and Albert Molinaro: *The Fender Bass, An Illustrated History*, 2001, Hal Leonard.

By Klaus Blasquiz: *The Fender Bass*, 1990, Mediapresse.

By Bob Brozman: *The History and Artistry of National Resonator Instruments*, 1993, Centerstream.

By Dave Burrluck: *The PRS Guitar Book*, 1999, Outline Press.

By Bob Carlin: *Regal Musical Instruments 1895-1955*, 2011, Centerstream.

By Walter Carter: *Epiphone: The Complete History*, 1995, *The History of the Ovation Guitar*, 1996, both Hal Leonard; *Gibson Guitars: 100 Years of An American Icon*, 1994, W. Quay Hays.

By Paul Day: *The Burns Book*, 1990, PP Publishing/Bold Strummer; *The Classical Guitar Book*, 2002, Balafon.

By Michael Doyle: *The History of Marshall*, 1993, Hal Leonard.

By Andre Duchossoir: *The Fender Telecaster*, 1991; *Gibson Electrics, The Classic Years*, 1994; *Guitar Identification: Fender-Gibson-Gretsch-Martin*, 1983, all Hal Leonard; *The Fender Stratocaster*, 1988, Mediapresse.

By Jim Elyea: *Vox Amplifiers, The JMI Years*, 2009, The History For Hire Press.

By Steve Evans and Ron Middlebrook: *Cowboy Guitars, 2002*, Centerstream.

By Jim Fisch & L.B. Fred: *Epiphone: The House of Stathopoulo*, 1996, Amsco.

By Paul Fox: *The Other Brands of Gibson*, 2011, Centerstream.

By Frank W/m Green: *The Custom Guitar Shop and Wayne Richard Charvel*, 1999, Working Musician Publications.

By George Gruhn and Walter Carter: *Acoustic Guitars and Other Fretted Instruments*, 1993; *Electric Guitars and Basses*, 1994, both GPI Books; *Gruhn's Guide to Vintage Guitars*, 3rd Ed., 2010, Backbeat.

By Philip F. Gura and James F. Bollman: *American's Instrument, The Banjo in the 19th Century*, 1999, University of North Carolina.

By Hal Leonard Publishing: *The Boss Book*, 2001.

By Robert Carl Hartman: *The Larson's Creations, Guitars & Mandolins*, 2007, Centerstream.

By Gil Hembree: *Gibson Guitars: Ted McCarty's Golden Era: 1948-1966*, 2007, Hal Leonard.

By Gregg Hopkins and Bill Moore: *Ampeg - The Story Behind The Sound*, 1999, Hal Leonard Publishing.

By Tom Hughes: *Analog Man's Guide to Vintage Effects*, 2004, Musicians Only Publishing.

By Dave Hunter and Walter Carter: *Gibson Bible*, 2008, Jawbone.

By Dave Hunter and Paul Day: *Fender Bible*, 2007, Jawbone.

By J.T.G.: *Gibson Shipping Totals 1948-1979*, 1992.

By Richard Johnston and Dick Boak: *Martin Guitars, A Technical Reference*, 2009, Hal Leonard.

By Mark Kasulen & Matt Blackett: *The History of Yamaha Guitars*, 2006, Hal Leonard.

By Robb Lawerence: *The Les Paul Legacy 1968-2009*, 2009, Hal Leonard.

By Mike Longworth: *Martin Guitars, A History*, 1988, 4 Maples Press.

By Wallace Marx Jr.: *Gibson Amplifiers, 1933-2008*, 2009, Blue Book.

By John Morrish: *The Fender Amp Book*, 1995, Balafon/GPI.

By Hans Moust: *The Guild Guitar Book: The Company and the Instruments 1952-1977*, 1995, GuitArchives.

By David Peterson and Dick Denney: *The Vox Story, A Complete History of the Legend*, 1993, Bold Strummer.

By Jim Roberts: *American Basses*, 2003, Backbeat.

By Paul William Schmidt: *Acquired of the Angels*, 1998, Scarecrow Press.

By Norbert Schnepel and Helmuth Lemme: *Elektro-Gitarren Made in Germany*, 1987, Musik-Verlag Schnepel-Lemme oHG.

By Jay Scott: *The Guitars of the Fred Gretsch Company*, 1992, Centerstream.

By Michael John Simmons: *Taylor Guitars, 30 Years of a New American Classic*, 2003, PPVMedien.

By Richard R. Smith: *The Complete History of Rickenbacker Guitars*, 1987, Centerstream; *Fender: The Sound Heard 'Round the World*, 1995, Garfish.

By Joesph E. Spann: *Spann's Guide to Gibson 1902-1941*, 2011, Centerstream.

By Paul Specht, Michael Wright, and Jim Donahue: *Ibanez, the Untold Story*, 2005, Hoshino (U.S.A.) Inc.

By John Teagle: *Washburn: Over 100 Years of Fine Stringed Instruments*, 1996, Amsco.

By John Teagle and John Sprung: *Fender Amps: The First 50 Years*, 1995, Hal Leonard.

By Art Thompson: *Stompbox*, 1997, Miller Freeman.

By Doug Tulloch: *Neptune Bound, The Ultimate Danelectro Guitar Guide*, 2008, Centerstream.

By Thomas A. Van Hoose: *The Gibson Super 400, Art of the Fine Guitar*, 1991, GPI.

By Jim Washburn & Richard Johnston: *Martin Guitars: An Illustrated Celebration of America's Premier Guitarmaker*, 1997, Rodale.

By Tom Wheeler: *American Guitars, An Illustrated History*, 1992, Harper Collins; *The Dream Factory*, 2011, Hal Leonard.

By Eldon Whitford, David Vinopal, and Dan Erlewine: *Gibson's Fabulous Flat-Top Guitars*, 1994, GPI.

By Hans-Peter Wilfer: *Framus Vintage*, 2009, Framus.

By Michael Wright: *Guitar Stories, Vol. I*, 1994; *Guitar Stories, Vol. II*, 2000, both Vintage Guitar Books.

Magazines (various issues): *Acoustic Guitar, Guitar Player, Guitar World, Musicial Merchandise Review, The Music Trades, Vintage Guitar.*

Various manufacturer catalogs, literature, and web sites.

DEALER DIRECTORY
A GEOGRAPHICAL GUIDE

Australia
Guitar Emporium
Darren Garth
155 Victoria Avenue
Albert Park, Victoria,
Australia, 3206
Phone 61.3.9696.8032
emporium@ozemail.com.
au
guitaremporium.com.au

Canada
Folkway Music
22 Dupont Street East
Waterloo, Ontario
Phone: 855-772-0424 (toll
free)
folkwaymusic.com

Surfside Music
Robbie Keene
1645-140th St.
Unit 103
Surrey, BC, Canada V4A
4H1
Phone: 778-294-1088
gtrman@shaw.ca
surfsidemusic.com

The Twelfth Fret Inc.
Grant MacNeill/Chris
Bennett
2132 Danforth Avenue
Toronto, Ont., Canada
M4C 1J9
Phone: 416-423-2132
Repairs: 416-423-1554
sales@12fret.com
12fret.com

England
Ampaholics
Authentic British Vintage
and Rare Guitar products
to inspire
Musicians and Collectors
Paul Goodhand-Tait
P.O. Box 542
Surrey, GU1 12F, England
Phone: +44-1483-825102
ampaholics@aol.com
ampaholics.org.uk

United States
Alabama
CnC Music & More
Chris Stephens
3864 Hwy 59 S.
Foley, AL 36535
Phone: 251-943-0678
cncmusicandmore@gmail.
com

cncmusicandmore.com

Arkansas
Blue Moon Music, Inc.
Les Haynie and Tim
Grear
3107 North College Ave.
Fayetteville, AR 72703-
2609
Phone: 479-521-8163
blumnmus@aol.com

California
Burst Brothers
Drew Berlin or Dave
Belzer
Mailing address:
13351-D Riverside Dr. #502
Sherman Oaks, CA 91423
Phone: 310-325-4111
info@burstbrothers.com
burstbrothers.com

**California Vintage
Guitar and Amps**
Dave Schwartz
5244 Van Nuys Blvd.
Sherman Oaks, CA 91401
Phone: 818-789-8884
sales@californiavintage-
guitarandamp.com
californiavintageguitaran-
damp.com

**Drew Berlin's Vintage
Guitars**
Drew Berlin
Phone: 310-325-4111
DrewBerlin.com
drewberlin@mac.com

**Eric Schoenberg
Guitars**
Eric Schoenberg
106 Main Street
Tiburon, CA 94920
Phone: 415-789-0846
eric@om28.com
om28.com

Freedom Guitar, Inc.
Dewey L. Bowen
6334 El Cajon Boulevard
San Diego, CA 92115
Phone: 800-831-5569
Fax: 619-265-1414
info@freedomguitar.com
freedomguitar.com

Fretted Americana
PO Box 9029
Calabasas, CA 91372
Phone: 818-222-4113

Fax: 818-222-6173
info@frettedamericana.
com
frettedamericana.com

**Gryphon Stringed
Instruments**
Richard Johnston
211 Lambert Ave.
Palo Alto, CA 94306
Phone: 650-493-2131
VintageInstruments@
gryphonstrings.com
gryphonstrings.com

Neal's Music
Neal Shelton
6916 Warner Ave.
Huntington Beach, CA
92647-5316
Phone: 714-842-9965
guitardcalsinfo@aol.com
nealsmusic.com

Rumble Seat Music
Dolores SW of 7th
Carmel, CA 93921
rumble@rumbleseatmusic.
com
rumbleseatmusic.com

TrueTone Music
Ken Daniels
714 Santa Monica Blvd.
Santa Monica, CA 90401
Phone: 310-393-8232
310-260-1415
sales@truetonemusic.com
truetonemusic.com

Connecticut
AcousticMusic.Org
Brian Wolfe & Leonard
Wyeth
1238 Boston Post Rd
Guilford, CT 06437
Phone: 203-458-2525
brian@acousticmusic.org
acousticmusic.org

Florida
Crescent City Music
Allen Glenn
111 North Summit Street
Crescent City, FL 32112
Phone/Fax: 386-698-2873
Phone: 386-698-2874
Cell: 386-559-0133
ccag@windstream.net
crescentcitymusic.biz

**Kummer's Vintage
Instruments**
Timm Kummer
Phone: 954-752-6063
prewar99@aol.com
kummersvintage.com

**Stevie B's of
Clearwater**
Joe Payne
30111 US Highway 19 N.
Clearwater, FL 33761
Phone: 727-785-9106
steviebs@verizon.net
steviebs.com

Georgia
Atlanta Vintage Guitars
"Serving Atlanta Guitar-
ists for Over 20 Years"
We Buy, Sell, Trade and
offer Consignments, Ebay
Contact: Greg
3778 Canton Rd, Ste 400
Marietta, GA 30066
Phone: 770-433-1891
Greg's cell: 770-324-3031
atlantavintageguitars@
gmail.com
atlantavintageguitars.com
http://stores.ebay.com/
Atlanta-Vintage-Guitars
http://www.gbase.com/
stores/atlanta-vintage-
guitars

Blue Sky Guitars
Robbie Cantrell
Canton, GA
Phone: 404-556-8858
770-479-9086
blueskyguitars@aol.com
blueskyguitars.com
By appointment only.

Hawaii
Coconut Grove Music
Mark Scrufari
167 Hamakua D., #200
Kailua, HI 96734
Phone: 808-262-9977
cgmusic@Hawaiiantel.biz
coconutgrovemusic.com

Illinois
**Chicago Music
Exchange**
David Kalt
3316 N. Lincoln Ave.
Chicago, IL 60657
Phone: 773-525-7775
Fax: 773-477-2775

info@chicagomusicex-
change.com
CME6.com

**Class of '67 Vintage
Guitars**
Terry Pekny
Phone: 312-813-0097
co67tp@aol.com
Classof67vintageguitars.
com

Guitar Works Ltd
Steve or Terry
709 Main Street
Evanston, IL 60202
Phone: 847-475-0855
Fax: 847-475-0715
guitarworksltd@aol.com
guitarworksltd.com

Make 'n Music
Contact: Teddy
780 W. Frontage Rd
Northfield, IL 60093
Phone: 312-455-1970
info@makenmusic.com
makenmusic.com

Make 'n Music
Downtown Showcase
159 N. Racine
Chicago, IL 60607
Phone: 312-455-1970
info@makenmusic.com
makenmusic.com

RockNRoll Vintage
Heith Jensen
4740 N. Lincoln Ave, Ste
2N
Chicago, IL 60625
Phone: 773-878-8616
rocknrollvintage@gmail.
com
rocknrollvintage.com

RWK Guitars
P.O. Box 1068
Highland Park, IL 60035
Phone: 847-432-4308
Bob@RWKGuitars.com
RWKGuitars.com

Kansas
Mass Street Music, Inc.
1347 Massachusetts St.
Lawrence, KS 66044-3431
Phone: 800-747-9980
sales@massstreetmusic.com
massstreetmusic.com
facebook.com/massstreet-
music

twitter.com/massstreet-music

Louisiana
International Vintage Guitars
Corner of LA Ave. &
Magazine St.
New Orleans, LA 70115
Phone: 504-442-0696
steve@webcorral.com
webcorral.com

Music Inc of Louisiana
Brandt Bourque
313 E. Cornerview Rd
Gonzales, LA 70737
Phone: 225-647-8681
musicinc.com

Maryland
Garrett Park Guitars
New-Used-Vintage-Collectible-Gear Since 1991
Rick
7 Old Solmons Island Rd.,
Ste 102
Annapolis, MD 21401-2421
Phone: 410-571-9660
gpguitars.com
gpguitars@gmail.com

Nationwide Guitars, Inc.
Bruce or Brad Rickard
P.O. Box 2334
Columbia, MD 21045
Phone: 410-489-4074
nationwideguitars@
comcast.net
nationwideguitars.com

Southworth Guitars
Gil Southworth
southworthguitar@aol.
com
southworthguitars.com

Massachusetts
Bay State Vintage Guitars
Craig or A.J. Jones
295 Huntington Avenue,
Room 304
Boston, MA 02115
Phone: 617-267-6077
info@baystatevintageguitars.com
baystatevintageguitars.
com

Luthier's Co-op
Steven Baer
108 Cottage St.
Easthampton, MA 01027
Phone: 413-527-6627
info@luthiers-coop.com
luthiers-coop.com

Michigan
Elderly Instruments
Stan Werbin
1100 North Washington
P.O. Box 14210 -VGF
Lansing, MI 48901
Phone: 517-372-7890
Fax: 517-372-5155
elderly@elderly.com
elderly.com

Huber & Breese Music
33540 Groesbeck Highway
Fraser, MI 48026
Phone: 586-294-3950
Fax: 586-294-7616
info@huberbreese.com
huberbreese.com

Lakeshore Guitars
Rich Baranowski
Troy, MI
Phone: 248-879-7474
richbaronow@aol.com
lakeshoreguitars.com

Minnesota
EddieVegas.com
Ed Matthews
Duluth, MN
Phone: 218-879-3796
e.matthews@mchsi.com
eddievegas.com

Willie's American Guitars
254 Cleveland Avenue
South
St. Paul, MN 55105
Phone: 651-699-1913
Fax: 651-690-1766
info@williesguitars.com
williesguitars.com

Missouri
Fly By Night Music
Dave Crocker
103 South Washington
Neosho, MO 64850-1816
Phone: 417-451-5110
Show number: 800-356-3347
crocker@joplin.com
texasguitarshows.com

Killer Vintage
Dave Hinson
P.O. Box 190561
St. Louis, MO 63119
Phone: 314-647-7795
          800-646-7795
Fax: 314-781-3240
killervintage.com

Nevada
AJ's Music In Las Vegas
Contact: Peter Trauth
2031 W. Sunset Rd.
Henderson, NV 89014-2120
Phone: 702-436-9300

Fax: 702-457-8764
ajsmusic@earthlink.net
ajsmusic.com

J&E Guitars
Jesse or Eric
3460 E. Sunset Rd., Ste. P
Las Vegas, NV 89120
702-522-8484
info@jeguitars.com
jeguitars.com

New Hampshire
Retro Music
Jeff Firestone
38 Washington Street
Keene, NH 03431
Phone/Fax: 603-357-9732
retromusic@myfairpoint.
net
retroguitar.com

New Jersey
Kebo's Bassworks
Kevin 'KeBo' Borden and
'Dr. Ben' Sopranzetti
info@kebosbassworks.com
kebosbassworks.com

Lark Street Music
479 Cedar Lane
Teaneck, NJ 07666
Phone: 201-287-1959
Larkstreet@gmail.com
www.larkstreet.com

New Jersey Guitar & Bass Center
Jay Jacus
995 Amboy Avenue
Edison, NJ 08837
Phone: 732-225-4444
Fax: 732-225-4404
NJGtrBass@aol.com
newjerseyguitarandbass-center.com

New York
Bernunzio Uptown Music
John or Julie Bernunzio
122 East Ave.
Rochester, NY 14604
Phone: 585-473-6140
Fax: 585-442-1142
info@bernunzio.com
bernunzio.com

Imperial Guitar and Soundworks
Bill Imperial
99 Route 17K
Newburgh, NY 12550
Phone: 845-567-0111
igs55@aol.com
imperialguitar.com

Laurence Wexer Ltd.
Larry Wexer
251 East 32nd Street #11F
New York, NY 10016
Phone: 212-532-2994

lwexer@gmail.com
wexerguitars.com

Rivington Guitars
Howie Statland
73 E. 4th St.
New York, NY 10003
Phone: 212-505-5313
rivingtoninfo@gmail.com
rivingtonguitars.com

Rudy's Music (Soho)
Rudy Pensa
461 Broome St.
New York, NY 10013
Phone: 212-625-2557
info@rudysmusic.com
rudysmusic.com

Rumble Seat Music
Eliot Michael
121 West State St.
Ithaca, NY 14850
Phone: 607-277-9236
Fax: 607-277-4593
rumble@rumbleseatmusic.
com
rumbleseatmusic.com

Sam Ash
Sammy Ash
Phone: 516-686-4104
sam.ash@samashmusic.
com

Sam Ash
Mike Rock
Phone: 516-435-8653
mike.rock@samashmusic.
com

We Buy Guitars
David Davidson
705A Bedford Ave.
Bellmore, NY 11710
Phone: 516-221-0563
Fax: 516-221-0856
webuyguitars1@aol.com
webuyguitars.net

We Buy Guitars
Richie Friedman
705A Bedford Ave.
Bellmore, NY 11710
Phone: 516-221-0563
Fax: 516-221-0856
webuyguitars@aol.com
webuyguitars.net

We Buy Guitars
Tom Dubas
705A Bedford Ave.
Bellmore, NY 11710
Phone: 516-221-0563
Fax: 516-221-0856
webuyguitars2@aol.com
webuyguitars.net

North Carolina
Bee-3 Vintage
Gary Burnette
PO Box 19509
Asheville, NC 28815

Phone: 828-298-2197
bee3vintage@hotmail.com
bee3vintage.com

Coleman Music
Chip Coleman
1021 S. Main St.
China Grove, NC 28023-2335
Phone: 704-857-5705
OR120@aol.com
colemanmusic.com

Ohio
Fretware Guitars
Dave Hussong
495 Miamisburg Center-ville Rd.
Dayton, OH 45459
Phone: 513-257-5193
fretwaregtrs@gmail.com

Gary's Classic Guitars
Gary Dick
Cincinnati, OH
Phone: 513-891-0555
Fax: 513-891-9444
garysclssc@aol.com
garysguitars.com

Mike's Music
Mike Reeder
2615 Vine Street
Cincinnati, OH 45219
Phone: 513-281-4900
Fax: 513-281-4968
mikesmusicohio.com

Oklahoma
Guitar House of Tulsa
Todd Cooke
6924 E. Admiral Pl
Tulsa, OK 74115-8709
Phone: 918-835-6959
info@guitarhouse.net
guitarhouse.net

Strings West
Larry Briggs
P.O. Box 999
20 E. Main Street
Sperry, OK 74073
Phone: 800-525-7273
Fax: 918-288-2888
larryb@stringswest.com
stringswest.com

Oregon
McKenzie River Music
Artie Leider
455 West 11th
Eugene, OR 97401
Phone: 541-343-9482
Fax: 541-465-9060
staff@mrmgtr.com
McKenzieRiverMusic.com

Pennsylvania
Guitar-Villa – Retro Music
We Buy Trade Appraise &
Consign

John J. Slog/Owner
Operator
228 Nazareth Pike
Bethlehem, PA 18020

Heritage Insurance Services, Inc.
Ellis Hershman
826 Bustleton Pike Ste 203
Feasterville, PA 19053
Phone: 1-877-853-6997
Ellish@musicins.com
musicins.com

Jim's Guitars, Inc.
Jim Singleton
2331 East Market St. STE A
York, PA 17402
Phone: 866-787-2865
Fax: 410-744-0010
sunburst549@aol.com.
jimsguitars.com

Northeast Music Center
Jack Gretz
713 Scranton
Carbondale Hwy
Siniawa Plaza II
Dickson City, PA 18519-1750
Phone: 570-909-9216
Fax: 570-909-9576
jgretz@nemusiccenter.com
nemusiccenter.com

York Music Shop
2331 East Market St. STE A
York, PA 17402
Tel: 866-787-2865
Fax: 410-744-0010
jimsguitars@comcast.net
yorkmusicshop.com

Tennessee
Carter Vintage Guitars
Christie and Walter Carter
625 8th Ave. S.
Nashville, TN 37203
Phone: 615 915-1851
walter@cartervintage.com
cartervintage.com

Gruhn Guitars
George Gruhn
2120 8th Ave. S.

Nashville, TN 37204
Phone: 615-256-2033
Fax: 615-255-2021
gruhn@gruhn.com
gruhn.com

Rick's Guitar Room
Rick Mikel
6415 Hixson Pike Ste B
Hixson, TN 37343
Phone: 423-842-9930
ricksguitarroom@bell-south.net
ricksguitarroom.com

Texas
California World Guitar Shows
Larry Briggs
Phone: 800-525-7273
Fax: 918-288-2888
larryb@stringswest.com
texasguitarshows.com
Custom Shop Guitars
17803 La Cantera Ter #1
San Antonio, Texas 78256
Phone: 210-560-2700
info@customshopguitars.com
customshopguitars.com

Chicago/Austin Guitar Show
Dave Crocker
Phone: 800-356-3347
Fax: 817-473-1089
crocker@joplin.com
texasguitarshows.com

Ellis Music
John Ellis
11008 Salado Springs Circle
Salado, TX 79571-5298
Phone: 951-347-5197
jolinmusic@earthlink.net
ellisvintage.com

Eugene's Guitars Plus
Eugene Robertson
2010 South Buckner Boulevard
Dallas, TX 75217-1823
Phone: 214-391-8677
pluspawnguitars@yahoo.com
texasguitarshows.com

Heritage Auctions
Isaiah Evans
3500 Maple Ave
Dallas, TX 75219
Phone: 214-409-1201 | 877-HERITAGE
IsaiahE@HA.com
HA.com

Heritage Auctions
Mike Gutierrez
3500 Maple Ave
Dallas, TX 75219
Phone: 214-409-1183 | 877-HERITAGE
MikeG@HA.com
HA.com

Hill Country Guitars
Dwain Cornelius
1716 San Antonio St.
Austin, TX 78701
Phone: 512-432-5051
info@hillcountryguitars.com
hillcountryguitars.com

Southpaw Guitars
Lefties Only
Jim
5813 Bellaire Blvd.
Houston, TX 77081
Phone: 713-667-5791
Fax: 713-667-4091
info@southpawguitars.com
southpawguitars.com

Texas Amigos Guitar Shows
Arlington Guitar Show
(The 4 Amigos)
Contact: Ruth Brinkmann
Phone: 800-473-6059
Fax: 817-473-1089
texasguitarshows.com

Van Hoose Vintage Instruments
Thomas Van Hoose
2722 Raintree Drive
Carrollton, TX 75006
Phone: 972-998-8176
tv0109@yahoo.com
vanhoosevintage.com

Utah
Intermountain Guitar

and Banjo
Leonard or Kennard
712 East 100 South
Salt Lake City, UT 84102
Phone: 801-322-4682
Fax: 801-355-4023
guitarandbanjo@earth-link.com
guitarandbanjo.com

Vermont
MusicStoreLive.com
Bringing the guitar shop into your livingroom.
Free Return Shipping!
27 Berard Dr. - Ste 2701
S. Burlington, VT 05403-5854
Phone: 888-260-5197
info@musicstorelive.com
facebook.com/musicstorelive

Virginia
Action Music
7 miles south of Washington DC
Matt Baker
212-B N. West Street
Falls Church, VA 22046
Phone: 703-534-4801
action.music@comcast.net
actionguitar.com

Vintage Sound
Bill Holter
P.O. Box 11711
Alexandria, VA 22312
Phone: 703-300-2529
bhvsound@vintagesound.com
vintagesound.com

Washington
Cole Music Comany
816 W. Garland Ave.
Spokane, WA 99205
509-244-3001
eben@colemusiccompany.com
colemusiccompany.com

Guitarville
Vallis Kolbeck
19258 15th Ave. North East
Seattle, WA 98155-2315
Phone: 206-363-8188
Fax: 206-363-0478

sales@guitarville.com
guitarville.com

The Trading Musician
5908 Roosevelt Way NE
Seattle, WA 98105-2744
Phone: 206-522-6707
mrv@trading musician.com
tradingmusician.com

Thunder Road Guitars
Specializing in fine vintage and modern guitars and amplifiers
3916 California Ave SW
Seattle, WA 98116
Phone: 206-678-5248
hello@thunderroadguitars.com
thunderroadguitars.com

Wisconsin
Bizarre Guitars
Brian Goff
3601 Sunset Drive
Shorewood Hills, WI 53705
Phone: 608-235-3561
bdgoff@sbcglobal.net
bizarreguitars.net

Cream City Music
John Majdalani
12505 W. Bluemound Rd.
Brookfield, WI 53005-8026
Phone: 262-860-1800
johnm@creamcitymusic.com
creamcitymusic.com

Dave's Guitar Shop
Dave Rogers
1227 South 3rd Street
La Crosse, WI 54601
Phone: 608-785-7704
Fax: 608-785-7703
davesgtr@aol.com
davesguitar.com

Gretschworld
John Majdalani
12505 W. Bluemound Rd.
Brookfield, WI 53005-8026
Phone: 800-800-0087
johnm@creamcitymusic.com
creamcitymusic.com

TECH/REPAIR

California
National Guitar Repair
Restoration of all fine resonator instruments, Nationals & Dobros a speciality

Marc Schoenberger
Phone: 805-481-8532
805-471-5905
Luthier17@aol.com
nationalguitarrepair.com

Skip Simmons Amplifier Repair
Skip Simmons
4827 Bevan Road
Loma Rica, CA 95901-9437

503-771-7345
skip@skipsimmonsamps.com
skipsimmonsamps.com

Soest Guitar Shop
By Appointment Only

Steve Soest
Phone: 714-538-0272
soestguitar@earthlink.net
soestguitar.com

Illinois
Third Coast Guitar
Chris Eudy
159 N. Racine Ave.
Chicago, IL 60607
Phone: 312-275-0095
thirdcoastguitar@ameri-tech.net
thirdcoastguitar.com

Iowa
AM Guitar Works
Alan Morrison
5259 Jersey Ridge Road
Davenport, IA 52807
Phone: 563-370-6810
amguitars@mchsi.com
amguitarworks.com
guitarupgradesonline.com

New York
The Guitar Specialist, Inc.
Doug Proper
307 Route 22
Goldens Bridge, NY 10526
Phone: 914-401-9052
doug@guitarspecialist.com
guitarspecialist.com

Ohio
Lay's Guitar Restoration
Since 1962
Dan Shinn
974 Kenmore Blvd.
Akron, OH 44314
Phone: 330-848-1392
Fax: 330-848-3727
laysguitar.com

Oklahoma
MandoAiki
Ed Cunliff
3433 Baird Dr.
Edmond, OK 73013
Phone: 405-341-2926
mandoaiki@yahoo.com
mandoaiki.com

MANUFACTURER
DIRECTORY

A Little Thunder
Los Angeles, CA 90026
info@alittlethunder.com
alittlethunder.com

Alembic
3005 Wiljan Ct.
Santa Rosa, CA 95407-5702
Phone: 707-523-2611
alembic@alembic.com
alembic.com

Amalfitano Pickups
Jerry Amalfitano
Phone: 817-917-8707
amalfitanopickups@gmail.com
amalfitanopickups.com

Analog Man Guitar Effects
Mike Piera
Route 6
Bethel, CT 06801
Phone: 203-778-6658
AnalogMike@aol.com
analogman.com

Bourns Inc.
1200 Columbia Ave.
Riverside, CA 92507-2129
proaudio@bourns.com
bourns.com

Callaham Guitars
Bill Callaham

217 Park Center Dr.
Winchester, VA 22603
Phone: 540-678-4043
Fax: 540-678-8779
callaham@callahamguitars.com
callahamguitars.com

Carr Amplifiers
Pittsboro, NC 27312
Phone: 919-545-0747
info@carramps.com
carramps.com

CaseParlor
23 South Beaver St.
Flagstaff, AZ 86001
staff@caseparlor.com
caseparlor.com

Chandler Musical Instruments
Paul or Adrian
236A W. East Ave., Box 213
Chico, CA 95926-7236
Phone: 530-899-1503
info@chandlerguitars.com
chandlerguitars.com
pickguardheaven.com
pickguards.us

Curt Mangan Strings
Curt Mangan
Phone: 970-564-5935

411@curtmangan.com
curtmangan.com

Demeter Amplification
James Demeter
6990 Kingsbury Rd.
Templeton, CA 93465
Phone: 805-461-4100
Fax: 805-267-4079
sales@demeteramps.com
demeteramps.com

Eric Schoenberg Guitars
Eric Schoenberg
106 Main Street
Tiburon, CA 94920
Phone: 415-789-0846
eric@om28. com
om28.com

Fleishman Instruments
Harry Fleishman, luthier
7771 Healdsburg Ave, #34
Sebastopol, CA 95472
Phone: 707-823-3537
hfguitars@gmail.com
fleishmaninstruments.com

Fuchs Audio Technology
Annette Fuchs
407 Getty Ave.
Clifton, NJ 07011

Phone: 973-772-4420
sales@fuchsaudio.com
fuchsaudio.com

Godlyke, Inc.
46 Marlboro Rd.
Clifton, NJ 07012
Phone: 866-246-3595
info@godlyke.com
godlyke.com

Harry Joyce USA
Phone: 941-584-5962
info@HarryJoyceUSA.com
HarryJoyceUSA.com

Mercury Magnetics
Patrick Selfridge
Chatsworth, CA
Phone: 818-998-7791
Fax: 818-998-7835
patrick@mercurymagnetics.com
mercurymagnetics.com

Mirabella Guitars & Restorations
Cris Mirabella
PO Box 482
Babylon, NY 11702
631-842-3819
mirguitars@ aol.com
mirabellaguitars.com
facebook.com/#!/profile.

php?id+623520277
facebook.com/#!/pages/
bBabylon-NY/Mirabella-Guitars/141766067458

RecycledSound.net
Greg Perrine
Conway, AR
glp@conwaycorp.net
recycledsound.net

Reverb.com
Reverb.com

ScreaminFX
Seth Wilk
3316 Tavistock Dr.
Austin, TX 78748
Phone: 512-380-1821
swilk@screaminfx.com
screaminfx.com

WD Music Products
17570 N Taminami Trail Ste. 1
North Fort Myers, FL 33903
Phone: 239-543-3625
sales@wdmusic.com
wdmusic.com

Xotic Guitars and Effects
info@xotic.us
xotic.us

For dealer directory advertising info contact
Jeanine at Jeanine@VintageGuitar.com or 1-800-844-1197.